THE WEST

A NEW HISTORY

ANTHONY GRAFTON
DAVID A. BELL

THE WEST

A NEW HISTORY

W. W. Norton & Company

NEW YORK • LONDON

EDITOR Steve Forman
ASSOCIATE EDITORS Scott Sugarman and Justin Cahill
PROJECT EDITOR Melissa Atkin
EDITORIAL ASSISTANTS Lily Gellman, Kelly Rafey, and Travis Carr
DEVELOPMENTAL EDITORS Alice Vigliani and Harry Haskell
CARTOGRAPHIC EDITOR Charlotte Miller
COPYEDITORS JoAnn Simony and Alice Vigliani
MANAGING EDITOR, COLLEGE Marian Johnson
MANAGING EDITOR, COLLEGE DIGITAL MEDIA Kim Yi
ASSOCIATE DIRECTOR OF PRODUCTION, COLLEGE Benjamin Reynolds
MEDIA EDITOR Laura Wilk
MEDIA PROJECT EDITOR Rachel Mayer
MEDIA ASSOCIATE EDITORS Michelle Smith and Sarah Rose Aquilina
MEDIA ASSISTANT EDITOR Chris Hillyer
MARKETING MANAGER, HISTORY Sarah England Bartley
PHOTO EDITOR Stephanie Romeo
PHOTO RESEARCHER Lynn Gadson
DESIGNER Jillian Burr
PERMISSIONS MANAGER Megan Schindel
PERMISSIONS ASSOCIATE Elizabeth Trammell
LAYOUT ARTIST Brad Walrod/Kenoza Type, Inc.
CARTOGRAPHER AND ILLUSTRATOR Mapping Specialists—Fitchburg, WI
MANUFACTURING Transcontinental Interglobe Inc.—Beauceville QC

This edition:
ISBN: 978-0-393-62325-3 (pbk.)

W. W. Norton & Company, Inc., 500 Fifth Avenue, New York, NY 10110

wwnorton.com

W. W. Norton & Company Ltd., 15 Carlisle Street, London W1D 3BS

1 2 3 4 5 6 7 8 9 0

W. W. NORTON & COMPANY has been independent since its founding in 1923, when William Warder Norton and Mary D. Herter Norton first published lectures delivered at the People's Institute, the adult education division of New York City's Cooper Union. The firm soon expanded its program beyond the Institute, publishing books by celebrated academics from America and abroad. By midcentury, the two major pillars of Norton's publishing program—trade books and college texts—were firmly established. In the 1950s, the Norton family transferred control of the company to its employees, and today—with a staff of four hundred and a comparable number of trade, college, and professional titles published each year—W. W. Norton & Company stands as the largest and oldest publishing house owned wholly by its employees.

TO OUR STUDENTS

ABOUT THE AUTHORS

ANTHONY GRAFTON is the Henry Putnam University Professor of History at Princeton University. A specialist in the cultural history of early-modern Europe, he is the author of many acclaimed books, including *The Footnote: A Curious History*, and *New Worlds, Ancient Texts: The Power of Tradition and the Shock of Discovery*, which won the Los Angeles Times Book Award in History, as well as intellectual biographies of Leon Battista Alberti, Girolamo Cardano, and Joseph Scaliger. Among his many honors from universities and cultural institutions around the world, Professor Grafton was awarded the Balzan Prize for History of the Humanities and the Andrew W. Mellon Foundation's Distinguished Achievement Award. At Princeton, where he regularly teaches the survey of Western Civilizations, he was honored with the President's Teaching Award. He is a member of the American Philosophical Society, the British Academy, and has served as president of the American Historical Association.

DAVID A. BELL is the Sidney and Ruth Lapidus Professor in the Era of North Atlantic Revolutions in the history department at Princeton University. His specialty is modern Europe with a focus on political culture in the age of revolutions. Among his recent works, *The First Total War: Napoleon's Europe and the Birth of Warfare As We Know It* was a finalist for the Los Angeles Times Book Award in History. Professor Bell regularly teaches undergraduate surveys of early-modern Europe, the Enlightenment, and the French Revolution. He is a regular contributor to *The Nation* and other general-interest periodicals. Professor Bell's current project is a transnational history of political charisma in the Atlantic revolutions of the late eighteenth and early nineteenth centuries.

CONTENTS IN BRIEF

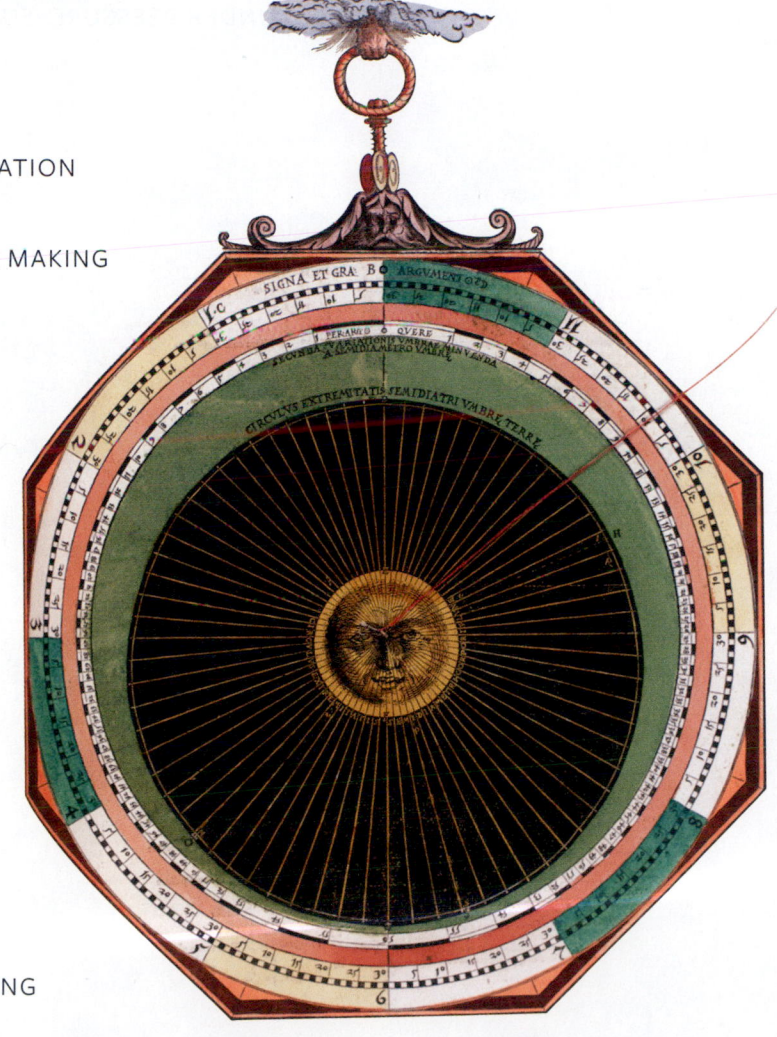

CONTENTS

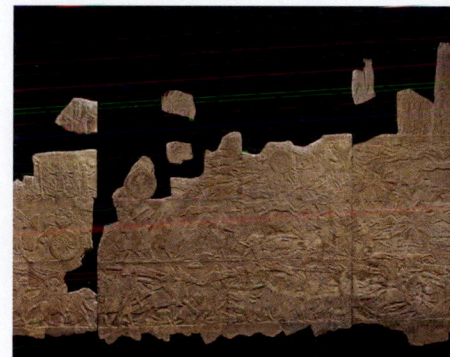

3. From Classical Greece to the Hellenistic World: Cultures in Contact, 400–30 BCE   77

6. The Late Roman Empire and the Consolidation of the Church, 312–476

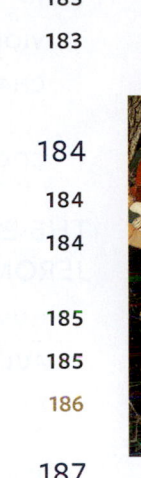

9. Consolidation and Crisis: The High Middle Ages, 1200–1400 287

11. Reformations: Protestant and Catholic, 1500–1600   371

13. Ordering the World: New Forms of Authority and Knowledge, 1640–1680   441

14. From Court to City: Emerging Cultures, 1680–1740   473

15. Enlightenment: Challenging the Prevailing Order, 1740–1780

19. Growing Pains: Social and Political Upheavals, 1845–1880 — 637

22. Ideologies: The Triumph of Political Extremes, 1922–1940   741

24. Recovery and Cold War: Rebuilding a Divided Continent, 1945–1973

25. Reunion: European Unification and the End of the Cold War, 1973–1999 845

26. Under Pressure: Europe's Uncertain Present, Since 2000   877

MAPS

PRIMARY-SOURCE FEATURES

A mural by Bansky on Brexit and the EU: May 2017; Dover, England.

PREFACE

The story of the West is an epic. This might seem strange to say, because there has never been a single, unified, easily defined place called "the West." Even the Roman Empire at its height did not control all of the territories that have come to form part of the West, and its hegemony lasted only a few centuries. The boundaries of the West have never been fixed or agreed upon. Moreover, whether in imperial Rome or Europe today, these borders have always been porous. People, goods, and ideas have constantly flowed across them in both directions, sometimes peacefully and often violently. What we today call "the West" is in significant measure a product of this unending process of exchange.

Even so, there is something we can call "the West." It is a web of societies, centered in Europe and its extensions, loosely linked by shared and interacting histories. These histories incorporate debts to other societies around the world and the results of conflicts both internal and global.

At their core are ideas and institutions—cultural, political, social, and economic—that have outlasted the individual societies that gave them birth and been developed and transformed to meet new needs. The story of the West is not one of repeated triumph or unbroken progress. It is not a story of a single tradition. But it is a story of epic proportions. It has been a story of hatred and intolerance, but also one of men and women fighting hatred and intolerance, and finding ways to rise above them. It has been a story of people who rejected the earth for heaven, and of people who wanted to build heaven on earth. It has been a story of breathtaking idealism and breathtaking cruelty, of innovation and competition, creation and destruction, new habits of thought, and of centuries-long conversations that we call "traditions."

The story is full of dramatic moments: moments when individuals and movements challenged established authorities and customs, when reformers transformed legal codes

and religious practices, and when revolutionaries over-turned governments. It is a story of individuals of titanic achievement: people who have given their names to ways of thinking and arguing, understanding the universe, and building and maintaining states. It is a story of blinding new insights into what justice really means, and one of blindness to the exploitation and persecution of others.

But it has also been a story of daily life: of men and women whose names we usually do not know who struggled to survive and raise children under the shadows of hunger and illness, war and displacement. It is the story of how daily life remained the same in many ways for thousands of years: of how most people lived close to the soil, trying to scratch out sustenance from it with their own muscle power and that of animals, according to the rhythm of the seasons. But it is also a story of how, starting in the seventeenth and eighteenth centuries, individuals and groups slowly developed new ways of wringing more food from the land—and how, by doing so, they changed the world.

Last, but by no means least, it is a story about how, in the last centuries, virtually everything about daily life changed, often at dizzying speed: factories rose, cities grew to sizes never seen before, gender roles were challenged and transformed, religion lost its commanding place in society, governments became newly pervasive, education

spread, new technologies emerged, new media flourished, and vast new forms of wealth were created. It is a story of how modern nation-states were forged and of how populations migrated into and out of Europe.

The story was not the work of Europeans alone. Indeed, the civilization that took shape in Europe has arguably been more dependent than any other on what it could borrow, beg, or steal from the rest of the world. For much of its history—amid the competing city-states of ancient Greece and the fierce rivalries of the western Middle Ages and Renaissance—the West has been smaller, poorer in resources, more politically divided, and less sophisticated than rival civilizations elsewhere in the world. Only with the capture of the immense resources of the Americas in the early modern period, and the harnessing of fossil fuels during the Industrial Revolution, did the natural resources that Europe possessed make themselves fully felt in the worldwide balance of power. Yet precisely as a result of the West's relative poverty and political fragmentation, Western politicians and thinkers, soldiers and tinkerers were driven constantly to innovate with the resources they had and with the ideas and techniques they borrowed from other cultures. Writing came to the West from the Near East—from the Phoenicians, a Semitic people who lived in Palestine and the Fertile Crescent. So did the idea of setting down in writing massive works that described the adventures of humans and the hierarchies of gods. But the two Greek epics traditionally ascribed to the poet Homer are distinctively different from the great Near Eastern epic *The Song of Gilgamesh*, in the ways that they portray relations between gods and humans and in the voices that they give to their own societies.

Many elements of this story will seem strange to young people who live in the West today. The physical and mental worlds of an ancient Greek soldier, a medieval nun, or an African slave in an early-modern European colony were all enormously distant from those of today's students. Indeed, the scale of change in every area of life in modern times—political, economic, cultural, religious, technological—can easily lead to the conclusion that an unbridgeable gulf separates the more distant past from the present. Can a cohesive story encompass present-day Europeans, the poorest of whom can generally count on living to old age in conditions of relative physical comfort, and their predecessors of whom half did not live beyond adolescence, with the remainder at constant risk of death from infectious disease and possibly starvation, not to mention chronic, debilitating pain? Is it possible to draw connections between the Europeans of today, almost entirely literate and able instantly to summon vast libraries of text, image, and sound on devices they carry in their pockets, and predecessors who learned about the world principally from oral tradition, religious authority, and travel limited by the speed of wind, animals, or their own legs?

We think it is possible. If you live in the West today, and particularly if you are a student, this story is your story. It is not by any means the entirety of your story, but it is a critical part of it, and for two reasons. First, it is the story of how significant parts of your world came into being. The political systems that exist in the West today, nearly all of which claim the mantle of democracy, trace their origins back to the ancient Greek world in which the word "democracy" itself was invented. They are part of a tradition—a long process of evolution, debate, and conflict—in which the meaning of democracy has changed radically to include new conceptions of rights, political representation, civic and social equality, and a separation between the realms of politics and religion. This long process did not take place solely in the West, but it was centered there. It was also shaped by forms of political competition and fragmentation that have been characteristic of the West throughout most of its history and that distinguish the West from many other historical regions of the world.

Similarly, the capitalist system that most of the West lives under today has roots that reach far back: to the trading cities that developed in the ancient world, to patterns of commerce and banking that developed in medieval Europe, and to ideas about the organization of societies and the operations of markets that were formulated during the European Renaissance and Enlightenment. This system depended, from the start, on currents of trade, exploration, and exploitation and conquest that stretched far beyond the West, and it has subsequently developed strongly on a global scale. But at its core this system was centered in the West.

More broadly, the very ways in which we learn to read, think critically, devise arguments, innovate, and express ourselves creatively derive in significant measure from millennia-long conversations that began in the ancient Near East, were carried on throughout the classical Mediterranean world, and thence into other parts of Europe and the world. These conversations were rarely harmonious. Their basic assumptions were challenged, in fundamental ways, by new voices from both within and without. Their subjects and forms changed repeatedly. But as this book will show, important continuities can still be traced within these conversations.

And this is the second reason why the story of the West is your story. The habits and practices of learning, critical thinking, and effective expression that are necessary for citizens of contemporary Western industrial democracies are intimately related to the complex history that produced them.

History does not just help us better understand the world around us; it helps us function more effectively in it. This lesson, and this awareness, are themselves part of the Western story, and they lie at the heart of one of the most important Western traditions: the tradition of higher learning that is today carried on in colleges and universities. Ancient Romans trained for positions within their own society by learning Greek and studying important works of Greek philosophy and literature. During the Renaissance, so-called humanists sought to revive ancient Greek and Roman learning not just for the sake of learning, but in order to train young men as civil servants and diplomats, lawyers, and doctors. These systems of education could function as forms of social discrimination, excluding from desirable careers those who lacked the means to study Latin and Greek—a category that included virtually all women. But learning about Western history and traditions can also serve as a means of social inclusion, drawing diverse student populations into conversation with peers from all corners of their own society, with their own predecessors from centuries past, and with some of the most brilliant and creative minds the world has known.

As historians who have both taught Western history for decades, we recognize that the story of the West is complex and often challenging for introductory students. It ranges across the fields of politics, society, economics, war, religion, philosophy, science, culture, and much else. It is a story marked by discontinuities such as the sharp differences among different regions of the West, and by the many different forms of exchange and contact between the West and other areas of the globe. But precisely because of these complexities, we believe in the importance of integrating the history with strong narrative threads and telling the story in as cogent, engaging, and fluid a manner as possible.

We have therefore chosen to proceed in as close to a strictly chronological manner as possible, presenting subjects like the development of Christianity or the scientific revolution as they unfolded alongside other contemporary events, rather than cordoning them off into separate chapters. We believe it is important for the chronology of events to be clear and visible for beginning students. We wish also to show students the mutual interplay over time of politics and society, ideas, beliefs, and material conditions. These many overlapping layers of history should be understood together, developing over time, rather than as disconnected strands of the story. We have done our best to achieve the right balance in attending to these many dimensions of history. We have also tried to incorporate the best new scholarship in these fields along with the insights of previous generations of scholars.

The book covers as broad a sweep of history as is practical in two volumes designed for a year-long survey course. Volume One, written primarily by Anthony Grafton, begins with a Prologue on prehistory and takes the story from the ancient Near East up through the Reformation. Volume Two, written primarily by David Bell, begins with the Renaissance and continues to the present day. Both volumes range in scope far beyond Europe. Volume One

emphasizes the origins of the Western story in the Middle East and gives due attention to the societies around the Mediterranean basin during antiquity and the Middle Ages, including the rise, expansion, and cultural flourishing of Islam. It also deals with patterns of global exchange and the expansion of European political power that began in the fifteenth century. Volume Two centers its narrative on Europe and its extensions, focusing on the continuing dynamics of disorder and order, cohesion and fragmentation, as they played out in politics, culture, and society over the modern period.

THE WEST comes equipped with a full complement of illustrations (more than 500), newly drawn maps (more than 130), and useful pedagogical features described in the coming pages. But at the core of history is narrative, and we hope that THE WEST demonstrates our belief that clear, engaging prose remains the most effective means of introducing students to history.

Anthony Grafton
David A. Bell

ACKNOWLEDGMENTS

Heartfelt thanks to Steve Forman, our eagle-eyed and ever cheerful editor, and to his colleagues at W.W. Norton, who inspired me, prodded me, and turned sometimes inchoate drafts into a finished book; to my colleagues at Princeton, who have taught me so much about history; and, above all, to the students who have taken History 211. Many of the tales told here were first spun for them, and their lively responses, in class and out, to lectures, readings, and expeditions to the Rare Book Room have given me both pleasure and enlightenment over the years. It is a pleasure to join David Bell in dedicating this book to our students.

Anthony Grafton

Many thanks to all the colleagues at Johns Hopkins and Princeton who helped me over the years with suggestions and comments. I am grateful to the terrific staff at W.W. Norton, and especially our wonderful editor, Steve Forman, for everything they have done to bring this project to fruition. As always, my deepest gratitude to my wife, Donna Farber, and to my children, Elana and Joseph Bell, for their love and support. One of the greatest joys of the profession I am in comes in the moments of one's students' discoveries, watching them see into the past in a new way. It is in memory of these moments, and in gratitude to those who have passed through my classrooms, that I am delighted to join Anthony Grafton in dedicating this book to our students.

David A. Bell

THE WEST is a collective work in many respects, most pleasurably in its reflection of the commitment we share with many of our colleagues to the introductory course and its students. We would like to thank the following scholars for reading and commenting on our draft chapters. We have benefitted enormously from their criticisms and suggestions.

Megan Armstrong, McMaster University
Kenneth Bartlett, University of Toronto
Jean Berger, University of Wisconsin at Fox Valley
Hilary Bernstein, University of California, Santa Barbara
Nick Bomba, Northern Virginia Community College
Curtis V. Bostick, Southern Utah University
Jonathyne Briggs, Indiana University Northwest
Tobias Brinkmann, Pennsylvania State University
Bill Bulman, Lehigh University
Jeremy Caradonna, University of Victoria
Shawn Clybor, Utah State University
Susan Cogan, Utah State University
William Connell, Seton Hall University
Alix Cooper, State University of New York at Stony Brook
Mairi Cowan, University of Toronto at Mississauga
Andrew Daily, University of Memphis
Leah DeVun, Rutgers University
David Dorondo, Western Carolina University

Mary Duarte, Cardinal Stritch University
Bonnie Effros, University of Florida
John Eglin, University of Montana
Kyle Fingerson, University of Wisconsin, Rock County
Christopher Frank, University of Manitoba
Andrew Gallia, University of Minnesota
Phil Haberkern, Boston University
Amanda E. Herbert, Christopher Newport University
Rowena Hernández-Múzquiz, Broward College
Laura Hutchings, University of Utah
Bruce Janacek, North Central College
Erik Johnsen, Portland Community College
Donald Johnson, University of North Carolina at Wilmington
Edward Kolla, Georgetown University in Qatar
Jodie Kreider, Colorado State University
Greta Kroeker, University of Waterloo
Matthew Laubacher, Ashford University
Anne E. Lester, University of Colorado, Boulder
Yan Mann, Arizona State University
Benjamin Marschke, Humboldt State University
Bruce McCord, Aiken Technical College
Jeri McIntosh, University of Tennessee, Knoxville
Murat Menguc, Seton Hall University
John Patrick Montaño, University of Delaware
Rosemary Moore, University of Iowa
Seán Farrell Moran, Oakland University
George Munro, Virginia Commonwealth University
William Myers, University of Alaska, Anchorage
Lawrence Okamura, University of Missouri
Katrina Olds, University of San Francisco
John Powers, Virginia Commonwealth University
Jennifer Purcell, Saint Michael's College
Andrew Reed, Arizona State University
Walter Roberts, University of North Texas
Nicholas L. Rummell, Trident Technical College
Emily Rutherford, Columbia University
Linda B. Scherr, Middlesex County College
Edward Schoolman, University of Nevada, Reno
Colleen Shaughnessy Zeena, Endicott College
Linda Smith, University of Alabama at Birmingham
Ginger Smoak, University of Utah
John Swanson, University of Tennessee at Chattanooga
Emily Sohmer Tai, Queensborough Community College, CUNY
Paul Teverow, Missouri Southern State University
Corinna Treitel, Washington University in St. Louis
Liana Vardi, State University of New York at Buffalo
Corinne Wieben, University of Northern Colorado

PEDAGOGY AND FEATURES

The West offers an array of pedagogical features to guide students through the chapters and enrich their understanding of people and events.

All chapters open with a list of **focus questions** that correspond to the major section headings in the chapter. These questions, which appear also in the relevant running heads at the tops of pages, are meant to keep students alert to the key developments in each section. All chapters also open with a **chronology** of major events and an **immersive narrative vignette** to draw students into the reading. The chapters end with a review page that includes **study questions**, a list of the **key terms** (with page references) that appear in bold in the chapter, and a set of **Core Objectives**—key points that students should take away from the chapter. These Core Objectives are reinforced in the exercises provided in the online Student Site for *The West*. The key terms are all defined in the Glossary located in the Appendix, which also includes the authors' lists of **Further Reading** for each chapter.

Since one of the most important course goals in the introductory survey is to train students in the use of primary sources, each chapter also includes three **primary-source features** intended to introduce students to different types of documents and help build their critical-thinking skills.

The first of these features, **Making Connections**, consists of paired primary documents that connect to each other and the text itself. Brief headnotes and questions focus students on the issues to consider. The **Documenting Everyday Life** feature, comprising a source, a headnote, and questions, helps students understand an aspect of the everyday life of the period. The **Understanding Visual Culture** feature presents an image as a primary source to be examined critically by students.

The West also presents an innovative feature entitled **City Life**, intended to enhance the text's theme of cultural change and give students further work in developing history skills. We have eight of these full-page features in the text, four in Volume I and four in the non-overlap chapters of Volume Two. Each one focuses on a city at a critical moment, from Fifth-Century Athens and Imperial Rome to Renaissance Florence and fin de siècle Vienna. Through source quotations, images, a central map, and short questions that connect to text discussions, the features ask students to reflect on distinctive aspects of life in the cities, whether the ways in which the emperors reshaped the city of Rome or the commercial context of art in Renaissance Florence. The digital resources connected to the City Life features further enhance student history skills.

Understanding Visual Culture

City Life

DIGITAL RESOURCES FOR STUDENTS AND INSTRUCTORS

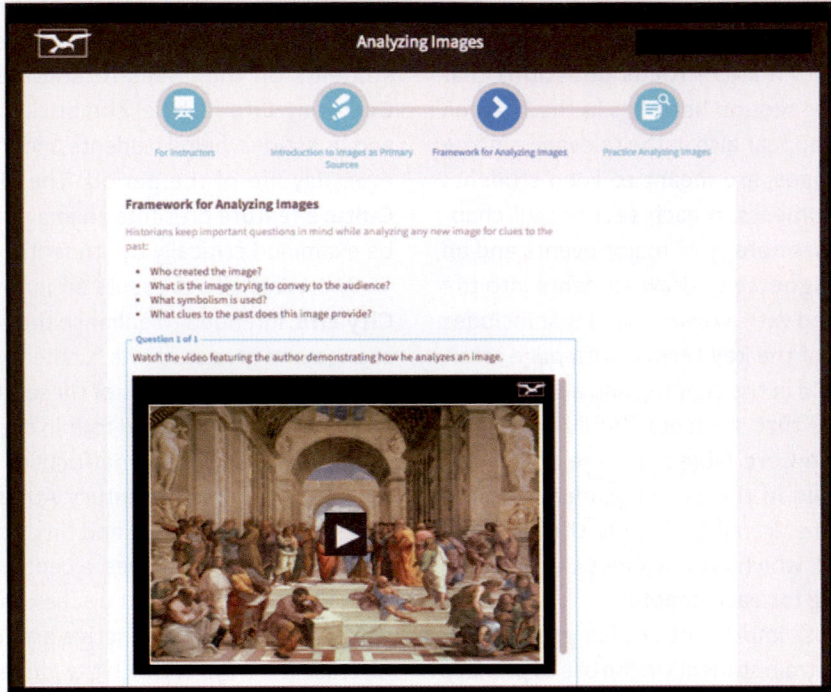

W. W. Norton offers a robust digital package to support teaching and learning with *The West*. These resources are designed to make students more effective textbook readers and to develop their critical thinking and history skills.

RESOURCES FOR STUDENTS

Resources are available at digital.wwnorton.com/thewest with the access card at the front of this text.

Norton InQuizitive for History

Norton InQuizitive for history is an adaptive quizzing tool that improves students' understanding of the themes and objectives from each chapter, while honing their critical analysis skills with primary-source, image, and map analysis questions. Students receive personalized quiz questions with detailed, guiding feedback on the topics in which they need the most help, while the engaging, gamelike elements motivate them as they learn. InQuizitive for *The West* was developed by Christopher Brooks, Portland Community College.

History Skills Tutorials

The History Skills Tutorials feature three modules—Images, Documents, and Maps—to support students' development of the key skills for the history course. These tutorials feature videos of the authors modeling the analysis process, followed by interactive questions that will challenge students to apply what they have learned.

Student Site

The free and easy-to-use online Student Site offers additional resources for students to use outside of class. Resources include interactive iMaps from each chapter, author videos, and a comprehensive Online Reader featuring more than 300 additional primary-source documents and images.

Ebook

Free and included with new copies of the text, **the Norton Ebook Reader** provides an enhanced reading experience that works on all computers and mobile devices. Features include intuitive highlighting, note-taking, and bookmarking as well as pop-up definitions and enlargeable maps and art. Direct links to InQuizitive also appear in each chapter. Instructors can focus

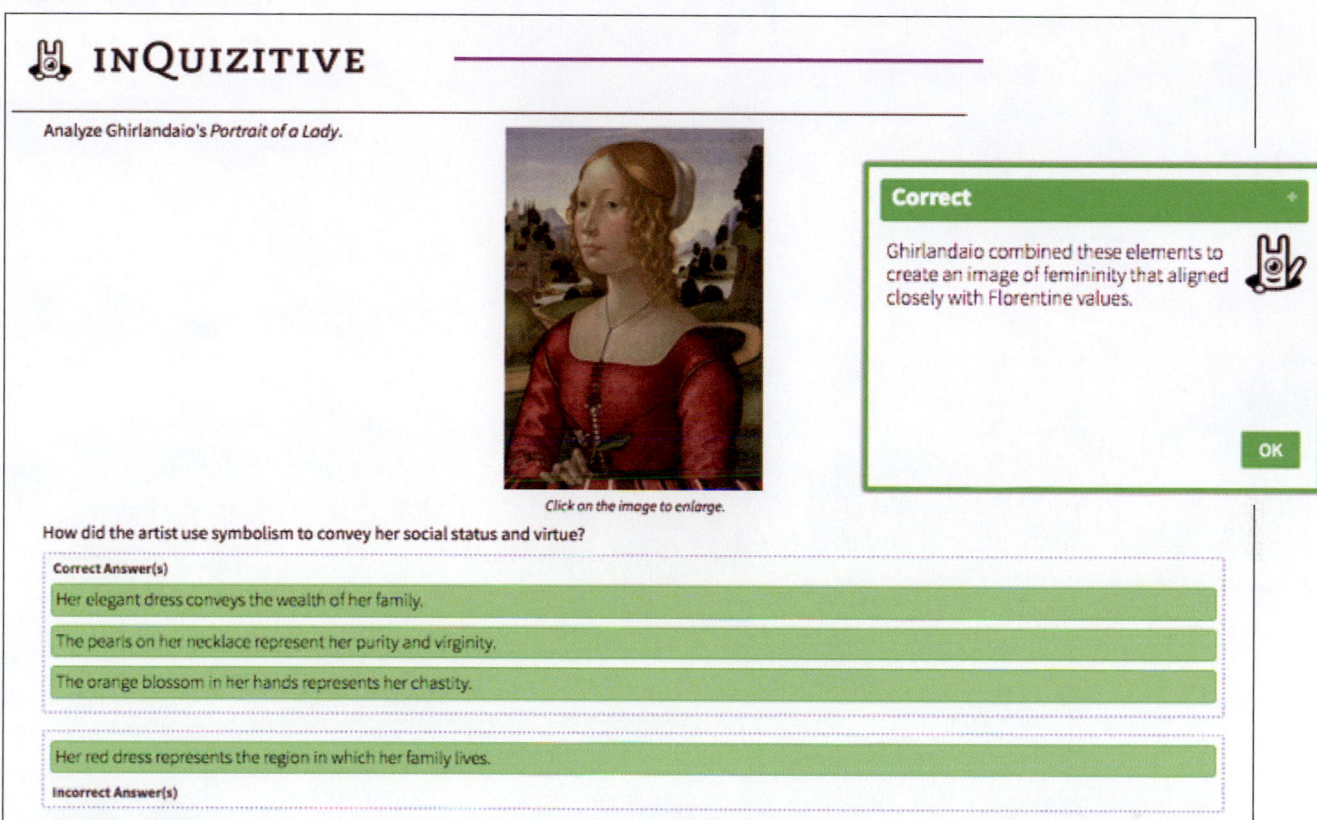

InQuizitive

Analyze Ghirlandaio's *Portrait of a Lady*.

Click on the image to enlarge.

Correct

Ghirlandaio combined these elements to create an image of femininity that aligned closely with Florentine values.

OK

How did the artist use symbolism to convey her social status and virtue?

Correct Answer(s)

Her elegant dress conveys the wealth of her family.

The pearls on her necklace represent her purity and virginity.

The orange blossom in her hands represents her chastity.

Her red dress represents the region in which her family lives.

Incorrect Answer(s)

student reading by sharing notes with their classes, including embedded images and video. Reports on student and class-wide access and time on task allow instructors to monitor student reading and engagement.

RESOURCES FOR INSTRUCTORS

All resources are available through digital.wnorton.com/books/instructors.

NORTON COURSEPACKS

Easily add high-quality digital media to your online, hybrid, or lecture course—all at no cost to students. Norton's Coursepacks work within your existing Learning Management System and are ready to use and easy to customize. The coursepack offers a diverse collection of assignable and assessable resources: **Primary-Source Exercises, Guided Reading Exercises, Review Quizzes, Flashcards, Map Exercises, and all of the resources from the Student Site.** The resources were developed by Matthew Mingus, University of New Mexico, Melanie Bailey, Piedmont Virginia Community College, and Gregory Vitarbo, Meredith College.

Test Bank

The Test Bank was authored by Rosemary Moore, University of Iowa, John Patrick Montano, University of Delaware, and Curt Bostick, Southern Utah University, and contains 2000 multiple-choice, true/false, and essay questions.

Instructor's Manual

The Instructor's Manual contains detailed Chapter Summaries, Chapter Outlines, Suggested Discussion Questions, and Supplemental Web, Visual, and Print Resources. This resource was authored by Craig Pilant, County College of Morris, Joel Anderson, University of Maine, and Mark Ruff, Saint Louis University.

Lecture and Art PowerPoint Slides

The Lecture PowerPoint sets authored by Nicholas Rummell, Trident Technical College, and Matthew Laubacher, Ashford University, combine chapter review, art, and maps.

THE WEST

A NEW HISTORY

Humanity Before History

The early history of human life is a long and complex story. It rests on physical evidence rather than the words of past humans, and has been told by geneticists, climatologists, and archaeologists rather than historians.

It starts in Africa, sometime after 200,000 BCE, when human beings anatomically identical with us—*Homo sapiens*—evolved from primate ancestors. By 130,000 BCE, these humans were migrating out of Africa, north and west into the Near East and Europe. A second wave, sixty or seventy thousand years later, moved eastward along the southern shore of Asia and eventually populated Australia and Micronesia. By 50,000 BCE—possibly long before, though the known archaeological record does not prove this—these humans learned how to make tools—stone blades, for example, in multiple regular shapes—and personal ornaments for men and women. Craft and art, in other words, existed long before humans developed writing.

The blades, scrapers, and brooches that survive from this period reveal a great deal about their makers. *Homo sapiens* was not alone. Earlier forms of human also populated the world—Neanderthal peoples in Europe and the Near East and *Homo erectus* in Africa and Asia. More than a million years ago, these species were using stones that they had shaped to fight one another, butcher animals, and cut wood. As they moved from Africa across the other continents, *Homo sapiens* learned from these older species that different materials, including human and animal bones as well as stones, could be shaped in different ways. They worked out how to strike one stone with another in order

▲ **Cave Painting** The walls of the Chauvet cave at Vallon-Pont-d'Arc, France, preserve a glimpse of early human culture: paintings made by Paleolithic humans around 30,000–28,000 BCE. This scene depicts horses, rhinoceroses, and aurochs (ancestors of modern domestic cattle), and may have served a religious purpose.

to produce a sharp implement for cutting or stabbing, and how to finish that weapon's edge. And they invented ways of teaching these skills to their young. Humans are not genetically programmed to make tools or wear bracelets. But they are programmed, evidently, to develop sets of skills—some of which they borrow from others. By 50,000 BCE or so, in other words, human beings were changing places and learning as they did so. But they were learning slowly. Human culture developed as a glacier moves, very slowly: similar tools are found in deposits separated by thousands of miles and thousands of years.

After 50,000 BCE, in the period known as the Upper Paleolithic, the last period of the Old Stone Age, history began to move more rapidly. Living conditions were hard, especially during the Last Glacial Maximum—the period, lasting approximately from 24,500 to 18,000 BCE, when an ice sheet covered most of northern Europe, forcing most humans to retreat south into Italy, the Iberian Peninsula, and the Balkans. Yet the signs of change were everywhere. Soon after 40,000 BCE, men and women were decorating the walls of caves with paintings of horses, rhinoceroses, and other animals. By 32,000 BCE, they were making and firing human figures out of clay. Some of these images, painted and sculpted, may portray gods or reflect religious visions and practices: evidence that their makers asked questions about the world and devised answers. Soon after 30,000 BCE, they learned how to make and shoot bows and arrows. As the ice retreated, the pace of change picked up. Humans learned to tame and live with animals: herders domesticated reindeer, farmers domesticated dogs, and both were portrayed on the walls and ceilings of caves.

Human ingenuity was already powerful—but not yet powerful enough to overcome the hardships imposed by nature. Sometime around 10,000 BCE two new epochs began. The Neolithic, a period in human history beginning around 10,000 BC and lasting 5000 to 7000 years, marked a transition in human culture. As we will soon see, settled societies took shape and their inhabitants intensively developed techniques for exploiting nature. The beginning of this historical era corresponded roughly with the start of a new geological period, the Holocene, which continues to the present. After thousands of years of violent fluctuations, temperatures stabilized at a new high level, where they have generally remained ever since. Such periods of warmth have been relatively short by the measure of geologic time. They come about, seemingly, every

▲ **Stone Tools** These sharp-edged tools from the Upper Paleolithic may have been used to tip spears, carve bone and horn, or fashion other tools.

hundred thousand years or so. Their effects are dramatic, and not always benign. The opening of the Holocene was accompanied by the extinction of such large mammals as the Mastodon and the Mammoth.

For humans, however, the new climate system offered unique opportunities to apply their skills and ingenuity in new ways. In the first place, agriculture—intensive, systematic cultivation of plants and animals—now became possible. In the Near East—as we will see in more detail in the first chapter—farmers cultivated cereals and raised animals for multiple purposes. Gradually, evolution cooperated with culture. At first, wild grasses were cut and their seeds pounded in mortars. Over time, systematic harvesting favored grasses like wheat and barley, the seeds of which lent themselves to human use. Herbivores—cattle and sheep above all—living in symbiosis with humans spread across the Eurasian land mass. Farming for cereals and dairy products developed with them.

In many cases, techniques passed from one place and people to another. Near Eastern farming techniques moved in all directions, reaching all the way east to India by 5000 BCE and all the way west to Britain by 4000 BCE.

EARLY HUMANITY

PLEISTOCENE EPOCH ca. 2,600,000–10,000 BCE	**PALEOLITHIC PERIOD (CA. 2,500,000–10,000 BCE)**	
	ca. 200,000 BCE	*Homo sapiens* evolve from primate ancestors
	ca. 130,000 BCE	Migration out of Africa
	By ca. 50,000 BCE	Invention of tools
HOLOCENE EPOCH ca. 10,000 BCE–Present	**NEOLITHIC PERIOD (CA. 10,000–4000 BCE)**	
	ca. 10,000 BCE	Invention of agriculture
	By ca. 8000 BCE	Settlement of first towns
	By ca. 4000 BCE	Near Eastern farming techniques reach Britain

In other cases, though, humans showed their ability as independent inventors. The natives of the Americas were nomads when, around 20,000 years ago, they crossed the land bridge that connected Asia with North America. In the Americas, they developed their own systems of cultivation in the fourth millennium BCE, growing maize (corn) and domesticating the llama, neither of which came from Eurasia. Did culture cross continents through colonization, through peaceful contact, or by independent inspiration? All of the above.

By now, inventions were radically changing the texture of human life. Consider the clay pot and the storehouse. By 8000 BCE at the latest, cultivators had begun to settle down in towns like Jericho, in Palestine. They were accumulating large amounts of seed and food, which they had to protect against both the elements and hungry animals. Large clay pots, crude and unadorned, provided a more-or-less airtight and rodent-free form of storage for grain and other edibles. Other inventions followed: the wheel, the cart, and the plow. The culture of sedentary cultivators became more and more complex—and more and more different from that of the nomads who still wandered with their herds, gathering and hunting what they needed rather than winning it from the earth. In settled communities, living standards rose. So did social hierarchies and diseases, like technologies, spread rapidly from one settlement to another.

Stone and clay were highly adaptable, but they had their limits. When points or blades were fashioned thin enough to cut well, they became fragile. Pottery lasted well unless struck by hard objects, but was often thick and clumsy. Neither was well suited for jewelry. Early in the Holocene, individuals learned that hammering could change the shape of metals—especially copper and gold. Later they found that heat could be applied to make metals thinner without depriving them of all their strength. Copper, for instance, abundant and relatively easy to work, could be made stronger when alloyed with tin to form bronze. In

▲ **Neolithic Pottery** This pottery bowl was handmade around 5500–5000 BCE by the Halaf people of what is now Iraq. The pattern is an early example of painting on pottery in the Near East.

time, techniques for smelting and working iron ore in large quantities were developed. The forge, with its anvils and hammers, became a central feature of social life, and a new world of weapons, tools, and ornaments appeared.

Soon the settled people would be writing. That is another story—the story with which this book properly begins. It is, as we will see, rich and dramatic, and involves many changes as well as some continuities. Many of the characteristics that humans had acquired in the early centuries of the Holocene would continue to shape their lives. They moved, endlessly, in search of new places to settle and new resources to exploit. They enslaved others and appropriated their labor. They were inventive, both at devising new tools and decorations and at passing them on to further generations. But they were also receptive: where one people devised its own ways of breaking the earth, five more borrowed them from others.

They recognized no limits to their power. The smoke of their forges and kilns blackened the skies, leaving a trail of dirt that can still be detected in the thick ice cap of the North Pole—though possibly not for very much longer. In some areas—such as Palestine, which was denuded of trees by 6000 BCE—their needs led to disastrous deforestation and other environmental damage. Humans were no longer simply the victims of their natural environments, forced to move as ice sheets covered what had once been habitats they loved and decorated. They were actively changing the environment they lived in—a process that has continued through the Holocene, transforming the face of the world over and over again. The continuity between human life before the invention of writing and after is nowhere clearer than in the endless social and technological innovations that have made possible our exploitation of the earth.

5900–4300 BCE
Mesopotamians irrigate land
between Tigris and Euphrates Rivers

ca. 4000 BCE
Sumerians establish
city of Uruk

From 4000 BCE
Semitic peoples
settle in Near East

By 3000 BCE
Writing developed
in Mesopotamia

ca. 3000 BCE
Egyptian kings unite
Upper and Lower Egypt

By 2700 BCE
Minoan civilization
emerges

19th century BCE
Amorites found
city of Babylon

ca. 1754 BCE
Hammurabi writes
his code of laws

16th century BCE
Horse-drawn chariot
becomes common
in battle

2300–1200 BCE
Mesopotamian empires
Sumer, Akkad, Assyria,
and Babylon form

By 1450 BCE
Mycenaean civilization
forms in Greece

12th century BCE
Bronze Age Crisis

1100–700 BCE
Greek Iron Age

From 11th c. BCE
Assyrians reemerge as
leaders of a massive
military empire

Origins

THE NEAR EAST, EGYPT, AND GREECE

12,000–600 BCE

On a winter day sometime around 700 BCE, a Greek chieftain sat with his family and retainers in the smoky main hall of his house. They had sacrificed an ox; burnt its bones, along with barley and cakes, as an offering to the gods; and roasted the rest for themselves. The men had eaten the meat and drunk large cups of wine diluted with water. Still reclining, as they had while eating, they discussed the things that mattered to them most: prospects for trade and warfare, the family histories of friends and enemies, the chances of marriage among members of their class, and the like. The women, after serving them, had remained, silent but present.

A bard began to recite:

> When early dawn appeared, rosy-fingered,
> The dear son of Odysseus rose from his bed,
> Put on his clothing, hung a sharp sword from his shoulder,
> And laced his handsome sandals to his shining feet.
> He left his room, his face like a god's.
> Immediately he asked the clear-voiced heralds
> To call the long-haired Greeks to an assembly.

Reliefs from King Assurbanipal's Palace These large panels relate a vivid narrative of a great Assyrian victory over their long-standing enemies, the Elamites, around 653 BCE. The battle's climax is depicted here, with Assyrian soldiers brutally killing the Elamite leader and preserving his head as a trophy.

goddess who transforms Odysseus's crew into pigs with her magical potions. Later in this chapter, we will come back to Homer and examine his work, as well as the eighth-century BCE revolution in Greek culture that it belonged to. For now, we will look—as the characters in his stories did—outside the Greek world, to the south and east, where, as the Greeks knew well, societies far older than theirs had built great cities and powerful empires.

THE NEAR EAST TO THE BRONZE AGE CRISIS

It was in the ancient Near East—a vast territory in southwestern Asia that now makes up parts of Iran, Iraq, Syria, Palestine, and the northern region of Egypt—that much of **civilization** as we know it came into being. This immense, open landmass attracted migrants and invaders of many kinds. From the fourth millennium BCE, Semitic peoples—groups that spoke the ancestral languages of modern Arabic and Hebrew—settled here, coming into contact and, often, into conflict. Here plants and animals were **domesticated**, clay was transformed into pottery, wheels were fashioned and used for chariots and carts. Cities were built—and then assembled, sometimes by force, into empires. Here **monotheistic** religions and mathematical sciences both took shape for the first time. Without these diverse inheritances, our own civilization could never have come into being.

This region was defined to the east by the mountains that bound the Iranian plateau, to the west by the Mediterranean Sea and the border of the cultivated area of Egypt, to the north by the Black Sea and the Caucasus Mountains, and to the south by the Arabian Desert. The core area of settlement within it, the so-called Fertile Crescent, stretched from the Persian Gulf in the southeast, through Egypt, to the Levant (an area corresponding to modern Palestine, Syria, and western Jordan) in the northwest. For thousands of years, as late as the Mesolithic Period (20,000–12,000 BCE), individuals and small groups with their herds ranged across the vast plateau and hills, never remaining long in one spot. Groups came from the northwest (Asia Minor and beyond) and the southeast (the area known today as India), some passing through and others remaining to establish footholds.

> The heralds called, and the Achaians quickly assembled.
> When the gathering had come together,
> He came straight into the assembly, a bronze spear in his hand,
> Not alone, for two swift dogs followed him,
> And Athena rained grace upon him.
> When he arrived, the people stared at him,
> As he sat in his father's throne, and the elders yielded to him.

This traditional story is one episode from a long series of tales about an older world in which men and gods mingled freely. In this case, Telemachus, son of the Greek hero Odysseus, has become a man during his father's participation in the long siege of Troy, a city-state on the distant coast of Asia Minor. Idle noblemen have gathered in Odysseus's house to feast and drink. Believing Odysseus must now be dead, they demand that Telemachus's mother marry one of them. Telemachus calls an assembly of the Achaeans—the men of Ithaca, the land his father had ruled. Because Athena, goddess of wisdom and daughter of Zeus, loves Odysseus, she helps his son by giving him a powerful, almost divine presence. The assembly eventually breaks up in disorder, but Telemachus takes the opportunity to outfit a ship and sail away in search of information about his father.

With that action the *Odyssey*—one of two Greek epics ascribed to a poet named Homer—was under way. Other parts of the poem take its characters—and its listeners—across the Aegean Sea, where they visit strange settlements and encounter everything from storms and monsters to a

NEOLITHIC AGRICULTURAL SETTLEMENTS (12,000–4300 BCE)

As early as 12,000 BCE, settlements of a new kind sprang up in the region. Earlier societies had moved, slowly but constantly, in search of grazing land for their herds. Now, in the period known as the Neolithic or New Stone Age, people began settling in one place, mostly in hillside villages: clusters of a few dozen mud houses, each with a few rooms and an open area around it, surrounded by cultivated land. Gradually these groups learned that they could improve both plants and animals by choosing seeds or particular animals and cross-breeding them. They began to grow barley with larger, softer grains and to raise sheep with richer meat and thicker, softer wool.

They also began to make more sophisticated tools and utensils, which enabled them to cultivate the land more intensively and to keep any surplus from what they grew. Seeds and other supplies had traditionally been stored in leather bags, which were vulnerable to moisture. Now the villagers worked out how to turn, fire, and glaze clay vessels. The decorated pottery that this new technology produced enabled them to store seeds and other products for much longer periods. The wheel, also invented around this time, was put to use in plows and carts.

Most of these **agricultural** settlements remained small during this period. They were largely populated by clans of connected families, which likely managed their business by making collective decisions.

IRRIGATION IN MESOPOTAMIA

Between roughly 5900 and 4300 BCE, the new agricultural civilization moved down into the plains. The southern

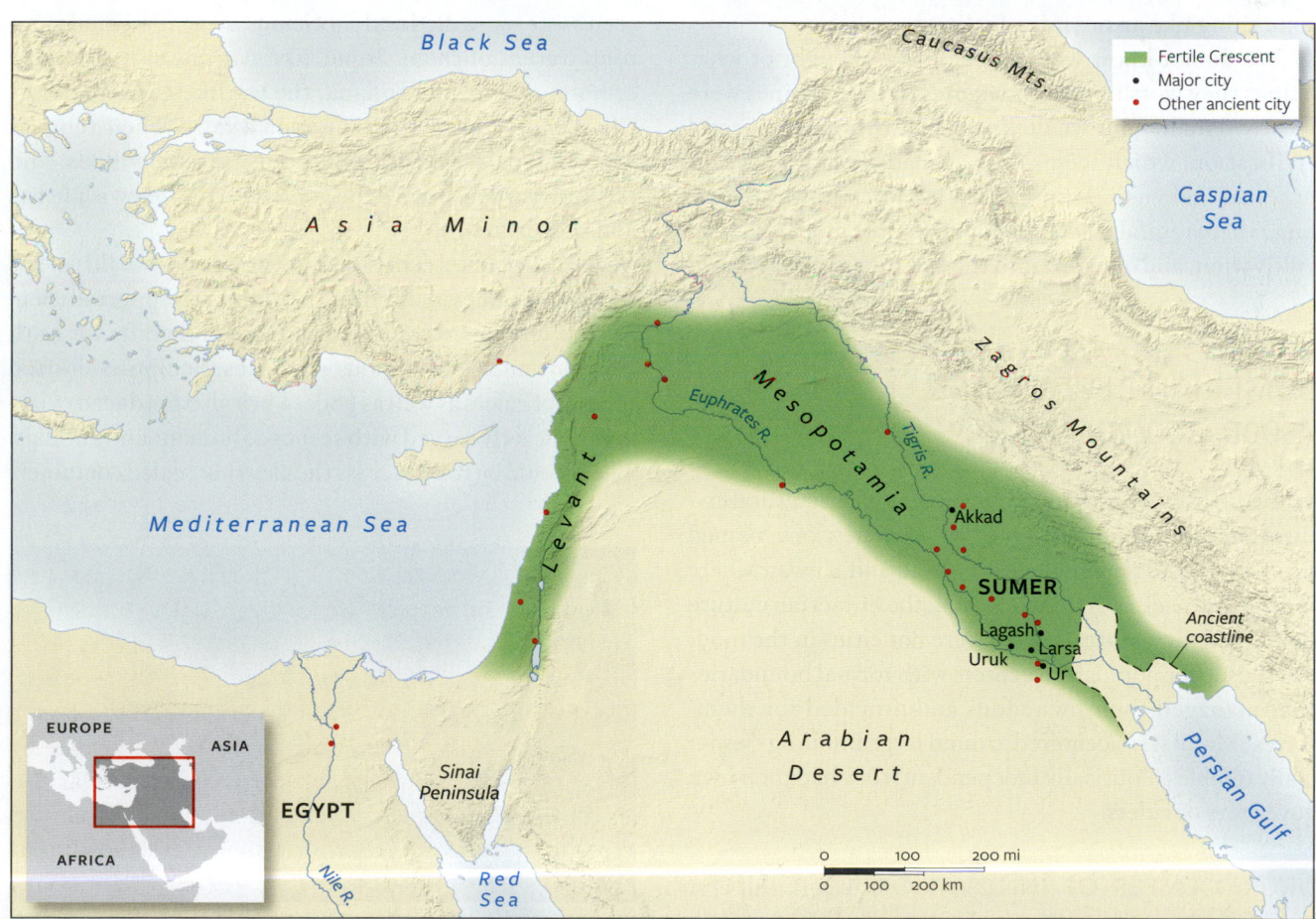

The Ancient Near East, ca. 3000 BCE The innovative Sumerian culture in southern Mesopotamia centered on the major city-states of Ur, Uruk, Lagash, and Larsa. But other cities lined the Tigris and Euphrates Rivers throughout Mesopotamia; and soon after, monarchs ruled a unified Egypt. Throughout the Near East, settlements were built along rivers, where irrigation allowed for agriculture and the support of large populations.

flatlands of southwestern Asia receive little or no rain, but in Mesopotamia—the alluvial plain created by the Tigris and Euphrates Rivers—new possibilities for agriculture existed. Natural flooding occurred each spring, depositing rich sediment along the riverbanks. Irrigation controls were then needed to draw the springtime floodwaters away from the new seedlings and bring water back to the fields after flood season to nourish the crops through the arid summer.

The land, once treated in this way, became astonishingly fertile: in some areas, it returned as much as ten times the amount of grain used to seed it (for comparison, normal land fertilized in a traditional way might return two to four times the amount of seed sown in it). To dig and maintain the necessary irrigation trenches, specialized, stable labor forces developed, and some villages grew much larger than others. Surplus grain was collected and sold, and the profits supported new, larger projects. Shrines arose, built on raised platforms—a first sign of something like an organized religion.

We do not know what these people thought or what beings they worshipped (the figures in their shrines were mostly female). But we do know that this new, peaceful civilization, which seems to have made few or no weapons, had real vigor. It spread to the north in Mesopotamia, where rainfall and wells could support more intensive cultivation, and outward into the Levant and Asia Minor.

SUMERIAN CITY-STATES (5000–3000 BCE)

In the fifth and fourth millennia BCE, this agricultural civilization of Mesopotamia gave way to a new one, named for Sumer—the region in modern Iraq and Kuwait where it came into being. After 5000 BCE, the Sumerian culture developed **city-states**. These were not cities in the modern sense, but population centers with formal boundaries that managed their own lands and provided for themselves. Many were centered around large buildings, especially temples. Politically independent, they had their own governors or rulers.

URUK: CENTER OF INNOVATION Uruk, the first great Sumerian city, arose after 4000 BCE in the far south of Mesopotamia, near the Persian Gulf. Varied ecologies came together there: soil fertilized by floods for farming, steppes for flocks, and marshes where fish and birds could be hunted. The relative abundance of food enabled some

inhabitants to specialize in crafts, which in turn allowed the settlement to develop on a scale never seen before. The walls of Uruk, at their greatest extent, were more than six miles in circumference, and the city probably had 50,000 or more inhabitants. At the beginning of the third millennium BCE, it was the biggest city in the world. Uruk may have established colonies as well: other cities, often on water routes, from the Mediterranean to areas of modern Iran, were built on similar lines and likely engaged in trade with Uruk. Perhaps these cities supplied materials that were in short supply in Uruk, such as timber and stone.

In place of modest shrines, Uruk had temples— vast complexes of buildings set on platforms, known as **ziggurats**, their walls decorated with colored clay cones set in patterns. The temples administered extensive lands of their own, which were cultivated by a large labor force, its members apparently free, whom the temples paid and fed. Their work sustained the priests and the artisans. The gods, male and female, were imagined in human form and seen as strong-willed and capricious. Artists created stunning statues of them. Some, like An, the sky god, were remote; others, like Innana, the warlike goddess of fertility, engaged directly in human affairs. Their temples were like palaces, with bedrooms, assembly halls, and pleasure gardens where the gods were regaled with feasts and concerts.

Uruk became a center of innovation. The wealth of the city's rulers attracted skillful artisans and supported them as they developed sophisticated arts and crafts for both religious and nonreligious purposes. Sculptors crafted images of rulers as well as gods. They also produced cylinders delicately carved with scenes of humans and animals. These could be rolled across the clay that sealed containers

Ziggurats Religious life in Sumerian cities centered on the large temples called ziggurats. They featured stacked terraces accessible by several sets of steps, often with a shrine at the top. This temple of Nanna, built in Ur around 2100 BCE by King Ur-Nammu, was one of the largest.

and storerooms to assert a person's ownership of the contents. New skills developed: the inhabitants experimented with new ways of fabricating uniform bricks for building and laying out plots of land for cultivation. Large households supported staffs of workers—legally free men and women who were paid for their labor, the scanty records suggest, in food and housing. This seems to have been the condition of most of the ordinary men and women who built the temple walls and grew the crops.

URUK AND THE DEVELOPMENT OF WRITING

Most remarkable, Uruk's inhabitants invented writing. For the first time in human history, people could keep formal records, and thus preserve the memory of their political and economic achievements long after the physical traces of them had been obliterated. It all started, in the fourth millennium BCE and perhaps before, with counters—little clay spheres or tokens marked with symbols of possessions to be inventoried. Throughout Mesopotamia, these were assembled in clay envelopes, which were then inscribed with the number of tokens they contained. The earliest symbolic representations were not as consistent as later writing, and they did not yet rest on coherent abstract understandings of, for example, numbers. The same sign could stand for different numbers of different commodities.

By the beginning of the third millennium BCE, these methods developed into the "Uruk system"—writing in the full sense. Both pictures and abstract symbols represented Sumerian words on the same clay spheres, almost 6,000 of which survive. The scribes who made them used their complex system—comprising more than 1,900 characters—for many purposes, from maintaining receipts to managing account books. They compiled lists of the names of animals, tools, and professions into the first dictionaries, probably to train the professional scribes who were the only ones to master this difficult but powerful early form of writing. Scribes made themselves indispensable to temples and other authorities, and were rewarded accordingly, as one noted: "The scribal art is a good lot, one of wealth and plenty."

The Uruk system was complicated and difficult to use because it is hard to draw lines and curves in clay. Over time, the scribes developed a system of writing that used combinations of wedge shapes, called **cuneiform**, which was both more practical and more abstract. The wedge shapes were used to represent individual sounds and, in combination, whole words, rather than to depict objects. The thousands of surviving tablets from Near Eastern cities preserve everything from treaties and other official

Cuneiform On a clay tablet dating from 2100–2000 BCE, the barley ration allocated to seventeen gardeners was recorded by a scribe using the complex cuneiform writing system.

documents to prayers and epic poems, in Sumerian, Akkadian, and other languages—the work of generations of highly trained scribes, who played central roles in the government of all Near Eastern states.

MESOPOTAMIAN EMPIRES (2300–1700 BCE)

During the third millennium BCE, powerful states formed in the region: Sumer and Akkad, Assyria and the Amorite kingdoms, and Babylon. The earlier city-states of Mesopotamia had competed for resources and clashed when their interests dictated. But Akkad, Assyria, the Amorite kingdoms, and Babylon were different. The rulers of these great empires set out not only to conquer other states but to incorporate them in their own domains, installing their own governors. They amassed precious metals through conquest and tribute, and displayed them lavishly to buttress their claims to power. Above all, they claimed divine status for themselves. Reliefs portrayed emperors wearing

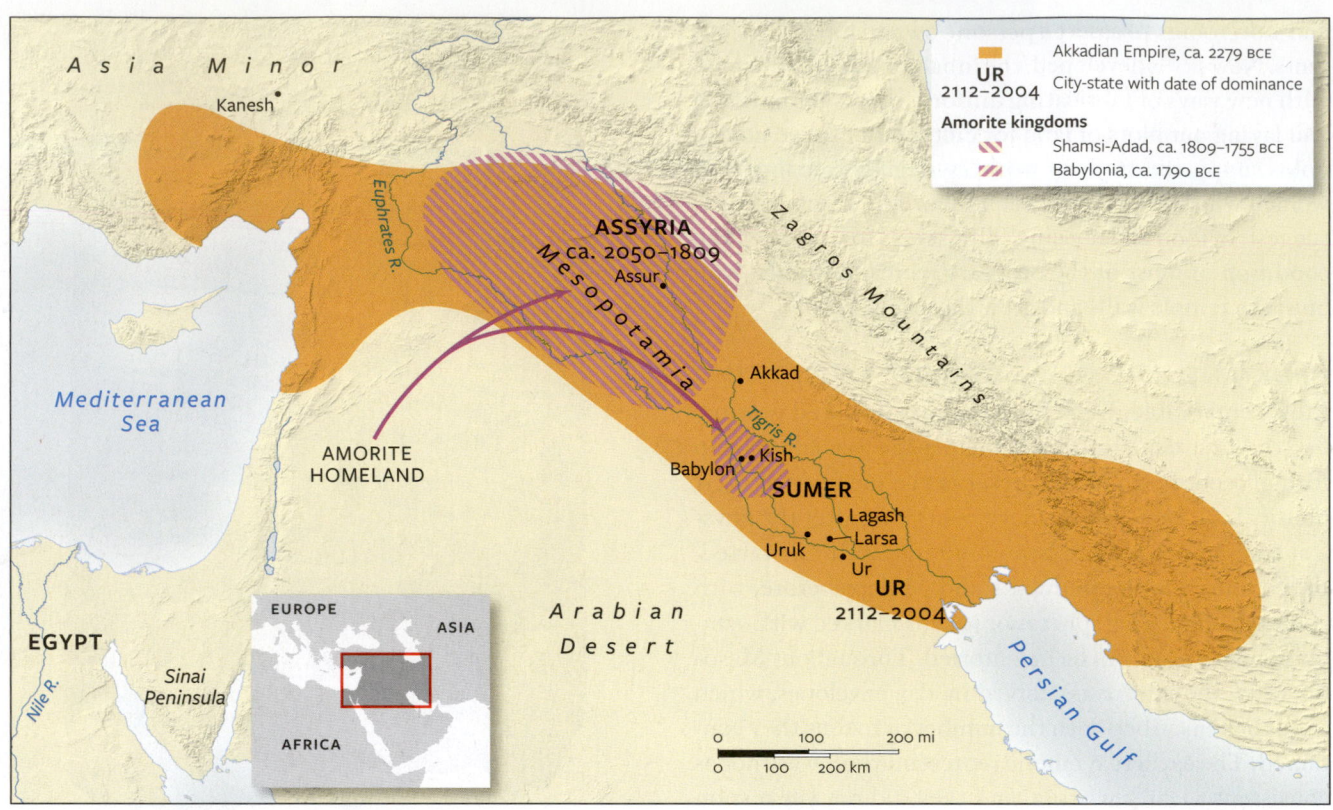

Mesopotamian Empires, 2300–1700 BCE The Akkadian Empire spread from the city of Kish to govern vast territory across Mesopotamia. When the empire collapsed (by 2154 BCE), smaller empires centered on capital cities took shape: Ur in southern Mesopotamia and Assur in Assyria. Some 350 years later, the Amorites came from Syria to establish kingdoms in northern and central Mesopotamia. Economic, political, and military links allowed rulers to control large areas outside their capitals.

the signs of divine status and ascending into the realm of the gods. These states did far more than maintain order and protect cultivation; they were aggressive, fast moving, and unwilling to recognize any limits to their power and authority.

SARGON AND THE AKKADIAN EMPIRE (2334–2112 BCE)

The greatest of the early emperors—Sargon (r. 2334–2279 BCE) of the central Mesopotamian city of Akkad—usurped the throne of the Sumerian city of Kish, and then embarked on a comprehensive program of invasion and conquest. Leading lancers and bowmen who moved far more quickly than the Sumerians with their heavy battle wagons, Sargon defeated them and amassed power across Mesopotamia.

Sargon also seems to have conquered the rulers of Asia Minor and Arabia. He appointed a force of soldiers and administrators, some 5,400 strong, whom he fed every day and on whom he could rely absolutely. His Akkadian Empire ruled Sumeria and maintained diplomatic relations with other lands as far away as the Mediterranean.

He was remembered as a great general who conquered all opponents, destroying one city that opposed him, according to a chronicle, "to the last spot on which a bird could perch." Sargon also replaced Sumerian, the dominant language of the area, with Akkadian, a Semitic language, so far as practical affairs were concerned. (Sumerian continued to be used for religious purposes.) For the first time in known human history, a brilliant military leader had set out, successfully, to build an empire.

UR (2112–2004 BCE)

After Sargon's death in 2279, revolts broke out, and though his sons extended the Akkadian Empire's territory, it collapsed by 2154. For nearly a century, from 2112 to 2004 BCE, the Sumerian city of Ur in the far south of Mesopotamia held dominance. Ur-Nammu, brother of the king of Uruk, made Ur his capital. He claimed to be king "of Sumer and Akkad," and he founded a dynasty, now known as the Third Dynasty of Ur. Like the Sumerian kings, those of Ur claimed divine favor and superhuman abilities: "When I sprang up," a hymn about a later king reads, "muscular as a cheetah, galloping like a thoroughbred ass at full gallop, the favor of the god An brought me joy." The kings of Ur ruled a large state composed of what had formerly been independent cities. Governors, chosen from prominent local families, administered those in the heartland. Others were ruled directly by military garrisons.

The state of Ur was powerful. Each province paid heavy taxes in goods particular to it: grain in one case; wood, reeds, and leather in another. Military provinces were forced to pay tribute in cattle, sheep, and goats. Some of the revenues went to support local governments. More, however, went to the kings, who used their wealth to maintain and extend the canals that irrigated the land. Most labor was legally free, but the state conscripted hundreds of men and women, some to work on the canals year-round, paying them with food and other necessities. The state also maintained substantial armies and a corps of scribes that kept elaborate records of its income, expenses, and diplomatic correspondence.

ASSYRIANS AND AMORITES (2050–1700 BCE)

Yet conditions were not stable. In the middle of the twenty-first century BCE, the Assyrians threw off the domination of Ur, whose empire broke up, and established their freedom. Assur, in northern Mesopotamia, became a prosperous merchant city with a distinctive constitution. A council of elders served as a brake on the power of the king of Assur. Even more unusual, every year a citizen was selected by lot to collect the taxes. In much of Mesopotamia, years were named after rulers; in Assur, they were named after this official. The merchants of Assur built family partnerships. Using their own resources, not state support, they spun extensive networks. In the city of Kanesh in central Asia Minor, as far from Assur as Chicago is from New York City, they built their own settlement, where they successfully sold rich fabrics from Mesopotamia. Constant correspondence maintained both trade and family relations across long distances.

For two centuries, the Assyrian kings successfully defended and enlarged their kingdom. But the Amorites, a Semitic pastoral people, came into the land from Syria during the period of Ur's hegemony. Seminomadic, they lived with their flocks of sheep and goats, staying with them in river towns in the summers and moving out into the steppe in the winters. Organized in tribes, the Amorites seemed uncivilized to city dwellers: "He is dressed in sheep's skins; He lives in tents in wind and rain; He doesn't offer sacrifices." Gradually, however, they integrated themselves into southern Mesopotamia, taking up residence in cities as well as in the countryside. In 1809

Standard of Ur This mosaic of shell, limestone, and lapis lazuli buried in a large grave at the Royal Cemetery of Ur around 2550 BCE depicts the soldiers and chariots of Ur.

BCE the Amorite Shamsi-Adad I deposed the native king of Assyria, took his place, and created an empire across northern Mesopotamia.

After the breakup of Sumerian rule in the south, other kingdoms whose rulers bore Amorite names were established throughout Mesopotamia. The Amorites divided large blocks of land devoted to supporting the temples and claimed that they had "freed the inhabitants of cities"—a process that remains mysterious. Larsa and other Amorite kingdoms depended on local tribal leaders to maintain herds and farms and to collect taxes on their behalf. A free-wheeling economy developed in the Amorite cities: individuals bought and sold properties and joined together to invest, for example, in merchant ships that sailed the Tigris and Euphrates Rivers down to the Persian Gulf.

The Amorite kings continued to claim divine status, and in their temples the old gods were worshipped in the traditional way. Slowly—we do not know exactly when or how—the idea grew up that kingship should be transmitted from one semidivine figure to his son, and onward in the direct male line of descent. Dynasties—series of monarchs from the same family—now took shape, and new rulers, especially those whose authority might be shaky, liked to claim that they, too, were descended from an ancient lineage of kings.

In the nineteenth century BCE, an Amorite dynasty

founded the city of Babylon in the center of Mesopotamia. The city rose to great wealth and power, and under Hammurabi in the eighteenth century BCE it became the capital of an empire in its own right. It became, as we will see, one of the principal centers of the distinctive civilization of the ancient Near East, playing a central role in the development of law, religion, and divination.

STATE AND ECONOMY IN THE ANCIENT NEAR EAST

These new states of the ancient Near East mobilized resources on a vast scale. Tens of thousands of tablets record official efforts to build and administer a command economy. They drew together large numbers of workers, not by enslaving them but by requiring them to put in a month or two a year as laborers on state projects such as irrigation systems. Even scribes and other individuals of high status could find themselves forced to provide labor in this way.

Conscripted workers built enormous temples out of durable materials, such as blocks of limestone, which were transported from quarries in the desert to create façades of sufficient strength and dignity. Their lot must have been hard: occasionally individuals or small groups tried to flee rather than work. In addition to conscript labor, slavery was a presence throughout the ancient Near East. Institutions and families held slaves, whose status was clearly lower than that of free people. Official documents assumed that Mesopotamians would not enslave other Mesopotamians, and warned the young against capture by slavers who worked from the mountains to the northeast. Many slaves were captured in war.

New technologies helped the developing states of the region to thrive. The plow adopted at Uruk, which had an automatic feeder to place seeds at proper intervals in the furrows it dug, made the soil of the Fertile Crescent live up to its modern name. The smiths of Mesopotamia became expert at working copper and tin into durable bronze, the material of choice for both weapons and tools. This favorite metal gave its name to the larger historical period in which the societies of the ancient Near East and early Greece took shape. The Bronze Age, as we will see, would last until almost the end of the second millennium BCE. The restless ingenuity of the artisans whom the state employed helped create the splendor of the Mesopotamian states.

These states had more in mind than displaying their wealth and the brilliance of their crafts. They devoted massive resources to supporting military professionals, especially after the rise of the horse-drawn chariot in the sixteenth century BCE. But at the same time, aristocratic families built up vast land holdings, which could escape the control of central authorities. Basic institutions could spin into disorder, as sheer scale and weight pulled them apart. Instability and defeat always threatened. Rulers and diplomats did their best to maintain alliances and respond immediately to threats, but the second duty often canceled the first: "He makes peace with one king"—so a ruler wrote of one of his fellows—"and swears an oath, then he makes peace with another king and swears an oath, then he repudiates the previous king he made peace with, as well as the new king he made peace with." Again and again, assassinations toppled royal dynasties.

NEAR EASTERN RELIGIONS

Mesopotamian cities were sacred as well as political spaces. Near Eastern religions were **polytheistic**—a form of belief and practice that can be hard for many in the West today, used to the exclusive claims of monotheism, to appreciate. Mesopotamian men and women acknowledged multiple gods, whose cults were supported by public rather than individual action. Though more powerful than human beings, these gods were not omnipotent or omniscient: each one carried out particular tasks, and gods and human beings could in some cases conceal their deeds from the divine view. Some gods died, especially those whose function had to do with fertility. Others entered battle on behalf of their supporters—a relief at Lagash shows one god capturing the city's enemies in a net and striking them with a mace. The gods of Mesopotamia were believed to inhabit the statues that represented them in the temples. When a city was defeated and its conquerors carried the statues away as booty, its inhabitants knew that the gods were angry with them and had departed.

As peoples traded goods, migrated, and fought, they began to notice one another's gods and temples, and to compare them—perhaps the first efforts to understand the universe. Polytheism is usually flexible: a common response to an encounter with a new and attractive god was to adopt his or her worship, enlarging one's pantheon. As a strategy this could prove especially helpful to monarchs trying, as so many did, to integrate foreign peoples into their expanding states.

DIVINATION Most Mesopotamian religions centered on **divination**—formal ways of predicting the future, especially that of the ruler and his people. With state power precarious and invasion often threatening, rulers sought ways to gain knowledge of what was to come, and priests did their best to supply this. They imagined the universe as a complex, buzzing web of messages about the future. Nothing was accidental, everything was predetermined, and the gods continually provided signs that revealed the future to those who could interpret them. Every time an animal was sacrificed, the form of its liver told informed interpreters what the kingdom could expect. In practice, interpreters often disagreed about particular signs, and temples competed to offer the most accurate predictions.

FROM ASTROLOGY TO ASTRONOMY Over a period of about a thousand years, from roughly 1800 BCE onward, Mesopotamian priests and scribes developed a sophisticated form of astronomy. From atop their ziggurats, they charted the stars and worked out that the motions of the sun, moon, and planets repeated themselves. In the belief that the motions of the stars also provided information about the future, interpreters at first declared what eclipses and the planetary positions portended for the kingdom as a whole. Eventually they decided that the heavens also determined the fates of individuals. In the fifth century BCE, diviners began compiling collections of individual horoscopes—charts of the positions of the planets at the day and time of a person's birth. The horoscopes that still flourish in newspapers and on the Web are a living remnant of an ancient Near Eastern vision of the universe. So, too, is the astronomy that scientists practice in observatories and teach in universities. The first quantitative science in history was born out of what today looks like superstition.

RULES OF CONDUCT: HAMMURABI'S CODE

It is not only agriculture, pottery, and mathematical science that we have inherited from the ancient Near East. For all the chaos and mutual distrust, the rulers of ancient Mesopotamia created fundamental features of Western political and administrative practice. From Uruk on, scribes developed systems for recording city revenues and expenses in publicly archived documents. Working together, rulers and scribes also recorded formal rules for governing conduct in public and private, with provisions for enforcement and punishment of violators.

Around 1754 BCE Hammurabi, the sixth king of Babylon, set out a code of specific statements about justice, couched in the everyday language of ordinary people. This **Code of Hammurabi** was probably not meant to govern the conduct of courts—contemporary legal documents do not refer to it—but to serve as a record of the ways in which Hammurabi had pursued justice. Some 300 laws and cases were copied on clay tablets and on at least one basalt stele, a tall stone slab. In this monumental form, the code makes a claim to divine sanction. Hammurabi himself appears in a relief sculpture at the top of the stone, wearing a royal headdress and showing reverence to the sun-god, who brings him his rod and ring, the symbols of authority. Modesty was not Hammurabi's vice: in an inscription, he claimed that he had led his people "into green pastures" and prevented them from ever having to worry.

Hammurabi's pronouncements were not meant to

Hammurabi's Code The top of this stele, or stone slab, from the eighteenth century BCE is a portrait of Hammurabi seated on a throne, receiving his rod and ring, the insignia of his power, from the sun-god. The text of the Code is carved in cuneiform at the bottom.

serve as a form of legislation in the modern sense. In normal Babylonian life, professional judges dealt with civil actions, such as lawsuits over property, for a fee, and judges working with a second body of elders presided over serious criminal cases. Verdicts imposing the death penalty—which was given for crimes ranging from burglary and encroaching on the king's highway to incest and adultery—could be appealed to the king, who had an absolute right to bestow pardons. There was not much place for a comprehensive legal code. But the fragments of earlier laws that archaeologists have unearthed make clear that Hammurabi followed Babylonian tradition when he tried to show how actions should be connected with their consequences.

A ruler with a passion for detail, Hammurabi examined relations between husbands and wives, sellers and buyers, masters and slaves. His code incorporated a strictly hierarchical vision of society. Individuals were classified, and penalties assessed, by social standing: "If anyone strikes the body of a man higher in rank than he, he shall receive sixty blows with an ox-whip in public"; "If a freeborn man strikes the body of another freeborn man of equal rank, he shall pay one gold mina"; "If the slave of a freedman strikes the body of a freedman, his ear shall be cut off." Hammurabi's rules made no evident allowances for mitigating circumstances: "If anyone commits a robbery and is caught, he shall be put to death." But by providing procedures for investigation when the truth of a matter was in doubt, they showed a clear concern for justice.

One could, Hammurabi believed, also do harm to others by engaging the help of malevolent supernatural powers. Fortunately, nature itself could be enlisted to determine whether this had occurred. If one man accused another of putting him under a spell, the accused had to dive into the sacred river. If he drowned, his accuser could take his house. But if he survived, "his accuser shall be put to death. He that plunged into the sacred river shall appropriate the house of him that accused." Perjurers should be liable to appropriate punishment, even if it could not be proved that they had deliberately lied: "If a man has borne false witness in a trial, or has not established the statement that he has made, if that case be a capital trial, that man shall be put to death." Proposed penalties for corrupt officials were severe: large fines and expulsion from office.

Hammurabi had every reason to portray himself as a defender of divine justice. How his subjects responded to these enactments, and how far they were put into practical effect, we cannot know, since he himself provides the little bit of evidence that survives. But it seems clear that Hammurabi, in his passion to represent himself as a just ruler and a servant of the gods, began the process of creating what we now know as legal codes.

EVERYDAY LIFE IN THE ANCIENT NEAR EAST

Like the Code of Hammurabi, much of the evidence of the Mesopotamian archives takes the form of official documents, which tell us more about how kings and elites wished others to behave than whether poor people and slaves actually did as they were supposed to. But enough documents survive to enable us to make some contact with the individual men and women who lived and worked in the region's sophisticated urban societies. Many of them are letters written not by the individuals whose voices they preserve, but by professional scribes following instructions or taking dictation.

VOICES Officials write to subordinates as they try to maintain order and justice: "I have written you repeatedly to bring here the criminal and all the robbers, but you have not brought them here nor have you even sent me word. And so fires started by the robbers are (still raging) and ravaging the countryside. . . . I am holding you responsible for the crimes which are committed in the country." Merchants appear, looking for accurate commercial intelligence and working with partners to avoid losses: "When I stayed there, they (two debtors) told me the following: 'No sale can be made on the market.' Today I hear, however, that many sales are being made on the market. Therefore, make them pay the silver."

Women speak, too—for example, a Sumerian who casts herself on the mercy of her lover: "When I saw you recently, I was just as glad to see you as I was when (long ago) I . . . saw (for the first time) the face of my Lady (the goddess Aja). And you too, my brother, were as glad to see me as I to see you. You said: 'I am going to stay for ten days.' . . . But you left suddenly and I was almost insane for three days. . . . I was more pleased with you than I was ever with anybody else." Even a female slave writes to her master to beg for help because the baby she has been carrying is dead: "May it please my master (to do something) lest I die. Come visit me and let me see the face of my master!"

WORK Many of these men and women worked in the palaces, as slaves captured in war or inherited by members of royal families. Every court needed finely woven and embroidered clothes for rulers and courtiers. Groups of women spun wool and wove it into cloth. Men provided the wool that the women worked, and likely carried out other processes, such as dyeing and finishing the cloth. Women also ground grain, baked bread, and prepared cooling drinks in the summer. Others might serve as entertainers or—in at least one documented case—as a doctor.

Outside the palaces, in the cities, the citizens who inhabited mud-brick houses were legally free and maintained impressively active lives as artisans and traders. Women came to marriage with dowries, carefully listed in binding documents that enabled them to reclaim their property if their husbands died or divorced them. Dowries might include household equipment such as beds and chairs, livestock, or wool. In many merchant households, women and men collaborated effectively. Women bought raw materials and oversaw the making of cloth, while their husbands undertook long treks, either in caravans carrying loads of wool and tin or on ships bearing cargoes for exchange as far away as Bahrain. There they traded grain, wool, silver, and resin for tin and copper. Poets celebrated the island city of Bahrain as a paradise where the ferries ran all night and no servant ever dared to empty dirty bathwater into the street.

A FOUNDATIONAL EPIC: GILGAMESH

In Babylon, which fostered the arts, erotic sculpture and poetry flourished. Here an unknown author of the time of Hammurabi composed the oldest epic that we have—the story of Gilgamesh, a king with almost divine powers who travels the universe, refuses to marry a goddess, and kills the Bull of Heaven when she sends it to avenge the slight. After his traveling companion dies, Gilgamesh sets out on another long and dangerous voyage, in the hope of finding the secret of immortality. He fails—but the failure is a great lesson in itself, since his journey gives him knowledge of the human condition in all its tragic limitations.

Like the Code of Hammurabi, the **Epic of Gilgamesh** was a compilation—a new, comprehensive version, written in Akkadian, of shorter tales that had originally circulated in Sumerian. Both reveal the extraordinary extent to which scribal culture flourished in Babylon: though most scribes spent their lives composing contracts and administrative records, others wrote and rewrote hymns, stories, and religious texts. Many of these were lost for thousands of years because of continued political turmoil. As cities were abandoned, the scribes' tablets were left behind, to be rediscovered and deciphered only in the nineteenth and

twentieth centuries. They provide further proof—if any is needed—that central elements of Western history have their roots in the earliest history of the ancient Near East.

THE HITTITES AND THE ASSYRIAN EMPIRE (1700–1200 BCE)

The Babylonian Empire of Hammurabi briefly dominated Mesopotamia, but dissolved soon after its creator died in 1750 BCE. Alliances between the rulers of the major Amorite kingdoms shifted endlessly, as they challenged one another for supremacy. A revived Assyria conquered much of the territory that had belonged to Babylon, and though the Amorite dynasty retained control of Babylon for a time, it ruled little more than the city.

New peoples—including some who spoke Indo-European languages, which are directly related to the ancestor language of modern English—entered central Asia Minor. Though it is not clear if the Hittites were originally one of these peoples, they adopted the region's Indo-European language as the official language of their court and administration. Their first kingdom took shape around a capital in Hattusa in the eighteenth century BCE and after. A conglomeration of vassal states, the Hittite Empire shifted borders constantly.

While the Hittites engaged in trade and esteemed their merchants highly, they were known above all as fierce and effective warriors. Their armies were a mixture of infantry, drawn from the free Hittite population with added levies from neighboring states, and charioteers. Three-man teams rode and shot their bows from two-wheeled chariots, which were quick but required great skill to manage. These men became professional soldiers, elaborately trained and bound by oaths to their rulers. They learned to fight at night, and when necessary knew how to attack and conquer walled cities using battering rams. And although the Hittites pioneered the forging of iron, a harder metal that would eventually replace bronze for use in weaponry, they used the results mostly in ceremonies, and continued to make their own weapons from bronze.

In 1595 BCE the Hittites conquered Babylon, which they sacked again in 1531, and their allies the Kassites took over rule of the city. Although urban growth slowed under their rule, the Kassites reconstructed older cities across Babylonia and even built a new capital, Dur-Kurigalzu (Fortress of Kurigalzu), with an enormous central palace and temple, in the far north. After 1500 the Hittite kingdom

Mesopotamia to the Bronze Age Crisis, ca. 1400–1200 BCE In the latter half of the second millennium BCE, powerful empires covered a wider area of the Near East: from the Egyptian Empire in the west, stretching all the way to the Levant; to the Hittite Empire in Asia Minor, and their allies the Kassites in Babylonia; to the powerful Assyrian Empire, which by 1200 BCE controlled all of Mesopotamia.

entered a phase of weakness, but in the next century it revived and acted as a great empire.

More and more, however, it was the Assyrian Empire that dominated the area. Ashur-uballit I (r. 1365–1330 BCE) began the process of recovery and expansion. The Assyrians, like the Hittites, made effective use of the chariot in warfare. By the thirteenth century BCE, they had repeatedly prevailed over the Hittites and conquered Kassite Babylon. Assyrian rulers built enormous new palaces and temples at their capital of Ashur and created massive new cities on the Tigris and elsewhere. Their royal servants, rewarded with grants of land, became an aristocracy, while free farmers were largely forced into slavery.

THE BRONZE AGE CRISIS (12TH CENTURY BCE)

At the beginning of the twelfth century BCE, the Near East—like other cultures of the time—entered what historians call the Bronze Age Crisis. The causes of the crisis are controversial: though there is evidence of earthquakes and drought, for example, it is not clear that either had dramatic effects. Those who lived through these great transformations, and others who looked back on them in later centuries, point to disruptive movements of populations. Egyptian observers in the first half of the thirteenth century BCE recorded the attacks of "sea peoples" whom no one seemed able to resist. These powerful invaders—including the Philistines and other nations, their place of origin as uncertain as their reasons for migration—fought their way across the Near East, and continued doing so in the twelfth century. Layers of dateable ash show that cities around the region, including the historical city of Troy, fell to the invaders. The Hittite kingdom collapsed. But the Assyrian Empire, the dominant power in its region, survived and flourished. Nebuchadnezzar I of Babylon (r. 1125–1104 BCE) defeated a rival power to the east, the Elamites, only to be defeated by the Assyrians. Thereafter Assyria dominated Babylon for centuries, even as new Semitic peoples entered and settled in what had been Babylonian territory.

LIFE AND DEATH IN EGYPT (3000–332 BCE)

The states of the ancient Near East were not the only great powers and cultures to take shape in the years after 3000 BCE. Egypt was connected to the Near East by the ecology of the Fertile Crescent and by constant contact, which took every form from brutal warfare to delicate diplomacy. Like the Near Eastern states, Egypt was ruled, from the beginning of the third millennium, by monarchs—the kings, later known as pharaohs—who were thought to have the gods' support and themselves to be divine. Like the Assyrians and Babylonians, the Egyptians built vast temples and other ceremonial buildings. Like them, too, they kept elaborate records using a difficult form of writing practiced by specialized scribes. And like the Near Eastern states, Egypt looked back to origins so ancient that no record described them.

UNIFICATION

In other respects, though, Egypt was distinctive—even unique. The king unified two very different worlds: southern or Upper Egypt, where a narrow band of agricultural land stretched along the Nile River, surrounded by immense deserts; and northern or Lower Egypt, where the Nile branched out into its delta and watered a vast territory of fields and marshes. At some point around 3000 BCE, as the Egyptians themselves remembered, the Nile Valley was fully settled. Mass immigration from Upper Egypt brought peoples from the south into the fertile lands of the Delta, in Lower Egypt.

Somehow—we do not know how—kings took advantage of Egypt's unique topography and unified these peoples. Their achievements were celebrated in powerful images: for example, the Narmer palette (ca. 3000 BCE), a rock slab used to hold pigments for painting, is inscribed on one side with an image of King Narmer the Hawk wearing an Upper Egyptian crown and leading an attack. The reverse shows his soldiers marching and enemy leaders being beheaded. Although there is no evidence that Narmer actually conquered Lower Egypt, the powerful imagery of the palette—which must have taken a skilled artisan hundreds of hours to carve and polish—suggests that to Narmer and his followers, he was the aggressive ruler of a unified country. In the lower part of the Delta, large settlements took shape, with warehouses, threshing

Narmer Palette Dating from the thirty-first century BCE, this large ceremonial palette depicts King Narmer of Upper Egypt conquering his enemies, perhaps a representation of the mythical battles that unified Upper and Lower Egypt. Archaeologists have interpreted some symbols on the palette as the earliest form of Egyptian hieroglyphs.

floors, and slaughterhouses large enough to support a massive population. Eventually—it is not known exactly when—Memphis, at the mouth of the Delta, became the capital of a united Egypt.

A DURABLE MONARCHY

The Egyptian monarchy survived, with intervals of disorder, through thirty dynasties that lasted almost 3,000 years. By the time of the Old Kingdom (2649–2150 BCE), the Egyptians were already building the enormous pyramids for which they are still famous. Through the Middle Kingdom (2030–1640 BCE) and the New Kingdom (1550–1070 BCE), the monarchy remained mostly united. Egypt's strong social and cultural unity prevailed even when a foreign people, the Hyksos, conquered the country around 1650 BCE, and when the pharaoh Akhenaten briefly

Ancient Egypt, 2700–1070 BCE In Egypt, population was centered in fertile areas along the Nile—in the kingdoms of Lower Egypt near the Nile Delta and in Upper Egypt farther upstream, which were unified in 2700 BCE. The Egyptians then spread north as far as the Euphrates during the Middle Kingdom period and farther up the Nile during the New Kingdom, despite challenges such as the invasion of the Hyksos people in 1650 BCE.

introduced a monotheistic religion in the fourteenth century. During the early Bronze Age Crisis, the Egyptians fought off the Sea Peoples again and again. Rameses III (r. ca. 1186–1155 BCE) conducted three victorious campaigns against them, but at great cost: he was assassinated and his successors proved weak. Attacks by Libyan and other

African peoples, and a revolt by Canaanite peoples whom the Egyptians had conquered, took a further toll. Yet even in the centuries of relative weakness that followed, Egypt continued to challenge the power of Assyria and to maintain its own religious and artistic traditions.

Amid its remarkable longevity, the Egyptian state experienced change. After the collapse of the Old Kingdom, power passed to local governors and priests. One reason that the kings of the subsequent Middle Kingdom built extraordinarily lavish temples and tombs was that they had to convince important local officials to accept them as divinely appointed monarchs and to recognize their prerogatives. But even in Egypt's last period of native rule (664–332 BCE), which was interrupted twice when the Persian Empire (a powerful state that emerged in modern Iran) conquered and occupied it, the Egyptians saw their land as the oldest and grandest of states, favored by the gods. They passionately argued that their traditions had lasted seamlessly over the millennia—and never more passionately than after they had suffered a defeat. In the first millennium BCE, when Egypt was conquered by Assyria in the seventh century and then by Persia in the sixth and fourth, their sculptures of pharaohs made clear that the kingdom had not suffered any substantial change. More even than the ancient Near East, Egypt offered a powerful political and social model: a single land, vast in extent and varied in its terrain, unified under the rule of a single king who enjoyed divine sanction.

THE NILE AND EGYPTIAN POWER

The Egyptian state had to wrest food for its people from an environment that could be both generous and unpredictable. The Nile made agriculture possible in Egypt by annually flooding and fertilizing the land along both banks in the late summer. But the extent of the flooding and how much land was fertilized varied from year to year. As the story of Joseph in the biblical book of Genesis makes clear, Egypt's rulers and inhabitants faced lean as well as fat years, and had to prepare for them. For much of the third millennium, the kings and their officers addressed these problems by centralizing the state and organizing the life of its people. The kings installed their own chosen followers as local administrators, heads of temples, and military commanders, and extended their command down into every sphere of life.

Egypt's officials took action to reinforce the operations of nature. They built canals to move the Nile floodwaters more effectively, and dug basins to retain water in the plains. The laborers who did this work, as slaves or free

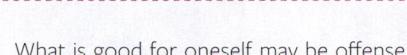

RELIGION AND NATURE

The ancient Mesopotamian and Egyptian civilizations had widely disparate ideas about religion, especially as it pertained to the natural world. In Mesopotamia the Tigris and Euphrates Rivers flooded unpredictably. In some years, flooding damaged crops and cities; in others, the flood was not sufficient and crops could not grow. This irregularity led Mesopotamians to a pervasive feeling that poor floods meant they were being punished by the gods for their misdeeds. Egyptians, on the other hand, saw themselves as blessed by their gods with a predictable and regularly flooding Nile. Egyptians generally believed that their deities wanted to help and protect them by providing what they needed to thrive and prosper. Expressing less anxiety than the Mesopotamians, the Egyptians composed hymns and poems lauding the benevolence of their gods.

Poem of the Righteous Sufferer

Mesopotamian people were constantly trying to determine how best to please their gods to avoid punishment in the form of natural disasters or illnesses. This source, from Mesopotamian wisdom literature (ca. 1700 BCE), illustrates this uncertainty and fear.

> I survived to the next year; the appointed time passed.
> I turn around, but it is bad, very bad;
> My ill luck increases and I cannot find what is right.
> I called to my god, but he did not show his face,
> I prayed to my goddess, but she did not raise her head.
> Even the diviner with his divination could not make a prediction,
> And the interpreter of dreams with his libation [offering of wine] could not elucidate my case…
> Like one who has not made libations to his god,
> Nor invoked his goddess when he ate,
> Does not make prostrations nor recognize (the necessity of) bowing down…
> Who has even neglected holy days, and ignored festivals,
> Who was negligent and did not observe the gods' rites…
> And abandoned his goddess by not bringing a flour offering…
> What is good for oneself may be offense to one's god,
> What in one's own heart seems despicable may be proper to one's god.
> Who can know the will of the gods in heaven?
> Who can understand the plans of the underworld gods?…
> He who was alive yesterday is dead today…
> Debilitating Disease is let loose upon me;
> An Evil Wind has blown (from the) horizon,
> Headache has sprung up from the surface of the underworld…
> (They all) came on me together,
> (They struck) my head, they enveloped my skull…
> My symptoms are beyond the exorcist,
> And my omens have confused the diviner.
> The exorcist could not diagnose the nature of my sickness,
> Nor could the diviner set a time limit on my illness.
> My god has not come to the rescue nor taken me by the hand;
> My goddess has not shown pity on me nor gone by my side.

Hymn of Praise to Ra

In this hymn (ca. 1550 BCE) from the Book of the Dead, an ancient Egyptian funerary text, the sun-god Ra is portrayed as the "god of life" and "king of the gods," who bathes the earth in his rays and creates joy and happiness for the people. (This excerpt's formal style reflects the translation, not the original text.)

> Homage to thee, O thou glorious Being, thou who art dowered [with all sovereignty]…. When thou risest in the horizon of heaven, a cry of joy cometh forth to thee from the mouths of all peoples. O thou beautiful Being, thou dost renew thyself in thy season in the form of the Disk within thy mother Hathor; therefore in every place every heart swelleth with joy at thy rising, for ever. The regions of the North and South come to thee with homage, and send forth acclamations at thy rising in the horizon of heaven; thou illuminest the two lands with rays of turquoise light. O Ra…the divine man-child, the heir of eternity, self-begotten and self-born, king of earth, prince of the Tuat [the Other World]…O thou god of life, thou lord of love, all men live when thou shinest; thou art crowned king of the gods….Those who are in thy following sing unto thee with joy and bow down their foreheads to the earth when they meet thee, thou lord of heaven, thou lord of earth, thou king of Right and Truth, thou lord of eternity, thou prince of everlastingness, thou sovereign of all the gods, thou god of life, thou creator of eternity, thou maker of heaven wherein thou art firmly established! The company of the gods rejoice at thy rising, the earth is glad when it beholdeth thy rays; the people that have been long dead come forth with cries of joy to see thy beauties every day.

QUESTIONS FOR ANALYSIS

1. In "Poem of the Righteous Sufferer," what are some of the actions the writer takes to placate the gods?
2. In "Hymn of Praise to Ra," how is the sun-god Ra portrayed as a life-giver?
3. What are the contrasting religious ideas about the world and the gods evident in these two sources?

Sources: Robert D. Biggs, trans., *The Ancient Near East, Volume II: A New Anthology of Texts and Pictures* (Princeton, NJ: 1975); E. A. Wallace Budge, trans., *The Book of the Dead: The Chapters of Coming Forth by Day* (London: 1898), pp. 10–11.

Nile Agriculture Egyptian agriculture was state-planned and highly organized. In this wall painting from a late-fifteenth-century BCE tomb, surveyors measure a wheat crop to determine whether it can be harvested. A couple offers gifts to the surveyors, and a scribe holding a palette waits to record the measurements.

conscripts, suffered terribly: many skeletons show slipped disks, teeth ground down by stony bread, and poor nutrition. Yet by the beginning of the third millennium, agriculture in the Nile Valley was immensely productive. Its regular, cyclical work fed masses of stonecutters, scribes, potters, and other craftsmen while they labored on the large projects thought appropriate for divine kings, such as the immense tombs on the Giza Plateau.

Great Pyramids Towering over the landscape, the vast pyramids at Giza are a testament to the wealth and power of the Egyptian kings.

THE PYRAMIDS OF GIZA By the middle of the third millennium BCE, it must have seemed as if the king of Egypt ruled the universe. This sense of cosmic power was reflected in the kings' greatest projects: the pyramids of Giza. Egyptian technology, less inventive than that of the Mesopotamians, boasted relatively few machines. Yet the wealth and power of the Egyptian state made it possible to muster the enormous teams of workers that created these immense structures. The sides of these great tombs were aligned precisely on north-south and east-west axes, staking a claim for the relation between the ruler's power and accomplishments and the order of the cosmos itself.

EGYPTIAN WRITING

In Egypt, perhaps thanks to the Sumerian example, symbols that first appeared in art were recast early in the third millennium BCE as the characters of a complex, expressive written language. These symbols played many roles: they represented the sounds of individual characters, stood for whole words and parts of words, and clarified the meanings of ambiguous terms. The Egyptians used these characters—which the Greeks later called **hieroglyphs** ("sacred carvings")—to inscribe the great monuments that they began to construct during this period.

A second form of writing called hieratic—more cursive than the formal hieroglyphs, with characters connected as they were written—was often used to compose the texts of books on **papyrus**. This writing material, made from reeds that grew along the Nile, became the standard not only in Egypt but throughout the ancient Mediterranean world. The oldest surviving surgical text, which describes the sophisticated operations carried out by Egyptian surgeons, was written on papyrus as early as 1600 BCE. Different forms of hieratic writing were used for administrative documents and for literary works.

Although Egypt was a highly sophisticated society, literacy remained confined to limited groups, and literature tended to be their exclusive property. Like the writing of the Mesopotamian scribes, hieroglyphs and hieratic script were difficult to master. They could not even be read without the formal training scribes gained in schools. Even those monarchs who dictated their words for preservation were often illiterate. In the seventh century BCE and after, a much simpler system of writing known as demotic ("popular") script was devised for keeping official records and other practical purposes.

EGYPTIAN RELIGION

Egyptian religion, like that of the Mesopotamian states, was polytheistic and public. Egyptians believed that the falcon-headed Re or Ra, the god of the sun, created all life. With Horus he ruled the world and protected the Egyptian kings. The jackal-headed Anubis presided over the judgment of the dead. Isis, the powerful female deity, was connected with the giving and preservation of life, and she protected women in childbirth. These and other gods were worshipped in the state temples. They were also seen as the protectors of the individual kings, not only in this life but in the next, for Egyptians envisioned their monarchs as enjoying a new life after death in a separate realm.

The pyramids of Giza were dedicated to commemorating dead kings and, even more, to protecting them and the retinues and goods interred with them for use in the world of the gods. The elaborate techniques—as complex as the surgical ones—by which the Egyptians preserved bodies from decay, turning them into mummies, were inspired by this fascination with death. More than in any other society known to history, Egypt's rulers continued, over the millennia, to see life above all as a preparation for death—a second life that would last much longer and, ultimately, matter far more than life on earth.

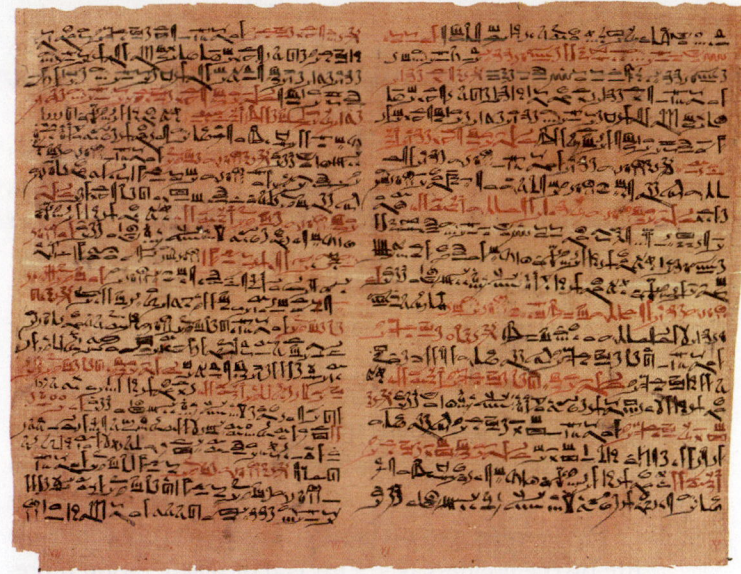

Hieroglyphs This papyrus, dating from around 1600 BCE, is the world's oldest surviving surgical text. Written in cursive hieratic script, with the main text in black and explanatory notes in red, it details forty-eight kinds of injury and how to treat them.

ROYALTY AND VIRTUE IN THE MIDDLE KINGDOM

From early on, Egyptian kings professed that their absolute duty was to maintain a just order in society and the state—*ma'at* was the term both for justice and for the goddess who represented it. During the Middle Kingdom, when royal authority had to be reestablished, the kings referred increasingly to ideals like *ma'at* to prove that their power was legitimate. Like their predecessors in the Old Kingdom, the Middle Kingdom rulers built great temples and necropolises (cities of the dead) that established their power in the civil and cosmic orders. But they relied more and more on elaborate official rituals and public records to convey a new vision of what royalty and virtue meant.

Some rulers exemplified this vision through their skill and independence. Hatshepsut was the strong-minded queen who took a throne name and ruled Egypt for more than twenty years early in the fifteenth century BCE. She built a massive palace and new temples at Karnak, near Luxor in Upper Egypt. Hatshepsut sent expeditions to Nubia, in what is now southern Egypt and northern Sudan. She traded with the mysterious land of Punt in the Red Sea, and with Cyprus and the Levant. But even this steely woman warrior had to manipulate the symbols of rulership, such as the beard she wore in some official sculptures, to maintain her power. (In other images she appears as a beautiful woman.) After her death, her charms ceased to work. Her monuments were desecrated at the orders of one of her successors, and her name was erased from public inscriptions—a fate that would have horrified any Egyptian ruler.

Kingship and virtue drew closer together with changes in Egyptian visions of the afterlife. In the Old Kingdom, kings and priests imagined that rulers would live on after death, but in their tombs on earth. In the Middle Kingdom, by contrast, rulers and their officials treated the afterlife as taking place in the realm of the gods. And the nature of one's afterlife would depend on the life that he or she had led. Each individual would be judged after death—and, if successful, vindicated against death itself. During this period, the god Osiris became prominent in Egyptian religion as the ruler of the underworld. His myth held that he was murdered by his brother, but then brought back to life by the goddess Isis. This god of regeneration represented the possibility of a spiritual rebirth for the virtuous.

Rulers and officials now had to demonstrate that they had disciplined their lives to the pursuit of virtue. Epitaphs from the Middle Kingdom period reveal this new commitment in the ways that they describe particular careers. Officials boasted that they had provided grain for widows and orphans, given wise advice to those who asked their counsel, and protected the land of Egypt. Yet

virtuous conduct alone was not enough. Motives mattered, too. Even great men and women must demonstrate, as their actions were weighed against ma'at in the cosmic scales, that they had been wholly dedicated to the pursuit of good ends. As one official carefully explained:

> My heart it was that urged me
> To do [my duty] in accordance with its instructions.
> It is for me an excellent testimony,
> Its instructions have I not violated,
> For I feared to trespass against its directions
> And therefore have I thrived mightily.

RELIGIOUS CHANGE IN THE NEW KINGDOM

In the first centuries of Egyptian history, only the ruler could aspire to union with the gods after death. During the Middle Kingdom (2030–1640 BCE), however, burials of many kinds were equipped with "coffin texts"—guides to life after death. Even individuals who did not belong to the court elite came to see the god Osiris as a kind of personal savior and to judge themselves and their careers by their success—so far as they could estimate it—in earning an afterlife.

For all its rich ritual, the Egyptian religious order could be burdensome. It demanded a life lived without feeling excessive desire or showing partiality, and it exerted pressure to find a god and win his or her favor. It provoked at least one great protest, led by the Middle Kingdom pharaoh Akhenaten in the fourteenth century BCE. When Akhenaten took responsibility for the divine and human order, he dismissed the ancient gods and all their works. Only the sun, he claimed, ruled the universe, and its only role was to provide the world with light. Akhenaten created a new capital city called Akhetaten (now Amarna), built new temples, and wrote new liturgies. When he died, he and his teachings were suppressed and literally removed from public memory by the destruction of many monuments and inscriptions that recorded what he had done. In this way, the dense and complex Egyptian religion successfully repelled the effort of the first great reformer in Western religious tradition to transform it.

Egyptian Deities Representations of gods and goddesses in tombs, such as this relief of the goddess Isis, granted protection and safe passage to the afterlife for interred rulers.

EGYPTIAN SOCIETY

Life in ancient Egypt revolved around the Nile. Egyptian farmers used the fertile soil of the Delta to grow the barley, wheat, and other cereals needed for making bread and beer, as well as fruits, beans, and salad vegetables.

EGYPTIAN FUNERARY STELES

Egyptian funerary steles were upright slabs placed as monuments in burial chambers. Through the period of the New Kingdom (1550–1070 BCE), they were carved in stone. Later steles, such as this one, carved around 946–712 BCE, were made of wood. Their purpose is still uncertain, but they may have served to immortalize the spirit of the deceased.

This stele commemorates a noblewoman supplicating Re-Harakhty, a form of the ancient Egyptian sun-god. Her sheer gown, trimmed in ornate detail, reveals her body, ideal according to the standards of Egyptian society. Her headdress of perfumed beeswax and a water lily demonstrate her wealth and high status. She pours a cup of wine on a table laden with food with one hand and raises the other in greeting and salute to a seated Re-Harakhty, who is taller than she is standing. The inscription behind them asks that the god present the food to Osiris, the god of the underworld, so that the noblewoman's spirit will be provided with the food it needs to survive in the afterlife.

This funerary stele portrays how Egyptians used the material aspects of their lives, such as clothing and food, to help them understand and navigate timeless, eternal questions of life and death.

QUESTIONS FOR ANALYSIS

1. How does this stele convey the noblewoman's social status?
2. What does the stele show about the relationship between the ancient Egyptians and their gods?
3. What does the noblewoman's request reveal about how ancient Egyptians understood the afterlife?

Irrigation systems kept the water from flooding specialized gardens and destroying the medicinal plants and other valuable flora that they contained.

The river was vital in other ways as well. The papyrus reeds that grew in the Nile were harvested and cut into long strips, which were then hammered into a smooth, durable writing material. Men were primarily responsible for this sort of outdoor work, toiling on the teams of builders and artisans that the kings mobilized for their projects. In the sandy soil of the upper Nile the Egyptians grew flax, a tall plant with extremely strong fibers. Once the flax was harvested and boiled, the fibers could be extracted. Men wound them into rope, and women, working indoors, carded the fibers and spun them into yarn. Both men and women worked in large-scale shops to make linen, a delicate fabric—normally white and often patterned—that was perfect for clothing in a hot, dry climate. Egyptians used it for many other purposes as well, including wrapping mummies.

The life of most workers was hard. Even those who worked directly for the kings lived in long rows of tiny, one-room houses, sleeping—probably—on the roofs. The linen weavers, male or female, crouching before their looms on little stools, suffered discomfort and other indignities. The words of an Egyptian text reveal much about attitudes toward gender as well as working conditions: "The weaver inside the weaving house is more wretched than a woman. His knees are drawn up against his belly. He cannot breathe the air. If he wastes a single day without weaving, he is beaten with 50 whip lashes. He has to give food to the doorkeeper to allow him to come out to the daylight." Vast quantities of linen were produced by these brutally efficient fabrication centers.

A DISTINCTIVE ORDER

Egypt astonished ancient visitors with its vast scale, enormous wealth, and immense ceremonial buildings. It offered a distinctive model of political and social order. Egypt sent expeditions to Nubia seeking cattle and slaves and intervened at times in politics in the Levant, but it was generally more oriented toward feeding its huge population and creating great temples and tombs than to conquering other lands—the enterprise that occupied so much of the energies of the Near Eastern states. Egypt often served as a target for its more aggressive neighbors. Most strikingly, in the Middle Kingdom period it taught its inhabitants, as we have seen, the powerful idea that individuals are responsible for their actions and will be rewarded or punished systematically for them—an idea in sharp contrast with the determinist vision of the universe represented by the diviners and astrologers of the Near East. Strange though Egypt seemed, and sometimes vulnerable, it was also a brilliant experiment in social order and human values.

THE NEAR EAST: GREAT POWERS AND A DISTINCTIVE PEOPLE (1100–330 BCE)

Until almost the middle of the first millennium BCE, the great powers of the Mediterranean world continued to be located in Egypt and Mesopotamia. After sharing in the collapse of the Near Eastern powers in the twelfth century, the Assyrians, in northern Mesopotamia, reemerged in the eleventh. Their kings became the rulers of a mighty military empire that dominated much of Mesopotamia. Great military leaders like Shalmaneser III (r. 858–824 BCE) led organized, effective campaigns. The states that had succeeded the Hittites, and other states as distant as the Levant, were conquered and governed as provinces of a new Assyrian Empire.

Expansion of the Neo-Assyrian Empire, ca. 900–680 BCE
Successful military campaigns propelled the Neo-Assyrian Empire. From the royal palaces at Assur and Nineveh, kings appointed governors to provinces as far away as Israel and Egypt.

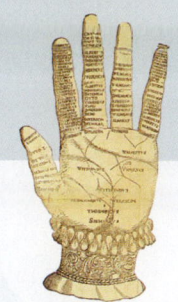

WOMEN AND INHERITANCE

In ancient Egypt, women had certain legal rights, including the right of inheritance. A woman's inheritance was at least her dowry plus one-third of the property gained during the marriage. We know this from reading legal texts, which give a glimpse into women's rights and familial relationships. These wills from two brothers were recorded on a single papyrus scroll around 1900 BCE, during the Middle Kingdom. In the first, Ankh-renef bequeaths property to his brother Wah. The second will is Wah's; it in turn bequeaths to his own wife, Teti, the property given to him by his brother, which Teti may give to their children as she pleases. Wah also assures that Teti will be able to continue living in their house.

First Will

Copy of the will made by the Trustworthy Sealer of the Controller of Works Ankh-renef.

Year 44, Month 2 of the Summer Season, day 13. Will made by the Trustworthy Sealer of the Controller of Works Ihy-seneb, nick-named Ankh-renef, son of Shepsut, of the Northern District.

All my possessions in field and town shall belong to my brother, the Priest in Charge of the Duty-shifts (of priests) of (the god) Sopdu, Lord of the East, Ihy-seneb, nick-named Wah, son of Shepsut. All my dependents shall belong to my brother.

A copy of these matters has been given to the Bureau of the Second Recorder of the South in Year 44, Month 2 of the Summer Season, day 13.

Second Will

Year 2, Month 2 of the Inundation Season, day 18. Will made by the Priest in Charge of the Duty-shifts (of priests) of (the god) Sopdu, Lord of the East, Wah.

I am making a will for my wife, a lady of the town of Gesiabet, Sheftu, nick-named Teti, daughter of Sit-Sopdu, concerning all the property that my brother Ankh-renef, the Trustworthy Sealer of the Controller of Works, gave to me along with all the goods belonging to his estate that he gave to me. She may give these things as she pleases to any children of mine she may bear.

I also give to her the four Canaanites that my brother Ankh-renef, the Trustworthy Sealer of Works, gave to me. She may give (them) as she pleases to her children.

As for my tomb, I shall be buried in it with my wife without anyone interfering therewith. As for the house that my brother Ankh-renef, the Trustworthy Sealer, built for me, my wife shall live therein and shall not be evicted from it by anyone.

The Deputy Gebu shall act as the guardian for my son.

QUESTIONS FOR ANALYSIS

1. What kinds of property are handed from person to person within the family, and what does this exchange tell you?
2. What does Wah's will tell you about Teti's legal and social status?
3. What do these wills tell you about the strength of government in Egypt?

Source: William Ward, trans., Pap. Kahun I, 1 (ca. 1900 B.C.E.), www.stoa.org/diotima/anthology/wardtexts.shtml.

THE NEO-ASSYRIANS AND NEO-BABYLONIANS (11TH–6TH CENTURIES BCE)

In this period, the kings of the Neo-Assyrian Empire built on a magnificent scale. Assurnasirpal II, early in the ninth century BCE, decorated his immense Northwest Palace at Kalhu with huge statues of winged elephants and lions, their heads human, carved from stone that had been carried from hundreds of miles away. His workers covered the palace walls with colorful glazed brick and spectacular sculpted reliefs. He also created schools of scribes and a vast library at Nineveh, a city north of Assur. Great powers, including Egypt itself in the seventh century BCE, fell to the Assyrians or fiercely resisted siege after siege.

But these wars and others—especially with the Medes, an Iranian people whose archers and cavalry could outmaneuver the Assyrians' slower infantry and chariots—eventually exhausted them. At the end of the seventh century, the Chaldeans, a Semitic people who had gained control of Babylon, formed an alliance with the Medes and defeated the Assyrians decisively, even though Egypt

Stele of Assurbanipal A stele from around 669–655 BCE depicts the king Assurbanipal in the traditional headdress of the Assyrian rulers. He carries a basket of earth on his head to symbolize his contributions to the rebuilding of Babylon, the great city sacked by his grandfather. A cuneiform inscription praising Assurbanipal runs over the stele.

Ishtar Gate Babylon's Ishtar Gate, built around 570 BCE, was decorated with glazed tiles forming designs such as this dragon, a symbol of Nebuchadnezzar II's power and authority. Merging features of various dangerous animals, including a viper, lion, and scorpion, the dragon stood as a warning to enemies of the city.

THE MEDIAN AND PERSIAN EMPIRES (678–330 BCE)

Yet Babylon in turn soon fell—as did the kingdom of the Medes, a short-lived Persian state established in 678 BCE—to the larger group of nomadic peoples who came together in the Persian Empire from the middle of the sixth century BCE on. Under the leadership of Cyrus the Great (r. 558–529 BCE), Persia would dominate more of the world than any other power before it.

The Persians settled in the area of modern Iran around 1000 BCE. By the end of the eighth century BCE, King Achaemenes founded the Achaemenid dynasty, whose later members built the empire. Persepolis became the ceremonial center of their realm, and other cities developed as administrative centers. The empire's vast armies, made up of peoples from many lands, were always anchored by highly trained Persian archers and infantry and supported by war wagons and scythed chariots. Cyrus and his successors wielded power that no other monarch could rival. He conquered the kingdom of the Medes and then the Neo-Babylonian Empire in turn, and his son, Cambyses II, conquered Egypt in 525 BCE. Their kingdom

tried to help Assyria in an effort to maintain the regional balance of power. Under Nebuchadnezzar II (r. 605–562 BCE), the Chaldeans consolidated a Neo-Babylonian Empire that enjoyed a brief period of preeminence in the Near East.

Nebuchadnezzar made Babylon perhaps the greatest city in the world. The huge Ishtar Gate, covered with brilliant deep blue tiles and vivid images of lions, bulls, and dragons, was only one of the formal entrances to the city. During this period Babylonian astronomy and astrology reached their peak, as we know from the lists of accurately dated eclipses of the moon and sun, and conjunctions of the planets, recorded over hundreds of years.

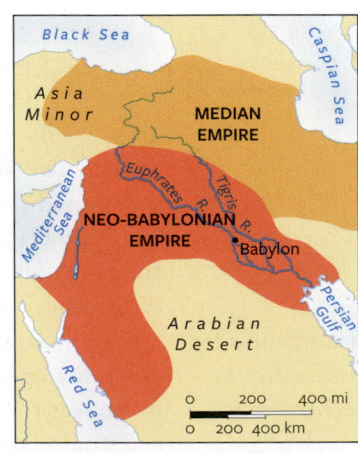

The Neo-Babylonian and Median Empires, 625–560 BCE

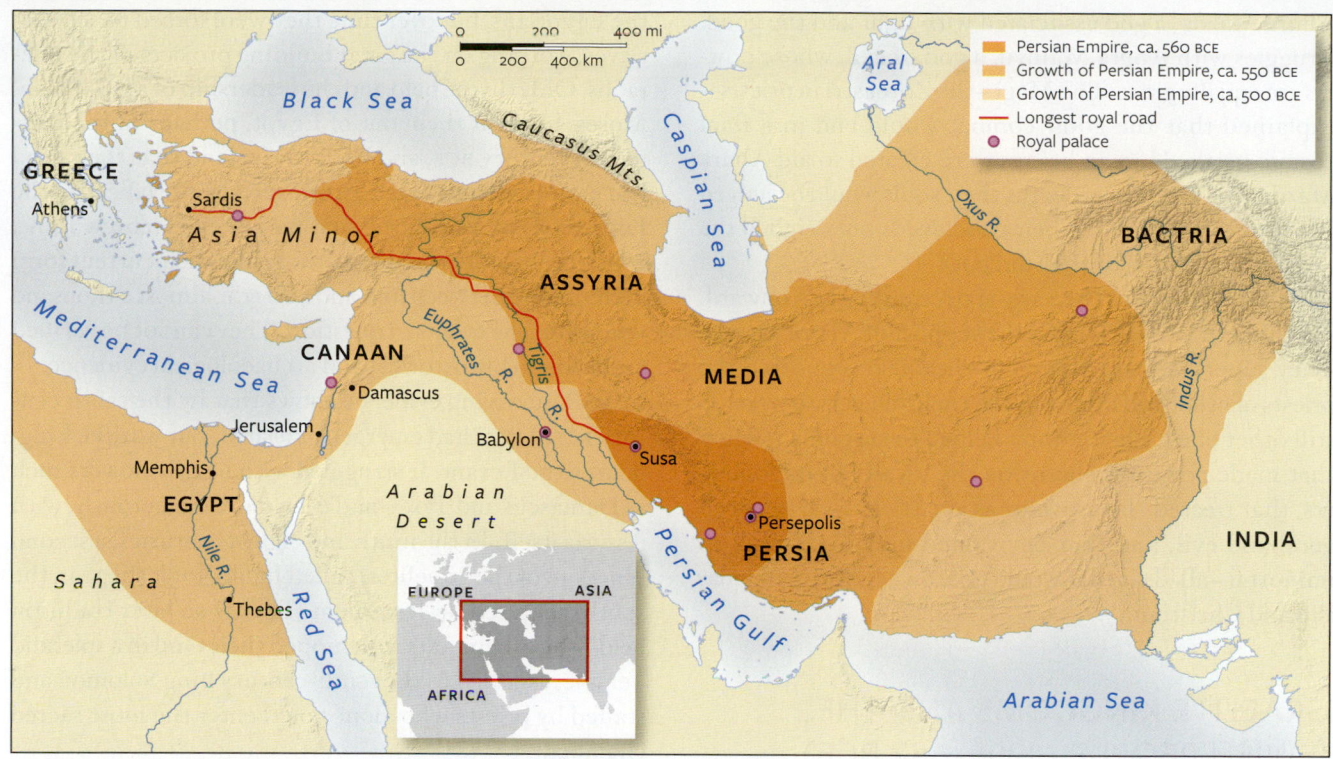

Expansion of the Persian Empire, 557–500 BCE Under the leadership of kings such as Cyrus the Great, the Persian Empire spread from its ceremonial center at Persepolis to cover a vast area, from the Nile to the Indus.

would remain a great power until 330 BCE, when it fell to Alexander the Great.

GOVERNANCE UNDER CYRUS AND DARIUS The Persian Empire at its height stretched from the Nile to the Indus. It was divided into administrative districts, each ruled from a palace by a Persian nobleman known as the satrap, who had his own staff of scribes and his own treasury. Royal roads, with rest houses to make travel easier, connected the satrapies to the capital: the longest one, from Sardis to Susa, stretched more than 1,550 miles. Personal representatives of the king, known as his "eyes," ensured that these local powers did not grow too independent. Every province had to contribute its share of tribute to the royal treasury. This payment chiefly took the form of gold and silver but could also include horses, grain, and eunuchs (men castrated as boys). The Persian kings were immensely rich: when Darius, the third king of Persia, built a palace in the decades around 500 BCE, he imported craftsmen from Egypt and Greece alike, while Babylonians were hired to make the bricks.

For all its demands, the Persian Empire seemed to many of its subjects a model of good government. Kings improved agriculture by maintaining and developing irrigation systems and promoted trade. More important, perhaps, it was Persian royal policy to leave each subject people in possession of its gods and customs, and to communicate with them in their own languages—or at least in Aramaic, the Semitic language that was gradually replacing Akkadian as the common language of the Near East. In the palace at Persepolis, reliefs showed representatives of multiple peoples carrying the royal throne. In Babylon, Cyrus had himself represented as a Babylonian king. Cultural sensitivity and language skills—as well as efficient and honest administration, stern policing, and good roads—made the Persians more desirable rulers than most.

ZOROASTRIANISM It was within Achaemenid Persia that Zoroastrianism, a new religion with a powerful vision of the universe, took shape. In its earliest form, Zoroastrianism identified the god Ahura Mazda as a single "wise lord" who ruled the universe. Certain lesser figures aided him; others, the *devas*, came to be seen as evil. Early Zoroastrianism is often considered to be one of the first monotheistic religions.

In its later form, Zoroastrianism became dualist.

Ahura Mazda, a god associated with light and the good, struggles with Angra Mainyu, a god of evil, whose powers are equally great. The Magi—the Zoroastrian priests—explained that the gods' combat would end in a final cosmic battle. Human beings were created to aid Ahura Mazda, and after their deaths their souls would be judged and sent to paradise (if their good deeds outweighed the evil ones) or to hell (if they did not).

From Darius I in the early sixth century BCE onward, the rulers of Persia claimed the support of Ahura Mazda. They supported the Magi, but they also supported the priests of other gods and allowed their subjects to worship still other ones. Their efforts helped to sustain a religion that made powerful claims on the loyalty of its followers, that treated the universe as a battleground between good and evil, and that envisioned individual souls as immortal—all ideas that would take on new forms in Judaism and Christianity.

ISRAELITE KINGDOMS AND THE JEWISH PEOPLE (1200–582 BCE)

In the later centuries of the second millennium BCE, a new Near Eastern civilization began to take shape in Canaan, part of the Levant. This area, once studded with relatively wealthy Canaanite cities, was now partly in decline. It was largely controlled by New Kingdom Egypt, though the **Phoenicians**, based on the coast, used their position and their skills as navigators and sailors to become prosperous as trading intermediaries between the empires to their east and west. Jerusalem was a Canaanite city that recognized Egypt as its overlord. In the years around 1200 BCE, new peoples—some of whom came from near the Aegean Sea—established settlements in Canaan. So, apparently, did another one: a Semitic people who called themselves the children of Israel.

ISRAEL AND JUDAH (1000–582 BCE) Centuries later, the children of Israel would recall that this arrival in Canaan was not the first. Their ancestors had already inhabited the Levant, but in the seventeenth century BCE, they believed, they had moved to Egypt, impelled by drought. There they had originally lived in peace with

the Egyptians, but over time they were forced to serve as slaves, working on the great building projects of the pharaohs. Only divine help and the leadership of a great man, Moses, brought them out of Egypt, perhaps in the thirteenth century BCE, and back to the land that their God had promised them. These stories are memorialized in the Five Books of Moses, the first part of the Hebrew Bible, which probably reached something like their current form in the period between 600 and 400 BCE, almost a thousand years after the events in question. They cannot be verified (or falsified) by historical and archaeological evidence.

Still, surviving evidence shows that by the tenth century BCE, Israel had emerged as a small but warlike kingdom in the Levant. It struggled with nearby powers such as Damascus and Tyre—and even more dangerously, with Assyria itself. In the ninth and eighth centuries, a second kingdom of the Israelites, called Judah, took shape in the south, centered on Jerusalem. There—so later tradition held—the inhabitants worshiped their God in a splendid Temple, ascribed to the tenth-century king Solomon and staffed by priests who alone could enter the most sacred chamber.

Originally, the Israelites lived simply, in families and tribes ruled by patriarchs. They supported themselves by a combination of pastoral activity and agriculture. Land was passed down through the male line, and women—who were often married off by their families for economic advantage—lived with their husbands' kin. As the kingdoms developed, Israelite society became wealthier and more sophisticated. Potters developed new skill in turning and polishing their wares. Families, which had once lived in small houses with several generations in three or four rooms, began to split up, and a distinct group of leading figures who served as warriors and royal counselors took shape. To some extent, the Israelite states came to look like much smaller versions of other Near Eastern societies.

Late in the eighth century BCE, the Assyrians repeatedly invaded and finally shattered the Israelite kingdom, transporting its population to other parts of the empire—a standard imperial policy. Judah survived, probably by becoming an Assyrian vassal state, and the city of Jerusalem grew rapidly as Judah's capital. The remains of walls, aqueducts, and jars with seals reveal an increasingly

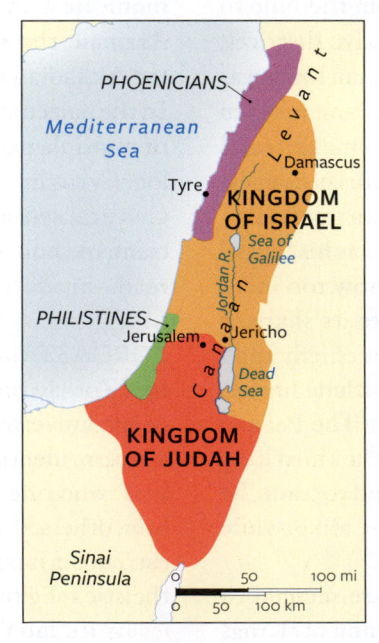

Israelite Kingdoms, ca. 900 BCE

vibrant society. After Assyria finally collapsed, however, the Egyptian and Neo-Babylonian Empires fought over the Levant. Between 597 and 582 BCE, the Babylonians destroyed the kingdom of Judah. When Jerusalem fell, the Temple was destroyed—a calamity that Jews still remember and mourn today. Under Assyrian rule, Judah had been a major producer of olive oil, but the conquest destroyed this prosperity.

MONOTHEISM AND JEWISH RELIGIOUS CULTURE

In one vital way, the Jews differed from virtually every other people. They believed, passionately, in a single deity who ruled the entire universe. Their God was not simply the most powerful among many, he was their only deity, and a being so radically superior to humans that he could not even be imagined in human form. In a world in which most states acknowledged and sacrificed to many gods, even Jews found it hard to maintain an active commitment to their hidden, abstract deity. From Moses to the kings of Israel and Judah, leaders found their followers all too eager to set up idols and sacrifice to them. And yet, monotheism became the very core of the Jews' historic identity.

Priests and scribes held that God had chosen the Jews as his special people, leading them out of exile in Egypt and appointing the dynasty of Kings David and Solomon to rule them. The hand of God led and protected his people at all times. This vision of political theology gave the kings legitimacy and supported those kings and priests who insisted that their God was a jealous one who would not allow his people to worship idols at the shrines of the Canaanites.

By 582 BCE, once the Jewish states had been destroyed and the kings had been driven from their thrones and become vassals of the Babylonians, this comprehensive theology and history no longer matched reality. **Prophets**, priests, and scribes gradually came to grips with the new situation. Although they continued to believe in a single deity, the prophets asserted that it was wrong to expect that God would intervene at all times and places in favor of a single people, however dear to him they might be. According to the prophets, the Jews—as the histories that were woven together in exile showed—had often rejected their God and his teachings, and had suffered the punishment they deserved. The Jews must learn, so the prophets insisted, to maintain purity: to practice circumcision on all males, observe the Sabbath, and so on. Eventually God would send a Messiah, an anointed king, to rule over the world. For now, however, salvation lay in meticulous observance of the laws laid down by Moses and conveyed in his Five Books.

House of David An Aramaic inscription on a ninth-century BCE stele from Tel Dan in present-day Israel celebrates the victories of an Aramean king. It includes the words "House of David," the earliest archaeological evidence of the Davidic dynasty.

In a sense, two foreign rulers did as much as any Jewish ones to shape the religion of Israel and Judah. The Babylonian king Nebuchadnezzar II, who conquered Jerusalem in 587 BCE, forcibly transferred the Hebrew elite—from kings to priests and scribes—to his own country. The experience of Babylonian exile probably inspired these men to shape the Hebrew Bible into the series of richly human stories of departure and exile that it became in these centuries. They enriched it as well with the profound reflections of the prophets and the psalms—the sacred songs that the Israelites believed had been composed by King David.

The other foreign ruler who helped to shape Jewish tradition was the Persian Great King, Cyrus. In 538 BCE, for reasons that remain unclear, he released the Jews from their captivity in Babylon. Over time, the returned Jews reestablished their worship and compiled, from older sources, the books of the law of Moses, with which they tried to govern Jerusalem and Judah. The exact process by which scribes and priests restored these books is impossible to reconstruct in detail. But it seems likely that they gave the early books of the Hebrew Bible something like their final form. These books, and the larger Bible that took shape in Palestine over the next centuries, would influence the thinking and belief of readers in vastly different circumstances, as we will see, for thousands of years.

THE EMERGENCE OF GREECE: BUILDING A CULTURE (2700–600 BCE)

The kingdoms of the Near East were ancient by the early centuries of the third millennium BCE—the time at which the first substantial states took shape in what would later become Greece. Located on Crete, a large island in the Aegean Sea, the centralized Minoan state resembled, in some ways, the older and larger polities of the Near East. In contrast, Mycenae, the stronghold of a society based on the southern Greek mainland that flourished after the Minoan state fell, was one of several small states that cultivated alliances with similar states nearby. The Minoan and Mycenaean settlements marked the beginning of Greek society during the Bronze Age; but it was Mycenae, with its multiple small states, that first provided one of the central patterns of organization that the West would follow, in ever-changing conditions, through the centuries to come.

BRONZE AGE GREECE: MINOANS AND MYCENAEANS (2700–1200 BCE)

The Minoan and Mycenaean cultures were as complex and creative, in their own ways, as the empires of the Near East. By 2700 BCE, the Minoans had developed centers of trade and commerce on Crete, and built palaces at Knossos, Phaistos, and elsewhere. We know little about these early kingdoms, which went into crisis around 1700 BCE, when the palaces were destroyed and population fell. In the seventeenth and sixteenth centuries BCE, the Minoans rebuilt their palaces and developed a dazzling culture.

MINOANS Named after their legendary king, Minos, the Minoans were literate, but the script in which they kept records, Linear A, has not yet been deciphered. Their archaeological remains indicate that their society—the new as well as the old—centered on palaces. Centralized storehouses for grain ensured that there would be enough food for courts and for consumption in festivals. Gifted at crafts such as multicolored pottery and needlework, the Minoans were also skilled sailors. They traded with cities in Syria and Asia Minor, Egypt, and Sicily. But the products of their crafts were largely reserved for use in their own palaces.

Decorated with magnificent frescoes depicting dances and religious rituals, the Minoans' palace at Knossos rivaled the splendor, though not the size, of its Near Eastern and Egyptian counterparts. The palace incorporated an impressive stage for rituals and comfortable living conditions for its inhabitants: the Minoans devised ways of admitting fresh air and even created the first indoor plumbing. Smaller structures elsewhere on the island, especially along its coasts, indicate that the society had an extensive reach. In one respect in particular, Minoan society may have been distinctive: numerous statues of priestesses, and paintings of women taking part in the same sports as men, suggest that women's status was higher there than anywhere else—perhaps on an equal level with men.

Palace at Knossos The royal apartments in the Minoan palace on Crete (ca. 1500 BCE) were magnificently decorated with frescoes, such as this one of dolphins (right), and paintings, such as this portrait of women of high social status (left). The courtyards and patios were carefully designed to allow for the circulation of light and cool air.

Minoan and Mycenaean Greece, ca. 1500–1200 BCE The Minoan people on the island of Crete had a strong centralized state, based primarily in the royal palace at Knossos. Later, the Mycenaean culture accumulated power by building alliances with similar, smaller city-states across the Peloponnesus and Greek mainland. But both civilizations collapsed around 1200 BCE, when the Dorian people invaded from the north.

MYCENAEANS Between 1450 and 1380 BCE, Knossos and the other Minoan palaces fell, probably to invaders from the Greek mainland. By then, however, another set of states centered on more modest palaces had come into being on the Greek mainland, in the Peloponnesus (the large peninsula that constitutes most of southern Greece), and on other islands in the Aegean Sea. At Mycenae, Tiryns, Thebes, and Pylos, the palaces—often heavily fortified—guarded the central administrations of small states. They were equipped with guardrooms and archives, and centered on a megaron (a great hall) surrounded by storerooms for oil, wine, and grain. The typical Mycenaean palace resembled nothing more than the large house Homer describes in the *Odyssey* as belonging to Odysseus.

The Mycenaean palaces, like those of the Minoans, were splendidly decorated, many with images of the Mycenaeans fighting wild men, a legend from a now-lost past.

On Crete, as well, the old palaces came back to partial life. This time, though, like the Mycenaean ones, they used Greek as their language of administration, perhaps because of conquest by or intermarriage with the leaders of the mainland states.

The inhabitants of these states worshipped some of the same gods who would emerge centuries later, in the writings of the poets Homer and Hesiod (ca. 750–700 BCE), as the gods of the Greek pantheon: Poseidon, god of the sea; the earth goddess, Demeter; and her daughter, Persephone. These Greek societies were aristocratic, ruled by men of high birth, and supported by sophisticated craftspeople and productive farmers. Artisans turned out handsomely decorated pottery, which would remain a specialty of the Greeks for centuries to come. Great men and women were buried sitting up, in beehive tombs (large circular chambers), with splendid gold masks and jeweled weapons.

These states were connected with the greater powers to the east and to the south by alliances maintained through complex diplomatic relations. And they made war, as those other powers did, with bronze arms and armor, using fighters on chariots as well as infantry and bowmen. Unlike the Near Eastern kingdoms and Egypt, however, the Mycenaean and Minoan kingdoms did not leave behind

Gods in Archaic Greece An early-seventh-century BCE bronze drum from Heraklion in Crete depicts the mythological ancestors of the Cretan people. The central figure's long hair and rectangular beard suggest an Assyrian influence.

any body of literature—no poetry, no religious texts, no fables, no codes of law. Interpreting sites without written texts to illuminate the beliefs of those who lived in them is very difficult. There is no way to know, for example, if any or all of these states actually mounted an expedition to Troy, as depicted by the eighth-century BCE Greek poets, though some scholars insist that they did.

THE BRONZE AGE COLLAPSE (1250–1100 BCE)

We do know that the Minoan and Mycenaean kingdoms underwent a final, shattering crisis in the thirteenth and twelfth centuries BCE, in much the same period that crises brought down Kassite Babylon and New Kingdom Egypt. Centuries later, Greeks told the story that the Dorians—one of the main groups of Greeks in later historic times—had come south to Greece from Macedonia and Epirus during this period, and that their arrival had meant war and dislocation. Raids and invasions certainly took place, as did natural disasters. The fragmentary surviving evidence does not as yet support any single explanation for the simultaneous collapse of so many societies. One point is clear: the world that the eighth-century BCE bards looked back to had been dead for a couple of centuries before they began composing their poems about it. Until more documents come to light and are deciphered, we will not know the Mycenaeans and Minoans nearly so well as we know those who lived in the cities of Babylon and Egypt.

DARK AGE GREECE (12TH–9TH CENTURIES BCE)

Starting in the twelfth century BCE, the Greeks lived, for the next three or four centuries, on a far simpler level. This period is often called the Dark Age of Greece. The *Odyssey,* written at the end of this time, includes details that correspond in part with what archaeologists have learned from Greek sites of this period. Telemachus is the son of a chief. His house has servants—women who maintain supplies and ply their crafts, and men who cultivate the land and look after the livestock. Its rooms include his father's high-roofed treasure room, a broad space where bronze and gold lay in heaps

> with clothing in chests and much fragrant olive oil.
> There stood jars of old sweet wine,
> full of drink unmixed and fit for the gods—
> neatly laid out along the wall . . .

The Greeks' society was made up of clans, their chiefs bound to one another by complex family connections and rules of hospitality, and educated above all for war. Noble men and women were buried, like Mycenaean lords, with jewelry, arms, and gold.

This world of small-scale communities dominated by powerful noble families was not narrow. Men like Homer's hero Odysseus traveled both to trade and to raid. But communities were small, unlike the vast Mesopotamian cities of Nineveh and Babylon, and institutions were simple. After Telemachus calls a meeting in which the adult men of Ithaca discuss what to do about their king's absence, a herald gives his staff to each speaker in turn, as a sign that he has the floor. But there are no governors or monarchs, no generals, and no police authority.

Religion also remained simple. During Telemachus's assembly, Zeus—for Homer, the most powerful of the gods and the one who strives to preserve justice—sends two eagles as an omen after Telemachus finishes speaking. They wheel across the sky, attack one another, and disappear. Like other ancient peoples, Greeks saw the actions of birds as potentially freighted with meaning. In this case the poet leaves no doubt that Zeus had sent them. But there is no temple staffed with priests to interpret what the eagles' conduct portended. One member of the assembly, Halitherses, warns the others that the gods are displeased. But one of the suitors mocks him, insisting that not all the motions of birds mean something. By the end of the poem—when Odysseus returns, reestablishes his marriage, and slaughters the suitors—it becomes clear that Halitherses had been correct. From the historian's standpoint, though, the absence of institutions that could issue a strong verdict is even more striking. Families had their divine patrons, and family heads, rather than specialist priests, sacrificed to these patrons and invoked their aid.

THE IRON AGE AND REVIVAL: TOWARD ARCHAIC GREECE (1100–700 BCE)

From the tenth century BCE onward, the world of Dark Age Greece began to change, for reasons that are not entirely clear. Graves increased in number, showing that the mainland population, which had collapsed after the fall of the Mycenaean kingdoms, began to expand again. By the beginning of the eighth century, burials—which had traditionally taken place within community boundaries—were pushed to the margins of settlements

Proto-Geometric Pottery The development of new tools inspired precise designs, such as the concentric circles on this Proto-Geometric jar from Athens (ca. 975–950 BCE).

such as plows were tipped with the new, harder material. They proved more effective and durable than those made with bronze had ever been. Farming became more intensive. Warfare became more violent, as iron weapons with their hard edges became available to more warriors. So began the Greek Iron Age, which extended from roughly 1100 to 700 BCE.

As the recovery proceeded, the texture of Greek life began to change. The noble households of the Dark Age described in Homer maintained substantial herds of cows and pigs, and the inhabitants sacrificed—and ate—a fair amount of meat. In the Archaic period, however, when populations grew, Greek communities turned increasingly to agriculture, raising the barley that was the staple of their diet and the flax that could be spun into linen cloth. The herds and the men who followed them decreased in number and moved into the hills.

Greek trade also revived. At the beginning of the first millennium BCE, Greeks were shipping their pottery to Cyprus and the Levant. Phoenicians and Greeks settled together in some trading stations. It is possible that the Phoenicians brought the Greeks back into international exchange networks in the tenth century and thereafter.

ARCHAIC GREECE (800–479 BCE): NEAR EASTERN AND EGYPTIAN INFLUENCES

The impact of Near Eastern and Egyptian developments on Greek society and culture, sometimes mediated by the Phoenicians, was profound. We have seen that the states of Mesopotamia and Egypt had created systems of theology and law, built temple complexes, and produced works of art on a vast scale. From the ninth century BCE at the latest, the Greeks began to emulate their neighbors.

PHOENICIANS AND THE GREEK ALPHABET The alphabet came early from the Phoenicians, who spoke a Semitic language. As early as the middle of the second millennium BCE, the Phoenicians had devised a nonpictographic alphabet to represent the consonants in their language. They used it in inscriptions—for example, on the sarcophagi (stone coffins) of their rulers. Phoenician merchants used their form of writing for recording their transactions, thereby bringing it to the attention of other peoples. The Greeks, who had traded actively with the Phoenicians for centuries, adapted the alphabet to the sounds of their own language, including the vowels, which

or beyond, as larger numbers of the living put pressure on the space once reserved for the dead. Cultivation of two crops that became central to Greek culture—olives and grapes—expanded. Pottery, which had degenerated after the collapse of the Mycenaean kingdoms, improved as well. Faster, more efficient wheels allowed potters to shape their vases more elegantly. New implements, such as compasses, enabled them to decorate their work with perfectly geometrical designs. Glazes became smoother and clearer. The pottery of this period, known as Proto-Geometric, was as elegant as it was simple.

A change in technology contributed to the general revival. In the Mycenaean world, as in the Near East and Egypt, the metal normally used for arms and armor had been bronze, an alloy of copper and tin. But new methods for molding bronze now developed. More consequential, smiths in Cyprus and the Levant learned how to smelt iron, which the Hittites had valued as a precious metal rather than for its practical applications. The Greeks adopted these techniques and began to make practical use of local deposits of iron ore. First weapons and then tools

their ability to observe and raise questions about the universe and human society.

THE INVENTION OF AUTHORSHIP: HOMER AND HESIOD
It is possible that the poet of the *Iliad* actually invented the Greek alphabet, and it is certain that poets applied this new tool in a highly imaginative way. As bold and willing to experiment as the artisans and traders who were bringing Greek pottery to other peoples, the singers of tales not only wove stories far longer than ever before but also recorded them for others to read. Too long to memorize or to perform in one sitting, these **epics** were committed to writing. A new kind of literary creation had become possible—authorship, in which a single poet crafted a work, episode by episode, and then recorded it, word for word, for everyone else to read. This invention marked the origins of a development as astonishing as it has been fruitful—the beginning of a self-conscious, independent, rambunctiously creative society and culture in Greece.

The society that Homer describes in his epic poems is centered on older values of hospitality and courage in warfare, the values that had sustained Greek communities at a time of poverty in resources and technologies. But his

Intersecting Cultures On this tenth- or ninth-century BCE bust of a pharaoh, his name is inscribed in Egyptian hieroglyphs on the chest, surrounded by a Phoenician inscription dedicating the bust to the patron goddess of a Phoenician city.

made their written language easier to read and write than the Semitic ones. Soon they had worked out how to use these letters for everything from signing their names on pots to chiseling inscriptions into stone.

The Greeks' fuller set of letters proved easy to master. Within fifty years after the alphabet came to Greece, early in the eighth century BCE, it had been used to create and record great poems. By the end of its first hundred years of existence, ordinary Greeks were using it to keep records, to label the mythological figures represented on their clay pots, and to sign their names as graffiti on the structures in Egypt and elsewhere where they served as mercenaries. Greece never developed a class or order of professional scribes like those who taught and practiced writing in the older states. It never needed to. Texts were written and read by ordinary people—and almost certainly sharpened

Odyssey A jar from fifth-century BCE Athens vividly depicts an episode in Homer's *Odyssey* in which the Sirens, winged women with beautiful voices, attempted to lure Odysseus and his men into wrecking their ship on the rocks. Odysseus had his men plug their ears with beeswax and then tie him to the mast so he could listen to the Sirens' singing.

Geometric Pottery This eighth-century BCE terra-cotta krater, a large vessel used to mix wine and water, demonstrates the intricacy of designs found in Greek Geometric pottery. It is decorated with a common Near Eastern motif: two goats on either side of a tree.

characters have varied qualities, reflecting a more complex morality. In the *Iliad* the warrior Achilles shows a passionate determination to pursue honor and a burning capacity for anger. His enemy, Hector, displays resolute courage in the defense of his home. And in the *Odyssey*, Odysseus reveals a dazzling wiliness—as well as formidable strength—in his pursuit of the conquest of Troy and then during his journey home. The complicated, often ironic ways in which their fates play out make the two poems surprisingly accessible today.

Homer's work as a whole—and even more, that of his near contemporary Hesiod—also show what contact with older civilizations meant to the Greeks. The Greek writers composed and performed as individuals, supposedly inspired by goddesses (the nine Muses), but still speaking on their own authority and in their own voices. Hesiod even introduced his own name to his poems, making clear his personal responsibility for them. Some Near Eastern writers had done the same. But others had written as scribes and priests, explaining how the gods were related to one another, laying out the history and structure of the universe, and striving to convey the ways in which divinity and humanity interacted. The Hebrew Bible gives a sense of what this literature was like.

Greeks, so far as we know, had never attempted to put the stories of their many gods in any sort of formal order

before this time. Now Homer, in a poem aimed at aristocrats who loved to hear about family histories so complex that modern readers find them almost impenetrable, traced the connections among the Olympian gods in passing comments. Hesiod devoted one of his major works to explaining the generations of the gods and their relationships to one another, in a scripture, of a sort, for a people who lacked one. More striking still, in a bitter poem on the life of the farmer, he insisted as sharply as any Egyptian that the duty of the authorities was to maintain a moral order, to preserve justice in the universe. In their hunger for the bribes that only the rich could provide, Hesiod observed, they often failed to carry out this duty. In his poetry we can hear the voices of those who lacked status and power, and earned their living by the hard work of the plow or by risking dangerous voyages on ships.

GREEK ARTS AND CRAFTS: BUILDING ON NEAR EASTERN AND EGYPTIAN MODELS Greek artists and artisans also explored the new possibilities that commerce with other cultures offered. In the age of Homer, as for centuries before, potters in Greece had decorated their wares with the abstract patterns that gave their style its name: Geometric. In the seventh and sixth centuries, by contrast, they followed models from the Near East

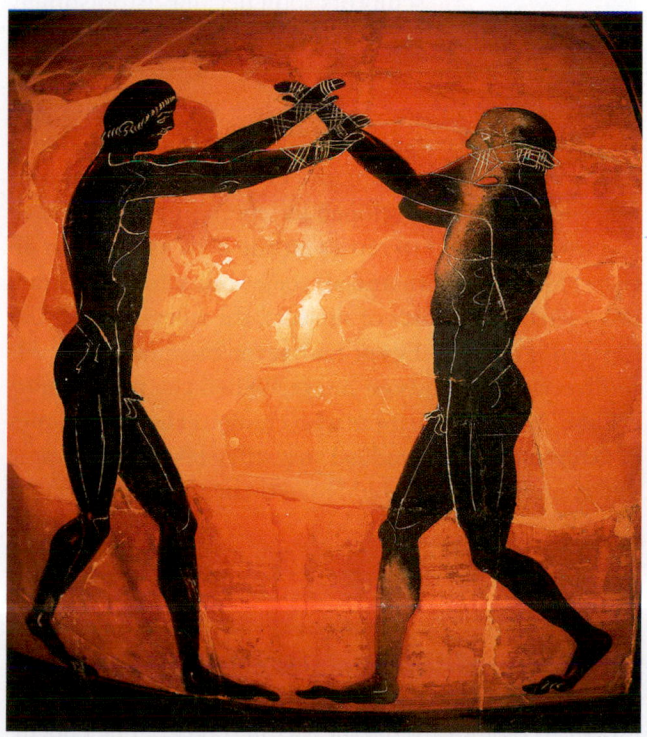

Athletics in Art A black pottery jar (525 BCE) from a Greek colony in Italy depicts two athletes engaged in a wrestling match.

Kouros The rigid arms and advancing stance of this life-size sixth-century BCE statue reveal the influence of Egyptian sculpture.

and Egypt, and experimented boldly with new forms—animals, both real and imaginary, and humans engaged in rituals and social life. On the black vases of this period—so called because their figures were portrayed in black against the bright orange background of the clay—vivid figures of the gods appear. So do human athletes throwing the discus and the javelin to the sound of music made by a flute player, women gathering at a public fountain, and animals locking horns.

Greek sculptors, similarly, learned from their skilled Egyptian colleagues to create life-size statues, in bronze and stone alike, of human figures. Again, they rang changes on foreign innovations. Statues of young men—kouroi—were represented in the nude, and the sculptors dwelled with pleasure on every detail of the human form. Statues of women were clothed, the sculpted fabric falling in stiffly stylized drapes and folds. Using Egyptian conventions, Greek sculptors soon became astonishingly skillful at producing realistic figures that seemed balanced on the balls of their feet and ready to move.

In the eighth century BCE, Greeks began to build substantial temples to their gods. The same sculptural conventions they had developed to represent beautiful men and women served to represent the gods as well. For all their glorious wealth and all their ability to orchestrate the work of thousands of subjects, the rulers of the Near Eastern lands and Egypt had never imagined the gods so directly in their own image. When the poor seafarers and marginal farmers who clung to the bony slopes of Greece took this radical step, they revealed a cosmic self-confidence that would take them a very long way, as we will see.

GREEK EXPANSION: THE COLONIES (9TH–6TH CENTURIES BCE)

As the Greeks' social and intellectual universe expanded, they set themselves in motion. From the early ninth century BCE on, the old city-states began to establish colonies around the Mediterranean. The Phoenicians, whose trading cities survived and prospered during the Bronze Age Crisis, also founded trading posts in the western Mediterranean in the same centuries when the Greeks did. Apart from Carthage in northern Africa, which became a powerful city-state in its own right, they stayed largely aloof from local politics. They came to trade. The Greeks built some of their colonies as trading posts, but they also set out from their home cities looking for sites to settle as independent cities. They searched for harbors well protected from bad weather and flanked by high headlands that could easily be fortified. Though they maintained contact with their home communities, the new settlements were politically independent.

In two bursts, one in the eighth and one in the sixth centuries BCE, the Greeks established colonies on the coast of Asia Minor, on Sicily, and in mainland Italy and Gaul (modern France). Some of these, like the Sicilian city of Syracuse, would become bigger, richer, and more powerful than many of the home cities their inhabitants had left behind. Greek civilization thus expanded to the east and to the west alike—a process that would last, in different ways, for hundreds of years and play a central role in the making of Western history.

HELLENIC CULTURE: CONVERSATION AND COMPETITION

Even as Greeks scattered from the western coast of Asia Minor to the far western Mediterranean, new institutions were developing that helped them to form a collective identity. The Greeks called their lands Hellas and themselves Hellenes, and these new forms of sociability and competition came to define Hellenism. Some of these practices were rooted in the customs of the Dark Age communities, and perhaps in Mycenaean life before that. None was more durable or proved more fertile than the **symposium** (literally, "drinking together"), which became the central form of Greek social life.

The *Iliad* and the *Odyssey* already depicted groups of men and women reclining together on couches, drinking wine, and listening to a bard or talking. Over time, the symposium came to be a male event, one in which women appeared only as servants or entertainers. But it also became a model of free and open discussion in which philosophers and generals, men of inherited rank, and self-made men could take part. For centuries to come, Greeks were set apart by their passion for these meetings, which often launched new kinds of literature and new ideas.

Even more than the Greeks loved gathering to drink and argue, they loved to compete: "Strife," Hesiod

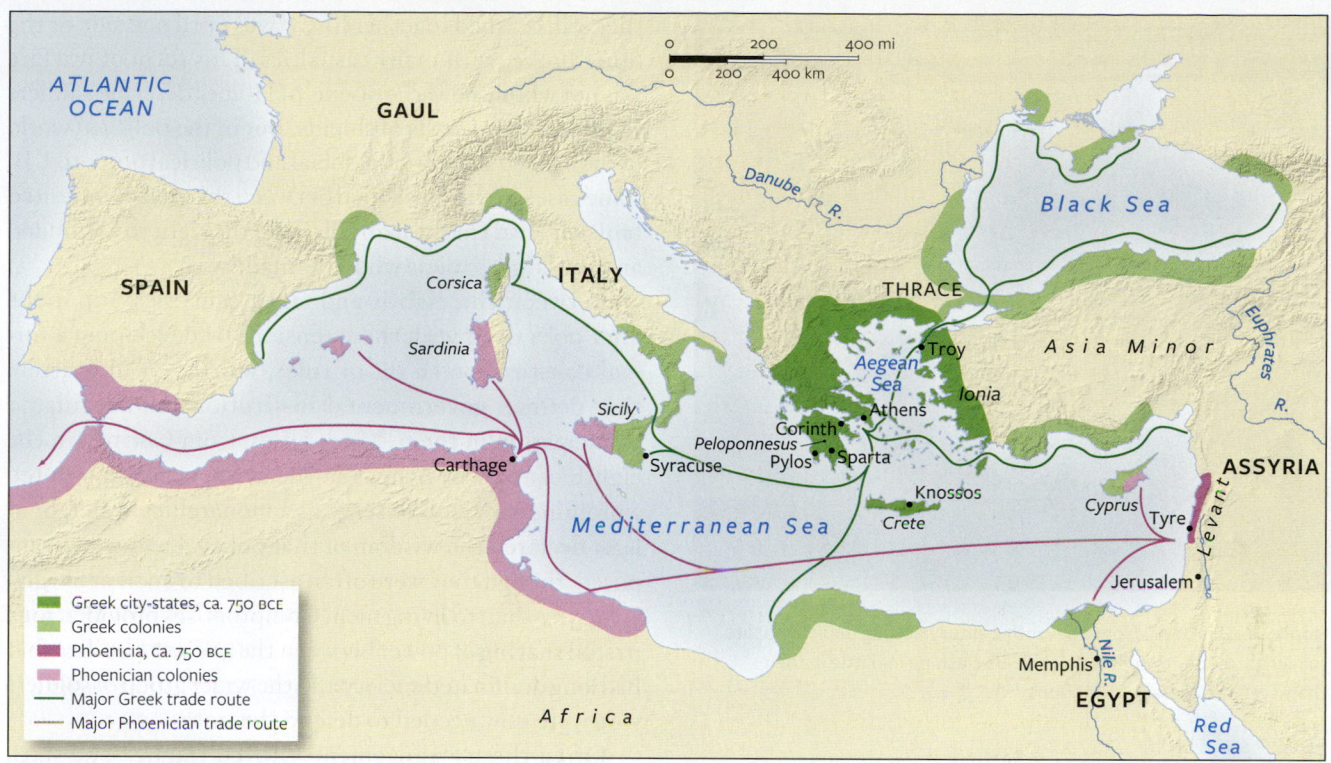

Greek and Phoenician Colonization, ca. 750 BCE From the early ninth century BCE, Greek city-states established trading posts, which ultimately became colonies, across the Mediterranean and the Black Sea. Together with the great maritime trading culture of the Phoenicians, the Mediterranean became a space in which goods, ideas, and even alphabets were exchanged, forming the basis of an enduring Greek linguistic and material culture.

explained, "is wholesome for men. And potter is angry with potter, and craftsman with craftsman, and beggar is jealous of beggar, and minstrel of minstrel." Homer has his heroes compete with all their strength, not only in warfare but also in the games that follow the deaths of their comrades, in which they race, wrestle, and box. In the ninth and eighth centuries BCE, these pursuits became the core activities at formal athletic competitions to which all Greeks were welcome. These were first held at Olympia, in the Peloponnesus, under the auspices of a great temple of Zeus, and then also at other sites.

Greek athletics took many forms, from boxing with hands wrapped in leather straps to racing chariots, and could be almost as dangerous as warfare itself. In 720 BCE, according to legend, one competitor lost his loincloth while running in a footrace. From then on, Greek athletes competed naked. As their contests began to occur regularly every two or four years, they developed into a pan-Hellenic institution. Special truces among warring groups enabled all contestants to attend the Olympics and other games. Poets celebrated the winners with elaborate verses of praise, and cities supported victors in comfort for the rest of their lives.

Conversation and competition both remained among the chief characteristics of Greek life for hundreds of years. Greeks were coming to have an identity as clear-cut as that of Babylonians or Egyptians—one centered on continual competition. The civilization that was beginning to take shape in the West already looked radically different from the older, wealthier, and more powerful societies with which it was in contact—and from which it learned so much.

GREEK CITY-STATES (12TH–6TH CENTURIES BCE)

In ancient times, most Greeks identified less as members of a great Hellenic world that stretched across oceans and continents than as citizens of individual communities. Independent city-states—settlements that recognized no superior and governed themselves—became the norm

Hoplites This detail from a seventh-century BCE jug depicts hoplite soldiers armed with spears and shields clashing in battle in their characteristic phalanx formations.

in Greece during the Dark Age and Archaic period, and would remain the standard form of Greek settlement until centuries later, when Greece finally became part of one larger empire after another. Called the **polis**, the Greek city—as we will see—followed a very different path of development than the cities of the Near East had.

HOPLITE WARFARE AND SOCIAL TENSIONS
Transformations in the city-state were the most consequential development of this consequential time. Bitter, prolonged warfare—consisting partly of pitched battles in which one side might rout and slaughter the other, and partly of long series of raids and crop-burnings in the countryside outside the enemy's walls—became the city's central activity during the Iron Age. The little communities controlled by noblemen now became larger settlements dominated by a class of fighting men called **hoplites**.

These soldiers mobilized in the warm weather to wage their campaigns and, in the fierce rivalry of Greek life, were called into action again and again. Each of them wore a helmet and carried a spear in his right hand and a large, round wooden shield in his left. Moving forward in a dense, coordinated formation called a phalanx, each hoplite was supposed to protect the man on his left with his shield, and trust the man on his right to do the same for him. These formations loosened as armies ran toward one another, but

they still crashed together like waves until one side or the other broke, with many casualties. This form of warfare was not wholly new: the poems of Homer describe soldiers fighting behind walls of shields. But in the political world of the city, it had powerful social and political potential. In some cases, strife developed between the men of inherited rank who had traditionally claimed the right to command and the larger groups who now made war.

Between the eighth and sixth centuries BCE, polis after polis dealt with these tensions by developing a formal constitution—a set of rules, written or unwritten, that defined governmental institutions and regulated participation in them. Many cities, from Corinth in the eighth century to Athens in the sixth, either appointed a prominent person to serve as a monarchical ruler, or at least declared the wisdom of that policy. Laws were composed, though they were often ascribed to ancient lawgivers rather than to living men. Compromises provided for a partial sharing of power between the ancient families that had long dominated society and the wider group of soldiers who were now needed to defend the state.

Often these arrangements proved fragile. The sixth century BCE saw "tyrants" take power in Athens and many other cities. Not despots in the modern sense, tyrants were individual rulers who could not necessarily claim that their rule was legitimate, but who could offer efficiency in government. History now took place, at different tempos, on individual urban stages. Across the Greek world, as much in the colonies as on the mainland, Greeks thought of themselves first as Spartans or Athenians, Corinthians or Megarians, and only then as members of a coherent larger culture.

SPARTA: A DISTINCTIVE ORDER The Greek *poleis* (cities) varied widely in physical form and political constitution. But a small city on the Peloponnesus in southeastern Greece—Sparta—stood out as a model that others could only aspire to. It developed a distinctive constitution—traditionally attributed to the lawgiver Lycurgus—in the eighth and seventh centuries BCE, after a time of civil strife. The city had two hereditary kings—members of ancient families who led its armies in wartime and performed religious rites. Another set of officials, called *ephors*, had the right to challenge royal decisions, and they often did so. A council of elders, the *gerousia*, also took an active part in making policies and negotiating treaties. In addition, an assembly of men of military age had the right to vote on enactments proposed to it, but not to stage formal debates. In Greek terms, Sparta exemplified **oligarchy**: the state was ruled by the few, rather than a single monarch or a mass of citizens.

What made the Spartan state distinctive, much more than these institutions, was its social order—and the sheer power that it enabled the city to unleash when the multiple governing bodies agreed to make war. The core of the city's strength lay in its fighting men, who called themselves *homoioi* ("men of the same kind"). Much of the social order was organized to train these men to be fighters of extraordinary skill and courage.

Spartan boys, who were taken from their families and raised for a time as members of age groups, were required to steal the food they needed to eat but punished severely if they were caught. For centuries after the city had ceased to exist, Greek writers told the story of a Spartan boy who, in his hunger, stole a live fox but had to come to the muster with it under his clothing. He proved his mettle by remaining silent, muffling his own cries, as the fox gnawed at his vital organs.

While growing up, each Spartan boy normally had his closest relationship with an older male lover, who would teach him the skills of warfare and the traditions of the city. Eventually the men would marry their female counterparts: Spartan women, who unlike those in the rest of Greece practiced gymnastics to make themselves fit wives and mothers for Spartan men. But even once they had reached adulthood, Spartan men lived more with one another in military messes—groups of men who ate together, feasting on the notorious Spartan blood sausage—than with their families. Male lovers marched into battle together, and their deep affection helps to explain the cohesion of Spartan armies, which astonished their enemies.

Sparta had its manufactures, but it never became an actively commercial society. The city never even minted its own coins, but used those of other states. The labor of slaves called **helots** provided the material support that sustained the system and the state. Tradition connected the helots to the wars that the Spartans waged in the eighth century against their Messenian neighbors in the southwestern Peloponnesus, though these accounts disagreed as to whether the helots were descended from the Messenians themselves or from Spartans who had not fought. The helots, who far outnumbered the free Spartans, worked at many jobs, from household service and sharecropping the farms of their masters to trade and crafts. Some reports stress how the helots were humiliated by their masters—for instance, being harassed by free citizens' youth groups, forced to wear demeaning clothing, or made to drink wine with no water. Others point out that some helots owned considerable property and saved enough money to buy their own freedom.

Despite these uncertainties, it is clear that like later slave societies, Sparta was regularly threatened by rebellions of the helots. The city responded with ferocity. Young Spartans learned part of their craft as soldiers as they prowled Spartan territory, doing their best to terrify the slaves and catch and kill any who resisted. Rebellious helots were killed even when it meant removing them from shrines where they had sought sanctuary—itself a religious crime. Yet the Spartans also allowed helots to serve as soldiers, when numbers required it, and to deliver food and supplies to hard-pressed Spartan units—hardly the sort of duty one would normally assign to bitter enemies. Success at jobs like this often brought freedom.

In retrospect it seems an austere and frightening society. Yet for centuries most Greeks acknowledged that Sparta was the most virtuous society they knew or could imagine. Small though it was, without massive buildings or stunning works of art, Sparta took pride in the prowess of its relatively small class of citizen soldiers—who dominated most of the battlefields on which they appeared until the fourth century BCE—and in the stability of its social and political order.

Other Greeks respected Sparta, especially what they considered its excellent constitution. But the stability of the Spartan ruling class was an ideal to be admired rather than a model to follow. By the time the Spartan constitution took on its definitive shape in the sixth century BCE, Greece was embarking on a series of extraordinary experiments in every realm, from the state to speculative thought. The era of the mature Greek city-state had arrived. Forms of society and government unlike anything the Near East and Egypt had brought into being would take shape on Greek soil.

CONCLUSION

Imagine an observer using a retrospective form of Google Maps to survey the Mediterranean world sometime between 800 and 580 BCE. If the technology had existed, it would have been possible to survey the vast buildings of Babylon, the pyramids of Egypt, the enormous armies of the Neo-Babylonian Empire, and the even bigger ones of the Persian Empire that succeeded it. On the Mediterranean and in the Aegean Sea, Phoenician ships would have appeared, dominating the main traffic routes. In the Levant, the observer might have watched the downfall of Israel and Judah result in the siege and capture of Jerusalem and the exile of national leaders. In Greece, small cities would be rising, their expansion limited by geography. It would have been especially hard to see that Sparta, which lacked thick walls and large buildings, was already embarking on its aggressive program of expansion.

Yet the Greeks were learning from the older civilizations—learning, for example, how to fuse their ancient stories of the gods into a coherent form. And they were developing new forms of warfare, civic life, and colonial expansion that would soon transform the Mediterranean world. Their society afforded space for competition, for the unfolding of individual powers, and for the creation of institutions that are still with us today. In Babylon the exiled Jews were editing and completing what would eventually become the West's single central account of how the universe was made and how human beings should understand it and worship its creator. Though they would have been hard to discern, the roots of new institutions and beliefs were growing and taking hold.

[CHAPTER REVIEW]

KEY TERMS

civilization (p. 8)

domesticated (p. 8)

monotheistic (p. 8)

agricultural (p. 9)

city-state (p. 10)

ziggurat (p. 10)

cuneiform (p. 11)

polytheistic (p. 14)

divination (p. 15)

Code of Hammurabi (p. 15)

Epic of Gilgamesh (p. 17)

hieroglyphs (p. 22)

papyrus (p. 23)

ma'at (p. 23)

Phoenicians (p. 30)

prophet (p. 31)

epic (p. 36)

symposium (p. 38)

polis (p. 40)

hoplite (p. 40)

oligarchy (p. 40)

helot (p. 41)

REVIEW QUESTIONS

1. In the ancient Near East, what were the preconditions necessary for the development of agricultural societies?

2. What were the most important innovations of the early Sumerian city-states?

3. What distinctive features gave Egyptian civilization its relative stability from the Old Kingdom until its conquest by the Persians in the fourth century BCE?

4. What were the Egyptian views about life and death, and how did these ideas shape cultural practices?

5. What made the Hebrew religious tradition distinctive in comparison to other ancient belief systems?

6. What are the most notable similarities and differences between the Minoan and Mycenaean cultures?

7. What important developments helped to lead Greece out of its Dark Age?

8. What do the art and architecture of the Archaic period tell us about Greek values?

9. Why were conversation and competition such an integral part of early Hellenic culture, and how did they help to shape Greek identity?

10. How did the need for hoplite armies affect Greek politics and society?

CORE OBJECTIVES

After reading this chapter, you should have a solid understanding of the following core objectives. To strengthen your grasp of the core objectives, use the resources on the Student Site for The West.

- Identify cultural, technological, and political innovations that arose in the ancient Near East.

- Explain how Egyptian society remained stable for such a long time.

- Describe what made the Hebrew religion distinct from other ancient religious beliefs.

- Analyze how the Greeks adapted non-Greek art, culture, and technology during the Iron Age.

 GO TO **INQUIZITIVE** TO SEE WHAT YOU'VE LEARNED—AND LEARN WHAT YOU'VE MISSED—WITH PERSONALIZED FEEDBACK ALONG THE WAY.

CHRONOLOGY

621–620 BCE
Draco draws up first
legal code for Athens

594–593 BCE
Solon's reforms

6th century BCE
Athenian Agora established

561 BCE
Peisistratus establishes
a tyranny

510 BCE
Cleisthenes frees Athens
from tyranny;
lays foundations of democracy

490–479 BCE
Persian wars

465 BCE
Slave revolt in Messenia;
Sparta expels
Athenian soldiers

454 BCE
Athenians transfer Delian
League's treasury from
Delos to Athens

459 BCE
Athens allies with
Megara to fight Corinth

451–450 BCE
Pericles excludes nonnative
Athenians from citizenship

447–432 BCE
Athenians build
the Parthenon

2

"The School of Greece"

GREEK POLITICS, SOCIETY, AND CULTURE

600–400 BCE

390S BCE
Athens rebuilds Long Walls
404–403 BCE
Rule of Thirty Tyrants in Athens
431–404 BCE
Peloponnesian War

Winter 431–430 BCE
Pericles delivers funeral oration
399 BCE
Death of Socrates

In the winter of 431–430 BCE, the Athenian statesman Pericles gave an unforgettable speech. Athens and a group of allied city-states had been at war with Sparta and its allies for a year, and the city's inhabitants were beginning to feel the impact of this conflict. Shut in behind the great walls that protected the city and its ports, Piraeus and Phalerum, a few miles away, the Athenians had seen the superior Spartan armies ravage their crops and property in the countryside while Pericles led a campaign against a Spartan ally. Frustrated, the Athenians had begun to question the wisdom of Pericles' strategies.

Pericles chose to meet his critics head-on at a prominent public occasion. Every year, the Athenians held a funeral ceremony for their fellow citizens who had died in battle. After a great procession in which the bones of the dead were carried in cypress coffins, "a man chosen by the state, of approved wisdom and eminent reputation," gave a speech. Standing on a high platform so that many could hear him, Pericles defended his decisions and described Athens as a city like no other in the world.

After praising the city's ancestors, Pericles singled out the city's distinctive form of government: democracy. Athenian citizens ruled their city collectively, and individuals who were born poor could rise to power so long as they showed ability in war or politics: "Our

The Parthenon Frieze Designed by the great sculptor Phidias around 438 BCE, the marble frieze that wound around all four sides of the Parthenon depicted a festival procession of horsemen, chariots, city elders, musicians, and religious celebrants. The animated beauty of these figures embodied the vitality, wealth, and power of Athens.

[FOCUS QUESTIONS]

- What social pressures led to the transformation of Athens from domination by aristocrats to democracy?
- How did the Persian wars transform Athenian power?
- What caused Athenian defeat in the Peloponnesian War?
- How did the physical city embody Athenian political ideals?
- How was Athenian society democratic, and how not?
- How did Athenian culture express the basic social and political conflicts of the Greek world?

administration favors the many instead of the few; this is why it is called a democracy."

This unique constitution enabled Athens to surpass the rest of Greece in every vital area, Pericles claimed. Though the Athenians did not live in the sort of tyrannical city-state that forged the rugged Spartans, they remained just and honorable because they feared the law more than they feared men. Though the Athenians opened their city to strangers and spent their time as much on trade and holidays as on military training, they had shown repeatedly that they were also great fighters, unbeaten in battle. And although the Athenians discussed every important issue in public before deciding on a policy—and by doing so had earned the contempt of the taciturn and warlike Spartans—their love of debate made them independent thinkers, politically aware at all times and decisive when necessary. The Athenians' openness, their civic spirit, and their generosity, Pericles argued, made them supremely adaptable and effective in emergencies—so much so that they dazzled all rivals. "As a city," Pericles claimed, "we are the school of Greece."

But serving this democracy was hard. Pericles admitted that he could not praise the young Athenians who had died for their country in terms that could ever satisfy those who loved them. But he insisted that they had chosen to make their sacrifice and that they had been right to do so, and he urged all Athenians to continue to support the war as much as their age, position, and gender allowed. Fathers should produce more sons if they still could, and brothers should strive to match their fallen siblings' great deeds. Male citizens

and residents of Athens, in other words, could achieve heroism as the dead had—through sacrifice.

Many others, excluded from the public sphere, could not. Women, for example, heard only a message of self-discipline from Pericles: "Great will be your glory in not falling short of your natural character; and greatest will be hers who is least talked of among the men, whether for good or for bad." Even as Pericles uttered the grandest praise of democracy and the open society ever heard in the ancient world, he essentially admitted that public life excluded many.

Pericles had no doubt that the prize was worth all the suffering it required. For the city of Athens itself deserved no less. In giving up their lives or those of family members to serve it, the Athenians were showing something extraordinary: that they had learned to love their city above all else. Like Homer's Greeks of antiquity, the Athenians of the fifth century BCE saw valor in war as the highest of human virtues, and they prized the honor it could enable a man to win. But unlike Homer's Greeks, they practiced this virtue in the service of a higher, civic end. What gave the soldiers' sacrifice meaning was that they had made it to preserve a city that they loved.

In his speech, Pericles defined the new society that the Athenians had created, and he offered a new ideal of patriotism as the highest ideal that men could strive for. He thus helped to create a tradition that would last for millennia after his time. In every republic and democracy that the world has known, from the Roman Republic to the modern American one, language has been the most important tool in politics. The power of language has made it possible to create new states, defend old ones, negotiate changes in policy, and—in some ways most remarkable, and most like Pericles—to redefine constitutions in ways that transformed civic life. When Abraham Lincoln redefined Americans' vision of their country in his Gettysburg Address in 1863 and Martin Luther King Jr. did so a century later in his speech at the Lincoln Memorial, they drew on a tradition that began in Pericles' Athens.

Yet language is only as strong as those who create and use it, as the Athenians learned when Pericles died and they found themselves embarked on a long, bitter war that seemed to offer no way out. As civil strife broke out across Greece and politicians debated fiercely in Athens and elsewhere, political language degenerated into demagoguery. What Pericles had used as a tool to create a new consensus became a weapon for defaming and dehumanizing enemies.

The story of political language in the West—in both its creative and destructive forms—begins here.

ATHENIAN DEMOCRACY: THE FOUNDATIONS

The Athenians that **Pericles** addressed inhabited a sophisticated commercial society with complex institutions. They believed that they had always inhabited their land, and it is true that Athens was not invaded in the centuries after the fall of Mycenae and the other early states. The city ruled a substantial territory called Attica, a large triangular peninsula that juts into the Aegean Sea. With rich uplands and coastal plains for farming, Attica produced enough foodstuffs not only to support its population but also to enrich the elite landowners who dominated rural life. When its population expanded, it did not need to found colonies to provide for its citizens. The countryside offered room enough.

THE ANCIENT CONSTITUTION (900–600 BCE)

In the Archaic period, Athens was already rich. Its potters made the most elaborate and sophisticated vessels in Greece. It even attracted craftsmen from the wealthy lands to the east, such as Syria. During the eighth century BCE, the population of Attica exploded and Athens shrank in importance. A group of noble families, the Eupatridae ("the well-born"), dominated the city. Only members of this aristocratic group could serve as archons, the magistrates responsible for civic, military, and religious affairs. Nine archons served at a time in one-year terms. Noble ex-archons also filled the membership of the Areopagus, the city's council, which prepared legislation for the Assembly. This latter body could at this point only accept or reject laws and proposals, and cannot have been large.

Prosperity did not bring peace to Greece. In the second half of the seventh century BCE, the tribes that dominated particular parts of Attica fell out with one another. It also seems that conflict developed between older aristocratic families and newer groups—particularly, perhaps, those who were prosperous and bore arms for the city, but were excluded from power by the traditional constitution. As city-states, such as Sparta and Thebes, competed for space and resources, wars regularly broke out, and Athens found itself compelled, somewhat later than many of its rivals, to adopt hoplite tactics. As elsewhere, the hoplites of Athens had to be rich enough to arm themselves and devote time to training. It is likely that many of these men, who were and saw themselves as the protectors of the city, were not able to participate in the Assembly and protested the power enjoyed by members of the older families.

During this period of conflict, disturbances often took place at public events. Around 630 BCE, an aristocrat tried to establish a tyranny at Athens. He was defeated by heavily armed peasants from the countryside who entered the city and slaughtered his followers. Soon thereafter, in 621–620, a lawgiver (perhaps of noble birth) named Draco drew up a legal code for the city. Whether his legislation represented an effort to consolidate or to moderate the power of "the well-born" is not clear. In later tradition, his code was remembered as extremely strict. The word *draconian* is still used for severe laws. In fact, Draco tried to make the legal system fairer and more efficient. His code was discriminating in its identification of crimes and assessment of penalties, distinguishing, for example, between murder and manslaughter.

SOLON: THE FOUNDATIONS OF A JUST SOCIETY (600–580 BCE)

Despite Draco's legislation, social conflict continued in Athens until **Solon**—an aristocrat who served as archon in 594–593 BCE—made a new set of laws. These were inscribed on wooden tablets and set into rotating frames so that everyone could inspect them.

The exact nature of Solon's reforms is uncertain. It seems likely, though, that they put an end to the system that had obliged many Athenian farmers to give a share of their produce to aristocratic landowners. Resentment of this duty, especially on the part of hoplites who were now key protectors of the city, had been growing until Solon ended it. He also divided the population into four categories according to property ownership, and allotted

Attica, ca. 700 BCE

public offices to members of the three highest ones. He may even have created a new system for choosing archons by lot—a method that would later prove essential, in a different form, to Greek **democracy**. Though he gave the Areopagus the right to try certain major crimes against the state, he also created a second council that prepared legislation for the Assembly—a change that would lead to the Areopagus's gradual loss of power.

More important than the details of Solon's reforms were the ideals that motivated them. In poems describing his achievements, he made clear that his enactments were based on compromise and that he tried to serve justice by giving each side its due. He stated that he had protected the aristocrats' rights but had also given ordinary people the privileges that were theirs—a new concept in Greece. By doing so, he explained, he had brought about "good order"—a just constitution—and avoided civil war, which he described as the worst threat to any city. From now on, Solon claimed, Athenians could see their laws and institutions as the creations of human beings like themselves, and could examine them to determine whether they in fact preserved justice.

Solon's reforms did not immediately bring social peace. In 561 BCE, shortly before Solon's death, the aristocrat Peisistratus (against whom Solon had warned the Athenians) established a tyranny. Though Peisistratus was expelled from the city twice, he finally established power with the help of mercenaries (paid soldiers) from other cities. And yet, his rule was effective. He fostered the Athenian economy by expanding the use of money, developed the city's public spaces, and played a role in the wider sale of Athenian pottery. He promoted the city's public religion as well, building a temple to **Athena**, the city's patron goddess, and adding her image to Athenian coins.

It was only the incompetence of Peisistratus's son, Hippias, that brought an end to the regime he had created. The king of Sparta allied with another Athenian aristocrat to expel Hippias in 510 and tried to bring Athens under Spartan influence. But the Athenian aristocracy split, and a second faction, led by Cleisthenes, a member of a powerful noble family, successfully resisted the first faction's effort to disband the Areopagus. As a result, Athenian independence was restored.

CLEISTHENES: THE INSTITUTIONS OF DEMOCRACY (510–500 BCE)

Cleisthenes did much more than free his city from tyranny. Late in the sixth century BCE, he also transformed its institutions, laying the foundations of democratic government. He reorganized the population, which had traditionally been divided into four ancient tribes, into 139 **demes**—local units or wards of Athens. These were then organized into ten new tribes, each one reflecting a cross section of the population. By doing so, it seems, Cleisthenes broke the oligarchic power of the small group of aristocratic families that had traditionally ruled the city.

Cleisthenes also enlarged the council created by Solon to 500 members, with the ten tribes each supplying fifty representatives. It met every day, except for the many feast days. Fifty members at a time, tribe by tribe, lived and ate in a public building, acting as a standing committee. The council prepared the agenda and proposed laws to the Assembly, which was expanded to include all male citizens. Finally, Cleisthenes set up new courts, with juries ranging in size from 201 to 401 for private cases and 501 for public ones. Their members were chosen by lot from a pool of 6,000 potential jurors, drawn each year from the ten tribes. The newly chosen jurors swore an oath to uphold the laws, and each of them received a ticket (initially made of wood, and later of bronze) to indicate his status. Archaeologists have found many of these tickets in Athenian graves—evidence of the pride people took in their right to serve. The system demanded widespread participation. Over the years, thousands of citizens cycled through the council (on which they could serve only twice in a lifetime) and the juries.

One of Cleisthenes' radical innovations, **ostracism**, reveals the difference between the direct democracy of the Athenians and modern representative democracy. Nothing was more likely to poison the political life of a Greek city than the growth of factions—groups that were so unwilling to compromise that they might cause what the Greeks feared most: civil war. Cleisthenes found an ingenious way to let off these pressures, which might otherwise have undermined the constitution.

The rules governing ostracism were simple. Once a year the members of the Assembly were asked if they would like to expel any prominent citizen who had become a danger to the state. Those voting yes scratched the name of the person on a piece of pottery called an *ostrakon* and placed it in an urn. Any

Ostrakon Members of the Athenian Assembly used clay tablets to record votes in favor of ostracizing prominent citizens who had become dangers to the state. This ostrakon from 482 BCE records a vote against the accused tyrant Themistocles.

individual who received 6,000 or more votes had to leave the city for ten years. No appeal was permitted, although the Assembly had the right to recall the ostracized man if public safety required it. Ostracism proved an effective way to resolve political tensions while avoiding violence. The ostracized citizen was not harmed or outlawed, simply forced to emigrate. The system rested on a popular consensus that did not require any individual to expose himself by bringing an accusation, as the courts did. Ostracism did not happen often, though archaeological evidence proves that it did take place. The practice itself indicates just how seriously the Athenians took the idea that the city and its laws mattered more than any individual did. And it commanded obedience even from the most prominent Athenians. Cleisthenes' own nephew was ostracized in 486 BCE.

THE DEVELOPMENT OF DEMOCRATIC INSTITUTIONS

Direct democracy found its fullest expression in the Assembly, which had ten annual meetings in addition to other sessions when necessary. All male Athenians older than twenty were eligible to take part in the Assembly and to speak. To vote, one had to be at the Assembly on the day when a measure was debated. Meetings took place on the Pnyx, a small hill in the center of the city, where the remains of the speakers' platform are still visible. The whole citizen body could not have assembled at the Pnyx or even heard the speeches that were given there. But the quorum of required voters for some measures was 6,000—evidence that large numbers regularly attended.

The democratic changes that began with Cleisthenes had many causes. But a central one was the new military role played by ordinary Athenians in the fifth century. As we will see, when Persia invaded Greece at the beginning of the fifth century BCE, Athenians—many of them men of low rank—played a central role in defeating the Persians. The ordinary men who served as hoplites in the army and as sailors and marines in the navy were responsible for the victories and likely proud of their role in defending the state. The generals—ten military leaders who could come from any income level in society and were nominated for their abilities by their tribes and then chosen by lot—became more important as they won the great battles in the Persian wars. They took political power from the archons, the older officials who came from great families and who now served in religious and judicial roles. In

462–461 BCE Ephialtes, an Athenian politician who seems to have been a firm democrat, proposed to the Assembly that the old council of the Areopagus be stripped of its powers as a kind of appeals court and left in charge only of homicide cases and a few other crimes. His law passed.

ATHENS AND THE PERSIAN WARS (490–479 BCE)

Athens was becoming not only a democracy but also the most powerful city-state in Greece. For generations, Sparta had seen itself as the dominant power in Greece and had combined diplomacy with force to settle affairs in other cities—even Athens. But when the Greeks found themselves facing the much greater power of Persia, they experimented with new forms of cooperation, which served them well in combat. During the Persian wars, Athens came to regard itself as Sparta's equal and as the leader of the Greek states.

CONFLICT IN IONIA

Long before, in the tenth century BCE and after, Greeks had established numerous independent city-states in Ionia, at the far western edge of Asia Minor. These lively and sophisticated cities were on the border of the empire of the Medes and then, after it was conquered and absorbed by Persia, that of the Persians. The massive Persian Empire, centered on the magnificent royal ceremonial capital of Persepolis in southwestern Iran, was far wealthier than Greece and saw itself—as most Greeks saw it—as the greatest power in the known world. Later, in the 540s, the Ionian Greeks had watched as Cyrus, the king of Persia, defeated their overlord, Croesus, the powerful king of Lydia in western Asia Minor. With this defeat, the western edge of the Persian Empire encompassed all of Ionia, including the Greek colonies.

Late in the sixth century BCE, Persians and Greeks began to come into direct conflict. In 500, Darius, the Persian monarch, sent a naval expedition into the Aegean to invade the wealthy island of Naxos, which would have given him a base near mainland Greece. This expedition was actually proposed by a Greek: Aristagoras, tyrant of the Greek city of Miletus in Asia Minor. When it failed, Aristagoras feared that the Persians would attack his city. He urged the citizens of Miletus and other Ionian Greek cities to join him in rebellion.

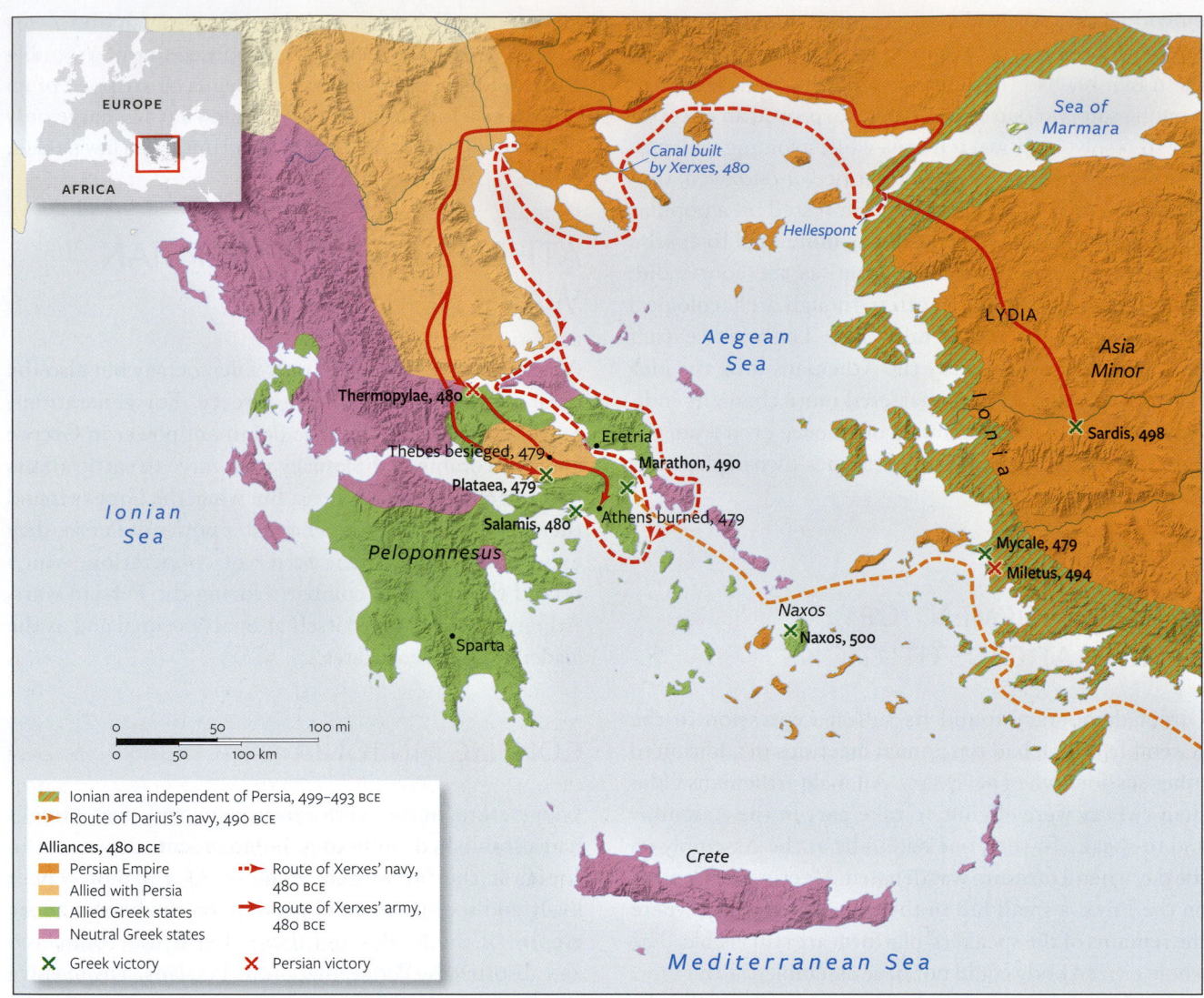

The Persian Wars, 499–479 BCE When the Persian king Darius invaded mainland Greece from the south with a navy of 600 ships, a Greek army decisively beat the Persians at the battle of Marathon on the southeast coast of mainland Greece. But when Darius's successor, Xerxes, invaded from the north, covering a vast amount of territory with a much larger army, the Persians won major victories—until they advanced far enough south to meet with Athenian naval power.

Despite the good advice of Hecataeus, a geographer who explained to the Ionian Greeks how powerful the Persians were, they went to war in 499 BCE. After destroying the Persian city of Sardis in 498, the Greek fleets and armies were decisively defeated. The Persians built vast siege mounds to take the Greek cities and also conquered several of the Greek islands off the Ionian coast. After their final victory in 493, the Persians burned the Ionian cities to the ground, made the Greek boys into eunuchs, and sent the girls to the royal harem.

The mainland Greeks took only a small part in this struggle. The Spartans had warned the Persians to leave their fellow Greeks alone, and the Athenians sent twenty ships to support their allies, the Eretrians, whose city, in mainland Greece, lay just across a narrow gulf from Athens. But after Darius crushed the Ionians' rebellion, he decided to invade mainland Greece to punish its inhabitants for their meddling, and in 490 BCE he crossed to Eretria.

WAR IN THE MAINLAND

Darius arrived with a massive fleet of some 600 ships and a substantial army. The Greeks were horrified by the scale of the invasion. Many years later, the poet and philosopher

Xenophanes described how Greek men would often ask one another when they first met, "How old were you when the Mede came?" Like the assassination of John F. Kennedy in 1963 or the attacks on New York and Washington, DC, in September 2001, the invasion became an unforgettable marker, a point at which time itself seemed to change.

The Spartans, whom the Eretrians asked for help, delayed until a religious festival was over. (Although they did not say so, they may still have resented the way that Cleisthenes had made Athens independent of them.) But Athens sent its hoplites, and one other city also sent troops. Apparently the Greeks were far fewer than the Persians—perhaps 10,000 Greeks arrayed against 20,000 or more Persians. After feeling out the enemy, the Greeks attacked, led by the Athenian general Miltiades, near the settlement of Marathon.

MARATHON New tactics gave the Greeks an advantage. The Persians, lightly armed, carried missile weapons—bows and slings. To avoid heavy losses early in the battle, the Athenian hoplites ran toward the enemy as soon as they came within missile range at about 200 yards from the Persian line. Giving the Persians little time to fire, the Greeks pressed their vulnerable enemies hard. The wings of the Greek army, deeper than the center, overran the Persian units that faced them. When the Persians pushed forward in the center, the Greek wings, instead

In Battle In a Persian cylinder-seal impression probably created at the time of the Persian wars, a lightly armed Persian soldier pierces the heavy armor of a Greek opponent.

of pursuing those they had beaten, enveloped the center and put the Persians to flight—as always, in Greece, the decisive moment of a battle.

Several thousand Persians died at Marathon, as opposed to only 192 Athenians and 11 allies, most of whom were hindered by their heavy armor as they chased the Persians. The Athenians then marched quickly back to Athens, ready to defend the city. Much later, a legend grew up that a single Athenian, Pheidippides, had run the whole distance from Marathon to Athens, announced the Athenian victory, and died—thus creating the legendary basis for the modern marathon run. The Athenians considered the victory a tremendous achievement and a testimony to the power of their people. They buried their dead under a great mound of earth at the battlefield. The war with Persia would continue, but soon after the victory at Marathon the Athenians showed their sense of political autonomy by carrying out the first ostracism of a powerful politician.

THERMOPYLAE AND SALAMIS Darius's successor, Xerxes—a harsher ruler than his predecessors, who campaigned brutally against the Babylonians when they rebelled against him—returned to the attack in 480–479 BCE. He brought a vast force against Greece: supposedly more than 1,200 ships and perhaps as many as 100,000 men. He had bridges built across the Hellespont (the strait between the Balkans and Asia Minor now known as the Dardanelles). The Spartans and a few of their Greek allies tried to cut off his advance at Thermopylae, where mountains on one side and the sea on the other left only a narrow, defensible pass. After a few days of savage fighting in which the Greek hoplites once again defeated the lighter Persian troops, a Greek traitor showed the Persians a path that led to the rear of the Greeks' position. This flanking tactic made the Greeks' situation hopeless, and most of them abandoned the fight. Three hundred Spartans, commanded by Leonidas, one of their two kings, remained with a few allies and died fighting heroically. Their epic last stand could not stop the Persian advance, though it may have bought the Athenians some time to prepare their ships for a decisive confrontation. But it became the first great model of what has remained the West's standard for absolute heroism: the last stand of a rear guard.

At this point the Athenians, led by Themistocles, an aristocrat who had served as archon, made one of those decisions that show how people of the past—even those who invented our system of government—often thought in ways that seem alien to us today. Leaders and common people routinely consulted **oracles**—sites where a god or a dead hero answered questions of all kinds, sometimes

The Greek Perspective The face of a terrified Persian soldier on the body of this drinking cup, made in Athens between 410 and 400 BCE, commemorates Athenian victory in the Persian wars. On the rim, a Persian servant ministers to her Greek mistress.

through the mouth of a priest or priestess. In this case an oracle predicted that wooden walls would someday protect the Athenians. So they followed Themistocles and left their city, which Xerxes burned, and entrusted their safety to their wood-hulled ships. In a momentous naval battle, a Greek fleet defeated the Persians at Salamis in 480 BCE. Xerxes then left the war in the hands of his commander, Mardonius, and returned to his capital, while the Greeks won a second victory at Mycale in 479. Greek hoplite armies did the same at Plataea and killed Mardonius. After his death, the Persians—although they continued their struggle with the Greeks in the Aegean for decades to come—would never again threaten the mainland.

MEANINGS OF WAR The meaning of these confrontations depends on the

The Delian League, ca. 454 BCE

point of view of those who interpret them. Persia not only survived its defeat but prospered. The Spartans remembered the heroic example set by the 300 fallen at Thermopylae and commemorated their brothers-in-arms by an inscription: "O stranger, tell the Spartans that we lie here, obedient to their word." The Athenians saw themselves—especially their navy—as the saviors of Greece and set out to play the leading role in Greek affairs that they thought they had earned. By modern standards, they treated their triumph with modesty. The oldest surviving Greek tragedy, *The Persians*, is the work of Aeschylus, who fought at Marathon. Performed less than ten years after the battle, the play re-creates the response of Xerxes' mother, and then of Xerxes himself, to the news of the Persian defeat at Salamis. The play shows both disdain for the Persians and a remarkable ability to imagine their suffering. But the Athenians also rebuilt their devastated city on a grand scale and looked for ways to expand their power.

THE ATHENIAN EMPIRE (479–433 BCE)

Over the first half of the fifth century BCE, the Athenians made themselves the heads of what began largely as an alliance among equals but soon became an Athenian naval empire. After the Persian wars, the Athenians collected tribute from the other Greek states—supposedly to support expeditions to harry the land of the Persians. However, the Athenians seemed to do little with the gold that piled up on the island of Delos under the supervision of an Athenian treasurer. The **"Delian League"** came to seem increasingly like an instrument of Athenian power—especially after the Athenians, around 454 BCE, transferred the league's treasury from Delos to the temple of Athena at Athens, a powerful symbolic change.

TRADE AND POWER More than symbols were at issue. Athens was developing its military power in a new and dramatic way. In 482 BCE, rich silver deposits were discovered in Laureion, near the eastern coast of Attica. The Athenian government leased these to entrepreneurs, who used a workforce of some 20,000 slaves to dig and purify the silver. Most important, Themistocles persuaded his fellow citizens not to divide the new treasure among themselves but to invest the revenue from the mines in the navy, and they continued to do so throughout the century. The Athenians also continued to collect tribute from allied city-states in return for protection against the Persians. Athens now dominated the ocean as no previous power had.

Trade flourished. Athens built the "Long Walls," several miles in length, to ensure safe transport to and from its ports, Piraeus and Phalerum. Both ports were crammed with ships and swarmed with middlemen. Many of these were resident foreigners called *metics* ("co-dwellers") who specialized in the activities vital to maintaining international trade, such as the manufacture of jars, the shipment of grain and wine to Athens, and the payment of Athenian silver to its suppliers.

Observers noted the vast range of goods available at Athens. Some of these—such as timber, which the bare hills of Attica did not produce—had to be imported if Athens was to sustain its naval power. The city depended on the rulers of Macedonia to the north for this vital raw material. Trade therefore was a matter of state, and the Athenians did their best to ensure that no other power interfered with their ability to obtain the raw materials on which their power rested. These included not only timber but pitch, rope, and all the other materials needed to outfit their warships.

Other Greek cities within the Delian League, such as Thebes and the island city of Thasos, found themselves compelled not only to pay Athens tribute but also to obtain its permission to engage in trade. One resentful aristocrat observed, "If a city is rich in shipbuilding timber, where will it dispose of it unless it wins the consent of the Athenians? What if some city is rich in iron or bronze or cloth? Where will it dispose of it unless it wins the consent of the rulers of the seas?" Athens was a democracy and favored democratic governments in other cities, yet its conduct seemed increasingly imperial. The Spartans saw themselves as the leading power in Greece, but the Athenians now made clear that they claimed to be, at the very least, the Spartans' equals.

THE NAVY AND SOCIETY: TRIERARCHS AND OARSMEN

What really mattered—and what made the expansion of trade possible—was the powerful navy that the Athenians built with their new wealth. They created a fleet of armed **triremes**—large galleys powered by muscular oarsmen sitting in groups of three, one above the other, all working to the limits of their strength. The Athenians developed sophisticated naval tactics. They practiced rapid rowing, probably reaching speeds higher than ten miles per hour, and sudden changes of course. They used the rams at the front of their ships to break enemy fleets, attacking them from the vulnerable flank. The marines and archers whom they carried made each trireme an even more fearsome weapon.

Later in the fifth century BCE, the Athenian democracy devised a new social and economic system to sustain the navy. This system required both the rich and the poor to contribute, and ultimately gave the poor what critics of democracy described as a preponderance of power. The wealthiest Athenians were required to use their fortunes, for a year at a time, to provide public services. Some served as trierarchs, responsible for outfitting and commanding triremes. The trierarchs worked with expert contractors who took care of the technical and military details; but the trierarchs still had to see to it, at their own expense, that one or more ships provided by the state had all the necessary equipment, and that the most skillful officers were employed to command the crew.

Triremes In a fourth-century BCE Athenian relief of a trireme, the top row of oarsmen is visible, along with the oars of the second and third decks of rowers below.

Like Sparta, Athens defined itself largely by the military that it maintained. Equipped by the wealthy, Athens' military drew its forces from the populace. Poor Athenians rowed the galleys, and were paid for doing so out of the public revenues. Men who could afford arms served as marines, fighting from the ships, and they too were paid. In a society in which aristocrats still commanded armies and navies, men of low birth provided vital manpower and demanded respect for doing so. As a fifth-century critic of the regime explained, ironically expressing admiration for a system that he could neither accept nor change, "at Athens the poor and the commons seem justly to have the advantage over the well-born and the wealthy; for it is the poor who man the fleet and have brought the state her power."

THE PELOPONNESIAN WAR (431–404 BCE)

In the decades after the Persian wars, relations between Athens and Sparta—never easy—deteriorated. Sparta tried to prevent the Athenians from rebuilding their city's walls

RIACE WARRIOR STATUE

Although far removed from the Bronze Age, Hellenic artisans and their patrons retained a long-standing affinity for bronze, the alloy of copper, tin, and other metals that formed a key technology in the Near East and Greece between the fourth and second millennia BCE. In the eighth century BCE, the poet Hesiod spoke of men who not only used weapons of bronze but were themselves made of the metal. In Homer's epics, "brazen-hearted" men wield "pitiless" bronze weapons. In the fifth century BCE, Greek artisans favored bronze as a malleable material that could be sculpted to give full expression to the human form. They used chisels or tracing tools to carve lifelike details and added color by incorporating paint, other metals, and stone.

This rare example of a large-scale Greek bronze statue (many were later melted down so the metal could be used for other purposes) was one of two warrior statues recovered off the coast of Riace, Italy in 1972. It was completed at the height of Athenian power, around 460 BCE. A shield strap on the subject's left arm reveals him to be a warrior; the right hand might have held a spear. Greek artists of this period often depicted men in full-length sculptures because it was believed that the body was as expressive as the face. Here, the warrior's imposing musculature matches his fearsome facial features, which are accentuated by silver-coated teeth and copper lips and eyes. Though the hair and beard are sculpted in lifelike detail, their careful arrangement emphasizes the idealized nature of this figure.

QUESTIONS FOR ANALYSIS

1. In what ways does this sculpture strike you as realistic?
2. How does it also embody Greek ideals of masculinity?
3. In what ways does this sculpture represent the Athenian values articulated by Pericles in his funeral oration of 431–430 BCE?

after the Persians left, a decision that would have dramatically weakened Athens. The continuing buildup of Athenian naval power greatly worried the Spartans and their allies. In 465 BCE, a slave revolt broke out in Messenia, a region ruled by Sparta, and the helots seized a mountainside city that they could defend. The Spartans appealed to the Athenians, who were experienced in siege warfare, for help. The Athenians sent soldiers, but the Spartans ordered them away, fearing that they might join forces with the helots. This marked the end of the alliance between the two cities and the beginning of the final long slide into open conflict.

In 459 BCE Athens joined with a neighboring state, Megara, traditionally a Spartan ally, to fight Corinth, another Spartan ally. Sparta joined the war on Corinth's side. The war lasted until 446/5 BCE, and the peace that followed was continually disturbed by conflicts over the great powers' dependent cities. In 431, a full-scale war broke out, as Corinth pushed the Spartans to resist the growth of Athenian power.

SOCIAL AND POLITICAL CATASTROPHES

Agitation and argument were constant during the Peloponnesian War, which stretched from 431 to 404 BCE. Pericles, who first led Athens into war but also cautiously recommended that the Athenians not battle the Spartans on land, died in a plague outbreak soon after the war began. The plague killed thousands of other Athenians as well, perhaps enough to undermine the city's power and explain its eventual loss of the war. It also caused a breakdown in social customs. The great Athenian historian Thucydides tells us that the sick were abandoned, and the dead—in a radical violation of Greek tradition—were left unburied.

Yet even this disaster paled next to the other catastrophes that the Athenians endured. Through the second half of the fifth century, the pressures of the Peloponnesian War kept Athens in a state of agitation punctuated by emergencies. These occurred, for example, when the Spartans destroyed Athenian crops or when some internal enemy mutilated the statues of the god Hermes placed at crossroads in the city, causing a public panic. Although the wealthy, aristocratic general Nicias tried to carry on where Pericles had left off, he never won the favor of the people. They preferred Cleon, a politician who shouted and gesticulated in public, raised the pay of the jurors, and used the courts to attack his enemies.

ATHENS' DEFEAT

Cleon's aggressive policies scored some successes, but in 422 BCE he was defeated and killed by the Spartans in northern Greece. Nicias made peace with the Spartans, but the two cities and their allies continued to struggle. A young Athenian politician, the brilliant and aggressive Alcibiades, pressed for renewed conflict. The Athenians lost this encounter in 418, but Alcibiades continued to enjoy wide support. Politics in Athens was now pitched in a new key, in which demagogic forms of expression—violent words and gestures—seemed more effective than the more moderate language and gestures of a Pericles. War, as Thucydides would remark, proved to be a harsh teacher.

Athenian policy became more radical. In 415 BCE an Athenian army destroyed the city of Melos, which refused to become an ally, and massacred its male inhabitants. In the same year, Alcibiades persuaded the Athenians to undertake a bold but ill-planned expedition to help allies in Sicily against the powerful Greek city of Syracuse. Nicias, who thought the expedition foolish, was forced to take command, and the Athenian forces were defeated on both sea and land. Though weakened, the city fought on. During the last years of the war, Persian satraps forged an alliance with Sparta. A naval loss at Aegospotami in 406 was the final blow, and two years later the Athenians and their allies surrendered to the Spartans. The long conflict had cost the Athenians thousands of their fellow citizens, dozens of ships, and much of their wealth. The Spartans removed the Long Walls, which were torn down to music played by flute girls. Athens could no longer wait out sieges, confident that it could import the grain its population needed.

THE THIRTY TYRANTS

The period after the war's end was hard for the Athenians. The Spartans had damaged Athenian farms and destroyed olive groves, which took a generation to replace; and they had allowed many of the slaves who worked in the state silver mines to escape. Less prosperous than they had been for generations, the Athenians had to import more of their food than ever.

Moreover, after the Athenians begged for peace in 404 BCE, a short-lived aristocratic junta, the Thirty Tyrants, took over with Spartan backing. This oligarchical government did more than rule the city; it declared its opponents public enemies, executed them, and confiscated their goods. This was a radical form of attack on fellow citizens that would be repeated during hard times in the

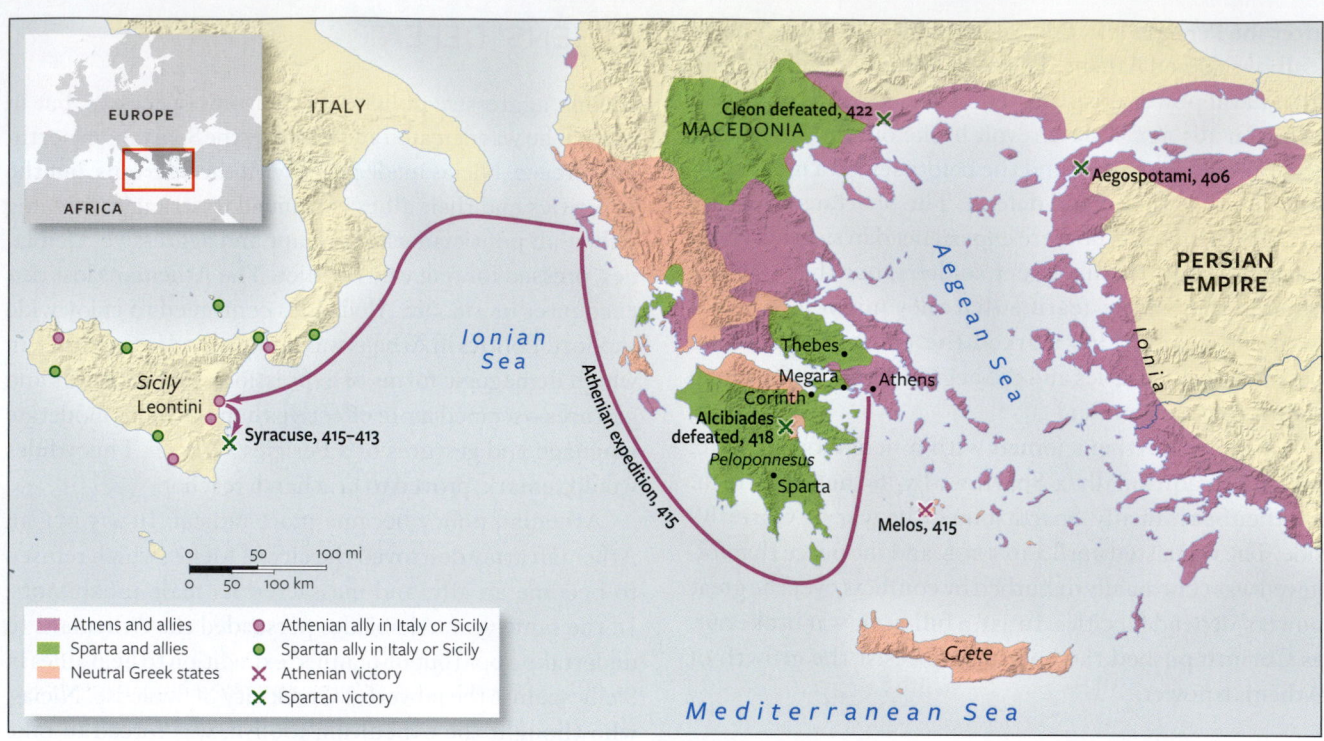

The Peloponnesian War, 431–404 BCE The Peloponnesian War mainly involved the two city-states of Athens and Sparta, but it raged across the entire Mediterranean region, from the massacre at the island of Melos in the Aegean Sea, to Alcibiades' ill-fated naval expedition to Syracuse, in Sicily, to the Spartan naval victory at Aegospotami.

Roman Republic and elsewhere. Opposition to the Thirty grew, and a small force of Athenian exiles seized a border fort. In bitter street fighting, the exiles defeated the leader of the Thirty, who died in the battle.

After further struggles, in 403 BCE the Thirty were expelled from Athens and the old laws and government restored. The democrats eventually declared an amnesty for the followers of the oligarchic regime, proclaiming that "we will remember past offenses no more." With its citizens reunited, Athens regained much of its strength. In the 390s the Athenians rebuilt the Long Walls under the protection of a fleet sent by the Persians, who wanted to counter the growth of Spartan power. The Athenian state began minting silver coins again, instead of the bronze ones issued during the war. Prosperity gradually returned, but Athens struggled against Thebes and other states for power over Greece. None managed to establish its power in a lasting way.

THE MEANING OF DEFEAT

The world's first great democracy was defeated in warfare by oligarchic Sparta. Those who have reflected on the story, from the historian Thucydides onward, have often suspected that the city's ruthless pursuit of power over others brought about its defeat and the temporary overturning of its institutions—an outcome to worry supporters of democracy. The city and its institutions survived the turmoil, and a more or less democratic constitution lasted for some decades, but Athens would never again dominate the Greek world as it had.

THE ATHENIAN EXPERIMENT (490–406 BCE)

Culturally, the Athenian experiment succeeded beyond anyone's dreams. An extraordinary range of new artistic and intellectual forms, new ideas, and new ways of understanding the universe took shape in the city over the century that separated Cleisthenes' leadership from the end of the Peloponnesian War. The Athens of this period—in which, as we will see, Sophocles wrote his tragedies, Socrates inspired Plato to compose his dialogues, and Phidias and others created the magnificent complex of buildings and statues on the Acropolis—was not a quiet marble wonderland but a vast, messy debating hall, as agitated as Paris during the French Revolution of 1789.

THE AGORA

The city itself underwent a radical transformation during the sixth and fifth centuries BCE. When the Athenians began rebuilding after the second Persian invasion, they set to work on providing their city with public buildings worthy of a great power. The Agora had been established in the sixth century in a central area where three roads joined the city's main road, the Panathenaic Way. Peisistratus built a temple and a drainage system there. In the fifth century, the Agora became the site of a council chamber for meetings of the smaller body tasked with steering debate and legislation in the Assembly. Nearby, in a colonnade known as the Royal Stoa, the archon served as the state's chief officer of justice, and the laws of Solon, carved on stone, reminded Athenians that all men had the duty to take part in politics. By the end of the century other structures joined these buildings, including temples dedicated to Hephaestus, the blacksmith god, and Athena, the goddess whom the Athenians saw as their protector, as well as a debtors' prison. Perhaps the most splendid of all was the Stoa Poikile ("painted colonnade"), the walls of which were decorated with murals said to have been extraordinarily lifelike and beautiful. One of them depicted the battle of Marathon.

THE ACROPOLIS

Especially magnificent were the projects that the sculptor Phidias carried out, with the political and financial support of Pericles, on the **Acropolis**, the steep hill at the center of the city that is visible for miles and dominates the region. After they made peace with Persia in the middle of the century, the Athenians, between 447 and 432 BCE, built on the foundations of an earlier structure (destroyed by the Persians) what has come to be seen as the classic Greek building, the Parthenon. This structure was a subtly elegant rectangular temple to Athena Parthenos ("Athena the maiden"), one of the avatars of Athens' patron goddess. Built to house a huge gold and ivory statue of the goddess sculpted by Phidias, its roof was supported with columns of extraordinary elegance and its interior crowded with the treasures that belonged to the Athenian state—everything from Persian daggers and a gilt lyre to six thrones, more than seventy shields, and an

The Acropolis The steep Acropolis hill and its temple complex dominated the city of Athens from the mid-fifth century BCE on.

ivory figurine of a cow. The temple was also a strongbox—the Athenian counterpart to Fort Knox.

The same rebuilding campaign created other structures in Athens. One was the temple of the mythic hero Erechtheus, where graceful caryatids (columns carved in human form) supported part of the roof. Beneath it sheltered the ancient wooden image of Athena that the citizens had carried with them when they abandoned Athens to the Persians. In the same years, the theater on the southern slope of the Acropolis was rebuilt. Later still, after the crisis years of the late fifth century, the complex on the Agora was expanded further, with a mint, a new courthouse, and large inscriptions that evoked the city's democratic past.

GRAND STRUCTURES AND IDEALS

The public buildings of fifth-century BCE Athens resembled those of Near Eastern states in their scale and beauty. But their purposes, reflecting the society that created them, were different. For decades to come, Athenians described these public buildings as the clearest evidence of their ancestors' patriotism and virtue. In those days, as a fourth-century orator recalled, the Athenians' leaders had lived in modest houses exactly like those of their neighbors. In the orator's day, by contrast, wealthy men built themselves houses larger than the ancient public buildings—as clear a sign of ethical and political decay, in his view, as the public opulence of the old city had been indicative of ethical and political strength.

Yet Pericles' great buildings are ambiguous, at best, as symbols of the democratic state. They were built by a direct democracy, but the actual decisions were taken by Pericles and other male leaders, since the democracy excluded women, metics, and slaves from participation. The Parthenon served a religious purpose, showing that the Athenians felt gratitude to their gods for the victory over the Persians, who had burned the older temples and public buildings. But Pericles used the funds of the Delian League to pay for it. This must have given a clear sign to the other member cities that Athens saw itself as their leader—even, potentially, their ruler. Still, in this case, a city created public buildings on a scale that previously only monarchical states had constructed. The idea that a popular government should house itself and its gods with such grandeur also belongs to the heritage of Athenian democracy.

THE BOISTEROUS REALITY OF POLITICS

If the setting for public life was grand and orderly, its reality was often awkward and messy. The Greek comic poet Aristophanes (ca. 450–ca. 388 BCE) created the character of a poor countryman whom he used to describe what public life was like in the early years of the Peloponnesian War. Coming into the city at daybreak, the poor rustic finds the Pnyx, where the Assembly met, deserted because the city folk are still gossiping in the Agora. Bored and restless, he spends his time yawning, stretching, farting, and longing for his place in the country—only to be shocked at noon when the citizens, led by their tribes' representatives, crowd into the Assembly and fight for the places closest to the speakers' platform.

The boisterous process that Aristophanes ridiculed was the core of Athenian direct democracy. Every time a public debate broke out, the Assembly had to meet. This occurred, for example, in 406 BCE after the Athenian navy won a sea battle but failed to save the survivors from sinking ships. At a meeting of the Assembly, the commanders addressed the citizens and defended themselves. The council proposed a vote by tribes, which would allow the people to express approval or disapproval of the commanders' conduct. Savage debate broke out as to whether the motion itself was legal, ending only when the motion's author threatened to prosecute the officials who opposed it. After further debate, the Assembly voted to condemn the commanders, and six were executed. Soon after, however, the Assembly reversed itself and voted to prosecute those who had brought the commanders to trial.

Political and juridical processes in this system were noisy, chaotic, and subject to manipulation. Lies, threats, and unrealistic promises could sway the Assembly. No wonder, then, that Socrates' pupil Plato, the most brilliant and eloquent of ancient thinkers, despised his city's democratic government, especially after one of its juries condemned his teacher to death. And yet, as Pericles pointed out in his funeral oration, the Athenians' constant exposure to political and military debate, and their incessant involvement in deciding how the city should ensure its food supply or avoid secession by its subjects, gave even ordinary citizens a form of political education unique in the ancient world.

RELIGION AND CITY LIFE

Although it took the political genius of Pericles to rebuild the Acropolis, its buildings were dedicated not to public administration but to the gods who, Athenians believed, protected their city. The Greeks loved telling stories about these gods—from the traditional family of Olympian divinities headed by Zeus and including Ares, the god of war, and Aphrodite, the goddess of love, to the grimmer gods Hades and Persephone, who ruled the realm of the dead.

Oracle at Delphi On this fourth-century BCE vase fragment the god Apollo consults the oracle, a priestess in the Temple of Apollo, at Delphi in the southern Greek mainland. Even gods—but more often generals and statesmen—listened to the oracle's enigmatic advice.

The Athenian pantheon was never fixed. As one observer noted, "Just as in other respects the Athenians welcome foreign things, so too with the gods." Over time they continued to accept new divinities—from Dionysos, the god of wine, to Boreas, the wind god—as well as human heroes such as Theseus, the legendary king of Athens, and the two young men who killed the tyrant Hippias. Like other Greeks, too, Athenians recognized the gods of other cities and nations as divine. They were as eager as residents of any other city to consult the oracle of the god Apollo at Delphi, which gave notoriously ambiguous answers to the questions sent by rulers and ordinary people.

RITUALS The Greeks believed the gods inhabited the temples dedicated to them. They often referred to the statues of the gods, like the gigantic Athena in the Parthenon, as if they were the gods themselves. The interiors of these temples were not used for religious services, but important rituals were performed in them nonetheless. The old noble clans of Athens produced men and women who served as priests and priestesses, presiding over public rituals. Sometimes these involved dramatic sacrifices of animals. A young woman would carry a basket containing a sacrificial knife, and women would wail as the animal was killed, always by a male sacrificer. Occasionally the whole animal was burned; sometimes only parts, while the rest was shared out and eaten. In still other cases, the sacrifice involved no bloodshed but rather the offering of cakes, milk, and honey at the god's altar. Individuals also

dedicated tripod vessels, vases, and even marble or bronze statues of young men and women, often with inscriptions explaining why they had done so.

Religious acts took place not only in temple precincts but throughout the city. When Greeks made a treaty or just organized a symposium (a party for drink and talk), they always began by pouring a little wine on the ground as a sacrifice to the gods. They also prayed, reminding individual gods of the long relationships between them and particular families, and expressing their hope for future favor. As one fifth-century Athenian wrote to the goddess Athena in an inscription that accompanied an offering, "Do you, daughter of Zeus, returning the favor, preserve [my] prosperity." Once a year, Athenians flocked to a massive shrine at nearby Eleusis, where they had the chance for a more personal religious experience involving rituals of initiation, after which the individual could lose himself or herself temporarily in a union with a divine being.

FESTIVALS The most striking feature of Athenian religion, however, was probably its public face. Life in any modern society is interrupted, throughout the year, for various purposes: holidays close schools, jury duty demands time away from work, and the like. But the interruptions are fairly uncommon. Ancient Athens, by contrast, enjoyed as many special days as normal ones.

Everyone knew that the calendar was thronged with religious festivals—as many as 150 in a year—and everyone knew, from the grand celebrations that accompanied

Religious Festivals At the annual festival of Dionysos, children aged two or three were given a first drink of wine from a child-size jug to celebrate their survival of infancy. These miniature wine jugs from Athens were made around 440–400 BCE.

them, when they took place. Varied in form and purpose, these rituals were dedicated to everything from celebrating the progress of the agricultural year to driving scapegoats out of the city. In some cases, they were as competitive as other Athenian activities, with teams competing in mock cavalry fights, exhibitions of skill at arms, and races. In other cases—especially those of the male and female groups that worshipped Dionysos—they practiced ecstatic rituals, leaving the city to do so. During these religious festivals the population did not work. The Athenian principle of equality also applied to the butchering of sacrificial animals, which were cut up into packages of equal size—some full of meat, others of bone and fat—and parceled out to every citizen for feasting. Although the public exercises of religion may have been more decorous than meetings of the Assembly, they embodied—and probably celebrated—the same democratic principle.

ATHENIAN SOCIETY

In the fifth century BCE, Athens dwarfed the other cities of mainland Greece. Covering some 1,000 square miles of Attica, its total population likely numbered more than 300,000 men and women: citizens, foreigners, and slaves. Much of its land was rural, with a large part devoted to the cultivation of staple crops such as olives, grapes, and barley. But the city depended on trade as much as cultivation. The Athenian climate made it hard to grow wheat, which was imported from the Black Sea region to the north through a system carefully overseen at tollbooths along the route. The richest citizens owned large amounts of land and earned their income by selling their surplus through middlemen in the city. The city also depended on a wide variety of artisans who constructed its buildings, adorned its temples, and manufactured arms and armor for its soldiers. Inscriptions on stone and passages in Greek comedy mention almost seventy different occupations, from the fullers who finished cloth to knife-makers and carpenters.

DAILY LIFE: DIVERSE GOODS AND PEOPLE

During the fifth century BCE, most of the 200,000 or so free Athenians lived and worked in the small households that were the basis of social life. The majority inhabited small stone houses with courtyards, constructed rapidly

Bounty of the Sea A fisherman holds small fish in his right hand and a basket of eel and oysters in the other. This Roman statue from the late first century BCE is likely a copy of a Greek original, suggesting the importance of the maritime economy to Greek city-states such as Athens.

after the Athenians reoccupied the city that the Persians had burned. Even the rich lived simply, as Athenians disapproved of excessive displays of private wealth.

With the seaport of Piraeus developing into the greatest market in the Aegean, Athens revived as a center of both manufacture and trade. Its workshops produced the goods for which the city had long been known, such as the red-figure pottery developed in the late sixth and fifth centuries, in which figures were left in the color of the clay, against a black background. Images on these vases show well-born men reclining and drinking at symposia, boys reading aloud from their books to their teachers and parents, women practicing mainly female crafts such as weaving, and the arms and armor that enabled the city to maintain its position in the Aegean.

Investors and traders saw to it that the city enjoyed all the goods it needed. A system of high-interest loans, which included an early form of maritime insurance, enabled traders to buy cargos of papyrus and rope from Egypt or

FIFTH-CENTURY ATHENS

❝ WE DO NOT COPY OUR NEIGHBORS, BUT ARE AN EXAMPLE TO THEM.....I SAY THAT ATHENS IS THE SCHOOL OF GREECE, AND THAT THE INDIVIDUAL ATHENIAN IN HIS OWN PERSON SEEMS TO HAVE THE POWER OF ADAPTING HIMSELF TO THE MOST VARIED FORMS OF ACTION WITH THE UTMOST VERSATILITY AND GRACE. ❞

PERICLES, FUNERAL ORATION, FROM THUCYDIDES, *HISTORY OF THE PELOPONNESIAN WAR* 2.41.1

Built atop the Acropolis in 447/6–433/2 BCE, the Parthenon was a magnificent temple dedicated to the goddess Athena, a storehouse for the city's wealth, and a monument to Athenian triumph. This detail from the Parthenon's frieze depicts the gods Poseidon, Apollo, and Artemis.

❝ THE GREEKS TEND TO HAVE THEIR OWN DIALECT, WAY OF LIFE, AND TYPE OF DRESS, BUT THE ATHENIANS USE A MIXTURE TAKEN FROM ALL, WHETHER GREEK OR BARBARIAN. ❞

PSEUDO-XENOPHON, *CONSTITUTION OF THE ATHENIANS*

❝ TELL ME NOW...
OF THE GOOD THINGS THAT DIONYSUS BROUGHT HERE FOR MEN IN HIS BLACK SHIP....FROM CYRENE HE BROUGHT SILPHIUM STALKS AND OX-HIDES, FROM THE HELLESPONT MACKEREL AND ALL SORTS OF SALT FISH, FROM THESSALY CRUSHED WHEAT AND BARLEY AND OX RIBS. ❞

HERMIPPUS, *BASKET-BEARERS*

A Panathenaic prize amphora, showing Athena as goddess of military victory with spear and shield. The victor in the chariot race at the Panathenaic Games was awarded 140 of these vessels filled with olive oil (roughly five tons).

POPULATION

Approximately 300,000 (including 200,000 free inhabitants, 50,000 of whom were adult males; 25,000 metics; 80,000–90,000 slaves)

THE PANATHENAIC FESTIVAL

The most important of the 150 holidays in the city calendar, a week-long celebration of the city held every August with athletic competitions, musical performances, a male beauty contest, and a ceremonial procession through Athens to the Acropolis, culminating with the presentation of a sacred woven fabric to the city's patron goddess, Athena

QUESTIONS FOR ANALYSIS

1. What evidence do the quotations provide for the adaptability and grace that Pericles attributes to the Athenians?
2. Considering the map and the city calendar, what role do you think the Panathenaic procession and other festivals played in the life of the city?
3. How did the Parthenon and its remarkable art announce what it meant to be Athenian?

pork and cheese from Syracuse. If their ships returned and the traders sold the goods, they immediately paid off their creditors. If a ship sank (the floors of the Black Sea and the Mediterranean are littered with wrecked Greek ships), the trader was no longer liable for the money—a system that, like more modern ones, invited abuse.

Athens also became a center of consumption. Athenians loved to eat—especially fish—and they indulged in the rich eel, red snapper, tuna, and other delicious sea creatures that were available in Athenian fish markets. A poet of the fifth century listed the splendid things to be found on sale in Athens, as well as their far-flung sources: mackerel and salt fish from the Hellespont, frankincense from Syria, cypress from Crete, ivory from Africa, and colorful carpets from Carthage.

No wonder the Athenians, unlike the citizens of some other city-states, allowed foreign residents of their city to establish temples to their own gods—as, for example, local Egyptians did for Isis, whom they worshipped as the ideal wife and mother and the protector of the poor. The citizens of Athens expected to have access to a vast range of goods and were willing to accept the presence of many foreigners if that was necessary. This tolerance for diversity in goods and peoples gave the city a striking, if partial, resemblance to a modern metropolis.

husband divorced his wife (divorce was easy to obtain in Athens), he had to repay the dowry to her father. If the husband died, she did not inherit his estate. Instead, one of his male relatives would marry her and administer the estate until his own male heir could inherit it. If a man caught another man having sex with a woman over whom he had authority—a wife or a daughter—he could kill the adulterer himself or inflict a variety of punishments, from taking his property to abusing him physically in public. Women caught committing adultery were forbidden to enter public temples or to wear ornaments of any kind.

In a society in which paternity mattered greatly, it was important that a bride be a virgin. To preserve their daughters from threats and temptations, Athenians tried to marry them off soon after they reached puberty. A woman of property might marry an older man when she was fourteen or fifteen years old. Immediately—as the writer Xenophon tells us in a manual on how to run a proper household—she was expected to make her house as neat and efficient as the captain of a well-ordered ship would make his cabin. Like Pericles, Xenophon insisted that women not attract attention outside the house: "Your business," his spokesman in the treatise said, "will be to stay indoors." Yet he also indicated that a woman needed a set of advanced skills to carry out the tasks mandated by

WOMEN'S LIVES

Athens of the fifth century BCE was certainly no democracy in the modern sense. Women were formally excluded from all forms of public life and, so far as possible, from all male company. Women of the upper and middle classes (as we learn from the male writers and orators who are our chief sources) were supposed to remain confined to their houses. When Pericles praised the Athenian dead in the first year of the Peloponnesian War, he told the women in his audience that the best way for them to earn praise would be to not become the objects of gossip. Although this sounds horrifying now, he probably meant that women who were never mentioned in gossip would win reputations for virtue. Poorer women certainly could not have observed such traditional strictures.

THE FAMILY AND THE HOUSEHOLD Athenian

men had considerable power over women. When a woman married, she and her dowry, the one substantial piece of property she was ever likely to own (even if only in a formal sense), were given by her father to her husband. If the

Women's Work This water jar, probably from fifth-century BCE Athens, suggests the gendered division of labor fundamental to Athenian culture. The seated woman is weaving, suggested by the wool basket at her feet, while a nursemaid hands her child to her.

Companions A detail from red-figure pottery (fifth century BCE), depicting a woman entertaining a man with music. Hetairai were professional women who provided elite men with music, conversation, and more intimate pleasures, and could count on a kind of social freedom that wives could not.

her separate sphere: she must keep the accounts, supervise indoor and outdoor slaves, look after slaves who became ill, and receive and store such necessities as wool and grain. Even as Xenophon praised the ideal household, he made clear that being in charge of it was a complex task.

Though women were confined, they worked at jobs that we know better from Athenian vase paintings than we do from any written texts. Most cloth, for example, was apparently made in the household. Paintings show women spinning raw wool into yarn and weaving it on looms. Even vessels made for men's symposia depict women making wool, which suggests that men esteemed this sort of work. Beautifully embroidered textiles might be displayed on cushions and chairs or as the clothing of statues of gods and goddesses to prove that the household's women were virtuous. Rich women would have been expected to supervise the female slaves who did this work.

PUBLIC APPEARANCES Naturally, not all women followed the purely domestic course that Pericles recommended. Young women marched together in some of the festival processions that Athenians loved to stage, and women of all ages attended funerals. **Hetairai** ("companions") were professional women who, from the sixth century BCE on, served as entertainers and companions for elite men. They appeared in public and attended symposia, where they played musical instruments, sang, and apparently took part in conversations. Collections of their witty remarks circulated in Greece. A hetaira named Aspasia was the chosen female companion of Pericles after he

divorced his wife. She bore him a son, entertained his friends, and supposedly gave him political advice. And he embraced and kissed her whenever he left or returned to their house, a warm gesture that other Athenian men are not recorded as offering their female partners.

Poor married women appeared in public by necessity. Those who had no slaves hauled their own water from the well and might have had to work as midwives or house servants. In less urban districts, women tended gardens and livestock. In the denser parts of the city, our sources offer glimpses of women assisting friends who had gone into labor, borrowing food and spices, helping to relight a lamp, and simply visiting one another as friends.

One exceptional source describes a woman named Hagnodike who cut off her hair, wore men's clothing, and trained as a doctor. After becoming a success at obstetrics, she was indicted for seducing her female patients. Brought into court, she raised her tunic to prove that she was a woman. Her prosecutors then denounced her even more fiercely—until their wives came to court and insisted that they stop bothering this woman who had helped so many others. Supposedly, the Athenians then changed their laws to allow women to study medicine. Stories like this are as rare as they are intriguing.

EDUCATION

Traditional Athenian education, which was chiefly aimed at boys, was not complex. They learned to read: vases show boys working with slates or scrolls in the presence of a tutor. As they grew older, they might go to a school. We know little about these, except that the law required they be open only between dawn and dusk. There or at home, boys would study the poems of Homer, from which, they believed, they could learn not only heroic ideals but also much practical information about everything from managing horses to fighting. From the seventh century BCE onward, music and movement formed an important part of many boys' education. Later accounts suggest that many learned to play the lyre and to set poetry to its music. Several hundred boys took part each year in formal choruses, and they were trained to sing and dance by *choregoi*—individuals from certain families chosen by the state to carry out this duty.

The point of all this preparation was to enable boys to emerge as young men able to play their roles in public life. Physical exercise was central to this form of training. Naked young men exercised at the gymnasium, learning

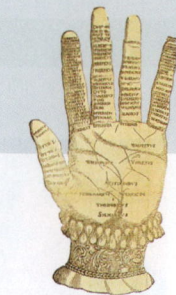

ATHENIAN FUNERAL LAW

This source from the late fifth century BCE, traced to the island of Keos near Athens, is a law governing burial practices in Athens. It is thought to be a copy of an earlier law enacted by the Athenian archon Solon. Throughout Greece, similar laws limited the expense of funerals and mourning at them. This was done partially as a democratizing measure: expensive or elaborate funerals could imply that the wealthy were more important in death than the poor. Another goal was to restrict women's attendance at funerals to the female relatives of the deceased, thereby reducing opportunities for women to gather outside the home. This source describes how Greek women washed the body and laid it out for burial, covering it with a shroud.

These are the laws concerning the dead: bury the dead person as follows: in three white cloths—a spread, a shroud, and a coverlet—or in fewer, not worth more than 300 drachmas. Carry out [the body] on a wedge-footed bed and do not cover the bier with cloths. Bring not more than 3 *choes* of wine to the tomb and not more than one *chous* of olive oil, and bring back the empty jars. Carry the shrouded corpse in silence all the way to the tomb. Perform the preliminary sacrifice according to ancestral customs. Bring the bed and the covers back from the tomb inside the house.

On the next day cleanse the house first with sea water, and then cleanse all the rooms with hyssop [an herb]. When it has been thoroughly cleansed, the house is to be free from pollution; and sacrifices should be made on the hearth.

The women who come to mourn at the funeral are not to leave the tomb before the men. There is to be no mourning for the dead person on the thirtieth day. Do not put a wine-cup beneath the bed, do not pour out the water, and do not bring the sweepings to the tomb.

In the event that a person dies, after he is carried out, no women should go to the house other than those polluted [by the death]. Those polluted are the mother and wife and sisters and daughters, and in addition to these not more than five women, the daughters' children and cousins; no one else. The polluted when washed with water poured out [from jugs] are free from pollution....

This law has been ratified by the council and the people. On the third day those who mourn on the anniversary of the death are to be free from pollution, but they are not to enter a temple, and the house is to be free from pollution until they come back from the tomb.

QUESTIONS FOR ANALYSIS

1. Why does the law limit the amount of money one can spend on funerals, and how might that restriction reflect Athenian democratic ideals?
2. What does "pollution" mean in this context, and how and why were women thought to carry that pollution?
3. What does this source tell us about Greek ideas about death?

Source: Mary R. Lefkowitz and Maureen B. Fant, "77. Funeral Law. Ioulis on Keos, Late 5th Cent. B.C.," *Women's Life in Greece and Rome* (website), www.stoa.org/diotima/anthology/wlgr/wlgr-greeklegal.shtml.

the arts of combat and competing in many forms of athletics. Eventually, an older man would become a young man's mentor and lover, teaching him the military skills of an adult and cultivating his mind. These relations were expected to follow a strict code. The older man had to maintain his dignity and not "fawn" on the boy or disgrace himself in other ways, and the boy was meant to learn to behave in a manly way. Unlike Sparta, Athens did not institutionalize these relationships in a formal, systematic way. But the similarities seem clear.

Technical education normally took place within the family. Healers and seers, carpenters and tailors taught their technical skills to their sons. Vase paintings show women reading scrolls, and many must have learned to do so. A few did that and more: Aspasia, the hetaira who was Pericles' companion, supposedly mastered and taught the art of rhetoric. Educated at home, most girls—at least according to the idealized description given by Xenophon—learned about diet and the various arts involved in making clothing.

Women Readers An olive oil jar from 450–425 BCE shows a woman reading a papyrus scroll. Women needed to learn to read, write, and do basic math in order to manage their households, but only a few exceptional women pursued their studies further.

METICS: RESIDENT ALIENS

As we have seen, many foreigners were attracted by Athens' wealth and power and settled there as metics. The city offered them work of every kind, especially when the great rebuilding program began after the Persian wars. At the same time, though, they were excluded from citizenship. In 451–450 BCE, Pericles introduced a citizenship law stating that no one who lacked two citizen parents could have "a share in the polis." Athenians, as a later historian put it, were the children of Athenians. Metics could and did serve as oarsmen and soldiers, but they could not own land, vote, hold office, or play any role in decision making. They could use the Athenian courts, but they were more vulnerable than citizens to summary arrest.

Citizenship could in exceptional cases be conferred on non-Athenians, as it was for the metic Pasion. A slave dealer who had been a slave himself, Pasion was freed by the bankers who owned him, and he prospered as a metic. He owned a factory that made shields. Showing an acute sense of diplomacy, he spent his profits freely on the needs of the Athenian people, who repaid him by making him a citizen. His son was an established Athenian who regarded himself as a guardian of the city's traditions. Most metics probably lived more modestly. Yet they too could win their way to citizenship. A list of men, probably metics, who were made citizens for helping to expel the oligarchic Thirty Tyrants in 403 BCE includes a farmer, a cook, a carpenter, a donkey driver, and a nut seller.

SLAVES

Even further from the status of citizens—and from enjoying the freedom and other rights that came with citizenship—were the thousands of slaves who kept the households and workshops of Athens functioning. Every bit as much as Egypt and Persia—as well as other Greek cities like Sparta—Athens was a slave society that depended on the work of unfree men and women. Most male slaves were purchased from a wide range of regions across Eurasia, from Syria to Scythia (the lands to the north and east, roughly from the Danube to the Don and Volga Rivers) and beyond. In the time of Pericles, Athens may have had as many as 80,000 or 90,000 slaves. Nicias, the aristocratic Athenian general who led the Sicilian expedition in 415 BCE, owned more than 1,000 slaves, whom he rented out to work in the mines. Even poor households probably had a few slaves, especially maids to perform basic household tasks.

Treatment of Slaves The working conditions of slaves varied widely: those depicted in this sixth-century BCE pottery fragment labored in a clay quarry.

COMPETING IDEAS OF SLAVERY IN HELLENIC SOCIETY

Slavery may be seen as a function of a society's cultural and political systems. Slavery was ubiquitous in Hellenic Greece, and some considered it necessary for the development of Athenian society. Most slaves were owned by and worked for Athenian families of all economic classes. These two sources, one from Athens and the other from a Greek outpost on the Black Sea, reflect differences in the ways slaves were defined and treated—socially, economically, and legally.

Constitution of the Athenians

The anonymous author of this treatise from the fifth century BCE is not Xenophon but is writing under his name. The treatise as a whole offers a critical interpretation of Athenian democracy. In this excerpt, Pseudo-Xenophon objects to the Athenian treatment of slaves as trusted and integrated members of society, and complains that it was essentially impossible to distinguish slaves, *metics* (resident aliens), and free persons.

Now among the slaves and metics at Athens there is the greatest uncontrolled wantonness; you can't hit them there, and a slave will not stand aside for you. I shall point out why this is their native practice: if it were customary for a slave (or metic or freedman) to be struck by one who is free, you would often hit an Athenian citizen by mistake on the assumption that he was a slave. For the people there are no better dressed than the slaves and metics, nor are they any more handsome. If anyone is also startled by the fact that they let the slaves live luxuriously there and some of them sumptuously, it would be clear that even this they do for a reason. For where there is a naval power, it is necessary from financial considerations to be slaves to the slaves in order to take a portion of their earnings, and it is then necessary to let them go free. And where there are rich slaves, it is no longer profitable in such a place for my slave to fear you. In Sparta my slave would fear you; but if your slave fears me, there will be the chance that he will give over his money so as not to have to worry anymore. For this reason we have set up equality between slaves and free men, and between metics and citizens. The city needs metics in view of the many different trades and the fleet. Accordingly, then, we have reasonably set up a similar equality also for the metics.

Achillodoros, The Berezan Letter

This rare source, scratched on a thin piece of lead, comes from the Greek outpost on Berezan Island in the Black Sea. It was written by the merchant Achillodoros to his son Protagoras around 500 BCE. Achillodoros entreats his son to inform Anaxagoras of a dispute that has arisen between himself and Matasys about both the loss of property and the threat of enslavement.

Protagoras, your father sends you these instructions. He is being wronged by Matasys, because he is trying to enslave him and has deprived him of his cargo-vessel. Go to Anaxagoras and tell him, because he [Matasys] insists that he [Achillodorus] is the slave of Anaxagoras, claiming "[Anaxagoras] has my property, male and female slaves and houses." But he [Achillodorus] complains loudly and denies that he and Matasys have any business with each other, and insists that he is a free man, and [Matasys] and he have no business with each other. But if he [Matasys] and Anaxagoras have some business with each other, they know it between themselves. Tell this to Anaxagoras and his wife.

QUESTIONS FOR ANALYSIS

1. What does Pseudo-Xenophon mean when he says that Athenian society had "put slaves and free men on equal terms"?
2. Why might Matasys want to enslave Achillodoros?
3. How do these two documents illustrate the fluid status of slavery in Greece during this period?

Sources: Pseudo-Xenophon, *Scripta Minora*, in *Xenophon*, vol. VII, trans. E. C. Marchant and G. W. Bowersock (Cambridge, MA: 1925), pp. 479–81; Michael Trapp, ed., *Greek and Latin Letters: An Anthology, with Translation* (Cambridge: 2003), p. 51.

The conditions in which slaves labored varied widely. Many worked in agriculture at every level, from field laborer to overseer. Pericles owned a highly educated slave who kept "meticulous" accounts for his household. Many slaves performed the same functions as free men and women, working beside them doing everything from weaving cloth to fluting columns. The workmen who built the complex on the Acropolis under Pericles included carpenters, metalsmiths, workers in gold and ivory, painters, and many more. Surviving records for one of the Acropolis buildings list eighty-six workmen whose status is clear: twenty-four citizens, forty-two metics, and twenty slaves toiled side by side, doing the same jobs. In theory, warfare was reserved for citizens. In practice, though, the Athenians were ready to abandon this rule in emergencies. In 406 BCE, when one fleet had been destroyed and another had to be fitted out by rapid improvisation, the Athenian Assembly used slaves to man the ships and granted them pay, freedom, and equality, not with Athenian citizens but with their allies, the Plataeans.

Other slaves worked in conditions as horrifying as those of the helots whose rebellions so worried their Spartan lords. Thousands, many of them children, not only worked in the Laureion silver mines in eastern Attica at terrible cost to their bodies but slept and ate below ground level. And in 413 BCE, when the Spartans invaded Athenian land in central Attica, some 20,000 slaves, mostly skilled workmen, deserted to the Spartan side—plausible evidence that they found their lives oppressive. All slaves, moreover, suffered indignities. Slaves belonged to their masters, who could sell them, rent them out, or bequeath them to others. Though they could marry, the master had an absolute right to break up their families. Protection from arbitrary violence and the legal right to purchase one's freedom, if one could assemble the necessary means, could not compensate for these hardships.

The prevalence of slaves in a state that stood for democracy and freedom seemed so awkward that the fourth-century philosopher Aristotle tried to explain it. Slaves, he insisted, naturally deserved their status because they were weaker and less intelligent than their masters. This argument would be revived almost 2,000 years later, during Europe's first age of colonial expansion.

ATHENIAN CULTURE: MASTERING THE WORLD

In the sixth century BCE the inhabitants of Ionian Greek cities, more quickly than their fellow Greeks on the mainland, became curious about the physical world and its many different inhabitants. Philosophers tried to understand how the physical universe operated: they offered explanations for earthquakes and the movements of the planets. Others tried to map the world and describe its peoples. After 500 BCE, philosophers and philosophy came to Athens, which gradually became the center of innovative thought in Greece. The Athenians learned much from Ionian thought, but they put their own twist on everything from poetry to philosophy.

This remarkable city created tragedy and comedy, and transformed rhetoric, philosophy, history, and more—forms of writing and thinking that have had lasting and pervasive effects. In medieval Baghdad and Paris, Athens was remembered only as the former residence of important thinkers. Even people who had no idea what the Parthenon looked like or any knowledge of Greek tragedy or history recognized words like *oligarchy* and *democracy* as keys to political life.

WAYS OF HEALING: HIPPOCRATES AND ASCLEPIUS

Athens in the fifth and fourth centuries BCE was a pressure cooker of political debate and intellectual inquiry. Native and foreign thinkers struggled to solve the problems of democracy and war and to understand their larger world. Medicine was one of the new ways of understanding that flourished in the fifth century BCE. The medical men—a group, rather than an individual, who wrote the works attributed to the single doctor Hippocrates (ca. 460–ca. 377 BCE)—were based outside mainland Greece. But they crossed and recrossed the Greek world in search of information about the human body and its ills, and of patients to treat.

Some of these medical men gradually developed new ways of dealing with disease. They insisted that a doctor must observe patients and record case histories precisely and unemotionally. They devised a system for explaining human physiology, which they claimed largely comprised four competing substances called humors: black bile, yellow bile, phlegm, and blood. Health depended on the balance among these, which the physician hoped to maintain. But because each city had its own seasons, winds, and water, the medical man must observe these closely to explain the illnesses that affected a particular people.

Hippocratic practitioners regarded all diseases as natural. Their empirical, fact-based method found a home in the skeptical, argumentative culture of the Athenians. Yet other sorts of healers also found a market there. After the plague of 430–426 BCE the god of healing, Asclepius, was eagerly received. A great shrine was built for him in Epidauros, where the sick, blind, and deaf could sacrifice, pray, and spend the night, in the hope that the god would visit them and heal their affliction. When he did appear, the temple priests interpreted his advice. More successes were recorded in the temple of Asclepius, carved into stone, than in the Hippocratic doctors' case histories.

TRAINING FOR PUBLIC LIFE: THE SOPHISTS

The Athenians fiercely debated the diverse ways of understanding the world. In the homes of the well-to-do—especially in the *andron* ("men's room," the Greek version of the man cave)—guests lying two to a couch would drink wine and carry on discussions. Public argument was equally fierce and mattered more, at least in practical terms. Anyone who hoped to survive politically had to be able to speak effectively to the Assembly, in order to convince his audience that his proposals would serve their interests.

In 427 BCE, a brilliant orator named Gorgias arrived in Athens from the city of Leontini in Sicily, hoping to gain assistance in a struggle with a more powerful city, Syracuse. Athens agreed to help Leontini—a decision that would lead in the end to catastrophe, when the Syracusans routed the Athenian expedition in one of the gravest Athenian defeats of the Peloponnesian War. More important, Gorgias himself inspired fascination for the seductive power of his speeches, which were cast in language rich in alliteration. He became the first in a series of specialists who offered instruction in the art of public speaking.

These men, known as **sophists**, educated young statesmen for public life. They had a sharp ear for current debates over what sort of medicine or government worked best in which circumstances. And they knew

that absolute truths could rarely be established. So they trained their young pupils to argue both sides of almost any case and to be well informed, quick on their feet, and eloquent. Sophists also taught the technical skills needed to speak effectively: memory training for speakers who had no teleprompters to rely on, and elocution lessons so that they could be heard, unamplified, by a crowd of several thousand.

Education in rhetoric, the art of persuasive speaking, involved more than style and elocution; it emphasized content and form. Ideally, every statesman needed a grounding in moral philosophy and a treasury of historical examples at his fingertips, ready to cite at appropriate points. More important, he needed to know how to compose and deliver a speech. Aristotle (384–322 BCE) may have drawn on textbooks written and used by the sophists, which have not survived, when he divided speeches into three kinds: (1) deliberative or political, (2) forensic or judicial, and (3) demonstrative—straightforward praise or blame. Each kind of speech had a goal: to convince the audience where its advantage lay, in politics; where justice lay, in law; or who or what deserved honor and shame.

The sophists prepared their students to keep an open mind and figure out, as circumstances dictated, what approach to a problem would work best. At their most radical, the sophists denied that human beings could ever know absolute truths, and insisted instead that a practical education should limit itself to teaching students how to make arguments that others would find convincing. "Man," the philosopher Protagoras explained, "is the measure of all things." At their most ambitious, they claimed that they could master and teach all of the arts: one of them turned up at the Olympics wearing clothes that he had made himself and playing a musical instrument of his own manufacture. The sophists were the first Western teachers to offer what we would now call a liberal education, concentrated not on technical skills but on the range of arts needed by the free men who ruled Athens and other city states. Again and again, later societies from republican Rome to revolutionary America would treat the skills that the sophists taught as the core of a practical education for public life.

STAGING CONFLICT: CIVIC LIFE AS LITERATURE AND PERFORMANCE

Sophists wandered the roads of Greece looking for clients in all the city-states that welcomed political or judicial debates. Tragic and comedic drama, by contrast, were

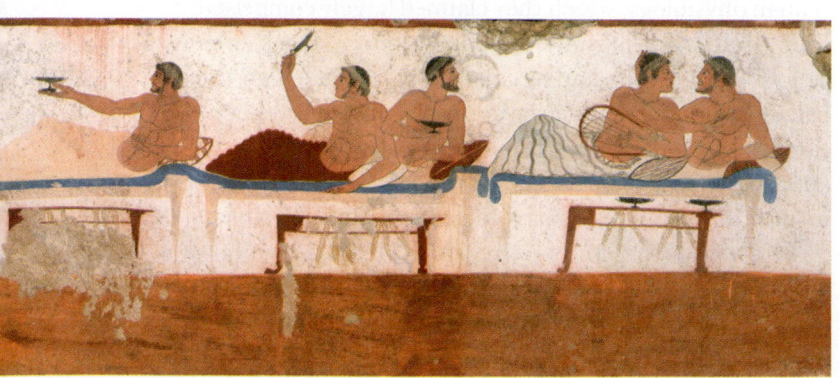

The *Andron* In this wall painting from 480–470 BCE, a group of men have retreated to the *andron* for a symposium, a gathering centered around wine-drinking and conversation. The men on the left are playing a popular drinking game, while the age-difference between the couple on the right suggests a kind of erotic relationship associated with the educated elite.

Athenian inventions. They emerged during the late sixth and early fifth centuries BCE, when the great celebration of the god Dionysos underwent a slow transformation with extraordinary results. Like the Homeric epics of centuries earlier, Athenian drama became the common property of all Greeks, as theaters were built and performances of Athenian plays were held across the Mediterranean world.

THE FESTIVAL OF DIONYSOS The cult of Dionysos, the Greek god of the grape harvest, wine, and ecstasy, existed in archaic times and was celebrated by groups of men and women in rituals about which little is precisely known. In the sixth and fifth centuries BCE the festival of Dionysos became the grandest event of the Athenian civic year. It began with a procession of priests carrying images of the god, citizens, and metics, and involved sacrifices and offerings to the god. What made the occasion distinctive was that it came to include competitive dramatic performances. Every year, authors would compete to write the best tragic and comic dramas. Three authors would compose four plays each: three tragedies and a satyr play (a comedy involving imaginary wild men). Five more authors would enter comedies. Each would receive support from a sponsor, who paid for and trained the chorus and actors, and each one's plays were performed during the festival. A panel of judges selected the winners.

The plays were staged in the Theater of Dionysos, originally a simple dirt amphitheater that later became an impressive structure in the shape of half a bowl, its seats carved from stone, on the side of the Acropolis. The plays formed part of a civic ritual. The sons of Athenians killed in war paraded before the audience, and the tribute won in war was exhibited. Then, in front of a vast crowd that included women as well as men, actors and a chorus performed their parts. Formal and stylized, the tragedies never entirely lost their ritualistic character. Men took all roles and wore high shoes and masks, which defined the ways in which they could move and speak. Violent action took place offstage and was described as if witnessed by the characters in the play. And the choruses—groups of actors who danced, sang, and spoke commentaries on the action of the dramas—moved and pronounced their lines in an even more formal manner, befitting the origin of tragedy in religious ritual.

Yet these plays became works of art of great power and individuality, addressing many different subjects in radically different modes. Like the Jews in their exile, the Athenians at their cultural peak found ways to reflect on the relation between gods and humans, the nature of

Festival of Dionysos A large fifth-century BCE vase depicts a procession of followers of the god Dionysos, including a goat-tailed satyr. The grand religious festival in honor of Dionysos was the highlight of the Athenian year.

justice, and the weakness of humanity that retain their power even today.

TRAGEDY AND THE ANCIENT PAST Aeschylus (525–456 BCE), the first of the three great tragedians whose work survives, used **tragedy** to explore the meaning of human life and the origins of such institutions as law and justice. Setting a succession of plays in the world of Homer's poems, Aeschylus followed the sequence of events—as inevitable in his depiction as the cycle of seasons—that begin when Clytemnestra, wife of the Mycenaean king Agamemnon, murders him on his return to Troy. Orestes, their son, feels compelled to kill Clytemnestra in revenge, though he knows that he will be pursued by the terrifying Furies, the ancient gods of earth whose task was to avenge the spilling of blood—especially that of a blood relative. Only in the last play of the sequence, *The Eumenides* (*The Kindly Ones*, a euphemism for the Furies), does the goddess Athena intervene to create a human court, the Athenian Areopagus, which can judge cases of murder and declare them justified or not. Aeschylus's tragedies thus trace, in mythical form, the conflict between divine and human justice and the way in which a long chain of revenge killings was finally replaced by courts designed to reach just verdicts. Aeschylus's formal, often difficult language, like the plots of his plays, looked back to the mythical past and the foundations of those very Athenian institutions, such as the Areopagus, that lost or gained importance in the fifth century.

Sophocles (ca. 496–406 BCE) also set many of his plays in the deep past of myth, especially that connected with the city of Thebes. He portrayed Thebes as an imaginary, ancient Athens, a republic that had somehow come into being during an archaic age of kings and jealous gods. These gods tended to destroy any man who became too powerful by using his own abilities against him. As in the world of Aeschylus, curses—those imposed, for example, on individuals who kill their parents—are still effective.

In *Oedipus the King*, the main character unknowingly kills his father and marries his mother. Gloom hangs over Thebes. The smoke of sacrifice no longer rises to the gods, and the city's ancient, honest prophet can no longer interpret their messages. Oedipus is, in modern terms, not guilty, because he never intended to commit a crime. He killed his father, not knowing who he was, after severe provocation, and has ruled his state well. Yet he must tear out his too-sharp eyes, confess his crime, and leave the city to others in order to lift the curse he has brought upon the citizens whom he has tried to help. Oedipus—a good ruler who loves his people and proclaims his intention to punish whoever is polluting his country—finds that he himself is the source of the disaster and must suffer banishment. One wonders what implications Athenians—who often treated formal punishment as appropriate for political opponents—drew from this story.

Euripides (ca. 485–406 BCE), by contrast, concentrated less on questions of eternal justice and blood curses, and more on the psychology of individuals. His re-creations of ancient myth convey with shocking vividness the power of the gods to force those who worship them to commit terrible deeds. When Euripides decided to portray Orestes and Electra as the killers of their mother and her lover, in his own version he did so more to understand their emotions than to present them as adults struggling with the bloody commands of a human law that seems to conflict with the divine law.

TRAGEDY AND PUBLIC LIFE For all its apparent remoteness from contemporary themes and concerns, tragedy provided a way for Athenians to see, enacted on stage, some of the conflicts that provoked the sharpest political debates in their society. In *Antigone*, Sophocles depicts one of these through the actions of the brilliant ruler, Creon. Having just saved Thebes from chaos after an invasion, during which both the Theban leader Eteocles and his brother, the invader Polyneices, have died, Creon has taken command. Like a well-schooled sophist, he develops an elaborate metaphor—one familiar to thousands of Athenians from their time in the fleet—to justify his claim to absolute power: "Sirs, the vessel of our State, after being tossed on wild waves, has once more been safely steadied by the gods." Creon demands (and here the tones of fifth-century BCE Athens can be heard) absolute loyalty to the state: "if any makes a friend of more account than his fatherland, that man has no place in my regard." Then he proclaims that Eteocles will receive the heroic funeral appropriate to one who has died for the city. The invader Polyneices, by contrast, will receive no burial, even though leaving the dead unburied, by Greek tradition, would pollute the city and invite the condemnation of the gods.

Antigone, the sister of Polyneices, insists that an ancient, divine law requires her to sprinkle dust on his corpse. Caught in this forbidden act, she accepts condemnation to death; this terrible fate, vividly described, is rapidly followed by the death of her lover, Creon's son, and the total collapse of his father. Both Antigone's sister Ismene and Creon denounce Antigone for violating the boundaries of female conduct. Yet the further progress of the play seems to show that she was right and they were wrong.

When read today, *Antigone*, first performed before the Peloponnesian War, seems a prophecy of central tensions in the Athenian polity: (1) the appropriation of the task of mourning for the war dead by male orators like Pericles speaking in public, and (2) the conflict between the Athenians' intention to defend liberty across Greece and the savagery of their actual conduct when smaller states refused to work with them. In its own time, it celebrated the woman's role as the guardian of sacred law in a society that seemed to be transforming some of its central customs and traditions.

Tragedy, then, did more than let individuals watch the terrifying but strangely gratifying stories of great men bringing themselves down by overreaching. It also made possible the literal staging—before a crowd of 15,000 that mirrored the population—of the dilemmas that afflict any organized society. Tragedy could not answer timeless questions such as how to reconcile the desire for revenge with the existence of a rational justice system. Its role was different: it literally dramatized the conflicts that no society could ever finally resolve.

COMEDY Unlike tragedy, comedy was set in the Athenian present, and it disregarded the complex rules that required tragedies to be dignified. The actors—all male—wore long phalluses to indicate the nature of the enterprise. The parts they played ranged from a slack-jawed yokel giving a comic perspective on the rituals of Athenian politics, to the politicians themselves.

Aristophanes (ca. 450–386 BCE), the greatest of the fifth-century BCE writers of comedy, offered commentary on the demagogic politics that corrupted Athenian

Comic Actors These terra cotta statuettes from the late fifth or early fourth century BCE, found near Athens, illustrate two characters commonly seen in comedies of the period: a grotesque, angry-looking man and a nurse holding a baby. All roles were played by men, who wore masks, and often padded costumes, to make the characters look bizarre and comical.

life as the Peloponnesian War raged on. At times, as in *Lysistrata*, he indulged in comic fantasy wild enough to convulse an audience. In this play, the women of Athens and other Greek cities, desperate for peace, conspire not to have sex with their husbands until peace is concluded. Their discussions—in which they decide to act as provocatively as possible, while still refusing to make love—parody the pragmatic arguments and calculations of Athenian political debate. At first the strike has ludicrous consequences (the actors' long phalluses play prominent roles in this particular comedy), but eventually the men of Sparta and Athens are forced to make peace. Like the tragedians, Aristophanes crafted models—indecorous and witty ones, rather than severe and tragic—that remain surprisingly powerful 2,500 years later.

HISTORY: CONNECTING PAST AND PRESENT

As grand and novel as Athenian drama, in its own way, was history—the effort, which came to center on Athens in this period, to explain the course of human affairs, using the same skills that had enabled the medical men to understand disease and the sophists to forge the rhetorical tools of politics. In the poems of Homer and Hesiod, great households and important cities employed experts who could recite the genealogies of kings and aristocratic families. But in the fifth century BCE, history became something new: a form of writing cast in prose, not poetry, that connected the past to the present in a detailed, systematic way. Resting on inquiry as well as tradition, history was analytical as well as celebratory.

Like Hippocratic medicine, history began not in Athens but in the Greek cities of Ionia. Its name, the Ionian word *historie*, originally referred not to narrative history in the sense it does now, but to any systematic effort to understand the world through observation. The Ionian Hecataeus (sixth century BCE) not only made inquiries but recorded them, traveling as far as Egypt, known as a land with real historical records, to do so. And after learning about the deep past from Egyptian priests, he was a pioneer in subjecting earlier writers to sharp critique: "Hecataeus of Miletus speaks thus: I write what seems to me to be true. For the accounts of the Greeks are various and foolish, in my opinion." For Hecataeus, history would always be presented in the key of personal, human argument.

HERODOTUS: HISTORY ON A GRAND SCALE

The scale of the Greek wars against Persia and the Athenian war against Sparta called for a new sort of historical consciousness, cast in a new kind of writing. Herodotus (ca. 484–425 BCE), born in Halicarnassus, in Ionia, provided it. Cosmopolitan from birth, he had relatives outside as well as inside the Greek world. He tried to come to terms with the amazing Greek victories over Persia, not only as a tale-teller but also as a reporter of a new kind. Herodotus traveled throughout the Mediterranean world, interviewing everyone he could. Once he had established the complex background of alliances that led up to the wars, he completed his work—which he eventually read aloud at the Olympic Games, to the Athenians' vast satisfaction.

If Herodotus strove to match the ancient epics in the sheer size of his work and the range of characters it embraced, he made clear that unlike the poets, he had no Muses to inspire him: "Herodotus of Halicarnassus, his *Researches* are here set down to preserve the memory of the past by putting on record the astonishing achievements both of our own and barbarian peoples." He told the story of the Persian invasions and the victorious Greek defense with drama, irony, and wonderful descriptions of the decisive battles. But he also expanded his inquiry to the entire Mediterranean world, setting the wars in a vast

Persian Wars A fifth-century BCE drinking cup from Attica shows a swordfight between a Greek hoplite and a Persian soldier. Produced at the time of the Persian wars, it represents the Greek view of the conflict on an individual scale—similar to the approach Herodotus often took in writing his histories. The better equipped Greek soldier dominates the scene, looming over his ineffective Persian opponent.

geographical and historical context that included everyone from highly civilized Egyptians to Scythian nomads on the steppes of what is now Russia. Finally, he tried to explain why the wars had taken place—and found himself hard put to offer a hypothesis that went beyond the recitation of ancient myths.

Herodotus's work is a mixture of elements. At times—especially in his descriptions of the rise and fall of Croesus of Lydia, the overlord of the Ionian Greeks—he reads like the tragedian Sophocles. He explained the fall of Croesus's kingdom partly as the result of the gods' envy of great human achievement, partly as retribution for ancestral crimes. Yet when he narrated the events of the Persian wars, he devised vivid ways to represent the clash not only of individuals, as Homer had done so well, but of whole armies. And in setting out the background to the war, he managed to describe whole civilizations—for example, that of Egypt—in great depth, not only chronicling kings but also analyzing customs and institutions. He realized that peoples differed in what they ate, who they married or worshipped, and how they dealt with the bodies of the dead, all of which he recorded in detail.

As the first author of a political and military narrative on the grand scale of epic, Herodotus was the intellectual ancestor of all those who have since tried to document the history of great events. Herodotus was also the first writer we know of who used systematic, oral inquiry to find out what people thought, in his own world and outside it, thus making him the intellectual ancestor of all travel writers, ethnographers, and social scientists. At times, as in his dazzling narrative of the battle of Thermopylae, he managed to bring these forms of inquiry and writing together.

In his account of the brave Spartans' stand against the cowardly Persians at Thermopylae, Herodotus began to create what would be one of the longest-lasting and problematic legacies of Greek thought: the set of ideas and prejudices that depicted non-Greeks as less manly, less warlike, and less capable of free and civilized life than the Greeks. The term *barbarian*, which was originally just a description of non-Greek–speakers, gradually became pejorative in the fifth century BCE and after. Yet like Aeschylus, Herodotus, who had non-Greek relatives of his own, also considered events from the side of non-Greeks and made clear that, in the end, every civilization followed its own rules.

THUCYDIDES: HISTORY AS PAST POLITICS

Remarkably, another historian soon overshadowed the achievement of Herodotus. **Thucydides** (d. ca. 401 BCE), an Athenian, served as a general in the Peloponnesian War but went into exile when he failed to prevent the Spartans from taking a city held by the Athenians. Like Herodotus, he inquired as widely as he could, talking to participants on both sides in the war. Like Herodotus, he depicted the war on an epic scale, placing it in the broad context of Greek politics and tracing it across the Mediterranean to Sicily. And like Herodotus, he became a great writer whose prose retains its ability to move and shock.

Like many historians after him, Thucydides denied the debts that he owed to his greatest predecessor. Early in his work, he explained that he had set out to write his book "not as an essay which is to win the applause of the moment, but as a possession for all time"—a clear attack on the entertaining ethnographies and other digressions in Herodotus's work. By critically weighing each report against others, and by verifying so far as he could what his witnesses told him, he claimed to establish a reliable narrative of events—something Herodotus, in his view, had failed to do. And he made clear why it mattered to know the past.

Human nature would not change, Thucydides claimed. Accordingly, his history would provide not just a reliable narrative of the past but a key to understanding the events of the future. By collecting the speeches given by each side and inserting them into his work—or at least inserting the speeches that each side should have given—he made it possible, as Herodotus had not, to understand the real reason why the war had occurred. That reason was not divine retribution, but Spartan fear of growing Athenian power. At the same time, though he did not say this, he made his book a handbook for statesmen and generals who would have to meet similar challenges and would need to know what to say. It is thanks to Thucydides that we know, so far as we do, what Pericles said at the funeral of the first year's dead.

Thucydides' work established the principle—one still observed by leaders worldwide—that the most effective way to justify a policy or a decision is to cite an appropriate historical precedent. Along with rhetoric, the form of history forged at Athens by Thucydides became the core of elite education for centuries to come.

FINDING THE LESSONS THAT HISTORY CAN OFFER During the course of the Peloponnesian War, which we still portray more or less as Thucydides did, the Athenians started treating other cities in an increasingly tyrannical manner, demanding their support and destroying them if they refused it. In 416 BCE, the Athenians insisted that the tiny Spartan colony of Melos join them in their war against Sparta. When the Melians refused, in Thucydides' account, the two sides met to confer. Thucydides laid out the Athenians' demands and the Melians' reply. Every time the Melians appealed to justice or to the gods, the Athenians dismissed their arguments with outright contempt. The harsh tone of their remarks caused an ancient critic, in the first century BCE, to comment that it was "indecorous" for Thucydides to make Greeks address other Greeks in a fashion appropriate only for Persians.

Thucydides likely thought the same. The last books of his history describe the defeat of the Athenians in Sicily. During this debacle, the Athenians' leader makes the same ineffectual appeals to the gods and justice that the Melians had made when Athens was at the height of its power. In another section of the book, moreover, Thucydides draws one of his rare general conclusions. Just as he had described the plague to enable others to recognize it when it occurred again, so he described what happens in war to the language of politics: "Words had to change their ordinary meanings and to take those which were now given them. Reckless audacity came to be considered the courage of a loyal ally; prudent hesitation, specious cowardice; moderation was held to be a cloak for unmanliness; ability to see all sides of a question, inability to act on any."

In this first and greatest of military histories, Thucydides made clear the lesson that many later political and military historians have not been willing to face: that war, however necessary, can and often does destroy the moral and civil world of those who wage it. Sophocles had made a

similar point in his own way, but what tragedy portrayed as a dilemma, history narrated as a story that could have been given a different ending by wiser and more just decisions. To read Thucydides is to gain not only a training in the arts of rule but also a moral education in their destructive capacity.

PHILOSOPHY IN ATHENS

Perhaps the most distinctive and powerful Athenian creation of all was systematic philosophy. In the second half of the fifth century BCE, the city became the stage for a new kind of debate about everything from the shape of the universe to the purpose of human life. In the fourth century BCE, Athens became the home of permanent institutions for research and teaching founded by the most famous of ancient philosophers, Plato and Aristotle. The foundations for what they created were laid, however, in the great age of Athenian democracy—which, as we will see, ultimately proved unwilling to tolerate thought that accepted no bounds.

SOCRATES More critical of Athens than Thucydides—and more influential in the millennia to come—was another veteran of the wars, **Socrates** (ca. 469–399 BCE). He was not a member of the Athenian elite, although he inherited enough property to serve as a hoplite. In many ways he lived the ordinary life of an Athenian citizen, distinguishing himself for courage in battle and during political crises. But he turned his life into a unique quest to find the truth—or at least to establish how little of it humans could ever attain.

Supposedly inspired by the revered Oracle of Delphi, which once told a friend of his that no man was wiser than Socrates, he began to interrogate his fellow citizens. He expected to show that many were actually wiser than he. Gradually Socrates developed a distinctive approach that sought the truth by posing questions. This Socratic method showed, in almost every case, that the answers Athenians gave to the great questions about life and the universe were actually full of unstated assumptions and hidden contradictions.

Like the sophists, Socrates haunted the Agora at the center of the city. Trees, he contemptuously remarked, could not teach him anything, but his fellow humans might. Like the sophists, too, he knew how to apply the destructive tools of critical reason. During the Peloponnesian War he became the center of a group of aristocratic disciples that included the politician Alcibiades and two eloquent writers, Plato and Xenophon, whose works

Socrates This marble statue of Socrates from the Hellenistic or early Roman period suggests the continuing influence of Hellenic culture in the centuries that followed.

present him and his views in detailed (and contrasting) ways.

Unlike the sophists, however, Socrates refused to accept any payment for his teaching; at the end of his life he insisted that his special wisdom consisted only in the recognition of how little he knew. As happy to pose questions to a slave as to a sophist, he became the scourge of the respectable men who had never thought hard about the beliefs that they overconfidently professed. A passionately urban intellectual, Socrates seems never to have tired of the city squares where he could ask his questions.

It is difficult to know exactly what Socrates believed. At times, he seems to have believed that wisdom could be attained only by an intense process of ever sharper questioning; at other times, he seems to have felt that the gods might provide knowledge of certain kinds by direct revelation. According to Plato, Socrates disapproved of democracy and thought that the ideal society would be one ruled by a philosopher-king. But Socrates not only fought for democratic Athens; he also opposed the Assembly when it condemned a group of Athenian generals, in his view a violation of the law. Later he refused to obey the orders of the Thirty Tyrants when they commanded him to take part in a judicial murder, even though these aristocratic rulers included some of his supporters.

THE DEATH OF SOCRATES In the bitter years after the Peloponnesian War, Socrates became unpopular—so much so that he was brought to trial on charges of corrupting Athenian youth and introducing new gods to the city. Plato records in his *Apology* what he describes as Socrates' speech to the jury in his own defense: a brilliant exercise in defiance, in which Socrates not only refuses to apologize for his conduct but demands that the city support him for the rest of his life, as it supported other benefactors. Condemned to execution by a majority of the jury, he accepted the sentence and died (if we can trust Plato's account) among his friends, who wanted to spirit him away—a measure Socrates refused.

Socrates's death, like the example of his thought, has inspired artists and thinkers ever since his own time. His decision to die, like the inquiries to which he devoted his life, derived from one basic belief: that the philosopher must pursue wisdom not only with his mind but also in his life, which should become a disciplined, ascetic pursuit of virtue as well as wisdom. The tragic outcome of Socrates' decisions, moreover, has often been seen as a condemnation of the city in which he lived and which he criticized so sharply, demonstrating the limits of tolerance in the world's first democracy.

CONCLUSION

In a world dominated by great empires, and in a Greek mainland split among multiple states, the Athenians built a state ruled by its own citizens. Decisions about war and peace, life and death, hinged on speakers' abilities to convince ordinary people that they were right. Though women were excluded from public life and the city depended on slave labor for sustenance, Athens was a direct democracy for its free, native, male inhabitants. Athens was also Greece's dominant naval power, the leader of the coalition that had defeated Persia in two great wars. No other city could rival its private and public wealth, the splendor of its temples on the Acropolis, or the brilliance of the philosophers and orators who debated in its streets and assemblies.

Yet in later centuries the city has also been emblematic for its loss of equilibrium and tolerance. Its drive for power over the other Greek city-states in the years before the Peloponnesian War allowed demagogues to dominate the political scene. In the late fourth century BCE, Athens would fail to sustain its independence and its constitution against a brilliant conqueror, Philip of Macedon, and the democracy would come to an end. Still, for almost 200 years—a longer span than virtually any modern state except the United States—Athens remained both a working democracy and an unparalleled cultural center.

The fate of the Athenian experiment in politics has been a subject of debate ever since the time of Pericles himself—debates carried on in public speeches before the Assembly as well as in histories like that of Thucydides. For more than 2,000 years, Athens served as an example of the chaos that democracy can cause. Not until the nineteenth century did Athenian democracy win the admiration of political leaders and historians, which it still largely holds. In either perspective, the forms of expression created in Pericles' city have remained, like the word *democracy* itself, central to the Western tradition.

[CHAPTER REVIEW]

KEY TERMS

Pericles (p. 47)
Solon (p. 47)
democracy (p. 48)
Athena (p. 48)

deme (p. 48)
ostracism (p. 48)
oracle (p. 51)
Delian League (p. 52)

metics (p. 53)
trireme (p. 53)
Acropolis (p. 57)
hetairai (p. 63)

sophist (p. 68)
tragedy (p. 69)
Thucydides (p. 72)
Socrates (p. 73)

REVIEW QUESTIONS

1. What specific steps led from aristocracy to democracy in Athens?

2. What drove Sparta and Athens to war in 431 BCE?

3. What types of activities took place in the Agora, and what do they tell us about Greek society?

4. How did Greek religious culture compare with that of other societies in the ancient world?

5. What roles did women play in Athenian society?

6. How important was slavery in Athenian society?

7. What was the key contribution of the sophists?

8. How did tragedy allow Greeks to explore the tensions in society?

9. What innovations did the Greeks make in the study of history?

10. What are the most lasting intellectual, social, and political innovations of Hellenic culture?

CORE OBJECTIVES

After reading this chapter, you should have a solid understanding of the following core objectives. To strengthen your grasp of the core objectives, use the resources on the Student Site for The West.

- Describe how social pressures led to the growth of democracy in Athens.

- Analyze how and why Athens emerged from the Persian War in a position of political power and prestige.

- Explain the causes and the results of the Peloponnesian War.

- Show how the practices of Athenian political life differed from its lofty ideals.

- Evaluate the ways in which Athenian society was, and was not, genuinely democratic.

 GO TO inQuizitive TO SEE WHAT YOU'VE LEARNED—AND LEARN WHAT YOU'VE MISSED—WITH PERSONALIZED FEEDBACK ALONG THE WAY.

CHRONOLOGY

387 BCE
Persia imposes "common peace" on the Greek world

336 BCE
Philip II dies; Alexander succeeds him

334–330 BCE
Alexander invades and conquers Persia

323 BCE
Alexander dies; successor state takes shape

3rd century BCE
Hebrew Bible translated into Greek (the Septuagint)

274–168 BCE
Seleucid-Ptolemy wars

338 BCE
Philip II of Macedon defeats Athens and Thebes at Chaeronea

335/334 BCE
Aristotle founds his Lyceum

282–133 BCE
Pergamum flourishes

305–30 BCE
Ptolemies rule Egypt

238 BCE
Ptolemies call for new religious feast in Alexandria, fusing Greek and Egyptian religions

3

From Classical Greece to the Hellenistic World

CULTURES IN CONTACT

400–30 BCE

196 BCE
Rosetta Stone created

167–166 BCE
Maccabees rebel against Antiochus

Sometime between 297 and 280 BCE, Demetrius of Phalerum, who oversaw the world's greatest library, sent a memo to his ruler, King Ptolemy II Philadelphus of Egypt. The library in question was a vast collection of Greek books stored in the new city of Alexandria, on the Mediterranean coast of Egypt. Demetrius thought that the collection also needed the laws of the Hebrews. The king agreed. He set free a number of Jewish prisoners and sent them as an embassy, bearing rich gifts, to the Temple in Jerusalem. There the high priest chose six men from each of the twelve tribes of Israel and sent them to Alexandria. Ptolemy spent a week discussing philosophical questions with them. They then translated the Hebrew Bible into Greek, taking exactly seventy-two days. The Jews of Alexandria examined the new version of their holy book and cursed anyone who would change it, indicating that they accepted it as authoritative. Then the translators returned home.

This story—though often repeated, in different versions, by Jews and Christians—is a myth, not history. Yet the core of the story is absolutely true. At some point in the third or second century BCE, the Hebrew Bible was translated into Greek, and the myth was popular enough to ensure that the most widely used version was called the Septuagint ("of the Seventy"). For centuries before this, Greek inquiries into other civilizations had

The Hellenistic World An 80 BCE floor mosaic from the Italian city of Palestrina depicts scenes of the animal and material wealth of the Nile River. The classical structures in this detail evoke the Greek-speaking people of Ptolemaic Egypt.

FOCUS QUESTIONS

- How did Plato and Aristotle transform the Greek understanding of the world?
- How did the dynamics of power change in the Greek world in the fourth century BCE?
- How was Alexander able to conquer, and rule, so much of the known world?
- Why were the Hellenistic monarchies so vibrant economically?
- What were the most important components of social change in the Hellenistic period?
- What were the new elements of Greek culture in the Hellenistic period?
- In what ways did the meeting of Greek and non-Greek cultures produce new understandings and beliefs?
- How did the Jews respond to the social and cultural changes of Hellenism?

Mediterranean, began to give way. Greek became both a tool of empire and a language that crossed borders, enabling Greeks and non-Greeks to exchange objects, ideas, and beliefs. Greek institutions such as the agora (an open space, its sides lined with colonnades) and the gymnasium spread to new parts of the Mediterranean world and well beyond its borders. Athletic grounds and pillared temples made these cities look typically Greek, and the culture that developed in them derived from Greek religious, philosophical, and literary traditions. Historians call this period Hellenistic, both because it witnessed the high-water mark of Greek ("Hellenic") influence over the Mediterranean world and beyond, and because its societies and cultures differed in many ways from those of Greece's Classical period (fifth and fourth centuries BCE).

Greek culture did not simply replace long-held beliefs and traditions. Egyptian, Jewish, and Mesopotamian peoples tried to maintain their own beliefs and practices while under Greek rule. In this chapter we will focus on two examples: the society of Ptolemaic Egypt, which was the largest and richest Hellenistic state, and that of Israel. We will see that Greek understandings of the world penetrated both societies and mingled with their native traditions, with tremendous consequences for the development of the West.

been the work of curious individuals such as Hecataeus and Herodotus. No Greek had managed to obtain a holy book from another culture, much less translate it. But in the Greek world of the third and second centuries BCE, as we will see, kings supported scholarship and science, and societies came into direct contact. The new understandings that emerged fundamentally transformed the development of Western literature, science, and religion.

These changes began in the course of the fourth century BCE, when the center of gravity of the Greek world shifted, slowly at first and then with a speed that stunned contemporaries. For hundreds of years, independent city-states had been the stages on which the political, social, and cultural dramas of Greek life had played out—not only in mainland Greece but also in areas as far-flung as southern Italy, France to the west, and the shores of the Black Sea to the north. By 300 BCE, though, foreign powers ruled many of these cities, as well as a range of territories outside the former Greek world. Massive kingdoms originating in Macedonia and incorporating Greek ways overspread the region.

Now Aramaic, which for centuries had been the language of trade and empire in Asia and much of the eastern

NEW WAYS OF UNDERSTANDING THE WORLD

The original Greek cities would never again be so rich or so powerful as they had been in the fifth century BCE. But over the century that followed, one of them—Athens—continued to play a central part in Greek culture. Tragedies and comedies were still composed and performed; speeches were still delivered in the Agora; and charismatic teachers could still find brilliant, receptive pupils. For eight or nine centuries to come, ambitious young men (and a few equally determined women) from outside Athens and even from outside mainland Greece would come to the city in search of enlightenment.

PLATO AND THE ACADEMY

In the first half of the fourth century BCE, Athenian philosophy reached a high point of ambition and brilliance.

Socrates' disciples, above all Xenophon and Plato, departed from their teacher's model in vital ways after his execution in 399 BCE. Whereas Socrates, who feared that writing could harm the memory, had taught only orally, his pupils composed elaborate written dialogues and memoirs in which they offered vivid portraits of Socrates as he had lived, taught, and died. Theirs are the only works in which we hear Socrates speak. And although Xenophon (ca. 431–ca. 352 BCE) depicted Socrates as a great but rather conventional moralist, **Plato** (429/8–348/7 BCE) developed the dialogue into a powerful form of philosophical writing.

Plato also established philosophy on a new basis. Socrates had simply talked with anyone who wanted to listen to him. Plato turned the subject into a group pursuit with a firm location. When he inherited property in the 380s BCE, he created an institution for study at the site of an olive grove a mile or so outside the walls of Athens. Known as the Academy, a site sacred to the legendary hero Akademos, this club was a private association that admitted only an elect group to study. It became the ancestor of, and gave its name to, the long series of educational institutions—including the modern university—that have existed in the West.

Plato's Academy A mosaic from a house at Pompeii (early first century BCE) imagines Plato's Academy: men under a tree reading and talking, with the Acropolis distantly visible in the background.

THE WORLD OF FORMS

Building on Socrates but going far beyond him, Plato envisioned the universe of our daily experience as only the shadow of the true world of **forms**—the preexisting ideas that the creator of the universe used as patterns when assembling the planets and the earth. Human beings, Plato argued, were born with memories of this higher world that could be reawakened. In this ideal realm humans were ethically required to pursue truth and virtue, which for Plato, as for Socrates, were closely connected. But because people had to carry out this quest in the turmoil of the everyday world, they could never do more than approximate the highest truths and harmonies. And most would never even realize that a higher world existed outside daily reality.

In Plato's ideal world there is a form for the city, a society in which men and women carry out the tasks for which they are suited by nature. Most do humble, repetitive work. But women, as well as men, of high ability serve as the "Guardians," who see to it that justice is done for all. Plato was at times pessimistic about whether a society that approximated this ideal one could exist in reality. In his great work of political philosophy, *The Republic*, Plato has Socrates describe everyday humanity as the prisoners of illusion, their world a cave and their lives projected images on the wall. If a philosopher escapes the cave and reaches the light of the higher world, he will at first be dazzled; and even when he has achieved understanding, he will find it impossible to descend back into the cave and convince his fellows of what he has seen.

PHILOSOPHY IN THE WORLD

Yet Plato visited the great city of Syracuse in Sicily twice, hoping to convince the city's tyrant, Dionysius II, to restructure it on ideal lines. By teaching the ruler, an adviser suggested, Plato would introduce "the true life of happiness throughout the whole territory." But he could not persuade the ruler to listen, and his efforts ended in failure. In the end, the government of Athens, which he disdained, had to arrange for him to be freed from arrest.

In Athens, however, Plato's teaching won disciples. He argued that the study of certain disciplines, especially mathematics, could yield insight into the realm of pure forms. And he proposed that the heavens, in which the stars and planets moved regularly and permanently around the earth, were more perfect than the earth, and the animals and humans who live on it. Many of his followers—especially the pioneering astronomer Eudoxus (ca. 390–340 BCE)—were inspired by him to study the mathematical disciplines, which became a hallmark of the Academy.

ARISTOTLE AND HIS SCHOOL

Aristotle (384–322 BCE), a native of Stagira in what is now northern Greece, moved to Athens to become Plato's pupil in the Academy. But in the well-established Greek tradition, he soon disagreed with, and distanced himself from, his teacher. Whereas Plato emphasized formal argument and mathematics, Aristotle favored the **empirical** study of reality. A gifted student of biology, he waded into tide pools to study starfish. He discussed the habits of animals with expert hunters and fishermen, who taught him that sharks produce not eggs but baby sharks, as if they were mammals; and he conferred with beekeepers, who described the belly dance with which their bees deposited pollen. (These two observations were either mocked or misunderstood until they were verified in the nineteenth and twentieth centuries.) As a student of living beings, Aristotle believed that the forms governing their development existed within them, not in a separate world of perfect ideas.

THE LYCEUM Aristotle used the same basically empirical approach when studying other areas, such as literature and politics. In 335 or 334 BCE he, too, founded a school—in the **Lyceum**, a public meeting place in a grove outside Athens, which also housed a gymnasium where hoplites exercised. The school was dedicated to Apollo, the god of sun, light, and music. Aristotle equipped his new institution with a portico in which students could walk as they carried on their discussions and with a library, which became a research tool of a new kind. To understand the effects of tragedy, he inspected many examples and identified the formal qualities that could produce a purge of emotions in the viewer, called catharsis. And to understand the different forms of civic life, he and his pupils collected dozens of accounts of constitutions. Only one of these, a detailed investigation of the development of government at Athens, survives.

POLITICS Aristotle used these collected materials to create a systematic work, *Politics*. He argued that all governments can be assigned to one of six categories, three good and three bad: democracy, aristocracy, and monarchy on the one hand; ochlocracy (mob rule), oligarchy, and tyranny on the other. Even as the age of the independent city-state drew to a close, Aristotle stuck to the belief that the typical small Greek community, in which citizens all knew one another, was the natural, and thus the ideal, form of state for human beings. People were, he explained, "political animals"—beings whose natural dwelling place was the city.

TWO PHILOSOPHERS, TWO WORLD VIEWS

Plato and Aristotle disagreed on central points. For Plato, the deepest truths lay outside the universe that humans inhabited and could observe, whereas for Aristotle these truths could be found inside it. But both men envisioned the physical universe in terms of hierarchies and saw the world of the heavens as changeless, permanent, and more perfect than the world of matter below.

Both believed in social hierarchies as well. Plato imagined a perfect society in which everyone carried out the tasks for which nature had fitted him or her. Aristotle held that some peoples, especially the Persians, were servile by nature and therefore well adapted to monarchical states. But he also believed that many Greeks were destined by nature to be slaves. This argument would find eager acceptance in many slave societies over the centuries.

Above all, both men insisted that philosophy, as they pursued it, was a comprehensive—even encyclopedic—inquiry and a way of life. Over the centuries to come, their followers would accept this ideal even as they continued to comment on, and sometimes alter, the founding texts of their schools.

THE TRANSFORMATION OF GREECE IN THE FOURTH CENTURY BCE

The philosophers explained the world as if nothing had changed since the time of Socrates, or even before. In fact, though, the political and military world of the city-states had been transformed by the Peloponnesian War (431–404 BCE). In the years that led up to the war, local rivalries and quarrels were largely suppressed by the formation of the Athenian and Spartan power blocs, which most of the independent city-states joined. After the war, Athens and Sparta were both poorer and less powerful than they had been, and powerful smaller states such as Corinth and Thebes could change the balance of power by switching alliances. In this new situation, conflicts between city-states flamed up more frequently than in the past.

POWER IN THE REGION

In the 390s, Corinth, Argos, and Boeotia, the northern Greek region around Thebes, joined Athens in a league against the Spartans, whom they defeated at sea, thanks to a rebuilt Athenian fleet. In 387 BCE, however, the Spartans defeated the Athenian navy near Asia Minor. Thereafter the Spartan commander opened negotiations with the Persians, again a formidable power in the region. A year later, the king of Persia, Artaxerxes II (r. ca. 404–ca. 358 BCE), a ruthless ruler who was as deft at murdering rivals at court as he was at making war with the Greeks, imposed a "common peace" on the Greek world, with Sparta in a dominant position.

This settlement did not last long. Thebes soon asserted itself as a new regional power, rising to leadership in a confederacy of states grouped against Sparta. Its "Sacred Band"—an elite infantry corps comprising 150 pairs of male lovers supported by the state—played a particularly important role when the Thebans defeated the Spartans at Leuctra in 371 BCE. Theban forces killed more than half of the 700 Spartan hoplites who took part in the battle, a crippling blow. Between 371 and 362, a rebellion of some of the Persian **satraps** (provincial governors) and conflicts with Egypt occupied Artaxerxes. Thebes dominated Greece until the battle of Mantinea in 362, when an alliance of Spartans, Athenians, and others defeated a league led by the Thebans.

Sparta never recovered its former strength, however, and even Athens had only a fraction of the material and human resources it had possessed in the age of the Delian League. Athens now claimed fewer than half of the 200,000 or so citizens it had once boasted. The Persian Empire continued to be the greatest power in western Asia and the Mediterranean, incomparable in wealth and in the scale of its army and administration.

CHANGES IN THE CITY-STATE

In this period of decline, many city-state institutions survived. Athenians continued to serve for pay on state juries. A new system of indictments made the positions of

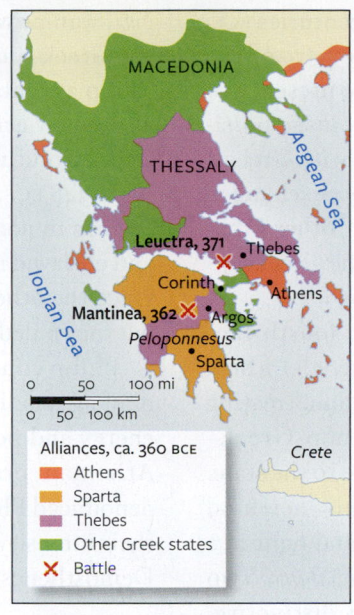

Greece in the 4th Century BCE

(Map labels: MACEDONIA, THESSALY, Aegean Sea, Leuctra, 371, Thebes, Ionian Sea, Corinth, Athens, Mantinea, 362, Argos, Peloponnesus, Sparta, Crete)

Alliances, ca. 360 BCE
- Athens
- Sparta
- Thebes
- Other Greek states
- ✗ Battle

officeholders even more precarious than they had been in the fifth century BCE, when ostracism sometimes rid the city of overly powerful men. Professional orators still dominated public life and continued to address large crowds in the Assembly, where they evoked the glories of the ancestral democratic constitution of Athens.

In other respects, though, the city-state system was no longer what it had been. Persia regularly intervened in Greek affairs, threatening the autonomy of individual cities that the Greeks had preserved from Persian aggression, at least in the Greek mainland, in the fifth century. In the perpetual warfare of the period, Athenians and other Greeks who would once have served in their own cities' armies found themselves fighting as mercenaries for anyone who would pay. Whereas hoplites could fight only during the warm months, when they could leave their farms, mercenaries could fight all year, weather permitting. Moreover, new tactics—especially the use of *peltasts* (lightly armed foot soldiers equipped with javelins) and cavalry—began to prove more effective than the traditional hoplite army. Warfare now assumed a professional form and took place on a vast scale.

THE RISE OF MACEDON

As the Greek city-states struggled for preeminence, a new power was rising in the north, one that they could not resist even when they formed alliances against it. Macedonia was a kingdom ringed by mountains and endowed with rich natural resources, including gold, silver, and timber. Situated between mainland Greece and the Balkans, Macedonia developed around the capital at Aigai, which was less a city than a palace complex like those of Mycenae long before.

Archaeological evidence shows that the Macedonians built a wealthy warrior nation that produced arms and jewelry far more splendid than anything seen in the Greek cities. But they adopted the Greek gods of Olympus as theirs, and their rulers traced their ancestry back to the Greek hero Heracles. It was Heracles who carried out the miraculous task of cleaning the legendarily filthy Augean stables by diverting a river to run through them.

Macedonian Currency
A silver coin from fourth-century BCE Macedon bears the name of Philip II and an image of a horseman.

By the fifth and fourth centuries BCE, Macedonia had become part of the larger Greek world. The presence of precious metals made coinage possible, and trade developed with Greece. Timber and minerals were exchanged for red-figure pottery and other Athenian consumer goods. The Greek language came into common use.

In the middle of the fourth century, **Philip II** (r. 359–336 BCE), a brilliant ruler, united Macedon, treating Greek-speakers and non-Greek–speakers as of equal value to the state. He forged his subjects into a new kind of fighting unit: infantry schooled to drill and fight in a formation called by the traditional term *phalanx*. Two innovations made this particular version distinctive. Philip introduced a new kind of spear, the *sarisa*, thirteen to twenty feet long and made of flexible dogwood. Each spear extended several feet beyond the man who held it. When the rows of spearmen who made up the phalanx marched, the sharp-edged metal points of their spears preceded them, row after row, like a terrifying metal hedge. Equally vital was the intensive training that disciplined the Macedonians so that they could march or attack at great speed in any direction, or stick together and hold off cavalry attacks that would have scattered other infantry forces. The Macedonians became a tightly packed, swiftly moving, and powerful striking force. The phalanx could not turn easily, but when it attacked an enemy line, its force was almost irresistible.

Philip, moreover, coordinated infantry with cavalry in new ways. Once the phalanx had broken the front of an opposing army, the horsemen—too lightly armed and, because they had no stirrups, too lightly attached to their horses to mount an effective frontal assault—moved in and slaughtered the enemy infantry. In former times, the Macedonians had chosen their rulers for their prowess as soldiers. Philip followed this tradition. He served as a commander and fought ferociously himself, losing an eye as the price for one major victory.

THE CONQUEST OF GREECE

Military action in northern Greece won Philip access to still greater resources. Thrace, which he conquered, gave him rich gold mines. Thessaly, where he intervened in a civil war, provided him with the most skillful cavalry in the Greek-speaking world. A brilliant recruiter of talent, Philip assembled not only a superb mercenary army but also a new aristocracy of adventurers from all over the Greek world, many of whom he settled in conquered lands.

In 348 BCE, when he took Olynthus, a powerful ally of Athens in northern Greece, he confiscated its territory and enslaved its population. The Athenians tried to convince the other Greeks to ally with them against Philip, but they failed and made a grudging peace with him in 346.

Philip continued to expand his power and territory, moving steadily into southern Greece. Even the demonic energy and fiercely democratic convictions of the great Athenian orator Demosthenes (384–322 BCE), who denounced Philip in speeches that became proverbial for their intensity and power, were not enough to resist him. Demosthenes' contemporary, Isocrates, a brilliant writer

The Rise of Macedon, 359–336 BCE Philip II waged a brilliant military campaign to conquer Thessaly and Thrace, defeating Athens and its allies at Olynthus and Chaeronea and subjecting native populations to his control. By the time Philip was killed, his domain reached across Thrace, where he challenged the borders of the powerful Persian Empire.

and a renowned teacher of oratory, hoped to see Greece unified and at peace. He appealed to Philip, whom he tried to convince to make peace with the Greek states, and he may have helped to inspire in Philip the idea that he might eventually challenge Persia. But the outcome was far from the Greek union Isocrates had had in mind. In 338 BCE, Philip challenged and defeated Athens and Thebes at Chaeronea, in the northern Greek region of Boeotia.

Thereafter a conference in Corinth proclaimed the creation of a new league of Greek states, led by Philip. He now declared war against Persia and sent an invading force across the Hellespont, the strait between Europe and Asia that Xerxes had bridged when he invaded Greece in 480 BCE. From now on, foreign rulers would be the masters of Greece. Even Isocrates, who had hoped to see the Greek cities unified, acknowledged that this change was tragic and starved himself to death.

ALEXANDER THE GREAT: THE WORLD TRANSFORMED

Philip was killed by an assassin in 336 BCE, and his son **Alexander** (356–323 BCE) took power at the age of twenty. Though he ruled for only thirteen years before his own death, the prodigiously talented Alexander transformed much of the known world—even areas that had previously been largely unknown to the Greeks.

THE YOUNG CONQUEROR (334–326 BCE)

Alexander began by establishing his position in mainland Greece. When Thebes rebelled against him in 335 BCE, he demolished the city and enslaved its citizens. This shocked the other Greek city-states and revealed the costs of resistance. In 334 Alexander crossed the Hellespont with an army of 32,000 infantrymen and 5,000 cavalry to attack Darius III of Persia (r. 336–330 BCE). An advance force of 10,000 more Greeks awaited Alexander in Persia. Still, he had far fewer soldiers than his opponent, who mustered as many as 100,000 infantrymen and 20,000 cavalry. But Alexander's mastery of tactics, speed in action, and determination gave him the advantage.

BATTLING PERSIA In his first confrontation with the Persian armies, at the river Granicus in northwestern Asia

Alexander the Great A mosaic from Pompeii depicts Alexander leading the cavalry charge against Darius's Persian forces at Issus in 333 BCE.

Minor in 334 BCE, Alexander faced superior numbers on high ground across the river. But the Persians had put their cavalry in front of their 20,000 Greek mercenaries, who could otherwise have prevented Alexander's men from crossing. Alexander led a cavalry charge across the river, visible to all in polished armor and a helmet with a white plume. Though he risked and almost lost his life, he inspired his infantry, who punched through the Persian cavalry and slaughtered almost all of the Greek mercenaries. At this, most of the Greek cities under Persian rule came over to Alexander.

After much maneuvering, Darius himself confronted Alexander in 333 BCE at Issus, a narrow plain between the mountains and sea in southeastern Asia Minor. This time Alexander used his cavalry to flank and disrupt the Persian battle line. Darius fled in his chariot and then, when it stalled, on horseback. Alexander captured the treasures with which the Persian ruler traveled, as well as the women of his household, whom he treated with humanity and respect. Ignoring a peace offer from Darius, Alexander went on to conquer Egypt and then turned back eastward, intent on a final victory against the Persian king, who had regrouped his forces in Babylon.

In the autumn of 331 BCE, Greeks and Persians met in a climactic battle at Gaugamela in what is now northern Iraq. The Persians had war elephants and terrifying chariots armed with sharp scythes. But the disciplined Macedonians opened holes in their lines, let the chariots through, and then isolated them and slaughtered their crews. Alexander once again disrupted and annihilated the Persian line of battle, and Darius fled once more, leaving the Macedonian master of the field.

CONQUERING PERSEPOLIS (330 BCE)

Alexander systematically stamped out opposition. When cities resisted him, as the Phoenician ports of Tyre and Sidon did, he stopped, laid siege, and did not move until he had crushed his opponents. He conquered not only the ancient cities of Babylon and Susa, which the Persians had ruled for centuries, but the ancient Persian capital of Persepolis, which he looted and burned in 330 BCE. From Persepolis he took the entire Persian treasury—a vast quantity of bullion worth the equivalent of more than $1 trillion today. He turned the bullion into coin, sharply expanding the money supply in the region. This not only strengthened Alexander's war machine but also transformed the economy of central and southern Asia. Realizing the futility of resistance, Darius's followers murdered their king, and

Alexander suddenly dominated the Mediterranean world and western Asia like a colossus.

Challenges soon arose—in the first instance, from the Persian who had killed Darius. But Alexander assigned his own satraps to deal with this revolt. He himself moved through the extraordinarily difficult terrain of what are now eastern Iran and western Afghanistan, crossed the high passes of the Hindu Kush, and invaded Bactria (modern Afghanistan).

TECHNIQUES OF RULE

Though revolt followed revolt and Alexander suffered some major reverses, he soon developed an effective technique for establishing control of the nations he conquered. As the ruler of Macedon, he continued to rely on the Macedonians and Greeks who fought for him. But once he took control of Persia, he kept Persian officials in office as well, demanding that they prostrate themselves before him as they had done before their Persian rulers. At the end of his life, he supposedly

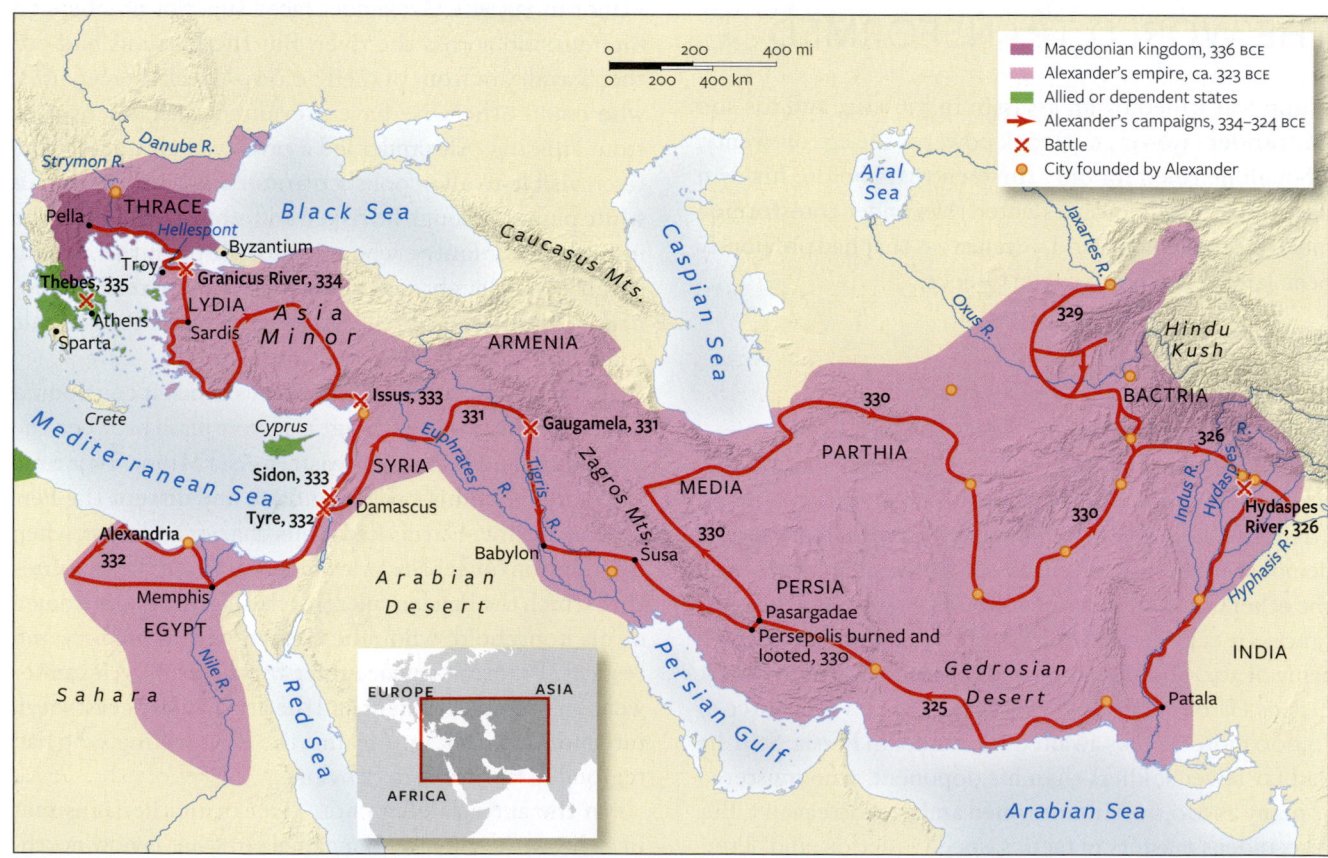

Alexander's Conquests, 336–323 BCE In 334 BCE Alexander crossed the Hellespont and engaged the Persian army in battle. His army defeated Darius III's forces repeatedly as they marched across the Near East and Central Asia, conquering Egypt, Babylon, and Persepolis, and territory as distant as Bactria (present-day Afghanistan). In just ten years, the entire area from Greece and Egypt to the borders of India was under Alexander's control, and contained many newly established cities, including several named Alexandria.

Hellenistic Affluence After Alexander conquered the Persian Empire, the taste for Hellenistic luxury goods spread as far as India. Jewelry like this delicate gold armband, decorated with the characteristically Hellenistic "Herakles knot," spread around the Greek-speaking world.

planned to move whole populations from Europe to Asia and vice versa to encourage intermarriage. He did establish many new settlements: about twenty new Greek cities, from Alexandria on the river Strymon in modern Bulgaria to Alexandria on the Indus in modern Pakistan. To these cities, a Greek ruling class brought not only the use of coinage but many other Greek customs. By working with different subject peoples and by fostering the spread of Greek culture in new territories, Alexander set the tone for the Hellenistic period.

Astonishingly, Alexander did not stop once he had defeated Greece's traditional enemies. Instead, following reports of the wealth and other marvels to be found at what Greeks considered the edge of the world, in India, he moved onward. In 326 BCE he defeated the Indian king Porus (d. 318 BCE), who ruled a state in what is now Punjab and whose vast army included war elephants, at the river Hydaspes. Even when his exhausted soldiers finally mutinied, Alexander continued his career of adventure. He turned south and fought his way, with great brutality, to the Arabian Sea. There he built a fleet, which he sent home under the command of a trusted admiral. He himself led his armies overland back toward the countries they had first conquered, in an epic journey through the deserts, to Persepolis and Susa.

RULING CULTURES (325–323 BCE)

From 325 BCE to his death in 323, probably from disease, Alexander established himself as absolute monarch of much of the known world: at least of Greece, Persia, and—as he claimed with more optimism than accuracy—Asia. Some modern historians have credited Alexander with a conscious policy of ethnic tolerance. He certainly showed none of the sense of Greek superiority that had established itself in the fifth century and that Aristotle, with whom he studied, had incorporated into his philosophy. Throughout his career Alexander worked effectively with men of many different origins. But the egalitarian interpretation of his thought goes beyond the contemporary evidence.

A PERSIAN GREAT KING What seems most likely is that Alexander saw himself as the successor of the Persian Great King. At the wedding ceremony that Alexander held in 324 BCE in the Persian city of Susa, where he married Barsine, eldest daughter of Darius, he wore court dress that was largely Persian. He also followed Persian court ceremonies and began to claim not only descent from Heracles but also divine status on the basis of his stupendous achievements. Persians had prostrated themselves before their king; now not only former Persian subjects but Macedonians and Greeks were ordered to prostrate themselves before Alexander, and only a few refused. His Macedonian supporters were married to Persian women and supplied with large dowries.

HELLENISM Even as Alexander emulated the manners of conduct of Persian Great Kings, the language and culture of his empire continued to be Greek, and his conquests spread the Greek language and Greek styles of city planning and religious observance, art, dress, and literature. This is what scholars mean when they call the last three centuries BCE **Hellenistic**: it was the time in which Greek language and culture extended farther than they ever had before, or would again.

Still, the new form of empire was not glued together by any clear common vision or ideology, or by any newer counterpart to the civic sentiments that had grown up with the rise of hoplite warfare in the Greece of the early city-states. Alexander ruled by force, and over time, force came to rule many of his actions. Always hot-tempered, he could become a despot when he felt challenged or provoked. He killed favorite commanders when they opposed him, and soon enough faced real enemies and their plots. In 324, when he issued a decree that required the Greek cities to take back many of their political exiles, he essentially forced them to rebel even though they knew the consequences that they risked by doing so. When Alexander died in 323, he was contemplating another invasion, this time of the western Mediterranean, where wealthy Syracuse and other Greek cities remained independent.

CULTURAL CHANGE

Alexander's conquests in Asia opened the way for thousands of Greeks to leave their homelands for cities in the East, bringing with them their language, religious beliefs, and cultural practices. The result was a Hellenistic culture that drew on Greek, Macedonian, Egyptian, Persian, and other Asian traditions. Alexander himself worked effectively with subjects of different origins. He adopted Persian court customs and married his Macedonian supporters to Persian women. He sparked controversy, though, when he ordered Greeks and Macedonians to prostrate themselves before him as his Persian subjects did. These two documents, written after the events described, illustrate the advantages and pitfalls of Alexander's cultural flexibility.

Arrian, *The Campaigns of Alexander*

Written in the second century CE by Arrian, a Greek-born Roman historian, this passage conveys the arguments of Kallisthenes, one of Alexander's advisers, against adoption of the Persian practice of bowing full-length before the ruler.

[Kallisthenes addressing Alexander:] "Perhaps, one must think like a barbarian[1] because our discussion takes place in a barbarian land. Even so I think it fit to remind you, Alexander, of Greece, for the sake of which you made this entire expedition—to annex Asia to Greece. And consider this: will you, on your return there, also compel the Greeks, the freest of men, to bow before you, or will you keep your distance from the Greeks but impose this dishonor on the Macedonians? Or will you make some final distinction when it comes to honors, and be honored by the Greeks and Macedonians in the human and Greek manner, while receiving barbarian honors only from the barbarians? But if it is said about Cyrus[2]…that he was the first man to have his subjects bow down to him, and that after him this indignity

became an institution among the Persians and Medes[3], one should bear in mind that the Scythians[4], men who were poor but independent, taught that very Cyrus a lesson—a lesson other Scythians later taught Darius[5], and the Athenians and Spartans taught Xerxes[6]…and Alexander—without having his people bow down before him—taught this Darius."

In making these and similar remarks Kallisthenes greatly vexed Alexander, though what he said pleased the Macedonians. Realizing this, Alexander sent word to the Macedonians telling them to think no more of the bowing ritual. But in the silence that followed these words, the most distinguished Persians stood up and one by one performed their bows.

Plutarch, From *Lives*

In this passage, Plutarch (46–120 CE), also a Greek-born Roman and author of biographical profiles of Alexander and other great figures of Greece and Rome, describes Alexander's purposes in cultural accommodation. Plutarch offers two examples of Alexander's prudent cultural policies.

Now, also, he more and more accommodated himself in his way of living to that of the natives, and tried to bring them, also, as near as he could to the Macedonian customs, wisely considering that whilst he was engaged in an expedition which would carry him far from thence, it would be wiser to depend upon the goodwill which might arise from intermixture and association as a means of maintaining tranquillity, than upon force and compulsion. In order to [do] this, he chose out thirty thousand boys, whom he put under masters to teach them the Greek tongue, and to train them up to arms in the Macedonian discipline. As for his marriage with Roxana, whose youthfulness and beauty had charmed him at a drinking entertainment, where he happened to see her, taking part in a dance, it was, indeed, a love affair, yet it seemed at the same time to be conducive to the object he had in hand. For it gratified the conquered people to see him choose a wife from among themselves, and it made them feel the most lively affection for him, to find that in the only passion which he, the most temperate of men, was overcome by, he yet forbore till he could obtain her in a lawful and honorable way.

QUESTIONS FOR ANALYSIS

1. Why does Kallisthenes object to Alexander's adoption of the Persian court practice in which subjects prostrate themselves before their ruler?
2. According to Plutarch, why was it wise for Alexander to accommodate the cultural practices of his foreign subjects?
3. How do these documents differ on the value of Alexander's adopting foreign ways?

[1] Barbarian: Non-Greek-speaker or foreigner, with a pejorative connotation.
[2] Cyrus: Persian King, mid-to-late-sixth century BCE.
[3] Medes: A Near Eastern people, conquered by Persia, mid-sixth century BCE.
[4] Scythians: A nomadic people living on the steppes of Eurasia.
[5] Darius: Darius III, Persian King, 336–330 BCE.
[6] Xerxes: Persian King, first half of the fifth century BCE.

Sources: Arrian, *The Campaigns of Alexander*, trans. Pamela Mensch, ed. James Romm (New York: 2010), pp. 168–9; Plutarch, *Lives*, vol. 4, trans. John Dryden, ed. Arthur Hugh Clough (Boston: 1888), p. 219.

THE ALEXANDER LEGEND

Decisive in real life, Alexander was portrayed as even more so in the myths that arose during his own lifetime. According to one legend, when challenged by an oracle stating that the conqueror of Asia Minor must untie a complex knot tied by a previous king of Phrygia (a region in central Asia Minor), Alexander could not find an end to pull, so he simply sliced the "Gordian knot" in half with a sword. This and other fictional exploits became the subject of hero cults and a vast body of art and literature. For centuries after the end of the ancient world, courtiers in Persia, Arabia, and medieval and Renaissance Europe grew up on a diet of Alexander's real and legendary adventures. He himself boasted that he had conquered the world, and he wept at the thought that there were no other worlds for him to conquer.

THE HELLENISTIC MONARCHIES (305–30 BCE)

Soon after Alexander's death, it became clear that only his energy and personal dominance had welded the vast range of peoples that made up his empire into a single political unit. Though a regent took control of the empire, the satraps of individual areas soon went to war, both with the emperor and with one another.

THE SUCCESSOR STATES

In the end, three large new states took shape among the ruins of the Macedonian Empire: (1) that of the **Ptolemies**, which extended from Egypt into Palestine, Libya, and Cyprus; (2) that of the Seleucids, in Palestine, Turkey, Mesopotamia, and parts of Afghanistan and India; and (3) that of the Antigonids, in Macedonia and northern Greece. But the crystallization of these larger states did not bring peace. Between 274 and 168 BCE, for example, the Seleucids and the Ptolemies fought no fewer than six wars in Syria.

Smaller states also sprang up, like that of the Attalids in western Asia Minor. One of Alexander's generals, Lysimachus, had built a small empire between the Black Sea and the Mediterranean, which he ruled from the city of Pergamum. He maintained independence by adroitly switching allegiances. On his death, his realm fell apart. But the Attalids took over Pergamum and gradually built it up as a splendid city—a rival version of Alexandria, with great temples and libraries, and a fan-shaped upper city centered on the vast royal palace. Their kingdom survived until 133 BCE, when it was bequeathed to Rome.

AUTOCRACY AND AUTONOMY

The Hellenistic states basically followed the model that Alexander had sketched out—itself partly derived from the Persians. Unlike most of the Greek states of the last several centuries, all of the Hellenistic states were monarchical in form and sharply hierarchical in character. Greek elites, separated by language and customs from the natives, occupied the top levels, with native elites below them.

The workings of Hellenistic government are best known from the Egyptian kingdom of the Ptolemies (305–30 BCE). Emulating the ancient Egyptian pharaohs, whose kingdom the Macedonians had shattered, the Ptolemaic kings claimed godly status and used everything from public ceremony to coinage to teach subjects to see them in that light. The Ptolemies dealt with their Greek subjects as Greek rulers, communicating with them in Greek and allowing them to build and administer the normal Greek institutions, such as public gymnasia, in their cities. They dealt with their Egyptian subjects as the pharaohs had, using the Egyptian language for decrees that affected them. Two systems of justice applied—one Greek, and one Egyptian. The Egyptian state of the Ptolemies was thus bilingual and in large part bimodal.

The other successor states developed variants on this model. The Seleucids inherited the largest single share of Alexander's empire—Turkey, Syria, and Iran. With a population of 50 or 60 million, these lands were immensely rich. Unlike the Ptolemies, the Seleucids employed natives in the administration and the armed forces, and encouraged their soldiers and other Macedonians to marry Asians. The children of these unions served in the Macedonian phalanx that was the core of the Seleucids' army, along with native light infantry, archers,

Hellenistic Currency A silver talent issued by King Attalus I of Pergamum in the third century BCE carries a picture of Athena and an inscription in Greek. Pergamum, capital of the Attalid kingdom in western Asia Minor, was modeled on Athens.

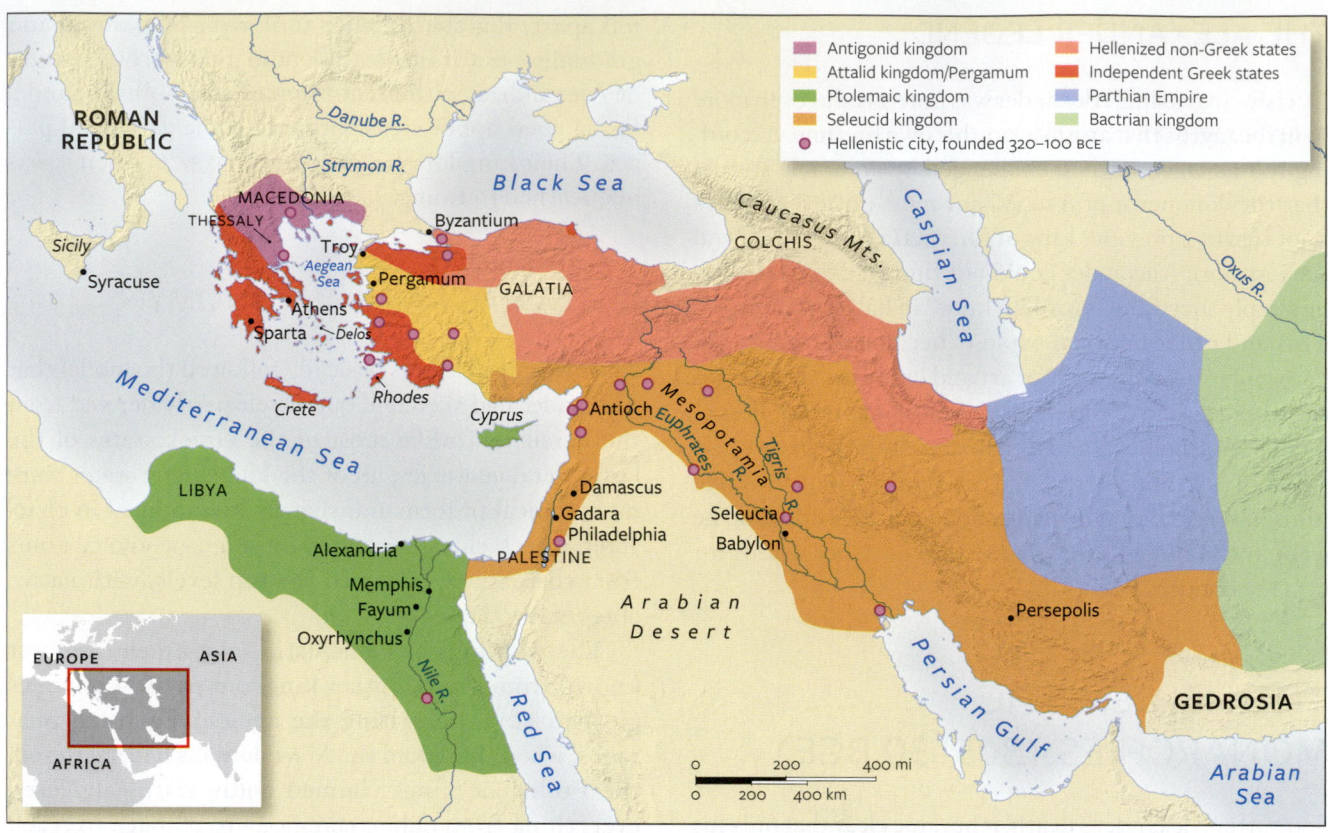

The Hellenistic World, Early 2nd Century BCE After Alexander's death, his empire broke up into three large kingdoms under the Ptolemies in Egypt, the Seleucids in Persia, and the Antigonids in Macedonia. These were joined by smaller states such as Attalid Pergamum in western Turkey and some of the original Greek city-states. Many new cities were founded in this period, particularly in Persia and Asia Minor.

and javelin-throwers. In 305 BCE, after initial efforts to establish satraps in the Indus Valley failed, Seleucus I (r. 321–281 BCE) made a deal with Chandragupta Maurya (r. 322–298 BCE), an Indian who was founding his own dynasty. Seleucus abandoned all claims to Indian territory in return for war elephants. Yet with all their military resources and native helpers, the Seleucids could not establish an effective administration for their immense domains. They established a ruler cult, in which cities worshipped the ruler "as if he were a god," and hoped that this could provide some of the unity that was imposed in Egypt by the nature of the Nile Valley.

The Antigonids, for their part, ruled as something like constitutional monarchs. Their authority was unchallenged because they respected the traditions of their Macedonian subjects. They had the strongest army of the successors and used massive fortresses not so much to dominate Greece as to ensure that it would serve as a buffer, preventing the Seleucids and Ptolemies from invading their territory.

THE ECONOMIC FOUNDATIONS OF POWER

AGRICULTURE The Hellenistic kingdoms, whether Ptolemaic Egypt or Seleucid Babylon, relied on the work of rural villagers to produce vast amounts of grain—the foundation of the state's prosperity. The Ptolemies considered themselves the true owners of all the land in Egypt. Lands outside their own estates, and those designated for use in the maintenance of temples, they assigned to officials who had served them well and to soldiers. Government officials introduced more effective agricultural methods, including irrigation, into the cultivation of especially fertile areas, such as the Fayum in north-central Egypt. They managed to push the desert back, improve yields, and create new settlements. Tax-farmers—entrepreneurs who bid for the right to gather taxes—maintained close oversight over the production, storage, and sale of wheat and other crops. Standing between landlords and villagers on the one hand and the kings on the other, tax-farmers made as much profit as possible by squeezing the taxpayers. The concerns of peasants reached the throne only in especially hard times, when mass flight from the land threatened the monarchy's economic foundations.

A MONEY ECONOMY
The grain economy and its structures were in part ancient, determined as much by the climate and geography of the Mediterranean world as by human decisions. But they now functioned within a new framework. Alexander's successors followed his example by continuing to mint the Persian monarchs' fabulous hoards of bullion into coin which they used, as Alexander had, to pay their troops, who came mostly from the Greek cities in the mainland and elsewhere. As precious metals filtered into the economy, each state began to depend on large amounts of coinage to maintain its military power. To ensure this supply, states and their tax-farmers insisted on collecting taxes in money rather than in kind. State revenues swelled. Alexander's kingdom produced an income of 30,000 silver talents annually (a talent, during the Peloponnesian War, would pay the wages of a trireme's crew for a month); Egypt, almost three centuries later, had an annual income of 12,500 talents. Sophisticated systems of exchange developed, and it was possible to write a wheat check in one part of Egypt that could be drawn from a wheat account 300 miles away.

TRADE
A lively trade developed across the Mediterranean. Roads were bad during the Hellenistic period, but ships were the major carriers of cargo, and their numbers exploded. In the three centuries after Alexander's death, the number of dateable wrecks on the floor of the Mediterranean went up 600 percent. Ship-borne commerce made possible the carriage of expensive goods from distant lands: African elephants for the Ptolemaic armies, spices from Yemen for the kitchens of the rich, olive oil and wine from Greece for homesick mercenaries and officials in Egypt, and other luxury goods from the Persian Gulf and southern Africa.

The monarchs taxed this trade, and by one scholar's calculation the Ptolemaic government controlled as much as 40 percent of the gross national product of Egypt—as much as a typical twentieth-century government. This enormous income stream enabled the Ptolemies to build the lighthouses, fortifications, docks, and warehouses needed to create safe and efficient ports. They also developed huge warships with many banks of oars and solid decks designed to hold catapults. As ships grew larger, armies did the same. Not all of the Hellenistic states could

match Egypt's resources. But all of them could muster more sheer military force than any previous Greek state had possessed—even Athens at the height of its power.

NEW GREEK CITIES

Within these powerful new states, Greek ways thrived as never before. The spread of the Greek language and the development of a money economy helped people, goods, and ideas to circulate rapidly. The Seleucids, in particular, encouraged immigration, and thousands of Macedonians and Greeks settled in Turkey and Mesopotamia, where they founded cities by the dozen. New cities, in fact, sprang up everywhere from northern Africa to northern Afghanistan, and some turned into metropolises, such as Alexandria in Egypt and Antioch in Syria.

These cities became models of Greek architecture and town planning as well as centers of administration and culture. Massive temples, their roofs supported by great columns and their precincts adorned with sculpture, honored each city's patron god or goddess. An agora was dedicated to public assemblies. Beside it stood a government building and a public auditorium. A second agora served merchants as a center for the exchange of goods and money. Often, the grandest complex in the city was a gymnasium or a theater, each a central Greek institution.

Alexandria, the Egyptian city founded by Alexander (who was buried there), had a Mediterranean port protected by an island, which made it a natural trading center. As the Ptolemies poured money into the city, massive public buildings took shape. These included the 400-foot-high lighthouse that took its place, in the first or second century CE, on the unofficial but widely circulated lists of the seven wonders of the ancient world. The city's rectangular grid design was in place by the first century BCE, and probably much earlier. Two main streets more than 100 feet wide crossed the city. Immigrants whose languages and ways differed sharply from those of the Egyptian residents poured in as well, especially from Greece but also from Macedonia and Persia. A substantial Jewish population worshipped in a massive, spectacular temple. With 300,000 free inhabitants, according to one ancient account, Alexandria dwarfed even the Athens of Pericles. So did Antioch in Syria and other Hellenistic cities.

URBAN NETWORKS
Whereas the Greek cities of the fifth-century BCE Classical period regarded one another with suspicion or hostility, those of the Hellenistic world

did their best to support one another. They recognized one another's gods, extended common privileges to one another's citizens, and copied one another's legislation. City walls fell into disrepair or were even torn down, and instead of joining military leagues, cities formed federations to maintain trading relations and protect one another against bandits and raiders. A group of Greek cities in Syria and Palestine, including Damascus, Philadelphia, and Gadara, formed the Decapolis (League of Ten Cities). Others formally recognized one another as friends, and when disputes and wars broke out, they sent their judges to serve as arbitrators. Cities also extended their power into the countryside around them, creating networks of substantial villages. The cosmopolitan urbanism of the Hellenistic period would have seemed strange to the Athenians and Spartans of the fifth century BCE.

URBAN BENEFACTORS

Hellenistic cities drew creatively on Greek tradition. Athens had long depended on the trierarchs who fitted out its warships and the benefactors who staged and directed its plays. Now, in the Hellenistic period, cities also depended on "doers of good deeds." Greeks had always loved to compete; now rich men competed to do good for their cities. They might pay for gymnasia or theaters; give the city financial capital, the interest on which could cover public needs; or help to float a loan. Individual benefactors built fountains for people and animals, and endowed the massage oil needed by athletes. Public inscriptions recorded communal gratitude for these essential services.

SOFT POWER IN THE HELLENISTIC WORLD

The tradition of "doing good deeds" also governed relations among the Hellenistic rulers and their cities. Each king had a duty to support the cities in his realm, and as he did so, he set his stamp on each city. The Ptolemies, for example, made Alexandria a center for Greek thought and letters—a new Athens. Inspired in large part by Aristotle, they accomplished this by creating institutions for the pursuit of knowledge based on the model of his Lyceum, equipping them with the resources needed for research. Late in the fourth or early in the third century BCE, one of the Ptolemies founded a Museum—literally a temple of the Muses, the Greek goddesses who supposedly inspired poets, historians, and artists. There they established a learned society of literary men and philosophers who were paid not to teach but to carry out research on a broad range

of questions, from the size of the earth to the meaning of obscure passages in Homer's epic poems.

THE LIBRARY OF ALEXANDRIA

The vast library that the Ptolemies created, and where some of these scholars worked, has become, like Alexander the Great, a legend—one far greater, in many of its versions, than the historical original. Yet the reality was extraordinary enough. The Ptolemies and their agents tried to assemble the entire corpus of Greek literature, and they succeeded in amassing some 700,000 papyrus scrolls. (Parchment—paper made from the skins of animals—was made from the second century BCE onward, but papyrus remained the normal writing material.) A law required ships calling in Alexandria to surrender all their books to the library. Those that were not already in the collection were kept, and the library provided copies for their original owners. To obtain the

Library of Alexandria From Ptolemaic Egypt around 285–250 BCE, this papyrus fragment is part of a copy of Homer's *Odyssey*. Alexandria's library was the most important repository of Homeric texts in the Hellenistic world, and its scholars sorted through variant readings to establish standard versions.

most accurate texts possible of the three great Athenian tragedians—Aeschylus, Sophocles, and Euripides—the library made a huge deposit, borrowed the official copies from the city of Athens, and then cheerfully forfeited the money in order to retain the precious Athenian books. Forged books, some created specially to meet the new demand for works of literature by the most famous Greek writers, accompanied the genuine ones into the library's warehouses, and then into the cupboards where scrolls were kept.

The Ptolemies found ways of dealing with efforts at deception. They appointed expert scholars to catalogue the collection—a first—and to sort the genuine from the forged works attributed to each author. One of these men, the poet Callimachus (ca. 305–ca. 240 BCE), is remembered as the patron saint of librarians for his remark, "A big book is a big pain." Several of them worked especially hard on the *Iliad* and the *Odyssey*, trying to correct the errors and remove the inauthentic verses that had entered both texts over the centuries.

FESTIVALS The Ptolemies undertook all this religious and literary activity partly because they, too, believed in the value of "doing good deeds." Yet they also saw such patronage as a way to establish the prestige and power of their royal line, which was a new dynasty, after all, in a land that prided itself on being ancient and never changing. From early in the third century BCE, the Ptolemies staged a spectacular procession in Alexandria every four years to honor the Olympian gods. The procession in honor of Dionysos, the god of wine, was particularly spectacular. Men dressed as creatures from Greek myth were sent out in scores to restrain the crowd. They were followed by the priest of Dionysos, musicians, and a train of decorated carts, each grander than the last. One bore an eighteen-foot statue of the god reclining on an elephant; another carried a mechanical contraption in the form of a woman who stood up, poured a libation of milk from a gold vessel, and sat down again. Hordes of animals—including birds, Indian and Ethiopian cows, a pride of lions, and an Ethiopian rhinoceros—and staggering crown jewels filled in the display.

Though costly, such festivals were effective ways for the Ptolemies to assert their wealth and power—both to the Egyptians who watched their new Greek masters and gods parade through the streets of Alexandria, and to foreign nations whose diplomats witnessed the magnificent show. The Ptolemies used such displays to support the cult of their dynasty, each member of which claimed the status of a god. This was the foundation of the loyalty they commanded from aristocrats, soldiers, and priests.

A NEW GREEK WORLD

Royal support and trade made Alexandria into something like an ancient counterpart to twentieth-century Paris or New York—a world city, rich, impressive, and cosmopolitan. No other city matched it. Throughout the Greek world, rulers saw, as the Ptolemies did, that the soft power of culture could solidify their hold on their thrones. The Attalids, for example, although they asserted their independence from the Seleucid dynasty, also emulated the direct descendants of Alexander. They built a vast temple complex and an enormous library at Pergamum. They, too, employed scholars to study the Greek poets. As Greek styles of building spread across Central Asia to India, across Egypt to northern Africa, and up into Afghanistan, Hellenistic institutions accompanied them.

Though Greek in language, systems of exchange, and literature, the Hellenistic world was genuinely new. Hellenistic states differed fundamentally from earlier Greek states. They were massive, exerted control over many spheres of activity, and squeezed vast resources from their subjects. The royal will was decisive in a way previously unfamiliar to the Greeks. The distance between subjects and rulers was greater than before. In some ways the Hellenistic states resembled those of the ancient Near East more than the earlier Greek states. In other respects, though, Hellenistic life offered new possibilities for segments of society—especially, as we will see, for well-born women.

HELLENISTIC SOCIETY

GLIMPSES OF THE EVERYDAY

The hundreds of documents, official and private, that have survived from Hellenistic Egypt paint a vivid portrait of urban life. Even a relatively small city such as Oxyrhynchus, with a population of some 20,000 about 100 miles southwest of Cairo near the Nile, had a lively, varied economy. The city maintained a central market with rental spaces for shopkeepers and artisans, including bakers; sellers of olives, rushes, and wool; makers of clothing and shoes; garland-weavers; and tinsmiths. Aristocratic women, who apparently enjoyed more freedom of movement than their Athenian counterparts, shopped for fine cloth and even ready-made clothing, rather than producing their own. Those with more money could go to a stall and drink "wine of Oxyrhynchos"; those with less money had to content themselves with "sour wine of Oxyrhynchos."

Some of these marketplace businesses became quite elaborate and needed a fair amount of equipment. Hellenistic bakers, for example, did everything from milling wheat into flour to baking coarse and fine bread and cakes to marketing them to consumers. Others, such as the fast-food sellers who offered customers bean and lentil pastes, worked on a tiny scale.

A sophisticated money economy, powered by consumption, offered commercial opportunities for nonelites with the energy and resources to capitalize on them, such as the third-century entrepreneurs Apollophanes and Demetrius. They were brothers who offered to set up shop in a new city and produce "cloaks, tunics, girdles, dresses, belts, ribbons, split tunics, everything to size," and promised that they could supply letters of recommendation to guarantee their abilities. Their documents were written in both Greek and demotic Egyptian, since the state used both languages. Greek proved especially helpful for the many craftspeople and merchants whose trade networks were not merely local. The spread of money and specialized trades carried the Greek language into new areas throughout the Hellenistic world.

SLAVERY

The Greeks, in modern times, have often been remembered as the defenders of freedom. But as we have seen, even the democracy of classical Athens depended on slaves at every level, from the ordinary household and farm to the silver mines that paid for the fleet. The societies conquered by Alexander and his successors also had slaves, especially in the temples, where they served the priests and sometimes engaged in a sacred form of prostitution. The people who worked the land in rural regions, however, were for the most part legally free, though they were often bound to remain on the ground they tilled unless they had official permission to leave (to attend the festival of a goddess, for example).

As Greek cities rose and Greek families settled in the conquered lands, slaves came with them. One in seven Greek families in Egypt—many of them recent settlers—owned slaves. Egyptian archives record that they were treated as property: bought and sold, bequeathed to others in wills, or set free (usually on condition that they remain with their master until he or she died). Laws established harsh penalties for any slave who dared to harm a free person. In Alexandria, a free man who threatened another

Slavery This third-century BCE fresco from a Hellenistic tomb in present-day Bulgaria depicts a slave leading a chariot and horses. Slavery was one of the many institutions that spread throughout the Greek-speaking world.

free man with a weapon of metal or wood had to pay a fine. A slave who did the same received 100 strokes of the whip, which could easily amount to a cruel form of execution.

Slaves were registered, like other forms of property, and sometimes they seem to have been marked on the face to make their status clear and indelible. Professional slave dealers brought cargoes of fresh workers from Syria and elsewhere to Egypt, and even bred some slaves especially for sale. An ancient geographer reported that tens of thousands of slaves came through the Greek island of Delos every day. A vast two-story colonnade, the largest structure on the island and situated conveniently near the harbor, has been identified by some scholars as the slave market, but others claim it was a park or a space for exercise.

For all their suffering, slaves were also vital to the economic expansion that made cities so prosperous. Many tax declarations and wills describe household workshops run by slave labor. For example, a Greek named

WOMEN'S LEGAL RIGHTS IN THE HELLENISTIC WORLD

This document is a legal complaint from a Greek woman living in the Egyptian village of Trikomia, which had a large Jewish population in the third century BCE. Lysias seems to have been a military settler there; his daughter Philista documents her injury in the baths, a Greek cultural practice exported to Hellenistic cities. Although addressed to Ptolemy, as most petitions were, it would have gone to Diophanes, the military general of the district. The bath attendant was turned over to the custody of the Egyptian police chief in the presence of Simon the *epistates*, an administrative official who was most likely Jewish. This document allows us to see not only the everyday practices of Hellenized Greeks but also gives us information about the mixed population of Ptolemaic cities.

To King Ptolemy, greeting from Philista daughter of Lysias, one of the settlers in Trikomia. I am wronged by Petechon. For while I was bathing in the bath of the aforesaid village on Tybi 7 of year 1 (he being bathman in the women's rotunda), and had stepped out to soap myself, when he brought in the jugs of hot water, he emptied one (?) over me and scalded my belly and my left thigh down to the knee, so as to endanger my life. On finding him, I handed him over to the custody of Nechthosiris, the chief policeman of the village, in the presence of Simon the *epistates*. I beg you, therefore, O king, if it please you, as a suppliant who has sought refuge with you, not to allow me, a woman who earns a living with her hands, to be so lawlessly treated, but to order Diophanes to write to Simon the *epistates* and Nechthosiris the chief policeman that they are to bring Petechon before him in order that Diophanes may inquire into the case, hoping that having sought refuge with you, O King, the common benefactor of all, I may obtain justice. Farewell.

QUESTIONS FOR ANALYSIS

1. This source includes a Greek woman, an Egyptian policeman, and a Jewish official. What does this suggest about Hellenistic society?
2. In addition to baths, what other Greek cultural and social practices were found in Hellenistic cities and villages?
3. What can you infer about Philista's status in relation to the male bath attendant, and what does this illustrate about the status of women in the Hellenistic world?

Source: Jane Rowlandson, ed., *Women and Society in Greek and Roman Egypt: A Sourcebook* (Cambridge, UK: Cambridge University Press, 1998), pp. 172, 174.

Apollonis, who managed the finances of Ptolemy II in the third century, owned small textile workshops in the Lower Egyptian city of Memphis, which had once been the national capital. One of them was operated by two male weavers, who may have been legally free, and three slave girls. Surviving letters show that one of the men had his master's trust and undertook voyages on his behalf, and that one of the female slaves gave orders to the men. When she suffered a robbery and lost a load of wool, she felt able to ask her master for help. Another will leaves the writer's property to his wife and children, but also sets free a female slave and her son, "whose father I am"—revealing another job that female slaves had to perform for their masters.

THE LIVES OF FREE WOMEN

In the cities of Hellenistic Egypt and Syria, free women enjoyed distinctive opportunities. Macedonian laws had given women far more freedom and power than Greek ones, and the laws did not change when men and women of Macedonian descent suddenly found themselves ruling much of the known world. Although the queens of the Hellenistic states often had to contend with dangerous court rivalries, court life also offered possibilities for attaining power. In the second and first centuries BCE, Egyptian queens became more powerful, until Cleopatra VII (r. 51–30 BCE) eliminated all of her siblings and became the last sole ruler of an independent Egypt.

Outside the Home Women in the Hellenistic world had more freedom than their Greek counterparts of the Classical period, and many worked outside the home. The dancing woman depicted in this bronze statuette from Alexandria (third or second century BCE) was likely a professional entertainer.

Queens amassed enormous amounts of property—much of which their husbands actually gave to them. And they used it for all the same things that kings did: to pay for great shrines to their favorite god, to sponsor chariots to compete for them in the Olympic Games, and to support poets who would praise them. Callimachus, the scholar at Alexandria, wrote a poem to celebrate the lock of hair that Berenice II, a Ptolemy by birth, had dedicated to the goddess Aphrodite to ensure that her husband would come back safe from Syria. He described Berenice's hair as ascending to the heavens and becoming a constellation. But Hellenistic queens also used their resources for purposes that reflected their gender, such as providing dowries for poor women.

Some Hellenistic women became poets, as a few Greek women had in the Archaic period. But they pursued many other vocations as well, often with the encouragement of fathers with careers in the same fields. Some became artists: Helena, the daughter of a painter who lived at the end of the fourth century BCE, painted a famous panorama of the battle of Issus that was taken to Rome and exhibited centuries after her death. Many women went far beyond elementary literacy, and some studied philosophy, especially within the tradition of Pythagoras, the mathematician and philosopher who lived in the sixth century BCE. Writers who called themselves Pythagoreans encouraged women to pursue wisdom. Some Pythagorean treatises, which emphasize that women must attain purity, avoid adultery, and lead a considered, moral life, are ascribed to female authors. A few women joined the Academy in Athens. Others became scholars and worked at the correction of texts. Many women worked at traditionally female jobs such as wet-nursing, textile production, and the production and sale of food. Some owned slaves and ran their own textile workshops.

All free women benefited from the Macedonian legal tradition, and in one sense ordinary women benefited more than queens. Perhaps because women as well as men had defined rights, marriage in the Hellenistic world came to be governed by contracts, many of which survive. These contracts regulated the conduct of both husbands and wives: husbands promised to take no further wives, and wives pledged to refrain from affairs with other men. Generally, women were more restricted than men in their movements. Contracts allowed husbands to travel freely, wives hardly at all. But in some parts of the Hellenistic world, such as the Fayum in Egypt, wives were as free as husbands to initiate divorce proceedings.

Literature reflected women's new freedom, if indirectly. It was in the Hellenistic period that poets began to compose love lyrics, and that both lyric and tragic poets began to imagine women as subject not only to duty (as Antigone had been in Sophocles' fifth-century BCE play) but also to personal passion. A more direct reflection appears in the world of legal documents, in which women often spoke—and still speak—for themselves, rather than being represented by men.

EDUCATION

For centuries, Greek cities had had their teachers—from slaves who taught children how to write on wax tablets to the sophists and philosophers who competed to train well-placed young men. In the Hellenistic period, official support enabled one kind of teaching—that of the Greek language and literature—to spread across the Mediterranean world and beyond.

In cities and towns, literacy offered vital possibilities: a way to emphasize the distance between city people and the illiterate peasants of the countryside, and a way to gain access to jobs in higher places. Hellenistic cities—and the kings and wealthy men who felt responsible for them—endowed positions for teachers, based in gymnasia. Public money paid for grammarians, who taught boys to read their way through the Greek classics, and rhetoricians, who taught them to compose speeches. There was no uniform system or curriculum, and each city had its own methods. But from Iran to the coast of Egypt, any cultured mother would have understood that when her son's teacher said he was reading the sixth book, this referred to what we call book VI of Homer's *Iliad*.

Greek theaters rose in Iran and Babylon, the epic poets were taught in Ceylon and India, and children in what is now Uzbekistan learned to love the story of the Trojan horse. Royal patronage enabled certain especially skillful poets and historians to make glamorous careers at court, while public contests gave poets and orators a chance to win fame. Greek education became one of the most widespread, shared features of Hellenistic society.

A COSMOPOLITAN CULTURE

The spread of public teachers and schools helps to explain how in many cities, both new and old, a Greek-speaking elite came into being. Its members were diverse in their origins but unified in their culture, and they exercised in the nude, practiced rhetoric and gymnastics, and produced a Greek literature of their own. This was a literature that never ceased to model itself on the great works handed down from classical Greece, but that also developed new ways of expressing the broadened experience of the societies formed by the Macedonian conquests.

NEW TYPES OF LITERATURE

From Athens to Alexandria, a new literature addressed the comic qualities of everyday life. Aristophanes, whose subversive, sometimes brutally personal comedies had amused and enraged the citizens of Athens in the fifth century BCE, had concerned himself with weighty issues such as war and peace. Menander (d. 290 BCE), his prolific successor in the late fourth and early third centuries, staged everyday life in exaggerated form. His gallery of characters included rude misers with pretty, marriageable daughters; eager, clumsy young lovers; and slaves deftly acting as intermediaries between lovers and maidens.

Menander responded shrewdly to the taste of his contemporaries. So did Theophrastus (ca. 372–ca. 287 BCE), a student of Aristotle's who applied his teacher's methods of classification to the characters of individuals, and the quirkier the better. He turned out Monty Pythonish character sketches of the fools and boors who people the streets of any big city: "The tiresome man is the one who will walk in when you have just dozed off and wake you up to have a chat. He will arrive for an appointment and then ask you to wait until he has taken a walk." Even at meals, this character can't stop talking about matters no one would want to hear about while eating: "You should have seen the color of the bile in my excreta," he says. "Darker than that gravy you've got." The city that Theophrastus observed was as funny, in its own way, as Athens had been when observed by Aristophanes.

This cosmopolitan new world inspired other sorts of literary exploration. Apollonius of Rhodes (third century BCE), from a Greek island in the eastern Aegean, devoted an epic poem to the mythical expedition that Jason and other heroes undertook in a ship named the *Argo* (which gave them the collective name Argonauts). To win a throne in Thessaly, Jason had to bring back the golden fleece of a winged ram from Colchis on the Black Sea. Apollonius took a deep interest in human psychology, especially in extreme situations. Building on the precedents set by Euripides centuries before, he developed complex internal monologues in which his characters revealed the emotions that wrenched them. Medea, daughter of the king of Colchis, pondered her plan to betray her father for the sake of her lover, Jason: "this pain of mine, it burns without end: how I wish / I'd been killed already by the swift shafts of Artemis." Hellenistic poets did not address great political and religious themes as often as the tragedians of classical Athens had. But they staged difficult emotional situations with a precision, insight, and empathy that lent their work much charm.

Charm, in fact, became one of the central characteristics of Hellenistic literature. The Sicilian Theocritus (310–250 BCE), whose talent took him from Syracuse to Alexandria, created a new genre called pastoral, the escapist literature of a sophisticated urban society. In Theocritus's dreamy idylls, shepherds and goatherds played reed pipes and told sad stories of unhappy lovers tormented by the gods. Allusive, sophisticated poetry like this appealed to the rulers and courtiers of the new cities. It attracted readers whose education enabled them to recognize allusions to older texts and who appreciated word games and riddles. The fifth-century comedies of Aristophanes were packed with allusions that called attention to the physical

Laocoön and His Sons According to Greek legend, the Trojan priest Laocoön and his sons met with a painful death from venomous snakes. This statue, a Roman copy of a Hellenistic original, displays the visceral emotion that found expression in Hellenistic literature as well.

appearance and personal foibles of public figures, as his audience knew. Poetry at that time had been part of a local, public life. In the Hellenistic world, by contrast, poetry was written for the highly cultivated members of courts. No Hellenistic thinker could have blamed a comic playwright, as Socrates had once blamed Aristophanes, for destroying his reputation.

NEW PHILOSOPHIES: EPICUREANS AND STOICS

However artificial, this elegant new literature speaks of a Greek culture that stretched across the Mediterranean, one in which poets and playwrights read and responded to one another. This new environment fostered Greek philosophy as well. Athens was still a central spawning ground for new ideas. Plato's Academy and Aristotle's Lyceum existed through the Hellenistic period, but new schools of philosophy flanked them. These schools addressed themselves to Athens and to the great monarchies and sophisticated cities of Egypt and the Near East.

The philosopher Epicurus (341–270 BCE) founded a school in Athens called The Garden. He and his followers insisted that the entire universe consisted of matter in motion. They traced the creation of the cosmos back to an accidental collision of primary particles, some of which swerved by chance as they fell through the great emptiness that preceded the universe. As more and more particles hit one another, the original chaos dissolved, and the earth, planets, and stars took shape. This vision of the world, radically different from the ordered, hierarchical ones that Plato and Aristotle had imagined, filled the **Epicureans** not with despair but with hope. They found no reason to fear the vengeful gods of earlier Greek myths, or the Furies that had appeared so terrifying on the Athenian tragic stage. Instead they devoted themselves to the pursuit of pleasure—rationally understood, of course.

Zeno (ca. 335–262 BCE) and Cleanthes (ca. 331–232 BCE), who taught in the Athenian building known as the Stoa Poikile ("painted colonnade"), came to be known as **Stoics**. Unlike the Epicureans, they saw the universe as animated by a divine spirit. They, too, however, insisted that the reasonable person should abandon fear and all other excessive emotions. Once one realized that the universe is ordered by a superhuman fate, one could cease to hope for mastery or struggle for the unobtainable.

Epicureans and Stoics differed in more ways than this one. The Epicureans formed something like a religious brotherhood, whose members followed detailed instructions for dress and diet. The Stoics, more loosely organized, insisted on the brotherhood of all men, in theory at least, and formulated natural laws that they held as superior to human laws. Yet both offered their followers not only an intellectual system but a guide to life. Like Socrates, they saw the pursuit of wisdom as a disciplined way of life to which the philosopher must dedicate himself, doing his best to put aside lesser concerns. Unlike Socrates, they derived strikingly similar moral codes, precise and humane, from their radically divergent underlying principles. They taught their followers to pursue their human duties so far as possible, and to avoid emotions that might spoil the calm enjoyment of the world that was the proper pursuit of a philosopher.

HELLENISTIC SCIENCE

In Alexandria, Syracuse, and other great Hellenistic cities, royal patronage enabled scholars to devote themselves for years at a time to solving highly technical problems in their fields. This fostered something like research centers

LADY OF KALYMNOS

The "Lady of Kalymnos" is a magnificent Greek sculpture whose features express values shared across the cultures of the Hellenistic world. This larger than life bronze sculpture, found on the seabed near the Greek island of Kalymnos in 1994, is a variation on the Herculaneum Woman, a type of draped, gracefully poised female figure found in Roman and Greek culture beginning in the fourth century BCE. The head of this sculpture also resembles the portrayal of Ptolemaic queens on coins, particularly in the framing of the face and hair by a veil.

The pose and clothing of the figure suggest that she is a noblewoman. She possesses a calm dignity as she seems to gaze at a distant point. Her dress, with its voluminous folds, makes the strongest statement of her wealth and social position. The shimmering drapery of her tunic wrapping around her full-length skirt indicates her domesticity and sober modesty.

QUESTIONS FOR ANALYSIS

1. How does this sculpture portray an ideal view of femininity in the Hellenistic period?
2. How does this statue represent the way cultures intermixed in the Hellenistic world?
3. Do you see in the sculpture signs of the greater autonomy that women experienced in this period? Explain.

Hellenistic Inventions Built in Athens around 150 BCE, the Tower of the Winds drew its name from the friezes of the wind gods at the top of its eight walls. Its weather vane and sundial—both since removed—indicated wind direction and the time of day, respectively, while an intricate system of pipes inside fed a water clock, which could keep track of the hours at night.

an object is placed in a fluid, it is subject to an upward pressure, known as buoyancy, equal in magnitude to the weight of the fluid it displaces. Eratosthenes (third century BCE), an Alexandrian scholar with an interest in quantification, ingeniously calculated the circumference of the earth by extrapolating it from the lengths of the shadows cast by the sun at noon.

In their quest for knowledge as well as power, Hellenistic rulers sponsored new forms of inquiry. Medical men in early-third-century Alexandria received permission to dissect human bodies and even to vivisect condemned criminals. A dizzying amount of new information emerged from what must have been investigations of unspeakable cruelty. The Alexandrians did not realize that the veins and arteries formed a single circulatory system, but they did establish that the arteries transmitted not air, as Aristotle had thought, but blood. At the same time, and in the same city, other scholars used royal support to craft ingenious devices. Inventors devised spectacular machines that used water or water vapor to make artificial birds sing and statues move. Archimedes not only worked on the theory of statics and mechanics but also created practical military devices such as the burning mirrors with which he supposedly reduced invading Roman ships to cinders in 212 BCE.

CONVERSATIONS ACROSS CULTURES

For centuries, Greeks had traveled around the Mediterranean world and the Near East, marveling at the age of Egyptian and Babylonian tradition. As knowledge of the Greek language spread, it now became possible for scholars and scientists to draw ideas and information from the vast catchment area that the Greeks ruled. These learned men began to engage in substantive conversations across cultures—for example, with the teams of astronomers and diviners who had worked competitively in Mesopotamian temples over the centuries.

CULTURAL FUSION: ASTRONOMY

Since the time of Plato, many Greek thinkers (though not the Epicureans or Stoics) agreed that sets of hard, nested, transparent spheres carried each planet around the earth, while also accounting for the apparent irregularities of its motion. These thinkers, less interested in predicting

and an international scientific community. Greek mathematicians had already developed their subject to a high level by Plato's time, and in the following centuries they composed systematic treatments of individual branches of the field. One of their textbooks, the *Elements* of geometry of Euclid (ca. 325–250 BCE), remained the standard for centuries to come.

These scholars also innovated radically, posing and solving problems that could not be directly answered by the mathematical means available. The Syracusan mathematician and scientist Archimedes (ca. 287–212 BCE), for instance, reckoned the number of grains of sand that would be needed to fill the universe and found ingenious ways to explain the behavior of objects in water. One of his principles, still named after him, holds that when than explaining planetary events, had not tried to correlate their geometrical models with the observed positions of the planets. As early as the eighth century BCE, in contrast, the priests who predicted eclipses and planetary positions for the rulers of Mesopotamia had decided that the planets and their movements determined the fates of kingdoms and individuals on earth. They based their predictions on mathematical tables that enabled them to forecast the positions of the known planets, the sun, and the moon for any given day and time.

On a day—and in a century—that we cannot precisely specify, a momentous conversation must have taken place. This exchange, in Greek or perhaps in Aramaic, was between a Greek who could use geometry to explain why the planets move as they do and a Mesopotamian diviner who could work out their future motion from tables. They realized that the tables drawn up in Mesopotamia could map onto the geometrical models of the Greek tradition. Conversation and inquiry continued. By the second century BCE, Hipparchus, an astronomer from Rhodes, and others fused these two sets of methods into a single, comprehensive mathematical theory that offered both explanations and predictions of planetary motion. For the first time in human history, at least in the West, precise statements about how the natural world works were cast in the language of mathematics and tested and refined against the results of observation.

Alexandria became the central place for the application of the new quantitative skills to astronomy, cartography, musical harmony, and many other fields. The methods created in Alexandria would continue to be employed for almost two millennia in the Islamic world to the East as well as in the West. As in early Greece, so in the Hellenistic world: the fusion of Western with non-Western skills, methods, and beliefs created what came to be seen, in retrospect, as the core achievements of the Western tradition.

NON-GREEK PERSPECTIVES

Greeks and non-Greeks did not confine their contact to the dining hall of Alexandria's Museum and similar spaces, where scholars literally compared notes. Sometimes their meetings were indirect. Few, if any, Greek scholars in Alexandria learned to read Egyptian hieroglyphs or cuneiform tablets from Mesopotamia. Interpreters— many of them Egyptians and Mesopotamians who had learned Greek—explained the histories of their peoples

and traditions to the literate, Greek-educated elites who ruled their kingdoms.

These non-Greeks keenly felt the loss of political independence, even if their rulers adopted local customs and rituals. They tended to insist, as the Egyptians had done some centuries before, on the age, stability, and profundity of their cultures. By showing that their historical records stretched far back in time, long before Homer or the Trojan War, Egyptians and Mesopotamians could avenge, in the study, the defeats their kings had suffered on the battlefield. And though only a few Hellenistic Greeks read these works attentively, and they did so in Greek translations that they could not verify, many of them came to understand themselves as newcomers to ancient lands, which they ruled but whose mysterious religions and traditions they might not be able to understand.

THE PTOLEMIES: MANAGING RELIGIOUS DIVERSITY

When the Macedonian dynasty of the Ptolemies took charge of Egypt, they introduced the Greek language and Greek cults. But, like the Persians and other ancient rulers before them, they made no effort to abolish the existing public religion. On the contrary, they accepted responsibility for it, made massive contributions to the priests and temples of the ancient Egyptian gods, and even created

Hellenistic Egypt Along with retaining Greek language, laws, and institutions, the Ptolemaic kings incorporated Greek stylistic influences in their architectural projects. Along the colonnade of the Isis Temple, built by a Ptolemaic king in 358–345 BCE, the carved faces gaze forward, rather than in traditional Egyptian profile.

Religious Diversity A grave stele from the Ptolemaic period combines Greek and Egyptian elements: from the bottom, the goddess Isis in the form of a snake; the Greek god of silence, Harpocrates, a Hellenization of the Egyptian god Horus; and an image of the deceased.

is now Cairo, had already begun to worship at the great temple of the god Apis, whom the Egyptians connected with Osiris, their god of fertility and the underworld. Osiris was a mysterious figure whose identity and attributes the Greeks did not fully grasp. Within a few years, however, this divinity took on a new, Hellenic form as Sarapis—a being whom the Greeks came to identify with their own fertility god, Dionysos, the very one who formed the focus of the Ptolemies' magnificent celebrations. Ptolemy I (r. 323–283 BCE) had a temple built in honor of Sarapis in Alexandria. Equipped with bilingual inscriptions that identified its founding god and goddess, the temple also held a massive library of Greek texts—a kind of annex to the main Alexandrian library. As the center for the cult of a divine couple, it soon became strongly identified with the Ptolemaic royal cult.

A few decades later, Ptolemy III (r. 246–221 BCE) went much further in the same direction. By now it was customary for the Egyptian priests to meet once a year in solemn assembly with their Greek king. In the winter of 238 BCE, the priests came to Alexandria to celebrate the king's birthday. The assembly yielded a series of decrees, recorded in both Greek and hieroglyphs, that called for the creation of a new religious feast in honor of the Ptolemies. It would take place, significantly, just when the Nile flooded and the land's fertility was assured for another year. From this point on, the priests identified themselves and their religion ever more strongly with their Greek rulers, whose epithets and titles were translated into Egyptian and frequently celebrated.

Lords of a double society and culture, the Ptolemies made a point of issuing their decrees in Greek as well as in Egyptian. This tradition gave rise to, among much more, the Rosetta Stone, an Egyptian record inscribed in 196 BCE on a massive piece of black stone in Egyptian hieroglyphs and demotic script, as well as ancient Greek. When unearthed in the late eighteenth century CE, the stone provided scholars with the key to deciphering the long-forgotten hieroglyphs. Even the Persians of the fifth century BCE had not managed religious and cultural diversity more skillfully than the Ptolemies.

CULTURAL TENSIONS AND NEW BELIEFS

Despite the Ptolemies' tolerance of diversity in Egypt, the Hellenistic world was hardly peaceful. The Seleucids, who

new temples—like a spectacular one built late in the third century BCE and graced during its construction, according to its hieroglyphic inscriptions, by the presence of the Ptolemaic king and queen.

In the course of the third century BCE the Ptolemies began to transform the religious and cultural systems that they began with, one Greek and one Egyptian, into something more coherent. Greeks in Memphis, south of what inherited Syria and parts of Asia Minor from Alexander, warred with the Ptolemies over and over again. The origins of the Greek dynasties in conquest often aroused terrible bitterness. Some writers adopted the Persian belief that history would end in a great confrontation between good and evil and turned to prophecy. They put into the mouths of the Sibyls, prophetesses known throughout the Mediterranean world, the prediction that at some future date history would reverse itself and the hated Greek invaders would either be cast out and the ancient kingdoms restored, or the great kingdoms would finally disappear in flood or fire.

The Greeks, as we have seen, had always been curious about the peoples they encountered. Herodotus learned much about the nomadic Scythians who lived in the steppes of Eurasia from Greek traders settled around the Black Sea. But this interest had never been universal or systematic. During the Hellenistic period, however, some Greeks began to believe as fervently as the Persians and Egyptians that non-Greek traditions might harbor vital teachings unknown to Greek thought. Alexander the Great himself is said to have been deeply impressed by the austere, loincloth-clad Brahmins whom he encountered in India and whom the Greeks called gymnosophists ("naked philosophers"). Still other Greeks collected mysterious stories and magical recipes associated with "thrice-great Hermes," the ancient sage who had supposedly taught the Egyptians how to write, or the Persian prophet Zoroaster, about whom Plato and others spun rich fables.

Many inauthentic texts came into circulation—supposed revelations of the non-Greek gods and prophets, stuffed with fragments of genuine Egyptian or Persian tradition but designed to show that these had anticipated, or were the source of, the Greek philosophies of Plato and Aristotle. Small sects formed, creating pseudo-Persian and pseudo-Egyptian rituals. Magical practitioners and astronomers who offered predictions of the future often described themselves as "Chaldeans" (Mesopotamians), even when they were Greek by birth, and sprinkled their writings with foreign words that gave them a mysterious appeal. The culture of the Hellenistic Mediterranean, for all the rigorous and lively scientific experimentation and scholarly debate that took place in Alexandria, also fostered abundant crops of new superstitions. These were as loosely connected to the peoples with whom they supposedly originated as the "Druidic" and "Egyptian" magical texts in a modern occult bookshop. This mixture of beliefs and practices became fertile ground for

Rosetta Stone From 196 BCE Ptolemaic Egypt, the Rosetta Stone is inscribed with a decree from King Ptolemy V written in the kingdom's three official scripts: Egyptian hieroglyphs, demotic (or "popular") Egyptian, and Greek.

the development of new religions—including, as we will see, Christianity itself.

THE JEWS IN THE HELLENISTIC WORLD

One of the ancient Near Eastern peoples, however, did learn to speak for itself, even under Hellenistic rule. Jews and Greeks had come into contact for centuries, especially in Egypt, where both nations' mercenary soldiers served. In the second half of the sixth century BCE, Cyrus, the king of Persia, had conquered Babylon and allowed the Jews, who had been forced to migrate there earlier in the century, to return home to Judah. There, as we will see, they were brought for a time under the control of one of the Hellenistic monarchies, the Seleucids, with explosive results.

SECOND TEMPLE JUDAISM (6TH–2ND CENTURIES BCE)

Jerusalem, the former capital of Judah, became the center of Jewish life and worship in the fifth and fourth centuries BCE. There, on a hill called the Temple Mount, the Jews had rebuilt their Temple. This **Second Temple**, an impressive structure, gradually became a vast complex of buildings. At the end of its existence, in the first century CE, it grew big enough to encompass some twelve modern soccer fields.

The Second Temple was uniquely central to Jewish life. It was the only place where Jews could perform sacrifices to their god, as their law mandated. Three times a year, at Passover, Pentecost, and Sukkot, Jews came to the Temple to make ritual sacrifices. For the rest of the year, the priests carried on services and made sacrifices. The Temple bustled with people, especially on the three great holidays, when moneychangers and butchers offered travelers help in buying and slaughtering ritual animals. This large and richly decorated house of God, which only Jews were deemed clean enough to enter, was also a central slaughterhouse where thousands of animals were butchered and

The Second Temple This Roman public notice displayed in the Second Temple is in Greek, the most common written language shared by Temple visitors from outside of Palestine. It reads, "No Gentile may enter beyond the dividing wall into the court around the Holy Place; whoever is caught will be to blame for his subsequent death."

eaten at every holiday. By charging for its services and soliciting donations, the Temple became as rich as it was elaborate.

THE PEOPLE OF THE BOOK Splendid though the Temple was, it did not dominate all of religious life in Israel. The Jews had long stood out as monotheists, bound to a single god by a national covenant, which they believed their ancestors had entered, and forbidden to worship others. Like other Near Eastern peoples, they had created some texts that recorded their laws, but as late as the fifth century BCE there was no set body of texts that corresponded to what we know as the Hebrew Bible. The Persian monarchy, however, pushed subject peoples, including the Egyptians and the Jews, to systematize their laws. A plan of this kind likely led the Persians to send Ezra, a professional scribe trained in Babylon, to Jerusalem in the middle of the fifth century BCE. He was instructed to collect and organize the laws of his people.

Ezra, so it seems, compiled what is now the first part of the Hebrew Bible: the Pentateuch, or Five Books of Moses (Genesis, Exodus, Leviticus, Numbers, and Deuteronomy). By doing so, he provided an authoritative account of the origins of the universe and the history of the Jews, as well as a summary of their laws and observances. He also brought the Jews together and presented their law to them, dramatically reading it aloud from a platform, after which a great celebration took place. Jewish worship after the Babylonian exile still revolved around sacrifice and prayer, but it added something radically new as well: the public reading of "the book of the law," presumably the Five Books of Moses, which was assembled in official copies and made accessible to the whole people, women as well as men.

Over the coming centuries, the Hebrew Bible took shape as further texts—especially the writings of the prophets and the Psalms—were added to the Five Books of Moses. Bible scrolls were kept in the Temple, and other copies in synagogues—religious gathering places that became increasingly central to Jewish life. On the Sabbath, Jews came together in synagogues to read from the Bible, first in Hebrew and then in Aramaic, the language of everyday Jewish life in Babylon. By the third century BCE, when the massive Hebrew Bible was translated into Greek, even Greeks could find out that the Jews were "the people of a book."

JUDAISM TRANSLATED—AND REVISED The Temple, with its wealth and power, and the scriptures, with their authoritative narrative of early history and their detailed codes and commandments, helped to maintain the unity of the Jewish tradition. Yet in this culturally fertile period, religious beliefs continued to change. The Bible could divide as well as unite. In a culture in which every text was produced by copying, it took centuries to stabilize the Hebrew Bible completely. And whereas most Jews in Palestine encountered the Bible through readings in Aramaic, others there and many in other areas spoke, read, and worshipped in Greek. They also needed a Bible in the familiar language that they could follow. By the second century BCE, a Greek translation of the Hebrew Bible was in circulation.

From translation to interpretation was only a short step. The **Septuagint**, the Greek translation of the Five Books of Moses made in the third century BCE, incorporated changes that rationalized and softened parts of its message. Writers whose identity we do not know went so far as to add new books of history, prophecy, or reflection, which they claimed also deserved to be treated as scripture. From Genesis 6, for example, writers in the third and second centuries BCE crafted the book of Enoch. This new book tells the story of the fall of the Watchers—angels sent by God to watch over the universe—and Enoch's efforts to intercede on their behalf with God. Over time the sacred history of Israel became more complex and rich than the narrative of it in the Five Books of Moses. The mental universe that believing Jews inhabited gradually filled up with superhuman beings not explicitly mentioned in the Bible.

SOCIAL AND ECONOMIC CHANGE IN HEBREW SOCIETY

The Hellenistic period was fertile materially as well as culturally for the people of Palestine. Though Judea itself, the area around Jerusalem, was rocky and poor, other parts of the country lent themselves to cultivation of grapes and olives. The peaceful conditions fostered by the Ptolemies encouraged trade with Egypt, and the vast expansion of money set loose by Alexander and his followers expanded economic activity. Lending came to be seen not as usury (a sin) but as a normal transaction. Caravans brought trade goods to Jerusalem, which became by the second century BCE, as a contemporary noted, a city "skilled in many crafts." Using devices for scattering seed and irrigating crops—technology well established elsewhere but new to Palestine—successful landlords accumulated extensive holdings and became rich.

The fast-moving, trade-centered Palestine of the third century BCE appears in Ecclesiastes, a later book of the Hebrew Bible. Kohelet, the author of the text, describes his decision to invest in vineyards and olive groves, which were far more profitable than fields of grain: "I made me great works; I builded me houses; I planted me vineyards: I made me gardens and orchards, and I planted trees in them of all kind of fruits." In this world, successful entrepreneurship on the land could make one, literally, as rich as a king.

Like other moralists, Kohelet dismissed his gains as "vanity and vexation of spirit." In memorable words he called for the restoration of a simple, traditional morality that would teach men to love God, enjoy their lives, and do good. Yet the world he described, and took for granted, was one in which rich men like him ground the poor under their feet: "If thou seest the oppression of the poor, and violent perverting of judgment and justice in a province, marvel not at the matter." Many of the new rich had slaves to work their land or serve in their households.

WOMEN'S LIVES The status of women changed as radically in Jewish society as it did in Egypt in the third and second centuries BCE. The older books of the Bible describe a polygamous society in which the prospective groom offered his future father-in-law a bride price: cattle and other goods, or money, which could support the bride if the marriage did not last. In the Greek world, brides brought property and money with them to their marriages in the form of a dowry. During the third century BCE, Jewish women also began to bring dowries with them to their marriages: goods and money to be managed by the husband and used, with his resources, to support the family. Scribes now drew up contracts to regulate this complicated system and to ensure that the interests of both sides were protected—for example, by ensuring that widows had the right to inherit their husbands' property. The new Jewish system of marriage was monogamous, and contracts required husbands to promise not to take further wives.

Women did not attain full equality, and only men could initiate divorce proceedings. But as the development of the marriage contract shows, women now had more property and power than ever before in Jewish history. Some were richer than their husbands and maintained them in better style than the men could have afforded on their own. And some women worked. Chapter 31 of the biblical book of Proverbs, written in the Hellenistic period, describes the ideal wife: she plants vineyards and trees, spins wool and weaves cloth, makes fine linen and sells some of it to merchants. Instead of eating "the bread of idleness," she rises before dawn to work, and the fine things she makes "praise her in the gates."

Other biblical passages written in this period praised women for their intelligence as well as for their beauty. And still others warned fathers to watch their daughters carefully, because too much independence could make them wicked. Unlike the soil of Egypt, that of Palestine has not preserved individual legal documents and contracts to illustrate these changes. But they mattered greatly—especially when a new prophet, named Jesus, began to preach a radical new message in Palestine.

ADOPTING GREEK WAYS

As trade and migration brought Jews into regular contact with the Greek world, the Greek language—and Greek culture—inevitably attracted them. Jews who moved to Egypt and elsewhere, as tens of thousands did, began to use Greek as well as Aramaic. Not only did Jews read their Bible in Greek, as we have seen, Greek eventually became a language of Jewish prayer in the great synagogue at Alexandria and in others across the Mediterranean. In the second century CE, rabbis in Palestine would hear the holiest Jewish prayer, the Shema, recited in Greek. In Palestine itself, moreover, the Greek language and Greek customs began to spread. For example, families that could afford it began to bury their dead in lavish above-ground tombs, which they equipped with Greek inscriptions praising the virtues of their dead relatives.

Greek artistic forms and ideas followed the language and infiltrated every area of life. The biblical book of Judith is a narrative originally written in Hebrew in the second century BCE, which survives now only in Greek. It describes how the virtuous widow Judith and her loyal maid enter the camp of an Assyrian general. Judith promises him sexual favors, tricks him into becoming drunk, and beheads him, maintaining her chastity and saving her fellow Jews. An inspiration to painters and musicians for centuries, the story clearly shows the impact both of the new position of women in Israel and of Greek tragedy.

Jews also came to appreciate the Greek custom of the symposium—the evening meeting at which men, and sometimes women, reclined, drank, recited poetry, and argued about philosophy. Eventually they took it over for themselves, and the Passover seder, which had been a rapid ritual, performed standing up, in memory of the ancient Jews' escape from Egypt, became a long celebration performed by Jews who reclined at the table and debated every aspect of the Passover experience.

SELEUCIDS AND MACCABEES: THE LIMITS OF CONVERGENCE (2ND CENTURY BCE)

What did it mean to live as a Jew? The Seleucid rulers of Palestine, like their Persian predecessors, allowed their Jewish subjects to follow their own ways of life and worship. But in the third and second centuries BCE, many Jews began to believe that turning away from the beliefs and practices of the rest of the world had been a mistake, the origin of centuries of misfortune. Young men began to practice athletics in the nude, as the Greeks did. Others began to worship the gods of the invaders. At the request of these Jewish reformers, in 176 BCE the Seleucid ruler of Syria, Antiochus Epiphanes, imposed the worship of the god Baal—a Semitic name for Zeus—whose idol he introduced into the Temple itself.

DANIEL'S VISION: RESISTANCE TO CULTURAL MINGLING

A resistance movement sprang up, one powered (at first) by the hope that divine vengeance would put matters right. The unknown author of the prophetic book of Daniel, horrified to see "the abomination of desolation" in the Temple, looked back to the earlier history of Israel and Judah for precedents to follow. Like the earlier prophets, he denounced the sin, corruption, and irreligion that he saw around him, and insisted that God would avenge himself.

The text of Daniel also offers a dramatic vision of the future. The king of Babylon dreams of a gigantic statue of a man, its head made of gold, its chest and arms of silver, its belly of bronze, its legs of iron, and its feet of iron and clay. A stone smashes the statue, whose remains are swept away by the wind while the stone fills the whole earth. The prophet explains that the metals of the statue represent the different kingdoms that succeeded one another in the past. The great stone stands for the new, universal kingdom that God will create.

Daniel and other Jewish writers found consolation for their present sorrows in the belief that history would soon come to a magnificent, terrifying close, as God smashed the oppressors of the true God and his people

EUROPE

ASIA

AFRICA

Sidon

Damascus

Tyre

PHOENICIA

Sea of Galilee

Palestine

Jordan R.

Mediterranean Sea

Jerusalem

Dead Sea

- Seleucid kingdom, 188 BCE
- ✕ Center of the Maccabean revolt, 167–166 BCE
- ✕ Maccabean victory, 167–166 BCE
- Kingdom of Judea, 76 BCE

0   50   100 mi
0   50   100 km

The Seleucids and Maccabees in the 2nd Century BCE

central to Judaism. In one of these books, the Jewish mother of seven sons, whom Antiochus puts to death for refusing to betray their religion, encourages the last one to die rather than to violate the commands of Judaism: "Accept death, so that in God's mercy I may get you back again with your brothers." He dies well, and she does the same. Belief in the sanctity of martyrdom—that a heroic death in defense of religious purity is the highest imaginable fate and means certain salvation for the martyr's soul—would become a central feature of Jewish tradition, and then of Christian and Islamic religious life as well. It was not only the belief in one god that these monotheistic religions had in common.

The victorious Maccabees did not prohibit all Greek influences. They issued public documents in Greek and minted coins that followed Greek models. They also used Greek to recount their own history in the second book of Maccabees. Even as the Maccabees restored the Temple and the worship of the God of Israel, Jews were beginning, for the first time, to think about how to explain themselves to non-Jews.

CONCLUSION

By the end of the second century BCE, the world had changed. A single, Greek-speaking culture had spread across the entire Mediterranean world and beyond it. A single pattern of urban settlement, a uniform kind of temple to the gods (though not the God of Israel), and a clearly chosen set of literary classics had imposed themselves from Bactria to Marseilles, and from Egypt to the Black Sea.

Greek culture had immense prestige. Everyone from the rulers of Egypt to the leaders of Jewish society in Palestine wanted to exercise in gymnasia, take part in athletic contests, write poetry in Greek, and—in most cases—worship Greek gods. Thanks to Persian gold and Macedonian conquest, the market society pioneered by the Phoenicians and expanded by the Athenians and other Greeks had become the normal form of urban life. The Greek language had spread across the Mediterranean world with the conquering armies and merchants, enabling distant peoples to communicate and supporting the creation of great states. A policy of tolerance, coexistence, and multilingual government had enabled the survival, in Egypt and elsewhere, of native priesthoods, religions, and customs.

At the same time, another power—one almost as old as

in one climactic confrontation or battle. Paradoxically, these opponents of cultural mingling between Jews and non-Jews may have drawn this vision from the Zoroastrians, with their visions of cosmic confrontations between good and evil. The Jews' convictions underpinned resistance, first to the Seleucids and then, as we will see, to Rome. They also provided a vital part of the framework on which Jesus and his followers created what would become the Christian church.

THE MACCABEES The **Maccabees**, a group of pious Jewish rebels, resisted the Seleucids in a more practical way, rising up against Antiochus Epiphanes in 167–166 BCE. Using guerilla tactics they defeated the Seleucid armies, cleansed the Temple, and reestablished worship there. Antiochus's death in 164 BCE prevented him from trying to regain control, and the Maccabees founded the Hasmonean dynasty, which ruled Judea for the next century. Religious ideology could, evidently, rally a people as effectively as the political ideologies that had long before united Athenians and Spartans.

The books of Maccabees, which recorded these events, offer the earliest testimony to beliefs that would become the Greek city-states and far stronger—had risen to challenge the Hellenistic states and some of their rivals. The Romans, whose state had grown up over the centuries in the center of the Italian peninsula, regarded themselves as the descendants of the Trojans, not of the Greeks. In that respect, as in many others, they posed a formidable challenge to the existing order as they entered it in the third and second centuries BCE.

[CHAPTER REVIEW]

KEY TERMS

Plato (p. 79)
forms (p. 79)
Aristotle (p. 80)
empirical (p. 80)

Lyceum (p. 80)
satrap (p. 81)
Philip II (p. 82)
Alexander (p. 83)

Hellenistic (p. 85)
Ptolemies (p. 87)
Epicureans (p. 96)
Stoics (p. 96)

Second Temple (p. 102)
Septuagint (p. 103)
Maccabees (p. 105)

REVIEW QUESTIONS

1. In what ways did Plato establish a new basis for philosophy?

2. What are the most important differences between Plato's and Aristotle's thinking?

3. What steps did Philip II take to conquer the Greek city-states?

4. How did Alexander consolidate his rule over the eastern Mediterranean and western Asia?

5. How did trade and commerce help to connect the Hellenistic world?

6. What types of "soft power" were used by Hellenistic monarchs to solidify their rule?

7. How were the lives of women different in the Hellenistic kingdoms as compared with those in fifth-century Athens?

8. How did the Hellenistic world contribute to the development of science and philosophy?

9. How did the Ptolemies draw on Egyptian and Greek traditions in their rule of Egypt?

10. What were the most important developments in Hebrew religious culture during the Second Temple period?

CORE OBJECTIVES

After reading this chapter, you should have a solid understanding of the following core objectives. To strengthen your grasp of the core objectives, use the resources on the Student Site for The West.

- Identify the distinctive approaches of Plato and Aristotle in understanding the world.

- Explain Alexander's approaches to non-Greek cultures as he conquered and ruled foreign lands.

- Analyze the causes of economic prosperity in the Hellenistic kingdoms.

- Describe the transformations in Greek culture brought about by contact with foreign cultures during the Hellenistic period.

- Evaluate the intellectual and religious innovations that arose from the mix of Greek and non-Greek thought in the Hellenistic period.

- Explain how Jewish culture and religion both accepted and resisted Hellenism.

 GO TO inQuizitive TO SEE WHAT YOU'VE LEARNED—AND LEARN WHAT YOU'VE MISSED—WITH PERSONALIZED FEEDBACK ALONG THE WAY.

CHRONOLOGY

753 BCE
City of Rome is
founded as a monarchy

280–276 BCE
Romans defend against invasion
by Greek King Pyrrhus

218–201 BCE
Second Punic War

149–146 BCE
Third Punic War

509–508 BCE
Romans establish Republic

ca. 500 BCE
Law of the Twelve Tables
Early fifth century–ca. 287 BCE
Struggle of the Orders

264–241 BCE
First Punic War

214–140 BCE
Romans war against
and defeat Macedonians
and Greeks

4

Rome

MONARCHY, REPUBLIC, AND THE TRANSITION TO EMPIRE

1000 BCE–14 CE

31 BCE
Octavian assumes sole
power as Augustus

133–121 BCE
Gracchi brothers
attempt reforms

91–87 BCE
Social War

73–71 BCE
Spartacus leads
slave revolt

63 BCE
Cicero delivers orations
against Catiline

After 50 BCE
Caesar becomes
sole ruler of Rome

44 BCE
Brutus and Cassius murder Caesar

I n the autumn of 63 BCE, the politician Marcus Tullius Cicero stood before the Roman Senate, the city's official body of elders, at a special meeting held in the Senate House, located in the Forum at the center of the city. Rome was an old city, traditionally dominated by great aristocratic clans that had been established for centuries. But it was also a republic, in which politicians of lower origins who had a gift for public speaking and organizing could attain power. Cicero was born to a rich family with noble status, but one based in the hill town of Arpinum, sixty miles southeast of Rome. As a so-called new man (the first in his family to win high office), he had established his authority through his accomplishments as a lawyer, orator, and official. In a series of fiery speeches, powerfully delivered, he now denounced the aristocrat Catiline, whom he had beaten in an election for consul, the supreme office in the Roman Republic. For the last century, as Rome became more and more prosperous, the poor had suffered and thousands lost their farms. Catiline, like other Romans of high standing before him, had wooed them by offering a program of land distribution.

Cicero proclaimed that his spies had caught Catiline and his followers conspiring to assassinate Cicero and take over the city of Rome. He described Catiline as a

Pompeiian Frescoes Well-preserved objects and artwork from the city of Pompeii, which was buried under ash after the eruption of Mount Vesuvius in 79 CE, offer some of the best clues to everyday life in the Roman world. This colorful fresco in a lavish Pompeii villa constructed around 40 BCE may show an initiation ritual in the cult of the Greek god Dionysos. It indicates how closely the gods were entwined in ordinary life, and how much the Romans embraced Greek culture.

FOCUS QUESTIONS

- What do Roman myths and modern archaeology reveal about the origins of Rome?
- How did social tensions find expression in Roman politics?
- Why did the Roman Republic expand throughout the Italian Peninsula and beyond?
- What were the core Roman values, and how were they transmitted through society?
- Why did the republican system become increasingly unstable in the second and first centuries BCE?
- What led the Republic into its century of crisis?
- How did Rome make the transition from republic to empire under Augustus?

monster in human form, a murderer of his own wife and son, a violator of the Senate's rules, a political assassin, and a reprobate—someone so visibly marked with the stamp of evil that his fellow senators shrank away as he walked among them. Cicero went on to compare the Rome of his own day, gripped by terror as political murders spread fear among the population, with the city in its former days, when "brave men did not lack the courage to strike down a dangerous Roman citizen more fiercely even than they struck down the bitterest of foreign foes." And he insisted that the Senate was at fault because it had tolerated the presence of a criminal: "This man still lives! Lives? He walks right into the Senate. He joins in our national debates. He watches and notes and marks down with his gaze each of us he plans to assassinate."

Catiline, overwhelmed by Cicero's opposition, left Rome and eventually died fighting alongside his followers. Cicero's speeches became classics, translated and memorized by schoolchildren for more than 2,000 years. His words deserved the fascination of posterity. Like the politicians of fifth-century Athens—but working in a far larger society and state—Cicero showed how a leader could win support and stamp out opposition by mobilizing effective language and using it to appeal to historical traditions that still had deep meanings for his fellow citizens. And like the Athenians, Cicero could use language to destroy as well as to create—wielding words as if they were edged weapons to practice the politics of personal destruction.

But if Cicero won his battle against Catiline, he lost the war, which he and others waged, to preserve the Roman Republic. In the end, Cicero would die by violence, assassinated by the agents of one of his political enemies, Mark Antony. A great empire would replace the Republic that he claimed to stand for, the largest state in the ancient world that was ruled by a group of citizens rather than a monarch. In his speeches against Catiline, Cicero argued that the keys to understanding and solving Rome's problems lay in Roman history, which offered a rich set of models for emulation and precedents for prudent action. Let us follow his example and turn back to the Roman past, to see how the Republic took shape, and why—in the end—it could not be sustained.

ORIGINS (1000–509 BCE)

The rise of Rome is different, in crucial ways, from the histories we have followed up to this point. Like Athens and Sparta, Rome began as a city, and though it was a monarchy at the start, it became, like them, a republic. But where the Greek cities fought and developed alliances with other city-states, Rome expanded into a vast national state, merging first with local peoples and slowly filling the entire Italian Peninsula. And whereas the Greek republics were eventually subjugated by the Macedonian monarchy, Rome not only remained independent but also became a world empire that long outlasted Alexander's. Like the Hellenistic empires, it had a common language—Latin— that spread as far as England, Spain, North Africa, and Syria; unlike them, it retained its possessions in all of these lands. But even as the Romans became masters of the world, they lost the republican liberty that they had prized for centuries, as Julius Caesar and those who followed him transformed their society into the greatest empire the world had known.

THE ITALIAN PENINSULA

Early in the first millennium BCE, many peoples inhabited the Italian Peninsula, a landscape that favored the development of multiple societies. In this narrow landmass stretching from the Alps in the north to a heel only one

The Italian Peninsula, 700–500 BCE The Latin people shared the Italian Peninsula with several other peoples: the Etruscans to the north; the Greeks to the south; their allies, the Sabines; and the Samnites, with whom they warred for centuries. Carthage and its colonies also proved a threatening local power. Rome was founded around 1000 BCE, but only slowly expanded its territory over the centuries.

would reach the far-flung borders of the Roman Empire. In the early centuries of the first millennium BCE, however, the Latins had many other peoples as near neighbors, including the Sabines, an Italic people, most of whom would eventually join the Latins; and the Samnites, who spoke a now-lost language and would fight the Latins for centuries.

THE ETRUSCANS

The **Etruscans**—a highly sophisticated people governed by aristocratic families—founded cities from the Po River valley in the north and what is now Tuscany down to the area around Rome. The Etruscans' language is not yet fully understood, and their origins are uncertain. But archaeologists have shown that they developed an urban culture with massive buildings, sophisticated painting, and free-standing sculptures of human bodies. They had a special gift for elegant metalwork that served for everything from fine hand mirrors to delicate dental bridges. Women enjoyed greater equality in the family and beyond. A Greek historian of the fourth century BCE remarked that "Etruscan women take particular care of their bodies and exercise often, sometimes along with the men, and sometimes by themselves. It is not a disgrace for them to be seen naked. They do not share their couches with their husbands but with the other men who happen to be present, and they propose toasts to anyone they choose."

The Etruscans worshipped multiple gods, believed in an afterlife in which the virtuous feasted and the vicious

hundred miles from the coast of North Africa, landscapes and ecologies vary sharply. The Apennines—the mountain chain that forms the peninsula's spine—divides east from west. Navigable rivers such as the Tiber, and wonderful natural bays, favor trade and exchange.

THE LATINS

The Latins, an Indo-European people, lived in Italy from the early centuries of the second millennium BCE. They settled a central Italian plain punctuated by hills that could be fortified, and bordered by the Tiber as well as the Tyrrhenian Sea to the west. They became the founders of Rome, and their language and traditions

Etruscan Houses Etruscan cremation urns—like this one from the seventh century BCE—were often modeled as houses, giving us an idea of what Etruscan and early Roman dwellings may have looked like. These homes were typically oval and made of clay, with a wooden roof in which a hole was cut to let the smoke from the central hearth escape.

An Etruscan Couple This Etruscan sarcophagus (ca. 600–500 BCE) depicts in expressive detail a married couple on a banqueting couch. It is an example of the Etruscan culture's relative gender equality: the couple are the same size and assume similar postures, with the woman in the foreground, and they participate together in a banquet, which in the Greek tradition was a distinctively masculine activity.

were punished, and possessed elaborate techniques for warding off evil in the present and divining the future. Their traditions were recorded in verse scriptures, some of which survive and can be read in part. Etruscan kings ruled Rome in the sixth century BCE, and over time many Etruscan cities became Roman.

GREEK COLONIES To the north, Celtic peoples, moving out from the area of modern Austria, expanded over the Alps into Italy. In the deep south, on the tip of the peninsula and in Sicily, Greek cities founded colonies as early as the eighth century BCE. In the fertile soil of Sicily, olive trees and grape vines grew readily, and the island soon began to produce oil and wine. Some of the colonies were as large and powerful as any city in the Greek homeland—especially the port of Tarentum, on the southern coast of Italy, and Syracuse, in Sicily, which as we have seen defeated an Athenian invasion during the Peloponnesian War. Hoplite warfare, magnificent temples to the Greek gods, and massive amphitheaters, all built in the best Greek style, spread across the lower portions of Italy. To this day, southern Italy possesses Greek ruins as magnificent as any in the Greek mainland.

CARTHAGE For all their wealth, the western Greeks did not control all of southern Italy. **Carthage**, a Phoenician settlement on a North African peninsula, sent its trading ships around the Mediterranean to import vital goods such as wheat and metals. The Carthaginians were brilliant navigators—around 500 BCE they sailed ships southward along the western coast of Africa, eventually reaching what is now Senegal. They aggressively set up colonies in Sicily and Spain that, unlike Greek colonies, were designed to serve the home city. And they defended these colonies with their expert seamanship and the military skills of their Numidian cavalry—Berbers who came from the region of modern Algeria and Tunisia. The Carthaginians would eventually prove the most dangerous of Rome's rivals.

ORIGINS AND MONARCHY: WHAT THE ROMANS BELIEVED

The city that became Rome—and that would eventually dominate or defeat the Etruscans, the Carthaginians, and many other Italic peoples, often learning from them at the same time—was first settled around 1000 BCE. The Romans themselves did not know this. They told two stories about the origins of their city. Like other Mediterranean peoples who wished to show that they were as venerable as the Greeks, the Romans traced their ancestry to the Trojan exiles who, led by the hero Aeneas, had left the city in Asia Minor after it fell to the Greeks and eventually settled in Italy. There, in the twelfth century BCE, or so they thought, the Trojan leader and his followers intermarried with the Latins who already inhabited the center of the peninsula. The other story held that the real founding of the city had taken place later, in the middle of the eighth century BCE, when Romulus—who was supposedly reared, along with his brother Remus, by a she-wolf—brought male settlers together at what would become Rome and then stole wives for them from the Sabines and the Latins.

From the start, these legends claimed, the Romans both fought and allied with other Italian peoples. The traditional narrative held that seven kings ruled the city for two and a half centuries, from 753 to 509 BCE: Romulus, Numa Pompilius, Tullus Hostilius, Ancus Marcius,

Lucius Tarquinius Priscus, Servius Tullius, and Lucius Tarquinius Superbus. This story cannot be literally true, as there is no known case in which an unbroken series of rulers all lived so long. And according to the stories, each of the early monarchs supposedly contributed something vital. Numa, for example, created the state's calendar and its public religion, and Servius Tullius built the wall that ringed the entire city. The last king, Lucius Tarquinius Superbus ("the Proud"), infuriated the city's inhabitants by taking tyrannical measures—starting, supposedly, with the assassination of his predecessor. When his son forced a virtuous woman, Lucretia, to sleep with him, she revealed the crime and then killed herself. In 509 BCE a rebellion broke out, led by Lucretia's husband and Lucius Junius Brutus. The rebels not only defeated the king but also transformed the state into a republic.

These vivid stories would be told and retold for centuries by everyone interested in the history and fate of Rome. They were created by well-born Roman writers centuries after the events they purported to describe, and they offer a mixture of myth and history, the original components of which are hard to pull apart. Yet it is possible to tease out of these stories the values that meant the most to the Roman elite—for example, that the survival of the state mattered more than any individual life. And behind those values one can sense something of the historical struggles, some of them violent, that led to the creation of Rome's republican institutions.

ORIGINS AND MONARCHY: WHAT THE RECORD SHOWS

In keeping with these narratives of the city's past, early Rome did reach a peak of grandeur in the sixth century BCE, which Romans remembered as a time of Etruscan kings. And the Romans did adopt central customs from the Etruscans: from the wearing of the toga, the long woolen garment that adult males wrapped around themselves, to the fasces—the bundle of rods, sometimes surrounding an axe, that was carried before Roman officials as a sign of their authority.

The period of the monarchy did witness the creation of the city's calendar and the building of the Cloaca Maxima, the great sewer that helped drain Rome's swampy central region. From the start, the city's public life revolved around a central marketplace, the Forum. But archaeologists and historians have discovered a great deal more, in the last several decades, about the rise of Rome.

Romulus and Remus Many Romans believed that twin brothers, Romulus and Remus, had founded their city. According to legend, they were abandoned at birth but rescued by a she-wolf. A medieval Italian artist added suckling infants to an ancient sculpture of a wolf to create this evocative visualization of the founding myth.

Though much remains uncertain, it seems clear that settlement in Rome began around the year 1000 BCE, when villages were founded on some of the seven hills surrounding that low-lying, swampy area. Much later—in the eighth and seventh centuries BCE—Rome's advantageous position near the mouth of the Tiber, which made it a natural center for trade, may have been decisive in transforming the small settlements into a single, larger city. Rome's craft production became more sophisticated, its trade more developed. A colony of Phoenician merchants from Tyre lived there, selling valuable silver and ivory objects to the Romans and to the Etruscans to the north.

The population was mixed: it included Latins and Sabines, and by the sixth century BCE there was also an Etruscan quarter. But Latin provided a common language, and inscriptions carved on stone show that some Romans were literate by the sixth century. Even before that, the city's inhabitants had collaborated on projects. A wall on the Capitoline Hill was raised in the eighth century (exactly the period in which legend set Rome's founding), and later projects included the paving of the Forum and construction of the first public buildings.

By the end of the sixth century BCE, Rome had taken on the form of a full city, though not one as grand or as elegantly laid out as a Greek city of comparable wealth and power. The Romans found ways to obtain vital resources: their city was on an existing road that the Sabines used to transport salt, essential for city life, from marshes at the mouth of the Tiber. Trade brought in luxury goods,

Fasces A sixth-century BCE relief depicts an Etruscan official holding *fasces,* a bundle of rods carried as a symbol of a ruler's authority—a custom the Romans later adopted.

including Greek vases of high quality, and local artisans began to construct temples out of stone with elaborate terra-cotta ornaments.

THE EARLY REPUBLIC (509–146 BCE)

From the traditional narratives we know that sharp tensions developed between the last kings, whose actions were seen as tyrannical, and some well-born and powerful Romans. When the last king of Rome, Lucius Tarquinius Superbus, was forced to leave the city in 509 BCE, Rome was transformed from a monarchy, as the much later historian Livy wrote, to "a free Rome under magistrates elected for a year and under laws whose authority exceeds that of men."

The first decades of the Republic were anything but peaceful. The city fought a long series of wars—with Tarquinius Superbus and his supporters (508 BCE); with the Latin League, a confederation of villages outside Rome; and with the powerful Etruscan city of Veii. The wars caused crises at home that threatened to divide Roman society. In the end, though, the city survived, making a treaty with the Latin League in 493 in which both sides were recognized as equals. Rome began to develop a constitution that could accommodate the stresses that came with expansion.

POLITICAL INSTITUTIONS AND SOCIAL TENSIONS

Some of republican Rome's central institutions took shape in this early period. Roman tradition held that the **Senate** came into existence with the city, as a body of 100 who advised Romulus, the city's mythical founder. Its membership was mixed, consisting of aristocratic men and men of lower birth. The Senate met in or near Rome when magistrates summoned its members. Meetings were private. After the presiding officer explained the issue to be discussed, each senator spoke in order of rank. The senators enjoyed complete freedom of discussion, each addressing the assembly from his seat. The right to wear a special striped tunic and boots, as well as other privileges, set the members of this great assembly apart from other Romans. Once the kings were expelled, the Senate took on greater responsibility for the state as a whole—but also proved unable to manage the social and political conflicts unleashed by the fall of the monarchy.

Rome's population as a whole was divided at an early stage into **patricians**, members of aristocratic families that enjoyed special political privileges, and **plebeians**—that is to say, everyone else who was free. Patricians were easy to identify: they derived their rank from their birth and held the monopoly, for example, on priestly positions. The category of plebeian was less neatly defined. It included both owners of small properties, who probably farmed their estates for a living, and providers of the crafts and services necessary to maintain the city. Many artisans and small shopkeepers were based on the Aventine Hill, near the Tiber, which became Rome's first river port.

The creation of the Republic was only the beginning of a long contest between these two social classes. The plebeians were excluded from priesthoods, magistracies, and the Senate. Over time the conditions in which they lived became harder: bad harvests and accumulated debt harmed small landholders. Continued wars with

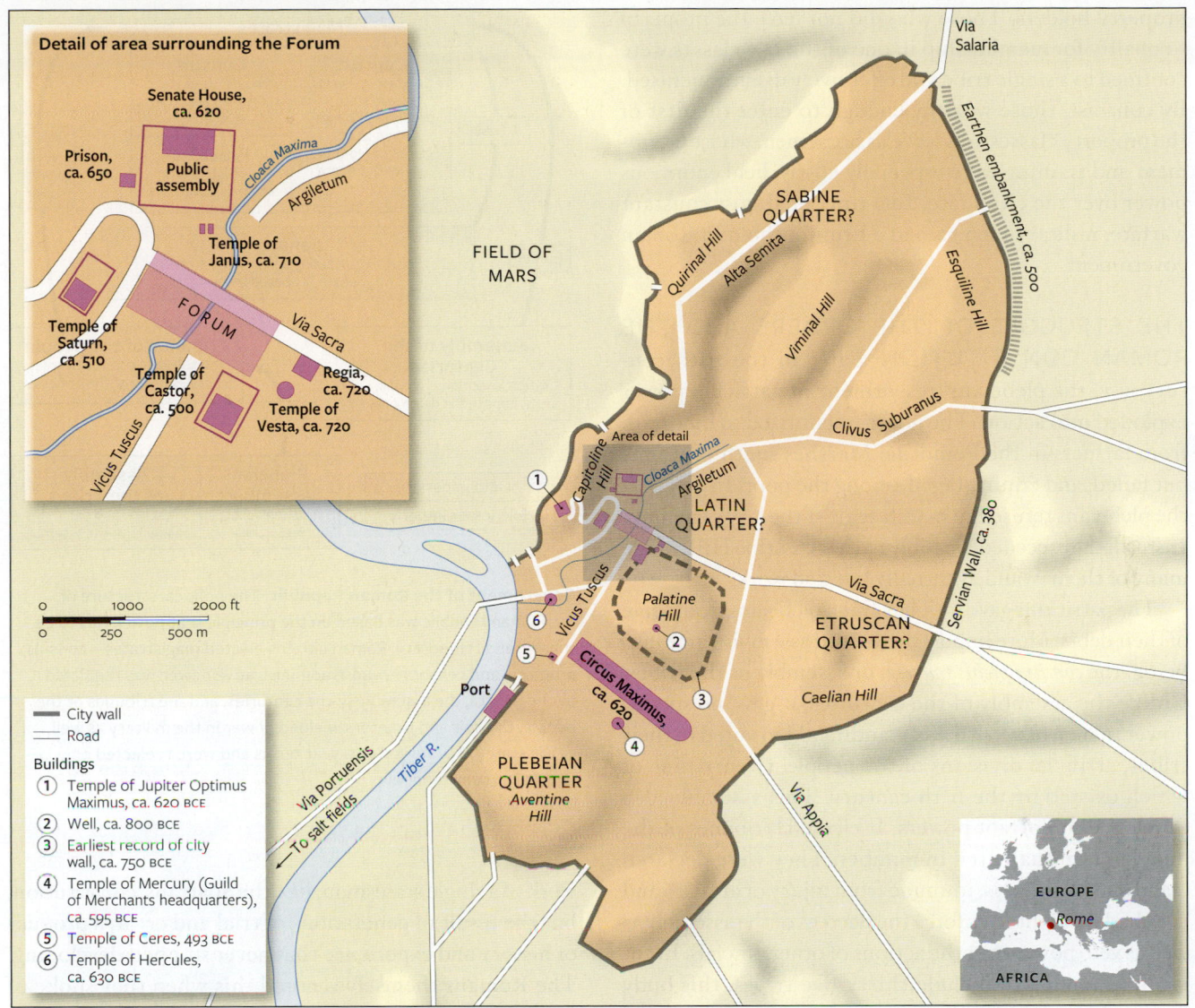

Detail of area surrounding the Forum

Senate House, ca. 620
Prison, ca. 650
Public assembly
Cloaca Maxima
Argiletum
Temple of Janus, ca. 710
FORUM
Via Sacra
Temple of Saturn, ca. 510
Temple of Castor, ca. 500
Regia, ca. 720
Temple of Vesta, ca. 720
Vicus Tuscus

Via Salaria
Earthen embankment, ca. 500
SABINE QUARTER?
FIELD OF MARS
Quirinal Hill
Alta Semita
Viminal Hill
Esquiline Hill
Capitoline Hill
Area of detail
Cloaca Maxima
Argiletum
Clivus Suburanus
LATIN QUARTER?
Via Sacra
Servian Wall, ca. 380
Palatine Hill
ETRUSCAN QUARTER?
Vicus Tuscus
Circus Maximus, ca. 620
Caelian Hill
Port
Via Appia
PLEBEIAN QUARTER
Aventine Hill
Via Portuensis
Tiber R.
To salt fields

0 1000 2000 ft
0 250 500 m

City wall
Road
Buildings
1 Temple of Jupiter Optimus Maximus, ca. 620 BCE
2 Well, ca. 800 BCE
3 Earliest record of city wall, ca. 750 BCE
4 Temple of Mercury (Guild of Merchants headquarters), ca. 595 BCE
5 Temple of Ceres, 493 BCE
6 Temple of Hercules, ca. 630 BCE

EUROPE
Rome
AFRICA

Republican Rome, ca. 350 BCE The Romans initially built their city on the Palatine Hill, above the banks of the Tiber River, but it soon spread outward to cover seven hills with densely packed roads and apartment buildings. In the center of the city, significant public buildings such as the Senate House and temples to deities such as Hercules, Jupiter, and Mercury were clustered around the Forum.

Rome's neighbors were also costly. The resulting conflicts between the plebeians and the patricians—known as the **Struggle of the Orders**—shaped the city's development. The history of Rome's political assemblies enables us to follow these tensions and their sometimes creative effects over time.

THE ASSEMBLIES The earliest Roman assembly, the *comitia curiata*, rested on a division of the entire population into thirty groups, or *curiae*, ten for each of the three tribes that Romulus had fused when founding the city. Each was headed by a magistrate called the *curio*, who mustered the city's armies. Later, a second, more complex organization,

the *comitia centuriata* ("assembly of the centuries"), was created, supposedly by the next-to-last of the legendary kings. This assembly took responsibility for enacting laws, choosing senior magistrates, and inflicting the death penalty on Roman citizens.

Citizens in Rome were divided into five classes by property and assigned to centuries (groups of 100 men) for military purposes. As in most Greek cities, only male property-holders could serve in the army. The smallest and richest of these five groups voted first in the assembly, and voting ended when a majority agreed. Thus, though all males who bore arms had a formal right to vote, the system gave predominant power to the wealthiest property-holders. Those who did not have the property to qualify for membership in one of the five classes were confined to a single tribe and effectively disenfranchised. By contrast, those wealthy enough to enter the first of the property classes and serve as horsemen, whose equipment and training were especially costly, held enormous power over the city's fate. In a time of almost constant warfare, military men gained a firm foothold in Roman government.

THE STRUGGLE OF THE ORDERS AND THE ROMAN CONSTITUTION

Early in the fifth century BCE, the plebeians' resentment of patrician power exploded into action. The government tried to buy grain from farmers in the Pomptine Marshes south of Rome, but failed, and famine raged among the poor. In 494 BCE, the plebeians refused to march against the city's enemies. Instead, they seceded, possibly to the Aventine Hill, where many of them would eventually live and work.

The patricians gave in. They freed plebeians from some of their debts. More important, a third assembly came into being: the *comitia plebis tributa*, or assembly of the tribes. Unlike the assembly of the centuries, it gave no special power to men of wealth and standing. Men voted in their tribes, artificial divisions of the people, twenty-nine of which existed by the fifth century. This assembly also developed important powers. It elected "tribunes of the people," eventually ten in number. They were declared "sacrosanct"—that is, immune from injury or attack—and they had the right to enforce the decrees of the assembly as well as veto power over the actions of other officials. Eventually extended to include thirty-five tribes, this body became Rome's legislative assembly. After a long series of further struggles, the Hortensian Law (ca. 287 BCE) gave the acts of the plebeian assembly, known as plebiscites, absolute authority over all Romans.

From early on, the Roman constitution took shape in the course of political struggles between groups that saw themselves as pursuing separate interests—and whose differences were sharpened when, as often happened, they were waging war with other peoples. To that extent, the Greek general and historian Polybius (ca. 200–ca. 118 BCE) was perfectly right when he said, in a passage later quoted by Cicero, that the Roman constitution differed from the others known to him. It was not, he explained, the

Voting On a coin we can date to 63 BCE, a man—presumably a propertied one—casts a vote in a legislative assembly.

Government of the Roman Republic The political structure of the Roman republic was based on the principle that power was to be shared, and temporary. Roman citizens elected magistrates—consuls, praetors, and censors—whose administrative power was regulated by the Senate, the assembly of the centuries, and the tribunes of the people. Consuls and praetors wielded power in the military as well as the state. They served one-year terms and were reelected only in unusual circumstances.

[Diagram: Government of the Roman Republic]

Magistrates

Censors Conduct censuses, lease state properties, identify men to be removed from the tribes or Senate

Consuls Two heads of state serve one-year term, lead army

Praetors Rank high in army; serve as governors

Advises

Have veto power over

Elects

Senate Senators (including senior magistrates) debate proposed laws

Assembly of the Centuries Citizens enact laws, serve in the army, impose the death penalty

Tribunes of the people Ten tribunes enforce decrees of Assembly of the Tribes

Elects

Hold imperium
Hold lesser imperium

Plebeian assembly Plebeians enact plebiscites

Assembly of the Tribes Plebeians and patricians pass acts of the assembly

work of a single statesman, like the Spartans' constitution, but the result of generations of trial and error, a product of history and experience that never stopped developing. The Romans themselves noted this when they spoke of the Struggle of the Orders and its significance.

MAGISTRATES

From around 509 BCE administrative and legal power lay in the hands of the magistrates—and would remain there until the end of the Republic half a millennium later. Two consuls—elected once a year by the centuriate assembly, which continued along with the plebeian assembly—possessed imperium, or supreme power. This was symbolically represented by the bundles of twelve rods, or fasces, that were carried before officials in public. The consuls—some of whom were patrician, others plebeian—ruled the state and led Rome's armies in the field, where they had almost unlimited authority.

Below these two rulers, a hierarchy of additional magistrates carried out other administrative and legal duties. Praetors, who held a lesser level of imperium, also wielded impressive power in the state and army. Later, as Rome came to rule other states as provinces of a single empire, praetors served as governors. Censors not only carried out formal censuses but also identified men of bad character, who were removed from their tribes and from the Senate. The censors also took responsibility for leasing the state's properties so that they brought in revenues. A patrician "king of the rituals" oversaw the sacrifices carried out on the Kalends, or first of the month, and announced the dates of other holy days. Other patricians continued to dominate the city's priesthoods. Meanwhile, the tribunes of the people represented the popular interest and gradually won a place of their own in the state's constitution.

MANAGING SOCIAL TENSIONS AND CONFLICT

Yet even as these institutions helped to stabilize the Roman Republic, it found itself enmeshed in conflict with other peoples. The causes of war varied. At times Rome acted when it saw a chance to gain more territory and resources. In the 440s, for instance, while helping to arbitrate a dispute between Latin powers, Rome annexed a town to the south that opened the way to the rich grain-producing area of the Pomptine Marshes. During the period of 437–434 BCE, Rome fought with the Etruscans at Veii to secure a city needed to protect the salt road. But later wars with Veii and other Etruscan cities seem to have been motivated more by the two sides' distrust of one another's designs for the future. In the early fourth century, Celtic peoples drove rapidly south over the Alps, sacked Rome, and held it for ransom—a traumatic event that destroyed the city's early records and shattered its citizens' confidence. Yet the city recovered rapidly from this shock, leaving new and skillful leaders in charge and giving their soldiers a new sense of self-confidence.

The Roman Republic continued to expand by either destroying enemy cities or offering them a place in the Roman state, and their inhabitants Roman citizenship. By the early fourth century BCE, it had become by far the largest state of its kind ever seen and too big to be considered a city-state in the classical sense. Aristotle had believed that a true state could not be much larger than a normal Greek city; otherwise its citizens could not all know one another. The Roman Republic occupied a vast amount of territory in central Italy, and the number of males legally entitled to take part in the assemblies approached 35,000.

Formal citizenship continued to expand, and

The Census In this second-century BCE relief, an official conducting the census registers young men for the army as a soldier looks on.

throughout Roman history many talented men born in the countryside, like Cicero himself, would rise to power and wealth in the city. But even as expansion and opportunity did much to power Rome's rise, problems remained. In practice, most of those who lived in the countryside outside Rome would not have been able to join in the actual voting, which was always held in the city. As stresses worsened in the centuries ahead, opportunities to manipulate the aging institutions of republican politics also expanded.

THE LAW OF THE TWELVE TABLES In the mid-fifth century BCE, the continuing struggles between patricians and plebeians led to the creation of the *decemviri*, a board of ten men charged with drawing up a law code that both groups could adhere to. Supposedly the board sent an embassy to Greece to study the laws of Solon at Athens; more likely they examined the laws of nearby Greek cities in southern Italy. After further struggles and another secession of the plebeians, the laws were finally passed and published, around 450 BCE, as the **Law of the Twelve Tables**. They were a set of definitions of legal rights and procedures posted in the Forum on twelve tablets of ivory or bronze, so that all Romans could see them.

The Twelve Tables prohibited intermarriage between patricians and plebeians, and dealt with general problems of marriage, inheritance, and real estate law. They defined the power of the Roman **paterfamilias**, or head of household, as absolute: the life and death of his children and his wife were in his hands. The Tables did not put an end to the Struggle of the Orders: the ban on intermarriage was abrogated as early as 445 BCE, and conflict continued for two more centuries. But the Tables showed the way to an eventual resolution: the creation of formal laws, which came to be a central feature of Roman government.

THE ROMAN LEGIONS Rome was also becoming more skillful at managing conflict with other peoples. As part of its response to the Celtic sack of Rome and the second invasion that followed half a century later, the Romans founded military colonies, settling citizen soldiers farther and farther from the seven hills. At times, these provocative measures sparked wars, as with the Latins and Volscians from 340 to 338 BCE. But Rome was also ready to respect and support the power of local elites if their members were willing to join the Roman state. After 338 BCE, all Latins shared the so-called **Latin right**: they could marry and trade with Romans, and even gain citizenship if they settled in Rome, while Romans who settled in Latin cities could become citizens there as well. Rome's continued growth gave opportunities to the poor and ambitious who lived far beyond the city's perimeter. Military service was one way for those ambitions to be realized.

The Roman armies grew with the city. Gradually they developed an organization that would remain standard, even as it evolved, until the end of the empire. The army was divided into detachments known as **legions**, which enrolled around 5,000 foot soldiers each. Soldiers of the same rank had uniform clothing and equipment, which a small allowance helped them to purchase. Each legion made camp in the same way, laying out its tents in the form of a square with streets to divide them and a ditch and palisade to protect them from attack. Uniform commands and a body of experienced noncommissioned officers, the centurions, gave the legion coherence and enabled it to march and take up positions for battle in a uniquely disciplined way. Archers and other support troops were mercenaries, paid for their service.

In 282 BCE the city of Tarentum, a Greek colony in southern Italy, appealed to King Pyrrhus of Epirus in northwestern Greece for help against the Romans. Pyrrhus knew that the Romans were powerful, and he hoped that once he had defeated them he would be able to conquer Macedonia. He arrived in Italy at the head

Pyrrhus This bust of King Pyrrhus of Epirus—whose invading army Rome eventually defeated, thereby establishing authority over the Italian Peninsula—is a first-century BCE copy, but the original, made during Pyrrhus's lifetime, is one of the earliest-known portraits of a Roman historical figure.

Legions This gold coin, issued sometime between 225 and 212 BCE, shows a Roman soldier and a soldier from an Italian ally swearing an oath of alliance.

of a professional Hellenistic army with 25,000 infantry and 3,000 cavalry. At first Pyrrhus was surprised by the discipline the Romans showed as their infantry and cavalry crossed a river to meet him in good order at Heraclea. Though the legion proved able to fight Pyrrhus's phalanxes on more or less even terms, his twenty war elephants broke up the Roman lines and made them vulnerable to attack by his cavalry. Still, the Romans continued the war. Four years later, Pyrrhus (whose name became proverbial for winning victories too costly to be justified, known ever after as "Pyrrhic victories") found himself so low on resources that he had to leave Italy and return to Greece, with only a remnant of his original force. Once Rome defeated this major Hellenistic Greek opponent, it was generally recognized as a great power in the Mediterranean, sovereign over the entire Italian Peninsula.

THE WARS WITH CARTHAGE

The peninsula, however, was not enough. Needing more land for agriculture and more citizens for soldiers, Rome was soon involved in wars in Macedonia and Greece. But the rival power of Carthage, the great Phoenician trading city in North Africa, challenged the Romans most powerfully—and did the most to make them the rulers of an empire. Because the Latin word for Phoenician is "Punic," Rome's long, exhausting series of wars with Carthage is called the **Punic Wars**.

THE FIRST PUNIC WAR (264–241 BCE)

For centuries, Rome and Carthage had coexisted without major conflict. But in the 260s, the tyrant of Syracuse made war against the Mamertines, mercenaries from the Italian mainland who had seized the Sicilian city of Messana. The Mamertines appealed for help, first to the Carthaginians and then to the Romans. In this case, most of the senators hesitated to go to war, but the plebeian assembly, eager for booty, voted to intervene. Syracuse allied with the Carthaginians, relying on the power of their fleet to protect them against Rome.

The war proved grueling. The Romans, inexperienced in naval matters, lost a series of fleets to storms and to the Carthaginians, whose seafaring skills were renowned. Though the Roman general Marcus Attilius Regulus, who was sent to North Africa with a small army, scored initial successes, at length he was defeated and captured. Yet the Romans persisted, and eventually they ground down the Carthaginians' brilliant commander in Sicily, Hamilcar Barca. In 241 BCE, after a war of twenty-three years, the Romans forced their enemies to make peace, and Rome was left in command of Sicily. This vast island, famous for its grain and other natural products, and rich in minerals as well, became Rome's first official province—the beginning of what would soon grow into an empire. Rome had also become, for the first time, a naval power—a development that would prove crucial for its empire.

Expansion and War, 390–133 BCE In the later centuries BCE, Rome expanded rapidly, sparking conflict with Carthage. In the ensuing series of wars, Rome gained control of Sicily and, ultimately—despite Hannibal's land invasion over the Alps and numerous Roman defeats—territory as far east as Macedonia and Asia Minor, as well as much of the Iberian Peninsula.

THE SECOND PUNIC WAR (218–201 BCE)

Soon after the end of the First Punic War, Carthage recovered enough strength to wage a long war against rebellious mercenaries. Rome, though it aided Carthage at first, became increasingly concerned at the signs of revival, especially as the Carthaginians began to negotiate with Celts in the Po River valley in northern Italy. The Romans used a rebellion in Sardinia as a pretext to take that island, which had been Carthage's granary. In response, the Carthaginians, anxious to ensure their supply lines and to regain leverage, invaded Spain—not a nation as yet, but a vast region inhabited by Celts, Greeks, and Phoenicians.

There Hamilcar Barca, his son-in-law Hasdrubal, and his eldest son, Hannibal, established a strong Carthaginian presence. According to tradition, Hannibal swore an oath to his father never to be a friend to Rome. For a time, peace held; but in 219 BCE Hannibal besieged and took the city of Saguntum in Valencia, in eastern Spain. Although Rome ignored the city's appeals for help, Hannibal decided that war was inevitable; moving with a speed and determination that shocked the Romans, he rapidly made his way from Spain to Italy.

The Second Punic War involved a confrontation between two of history's most brilliant commanders. Hannibal is still famous for his decisiveness, speed in action, and willingness to take great risks. His Roman opponent, Publius Cornelius Scipio Africanus, was equally renowned, not only for his absolute commitment to Rome and his tactical daring but also for his humanity. Hannibal led a powerful force, including elephants and, according to tradition, more than 100,000 infantry and cavalrymen. Dodging Scipio, who came to meet him in Gaul (modern France), Hannibal crossed the Alps, though his forces suffered terrible losses in doing so. He routed the Romans at Lake Trasimene in 217 and at Cannae in 216, where he encircled and killed tens of thousands of Romans and their allies. The losses were devastating: almost as many Romans died in one day at Cannae as British soldiers died, under a hail of German artillery and machine-gun fire, on the first day of the Somme, one of the deadliest battles of World War I.

A brilliant tactician, Hannibal was also politically gifted. He made a point of releasing all the Latins whom he took captive. Impressed by his generosity, several cities—including Capua, the second largest in Italy—seceded from Roman rule and joined him. He also formed an alliance with the king of Macedonia. But the Romans once more showed their powers of recovery. A Roman commander, Fabius Maximus, nicknamed Cunctator ("the Delayer"), kept Hannibal busy without allowing him many chances for formal battle. Hannibal scored tactical successes, defeating Roman armies at Herdonia and Locri in southern Italy. But he never managed to conquer the critical port city of Tarentum. Moreover, newly developed Roman sea power prevented Carthage from sending reinforcements to Italy.

Eventually, Scipio gained permission to take the war to Africa—a stroke as brilliant as Hannibal's march across the Alps. After Scipio defeated Hasdrubal, Hannibal was recalled to defend the homeland. Scipio had learned to leave open spaces in his battle array to avoid letting Hannibal's elephants throw his soldiers into confusion, and to coordinate Numidian cavalry with his Roman foot soldiers. In 202 he defeated Hannibal at Zama, in Carthage. Hannibal advised his masters to make peace, and they surrendered in 201.

Rome emerged from the Second Punic War, as from the first, as undisputed victor, with an enormous military. Rome commanded more than 100,000 soldiers by the end of the war and faced engagements in new areas, such as the Balkans, where they had fought an ally of Carthage, Philip V of Macedonia. Carthage, by contrast, had to hand over all but ten of its ships and all of its elephants, and to pay an enormous fine. The crushing burden of this peace did much to ensure the coming of a third and final war.

Hannibal's Elephants A Roman plate from the third century BCE depicts an elephant carrying soldiers and a military fortification, conveying an idea of the terror that Hannibal's elephants may have inspired.

Rome's expansion continued, now on a far grander scale. In 196 BCE a Roman general who shared what would soon be a fashionable attitude of warm respect for the Greeks defeated Philip V, confined him to the Macedonia north, and proclaimed that Greece was free. Warfare continued intermittently until the 140s, when the Romans, having defeated the Macedonians and the Greeks themselves, declared the former Greek world another province of their empire.

THE THIRD PUNIC WAR (149–146 BCE)

In the years that followed Rome's victory in the Second Punic War, Carthage came under continuing attack by Massinissa, king of Numidia and a Roman ally in North Africa. Rome tried at first to mediate, but then sided more and more with Massinissa. In 153 BCE, a Roman embassy led by the censor Cato was struck by Carthage's wealth and by its efforts to rearm. Cato led a campaign for invasion in the Senate, and in 149, after the Carthaginians attacked the Numidians, the Romans invaded the attackers' homeland. The invasion started poorly. But Scipio Aemilianus, the adopted grandson of Scipio Africanus, became consul in 147, and his leadership proved decisive. Carthage fell after a long siege and some vicious street fighting. The city was partly burned, but the Romans did not, as legend holds, sow salt in its territory so that nothing would ever grow there again. Eventually Carthage recovered to become a prosperous regional capital in what was now the Roman province of Africa.

Through the next decade and after, Roman armies carried out massive operations in Spain and Gaul, conquering most of each. The city that had been hamstrung by civil strife two centuries before found itself the ruler not only of Italy but also of an empire that stretched across much of the Mediterranean world. For the next century and more, Rome would never be at peace: a long series of wars, abroad and in the Italian Peninsula, would continue to reshape the Roman state and society.

THE EXPANDING REPUBLIC: CULTURE AND SOCIETY

Rome's rise to regional dominance brought with it vast cultural change. Romans began to write about their past. And Greeks realized that they were face to face with something they had not experienced before: a state as aggressive and powerful as Macedonia had been, but ruled as a republic rather than a monarchy. Their efforts to understand how this was possible also help us to understand the nature of the Roman Republic as it rose to dominance in the time of the Punic Wars and after.

POLYBIUS: EXPLAINING ROME

In the third century BCE, members of the Roman elite were beginning to learn Greek and write in the forms that the Greeks had created. By the second century, young Romans—some, but not all of them, patricians—were studying grammar and rhetoric in the Greek manner and using their skills to compose tragedies, comedies, epics, elaborate formal histories of the city, and technical treatises on subjects as dry and practical as husbandry.

In the mid-second century BCE the Greek general Polybius (ca. 200–ca. 118 BCE), who became a close friend of the younger Scipio during a long stay in Rome as a hostage, decided to learn how Rome had become great. Roman leaders could now entertain—and impress—a visitor with their long experience of politics and warfare. A sophisticated and widely read man, Polybius believed that one could survive the trials of the present only by finding patterns in the past—patterns created not, as the Jewish author of the book of Daniel thought, by divine intervention, but by human nature in action. Polybius set out to take apart Rome's institutions, in order to work out exactly what made them function so well.

POLITICS Following Aristotle, Polybius noted that all states seemed to fall into six types: monarchy, aristocracy, and democracy, and their evil twins, tyranny, oligarchy, and mob rule. Whatever form a society took, it had little hope of attaining real stability. Human nature destined most cities to move through the entire set of forms of government in sequence, as each of the sound forms gradually failed and gave way to its own dark side.

Rome, however, seemed to have worked out a uniquely stable form of government. By allowing monarchical and democratic elements to temper its basically oligarchical constitution, it

Polybius A second-century BCE stele depicts the Greek general and historian Polybius, whose writings illuminated the history of Roman society and politics.

had hindered the processes that normally made governments deteriorate from working as quickly and destructively as elsewhere. When foreign powers menaced Rome, the consuls, the Senate, and the plebeian assembly competed to serve the public good by cooperating as effectively as possible. And when the consuls or the Senate tried to make the state serve the one-sided ends of a monarchy or an aristocracy, the other elements in the constitution resisted. Rome's unique constitution created a system of checks and balances, one so smoothly machined and precisely balanced that it might preserve the city for a long time against the corruption that was inevitable in the long run.

SOCIETY Roman society as a whole, moreover, was organized in ways that promoted courage and patriotism. Family rituals, for example, helped to initiate the young into the values that made this republic uniquely durable. Great houses displayed masks that reproduced the features of their accomplished men. These served not only, like modern family photographs, as a record but also as an educational tool. At funerals, living men who resembled the distinguished dead donned these masks, and speakers connected the achievements of the deceased with those of his ancestors.

The experience of growing up in such families, Polybius explained, was powerful: it explained why Roman heroes had proved willing, over the centuries, to sacrifice their lives or even those of their sons, "setting a higher value on the interest of their country than on the ties of nature that bound them to their nearest and dearest." The virtues that the Spartans tried to instill in young men by taking them out of their families, and that Pericles had tried to teach by oratory in Athens, were integrated into Roman domestic life in a way that no Greek city had achieved. This helped to explain how the Romans could recruit enormous armies and navies not from mercenaries but from citizens, who fought "for their country and their children."

A MIXED CONSTITUTION Polybius was not starry-eyed, though. He found the Romans greedy and cruel. When they captured a city, he observed not only human corpses but also those of dogs and other animals, cut to pieces. His understanding of Rome, moreover, was that of a foreigner, who sometimes applied Greek ways of thinking about society inappropriately to what remained a foreign world. He did not see—as we soon will—that Rome was undergoing an economic transformation while he lived there, which would add new sources of strength and strain to those he appreciated. Nonetheless, Polybius's

vision of the Roman constitution and of Roman society captured something that would fascinate readers and political philosophers for centuries. When the American Founding Fathers needed a model for the constitutional order of their new country, they found it—so they believed—in the Roman mixed constitution that Polybius described.

ROMAN VALUES

Few if any Romans could have rivaled Polybius in producing a sophisticated explanation of what made their state so special. But most would have agreed with his emphases, and by the mid-second century BCE, Romans themselves were giving expression to what they considered distinctively Roman beliefs and values.

THE INTERESTS OF THE STATE Just as Polybius argued, special traditions nourished Roman abilities in politics and warfare. Like Athenians and Spartans, ordinary Roman men served as their country's soldiers, and men of family and position as cavalrymen and officers. The great Roman commanders saw the giving of counsel as an essential duty, and tradition held that they were bound to advise the Republic to the best of their ability, even if doing so might lead to their own deaths. When Regulus, the Roman commander sent to attack Carthage during the First Punic War, was captured by Spartan mercenaries, the Carthaginians sent him back to Rome on parole. They demanded that he advise the Romans to make peace or exchange prisoners. Instead, Regulus told the Romans to continue waging war against their enemies. He then returned to Carthage, although he knew that he would be savagely put to death for doing so. (The Carthaginians supposedly placed him in a barrel full of spikes and rolled it down a slope.)

Central to the exalted behavior of Romans like Regulus was the belief that the state and its good health mattered most, individual ambition not at all. True, the ancient families that dominated the Senate and the consulship were the ones that celebrated their members' accomplishments with the funerals that so impressed Polybius. But Romans imagined themselves as a people of virtuous farmers, more or less equal.

Tradition heralded heroes like Cincinnatus (b. ca. 519 BCE). A consul, a patrician, and a staunch opponent of all efforts to improve the standing of the plebeians, Cincinnatus had lived plainly, so the story went, farming his own land. When an emergency arose during one of

Rome's wars, he agreed to serve as military commander at the request of one of the consuls and the Senate. Cincinnatus carried out his task brilliantly and defeated the enemy, against whom he himself led the infantry. But as soon as the enemy surrendered, he spared them; and as soon as he had accomplished his task, he returned to his farm.

THE TRIUMPH Though the story of Cincinnatus is a bit too good to be true (and probably took shape some centuries after the events it describes), it accurately conveys the values of those who told it. So did many of the rituals that the Romans used, along with tales of the mighty dead, to give expression to their values. For example, the triumph—a great procession derived from Etruscan ritual—was held in honor of Roman generals who returned from the field after defeating the city's enemies. Only commanders who had killed some 5,000 of the enemy and held the rank of praetor or consul could enjoy a triumph.

Those who did receive this signal honor—starting, according to Roman tradition, with Romulus himself—might ride in a four-horse chariot through the city to the temple of Jupiter on the Capitoline Hill. Accompanied by his sons, if any, as well as the members of the Senate, enemy captives dressed for sacrifice, musicians, torchbearers, and colorful banners and paintings, the *triumphator* passed through large public places where the entire city could see him. Nothing could have emphasized the primacy of military virtue more effectively.

RELIGION

Rome was also a devout city. It revered a rich panoply of gods, both the older Roman ones and newer ones from

Roman Gods A second-century CE relief—perhaps part of a model of the temple of Jupiter on the Capitoline Hill—portrays the three gods most central to Roman religion: Jupiter, ruler of the universe, in the center; Juno, mother of the earth, on the left; and Minerva, goddess of wisdom, on the right.

Vestal Virgins This first-century CE relief depicts the goddess Vesta (seated on the left) and her Vestal Virgins, full-time priestesses who took vows of chastity and who could be punished by death if the vows were broken.

Hellenistic Greece. At the start of the Republic, the cult of the three great Roman gods, Jupiter Optimus Maximus, Juno, and Minerva, was moved to the Capitoline Hill, where a stone temple with terra-cotta decorations, in the Etruscan manner, was built for them. Jupiter was officially worshipped as ruler of the universe; Juno as mother of the earth; and Minerva, the goddess of wisdom, presided over the arts and crafts. Temples to other gods—Saturn, Ceres, Mercury—spread out below the Capitoline Hill. Of these the temple of Janus was especially important. Janus was the two-faced god of beginnings and endings, war and peace. The gates of this small, rectangular temple in the Forum were opened when Rome was at war and closed—a rare event—only when it was completely at peace.

Priests and priestesses were organized into groups called colleges: the Vestal Virgins served Vesta, the Roman goddess of the hearth. Male specialists scrutinized every piece of evidence they could find to determine what the gods desired them to do and had in store for them. Priests charged with divining the future used ancient methods to interpret the entrails of sacrificial animals, as well as certain forms of animal behavior. Eclipses, earthquakes, and the births of strange fetuses, human or animal, were recorded and then connected with later events to show that the gods had sent omens in advance. Ancient ritual brotherhoods continued to perform their rites, and new priesthoods—like those of the orgiastic mystery religion of Dionysos, imported from Greece—offered new forms of religious experience. Like the Athenian calendar, the Roman one was dotted with holy days—some forty-five of them.

In some ways, though, the core of Roman religion was private, not public, based in the household, with its own lares and penates—the gods who protected households and certain other realms. The head of the family was responsible for seeing to it that these gods were fed by sacrifices, and their statues attended banquets and other family occasions. A wealthy household might include a handsome shrine to its gods, with fine reliefs sculpted to represent the protector and the protected. Even the poorest plebeian house would have its own more modest version.

THE FAMILY

The family—the large kin group that Polybius had seen as essential to the preservation of Roman values—was the core of Roman society. Each head of household, or paterfamilias, ruled his family, at least in theory, absolutely. The Roman father had the power of life and death over his children, as the Twelve Tables had stated (in practice, he exercised this only when deciding if a particular baby, perhaps one born with a deformity, should be exposed—left outdoors to die—or accepted). Yet mothers also mastered the stern tradition of Roman virtue and lived by it when called on to do so—as Regulus's wife supposedly did by torturing Carthaginian prisoners to death on learning of her husband's fate.

Sons and daughters grew up listening to the same tales of family tradition, and both passed to maturity through carefully marked stages of life. For sons, this meant changing from the boy's toga with its purple stripe to the manly toga, which was all white, at the age of fourteen, when they might also receive permission to attend their fathers, if they were senators, on official business. Girls entered maturity by marrying, for which they were considered ready by the age of twelve.

EDUCATION

The sources do not tell us much about the ways in which Roman children were educated in the first centuries of the Republic. Though the state provided no official schools, it seems that schools of some kind existed by the second century BCE, and that girls as well as boys attended them. The children apparently studied Greek poetry, which probably means that their families could afford tutors to teach them the elements of the language. Formal education became one more way in which the boys and girls of the upper class were separated from the rest of society. The early teachers were men of low status, slaves, or freedmen—one reason, probably, that we know relatively little about them.

Boys engaged in physical education: not the naked gymnastics of the Greek tradition, which the Romans tended to look down on, but training in horseback riding and the use of weapons. Hunting was highly valued as both a form of exercise and a training in boldness and dexterity. Both boys and girls, finally, learned by watching their parent of the same sex: boys about the public life of politics, law, and war-craft; girls about the skills of household management.

WOMEN'S LIVES

When Roman men spoke about women—for example, in the stone epitaphs with which husbands celebrated the virtues of their honorable, loving wives—or represented them in paintings and sculpted reliefs, they emphasized female docility and removal from economic life. In fact, though, many women lived more active and visible lives in Rome than had been possible in Athens. In the Greek city, women were supposed to occupy separate quarters, or at least to seclude themselves when male visitors arrived. In Rome, by contrast, women and children inhabited every corner of their houses. When guests arrived, the mother of the family might be working at her loom—a useful occupation and a symbol of her virtue and commitment to overseeing

An Ideal Wife This grave marker from around 80 BCE includes a portrait of a Roman husband and wife. The husband is identified by his trade as a butcher; the wife, by feminine virtues typically valued by Roman men: she is "chaste, modest, and not gossiped about."

POMPEII'S VILLA OF THE MYSTERIES

This painting is part of a large fresco featuring life-size figures that decorates all four walls of a grand room in the Villa of the Mysteries in Pompeii. The name of the house reflects the idea that the fresco depicts the "mysteries" of initiation into the religious cult of Dionysos. Scholars disagree on this interpretation of the fresco, however; some believe that it shows preparations for marriage rites. In any case, this lavish wall decoration clearly indicates that the household was a prosperous one. The red color of the background was made from cinnabar, an expensive pigment, and its extensive use announced the prestige of the villa's occupants.

In the detail shown here, a fully dressed, veiled woman enters a room at left. A naked boy reads from a papyrus scroll under the watchful eye of a female figure, perhaps his mother, who also holds a scroll. Another woman, wearing a wreath and carrying a plate of what may be bread, glances back while she walks out of the scene. Throughout the fresco, the use of shading and perspective creates an illusion of depth.

QUESTIONS FOR ANALYSIS

1. What clues to everyday life in ancient Rome do you see in this section of the fresco?

2. What details in the fresco suggest that the family living in the villa were of the elite?

3. Historians disagree about the fresco's meaning. Drawing on your reading of the chapter, what is your interpretation of it?

her household. But she would speak to male visitors and might well join them, reclining, at the banquet table. Roman women could own property and initiate divorce proceedings. Many women owned agricultural land, and some of them chose their tenants and collected the rents. And although paternal authority could weigh heavily on them, many had no father by the time they married: most women married by the age of twenty, whereas men waited until they were around thirty—and were thus likely to die before their daughters reached marriageable age.

Poorer women worked at every imaginable job. They served as nurses and as maids; they became butchers, fishmongers, and bakers; they wove cloth or laundered clothing. Others sold everything from beans to nails. Many were employed as waitresses in taverns, jobs that may have included prostitution as a side activity. Anyone who walked through Rome, or any Roman city, passed dozens of *tabernae*—little square rooms, with open fronts facing the street, where artisans and merchants had their shops—in which women earned their own livings. Roman law assumed in theory that women were weak-minded

Women's Work Women whose families relied on their income worked in a wide range of jobs. In this relief from second-century BCE Rome, a woman in a butcher shop writes on a wax tablet—perhaps recording the shop's accounts.

and needed male protection; Roman writers argued at length that women were fickle and unreliable. But the social reality was more complicated than law or literature portrayed.

SLAVERY

In one case especially, social reality came close to undermining Roman ideals. The Punic Wars transformed the Roman state, as we have seen. But they also transformed Roman society. Romans had always owned slaves, but after the Punic Wars their numbers rose dramatically. Slaves began to play vital roles in almost every sphere of Roman life.

Rome's victories produced captives by the thousands. The wars against the Samnites in the early third century BCE, for instance, were said by the historian Livy to have yielded 50,000 slaves. Scipio Africanus sent 2,000 skilled artisans back to Rome after he captured New Carthage (Cartagena, in Spain). This enormous stream of captives was swelled by a second one provided by brigands and pirates, who kidnapped men and women—including Roman citizens who ventured onto lonely roads—and sold them to feed the labor market.

Slaves—and freed slaves—were soon working throughout Rome and the other Roman cities. Town slaves probably worked shorter hours than farm slaves and were normally paid a wage. In households, they served as stewards, cooks, and maids; in shops, they worked as artisans and salespeople. Those with particular talents, or whose callings required them to master special skills, could become famous and rich: Publius Terentius Afer, a slave from Africa who became a successful playwright, ended his life as a free Roman. So did star actors, who used their earnings to buy their own freedom. Town governments bought slaves, who served as clerks, attendants at baths and temples, and assistants to the officials charged with maintaining buildings, roads, and sewers.

Amid these variations were important uniformities: Roman slaves had no civil rights. They could not serve in the armed forces, vote, or own property (slaves who saved their salaries did so with their master's permission). Marriage was also prohibited, though again, if the master permitted them, they could enter a form of marriage. On funeral monuments, slaves sometimes spoke of their dead partners as husbands or wives, but they did so at the sufferance of their owners. Discipline was harsh, especially for those who worked in the most dangerous jobs,

Slave Society This first-century CE Pompeiian fresco depicts a mythical scene with an element of everyday life included: to the left, a slave washes the floor, a common occurrence in wealthy Roman households.

THE REPUBLIC IN FLUX: ECONOMIC AND SOCIAL CHANGE (218–180 BCE)

No Roman spoke more powerfully for what had become the city's values in the second century than Marcus Porcius Cato (234–149 BCE). A disciplined and effective military commander of humble origins, he served in Spain but accepted none of the loot from his conquests there. Austere and demanding of others, he wore the simplest Roman clothing and normally drank only water, or wine of the same quality that he gave his slaves.

Cato's *Origins* was the first account of Roman history written in Latin by a Roman. More revealing of a new Rome, though, is his book on agriculture. Also written in Latin, this impressive manual on how to run a farm presents farming as a primary business for Romans, one that they should enter while young. But what Cato offered readers was not advice on how to cultivate one's own small plot, in the manner of Cincinnatus. Rather, it was a handbook on how to flourish in the new economic and social world that was taking shape.

as gladiators or in the mines. A well-ordered farm was supposed to have an underground prison where masters could confine slaves who displeased them.

In some cases, masters developed warm relationships with their slaves. Cicero worried when his slave secretary, Tiro, was sick, and sent him another slave to keep him company. Eventually he gave Tiro his freedom and made him—as Cicero's brother Quintus wrote in a congratulatory letter—"a friend rather than a slave." The two men in fact continued to be close. Women, similarly, could feel real affection for their maids.

But as the number of slaves rose—to 10 percent or more of Rome's total population—Rome showed all the features of a slave society. Masters were told to treat their slaves gently in order not to provoke them, as that could result in their own murder. Runaway slaves who were recaptured could be branded on their foreheads or have metal chains forged around their necks, and when slave revolts broke out, as we will see, they were put down without mercy. The new Roman household, with its slaves for cleaning and serving, and its income from farms run by slave labor, had little in common with the ancient Roman ideal of virtuous poverty.

THE LATIFUNDIA: INEQUALITY IN THE COUNTRYSIDE

Rome's new society and economy had its roots in the long wars against Carthage and Macedonia, which transformed the nature of military service. Instead of joining the army for the duration of a short, traditional campaign, soldiers now spent decades traveling and fighting with their commanders. When they finally returned home, some found that a neighboring landowner had appropriated their family's small farm; others, unable to settle back into rural life, sold their plots of land and moved to Rome or another city. The farms of the wealthy became larger and larger, requiring newly massive labor forces to herd flocks, tend vines and olive trees, and plant grain.

These large agrarian estates, known as **latifundia**, were assembled by entrepreneurs, many from the class known as *equites* ("knights"), below the senatorial aristocracy. On these properties, using free tenant laborers as well as slaves, the equites cultivated the crops that the army, and the growing city of Rome, needed. Reaping machines and other technology were essential to farming on this scale. In his plainspoken book, Cato describes

Latifundia Vast estates outside Rome cultivated the crops and livestock needed to feed the city's growing population. This first-century CE mosaic from present-day Algeria possibly depicts such an estate, with laborers cultivating its grapevines.

a substantial estate, well equipped and staffed, run by a manager and designed to yield cash crops in substantial quantities.

Cato's inventory of the people and equipment needed to make olive oil on this estate conveys a large-scale operation with specialized craftsmen whose products support the ongoing work. Cato lists everything: staff members, draft animals, oil presses, other equipment and tools, all the way down to mattresses, pillows, and towels. His recommendation that slaves too old to work simply be discharged, so that they do not burden the estate, reveals more cold-eyed efficiency than old-fashioned Roman values. Cato, the heroic defender of Roman tradition, was a precise, passionless modernizer when it came to extracting money from the land. He and others like him helped to turn Rome into a more cash-centered society, in which rich and poor were widely separated.

CITY LIFE

Rome was changing not only in the countryside but in its cities as well. By 100 BCE the city of Rome itself had as many as 750,000 inhabitants. The new urban life that took shape in this period had little in common with Rome's vision of its past. Improved building technologies that made use of stone, brick, and concrete spanned the valleys that separated the city from mountain springs with aqueducts and brought fresh, clean water to Romans. But as they grew, Rome and its subject cities were anything but neat and clean. City dwellers had to navigate labyrinths of narrow streets caked with dirt and animal dung, frequently blocked by benches and shop stalls—features of a newly vibrant economic life.

URBAN INEQUALITY In this bustling urban setting, wealthy families lived in individual houses built around an atrium, or open space, with a pool in its center where the head of the house would meet visitors. An opening in the roof let in light and air as well as rain to fill the pool, channeled by ornamental downspouts. One room might be given over to the household gods and to images of distinguished ancestors; another to the library and records of the paterfamilias. Well beyond the atrium, in the public part of the house, the family would enjoy its own garden, very likely with pools for fish and swimming. A lavatory with running water awaited those who needed to relieve themselves after the many courses of a banquet, which the guests, reclining on couches, would eat in the garden in warm weather.

Most Romans, however, lived on a much more modest scale than the rich. Republican Rome became a city of *insulae* ("islands")—apartment houses built of wood and mud bricks that took their name from their appearance: they stood out like islands in the city. Often five or six stories

Aqueducts Improvements in technology allowed Rome to create irrigation systems that spanned vast distances. The Pont du Gard aqueduct was part of a thirty-mile irrigation system in southern France built in the mid-first century BCE or CE.

high, these apartment houses were built, like the houses of the wealthy, around central courtyards. Their ground floors were pierced with niches, in which shops operated. From the courtyard, stairways gave access to corridors on the higher floors. Even the bigger, more expensive apartments on the second floor had no lavatories or kitchens, and little privacy, since rooms opened into one another. On higher floors, the corridors were lined with single rooms, each of which might have a small balcony and a single window, unglazed or covered with thin sheets of mica, and each of which might house an entire family. Inhabitants could buy cooked food from shops or prepare their own meals on small coal braziers—a risky process that often caused fires. Collapses were also common, even though building regulations limited the height of these structures and mandated the thickness of their walls.

GRAFFITI: URBAN VOICES

Craftsmen and small merchants lived high in the air—except when they had to run downstairs to buy food or relieve themselves. Their wishes, beliefs, and political ideals were expressed not in eloquent speeches but in passionate and often ungrammatical graffiti, which are still a major Roman art form. The walls of another large Roman city, Pompeii, preserved by volcanic ash after the eruption of Mount Vesuvius in 79 CE buried the city, bear every kind of message—from homespun wisdom ("A small problem gets larger if you ignore it") to wild boasts ("Floronius, privileged soldier of the 7TH legion, was here. The women did not know of his presence. Only six women came to know, too few for such a stallion"). There are humble confessions ("We have wet the bed, host. I confess we have done wrong. If you want to know why, there was no chamber pot") and messages

Wealthy Households The House of Menander in Pompeii, likely owned by a rich merchant, includes all the hallmarks of a Roman mansion, including a central atrium with a pool, a skylight, and vivid mosaics decorating the walls.

of support for candidates in elections. As one unusually critical writer put it, "O walls, you have held up so many tedious graffiti that I am amazed that you have not already collapsed in ruin."

The lives of the urban poor—small shopkeepers and laborers, to say nothing of slaves—had little to do with traditional Roman values, the virtuous life of the farm, or even the lives of established plebeian families. The upper classes saw them less as fellow Romans to be helped than as mouths to be fed and voters to be manipulated—and as potential support for revolutionary movements.

SPECTACLE AND ENTERTAINMENT

Like other great cities, Rome devised its own public spectacles—partly designed to divert city-dwellers from the difficulties of daily life.

GLADIATORS

As early as the third century BCE, great men in Rome sponsored what became a central form of urban amusement: combats between matched pairs of professional fighters, or gladiators. These were held at

Urban Voices Graffiti covered the walls of Pompeii, giving popular expression to views on all kinds of issues, from sex to politics. This inscription endorses a local political candidate.

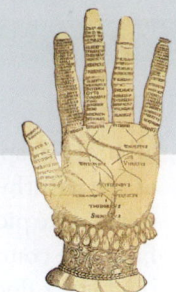

GRAFFITI AND WALL INSCRIPTIONS FROM POMPEII

Graffiti provide an unexpected and delightful source for social, economic, and even political history, as evident in these inscriptions from the Roman provincial town of Pompeii, destroyed by the eruption of Mount Vesuvius in 79 CE. They offer an intimate look at the everyday concerns of Pompeii's people, sometimes expressed in poignant ways. The wall inscriptions were used as bulletins and notices, campaign posters, message boards, and confessionals to express emotional declarations and pieces of advice.

Market days: Saturday in Pompeii, Sunday in Nuceria, Monday in Atella, Tuesday in Nola, Wednesday in Cumae, Thursday in Puteoli, Friday in Rome.

A copper pot is missing from this shop. 65 sesterces reward if anybody brings it back, 20 sesterces if he reveals the thief so we can get our property back.

Take your lewd looks and flirting eyes off another man's wife, and show some decency on your face!

Anybody in love, come here. I want to break Venus' ribs with a club and cripple the goddess' loins. If she can pierce my tender breast, why can't I break her head with a club?

Twenty pairs of gladiators of Decimus Lucretius Satrius Valens, lifetime flamen of Nero son of Caesar Augustus, and ten pairs of gladiators of Decimus Lucretius Valens, his son, will fight at Pompeii on April 8, 9, 10, 11, 12. There will be a full card of wild beast combats and awnings [for the spectators]. Aemilius Celer [painted this sign], all alone in the moonlight.

The dyers request the election of Postumius Proculus as Aedile.

Vesonius Primus requests the election of Gaius Gavius Rufus as duumvir, a man who will serve the public interest—do elect him, I beg of you.

His neighbors request the election of Tiberius Claudius Verus as duumvir.

The worshipers of Isis as a body ask for the election of Gnaeus Helvias Sabinus as Aedile.

The inhabitants of the Campanian suburb ask for the election of Marcus Epidius Sabinus as Aedile.

At the request of the neighbors Suedius Clemens, most upright judge, is working for the election of Marcus Epidius Sabinus, a worthy young man, as duumvir with judicial authority. He begs you to elect him.

The sneak thieves request the election of Vatia as Aedile.

The whole company of late drinkers favor Vatia.

Inn to let. Triclinium [dining room] with three couches.

Here slept Vibius Restitutus all by himself his heart filled with longings for his Urbana.

To rent from the first day of next July, shops with the floors over them, fine upper chambers, and a house, in the Arnius Pollio block, owned by Gnaeus Alleius Nigidius Maius. Prospective lessees may apply to Primus, slave of Gnaeus Alleius Nigidius Maius.

To let, for the term of five years, from the thirteenth day of next August to the thirteenth day of the sixth August thereafter, the Venus bath, fitted up for the best people, shops, rooms over shops, and second-story apartments in the property owned by Julia Felix, daughter of Spurius.

He who has never been in love can be no gentleman.

Health to you, Victoria, and wherever you are may you sneeze sweetly.

Restitutus has many times deceived many girls.

If any man seek / My girl from me to turn, / On far-off mountains bleak, / May Love the scoundrel burn! / If you a man would be, / If you know what love can do, / Have pity and suffer me / With welcome to come to you.

At Nuceria, I won 855½ denarii by gaming—fair play!

On October 17 Puteolana had a litter of three males and two females.

The smallest evil if neglected, will reach the greatest proportions.

If you want to waste your time, scatter millet and pick it up again.

QUESTIONS FOR ANALYSIS

1. How can these graffiti help us to discover what life was like in this Roman provincial town?
2. What kinds of information do these notices give us about political life in the late Republic and the early empire?
3. How do the rental notices illustrate how and where people lived and worked?

Sources: Naphtali Lewis and Meyer Reinhold, eds., *Roman Civilization: Selected Readings*, 3rd ed., 2 vols. (New York: 1990), p. 276ff; William Stearns Davis, ed., *Readings in Ancient History: II. Rome and the West* (Boston: 1913), pp. 261–4.

Gladiators A terra-cotta relief from the first century BCE depicts one of the public spectacles staged throughout the empire: gladiators fighting lions in an arena.

first as games to commemorate the death of a male relative. Armed with fearsome weapons—some with short swords and shields, some with net and trident, some with scimitars—the gladiators fought to the death. They were recruited in many ways. Some were criminals or prisoners of war, sentenced to fight; others were volunteers, both slaves and freemen, who fought as professionals and were trained by experts. With increasing frequency, gladiatorial combats were held in the Forum and other public places, and the tickets distributed, as a sign of favor, to prominent plebeians. Men and women sat together to watch the blood flow.

In 186 BCE, another form of public slaughter was introduced to Rome: the *venatio* ("hunt") of animals, the rarer and wilder the better: lions, tigers, bears, elephants, leopards, and crocodiles. Crowded into amphitheaters, the citizens of Rome could now enjoy watching the sort of exciting combat between men and beasts that had once been accessible to the rich and powerful alone. Rome's new public culture of violence spread throughout the rest of the Roman world. Schools for gladiators opened in Capua, in southern Italy, and other cities. We cannot know exactly what these combats meant to those who watched them, but they were almost certainly seen as celebrating the military virtues that were central to Roman society. Perhaps they also helped exorcise the fear inspired by the massive defeat the Romans had suffered at Cannae in 216 BCE during the Punic Wars.

THEATER Another form of public entertainment also took shape in the third and second centuries BCE: Roman theater. As Romans traveled to and traded with the Greek cities of southern Italy, they saw Greek plays performed. By the mid-third century BCE, the Greek poet Livius Andronicus was translating and adapting Greek works into Latin, notably Homer's *Odyssey*. In 240 BCE he staged the first of what became a series of plays in Latin, both tragedies and comedies.

Following Livius Andronicus, the Roman Plautus (who may have begun life as a stage technician) and the African Terence (who, like Andronicus, came to Rome as a slave and was eventually emancipated) composed massive series of plays. Theatrical performances became a standard element in Roman religious festivals, taking place at first in temples. Typically, the actors were slaves and the plays were produced by officials of patrician blood who hoped that they could rise, with popular support, to higher office.

Plautus (ca. 254–184 BCE) made comedy Roman. He filled the stage with characters who were familiar to Romans, from boastful soldiers to slaves who often outwitted their masters. Terence (ca. 186–ca. 159 BCE), whose comedy was less broad than that of Plautus, adapted Greek plots and cast them with characters who were more complex, though his female characters tended to be stereotypically submissive. The plays of Plautus and Terence were enormously popular with Roman audiences. These grew from the couple of thousand who could have seen the original comedies in temples to much larger assemblies. Roman theater attracted patricians, equites, ordinary men and women, and slaves, seated (or standing in the case of the slaves) in positions determined by their status.

Roman Theater Vast audiences flocked to see the plays of authors such as Plautus and Terence. This second-century BCE relief of a scene from a Terence comedy suggests the rudimentary stage set and the masks the actors wore, conventions borrowed from Greek drama.

THE CRISIS OF THE REPUBLIC (133–31 BCE)

As ordinary Romans in their thousands left the land and large, unruly cities took shape, the Republic entered what would prove to be its last century—a century of crisis. Rome's new imperial reach had introduced instability into the constitution that Polybius had praised for its balance. Thanks to the Hortensian Law that had concluded the Struggle of the Orders around 287 BCE, decisions made by the plebeian assembly carried the force of law. Nonetheless, the great aristocrats continued to dominate politics, maintaining a near monopoly over high office. Of the 256 consuls elected between 262 and 134 BCE, only 16 were "new men": the rest belonged to an inner circle of some twenty families. The aristocrats who, despite the growing numbers of slaves and poor city dwellers, remained committed to the belief that they were best qualified to manage Rome's political and military affairs were known as *optimates*. Others, known as **populares**, argued that it was vital to help the poor, to whom they turned for support.

Roman officials also incited disorder in the provinces. For many years, Roman governors could extort cash and booty from the provinces entrusted to them, almost at will. Even if convicted of extortion, they would only have to reimburse what they had taken. Meanwhile, Roman tax-farmers (officials, often from great families, appointed to collect the taxes as contractors) extracted not only the legally required revenues but much more—from Sicily, from Spain, and after 167 BCE, from Macedonia. Those in a position to enrich themselves became wealthier, and their interests increasingly diverged from those of ordinary Romans.

THE GRACCHI

The members of one noble family, **the Gracchi**, set out to reform the system—to recast Roman society on lines more in keeping with the austerity and general egalitarianism of the city's traditional beliefs and values. Or so they claimed.

TIBERIUS
Tiberius Gracchus (163–133 BCE), the son of a man who had served more than once as consul and won a triumph, introduced legislation when he was tribune in 133 BCE to restore the limits on how much of the state's public land any Roman could own, and to redistribute the land thus freed to landless men. The measure passed the plebeian assembly, but another tribune, Marcus Octavius, vetoed it; and when it went to the Senate for adjudication he vetoed it again, both times violating the traditions of Roman politics.

Tiberius promptly removed Octavius from office—another innovation, but one that the other tribunes did not contest—and created a land commission that began work on a redistribution project. When the ruler of Pergamum in Asia Minor left his kingdom to the Roman people in 133 BCE, Tiberius accepted the legacy without consulting the Senate and proposed to divide it among the landless. He then broke with tradition even more sharply by running for the office of tribune again, in order to gain immunity from a charge of treason. Terrified by these radical measures, the *pontifex maximus* ("chief priest") led a crowd of senators and others to the Capitoline Hill, calling on them to save the Republic. They murdered Tiberius and some of his followers, though the land commission continued to operate.

GAIUS
A decade later Tiberius's younger brother Gaius Gracchus (153–121 BCE), elected tribune in 123 and 122 BCE, introduced even more systematic legislation. This included a grain law designed to ensure that the people received a guaranteed supply of wheat at subsidized prices, as well as regulation of recruitment into the military and expansive public works programs. No radical, Gaius seems to have been most concerned with spreading the risks—and the responsibilities—of government more widely among the inhabitants of what had become essentially a Roman Empire. He fought to have senatorial legislation exempted from control by the tribunes. But he also sought to give the equites, who were ineligible for service in the Senate but whose wealth gave them considerable power, a monopoly over membership in criminal juries. He did this to ensure that they exercised real control over the notorious abuses of Roman governors in the provinces, by judging them when accusations of corruption or cruelty arose. Finally, he tried to extend the political rights of full citizenship to all Latins, and Latin status to all allies, who would thus be protected from the worst horrors of Roman government and made eligible for the land distribution that his brother had introduced.

At this point Gaius's allies began to defect. He failed to win reelection as tribune in 121 BCE and raised an armed revolt. The Senate responded by passing, for the first time, the *senatus consultum ultimum* ("final decree of the Senate"), which allowed the consul to deal with enemies of the state violently, if necessary, without worrying about strict legality. Gaius and his followers were killed—as the *popularis* Catiline would be, just over half a century later. Ironically, one effect of Gaius's legislation was to put the vast wealth of the province of Asia (southwestern Turkey) into the hands of the already wealthy publicans, or tax-farmers, who collected taxes for the state and paid a fee for the right to do so. The Gracchi, in other words, failed. But their policies would be revived again and again by later *populares*.

CONTINUING UPHEAVAL (108–51 BCE)

The suppression of the Gracchi and their programs did not restore order and tranquility. Warfare continued. Slaves rose against their Roman masters from 138 to 132 BCE and 104 to 101 BCE. The senatorial elite performed feebly against Numidian forces who fought hard against Rome's armies in North Africa in the last two decades of the second century BCE. An even tougher opponent was Mithridates of Pontus, an area on the southern coast of the Black Sea in Asia Minor. Known for his command of languages (he could speak those of all twenty-two countries he ruled), Mithridates (r. 120–63 BCE) played effectively on local discontent with Roman taxes. He began hostilities by organizing the slaughter of some 80,000 Romans and Italians living in Asia Minor. And when he represented himself as the defender of Greek freedom against Roman oppression, he gained support from Athens and other Greek cities.

THE SOCIAL WAR
Most threatening of all was the **Social War** of the early first century BCE. Over time, the inhabitants of Italy had come to be classified in three ways: (1) as full Roman citizens, with all the attendant rights, including freedom from direct taxes; (2) as "Latins," who had an intermediate status, enjoying the civil and legal but not the political rights of citizens; or (3) as "allies," who supplied many of Rome's soldiers but were not allowed to possess the lands they helped Rome to conquer. When Gaius Gracchus proposed, in 123 BCE, to grant the Latins full citizenship and the allies Latin status, the Senate rejected the measure and expelled the Latins and allies who did not have voting rights from the city of Rome. In 91, a nobleman who belonged to the populares, Marcus Livius Drusus, proposed a law that would have made the Latins citizens. The senators, furious, rejected his proposal and murdered him in his own house.

At this point the Marsi (a Latin people who had sent soldiers, ineffectively, to help Drusus), the Samnites, and soon most of central and southern Italy erupted in a bitter revolt against the Romans. They even created their own state, which they called "Italia," with a new capital and its own coinage. Atrocities were committed on both

sides. Though Rome sent its best generals to deal with the enemy, the elite decided in the end to compromise, and in 89 BCE Latins and allies who had not risen against Rome or who were willing to lay down their arms were granted citizenship. For the rest of the history of the Republic, Rome would struggle to assimilate these new citizens, some of whom became prominent.

Social War The Latins and their allies minted this coin in the early first century BCE. The Italian bull trampling and goring the Roman she-wolf is a metaphor of the Social War.

MARIUS AND SULLA
As confidence in Rome's future and its safety dimmed, great military bosses began to play central roles in public life and politics—and not only, in the traditional way, as holders of elective office. Gaius Marius (157–86 BCE), a "new man" from outside the Roman elite, and Lucius Sulla (138–78 BCE), an aristocrat who started out as one of Marius's officers, fought more successfully than the older members of the elite. But they did so by abandoning traditional restraint. Marius gave up on the ideal of the citizen army. With the latifundia expanding, fewer citizens could afford to serve, and recruitment dwindled. Marius set no property qualification for military service and enrolled his own forces, whom he paid and who were

Sulla Lucius Sulla, who won a reputation for his violent methods of "proscribing" and hunting down his enemies, is portrayed in this bust from about 50 BCE.

loyal to him alone. Suddenly, Romans were joining the army less to preserve what they and their fellow citizens had than to win property and money. Marius's campaigns in Africa and against the Cimbri (Germanic tribes that invaded Italy in 102 BCE) proved so successful that equites and members of the senatorial elite supported him and helped to elect him consul time after time. Sulla, for his part, fought brilliantly against Mithridates, whose armies he destroyed, and against the Latins in the Social War.

But in addition to winning great victories for Rome, Marius and Sulla introduced a new level of violence into Roman politics. Each in turn found himself expelled for a time from the city. Sulla actually fought his way back in. And each responded by massacring his opponents. Marius simply had them killed. Sulla used a more terrifying means: like the Thirty Tyrants of Athens, he "proscribed" his enemies, listing their names on tablets in the Forum and sending squads of soldiers to hunt them down. Sulla promised rewards to slaves and members of their families if they would betray the outlaws, and barred their descendants from holding office. Though Sulla proscribed and killed only a few hundred people, no citizen could feel secure in the protection of laws and officials after these extralegal measures had been taken. He consolidated his power by settling his veteran soldiers on confiscated lands in Italy. This was the world in which Cicero would grow up and form his political convictions.

In the end, Marius voluntarily gave up his dictatorial power. Sulla, who turned out to be a genuine traditionalist, did his best to prevent imitation of the radical Gracchi. He ruled that men who had served as tribunes could not take on more prestigious magistracies and that they could no longer veto legislation—an effective way to discourage would-be tribunes of the people. He also increased the number and activities of the courts, doubled the size of the Senate and enhanced some of its powers, and then retired—to die, almost immediately. Yet violence continued. The most alarming outbreak came in 73 BCE when a former Roman soldier named Spartacus, who had become a gladiator, led a small group of hard-bitten followers who soon raised a massive slave revolt. Spartacus destroyed a number of Roman legions before he was finally defeated and killed in 71 BCE.

THE FIRST TRIUMVIRATE

Although the forms of republican government continued to exist and function, all efforts to stabilize Roman politics seemed to have failed. Politics looked more and more like a game dominated by power and money, as great men fixed elections by telling their many dependents, known as clients, how to vote. At last, three of the great Roman military bosses—Julius Caesar, Pompey (Gnaeus Pompeius Magnus), and Marcus Licinius Crassus—formed an informal alliance in 60 BCE, retrospectively known as the First Triumvirate. These men were powerful generals and effective diplomats who had fought in all corners of the Roman world and beyond. Their massed military power enabled Caesar to force through legislation. But this alliance also fell apart as the ambitions of its three leaders clashed.

MODELS OF LEADERSHIP

In the continuing efforts of Roman elites and ordinary citizens to stabilize the chaotic situation, two powerful models of leadership emerged, each best personified by a single man.

CICERO

The statesman and orator Marcus Tullius Cicero (106–43 BCE), whom we met at the start of the chapter, fought to preserve what he saw as the core of Roman tradition. A new man himself, he could not point to distinguished ancestors when he sought public office. Instead, he honed his skill in using language. This was the art that he deployed against Catiline in 63 BCE, in speeches that utilized every tool in the rhetorician's kit with matchless brilliance. It enabled him to defend the traditional preeminence of the Senate—and the power of the families that had dominated it for centuries—against those who sought to transform Rome. It gave him the ability to flatter those whose views he opposed, such as Caesar, one of the aristocratic populares.

CAESAR

The general and statesman **Julius Caesar** (100–44 BCE) represented the other great model of political action. Born in Rome to an ancient family, Caesar could call on the distinguished ancestors that Cicero lacked. As gifted a writer as Cicero ("Avoid an unfamiliar word," he advised, "as a sailor avoids the rocks"), Caesar practiced a very different craft: the precise, lucid, and matter-of-fact description of his achievements on the battlefield. Caesar made those achievements the basis of his authority. His conquests were quick and dramatic: in the years between 58 and 50 BCE, his forces killed more than a million Gauls, enslaved a million more, and conquered the whole vast area they inhabited (basically all of modern France and Belgium). Caesar's powerful histories of the wars he waged against the Gauls and his fellow Romans were exercises in propaganda that became literary classics.

Like Marius and Sulla, Caesar took personal

Julius Caesar This bust may date from 46 BCE and could be the most reliable indication of what Caesar might have looked like.

they made the fabulously rich general drink molten gold.) Caesar made himself master of Rome just after 50 BCE. Like Cicero, Caesar often looked back to past precedent. As *pontifex maximus* ("chief priest") of the city, he did his best to reestablish traditional Roman morality in what many saw as a decadent time. But Caesar picked very different precedents to follow. Like the Gracchi, he saw that stability could be obtained only if the thousands of poor men whom military service and economic growth had thrown off their lands were granted new lands by the state. After he conquered Gaul in 50 BCE, he resettled almost 200,000 poor Romans there, to the fury of the natives.

command of what became not the armies of the Republic but his own armies. Locked in a tense alliance with the other members of the First Triumvirate, he broke with them and then defeated and killed Pompey. (The Parthians, who controlled a vast territory in western Asia, did as much for Crassus: showing a sense for poetic justice,

CAESAR IN POWER

Over time, Caesar secured his hold on power through a series of bold innovations. In 49 BCE he entered Italy, famously crossing over the Rubicon River, in defiance of the law that forbade a commander with imperium, the right of command, to come into Italian territory with soldiers. Leading his legions, Caesar used military

Rome in 44 BCE Under Julius Caesar, the Roman army conquered large territories, including all of Gaul, and Numidia in North Africa. The rulers of several client states, such as Egypt, also owed allegiance to Caesar. By the time Caesar was assassinated in 44 BCE, Roman territory encircled the Mediterranean Sea.

force, and the threat of force, to dominate Roman politics. He depended on men whose loyalty was not to the state but to him alone, even giving his former slaves official positions in the mint. He enlarged the Senate to 900 members, inviting allies from as far as Gaul to join, in order to solidify his base of support. Caesar expanded the public games to include such magnificent spectacles as mock naval battles—a precedent that the emperors would build on for centuries to come. He replaced the republican Roman calendar—a complex system that had been manipulated for political purposes by the Roman priests—with a new one based on the observed course of the sun through the heavens. His Julian calendar is basically the one still in use today in most of the world.

More generally, Caesar began to treat Rome in a new way: not just as the ancient capital of what had become a new empire but as a world city, as Alexander had treated his new city of Alexandria in Egypt hundreds of years earlier. In 47 BCE Caesar restored Cleopatra, the last of the Ptolemies, to the throne of Egypt. Though he himself rejected the title of king, which Romans disliked, he agreed to be made a god (Mark Antony, his relative and ally, became his priest). There was every reason to suspect that Caesar meant to turn Rome into a monarchy.

THE SECOND TRIUMVIRATE

In 44 BCE, Marcus Junius Brutus and Gaius Cassius Longus, senators and politicians as loyal to the old Roman order as Cicero had been, but more decisive, murdered Caesar in the Forum and tried to reconstruct the Republic. Unable to find wide popular support, they lost the ensuing civil war to Caesar's nephew Octavian (63 BCE–14 CE), who had formed a Second Triumvirate with Mark Antony and another patrician, Marcus Aemilius Lepidus in 43 BCE. Proscribed after Caesar's assassination, Cicero might have been saved by Octavian, who admired him; but Mark Antony, whom Cicero had denounced as the chief threat to the Republic, insisted on his death.

Over time, Octavian eliminated all threats to his power. When Mark Antony married Cleopatra and began to act independently, suspicion grew that he hoped to set himself up as ruler of the Roman Empire, using the wealth and power of Egypt to rule the rest. Though the fleets and armies that Octavian and Mark Antony mustered were comparable in size, Octavian defeated his rival in a naval battle near Actium in Greece in 31 BCE. Mark Antony was a highly competent general and even won one victory on land at Alexandria, but his troops melted away, and first he and then Cleopatra committed suicide.

OCTAVIAN: LAST REPUBLICAN OR FIRST EMPEROR?

Octavian created a new system, known to historians as the principate: the rule of a single chief, or *princeps*. From 31 BCE on, a single ruler would hold the reins of power in Rome. Yet it would take a century and more before Roman rulers were ready to abandon the pretense that the Republic still functioned.

Throughout his life, Octavian insisted that he was no

The Ides of March The silver coin, minted in 43/42 BCE, bears the legend "EID MAR," two daggers, and a cap worn by freed slaves. The message is clear: on the Ides of March, the day Brutus and Cassius assassinated Caesar, they liberated Rome from his tyranny.

Cleopatra This is a first-century BCE marble portrait of Cleopatra VII, whom Julius Caesar restored to the throne of Egypt in 47 BCE.

more than the first among Roman equals. As a sole ruler, he preserved and respected the institutions of the Republic, above all the Senate; lived simply, in the manner of Cato and other earlier Roman heroes; and expanded the empire. Even more than Caesar, **Augustus**—as Octavian was renamed—set the style for the transformed Rome that would rule the western Mediterranean world for almost 500 years. His Rome was a full-scale empire ruled from a court rather than the republican capital of a territorial empire formed by conquest. Historians and poets, politicians and pundits have debated the lessons of this transformation for centuries—ever since the greatest Roman historian, Tacitus, writing in the early second century CE, identified Augustus as the one who subverted the Republic while pretending to maintain it.

AUGUSTUS: BUILDING AN EMPIRE (31 BCE–14 CE)

Augustus's policies were the most potent mixture of tradition and innovation that Rome had seen. Dignified and austere in the old Roman way—one of his favorite sayings, according to his ancient biographer, was the homely "quicker than you can boil asparagus"—Augustus cut a powerful figure. At first he held only traditional offices, such as the consulship, and insisted on showing deference to the Senate and to the ancient customs of the Republic. Many important responsibilities actually remained with the Senate: for example, the administration of large parts of the empire, from Asia Minor and North Africa to nearby Sicily and Sardinia. Just as under the Republic, praetors governed all of these. But the city of Rome panicked when he threatened to cease serving as consul, and he eventually took on a new role, accepting the powers of a tribune, but without the formal title.

RESTORING ORDER

Augustus made massive efforts to restore order at all levels. Newly precise rules of dress sorted out the "orders" of Roman society, distinguishing senators from equites by the decoration of their cloaks and togas. He paid special attention to religion. Augustus brought back ancient orders of priests, served in them himself and urged others to do so as well, and started a massive program to restore the formal temples of the city of Rome. In one year, he

Augustus In monumental public statues, Augustus expressed different visions of his authority: as a heroic warrior, with the figure of Cupid suggesting his divine lineage; and as a somber statesman, wearing the toga of the Roman citizen.

rebuilt some eighty-two of them, which had fallen into ruin during the civil wars, and he created particularly magnificent temples to Jupiter on the Capitoline Hill, and to Apollo, whom he saw as his special patron, on the Palatine Hill. The private worship performed in Roman families had never ceased, but Augustus put new emphasis on the public cults of the state, which would become central to the empire.

Following the example set by Caesar, Augustus insisted that he stood for peace. In his monumental autobiography he noted that he had ended wars in region after region: Gaul, the Iberian Peninsula, Germania. Nothing pleased him more than the moment in 29 BCE (and two other occasions) when the doors of the temple of Janus were formally closed, indicating that no war was being waged anywhere in the Roman world. One of the most splendid structures with which he enriched the city of Rome was an altar to the goddess of peace (Ara Pacis), decorated with splendid friezes showing the whole city in procession to celebrate his safe return from Gaul and the Iberian Peninsula. These measures were not mere gestures. After two centuries of almost continual conflict, Augustus's reign ushered in the long period of peace traditionally called the **Pax Romana** ("Roman Peace"), which lasted from 27 BCE until 180 CE.

Augustus reinforced the cult of peace by taking care, in the late-republican tradition, to display the value of clemency in his own conduct. He treated his political opponents with far more tolerance than the previous generation had shown. He refused to hunt down the authors of political lampoons against him posted around the Senate, though he did refute their charges and suggest that anonymous authors of such works should be condemned.

EXPANSION AND CONFLICT

Even as he celebrated his ability to keep the peace within the empire, Augustus spent vast energy and resources on expanding and consolidating its borders. Sometimes, he was able to do so without engaging in conflict. In 25 BCE, when the ruler of Galatia in central Asia Minor was assassinated, it was transformed into a Roman province without bloodshed. Following the death of Herod the Great, the client king who ruled Judea, Augustus deposed his successor and imposed direct Roman rule through an appointed prefect. But Augustus's vast armies waged war again and again: in the Iberian Peninsula, where Augustus himself took command in the field for the last time, from 27 to 25 BCE; in Africa, where Ethiopian and Berber

raids had to be met and retaliation proved necessary; in the east, where Armenia—a client state of Rome, important as a buffer between Roman-controlled Asia Minor and the Parthian Empire—fell into turmoil in 2 BCE, calling forth a massive Roman response.

Above all, though, it was in the western territories that Roman armies fought. A series of invasions between 12 BCE and 6 CE pushed deep into the land of the Germanic peoples, to the Elbe River and beyond. Publius Quinctilius Varus, who commanded Roman forces on the Rhine River, was deputed to establish the empire's authority in the new province of Germania, across the Rhine from Gaul. He was opposed by the Marcomanni and other Germanic tribes, led by Arminius, son of the chief of the Cherusci. In 9 CE Varus provoked a revolt in Germanic territory. Led by Arminius (ca. 19 BCE–21 CE), who had learned the craft of war serving in the Roman armies, the Germanic forces annihilated Varus's three legions in a running battle in the Teutoburg Forest. The bones and armor of the Romans slaughtered there have recently been recovered by archaeologists, scattered over several miles. Augustus, stricken with grief and fury, beat his head against the wall of the imperial palace, demanding that Varus give back his lost

First among Equals On this section of a frieze from the Ara Pacis ("Altar of Peace") a procession from left to right includes a group of priests; Augustus's son-in-law, Agrippa, his toga covering his head; and other members of Augustus's family. The size and detail of these figures match that of Augustus (not shown), echoing his pretense of being simply first among equals.

Building an Empire, 30 BCE–14 CE Augustus consolidated and expanded Roman rule, bringing Egypt and large parts of central Europe and Asia Minor under imperial control. Between 12 BCE and 6 CE, Augustus's forces engaged in protracted, bloody battles with Germanic tribes, but never fully succeeded in bringing their territory under Roman control.

legions. Augustus never admitted that this terrible defeat led him to abandon plans to make the Germania province Roman. In practice, though, he and his successors accepted that Roman power could not move far beyond the Rhine. The borders that Augustus established would remain the effective borders of the empire for some 300 years after his time.

AUGUSTAN ROME

The traditional Roman respect for established law and restraint in dealing with other nations—a tradition that had been deeply strained in the last years of the Republic—continued to exist. But it did so, from now on, less as the expression of a consensus than as the decision of a single, all-powerful individual. Even as Augustus and his counselors insisted that nothing basic had changed, he was laying the foundations for a fundamentally different constitution: an autocratic one, ruled by a court, in which once-great institutions like the Senate gradually became marginalized.

ECONOMIC REFORMS Augustus developed the operations of the empire on a new scale. He created a permanent imperial treasury. He developed a modest administrative apparatus for those parts of the empire, like Gaul and the Iberian Peninsula, that Caesar and he had conquered and that still had military garrisons. These Augustus claimed as imperial property and ruled directly. And as Augustus became responsible for the welfare of the Roman people, he regulated the city of Rome with a new precision. A massive program of resettlement, which Augustus worked on throughout his reign, provided land and livings for thousands of those who had been thrown off their original properties to provide land for Pompey's and Caesar's military veterans: Horace and Virgil, the greatest poets of the time, both of whom celebrated Augustus in powerful verse, were among those whose families he saved from homelessness and destitution.

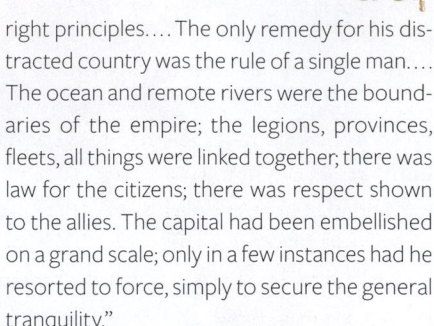

"RESTORING" THE ROMAN REPUBLIC

Octavian Caesar, better known by his honorific title Augustus (meaning "great" or "venerable"), was praised as a politician who repaired the most grievous political, economic, and social problems of Roman society and who "restored" the Republic after the assassination of his uncle and adoptive father, Julius Caesar. In actuality, Augustus created a monarchy by taking titles and ruling independently of other magistrates and even the Senate, while at the same time claiming to have preserved Roman identity and unity. Suetonius's text records the widely held view of Augustus as protector of the Republic, whereas Tacitus illustrates the more complex view of Augustus as both political savior and despot.

Suetonius, "Life of Augustus"

Gaius Suetonius Tranquillus, commonly known as Suetonius (ca. 69–ca. 122 CE), was a Roman equite and biographer who wrote *The Twelve Caesars* in 122 CE. In this excerpt, Suetonius frames Augustus's political actions as done for the good of the state and the happiness of the people.

His good intentions he often affirmed in private discourse, and also published an edict, in which it was declared in the following terms: "May it be permitted me to have the happiness of establishing the commonwealth on a safe and sound basis, and thus enjoy the reward of which I am ambitious, that of being celebrated for molding it into the form best adapted to present circumstances; so that, on my leaving the world, I may carry with me the hope that the foundations which I have laid for its future government, will stand firm and stable."

He corrected many ill practices, which, to the detriment of the public, had either survived the licentious habits of the late civil wars, or else originated in the long peace. Bands of robbers showed themselves openly, completely armed, under color of self-defense; and in different parts of the country, travelers, freemen and slaves without distinction, were forcibly carried off, and kept to work in the houses of correction.... The bandits he quelled by establishing posts of soldiers in suitable stations for the purpose; the houses of correction were subjected to a strict superintendence; all associations, those only excepted which were of ancient standing, and recognized by the laws, were dissolved. He burnt all the notes of those who had been a long time in arrear with the treasury, as being the principal source of vexatious suits and prosecutions....

He was desirous that his friends should be great and powerful in the state, but have no exclusive privileges, or be exempt from the laws which governed others....

The whole body of the people, upon a sudden impulse, and with unanimous consent, offered him the title of Father of His Country. It was announced to him first at Antium, by a deputation from the people, and upon his declining the honor, they repeated their offer on his return to Rome, in a full theatre, when they were crowned with laurel.

Tacitus, *Annals,* Book I

Publius Cornelius Tacitus (56–117 CE) was a Roman senator and historian. In his *Annals* (ca. 109 CE), Tacitus discusses the emperors who succeeded Augustus, but here he describes Augustus's funeral and reign. Tacitus records the popular ambivalence about Augustus's deeds, a mixture of praise and scorn that contradicts the idea that his actions were universally lauded.

Then followed much talk about Augustus himself.... People extolled, too, the number of his consulships ... and his other honors which had been either frequently repeated or were wholly new. Sensible men, however, spoke variously of his life with praise and censure. Some said "that dutiful feeling towards a father, and the necessities of the State in which laws had then no place, drove him into civil war, which can neither be planned nor conducted on any right principles.... The only remedy for his distracted country was the rule of a single man.... The ocean and remote rivers were the boundaries of the empire; the legions, provinces, fleets, all things were linked together; there was law for the citizens; there was respect shown to the allies. The capital had been embellished on a grand scale; only in a few instances had he resorted to force, simply to secure the general tranquility."

It was said, on the other hand, "that filial duty and State necessity were merely assumed as a mask. It was really from a lust of sovereignty that he had excited the veterans by bribery, had, when a young man and a subject, raised an army, tampered with the Consul's legions, and feigned an attachment to the faction of Pompey. By a decree of the Senate he had usurped the high functions and authority of Praetor ... wrested the consulate from a reluctant Senate, and turned against the State the arms with which he had been entrusted against Antony. Citizens were proscribed, lands divided, without so much as the approval of those who executed these deeds.... No doubt, there was peace after all this, but it was a peace stained with blood.".....

No honor was left for the gods, when Augustus chose to be himself worshipped with temples and statues, like those of the deities, and with flamens and priests. He had not even adopted Tiberius as his successor out of affection or any regard to the State, but, having thoroughly seen his arrogant and savage temper, he had sought glory for himself by a contrast of extreme wickedness.

QUESTIONS FOR ANALYSIS

1. What kinds of problems does Suetonius tell us that Augustus corrected, and what effect did his actions have?
2. Tacitus gives us two views of Augustus. What are they, and on what actions and ideas are they based?
3. What can these two documents tell us about Augustus's impact on the development of imperial Rome?

Sources: Suetonius, "Life of Augustus," in *The Lives of the Twelve Caesars*, trans. Alexander Thomson, rev. T. Forester (London: 1893); *Annals of Tacitus*, trans. Alfred John Church and William Jackson Brodribb (London: 1876).

Desiring to control the obligations of the state, Augustus limited the number of those entitled to distributions from the public granaries to 350,000. But to ensure supply, he had to create a formal system of grain imports and distribution, supported by fleets of transport ships and storehouses. It was ruled at the top by a new official—one of many whose posts Augustus created—from the equites. Because Italy itself could not supply the vast amount of grain that Rome required, it had to be imported, especially from Egypt and North Africa, which between them supposedly provided 80 to 90 percent of the city's needs. Docks, warehouses, and mills also had to be provided, and supplementary stocks of grain bought in Gaul and elsewhere in the empire.

SOCIAL CHANGE Under Augustus, divisions between the rich and the poor, the free and the unfree, became starker than ever before. Men like Marcus Vipsanius Agrippa, a general and statesman who became Augustus's son-in-law, amassed unlimited fortunes. With these they assembled properties on a vast scale, including urban palaces and magnificent villas in the Bay of Naples, on Capri, and elsewhere, where slaves staged elaborate banquets. Equites and freedmen who amassed fortunes by supplying the legions and the state also enjoyed lives of display.

By contrast, hundreds of thousands of ordinary Roman citizens lived on what they could bake from the three pounds or so of grain they received each day, with perhaps a little cheese or meat, or worked in the thousands of menial jobs that the city provided: cooks, porters, hairdressers, and other poorly paid positions. Near the bottom of the social scale, butchers and fishmongers, tanners and fullers (cloth-finishers) faced tasks that required them to work with the bodies of dead animals, apply noxious chemicals, or spend whole days standing in tubs of dirty water. Only the public baths provided by the state, which were freely available to all, enabled them to clean their bodies. Yet they and their families walked streets that were carpeted in animal dung and lived in tiny, ill-ventilated spaces.

In Augustus's time, as many as half of Italy's more than 7 million inhabitants may have been slaves. Though no longer seen as the threat they had been in the time of Spartacus, they were still subject to brutal discipline and were legally unfree. Even those who attained freedom, moreover, continued to be obliged to carry out certain tasks for their former masters.

WOMEN'S AUTONOMY In one respect at least, the changes that this period brought actually loosened the established structures of authority. For most of the history of the Republic, wives came under the absolute power of their husbands: their property was surrendered to their husbands, and they themselves could be divorced for any cause—including, in the case of the elder Cato, his desire to pass his wife on to a potential benefactor. In the late Republic, more and more families objected to the loss of property that the marriage of their daughters entailed. New legislation transferred power over dowries to wives, giving them a new independence of action. Meanwhile, the growth of a court society offered a few women of high standing a new level of freedom and authority. Augustus's own wife, Livia Drusilla, who divorced her previous husband to marry him, exemplified the traditional Roman matron and enjoyed his full confidence, so much so that her son from her previous husband, Tiberius, became Augustus's heir. Some suspected her of being a ruthless political intriguer.

Augustus did his best to exert paternal authority in the old way over the younger women in his family. His biographer Suetonius wrote: "In bringing up his daughter and his granddaughters he even had them taught spinning and weaving, and he forbade them to say or do anything except openly and such as might be recorded in the household diary. He was most strict in keeping them from meeting strangers, once writing to Lucius Vinicius, a young man of good position and character: 'You have acted presumptuously in coming to Baiae to call on my daughter.'" But his measures failed: he felt compelled to banish a daughter and a stepdaughter for their promiscuity and other vices, and wished that his daughter had committed suicide, as a more virtuous friend did, when disgraced.

THE CITY OF ROME Nothing was more obviously dramatic in Augustus's policies than his effort to transform the city of Rome. He laid special emphasis on improving the city's infrastructure. Augustus divided the city into fourteen administrative districts for more effective management. He gave the prefect of the city the power to supervise all guilds and corporations and to ensure that all necessary practical measures were taken. The city's walls, towers, and gates were rebuilt, and the roads that connected it with the rest of the empire repaved. Another official oversaw the dredging and draining of the Tiber and the maintenance of the aqueducts and sewers that were vital to Rome's public health. He also commanded the city's police force and its fire brigade—an innovation inspired by the example of Alexandria in Egypt. A special tax on the sale of slaves made it possible to station seven detachments of night watchmen (*vigiles*), who patrolled the city for fires, equipped with grapnels, ladders, and even with pumps pulled by horses. For more than half a century, Augustus's fire brigade prevented the outbreak of large-scale fires.

But Augustus's vision embraced more than the city's practical needs. As he also remarked, he turned the brick Rome that he inherited from his predecessors into a brand-new city of gleaming marble. His temple of Apollo, with its colonnades and public library, became a favorite meeting-place for the Senate. Grand as it was, though, it could not compete with the magnificent complex he built on the Campus Martius ("Field of Mars"), a spacious area in a bend of the Tiber that Augustus had embanked and graded. With a dazzling exhibition of the Roman mastery of resources and technology, he had an Egyptian obelisk floated across the Mediterranean and installed, upright, so that citizens could follow the shadow cast by the sun through the signs of the zodiac, which were inlaid on the pavement.

In addition to the new Forum that the emperor built, the statues of a dignified Augustus that appeared everywhere, and the Pantheon (temple of all the gods) and baths built by his son-in-law Agrippa, these projects turned the city into one great stone demonstration of the emperor's power and benevolence. Like Periclean Athens, Augustan Rome seemed to visitors almost to speak aloud of its greatness. But whereas the buildings and sculptures of Athens told a civic story, those of Rome celebrated a single person.

At age seventy-six, Augustus recorded his life in a testament written in Greek, copies of which he had set up around the empire—itself a practice of Julius Caesar and other great men of the Republic. Augustus boasted that he had refused the title of dictator when it was offered to him. In the conclusion, after reviewing a life of achievement that had begun with avenging Caesar's murder and led to the extension of the empire deep into Africa, far north into Germania, and far to the east, he stated proudly that he had never called himself a monarch. He insisted that the Senate continued to rule Rome, while he merely held traditional offices such as the consulate and did his best for his fellow Romans: "I exceeded all in influence," he admitted, "but I had no greater power than the others who

Mausoleum of Augustus Completed long before his death, Augustus's mausoleum was enormous in comparison to other elite tombs, and was fronted by bronze pillars that listed his many accomplishments. Despite Augustus's statement "I had no greater power than the others who were colleagues with me," the mausoleum, like so many other buildings he erected, proclaimed his power and importance.

were colleagues with me in each magistracy." No wonder that the Roman people had given him what he described as his proudest title: father of his country.

LATIN LITERATURE IN ITS GOLDEN AGE The last decades of the Republic and the first ones of the empire were remembered for centuries as a golden age of Latin literature. Highly educated Romans could now make creative use of Greek models. Writers like Catullus, Tibullus, and the female poet Sulpicia created a new kind of personal love poetry, which described in vivid detail what it was like to feel desire for a hard-hearted woman (or young man)—and, on occasion, to have it gratified. Ovid wrote in graphic detail about the techniques needed by a lover—and succeeded in irritating Augustus, who exiled him. As comedy had reflected the new social world of Rome during the Punic Wars, love poetry reflected that of the late Republic and early empire, in which wealthy Roman women enjoyed splendid educations and a remarkable freedom from constraint. But the highest praise—and the richest rewards—went to the poets and prose writers who used Latin to describe the epic rise of Rome to its new position. Horace (65–8 BCE), another very sophisticated poet, adapted many forms of Greek verse. A satirist and a philosopher, he also found ways to celebrate Rome's virtues of military heroism, piety, and moderation in power.

The most spectacular achievements were those of the poet Virgil and the historian Livy—both of whom turned their talents, so it seemed, on the Roman past. Virgil (70–19 BCE) made his name with short poems in the pastoral mode, modeled on Hellenistic verse, and a longer poem on farming. But his great achievement was the *Aeneid*—a magnificent epic, left incomplete at his death, in which he built on the models of Homer's *Iliad* and *Odyssey* to tell the story of how the Trojan Aeneas brought a remnant of his people to Italy and founded Rome. Livy (59 BCE–17 CE), for his part, wrote in prose, in which he produced a monumental survey of Roman history. He also drew heavily on earlier writers, especially Polybius. Both men's lives were shaped, like so many others, by Augustus's career and accomplishments. Virgil thought Augustus had revived Rome. A prophecy in the *Aeneid* proclaims that he, "born of the gods, will again found the golden ages." A republican himself, Livy shared Augustus's love for Roman traditions, and treated the emperor as a restorer of the Republic.

For centuries, across the Roman Empire, ambitious young men and women would learn what it meant to be Roman by reading their way through these great depictions of the glorious present and past. Yet neither author simply praised everything that Rome had done. Virgil made clear, as he followed Aeneas through his wanderings and then through his bitter war with those Latins who refused to join the Trojans, how much suffering it had taken to create Rome. Livy indicated, as he looked backward to early Rome, that its society had been far purer and more virtuous in the distant past than it was in his own day: "the less wealth men possessed the less they coveted."

CONCLUSION

During the first centuries BCE and CE, Roman society and culture flourished, in some ways, as never before. Thanks to the Pax Romana and the vast wealth that emperors and other patrons could deploy, architecture and art blossomed: the most astonishing relics that the visitor sees today in Rome, from the Roman Forum and Colosseum to baths and theaters, come from this period.

Yet to Tacitus, the historian from the senatorial order who held many public offices, the story of the early empire was one of republican virtue lost under autocratic rule, as the free oratory of the Republic was transmuted into the gossip and flattery practiced in the imperial court. Augustus, in his view, had begun this process. As Tacitus wrote in his *Histories of Rome*,

> Many authors have written of the earlier period, the 820 years from the founding of the city of Rome, and they recorded the history of the Roman people with both eloquence and freedom. But after the fight at Actium, when it seemed vital that all power be granted to one man, those great minds disappeared. Truth was harmed in many ways: first of all, by growing ignorance of public affairs, which were seen as strange to them; then by the passion to flatter the masters, or, on the other hand, by hatred of the rulers. Some were opponents, others were servants, and between the two, neither worried about posterity.

Whereas Polybius had described the Roman constitution as a great balancing apparatus, Tacitus believed it had completely lost its equilibrium. And whereas the Romans Polybius knew taught their sons about their past so that they would become virtuous citizens, the Romans Tacitus knew turned away from their past and pretended it had not happened. They had ceased to worry about making Romans.

The terms Tacitus used here are important. He did not argue that there could have been another way to escape the calamities of the late Republic, another path that Augustus or other leaders could have taken. Peace could be restored, he admitted, only when one man held power in the state. The Republic had proved mortal, and the city that had freed itself from monarchs was a monarchy again.

The limited freedoms that survived under the empire depended on the will of absolute rulers. Yet Tacitus argued that Augustus and his rivals could not have preserved republican liberty in any measure without allowing the Republic itself to fall. No wonder that the story of Rome's tumultuous final century as a republic and first century as an empire has troubled citizens of all modern republics.

[CHAPTER REVIEW]

KEY TERMS

Etruscans (p. 111)
Carthage (p. 112)
Senate (p. 114)
patricians (p. 114)
plebeians (p. 114)

Struggle of the Orders (p. 115)
Law of the Twelve Tables (p. 117)
paterfamilias (p. 117)
Latin right (p. 118)

legion (p. 118)
Punic Wars (p. 119)
latifundia (p. 127)
populares (p. 132)
the Gracchi (p. 132)

Social War (p. 133)
Julius Caesar (p. 134)
princeps (p. 136)
Augustus (p. 137)
Pax Romana (p. 137)

REVIEW QUESTIONS

1. What peoples inhabited the Italian Peninsula before the founding of Rome, and how did they influence its origins?

2. What were the central political institutions of republican Rome, and how did they work together?

3. How was the class system reinforced in the Roman Republic?

4. What propelled the expansion of Rome under the Republic?

5. What were the benefits of being a Roman citizen, and how did Rome use the promise of citizenship to its advantage?

6. How did family and religious rituals help to foster such Roman values as courage and patriotism?

7. What types of inequality were prevalent in republican Rome?

8. What were the most important reforms of the *populares*, and what tensions were they responding to?

9. How did Julius Caesar seize power and create stability?

10. Was Augustus a republican or an emperor? Explain.

CORE OBJECTIVES

After reading this chapter, you should have a solid understanding of the following core objectives. To strengthen your grasp of the core objectives, use the resources on the Student Site for The West.

- What do both Roman myths and modern archaeology reveal about the origins of early Rome?

- Explain how Rome's strength and political skill enabled it to conquer the Mediterranean region.

- Evaluate how Roman cultural and political ideals were expressed in its social and cultural institutions.

- Explain why the republican system became unstable in the second and first centuries BCE.

- Describe what made Julius Caesar's rise to power distinctive.

 GO TO **inQuizitive** TO SEE WHAT YOU'VE LEARNED—AND LEARN WHAT YOU'VE MISSED—WITH PERSONALIZED FEEDBACK ALONG THE WAY.

CHRONOLOGY

14–68 CE
Julio-Claudian
dynasty

ca. 30 CE
Crucifixion
of Jesus

46–62 CE
Paul travels
throughout
eastern empire

66–73 CE
Jewish war

70 CE
Romans conquer Jerusalem
and destroy Second Temple

79 CE
Mount Vesuvius erupts,
destroying Pompeii and Herculaneum

96–192 CE
Nerva-Antonine line

After 122 CE
Hadrian's Wall built

166 CE
Plague strikes across empire

Early 3rd century CE
Imperial persecution of
Christians becomes systematic

By 200 CE
Codices in widespread use

5

The Roman Empire and the Rise of Christianity

14–312 CE

A Christian woman named Perpetua died in 203 CE during an outbreak of persecution at the rebuilt city of Carthage. She recorded her experiences in prison as death approached. A well-born young Roman matron with a new baby, perhaps in her late teens, Perpetua belonged to a group of converts who were preparing to be baptized. Other members included one of her two brothers and a female slave named Felicitas. When Perpetua's father demanded that she leave the group, she explained to him, in the most graphic terms, that she now had a new identity and a new family: "'Father, can you see this vase that is lying here, for example, or waterpot or whatever?' And he said, 'I see it.' And I said to him 'Well, can this be called by any other name than what it is?' And he said, 'No.' 'That's it: I can only call myself what I am, a Christian.'" As Perpetua encountered it, Christianity was less a set of formal doctrines than a thick web of lived experience and loving community—a set of relationships far richer than those that bound her to her family. Nothing could make her abandon her beliefs and make offerings—as the authorities demanded—to the well-being of the emperor. The group was first subjected to surveillance and then arrested by Roman officials.

Arrest horrified the young mother: "I was terrified, because I had never experienced

A Mighty Empire As Roman troops conquered territory across Europe and the Mediterranean, they built grand and lasting infrastructure. This relief from Trajan's Column, erected in Rome in 113 CE to commemorate Emperor Trajan's victory against the Dacian people near the Black Sea, shows the ceremony at the opening of an arched bridge built over the Danube. The emperor himself stands to the right, preparing to sacrifice a bull.

such darkness. What a terrible day! The crowds made it unbearably hot. The soldiers demanded money. And then I was torn apart by worry about the baby." Partial relief came soon. Deacons—officers of the Christian community—bribed the guards to let the Christians go to a more comfortable part of the prison for a few hours. Later Perpetua gained permission to have her baby with her and to nurse him. More important, her brother made a request—one that shows that a Christian woman in 203 CE could be a figure of power in her church. He told her "you are highly honored," and asked her to request a vision. Perpetua complied. She asked for—and received—visions: a comforting vision of a heavenly shepherd, and an empowering one in which she defeated an Egyptian wrestler. She told her companions that martyrdom awaited them—but also, after that, victory over their enemies. Perpetua did not bend. When her father was beaten at an official's order, she "was as sorry for my father's plight as if I had been struck," but her pity for his wretched old age did not change her mind. Christianity somehow dissolved the paternal authority that had traditionally been a central feature of Roman society.

Perpetua and Felicitas died in the arena, their flesh torn by beasts and their throats cut. These were experiences of unimaginable terror, which they bore, according to the record, with remarkable dignity. Their story—including Perpetua's diary—became part of the church's official history, celebrated with sermons by great bishops.

Nothing is harder for historians than understanding the convictions that gave Christians the strength to do what Jesus had told his original followers that he expected: to leave their parents, spouses, and children and follow him. Roman Christians—many of them free, some of high standing—turned their backs on their families and their positions in society. They had to defy those whose authority they had been taught since birth to acknowledge: parents, officials, the emperor himself. And they had to do so in cities built to display the power of Rome and in courts and arenas that dealt out punishments that now seem inhuman. Unfortunately, most of the documents that describe events like these, accounts written in retrospect and designed to celebrate the triumph of the new church, give little sense of what Christianity meant to its first followers. But the words of Perpetua and other, anonymous, Christian writers—rare survivals, with the immediacy of everyday life—take us with them along the streets of the late Roman city, and into the courts, prisons, and circuses where they suffered. From them we can glean a sense of how effective the Christian message was, even as Roman authorities tried to stamp it out.

THE EARLY EMPIRE (14–96 CE)

By 203 CE, when Perpetua and her friends died in the amphitheater, the Roman Empire bestrode the Mediterranean world like a colossus, as powerful in Africa as in Italy or Gaul. Go back two centuries, and this development seems even more astonishing. For the early empire was as much a tangle of contradictions as a massive, powerful state.

Although republican traditions mattered deeply to Octavian and his subjects, they slowly became accustomed to thinking in monarchical terms. Octavian accepted new titles—including "emperor" and "Augustus"—that revealed, whatever his claims to the contrary, that he was more than the first citizen of Rome. His vast resources and his habit of micromanagement meant that the emperor dominated even in the older republican conquests, such as North Africa, which were legally subject to the Senate. Resistance to Augustus disappeared after the defeat of Antony and Cleopatra, and the empire, despite its unsuccessful effort to expand in Germania to the river Elbe, was now immense. It almost completely surrounded the Mediterranean, from Egypt and Judea in the east to Gaul and Spain in the west. The lands Augustus conquered in Africa stretched from the Sinai Desert all the way to Numidia, and the enormous income from land rents in Egypt, which effectively belonged to the emperor, supported the projects of many of Augustus's successors. Many areas that the empire did not directly control—such as Mauretania, on the northwestern tip of Africa—were ruled by Roman clients.

But like all monarchies, the Roman Empire faced difficult problems. It would have to maintain a vast population and an extensive apparatus of roads, fortifications, and officials, but it could not rely indefinitely on the enormous wealth that Augustus disposed of. And it would have to arrange for peaceful succession—a problem especially difficult if the emperor in question was not popular with the Senate or the people, or if the identity of the proper heir was problematic.

THE JULIO-CLAUDIANS (14–68 CE)

Until 68 CE, the emperors—four of them after Augustus—were chosen from two imperial families, the Julii and the Claudii. Their ability to follow the example set by Augustus varied. So did their claims to the throne, which depended on a complicated combination of adoption, marriage, and actual shared blood. None of them was succeeded by his own son. As their fortunes indicate, the great structure that Augustus reared was in part quite shaky, despite appearances.

No emperor could hold his throne in security unless he had the support of multiple parties: the Praetorian Guard, a special unit that the Claudian emperor Tiberius settled on the outskirts of Rome and tasked with protecting the palace; the armies, mostly on the frontiers; and the old senatorial elite, which supplied emperors with their chief administrators. Even a powerful ruler could find himself—or think himself—threatened if one or more of these pillars seemed to wobble.

For example, Tiberius (r. 14–37 CE), whom Augustus designated as his successor, was a man of high intelligence and education who shared Augustus's respect for Roman traditions, but he was hampered from the start by financial problems. Many of these were caused by a long and expensive series of campaigns in Germany. There his nephew Germanicus failed to take back the territories lost by Varus in 9 BCE. The growing suspicion that others

Praetorian Guard A marble relief from the second century CE depicts members of the Praetorian Guard, the special military unit tasked since the reign of Tiberius with protecting the emperor.

were plotting against him, made worse by his passion for astrologers' predictions, led Tiberius to institute trials in the Senate, sometimes for far-fetched reasons, and eventually to withdraw from Rome.

Tiberius's heir, Caligula, became emperor in 37 CE. He was also highly cultured, but after a popular start he demanded the sort of preeminence that Hellenistic rulers had enjoyed. He insisted on his own divinity, humiliated courtiers and senators, and even demanded that a statue of him be placed in the Jerusalem Temple—exactly the sort of humiliation of subject and allied peoples that republican Rome had traditionally avoided. The Praetorian Guard assassinated him in 41 CE and replaced him with his uncle Claudius (r. 41–54 CE), whom they found cowering behind a tapestry. An erudite man with a rich sense of Roman history and tradition, Claudius achieved considerable successes—he conquered much of Britain, enlarged the citizenship, and built a great harbor north of Ostia, at the mouth of the Tiber, southwest of Rome. But he did not win much love or respect. Dominated by his third and fourth wives, Messalina and Agrippina, Claudius allowed his only

Nero's Palace In 64 CE, Emperor Nero began construction of his extravagant palace on the Palatine Hill, the Domus Aurea ("Golden House"). Its lavish design drew on all the latest architectural advances, from concrete walls to a mechanical system operated by slaves that allowed this central courtyard's domed ceiling to revolve.

surviving son to be pushed aside by Nero, Agrippina's son by a previous marriage.

Nero (r. 54–68 CE) won golden opinions in the first part of his reign—during which he allowed his mother and then his chief advisers, the philosopher Seneca and the freedman Burrus, to counsel him—and made clear his desire to work with the Senate. But when Agrippina opposed his affair with the daughter of the Roman proconsul in Greece, he had his mother killed. Treason trials for Burrus, among others, soon followed. Nero's passion for the arts and for sport—he played musical instruments and competed in the Olympic Games—won him respect from the Roman crowd, as did his magnificent building program. However, after much of Rome burned in 64 CE, Nero used 125 acres of private land near the Palatine Hill to build a magnificent palace, its rooms decorated with glorious frescoes and a colossal statue of himself. Though always popular with the Roman plebeians, Nero gradually lost the senatorial elite and the armies. After a revolt in Gaul against his tax policies, Nero's support dwindled until he committed suicide, and the Senate acclaimed a governor in Spain, Servius Sulpicus Galba, as the next emperor.

THE FLAVIANS (68–96 CE)

Cruel, lazy, and unwilling to bribe soldiers for their support, Galba lasted only seven months of 68 and 69 CE before being assassinated. After a chaotic period in which four emperors succeeded one another within a year, the Flavians—Vespasian, Titus, and Domitian (all successful military commanders)—restored order. Vespasian (r. 69–79 CE) reformed the public finances, instituting new taxes. When his son Titus complained that it was undignified to charge for entrance to public urinals, Vespasian, a cold, efficient man, replied, "Money has no smell." He also began construction of the Flavian Amphitheater (now known as the Colosseum), the largest in the world, where crowds of 50,000 and more could watch gladiatorial combat, mock naval battles, and public executions. Titus, though he died in 81 after only two years in office, also won respect for the efficiency and generosity he showed in dealing with a great public disaster, the eruption of Mount Vesuvius in 79, which destroyed the cities of Pompeii and Herculaneum.

Domitian (r. 81–96 CE) avoided wars of aggression, managed trade and taxation effectively, and won popularity with the plebeians. But the price was high. Augustus had made Julius Caesar a god and became one himself, after his death in 14 CE. The Flavians took office after office, demanded to be called "lord and god," and formed a court society more docile than anything Rome had seen before. Domitian infuriated the senatorial aristocrats. After court officials assassinated him, the Senate formally condemned his memory, destroying all memorials to him.

The Colosseum In 72 CE, the emperor Vespasian began building the Flavian Amphitheater, now known as the Colosseum, just east of the Forum. When completed eight years later, it could hold more than 50,000 spectators and was the stage for many public events, including gladiatorial contests.

THE EMPIRE AT ITS HEIGHT

The emperors who came after Domitian—starting with one of his advisers, Nerva—were childless and appointed their successors, who consistently attained high levels of prosperity and military success. After the disorder of the first century, their rule through more than half of the second century reassured members of the aristocracy, who came to believe that a virtuous emperor could still preserve the core virtues of the Roman order. The hard-working, conscientious rulers of the Nerva-Antonine line—Nerva, Trajan, Hadrian, Marcus Aurelius, and Antoninus Pius—preserved the borders of the empire, maintained the roads and armies, and enabled the citizens of the empire to enjoy peace and prosperity for decades.

This long period of basic tranquility, interrupted by two brief civil wars, was a true Pax Romana. The empire's cities grew and prospered. Rome itself dwarfed the rest, but some ten other cities reached 100,000 or more inhabitants. The elite of every great city, moreover, tried to make its habitat over in the most up-to-date Roman image. They built gymnasia and baths, forums, colonnades, and amphitheaters. Their houses featured fine tiles, their tables wine, oil, and fish sauce. From these bright centers where members of the elite met in city squares to argue, there stretched sprawling suburbs where the much larger number of prosperous craftspeople and merchants lived and worked. And beyond these lay huge tracts inhabited by peasants cultivating extensive estates as sharecroppers or tilling small farms of their own.

Imperial Cities Throughout the empire, local elites designed their cities after the Roman model. This second-century theater in Palmyra, in present-day Syria, was built with ornate columns and terraced seating in the Roman style. The main entrance was even decorated with a bust of the emperor.

SOURCES OF UNITY

The stability of the second century made it possible for the Roman economy to grow—and, more particularly, for members of local elites to prosper. A uniform currency, a massive road system, and the protection of Roman arms fostered trade in regions from Gaul to Asia Minor.

Currency Gold coins, minted only in Rome but circulated throughout the empire, united all subjects under the image of the emperor. This coin bears Emperor Hadrian's name and profile.

COINAGE Local authorities were allowed to mint the small bronze coins of low value needed to purchase everyday necessities. But silver and gold coins were minted, for the most part, only in Rome. From Caesar on, coins carried new images: not the traditional bust of the goddess Roma, but a portrait of one of Rome's rulers, represented as a god on earth. These reinforced the legitimacy of the empire and the emperors, often connecting the latter with divine or heroic ancestors. But they also afforded help of a less transparent kind. Italy lacked precious metals, which had to be mined or captured elsewhere. Successive imperial governments debased the quality of the standard coin, the denarius, slowly but steadily—and thus managed to stretch their official budgets for the military and public works further than they could have done had the purity of the coinage been maintained.

ROADS An effective system of public transport—ports and docks on seacoasts and the enormous network of Roman roads—enabled Rome to stay in touch with its distant provinces. A permanent magistracy created by Augustus saw to the building and repair of this huge system, which at its height included some 50,000 miles of stone roadway, cemented in place and laid on top of a bed of stones to allow for drainage. Sometimes as straight as a ruler for miles, sometimes curving to follow the countryside, the roads enabled the legions to move their enormous baggage trains across the empire, a vital logistical support for Roman power. A postal system that could pass letters and information from the western end of the empire in Britain to Antioch in Syria had stations every twenty-five

Roman Roads This detail from Trajan's Column shows Roman soldiers building a road. Rome's excellent roads linked the empire from end to end, facilitating the movement of troops and supplies, and speeding up communication. They were crucial to the expansion of Roman power.

to thirty-five miles, and even more frequent points for changing the horses that pulled its carriages. The roads were never perfectly safe—brigands threatened travelers even in peaceful times. But the system was an immense achievement, longer in total than the American interstate highway system.

EVOLVING LEGIONS The empire supported massive armies to protect and occasionally to extend its borders. The Roman legions, always seen as the core of the military, were recruited in the first instance from citizens, the elite of the Roman plebeians, or from noncitizens who received citizenship when they joined up. Members of auxiliary infantry and cavalry forces received citizenship when they left the army after serving for twenty-five years. Gradually recruitment became more local. One African legion, for example, was made up of Italians and Gauls in the first century. In the second century, foreign recruits from Asia Minor, Syria, and eastern Europe dominated, but Africans joined as well. By the end of the century, most of the soldiers in the legion were Africans, from Mauretania and Numidia (where the legion was stationed). These disparate groups underwent rigorous training. In theory they had to remain single while they served. But though they slept in what were supposedly single-sex barracks, archaeologists have shown that women and children lived with them, evidence of long-term relationships.

The army not only maintained Roman power but also carried out vast engineering works, building camps, roads, and dykes from North Africa to northern Britain. When necessary, a legion could hunker down for as long as a year to build the siege ramp and equipment needed to take a fortress. And all members of the army learned to live as Romans, with Latin as the common language. In many areas—though not all—the army succeeded in Romanizing large numbers of subject peoples.

IDENTITY The empire continued to take in peoples whose identity was very far from Roman. Add up the importation of slaves, the recruitment of soldiers, and the movements of those engaged in trade, and it is likely that Roman populations were more mobile than any other before modern times. Yet there were limits to Rome's openness and flexibility. Like the Greeks, Romans spoke readily of "**barbarians**": in their case, members of the tribal societies that dominated Scandinavia, much of the Germanic world, and the steppes to the east. Some of them—such as the Gauls and the inhabitants of what is now England—proved willing to take up bathing, eating bread, and other Roman habits, along with Roman dress. But many of them—above all the Germanic peoples—seemed impossible to socialize in Roman ways. They clung to their gods, their languages, and their accustomed practices. Romans admired the courage of these "barbarians"

Barbarians A second-century CE sarcophagus depicts two barbarians—identifiable from their long beards and cloaks—surrendering to a group of Roman soldiers.

in battle, as Tacitus explained when he wrote a short treatise about Germania—but not their refusal to engage in commerce or productive work. Over time, the empire's Germanic neighbors would put immense pressure on its structure, opening what proved to be decisive cracks in its defenses.

REVENUES Support for this vast imperial system came from multiple sources. The empire taxed most of its subjects systematically. Indirect taxes were universal: customs duties on trade, a 5 percent inheritance tax, taxes on selling or freeing slaves. Outside Italy, in the first and second centuries CE, direct taxes were also imposed. Periodic censuses established the numbers of inhabitants in particular areas and the distribution of property in them—including slaves and houses as well as land. These served as the basis for a head tax and a property tax, which were paid in coin in the large mercantile cities of the Greek east, but paid in kind in the great agricultural provinces of North Africa and Sicily.

In addition, the emperors themselves contributed to the budget, sometimes—as in the case of Augustus—on an immense scale. During peaceful times, the treasuries of empire and emperor alike grew rich. Tiberius claimed that he saved more than Augustus himself had spent on gifts for citizens and veterans. But Caligula spent what Tiberius had hoarded, and major wars could empty the treasury rapidly. Nerva and Marcus Aurelius both had to sell off palace furniture and other imperial possessions to finance their campaigns. The evidence is fragmentary, but it seems that on the whole, taxes and duties on trade did not seriously damage the imperial economy in its first two centuries.

ROMAN LAW Equally important in constructing and maintaining the authority of the emperors was the legal system that reached its definitive shape in this period. For centuries, Roman lawyers had stated and generalized legal principles. Augustus licensed certain officials to give formal interpretations of legal questions, on his authority as *princeps* (ruler). By the second century CE, emperors treated the law as a central part of their function. The emperor was the source of law, which his edicts and instructions to provincial governors promulgated and clarified. His counselors included legal experts and he himself served officially as the final court of appeals (though these became so numerous by the third century that an assistant had to handle them). Roman law could be harsh, but it also recognized certain vital principles: for example, that one must assume a given person was free in status unless there was clear proof to the contrary. Even in the provinces, where Roman law coexisted with foreign systems—such as the law of the Jews—it was often seen as fair and incorruptible, even by citizens who had been raised by other customs.

THE REIGN OF THE "GOOD EMPERORS" (96–180 CE)

The talented emperors of the Nerva-Antonine line continued, on an even vaster scale, the Augustan program of transforming Rome into a city that spoke of the power of its rulers and inhabitants. Hadrian (r. 117–138 CE), for example, built a new palace on a plot of land almost as large as the city itself. He also designed and built a huge

The Pantheon Hadrian's ambitious transformation of Rome included the rebuilding of the Pantheon, with its vast dome, in 118–125 CE—a great achievement of Roman construction technology.

temple to Venus and Roma in the Forum. And he rebuilt the Pantheon—the enormous temple to all the gods that Augustus's son-in-law Agrippa had raised in 27 BCE. Hadrian equipped it with what was for centuries thereafter the largest dome in the world, a vast coffered expanse with a round window at its summit to admit the rays of the sun. To celebrate his conquest of Dacia, in what is now Romania, Hadrian used as many gladiators in four months of games as Augustus had used in forty years. The enormous structures built in Rome by Trajan and Hadrian, many of which survive, were the greatest civic benefactions that had ever been seen in the Roman world.

Working with the Senate, dozens of whose members served him as military commanders and provincial governors, Hadrian devoted most of his attention to the imperial provinces. Traveling most of the time with a large retinue of soldiers, officials, and technical specialists, he inspected legions, negotiated with both local inhabitants and the empire's neighbors, and expended funds and effort on massive public works. Across the northern expanse of Britain after 122 CE, he built an eighty-mile wall to separate the "barbarians" of Scotland (defeated in battle but impossible to conquer) from the Romans to the south. This ambitious project—with towered gates at intervals of a mile, and sixteen larger forts to protect it—housed a multinational, multi-ethnic force of Roman soldiers who watched their lively frontier for more than 200 years.

Marcus Aurelius's Campaigns Marcus Aurelius erected a monumental column in Rome in 180–195 CE to memorialize his victory in battle against Germanic tribes. This detail shows Roman soldiers beheading Germanic nobles, an undeniable symbol of the emperor's conquest.

A passionate enthusiast for Greece and Greek traditions, Hadrian attended the Eleusinian mysteries more than once and supplied the funds to complete the enormous Temple of Olympian Zeus at Athens.

Like his predecessors, Hadrian found that the person of the emperor was a great source of authority. He spent relatively little time in Rome, but crossed and recrossed the empire from Britain to the frontier of the Parthian Empire, with which he made peace. When necessary, he went to war—as in Judea, where Simeon bar Kokhba led a massive revolt in 132 CE, which Hadrian suppressed only with difficulty and the loss of many soldiers. Still, he held the loyalty of the Roman armies, and when he died he was entombed in the vast mausoleum that he had created for himself on the bank of the Tiber.

Antoninus Pius and Marcus Aurelius smoothed the rough edges of Hadrian's imperial system. Antoninus (r. 138–161 CE) pushed farther north into Scotland, even building a new wall; mended some fences with the Senate; and tried for economies in public expenditure. Marcus Aurelius (r. 161–180 CE), the first emperor to be challenged seriously by barbarians, fought bitter but eventually successful campaigns against peoples from what is now Romania. Eventually he established and fortified the northeastern frontier of the empire. He also spent much time away from Rome, touring the eastern provinces and defending the frontiers.

A SYNTHESIS OF ROMAN AND GREEK TRADITIONS

As the imperial frontiers expanded, the great emperors of the second century CE increasingly saw themselves as representing—even embodying—a synthesis of the Roman and Greek traditions at their best. Devoted to the Roman gods, they maintained both ancient and recent traditions. Hadrian dedicated his Temple of Venus and Roma on April 21, traditionally celebrated as the day of Rome's founding. Marcus Aurelius had his successful campaigns against the barbarians recorded in stone reliefs, as Trajan had, on a monumental column. But they also pledged allegiance to Greek culture with a dedication that some of their predecessors had lacked. Hadrian completed the Temple to Olympian Zeus at Athens, which the Athenian ruler Pisistratus had begun several centuries before. Marcus Aurelius studied and wrote Stoic philosophy, in Greek. His *Meditations* expressed in pregnant, short passages his overwhelming sense of duty, his deep feelings of debt and gratitude to those who had trained him—and his

IMPERIAL ROME

> OTHERS, I AM SURE, WILL FORGE BRONZES THAT LOOK EVEN MORE LIKE BREATHING FLESH, / WILL PULL FACES THAT SEEM ALIVE FROM THE BRONZE, / WILL PLEAD THEIR CASES BETTER, WILL CHART THE MOVEMENTS OF THE SKY / WITH THEIR RODS, AND PREDICT WHEN THE STARS WILL RISE. / YOU, ROMAN, REMEMBER TO RULE THE PEOPLES WITH SUPREME POWER. / THESE WILL BE YOUR ARTS, TO CIVILIZE THE LIFE OF PEACE, / TO SPARE THE DEFEATED AND TO CRUSH THE PROUD.
>
> VIRGIL, *AENEID*

> THE PEOPLE, WHICH USED TO GIVE OUT MILITARY COMMANDS, CONSULSHIPS, LEGIONS AND THE REST, NOW PAYS NO ATTENTION AND EAGERLY DESIRES ONLY TWO THINGS, BREAD AND CIRCUSES.
>
> JUVENAL, *SATIRE 10*

Emperors mobilized extensive resources to build massive public baths, the largest of which could accommodate a few thousand guests. By 52 CE, Rome used 200 million gallons of water a day, much of it supplying public baths for a population of 1 million.

> WHAT WORSE THAN NERO? WHAT BETTER THAN NERO'S BATHS?
>
> MARTIAL, *EPIGRAMS*, BOOK VII

This coin (97 CE) shows Annona, goddess of the grain supply, and Ceres, goddess of agriculture. The grain dole, established in 58 BCE and distributed at the Temple of Ceres, provided free grain for all citizens older than ten in the city of Rome, some 220,000 tons of wheat per year.

The Circus Maximus (first century CE), with a capacity of 250,000 spectators, was the largest site for public games in Rome.

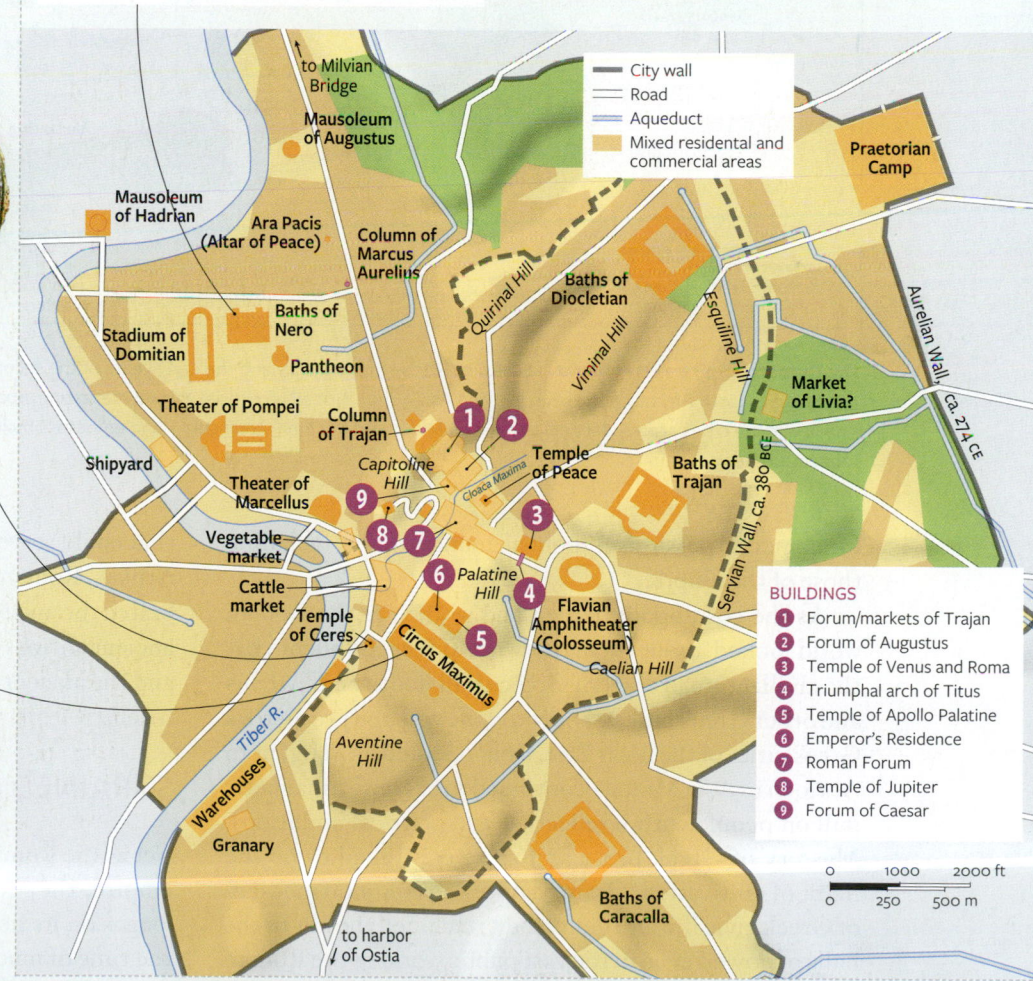

City wall
Road
Aqueduct
Mixed residental and commercial areas

to Milvian Bridge
Mausoleum of Augustus
Mausoleum of Hadrian
Ara Pacis (Altar of Peace)
Column of Marcus Aurelius
Quirinal Hill
Baths of Diocletian
Viminal Hill
Esquiline Hill
Praetorian Camp
Aurelian Wall, ca. 274 CE
Stadium of Domitian
Baths of Nero
Pantheon
Theater of Pompei
Column of Trajan
Capitoline Hill
Cloaca Maxima
Temple of Peace
Market of Livia?
Baths of Trajan
Shipyard
Theater of Marcellus
Vegetable market
Cattle market
Temple of Ceres
Palatine Hill
Flavian Amphitheater (Colosseum)
Caelian Hill
Servian Wall, ca. 380 BCE
Circus Maximus
Tiber R.
Aventine Hill
Warehouses
Granary
to harbor of Ostia
Baths of Caracalla

BUILDINGS
1. Forum/markets of Trajan
2. Forum of Augustus
3. Temple of Venus and Roma
4. Triumphal arch of Titus
5. Temple of Apollo Palatine
6. Emperor's Residence
7. Roman Forum
8. Temple of Jupiter
9. Forum of Caesar

0   1000   2000 ft
0   250   500 m

QUESTIONS FOR ANALYSIS

1. How did the power of the emperor shape the physical city of Rome?
2. How did basic aspects of everyday life in the city depend on Rome's imperial power?
3. How would you assess the opening quotation's comparisons of Rome to other cultures during this period?

155

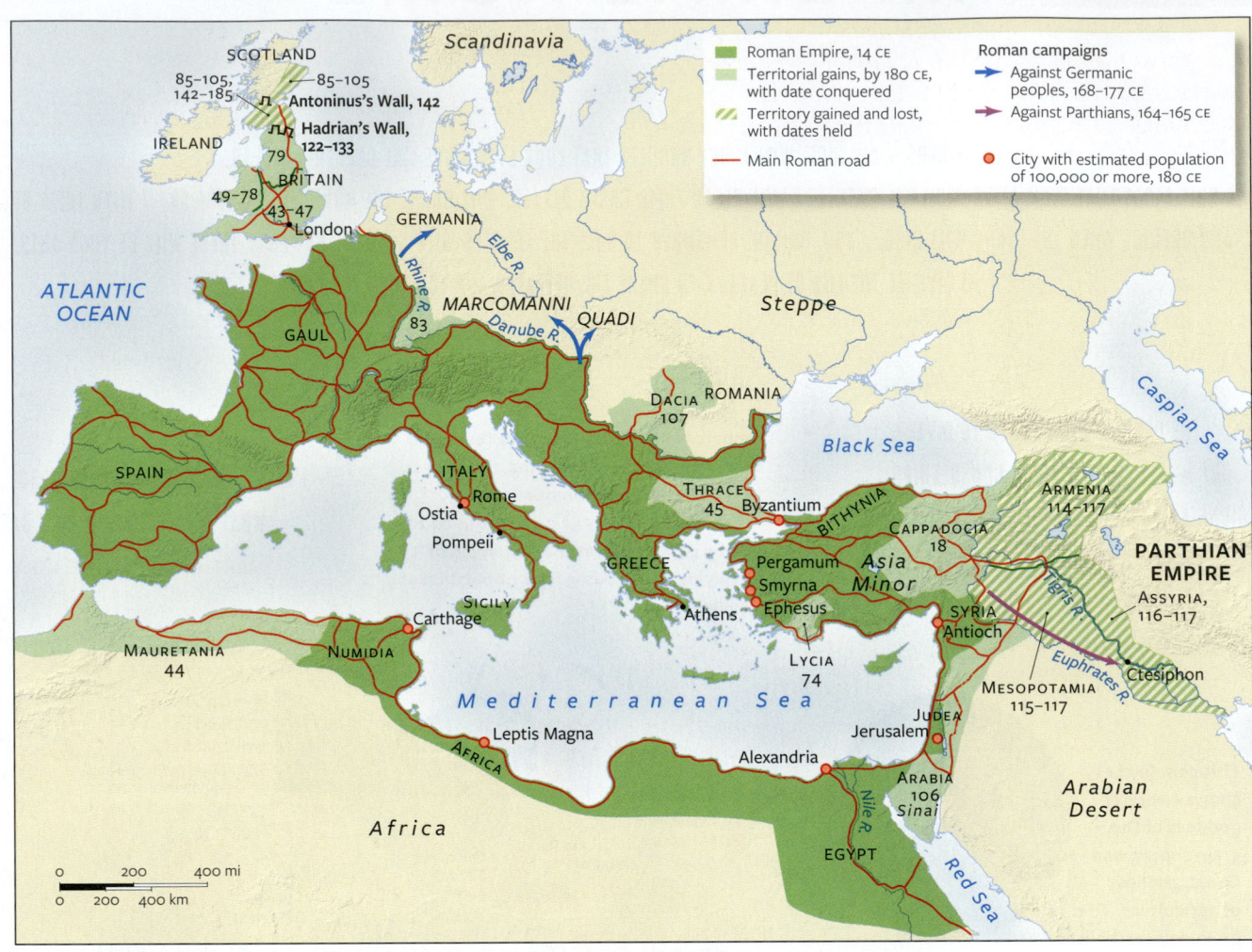

The Roman Empire at Its Height, 14–180 CE In the first century and the early years of the second, the Roman Empire expanded, pushing farther into Britain, North Africa, central Europe, and Asia Minor. Not all territorial gains were lasting. But during the long second-century period of stability, many cities grew—particularly in Asia Minor and the Sinai Peninsula—and emperors built new roads and other infrastructure projects that connected the vast empire.

fundamental pessimism about all human affairs, including those of the empire.

As the cosmopolitan men and women of the Roman world looked about them, they could feel confident that the civilization of ancient Greece still flourished. Athens and other Greek cities—above all, the vast and prosperous Greek cities of the Near East, from Alexandria in Egypt to Antioch in Asia Minor—continued to exercise a magnetic pull on people with intellectual and political ambitions. Mastery of Greek prose and verse continued to be the mark of cultivation. Oratory, once the common medium of Greek civic life and diplomacy, remained the key to the halls of power, even in the vast public world of the Roman Empire. Based on word-by-word imitation of classical Athenian orators such as Demosthenes, the oratory of the second century was a virtuoso exercise in reviving the past

that could serve real political purposes in the present. In Athens, Romans and Greeks also formed clubs that celebrated the ancient gods. And across the Roman world, the ancient shrines continued to make sacrifices to the gods and the ancient oracles to offer messages.

STRAINED BORDERS

Yet as the Romans consolidated their rule over their vast empire, they found themselves confronting new challenges on its borders. In 161 CE the Parthians—rulers at the time of much of Persia—attacked the Roman protectorate of Armenia and Roman territory in Syria, defeating the legions that mustered against them. Marcus Aurelius had convinced the Senate to accept his adopted brother,

Lucius Verus, as co-emperor, on an equal footing with him. Verus marched against the Parthians, transferring legions from the Rhine and Danube borders. He chose his commanders well, and they drove the Parthians out of Syria and invaded Mesopotamia. The Romans signed a peace treaty with the Parthians in 166 CE. In the same year, though, a plague struck one of the armies that had carried out this campaign. It spread rapidly through the Roman armies and eventually drove Marcus Aurelius from Rome. As much as 10 percent of Rome's population died.

The empire had no respite from border attacks and other afflictions. In 168, population pressure from Germanic peoples in Scandinavia forced the Marcomanni and Quadi tribes west across the borders into the empire. Verus died in 169, leaving Marcus Aurelius in sole charge. Faced with an empty treasury and a depleted army, he auctioned the imperial flatware to raise money and recruited brigands and slaves to serve in the army. War with the Marcomanni and Quadi continued until 175, when peace was made, but then broke out again in 177. Recurrences of the plague also hit the Romans hard. Marcus was about to begin yet another campaign when he died in March 180. In some ways, the empire never recovered from this series of strains.

THE JEWS OF IMPERIAL ROME

Yet it was a different set of enemies—the Christians—who would eventually undermine, and transform, the Roman Empire. Christianity was, originally, a Jewish sect. The Jews—some of them settled in what they saw as their divinely promised homeland, Palestine, under rulers indirectly controlled by Rome; others scattered across the world—had created a distinctive and powerful religion. By the end of the first century CE, the Jews of Palestine had fought and lost a disastrous war against the Romans. But they had also created the conditions under which a new, universal religion—Christianity—came into being.

PALESTINE

In the first century CE, there may have been as many as 5 million Jews. History had scattered them everywhere, from Babylon (where a large community flourished, descended from the ancient Judeans who had gone into exile there in the sixth century BCE) to Egypt (where another large community, partly descended from Jewish mercenaries, maintained an immense synagogue in

Jewish Settlements in the Roman Empire, 1st Century CE Millions of Jews lived throughout the Roman Empire, but particularly in Babylon, Egypt, and Palestine, where Jerusalem remained the center of Jewish life and worship. The old walled city surrounded the Hasmonean king Herod's palace, and the enormous Second Temple on the Temple Mount—which Herod rebuilt—towered over everything.

Alexandria). The center of Jewish life and worship, as it had been since the middle of the fifth century BCE, was Jerusalem, the largest city in Palestine. In the second century BCE, the revolt of the Maccabees against the Seleucids had won independence for Palestine, first as a semiautonomous monarchy and then as an independent one, ruled by the Hasmoneans. In 63 BCE, however, the Romans conquered Palestine, turning it into the province of Judea. After decades of troubles, Herod, the son of a Hasmonean official from southern Palestine, was made the king. He married a Hasmonean princess, murdered the last male heir of that dynasty, and embarked on an ambitious career that involved romanizing Palestine as

The Second Temple Found in a first-century CE synagogue near the Sea of Galilee, this large stone block bears iconography that may depict the Second Temple. Classical columns frame a seven-branched lamp, or menorah, and jars of oil like those kept in the Temple's inner chamber.

far as possible. Herod built a spectacular new city on the coast, Caesarea Maritima, planned in the Roman way with an aqueduct, forum, and amphitheater.

TEMPLE AND SYNAGOGUE But Herod also supported the Jewish religion, which he practiced. He reconstructed the enormous **Second Temple**, a wealthy center of learning and ritual in Jerusalem. Here the priests carried out regular prayers and animal sacrifices, officials collected and accounted for tithes, and scribes maintained official texts of the Bible and produced new scrolls. Great baths enabled women to undergo ritual purification. At the national festival of Passover, as many as 400,000 people flooded into the city from Palestine and beyond to take part in the Temple's public rituals. Perhaps only such modern pilgrimage rituals as the mass journeys of Muslims to Mecca every year can give a sense of the scale and drama of these celebrations.

For all its size and wealth, however, the Temple was by no means the Jews' sole religious institution or the dominant one in daily life, and others had a very different tone. Many communities in Palestine, including some Jerusalem neighborhoods—and all of the larger Jewish communities outside it—had synagogues, which were public halls where congregations held meetings, offered public prayers, and studied the Hebrew Bible. In synagogues built after 70 CE, archaeologists have discovered pulpits—evidence that a community member led the service and perhaps preached to the congregation. Unlike the Temple priesthood, the wealthy community members who built

synagogues did not necessarily see it as their job to set off and cleanse separate spaces or to keep them absolutely free from non-Jewish words and practices. Unlike modern Orthodox synagogues, ancient ones do not seem to have divided their congregations by gender. Jews simply met, prayed, and studied—at times using Aramaic, at times Greek. Sometimes their discussions led to new varieties of religious belief and practice.

VARIETIES OF JUDAISM

The Jews themselves exhibited diverse practices and beliefs. Rabbis (teachers) were beginning to formulate new ways of thinking about the requirements of Jewish law, but at this time they seem to have enjoyed limited authority. Judaism itself, after all, was divided into a variety of groups. The relatively wealthy Sadducees, a small group, saw the Bible as the sole religious authority and insisted that no human being had the right to interpret the text in any way. Sadducees served in important Temple offices, and they saw the Temple and its sacrifices as the core of religious life.

More numerous than the Sadducees—and more influential, in the long term—were the **Pharisees**. The Pharisees saw the observance of the Law—the maintenance of purity that set Jews apart as the people of a single, unique God—as central to Judaism. They formed associations whose members ate together to ensure that all the food they consumed met the highest standards of purity. But the Pharisees found that the text of the Hebrew Bible was too brief to tell them exactly what these standards required. Instead, they learned to interpret the scriptures and devised rules for doing so properly. The Pharisees, for example, extended the biblical prohibition against eating a calf boiled in its mother's milk into a firm rule against ever mixing meat and dairy products in a single meal—the basis of the system of kosher foods that many Jews still follow.

Another group, the Essenes, developed codes of diet and conduct even stricter than those of the Pharisees. Repelled by what they saw as the corruption of the Jerusalem Temple, they founded their own communities, which only those who committed themselves to their beliefs and practices were allowed to join. Some lived in cities, others withdrew into the Palestinian desert. Eating only vegetables prepared by their community's strict codes, using latrines far outside the perimeter of the inhabited space, refraining from sexual intercourse, and praying regularly by their own calendar, the Essenes dedicated themselves to the pursuit of purity and holiness. Those who could not sustain the discipline that the community demanded were excluded from it. Some starved, unable to bring themselves to eat foods not prepared by Essenes.

Groups like this one—coherent, strictly regulated, walled off from normal society—often teach the rejection of existing authorities in both politics and religion. The Essenes argued that the Temple and the ruling house of Herod had become so corrupt that the existing order would soon be overthrown. Only what one text called the "War of the Sons of Light against the Sons of Darkness" could restore righteousness. Drawing on the prophets of the Hebrew Bible, they awaited the end, not rebelling but praying.

OTHER JEWISH GROUPS

The Sicariots ("assassins," so called because they carried small daggers known as *sicae*) and Zealots took a militant political position. Convinced that Roman rule over Palestine represented, as the rule of Alexander's successors had, a violation of the divine order, they called for armed resistance and revolution. Meanwhile other prophets, especially in Galilee, north of Jerusalem, preached the coming of a new order, and magicians claimed their own kind of supernatural power, drawn not from divine help but from their sovereign abilities to command demons and transform the order of nature.

In Palestine as well as across the Roman Empire and beyond, finally, there were "Hellenists"—Jews who spoke Greek and used the language in their worship. No language barrier separated Hellenized Jews from their neighbors. They maintained a rich ritual life and an attractive set of communal institutions. Their scriptures offered a powerful account of the cosmos and history and a profound ethical literature. Though many pagans continued to mock the Jews for their stubborn insistence on parochial customs such as circumcising male babies, and their refusal to eat pork or fight on Saturdays, others found Jewish religion and custom magnetically attractive. Thousands converted or became "God-fearers"—sympathizers who attended synagogue services or even participated in communal institutions without formally converting to Judaism. Sometimes these sympathizers were wealthy and enjoyed prestigious positions as benefactors of the synagogues that they frequented.

In the decades around the beginning of the Christian era, Judaism was complicated and full of conflicts, expansive and vital. It was in this world—in a Palestine ruled by Rome, most of whose inhabitants practiced what claimed

to be a universal religion—that the tiny Jesus movement began to grow into a new religion.

THE LIFE AND DEATH OF JESUS

Jesus, whose life and death inspired Christianity, was born in Bethlehem, a city not far from Jerusalem, a few years before the beginning of the Common Era. He was a Jew, not only by birth but by upbringing and lifelong practice. Recognized early for his wisdom, he taught by giving direct advice and by offering parables (stories with a moral). According to those who knew him, he also performed wonders: at different times he healed the sick, raised the dead, and cast out the demons that haunted many of his contemporaries. So far, Jesus did not stand out. Other men of power—such as Honi the Circle-Drawer, a wise man who conjured rain from the skies when the sun baked the fertile soil of Galilee—walked the roads and villages where Jesus spent his early life. Other preachers, such as John the Baptist, urged men and women to forsake their sins and repent.

A RADICAL MESSAGE

Over time, however, Jesus became more radical than these other preachers of righteousness—even more radical than other dissidents among the Jews. Like the Essenes, he taught that the end of time was approaching rapidly, that the men and women alive in his own time would witness the final struggle between good and evil. Like them, too, he formed a small community of his own, one made up of men and women who acknowledged his spiritual power and followed him as disciples—though unlike the Essenes, his followers did not immediately establish settlements. They continued to live as other Jews of the time did: they followed the elaborate rules codified in the Law, which had become central to Jewish life after the return from the Babylonian exile, and which offered detailed rules for most aspects of life. But Jesus demanded more of them, much more. He forbade them to divorce their spouses, told them never to use violence against others, and urged them to give up their own families and follow him.

CONFRONTING AUTHORITY Jesus evidently could not make his peace with the priests of the Second Temple. He came to believe that he was the Messiah—the anointed king whose coming the Hebrew prophets had predicted

Jesus's Origins One of many sacred images from a third-century CE catacomb in Rome used for Christian burials, this mural of Christ as a shepherd is one of the earliest artistic portrayals of Jesus.

and whose reign would bring history to its conclusion. A central reason why this change was necessary, for Jesus, was that the Temple itself was corrupt. One spring, probably around 33 CE, he went to Jerusalem, as did thousands of others, for the great Passover ceremony—but in his case, also with the intention of confronting the religious authorities. In the immense forecourt of the Temple, Jesus denounced and attacked the moneychangers who helped pilgrims from abroad make their contributions to the priests. He also seems to have threatened the Temple itself with destruction at God's hands. Arrested and tried by the Romans—for reasons that historical sources do not directly state—he was executed in the Roman manner, by crucifixion.

EXECUTION As he hung on the cross dying, Jesus seems to have thought that he had failed: he cried out, "Lord, lord, why have you forsaken me?" But on the third day after his death, when his disciples came to claim his body—so they reported—it had vanished from the tomb. Soon Jesus appeared to many of them, apparently alive, inviting those who doubted his resurrection to touch his wounds. The terror and misery caused by his death made way, among his relatives and disciples, for new emotions: joy, excitement, and renewed commitment to his cause.

HISTORICAL QUESTIONS

Even this brief outline of Jesus's story—one based on generations of scholarly effort to analyze all the sources that survive in the same way that a historian would analyze any other source—is debatable at every point. All of our sources—the narratives that became the four **gospels** (literally "good news") in the **New Testament**, other rival gospels, the short and problematic account in the work of the Jewish historian Josephus (37–100 CE)—were written decades after Jesus's time. Their authors depended on earlier written accounts, which do not survive. In normal circumstances, eyewitness testimony could not have lasted unchanged until the gospels were written. The particular traditions about Jesus that went into the gospels were altered as they were retold and first written down, and each of the authors of the gospels selected and edited his material in a unique way.

When the gospels disagree, as they often do, and when they all diverge from what is known from other sources, no other historical authority can give certain guidance. Scholars disagree, accordingly, on whether Jesus was tried by the Jews or by the Romans; on the role played by Pontius Pilate, the Roman governor, in Jesus's condemnation and execution; on whether Jesus saw himself as an anointed human king of the Jews, a son of God, or a Jewish prophet like those of the Old Testament; and on whether any of these events actually took place.

THE JESUS MOVEMENT

It is certain, however, that after Jesus's death he became the beloved founder of a larger movement within the Jewish world—one led by his brother James and others in Jerusalem. His followers clearly believed that he had been chosen by God to transform the world. And when the heavens did not open up and the Temple did not fall after his death (as Jesus had warned would happen), they reinterpreted his call for change as the demand to begin a mission.

CHRISTIANS Some of Jesus's immediate followers and others who had not known him in the flesh began to preach in his name. By the late 60s CE, they would be known as "Christians"—followers of Christ, a word that means "the anointed one." With that choice of term they claimed divine status for Jesus. Like him, they healed the sick, raised the dead, and fed the hungry, and these wonders established their charisma and authority. Soon a number of Jews from different sects—and some non-Jews (known as Gentiles), including a few Roman "God-fearers"—joined the movement. Small congregations formed, meeting to celebrate the common meal—to eat bread and drink wine—in his memory. Before long they began to encounter opposition, and then persecution, from other Jews. Christian missionaries were denounced and stoned. At the same time, they began to debate certain issues: for example, the role of non-Jewish converts within the new movement. Should they be required to follow the Jewish law? Or could they simply accept Jesus and his teachings? After Jesus's death, the movement was tiny—so tiny that its growth seems to have stirred no discernible interest among the Roman authorities, ever alert for any signs of subversive meetings. How did this tiny seed take root?

A SPIRITUAL REVOLUTION

Historians no longer invoke the power of miracles to explain events in human history. But it is not irrational to think that the triumph of Christ over Rome had something miraculous about it. It was, in fact, the culmination of a unique and seemingly inexplicable sequence of events—a spiritual revolution that unfolded over the last two centuries before and the first three centuries of the Common Era.

A generation or two ago, historians argued that Christianity, like other revolutionary movements, appealed chiefly to outsiders caught in tumultuous social and economic change. In fact, however, Christianity appealed almost from the beginning to a strikingly wide range of individuals. And the church spread through the Roman Empire not only in the troubled first-century times of Nero and his immediate successors, but also in the prosperous and peaceful second century—the empire's high point of power and wealth. To find the sources of Christianity's strength, we must look within. Its success was the result of a shift in the way men and women understood the universe, and its past and its immediate future—and in the ways they hoped to find their own paths through the dark labyrinth of life on earth to a higher existence elsewhere.

EARLY CHRISTIANITY

In the fourth decade of the first century CE, the Christian movement underwent its first radical transformation—a world-shattering change that took place in the realm of the spirit and was the work, to a great extent, of one person. Saul, a Roman citizen and educated Jew who had helped to persecute the Christians, became one of them, changing his name to **Paul**. Soon he became a leader, one who unhesitatingly took positions on the great questions of organization and theology on which, like so many jagged rocks, the small Christian vessel seemed likely to founder. Paul's official letters to other Christians and Christian congregations are preserved in the New Testament, along with a number of letters that scholars agree he did not write. Paul's letters are the earliest Christian texts, older than the gospel retellings of the life of Jesus. The early history of the church can be traced in them and in the book of Acts, the New Testament book that describes the spread of Christianity after the death of Jesus.

THE CONVERSION OF PAUL

Saul was born in Tarsus, a bustling city near the Mediterranean coast of what is now southern Turkey. A mercantile center, Tarsus lay at the intersection of many trade routes, and it had a mixed and cosmopolitan population. Saul himself was a Pharisee. According to the book of Acts, Saul studied the Jewish law not only in his native city but also in Jerusalem. By his own account, he was "a Hebrew of Hebrews," passionately loyal to Jewish tradition, and worked against the first Christians whenever he encountered them.

Then one day, as Saul and his companions traveled to Damascus, they saw a brilliant light. Saul also heard a voice say: "Saul, Saul, why do you persecute me?" When Saul asked for the identity of the being who addressed him just as God had addressed the ancient Hebrew prophets, he learned that Jesus himself was speaking. Stunned by the experience and struck blind for three days, Saul was cared for by Ananias, a Syrian Christian who had also had a direct revelation. Ananias healed Saul by laying hands on him, and informed Saul of his mission as the prophet of Christianity. The bitter defender of Judaism suddenly became Paul, an eager, eloquent missionary who crossed and recrossed the entire Mediterranean world, converting many men and women to Christianity and helping the new churches overcome the problems they encountered.

A change of heart as radical as it was unexpected, the conversion of Paul is one of the exemplary dramas of Western history. For centuries, writers and painters have portrayed the moment of transformation—Saul, prone on the dusty Syrian road, struggling with his divinely assigned mission—as a metaphor for true conversion to any faith. Many Christians in much later times—one famous example is Martin Luther, the religious reformer who in 1517 began the Reformation—have seen Paul's conversion as the standard by which all decisions to join the Christian church should be measured.

PAUL AND THE TENETS OF EARLY CHRISTIANITY

Jesus's followers, as we have seen, believed that Jesus had come back to life and appeared to them. Paul never met Jesus in the flesh, but he understood his own conversion in the same terms. He was certain that he had encountered a living Jesus and that the meeting had changed him completely. Again and again, in his magnificent first letter to the Christian community in the Greek city of Corinth—a church Paul himself founded—he insisted that Jesus had literally risen from the dead and that his resurrection was the central guarantee of the truth of Christianity. The promise of eternal life, verified by Jesus's return, made clear, for Paul, that the Christian revelation was true.

What did it mean, then, to follow Jesus, the son of God? Must his followers also practice Judaism? Many of them—especially Jesus's brother James, who developed the church of Jerusalem—thought so. Paul never lost his respect for the Jewish law, which had provided a canon of upright conduct and belief for the Jews over the centuries. He seems to have remained an observant Jew himself. But when he saw the disorder and confusion caused in early Christian communities by those who insisted that the Jewish law continued to bind them—and that horrified

others who came to Jesus from the pagan world—he began to believe that those who accepted the new faith from the outside had no obligation to follow the Jewish rules of diet, conduct, and rest. After all, those rules, as the prophets and Jesus had both taught, were made by human beings, not for them.

Paul developed a powerful new theological doctrine to justify this argument, and he maintained it in the teeth of opposition from the family of Jesus himself. Sin, in traditional Judaism, required atonement, and atonement in turn required sacrifice. It was by making offerings that the Jews, as the Five Books of Moses explained, had reconciled themselves to God after they slipped back into idol worship on their way from Egypt to the promised land. In fact, Judaism revolved as much around ways to make amends as it did around obedience to positive commands. The willingness to sacrifice what was dearest to one, moreover, was the highest proof of one's love—as the biblical patriarch Abraham showed when he made clear, in the book of Genesis, that he would sacrifice his son Isaac at God's command.

Jesus, Paul now argued, had been the son of God—not just an anointed king, but a divine being. The human race, God saw, had become so corrupt, had committed so many sins, that it could never reconcile itself with him through ritual or prayer. He decided, accordingly, to sacrifice his only son and, by doing so, to make his son atone for the sins of the human race. All that one needed for salvation, now that this epoch-making event had taken place, was to have faith in Jesus and his sacrifice. Any non-Jew who had faith would be saved and had no need to follow Jewish laws or perform Jewish rituals. Any Jew could be saved as well, so long as that individual shared the faith.

A NEW MESSAGE, A NEW MEDIUM

This message proved sharply controversial, and Paul embraced the controversy. He argued with Jewish Christians who insisted on the necessity of following the Law, and with Christians who tried to combine the new teachings with such traditional practices as magic and astrology. And he argued with those who did not show enough respect for the Jewish law and its crucial role in the drama of human salvation—to teach people that they were sinners. Jesus had said that he came bringing not peace but a sword, and Paul repeatedly confronted, and overcame, opposition. He made himself an extraordinarily effective organizer and missionary, in perpetual motion around

Peter and Paul A second-century CE sarcophagus from the Roman Christian catacombs depicts Paul, the church's first leader; and Peter, one of Jesus's disciples. The imagery also includes the Greek letters *xi* and *rho*, the first two letters of "Christ."

People of the Book Christians were early adopters of the codex, which resembles the modern book. This second-century CE Greek-language manuscript, the oldest known copy of the Gospel of John, is written on separate, stacked sheets of papyrus instead of on a long, continuous scroll.

SPREADING THE MESSAGE: THE HOUSE CHURCHES

Paul wove his way up and down the trade routes of the eastern Roman Empire, moving from city to city in Asia Minor, Syria, Palestine, Greece, and Italy. He worked intensively with groups of those he called the Brothers—fellow believers. When Paul reached a new city, he began by preaching Jesus's message in the synagogue. Jewish responses were often harsh: "Five times," he told the Corinthians, "I have had forty lashes less one [thirty-nine blows of the whip] from the Jews. Three times I was beaten with rods; once I was stoned." At Damascus, he had to have himself lowered down the city wall in a basket to escape Jewish opponents. Evidently, then, Paul began each mission within the Jewish world from which he came, only to be expelled from it.

Yet the cities that Paul knew also harbored associations the cities of Asia Minor and beyond. After his arrest, he appealed, as a Roman citizen could, to the emperor, and traveled to Rome and elsewhere before he met his eventual martyr's death. Even after he died, his writings carried on his arguments with opponents on all sides.

Christians very soon began to copy Paul's work, and other texts, in a new kind of book—not rolls of vellum or papyrus, of the sort that had been used for centuries, but codices. The Romans had traditionally strung together wooden tablets and written on them. Soon they began to fold parchment and papyrus, their two forms of paper, and make books of the form we still use. Protected with bindings of wood and leather, codices could hold more content than scrolls and were easier to refer to if a debate sprang up. Such books were in use by the end of the first century, when the poet Martial described them: "If you want to have my books with you at all times on a long trip, buy the ones with small pages made of parchment." Paul's little books—which explained how Jesus had come to complete the historical experience of the Jews—and other texts began to make Christians, too, a people of the book.

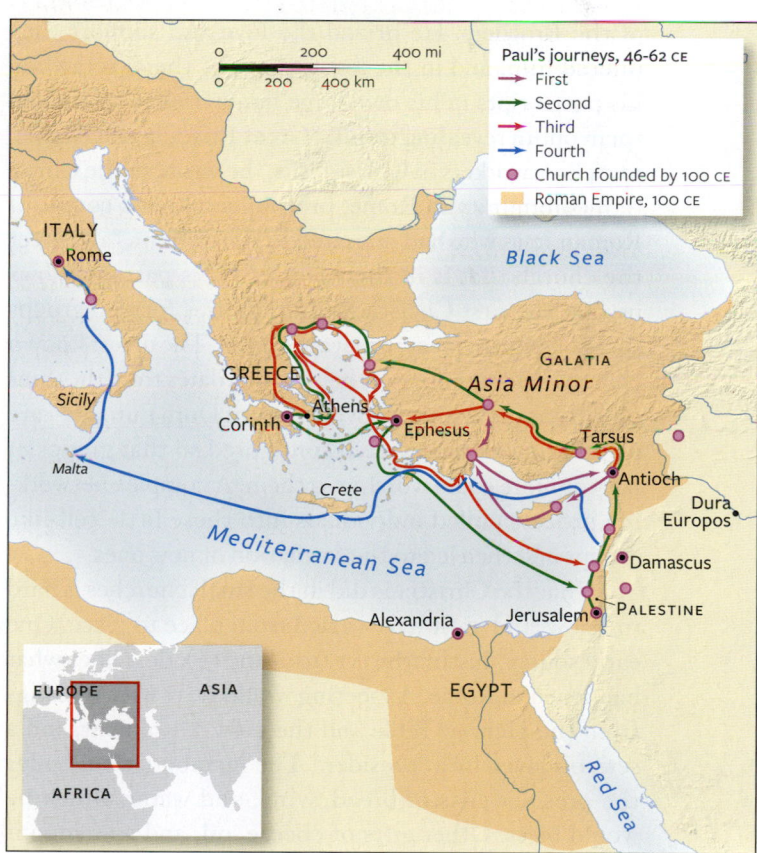

Paul's Travels through the Eastern Roman Empire, 46–62 CE After Paul converted to Christianity, he traveled repeatedly on the Mediterranean trade routes to spread its tenets. At first his journeys did not take him far from his native Tarsus, but later he went as far as Rome. He visited the Christian communities in the cities he passed through, and founded churches, such as the one at Corinth, himself.

An Early Church The house-turned-church at Dura Europos in present-day Syria, the earliest known church building, dates from 235 CE. The frescoes in its meeting room are probably the oldest existing Christian paintings. This one depicts Christ as a shepherd (on the left), accompanied by his flock.

of the Brothers. He prized the love and support they offered him, and in the letters he sent them, scrawling his postscripts in his own large handwriting, he singled them out in revealing terms: "Greet Priscilla and Aquila, my fellow workers in Christ Jesus," he wrote to the Christian community in Rome, praising a married couple of Roman Jews who had migrated to Asia Minor, "and greet the church that is in their house." This passage shows us that the first Christian communities formed groups small enough to meet in private homes. The oldest known church buildings—one of them, which dates from the third century, is in the ancient Syrian city of Dura Europos—are private houses that were reconfigured so that groups of fifty or more could worship in them. A complex networking process pulled individuals into these little cell-like groups and then led to the formation of new ones.

What the Christians did in the small churches is hard to know, and must have varied from place to place. One early source, Justin Martyr (100–165 CE), describes what happened in Rome. A meeting would start with readings from the Hebrew Bible and the New Testament, and a sermon given by a "presider." The members would offer the presider gifts of bread, wine, and water, which he would bless. Other gifts of cheese, oil, and wine might also be blessed. Then the gifts would be distributed to those present, and deacons would take them to those who could not come. It was a simple service, with very little set ritual or formal prayer, and it included the offering of the Eucharist—the holy meal of bread and wine at which Christians recalled the sacrifice of their savior by partaking, spiritually, of his body and blood.

EARLY CHRISTIAN SOCIETY

Paul's travels on the trade routes took him to cities of very different kinds. In Greece, he went from Athens, still grand and rich, where he found no footing, to Corinth, which the Romans had destroyed in 146 BCE. Julius Caesar had recently reestablished the city, and in this rapidly changing society Paul seems to have found many who were eager to hear his message about Jesus. The men and women who joined these early Christian communities, some of whom Paul identified by their callings, belonged to different social levels. Paul himself earned his living by making tents. This was a craft that he could pursue as he moved from city to city, since it required only skilled hands, a curved needle, and a few other tools. Many of those to whom he preached and with whom he worked also practiced modest crafts. But many of the Brothers to whom he sent greetings by name in his letters to the Romans and Corinthians were of higher social standing. Crispus, for example, whom Paul baptized at Corinth, had been the "ruler" of a synagogue—a wealthy man, entrusted by the congregation with responsibility for the upkeep of the building. Others held positions as local officials or engaged in what may have been quite substantial businesses. Some of them owned slaves.

What seems most striking about the individuals Paul singled out for greeting is the variety of their origins and fortunes. They included Jews like Paul, but also Hellenist Jews and non-Jewish God-fearers like the Roman centurion Cornelius, who is mentioned in the book of Acts. "There is neither Jew nor Greek," Paul told the Brothers of Galatia in central Asia Minor, "there is neither slave

The Eucharist From the Greek word for "thanksgiving," the Eucharistic meal was part of the ritual of early Christian churches. One of the first representations of the Eucharist is this early-third-century CE mural from the Roman catacombs. It shows men and women sitting together at a table to share the ceremonial bread and wine.

THE CHRISTIAN CATACOMBS

The proper burial of its members was an important function of the early Christian community. Since only Roman aristocrats could be buried in the city of Rome, Christian leaders arranged with Roman officials to bury their dead in tunnels constructed in the soft volcanic rock beneath the city. Beginning at the end of the second century, the Christian catacombs spread over some sixty-eight square miles and eventually housed almost a million burials.

The frescoes on the walls of the catacombs, which may have been indicators of the wealth or social status of the dead, depict episodes in the life of Jesus and the narratives of the New Testament. This wall painting shows a miracle in which a suffering young woman is healed by merely touching Jesus's clothing. As Jesus passes, she reaches out to catch a trailing thread of his simple white cloak, similar in appearance to her own. He then turns and blesses her with his right hand. Jesus appears as a youthful, clean-shaven, and compassionate figure.

Recent scholarship contends that Christians gathered in the catacombs to eat meals, worship, and celebrate Mass among their departed. The scenes depicted in the frescoes provide important evidence about the customs and beliefs of the young church.

QUESTIONS FOR ANALYSIS

1. How would an image like this have helped in the spread of Christianity?
2. What significance do you see in the similarities between these two figures?
3. What does the image of the woman suggest about women's status in the early church?

Women in the Church Paul's letters revealed that women numbered among the leaders of the early Christian church. Their importance was reflected in religious imagery, such as this fourth-century CE wall painting from the Roman catacombs. It illustrates a story from the Gospel of John in which a Samaritan woman gives Jesus a drink from a well, even though the Samaritans were traditional enemies of the Jews.

nor free, there is neither male nor female: for you are all one in Christ Jesus." Paul's letters show that he believed this passionately, and that the early church corresponded in many ways to his idealistic vision of an all-embracing spiritual community.

Women as well as men actively supported the movement. When Paul wrote to the Romans, he thanked a fair number of men by name for their help. But he showed equal gratitude and affection for Priscilla, who, with her husband Aquila, had risked her life to save him, and "Mary, who has done much work among you." Most striking of all are his warm words for Phoebe, "a deacon of the church at Cenchreae" (the eastern port of Corinth). Paul urged the Romans to "receive her in the Lord in a manner worthy of the saints, and help her in whatever she may need from you, for she has supported many, including me." Evidently, women played a very active part in the first years of the Christian movement.

And when Paul sent greetings to "those of the household of Aristobulus" and "those of the household of Narcissus," he was offering fellowship—not by name, and less warmly than he offered it to free men and women—to the domestic slaves who shared the religion of their Christian masters and mistresses. At the beginning of his first letter to the Corinthians, Paul noted that "not many of you were wise according to the flesh, not many were powerful, not many were of noble birth." As usual, he chose his words with care, to describe a loose set of congregations whose members could be found at all points on the social and cultural ladders of the time.

IMPROVISATION AND ORDER

As Paul moved from city to city and from synagogue to house church, he confronted a kaleidoscopic world of beliefs and practices, one in which even what later came to be seen as basic Christian ideas and institutions had not yet crystallized. His own first letter to the Corinthians describes the general order of services: "When you come together, each of you has a psalm, a lesson, a tongue, a revelation, an interpretation"—a varied, flexible, and unpredictable ritual. With complete acceptance, Paul notes that members of the congregation might speak in tongues—that is, give testimony in strange languages unknown to them or anyone else, a phenomenon still widespread today in evangelical Christianity. He cautions the Corinthians only that they should restrict the number of these testimonies in any given service, and reserve time for precise discussion of or quiet meditation on their meaning.

Whereas Judaism emphasized tradition, as embodied in what had become a fairly set canon of sacred books that were read and interpreted in the synagogue, the new house churches of the Brothers rang with improvisations and hummed with the silence that accompanies deep thought. A modern Quaker meeting may give some idea of the tone and quality of their services. No wonder that these lively churches, which offered fellowship to women and slaves, spread so rapidly throughout the empire.

In time, Paul and other leaders decided that they must formulate clearer rules to maintain order and discipline in the new church. Paul explained to the Corinthians that although it was important to have Christians who spoke in tongues, other offices and gifts mattered as well. Christians needed prophets to tell of the future, deacons to oversee community funds, and apostles to preach. Gradually, Christian worship took a coherent shape, centering on the Eucharist.

Paul himself clearly respected female colleagues—as we have seen in his support for Phoebe, a female deacon. Yet his first letter to the Corinthians demanded that women cease playing a public role in Christian services: "The women should be silent in the churches. For they are not permitted to speak, but to be subordinate, as the law also says. If they want to learn something, let them ask their own husbands at home. For it is shameful for women to speak in church." It is possible that Paul decided that women must keep silent—but more likely that a later writer, seeking as Paul had to impose order, inserted these words. Slowly, the church was developing a spiritual hierarchy.

ROME'S EARLY RESPONSES

As pagans became more aware of the existence of the Christians, they also grew more suspicious about the Christians' secret meetings, normally held at night, and the barbarous deeds that were rumored to be carried out in them. Wild accusations flew. Pagans whispered that Christians met, for example, to devour the flesh of babies and engage in promiscuous sex.

When in 64 CE the city of Rome suffered a devastating fire, which destroyed three of its fourteen districts completely and badly damaged seven more, the emperor Nero blamed the Christians. Many of them were put to death—some in a circus (an arena for sports and spectacles), wrapped in bloody animal skins and torn apart by wild beasts, and others nailed to crosses and set on fire. Tacitus (d. after 117 CE), the great historian of Rome who tells us this, also notes that many onlookers began to feel sympathy for the Christians who suffered so terribly.

Similar accusations against the Christians reached the emperor Trajan in the second century CE. Pliny the Younger, his official in Bithynia, a rich and strategically important province in northern Asia Minor, was puzzled by the apparent contradiction between the unpleasant but harmless rituals that the Christians actually performed and the savage deeds attributed to them. He asked his emperor for advice on how to treat the denunciations. Trajan replied that though he should not seek out individual Christians and should discourage anonymous denunciations, he should certainly punish zealous Christians with death. Although most Christians lived in relative personal safety much of the time, they often found themselves accused of overturning traditional beliefs and engaging in barbarous conduct. The accusations were hard to bear and harder to defend oneself against in a conservative society.

NEW SCRIPTURES

The last decades of the first century witnessed radical changes in the situation of both Jews and Christians. A Jewish rebellion against Rome in Palestine resulted in a disastrous defeat—including the destruction in 70 CE of the Second Temple, which Jesus had prophesied. Christians inside and outside Palestine responded to these events, drawing up accounts of the life of Jesus and other books that contrasted their traditions, beliefs, and practices with those of the Jews. These became, with Paul's writings, the core of their own new Bible.

THE JEWISH WAR (66–73 CE)

What gave the Christian movement its final push toward self-definition was a series of transformative events in the history of the Jews. In 66 CE, the Zealots, a faction of Jews in Jerusalem advocating rebellion against the Romans, slaughtered several hundred soldiers and drove out the Roman proconsul. Nero assigned the general Vespasian—later to be emperor himself—the task of conquering Palestine. The Jews mounted such powerful resistance that the Romans needed some years to conquer Jerusalem, which fell in 70 to Titus, Vespasian's successor in command. The Romans destroyed the Second Temple and carried away its great seven-branched candelabra, which they later paraded in triumph through the streets of Rome. Pockets of Jewish resistance elsewhere were eventually wiped out; at the rocky citadel of Masada, the Jewish garrison committed mass suicide when it could no longer resist. By 73, however, the Romans had completely defeated the Jews.

The consequences of this war—and the later outbreaks that followed it—were many. Jewish religious authorities lost their taste for religious war. The Sadducees and Essenes gradually disappeared. The Pharisees, at first few in number, survived to become the leaders of a new kind of Jewish life in which there was no Temple, the synagogue took its place as the center of Jewish communities, and the rabbis became the chief interpreters of the Law. As to the Jews more generally, they lost their independence in what they saw as their native land. Though they remained

Spoils of the Second Temple A relief on the Arch of Titus in Rome (82 CE) records the fall of Jerusalem and the destruction of the Second Temple in 70 CE. Here, Roman conquerors carry away spoils from the city, including the golden menorah that was lit every night in the Second Temple.

ROMAN POLICY ON CHRISTIANS: MEMO TO AN EMPEROR

When Christianity emerged in the Roman Empire in the first century CE, it aroused the suspicion of emperors and officials. Though Christians were often blamed for fires and natural disasters, the empire varied in its responses to those accused of practicing the new religion.

This exchange of letters between Emperor Trajan and Pliny the Younger, governor of the Roman province of Bithynia from 111 to 113, conveys the unsettled nature of Roman policy toward the early Christians. In the first letter, Pliny anxiously asks whether his various actions toward Christians have been proper in the emperor's opinion. Trajan's response, no doubt to Pliny's great relief, approves of his decisions. The emperor also stresses that former Christians who repent should be spared, and that anonymous accusations are improper.

Letter of Pliny the Younger to Emperor Trajan

Pliny's letter on the Christians (112 CE) was one of dozens he wrote to Trajan, describing matters ranging from the upkeep of aqueducts and theaters to public celebrations of the emperor's rule.

It is my normal practice, my lord, whenever I am not sure how to deal with a matter, to refer it to you. For who could be better to guide me when I delay or to instruct me in my ignorance? I have never taken part in the trials of Christians. Accordingly, I do not know what is normally investigated, or punished, and how far. I have also been uncertain whether any distinction should be made because of age, or whether the young should be distinguished from those who are fully grown; whether those who repent should be pardoned, or if it does not help a man, once he has been a Christian, to stop being one; whether the name Christian itself deserves punishment, if no crimes come with it, or the crimes that belong to the name. Meanwhile, in the cases when Christians were brought before me, I acted in the following way. I asked them formally if they were Christians. If they confessed, I asked them again and a third time, and threatened punishment. If they persisted, I ordered their execution. For I did not doubt that, whatever they might confess, obstinacy and unbending stubbornness deserve punishment.... An anonymous pamphlet was published, which contained many names. I thought that those who denied that they were or had been Christians, and at my dictation venerated the gods and worshipped your image, which I had ordered to be brought here with the statues of the divinities, with incense and wine, and cursed Christ—none of which those are truly Christians can be coerced into doing—should be released. Others whom the informer named said that they were Christians and then denied it. They said they had been but had ceased, some three years before, some many years, some even twenty years. All of them also worshipped your image and the statues of the gods and cursed Christ. They claimed that the sum total of their guilt or error had consisted in this: that they had regularly assembled on a particular day, before dawn, and sung responsively a hymn to Christ, and bound themselves by an oath, not to commit some crime, but not to commit fraud or theft or adultery, lest they break their word or refuse to repay their deposit when called upon to do so. After doing this it had been their custom to depart, and then to come together again to take food, but ordinary, innocent food. And they claimed that they had ceased to do this after my edict, by which, following your commands, I had forbidden associations. Therefore I considered it all the more necessary to find out the truth from two maids, who were called deaconesses, by torture. All I found was a wicked and wild superstition. Therefore I postponed the trial and immediately consulted you. It seemed worthwhile to consult you about the matter, because of the large number of those at risk. For many people of all ages, of all ranks and of both sexes are being, and will be, put in danger. And the plague of this superstition has spread not only through the cities, but also through towns and fields, and it seems possible that it can be stopped. For it is clear that the temples, which had almost been deserted, have begun to be frequented, and that the established rituals, which had ceased, are being performed again, and that the meat of sacrificial victims, for which hardly any buyers could be found, is coming from all sides. From this it is easy to grasp how many people may be freed from error, if there is some possibility of repentance.

Letter of Emperor Trajan to Pliny the Younger

Trajan was one of the conscientious, hard-working rulers of the Nerva-Antonine line. He governed effectively with his officials in the provinces, as this letter from 112 CE demonstrates.

You followed exactly the right procedure, my dear Pliny, in dealing with the cases of those who were denounced to you as Christians. For it is not possible to lay down any absolute, general rule. One should not go looking for them. If they are denounced and accused, they should be punished—with the proviso that anyone who denies he is a Christian and demonstrates that clearly, by worshipping our gods, should receive pardon because of his repentance even if he came under suspicion in the past. But anonymous denunciations should play no part in a prosecution. For this is a terrible precedent and does not fit our times.

QUESTIONS FOR ANALYSIS

1. Why does Pliny give alleged Christians several chances to reject their faith?
2. According to Trajan, under what circumstances should suspected Christians be punished?
3. How do these letters convey the unsettled policy of Rome toward the early Christians?

Sources: Translations by Anthony Grafton.

more numerous in the diaspora—the world of Jews scattered from East Asia to Gaul and Britain—their interest in the conversion of others died away. Jewish religious life became, as it has been ever since, an effort to live a virtuous and holy life in the absence of the Temple and—until recently—a homeland.

Above all, the consequences of the Jewish revolt against Rome proved dramatic for the Christians. Suddenly, the vast changes that Jesus had predicted seemed to have taken place. The Temple lay in ruins as he had said it would, its priests dead or scattered. In the decades after the Jewish war, Christians began to write down the first narratives of Jesus's teachings and life. As they did so, they redefined their Messiah. Collections of sayings attributed to Jesus were set into contexts in his life. At some time before 100 CE, the **gospels** took shape: accounts of Jesus's life, ascribed to many different writers. Four of them, which bore the names of Matthew, Mark, Luke, and John, were collected in what became the Christian scriptures.

THE GOSPELS

The Gospel attributed to Mark, probably the earliest of the four, portrayed Jesus as a prophet sent to preach to unbelievers—one who deliberately adopted a language they could not understand so that they would condemn themselves. In Mark, Jesus tells his followers, for example, a parable about a man who sowed seed—some of which was eaten by birds, some of which fell on rocky soil and died, and some of which "fell on good ground, and gave fruit that sprang up and increased; and one seed yielded thirty, and one sixty, and one a hundred." The story seems simple. Modern readers often see in Jesus's decision to speak in parables evidence of his homely, accessible approach to moral and theological teaching. In fact, Mark represented Jesus's stories as one tactic in a spiritual war that he waged against much of his original audience.

According to Mark, even Jesus's disciples found the parable about the seed puzzling. Jesus explained that the story referred to the ways in which different individuals received the word of God. More important, he told his disciples that only they, the few, would hear his message as they should: "To you it has been granted to know the mystery of the kingdom of God." Unbelievers would hear his stories but not understand them, and by failing to understand, they would condemn themselves. A remnant would understand and be saved—and even they would not share the disciples' direct access to the mysteries Jesus taught. The gospels described the Jesus movement itself

as hierarchical, as the church had in fact become already in the course of Paul's career.

Later writers conveyed Jesus's teachings in different ways. The author of the Gospel attributed to Matthew, for example, set out to show that the wisest of the pagans, the three Magi—eastern kings who came bringing gifts for the infant Jesus in the manger—had used their skills in astrology and other occult forms of knowledge to predict the birth of a Jewish messiah and then to find him. The Gospel of John used the terminology of Greek philosophy to argue that Jesus, as the son of God, was no mere holy man but a divine being who had existed from the very creation of the world. These later evangelists placed less emphasis on the rapid approach of history's end—which Mark saw as imminent, after the Temple's fall—and more on the individual Christian's duty to prepare his or her soul for death.

Christianity gradually created a rich religious literature of its own, one that combined in beautiful and original ways the sayings attributed to Jesus and the stories, developed from them, about his life and works. Christian beliefs continued to develop, with many branches of theology and ritual sprouting from the original trunk. But by the end of the first century a loose movement with tenuous borders had given way to a more structured organization.

Christianity had slowly begun to set itself apart from its Jewish roots. The Jewish branch of the early church would have largely died out by the early second century. The Christian gospels, moreover, as they were written and incorporated into what became a coherent and powerful new set of scriptures, made clear that Jesus had come not to fulfill but to replace Judaism. The gospel accounts also held the Jews—above all, the Pharisees and the Temple authorities—responsible for Jesus's death. The firm distinction between Jews and those who accepted Jesus became a condition of existence for the new religion—a condition that would, over the centuries, have some lasting and terrible results, especially for the many Jews who continued to live in Christian societies.

REVELATION: THE POWER OF THE WORD

Although Christianity defined itself against Judaism, it still retained many Jewish practices and traits. None of these proved more fundamental to the new religion than the belief that history was nearing its end.

PAUL AND THE END OF TIME Paul clearly believed that he was living in the last years of the world. "Behold," he told the Corinthians, in words that ring in the mind like the magnificent trumpet music that accompanies them in Handel's *Messiah* (1741), "I show you a mystery. We shall not all sleep, but we shall all be changed, in a moment, in the twinkling of an eye, at the last trump: for the trumpet shall sound, and the dead shall be raised incorruptible, and we shall be changed."

Paul expected to see the just fly through the air to greet the second coming of the Messiah, and the dead rise, in his own lifetime. But he also warned against any effort to compute the date and time when the last act of history's drama would take place, or to anticipate the transformation of the state and society by human action. In the perfect world to come, all would be different, starting with the bodies of the saved, and all believers would be equal in their saving faith. For now, though, slaves should remain slaves, and free men and women free, awaiting the moment when the mystery would be revealed in the heavens.

Others, however, were less content to wait, and more intent on the nature of that second coming and what it would mean for Christians and others. The expulsion of the Jews from Rome by Claudius around 50 CE, the catastrophic Jewish war against Rome from 66 to 73 CE, and the fall of Jerusalem in 70 all made these questions even more urgent. This series of disasters evidently suggested to many Jews and Christians that the end of time was near.

JOHN'S VISIONS Sometime in the second half of the first century, a Christian named John, who believed this, wrote another of the open letters that make up so much of the New Testament—the book of Revelation. A writer full of hatred against Rome and other centers of sin, John described himself as living in a time of trouble—an age when a "synagogue of Satan" (perhaps a group of Jewish Christians) flourished in Ephesus, a Greek city on the coast of Asia Minor, where John himself may have lived, and a prophetess named Jezebel told Christians that they were permitted to commit fornication and eat food that had been sacrificed to idols. Addressing himself to seven churches, John explained to them, as an angel had explained to him, how Jesus would return in splendor and violence to judge and then transform the world.

In Revelation, a spectacular series of visions explodes upon the page—of "one like the son of man, in the middle of 7 candlesticks . . . and he had 7 stars in his right hand, a sharp sword emerging from his mouth. And his face was as when the sun shines at its full strength"; of a royal figure with a sealed book, worshipped by beasts and elders; of a lamb with seven horns and seven seals, and many more

strange figures. The angelic revelation makes clear that the future holds a time of destruction, as the four horsemen of the apocalypse—terrifying mounted figures named Conquest, War, Famine, and Death—slaughter humanity. The martyrs, or "witnesses"—those who have died for the truth—emerge from their graves to cry for vengeance, and a cosmic war is waged in heaven. Finally Babylon, the great city of commerce, withers; Satan is chained for a thousand years and Jesus is resurrected; and then, after a still more terrible time of tribulation, the devil is loosed, to be destroyed in a final combat. Then, and only then, can the Last Judgment take place and a new heaven and earth take shape.

Neither the date when Revelation was written nor the identity of its author is certain. But John, whoever he was, clearly found beauty and consolation in the idea that Jesus was the Messiah and would come back, in the course of a cosmic war, to judge the dead and the living and to create a perfect society. In many ways, he harked back to Jewish writers of the last centuries BCE. John shared with them the conviction, perhaps drawn from the Persian Zoroastrians (who, as we saw, had similar beliefs), that the true history of the universe took the form of a battle between powers of good and evil. Like the Zoroastrians, John knew that in the course of history, God would right the wrongs inflicted by evil rulers on those who had remained faithful to the true religion.

WORDS TO OUTLAST STONE In other respects, however, Revelation marked something new in sacred literature. In the vividness with which John evoked the sufferings that would lead to the transformation of the world, and in the gloating passion with which he contemplated the mass deaths of those he condemned, he forged a new kind of religious feeling: steely, powerful, and deeply and absolutely self-righteous. His rich imagination enabled him to call up, from the language of biblical prophecy, a vision of the future, cast in words alone, that would outlast the marble and concrete of the imperial world around him, which he despised. The Roman Empire, from Augustus on, used urban complexes and great structures to tell stories about its power and glory to its subjects: monuments like the Testament of Augustus in Asia Minor, temples to the imperial cult, forums, and triumphal arches. The author of Revelation imagines away these massive stone symbols of power, offering believers a countervision of the future. His work—still read by millions of Christians, long after the Roman Empire is dust—attests to the evocative force of the word. The book of Revelation framed the Christian millennium in such powerful terms that it would become a permanent force in Western culture.

THE DEVELOPING CHURCH

The fiery visions of Revelation notwithstanding, Christian beliefs in the second century CE sometimes seemed as fragile as the empire seemed eternal. Even success created new problems. As more educated people joined the church, they began to read and respond to the scriptures in new ways.

VARIETIES OF BELIEF

All Christians believed that there was one God and that Jesus was his Son, but they understood what that meant in different ways. Was Jesus the same as God the Father? And what of the Holy Spirit, who was also mentioned in the Gospels? Opinions differed and debates broke out.

THE TRINITY
Gods who died, as Jesus had, were nothing new. Plenty of lesser divinities in Greek myth died, usually from unnatural causes, and plenty of Greek rulers and Roman emperors became gods once they were safely dead and out of office. But these were minor deities. Paul and other Christians, by contrast, insisted that the true God and Creator of the universe had become flesh and died. But some who saw themselves as Christians could not accept the notion that God had actually humbled himself to put on human flesh and undergo the torment and humiliation of the Crucifixion. Some insisted that Christ had not actually died on the cross.

One dissenting school devised a radical hypothesis: Jesus was divine; but like the Greek and Roman demigods whose mortality he shared, he had been a lesser god. Only in the early third century did Christians frame what became the definitive view for most of them: that God the Father, God the Son, and the Holy Spirit were the same yet different. Tertullian (ca. 160–ca. 225 CE), a Christian from Carthage, became the first writer to use the term *Trinity* for this God who was three in one.

GNOSTICS
Another group of early Christians known as **Gnostics** left a rich and sometimes wildly imaginative body of religious texts, many of them recovered in the twentieth century from the jars in which they had been buried in the Judean desert. Inspired by the philosophy of

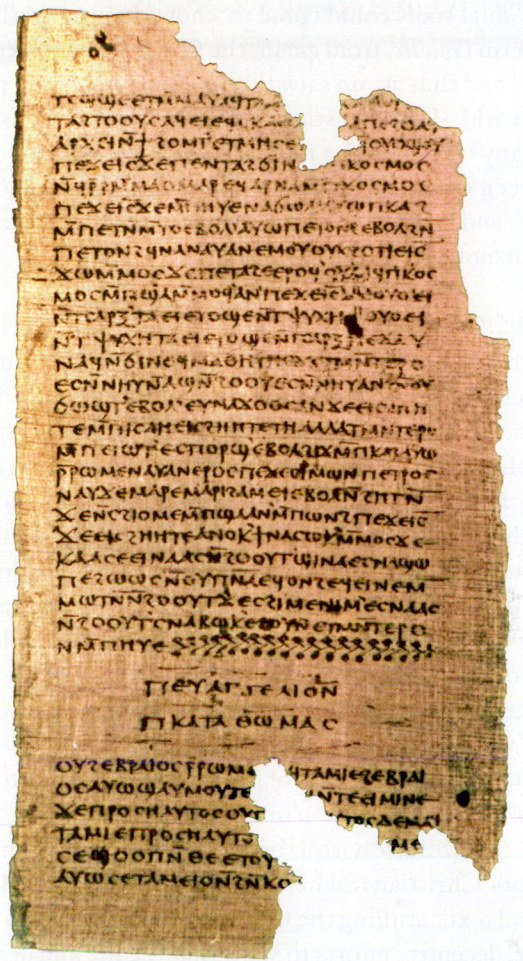

Gnostic Texts In the centuries after Jesus's death, accounts of his teachings were not limited to the texts preserved in the Bible. This is the first page of the gospel of Thomas, a record of sayings attributed to Jesus, from a papyrus codex of fourth-century Gnostic gospels.

the Platonists, which strictly separated the material world from the ideal, many Gnostics refused to believe that the true Creator could have anything to do with evil or suffering. They elaborated visionary cosmologies and theologies of great beauty.

The true Creator, the Gnostics believed, brought forth not the universe itself but emanations of himself—subsidiary beings. One of these was the feminine Wisdom, which they defined as the creator spirit. Wisdom, deluded and believing that she was the universal ruler, created the material world. Human souls roamed this world, with all its error, confusion, and darkness, like fireflies in a forest—pinpricks of light against a vast, turbulent, and threatening background. With the help of the Savior and other emanations from the divine Creator, individual souls could come to know themselves (hence the term *Gnostic*, from *gnosis*, the Greek word for knowledge), and thus attain salvation by rising out of the material world. The Gnostics challenged other Christians in many ways—by the radical separation they assumed between the world of matter and the higher world of the spirit, and by their insistence that salvation was an individual, not a collective, matter.

MARCION Even the most solid pillars of Christian belief and conduct sometimes shook under the impact of these controversies. In the first half of the second century, a Gnostic named Marcion (ca. 85–ca. 160 CE), son of a wealthy merchant family in Asia Minor, established a theology all his own—a revelation with which he challenged all other authorities. The God of the Old Testament—the Creator—Marcion insisted, could have nothing to do with the God of the New Testament. For the Creator was a bungler who had brought pain and suffering—for example, the pain of childbirth—into the world. The God of the New Testament, by contrast, promised salvation to those who had faith in him.

The Gospels and parts of Paul's Epistles seemed to contradict Marcion's version of Christian truth. But he overcame this obstacle with a simple application of his mighty scissors. Christian teachers, he insisted, had falsified their central texts, stuffing the Gospels and Epistles with irrelevant, deceptive efforts to show that the life and death of Jesus verified what the Old Testament prophets had foretold. In fact, Marcion claimed, the true New Testament consisted only of a few chapters from Luke's Gospel and the central letters of Paul, in which he had dwelt on the unique, saving nature of Jesus. All the rest was not only padding but ugly growths, grafted onto the authentic core texts by teachers of darkness. The new church that Marcion organized did not last long: his strict insistence that all members remain celibate ensured that.

MONTANISTS In the late second century CE, another creative misreader—Montanus, a cleric from Phrygia in central Asia Minor—posed a more serious challenge to those who would build an orderly church. In his thought, the established Christian expectation that the world would soon end took on new urgency. The city of God— New Jerusalem—would soon descend on the Phrygian hills, and those Christians who did not accept his revelations would be destroyed, along with the unbelievers. Montanus preached the coming of the end and attracted female prophets who had their own ecstatic visions and preached as effectively as he did. Their message appealed

to many, including the formidable theologian Tertullian. Montanist churches sprang up around the Roman world, and unlike those of Marcion, they survived for centuries.

SUFFERING AND STRENGTH

Christians not only disagreed with one another on central issues, they also had to contend with harsh treatment from outsiders, as they had earlier under Nero and other emperors. In 177 CE, for example, Christians in the cities of Lyon and Vienne, both on the Rhône River in Gaul, were rounded up, dragged into the city forum, imprisoned, and interrogated. One of them, Sanctus, repeated in Latin "I am a Christian" and held out even when red-hot metal plates were pressed against him. A tiny woman, Blandina, resisted with equal courage even though "her whole body was mangled and her wounds gaped." Later the two of them and others were sent to the circus, where they were

Early Christian Martyrs Early Christians venerated those of their number who held to their faith despite persecution. A fourth-century catacomb fresco celebrates the martyrs Marcellinus and Tiburtius, both executed in the early fourth century CE. Marcellinus was a priest; Tiburtius was a wealthy man who donated all his wealth to the poor when he became a Christian.

whipped, attacked by wild animals, and finally burnt to death. Even the ashes of their bodies were scattered to prevent proper burial.

A firsthand report of their death somehow survived, but it is not clear how literally we can take this and later accounts, few of which offer the graphic details found in the partly first-person documents about Perpetua. Martyrdom came to have its own scripts, and we cannot tell, at this distance, whether martyrs actually performed these as they were tortured and killed, or whether the patterns of heroic suffering were imposed on them by pious writers in retrospect. What is clear, though, is that the sense of identity and loyalty that these groups displayed was one of Christianity's chief sources of strength and stability. The tradition of the martyrs' deaths suggested that however sharply Christians might disagree about the nature of God or the proper order of the service, they could unite to resist the challenges presented by an empire that treated them as subversive.

Early Bishops In the second and third centuries CE, the clergy in large Christian cities increasingly chose leaders—bishops—to oversee all of the priests in their region. This fifth-century CE mosaic from Naples depicts a Carthaginian bishop carrying a holy text as a symbol of his authority.

THE CHURCH AS AN INSTITUTION

Yet even during this time of debate and persecution—the former of which never ended—Christianity crystallized into a church, a formal institution with a complex hierarchy of officials. During the second and third centuries CE, the local clergy in great cities such as Rome, Alexandria, and Antioch chose clerics to lead them. These men took chief responsibility for doctrine and worship in their city and in the smaller communities around it. They also represented their communities to the wider Christian world, exchanging letters with the heads of other communities. Gradually the term for their office, *episkopos* ("overseer" or "bishop"), took on a new meaning. These **bishops** established themselves as the formal leaders of the new Christian church.

CHRISTIAN LEADERSHIP Christian leadership soon became a specialized calling that required a range of skills and knowledge. In the first instance, the bishop preached. Indeed, for some centuries he was normally the only one to preach in a given cathedral, or main city church. His sermons became the preeminent source of religious instruction for ordinary Christians. But the bishop did more than that. He also chose young men to follow careers in the clergy, and he organized the collection of a treasury from his parishioners to cover the church's expenses. Gradually, too, certain bishoprics—especially that of Rome, which claimed that the apostle Peter himself had established it—developed a special preeminence in the church. Their

bishops came to have special titles as "archbishops" or "metropolitans." They not only administered their own dioceses, but also presided over all the others in a given district.

MATERIAL SUPPORT Once episcopal leadership was established, Christians became immensely successful at raising funds. Whereas the imperial government, when it promoted the ransoming of Roman citizens from captives, could only watch with regret as these citizens became the slaves of those who had paid for their freedom, Christian communities could pay for the release of their fellows and afford to impose no further bonds on them. By the middle of the third century CE, Christians were feeding some 1,500 poor people a day in Rome. In this and other ways, the church took over, for its flock, one of the traditional duties of the emperor—something that the "good emperors" of the second century would never have allowed.

THE CATACOMBS The church had also begun to take responsibility for proper burial of the dead. In Rome, by the end of the second century, the church had won permission to bury Christians in underground galleries called catacombs. Over the next several hundred years, almost 900,000 Christians would be interred in the Roman catacombs, which stretched over sixty-eight square miles. Christians did not fear the dead, and early services sometimes took place in small churches near these cemeteries.

Hundreds of years later, in the sixteenth century, Christian scholars would imagine that the early Christians had hidden underground from their persecutors. In fact, though, the government had allowed the Christians to create their buried city of the dead, long before they were permitted to build public churches for the living. Gradually, the church had developed a structure of institutions, a hierarchy of officials, and a body of art and literature—all before its existence won official approval from the empire.

INSTABILITY IN THE EMPIRE (180–312)

To Christians, the empire must often have seemed like a vast and immovable structure. In fact, however, the crises of the mid-second century had weakened it in crucial ways. For decades to come, military commanders competed with one another to seize power. Arbitrary rule sapped the empire's institutions and debased its coinage, leaving it without the resources to meet new threats on the borders.

MISRULE AT THE TOP

The emperor Commodus (r. 180–192 CE), who succeeded Marcus Aurelius, was the first emperor in decades not to be chosen for his abilities, but because he was the emperor's son. He brought with him a return to the frightening days of the Julio-Claudian emperors. Commodus ruled through favorites, had senators executed, and performed as a gladiator. When he renamed himself Hercules and gave other signs of megalomania, including an effort to transform the city's calendar, he was murdered. After a year of crisis in 193, during which five emperors claimed the throne, Septimius Severus became emperor and ruled until 211.

In this period the empire's main institutions continued to function: some of the greatest jurists in Roman history worked and wrote under Septimius Severus and his successors. But the vast system that had supported the empire was beginning to weaken. Septimius expanded the army and raised its pay, straining the treasury. He deliberately debased the basic Roman coin, the silver denarius, resulting in a rapid inflation that weakened the urban economy. The Severan emperors pushed urban elites hard to collect and pay the taxes the state badly needed, and Septimius tried experiments in border defense, but with little positive effect. Septimius's sons Geta and Caracalla

Septimius Severus This portrait of Emperor Septimius Severus, his wife Julia Domna, and his sons Caracalla and Geta was painted in Roman Egypt around 200 CE. Geta's face has been erased—perhaps after Caracalla had his brother assassinated in 211.

inherited the empire, but Caracalla had his brother murdered, and ruled until he was assassinated in turn by one of his bodyguards. For three-quarters of a century, emperors won their office and lost it at the point of a sword. In one period of forty-five years, the armies created twenty-seven emperors, only one of whom died a natural death.

AN ORGANIZING THREAT AT THE BORDERS

The same period saw the Germanic tribes along Rome's borders develop into a greater threat. The origins of these Germanic peoples are uncertain—late legends traced them back to Scandinavia, but the archaeological record connects them to northern Poland. When Rome first encountered them in the expansive years of the early empire, they were relatively few, poor, and disorganized: once they had used up the soil around a particular settlement, they moved on. But in the course of the second and third centuries CE, the **Goths** and other Germanic peoples who moved toward Roman territory learned to keep cattle and use manure to fertilize their farms. Their settlements grew larger and they began to trade more effectively with the Romans, providing them with slaves, military recruits, and amber (coagulated tree sap) for jewelry. Eventually, the tribes mastered the new ways of working iron to make tools and weapons, and of turning pottery on wheels.

Their society, once relatively egalitarian, became dominated by increasingly powerful and wealthy elites: burials, in which arms and armor appear ritually mutilated, suggest that warriors played an increasingly prominent role. Bands of young warriors—young men who had no land, or too little to cultivate—led their movement to the west, but women and children followed. By the second century they had reached the eastern shores of the Black Sea, and in the third century they spread through the region, raiding the Aegean coasts of both Asia Minor and Greece. They raided up to the walls of Thessalonica in northern Greece and planned to invade Greece. A Roman army defeated them at Naissus in Serbia, probably in 269,

but they remained in large numbers in parts of modern Ukraine and Poland.

Most important, permanent coalitions of the tribes came into being, with powerful leaders. We know relatively little about these small kingdoms, such as the Tervingi and the Greuthungi, but the confederations stayed together and posed an unmistakable threat to the empire. And to the east a new dynasty in Persia—the Sasanians—mounted newly aggressive campaigns against Rome.

PULLING APART

During this period the Roman armies assigned to prevent border incursions rebelled against imperial control more than once. Military commanders formed alliances, only to

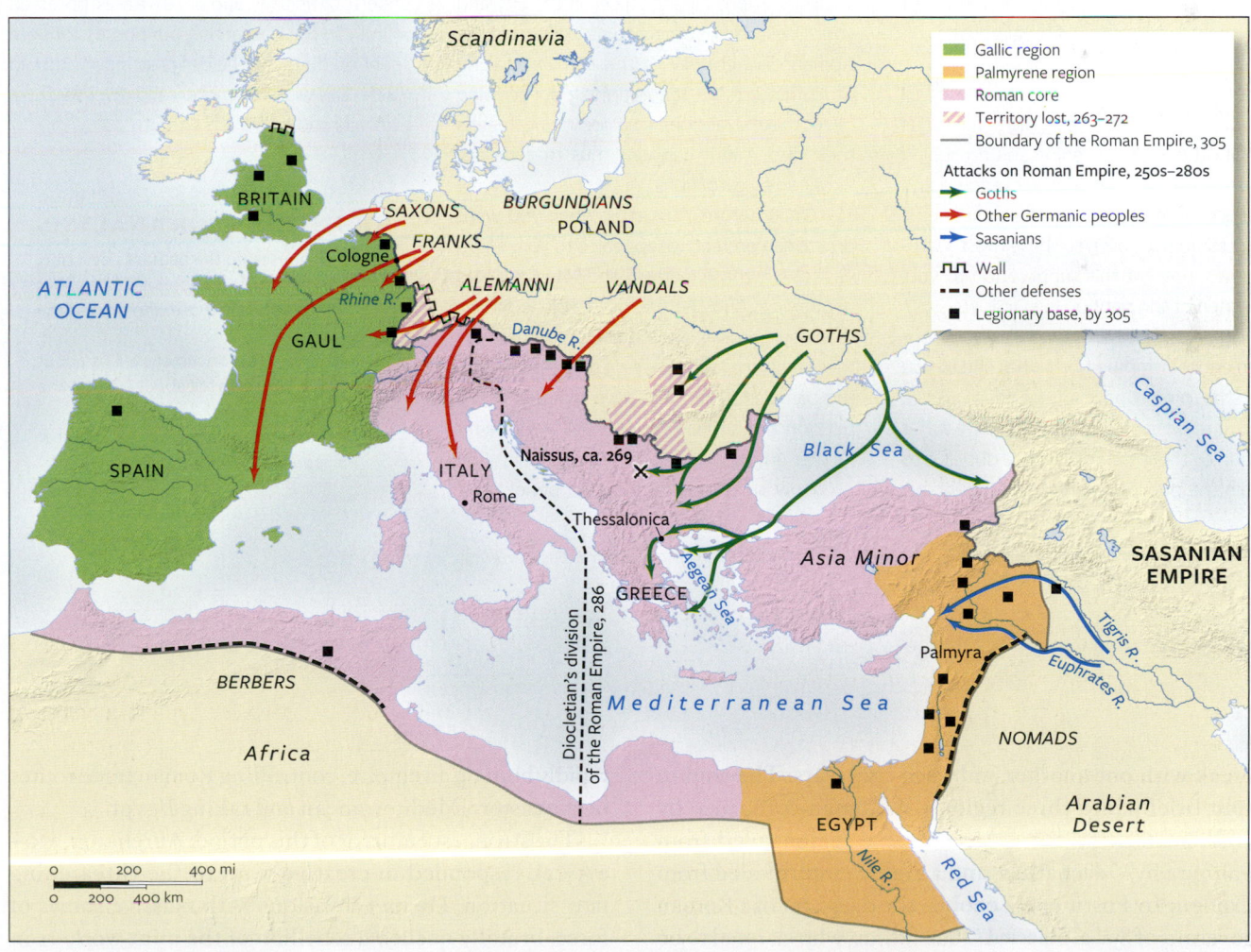

Instability in the Empire, 180–305 CE From the late second century on, the territorial integrity of the empire was increasingly under strain. Those with rival claims to territory, particularly the Goths and other Germanic peoples from northern Europe, pushed at the borders, clashing with the Roman armies despite defensive fortifications, and in some cases taking territory. In 286, Emperor Diocletian permanently split the empire in two.

PETITION OF PEASANTS TO EMPEROR MARCUS JULIUS PHILIPPUS

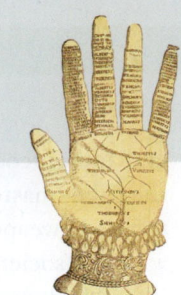

The crisis of the mid-second century had lasting effects on the empire. One result was a debasing of the coinage, causing inflation and difficulties for the tenant farmers living on agricultural estates. High-ranking political and military officials and soldiers took advantage of the weakness of these poor peasants to extort money, resources, and labor from them. In this document from 245 CE, peasants from Phrygia, in Asia Minor, petition Roman emperor Marcus Julius Philippus (r. 244–249) to protect them from such abuses, which he had apparently attempted to do previously as prefect of the Praetorian Guard.

Petition to the Emperor Caesar Marcus Julius Philip Pius Augustus and to the most noble Caesar Marcus Julius Philip [Philippus's son] from Aurelius Eclectus for the community of …your tenant farmers in…Phrygia, by the soldier Titus Ulpius Didymus.

Most reverend and most serene of all emperors, although in your most felicitous times all other persons enjoy an untroubled and calm existence, since all wickedness and oppression have ceased, we, alone experiencing a fortune most alien to these most fortunate times, present this supplication to you. The burden of the petition is as follows.

Most sacred emperors, we are your property, an entire community, that has fled to you and has become supplicants of your Divinity. We are unreasonably oppressed and we suffer extortion by those persons whose duty it is to maintain the public welfare. For although we live remotely and are without military protection, we suffer afflictions alien to your most felicitous times. Generals and soldiers and lordlings of prominent offices in the city and your Caesarians, coming to us, traversing the Appian district, leaving the highway, taking us from our tasks, requisitioning our plowing oxen, make exactions that are by no means their due. And it happens thus that we are wronged by extortions.

Once before, Augustus, when you were praetorian prefect, we appealed to your Highness about these matters, showing what was happening. And the enclosed epistle shows that your godlike spirit was disturbed about these matters: "We have sent to the proconsul the complaints that you have included in the petition and he shall provide that there be no further ground for the complaints."

Now since this petition no benefit has resulted and since it has happened that undue exactions are made in regard to our farm work when people descend upon us and tread us underfoot unjustly, and since we are oppressed willfully by the Caesarians, our possessions are spent on them, our fields are stripped and laid waste, and we live remotely and dwell far from the highroad.

QUESTIONS FOR ANALYSIS

1. What abuses do the peasants describe, and what do these abuses indicate about the conditions of those who worked the land?
2. What does this document tell us about how the peasants felt about political and military officials?
3. Did the petitioners believe that Emperor Philippus could and would help them?

Source: Allan Chester Johnson, Paul Robinson Coleman-Norton, and Frank Card Bourne, *Ancient Roman Statutes* (Austin, TX: 1961), p. 232.

break with one another and wage civil wars. The empire split briefly into three regions—a Roman core ruled by Gallienus (r. 253–268 CE), an eastern region ruled from Palmyra by Odaenathus, and a Gallic empire ruled from Cologne by Postumus. Zenobia, the daughter of a Roman governor of Syria, married Odaenathus, who claimed to be both "king of kings" in Palmyra and the holder of a Roman office. In 267, when he was assassinated, she took command, calling herself Augusta and her child Augustus. She rapidly built up an empire, controlling Roman trade routes in the eastern Mediterranean and taking Egypt.

The strongest emperor of this period, Aurelian (r. 270–275 CE), responded in creative ways to the threatening new situation. He met invasions with massive shows of force, brutally quelled a rebellion of the mint workers in Rome, and defeated and captured Zenobia, putting an end to her rival empire. To protect Rome—since the armies usually remained at the frontiers—he surrounded it with enormous brick and concrete walls, parts of which survive. Yet Aurelian was murdered by his own officers while marching to meet a Germanic invasion, and it took some weeks before an elderly commander named Tacitus (r. 275–276 CE) was chosen to replace him.

DIOCLETIAN

What remained of the old senatorial elite of Rome gradually disappeared, and provincial commanders dominated the empire. Only in 284 CE did the uncultured but effective **Diocletian**, a hard-bitten soldier, take office and restore order. Diocletian (r. 284–305 CE) defeated the Sasanians and other enemy peoples, and reinforced the empire's borders with a massive program of fortress building.

REFORMS Diocletian reorganized the administration of the empire's provinces, dividing the responsibilities of military and civil officers. He recast the tax system to take account of the productivity of land: more fertile areas and larger estates paid more than poorer ones. And he tried to stabilize the coinage by producing a new pure gold coin, the aureus. Diocletian also supported the codification of the law—an enterprise that later emperors would continue. Formidable though his energy and skill were, however, he brought on severe difficulties when he legislated wages and prices across regions. By eliminating the regional differences in wages and prices that had encouraged specialization and trade, these measures did fundamental harm to the Roman economy. Diocletian also tried to bind members of many occupational groups, such as soldiers, *coloni* (tenant farmers), and bakers, to their jobs and towns. In the end, he was reduced to accepting payment in kind, rather than coin, for taxes.

THE TETRARCHY At the same time, he began the process that would eventually split the empire. Diocletian appointed an able co-emperor, the general Maximian, who ruled the west while Diocletian ruled the east. Each emperor, or Augustus, was soon flanked by a caesar, who assisted him. The new form of imperial government—carefully designed to avoid many of the weaknesses of the old—was known as the **tetrarchy**, or rule of four. It was meant to provide effective administration of the empire by splitting it into coordinated regions.

SYSTEMATIC PERSECUTION From the beginning of the third century CE, imperial persecutions of Christians, long intermittent, became systematic in their execution

and serious in their impact—perhaps reflecting recognition of the power that the church had attained. In the middle of the third century, when the emperor Decius (r. 249–251 CE) ordered persecutions, Christians in many areas were forced not only to make sacrificial offerings to the emperor but to obtain certificates attesting that they had done so. Individuals found themselves compelled to make frightening and dangerous decisions, sometimes on the spur of the moment, and even those of greatest authority in the Christian world could not always be consistent in their actions. Cyprian, the bishop of Carthage, fled persecution under Decius. Afterward, however, Cyprian argued that those who had obtained certificates should be expelled from the community of Christians. Under the emperor Galerius (r. 305–311 CE) he gave himself up and suffered martyrdom. Confusion spread: How far could a Christian yield to the pressure of the persecutors and remain a Christian?

Diocletian's Tetrarchy A sculpture from Constantinople from around 300 CE personifies the tetrarchy Diocletian introduced. The two Augusti, with beards signifying their seniority, consult closely with the caesars who assist them.

In 303 CE, moreover, Diocletian launched the most sustained of the persecutions. After attacking the Manicheans—a group of dualists whose missionaries competed for a time, in the third and fourth centuries, with the Christians—he set out to eliminate the alternate hierarchy and authority of the Christian churches. In Palestine, a center of Christian activity, Christians were arrested, held for many years, and then enslaved in the copper mines or publicly executed. Throughout the empire, Roman authorities destroyed churches, confiscated Christian books, and rounded up Christians. By the time this **Great Persecution** came to an end in 311, it had cost the lives of half the early Christian martyrs whose names are known. The church had never faced a more serious threat.

THE ASCENT OF CONSTANTINE

Within a few years, however, the empire was transformed once more, in a way that thoroughly altered the condition of the church. The process began with a period of political turmoil. In 303 and 304, Diocletian's health collapsed, and he and Maximian abdicated in 305. The caesars, Constantius and Galerius, became the new Augusti. But civil war broke out between Constantine, son of the senior Augustus, whose mother was a Christian; and Maxentius, son of Maximian, who had ruled with Diocletian. In Rome in 306 the Praetorian Guard declared Maxentius *princeps*, and he then usurped full power. Constantine's power rested on the Roman legions in Britain, where he ruled. After long negotiations and struggles with Maximian and a series of campaigns against the Franks, who were threatening the empire's Rhine frontier, Constantine invaded Italy.

Once there, he defeated Maxentius's forces in the north and marched on Rome. Before a final confrontation on October 26, 312, near the Milvian Bridge across the Tiber, Constantine saw—or so he claimed late in life—a cross above the sun in the sky, with the words "Be victorious in this." His troops went into battle with crosses on their shields and won a decisive victory. Maxentius drowned and Constantine became the unquestioned senior emperor.

Convinced that he owed his victory to the Christian God, Constantine (r. 306–337) immediately put an end to persecution. On the site of what had been a military barracks, he built a church for the bishop of Rome—a vast, dark basilica, or hall, in the form traditionally used in Rome for public buildings. Crises would return in later years; but Christianity itself would become, as we will see, the religion of the empire and of regions far beyond it. The little movement of Jesus and his followers had transformed the world.

CONCLUSION

The Roman Empire, in its centuries of growth and consolidation, left a deep imprint on the Mediterranean world and the lands to the north and west. The Latin language, which spread with empire, would gradually develop into the Romance languages. Roman roads and fortifications survived, often in continued use, for centuries. And the memory of a great power that had stretched across what is now Europe would remain—and inspire repeated attempts at revival, not only in western Europe, but in many other lands as well.

In some ways, though, Christianity—modest though its institutions were in these centuries—proved even more durable, and even more powerful. The dramatic new understanding of the self and its place in the universe, and the vivid promise of salvation, amounted to a spiritual revolution, which also reshaped society across the Mediterranean world and beyond. What began as the creed of small groups of outsiders like Perpetua and her fellow martyrs became the theology of an institution that spread more widely than the empire itself, and that took over, as the empire fell on hard times, tasks that had once been central to the emperor's office. There is no Roman Empire today, and no one is trying to revive it. But Christianity continues—sometimes, as in Rome, within the same churches built by Constantine, the first Christian emperor.

Battle of Milvian Bridge The triumphal Arch of Constantine in Rome, built to celebrate the victory at Milvian Bridge, includes this frieze of Maxentius's troops drowning in the Tiber River.

[CHAPTER REVIEW]

KEY TERMS

barbarians (p. 152)   gospels (p. 160)   Gnostics (p. 171)   tetrarchy (p. 177)
Second Temple (p. 158)   New Testament (p. 160)   bishop (p. 173)   Great Persecution (p. 178)
Pharisees (p. 158)   Paul (p. 161)   Goths (p. 174)
Jesus (p. 159)   Trinity (p. 171)   Diocletian (p. 177)

REVIEW QUESTIONS

1. What were the most important sources of unity within the Roman Empire?

2. What made the "good emperors" of the Nerva-Antonine line so successful?

3. What was the importance of Greek culture in imperial Rome?

4. What made Jesus's message more radical than that of other dissident Jews?

5. Why did Christianity find such a receptive audience within the Roman Empire?

6. How did the apostle Paul help to shape Christian theology?

7. What were the hallmarks of early Christian communities?

8. How did Rome's persecution of Christians help make the early church stronger?

9. What threats did Rome face at the empire's borders in the second and third centuries?

10. What were the most important reforms made by Diocletian?

CORE OBJECTIVES

After reading this chapter you should have a solid understanding of the following core objectives. To strengthen your grasp of the core objectives, use the resources on the Student Site for The West.

- Identify the factors that contributed to the Roman Empire's stability and prosperity during its first two centuries.

- Trace the emergence of new sects and new beliefs among the Jews of the imperial period.

- Identify the major steps in the development of the small Jesus movement into early Christianity.

- Describe the characteristics of the mature Christian church of the second and third centuries.

- Evaluate the internal and external challenges to Roman power starting at the end of the second century, and Rome's response to them.

 GO TO inQuizitive TO SEE WHAT YOU'VE LEARNED—AND LEARN WHAT YOU'VE MISSED—WITH PERSONALIZED FEEDBACK ALONG THE WAY.

CHRONOLOGY

Early 3rd century
Origen and other Christian scholars
create canonical Old and New Testaments

325
Council of Nicea

324–330
Constantine founds
Constantinople

By 346
Some 3,000
monasteries
exist in Egypt

363
Jovian
reestablishes
Christianity

395
Theodosius I divides the
empire between west and east

380
Edict of
Thessalonica

313
Edict of Milan

337
Constantine is baptized
as a Christian

360–363
Julian re-creates paganism

378
Roman defeat at Adrianople;
Alaric unites the Goths

390s
Augustine writes
his *Confessions*

Late 4th century
Jerome begins
the Vulgate Bible

The Late Roman Empire and the Consolidation of the Church

312–476

476
Odoacer removes
Romulus Augustulus
from rule

413–414
Theodosius II constructs
giant walls around Constantinople

Early 5th century
Christians in Alexandria
expel the Jewish population

455
Vandals sack Rome

Byzantium, a small Greek city, had stood for centuries, a prosperous trading center on a peninsula at the well-placed point where Asia and Europe meet. There, between 324 and 330, Constantine founded a magnificent city that he named Nea Rom ("New Rome"). Soon renamed Constantinople ("Constantine's City"), it celebrated its official birthday on a day chosen by astrologers as propitious. Constantine, who considered raising great buildings to be central to his imperial role, equipped his new creation with every architectural feature of an important Roman city. He built a forum, a circus, and a splendid imperial palace, which subsequent rulers would enlarge and rebuild for centuries. Later, in 413–14, the emperor Theodosius II would construct twelve miles of thick walls around the city, with eighty-six gates and hundreds of towers, which protected Constantinople from invasion for almost a thousand years.

Constantine's city was a Christian capital, equipped with fifty churches, but its location made it something else as well: a shopping mall for the whole Mediterranean world. The city's arcaded main street was laid out on two levels, an upper one for pedestrians and a lower one for shops that sold everything from precious stones and purple silks to spices. Traders from all over the world came to Constantinople to exchange their goods—many

From Palace to Church When the fourth-century consul Junius Annius Bassus decorated his palace in Rome, he included this marble inlay showing him at the head of a procession of chariots. Around 150 years later (ca. 470), a Germanic general occupying Bassus's palace donated the building to the pope. It remained a church until the seventeenth century, with this image as a reminder of its pre-Christian history.

- How did Constantine strengthen Christianity in the empire?
- How did Constantine and his successors attempt to fortify the empire?
- What factors weakened the empire in the later fourth century?
- What major beliefs and philosophies competed in late imperial culture?
- How did Christianity respond to the rival beliefs of the period?
- What new developments in Christianity strengthened its position?
- How did imperial authority come under challenge?
- How did Jerome and Augustine set a new foundation for the Latin church?
- How can an empire fall and no one notice?

having traveled the Silk Road west from China across grassy steppes, mountain passes, and desert oases. They arrived to be astonished by the city's magnificent white marble buildings, which seemed to float above the waters of the Bosporus strait. For centuries, Constantinople would be the central node on trade and information networks that stretched over land and sea from Asia to western Europe. Apparently, the Roman city—one of the chief building blocks of the empire—still had life in it.

In some ways, Constantinople was simply the newest and largest of the great cities of Asia Minor, such as Antioch and Ephesus, in which Greek literature and culture flourished under Roman imperial rule. In other ways, though, it was distinctive: not exactly like the old imperial capital of Rome or the Greek cities of the empire. Its institutions, though Roman, were less elaborate than those of Rome. Constantinople was governed by a proconsul, one of the officials who normally governed provinces of the empire, and though it had a Senate, its members carried a lower status and less grand titles than their counterparts in Rome. The complex web of institutions that looked after streets and sewage, cared for temples, and preserved public order in Rome did not exist in Constantinople. Constantine himself used grants

of land to encourage settlers and provided free food for citizens. For all its wealth, Constantine's great city had an improvised character. The columns and statues that made the city so splendid were, for the most part, brought from elsewhere in the empire rather than fabricated there. Constantinople's mixture of public grandeur and institutional weakness was typical of the late Roman Empire as a whole, from its restoration in the decades just before and after 300 until it finally flickered out of existence a few centuries later.

Constantinople was typical of its period, also, in the way in which cultures and traditions mingled in it. The city's inhabitants spoke Greek, but Latin continued to be used in the legal system, and bureaucrats prided themselves on their knowledge of ancient Roman and Etruscan customs. Constantine, who favored Christianity, prohibited the building of new pagan temples, but the existing temples continued to be active, and the goddess of Fortune was not only invited into the city but celebrated. The statue of Constantine atop a colossal column held a smaller statue of Fortune in his hand. The emperor cared for the preservation of other Roman customs, such as chariot racing, for which he greatly expanded the city's existing racecourse, the Hippodrome. Like the eastern empire that would eventually have its capital in Constantinople, the city was a newer and more distinctive community than its inhabitants liked to admit.

CONSTANTINE AND CHRISTIANITY

Constantine himself is a mysterious figure, his embrace of Christianity ambiguous. He held off from formal baptism until 337, when he was nearing death. He destroyed a few pagan temples and eventually prohibited sacrifice, yet he generally allowed temples to remain. His image continued for many years to appear on coins decorated with the image and name of the sun-god. The arch built in Rome to commemorate his triumph discreetly omitted the names of both the pagan gods and the Christian God. Historians have sometimes been quick to point out what look like contradictions in Constantine's policy, and to condemn him as a hypocrite—someone who chose to throw his weight behind the new church for solely political reasons. But they overlook the fluidity of belief in this period, when as we will see, pagan and Christian practices often overlapped. They also overlook the differences between modern and ancient customs, both Christian and non-Christian. Many Christian converts postponed baptism until they were near death, and rulers in the ancient world often chose to follow a particular divinity for pragmatic reasons. Seen in this framework, Constantine's decision to cast his lot with the divinity that had led his troops to victory at the Milvian Bridge was a plausible response to his own experience. What we can say about Constantine is that from 312, he supported Christianity.

BUILDING NEW CHURCHES

That support came first of all in material form. The **Edict of Milan**, which Constantine issued in February 313, ordered the return of meeting places and other property that had been confiscated from Christians during the Great Persecution initiated by Diocletian. In the years

to come, he endowed the church with more lands and properties.

At the same time, he set out to build the first great public churches for what had been a persecuted religion— for example, the Lateran and the Vatican churches in Rome, which he began and his successors completed. These basilicas were immense halls modeled on the public spaces of Roman political life and designed to give the church the visible authority of great Roman institutions. As the faithful entered through the basilica doors, the bishop and the priests, standing at the altar at the opposite end, looked like high Roman officials. Brilliantly colored mosaics portrayed the members of the Holy Family and the saints and retold in visual form the stories of the Hebrew Bible and the New Testament. These new churches became centers of Christian life, teaching, and worship, some of which have remained to the present day.

As Rome's prestige grew, the bishops of Rome came to see themselves as the successors of Saint Peter, the apostle who had evangelized Rome and died there in or after 64 CE. They began to claim precedence over other bishops: eventually the title *papa* ("pope"), originally used for all high clerics, became exclusively theirs. And the Roman church began to use Latin, not Greek, as its language—and not just any Latin, but that of the Roman Empire, in which the **pope**, like the emperor, spoke of himself as "we."

The Church of the Nativity and the Church of the Holy Sepulcher, which Constantine had built in Bethlehem and Jerusalem, respectively, also became centers of the Christian cult. And Palestine itself became, for the first time, the imaginative center of Christianity—the goal for those who embarked on a new sort of travel, known as pilgrimage, to see the great sites of Christianity's early dramas, and for thousands more to dream about.

Constantine This sculpture of Constantine's head was part of a colossal statue that once stood in the basilica the emperor built in Rome to commemorate his victory at the battle of Milvian Bridge.

Constantinople and Other Cities in the East, 324 Founded by the emperor Constantine on the site of the Greek city of Byzantium, Constantinople was located at a key point along networks of trade, ideas, and Christian beliefs.

A NEW STATUS

Constantine did more than make the church richer and grander. Like Augustus, Constantine reoriented time itself, ordering the empire to adapt its public calendar to the seven-day week of the church and respect the Christian day of rest, on Sunday. By doing so, he dramatized the new status of Christianity in the empire. He did the same, as we will see, even more effectively in 325 when he convoked a council of the church at Nicea. Arius (ca. 250–336), a priest in Alexandria, had been arguing, in defiance of his own bishop, that only God the Father (and not Jesus) had existed eternally. On this and other points, the council laid down what would become central beliefs of Catholic Christianity.

Yet even the emperor could not impose unity on the entire church. The position that only God is divine, which came to be known as **Arianism**, remained influential in the empire and beyond, and compromise positions continued to be proposed. The late empire remained home to a lively and diverse array of religious beliefs and practices. For all his power and his capacity to innovate, Constantine could not change that.

THE EMPIRE RECAST: FROM CONSTANTINE TO THEODOSIUS I (312–395)

The late empire, as Constantine consolidated it in the early fourth century, rested on foundations laid by Diocletian. His policies had enriched the imperial treasury, and Constantine used the accumulated wealth for his own enterprises. Diocletian had also been a great builder, who provided Rome with an enormous new public bathhouse and reared a grand palace for himself in Split, in modern Croatia. He, too, had spent much of his time campaigning and ruling in the eastern territories of the empire. Above all, Diocletian set the tone for the reconfiguration of the empire. Whereas Augustus and other early rulers of Rome had refused titles that reflected their power, Diocletian took the title *dominus* ("lord") and wore a diadem.

Solidus On this gold coin from 326, Constantine wears the laurel wreath crown, an old Roman symbol. The Latin inscription proclaims that his power is ordained by God.

A VAST BUREAUCRACY

Constantine and his successors continued to make the empire more splendid, formal, and elaborate. The civil service had been small and rickety in the age of Augustus and his immediate successors. Local notables across the empire had mostly concentrated on their home cities, which they defended at court when necessary and enriched with gifts of public buildings. After the violence and dislocation of the third century, however, this local elite was slowly replaced by a new one of imperial servants, who looked to the emperor and his representatives. The late empire employed some 30,000 administrators, divided into military and civil services and responsible for oversight of everything from the imperial armies to the local affairs of cities. A detailed gazetteer lists them all, with their titles and duties, the hierarchy of their offices, and even the postal privileges each of them enjoyed. The empire had become a vast bureaucracy.

The emperor himself became a grander and more distant figure than ever before. Only foreign rulers, diplomats, and members of the imperial family could gain access to the emperor and his successors, figures as stately and splendid as animated statues in their official costumes, richly worked in purple and gold. As the court moved, the cities where it came to rest—Arles, in what is now the south of France, and Trier, in western Germany, as well as Constantinople—became splendid ceremonial centers.

ECONOMIC REFORMS

Constantine worked hard to promote prosperity. Drawing gold from the treasuries of pagan temples, he created a new gold coin, the solidus, which stabilized the currency and continued to be minted for centuries. Through legislation he provided tax exemptions for cities that had been hit especially hard by the disturbances of the last century. Constantine did his best to restore agricultural labor forces where civil war had created "deserted fields," as abandoned lands were called. He settled military veterans in some areas and gave tax concessions to help landlords in others.

PROSPERITY Romans in many regions of the empire prospered for much of the fourth century. In Britain, Romans living both in towns and in country villas laid down splendid mosaic floors in their houses. Favored cities in the western empire grew with stunning speed. So did the cities of Asia Minor, stimulated by the building of Constantinople. In North Africa and in Palestine as well, landowners prospered as the eastern cities boomed. And trade flourished, as indicated by the new wrecks full of wine and wheat that joined the dozens of older ones on the floor of the Mediterranean, and by the continued distribution around the empire of goods such as pots made in Gaul.

STRESS Yet there were signs of stress as well. Constantine's government weighed heavily on its subjects. The solidus, which made the imperial currency the literal gold standard for all transactions, also, as contemporaries noted, increased the gap between rich and poor. Higher taxes were needed to maintain armies large enough to protect the frontiers and to support the massive civil service. And because the armies had to be mobile to combat threats on the frontiers, the government needed its revenues in currency rather than grain, so far as possible. Some provinces of the empire—Asiana, for example, in western Asia Minor—were overwhelmed by garrisons of soldiers and demands for taxes in the form of tithes on locally produced grain. A new tax on business transactions, collected every four years, and a new head tax brought choruses of complaint that the government was stifling enterprise in every field.

THE *COLONI* Most consequential in the long run, though, was Constantine's decision to bind many groups of Romans to the places where they lived and worked. Again following Diocletian, he required that *curiales* (local officials) make up any shortfalls in the expected tax revenues. As notable families began to try to evade these offices, legislation tied them—and their descendants—to their posts. Agricultural workers were legally bound, first on imperial lands and then throughout the empire, to the land they cultivated. Forced to stay in place as laborers on the great estates, liable to taxes as well as exactions from their landlords, these *coloni* were legally free, but substantively as confined as slaves. So were artisans in the cities, who were bound to their crafts.

CONSTANTINE'S SUCCESSORS

Some of the fourth-century emperors carried on the fratricidal tradition that Diocletian had tried to end with the advent of the Tetrarchy in 293. After Constantine died, two of his nephews were murdered. But other emperors worked as intensively as Constantine to improve their inheritance. Julian (r. 360–363), another of Constantine's nephews, reversed what seems in retrospect the normal pattern of conversion. He left Christianity, in which he had been raised, for paganism, which he tried to restore

Coloni A detail from a fourth-century Carthaginian mosaic shows agricultural laborers—possibly *coloni*—delivering ducks and other produce to the owner of the estate, a lounging, richly dressed woman. In the background, child workers harvest olives from a tree.

throughout the empire. The version of pagan religion that Julian favored was much tighter and less tolerant than paganism had traditionally been—a religion in a new sense: more like Christianity, which demanded more than formal adherence. After dismissing the Christian bishops and priests who had received official support from Constantine, Julian reestablished the pagan temples that had ceased to function. Splendidly educated, he took pleasure in using his excellent classical Greek to denounce anyone who ventured to criticize or disagree with him. Julian also set out to stabilize Rome's frontiers. But in 363, in the course of a border war with the Sasanian Empire, he received a mortal wound, and the revival of paganism came to a halt, though not quite to an end.

Julian's successor, Jovian, who ruled for less than a year, reestablished Christianity as the imperial religion. Jovian's successor, Valentinian I (r. 364–375), was an effective soldier who seemed to restore the prestige and power of the empire everywhere at once. A long series of campaigns across both the Rhine and the Danube repelled threatened invasions and enabled Valentinian to strengthen both frontiers with further fortifications. Through effective mobilization of resources he defeated a massive invasion of Roman Britain by three allied Germanic peoples, and ran his own successful campaign in North Africa. By the end of his reign, Rome was again the greatest power in the Mediterranean world.

THEODOSIUS I

Theodosius I (r. 379–395), Valentinian's chief general, was almost as effective when he himself became emperor

THE OBELISK OF THEODOSIUS

In 390, the Roman emperor Theodosius I raised an ancient Egyptian obelisk in the Hippodrome, the racetrack in Constantinople. Two inscriptions on the monument's base proclaim the power of Theodosius. The writing on the southeast side, visible from the seats of the emperor and his officials, is in Latin, the official language of Roman law, government, and the army. The northwest inscription, facing the crowd, is in Greek, the common tongue of the eastern empire. The obelisk also features hieroglyphs that commemorate the victory of an early Egyptian king.

The southwest side, pictured here, shows a chariot race on its lower half. Above the race, orderly rows of officials and guards occupy the imperial box. Although damaged, the four seated figures are probably of high rank, as every other figure is standing. Two officials flank what may be a staircase that leads from the Hippodrome up to Theodosius's box. The obelisk's inscriptions and imagery announce the stability of the emperor's rule at a time of declining imperial strength.

QUESTIONS FOR ANALYSIS

1. What cultural and class intersections are present in the inscriptions on the obelisk and its base?
2. Why was the Hippodrome a politically useful place to raise this obelisk?
3. Why would the message of the obelisk have been particularly important in the context of the declining Roman population and the pressures on the empire's borders in the late fourth century?

in 379, not long after the death of his old master and his brother Valens. (Valens ruled the eastern empire from 364 to 378, when, as we will see, he died in combat against Gothic invaders.) Like Valentinian, Theodosius was a ruthless and effective commander. He defeated and killed Magnus Maximin, a western commander who usurped power in Gaul and Italy. Like Valentinian, too, he moved back and forth between Constantinople and Milan, now the capital of the western empire, and maintained his power in the west by promoting Latins and wooing the

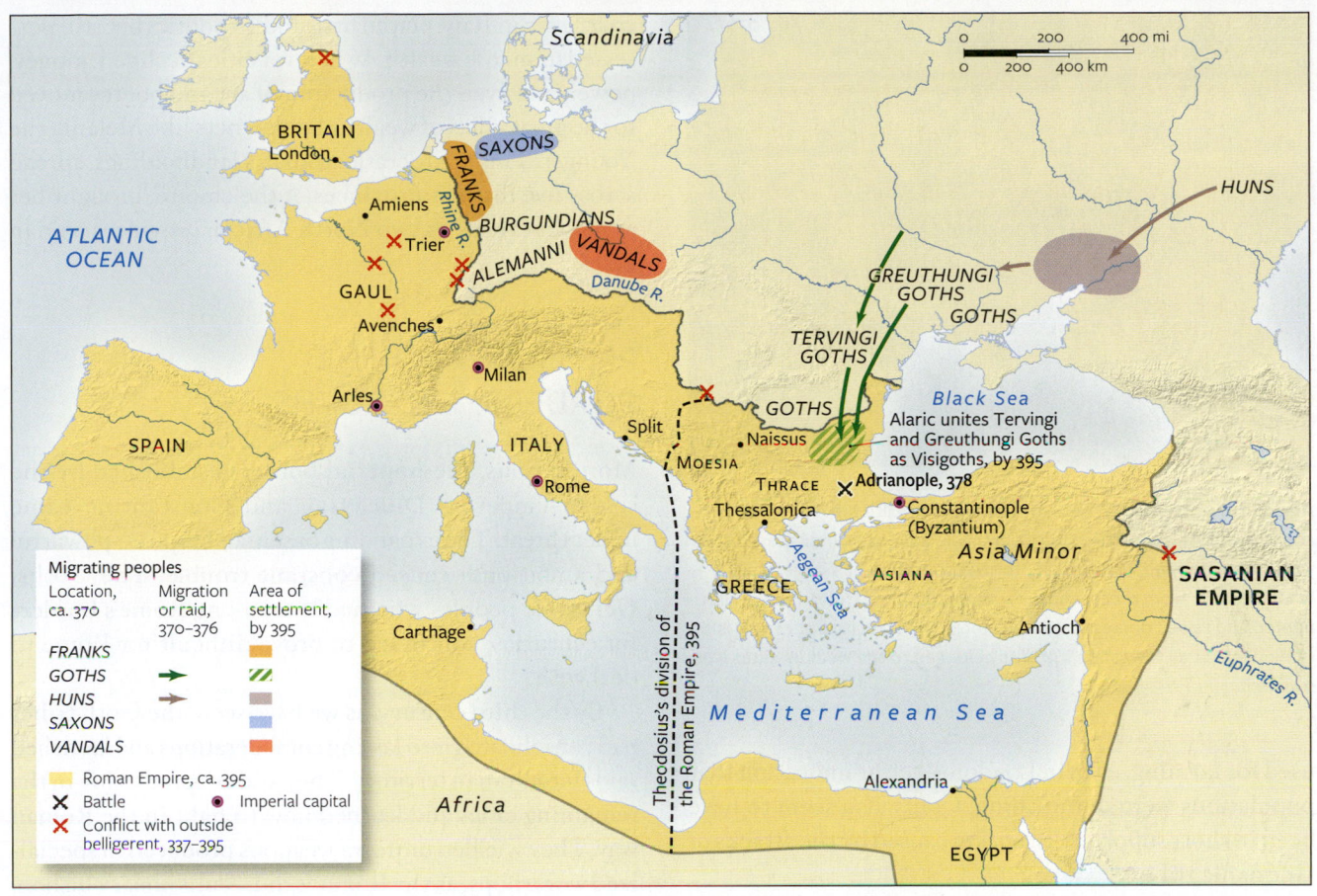

The Empire in Reverse, ca. 337–395 Beginning in the late third century, rival forces began to put pressure on the Roman Empire's borders. The Sasanian Empire was a major threat in the east, while Germanic tribes such as the Goths, Franks, and Vandals began to push into Roman territory from the north. In 378, Roman forces suffered a devastating defeat at Adrianople after confronting a group of Goths who had moved into Roman territory.

old senatorial families in Rome—even those that had supported Magnus Maximin. The Edict of Thessalonica, which Theodosius issued in 380, declared the form of Christianity that had been established by the Council of Nicea the official religion of the empire. He deposed Arian bishops and declared the pope in Rome—Damasus, who held office from 366 to 384—the guardian of orthodoxy. Though Theodosius did not destroy pagan temples by direct action, he did not punish those who did, and he abolished the order of Vestal Virgins at Rome and the Olympic Games.

Yet even Theodosius could not always impose his will. Unable to defeat the Germanic peoples who had entered imperial territory, he settled them as allies in Thrace and Moesia (Serbia). He also made a treaty with the Sasanian Empire. Though he celebrated both events as military victories, they showed the limits of his power. It may have been his realization of those limits that led him to divide the empire again, at his death in 395, between his sons Arcadius (in the east) and Honorius (in the west).

THE EMPIRE IN REVERSE

Slowly, over the later fourth century, the great imperial project went into reverse gear. The area of settlement in many cities shrank—Amiens from 250 acres to 25, Avenches from 370 to 22. Large-scale projects such as Diocletian's baths were few, and such resources as were available were often spent on surrounding the shrunken city cores with walls. By the end of the fourth century, even areas that had recently shown great prosperity—such as Roman Britain—saw their cities shrink. Archaeologists have found evidence of squatters in possession of buildings, blocked ditches and sewers, and urban land being

Agricultural Estates When cities declined, wealth moved to the countryside. This fourth-century Carthaginian mosaic indicates the vast number of people necessary for the operation of a large-scale landed estate, from those who grew vegetables and fruit to those who hunted and raised domesticated livestock. The structure at center is a reminder that all the estate's profits belonged to the wealthy elites who owned it.

used for farming, even in London—a clear indication that populations were diminishing. Coins also seem to have been in short supply, a disruption caused by the attacks of Germanic tribes.

POVERTY AND WEALTH IN THE COUNTRYSIDE

On the land, latifundia, large agrarian estates with bound labor, continued to develop, and small-scale farming to decline. More and more of the poorer population found itself attached to the land. Conditions varied: in some cases, laborers voluntarily agreed to become coloni in return for protection; others tried to escape. In 419, it was discovered that a number of high imperial officials were runaway coloni. The restrictions on them were tight. Male coloni had to marry daughters of coloni. They could not sell their property without their landlord's permission. They paid their taxes through the landlord, as well as paying him rent. And they could not sue him. In the ninth and tenth centuries and after, the majority of Europe's agricultural workers would become serfs, legally unfree and bound to the land. Though the coloni were not their direct ancestors, their attachment to the land marked the beginning of a period of many centuries during which most of Europe's inhabitants would be unfree.

The great senatorial families, far from the imperial court even in Italy, played little role in politics but still possessed immense wealth. Wherever cities declined, money, power, and even the production of art and poetry moved to the great villas of wealthy landowners like Melania the Younger. This aristocratic woman's landholdings, spread across five distinct provinces of the empire, brought her as much revenue as two North African provinces paid in taxes.

PRESSURES ON THE BORDERS: THE GOTHS

More serious, the imperial borders established by the soldier-emperors Diocletian and Constantine came under threat. The expanding Sasanian Empire—powerful and ambitious—caused constant trouble. The Goths, Germanic peoples who had lived along Rome's borders for centuries, continued to prove difficult for Rome to deal with.

By the third century, as we have seen, the Goth tribes had consolidated into lasting confederations and launched raids into Roman territory. They also adapted to life in the remaining cities and learned how to fight in the Roman way. They wielded uniform weapons produced in specialized workshops, as the Romans did. A missionary bishop, Ulfila, had converted them to Christianity—though they adopted a theology that was close to Arianism—and even provided them with an alphabet, with which a translation of the Bible could be written down. Constantine and later emperors made them *foederati*—formal allies.

Goths As the Goths moved into western Europe, they increasingly encountered and came into conflict with the people of the Roman Empire. This chaotic marble relief from a mid-third-century sarcophagus shows Romans locked in fierce combat with Germanic tribesmen, identifiable by their thick beards and bare chests.

ADRIANOPLE In the later fourth century, the **Huns**, horse-borne nomads from the east who were skilled archers, began to devastate the Goths' settled agrarian communities, situated outside the Roman walls and fortresses. In 376 the Goths asked for permission to cross the border and enter the Roman Empire. The eastern emperor Valens agreed. Two years later he decided that he had made a mistake and confronted the Goths—and perhaps some of the Huns—in Thrace. He did not wait for the troops of his western fellow emperor, Gratian, to reach the field, and faced an army as large as his near **Adrianople** in 378. Pulled out of line and surprised by the cavalry of the Goths' allies, the Romans suffered a devastating defeat. Valens himself died in the rout, along with 20,000 of his 30,000 soldiers. It was in the aftermath of this decisive battle that the Goth leader Alaric united the Tervingi, the Greuthungi, and others into a single people, who came to be known as the Visigoths.

THE AFTERMATH From now on, even such strong emperors as Theodosius I had to treat the Goths more or less as equals, using their military power to supplement that of the shrinking Roman armies. Gothic kingdoms began to develop inside what had been Roman territory.

Gothic Alliances As the Goths became more powerful and settled inside the boundaries of the empire, Romans had to make alliances with them to ensure peace. Even the daughter of Emperor Theodosius I, Galla Placidia—shown wearing a pearl necklace and earrings in this fifth-century portrait with her son and daughter—was briefly married to a Gothic king after she was captured by Alaric.

The emperors found no way to resist any given group of "barbarians"—as the Romans of the time of Augustus or Marcus Aurelius would have called them—except by forming alliances with other ones. By the end of the fourth century, Vandals, Franks, and other Germanic peoples warred with one another in northern Gaul. Over the next hundred years, they took over more than half of the former territory of the empire. Meanwhile, the Huns continued to harry Romans and Goths alike. The western empire—with longer and more dangerous borders to defend than the east, and poor revenues with which to pay for its armies—was in clear decline.

The eastern empire had its share of defeats. The army that the Goths destroyed at Adrianople belonged to the east, and the Huns sacked the eastern fortress city of Naissus in Serbia in 441. Eastern emperors paid a heavy tribute to Attila, leader of the Huns—so heavy, according to one source, that providing the revenue for it drove some hard-pressed taxpayers to commit suicide. In the end, though, the sea and the walls of Constantinople protected the heartland of the eastern empire in Asia Minor from the resettlements, invasions, and wars that transformed the western empire.

A DYNAMIC CULTURE: COMPETING BELIEFS AND RIVAL PHILOSOPHIES

In these conditions, it did not come as a surprise to the well-informed clerics and senators of Rome when the Visigoth leader Alaric besieged their city in 408 and sacked it in 410. But some found in this event confirmation of their fears that the empire was collapsing. After Julian, the emperors had sided more and more completely with the Christian church. Pagan sacrifices were prohibited. The great altar of the goddess Victory, at which Roman senators had been initiated into their duties for centuries, was removed. Some of those who had never converted blamed Christians for the city's fall from its former greatness. As we will see, the same period in which the western empire lost so much of its power and cohesion saw the church reach a new level of organization and stature. But even as Christianity became the imperial religion, it faced competition at every level—from long-established forms of philosophy and from newer revelations that circulated through the vast and rapid communications systems of the empire.

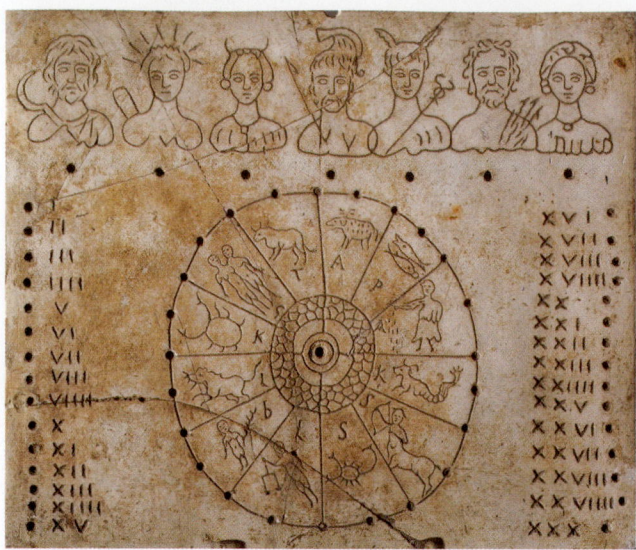

Roman Astrology A first-century Roman calendar associates each month with a sign of the zodiac, and each day of the week with a god from the Olympian pantheon linked to one of the planets, indicating the importance of astrological symbolism in daily life.

ASTROLOGY: GODS IN THE PLANETS

In the Hellenistic centuries, Babylonian diviners, who used the positions of the planets to predict the future of everything from individuals to nations, brought their techniques into the Greek kingdoms, where they fused with Egyptian ideas about time and Greek astronomical methods. By the first century BCE, astrological beliefs and practices were rapidly spreading through the Roman world as well. Learned Greeks and Romans practiced astrology as a complex, demanding art, and even men and women of great power turned to astrologers for advice on critical matters. The emperor Tiberius (r. 14–37 CE), for example, relied on the counsels of a professional astrologer, Thrasyllus, who may not have read the stars but certainly understood his employer. When Tiberius had him stand at the edge of a cliff, next to a powerful slave, and asked what he thought of his own future, Thrasyllus replied that everything looked dark. Struck by the accuracy of the astrologer's prediction, the emperor relied on his advice, which sometimes moderated Tiberius's cruelty.

THE SEARCH FOR PERSONAL REVELATION AND GUIDANCE

People at every social level sought advice not only from diviners, but also from traditional oracles like the one at Delphi in Greece, from specialists in explicating dreams, and from magicians and charmers. Many searched for gods who could provide them with a satisfactory understanding of the universe and intimate personal guidance. In the middle of the second century, for example, a previously successful Greek orator named Aelius Aristides became ill. For twelve years he lay in bed unable to move, tormented by strange dreams. When Aelius did manage to get up, he subjected himself to violent exercise routines, running barefoot in the mud or swimming in the ocean in midwinter. He did all this because the god Asclepius, who specialized in healing, appeared in his dreams and gave him instructions. Asclepius comforted Aelius and prescribed mild therapies as well as the violent ones: suffering from a sore throat, Aelius dreamed that the god instructed him to gargle.

Aelius tried to lead an old-fashioned life. Like most Greek writers during this period, he did his best to use the traditional vocabulary and language of Greek prose at its classic height. In religion, too, he saw himself as a traditionalist. Yet he forged a personal relationship with his protective divinity, whose immediate presence he felt, while Zeus and the other Olympians remained distant figures, irrelevant to his everyday needs and problems. Many other residents of the vast Roman Empire felt similar needs and, like Aelius, found themselves unable to fulfill them by joining in the traditional temple cults.

EASTERN CULTS

The search for insight into the larger meaning of life, moreover, took place at a time when individuals—not only well-born Romans, but also much poorer men and women—could see and experience a wide range of religions. They could watch animal sacrifice and listen to prayers being offered at the ancient cult centers of their own cities, since the Romans allowed traditional priesthoods to carry out their rituals so long as they acknowledged the supremacy of Roman gods and the Roman emperor.

And while emperors battled to keep foreign powers from invading Roman territory, the imperial borders yielded to individual travelers and their beliefs. Egyptian and Syrian temples enticed pilgrims with spectacular rituals couched in mysterious Eastern languages. Newer Eastern cults and Westernized versions of them, like the Egyptian cult of Isis, also spread. Often these revelations rested on little direct knowledge of the traditions that had spawned them. After the defeat of Antony and Cleopatra

Eastern Cults Religious practices from distant reaches of the empire also shaped belief at its center. A fresco from first-century Naples portrays Isis-Fortuna, a Roman interpretation of the Egyptian goddess Isis. She is decorated with celestial motifs and attended by a winged cupid and by her son, Harpocrates—a Hellenistic rendering of the Egyptian god Horus—on horseback.

in 31 BCE, the Egyptian priests gradually lost their command of the ancient hieroglyphic texts that preserved the rituals and beliefs of their ancient nation. Few priests could write a text, even when a Roman emperor wanted one to adorn an obelisk.

Around the second or third century a new cult, centering on the revelations of an ancient prophet named Thrice-Wise Hermes, found adherents in Egypt and elsewhere. Its founding texts were stitched together in Greek from mixed remnants of Egyptian religion, recalled in fragments, and Greek philosophy. Throughout the Mediterranean, at the same time, magical texts attributed to Hermes provided readers with astrological, alchemical, and magical recipes. It was an extraordinary moment. Any citizen of a fairly cosmopolitan Roman city in, say, Asia Minor could read about, and some could experience, half a dozen revelations and their associated rituals. Christianity developed—and soon found its most learned and powerful supporters—amid this extraordinary cultural ferment.

RIVAL PHILOSOPHIES AND THE VIRTUOUS LIFE

Those in search of guidance could find philosophies, as well as cults, that offered what they needed. The search for an understanding of the universe, and the passion to lead a virtuous life, were deeply rooted in the civilization of the Romans. For centuries, Greek philosophers had offered their own form of guidance to the virtuous life. From Pythagoras and Socrates on, they had not only offered definitions of virtue but provided examples of it in action, and even organized communities whose members could pursue the truth and the good life. Romans such as Cicero offered introductions to the beliefs of Platonists and Aristotelians, Stoics and Epicureans, in accessible Latin works. Here, too, inhabitants of the empire could hope to find personal guidance.

Two forms of Greek philosophy in particular—Stoicism and Epicureanism—were popular in the Roman world. In his *Meditations,* Marcus Aurelius, one of Rome's highly effective "good emperors," examined his daily life and work in the light of his Stoical convictions. Doing so, he learned how little his grand military successes mattered in the universe at large. Warfare, he realized, was nothing more than "dogs fighting over a bone." By learning to see his own deeds from a critical distance, he shaped his self as rigorously and virtuously as—and more effectively than—he shaped his larger society. And the Stoic emperor was only one of many who tried to live a life of both action and contemplation.

NEOPLATONISM: PHILOSOPHY AS CULT

The Platonic tradition also drew thought and action together in ways that remained influential in Rome. In the centuries after Plato's death, the members of his Academy explored philosophical positions very different from Plato's own. In the second and third centuries, a new version of Platonism took shape that owed as much to Aristotle as to Plato.

Plotinus (204/205–270), the most charismatic advocate of **Neoplatonism**, believed that he was restoring the ancient core of the philosopher's teachings. His synthesis would dominate the reading and teaching of Plato for centuries to come. Deeply committed to living the tenets of his philosophy, and idealistic in the extreme, Plotinus regretted that he even had a body. Still, he saw the universe as a great and beautiful chain that stretched, each link in place, from the divine being that had created it all the way down to the earth. The gods, Plotinus held, ruled this universe, as its symphonic beauty made clear. The sage should seek an understanding of the cosmic order and its purpose by mastering mathematics and the other central disciplines, and by learning to apply them with discipline and imagination. Knowledge, for Plotinus, must be pursued not only for its own sake but also because it was the path to virtue. As the wise had long understood, philosophy was not only an intellectual but also a moral discipline, one designed to lead those who followed it to the good life. So far Plato himself might well have agreed.

But Plotinus's practices were not all traditional. The philosopher, as Plotinus embodied him, still used reason to seek the truth, but he was now a holy, as well as a wise, man. Gods spoke to him directly, and he used techniques of incantation to exploit their powers. The form of philosophy that he and his followers stood for, moreover, was very different from Plato's. Plato had cast his arguments as dialogues, which mimicked the form of living speech and suggested that there might be more than one side to a debate. Plotinus, by contrast, read widely in many traditions beside his own and, like Aristotle, composed formal treatises. His chief disciple, Porphyry (245–ca. 305), arranged his teacher's works in systematic form and used it to wage war against rival revelations—notably that of the Christians.

Other Neoplatonists followed up on hints in Plotinus and argued that his thought was the culmination not only of Greek but also of ancient Near Eastern history—that it encapsulated the revelations of the ancient Egyptian and Babylonian priests. In the Mediterranean world of the third century, antiquity was still the source of authoritative patterns in thought, in literature, and in the arts. Philosophy itself now became a learned, encyclopedic pursuit.

PAGAN CRITICS OF CHRISTIANITY

Over the second and third centuries, these multiplying philosophies and cults, with their many rewards, posed a serious challenge to Christianity. Though Christian numbers grew, the majority of Romans were still pagans, who had never regarded Christians with special favor. Like the Jews, after all, they practiced a religion whose tenets prevented them from taking part, as all citizens and subjects should, in the public forms of sacrifice and ritual staged in great temples across the empire. Neither group was willing to sacrifice to the emperor. Like the Jews, the Christians observed a day of rest. Worse still, rumor held, they emulated the worst deeds of the heroes of ancient Greek myth: they had sex with their mothers, like Oedipus, and

ate their children, like Thyestes. What more could one expect, some pagans asked, from men and women whose God had died the most humiliating death, like a slave, on a cross?

Better-informed pagan critics of Christianity, such as Porphyry, wielded more sophisticated weapons. A trained scholar, Porphyry studied the Old and New Testaments as if they were Greek histories. The results were striking. The biblical books, he argued, swarmed with obvious errors and contradictions. It was clear, for example, that the book of Daniel, with its prophecies of events to come, had actually been written in the second century BCE, long after the events it described. As to Christ's commandments, they were perverse and foolish. To follow them, Porphyry stated, would be in itself clear evidence of folly.

FORGING A NEW CHRISTIAN CULTURE

From the second century on, Christian writers had found ways to answer at least some of these attacks. But in the third and early fourth centuries, a new Christian culture took shape—one that applied the tools of ancient scholarship and philosophy to defend the church. Throughout the Roman world, Christian communities were growing in towns that also harbored Greek and Roman temples, their cults in full operation, as well as Jewish synagogues, many of whose members saw the new religion as a perversion of their true one. Certain cities offered special opportunities for Christian missions—for example, Caesarea, a port town in Palestine that Herod had rebuilt in the first century BCE as the model of a Roman urban paradise with fine roads, temples, baths, a circus, and a theater. Caesarea had lively communities of every kind: Greeks and Romans loyal to their gods, Jews who prayed and read their Bible in Greek, Jews who prayed in Aramaic and read the Bible in Hebrew, and Christians.

These people of different languages and ideals lived side by side, walked the same streets, and argued in the same markets. In one case they even witnessed the same miracle—an outbreak of perspiration on temple pillars, which was reported independently by a Christian and a Jewish source, who interpreted the event very differently. In Caesarea, throughout Palestine, and in other eastern areas where many traditions intersected and interacted, Christianity took on new ideas and practices that redefined its relation to ancient culture.

ORIGEN OF ALEXANDRIA

If Porphyry became the charismatic leader of a new pagan philosophical school, his counterpart, **Origen** of Alexandria, became one of the first Christians who wielded the pagans' weapons as effectively as they did. Born into a Christian family around 175, Origen received traditional training in Greek scholarship and philosophy in his native city. A passionate Christian whose father died a martyr, he was devoted to the teachings of Jesus—so much so, according to some accounts, that when he found himself tortured by lust, he castrated himself to remove the cause of the problem. Steeped in the writings of the Jewish philosopher Philo (ca. 13 BCE–ca. 45 CE), as well as the works of Greek thinkers, Origen became a profound reader of the scriptures and an original theologian. In Alexandria, he mastered pagan learning but seems to have found little support. Once he moved to Caesarea, however, Origen set out to show that Christianity represented not the denial but the culmination of the best parts of ancient culture, Greek and Jewish alike.

To make this case, Origen had to clarify what Christianity stood for. Heretics, Gnostics, and even conventional Christians disagreed about what belonged in the Bible. During the second and third centuries, most Christians read not what we now call the Bible—a set group of texts, presented in a systematic order—but a more or less random collection of biblical books that circulated independently in scrolls. These were too small to hold more than a fraction of the New Testament, to say nothing of the Old. Many read texts that did not become part of the Christian biblical canon, or that were even declared heretical in later centuries, but which they had no particular reason to exclude from study and contemplation.

ASSEMBLING THE BIBLE

Origen was one of many Christian scholars who collaborated to establish a canon: a set of texts generally recognized as orthodox. In twenty codices, Origen laid out the Old Testament, word by word, in Hebrew, then in Hebrew transliterated into Greek, and in four different Greek versions, none of them his own. And he dressed the texts of the Old and New Testaments in the protective garment of his commentaries, which were designed to lead readers who were not theologians through difficult passages to the hidden truth. The Bible,

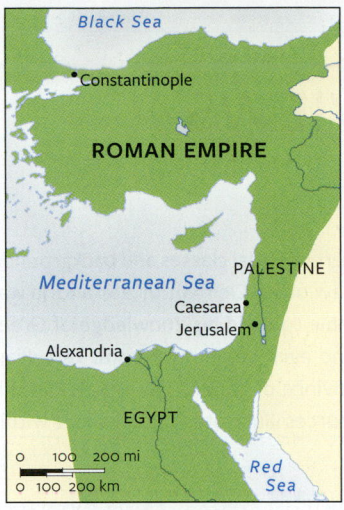

Caesarea and Alexandria, 3rd Century

as Origen tried to recast it, became a source of central authority—authority of a new kind, in an organization that was equally novel.

But bringing the texts together caused new problems, for it showed that the Hebrew Bible and the Septuagint, the most widely used Greek translation made by Jews long before, often disagreed, as did manuscripts of the New Testament. If, as Origen believed, the Hebrew Bible and the New Testament were God's divine revelation, they could not contain serious mistakes or real contradictions. Wherever they seemed to err, accordingly, he read them as Greek scholars of his time often read Homer: allegorically. The tale of Jonah and the whale that swallowed him might seem problematic in the literal sense—but this meant only that it stood for a hidden, higher sense, which the puzzling narrative challenged the Christian reader to discover. In a massive series of editions and commentaries derived from his famous lectures on the biblical text, Origen assembled the first systematic Christian explication of the Bible.

A CHRISTIAN VIEW OF HISTORY

Origen's reading of the Bible, in turn, underpinned an account of the order of the universe as stately and beautiful as those of the pagan Neoplatonists, with whom he had much in common. God, he explained, though one in nature, had three persons. Origen used a different terminology, but he accepted and defended the earlier Christian doctrine of the Trinity—the Father, the Son, and the Holy Ghost. He went on to connect God to the created world in novel and powerful ways. In the beginning, God had created not only the universe, but minds worthy to contemplate it and know it—and, by knowing it, to attain salvation. These created minds had had free will, which enabled them to choose not to know the truth and to fall into error in their ignorance. Like fallen stars, they lost their brilliance as they plunged into the darkness of the world of matter. But over time, Origen argued, as these souls lived and died (and he firmly believed in reincarnation), they would come to know the truth and then to follow it.

World history, accordingly, followed a clear arc—one that led from the confusion and disorder of the present to a future "restoration" when all things would be made simple and true once more. This idea, which Origen borrowed from the Stoics, he generalized into the first Christian

EARLY CHRISTIAN VIEWS OF MARRIAGE

Early Christians were adult converts who came from different social classes and backgrounds, and often combined their previous beliefs with their new ones. Clement of Alexandria was an early "Greek Father" and a Neoplatonist who was able to meld his knowledge of Greek Platonic philosophy with ideas from Christian belief and even some mysticism. Tertullian, a Latin church father from Carthage in the Roman province of Africa, saw Greek Platonic philosophy as misleading and suspect. This pairing of sources illustrates the presence within Christianity of competing social and religious views.

Clement of Alexandria, *Stromateis*

In *Stromateis* ("Patchwork"), Clement of Alexandria (150–215) discusses a variety of topics, including the scriptural exhortation to marry for procreation. He believed that marriage was a good and necessary institution, providing order in love and in the Christian's life.

Marriage is a union between a man and a woman; it is the primary union; it is a legal transaction; it is a spiritual transaction; it exists for the procreation of legitimate children.... So there is every reason to marry—for patriotic reasons, for the succession of children, for the fulfillment of the universe (insofar as it is our business). The poets regret a marriage which is "half-fulfilled" and childless, and bless the marriage which is "abundant in growth." Physical ailments demonstrate the necessity of marriage particularly well. A wife's care and her patient attention seem to surpass all the earnest devotion of other family and friends; she likes to excel all others in sympathy and present concern; she really and truly is, in the words of Scripture, a necessary "helper."...

It is a sign of weakness and unmanliness to try to escape from a partnership in life with wife and children. A state which it is wrong to reject must be totally right to procure. So with all the rest. In fact, they say the loss of children is one of the greatest evils. It follows that the acquisition of children is a good thing. If so, so is marriage. The poet says, "Without a father there could be no children, without a mother, not even conception of children." Marriage makes a man a father, a husband makes a woman a mother.... Marriage must be kept pure, like a sacred object to be preserved from all stain.

Tertullian, *Ad Uxorem*

Tertullian (ca. 160–ca. 225) produced an extensive body of literature in defense of Latin Christian beliefs and practices. He praised marriage but considered the celibate, unmarried state of Christians like the apostle Paul to be superior, arguing that though it is "better to marry than to burn," chastity is preferable because it allows a Christian to remain more pure and be closer to God. *Ad Uxorem* ("To His Wife") was written on the occasion of the remarriage of a Christian widow to a non-Christian, a union abhorrent to Tertullian.

[T]here is no place at all where we read that nuptials are prohibited; of course on the ground that they are a good thing. What, however, is *better* than this good, we learn from the apostle [Paul], who *permits* marrying indeed, but *prefers* abstinence; the former on account of the insidiousnesses of temptations, the latter on account of the straits of the times. Now, by looking into the reason thus given for each proposition, it is easily discerned that the ground on which the power of marrying is conceded is *necessity*; but whatever *necessity* grants, she by her very nature depreciates. In fact, in that it is written, To marry is better than to burn, what, pray, is the nature of this good which is (only) commended by comparison with evil, so that the reason why marrying is *more* good is (merely) that burning is *less*? Nay, but how far better is it neither to marry nor to burn?

But if we listen to the apostle, forgetting what is behind, let us both strain after what is before, and be followers after the better rewards. Thus, albeit he does not cast a snare upon us, he points out what tends to utility when he says, the unmarried woman thinks on the things of the Lord, that both in body and spirit she may be holy; but the married is solicitous how to please her husband. But he nowhere permits marriage in such a way as not rather to wish us to do our utmost in imitation of his own example. Happy the man who shall prove like Paul!"

QUESTIONS FOR ANALYSIS

1. In *Stromateis*, how does Clement of Alexandria argue in favor of marriage and the family?
2. In *Ad Uxorem*, why does Tertullian argue that although marriage is good and a necessity, abstinence is better?
3. How and why do the early Christian writers feel conflicted about the relative values of marriage and celibacy?

Sources: Clement of Alexandria, *Stromateis* 2.23.137(1), 140(1), 142(3), 145(1), trans. John Ferguson (Washington, DC: 1991), pp. 249–54; Tertullian, *Ad Uxorem* 1.3, trans. S. Thelwall, in *The Ante-Nicene Fathers*, vol. 4, ed. Alexander Roberts, James Donaldson, and A. Cleveland Coxe (Buffalo, NY: 1885), p. 40.

philosophy of history. The great restoration, though inevitable, would happen only in the future—perhaps only after centuries. In the meantime, the Christian should lead, as Origen did, a life of extreme austerity, ideally in celibacy, poverty, and dedication to one's fellow Christians.

In Origen, the Christians at last had an exponent equal in learning and eloquence to the greatest of their opponents. He and his disciples—who were many and passionate—found that their faith sustained them through persecutions. During a savage campaign that the emperor Decius (r. 249–251) mounted against Christianity in the middle of the third century, Origen was arrested and tortured, and his sufferings probably hastened his death. But his books and his model of a new kind of Christian thought and scholarship survived.

INTERNAL DIVISIONS: MANICHEISM

By the third century, Christianity was becoming a learned, even a cultured, religion—the sort of religion that could appeal to highly educated men and women. But it was also threatened by new internal divisions. Even as Christian scholars debated with those pagan scholars who noted their existence—probably still a small minority—they also found themselves challenged, yet again, by rivals from within their ranks. The most powerful challenge came from the east—from outside the Roman Empire.

Mani (216–276), a Persian Christian a generation younger than Origen, began in the mid-third century to preach what he believed God had revealed to him. He knew the traditional Persian religion of Zoroastrianism, according to which the cosmos was the object of a great struggle between two great powers, being and not-being. In the course of his travels, which took him as far as India, he encountered Buddhism and Hinduism as well. Drawing on all of these traditions, as well as Christian Gnosticism, Mani explained the cosmos in a much more pessimistic way than Origen or the Zoroastrians had. His dualist vision distinguished sharply between the realm of spirit, which was good, and that of matter, which was evil. Before the world was created, matter had invaded spirit: the realms were mingled. Since then, souls had been locked in matter, and humans had been doomed to commit sins and then to expiate them by being reborn in the same condition, again and again, rather than escaping to the realm of pure spirit.

As the successor to Jesus, who had been pure spirit, Mani claimed, he could offer his followers not only an explanation of the universe, but a guide to life, which could release them from matter. He demanded that the "elect"—his most loyal followers—lead an ascetic life, for which he provided detailed rules. Prohibitions against eating certain foods, for example, enabled the Manichean to avoid harming any human spirit that might have entered a lesser being, such as a plant, in the course of reincarnation. These views and precepts had something in common with Origen's. Mani presented them, however, as the culmination not only of Christianity, but of the teachings of all wise men at all times. And he charged his ordinary followers, known as "hearers," not only with learning the true doctrines but also with providing for the elect.

Mani and Manicheans
The Persian mystic Mani used this rock-crystal seal to sign documents. Its design shows Mani flanked by two followers, and the Syriac inscription reads, "Mani, apostle of Jesus Christ."

Mani himself seems to have been executed by the Persian king. But Manichean monks, male and female, put his teachings into practice. A Manichean church grew up, with its own structure and offices. Missionaries soon took to the roads, bearing the scriptures and teachings of Mani everywhere from Spain, Italy, and Roman North Africa to China, where for hundreds of years Manichean churches continued to teach their dualist method and prescribe their rules for a truly holy life. In city after city, the Manicheans and other opponents from within the Christian camp challenged conventional Christians and their beliefs in public debates.

CHRISTIANITY: NEW SOURCES OF STRENGTH

In the fourth century the Christian church grew and changed rapidly. New bishops and clerics, called to replace those who had died in the persecutions and convulsions of the last hundred years, needed training. New churches needed correct, orthodox books with which to conduct services. And many Christians sought new, more intensive forms of spiritual life, which required further innovations. From Constantine on, emperors (except for Julian) transformed Christianity from a dissident sect—in radical opposition to official culture if not engaged in political rebellion against it—to the official religion of the empire. But it still needed defense against enemies, especially those, like the Manicheans, who seemed to have much in common with the Christians.

EUSEBIUS: ENVISIONING THE CHRISTIAN EMPIRE

Eusebius (ca. 260–ca. 339) was the most prominent of the Christian thinkers and writers who met these needs. A cleric from Caesarea, the cosmopolitan city in Palestine where Origen flourished, he came to maturity under the guidance of the saintly Pamphilus, with whom he corrected manuscripts of the Bible, even as his teacher awaited martyrdom in prison. Eusebius assembled all the information he could about the pagan and Christian past, and collected manuscripts of the Greek Old and New Testaments, the acts or records of the sufferings of martyrs, and the writings of Christian teachers. In Caesarea, a wealthy town and diocese, Eusebius had access not only to books but also to skilled scribes who could make multiple copies of them on command. He used these resources effectively to outdo all of his predecessors—including Origen, whose library he used intensively—in fashioning versions of the Bible and accounts of the Jewish and Christian past for Christians to use. He turned the local church into something like a media center for the new Christianity and the Christian empire.

REIMAGINING HISTORY

Even before Constantine's victory in 312, Eusebius drew up the *Chronicle*, a long and complex series of comparative tables of world history—Egyptian, Assyrian, Persian, Jewish, and Roman. These showed Christianity—and its elder sibling, Judaism—to be far older than the culture of the Greeks. The tables also showed, in graphically clear form, that after older empires rose and fell, Rome had unified the world under a single empire just in time for the message of Christ to reach all of its citizens. Evidently, the Christian God was guiding the course of history.

After Constantine rose to power, Eusebius composed an equally innovative history of the church. This work, which unlike pagan histories was largely made up of older documents that gave it the ring of absolute authenticity, argued that true Christians had always accepted a core of canonical texts and doctrines. It vividly portrayed the sufferings of Christian martyrs, often in their own words, and it dismissed even the most serious challenges to Christian orthodoxy, such as the Manicheans, as madmen who "patched together false and godless doctrines." Two more works, both compiled from a vast range of pagan sources, argued that the best pagan thinkers had agreed with Christianity on basic points. A generous God had given them partial revelations of the truths made fully accessible only to Jews and Christians.

THE EMPEROR AS CHRISTIAN HERO

Faced with the need to explain how the Roman emperor could be not a figure of darkness but a hero of the true religion, Eusebius took advantage of ideas first developed during the Hellenistic age of Alexander the Great and his followers. In an elaborate biography, Eusebius portrayed Constantine as the ideal monarch. This almost superhuman figure, as pious as he was strong and virtuous, deserved the help of God and the loyalty of his Christian subjects. The new rhetoric that Eusebius developed, which portrayed the emperor as a godlike figure who ruled the church as well as the state, remained standard in the Eastern world for

A Christian Ruler Many sources other than Eusebius highlight Constantine's devotion to his faith. On this sarcophagus from the late fourth century, Constantine holds a crucifix and what may have been an orb, a symbol of office carried by Christian rulers since Constantine's time.

hundreds of years to come. And the novel texts that he composed became the models for Christian writers for generations.

MONKS AND HERMITS: NEW WAYS OF CHRISTIAN LIFE

Imperial support and theological scholarship were not the only foundations for Christianity's new strength in the fourth century. For some time, individual Christians had left their communities and families to live an especially religious life. Such men and women pursued holiness by dedicating themselves to disciplined and celibate lives. As they did so, they provided the church with new and lasting forms of organization and of spiritual life.

CHRISTIAN MONKS In Upper Egypt, early in the fourth century, a military veteran named Pachomius organized new Christian communities: groups of men, and then of women, who lived together, wore uniform clothing, and followed a simple set of rules for life. Some, like Pachomius himself, had been conscripted into Roman armies and needed a place to settle once peace returned and they were released. Some were poor farm workers seeking a life with meaning. But some were men and women of high family who read Pachomius's writings and sought him out. Whatever their origins, they joined a rigorously ordered community—one perhaps modeled in part on the camps Pachomius had known in the army.

Their day began at dawn, with prayer. Thereafter the members worked, weaving ropes and baskets from rushes, or gardening and baking to produce the simple bread and cooked vegetables that they ate twice a day, in silence, at common meals. At evening came further prayers and a brief discourse by the head of the house, which the others would then discuss among themselves in small groups. A humble, quiet existence, the new **monastic** form of Christian life spread quickly. By the time Pachomius died in 346, some 3,000 monasteries dotted Egypt. These modest houses were the direct ancestors of the thousands of monastic houses, with their extensive libraries and rich liturgical life, that would become one of the central institutions of Christian Europe for centuries.

DESERT HERMITS In Lower Egypt, by contrast, a different sort of Christian life took shape: that of the so-called Desert Fathers and Mothers, many of whom

A Desert Monastery These frescoes of Christ (bottom), Mary (left), and John (right) date from the eleventh century, but the church itself was built in the fourth century for a monastery founded in Lower Egypt by one of the Desert Fathers, at a time when Christian monks in the region became known for their asceticism.

actually lived on the borders of towns. Like the Pachomian monks, the hermits of Lower Egypt chose a life of hard and unremitting work. They, too, wove ropes to earn their keep. But they led severely ascetic lives, often choosing to live entirely on their own, outside civilization, or in tiny groups of individual cells, rather than in communities. They found a strange comfort in the stark lands on the edge of the desert. Syncletica, a fourth-century female ascetic born to wealth, lived in a crypt, among tombs. And they devoted themselves with a silent, radical passion to the pursuit of holiness.

Those who stood out for their piety became spiritual masters, to whom apprentices would come in search of an apparently simple spiritual instruction, which might take years to explore. Their experiences found a unique record in the so-called *Sayings of the Desert Fathers and Mothers*—a long series of stories about the masters, their practices, and the ways in which they initiated younger and less certain believers into the full demands of the desert life. The most stringent of these demands was that the desert way be lived not only in the body but in the spirit. "There are many who live in the mountains," Syncletica told her disciples, "and behave as if they were in the town. They are wasting their time. It is possible to be a solitary in one's mind while living in a crowd." Here was a faith for the toughest of Christians, those men and women who could settle into desert ravines on the edge of cultivated land

and master the snakes and scorpions, demons, and attacks of temper and indigestion that haunted all who tried to live this scrupulously pure Christian life, scraped clean of all temptation. "Those who are great athletes," Syncletica warned, "must contend against stronger enemies."

The dedicated lives of these monks and hermits exercised something of the same magnetic attraction on a particular kind of believer that the small, persecuted groups of the early church had had for believers like Perpetua and Felicitas. Many hoped to make God the center of their lives on earth, thereby finding a peace of the spirit that no other life could offer. For centuries to come, male and female ascetics would serve as core supporters of the church. They offered an example of a more consistently Christian life than anyone could hope to attain in the public life of cities, and of a deep emotional commitment to one another that turned the desert caves they inhabited into a warm and loving community. The desert, the biographer of the hermit Antony wrote, became in their settlements a kind of city.

SIMEON STYLITES The new asceticism was not, of course, for every Christian. This was true even of the more

Simeon Stylites A fifth- or sixth-century Byzantine relief carving depicts Simeon Stylites atop the column where he spent much of his life. The man ascending the ladder, perhaps a priest, carries a censer, the container in which incense is burned during the Mass.

modest forms in which it was practiced by the Egyptian monks of Pachomius or the Palestinian monks who later filled the outskirts of Jerusalem and other cities with their clustered cells. But it could be witnessed and appreciated by thousands, such as the crowds drawn to a curious spectacle in the desert near the Syrian city of Aleppo.

There Simeon Stylites—a Syrian Christian of the late fourth and early fifth century—devoted himself to an increasingly harsh regimen that included fasting and wearing clothing so tight as to cause severe pain. He began to live on increasingly tall pillars (Stylites means "of the pillar") and took up permanent residence on a small platform atop an ancient column some thirty feet high. Simeon stayed there for thirty-six years, leading a stunningly austere life. Though Simeon insisted he was an ordinary mortal, the fascinated crowds that gathered under his pillar regarded him as a man of superhuman purity and power. They cheered and counted as he prostrated himself over and over again, and listened eagerly to his twice-daily sermons urging them to fight heresy, repress the Jews, or demand greater dedication and piety from the leaders of the church.

THE RELIGION OF EMPIRE

When Constantine defeated his chief rival and established his imperial power under the sign of Christianity in 312, the religion that he sought to favor and regulate was complicated and contentious. Holy men rivaled bishops for authority, and heretics challenged orthodox theologians. Moreover, Christianity was but one feature of the late empire's rich and fluid culture, which was still steeped in the pagan practices and classical learning of the Roman Republic and early empire. How was the first emperor to give Christianity legal standing to deal with these pressures?

ARIANISM AND THE COUNCIL OF NICEA It was one of the many challenges to orthodoxy that moved Constantine, as we have seen, to take a direct hand in governing the church. A priest from Alexandria named Arius had been putting forward arguments about God and Jesus that troubled many. Arius had challenged his bishop, who argued for the absolute divinity of Jesus, with the argument that God the Father had, in fact, created his Son. If the Son was created, then he was not eternal and could not be identical in his essence to the Father. The compelling logic of this position, called Arianism, appealed to a

Council of Nicea A twelfth-century fresco from a monastery in present-day Bulgaria imagines the Council of Nicea in 325. Constantine, flanked by members of the clergy, passes judgment on the Alexandrian priest Arius, who lies prostrate in the foreground.

number of respected thinkers, including Eusebius himself. A local gathering of bishops suggested to Constantine that he assemble the senior clergy to debate it. He did so, assembling the first general council of the church in 325 at Nicea, not far from Constantinople.

At this **Council of Nicea**, the vast majority decided against Arius, and almost all of the bishops who had supported him accepted their opponents' view. The view of Jesus as divine, after all, had the authority of tradition behind it, as Origen and other Christian writers had generally espoused it. The council fathers hammered out a formula—one account holds that Constantine proposed it—according to which God the Father and the Son were "of the same substance," and they inserted this into the statement of the Christian creed that the council promulgated as an official statement of the church's core beliefs. This came to define the core beliefs of Catholic Christianity. Arius went into exile in Palestine.

Unity, however, was never fully achieved. Constantine gradually moderated his position, allowing Arius and his followers to return home. Constantine's last surviving son, who ruled as Constantius II from 337 to 361, was strongly attracted to Arianism and tried to establish a compromise position between it and what had become orthodoxy. The questions at issue would continue to be debated over the centuries.

THE DONATIST CHALLENGE

More serious—and much more threatening to the church's unity—was a second spiritual war, one that blazed up after the Great Persecution begun under Diocletian came to an end in 313. North Africa had long been a central area of the church, as it was of the empire: wealthy, productive, and closely connected to the western center of the empire in Italy. When the persecution of Christians ended there, debates raged about the status of those Christians who had surrendered books and other church properties to the authorities without seeking martyrdom. Donatus Magnus (d. ca. 355), who became bishop of Carthage in 313, insisted that sacraments administered by the clerics who had compromised themselves in the years of persecution were invalid. In Carthage and elsewhere, bishops who had managed to survive by making what they saw as necessary concessions were denounced by **Donatist** purists, who insisted that they should have died for the faith.

From the Donatist challenge a second church began to emerge—a church, like the earliest Christian ones, that admitted the faithful only, excluded all others, and chose its own bishops and clerics. Donatists had the moral and theological authority that comes with absolute adherence to a narrow, tautly drawn line of principle. Their preaching seems to have had a special appeal for the peasants of Roman North Africa. Their church challenged the imperial church to a competition that an established religion could hardly hope to win if it had to rely on the human qualities of its servants alone. The orthodox church was still trying to force the Donatists back into the fold by systematic persecution when the Vandals invaded Africa in 429 and conquered it within a few years.

CHRISTIANITY IN A DIVERSE CULTURE

In the late fourth century, as emperors fought unsuccessfully to keep Rome united, the religious and cultural scene in the empire was above all diverse. From the city of Rome to cities deep in the western and eastern provinces, a great many people continued to observe pagan rituals,

Hypatia of Alexandria A fifth-century terra-cotta statue portrays Hypatia, a scholar who was representative of the great intellectual and cultural diversity of the later Roman Empire. This diversity was dealt a blow when, caught in the middle of a conflict between Christians and Jews in Alexandria, she was murdered by a Christian mob.

to consult and sacrifice to pagan gods, and to believe that they lived in the religious and moral world of the great republican writers Virgil and Cicero. Education, after all, still centered on the study of the republican and early imperial classics. Grammar schools and state-supported public professorships of rhetoric trained ambitious young men in the skills of oratory. In the houses of great urban families, and in the villas of Roman aristocrats in Britain and Gaul, young men copied and corrected manuscripts of the Roman poets and historians under the severe eyes of tutors who insisted that they master every fine point of grammar, rhetoric, mythology, and history. In the cities of the east, the Greek classics were studied with equal care. Hypatia (d. 415), a female scholar and philosopher who learned mathematics and much more from her father, the mathematician Theon of Alexandria (d. ca. 405), corrected and edited the works of the greatest ancient astronomer, Claudius Ptolemy.

This way of life, with its passionate loyalty to the old texts and the old gods, coexisted surprisingly well with the Christian churches in much of the empire. Many—perhaps the majority—of members of the old pagan families attended churches, even as they also committed themselves and their children to a regime of purely classical literary education. Learned Christians studied Plato and his followers, consulted astrologers about the future, and had their villas frescoed with mythological images.

Ordinary Christians also studied the New Testament texts in the new kind of book—the codex—that Christians now preferred. One way to study was simply to copy the text, and women sometimes acted as scribes as well as men. Those who could not read the New Testament—and those who could read a little, but had no access to the works of learned authorities such as Origen and Eusebius—were mostly dependent on what they could learn when a bishop preached to the city's entire Christian community in simplified language. Christians sometimes married pagans,

Mixing Christianity and Paganism A third-century mosaic from a cemetery beneath Saint Peter's Basilica in Rome reflects the interwoven religious practices of many communities. The intermingling Christian and pagan imagery conflates Christ with the sun-god Apollo, who is drawn through the sky on a chariot.

and even pious ones engaged in practices that resembled those of the pagans. Monica, the North African woman whose son, Augustine, would become the greatest Christian thinker of the late empire, still brought small gifts of flowers and food to the shrines of Christian martyrs, as her ancestors would have to pagan temples. In many areas, though not all, the religious situation seemed diverse but stable—perhaps more stable than the empire itself as imperial authority came under increasing threat internally and externally.

IMPERIAL AUTHORITY UNDER THREAT (MID-4TH– MID-5TH CENTURIES)

Attacks at the borders continued to command the armies and resources of the empire over the mid- and late fourth century. What had been a network of great cities that stretched from Britain to Asia Minor was gradually

New Testament Codices In this fifth-century Italian mosaic, bound codices of the Gospels of Mark, Luke, Matthew, and John are displayed in a cabinet. Codices, the new literary technology so important to the spread of Christian texts, were stored flat to prevent warping.

reduced to a skeleton of more or less intact roads sustained by the tax collectors and garrisons who traveled them. City governments relinquished some of their traditional functions of public support to the church, especially as elite families departed for the countryside. And public disorder became a more serious threat in the cities of the empire.

VIOLENCE AND AUTHORITY

Never gentle to its subjects, the imperial state in the fourth century became increasingly violent to anyone who broke the law, threatened public order, or simply angered an emperor. Constantine, hailed by Christians for his tolerance, showed zeal and ingenuity in inflicting pain. He revived the old Roman punishment for parricide (the murder of a parent or close relative): sewing up the guilty party in a sack, with snakes, and throwing the bundle into a river. He also devised ingeniously appropriate penalties for other crimes, such as pouring molten lead down the throat of a slanderer. Members of the imperial court who fell into suspicion and public enemies were crucified or burned at the stake.

One document gives the flavor of this new imperial world. A conversational manual for Latin speakers who planned to travel in Greek-speaking parts of the empire in the fourth century includes in one of its vocabulary exercises this description of Roman justice in a provincial town: "The governor arrives to take his place on the platform between the guards. The platform is prepared. . . . The accused man stands, a brigand. He is interrogated as his doings deserve. He is tortured. The interrogator hammers him, his breast is torn. He is hung up . . . he is beaten with rods, he is flogged . . . he is led off to be beheaded." Imperial authority, in the world of this textbook dialogue, was not an abstraction. But enforcement of this kind required consistency: any sign of weakness could undercut such public shows of strength and provoke further resistance.

CHALLENGES TO IMPERIAL AUTHORITY

Yet the threat of official violence was not strong enough to maintain order. In the face-to-face world of the ancient cities, where news traveled quickly, crowds assembled on little notice: Christian flash mobs materialized when a Manichean and a Christian, or a Donatist and an orthodox bishop, were to debate. Sometimes they took it into their own hands to create, or restore, what they saw as true public order.

CROWD ACTIONS Early in the fifth century, some 500 Egyptian monks entered the city of Alexandria en masse. The two patriarchs of the local Christians were locked in confrontation with Orestes, the imperial prefect tasked to run the city. Amid these tensions brawls broke out between the city's numerous Jews and the local Christians. Orestes seemed to take the Jews' side when he ordered the arrest of a Christian teacher they detested. Violence on both sides followed, and eventually the Christians expelled at least a large part of the Jewish population from the city. They even attacked Orestes, himself a Christian, who barely escaped with his life. The crowd also murdered Hypatia, the female scholar and philosopher. Christians, once the victims of Roman crowds and imperial authority, now themselves challenged the empire's public order.

THE BISHOP AND THE EMPEROR

Emperors could use such mob actions to confront enemies and carry out policies, but they could also respond with savage punishments. In 390, the citizens of Thessalonica murdered an imperial official who had arrested a popular charioteer, along with some of his colleagues. Ambrose, a famously learned bishop of Milan, and others begged the emperor Theodosius I, who was then in Italy, to spare the sinners. He did so at first, but then decided to avenge the murders and massacred some 7,000 citizens.

The horrified bishop wrote formally to the emperor, to tell him that he must repent—and that he, Ambrose, could not allow the Christian emperor to attend Mass or take Communion until he did so: "I dare not offer the sacrifice if you intend to be present. Is that which is not allowed after shedding the blood of one innocent person, allowed after shedding the blood of many? I do not think so." Theodosius thus became the first in a long line of secular rulers who would, through the centuries to come, find themselves confronted by the demand of a religious authority that they recognize it as the higher power. Unlike some of those who came after him, Theodosius, after mourning for several months, accepted his punishment and did penance in public. Christians wept to see the emperor humbly repenting his sins in this way.

Theodosius, as we have seen, formally established the empire as Christian with the Edict of Thessalonica in 380. But the location of spiritual—and political—authority was less clear than ever. In the days of the Julio-Claudian emperors, the historian Tacitus had remarked that the "secret of empire" was that soldiers outside Rome could make an emperor. In the age of Theodosius I, it seemed that the Christian God and his human servants might be able to unmake one.

Saint Ambrose A fourth-century chapel mosaic depicts Ambrose, the influential bishop of Milan who convinced Emperor Theodosius I to repent for his massacre of citizens of Thessalonica.

CODIFICATION OF THE LAWS

Both the accomplishments and the weaknesses of the late empire are starkly visible in the figure of Theodosius II, emperor in the east from 416, when he took power in his own right, to 450. In 438, Theodosius issued a codification of the laws: 2,700 enactments of the emperors from Constantine to his own time, topically arranged. He made clear that part of the purpose of this legal project was to attack heresies, which he defined in some detail. Self-confident and pious, Theodosius thus completed what many would have seen as a project that began with Constantine: the full Christianization of the empire. For all his piety, though, Theodosius did not succeed in infusing the vast majority of the laws in his code with any Christian content. His own wars against Rome's enemies, from the Persians to the Vandals, were only indifferently successful. He could not prevent the loss of North Africa and other onetime imperial heartlands.

THE EMERGENCE OF THE LATIN CHURCH: JEROME AND AUGUSTINE

As the western empire disintegrated, great churchmen settled, in a definitive way, the church's organizational and theological problems. Having mastered the works of earlier Christian scholars and theologians, they confronted the rivals of Christian orthodoxy, from pagan philosophers and Manichean missionaries to the churches that claimed to enroll only true believers. Two late Romans in particular—Jerome and Augustine—placed what would become a distinctively Western, Latin church on its long-term foundations.

Both men were born far from what we now think of as the centers of the West—Jerome in Stridon, in what is now Eastern Europe, and Augustine in Thagaste, in North Africa. Both mastered the classics brilliantly, and both soon attracted favorable attention from those in higher positions. **Jerome** (ca. 347–419/420), a Christian from birth, achieved prominence in Rome, where the cultivated Pope Damasus (366–384), grateful for Jerome's support when his election was challenged by a rival and violence ensued, made him his secretary. But Jerome had to leave the city after Damasus died, when he was charged with having illicit relations with well-born female disciples. **Augustine** (354–430), the son of a Christian mother and a pagan father, became a highly successful orator, poet, and teacher of rhetoric, and he climbed the Roman career ladder from Carthage, to Rome, to the imperial capital of Milan.

Both men struggled, throughout their lives as Christians, to accommodate their love for the ancient writers with their commitment to the church. Jerome expressed this conflict in his account of what became a famous dream, in which he was dragged before the divine seat of judgment, flogged, and told that he was "a Ciceronian, not a Christian." Augustine portrayed it even more memorably in his spiritual autobiography, the *Confessions*, in which he tried to understand and explain why his younger self had loved Virgil's pagan heroine Dido so much.

HUMAN NATURE AND SALVATION

In the struggle to define Christian doctrine that continued to occupy much of the church's attention, both men came down, as they thought Paul had, firmly against those thinkers who held that the innate good qualities of human nature entitled at least some men and women to the award of divine grace. As Paul had preached, only faith in Jesus, given by divine grace, could save unworthy humans from the damnation that they deserved. Humanity without grace, Jerome and Augustine insisted, was a disgusting spectacle. With his customary ability to find the vivid detail that no reader can forget, Augustine remarked that a baby, glaring and shrieking in its furious desire for its mother's breast, feeling no desire to help or love anyone else, was a reflection of human nature after the sin of Adam and Eve, and only Christ could ransom it. Jerome would certainly have agreed.

Augustine went on to elaborate the doctrine of predestination. God, Augustine insisted, chose of his own volition both the elect, who had faith, and the reprobate, who did not. Yet the elect could still fall and the reprobate could still rise, if they willed it: "It depends on you to be elect," Augustine told his congregation. True, God knows who will be saved and who will be damned, but this is because he knows what each person will do. Predestination, Augustine believed, did not do away with human freedom.

Jerome and Augustine Despite their differing approaches to their faith, this miniature seventh-century painting of Jerome (left) and Augustine (right) places them side by side, emphasizing their shared pursuit of Christian scholarship. Both hold a book, symbolizing their notable learning.

AUGUSTINE'S CONVERSION

The two men differed in many ways and did not get on particularly well with one another. Jerome did not have to undergo anything like Augustine's protracted struggle to become a Christian in the first place. Augustine, though exposed to Christianity early in life by his mother, followed a long and winding spiritual journey. At one time a convinced Manichean and astrologer, he later decided that the canonical Manichean texts and those who taught them were superficial. Even then he dedicated himself at first to the reading of pagan philosophical works by Plato and others. Long attached to a woman whom he loved and with whom he had a son, he gave her up for a more

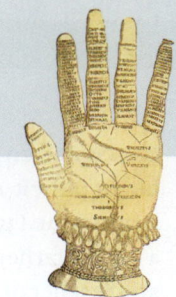

AUGUSTINE AND MONICA

In his *Confessions* (397–400), Augustine, Bishop of Hippo, describes the death of his mother, Monica. He conveys the sadness of the universal experience of losing a parent, but also the solace of his Christian faith in her salvation. Torn by these responses, he seeks to reconcile his identities as a Christian and his mother's son.

On the ninth day, then, of her sickness, the fifty-sixth year of her age, and the thirty-third of mine, was that religious and holy soul set free from the body.

I closed her eyes; and there flowed a great sadness into my heart, and it was passing into tears, when mine eyes at the same time, by the violent control of my mind, sucked back the fountain dry, and woe was me in such a struggle! But, as soon as she breathed her last, the boy Adeodatus burst out into wailing, but, being checked by us all, he became quiet. In like manner also my own childish feeling, which was, through the youthful voice of my heart, finding escape in tears, was restrained and silenced. For we did not consider it fitting to celebrate that funeral with tearful plaints and groanings; for on such wise are they who die

unhappy, or are altogether dead, wont to be mourned. But she neither died unhappy, nor did she altogether die. For of this were we assured by the witness of her good conversation, her "faith unfeigned," and other sufficient grounds.

What, then, was that which did grievously pain me within, but the newly-made wound, from having that most sweet and dear habit of living together suddenly broken off? I was full of joy indeed in her testimony, when, in that her last illness, flattering my dutifulness, she called me "kind," and recalled, with great affection of love, that she had never heard any harsh or reproachful sound come out of my mouth against her. But yet, O my God, who madest us, how can the honour which I paid to her be compared with her slavery for me?

As, then, I was left destitute of so great comfort in her, my soul was stricken, and that life torn apart as it were, which, of hers and mine together, had been made but one.

QUESTIONS FOR ANALYSIS

1. What does Augustine mean when he says that his mother did not "altogether die," and why then was it unfitting to cry at her funeral?
2. Why was Augustine so "full of joy" about her testimony of his dutifulness?
3. What does Augustine see as the real source of sadness after the death of a loved one?

Source: *Prolegomena: St. Augustine's Life and Work, Confessions, Letters,* trans. J. G. Pilkington, in *The Nicene and Post-Nicene Fathers of the Christian Church,* 1st ser., vol. 1, ed. Philip Schaff (Buffalo, NY: 1886) pp. 138–39.

---

advantageous marriage and found it achingly difficult to renounce his sex life and become celibate. It was only by traveling mentally through the harmonious universe of the Neoplatonists that Augustine finally found himself, in Milan, living with Christian friends and exposed to Christian classics.

Augustine described these spiritual adventures in his *Confessions*, written in the 390s. His story reaches its climax in a famous scene in a garden. Here Augustine recounts how he heard a child chant *Tolle, lege* ("Take, read"); opened the life of Saint Antony; and found inspiration for a new kind of meditation and, ultimately, a full

and final conversion. Augustine's experiences, and his narrative of them, became the preeminent model of Christian conversion in the Western church. Jerome, for all his eloquence and erudition, wrote no comparably classical work of Christian spirituality.

JEROME AND AUGUSTINE AS LEADERS

Their careers as leaders of Christian communities also diverged. Jerome had problems with male authority figures, from Pope Damasus, whom he criticized sharply, onward. He benefited from the patronage of wealthy Christian women, which enabled him to found a learned, monastic community in Palestine. With their help Jerome became one of the models of the Christian life of retirement and contemplation. He admired two of his benefactors, Paula and Eustochium, so much that he wrote letters under their names, which powerfully demonstrated their piety and learning. Augustine, by contrast, found mentors in the public men who led the church—above all Ambrose, whose learning, eloquence, and unshakable poise impressed him deeply. He watched as Ambrose regulated Christian life for the great city of Milan, admiring the rigor with which Ambrose enforced what he saw as pure Christian devotion. Augustine also noted the sharp sense of what worshippers needed that led Ambrose to introduce communal singing into the service. Women, in Augustine's vision of Christianity, played a more subordinate role than in Jerome's.

Later, Augustine was chosen by popular demand, first as a priest and then as bishop of Hippo in North Africa. There he spent the last three decades of his life administering a large diocese and defending his flock against heretics and invaders. Augustine's lived Christianity was active and engaged in the world: a model for later bishops, not for contemplatives.

JEROME AND AUGUSTINE AS SCHOLARS

Nonetheless, the two men's achievements were closely related. Both of them, to begin with, set out to establish Christian scholarship and theology, in the Latin-speaking western empire, on a still deeper and more solid foundation than the one Origen and Eusebius had provided in the east. Jerome, a scholar trained in Greek and even, to some extent, in Hebrew, set out, as Origen had, to provide his church with a reliable Bible. Working with the Hebrew original of the Old Testament, as well as the Greek version of it and the Greek New Testament, he produced an extraordinarily beautiful work in Latin that became, somewhat altered, the **Vulgate**—the Bible that came to be used throughout the Western church.

Augustine lacked Jerome's mastery of Greek, to say nothing of Hebrew. But he shared the same commitment to applying the finest tools of ancient philosophy and rhetoric to the needs of the Christian church. In *On Christian Doctrine*, he showed how each of the main disciplines of the ancient curriculum could be applied to the study of the Bible and the preaching of Christian doctrine. Augustine acknowledged that even the wisest pagans had not fully anticipated Christian truth. But he still found a place for their ideas and methods in the Christian curriculum. The Jews had robbed the camp of the Egyptians on their way to freedom, he argued, and made Egyptian treasure serve their needs. In the same way, Christians could rob the pagans of their ideas and methods, so long as they saw to it that these were used only for proper religious ends. Augustine himself used the philosophical skills he had learned from the Neoplatonists to show how inferior the wisdom and eloquence of human writers were to the simple, inevitable truths that his Christian mother, who may have been illiterate but whose piety was unshakeable, had always known.

A UNIVERSAL CHURCH

The more sharply Augustine was challenged, the more original and brilliant were his responses. When Rome fell in 410 to Alaric and the Visigoths, members of the senatorial aristocracy complained that the city had lost the favor of its ancient gods by adopting the Christian religion. Augustine replied with a massive and magnificent rereading of history, *The City of God*, in which he denied any effort to glean simple, providential lessons from historical events. Christians, he argued, could never be certain, in this world, who was saved and who damned. The two groups coexisted, in state and church, like good and bad fish hauled out of the ocean in a single net, all gasping, all sparkling, but only some of them edible and healthy. Only on the Day of Judgment would God's decisions be announced. Until then, Augustine argued, God's servants on earth—his priests and civil governors—must do their best to rule the church and the state.

As bishop of Hippo, Augustine scored some dazzling successes. The Manichean Faustus acknowledged his defeat in debate with Augustine and converted to Christianity. But when persuasion failed, as it did with the Donatists, Augustine urged the state to apply coercion. Even forced conversions were better than persistence in heresy and error. In Milan, Augustine had seen the great archbishop Ambrose at work—a bishop who did not hesitate to call the emperor himself to account when he thought it necessary. In Hippo, Augustine defined the church as a mixed body—a universal, not a gathered church limited to the saved—and made clear that the state must serve and protect it.

As Augustine lay dying, enemy Vandals who had invaded Christian North Africa and would eventually destroy its deeply rooted Roman civilization were besieging his city. The church he served had developed over two centuries from an archipelago of tiny communities spread across an empire that disliked, and sometimes tried to exterminate, them, into a great public institution, one that possessed buildings, treasuries, and libraries. Christian doctrines, built on but radically different from the philosophy and scholarship of the pagan empire, had reached a high level of precision and sophistication. The ablest men and women in the western empire, in fact, were choosing—for all sorts of reasons—to place their lives in the service of the church. Their decisions proved wise. For centuries to come—indeed, even now—their successors would continue to hold religious services and offer spiritual support to Christians in Europe and beyond.

THE FALL OF ROME (5TH–6TH CENTURIES)

Look up the fall of Rome and you will learn that it happened in 476, when the Gothic leader Odoacer removed Romulus Augustulus from the throne and took him captive. It sounds like the end: the leader of a Germanic tribe topples a Roman emperor—and one named after the founder of the city of Rome. In the fifth century, however, the fall of the last Roman emperor attracted very little attention: neither contemporary observers nor historians said much about it. Romulus Augustulus survived his downfall in good condition. Odoacer gave him a pension, and he lived on in a lavish villa built centuries earlier by a wealthy Roman. Can an empire fall if no one notices?

DEFEATS IN THE WEST

In fact, the quiet transformation of 476 was one in a long string of misfortunes that struck the city of Rome and the territories around it in the fifth century. These events definitively separated the declining western half of the Roman Empire from the eastern, which continued to flourish under the rule of Constantinople. Some of these events spread fear throughout the Mediterranean world. In 408, the Visigothic ruler Alaric besieged the city of Rome, holding out successfully for a massive ransom.

In 410, he returned, stormed one of the city's gates, and allowed his troops to sack and pillage. (As Christians, the Visigoths generally spared churches but ransacked the tombs of the pagan emperors.) In the 450s, Attila, leader of the Huns, a terrifying force of Eurasian warriors on horseback, ravaged Italy. Attila decided not to attack the city of Rome itself, and he died in 453 before he could attack Constantinople. But in 455 the Vandals, a Germanic tribe that had moved west from Poland to Spain and had taken North Africa from the Romans, sent a fleet that sacked Rome as effectively as Attila could have.

Disasters like these made clear that the massively fortified borders created by the emperors of the second and third centuries could no longer protect Rome's citizens and subjects. Roman Britain, suffering raids by another Germanic tribe, the Saxons, and unable to gain help from the imperial government in Italy, ceased to exist in 409 or 410, when Roman magistrates were expelled. Roman Spain fell to Germanic invaders in the same years. Life changed dramatically and permanently for the inhabitants of these former Roman provinces. Although the empire continued to mint new coins in the fifth century, they evidently did not circulate in the Iberian Peninsula and Britain, where these coins have not been found. Older coins were also taken out of circulation, hoarded, and buried by fearful owners desperate to preserve what they had and no longer able to buy the sorts of goods they had once routinely imported. Even before the Romans first invaded Britain, the British had regularly bought wine and pottery in large quantities from Gaul. In the fifth century, this trade ceased. The economy of Britain functioned at a lower level after the turn of the fifth century than it had 450 years before.

THE LAST GARRISON

As defeats multiplied, borders crumbled, and conditions inside the imperial heartlands worsened, it became clear that a definitive change had taken place. Long before 476, many realized that the western empire was no longer the powerful entity that it had been even in the fourth century. Surviving sources give us a glimpse of the end on the ground.

Severinus, a Christian from the east who became a saint, arrived in Noricum, near the Danube, an area that now belongs to Bavaria and Austria, in 453 and spent the next three decades there. Another Christian, Eugippius, wrote Severinus's biography. Eugippius was more

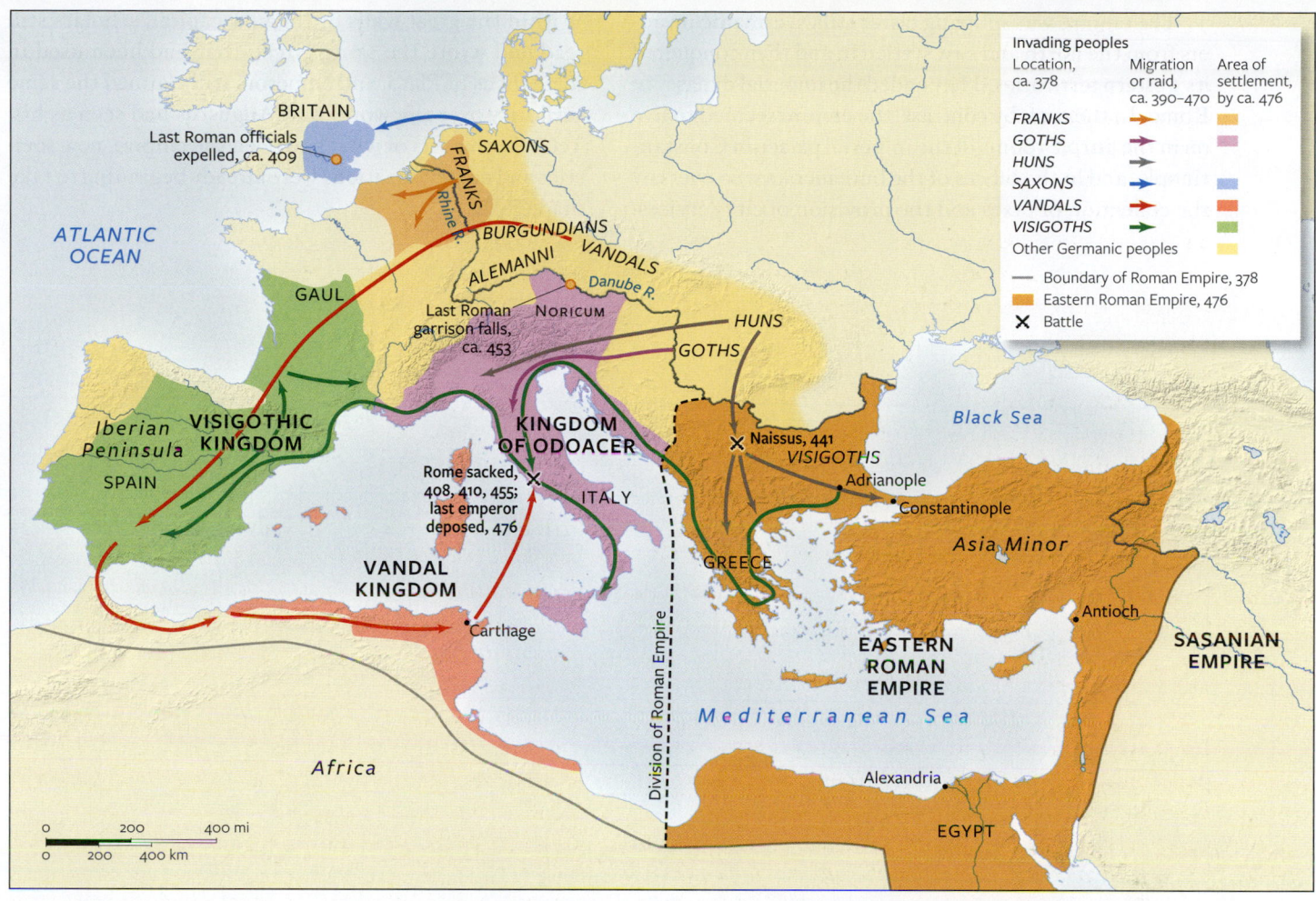

The Fall of Rome, 378–476 After the division of the empire, Roman rule gradually became less stable. Saxons invaded England, expelling Roman forces by 410. Franks, Vandals, Huns, Goths, and Visigoths pushed into Roman territory on all sides. Germanic tribes sacked Rome repeatedly, while the Huns made it as far as Constantinople. The last Roman garrison on the Rhine fell around 453, and by 476 the Gothic leader Odoacer ruled Rome.

interested in Severinus's holiness than in the melting away of Roman authority and power, but he described that as well. Eugippius's account of the last Roman garrison to guard the Danube frontier is especially revealing. Far too small to cover the entire stretch of frontier in any case, this garrison ceased, in the course of Severinus's life, to receive any pay. The empire, based in Italy, no longer maintained the old safe courier service to all its provinces. Detachments of soldiers were sent to collect the money owed, and for a while they succeeded. But a last group was killed by local barbarians, who threw the soldiers' bodies in the river, where they eventually washed up on the shore. This is the last we hear of the garrisons on what had been the Germanic front. Not with a bang but with a whimper, the imperial frontier ceased to exist.

CONCLUSION

In the fourth and fifth centuries, church and empire were both transformed. Christianity became the official religion of the whole vast territory Rome had ruled. The church found ways to take on the learned traditions of the Greco-Roman world, using scholarship and philosophy for its own ends. Its bishops became civic as well as religious leaders, capable of standing up to an emperor when Christian values demanded it. And the church had begun to create new institutions, which enabled Christians to pursue holiness outside the bonds of normal life, in ascetic communities or in solitude. Yet the church was also showing multiple fault lines, as disagreements over theological questions hardened.

The empire was splitting faster still. Germanic invaders from the north and east settled in and then conquered its western territories. They ended the imperial dynasty in Rome. In the east, by contrast, the empire seemed to live on in the purple rooms of the imperial palace in Constantinople, and in the offices of the bureaucrats who oversaw the collection of taxes and the provision of city services.

Within the great walls of the new capital, scholars still read and wrote the same Greek that had been used in the Athens of Plato, and emperors still claimed the same authority over the world that Augustus had seen as his. Yet in both parts of what had been the empire, new societies and new civilizations were already beginning to take shape.

[CHAPTER REVIEW]

KEY TERMS

Constantine (p. 182)
Edict of Milan (p. 183)
pope (p. 183)
Arianism (p. 184)
coloni (p. 185)

Huns (p. 189)
Adrianople (p. 189)
Neoplatonism (p. 191)
Origen (p. 193)
Mani (p. 195)

Eusebius (p. 196)
monastic (p. 197)
Council of Nicea (p. 199)
Donatists (p. 199)
Jerome (p. 202)

Augustine (p. 203)
Vulgate (p. 205)

REVIEW QUESTIONS

1. How did the city of Constantinople exemplify Roman traditions and new departures?

2. What role did Constantine play in the rise of Christianity?

3. What was the relationship between Rome and the various Germanic tribes during the late empire?

4. What other religions and philosophies competed with Christianity in the religious marketplace of the late empire?

5. What criticisms were leveled at Christianity by the pagans, and how did the Christians use scholarship to defend their faith?

6. How was the Christian Bible assembled?

7. How did the late empire use violence to assert its authority?

8. How did religious leaders try to assert their authority over secular rulers?

9. What role did Jerome and Augustine play in the development of the early church?

10. What weaknesses eventually led to the fall of the western Roman Empire?

CORE OBJECTIVES

After reading this chapter, you should have a solid understanding of the following core objectives. To strengthen your grasp of the core objectives, use the resources on the Student Site for The West.

- Analyze the religious and political changes introduced by the Roman emperors from Constantine to Theodosius.

- Identify the causes and effects of economic and social decline in the late Roman Empire.

- Describe the spiritual and philosophical movements and innovations in late Roman society.

- Analyze the evolution of Christian theology and practices in the late imperial period.

- Evaluate the political changes, and the ultimate collapse, of the western Roman Empire in the fourth and fifth centuries.

 GO TO **inQuizitive** TO SEE WHAT YOU'VE LEARNED—AND LEARN WHAT YOU'VE MISSED—WITH PERSONALIZED FEEDBACK ALONG THE WAY.

CHRONOLOGY

483
Clovis I establishes
Frankish kingdom

493
Theodoric the Great founds
a Gothic kingdom in Italy

523
Boethius composes
*The Consolation
of Philosophy*

527
Justinian becomes
Byzantine emperor

529
Benedict creates his monastic *Rule*

529–534
Justinian issues *Corpus Iuris*

532
Nika riots

540
Persian king Chosroes I
attacks eastern
Roman Empire

590
Romans unanimously
proclaim Gregory pope

By end of 6th c.
Saxons conquer
much of Britain

610
Heraclius ascends to Byzantine throne;
reforms and strengthens military;
Muhammad first receives his revelations

622
Hijra to Medina

672 and 711
Muslim troops fail to
conquer Constantinople

726–729
Byzantine emperor
Leo the Isaurian
forbids worship
of icons

By 720s
Umayyad Caliphate
extends from
Asia to Spain

Early 8th century
Bede writes his *Ecclesiastical
History of the English People*

7

Between Worlds

LATE ANTIQUITY AND THE MAKING OF THE MIDDLE AGES

476–900

Christmas Day 800
Pope Leo III crowns
Charlemagne Holy
Roman emperor

843
Treaty of Verdun

n 949 an Italian priest named Liutprand arrived in Constantinople, the capital of the Byzantine Empire. He represented a prince who effectively ruled Italy, and he was well prepared for the mission. Unlike most of those who now lived in central and northern Italy, Gaul, and the Iberian Peninsula, Liutprand not only spoke Latin but also learned Greek, the language used in Constantinople and the provinces it ruled. Well informed about the world, he could discuss the threats to peace in Italy and elsewhere in the west that were posed both by the Islamic rulers who controlled North Africa and the Iberian Peninsula, and by the barbarian peoples of northern Europe. By Liutprand's time the Vikings, seafarers from Scandinavia, were harrowing Atlantic and Mediterranean seacoasts and establishing settlements of their own. The great empire established in the west by Charlemagne was falling apart.

A sophisticated traveler, Liutprand was nevertheless astonished by Constantinople and the magnificent imperial court it housed. The immense buildings, obelisks, and columns that crowned its central ridges stunned visitors. Liutprand saw the Hippodrome built in antiquity for chariot races, the Senate House, and the great domed church of Hagia Sophia ("the Holy Wisdom") as he followed the central processional road that led to the imperial

Ravenna Mosaics After Byzantine forces led by Justinian's general Belisarius recaptured Ravenna, the capital of western Rome, from the Ostrogoths in the mid-sixth century, the city's bishops initiated the construction of magnificent churches decorated with colorful, intricate mosaics. This panel, from The Basilica of Sant'Apollinare in Classe, shows a group of holy virgins following the Magi to welcome the baby Jesus. Their beautifully patterned clothing was popular among noblewomen at the time.

palace complex. There he passed through the Chalke Gate, a large gatehouse covered with statuary, and entered the multiple suites of rooms for receiving visitors—the largest of which could accommodate 228 guests for dinner. The crowds in attendance maintained strict order, coordinated by officials called *silentiaries*—who, as their title suggests, were responsible for warning guests to keep the proper, respectful quiet as they ate.

When Liutprand entered the throne room of the Magnaura Palace, where the emperor awaited him, he saw the most breathtaking spectacle of all. Next to the emperor's throne was a metal tree on which mechanical birds perched and sang. Beside the throne, moving statues of lions roared and lashed the floor with their tails. Following the proper etiquette, Liutprand prostrated himself before the emperor. When he rose, the Byzantine ruler had apparently disappeared. Dazed, Liutprand looked around. Slowly he realized that the emperor, Constantine VII Porphyrogenitus ("purple-born"), and his throne had shot upward toward the ceiling. The emperor, who had somehow managed to change from one set of ceremonial clothing to another, now sat high in the air at a level with his mechanical singing birds—a feat of stagecraft that dramatized his power as no ordinary ceremony could have. The technology that amazed Liutprand had in fact first been developed in Hellenistic Alexandria, though the elaborate court rituals preserved in Constantinople had disappeared in the west. Liutprand could only wonder if the mechanism was something like that of a wine press.

After the death of Theodosius I in 395, the Roman Empire split definitively into its eastern and western components. As the western empire collapsed, the eastern empire gradually evolved into a new organism. Its name comes from

the ancient city of Byzantium, and its transformation from Rome to Byzantium took a couple of centuries, from the fifth to the seventh, to reach completion. Historians used to mark the beginning of the Middle Ages with the formal fall of Rome in 476. Now they refer to the fifth through seventh centuries, when ancient legacies in the East and West were creatively adapted into new forms of political and religious life, as "late antiquity," followed by the long process, from the seventh to ninth centuries, in which a new, medieval civilization took shape. The most dynamic force in this period of adaptive change was Islam, a faith that quickly established a political and cultural foothold in the western and eastern lands where Rome's legacies continued to unfold.

BYZANTIUM: EAST ROME TRANSFORMED (527–630)

Byzantium, as we have seen, was refounded by Constantine as New Rome, the eastern capital of the Roman Empire, in 330 CE. Constantine had equipped it with the aqueducts and roads, forums and law courts that a great Roman city needed, and after his death it came to be called Constantinople—"Constantine's city." Over the centuries to come, Constantine's successors expanded on what he had begun. They provided the city with palaces, churches, holy images, and miracle-working relics—objects that had come into contact with Jesus. One central institution was the Hippodrome, greatly enlarged by Constantine. Chariot races took place there six times a day, preceded by parades and interspersed with performances by singers, acrobats, and mimes. As at Rome, four teams—Reds, Greens, Blues, and Whites—competed, and factions of fans supported each of them with an enthusiasm that often bordered on mob violence. The most important long-term addition to the city's infrastructure came about in the fifth century, when the entire city was surrounded with two sets of immense limestone and brick walls, strengthened by a moat and 192 battlemented towers. These formidable defenses would protect the city from external enemies for some 800 years.

JUSTINIAN: REBUILDING AUTHORITY

The real transformation of Constantinople—and the empire it ruled—took place in the sixth century. For almost forty years, **Justinian** (r. 527–565), nephew and counselor

A Charioteer of the Hippodrome This funerary monument from the Hippodrome memorializes a famous charioteer, Porphyrius, who competed there in the late fifth and early sixth centuries. The relief shows Porphyrius in his chariot, flanked by two winged victories.

of the previous emperor, the childless Justin, ruled the empire. Justinian was an innovator—he took advantage of a new law permitting marriage between people of different rank to wed his mistress, an actress named **Theodora** (ca. 500–548). Of the many institutions he transformed, the central one was the law.

A NEW LEGAL CODE For centuries Roman law had grown, slowly and unevenly, as the Senate and the emperors issued edicts and jurists interpreted them. There were schools, at Berytus (modern Beirut) and elsewhere, to train future lawyers, but only a few collections of the laws existed. In 425 Theodosius II, worried that legal skills were declining in the eastern empire, founded a new law school in Constantinople. More important still, four years later he set up a committee of twenty-two jurists who organized and edited the decrees of the Roman emperors from

Constantine to Theodosius himself. This was the first official law code that the empire had issued in centuries.

Justinian, however, went much further than his predecessors. He declared that making and interpreting the law formed a central part of the emperor's job: "The imperial majesty should be armed with laws as well as glorified with arms, that there may be good government in times both of war and of peace, and the ruler of Rome may not only be victorious over his enemies, but may show himself as scrupulously regardful of justice as triumphant over his conquered foes." Justinian created a committee of jurists that, in only five years, updated the body of imperial legislation in a new *Code*; collected and edited the opinions of authoritative Roman jurists from over the centuries in the *Digest*; and compiled a textbook of legal principles, the *Institutes*. This book offered statements of basic principle, such as "Justice is the set and constant purpose which gives to every man his due. Jurisprudence is the knowledge of things divine and human, the science of the just and the unjust." The **Corpus Iuris** (*Corpus of Law*) as a whole was intended to embody these principles as well as to provide, in one place, the body of Roman law as emperors and jurists had developed it.

Like the codes of the ancient Near East, Roman law was not gentle. Following the precedent set by Constantine, Justinian introduced many new forms of penalty, notably bodily mutilations, into Roman legal practice. But the law still aimed at justice. It acknowledged the continued existence of slavery, but taught that men and women should be considered free until their slave status was demonstrated. Divorce, which Christianity condemned, was restricted more severely than ever before. Women's control of their own property was confirmed, and they were allowed to make bequests directly to their children, even if still minors. Though the *Corpus Iuris* was compiled in a Greek-speaking city, the laws and opinions it contained were in Latin. The continued use of Latin for legal purposes perpetuated the belief that the eastern empire was still Roman—a belief that Justinian's successors would cling to for centuries.

Yet the codification of the law transformed the nature of the empire. Copies of the *Corpus* were sent to provincial capitals. Barbarian rulers in the west, such as the kings of the Lombards, whom we will soon meet, took it as the model for compilations of their own laws. Imperial and royal authority was more solidly founded than ever before. It was rooted, the law made clear, in the sovereign power of the people, but that had passed, irrevocably, to the emperors. In time, as we will see, the mere statement that the people had once exercised power proved radical in its implications. For the moment, however, the emperor claimed a new kind of ideological supremacy, based in the first instance on law.

FISCAL REFORM Justinian also rebuilt the fiscal foundations and administrative organization of the empire. John the Cappadocian, a close ally who rose, as Justinian did, from relatively modest origins, served him as Praetorian prefect and legal adviser. John did his best to transform the existing tax system in the east, which had concentrated on collecting vast amounts of grain and other agricultural products, into one that brought in cash instead. He let no one—even the wealthy—escape their obligations. John's efforts aroused anger, even from some fellow members of the official service. John the Lydian, a learned lawyer and bureaucrat from Philadelphia in western Turkey, recalled those years in savage terms, with a nice classical allusion to the ancient myth of the Greek underworld (Hades) and the three-headed dog that guarded it: "This shark-toothed Cerberus, though he was the common plague of mankind, chewed up my Philadelphia so finely that after him ...it became bereft not only of money, but also of human beings." Archaeological evidence confirms that in the area of Asia Minor that John the Lydian came from, agriculture and city life both contracted in this period—though, as we will see, taxation was by no means the only destructive

Justinian This mosaic in the Basilica of San Vitale in Ravenna from 547 depicts Justinian in all his imperial grandeur, dressed in purple and accompanied by numerous courtiers. The halo around his head and his position beside a bishop (in the gold robe) symbolize that the Christian church sanctioned Justinian's rule.

force at work. Still, by the early 540s, when John the Cappadocian was dismissed, the state enjoyed far larger means than ever before.

THE NIKA RIOTS (532) Justinian's efforts to establish imperial authority and power on deeper foundations provoked resistance. In 532 he scheduled public executions of a member of each of the leading circus factions, the Blues and the Greens. Crowds gathered and a riot started. While faction members chanted "Nika, nika" ("Win, win"), much of Constantinople burned, including the massive old church of Hagia Sophia. The only account we have—the *Secret History* by Procopius, a contemporary historian who recorded the emperor's achievements but despised his character—claims that the emperor was terrified that the mob would murder him in his palace and almost abandoned the city. At this point Theodora played a crucial role.

In Byzantium—as in other court societies—women of high position could be central in political and social life. Theodora came of age as an actress, playing mythological characters in revealing costumes. The law forbade actresses, who had low status in Byzantium, to change their occupation or to marry men of higher standing, such as an heir to the empire. But Justinian fell in love with this tough, witty woman. When he became emperor, she became his partner, and when a new law permitted it, they married. Some later historians described their reign as a double monarchy.

Despite court gossip describing her as a prostitute, Theodora became essential to Justinian's success. Never losing her fellow feeling for poor women, she tried to eliminate prostitution in Constantinople and helped women who had been forced into that life by providing them with dowries. When Justinian wrote, in one law, that there was neither male nor female in the service of Christ, he showed his respect for her views. In the Nika riots crisis of 532, it was Theodora who stiffened her husband's back. "An empire," she supposedly remarked, "makes a beautiful shroud." Justinian held fast. His favorite commander, Belisarius, bribed one faction to leave the circus, then entered it at the head of an army and massacred thousands of members of the other factions. At the end of the day, public order was not only restored but more firmly founded than ever.

IMPERIAL GRANDEUR Justinian, moreover, deployed his wealth in creative ways, building on foundations that previous emperors had laid. Over the last two centuries, Roman men of power had abandoned their distaste for rich colors and fabrics. Silk became the fabric of choice, and

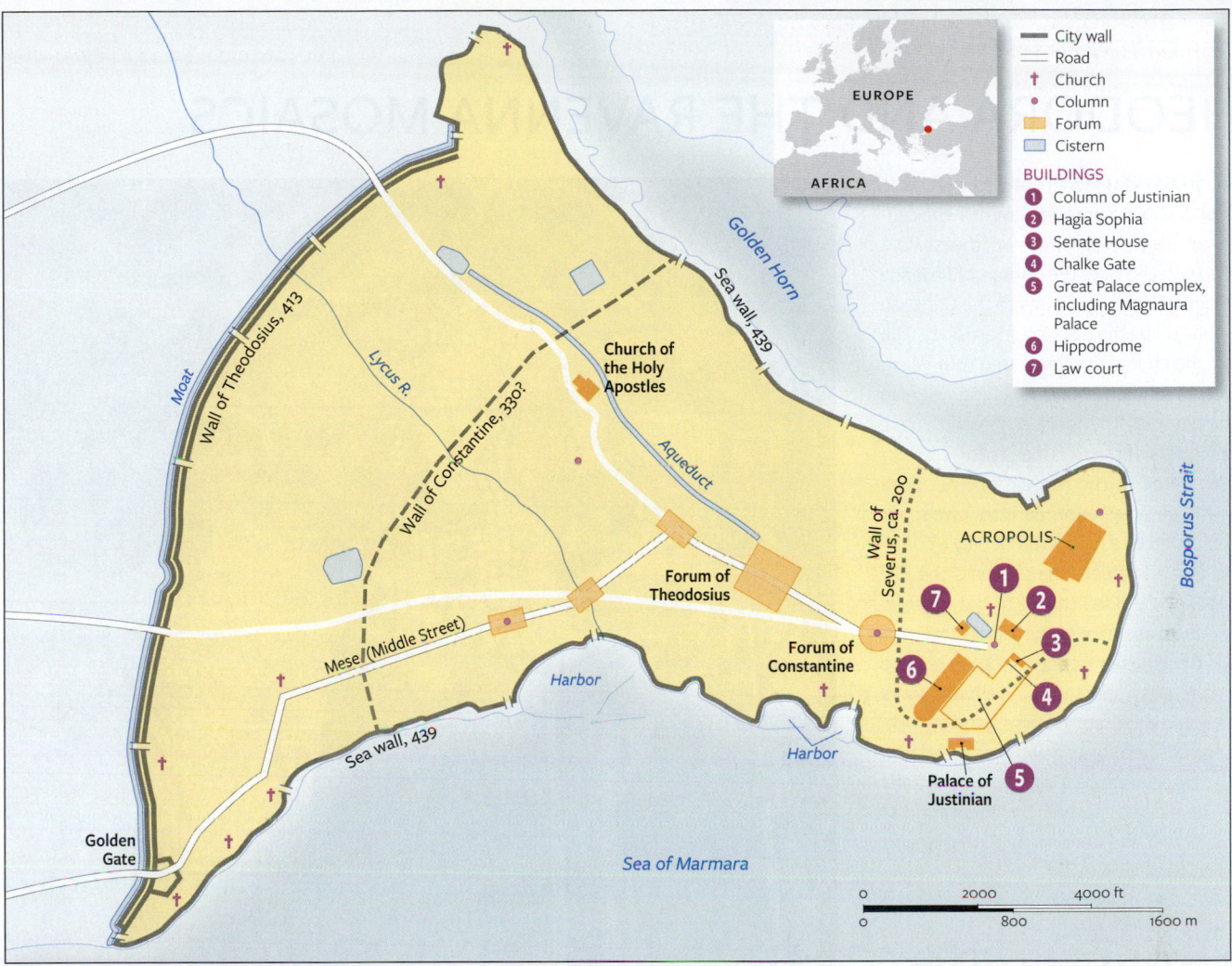

Constantinople under Justinian, ca. 560 Situated on a peninsula overlooking the Bosporus, Constantinople had expanded considerably since it was founded, with Theodosius's fortified wall of 413 marking the ultimate border of the city. The Roman institutions built by Constantine, such as the Hippodrome and law courts, were located in the old city center, at the tip of the peninsula. Roman infrastructure—roads, aqueducts, forums—spread throughout the city. When Justinian rebuilt Constantinople in the mid-sixth century, he added monumental building projects of his own, such as the Great Palace and the church of Hagia Sophia.

purple, the deep, glowing dye made from crushed shellfish, the most desired and enviable of colors, used only by members of the imperial family. Palace life became grander. The corps of eunuchs—men castrated as boys, who had long served as a buffer between the imperial family and the rest of the world—grew in number and importance. These beardless men held many positions in the imperial bureaucracy, in which they had their own career hierarchy. Narses, a court eunuch, would eventually become Justinian's second great commander.

Justinian played to the new respect for extravagance as he rebuilt Constantinople, making it the grandest of capitals. He placed an equestrian statue of himself on an immense column in the center of its largest square to celebrate his military achievements, all of which had been the work of his generals. Magnificent mosaics on the same themes sprawled across the walls and ceiling of the huge palace gate. By the end of his reign, the city had around half a million inhabitants—a radical contrast to Rome, where fewer than 50,000 inhabited a city that had been built for a million people. Like Hadrian and other successful emperors of ancient Rome, Justinian acted as a benefactor across his territories. As he fortified cities such as Athens and Corinth, which had become vulnerable to invaders from the north, and equipped them with baths and other public structures, the emperor seemed to be everywhere.

THEODORA AND THE RAVENNA MOSAICS

In 540, armies dispatched by the Byzantine emperor Justinian captured Ravenna, the capital city of the Ostrogoths in northeast Italy. Between 540 and 600, the bishops of Ravenna built magnificent monuments to the Christian empire, including the Basilica of San Vitale. The walls of the church are decorated with grand mosaics, completed in 547, depicting Justinian and the empress Theodora as imperial rulers and defenders of the Christian faith.

This detail of the mosaic of Theodora shows the empress adorned with jewels, her head encircled by a halo. Attended by a courtier and a handmaiden, she presents the gift of a bejeweled golden chalice to the courtier. The striking placement of the sacred chalice in front of the courtier's contrasting white robe accentuates its importance. All three figures are richly and elaborately dressed, and the bottom edge of Theodora's gown is embroidered with the three Magi bearing gifts to the baby Jesus. The mosaic captures the integration of imperial power and Christian faith that was so central to Byzantine rule.

QUESTIONS FOR ANALYSIS

1. How does this mosaic convey Theodora's faith?
2. How does it represent Theodora's power?
3. How does the image of Theodora suggest the strength of character she showed during the crisis of the Nika riots?

THE CHRISTIAN EMPIRE

Justinian strengthened the imperial embrace of Christianity. In 529, shortly after becoming emperor, he attacked pagan learning through a decree that forbade the teaching of philosophy at Athens; he also made it illegal for pagans to hold public office. This decree resulted in the closing, after almost a thousand years, of the Academy at Athens. Its philosophers, who saw themselves as carrying on the ancient tradition of Plato himself, supposedly went into exile in Persia.

From the start of his reign, Justinian also tried to impose religious unity on the church. Beginning in 325 with the Council of Nicea, the church had been attempting to identify the core doctrines that every Christian must accept. But debates continued. In Rome, and in the west more generally, official doctrine held that Christ was fully God, as well as fully human. In the east—which had been the heartland of Arianism—many disagreed, holding to the position that only God was divine. Since 451, when an ecumenical council had taken place at Chalcedon, near Constantinople, disputes over the relation between Christ's human nature and his divine nature had racked the church. Justinian did his best both to find a theological compromise and to expel heretics. In the end, he failed to stamp out the Monophysites, who held that Christ had only one, divine nature—and whose supporters included his wife, Theodora, as well as many bishops. Eventually, the term *catholic* (literally, "universal") would come to designate the Latin church of Rome. The churches of the east, whose chief officials were called patriarchs, would eventually declare independence from it.

THE CHURCH OF HAGIA SOPHIA
Above all, Justinian made Constantinople the grandest center of Christianity. The city already boasted many churches, a few of them imposing. But the church of Hagia Sophia, rebuilt by Justinian in the wake of the destruction caused by the Nika riots, not only outdid them but even surpassed the great domed Pantheon in Rome itself. Justinian imposed the task of creating the vast structure on two experts in both mathematics and architecture, Isidore of Miletus and Anthemius of Tralles. Setting some 10,000 men to work, they imported materials from all around the empire: porphyry from Egypt, marble of many colors from Thrace and elsewhere, columns from Hellenistic temples in Asia Minor. On an enormous square nave they reared an extraordinary dome, more than 100 feet across and almost 200 feet, at its peak, from the floor of the church.

A high arcade with forty windows let in a flood of

Hagia Sophia The great church of Hagia Sophia in Constantinople is a monument of architectural mastery. Its vast dome and many windows let in far more light and air than had been possible in earlier basilicas. The Arabic calligraphy was added after the church was converted to a mosque in the fifteenth century.

sunlight and made the golden dome, for all its size, seem, as Procopius wrote, "not to rest upon solid masonry" but to be "suspended from Heaven." Traditional basilicas were imposingly dark. Hagia Sophia, by contrast, was so bright it seemed that it was "not illuminated from without by the sun, but that the radiance comes into being within it." The multiple colors of the stones pulled the eye from surface to surface: "One might imagine that he had come upon a meadow with its flowers in full bloom. For he would surely marvel at the purple of some, the green tint of others, and at those on which the crimson glows and those from which the white flashes." The splendid marble blocks were smoothed and fitted together not with lime or mortar but with melted lead, which made the divisions barely visible. This delicate craftsmanship enhanced the beauty of the church and overpowered visitors. When Justinian himself first entered the church, he cried out, "Solomon, I have outdone you."

Hagia Sophia was indeed larger and more spectacular than Solomon's Temple at Jerusalem, as described in the Old Testament. Equally splendid were the services led there by the patriarch of Constantinople and often attended by the emperor and his court. When emissaries from the prince of Kiev, in Russia, came to Constantinople a few years after Liutprand, they reported that during services in Hagia Sophia, they could no longer tell if they were on earth or in heaven.

Justinian built and repaired churches and raised basilicas across the empire, from Jerusalem, to Ephesus in

Asia Minor, to Carthage in North Africa. In the church in which the monks of the fortified monastery of Saint Catherine at Sinai still worship, a millennium and a half later, the roof beams still bear the names of the church's patrons, Justinian and Theodora.

EMPEROR OF STATE AND CHURCH By creating so many structures in honor of God, and by supporting, as he did, the power of the bishops, Justinian represented himself as a Christian emperor in a new sense: one who held power of the same kind, divine in origin, over state and church. He introduced more and more religious elements into court art and ceremony. Sometimes he appeared to defer to religious authority. In processions, he walked while the patriarch rode. On the whole, though, the emperor emerged as the dominant figure. Hymns of a new kind were composed, which emphasized the unity of Christ and emperor. Images also celebrated the emperor in a new way. A double panel of ivory, carved in the 530s

Icons Divine images painted on wood or pieced together in mosaics became associated with the Christianity of the Byzantine Empire. This sixth-century icon of Mary and the baby Jesus comes from the Monastery of Saint Catherine in Egypt.

Barberini Diptych An intricate ivory carving from the 530s shows a triumphant Emperor Justinian on horseback. The heavenly realm of angels above him and the laboring peasants below suggest a divine order of creation.

and known as the Barberini diptych after its later owners, shows Justinian as a classical warrior on horseback, triumphing over his enemies. Angels appear above the emperor, holding a bust of Jesus, to emphasize the religious sanction that underpinned his authority.

RELIGIOUS ICONS: THE EASTERN TRADITION
In the long term, the effects of the new emphasis on religious images were profound. Eastern Christians had long created icons: flat panel paintings that depicted Jesus, the members of the Holy Family, or saints. The earliest surviving examples come from the time of Justinian, from the monastery of Saint Catherine at Sinai. Soon Constantinople became a city of icons, as well as relics, and the icons came to be charged with a miracle-working power. Many thought that the Virgin, images of whom were displayed during sieges, saved the city from barbarian armies. Later emperors went to war carrying icons of this divine

protector. Theologians explained that when worshippers prayed before an icon, they should venerate not the image but its subject. In practice, though, many came to these images to beg them for help in having children or healing illness. Images permeated personal as well as public religious life, and the religious practices that surrounded them deviated more and more from formal theological principles.

Even as the empire became solidly Christian, with the emperors clearly established as protectors of and authorities in the church, Christianity became imperial. The images of Jesus that Justinian's brilliant mosaic workers pieced together from millions of colored stones and tiny pieces of glass represented him not as a suffering human on the cross but as an exalted ruler in heaven, the Pantokrator, or ruler of the universe. A new form of Christianity—the ancestor of modern Orthodox Christianity—had come into being: one that identified rulership with holiness and treated the emperor as godlike.

ECONOMY AND SOCIETY

Constantinople was created as a ceremonial center and a fortified base for the rest of the eastern empire. Home to a thriving sector of artistic and craft production, the city also supported a massive population that had to be defended and provisioned even in difficult times. These identities did much to determine the ways in which the ordinary people of the city lived, worked, and died.

WORK Constantinople, the empire's capital, housed not only the court and the church, but the large population of artisans who realized Justinian's vision of what a church should be. Few made enough to own their own shops. Many earned wages, instead, in large workplaces owned by the imperial government or by churches. Some worked in the mint, creating coins that not only served as a medium of exchange but also enhanced the image of the emperor, shown being crowned by Christ or in the company of the Holy Family and the saints. A whole series of specialized crafts collaborated to make silk. The silk filaments had to be unraveled from cocoons, put onto reels, made into cloth, and finished and dyed—each step requiring a different craft workshop. Mosaics were the most painstaking of crafts. As many as 20,000 pieces were needed to compose one square meter of an image that, when complete, would cover an enormous wall. Foreign merchants traveled to the city from east and west, armed with safe-conduct documents. Glass, linen, and African ivory came from Greece

and Egypt; luxury goods, carried by Arab traders, came from China and India. A system of investments and loans financed large trading expeditions.

Outside the capital, most Byzantines worked the land. They sowed wheat in the late fall to take advantage of the rainy season, allowing half of their land to lie fallow each year to restore its fertility. As always in the Greek world, olive trees and grape vines were widely cultivated, as olive oil was used for cooking and for fuel in lamps. Life in the country was, for the most part, poor and simple. The tools farmers used had changed little, if at all, since Roman times, and crop yields were relatively low.

WOMEN'S LIVES Women's lives were sharply separated by their places in society. Noblewomen lived in palaces, traveled in litters (seats carried by servants), and seldom if ever saw the world outside their luxurious habitats. Like the women of ancient Athens, they were expected to remain at home except when joining a religious procession, going to the public baths, or mourning a death or celebrating a birth in their family. They were accompanied by male escorts and covered their faces with veils. Poor women lived and worked in shops and fields. When a wealthy woman lost her husband, she might enter an aristocratic convent. A poor woman in the same situation would go on working as she always had, unless a grown child could support her. Whatever her rank, a Byzantine

Byzantine Noblewomen In a mosaic from the early sixth century, a female figure is clad in the richly decorative clothing, jewelry, and hairstyle suggestive of the luxurious (though cloistered) lives of Byzantine noblewomen.

woman's destiny was normally assumed to be marriage and childbearing. Girls as young as seven could be engaged, and most married at thirteen or fourteen. Only women from the higher ranges of Byzantine society became literate. Yet—as the case of Theodora shows—the empire's extremely hierarchical order enabled empresses, and a few other highly born women, to shape public policy and religious life.

IMPERIAL STRENGTH AND DECLINE

As Justinian's triumphs in the east grew, he also tried to reunite the Roman Empire as a whole. He sent his general Belisarius, who had won his and Theodora's trust when he crushed the Nika rioters in 532, to North Africa the next year. There, with an armada of ships and a small army of some 15,000 men, Belisarius defeated the Vandals, a Germanic tribe, who had invaded the region in 429 and founded their own kingdom. Awarded the consulship and other honors, Belisarius then conquered Italy, taking Naples, Rome, and finally the capital of Ravenna back from their Gothic rulers. His later career was less dazzling

and he lost Justinian's confidence, retiring to Constantinople in 548. But he survived to defend the city in 559 against another set of invaders, Huns from north of the Danube. His clever tactics convinced them that the ragtag militia he had managed to raise was a massive army. Meanwhile, the eunuch general Narses, who followed Belisarius into action in Italy in 551, conquered the Goths and restored Byzantine power. He remained in Italy, rebuilding fortifications and defeating another Germanic tribe, the Franks, until he was dismissed and given a high title in 568.

Although the capital that Justinian built was still the city that astonished Liutprand four centuries later, the unified empire that Justinian thought he had brought back into existence in the 530s could be maintained only at the cost of long and destructive wars from Italy to Syria—and by paying subsidies to barbarians, which in turn engendered resentment, and even assassination plots, against the emperor. For much of Byzantine history, the great capital in Constantinople was the head of a much smaller political body than its architects had expected.

PLAGUE (541–542) Like his successes, Justinian's failures show that history often turns on unpredictable

Byzantium, 527–565 In 527, the Byzantine Empire held sway over the former eastern Roman Empire, including Greece, Asia Minor, and Egypt. By 565, it had expanded across North Africa, subsuming the Vandal Kingdom; gained territory as far as the southern coast of the Iberian Peninsula; and conquered former Ostrogothic lands in Italy and around the Adriatic Sea. Constantinople even withstood an attack by the Huns in 559.

events, big and small. Without Belisarius, for example, the timid Justinian would never have had a chance of winning back the western empire, even temporarily. Another contingency proved even more powerful and, in fact, decisive. In 541, plague struck the empire. Procopius recorded the terrifying, and puzzlingly varied, symptoms that manifested themselves: black swellings in the groin, armpits, and elsewhere, followed in some cases by deep coma and in others by wild excitement as patients threw themselves out of their beds onto the floor or tried to hurl themselves into the sea. The disease raged for three or four months in Constantinople, where mortality rose to 5,000 and then to 10,000 a day, and returned in later years.

Normal morality disappeared in these terrible conditions: "Now in the beginning each man attended to the burial of the dead of his own house, and these they threw even into the tombs of others, either escaping detection or using violence; but afterwards confusion and disorder everywhere became complete." Justinian appointed an official to see to the burial of the dead and put the army at his disposal. But the mounds of corpses grew too quickly for orderly disposal. Funeral rites were abandoned, corpses piled in ditches and fortifications, and finally the emperor himself fell ill. Throughout the empire and outside it, in Persia and elsewhere, the plague emptied farms, left crops unharvested, and harrowed the cities. Slaves melted away, and many houses were completely deserted. Although Justinian recovered, Theodora died. He never regained the energy and creativity of his early years, and his reunited empire soon cracked apart once more.

THE REVIVAL OF PERSIA

Another—and equally unexpected—cause for Byzantium's decline came, as the plague probably did, from outside the empire. In 224 a Persian nobleman, Ardashir I, overthrew the Parthian kingdom with which Rome had long waged war and created what became the Sasanian Empire (224–651), centered in Iran but encompassing much of the Near East and Central Asia at its height. This new, tightly organized Persian state now spread from the Euphrates to the Indus. It had its own Zoroastrian religion; its own priesthood, the Magi; and its own spectacular capital at Ctesiphon (not far from modern Baghdad), one of seven central imperial cities. An immense brick arch, more than 100 feet high, is all that remains of what was once a structure as spectacular as anything in Constantinople—an imposing palace, its floors covered with splendid carpets and its walls with mosaics and more carpets. Supplicants came here from all corners of the Sasanian Empire to plead their case to the *shahanshah*, an absolute monarch who ruled his empire,

as the kings of ancient Persia had, through satraps. He received them wearing a crown so heavy that it had to be suspended from the ceiling. In this tolerant kingdom, not only Zoroastrians but Christians, Manicheans, and Jews lived together peacefully. Under Sasanian rule, the Jewish academies of Babylon assembled the great body of legal principles and debates now known as the Babylonian Talmud, which would become the core of Jewish tradition and education in later centuries.

WAR WITH SASANIAN PERSIA (540–630)

The Romans warred with Persia from 230 to the end of the third century, and again from the 330s to the 380s and in the 520s. In 540 Chosroes I, the ruler of Persia, attacked the empire from the east, forcing Justinian to strengthen his frontiers. The Persians' heavily armed cavalry and skilled archers hit hard and fast, so terrifying the eastern Roman legions that they sometimes refused to fight. Chosroes reached Mesopotamia and Syria, where he sacked the ancient city of Antioch. In the second half of the sixth century, though, Persia—like Constantinople—suffered from plague and invasion by migrant peoples, as the Slavs, followed by the Avars, warrior nomads from the steppes north of the Black Sea, spread into the Balkans and beyond. Divided and relatively weak, the Sasanian Empire now posed little threat; in 591, the Byzantine emperor Maurice (r. 582–602) won concessions from the son of the monarch, Chosroes II, in return for installing him on the Persian throne.

But Maurice became unpopular with the troops when he insisted on cutting military pay and campaigning through the winter, and eventually an officer deposed and executed him. Civil war broke out in Byzantium just as Sasanian Persia was recovering strength. Persian armies moved into Roman territory, conquering Egypt and Syria and taking their great cities, Alexandria and Damascus. In 614 Persian troops captured Jerusalem, taking the True Cross—on which, tradition held, Jesus had been crucified—from its place in a Christian shrine. When the Byzantine emperor Heraclius (r. 610–641) asked for a peace treaty, Chosroes II imprisoned his diplomats. Soon the Persians besieged Constantinople itself.

REFORM UNDER HERACLIUS

In a whirlwind of activity following his accession in 610, Heraclius reorganized the empire. By cutting official pay, raising taxes, and melting down the treasures of the churches, he found the resources to buy off one set of enemies, the Avars, for a time. He remade the Byzantine army into an effective force. He schooled his soldiers in the belief that they

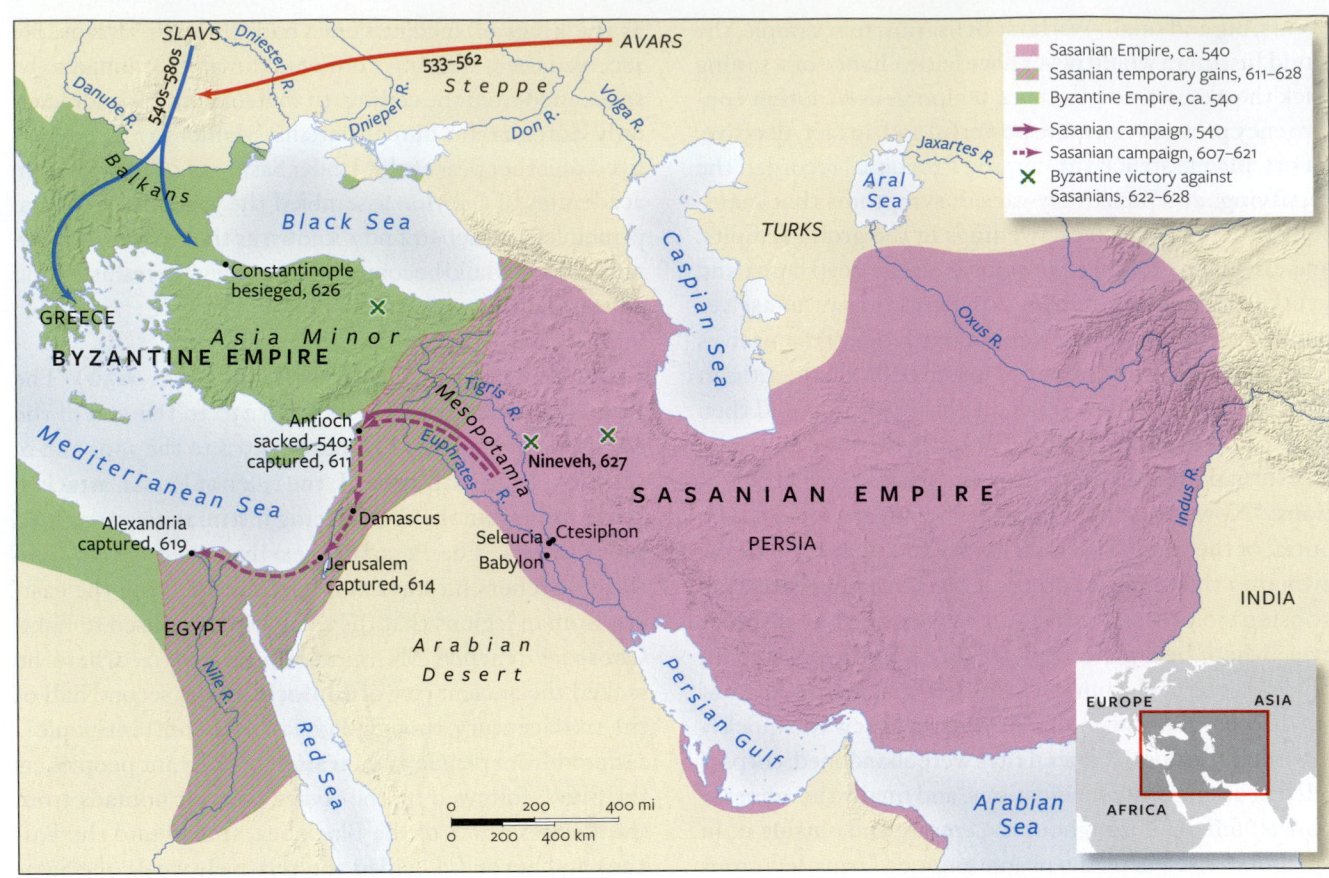

The Sasanian Empire and Its Wars with Byzantium, 540–628 From the mid-sixth century, the powerful Sasanian Empire put renewed pressure on Byzantium's eastern borders, conquering significant territory in Syria and Egypt and even besieging Constantinople in 626. To the west, Byzantium was threatened by the Slavs and Avars invading from eastern Europe and Central Asia. These migrant peoples also caused instability in Persia, and Heraclius's campaigns in the 620s succeeded in reversing Sasanian territorial gains.

represented Christianity against infidels—an idea that would have a long history—and trained them intensively in traditional Roman tactics. In a brilliant series of campaigns, Heraclius defeated three separate Sasanian Persian armies and formed an alliance with the Turks, a Central Asian people. Meanwhile, in 626 the great walls of Constantinople held off a siege force consisting of Persian ships and an Avar army. As Heraclius and the Turks ravaged the central lands of Persia, news came of a plot against Chosroes II, who was deposed and killed in 628. The previous frontiers of the Byzantine Empire were restored, and in 630 Heraclius brought the True Cross back to Jerusalem.

THE ORIGINS OF ISLAM (600–650)

The eastern empire had survived its most demanding test. Or so Heraclius believed. But he could not have been more

wrong. In their search for allies, both Byzantium and Persia had dealt with Arabs—inhabitants of the coastline and, in some cases, the central desert of the Arabian Peninsula. These lands now produced a new and lasting civilization, centered on a new religion: one whose quick expansion threatened the survival of the eastern empire far more radically than the Persians had.

ARAB SOCIETIES

The new religion of Islam took shape around oases in the Arabian Desert. The peninsula had been divided, for centuries, between coastal inhabitants and desert peoples. Along the eastern and southern coasts, great states grew up in the first millennium BCE. Once navigators mastered the Indian Ocean monsoon cycle, around the beginning of the Christian era, they used the winds that could take ships across the ocean in both directions to play a central role in world trade routes. Ivory and other goods were brought across the Red Sea from Africa and transported north to Persian and Roman territory. The **Silk Road**—the 4,000-mile-long series of trade routes along which goods and beliefs traveled from China and India to Constantinople and Rome, was reaching the peak of its activity, with caravans passing through Persia and the northern territory of the Arabian Peninsula. The Arabian kingdoms controlled the trade in spices, which were carried in ships across the Indian Ocean and north up the Red Sea. They also produced goods of their own—notably frankincense and myrrh. Readers of the Gospels would have understood that the Magi who came to see the baby Jesus were Persian wise men bringing precious gifts from Arabia.

Foreign cultures strongly influenced these coastal Arab societies. In Bahrain, an archipelago in the Persian Gulf, archaeologists have found villas and temples built in the styles of the Hellenistic Greeks, with fine stone pillars and

mosaics. Jews from Palestine and Christians from Ethiopia, as well as polytheists whose temples honored many gods, settled in these communities. Many religious messages circulated through the oases and along the caravan trails.

By the fifth century CE and after, however, these centers of trade were in decline. The west, in the last centuries of the Roman Empire, could buy fewer goods. Power in the Arabian Peninsula now rested not with traders but with the inhabitants of the desert: the many tribes of the Bedouin, migrants who lived as shepherds. Domesticated camels, which could move quickly through the arid center of Arabia living on stored water for days at a time, carried the desert migrants across country with a speed and security usually reserved, in the premodern world, for travel by water. Organized in kin groups and linked by polygamous marriages, the desert Arabs valued courage and honor above everything else. They dominated the caravan trade and settled at oases, where deeply buried water sources enabled them to build stable clusters of fortified houses and to raise idols to their gods. At Mecca, a busy and successful oasis and mercantile center, a group of them dominated the town. Like most Bedouins, they were polytheists, but they paid special reverence to a small, square shrine—the wall of which encased a meteorite—one of the typical forms of local religious practice. Here, in 610, a merchant named Muhammad began to receive messages from an all-powerful God. At first, these revelations terrified him. Gradually they became the core of a new religion and inspired the creation of a new society.

"THERE IS ONE GOD AND MUHAMMAD IS HIS PROPHET"

A boy of noble descent who was left a poor orphan when his father died, **Muhammad** (ca. 570–632) worked as a merchant. His success leading a caravan for a wealthy older woman won him her respect and affection. They married, and he grew in prominence. A traditional story records that when the four tribal groups that ruled Mecca wanted to repair the **Kaaba**, their square shrine, they could not agree on which of them should lift the sacred stone back into place in the structure. Muhammad suggested that they place the stone on a cloak and that members of each group should lift one corner of it. Then he himself set the stone back into place. The story—like the many others that grew up around Muhammad's early years—may not be literally true. But it makes clear that he developed a reputation as a man of fairness and integrity, one whom all

Cultural Exchange on the Silk Road Connecting Rome and Constantinople to far-flung China and India, the Silk Road enabled more than goods to circulate. This Buddha figure from third-century Gandhara (present-day Pakistan) combines Eastern religious imagery with a toga-like garment and tightly curled hairstyle indicative of Roman influence.

The Kaaba The Kaaba shrine in Mecca, the holiest place in Islam, is the most important destination for Muslim pilgrims to this day.

could trust. He and his wife had four daughters and two sons, both of whom died very young.

Gradually, Muhammad began to retreat to a cave not far from Mecca, where he camped on an arid hill for periods of several days to meditate and pray. One day, apparently when he was home in Mecca, a voice spoke to him, saying in Arabic, "You are the messenger of God." His experience seems to have been as dramatic—if not as unexpected—as the vision that transformed the Jew Saul into the Christian Paul on the road to Damascus. Terrified, Muhammad begged his wife to cover him. Eventually he began to receive regular visits from what he regarded as a powerful spirit, traditionally identified in the Islamic world as the angel Gabriel. He ran away and even thought about throwing himself off a mountain. But God himself confirmed the truth of the messages that Muhammad received. Soon the messenger commanded him to recite, and he found himself beginning to offer teachings in the form of rhymed verses.

EARLY TEACHINGS

Scholars believe that when Muhammad began to address the people of Mecca after 610, he started by announcing that the world was out of joint. God, whom he now called Allah, was eternally just and omnipotent. All should hear and follow the teachings of this true God. But many—especially the wealthy polytheists who controlled Mecca—did not do so. They attributed their gains to their own gods, when in fact Allah "has provided them against hunger and kept them safe from fear." They made no effort to maintain justice or to use their riches to help the poor. And they were oblivious to God, who had showed them "the two ways"—the hard way of justice and the easy one of vice.

Muhammad often spoke of the future. Like the ancient Hebrew prophets, he used it as a weapon, claiming that the sins that he saw everywhere in the present would be avenged in the future. A day of judgment awaited those who refused to believe in and obey Allah: "For when the trumpet is sounded, / That, at that time, shall be a difficult day, / For the unbelievers, anything but easy." Those who rejected Allah would have "an entertainment of boiling water / and burning in hell." Those who accepted God's teachings and followed them, in contrast, would enjoy an eternal life in paradise, which Muhammad vividly described. His teachings challenged the whole social world of Mecca and its merchants, with their worship of many gods. Soon Muhammad began to gain a reputation—a mixed one. Some, like his cousin Ali, found him and his teachings deeply impressive; others rejected his teachings. And as Muhammad gained followers, they attracted more and more unwelcome attention from the ruling groups.

FROM MECCA TO MEDINA

At first, Muhammad appealed to members of more than one group. His religious ideals clearly resembled those of the monotheists who already lived near him in Arabia and whose traditions he respected. Muhammad not only regarded the Jewish prophets and the messengers of the Christian revelation as divinely inspired, but also hoped he might win their followers to his message. Accordingly, he adopted certain Jewish customs, such as facing east while praying. Soon, however, he realized that Mecca's inhabitants were incurably hostile to his beliefs. His criticisms of the worship of idols apparently enraged local men of wealth, who mistreated those of his followers who could not retaliate. Though Muhammad's clan protected him from violence, the other inhabitants of Mecca boycotted his followers and finally began to threaten Muhammad himself.

After some exploration he found a new home a couple of hundred miles to the north, at an oasis called Yathrib. It was a community with many Jews, where a fair number of people already saw themselves as monotheists. After making preparations, he sent his followers there ahead of him. Only when all had left Mecca safely did he and Ali depart, moving at first in the opposite direction, and finally join their friends. This journey, or *hijra*, to the city that came to be called Medina, took place in 622. As soon as they could, Muhammad's followers built a small complex where the Prophet, as they now knew him, could live and develop his revelations. They also established in Medina a place where he and his followers could prostrate themselves before Allah: Islam's first shrine. For centuries, these events have been taken as the real beginning of Islamic religion, and of practices that would remain characteristic of it for centuries. It was in Medina, for example, that Muhammad received the revelation that he and his followers should worship facing Mecca, rather than Jerusalem. Muhammad also approved polygamy by his example in this period. After the death of his first wife he married two others, one of them a scholar and religious thinker in her own right, whom he brought with him to Medina; there he married another four women.

THE FORMATION OF ISLAM

During the next ten years, Muhammad built both a religion and a community in Medina. The process was not easy or peaceful—nor did Muhammad expect it to be. The term for the religion he founded, *Islam*, is connected to the Arabic word for peace. It means "voluntary submission to God," and the word *Muslim*—which comes from the same root— refers to one who engages in that form of religious activity. But like Jesus, Muhammad did not come to bring his followers an easy or a peaceful life. His revelations included the concept of jihad ("effort," or "labor"): Muslims, he told them, had the duty to strive, to struggle. The word could refer to an internal effort to fight evil and do good—or to an external struggle against those, whether Muslims or not, who refused followers of Islam the right to practice their religion in the proper way. Muhammad himself led an attack on a Meccan caravan, which provoked efforts at retaliation. His new city had to hold off more than one attack, including a full-scale siege in 627 known as the Battle of the Trench, after the defenses that the Medinans dug.

By 632—when Muhammad moved back to Mecca, on the invitation of the leading clans, only to die shortly after his arrival—the new religion had taken on many features of what would become its permanent form. Shaped by persecution and then by exile, the new faith was now not accommodating to older gods and other deities. Although it is common to identify the three faiths as "Abrahamic" because of their shared origins and principles, the followers of Allah now set themselves apart from Jews and Christians, even though they continued to respect those traditions and revere their prophets. Allah demanded sole allegiance. As Muhammad uttered the verses that went into the Qur'an and the Hadith (the body of "traditions"

The Rise of Islam, 600–632 Islam took shape in the busy and diverse atmosphere of the Arabian Peninsula. Populated by Bedouin nomads as well as Arab traders settled in oasis towns such as Mecca, Arabia was crisscrossed by trade routes to Europe and Asia.

also acknowledged as authoritative), his statements became longer and more complex, and the system of belief and conduct they commanded developed into an articulated whole. The Kaaba in Mecca—once a pagan shrine—became the central place of worship for Islam, the new faith.

LIVING BY ALLAH'S COMMANDS Muhammad taught a rigorous code of belief and conduct. In the central command of the **Five Pillars of Islam**, the followers of Allah must acknowledge that God is supreme in goodness, knowledge, and mercy, incomparable to any other being, and that Muhammad is his messenger. But worshippers of Allah must do far more than proclaim God's greatness and loving kindness. The Five Pillars of Islam also required that Muslims pray five times daily; practice charity; fast during Ramadan, the ninth month of the year; and make a pilgrimage to Mecca. Every Muslim knew that his day, his year, and his lifetime must reflect these commands.

The Prophet called for a radical transformation in many areas of behavior. The inhabitants of the desert had traditionally followed a code that required immediate action to redress any slight to one's honor. If one member of a clan killed or injured a member of another, acts of retaliation followed—often for years. By contrast, Islam called for self-control and submission to God. Whereas the members of tribes had been fearless, Muslims feared God and disciplined their actions to reflect that fear. The tables of penalties that Muhammad and his followers devised shared the harshness of ancient Near Eastern and Roman law: the amputation of a hand was the punishment for theft. The tables reflected a systematic effort to impose an economy on violence that had often spread without limit.

Islam shared some requirements with the other Abrahamic religions. Like Jews, Muslims were forbidden to eat pork. But the code of Muhammad imposed rules on new areas of human life. Muslims must not drink wine. They must not cut off one or more of their children from their estate. Men must treat women with respect, and women, though not the equal of men, possessed rights even in what became the established system of polygamy: they retained control of their dowries and, under certain circumstances, they could initiate divorce. Like Christians, Muslims could own slaves. But the teachings of Muhammad aimed at mitigating the worst consequences of the institution. Concubines were automatically freed on their master's death, and the child of a free man and a slave woman was automatically free. Islam treated manumission of slaves as a highly meritorious act. Slave owners were warmly encouraged to free their slaves when they themselves died, if not before, and many did—though other Muslims continued to trade in slaves.

AN EXPANDING STATE

Muhammad's demanding code, and the community that strove to live by it, rapidly attracted followers. Muhammad himself was a gifted diplomat and politician as well as a prophet. During his years in Medina and after returning to Mecca in 632, he acted not only as the head of a sect but also as the ruler of a state. Subsequent rulers of the Muslims bore the title of **caliph** ("successor"), meaning

that they had taken on Muhammad's authority. And worshippers began to see themselves as members of a single *ummah*, or nation—a community constituted not by membership in kinship groups but by adherence to a common set of religious beliefs and practices. By the end of Muhammad's lifetime, effective preaching and clever diplomacy had won him power over all of Arabia.

THE QUESTION OF SUCCESSION But the question of succession to the position Muhammad had occupied introduced a measure of instability into Islam. Who was to become caliph? Those who had had personal connections with the Prophet? Those who were formally related to him? Those who showed the greatest ability? Muhammad's first two successors, Abu Bakr (632–634) and Umar (634–644), had been his close associates. They argued that Islam meant that all followers of the religion were bound not only to Muhammad but also to one another, and after a short civil war their position was generally accepted. During Umar's term as caliph, the Muslims made the conquests in Persia, the Levant, and Egypt that turned their society into an empire. Uthman (644–656), whom Muhammad inspired to become one of the first converts to Islam, continued to expand Islamic territory and encouraged economic activity. He also presided over the production of a full written text of the **Qur'an**, Islam's scripture. But some of his policies—especially his habit of granting his own family lucrative positions—stirred opposition. In 656, rebels entered his house and assassinated him. The next caliph—Ali, the Prophet's cousin and son-in-law, whom the rebels put in place—tried to reestablish what he saw as the purer principles of Muhammad. But he also confronted rebellious armies and was murdered after five years in office. From that time on, faithful Muslims have disagreed radically, and sometimes violently, about who is the rightful successor of the Prophet.

SHIITES AND SUNNIS The Shiites, who derived their name from the term *shia* ("party"), held that only someone directly descended from Muhammad through his daughter Fatima (and her husband, Ali) should be caliph. Gradually they came to believe that the true caliph should also be a holy man, or *imam*. But agreement among them broke down after Ali's sons Hasan and Husayn struggled for the succession and Husayn was put to death. The Sunnis, who gradually became the dominant group in most of the Islamic world, saw the caliph as a political leader appointed by a general consensus. Though they agreed that Ali had been the legitimate caliph, they insisted that his status was no different from that of the other caliphs before and after him. They supported the **Umayyads**—the family that took over the caliphate in the later seventh century and consolidated the creation of imperial Islam.

THE EARLY CONQUESTS (633–719)

Though struggles beset the caliphate from the start, it expanded with great force, and it is not hard to see why. The original armies of Islam were made up entirely of Arabs and believers. United by their religion and their world view, ready to combat injustice and irreligion, they moved with great speed. Unlike the heavily armed Byzantine forces, Muslim soldiers traveled light, using camels to carry everything they needed over their desert highway. The early caliphs devised a military system that effectively

bound the tribal warriors to them. Regular salaries and gifts of conquered land won their loyalty and ensured that support for the caliphate spread into new territories. The continued prominence of tribal chiefs—and the practice of relocating members of the same tribe near one another in new lands—were also important in ensuring loyalty.

The Byzantine and Sasanian Empires—exhausted by their recent conflicts—could put up no effective resistance. Muslim forces invaded Syria in 634 and controlled the Levant within a year. Sasanian Persia, invaded twice, in 633 and 636, fell in 651. So did the breadbasket of the Mediterranean world, Egypt, which Muslim armies attacked in 639, and North Africa. As a result of these conquests, Byzantium and Rome were cut off from the ship-borne supplies that had supported the growth of the great cities since the conquest of Carthage by the Roman Republic in the third and second centuries BCE. By the second decade

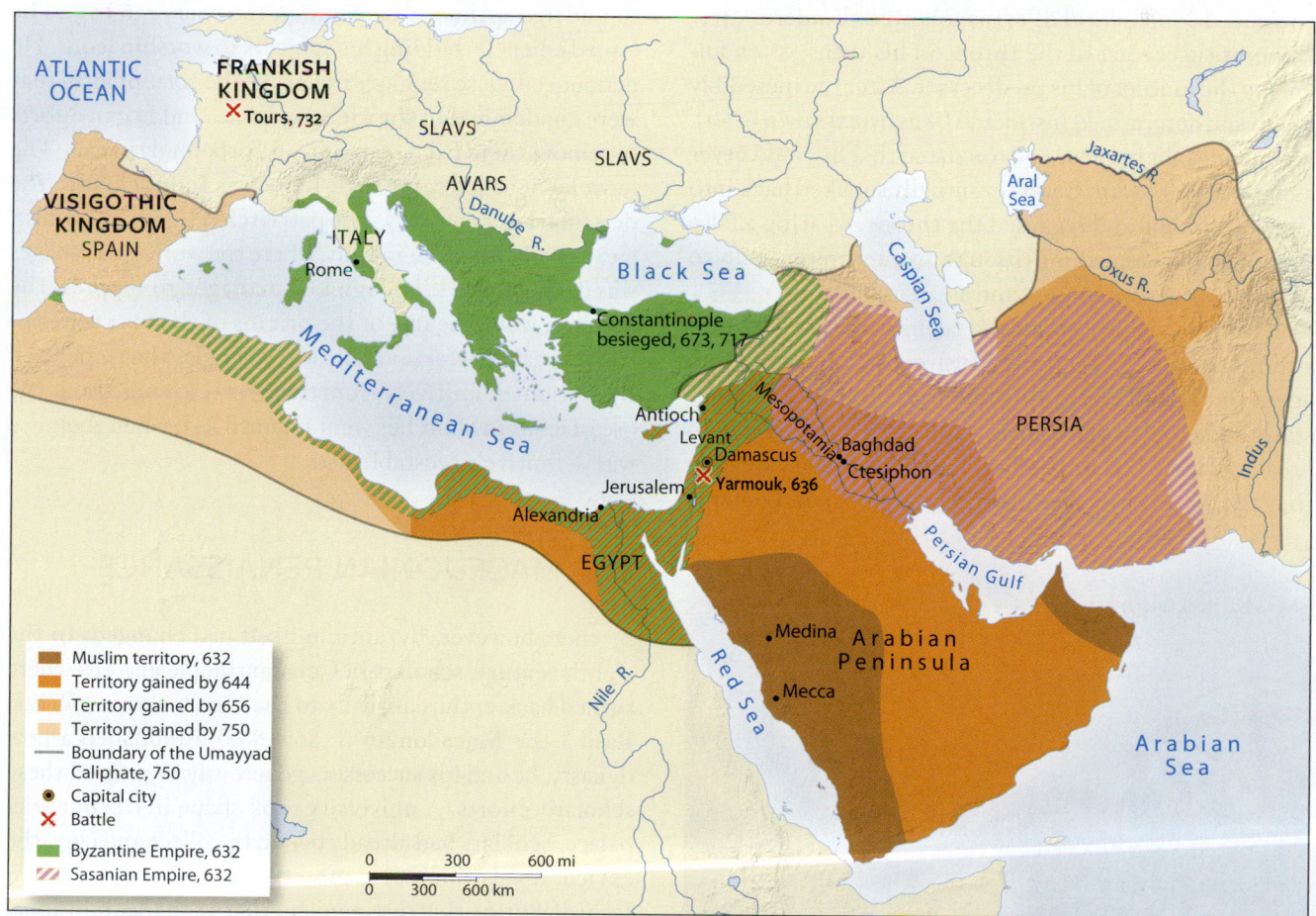

The Expansion of Islam, 632–750 Not long after Muhammad's death, the Islamic caliphate began to expand. Muslim armies spread first across the Arabian Peninsula into Egypt and southwestern Persia. By the middle of the seventh century, they had conquered the rest of Persia and large territories formerly ruled by Byzantium. By 750, the Umayyad Caliphate spanned from the Indus River in Asia to the Iberian Peninsula.

of the eighth century, the Islamic world, organized as the Umayyad Caliphate, extended from Asia to modern Spain. Eventually the faith and its followers would expand still farther, into sub-Saharan Africa, China, and India. Already, however, Islam had conquered all of the lands that would make up its core for centuries to come.

ISLAM AND BYZANTIUM: CULTURAL ADAPTATION (7TH–10TH CENTURIES)

As much of what had been the eastern empire, including the Holy Land itself, fell to the Arabs, Byzantium grew unstable. In the 620s, Heraclius had saved Byzantium from conquest by Sasanian Persia. But the armies of Islam proved superior to his. In 636, at Yarmouk, east of the Sea of Galilee, they inflicted a decisive defeat on the Byzantines. A long period of crisis followed. Emperor after emperor succeeded to the throne in his teens, often following the murder of his predecessor. After the incredibly tough and determined Justinian II was overthrown in 695, his enemies slit his nose and tongue so that he could never assume power again. But he eventually sneaked back into Constantinople and regained the throne, wearing a false nose of gold and speaking through an interpreter—only to be overthrown once more, and assassinated, in 711.

The Byzantines employed a mixture of tradition and innovation to keep the Muslims at bay. In 673 and again in 717 and after, Muslim efforts to conquer Constantinople failed. The great walls proved impossible to breach, and Greek fire—an oil-based incendiary weapon that the Byzantines shot, through siphons, onto enemy

Greek Fire A twelfth-century manuscript depicts the use of Greek fire by Byzantine forces. The Byzantines used this oil-based weapon to destroy the ships of Muslim invaders in 672 and 711.

ships—destroyed the Arab fleets. But the Muslim conquests continued in what is now Spain (711–718) and southern France (718–719). By this time, the Umayyad Caliphate ruled one of the greatest empires ever created. After these years, the westward progress of the caliphate's border slowed, and finally stopped, as the military situation in France grew stable.

ICONOCLASM

The challenge posed by Islam sent tremors through Byzantine society and culture. The emperor Leo the Isaurian (r. 717–741) fought the Umayyads to a standstill. He invited Slavs to settle in depopulated areas of the empire, freed large numbers of agricultural workers who had been tied to the soil, and reformed systems of taxation and law.

One of his most powerful innovations lay in the realm of religion. After forcing Jews and heretics in the empire to undergo orthodox baptism, in the years 726 to 729 he issued edicts forbidding his subjects to worship icons. He denounced these religious images as the sorts of idols that were condemned in the Hebrew Bible, and began efforts to remove them from churches and other holy places. The movement he led came to be known as **Iconoclasm** ("the destruction of images"). The patriarch resigned in protest, and a revolt broke out in Italy, where the worship of images was deeply rooted. Though Leo managed to suppress the revolt, it would be one of the origins of the long series of theological debates and political struggles that separated Byzantium definitively from the west. Debates about the use of icons in churches went on until 843, when their use was definitively reestablished.

THE MACEDONIAN RENAISSANCE

By then, however, Byzantium itself had changed. In the eighth century, scholars in Constantinople and elsewhere turned back enthusiastically to the Greek classics. When Basil I the Macedonian (r. 867–886) established a new dynasty, he and his successors generously supported these scholarly efforts. A university took shape in the imperial palace. Scholars had already begun to collect and copy the ancient texts, which were preserved in codices with a new form of writing that distinguished between the traditional capital letters and new, lowercase ones. In almost all cases, surviving texts of ancient Greek books descend from the copies made in this period. With official support, these scholars compiled immense encyclopedias of information about history, geography, technology, and other subjects useful for imperial purposes. The wealthy, technologically sophisticated Byzantium that Liutprand visited in the tenth century did not descend directly from the city of Constantine. Its culture was the product of deliberate efforts to revive and use the past—efforts so systematic that scholars have called this period the Macedonian Renaissance.

CALIPHATE CULTURE

The Umayyad Caliphate (661–750) founded its capital at Damascus in Syria—a place that had been inhabited for millennia and had the natural resources, as the oases of Arabia did not, to support a court and all that came with it. At first the Umayyads maintained the administrations of the lands they conquered, working with local officials of the former Byzantine government. They showed tolerance to Christians and Jews, even allowing churches to be built. By the end of the seventh century, however, their policies were changing. Arabic, which had been written for centuries, now became the official language of government. With administrators and judges appointed, and coins struck, the Umayyad Caliphate had become a massive, well-organized state. As its armed forces expanded—thousands of Persian soldiers converted to Islam and joined the Umayyad armies—the need for revenue increased, and government developed to cope with it.

SCRIPTURE AND INTERPRETATION Within the new state, a new culture took shape. Like the other Abrahamic religions, Islam developed a set of core texts: the fixed, canonical scripture of the Qur'an, and collections of the sayings and deeds of Muhammad not included in it, called the Hadith. Unlike the Hebrew Bible or the New Testament, the Qur'an does not follow a narrative structure. In rhythmic prose, it calls for worship of the one god, Allah; lays out his teachings and the code of conduct that his followers must accept; and evokes a future day of judgment. After Muhammad's death, as questions of interpretation arose, scholars gained prestige for their ability to solve these problems. Schools grew up around them—not only in Arabia but also in Syria, Palestine, and Egypt. More like Judaism in this respect than Christianity, Islam had no central religious authority, no pope or patriarchs who could claim widespread support for their own supreme status. Rather, the ulema, the body of learned men who forged theological and legal principles from the Qur'an and the Hadith, came to have a collective authoritative status.

Umayyad Mosque A mosaic from the western colonnade of the Umayyad Mosque in Damascus applies Byzantine style to new Islamic themes. The harmonious intertwining of huge trees, flowing water, and ornate buildings strung with hanging lamps or pearls evokes a heavenly or terrestrial paradise.

THE MOSQUE Formal religious services—and a system of institutions to support them—also came into existence as the caliphate became wealthy and powerful. As the Christians had taken over both Roman temples and the standard Roman form for a large public building, the basilica, so the Muslims began—in seventh-century Damascus, for example—to take over for worship the parts of a temple that had become a church, inside a vast enclosure. The temple structure was torn down, but its outside walls were preserved. Inside this enclosure and to the south, a vast prayer hall was erected. Facing it, a courtyard, surrounded by arcades, became the central space of the **mosque**—a new worship center that could easily expand when the need arose. Fountains cooled the air and enabled worshippers to wash. Magnificent mosaics depicted the landscape of paradise, a place of gardens and rivers. Muezzins called the faithful to prayer five times a day, led prayers, and in many cases became famous for the power with which they recited the rhythmic lines of the sacred text.

THE DOME OF THE ROCK Islamic architectural projects soon became at least as ambitious and splendid as Byzantine ones. As early as 685, the Umayyad caliph Abd al-Malik ibn Marwan began construction of a great shrine, the Dome of the Rock in Jerusalem. An octagon with an immense wooden dome, designed to rival the domed Church of the Holy Sepulcher built by Constantine, the Dome of the Rock was meant to house Muslim pilgrims on the Temple Mount. Its location was carefully chosen. For Jews, it was the site of the Second Temple, destroyed by the Romans in 70 CE during the siege of Jerusalem. For

Dome of the Rock Around 685, the Umayyad caliph Abd al-Malik ibn Marwan built the magnificent Dome of the Rock, its rotunda meant to rival the architecture of great Christian buildings. It still stands on the Temple Mount in Jerusalem, a site sacred to Muslims, Christians, and Jews alike. The complex tilework and the golden covering of the dome were added later.

Christians, it was the site of the Church of the Holy Wisdom, which Constantine's mother Helen had founded. For Muslims, however, it was the place where Muhammad had ascended to heaven, guided by the angel Gabriel.

The caliph rivaled the emperors of Byzantium as he exploited technology and art to create a new and spectacular sacred space. A work of engineering wondrous enough to compare to Hagia Sophia, the dome's gilt exterior reflected the sun so brilliantly "that no eye could look straight at it." Inside the shrine were brilliant marbles and mosaics—the latter executed by craftsmen from Byzantium. Inscriptions emphasized that Islam regarded Jesus as a true prophet but also denied that he was the Son of God. They stated that "God has no companion"—a clear attack on the Christian doctrine of the Trinity—and quoted the Qur'an for the first time, so far as is known. A century and a half after the Byzantine emperor Justinian's death, Islam had not only taken over much of his empire but also achieved a comparable mastery of art and nature. For all the questions about where authority did and would rest, the caliphate was clearly the most powerful, expansive organism in the bitterly competitive political ecosystem of the eighth- and ninth-century Mediterranean world.

THE HOUSE OF WISDOM Late in the eighth century, the caliph Haroun al-Rashid—perhaps imitating the rulers of Persia—created the House of Wisdom in Baghdad, a new city founded in 762 as the capital of the Abbasid Caliphate, successors to the Umayyads. In this institution, Muslims, Jews, and Christians studied a wide range of fields. They devised astrolabes and other tools for observing nature, collected maps and drew up new ones, and looked in books for ancient models of knowledge. Some of the inspiration for this work very likely came from a sense of rivalry with Byzantium, where scholars were also working to recover ancient texts. Many exchanges took place between Greeks and Muslims, with scholars from Constantinople taking part in diplomatic missions from the emperors to the caliphs. Collections of medical remedies and manuals on the interpretation of dreams were translated from Arabic into Greek: they may even have been commissioned by the imperial court.

ISLAMIC SCHOLARSHIP In the ninth and tenth centuries, scholars at the House of Wisdom and elsewhere collected, read, and translated many of the basic works of the ancient Greeks. This movement was first pursued systematically by Syrian Christians like Hunayn ibn Ishaq

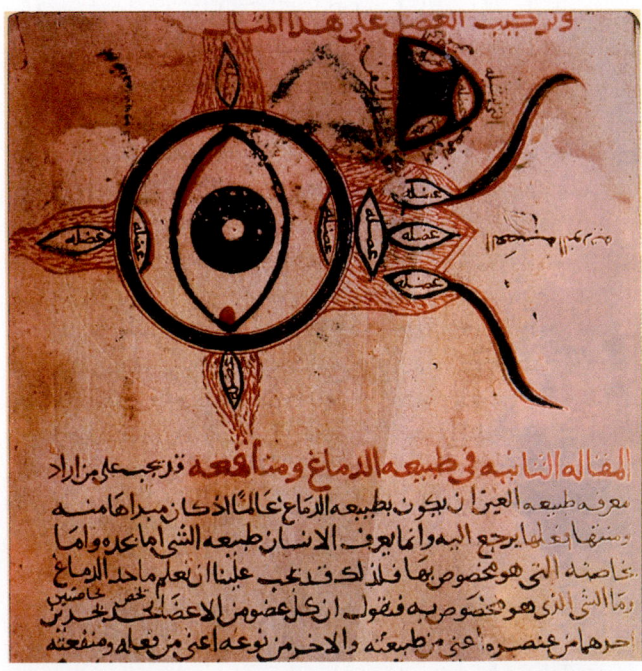

The House of Wisdom This illustration of the anatomy of the eye comes from a twelfth-century copy of the ninth-century *Book of the Ten Treatises on the Eye* by Syrian physician Hunayn ibn Ishaq. Like other members of the House of Wisdom, he translated the work of Galen and other Greek writers into Arabic, often adding important scientific insights of his own.

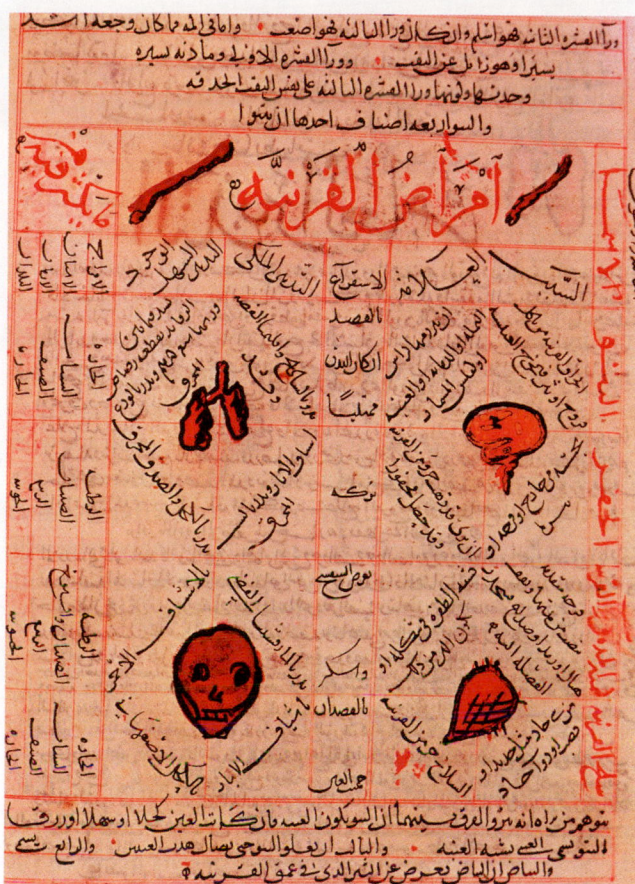

Islamic Learning A page from *The Canon of Medicine* (1025) by the Persian physician and scholar Avicenna (Ibn Sina) details the anatomy of the skull, lungs, stomach, and heart.

(809–873), who studied medicine in Baghdad and became the physician to the caliph. His interests embraced ancient Greek philosophy as well as medicine, and he translated Aristotle's works as well as those of the great Greek medical writer Galen. Islamic scholarship and teaching never embraced the whole of Greek thought: poetry, history, and tragedy did not win much interest in the Islamic world. Instead it developed its own forms of imaginative literature, such as the fantastic tales collected in *The Thousand and One Nights* and the philosophical novel written by Ibn Tufail in the twelfth century, *The Self-Taught Philosopher*. But the translation movement of the Abbasids brought the basic texts of Greek logic and philosophy, and the technical works of Greek astronomers and astrologers, cartographers, and medical scholars, into Arabic.

Within a few decades, Muslim philosophers were adding new ideas, methods, and discoveries to those of the Greeks. The Persian scholar Avicenna (Ibn Sina; ca. 980–1037), for example, wrote exhaustively on philosophy and medicine. His *Canon*, a massive medical textbook, brought together the heritage of Greek medicine. Where theories differed—Aristotle had insisted on the central role of the heart in human physiology; Galen on that of the liver—he weighed them and suggested solutions. His work became the standard textbook not only in Islamic but also in Christian medical schools, where it was studied for centuries. The Muslim mathematician Muhammad ibn Musa al-Khwarizmi (ca. 750–ca. 830) and his colleagues formulated many of the rules of algebra, the very name of which (from *al-jabr*, "restoration") still records its origins. Christian administrators and businesspeople learned from translated Arabic works how to do computations rapidly and simply and how to keep accurate quantitative records.

THE WEST IN LATE ANTIQUITY (475–843)

In the eighth century, the Umayyads, who held on to power in most of the Iberian Peninsula, except for a couple of northern regions, were hoping eventually to push north into the former territories of the western Roman Empire. Byzantine emperors, as we have seen, still hoped to regain the lands in Italy and North Africa that Justinian had managed, for a time, to rule. Neither would have seen the little monarchies and impoverished churches that still existed in their time in Italy, Gaul, and the British Isles as even potential rivals. Yet, for all their weaknesses, the western lands were already constructing a new social order and political and religious institutions that would, eventually, underpin their own claim to world power.

The societies of western Europe had been undergoing a slow transformation from the fourth century on. Relics of the Roman past—and many members of the old Romano-British and Gallo-Roman aristocracies—survived for centuries. Roman roads continued to serve for travel and transport of goods; Roman aqueducts, sewers, and baths continued to function; and leading men in Britain and Gaul continued to aspire to Roman ideals of both social life and government. Germanic peoples were also present in the former Roman territories, normally because they had provided paid military service. Late in the fourth century, in response to a king's request for aid in a dispute, Saxons, Angles, and Jutes from northern Germany entered Britain with threatening force. The Roman Empire did not respond to requests for help, and though the British won a number of battles, by the end of the sixth century these so-called Saxons had conquered most of Britain and established a number of small king-doms there. By then most vestiges of Roman social and economic life were gone.

THEODORIC'S GOTHIC REALM

The first systematic effort to re-create institutions in the Latin west—the kingdom of Theodoric the Great—was a remarkable attempt to continue and transform the Roman state. **Theodoric** (r. 475–526) led the eastern branch of the Goths, or Ostrogoths. Empowered by an agreement with the emperor in Constantinople to recapture Italy, which had been conquered in 476 by the Germanic leader Odoacer, Theodoric conducted an effective campaign. He defeated Odoacer with the help of the Visigoths, the western Goths who had established themselves in the Iberian Peninsula earlier in the century. Isolated in Ravenna, which he had made his capital city, Odoacer made peace with Theodoric in 493 and agreed to split Italy with him—only to have Theodoric murder him, with his own hands, at the banquet held to celebrate their pact.

From 493 until his death in 526, Theodoric ruled with considerable skill. Officially he served as *patricius* ("noble of senatorial rank"), representing the emperor in Constantinople, but effectively he ruled his own lands independently. Through astute marriage alliances and generalship—in military affairs Theodoric relied exclusively on the Goths and their allies—he made himself, in effect, the ruler of a Gothic realm that stretched from modern France to the Balkans, and included for a time the Vandal kingdom in Africa as well. Romans loyal to tradition appreciated Theodoric's support for the circus and its games. Like most Goths, Theodoric was an Arian—a believer in the view that because God the Father had created the Son, Jesus could not be divine. But Catholics and Jews were grateful for the tolerance that he extended to their forms of worship: "We cannot," he wrote to the Jews of Genoa, "order a religion, because no one can be forced to believe against his will."

Members of old Roman noble families—Symmachus, his son-in-law Boethius, and Cassiodorus—served Theodoric, combining such traditional offices as the consulship with the post

Theodoric the Great The Ostrogothic king Theodoric drew on memories of Roman authority to consolidate his reign in Italy. Following the Roman model of including an emperor's portrait on coins, he minted a solidus that was a close copy of a contemporary Byzantine coin.

of *magister officiorum* in the Ravenna court. They composed official rulings and drafted official correspondence for him. Early in the sixth century, when the pope and the Eastern Orthodox Church split on theological grounds, Theodoric even found himself allied with his theological opponents. By the end of Theodoric's reign, the synthesis he had brought into being was already showing deep signs of wear. His treaty with the Vandals broke down, the Visigoths reasserted their independence, and he left no adult heir. Angry, paranoid, and very likely surrounded by real enemies, Theodoric had Boethius and Symmachus arrested on suspicion of treason. Charged with aiming to restore the power of the Senate and with conspiracy with Constantinople, Boethius was executed with extreme cruelty in 524. Theodoric himself died soon after. Neither the female regent he left in command nor her cousin, who deposed her, proved capable of rallying the Gothic nobility against Justinian. Byzantine authority was restored in Italy and much of the west.

In most of the Iberian Peninsula, however, the Visigoths who had supported Theodoric maintained their independence. Leovigild (r. 568–586) fought fiercely against the Byzantines, and toward the end of his reign began to bring his people back into the Catholic fold. He also began the long, slow process of removing barriers between the Visigothic warriors who had invaded and settled in the peninsula and the older Roman families who had long cultivated the land. In the course of the seventh century, the Visigoths elaborated a sophisticated legal code. The king was described as a holy ruler, and though he did not interfere with the church on matters of doctrine, Visigothic kings not only appointed bishops but also excommunicated criminals. Fierce regulations and severe physical punishment were brought into play to force the peninsula's Jews to convert: failing to observe the Christian day of rest on Sunday, for example, could result in a Jew's being flogged and scalped. This warrior society, with its violent code of law, survived until the Islamic invasions transformed the Mediterranean world.

LOMBARD DUCHIES IN ITALY

But the Byzantine government in Ravenna did not enjoy authority for long. In the 540s, a Germanic people known as the Lombards—whom a Roman history memorably and paradoxically described as "a people fiercer than the fierceness of the Germans"—moved into Pannonia (now part of Hungary). In 568 a bold and effective ruler,

Germanic Kingdoms in 500 and 650 By the end of the fifth century, Germanic tribes ruled most of western Europe. Jutes, Angles, and Saxons had invaded Britain from northern Germany; the Gothic king Theodoric the Great controlled a large region reaching from Spain to the Balkans; and the Franks, Visigoths, and Vandals had established other independent territories. From 568, the Lombards invaded much of the Italian Peninsula, and the Franks began to significantly expand their rule in Gaul.

Alboin, led them and several other tribes across the Alps into Italy. They soon established what they called a Lombard "duchy" in the northeast and then proceeded to move south through Italy. Byzantine resistance was weak, and Milan fell in 569.

The Lombards terrified the Romans. With their striped clothing and long hair, they looked like the very image of barbarians. They starved out the Roman cities of Tuscany. Only ports, which the Byzantine navy could defend and supply, remained independent. Christian authorities claimed that the Lombards rifled churches and confiscated all the valuables. They established their capital at Pavia, while other communities, such as Naples

and Benevento, became the seats of the thirty-six Lombard dukes who ruled almost the entire Italian Peninsula. Groups of Lombard families, organized at first for combat, spread through Italy.

Some Italians decided it would be possible to live with the Lombards, and surrendered to them. Gradually the Lombards themselves became, to some extent at least, recognizably Romanized. Impressed by the coherence of Roman law, they began to codify the elaborate rules that regulated crime and the vendettas that followed, the manumission of slaves, and the relations between landowners and those who served them, in Latin codes of their own. Though they were Arians, one of their queens, the Bavarian Catholic Theudelinda, did her best to support the Latin church. At first her efforts met mostly with resistance. By the end of the eighth century, however, a Lombard monk from Monte Casino, Paul the Deacon, could write the whole history of his people from an impeccably Catholic point of view.

THE HERITAGE OF THE ANCIENTS IN THE LATIN WEST

Through the sixth and seventh centuries—while the Roman senatorial elite slowly lost its wealth and power, the Senate itself was disbanded, and such central Roman institutions as the circus ceased to exist—the foundations of a new culture were being laid. Members of the old elite played a crucial role in this project.

THE WORKS OF BOETHIUS
When Boethius (ca. 480–524), superbly educated in Greek and Latin, was imprisoned by Theodoric in 523, he composed a great dialogue, *The Consolation of Philosophy*. In it Philosophy, personified as a woman dressed in splendid clothing that has become worn and ragged, visits him in prison. In a magnificent set of speeches, she leads him through arguments that ease his suffering, not by improving his condition but by showing him the truth. As Boethius and Philosophy examine key moments in his past and stories from ancient history and literature, he learns that Fortune, the fickle force that bestows wealth and position, takes them away just as arbitrarily. In an image that painters and poets would elaborate on for centuries, Philosophy depicts Fortune as a goddess who turns a wheel that first raises the men who ride on it but then throws them down: "As thus she turns her wheel of chance with

Wheel of Fortune In this fifteenth-century French manuscript of *The Consolation of Philosophy,* Boethius encounters the goddess Fortune—portrayed here as a queen—and her wheel of fate.

haughty hand...fortune now tramples fiercely on a fearsome king, and now deceives no less a conquered man by raising from the ground his humbled face."

Happily, Boethius learns, it is not this frightening being but God who rules the universe. Being eternal, God has foreknowledge. Since all time—past, present, and future—is the same to him, he knows everything that will happen, including human mistakes and sins. But God does not cause these sins. From their own standpoint, humans, who live in time, freely choose between good and evil. Philosophy, in other words, teaches us both that the universe is ruled by divine Providence, and that humans make their own fates and have the duty to live virtuously.

Boethius's dialogue—composed in a mixture of prose and verse—is one of the most culturally revealing products of late antiquity. From the third and fourth centuries on, Christians searched for ways to make creative use of the ideas and writings of the best pagans. Boethius was definitely a Christian, but in *The Consolation of Philosophy* he never mentions the Christian God or Jesus. Instead, he argues that there is a divine order behind the apparent chaos and injustice of this world. The study of the liberal arts and of philosophy allow humans to understand this order and to live virtuously within it. As Latin Christianity began to develop a formal theology in the eighth century and after, Boethius's work remained essential.

CASSIODORUS: LEARNING AS THE PATH TO GOD

Even more significant was the work of another Roman aristocrat and government official, Cassiodorus (ca. 490–ca. 585). After the struggles that followed the death of Theodoric, he spent time in retirement in Constantinople and then, after 550, moved to his ancestral lands in southern Italy. There, on an estate that he named Vivarium ("fish-pond") after the ponds that Roman aristocrats stocked with fish on their estates, he created a monastic community. Cassiodorus's writings touched on many subjects. Like other writers in the fifth and sixth centuries who drew up compendia and syntheses, as if they glimpsed that the world would soon change and many of the books to which they had access would disappear, Cassiodorus wrote a history of the world. But his central achievement—the one that proved formative for the culture of the Latin west—was to define Christian culture, especially monastic culture, as bookish.

Cassiodorus had tried to establish a center of Christian higher learning in Rome but failed "because of continual wars and raging battles in the Kingdom of Italy." Accordingly, he set out to create with words what he had failed to build in three dimensions: a guide to learning that would lead Christians to "ascend without hesitation to Holy Scripture through the praiseworthy commentaries of the Fathers." In his *Institutes*, a treatise on the disciplines and their uses, Cassiodorus showed the reader how to master not only the Bible and its commentaries but also the ancient liberal arts, for each of which he provided a brief description and a bibliography. Cassiodorus adopted a classification created by a scholar from North Africa, Martianus Capella, who divided the seven liberal arts into two categories: the humanistic arts of language, grammar, and rhetoric, and the "scientific" arts of arithmetic, geometry, astronomy, and music. Cassiodorus added that dialectic, the art of argument, had both humanistic and scientific aspects.

The library that he assembled in his own monastery disappeared during the troubles that later afflicted the Italian Peninsula. But Cassiodorus made clear that the Christian life must center on a systematic, intensive encounter with the sacred texts: "Therefore, pray to God, the source of all that is useful; read constantly; go over the material diligently; for frequent and intense meditation is the mother of understanding." And he explained that Christian scholars must not just collect the scriptures and other texts but do their best to copy texts for future generations and ensure that they were correct. The path to God—for Cassiodorus, and for generations of later Christians—thus lay through learning.

FOUNDING THE MEDIEVAL LATIN CHURCH

In an age of invasion and political upheaval, late antique thinkers in the West worked hard to preserve classical texts, arts, and ideas in a form in which Christians could use them. Two more men, both of them as deeply connected as Boethius and Cassiodorus to the old Roman world, transformed the Christian church. Benedict of Nursia and Pope Gregory, later known as Gregory the Great, are fought over by historians precisely because they belong to two different worlds: the surviving ancient one that formed them and the early medieval one that they helped to create.

BENEDICT AND THE BENEDICTINES
Benedict (ca. 480–ca. 547), born to a substantial family and educated at Rome, decided while young to follow the monastic life. In 529 at Monte Cassino, on a hill overlooking the road from Rome to Naples, he created a new kind of religious community and drew on existing models to compose his *Rule*, a book that set down its principles. Benedict saw the monastery not, as the eastern Desert Fathers had, as a collection of brilliant spiritual soloists, each ascending to God in his own cell, but as a choir singing in harmony, a community governed by an abbot or father and linked in their pursuit of holiness.

Abbey of Saint Scholastica A sixth-century fresco from the Abbey of Saint Scholastica in Italy provides an early view of monks and nuns who, in their uniform clothing and plain surroundings, conformed to Benedict and Scholastica's prescriptions for a holy, ordered life.

Benedict at Monte Cassino This illustration from an eleventh-century Italian manuscript imagines Benedict seated in front of the Abbey of Monte Cassino, where the abbot presents him with books produced by the abbey's monks, symbolizing the lasting influence of the religious order that Benedict inspired with his *Rule*.

The monks were to lead an ordered life, divided into periods devoted to manual labor, study of the Bible and other texts, and performance of the liturgy—which was, and would remain, the central task of Benedictines over the centuries. Again and again through each day and night, at each of the eight canonical "hours" that began at midnight with Matins (the morning service), the monks would rise and chant the service, sometimes for hours. These prayers did not come to an end until nine in the evening, with Compline. The Lombards destroyed Monte Cassino, along with the other Italian monasteries, not long after Benedict died. But his model—which soon became an order, whose members founded houses across the Latin west—turned into the first great Latin model of the religious life, one that still survives.

SCHOLASTICA
Monasticism was not confined to men. According to Pope Gregory, whose *Dialogues* depicted many incidents from Benedict's life, Benedict's sister Scholastica was, if anything, more of a miracle-worker than her

brother. She founded a community of nuns not far from Monte Cassino, which was probably directed by Benedict as well. In the following centuries, double monasteries, in which a convent for nuns accompanied a monastery for monks, spread across Europe. Such houses attracted many women of high birth, like Scholastica, and it was common for the abbess to take charge of both houses, the male as well as the female. Some abbesses claimed to possess the power to hear confession and grant absolution. Nuns, like monks, sang psalms, fasted, and kept vigils at night; like monks, too, they carried out the administrative jobs that their houses required, such as overseeing the wine cellar, the making of cloth, and the gate where visitors were admitted. Those who could read were expected to teach the illiterate. Some became scribes. According to the life of a sixth-century French bishop, "the virgins of Christ lettered most beautifully the divine books." Others wrote lives of holy men and women. The abbey offered women of different origins the chance to pursue spiritual lives as systematically and intensively as male monks.

GREGORY: SUSTAINING THE CHURCH If Benedict created one of the medieval church's central institutions, **Gregory** (ca. 540–604) rebuilt the church as a whole. Born into an aristocratic Roman family whose ancestral house was near the Colosseum, he served as prefect of Rome. When he turned, still early in life, to the monastic vocation, he transformed his family estates into monasteries. Later he represented the Roman church to the Byzantine imperial court in Constantinople. In 590, Gregory was proclaimed pope unanimously by the clergy, nobles, and ordinary people of Rome. A man of great personal humility, Gregory preferred the title bishop of Rome to the grander one of pope. But he devoted unremitting energy to the interests of the church he worked for as *servus servorum Dei*—"servant of the servants of God."

As an experienced administrator, Gregory knew the importance of maintaining and preserving the church's lands and other properties, and he defended these by every means at his disposal against Lombard invaders and everyone else who hoped to dispossess the church. His motive for doing so was deeply Christian. As the Lombard invasions destroyed public order and thousands of once solid citizens and farmers found themselves wandering the roads of Italy, homeless and impoverished, Gregory used the church itself to sustain them. He organized public distributions of bread and other forms of poor relief and created hospitals to help cope with the devastation wrought by plague.

Gregory Pope Gregory, portrayed in this ninth-century Italian fresco, was celebrated for his humility and service to the church. He converted his family estates into monasteries, created hospitals in response to plague, and organized the distribution of bread among the poor.

To support all this activity, and to ensure that the church had the resources to sustain it, Gregory also created a new administrative structure. Elaborate records carefully kept by officials provided a foundation for the church's claims to lands and income. Always better equipped than any rival institution in Italy with records, and always better able to produce public documents, the church became the chief heir in the west to Rome's mastery of filing and control systems. Gregory was passionately committed to the church's spiritual tasks as well. He made long-lasting changes in the order of the Catholic Mass and helped to create the form of plainchant that came to be known as "Gregorian chant." He also collected the miracles of Benedict and other saints, and told their stories dramatically in his *Dialogues*—a work that represents the beginning of one of the church's most durable projects and one that goes on to this day: its massive effort to record, evaluate, and classify the deeds of the saints and identify those that were genuinely miraculous.

Finally, in his *Rule of Pastoral Care*, Gregory put forward a new ideal of the priestly life, aimed not at those who lived as monks in closed communities but at those who served Christians in the world. For centuries to come, most prelates such as bishops and archbishops, abbots and abbesses, would be, like Gregory himself, men and women of high birth. But Gregory insisted that social standing on its own did not make a bishop. The true prelate, like the true monk, must aim high: "The conduct of a prelate ought so far to be superior to the conduct of the people as the life of a shepherd is accustomed to exalt him above the flock." This was, of course, an ideal, but it inspired Gregory himself. He had hoped to go to Britain as a missionary when his career was interrupted by his elevation to the bishopric of Rome. By the end of the sixth century, despite the disruptions of the Lombard invasions, he was sending missionaries to bring the Christian message to the Angles and Saxons living in what is now England.

CHRISTIANITY IN IRELAND By Gregory's time the church's missionary enterprise was well established. Rome's effort to enlarge the frontiers of Christianity in northern Europe centered on Ireland, which was converted to Christianity when missionaries—most famously a Briton, Saint Patrick—reached the island in the fifth century and began to preach. An effective advocate, he ordained priests and presided over them as a bishop. Soon, noblemen and noblewomen founded monasteries, and the Irish monks mastered Latin with enthusiasm. They developed great skill in copying texts, which they wrote out in splendid calligraphic scripts and decorated with magnificent illustrations—everything from full-page portraits to drawings of technical concepts to whimsical flora and fauna sprawling in the margins. These illuminated manuscripts were beautiful to look at and made texts more accessible to readers. They also began to write their own Latin poetry—verse of great wit and skill in which they deployed an immense vocabulary in the service of acrostics, puns, and other forms of wordplay, as well as in the praise of God. Their work even shows acquaintance with Hebrew and Greek words—an extraordinary phenomenon at a time when most western clerics in Italy and Gaul knew only Latin.

Irish monasteries attracted students from England as well as their own land. In 563, Saint Columba transplanted their monastic system to Scotland, and from there it spread through the British Isles and to Gaul. To help

The Book of Durrow Irish monasteries became famous for their illuminated manuscripts. The Book of Durrow, a colorfully decorated text of the Gospels, was likely created in the second half of the seventh century by Irish monks. In this full-page illustration, a detailed geometric design interlaces various animals.

ordinary Christians come to terms with their sins, Irish monks composed penitentials: short treatises that listed the sins and prescribed prayers for repentance. This new spiritual tool made the Irish priests highly effective as missionaries and counselors.

BEDE: A NEW CHRISTIAN CULTURE Irish monks and Roman clerics disagreed, however, on vital points: for example, when to celebrate the central Christian feast, Easter. Each side claimed to follow the accounts in the

Gospels and the traditions of the church, and each found followers. Debate led to a synod, held at Whitby in northern Britain in 665, where the Roman side won—as Bede, a monk of the nearby Benedictine house of Jarrow, recorded with some satisfaction.

The Venerable Bede (d. 735) himself was an expert on time and the calendar, on which he wrote a detailed and useful book. More important, he had the intellectual resources to write, in the first decades of the eighth century, a magnificent *Ecclesiastical History of the English People*. This dramatic book recorded not only the debates about the calendar but the whole course of the Christianization of Britain, in rich and sometimes poetic detail. As Irish, Italian, Gallic, and British monks argued and swapped texts, a new Christian culture was taking shape: one that could do more than preserve the Bible and its commentators. Gradually—as Bede made clear in his history—the Roman church established its authority over the larger structure of the church's calendar and liturgy. But appointments to the important offices in the church remained in the hands of local rulers, whom clerics served as counselors.

THE FRANKISH KINGDOM: THE MEROVINGIANS (483–561)

As a new Christian culture spread through Britain, a new authority took hold in Gaul that blended Roman and Germanic traditions. Bands of **Franks**—Germanic warriors—had crossed the Rhine into Gaul since the third century. Some of them the Romans wiped out; others, however, joined the Roman army, and many of their leaders eventually gained high positions in the Roman administration. In the fifth century, Roman authority faded, and the Franks began a series of conquests that put them, by the end of the century, in control of northern Gaul, while the Ostrogoths still ruled in the south.

CLOVIS The Franks' historical tradition crystallized around a figure called Merovech, supposedly the founder of the Merovingian dynasty who led them in the fifth century and after. But the solidly attested part of their history begins with Clovis I (466–511), supposedly Merovech's grandson, who came on the scene in 483. Merovingian power rested on the ability to mobilize a large number of skilled and ferocious warriors. Clovis did this with exceptional skill. He defeated Visigoths, Ostrogoths, and Burgundians and created a Frankish realm that stretched, at its farthest extent, from the Pyrenees to the Danube. Paris served briefly as his capital, though he was always in motion. Even the Byzantine emperor recognized Clovis's rule over vast areas of the west. After Clovis's death in 511, his four adult sons divided the kingdom and established four separate capitals, in Reims, Orléans, Paris, and Soissons. Though Clothar, the son based in Soissons, reunited the kingdom in 558, a new division into three parts followed his death in 561.

FUSING GERMANIC AND ROMAN INSTITUTIONS

In the Frankish kingdoms, Germanic and Roman practices and organizations were fused into something new. Roman landowners continued to operate their great villas, using a labor force tied to the land. Members of the Frankish nobility also accumulated wealth and power. Free Roman and Gallic small farmers, arms-bearing men who had the right to settle their own quarrels in their own Roman courts, dominated the landscape in large parts of northern Gaul. Other cultivators were legally classified as "half free" and possessed only limited rights. Roman cities such as Lyon and Bordeaux, which continued to serve as centers of exchange, dwindled into small local capitals, their populations sharply reduced from what they had been in the first and second centuries CE.

The personal power of the Frankish kings continued to rest on their ability to mobilize a large retinue of free warriors. But they also took over vast amounts of public land, where estates cultivated by bound peasant labor had provided the basic revenues for the Roman administration. With this new wealth, and with the many Gallo-Roman inhabitants who continued to possess resources and influence, the Franks erected courts that followed Roman models in key ways. High officials who bore the title *comes* ("count") oversaw the royal treasury, transportation, and other practical matters, and administered the districts of the kingdom, independently for the most part. The *maior domus* ("head of the household") oversaw the royal court—a position that would become increasingly powerful in the sixth century, as king after king died leaving minors as their only heirs. Yet Frankish kings were still formally acclaimed by being raised on shields, in accordance with the ancient custom by which the assembly of free warriors had elected and proclaimed war-leaders. The traditions of the Franks were still preserved in songs, and their rulers—as we will see—did not master the writing of Latin, though they understood it. They concentrated on the traditional skills of hunting and fighting.

The church had survived more or less intact in the

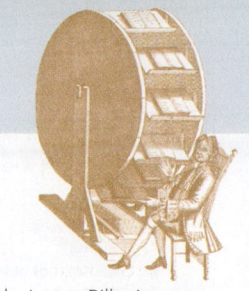

ROMAN AND GERMANIC LAW

The Germanic kingdoms had their own ancient laws, but their earliest written collections of laws were only created after contact with the Romans. When read in full, Roman and Germanic laws provide a wealth of information about regulations, everyday concerns of fairness and justice, and methods of dispute resolution in the societies that created them. Just the section titles alone, like the sampling given in the two sources here, provide a strong sense of each society's priorities.

From *The Digest of Justinian*

The *Digest* is a collection of writings over many centuries by Roman jurists, organized by topic into fifty books. It was promulgated by Emperor Justinian in 533.

I.
- I. On justice and law
- II. On the origin of law and of the different magistracies, as well as the succession of those learned in the law
- III. On statutes, decrees of the Senate and long usage
- IV. On Imperial enactments
- IX. Concerning Senators
- X. On the office of Consul
- XXI. On the office of one to whom jurisdiction is delegated

II.
- III. Where a man refuses obedience to the magistrate exercising jurisdiction
- V. Where one who is cited fails to appear; also where a man cites one whom, according to the Edict, he has no right to cite
- X. On one who contrives that a defendant shall not appear
- XIII. On statement of particulars and discovery of documents etc.

III.
- IV. On proceedings taken on behalf of any corporation or against the same

IV.
- II. Acts done through fear
- IV. On persons under twenty-five

V.
- I. On trials at law; as to where a man ought to take proceedings or be sued
- III. On the action for recovery of an inheritance
- IV. On suits for parts of an inheritance

VII.
- VII. On the Services of Slaves

VIII.
- II. On Servitudes of Urban Estates
- III. On Servitudes of Rustic Estates
- IV. Rules common to Urban and Rustic Estates

XI.
- III. On Corrupting a Slave
- IV. On Fugitive Slaves
- V. On Gamblers
- VI. When a Surveyor makes a false report as to Dimensions
- VII. On Things Religious and Funeral Expenses and on the right to conduct funerals

From *The Laws of the Salian Franks*

The laws of the Salian Franks, a Germanic group living in what is now the northern Netherlands, were probably recorded during the time of Clovis I in the sixth century, then later revised and expanded under the Merovingians and Carolingians.

- I. Concerning a Summons to Court
- II. Concerning the Theft of Pigs
- III. Concerning the Theft of Cattle
- IV. Concerning the Theft of Sheep
- V. Concerning the Theft of Goats
- VI. Concerning the Theft of Dogs
- VII. Concerning the Theft of Birds
- VIII. Concerning the Theft of Bees
- XI. Concerning Thefts or Housebreaking Committed by Freemen
- XII. Concerning Thefts or Breaking-in Committed by Slaves
- XIII. Concerning the Abduction of Freemen or Free Women
- XIV. Concerning Waylaying or Pillaging
- XV. Concerning Homicide or the Man Who Takes Another Man's Wife While Her Husband Still Lives
- XVI. Concerning Arson
- XVIII. Concerning Him Who Accuses Before the King an Innocent Man Who is Absent
- XIX. Concerning Magic Philters or Poisoned Potions
- XX. Concerning the Man Who Touches the Hand or Arm or Finger of a Free Woman
- XXIII. On Mounting a Horse Without the Consent of Its Owner
- XXIV. On Killing Children and Women
- XXV. On Having Intercourse with Slave Girls or Boys
- XXIX. Concerning Disabling Injuries
- XXXII. On the Tieing-up of Freemen
- XXXIV. Concerning Stolen Fences
- XXXV. Concerning the Killing or Robbing of Slaves
- XXXIX. On Those Who Instigate Slaves to Run Away
- XL. Concerning the Slave Accused of Theft
- XLI. On the Killing of Freemen
- XLVIII. Concerning False Testimony
- LV. On Despoiling Dead Bodies
- LX. Concerning Him Who Wishes to Remove Himself from His Kin Group
- LXIV. Concerning Sorcerers
- LXVe. On Killing Pregnant Women
- LXX. On Cremation
- LXLVIII. Concerning the Woman Who Joins Herself to Her Slave

QUESTIONS FOR ANALYSIS

1. How important were politics and civic life to the Roman jurists whose writings were consolidated into the *Digest*?
2. In what ways do the laws of the Salian Franks demonstrate an interest in limiting violence and vengeance in Germanic society?
3. What are the most significant areas of similarity and difference between Roman and Germanic law?

Sources: Charles Henry Monro, trans., *The Digest of Justinian* (Cambridge: 1904–9), pp. vi–xi; Katherine Fischer Drew, ed., *The Laws of the Salian Franks* (Philadelphia: 1991), pp. 59–63.

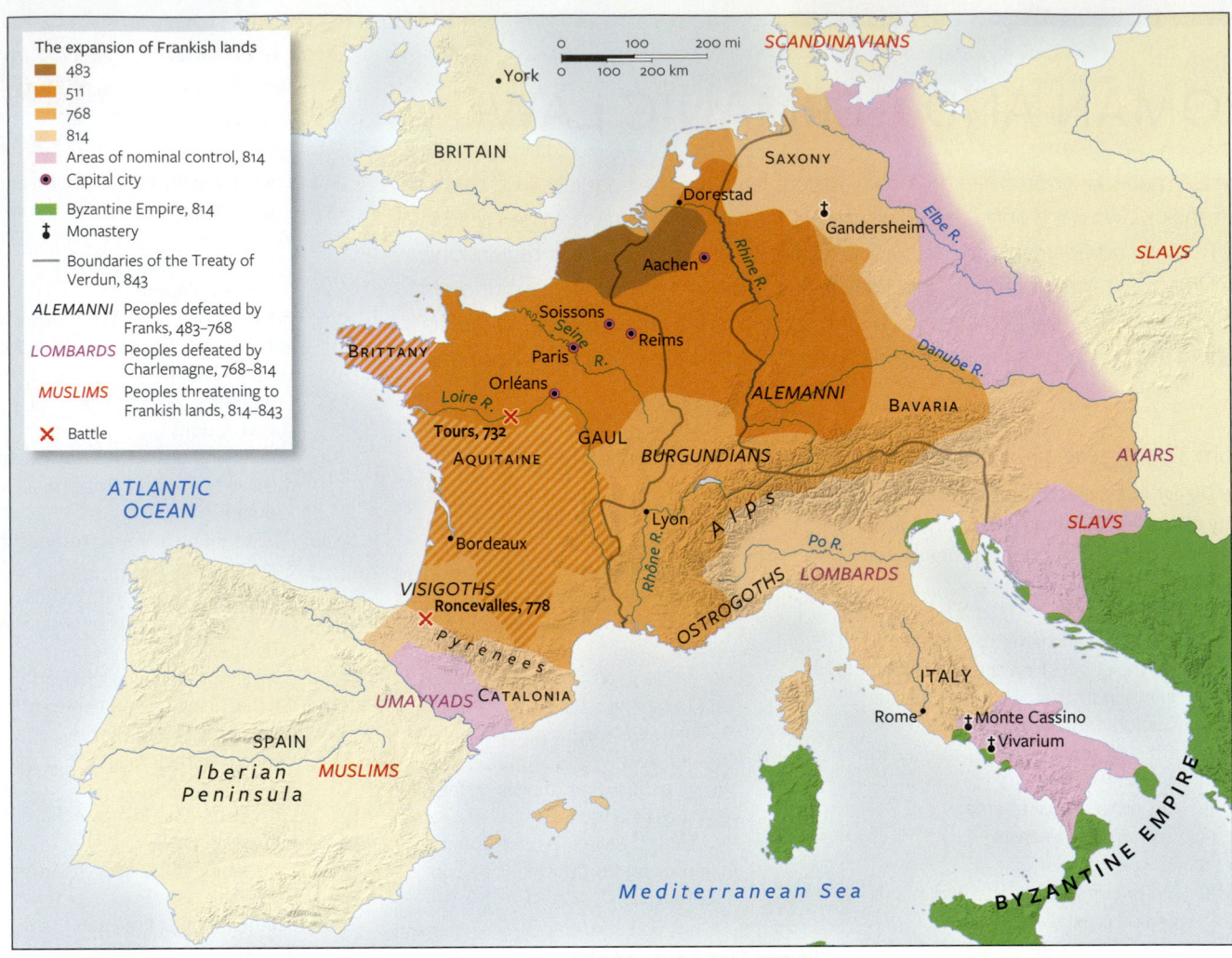

Frankish Kingdoms, 483–843 By the early sixth century, the Merovingian king Clovis I had defeated rival Germanic tribes to gain control of northern Gaul. His four sons divided the kingdom, governing separately from their capitals of Orléans, Paris, Soissons, and Reims. In 732, the Carolingian king Charles Martel defeated Umayyad forces at Tours. When his great-grandson Charlemagne acceded to the throne in 768, he began a program of expansion, ultimately controlling Frankish territory from the Umayyad borderlands in Catalonia, to the Italian Peninsula as far south as Rome, and to the Elbe and Danube Rivers in the east.

Frankish lands, and bishops based in cities still administered its dioceses. Inspired by his wife Clothilde, a Burgundian princess and a Catholic, Clovis converted to Christianity. A tradition, perhaps based on the life of Constantine, holds that he did so after praying for and winning a victory over the Alamanni, another Germanic tribe. From his time on, the Frankish rulers effectively exercised power over the church within their realms, more or less as the Byzantine emperors did in theirs. But though the Frankish churches were Catholic, they were also locally controlled. The lords who ruled their lands also appointed their clergy, without practical input from the pope.

THE FRANKISH EMPIRE: THE CAROLINGIANS (768–843)

In the course of the eighth century, the kings of the northeastern Franks—the Merovingians—gradually ceded more and more of their power to another family, the **Carolingians**, descended from noble Frankish clans. The Carolingians took possession first of the office of mayor of the palace, becoming dominant figures in the court and building a powerful army. In 732, one of them, Charles Martel ("the hammer"), defeated the forces of the Umayyad Caliphate that had crossed the Pyrenees between Tours and Poitiers, at what came to be called the battle of Tours. Though no one could have known it at the time, this eventually turned out to be the end of Islam's expansion from the Iberian Peninsula into Gaul. Charles also encouraged and protected missionaries from Britain, notably Saint Boniface (d. 754), who set out to convert the Germans. Charles's grandson, Pepin the Short, became king of a larger Frankish realm in 751. And Pepin's son, Charlemagne ("Charles the Great"), turned the Frankish kingdom into the largest and most successful empire the west had seen in centuries.

CHARLEMAGNE Charlemagne (r. 768–814) cut an impressive figure—in a world of relatively small men and women, he was more than six feet tall—and was an effective warrior. Though officially he shared his inherited crown with his brother Carloman, his preeminence became clear. He added vast stretches of territory to the domains of the Franks—from Aquitaine (eastern France), through Saxony and Bavaria (Germany), to Hungary.

Passionately committed to Christianity, Charlemagne

Charlemagne A ninth-century bronze statue of Charlemagne on a horse shows him wearing the crown and stately clothing befitting an emperor. The globe in his left hand is a symbol of his own power and of the new Holy Roman Empire's historic reach.

not only conquered the Saxons and Bavarians but also destroyed the shrines of their gods. He continued to recruit missionaries from Britain, though his own efforts took the form of smashing and burning idols and executing those who continued using pagan practices. He also defeated the Avars, nomads from Asia who had settled in and fortified much of what is now Hungary. By the 770s, Charlemagne was campaigning successfully in Italy, where he conquered the Lombard cities. He also moved forces across the Pyrenees into the Iberian Peninsula, most of it still ruled by the Umayyad Emirate of Córdoba. Though his rear guard was wiped out at Roncevalles, he and his sons took territory in Catalonia, beginning a struggle between Christians and Muslims for the Iberian lands that would last for hundreds of years.

VASSALS AND ENVOYS Charlemagne did his best to organize the vast territories that he ruled. Under the Merovingians, great lords were connected to lesser ones through a ritual. The **vassal**—the lesser nobleman or warrior who was to be the subject—placed his hands inside those of the lord. Then he swore an oath to serve the lord, who in turn swore to protect the vassal and to rely on him, both as a warrior and as a counselor. Charlemagne made intensive use of this practice, which came to be called **fealty**.

At the same time, though, Charlemagne used special officials called *missi dominici* ("the lord's envoys"). Traveling in pairs—one of them was normally a cleric, one a layman—they visited both the lords and communities ruled by Charlemagne and his own possessions. They systematically examined the administration of the laws, the collection of revenues due the ruler, and the governance of Charlemagne's own manors. They reported back directly to the emperor, who threatened severe punishment for anyone who harmed them or interfered with their work. As we will see, both of Charlemagne's ways of securing his power—the swearing-in of loyal vassals and the construction of new institutions such as his envoys—would be vital for centuries to the states that came after his.

A NEW EMPEROR At the end of the eighth century, Pope Leo III, supposedly mistreated by the Romans, appealed to Charlemagne for help. Charlemagne responded, calling a church council at Rome. On Christmas Day in 800 CE, the pope crowned him emperor. The act was dramatic: it indicated that the Roman Empire—which should mark, according to the book of Daniel, the last stage of history before the end of time—could be continued, as authority over it passed to a new dynasty. But the pope also saw himself as creating something new: a **Holy Roman Empire** that would act as the protector of the church. From this point on, Byzantium could no longer claim sole rights to be Rome's successor state. Charlemagne had become not only a claimant to power but also a world figure—one recognized both by the ruthless empress Irene of Byzantium, who proposed marriage (which he prudently declined), and by the learned Abbasid caliph of Baghdad, Haroun al-Rashid, who sent him an elephant (which he appreciated). Yet debates would also rage for centuries to come. Who was the master—the pope who crowned the emperor or the emperor who protected the pope? Was the emperor himself a holy figure, responsible for the church in his domains? The Holy Roman Empire that began—as later historians argued—with Charlemagne would confront these questions again and again.

ECONOMIC AND SOCIAL LIFE In many ways, the Carolingians laid the foundations on which European prosperity would rest for generations to come. Pippin set a precedent by legislating the exact quantity of silver that a denarius had to contain. Charlemagne, thanks to successful efforts at mining silver in what is now western France, was able to impose a new and heavier standard for the denarius, which he proclaimed legal tender in 794. This new currency—like that of the Byzantine emperor—advertised the power of the rulers who issued it. It also made possible the spread of trade. In the ninth and tenth centuries, public markets sprang up, held usually once a week, encouraged and protected by local lords. Wool cloth from England and high-quality weapons made by the Franks in the east could be bought in western towns like Dorstad, on the Rhine in what is now Holland. Rulers and clerics did their best to encourage trade and commerce by building bridges across the Seine and other rivers and repairing roads. They assembled craftsmen and artists, who worked on churches and palaces or on great estates, and consumed food, clothing, and other goods.

Women of noble birth played a central role in social and economic life. They were responsible for vital duties in the sizable households of estates and palaces: the provision of appropriate hospitality to guests, the preparation of food and drink, and the distribution of charity. Women oversaw the proper treatment of domestic animals and the cultivation of gardens. They took full charge of childbirth and the treatment of what were seen as women's characteristic ailments. And they specialized in one of the period's central art forms: the creation of the richly varied embroidered fabrics used for the decoration of churches, the proper vestments of priests, and gifts for hosts and

Saint Radegund and Charity Many noblewomen undertook charity as part of their household duties, but the sixth-century Frankish queen Radegund went so far as to found a monastery. An eleventh-century manuscript of an account of her life shows her washing the feet of the poor and serving them food.

guests. In the extraordinary colors and designs of these fabrics, we see one of the first art forms created by European women.

In the thousands of peasant households found on the great estates of the Franks, wives joined with husbands to work the land. Women produced and sold cloth, cheese, and milk, and raised and sold chickens and eggs, in large enough numbers that the laws took notice of them. A statute condemning those who violated rules for coinage included separate physical punishments for women, "because women too are in the habit of engaging in market transactions." Under the law, husbands had absolute power over their wives, whom they could repudiate or even kill. In everyday life, however, families recognized the nurturing and guidance of women by the appointment of godmothers for children, which became more common. And the vision of marriage offered by the church emphasized that spouses should both consent before wedding one another.

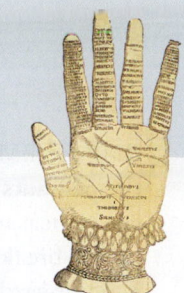

A CAROLINGIAN MOTHER'S HANDBOOK FOR HER SON

We know about the Frankish aristocrat named Dhuoda only through a short book she wrote in the 840s, during a period of discord and war, for her absent teenage son William. This text, called a handbook after its Latin title, *Liber Manualis*, is a book of religious education and moral advice, as well as a kind of literary mirror into which William could look to evaluate his faults and contemplate the salvation of his soul. It includes sections on God, death, prayer, proper relations within the family, and even interpreting numbers. Her writing shows that Dhuoda was highly educated. This excerpt is about the importance of able counselors.

There are some people who consider themselves advisors, and who really are not, for they believe they are wise although they are not. "If I speak as a person who is less wise, I am wiser." But this is not the fault of God, in whom all possible usefulness thrives. There are those who give good advice, but who do not give it well. This is of no use to them, nor does it inspire the other person. Why? Because such advice does not aim at the highest and principal virtue. And many give bad advice which has no bearing on the problem. There are different ways of reacting to various questions. In the old days there lived many honorable, practical, truthful people. Folk nowadays certainly differ from them in many respects. What is its relevance to us? The world reveals many things. Scripture says, "Evil abounds and charity is grown cold among many." In these turbulent times, a man doesn't know whom to choose as counselor, or someone he can trust above all. For many people the hope of finding help from any one remains dim....

But all the same, do not despair on that account, my son. There are still, among the descendants of our elders, several people who with God's help are good at and capable of giving advice, which I believe is useful, appreciated, and pertinent to them and their lords. All these things are unfolded in the One who is called the Most High. For Scripture says, "Is there no physician in Egypt, no balm in Gilead," no flowing water in Canaan, nor any counselor in Israel? and so forth. Surely there is. It's evident that many people have common sense. "The Lord knows his own." He is the light of the world, "angel of great counsel," dispenser of beneficent words and salvation to his own people. He existed then and now, he dwelt with the men of old and today he dwells among the living. He is in you as you go and come, and he exhorts you, as companion-at-arms to this noble and illustrious king, to accept the dominion of your overlord. May God lead you onward to become this king's high and upright counselor! Amen....

For you to become such a counselor, everything depends on the will and power of the Almighty God. If with help of the supreme Creator you reach the time of life I spoke about earlier, be on guard against the dishonest, choose the worthy. Shun the wicked, associate with the good. Don't take advice from a malicious, cowardly or wrathful man. Such a man will gnaw at you like a ringworm and he will never remain firm in his counsels. Wrath and his habitual envy very easily drag him headlong to his plunge into the abyss....

And you, son William, be wary, and so on. Flee from the type of wicked men I have described. Associate with wise people who pursue the good, those who with true submission to the will of their lords proffer good counsel, and so have earned from God and the world an honorable and great recompense. What was true for them in their time, I pray that now, today and always, may increase in you, dearest son.

QUESTIONS FOR ANALYSIS

1. According to Dhuoda, what are the qualities of good and bad counselors?
2. Why is it so difficult to distinguish between the two kinds?
3. What do we learn from this excerpt about the importance of good counsel in the Carolingian world?

Source: Dhuoda, *Handbook for Her Warrior Son, Liber Manualis*, ed. and trans. Marcelle Thiébaux (Cambridge: 1998), pp. 101, 103, 105.

IMPROVEMENTS IN AGRICULTURE The work life of the peasants was changing too. In parts of the Frankish world, peasants learned in the eighth and ninth centuries how to break the heavy, wet soil of northern Europe using a moldboard plow with a coulter, or vertical blade, that cut deeply into the ground. This device was not new: it had been used in parts of the Roman Empire. The deeper furrows made by the metal coulters allowed rainwater to drain away without drowning the seeds. Too hard for oxen to pull, the moldboard could be drawn effectively by horses, once proper harnesses were invented. Anonymous innovators brought plows and horses together in this period. Some of them began to rotate fields as well, planting both spring and winter wheat in different seasons, and devoting the rest of their land to beans and legumes, which provided vital protein for their diets and restored the soil's fertility at the same time.

After centuries in which European farmers recouped barely three times their original investment of seed—and thus had little more than enough to plant again and feed themselves—agricultural productivity probably rose, propelling the rise in population that becomes visible in the late tenth century. The agricultural foundations for Europe's eventual revival were laid in this period. But their full adoption would not be quick. Field rotation worked best if peasants could pool most of their lands and plow and cultivate them together. But it would take centuries for new forms of community to develop, in which the forms of collaboration necessary to support field rotation could be mastered, and for landowners and peasants to devise ways of making the investments in costly iron and draft animals that were needed to spread the new agriculture.

ALCUIN AND THE CAROLINGIAN RENAISSANCE

Though Charlemagne's empire did not prove durable, the changes that he introduced touched many areas. Illiterate himself, he loved to hear books read, and he deeply respected learning. He imported learned men from Britain, who created a palace school for him at Aachen, in modern Germany, where he established his capital. Alcuin of York was one of many learned clerics who came from England to the Continent and joined other erudite men to teach Charlemagne, his sons, and his courtiers. It was Alcuin who convinced Charlemagne that he should seek not only to kill pagans but also to convert them.

Charlemagne's scholars also created new traditions of learning at monasteries across Europe. Alcuin made clear that to become learned, one had to "hoist himself up with the help of seven pillars or steps"—that is, master the seven

Scriptoria This ninth-century Carolingian ivory relief depicts Saint Gregory and a group of monks working together in a scriptorium, the monastery's dedicated room for the production of manuscripts.

liberal arts. Monasteries, in earlier times, had not had special spaces dedicated to producing and storing books: this helps to explain why the original collection of Cassiodorus at Vivarium and the library of the Benedictines at Monte Cassino were eventually lost. Alcuin convinced his pupils—and his patron—that they needed to gather the ancient texts and ensure their survival. Charlemagne created a court library, where he had the classics collected so he could enjoy listening to them being read aloud. More important, in the late eighth century, monasteries began to devote fixed spaces, known as scriptoria, to the writing of books. Here scribes could devote themselves, over the years, to the slow, careful work of copying.

Alcuin's pupils, and their pupils in turn, collected

strenuously. They brought together almost all of the ancient Latin texts that we possess now, corrected them where they seemed corrupt, and multiplied copies of them. And they gave these copies a new form, producing the model of the book that we still use more than a thousand years later. This was not just a codex, but one with a single block of text on each page, with word divisions and punctuation to help readers who were not native speakers of Latin. The Carolingian scholars equipped ancient texts with their own commentaries and drew up textbooks on complicated subjects, such as the form of the universe and the nature of the calendar. And they used the Latin models creatively. Alcuin himself wrote a Latin life of Charlemagne, in which he cleverly adapted the life of Augustus written by an ancient Roman historian, Suetonius. The energy and intelligence with which these scholars used the ancient texts they knew has earned their work the title **Carolingian Renaissance**.

One of the many disciples of the Carolingian scholars was Hroswitha (ca. 935–1002), a German noblewoman who became a canoness of the Abbey of Gandersheim in northern Germany. She studied the ancient Latin comedies of Terence—himself an African who had become Romanized by culture—and wrote witty comedies in his manner about Christian martyrs. But Hroswitha's female characters defied authorities with a wit and independence more reminiscent of characters in Greek drama than of the submissive women in Roman plays.

In the end, the Carolingians studied the classics for religious ends. Alcuin himself argued that Saint Paul, whom he took as a model, had found Christian pearls in "the dregs of the poets." His followers used their new learning to draw up a massive commentary on the Latin Bible, which was also copied repeatedly and became the basic text used for educating priests in cathedral schools.

COLLAPSE OF THE FRANKISH DOMAINS

When Charlemagne died in 814, the political structure that he had assembled soon proved to be more fragile than it had seemed. His son, Louis the Pious, tried to preserve the empire while dividing it into semiautonomous areas ruled by his own three sons and a nephew. But he soon found himself confronting multiple problems: bitter rivalry among his sons; frontier attacks from Scandinavia, the Slavic peoples, and Muslim Iberia; and disaffection among some of his followers. He defeated his opponents and seemed to have settled the empire solidly when he died in 840. In fact, though, his surviving sons soon went to war with one another.

Carolingian Scholarship Charlemagne's enthusiasm for books and learning helped establish a tradition of collecting, studying, and updating the classics and religious texts. This illustration (845) celebrates the presentation of the Bible in which it appears (left) to King Charles the Bald, one of Charlemagne's grandsons, by the monks who painstakingly created the book.

The Treaty of Verdun, signed in 843 by the three grandsons of Charlemagne, ratified what now seemed inevitable: the permanent fission of Charlemagne's unified Frankish domains into smaller realms, which would eventually become the cores of modern France and Germany. For the first—but not the last—time after the fall of Rome, the immense difficulty of combining the many peoples of what is now Europe into a single empire or nation became clear. As the Frankish realms fell apart and Vikings and other nomadic peoples harried the coasts and borders of what had been Charlemagne's empire, the times seemed dark indeed. Yet like the action of the moldboard plow, these divisions prepared the ground for another revival soon to come.

CONCLUSION

By the tenth century, the Roman Empire that had once stretched from northern Britain to Syria and Egypt had been divided, more or less permanently, into three distinct civilizations: Byzantium in the east, the expansive realm of Islam, and the societies of western Europe. Each had its own vision of spiritual life, its own language of high culture, and its own ways of organizing politics and society. Each was, as we have seen, at times eager to borrow from the others. Though ancient texts continued to hold the keys to the kingdom of knowledge, new ways of organizing society, new forms of worship and religious life, and new forms of production had begun to take shape. We have moved from a late antique world, still largely shaped by the inheritance of Greece and Rome, into a new world—that of the Middle Ages.

[CHAPTER REVIEW]

KEY TERMS

Justinian (p. 212)
Theodora (p. 213)
Corpus Iuris (p. 213)
Silk Road (p. 223)
Muhammad (p. 223)
Kaaba (p. 223)

Five Pillars of Islam
  (p. 225)
caliph (p. 226)
Qur'an (p. 226)
Umayyads (p. 227)
Iconoclasm (p. 228)

mosque (p. 229)
Theodoric (p. 232)
Benedict (p. 235)
Gregory (p. 236)
Franks (p. 238)
Carolingians (p. 240)

Charlemagne (p. 241)
vassal (p. 241)
fealty (p. 241)
Holy Roman Empire
  (p. 242)
Carolingian Renaissance
  (p. 245)

REVIEW QUESTIONS

1. What were the most important reforms undertaken during the reign of Justinian?

2. What role did Justinian play in both strengthening the institutional church and furthering the connection between church and state?

3. What are the core tenets of Islam?

4. Why was Islam able to expand with such great force?

5. How did Muslim society utilize the knowledge of classical antiquity?

6. What peoples conquered the Italian Peninsula in the century after the fall of Rome, and how were they influenced by the empire's legacy?

7. How did Benedict create the blueprint for monastic life in Europe?

8. What is Pope Gregory's legacy in the history of the Christian church?

9. How were Germanic and Roman institutions and customs fused in the Frankish kingdoms?

10. What were the most important innovations of the Carolingian dynasty?

CORE OBJECTIVES

After reading this chapter, you should have a solid understanding of the following core objectives. To strengthen your grasp of the core objectives, use the resources on the Student Site for The West.

- Assess the political and cultural transformations of the eastern Roman Empire from the fourth through the seventh centuries.
- Analyze the threats and crises that affected the Byzantine Empire beginning in Justinian's reign.
- Describe the origins and spread of Islam.

- Compare the culture and scholarship of the later Byzantine Empire to that of the Islamic caliphates.
- Evaluate the intellectual and religious changes that took place in western Europe in late antiquity.
- Describe the political and social evolution of western European society in the early Middle Ages.

 GO TO **inQuizitive** TO SEE WHAT YOU'VE LEARNED—AND LEARN WHAT YOU'VE MISSED—WITH PERSONALIZED FEEDBACK ALONG THE WAY.

CHRONOLOGY

Late 9th century
Vikings found Kievan Rus' state

Early 11th century
Kings of Wessex rule
loosely organized
state in England

Mid-11th century
Reconquista begins

1054
Schism between Roman
and Orthodox Churches

1066
Battle of Hastings
and Norman conquest
of England

1085
King William I
commissions
Domesday Book

1091
Norman counts
control all of Sicily

1096–1099
First Crusade

12th century
Trade fairs begin
in northern France;
universities are established
in Italy and Paris

Europe Revived

Mid-12th century
King Henry II establishes common-law precedent in England

1147–1149
Second Crusade

1137
Louis VII begins to unify territories that would become France

1154–1155
Holy Roman Emperor Frederick Barbarossa establishes military authority in Italy

I n January 1077, the Holy Roman emperor Henry IV trekked south from Germany over the Alps to the fortress of Canossa, on the summit of a steep hill in northern Italy. Barefoot in the snow, dressed as a penitent in a hair shirt (a rough garment that abraded the skin), he spent three days outside the gates. Inside, Pope Gregory VII had taken shelter with Countess Matilda of Tuscany, a formidable ruler and one of the few successful female military leaders of the Middle Ages. She had offered to protect the pope from the emperor's troops. Like his predecessors, the emperor had insisted on the right to choose and install clerics in his dominions, a process known as investiture. But Gregory fought back, supported by a party of reformers within the Roman church who asserted its independence from imperial control. Gregory excommunicated the emperor (made it unlawful for him to take Communion) and declared him deposed. Though Henry resisted, German princes and aristocrats took advantage of the situation to push for greater independence from the empire. Henry decided to concede, for the moment, so that he could consolidate his position. After three days of public humiliation, Henry was allowed inside the gates. He begged the pope's forgiveness, Henry's excommunication was lifted, and Gregory, Matilda, and Henry shared Communion in the fortress's cathedral.

Medieval Court Culture In the Middle Ages, courts shaped new customs and expectations for the behavior of nobles and their retinues. The characters that populate these medieval playing cards include a lady-in-waiting—an attendant to a queen or noblewoman—plucking a musical instrument (left); an extravagantly dressed young man posing with a falcon trained to hunt (center); and a horseman blowing a trumpet adorned with a flag (right).

[FOCUS QUESTIONS]

- How was medieval society organized?
- In what ways were cities gaining in importance?
- What new features and powers did European states develop?
- How did the power of the Church find expression in this period?
- What were the major sources of cultural change in medieval Europe?

Making the journey to Canossa became a proverb, in more than one European language, for undertaking public penitence. Yet this dramatic moment had only limited practical consequences. Within a few years Henry reasserted his power to appoint clerics, and Gregory excommunicated and deposed him again. The Holy Roman Empire and papacy were locked in a contest that would last for more than two centuries, leaving both sides exhausted. Still, the meeting at Canossa indicated that radical changes had taken place in Europe in the late tenth and eleventh centuries. The papacy and the empire were now great powers, determined to assert their autonomy and authority. Both could muster resources, spiritual or political, from allies and supporters across Europe. They were flanked, moreover, by revived smaller powers—from the princes who owed allegiance to the emperor and the cities of Italy, to the states that were developing across Europe.

In the years from 1000 to 1200, the European world showed an expansive vigor that no one, observing the collapse of Charlemagne's successors and the harrying of Europe's borders a century or two before, would have expected. Trade and industry began to develop, cities grew and pushed for independence, and new states—large, coherent, and powerful—began to take shape. Religious men and women explored new forms of the devout life and helped build new kinds of churches. New ways of thinking about God, nature, and humanity developed and became established parts of the curriculum of Europe's first universities. Europeans mounted military expeditions to retake the holy lands of early Christianity from Islamic powers, and intellectual expeditions to learn what the Muslims knew about ancient philosophy and science. It was a time of radical innovation, desperate struggles, and fierce debates.

Yet most people who lived in this time did not think of their age as one of rapid change. In theory, at the end of this period as at the beginning, society consisted of three orders or estates: those who prayed (clerics), those who ruled and fought (nobles and armed knights), and those who worked (peasants, servants, merchants, and artisans). Each group had its own purpose and its own place in what was seen as a larger divine plan. And even when one group called for change—as many clerics did when they demanded reforms in the relationship between state and church—they often did so by insisting on a return to an ideal past or following the authority of ancient books. In the medieval world, even revolutions often began by looking backward.

THE SOCIAL ORDERS

Europe in the year 1000 was a society of scattered farms and tiny towns. Within the town walls, as well as just outside, large patches of ground were cultivated. The towns were inhabited not only by people but also by animals of many kinds, from the cows and pigs kept for milk and meat to the oxen and horses that served as beasts of burden. Noisy and chaotic during the day, towns were quiet and dark at night, when their gates were closed, street doors locked, and windows shuttered.

Between settlements there stretched vast tracts of forest—tangled masses of living and fallen trees and thick vegetation, home to bears, wolves, and wild boar, as well as smaller animals. Here and there a hermit or a group of monks might have built a small house. In clearings, fires burned all day as charcoal makers turned wood into coal. These patches of open space were more important than they probably looked. Slowly, tree by tree, the great forests of Europe were felled. As it became available, a lord would install serfs to farm the new land.

MANORIALISM: SERFS AND LORDS

In much of Europe, the way of organizing agriculture that had taken shape in Carolingian times—called

manorialism by historians—was spreading. Lords—nobles vested with local power by their overlords—ruled a population that consisted, more and more, of **serfs**: peasant laborers, male and female, bound to the land they cultivated. Serfs were not slaves—in fact, the percentage of slaves in the population gradually shrank. And the status of the farming population was never entirely uniform. The children of serfs sometimes gained permission to marry individuals who were legally free, for example. But the vast majority of peasants could not move from their land or marry without the permission of their lord. They paid their lord taxes on the crops they grew for themselves, and provided labor for their lord's farm.

In the central regions of France, in northern and western Germany, and elsewhere, serfs worked together, planting crops twice a year and rotating fields to maintain fertility. They rarely produced sizable surpluses in the thick, hard soils, but their shared fields yielded enough to sustain their communities and provide seed for the future. Meanwhile, intensive cultivation of the small areas around peasant houses, fertilized by human and animal manure, provided the variety that kept a diet healthy: legumes such as beans and peas, and vegetables.

Women worked beside men. They helped glean wheat and make hay in the lords' fields. Women also looked after poultry and cows, made cheese and other dairy products, and sold some of what they produced in village markets. Houses were small—usually one or two rooms, in which a whole family would share a single bed. But the village

Serfs at Work A richly illuminated page from a fourteenth-century English book of psalms includes an illustration of serfs laboring in the fields. Three women are harvesting grain with sickles, while a man gathers the cut grain into bundles.

well, where women drew water, and the village laundry, where they washed their family's clothes, offered spaces for sociability. This was the life of those who worked. It imposed many burdens.

The lords and ladies who ruled the land and lived on the work of others had demanding tasks of their own. In return for the right to establish and profit from their manors, they owed obedience to a higher ruler, whom—as we will see—they served in multiple capacities. In their own domains, they were expected to provide protection against raiders and thieves, and to offer justice when crimes took place or families fell out over the division of the lands assigned to them. Nobles used their revenues to build small fortresses—the castles that began to dot the European landscape—and to equip themselves and some of their followers with arms and armor.

Men of the knightly class, often nobles who as younger sons did not stand to inherit lands and wealth, learned to fight as boys. They prepared for lives as warriors in the service of kings or great nobles, which—if they were skillful and lucky—might earn them manors and titles of their own. Noblewomen learned to administer a complex household, maintaining stocks of everything from linens to spices and organizing feasts for visitors of high status.

Across Europe, members of this second order, those who ruled and fought, mastered similar skills and provided similar services for those bound to their lands. But the formation of a military class across Europe did not ensure peace. For knights, the normal way of settling disputes, after all, was by combat, and a simple slight could easily lead to a formal feud that involved all members of two houses and their allies. They also plundered and harried peasants and clerics who could not defend themselves.

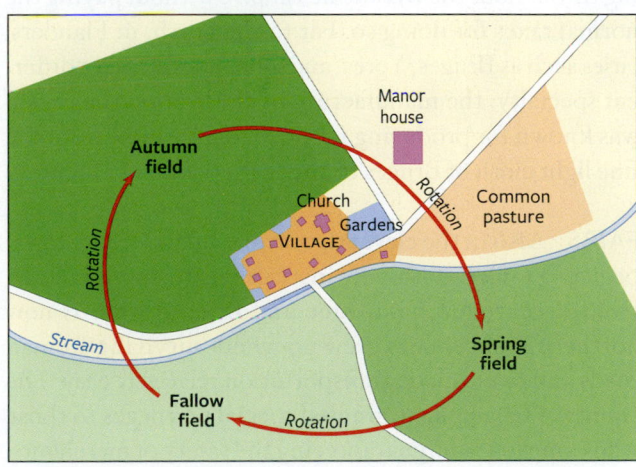

A Medieval Manor A manor might have consisted of the lord's house, a cluster of serfs' cottages surrounded by vegetable gardens, and three fields. Each year the fields were rotated: one field was planted in the spring and another in the fall, with the third lying fallow to restore its fertility.

THE PEACE OF GOD: THE CLERGY

As the end of the first millennium since the birth of Jesus approached, clergy in southwestern France devised what they hoped might be a way to prevent continual violence against the innocent. Local clergy and nobles met in councils called peace assemblies, which gathered around the relics of the saints that every church and monastery possessed. The presence of these bones and garments, charged with the sacred electricity generated by their onetime owners and vested with the power to do miracles, galvanized the crowds. The councils—made up, in many cases, of the same local authorities that had been responsible for at least some of the violence—called for a **Peace of God**. They issued rules and threatened those who broke them with powerful spiritual sanctions—the interdict (prohibition of divine services) or excommunication. In 989, one of these councils met at the Benedictine abbey of Charroux in western France. It condemned those "who break into churches," those "who rob the poor . . . of a sheep, ox, ass, cow, goat, or pig," and anyone who "attacks, seizes, or beats a priest, deacon, or any other clergyman, who is not bearing arms (shield, sword, coat of mail, or helmet), but is going along peacefully or staying in the house."

The peace movement won impressive support, and the coming of the year 1033—marking a thousand years since the Crucifixion—aroused new forms of religious enthusiasm. The formal rules became more precise: the Truce of God, for example, forbade warfare in the period from Thursday to Sunday. Yet it also became clear that spiritual commands alone would not stop the nobles from engaging in their feuds or doing violence to those who could not resist, and the movement gradually lost its force. Over time, as we will see, new political forms took shape that tasked those who fought to guard and protect the members of the other two orders.

THE REEMERGENCE OF CITIES (900–1200)

In 900, imperial Rome was a ghostly ruin. Some 20,000 inhabitants clung to parts of the historic city center and to the great churches—Santa Maria Maggiore, the Vatican, and the Lateran, where the popes actually lived. The Forum was deserted, as it would be for centuries, except for flocks of animals and their shepherds. Ancient monuments such as the Colosseum served mostly as quarries for *spolia* ("spoils") such as columns, dozens of which were taken from Roman temples and basilicas to be reerected in the naves of churches.

TRADE AND MANUFACTURING

Outside Rome, though, cities began to grow and take on new functions. On Italy's western coast, Amalfi had developed trade in the eighth and ninth centuries, selling local grain and timber in Egypt for gold, with which the merchants bought silk and other luxuries in Byzantium. In Genoa and Pisa, which rivaled and then overtook Amalfi, coins came back into circulation in large numbers—gold dinars from Egypt and Syria, and coins from Byzantium as well. Trade needed protection, especially from the raids launched by the Muslim Caliphate of Córdoba (Spain) on Christian ports, including Pisa itself. The cities developed fleets of galleys—long, narrow ships propelled by oars and manned by trained fighters. In 1015–16 Pisa and Genoa defeated Muslim efforts to invade Sardinia—only to fight over the island themselves, with the Pisans ending up victorious.

On the other side of the Italian Peninsula, Venice—a new city that had taken shape in the ninth century on islands and marshes in a lagoon on the Adriatic Sea—began to build trading networks in the central and eastern Mediterranean. Late in the eleventh century it entered into alliances with Byzantium. In return for its military aid against expanding Norman and Muslim power, Venice received support for its churches and the privilege of trading throughout the Byzantine Empire without paying the normal taxes for doing so. Far to the north, in Flanders, cities such as Bruges, Ypres, and Ghent developed a different specialty: the manufacture of cloth. Soon the region was known for producing fabric of many kinds, from the fine light cloth of Bruges to the scarlet cloth of Ghent.

FAIRS   Also in the eleventh century, inland trade slowly began to revive, with new institutions to support it. In twelfth-century Champagne and Brie, in what is now northern France, fairs grew up where surviving Roman roads and rivers made transportation relatively easy. The counts of Champagne granted special privileges to those who came to trade, guaranteeing the safety of merchants, enforcing agreements, and regulating weights and measures. What began as local centers for exchanging produce and livestock turned into trade fairs for many different kinds of goods. The spice trade played a central role, though not—as used to be thought—because spices preserved food or disguised the taste of meat and fish that had

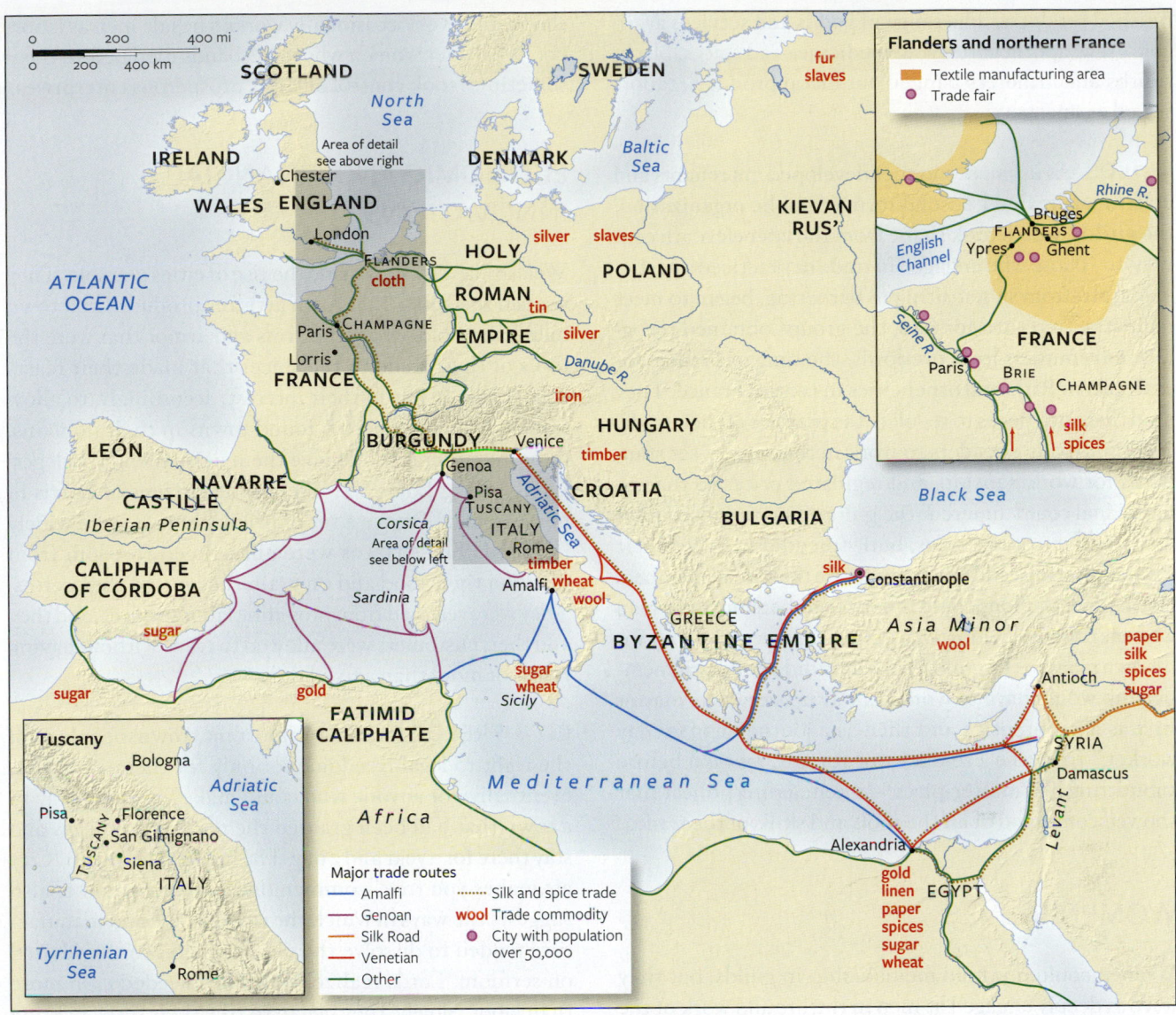

The New Cities and Commerce, ca. 1000 From the eighth century, new trade routes connected Europe's growing cities. Valuable commodities such as sugar and gold crossed the Mediterranean, while spices and silk came from farther east through Constantinople. Cities in Tuscany benefited from being at the center of this Mediterranean commerce. In Flanders, France, and England, trade fairs sprung up along major waterways, where townspeople could buy goods from across Europe and even Asia.

gone bad. Europeans in this period liked strongly flavored food, and almost all the spices that served their needs were produced in Asia. Italian merchants brought spices and silk (another Asian luxury product) overland to the fairs, where they could trade for Slavic and Baltic slaves, furs from the north, and the fine cloths of the Flemish. Once again—but now in a new way—western Europe was connected to trading networks that spanned Eurasia.

NEW TOWNSCAPES European towns, often sited where ancient Roman roads or more recent trails met,

gradually took on a new and characteristic form. Towns from Chester in western England to Bologna in Italy were identifiable from a distance by the walls that protected them and the gates where guards and city officials controlled traffic. In the town center, a market square offered space for the sale of food and other goods. Along the central streets, merchants and craftsmen built houses of a new pattern. On the ground floor a shop or workplace, open to the street, offered the space to produce and sell goods. The family that owned the shop normally lived above it, using attic space, if available, to store raw materials and finished products. The range of goods and services available grew: apothecaries sold medicines and spices, blacksmiths and armorers banged out metal products, tailors sewed garments.

GUILDS

As urban economies developed, merchants and craftsmen created a second form of public organization: the **guilds**, which took shape from the later eleventh century on. Those who engaged in trade or practiced a particular craft, from shoemaking to barbering, began to meet regularly. In return for fees, the groups obtained recognition from their legal overlords: the king of France, for example, in Paris and other cities in central France. They used these privileges to regulate the practice of their trade. Guilds forbade outsiders to work in their trade, set standards for workmanship, and regulated prices so that no individual could undercut the group. They imposed fines for violations of the rules, built splendid halls for their formal meetings and feasts, and gave their dead members lavish funerals. Sons could inherit membership, but a man who married the widow of a guildsman needed to pay for his own place in the guild. A boy who did not inherit membership would have to work his way up, serving a master first as an apprentice and then as a journeyman (a "day worker," from the French word for day, *journée*) before submitting his "master-piece"—a demanding project that showed command of all the tools and skills of the trade.

WOMEN'S LIVES

Women could not hold membership in guilds, but they were as deeply engaged as men in the life and work of the towns. Sermons and books of advice for women instructed them to confine themselves to their homes and, if they needed to leave home at all, to keep their eyes modestly fixed on the ground. Their main job, according to these books, was to administer their households—a complicated and demanding task for the wife of a prosperous merchant or craftsman. She had to see to it that the house's chests were full of clean linens, the kitchen stocked with food and utensils, and her own medicine chest fully equipped with remedies. These duties, though limited, were demanding enough. Maintaining the household took long hours and required expert knowledge of everything from washing fine cloth to overseeing childbirth (sometimes with the help of a paid midwife) to nursing sick children. Despite the advice books, the realities of city life placed women in many other roles as well. Poor women sold food and clothing in markets, carded and spun wool, wove cloth in shops, and even occasionally worked beside men as laborers. Wealthier women whose husbands died before them sometimes took control of large, prosperous enterprises.

ECONOMIC AND FINANCIAL INNOVATIONS

Wealthy landowners made the rise of cities possible. They needed the goods that town artisans produced and town merchants sold—from the arms and armor that were the tools of their trade to the spices that made their feasts appetizing. It was in their interest, accordingly, to allow traders and craftsmen to found towns in their domains, to protect them, and to give them permanent privileges. In 1155, King Louis VII offered the citizens of Lorris in north-central France a set of privileges that were widely imitated. The citizens were guaranteed freedom from taxes on their food and on grain they raised themselves. They were released from providing labor services, and they and their customers were allowed to trade without paying tolls—or more than a fixed rate.

CITY FREEDOM

Most important, townspeople won the right to legal freedom, not only for themselves but, eventually, for anyone who could make his or her way to a town that had been granted the normal privileges and stay there for a year and a day. The medieval proverb "City air makes you free" commemorates this system. It also suggests the ways in which the rise of trade and manufacture tended to dissolve the older landed economy based on serfdom. Lords realized that they needed cash more than labor. Slowly, they began to free their serfs, making them tenants—charging them rent rather than requiring specific tasks—and allowing some of them, and their children, to leave the land.

FINANCE

As trade grew in scale, so did costs and profits, calling forth new means of financing these activities. By the tenth and eleventh centuries, merchants in Italian cities were joining together to create ventures larger than any one of them could have financed alone. A form of contract developed in the Islamic world, the *commenda*, offered a template for an effective kind of association. Investors became "sleeping partners," venture capitalists who raised the money that enabled an active partner to outfit ships and buy trade goods. Liability was limited: if the enterprise failed, a ship's captain did not have to repay his investors. The very existence of these contracts shows that a new society was taking shape—one whose members were used to calculating prices in different currencies and knew about the goods that were for sale in cities hundreds of miles apart on the coasts of distant lands.

One new group of specialists, the notaries, produced the contracts and other forms without which a commercial society could not function, and maintained registers of them to document commercial agreements. Eventually banks took shape, often with headquarters in an Italian city and multiple branches in distant regions. Instead of carrying coins, always a risky business, a merchant could deposit money with the Bardi or Peruzzi banking families in Florence, receive a letter of credit, and withdraw the cash when needed—for example, to buy pepper in Alexandria or furs in Champagne.

THE COMMUNES: INDEPENDENT CITY GOVERNMENTS

As cities grew richer and more powerful, a second transformation took place. In the centuries after Rome fell, local bishops often ruled cities. But their powers were limited and the new cities proved violent—so violent that they undermined trade and defied control. In Italy, extended kin groups banded together to build towers in which members of allied families could take refuge and defend themselves during civil strife—notably by dropping tiles from the lofty roofs on their enemies. From a distance, these cities looked like forests, as San Gimignano in Tuscany and a

Italian Towns In San Gimignano, in Tuscany, fortified towers—built between the eleventh and thirteenth centuries by noble families for defensive purposes—still dwarf the town's other buildings.

few others still do. But these developments only worsened the dueling and feuding.

Throughout the eleventh century, groups of local noblemen came together in Pisa, Siena, and other cities, determined to devise a more stable form of government. When necessary, they negotiated or fought to remove themselves from the political and legal control of their bishops or local lords. They declared themselves **communes**, ruled by officials called consuls and by assemblies of "law-worthy men"—men whose noble status enabled them to seek redress for grievances in court. The city was coming back to political life—and not only as a central cog in a much greater machine, as in the Roman world, but as an independent organization, as it had been in ancient Greece.

The earliest form of city government did not last long in most cases. The merchants and bankers who were becoming increasingly prominent in urban economies generally found themselves excluded from the assemblies and public offices populated by noblemen. Struggles ensued, and by the first decades of the thirteenth century, new and more settled forms of government took shape. In some cities, such as Florence, members of the old noble families were legally excluded from political life. In others, such as Venice, nobles and merchants merged into a single ruling class. Whatever their decisions on this point, most Italian cities created central governments and housed them in fortified palaces that dominated the urban landscape. Foreign professionals, usually trained as lawyers, were hired to manage city finances, administer justice, and even lead their armies in war. After a one-year term, each incumbent, known as a *podestà* (chief magistrate), and his staff would leave for another city—but only after the books had been audited. Other tasks were carried out by committees of citizens who were chosen by lot and lived in government buildings while they served. Creativity was a hallmark of this new urban society.

THE MEDIEVAL STATE

The Middle Ages also saw the creation of territorial states: cohesive polities that gradually developed all of the powers we now ascribe to governments, from raising taxes to providing justice. In some cases—France, for example—these states began as mosaics, as rulers hastened to bind lesser nobles to them, though at the expense of giving them lands of their own to exploit and govern. In other cases—especially in England—right of conquest enabled the king to divide up the whole territory as he wished. In theory, subjects had to obey ultimate royal authority. In practice, obedience could be difficult or even impossible to compel. But over time, as we will see, new institutions took shape that could provide rulers with tremendous power and resources.

ORIGINS

Building on precedents that went back to Charlemagne and before, kings and great nobles constructed states, at first, not by creating institutions but by building networks of fighting men who could help them wage war or defend the realm. A nobleman or a knight was both a person of status and, in almost every case, a subordinate whose superiors might include a great noble, such as a duke or king. Like serfs, lords and knights were bound to their superiors. A dramatic ceremony sealed the pact: the inferior party placed his hands within the superior's, swore fealty, and entered a relationship—like the serf's relationship with his master—defined by a complex web of rules. A noble vassal would usually owe his lord defined obligations: thirty days' military service each year, for example, and help with large expenses, such as a daughter's dowry. In return, the vassal might be granted an estate, with its revenues, and a castle. Such compacts were endlessly modified: one vassal of the

Swearing Fealty An illustration from a thirteenth-century English book of psalms depicts a knight—equipped with armor, sword, and horse—kneeling before a king and extending his hands as he swears his oath.

king of England was bound to hold the head of his seasick lord as he vomited on Channel crossings. But all of these agreements were designed to provide the lord with the array of trained soldiers he would need to face an armed enemy in the field, and to provide those soldiers with the financial support they required to maintain themselves as fighting knights.

EARLY STATES: THE DUCHY OF NORMANDY

The supple system of political organization, grounded in the loyalty between lords and vassals, was even enlisted by former enemies of Christian Europe. From the ninth century onward, Vikings from southern Denmark, Norway, Sweden, and the island of Gotland in Scandinavia sailed the Baltic and Norwegian Seas in their slender longships. They sacked cities—Rouen fell to them in 840—and raided monasteries. In the ninth century, warriors from Denmark invaded England and conquered three of the four Anglo-Saxon states—Northumbria, East Anglia, and Mercia—leaving only Wessex under Anglo-Saxon rule. The territory they held, which came to be called the Danelaw, was gradually reconquered by the Anglo-Saxons, who drove them out of their last holding, Northumbria, in 954. In the early tenth century, after raiding and forming small colonies, warriors from Denmark and Normandy founded the duchy of Normandy in northwestern France. There they found their place in the local structures of authority. The Viking Rollo, appointed the first Norman duke by the king of France in 911, agreed to protect France from further raids. In the same period, the Vikings who had remained in Scandinavia created the kingdoms of Denmark, Sweden, and Norway.

Gradually the Normans adopted Christianity and became experts in the European form of warfare. From Normandy, warriors and traders soon moved out into the Mediterranean and Atlantic worlds. In the late ninth century and after, Norman traders played a role in the creation of the medieval state of Kievan Rus', while others settled Iceland.

Throughout the late tenth, eleventh, and twelfth centuries, rulers expanded the effective power of their states, finding ways to enforce the obligations of their vassals and to develop new powers alongside them. By the end of the tenth century, Richard II, Duke of Normandy (r. 996–1026), had the best-organized small state in Europe. His courts offered justice to subjects in all parts of his domain. Taxes and tolls gave him dependable revenue. And a

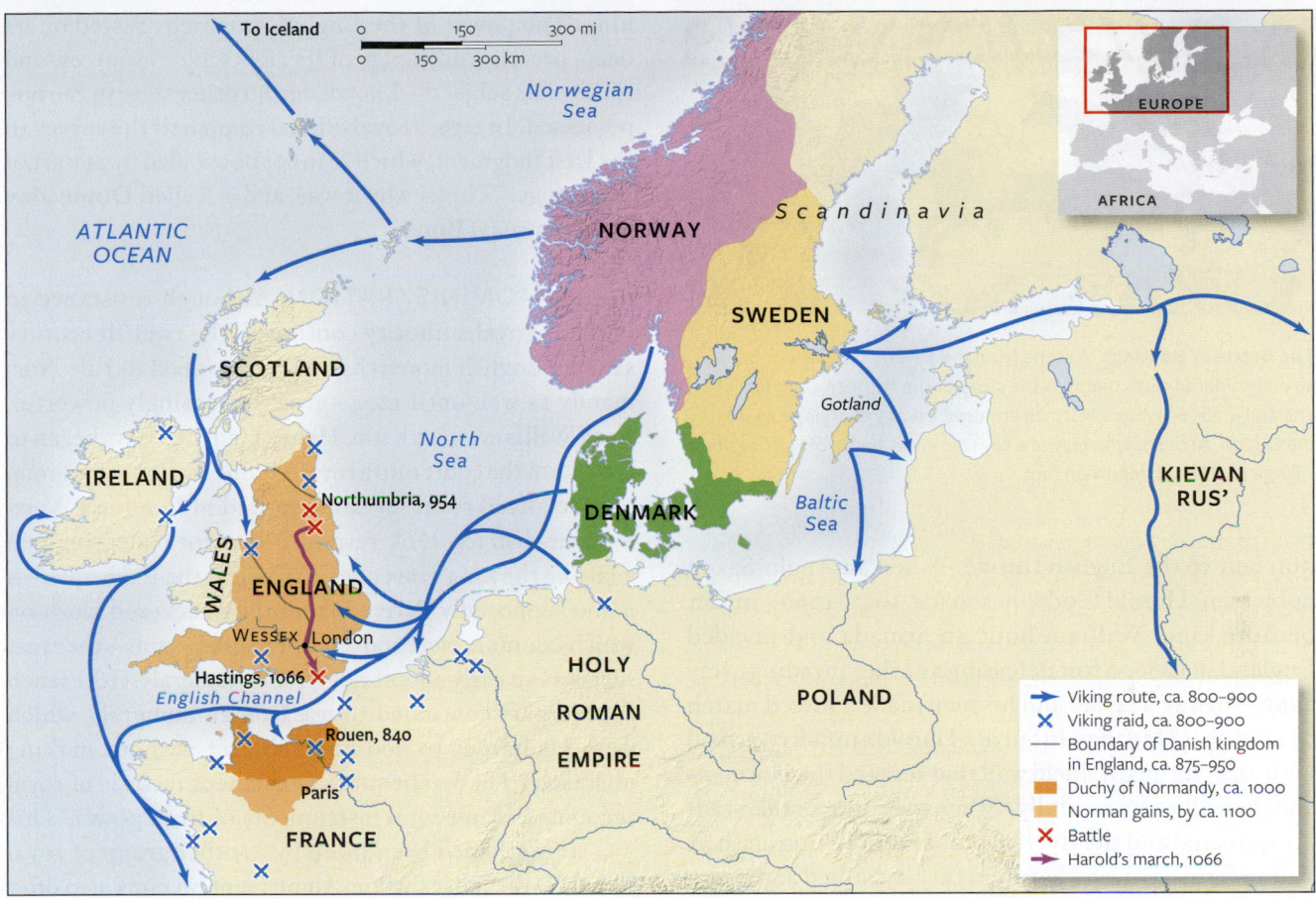

The Vikings, the Duchy of Normandy, and the Conquest of England, ca. 800–1100 In the ninth century, Vikings sailed out from Scandinavia to colonize new territories, from Iceland to Kievan Rus'. They raided towns and monasteries on the English, Irish, and French coasts, establishing the Duchy of Normandy in France in the early tenth century. In 1066, William II, Duke of Normandy, gained control of England after his military victory at Hastings.

precise set of rules governed the number of horsemen that each of his vassals was required to provide in times of war.

EARLY STATES: THE KINGS OF WESSEX

By contrast, the kings of Wessex in southern England ruled a much weaker state than the duchy of Normandy. Though they had also begun to extend their justice to all parts of the realm, they had little dependable revenue. More important still, many of the farmers who worked the land were free peasant landholders (as their descendants would remain until the Norman conquest). In wartime, the Wessex kings had to rely on a large but poorly trained militia of free farmers and a much smaller group of elite soldiers. Locally, the kingdom was divided into districts called shires and administered by "shire-reeves"—officials whose title would eventually evolve into the familiar word

sheriff. These men, powerful and hard to control, were responsible for local defense and the collection of revenues. Even more difficult to handle were the powerful lords of the realm, who gave little support to most English kings and took no interest in strengthening the realm as a whole. Though large and rich, England could not raise an army of armored men on horseback who were bound to their king by personal ties. A strong individual king such as Canute the Great (d. 1035), who was himself of Danish and Slavic rather than British descent, could assert royal authority for a time, but in the end the noble families reasserted their power.

Over time, the Normans developed tight connections with the Anglo-Saxon rulers of the House of Wessex—especially Edward the Confessor (r. 1042–1066), whose mother was the sister of a Norman duke. William II, Duke of Normandy (r. 1035–1087), seems to have thought that Edward, who had no children, promised to make

The Battle of Hastings A scene from the Bayeux Tapestry (1067)—an embroidered cloth that tells the story of the Norman conquest of England in 1066—shows Norman armored cavalry charging toward the English. Archers, who played a key role in the battle of Hastings by killing King Harold, follow on foot.

him heir to the English throne. When an Anglo-Saxon nobleman, Harold Godwineson (ca. 1022–1066), in fact became king, William built an armada and invaded England in 1066. After defeating another invading army from Norway, Harold and his men made a forced march to a hill near Hastings, in Surrey. Harold's infantry, armed with axes, formed a shield wall that resisted the Normans and their allies successfully. When the continental invaders retreated and the English pursued, breaking up their strong formation, the Norman cavalry rallied and counterattacked, supported by skillful archers who managed to kill Harold. Suddenly, Duke William II of Normandy was King William I of England, known thereafter as **William the Conqueror**.

ENGLAND: ESTABLISHING CENTRAL AUTHORITY

Over the next century and a half, England became a strong state. Because William had taken the entire country by conquest, he could parcel it out to his vassals in a single, coherent system. He carefully divided the land holdings given to his followers to prevent any of them from becoming too mighty. His court, made up of his chief noblemen and clerics, supported him in taking control of the new territory. In 1085, William's counselors took part in his decision to send agents throughout England and make a comprehensive assessment of the wealth of the whole land. The survey that resulted, though incomplete (London, for example, was omitted), was 2 million words long. It registered 13,418 settlements by order of their landholder—from the king, the clerics and religious houses, and the noble tenants-in-chief, down to the lesser servants of the

king. The power of the English monarchy rested on its deep, precise knowledge of its rights and resources, and those of its subjects—knowledge no other state in Europe possessed. In 1179, a royal official compared the survey to the Last Judgment, which "cannot be avoided by any art of subterfuge." This is why it was, and is, called **Domesday (or Doomsday) Book**.

ROYAL ADMINISTRATION Although resistance to Norman royal authority continued, the twelfth century saw the English monarchs—who continued to rule Normandy as well until 1204—grow increasingly powerful. King William's fourth son, Henry I (r. 1100–1135), began to transform the court into a royal administration. One group of specialized royal servants, settled in London's Westminster district, took responsibility for collecting and auditing the king's revenues. Known as the Exchequer—a name supposedly derived from the checkered cloth on which counters were moved to compute sums—the treasury was an early adopter of Arabic numerals. (Its French counterpart continued to use Roman numerals, which were far harder to add and subtract without making mistakes.) The Exchequer's permanent records of royal accounts became vital instruments of royal power. This was strengthened even more by another group of royal servants: the judges whom Henry sent on circuit to offer royal justice throughout the kingdom. Though civil war followed Henry's death, his grandson Henry II, Count of Anjou, not only restored the structures that Henry I had built but substantially improved them. During the Angevin Henry II's reign as king of England (1154–1189), the court became a royal council, whose support the king called on when he made legislation.

JUSTICE BASED ON LEGAL PRECEDENT Even more systematically than Henry I, Henry II exploited royal power to give justice to his subjects. In the eleventh century, most trials in England were conducted by ordeal or battle. The outcome revealed the judgment of divine Providence as to which side was in the right. But Henry II promoted the growth of juries—a dozen free men brought together at first simply to state whether a given person was lawfully in possession of particular lands. Henry sent out more justices to preside over the ordinary courts as well. By the end of the twelfth century, many English people thought of justice as something provided by juries, who determined questions of fact, and royal judges, who offered a form of justice based on legal precedent rather than divine intervention. The system seemed fairer and more transparent than the old one, and it extended royal

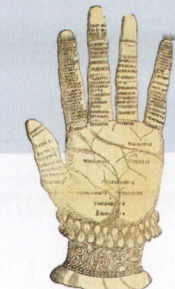

THE SURVEY OF HUNTINGDONSHIRE FROM DOMESDAY BOOK

Domesday Book was an extensive land survey commissioned by King William I of England in 1085 and conducted throughout the following year. The information collected allowed the king to estimate the revenues he could expect from his newly conquered lands and how many fighting men he could call up. It also helped him to settle land disputes between lords. All in all, it was an important tool for the administration of good governance.

The following excerpts are from the entry on Huntingdonshire, a county north of London. It describes the economic value of lands held by the king and by the Abbey of Ely, a prosperous Benedictine monastic community of importance to the Norman kings.

The land of the king

A manor.[1] In Hartford King Edward [r. 1043-1066] had 15 hides[2] assessed to the geld.[3] There is land for 17 ploughs.[4] Rannulf the brother of Ilger keeps it now. There are 4 ploughs now on the demesne[5]; and 30 villeins and 3 bordars[6] have 8 ploughs. There is a priest; 2 churches; 2 mills rendering 4 pounds; and 40 acres of meadow. Woodland for pannage,[7] 1 league in length and half a league in breadth. [In the time of King Edward the Confessor] it was worth 24 pounds; now 15 pounds....

[The land of the abbey of Ely]

In Spaldwick the abbot of Ely has 1 manor assessed at 15 hides to the geld...15 ploughs can plough this land.... Now the abbot of Ely has there 4 ploughs; 7 beasts; 30 pigs; 120 sheep...4 beehives; and 1 mill worth 2 shillings. There are 50 villeins and 10 bordars. Among them all there are 25 ploughs and 160 acres of meadow; 60 acres of woodland for pannage. It was worth [in the time of King Edward the Confessor]...16 pounds; and now it is worth 22 pounds.

QUESTIONS FOR ANALYSIS

1. What types of economic information are recorded in these excerpts from Domesday Book?
2. What comparisons can you make between the two properties described?
3. How did Domesday Book enhance the power of the Norman kings?

[1] manor: an estate or unit of lordship   [2] hide: the amount of land that would support a household   [3] geld: a tax collected by the Normans   [4] plough: the amount of farmland that could be plowed by a team of eight oxen   [5] demesne: the part of the manor held directly by the lord or farmed for the lord's profit   [6] villeins and bordars: unfree peasants who owed labor services to their lord and farmed some land for themselves   [7] pannage: food given to pigs in the autumn

Source: "The Survey of Huntingdonshire in Domesday Book," in *English Historical Documents 1042–1189*, 2nd ed., ed. David C. Douglas and George W. Greenaway (London: 1981), pp. 1036, 1075.

---

authority across the land. Though still a medieval monarchy, Henry II's England offered a new and powerful model of good government.

MEDIEVAL MONARCHY ON THE CONTINENT

The largest continental monarchies did not develop new institutions as quickly as England, partly because they did not have the unique opportunity to reorganize their institutions that the Norman conquest provided William I and his successors.

FRANCE France, for example, developed slowly. When Hugh Capet, a Frankish landowner, was crowned king in 987, he was actually chosen by his fellow noblemen in preference to a candidate from the Carolingian line. A weak monarch, he had to give away some of his own lands to win supporters. His successors, though often no stronger than he, benefited from good genetic luck: they had long reigns and produced sons to continue their line. Forgetting the

Catholic territory	⎯⎯⎯ Country boundaries, ca. 1200
Orthodox territory	········ Boundary of English holdings within France
Muslim territory	⎯⎯ Boundary of royal domain
Pagan area	
○ Papacy of Catholic Christianity	✕ Battle
○ Patriarchate of Orthodox Christianity	

Continental States, 1200 In the eleventh and twelfth centuries, new Christian monarchies developed across Europe. Catholicism held sway from the Iberian Peninsula, where Spanish kings had begun to push back the Islamic caliphate, to the Norman monarchies of England and Sicily, the Holy Roman Empire in central Europe, and networks of towns ruled by nobles in Poland and Hungary. The Orthodox Kievan Rus' and Byzantine Empire were strong, centralized states, though Turkish peoples pressured their borders from the east.

older principle of election, they came to see themselves as monarchs by inheritance, and more and more of their subjects agreed. Slowly, the French kings built up their control over what became the royal domain: the territories in and around the Île-de-France, which included the city of Paris, and for a time the duchy of Burgundy.

Slowly, too, other great nobles in Burgundy, Anjou, and elsewhere emulated the dukes of Normandy and established firmer states. French landholders loved to fight, but gradually they settled into a more orderly existence as a landed aristocracy. Though the French king Louis VII (r. 1137–1180) was less successful than England's Henry II, his contemporary and rival, he did manage to establish connections with vassals across France, and the court began to employ more educated men. For his part, Henry applied ferocious energy to holding and expanding the Angevin territories. In 1152, after Louis VII had his marriage to Eleanor of Aquitaine (ca. 1122–1204) annulled, Henry married her, and by doing so became duke of Aquitaine and Gascony. French armies attacked, but Henry fought them off and added Brittany and Toulouse to his holdings. He also conquered a large tract of Ireland and invaded Wales. Modern historians have sometimes described this vast collection of territories as an Angevin empire, though it seems more likely that Henry planned to distribute parts of it to his sons: he gave Aquitaine to Richard and Ireland to John to rule. By the end of the twelfth century, this "empire" was beginning to dissolve.

SPAIN In Spain, a number of small Christian kingdoms—Navarre, Aragon, Castile, and León, which ruled parts of the northern Iberian Peninsula from the ninth and tenth centuries onward—engaged in a long struggle to regain territory from the Muslim states. Effective warriors such as Sancho III of Navarre (1004–1035) and Ferdinand I of León (1037–1065) pushed the boundaries of Christian power to the west and south. They also encouraged Christians to settle on the land and developed networks of vassals. By the middle of the eleventh century, the northern half of the Iberian Peninsula was largely in Christian hands.

SICILY The best organized of the continental European states—Sicily—was, like England, governed by Normans. Two adventurous Norman brothers, Robert Guiscard (ca. 1015–1089) and Roger de Hauteville (d. 1101), had already conquered much of Calabria, in southern Italy, by 1061, when one of the three Muslim rulers of Sicily appealed to them for help against a rival. They captured the city of Palermo in 1072 and controlled the whole island by 1091. Drawing on the skills of Greek shipbuilders and sailors, Robert used Sicily, without much ultimate success, to war against Byzantine settlements. As the count of Sicily, Roger set up a unique government, partly based on the existing foundations of Muslim rule. He followed his predecessors' example in granting Greeks and Muslims, as well as the much smaller Latin population, free exercise of their religion, and their own courts and tax system. He ruled as absolute monarch over all.

THE HOLY ROMAN EMPIRE The Holy Roman emperors, in theory the superiors even of their fellow monarchs, claimed lands that stretched from Saxony in far northern Germany to Lombardy in northern Italy, and from parts of eastern France to the borders of Hungary. In practice, strong emperors such as Henry IV (r. 1084–1106) and Frederick Barbarossa (r. 1152–1190) a century later exercised power over vast areas, while official servants, called *ministeriales*, collected revenues and offered justice in parts of the empire that the emperor ruled directly. But when

struggles with the Roman church engaged imperial attention, or weak rulers inherited the title, the power of local princes and noblemen increased.

Henry faced many challenges after his submission to the pope in 1076. He spent much of his reign on inconclusive wars in Italy and the empire, and near the end of his life he was deposed by his son. But he retained strong support—made stronger by papal efforts to intervene on behalf of his enemies. He ended his days back on the throne, having established the imperial house as a center of loyalty, and in 1101 created the Landfrieden—a general peace agreement designed to eliminate feuding between local rulers and nobles.

Frederick Barbarossa In an illumination from a twelfth-century German chronicle, Frederick Barbarossa is depicted as emperor, crowned and seated on a throne, flanked by two of his sons.

Frederick advanced imperial authority beginning in 1154–55 with the first of what would eventually be six expeditions to Italy. He helped the papacy put down a rebellion in Rome, conquered the rich and strongly fortified city of Milan, and reasserted some of the imperial powers over the appointment of clerics that Henry IV had claimed. Fascinated by the traditions of Roman law, he hired jurists who described him as the lord of the world and the inheritor of the great Romans. But as Frederick grew older and the northern Italian cities became wealthier and more independent, the balance of forces changed, and in 1176 he was defeated by the cities of Lombardy at Legnano, not far from Milan. In the empire itself, he achieved considerable success at a more pragmatic level, pacifying and uniting the princes who ruled the German lands—only to drown in 1190, when crossing a river at the head of a military expedition to regain the Holy Land from Muslim rule. Frederick left behind the myth of a great emperor, whom many Germans believed would someday return to rule them again, but relatively few strong institutions.

POLAND

East of the Holy Roman Empire's German territory and north of Austria, Catholic central Europe was divided into massive kingdoms. Poland, which stretched south all the way from the Baltic Sea to the Carpathians, had been Catholic since the tenth century, when the first ruler of Poland, Mieszko (r. 963–992), adopted the religion of his Christian wife, Dobrava, who came from the empire's kingdom of Bohemia (now part of the Czech Republic). Once Mieszko and his court were baptized, determined preaching gradually brought the previously pagan Polish tribes into the Christian church.

Boleslaw, the duke of Poland from 992 to 1025, mounted an ambitious program to unify Poland and Bohemia. Over the next two centuries, however, Poland collapsed into rival duchies fragmented by a powerful peasants' revolt and the grinding pressures exerted by the Holy Roman Empire to the west and Kievan Rus' to the east. Poland was also the target of raids by Old Prussians and Lithuanians, Baltic tribespeople from the north and east, and threats by the crusading order of the Teutonic Knights, who conquered the Old Prussians and settled Prussia in the thirteenth century. During this period, Poland gradually developed towns, partly thanks to the immigration of German merchants and artisans. Though many formerly free Polish peasants were forced into servile dependency on their lords, others in border areas to the south were able to gain their freedom in return for settling new lands. Under Casimir III (r. 1333–1370), the last king of Poland from his dynasty, the state managed to consolidate its authority internally and began to expand successfully into Kievan Rus' and Lithuania.

HUNGARY

Hungary, too, had been Christian since the tenth century, but had been slow to develop the characteristic forms of western European urban life. A Christian chronicler who passed through in the first half of the twelfth century saw more tents than houses. But in Hungary as in Poland, the twelfth and thirteenth centuries witnessed German immigration; the development of towns, in which Muslim and Jewish as well as Christian merchants contributed to a flourishing economy; and the spread of manors and servile labor. As in parts of western Europe, struggles for supremacy between the king and the nobility led to the issuing of charters that began as statements of noble privileges and gradually came to be seen as statements of the rights of all free men. The invasion in 1241 of Mongol nomads from Central Asia destroyed the Hungarian army and devastated the country.

BOHEMIA

The most powerful and prosperous of these central European Catholic states was Bohemia. Cities grew rapidly there, powered in part by the success of local silver mining and supported by royal charters that specified the liberties citizens enjoyed. Prague, well situated on the Vltava River, became the largest city east of the Rhine, with more than 30,000 inhabitants after 1300. It developed skilled crafts and manufactures—notably that of arms and armor—and in 1348 it became the seat of the first university in central and eastern Europe, which soon attracted more than a thousand students. The rise of merchant capitalism affected rural as well as urban Bohemia. As in the west, peasant families lived in widely varied conditions, and the most successful and ambitious purchased their freedom.

KIEVAN RUS'

Farther east the Viking merchant-raiders who took part in the founding of Kievan Rus' moved south from Scandinavia along the Volga River, seeking to exchange slaves and furs from eastern Europe for Islamic silver coins. There they came into contact with the East Slavs, tribes driven from the lower Danube River basin in the sixth century into the vast forested lands that stretched from the Dnieper River in the south to the Baltic Sea and Volga River in the north. Russian tradition assigns the foundation of the first state, in the northern town of Novgorod, to Rurik (r. ca. 860–879), a Viking, and his followers, the Rus'. Some of Rurik's warriors moved south to Kiev. His successor, Oleg (r. 879–912), followed them, killed their leaders, and made Kiev his capital.

Cyril and Methodius This fifteenth-century manuscript shows Byzantine brothers Cyril and Methodius at their writing desks, inventing the Cyrillic alphabet used to record the Slavic language. The text below their portrait is written in Cyrillic.

For the next century, the Kievan state expanded, subjugating the East Slavic tribes and forcing them to pay tribute. Raids on Byzantium in 907 and 941–44 persuaded the emperors to make trade agreements with Kiev. Nomadic incursions and civil war slowed the growth of the Kievan Rus', but Grand Prince Vladimir I (r. 981–1015) consolidated the state. He also brought it into the world of Eastern Christianity.

In the ninth century, two Byzantine brothers, Cyril and Methodius, had invented a new alphabet for writing in the Slavic language. They translated Greek biblical and liturgical texts for the inhabitants of Moravia (now part of the Czech Republic) inhabited by Slavs. There they met with opposition from Franks who used a Latin text for the Mass and did not think the liturgy should be translated into the vernacular. The Byzantine emperor and the Orthodox patriarch, however, supported these efforts, and the Slavonic liturgy spread in Bulgaria and elsewhere. Eventually, Vladimir decided—perhaps in hope of unifying the diverse peoples in his enormous realm—to convert Kiev to the Orthodox Christianity of Byzantium, which became the state religion of Kievan Rus'. Grand Prince Yaroslav I (r. 1019–1054) encouraged the building of cathedrals in Novgorod and Kiev, and the Russian church eventually began to assert its independence from the patriarch of Byzantium.

Most Russians lived as free peasants, by farming and gathering fish and furs. What once had been a ruling order of merchant-warriors divided into a group of noble landholders, or boyars, and another of professional merchants. Fortified towns spread, and artisans began to supply a wide range of goods and services. For all its sophistication—under Vladimir, a law code was committed to writing—the unified Kievan state, beleaguered by raiders from the steppe, began to undergo fission into multiple principalities. The power of Kiev declined. Though a newer Baltic trade based in the wealthy and powerful city of Novgorod prospered, Kievan Rus' never regained the prominence it had possessed before 1050.

COURT CULTURE: CHIVALRY

The elaborate courts of the Holy Roman Empire and the new states of France, England, and Spain helped to create a culture that cultivated and celebrated the virtues of the nobility. Supported by monarchs who believed in military values—but also wanted their courts and retinues to live in a reasonable, disciplined way—knights and nobles of higher standing developed a new code, called **chivalry**. They began to describe the life they followed as a calling, blessed by God, for which one required formidable skills and elaborate training. The prospective knight had to learn his craft by serving an older knight as a squire. Then he must pray and hold vigil over his future arms before he could be formally dubbed a knight.

CODES OF CONDUCT Combat, and the skills it required, mattered most—as it always had—to younger sons who had to make their way as soldiers. But the knight also had to learn the pursuits of peacetime. Hunting, falconry, and the artificial combat known as jousting, which soon became a highly regulated and vastly popular practice, provided ways to maintain combat readiness. Weddings, visits from one monarch or noble to another, and diplomatic missions required skills of a different kind: the knight had to know how to stand, speak, dance, and sing with poise and elegance. Codes of knightly conduct were enforced by specialists such as heralds, who laid down the rules for what arms a nobleman could bear.

Women of the noble order had to master the skills of peacetime as well. Women usually did not fight, and they ruled, for the most part, only when no mature male heir was available. But in the world of the court, they presided at tournaments and feasts, and performed in public before large, attentive, and critical audiences. Books of advice—and satires of those who failed to meet the new standards—set the rules. Every aspect of the noblewoman's life—dress, movement, eating—became an art to be cultivated in a systematic way. Noblewomen must be at once lively and decorous, open and demure; must speak courteously with men of their own rank without doing anything to harm their reputations; and must certainly never be seen, as more than one book warned, eating greedily or smearing their mouths with food.

Courtesy, honor, love: these complex terms, rich and ambiguous, denoted the codes of conduct that developed to regulate aristocrats' conduct toward fellow warriors and noblewomen. The change was marked: the nobles of Europe learned to discipline their movements, restrain their appetites, and keep themselves clean—skills that would gradually spread through the rest of the European population.

COURTLY LOVE Most remarkable of all, the nobility began to practice a new form of love—courtly love. Marriages, as we will see, were typically arranged for political or financial advantage. But at courts, love blossomed between women and men of high rank. They modeled their relationships on that of lord and vassal. The woman was the sovereign: her will ruled, and her favors—from the award of a glove to a tournament victor, to the award of a kiss or an embrace—were the highest compensation a man could hope for. Perhaps these relationships were seen as a parody, an inversion of the natural order; or perhaps they were seen as a challenge to it.

What is certain is that conflicts arose. Many noblemen were vassals of more than one master, a situation that put the ties that supposedly bound society under intolerable stress. In the close-knit, ceremonious world of the court, conflict was common, and love—between a knightly vassal and his lord's wife, whose favor he might wear at a tournament—apparently even more so. What was a chivalrous man to do when his duties—or duty and "courtesy"—conflicted?

Courtly Love Enameled figures on this twelfth-century chest enact scenes from chivalric love poetry. At left, a troubadour plays a stringed instrument for a dancing woman; at right, a woman restrains a suitor with a leash, symbolizing the complex rules that governed relationships at court.

LITERARY INNOVATIONS These dilemmas could not be solved. But they found expression in what seemed a new poetic form, the epic, composed in the modern languages that were then taking shape—French, Spanish, and a type of German. As early as 1066, Norman knights waiting to fight at Hastings heard "The Song of Roland"—a poem about the defeat of Charlemagne's rear guard by Muslims at Roncevaux in 778. In the song, Roland, leader of the rear guard, dies heroically—but only after putting himself and his friends at the mercy of their enemies by his rashness. Even at this early stage, the epic form not only celebrated but also questioned noble values. Roland's courage was clear at every point, but it brought him to disaster. Wisdom and good counsel, which he lacked, would have served him, his men, and his king better. A Spanish epic, *The Poem of the Cid*, composed in the twelfth century, celebrated the deeds of Rodrigo Díaz (ca. 1043–1099), a Castilian nobleman who fought for both Muslim and Christian lords. In 1094 he captured the city of Valencia in eastern Spain, where he founded his own short-lived principality. The poem praises him as a great warrior, but it also elevates him fictionally, through the marriages he arranges for his daughters, into the catalyst of unity among the Christian kingdoms of Spain.

Chrétien de Troyes (ca. 1135–ca. 1190) explored the potential conflicts between skill at love and valor in war. In a series of romances—episodic poems based on ancient stories about King Arthur and his followers—he made clear his own view: the good lover could not be a good fighter. The brave Lancelot, obeying the orders of his lady, finds himself unhorsed and unconscious again and again. Marie de France (fl. late twelfth century) emphasized the violence implicit in the chivalric order. In the first of her lays, short romances that derived from a Breton tradition, the wife of a royal servant stuns the king with her beauty. She plots with him to kill her husband, only to have the knight turn the tables and kill them both.

Even more novel were the poems that celebrated love, especially illicit love, despite its violation of Christian codes of law and conduct. New conventions of behavior recognized that women, as well as men, nourished passions not recognized, much less accepted, by the formal codes of state and church. The troubadours—the love poets of southern France—recognized, as Marie de France did, that women harbored strong desire:

Fair, agreeable, good friend,
When will I have you in my power,
Lie beside you for an evening,
And kiss you amorously?

COURTLY LOVE

Fin' amor, or courtly love, was the name given to a form of chivalric love that was supposed to improve the lover by joining romantic passion to a reverence for the beloved. The ideal of courtly love had its origins in earlier Arabic and Latin love poetry, recent trends in Christianity toward a spiritual adoration of God, attempts by the Church to regulate marriage, and the formal relationship between lord and vassal. It was most clearly articulated by the troubadours of southern France, such as Bernart de Ventadorn and Marcabru. Both selections reveal the element of social power underlying professions of courtly love between men and women.

Bernart de Ventadorn, "When I see the lark move"

Bernart de Ventadorn was one of the most popular troubadours of the twelfth century, and his descriptions of courtly love were often imitated by other medieval poets. In this song, his love causes a loss of power over himself, for which he seems to blame all women.

When I see the lark move
for joy his wings in the sun,
and disappear and swoop
for the delight that comes to his heart,
great envy comes upon me
at one so joyful,
and I wonder that in an instant
my heart does not faint for desire.

Ay, alas! I thought I knew much
of love and I know so little!
for I cannot forbear to love her
from whom I shall have nothing.
She has stolen my heart and my being,
and for herself the whole world;
and when I am parted from her, there is
 nothing
other than desire and my yearning heart.

Never more have I power over myself
nor was I myself from the moment
that my eyes saw her
in a mirror that pleased me much....

Of ladies I despair;
never more shall I trust them
and as I once defended them,
so shall I forsake them.

Since I see that none help me against her
who destroys and confounds me,
I fear them all and mistrust them,
for I know they are all alike.

In this does show herself true woman
my lady, for which I blame her,
since she wants not what she should
and does what is forbidden.
I am fallen in disgrace
and have acted like a fool on the bridge;
and I do not know what is happening to me,
unless I have aimed too high.

Marcabru, "The other day, beside a hedge"

The troubadour Marcabru often used satire as social criticism. In the humorous "The other day, beside a hedge" (ca. 1130–50), the protests of a peasant woman against a nobleman's advances expose flaws in the ideal of courtly love. This excerpt is a prose translation of the original verse.

The other day, beside a hedge, I found a common little wench brimming with joy and wisdom: just like the daughter of a peasant woman, she wears a cape, a tunic lined with a pelt, a coarsely woven blouse, shoes and woolen stockings.

…

"My sweet, dear pretty one" said I, "I turned off the road to keep you company, for such a peasant wench as you ought never to have been looking after so many beasts without a suitable companion in such an isolated place as this."

"My lord," she said, "whoever I may be, I know wisdom or folly when I see it. Let your 'companionhood,' sir," thus said the peasant woman to me, "remain where it is fitting, for she who thinks she is the mistress of it has nothing more than the vain illusion of it."

…

"My pretty one," said I, "a noble fairy fashioned you when you were born: there is in you a pure and rarefied beauty, and it would be easily doubled with just one union, me on top and you underneath."

"Sir, you have praised me too much that I am very angry about this. Since you have exalted my reputation so much," thus said the peasant woman to me, "because of this you shall have me as your reward when you leave: gape fool, gape in your mid-day siesta!"

"Wench, one tames a cruel and savage heart with practice. I well know that a man can have a mighty good time when he has a chance encounter with such a little peasant wench, with noble affection, as long as one does not cheat the other."

"My lord, a man excited by the heat of folly swears and makes pledges and guarantees. You would pay such homage sir," thus said the peasant woman, "but I, for a small entrance fee, do not wish to exchange my maidenhood for the title of whore."

QUESTIONS FOR ANALYSIS

1. How does the lover in "When I see the lark move" connect matters of love and power?
2. In what ways does the woman in "The other day, beside a hedge" challenge the social assumptions of chivalry?
3. What do these poems tell us about the ideals and realities of romantic relationships between men and women in the twelfth century?

Sources: Bernart de Ventadorn, "When I see the lark move," *Music of the Troubadours* (CD liner notes), trans. Keith Anderson (Munich: 1999), pp. 10–11; Marcabru, "The other day, beside a hedge," in *Marcabru: A Critical Edition*, ed. and trans. Simon Gaunt, Ruth Harvey, and Linda Paterson (Cambridge: 2000), pp. 379, 381.

Marie de France An illumination from a thirteenth-century French manuscript depicts the poet Marie de France writing at a desk.

Within the complex codes that governed every aspect of noble life, some men and women refused to let any rules dictate what they desired and felt. As we will see, they were not the only twelfth-century Europeans who refused to subject themselves to the rules that normally governed Christian society.

THE MEDIEVAL CHURCH

Europe remained deeply Christian in the tenth, eleventh, and twelfth centuries, but the Roman church was evolving rapidly. The long-standing differences between the Greek church in Byzantium and the Latin church in Rome sharpened into a schism. On the doctrine of the Trinity, the western church held that the Holy Spirit proceeded through the Father and the Son, the eastern church that the Spirit proceeded through the Father alone. In 1014 Pope Benedict VIII (r. 1012–1024) added the Nicene Creed, which in 325 had affirmed the co-divinity of the Son, to the Mass. By the middle of the eleventh century, the papacy was insisting that Greek churches in southern Italy either conform to Latin practices or close. In response, the Orthodox patriarch Michael Cerularius closed the Latin churches in Constantinople. A papal legate sent to Constantinople in 1054 demanded that the patriarch recognize the supremacy of Rome. When he refused, the papal legate excommunicated him, and he excommunicated the legation in return. Reconciliation proved impossible, and from this time forward the Roman and Orthodox Churches were divided by what is known as the **East-West Schism** or the Schism of 1054.

CHURCH AND STATE

Relations between the Catholic Church and developing state authority were also changing. In the tenth century, as we have seen, the Holy Roman emperors, though far weaker than Charlemagne had been, routinely followed his example in choosing and installing popes, not to mention the bishops and abbots in their realms. Kings and other local lords also claimed the right to appoint clerics in their domains, as they had for centuries. Some saw themselves as heirs to the legacy of the Roman emperors as holy kings who were as much representatives of God on earth as any cleric. All rulers regarded high positions in the Church as powerful offices in the state and believed it vital to staff them with men, often of noble birth, who would offer good counsel and reliable assistance in crises—including military crises. For their part, many clerics saw it as normal to pay for their offices, as was often required.

Investiture On this twelfth-century enamel plaque, the Holy Roman emperor, carrying the cross and orb of royal authority, invests a monk as a bishop.

In the eleventh century, circles of reform-minded clergy who studied the scriptures and the historical record decided that these practices violated what they now saw as basic standards. They found it frightening that many clerics obtained their high positions by paying for them, for in doing so they were committing a clear sin, that of simony (named after Simon Magus, a character in the New Testament book of Acts who tried to buy the powers of Jesus's disciples). Priests who came to see themselves as God's representatives on earth, members of a separate and high estate, could no longer accept that even the highest clerics—most eleventh-century popes—were appointed by secular lords. They looked back to the Christian Roman Empire and saw, as they wanted to, that the clerical estate had then stood higher than the nobility, higher even than the emperor himself. When Ambrose had first condemned and then absolved Emperor Theodosius I in 390, he had set a precedent that should be revived. It was a pope, they noted, who in 802 had invested Charlemagne with his imperial crown.

Changes were made. In 1059, when Holy Roman Emperor Henry IV was still a boy and could not intervene, the College of Cardinals—a group of priests and bishops in Rome that would become increasingly central to the Church—elected the pope without consulting Henry. This firm move was intended to take the whole question of clerical election out of secular hands.

THE INVESTITURE CONTROVERSY (1075–1122)

Henry IV had assumed his full powers by the time a Roman cleric named Hildebrand, famous for his learning and holiness, was proclaimed Pope Gregory VII in 1073, to the wild enthusiasm of the Roman populace. Gregory strongly advocated clerical independence of secular authority. Two years later, conflict flared in Milan, a republic within the Holy Roman emperor's dominions. A candidate for the important archbishopric of Milan requested recognition of his appointment from Henry IV and paid a fee. Gregory condemned the transaction. Henry's clerical supporters condemned Gregory. Soon bishops and theologians on both sides were hurling anathemas (condemnations) and excommunications at the other side's leader and at one another. This **Investiture Controversy** became one of the great ideological disputes in European history.

POPE GREGORY VII Papal records claim that at the time of the Milan dispute, in 1075, Gregory VII drafted

a document entitled the Dictatus Papae ("papal dictation"). With radical simplicity he confirmed the preeminence of the pope over all others, both in the Church and outside it. Gregory claimed that only the pope, as the sole universal ruler appointed by God, could depose or reinstate bishops, divide or unite bishoprics, and use the imperial insignia, and even "that it may be permitted to him to depose emperors." These ferocious axioms, though not made public at the time, served as the basis of Gregory's policies. Gregory and his associates in the Church tried systematically to put his principles into effect—an enterprise that has come to be known as the **Gregorian Reform movement**. His views soon found their way into one of the Church's earliest written codes of ecclesiastical law. Imperial theologians drew up equal and opposite codes. They stressed the absolute authority of secular rulers, appointed by God.

Though Henry IV's penance at Canossa in 1077 gave Gregory a victory in the first skirmish, the war ran for another century and a half. Both sides won victories from time to time, and compromises were forged—above all in 1122, when Emperor Henry V (r. 1111–1125) and Pope

The Investiture Controversy A twelfth-century manuscript illustration captures a key moment in the drama of the investiture dispute: Henry IV kneels in supplication to the abbot of Cluny (left) and Countess Matilda of Tuscany (right), asking them to intercede with Pope Gregory on his behalf. Matilda and the abbot are larger than Henry to emphasize their power in the negotiation.

Calixtus II (r. 1119–1124) agreed that although rulers could invest bishops with their powers as secular lords, only the pope could confer spiritual authority on them by presenting them with a ring and a staff. This agreement, called the **Concordat of Worms**, ended the formal Investiture Controversy, but the great struggle between church and state continued.

THE CONTINUING CONFLICT: THOMAS BECKET

In England the conflict pitted the powerful monarch Henry II against Thomas Becket (ca. 1120–1170), a brilliant lawyer and state official, as well as Henry's personal friend. Becket rose to be Henry's chancellor, and in 1162 the king followed tradition and appointed Becket archbishop of Canterbury. Once a worldly man, Becket turned ascetic in his new office—another sign of the reforming inspiration so widespread in the Church. At a meeting in 1164 of the English clergy at Clarendon Palace in southwestern England, Henry demanded that the Church accept limitations on its privileges—especially the jurisdiction of its courts. Becket refused to sign the constitutions Henry issued. Summoned for trial, Becket fled to the Continent.

After the pope brokered Becket's return to England in 1170, four of Henry's knights made their way to Canterbury and murdered the archbishop. Tradition holds that he was wearing a hair shirt under his splendid official raiment. Within two years Becket had been made a saint,

Thomas Becket The story of Thomas Becket's assassination spread far beyond England. This Italian church fresco shows Henry II's soldiers murdering Becket in Canterbury Cathedral, with the cathedral's altar and columns clearly visible in the foreground.

and his shrine at Canterbury became a central focus of Catholic life in England. The murder cost Henry much of his popularity, and helped to trigger a revolt of the English barons against him in 1173–74. Though he did penance for Becket's assassination and defeated his enemies, the monarchy was left in a weakened position at his death in 1189. When church and state came into conflict, not even the most skillful of secular rulers could count on victory.

CHURCH AND STATE COLLABORATION: THE EARLY CRUSADES

For all their struggles, church and state often found it possible to cooperate. Great clerics never stopped serving as royal counselors and ministers. And church and state collaborated on some major enterprises. The first of these joint ventures was called into being by the Church's new energy and received strong support from secular rulers. For centuries, as we have seen, the original heartlands of Christianity in Asia Minor and the Levant had been in Muslim hands. In the course of the eleventh century, the era of the Peace of God, many Christians seem to have taken an increasingly strong interest in the Holy Land. Pilgrims traveled to Palestine sometimes in groups thousands strong, and parents named their daughters Jerusalem.

ORIGINS At the same time, the papacy actively encouraged the reconquest of Spain from the Muslims—an enterprise that began with the expansion of Christian kingdoms in the northern half of the Iberian Peninsula and that came to be known as the **Reconquista**. As early as 1064 Pope Alexander II (r. 1061–1073) offered an indulgence (remission of the normal penance for one's sins) to those who participated in the campaign to take the city of Barbastro in northeastern Spain. The expedition succeeded, but only temporarily; the city was retaken by the Muslims a year later. Christians of every social level shuddered as they heard about the sufferings of their fellows in the Holy Land and in Spain, where, Christians claimed, in 1086 Muslim soldiers had filled carts with the heads of the Christians they had defeated at Zallaqa.

The Muslim great powers—the Abbasid Caliphate in Arabia, Iraq, and Central Asia; their rivals the Seljuk Turks in Asia Minor; and the Fatimid Caliphate in North Africa, Egypt, and the Levant—could easily be represented as the natural enemies of all Christians. In Christian eyes, the Seljuk Turks posed an especially powerful threat. The

The Early Crusades, 1096–1192 In 1096, the Peasants' Crusade traveled from Cologne to Constantinople with the goal of retaking the Holy Land from Muslim rule. Along the way, they attacked communities of Jews, whom they also saw as enemies of Christianity. Later crusaders fought many battles in Asia Minor and the Arabian Peninsula, conquering the Seljuk Turks' capital at Nicea in 1097 and Jerusalem in 1099.

Byzantine Empire was beleaguered on many sides, from Norman invasions of Greek territory and rebellions by Christian sects and Turkic groups. In 1071 the Seljuks defeated the Byzantine army decisively at Manzikert in eastern Asia Minor, conquering almost all of the peninsula. The Byzantine emperor Alexius I (r. 1081–1118) managed to regain control of some coastal areas in the west, and courted the papacy in the hope of finding help against the Seljuks, whom the Byzantines represented as a common enemy.

In these same years, the Gregorian Reform movement inspired many nobles, especially in France, with the desire to serve Christianity. But the desire to serve the faith, as they interpreted it, did not always imply giving up their arms. Sometimes it implied adventure—as when they themselves undertook pilgrimages to the Holy Land. Sometimes it implied armed conflict. Princes, prelates, and nobles began to devise ways of arguing that a given war was itself just and pious—a campaign undertaken for Christian ends.

It seems probable that Odo of Lagery, the reforming cardinal who became Pope Urban II in 1088 and served until 1099, already had some kind of Christian expedition to the Holy Land in mind when he took office. In 1095 an embassy from the Byzantine emperor to the Council of Piacenza asked Urban for help against the Seljuk Turks. Later that year, at the Council of Clermont, Urban preached a sermon. The historical sources that report Urban's words on that occasion were written later, and their authors may well have modified their accounts of what he urged his audience to do in the light of later experiences. Supposedly, Urban urged Christians to band together and attack the "base and bastard Turks" who held the Holy Sepulcher, the tomb of Jesus. Supposedly, spontaneous shouts of "God wills this" from the crowd greeted his call to arms. Whatever the truth of these stories, Urban launched the first European efforts to wage a holy war: the **Crusades**, a term derived from cloaks marked with silk or woolen crosses that Christians from all orders of society donned as they vowed to make their way to the Holy Land and redeem it for Christians.

Preaching spread the crusading impulse through France, Italy, and western Germany. It was usually targeted on large cities such as Poitiers and Tours, where multiple churches could provide support and information. Crusaders had mixed motives. They wanted to strike a blow for the Church—and, by doing so, win freedom from their sins and the necessary penalties. But they also wanted to fight an enemy whom they increasingly saw as hateful. Two brothers from southern France said that they took the cross "on the one hand for the grace of the pilgrimage and on the other, under the protection of God, to wipe out the defilement of the pagans." For the first time in Christian history, war came to be defined as holy—and the destruction of a particular enemy as a virtuous act.

THE PEASANTS' CRUSADE

The first groups that actually took the crusader's cross were peasants and knights of low stature, badly organized and most of them poorly armed. They were led by Peter the Hermit, a preacher famous for his ascetic life and personal piety. This Peasants' Crusade, a mixed group of Franks and Germans, made their way in 1096 from Cologne to Constantinople, where the Byzantines transported them to Asia Minor. There they attacked the outskirts of Nicea, once a Christian center and now the Seljuk capital, and raided other cities. When they marched out to conquer Nicea, the Turks slaughtered most of them. Peter, who was in Constantinople when the battle took place, survived, as did a few thousand of the crusaders.

Another crusader group, led by a count named Emicho, made its way through the cities flanking the Rhine River. Emicho and the Christian citizens of Cologne and other German towns were struck by a powerful thought. On the way to deal a blow for Jesus against the Muslims who had taken the Holy Land away from Christianity, they decided it was both reasonable and proper (although the official

The Peasants' Crusade In an illustration from a twelfth-century French manuscript, Peter the Hermit stands at the head of a crowd of crusaders, boldly leading them forward—presumably to the Holy Land.

Church sharply disagreed) to attack those who had killed Jesus in the first place—the Jews.

THE JEWS AND THE CRUSADES

Communities of Jews had lived for centuries in western and central Europe, especially in southern France and the cities of the Rhineland. Well established, prosperous, and pious, they maintained synagogues, ritual baths, and the other necessities of Jewish communal life. For the most part they lived in an uneasy peace with their Christian neighbors, attending the same markets and practicing the same crafts. As cities developed and laws and guild ordinances were written, however, Jews were forbidden to engage in the same trades or crafts as Christians. Jews were allowed to serve as moneylenders—an activity that Church law prohibited Christians from practicing, and not one calculated to soften Christian attitudes toward Jews. Violence against the Jews began to spread into regions that had not known it. In Toulouse in southern France, a Jew was publicly slapped every year in retribution for an imaginary betrayal—hard enough that one of the victims died. Now the Jews realized that they were under threat, and they turned to the traditional ways by which Jewish communities had survived in the past. They prayed and fasted in the hope that God's anger might be turned aside. They asked local bishops for help—and in Speyer and other Rhineland cities, the bishops protected them.

But even bishops could not provide safe refuge everywhere. In 1096 in the Rhineland city of Mainz, where 700 Jews crowded into the bishop's great hall for protection, Emicho and his followers broke in and slaughtered them all—men, women, and children. Some of the Jews, reviving the ancient precedent of Masada, the last Jewish stronghold to fall to the Romans, killed their own families, "preferring them to perish thus by their own hands rather than to be killed by the weapons of the uncircumcised." The crusaders plundered their bodies and piled them in heaps. The stories of these Jewish martyrs would be commemorated for centuries to come on Yom Kippur, the Jewish Day of Atonement.

THE CRUSADER KINGDOMS

The Peasants' Crusade of 1096 was only the beginning of what is called the First Crusade. In the same year, noblemen such as the pious, hard-bitten warrior Count Raymond of Toulouse (d. 1105) and the Frankish knight Godfrey of Bouillon (d. 1100) led better-organized groups of professional soldiers to the East in what came to be called the Princes' Crusade. Helped by the element of surprise and by extraordinary luck, the crusaders won battle after battle, taking Nicea in 1097 and marching through Syria toward Palestine. In 1099 a much reduced crusader army succeeded in taking Jerusalem itself after a short siege. A brutal massacre of many of the Muslim and Jewish inhabitants of the city followed. Godfrey became the first king of a Latin Christian kingdom based there, though he died almost immediately after in battle.

Four new Latin Christian territories took shape in the East between 1098 and 1104: Edessa, Antioch, Jerusalem, and Tripoli. Each had its own aristocrats and knights who built castles on the best European models to serve as their bases of power. They captured ports—Haifa, Acre, Beirut, and Tyre—that enabled them, through Italian merchants and navies, to remain in contact with Europe. The spice trade, vineyards, and olive groves of the region provided valuable goods that they sold and shipped to Europeans. Venetian and Genoese merchants not only provided transport but in return for military help to the colonists, negotiated the right to build and fortify settlements of their own. Meanwhile, the Latin lords came to an accommodation with the inhabitants of their new lands—Jews, Muslims, and Eastern Orthodox Christians—whom they not only ceased to attack but treated, in the case of the Jews, better than they would have at home. Though the capture of the Latin East was motivated by religious zeal and hatred of

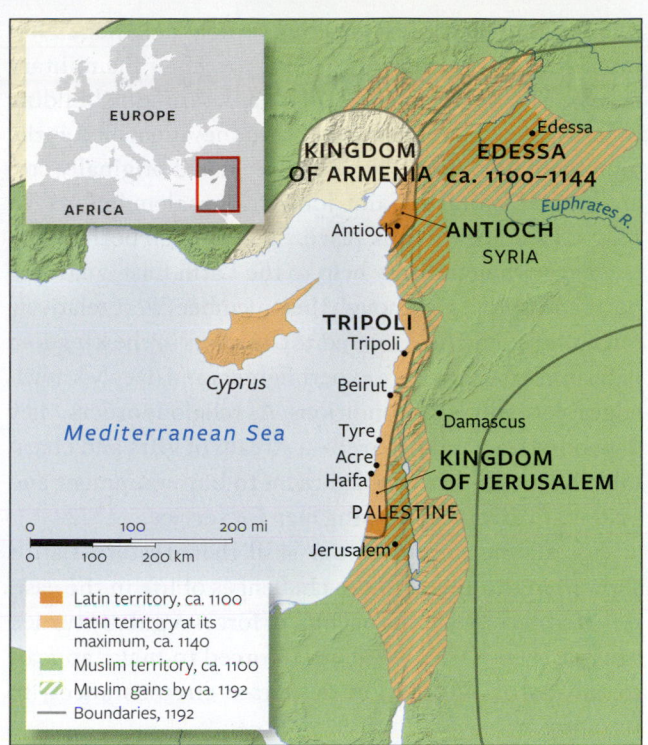

The Crusader Kingdoms, ca. 1100–1192 After conquering Jerusalem in 1099, Latin Christians established the kingdoms of Edessa, Antioch, Jerusalem, and Tripoli. Controlling port cities allowed them access to the Mediterranean and Europe. These kingdoms had expanded by 1140, but were never stable. By 1192, Saladin and other Muslim rulers had retaken almost all of these Latin Christian territories.

non-Christians, some Latins discovered there the pleasures of a cosmopolitan life.

The four Crusader kingdoms never became as solidly rooted as those of western Europe. A high mortality rate meant that male heirs were not always available for thrones or major fiefs. In such cases, lordships reverted to the rulers of the four settlements, reducing the power of nobles to resist their rulers—but also weakening the rulers' ability to muster the resources to defend the realm. Women from ruling families took advantage of this situation to take power. When the king of Jerusalem Baldwin II (r. 1118–1131) died, his eldest daughter, Melisende, and her husband, Fulk, were crowned. Though Melisende could not command in war, she successfully insisted on ruling with Fulk, and kept her son Baldwin III out of power for seven years after he came of age in 1145. Her younger sister, Princess Alice, made a similar effort to rule Antioch after her husband died, and succeeded for seven years.

Though the Latin kingdoms in the East cooperated effectively, they could never count on being strong enough to fight off the hostile forces that surrounded them. New institutions were created to help—above all the military orders. The Templars took their name from the building in Jerusalem where they met, which they identified as the Temple of Solomon. The Hospitalers had originally created the Hospital of Saint John in Jerusalem before the First Crusade even took place. Soon enough both orders were providing military help to the Latin East, guarding ports and borders. Although their members were relatively few—each could field around 300 soldiers in the kingdom of Jerusalem—they were expert fighters and deeply knowledgeable about local conditions. As religious orders, they depended on—and received—a stream of gifts and charitable bequests that enabled them to buy equipment and systematically recruit young men for service.

For all the improvisatory skill that western Latins showed in dealing with the challenges of life in the eastern Mediterranean, the balance of forces regularly turned against them. They were often forced to make appeals to the Latin West or, in desperate circumstances, to Byzantium.

SALADIN AND THE CRUSADES When one of the Crusader kingdoms fell in 1144, Pope Eugene III announced a Second Crusade (1147–49) to restore the territory to Latin control. Popular enthusiasm for this crusade—though perhaps less intense than for the first—was still widespread. To mobilize Christian forces, the French cleric Bernard of Clairvaux and King Louis VII of France held a public meeting at Vézelay in central France, at which the king appeared wearing his cross. The audience grabbed all of the premade crosses that Bernard had brought with him, and he had to tear his monastic habit into strips to meet the further demand. But both the French and imperial armies were defeated by the Seljuk Turks in Asia Minor, and an assault on Damascus failed as well.

The Crusader kingdoms faced even greater danger when Saladin (Salah al-Din Yusuf ibn Ayyub; 1137/8–1193), a Muslim of Kurdish ancestry, first became vizier of Egypt and then took over the state, ruled until then by the Fatimid Caliphate. Allying himself with the Abbasid Caliphate in Baghdad, Saladin invaded and conquered Syria between 1174 and 1182. In 1187 he defeated a crusader army and retook Palestine. A chivalrous ruler who granted amnesty to Christian soldiers (once they paid a substantial ransom), Saladin won the respect of opponents as well as allies. The English king Richard I, known as Richard the Lionhearted (r. 1189–1199), joined in a Third Crusade (1189–92) against Saladin, along with Holy Roman Emperor Frederick Barbarossa and Philip II (r. 1180–1223)

Saladin's Soldiers A mid-thirteenth-century history of the Crusades includes this illuminated initial "B," in which Saladin's troops take a group of Europeans prisoner while a city burns behind them.

of France. But Barbarossa accidentally drowned along the way, leaving Leopold V, Duke of Austria, to lead a much reduced imperial force. The others joined Guy of Lusignan, the king of Jerusalem, and once Richard arrived, they used the full range of medieval siege technologies to take the port of Acre. Quarrels broke out among the Christian rulers, and Philip and Leopold eventually left. Richard, a brilliant warrior, managed to defeat Saladin at Arsuf in 1191 and took Jaffa. Divisions in the Crusader army prevented Richard from retaking Jerusalem, which remained in Muslim hands, though unarmed Christian pilgrims and merchants were guaranteed the right to visit the city. Richard was captured by a Christian enemy on his way home and died soon after, as did Saladin.

Gradually the Crusader kingdoms were ground down. Still, Latin states and Roman popes continued to see themselves as having a vital stake both in the Holy Land and in other areas where Christians and Muslims confronted one another. As we will see, serious crusading enterprises continued for centuries to come, most successfully in Spain.

THE NEW CHRISTIANITY

As novel as the Crusades—and in some ways more durable—was the vast outpouring of religious feeling that inspired them. The old monastic houses that looked back to Benedict—with their well-born monks; their slow, stately life of religious services and manuscript copying; and their great wealth—had become hard to distinguish from other centers for the noble and rich. Newer and more energetic religious establishments flanked them. The Benedictine monk Bernard of Cluny drew up a massive indictment of the sins of his time in the long poem "On Contempt for the World." Bernard threatened his fellow monks and nuns—as well as the corrupt priests who lived in the world and pursued glory and gold there—with the wrath of the Savior, who would soon return and punish them: "The times are very bad, the hour is late, we must take heed: For the final judge will soon arrive." The monastery of Cluny in eastern France became the center of a federation of Benedictine houses devoted to piety and prayer and to the reforming ideals of the Gregorian movement.

THE CISTERCIAN ORDER   Not everyone agreed with the monks of Cluny, who held that monks should abandon physical labor for prayer. At Cîteaux, not far from Dijon, a Benedictine abbot and some twenty followers founded a new house in 1098. They called for a return to strict observance of Benedict's *Rule*. To pursue holiness as Benedict had hoped, they argued, monks must abandon the collecting of rents and the gathering of appointments to well-endowed priestly offices and go back to working the land.

Though these **Cistercians**—they drew their name from the location of their first house—regarded themselves as "perfect Benedictines," under the inspired leadership of Stephen Harding (d. 1134) they soon developed rules and customs of their own. They replaced the black Benedictine habit with a new one of white wool, which signified their commitment to lead an "angelic" life. They insisted that they would accept only gifts of unimproved land, which they would cultivate themselves. The Cistercians' rigorous pursuit of holiness inspired enormous enthusiasm. Gifts multiplied as Europe's prosperity rose, and by the middle of the twelfth century Cistercian houses had appeared everywhere—from Britain in the north, to the Iberian Peninsula in the south, to the Holy Roman Empire, Hungary, and Poland in the east. All houses sent representatives to the general chapters of the order, which took place once a year, and which maintained discipline throughout the new order.

Women of many social levels—daughters of minor nobles and urban merchants and craftsmen, but poorer women as well—looked for a way to turn from the world and live an "apostolic" life. In the twelfth and early thirteenth centuries, many formed small communities, living in houses on the edges of cities and tending the sick in hospitals or the lepers in their leprosaria. They sang hymns, prayed, and sometimes adopted habits. These initiatives could stir disapproval from the Church, but in rich towns such as Troyes in northern France, many of these small, informal women's religious organizations became Cistercian convents, whose members were allowed to frame their own austere lives in search of purity.

The leaders of the Cistercians—above all Bernard of Clairvaux (1090–1153)—promoted new forms of Christian spirituality and devotion. In profound treatises on pride and humility, Bernard explored the religious experience of monks like himself. More important for ordinary Christians, he believed passionately in the spiritual power of the Virgin Mary and helped to spread a new form of Christianity in which her intercession—and that of her Son—became central to religious experience. Many Christian men and women appealed to Mary and Jesus for help—just as they would have appealed, in ordinary life, not to the king but to their local lord or lady. Alongside the militant piety of the crusaders, a more personal piety took shape in the twelfth century.

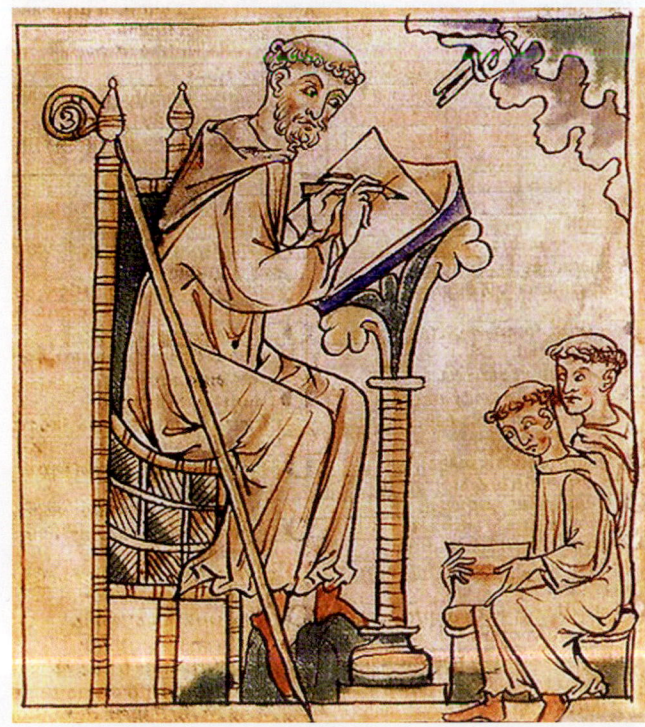

Bernard of Clairvaux   In this twelfth-century French woodcut, the Cistercian leader, wearing his order's white habit, composes a sermon while young monks study at his feet. The hand of God reaching down from heaven symbolizes that Bernard has received divine favor.

HILDEGARD OF BINGEN Ordinary Christians regularly interpreted experiences—especially those that seemed outside the order of nature—as evidence of supernatural intervention. And they valued, and searched for, sincerity and sanctity in those around them. Evidence of these qualities could enable their possessor to transcend what might otherwise have been the overwhelming limitations of birth and sex, and gain recognition as a teacher and scholar.

Hildegard of Bingen (1098–1179), the tenth child of a German noble family, was given as a "tithe" (a tax of 10 percent) to a Benedictine house in the Rhineland, where she was enclosed (cloistered). At the age of five she began to have visions "while awake and seeing with a pure mind and the eyes and ears of the inner self, in open places, as God willed it. How this might be is hard for mortal flesh to understand." At first, she talked about the revelations she received only to a trusted few. But gradually she developed a reputation for piety and began to gather supporters. A male cleric became her first secretary and recorded

Hildegard's Visions In a twelfth-century edition of Hildegard's *Visions*, a small portrait shows her sitting at a writing desk (bottom left), while the center of the page records her vision of the earth as God created it, as told in the story of Genesis: sea creatures, birds, and plants populate the world, which humans manage and cultivate.

her revelations. She also composed hymns, both the music and words. And when she could, she preached publicly in Trier and other cities in western Germany, converting her revelations into prophetic sermons.

By tradition only men could create liturgies or interpret the Bible. Hildegard, as she was the first to admit, had no formal education, and she suffered terribly throughout her life from physical pain and paralysis. She accepted her suffering as the direct work of God's hand, intended to prevent her from committing the sin of pride. Eventually, however, she found herself able to enter what had been largely male territory since the first generations of Christianity: "Heaven was opened and a fiery light of exceeding brilliance came and permeated my whole brain, and inflamed my whole heart and my whole breast, not like a burning but like a warming flame, as the sun warms anything its rays touch. And immediately I knew the meaning of the exposition of the Scriptures."

Hildegard corresponded with prelates and the Holy Roman emperor. As the extraordinary network of her contacts grew, so did the range of her speculations. By the end of her life, she had developed a coherent theory of the universe—one that was nourished by reading in her community's library and that followed the long-standing Neoplatonic tradition. She emphasized the connections between the higher realms of the angels and the stars and the lower one inhabited by humans. Adam, before he fell, had been able to hear "the voice of the living spirit," the cosmic harmony: "still innocent before his fault, he had no little kinship with the angels' praises." Music, now, might reach listeners and make them pious.

For five centuries, the form of music traditionally ascribed to Pope Gregory I (r. 590–604) and usually known as Gregorian chant—the chanting of psalms and other parts of the liturgy by male soloists and choirs—had spread through the Western Church, displacing older, local forms. No one expressed more vividly than Hildegard the power and beauty of the Latin Mass that had become the core of Catholic religious life. Her writings and compositions enable us to glimpse something of what the Cistercian nuns, who did not leave such rich testimonies behind, must have felt as they worshipped.

GOD'S ARCHITECTURE: CATHEDRALS The same passionate commitment to Christianity—and the same vision of an orderly, beautiful universe—that inspired Hildegard of Bingen also inspired the patrons and artists who began to transform the physical world of the Church. In late antiquity and after, as we have seen, great Christian churches took the standard form of Roman public

STAINED GLASS AT CHARTRES CATHEDRAL

As we have seen, Suger, the early-twelfth-century abbot of Saint Denis, wrote that the light inside his church, transformed by stained glass, "Should brighten the minds [of congregants], allowing them to travel through the lights / To the true light, where Christ is the true door." Suger proudly hired the most skillful artisans to create the church's windows.

By the mid-twelfth century, stained glass became a highly developed art form, exemplified by the windows at Chartres Cathedral. Of the 173 original windows completed in the early thirteenth century, 143 remain largely intact—the largest existing collection of medieval stained glass in the world. They provide a detailed visual archive of medieval culture and society.

The windows portray Christian figures such as Jesus Christ, the Virgin Mary, and the apostles. They also depict everyday life in the figures of bakers, butchers, furriers, masons, cobblers, and armorers. These workers are representatives of the guilds whose contributions helped build Chartres and other medieval churches.

In this detail from a window illustrating the story of Noah's Ark, a cooper nails hoops on a barrel. His labor in support of Noah's mission is a demonstration of artisanal skill and Christian faith.

QUESTIONS FOR ANALYSIS

1. How did the stained glass windows of medieval churches convey a sense of the sacred?
2. How did this art form reflect secular interests as well?
3. What does the depiction of a cooper in this great cathedral tell you about medieval society and its attitude toward work?

buildings: the basilica, a long hall flanked with columns. From the eleventh century on, in France and elsewhere, the clerics and builders who created cathedrals—the churches where bishops had their seats—began to aim for a different set of effects. A new form—the **Romanesque**—retained the design of the basilica but replaced its flat roof with an arched vault. Semicircular portals opened off the main church, but few windows pierced its thick walls.

In the twelfth century, another form—known as **Gothic**—developed. The nave—the long body of the church that led up to the high altar, lined with chapels—was now crossed by another, shorter segment: the transept. Sculptured reliefs, as varied and powerful as those of ancient Athens, surrounded the main entrance. New construction techniques made it possible to raise high, lightweight roofs supported by complex networks of rib vaults. Dramatic flying buttresses sprang from the walls to the ground, making it possible to raise spectacular towers and open up the walls for huge windows. Circular "rose" windows over the main entrance to the west, and sharply

Romanesque and Gothic Architecture In the eleventh century, churches such as Notre-Dame la Grande in Poitiers (left) were built in the Romanesque style, with its characteristic rounded arches, pointed roofs, and small number of doors and windows. In the twelfth century, Gothic constructions such as the Cathedral of Notre-Dame of Amiens (right) became popular. Built in the shape of a cross, Gothic buildings included high roofs, many pointed arches, and large stained-glass windows.

pointed ones along the nave—made of stained glass in deep, rich colors—told the stories of the Old and New Testaments and filled the interiors with multicolored light.

The first church to bring most of these features together was the basilica of Saint Denis, north of Paris, originally built in the Carolingian period. Suger, the early-twelfth-century abbot of Saint Denis, transformed the church's west facade. He turned it into a treble triumphal arch and pierced it with a massive rose window whose stained glass illuminated the church's nave—a feature that would soon be imitated in cathedrals in Chartres, Paris, and elsewhere. Clerestory windows pierced the upper sections of the walls, suffusing the church with light.

In his account of his time as abbot, Suger recalled with pride how he had spared no expense to bring the most skillful painters, sculptors, and bronze-casters to work on his church. Some of these skilled artisans proudly carved their names—and sometimes their self-portraits—into the stone panels and rich wooden pulpits of the cathedrals. Suger also noted the treasures he had lavished on the church, in the form of jewels and precious metals (Suger thought it a miracle, though a "humorous one," when monks from other abbeys turned up with gems for sale in the nick of time). Above all, though, he insisted that this material splendor served a higher spiritual purpose: "The noble work is bright, but, being nobly bright, the work / Should brighten the minds, allowing them to travel through the lights / To the true light, where Christ is the true door." Like the cosmic music that Hildegard of Bingen imagined, the visible harmony and light of the church's symphonic set of spaces, hierarchically ordered in praise of the Creator and his saints, was meant to bring Christian minds to God.

NEW DIRECTIONS IN MEDIEVAL CULTURE

In the years from 1000 to 1200, Christian minds also turned to a new kind of learning, often centered in the great cathedrals. Europeans rediscovered classical and Christian texts that had been preserved in monastic libraries. They learned that in the Islamic world, the heritage of Greek philosophy, mathematics, astronomy, and medicine had not only been preserved but developed and expanded in powerful and creative ways. In monasteries and cathedrals, in the centers of busy Italian trading cities, and in the seclusion of hermitages, Europeans began to rethink everything from the structure of the universe to the practical problems of everyday life. They also created institutions for the pursuit of learning that still exist—the universities that have been a central feature of Western society for a thousand years.

CLERICS AND THE FOUNDING OF SCHOOLS

The Gregorian Reform movement made it clear that clerics needed learning—everything from literacy in Latin to a sophisticated understanding of theology, depending on their offices and ranks—to fulfill their new responsibilities. Yet this education was not easy to find in tenth- and eleventh-century Europe. Without the support that Charlemagne and his immediate successors had provided for scholarship, classical learning had declined.

BEC ABBEY Nonetheless, the clerics of the eleventh century began to collect and study ancient texts in a newly systematic way—turning back to the ancients for knowledge, just as the Gregorian reformers turned back to the ancients for a model of a true Christian life. Lanfranc (ca. 1005–1089), a cleric from Pavia in northern Italy, made a great name for himself as a teacher in France. The school he founded at Bec Abbey became one of the first of a set of new institutions that took shape for the study, copying, and use of texts, especially the Latin Bible. Lanfranc used his knowledge to defend the doctrine of transubstantiation, which held that the Eucharist truly became the body and blood of Jesus, even though the bread continued to look like bread and the wine like wine. His learning and piety won the respect of King William I of England, who appointed him archbishop of Canterbury.

GLOSSING THE TEXTS Informal schools grew up, usually in cathedrals. At first, individual masters offered instruction for small groups of pupils, who stayed until they felt satisfied with their level of knowledge. Gradually, teachers forged new tools, such as a basic commentary—a set of marginal and interlinear notes—on the Old and New Testaments. These notes were assembled by Anselm of Laon (in northern France; d. 1117) and other teachers into what came to be known as the Ordinary Gloss. The gloss drew much of its content from the church fathers and other earlier writers, but it made their views far more accessible than they had been. It spread through the commented Bibles used by scholars, and it provided baseline interpretations of passages central to Christian ritual and practice. Long commentaries by scholars at Chartres explored the work of Augustine, in particular his view that Plato's account of the universe was largely compatible with Christianity. Soon the effort to show that faith and reason were not in conflict became the central focus of what came to be called scholastic philosophy and theology. Propelled by a new method of teaching and learning—formal argument, or at least no-holds-barred debate—**scholasticism** spread through the Christian world.

PETER ABELARD AND THE NEW METHOD

Paris emerged as a center, first of the new formal way of argument and then of the scholastic system that rested on it. Combative teachers and their pupils argued both about the method a Christian should follow in study and about specific problems in theology. Peter Abelard (1079–1142), the son of a French noble family who brought his family's martial spirit into the classroom, became one of the most celebrated Paris masters. He laid out, under the title *Yes and No*, what seemed to be contradictory statements in the Bible and in the church fathers' commentaries on a vast range of theological questions. Some authoritative texts treated God as one, for example; others as three, or three in one. Abelard pointed out that the more Christian scholars learned, the more of these problems appeared.

Many readers found Abelard's collection of materials shocking: it seemed to them that he had traced fault lines in the solid body of Christian authority. But Abelard pointed out that church fathers such as Augustine and Jerome had already worried, centuries before his time, about what they saw as contradictions in scripture. He made clear that the right kind of analysis could remove many apparent contradictions. The interpreter must begin by assuming that what looked like mistakes or contradictions in the texts were probably the result of his or her own failure to understand, or that scribes might have made errors when copying the texts.

Above all, Abelard showed, the teacher had to master the tools of dialectic—the logic used in formal argument. For it was by making distinctions—for example, between the different senses of some words—that the scholar could hope to gain control over the apparent chaos of the Christian textual universe. Abelard himself became a great logician. He set out to determine whether universals, such as "man," actually existed, and concluded that they did not: there were only actual individuals, the unique people and concrete things that populated the universe. As he applied these tools to the texts, some of the contradictions resolved themselves without a struggle. Abelard's teaching of logic made him an intellectual star to whom students flocked. Older scholars who could not master his method, including his own teachers, found themselves relegated to obscurity.

THEOLOGY AND CHRISTIAN PRACTICE

By the middle of the twelfth century, Abelard and his rivals and successors had made Christian **theology** into a formal discipline. It had its own textbook: the *Four Books of Sentences* by Peter Lombard, an Italian who became bishop of Paris. This work provided students of theology with endless propositions to debate. Theology also had its own method: the logic of Aristotle, as reconfigured and developed to fit the needs of Christian scholars anxious to understand matters such as the nature of the Eucharist, which Aristotle could not have imagined.

Though medieval theology seems abstruse, it was tightly connected to vital Church practices. The Bible and the church fathers had not revealed for certain where the majority of Christians would spend the centuries after their deaths. In the first half of the twelfth century, theologians built on earlier discussions to establish a solution. The dead did not go directly to hell or heaven, for the most part. Instead, ordinary sinners inhabited purgatory, a realm of long-term punishment where cleansing fires could burn away the sins that they had committed in their lifetimes.

PURGATORY AND PENANCE This vision of punishment and correction supported one of the Church's fundamental practices, the sacrament of penance. Since the third and fourth centuries, Christians had confessed their sins to priests (at first in public) and received absolution for them. Manuals for confessors helped bring Christianity into daily life as Europe was evangelized in the seventh and eighth centuries. The theologians now explained that by doing penance in the proper way, Christians could shorten the time they would have to spend after death making up for their failures. Heaven and hell had long played dramatic roles in the Christian imagination. They were now joined by a third realm, purgatory, where even after death, change could still take place.

Over the centuries to come, religious visionaries, artists, and poets equipped purgatory with a precise landscape and imagined its inhabitants and their sufferings in vivid detail. Theology laid the foundations on which these complex and vital structures of religious life and artistic imagination were built. Formal argument—mastery of the cut and thrust of logic—offered the keys to this intellectual kingdom.

Mapping the World Medieval European cartographic efforts offered a view of the known universe embellished with rich symbolism. In this detail from a thirteenth-century English map of the world, Jerusalem is placed at the center (marked with a large cross and dark circle), and the Mediterranean Sea is imagined as a large body of water separating Europe (bottom left), Africa (bottom right), and Asia (top).

THE FORCE OF TRADITION

In one sense, the European intellectual world of the eleventh and twelfth centuries remained highly traditional. Scholars still imagined the heavens in terms that the ancients would have recognized. The earth remained the center of the universe—the theater where the cosmic drama of salvation and damnation of the human race was enacted. At its core, the devil raged and ruled over the damned. Outside its atmosphere, the seven planets (the moon, Mercury, Venus, the sun, Mars, Jupiter, and Saturn)—perfect globes quite different from the messy earth—moved ceaselessly on their crystalline spheres, as did the fixed stars on an even larger sphere. Beyond them, the orders of the angels, as perfectly ranked as the heavens, made their celestial music in praise of God. Human beings inhabited the intersection between the changeable world of matter and the perfect world of the heavens—the one place where salvation could be won or lost.

These structures were slow to change. Even as Latin Christians came into contact—and conflict—with Muslims, Jews, and Greek Christians, Persians and Seljuk Turks, many of whom knew Africa and Asia far better than they did, Latin mapmakers continued to divide the face of the earth into three continents, which they represented schematically. They placed Jerusalem at the center of the world for theological reasons. They also knew only North Africa and depicted the Indian Ocean as enclosed by land, even though the Arab traders whose caravans crossed the Sahara and whose ships followed the trade winds across the Indian Ocean knew better. These mapmakers devoted huge effort to such symbolic, rather than empirical, enterprises as trying to fix the location of the Garden of Eden.

Pushing against the weight of tradition in the European intellectual world, the practical problems of an increasingly commercial society created new openings for innovation. Monarchs, merchants, and nobles all needed guidance as cities and their economies developed, and political conflict flared between states and with the Church. Laymen as well as clerics consulted the ancient books that covered everything from how to regulate commercial transactions to how to maintain the health of the human body.

INNOVATION IN THE LAW

One of these ancient works was the Roman *Corpus Iuris*. Although compiled under Emperor Justinian in Constantinople half a millennium before, it offered exactly the tools needed: powerful definitions of principles that could regulate relations, and clear statements about how they operated.

SECULAR LAW

By the beginning of the twelfth century, scholars in Bologna, a large and prosperous commune with a thriving textile industry and a sophisticated city government, were offering lectures on Roman law. Like the theologians, the lawyers taught by lecturing on texts and holding debates; and like the Bible, the Roman law was soon barnacled with a thick coating of explanatory comments.

Rulers and their advisers, merchants, and nobles scoured the Roman law for insights and detailed legislation they could adapt to their own purposes. It could be used to support the pretensions of central power: "the king," it declared, "is emperor in his own realm." But it could also support the privileges and autonomies of particular groups or cities. The Roman law made clear that the Roman people had transferred their power to the emperors—a statement that could be cited for support as readily by republicans as by monarchists. The revival of secular law helped to regulate trade and other urban practices, but it also helped to spawn new debates about the foundations of politics.

THE CHURCH, LAW, AND MARRIAGE

The Church, for its part, had substantial responsibilities in what would now be considered the realm of law. Marriage was a formal business in the Middle Ages—an opportunity for royal and noble families or established city merchants and craftsmen to form alliances with powerful counterparts. It was normally marked by an exchange of property, especially in the form of a dowry provided by the bride's family. The clergy, who were responsible for marriage, tried to convince ordinary Christians that marriage should be based on affection as well as political and economic strategy. They also gradually pushed people in northern Europe to give up the custom whereby a couple would become engaged and then have intercourse to seal their marriage, in favor of a marriage ceremony outside the church door, followed by a nuptial Mass inside the church presided over by a priest.

As the role of the clergy grew, priests became responsible for determining whether the prospective bride and groom could marry legally in the first place. With many noble families related by intermarriage, it was easy to mistakenly marry within the so-called prohibited degrees of kinship—especially when doing so might have the practical advantage of knitting together adjacent land holdings.

The rules for ending marriages were also complex.

Jesus had forbidden his followers to divorce their partners. But if a king or a wealthy merchant could not impregnate his wife, for example, he might seek to have his marriage annulled by the Church on the grounds that she was infertile. This accusation was humiliating, and the exchanges of property that had to follow the dissolution of a marriage were intricate. Laws and tables were drawn up to give priests—and, when appeals to Rome took place, archbishops and cardinals—guidance on how to decide all of the questions that could provoke disputes.

In addition, the Church had its own vast properties and prerogatives to protect. Accordingly, clerics used the Roman model to create a second body of law—canon law, or the law of the Church—and built a system of courts to administer it. Canon law rested on a textbook, the *Decretum*, assembled by the Benedictine monk Gratian, who taught in Bologna in the mid-twelfth century. Like the ancient Roman lawyers before them, the clerics compiled and taught these laws so effectively that by the end of the

Medieval Marriage An illustration from a twelfth-century Spanish manuscript displays the solemnity associated with marriage between nobles. The French viscount of Nimes (seated) formally sanctions the betrothal of his daughter Ermengarde—her hair uncovered to indicate that she is a virgin—to a Spanish count, while the viscountess looks on.

twelfth century the best way to rise to the highest positions in the Church was to study law. And like the Roman lawyers, the clerics provided arguments for partisans of radically opposed positions.

THE FIRST UNIVERSITIES

Alongside these changes in secular and canon law there came new institutions—institutions more formal, at first, than the Paris schools of Abelard's time—for pursuing practical studies. Bologna, as we have seen, became a center for legal studies early in the twelfth century. Salerno, in southwestern Italy, developed a medical school. As their numbers grew, the students in these cities emulated those engaged in other trades. They banded together and formed what they called a *universitas* (Latin for a corporation or guild) to regulate teaching and learning. Once organized and equipped with rules and privileges, they hired professors and insisted that they teach the full hour, until the bell rang to dismiss class. Students did not make all the rules. School faculties defined the texts that students must study to become qualified practitioners, laid out curricula, and set exercises to test mastery of particular subjects. By the end of the twelfth century, these Italian professional schools had crystallized as formal universities—one of the characteristic new institutions of medieval Europe.

The Early Universities, 1200

PARIS AND ITS STUDENTS In Paris, meanwhile, the professors did what the students had done in the south. They formed a university in the mid-twelfth century, established faculties, and drew up a curriculum for formal study. In Paris, theology, not law or medicine, became the central course of study. Students in Paris—and at the other universities soon formed in its wake, such as Oxford—were clerics. They mastered the liberal arts and logic, and carried out the exercises that made them first bachelors and then masters of arts. Most finished at that point, but an elite few continued and took doctorates in theology.

Many students came—as Peter Abelard did—from the nobility. But able students from farms and city streets also gravitated to the schools in Paris and elsewhere. They survived at first by begging, but systems of scholarship support gradually took shape, which enabled poor students to concentrate on their work. These students acquired a new status. At a time when most young people were bound to the land they worked, to the shops where they served as apprentices, or to the knights or ladies whom they served as pages or maids, students enjoyed great freedom. They lived in cities, in inns and halls, with little supervision. Often they spent their free time in taverns and brothels. Students became known not only for their intellectual skills but also for their willingness to fight when challenged by citizens whom their behavior annoyed, or innkeepers whom they refused to pay.

NEW AVENUES TO POWER For all their differences of emphasis and curriculum, these new universities had much in common. In the same years when poets created new forms of literature in the vernaculars, professors created new forms of lecture and treatise in Latin, devising technical terms that had not existed in the ancient world. In this case, as in others, a language with no native speakers proved so useful that it not only survived, it also developed in new and unexpected ways. The masters used their new technical language to teach students how to read and debate about authoritative texts. And they all recognized one another's degrees. Become a Master of Arts at Paris, and you could teach the liberal arts at any other university. A common culture of learning based in the new institutions spread across Europe, especially as it became clear that popes, kings, and city governments highly valued the graduates. For the first—but certainly not the last—time in European history, formal education offered access to political and economic power.

THE IMPACT OF ISLAMIC LEARNING

As the foundations of Western intellectual life were renewed, Latin culture also absorbed new information and new ways of thinking from the Islamic world. Specialized disciplines such as philosophy, astronomy, technology, and medicine flourished in the age of Saladin, as they had in Hellenistic and Roman Alexandria. Prosperous and sophisticated Islamic states created libraries, mosques, and formal institutions. Al-Azhar, the Muslim

MEDIEVAL PARIS, ca. 1200

> I PREFERRED THE WEAPONS OF DIALECTIC TO ALL THE OTHER TEACHINGS OF PHILOSOPHY, AND ARMED WITH THESE I CHOSE THE CONFLICTS OF DISPUTATION INSTEAD OF THE TROPHIES OF WAR.

PETER ABELARD, *HISTORY OF MY CALAMITIES*

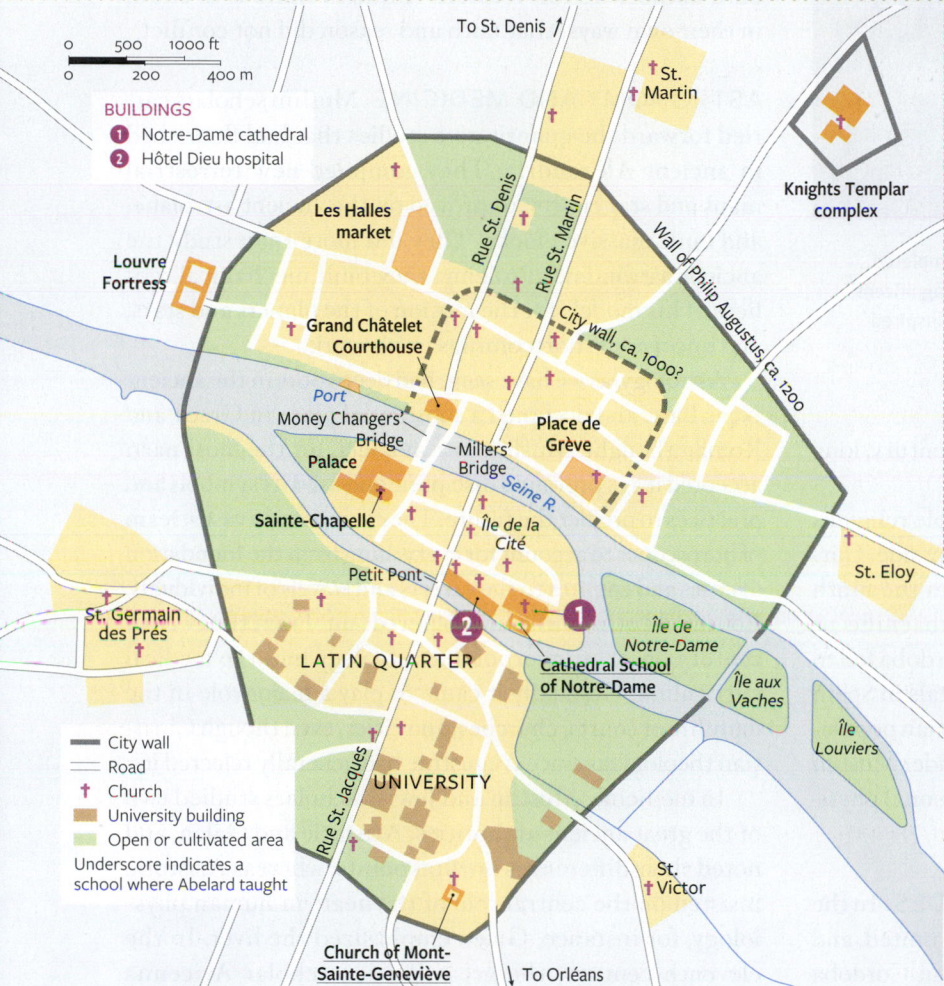

BUILDINGS
1. Notre-Dame cathedral
2. Hôtel Dieu hospital

To St. Denis
St. Martin
Knights Templar complex
Les Halles market
Louvre Fortress
Rue St. Denis
Rue St. Martin
Wall of Philip Augustus, ca. 1200
City wall, ca. 1000?
Grand Châtelet Courthouse
Port
Money Changers' Bridge
Millers' Bridge
Place de Grève
Palace
Sainte-Chapelle
Seine R.
Île de la Cité
Petit Pont
St. Eloy
St. Germain des Prés
LATIN QUARTER
Cathedral School of Notre-Dame
Île de Notre-Dame
Île aux Vaches
Île Louviers
Rue St. Jacques
UNIVERSITY
Church of Mont-Sainte-Geneviève
St. Victor
To Orléans

City wall
Road
✝ Church
University building
Open or cultivated area
Underscore indicates a school where Abelard taught

POPULATION
Early thirteenth century: ca. 50,000.

UNIVERSITY ATTENDANCE
2,000–3,000 students living and studying in the Latin Quarter.

STUDENT EXEMPTIONS
As clerics, all students were exempt from secular laws and the jurisdiction of city courts and lords, occasionally leading to friction with local residents.

A professor lectures on a theology text at a Parisian school in this fourteenth-century manuscript illustration. Professors used Latin in new ways to teach students how to read and debate their texts.

> I, A WANDERING SCHOLAR LAD, / BORN FOR TOIL AND SADNESS, / OFTENTIMES AM DRIVEN BY / POVERTY TO MADNESS. / LITERATURE AND KNOWLEDGE I / FAIN WOULD STILL BE EARNING, / WERE IT NOT THAT WANT OF PELF / MAKES ME CEASE FROM LEARNING.

ANONYMOUS STUDENT POEM, FROM *CARMINA BURANA*

This fourteenth-century French manuscript shows Parisian students at prayer. From the cathedral school of Notre-Dame to the University of Paris, schools were intimately connected to the Church, and theology formed the core of their curricula.

> SOME ARE GAMING, SOME ARE DRINKING, / SOME ARE LIVING WITHOUT THINKING; / AND OF THOSE WHO MAKE THE RACKET, / SOME ARE STRIPPED OF COAT AND JACKET; / SOME GET CLOTHES OF FINER FEATHER, / SOME ARE CLEANED OUT ALTOGETHER; / NO ONE THERE DREADS DEATH'S INVASION, / BUT ALL DRINK IN EMULATION.

STUDENT DRINKING SONG, FROM *CARMINA BURANA*

QUESTIONS FOR ANALYSIS

1. What made Peter Abelard's argumentative approach to teaching so exciting to students?
2. What can you say about student life in medieval Paris from the evidence here?
3. How did students in the medieval universities experience a new independence in their social and intellectual lives?

Mosque of Córdoba The Great Mosque of Córdoba (completed in 987), with its vaulted, striped archways, is not only a magnificent example of the architecture of the Islamic world but also inspired builders of Christian cathedrals throughout Europe.

university in Cairo, took shape in the tenth century, long before any Western one.

In many parts of the Islamic world, multiple religious and philosophical traditions flourished side by side. Córdoba had been the capital of Muslim Spain in the ninth and tenth centuries. It boasted an enormous, magnificent mosque—a building so splendid that, after Córdoba fell to Christian forces in 1236, architects of cathedrals in Spain and France did their best to copy it. The Christian population of Córdoba had their own bishop while under Muslim rule, and in the tenth century the caliph's personal physician was a learned and wealthy Jew.

CÓRDOBA: AVERROËS AND MAIMONIDES In the twelfth century, Muslim Spain was no longer united, and Seville replaced Córdoba as its leading city. But Córdoba still gave birth to extraordinary thinkers. Averroës (Ibn Rushd; 1126–1198), who served for many years as a judge, drew up commentaries on almost the entire body of Aristotle's works. Averroës argued that Aristotle offered a consistent, powerful understanding of the universe, and that his thought did not conflict with the revelations of Islam. Where philosophy and religion appeared to disagree, they were actually offering different kinds of truth. Moses Maimonides (1138–1204) also came from Córdoba. The most influential Jewish thinker of the Middle Ages, he too became an expert on law—in his case, Jewish law—and a medical man as well. In a massive philosophical work, *The Guide for the Perplexed*, he asked how a benevolent and omnipotent God could have created a universe that included evil of so many kinds.

Both men ended up in exile: Averroës was banished by the emir of Córdoba in 1195, and when a new dynasty from North Africa seized Córdoba and exiled its Jews in 1148, Maimonides was forced to leave with them. Yet their works became classics, not only in their original Arabic but in the Latin translations that made both of them standard authorities for Western thinkers anxious to show, in their own ways, that faith and reason did not conflict.

ASTRONOMY AND MEDICINE Muslim scholars carried forward the quantitative studies that had flourished in ancient Alexandria. They compiled new terrestrial maps and star charts, improved on the ancient astrolabe, and built massive clocks. They did more than study the ancient astronomer Ptolemy: they built mechanical replicas of his models for the motion of the planets and stars, and uncovered shortcomings in his work.

Astrology, as we have seen, had deep roots in the ancient Near East, and occupied a substantial place in Greek and Roman thought. Muslim astronomers, for the most part, accepted it as a profound discipline and used its symbols and practices to predict the future. They composed a vast stream of horoscopes to account for everything from the foundation of cities and empires to the careers and travels of individuals. Educated Latin Christians followed suit. From the twelfth century on, they incorporated astrology into the medical curriculum. Gradually it came to play a major role in the daily life of courts, churches, and cities, even though Christian theologians since Augustine had generally rejected it.

In medicine, Muslim and Jewish scholars studied two of the great ancient authorities, Aristotle and Galen, and noted their differences on vital points: whereas Aristotle insisted on the central role of the heart in human physiology, for instance, Galen emphasized the liver. In the eleventh century, the great Persian scholar Avicenna (Ibn Sina; d. 1037) confronted this problem of conflicting authorities and compiled a massive medical encyclopedia, *The Canon of Medicine*, which laid out the elements of Galen's system. Avicenna set out the basic causes of health and illness, described the constitution of the universe, and offered detailed discussions of anatomy, physiology, and therapy. Late in the twelfth century, the Italian scholar Gerard of Cremona (ca. 1114–1187) translated the *Canon* into Latin. It served as the basis of medical teaching in Christian universities for centuries.

TRANSLATING THE ISLAMIC CANON For Muslims as for Latins, knowledge mostly meant the contents

of books. As the Crusades and travel brought the two cultures into closer contact, educated Westerners realized how great a wealth of material was accessible to scholars in the Muslim lands. Scholar-explorers from all over the Latin West made the difficult trip to Sicily and the Iberian Peninsula in the first half of the twelfth century. There some learned Arabic and all gained access to the Islamic canon of philosophical and scientific texts. Often collaborating with local helpers, they rendered many of the classic, systematic works of ancient philosophy and science from Arabic into Latin: Aristotle's works, Euclid's *Geometry*, Ptolemy's major works, and much more. The Greek originals of these works had been translated in literal fashion, word for word, by the scholars of Baghdad's House of Wisdom in the ninth century. Now Latin scholars followed suit, rendering the Arabic translations word for word into Latin. The results were not elegant, but these translations gave Western thinkers direct access, for the first time in several hundred years, to many of the central works of Greek thought.

THE TRANSFORMATION OF LATIN THOUGHT

A wealth of technical books from the Islamic world became accessible in the West for the first time in the twelfth century, and their impact was profound. Western scholars hungrily seized on them. Latin libraries expanded to include their astronomical tables and medical textbooks. Arabic numerals spread alongside the traditional Roman ones. In the lively, urban world of the universities, the newly available ancient texts and the works of more recent Muslim scholars found a natural audience. Latin thinkers developed new skills and, even more important, a newly critical attitude toward many of the ancient authorities and their assumptions.

BEYOND TRADITION: ABELARD AND HÉLOÏSE

The rise of new sources and methods for intellectual life was accompanied by striking changes in its style and temper. Learning and brilliance assumed a value that they had never previously possessed in the Latin tradition. In this strange new world, Peter Abelard, the deft practitioner of the new style of formal argument, became a cultural hero of a new kind. As Héloïse d'Argenteuil (d. 1164), the young woman who knew him more intimately than anyone else, described in a letter to him, his brilliance as a philosopher had made him a celebrity, one whose presence called crowds into the streets: "For who among

kings or philosophers could equal you in fame?" Héloïse described Abelard as a glamorous poet who could "captivate the heart of any woman" with the songs he composed and sang—an art form, she noted, that philosophers had rarely pursued.

Héloïse's testimony has a special value. For she was not only Abelard's friend but also his philosophical pupil, his secret lover, and his equal as a writer. She became pregnant with his son, whom she named Astrolabe—a testimony to the passion for knowledge she shared with Abelard. Her uncle and guardian, Fulbert, who became increasingly angry at his niece's relationship with Abelard, eventually arranged to have him castrated—and thus inflicted not only a monstrous physical wound but also a terrible psychic one, since the event immediately became public. Abelard found himself not only mutilated but humiliated.

REVEALING VOICES What makes this story most remarkable—and most characteristic of the extraordinary world in which it unfolded—is that both Abelard and Héloïse recorded their story and their responses to it: Abelard in his *History of My Calamities* as well as in letters to Héloïse and others, and Héloïse in complex, spectacular letters to Abelard. Abelard related, with unsparing precision, the details of his earlier career—the passion with which he had first sought out great teachers such as Anselm of Laon, and the demonic pride with which he had waged intellectual war against them. It was in the full heat of pride, Abelard insisted, that he—who had always preserved his virginity and hated casual sex and prostitution—taught and then fell in love with Héloïse, and in doing so betrayed his calling as a teacher. Like Augustine, Abelard set himself on what proved a twisting path to peace and salvation. Unlike Augustine, he set down in detail the machinations of the unworthy and the enemies that he encountered, even after God had so powerfully drawn his attention to his own faults.

HÉLOÏSE: A NEW CONSCIOUSNESS Though Héloïse had been Abelard's adoring pupil and might have been expected, as a woman who had borne a baby out of wedlock, to remain silent from shame, she now spoke for herself—and did so even more powerfully than he did. After she became pregnant, Abelard suggested that they marry secretly. Héloïse, in a magnificent tirade that Abelard summarized, insisted that it would be wrong for either of them to marry, since by doing so they would enter a state of misery and distraction. The true philosopher, she argued, must embrace solitude and contemplation: "What possible concord could there be between scholars and

Abelard and Héloïse In this fourteenth-century illustration, the two lovers—Abelard wearing a scholar's garment, and Héloïse dressed as a nun—converse together. Their hand gestures indicate their passion for argument.

domestics, between authors and cradles, between books or tablets and distaffs, between the stylus or the pen and the spindle?" She could not imagine herself, any more than Abelard, combining the pursuit of wisdom with the cares of married life.

In an extraordinary passage—one closer in spirit to the new poetry of courtly love than to the Latin and Christian classics that Héloïse had studied with Abelard, but even more defiant of conventions and tradition—she transformed the bond between man and woman from a practical connection to a communion of souls. Héloïse explained herself with a moral clarity next to which Abelard's severest efforts at self-flagellation look flat and insincere. With characteristic originality, she reclaimed the abusive terms for women who lived with men outside the social bonds of marriage. These were more appropriate to the philosophical life she wanted to share with Abelard—a relationship of equals—than the standard role and position of wife:

> The name of wife may seem more sacred or more binding, but sweeter for me will always be the word mistress, or, if you will permit me, that of concubine or whore. . . . God is my witness that if Augustus,

Emperor of the whole world, thought fit to honor me with marriage and conferred all the earth on me to possess for ever, it would be dearer and more honorable to me to be called not his Empress but your whore.

In Héloïse's brave words we hear the voice of a new consciousness—that of someone who is absolutely committed to scrutinizing her own conduct and judging it by the highest standards of morality, but who frames those standards for herself rather than accepting the norms of a society that expected women to be silent and decorous. Christian Europe was witnessing the birth not only of a culture of higher education, but one of individualism as well.

CONCLUSION

At the end of the twelfth century, Europe was still collectively poor—far poorer than China, at the other end of the great Silk Road trade route—even if some Europeans were enormously rich. Society was still organized into three basic orders: those who prayed (the clergy), those who fought (the military aristocracy), and the great majority who worked (primarily as serfs tied to the land). European monarchs had developed new systems for gathering revenue and administering justice, but even the most powerful rulers still depended on their aristocratic and clerical vassals for political counsel and military support. Struggles for authority between rulers and popes, and between rulers and cities that wished to be independent of their authority, consumed vast resources.

Still, Latin Europe was now on the move. Cities were growing again, and bound laborers who made their way to them and managed to remain for a time became legally free. The merchants and craftsmen who built the cities also created new forms of self-government of lasting consequence. Europeans were developing trade routes and mounting military expeditions into areas that had not been part of the Latin world since Roman times. They were mastering ancient texts, many of which had been lost to Latin culture and preserved in Arabic in the Islamic world, and composing new ones, in both Latin and new vernacular languages. The social and cultural changes of this period enabled some Europeans to begin to see themselves as unique individuals, who could imagine lives outside the normal categories that seemed to organize society. The individualism of the modern era may have begun in this deeply Christian world that remains almost wholly strange to us.

[CHAPTER REVIEW]

KEY TERMS

manorialism (p. 251)

serf (p. 251)

Peace of God (p. 252)

guild (p. 254)

commune (p. 255)

William the Conqueror (p. 258)

Domesday Book (p. 258)

chivalry (p. 263)

East-West Schism (p. 266)

Investiture Controversy (p. 267)

Gregorian Reform Movement (p. 267)

Concordat of Worms (p. 268)

Reconquista (p. 268)

Crusades (p. 270)

Cistercians (p. 273)

Romanesque (p. 275)

Gothic (p. 275)

scholasticism (p. 277)

theology (p. 277)

REVIEW QUESTIONS

1. What means of control did lords have over their serfs in the manorial system?

2. What innovations helped to spur the development of commerce in the cities?

3. What types of freedom did city life afford that were not available on the manor?

4. What steps were taken to create new, independent city governments?

5. How did King William I establish his authority over England?

6. What were the most important elements of the chivalric code?

7. What issues sparked conflict between the European monarchs and popes?

8. What were the initial motivations for Christian Europeans to undertake the Crusades?

9. What were the most important spiritual innovations of the medieval period?

10. What intellectual contributions did the Islamic world make to Latin scholarship?

CORE OBJECTIVES

After reading this chapter, you should have a solid understanding of the following core objectives. To strengthen your grasp of the core objectives, use the resources on the Student Site for The West.

- Analyze the social and economic changes in Europe that began in the eleventh century.

- Describe the new political institutions that arose in medieval society.

- Evaluate the evolution of the medieval church and its relationship to secular power.

- Identify the origins and outcomes of the Crusades.

- Assess the developments in medieval religious practices.

- Trace the development of medieval scholarship and institutions of learning.

 GO TO **inQuizitive** TO SEE WHAT YOU'VE LEARNED—AND LEARN WHAT YOU'VE MISSED—WITH PERSONALIZED FEEDBACK ALONG THE WAY.

Early 13th century
Dominican and
Franciscan
Orders develop

1204
Crusaders sack
Constantinople

1202–1204
Fourth Crusade

1209–1229
Albigensian Crusade

1214
Philip Augustus completes
reclamation of Norman
lands from England

1215
Fourth Lateran Council;
King John of England
signs Magna Carta

1217–1229
Fifth and Sixth
Crusades

1238
Mongols invade Muscovy

1271–1295
Marco Polo journeys
throughout the East

1291
Last major Christian
stronghold in Palestine
falls to the Mamluks

1315–1322
Famine follows poor
harvests across Europe

1309–1377
Avignon papacy

1330s–1453
Hundred Years' War

Consolidation and Crisis

THE HIGH MIDDLE AGES

1200–1400

1381
Wat Tyler leads
Peasants' Revolt

1347–1350
Black Death
strikes Europe

1358
Jacquerie rebellion

1382
Oligarchical republic
takes control of
Florence

The Florentine merchant and banker Giovanni Villani (d. 1348) spent his last years composing a history of his city. His ambitious book began with the fall of the Tower of Babel. He traced the origins of Florence back to ancient Rome, and those of Rome back to Troy. It was normal for medieval historians to frame the history of their city or their monastery in this grandiose way. Late in the work, though, Villani offered a striking innovation. He broke off from his narrative, pulled his camera back from the day-to-day details of politics and war, and surveyed his city.

It was, to begin with, a vast community: "Careful investigation has established that at that time there were in Florence approximately 25,000 men capable of bearing arms, ages fifteen to seventy, all citizens, of which 1,500 were noble and powerful citizens.... There were then around seventy-five fully-equipped knights." Graphic details made clear what it took to support this immense male population—as well as the population of women and children, and the members of religious orders. All goods that passed through the city gates had to be registered and a duty paid. Every year, the records showed, Florentines consumed 4,000 oxen and calves, 60,000 sheep, 20,000 goats, and 30,000 pigs, and drank at least 5.9 million gallons of wine. Any contemporary reader could imagine the noise

Commerce and Guilds The High Middle Ages saw rapid increases in commerce and wealth in European cities. In this bustling scene from a Bolognese manuscript (ca. 1300), members of a merchants' guild display wares ranging from wine to horses, count money, and weigh goods to determine their value. An angel casts a benevolent eye over the scene, granting divine sanction to the hive of economic activity.

[FOCUS QUESTIONS]

- How did economic growth transform parts of high medieval Europe?
- What major changes transformed European states in the High Middle Ages?
- What were the major new directions for the Church in the high medieval period?
- What developments brought medieval society to crisis in the fourteenth century?

these hordes of animals made as they entered the city, their screams as they were butchered, and the smell of their meat and carcasses. Here was clear evidence, inscribed in blood and offal, of the scale of urban living in the fourteenth century. The magnitude of the slaughter had a certain grandeur. So did the thought of the 4,000 loads of cool melons that came through the city's San Friano Gate every July, as temperatures rose.

Villani did his best to show that the city was more than a vast mouth that consumed nature's resources. Its citizens took a special pride in their handsome public and private buildings, from the churches and monasteries inside the walls to the "large and rich estates" and mansions outside them. The "sumptuous buildings and beautiful palaces," towers, and walled gardens in the suburbs were so dense and impressive that they fooled first-time visitors into thinking the city even bigger than it actually was. A single, unified world of city and country, palace and villa, Florence as Villani portrayed it was something new: not the city as refuge from a violent countryside; not the city as Babylon, the den of evil from which those who sought peace, quiet, and an environment free from sin had to flee; but a kind of urban paradise—a community that inspired, as a whole, a secular version of the rapture that Abbot Suger had felt as he saw light streaming through the new rose window of the Saint Denis basilica.

Historians in the Middle Ages, as in antiquity, commemorated the past and recorded the present to instruct the men and women of the future. In most chronicles, examples of heroic and saintly deeds provided Christians with models for imitation. What Villani looked for, by contrast, were readers who shared his interest in the quantitative details

that measured the city's health, and could learn from these details how to maintain greatness in the future. His readers would be, like him, experienced in trade, banking, and city planning, and passionate analysts of balance sheets: "the wise and worthy citizens who [will] rule in future times." We do not know how precisely Villani's statistics reflected Florentine realities. But in the data we can see something striking: the textures of city life from the eleventh and twelfth centuries onward. The power and independence of these cities were among the most distinctive features of the civilization of the High Middle Ages.

Between 1200 and about 1350, European cities grew to sizes not seen since Roman times. Their citizens pursued finance and industry, art and craft. And they continued to show immense ingenuity and energy in developing effective forms of government and administration. In the same years, European monarchies built new institutions and exercised new powers. The Church adapted in creative ways to these changing conditions: efforts were made to ensure that both clergy and ordinary Christians acted in accordance with religious teachings, and novel forms of religious life were invented.

This confident, cosmopolitan world Villani knew so well would soon be swept away by the Black Death, the great plague that struck Europe in 1347 and very probably killed Villani himself, along with thousands of others. Yet long before this, as we will see, the problems that come with growth and the stresses of life in a new and complex society were starting to be felt.

TRANSFORMING CITY AND COUNTRYSIDE

The new urban society that filled Villani with such pride rested on foundations laid in the late twelfth and thirteenth centuries. The rise of the great abbeys and cathedrals required the mobilization of far more than spiritual energy, vitally important though that was. Vast quantities of stone had to be quarried. To build Notre-Dame Cathedral and other great structures in Paris, stonecutters excavated more than 180 miles of tunnels under the city (the entire modern Paris subway system, the Métro, is only two-thirds as long). To connect the stones and provide structural stability, vast amounts of iron had to be forged. Ten percent of the expense of building a cathedral went on iron ore and the forges where it was processed. Water-powered hammers replaced some of the human labor and accelerated the production of bars and fasteners.

As the crafts became more complex and productive, rulers began to compete for the best practitioners. Skilled miners were favored by royal houses: when King John exempted English tin miners from ordinary taxation and military service in 1201, he unleashed the growth of what became a vast industry. German miners, famed for their expertise at extracting iron, were encouraged to migrate into the Balkans and beyond by rulers anxious to extract the commodities and precious metals hidden in their own hills. Soon new towns grew up, such as Kutna Hora in Bohemia—a center for silver mining that exploded in size in the thirteenth century and soon rivaled Prague, the capital, in wealth and splendor.

SPECIALIZATION: FROM WOOL TO CLOTH

At first, as we have seen, medieval cities were less like their modern counterparts than collections of villages. Their inhabitants usually came from nearby regions, and most of them continued to do at least some small-scale farming if they could. In a world of masons, blacksmiths, miners, and carpenters, however, the old way of life, which mixed urban and rural pursuits, made way for a new system: one of division of labor, in which the inhabitants of towns mostly worked for money. Whole regions specialized. In Flanders and northern France, the first part of Europe to become a center of commerce and trade fairs, and in central and northern Italy, connected by sea to markets around the Mediterranean, a massive cloth industry developed in Ghent and Bruges, Florence and Milan.

When considering the High Middle Ages, it is important not to let an apparently familiar word such as *industry* delude us into thinking in terms of the nineteenth and twentieth centuries. There were, as yet, no large factories like those that developed in the modern world; medieval industry had its own ways of working. Wool was turned into cloth in a series of stages, most of which were carried out by specialized workers in their own homes.

Entrepreneurs guided and organized the process. In Florence, for example, some 200 firms, whose principals belonged to the guild of Linaiuoli, manufactured woolen cloth. Two or more partners would contribute the necessary capital. They would also hire a factor, or agent, who would follow the cloth through the stages of

Medieval Industry Northern Italy was one center of the vast European cloth industry in the Middle Ages. An illustration from 1390s Italy shows merchants at a market stall measuring, cutting, and sewing silk garments.

its manufacture. The factor ordered wool from suppliers as far afield as Spain and England, and hired workers to prepare it in his shop under the supervision of a foreman. Then brokers began to move the wool, at first back out into the countryside around Florence, where women, working in their own cottages, spun it into thread. The finished thread went to weavers, who turned it into cloth on their looms. The brokers would then take the cloth to fullers, who trampled it into a mixture of fuller's earth (a kind of clay that absorbed and removed the wool's natural grease) and urine (which helped to clean and whiten it) until it took on a thick, smooth texture. Dyers added color, sometimes to the yarn, but sometimes to the finished cloth.

Once the cloth was sheared, smoothed, and pressed, the entrepreneurs exported most of it. Bales went to the big ports at Venice and Naples, and from there to stalls in markets around the Mediterranean and in the north. It seems remarkable that these many transactions could all be governed and tracked not by computers but in simple handwritten ledgers.

This dispersed production process soon reached an astonishingly large scale—large enough to transform the uses of agricultural land across the English Channel. In 1273, the farmers of England—from smallholders who kept a few sheep, to the great abbeys of Fountains and Rievaulx that had flocks of thousands on their vast landholdings—sheared 8 million sheep and sent some 7 million pounds of wool across to the clothiers of Flanders. Town after town grew to 10,000 or 20,000 inhabitants, as specialist industries in everything from glassmaking to armor and weapon smithing took shape. Yet the increasing scale of production also brought with it a new vulnerability to external economic and political events—as in the years 1270–74, when the English monarchy embargoed exports of wool to promote the domestic cloth industry, a decision that shocked the Flemish.

A NEW ECONOMY

The thirteenth century saw massive economic development across much of Europe, and populations rose. In England, according to one historian's estimate, the population more than doubled, rising from 3.4 million to 7.2 million. Even in sectors of the economy that had remained more or less bound to traditional ways, new methods and attitudes became visible. Instead of depending on the incomes set by their traditional agreements with their serfs and tenants, landowners now sought to exploit their own properties for everything they were worth. They hired expert managers to organize the work and ruthlessly exploited the labor of their serfs. Everywhere, or so it seemed, buying and selling, exchanging one specialized product for another, replaced the old self-sufficient economy of the manor.

MONEY AND EXCHANGE Perceptive observers realized that a new world was taking shape—one in which money played a vital role. Even in the countryside, whole regions came to depend not on the crops and animals they could raise but on the income their products brought in. As commodities became more accessible and more varied, demand and supply both grew. Great monastic communities founded to provide a refuge from the cities of the twelfth century were now sucked back into the economic orbits of the bigger and more sophisticated cities of the thirteenth century, as they transferred large portions of the acreage they had once devoted to crops to the cultivation of grapevines (viticulture) and actively marketed their products.

In the middle of the thirteenth century, an Italian friar named Salimbene of Parma (1221–ca. 1290) traveled through northern Europe. A member of the new Franciscan religious order known for its strict pursuit of poverty, he was struck by the rise in consumption. Salimbene noted with interest that "the French delight in good wine." He showed understanding when he remarked that "we must forgive the English if they are glad to drink good wine when they can, for they have but little in their own country." What impressed this perceptive observer most, though, was the dramatic way in which, in some regions, viticulture had become a monoculture. In the Auvergne, a wine region in southern France, he noted that "these people sow nothing, reap nothing, and gather nothing into their barns. They only need to send their wine to Paris on the nearby river that goes straight there. The sale of wine in this city brings them in a good profit that pays entirely for their food and clothing."

BANKS AND INTEREST New financial systems and practices were needed to meet the needs of merchant capitalists and monarchs. As the trade networks that Salimbene described spread across Europe—with masses of raw material paid for in Britain and processed in Flanders by workers whose wine came from France—cash payments proved increasingly inadequate for the needs of the economy. Merchants needed to move money if they were to move goods. And, as we will see, kings and other rulers needed money if they were to muster their military forces, now made up of professional soldiers rather than vassals serving for the traditional—but often inadequate—term of forty days.

In theory, Christians were prohibited from lending money at interest. Philosophers and theologians argued that charging interest was, in essence, selling time, which belonged only to God. The Bible seemed to support their position. Hebrew prophets condemned usurers, and Christ drove the moneychangers out of the Temple in Jerusalem. In practice, however, Christians loaned and borrowed money. And during the course of the thirteenth century, Italians branched out from trade into banking, which became a specialty in Florence, Genoa, and elsewhere.

Early banks were small firms like any others: just a shop or market stall with a *banco* ("counter") where the proprietor met his customers. Money in the Middle Ages was local: in every city, artisans' private mints, licensed by the monarchs to use their official images, produced coins. Professional moneychangers were experts. They had to know

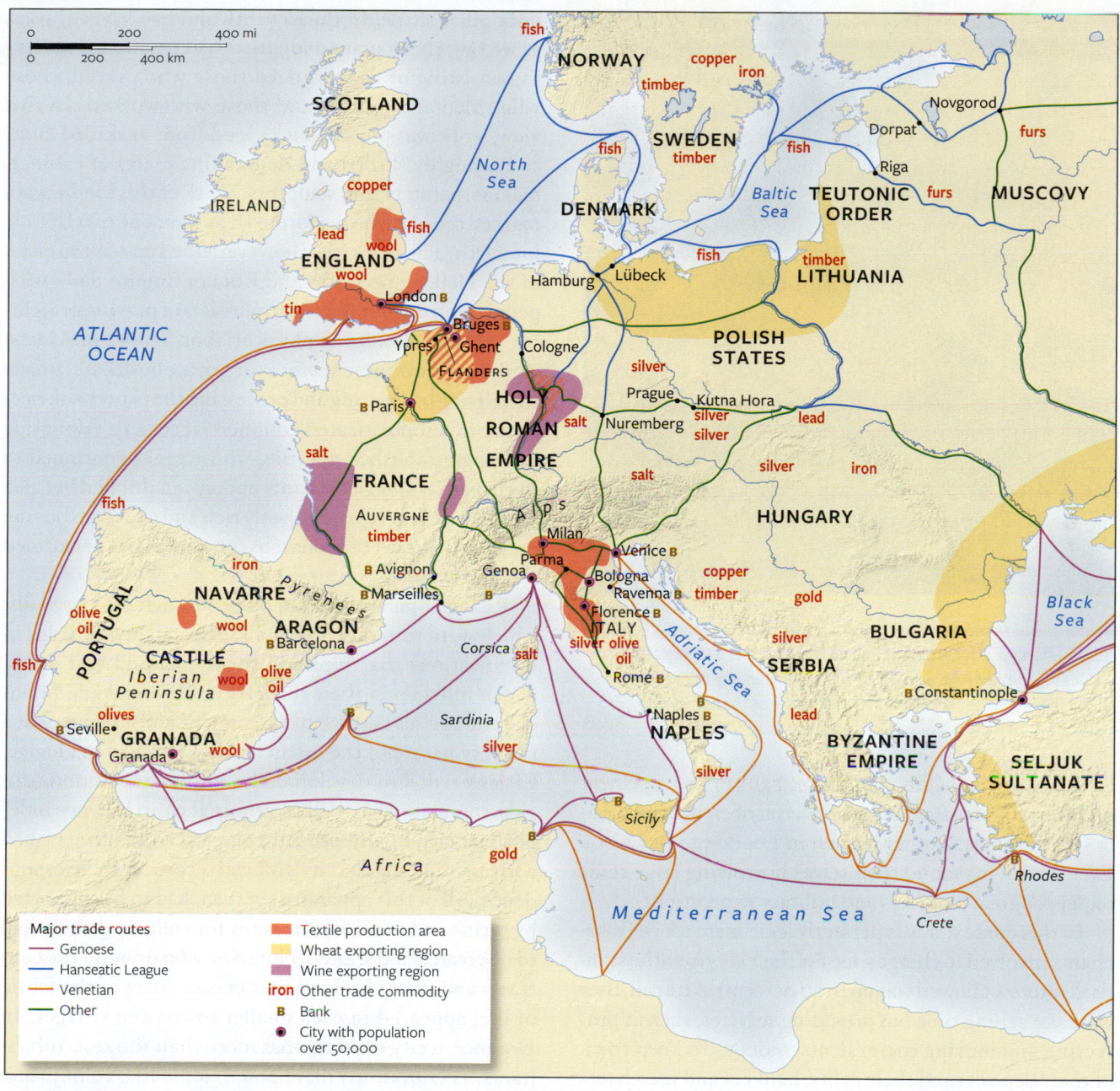

Economic Development in Europe, ca. 1300 Sophisticated trading and financial networks circulated raw materials and goods throughout Europe in the High Middle Ages. Ships plied trade routes across the Mediterranean and Baltic Seas, conveying precious metals, timber, silk, and wool. Luxury foodstuffs, such as wine, olives, olive oil, and salt, were transported to major cities and then exported. Branches of Italian banks opened in the larger cities, connecting merchants to an international financial system.

the value of every form of coinage and how to tell fake coins from genuine ones. They also had to keep abreast of monarchs' efforts to inflate their currencies and reduce their debts by cutting the amount of precious metal that their coins contained. Biting coins—the traditional test of genuineness—was only the beginning of the banker's work. Gradually, merchant firms that could provide such services—most of them beginning as family partnerships, such as the Bardi and Peruzzi of Florence—spread across Europe. Family members or trusted friends opened branches in cities from London to Constantinople. These banks and the networks of messengers that they maintained gave vital support to the new economy of long-distance, large-scale trade. A cloth manufacturer

Banking and Moneylending The coat of arms of the Moneychangers' Guild of Perugia, Italy, from the guild's 1377 Statutes and Register, includes a gryphon—an emblem of the city—standing atop a money chest, suggesting the security that banks offered to their clients.

could deposit money in a Florentine bank branch in Ghent or Ypres, travel to England with a letter of credit, and withdraw cash from another branch in London to buy wool. Even monarchs found themselves borrowing large sums to pay for great banquets and military expeditions.

In this context it was perfectly legitimate for the merchants involved to charge a fee for their services (the standard interest allowed was up to 20 percent). After all, they were not selling time but providing services, such as protecting and moving their clients' money. To keep track of their deposits and their debts, bankers and merchants adopted the more efficient Arabic numerals, and used them for double-entry bookkeeping (probably invented in thirteenth-century Florence). This system required that every transaction be recorded as both a debit and a credit, so that a partner could establish a firm's exact financial position at any moment by balancing the accounts. Though errors crop up in many medieval balance sheets, this method made the firms that adopted it—and the governments that eventually emulated them—more efficient than ever before.

SERVICE PROVIDERS With the rise of banks and commerce, the world that city-dwellers knew took on an unfamiliar shape. In the eleventh and twelfth centuries, as we saw, theologians and jurists had envisioned society as consisting of three orders: those who prayed, those who ruled and fought, and those who worked. In this view, work was physical: it ranged from unskilled labor to the highly skilled and demanding crafts of cabinetmakers, painters, and sculptors. Work of this kind always marked the one who performed it as someone of relatively low birth. The new cities, however, filled up—as the cities of the Hellenistic states and Roman Empire had—with people who did not make a profession of praying or fighting, but who also did no physical labor. Service providers, working in government offices or private businesses, made their living by creating and processing the paperwork necessary in a sophisticated commercial society. Alongside the long-established notaries, whose ranks continued to swell, bankers and merchants not only multiplied but also flourished. Some became vastly rich and ended up buying noble titles from the monarchs for whom they performed their services.

Rising populations soon burst through old city walls, which were torn down across Europe. The new rings of fortifications that replaced them enclosed vast areas, which filled up in their turn. As commercial and financial enterprises became more complex and larger in scale, the very nature of the urban legal system had to change. Cities needed to develop codes of private law and provide commercial as well as criminal courts. Every independent city, finally, needed a chancery—an office tasked with maintaining the city's official records and correspondence. All of this apparatus, in turn, had to be supported by tariffs and taxes, and systems for collecting them had to be created and staffed. Notaries, who drew up the contracts and deeds for land that became part of the fabric of life, appeared in ever smaller towns and villages. In Florence, a city of somewhat more than 100,000 inhabitants, as Giovanni Villani noted, some 10,000 boys and girls attended the so-called abacus school, where they learned to read, write, and do calculations. High medieval society was, among its other qualities, highly literate and numerate.

CITIES AND CULTURE: THE NEW WRITERS

Giovanni Villani was in many ways a typical member of this new urban elite. Starting out in the last years of the thirteenth century as a wool merchant, he invested in the Peruzzi bank, for which he undertook commercial travels across Europe. In later life he served Florence as a diplomat and skillfully led his city's delicate negotiations with its Tuscan rivals—though he also underwent public humiliation and even spent time in jail when the Buonaccorsi bank, to which he had transferred his business, failed. A cosmopolitan man who knew many cities and languages, Villani made sense of his complicated world, as we have seen, by describing it in vivid detail in his chronicle of Florentine history, which he composed in Italian, the language of daily life.

BRUNETTO LATINI Medieval cities produced many people who combined active political lives with serious writing, and who transformed the languages they spoke into vehicles for great literature. Brunetto Latini (ca. 1210–1294) was a Florentine notary who held high government offices. He was also a versatile writer who brought the learning of a scholar into the vernacular. In *On the Government of Cities*, written in prose, he explained why he thought it possible for a commune like Florence to govern itself as a republic, laid out the principles of justice and fairness that needed to inform the making and enforcement of laws, and provided guidelines for the podesta, whose job it was to translate ideals and principles into the everyday work of fair government. Latini also wrote a long poem in which he surveyed the universe, from God down to the globe of earth and water that humans inhabit. This wide-ranging work covered planets, elements, physiology, plants and animals, as well as human virtues and the nature of love. Latini's readers had access to a wealth of ancient learning and modern experience, all crisply conveyed.

DANTE ALIGHIERI No one read Latini more eagerly than **Dante Alighieri** (1265–1321), another Florentine of good family who served in the highest public offices until he and his allies lost out to a rival faction. Condemned for corruption in 1302, he insisted on his innocence and refused to pay the fine assessed. His sentence of exile was extended from its original two years to eternity. Dante served the prince of Ravenna, but devoted himself above all to writing in vernacular Italian. His *Divine Comedy* (1308–21) was a spectacular poetic triptych in which he portrayed himself voyaging through Hell, Purgatory, and Heaven, convoyed first by the Roman poet Virgil and then by Beatrice Portinari, the daughter of a Florentine banker, whom he had long admired. As sweeping and powerful as Virgil's *Aeneid*, Dante's series of poems amounted to a magnificent revenge, in the realm of the spirit, for his defeat in the city: a passionate, powerful demonstration that the universe is governed by a divine order that would

Dante Alighieri The Florentine painter Sandro Botticelli created this portrait of Dante 175 years after the poet's death. The laurel wreath attests to Dante's artistic greatness as well as his connection to the classical tradition.

eventually put Dante's enemies, as it had put the murderers of Julius Caesar, in the underworld.

GEOFFREY CHAUCER The works of Latini and Dante—and their chivalric predecessors—were read by the cosmopolitan, polyglot inhabitants of cities across Europe. Geoffrey Chaucer (ca. 1340–1400), scion of a prosperous London family, explored France as a soldier and visited Italy to negotiate a commercial treaty with Genoese merchants who wanted to trade in England. Still later he served as controller of customs, a vital job in the heyday of the British wool trade. A master linguist, he was a prolific writer whose output included a treatise on how to use the astrolabe as well as his great poem of love, *Troilus and Criseyde*, which he adapted from the influential Italian poet Giovanni Boccaccio. But Chaucer's greatest work was

Geoffrey Chaucer Though posthumous and idealized, this portrait in an early-fifteenth-century manuscript is the best likeness we have of Chaucer. His extended arm points at a verse that praises him.

the extraordinary set of narratives known as *The Canterbury Tales*, with their vivid portraits of a group of people from every part of society who meet at the Tabard Inn in Southwark, south of London Bridge, and embark on a pilgrimage to Canterbury. The twenty-three stories that he completed bring to life characters such as the Wife of Bath, with her passionate disdain for the opposite sex and her strong conviction that women want and deserve to rule in love and marriage.

A NEW SOCIETY

It was no accident that writers like Boccaccio and Chaucer found the lives of ordinary men and women—including their sexuality—to be fascinating subjects. Family life was growing more complex in cities. According to the male clerics and patricians who wrote the traditional books of advice for men and women, the family was a simple hierarchy. Marriage joined unequal partners. The husband possessed wisdom and moderation as well as property and power. The wife, by contrast, was possessed by forces beyond her control: her senses, which ruled her mind and made her less capable of reasoning; and the legal authority, first of her father and then of her husband, which gave them control over her life and property. Believed incapable of taking part in the wider worlds of work and politics, women were to remain indoors and devote themselves to running clean, efficient households. As one theologian put it, "a husband is to his

wife as a superior being is to an inferior, as perfect is to imperfect, as giver is to receiver."

These traditional attitudes were not completely disconnected from reality. Male bankers, merchants, and craftsmen normally waited to marry until they could maintain independent households. They chose wives who were young enough to produce multiple heirs and came from families that could equip them with adequate dowries. At a time when marriage was arranged by negotiation and designed to perpetuate the family as an economic and political enterprise, and regularly involved mature men marrying teenage girls, it was easy to imagine women as beings who existed only to support and give comfort to their male lords.

CITY WOMEN In fact, however, city women often participated as actively as men in the new urban economies. One-fifth of the *commenda* contracts issued in Genoa between 1200 and 1250 involved women, who invested almost 15 percent of the total capital involved. From Ghent and Cologne to Florence, women served as business partners to their husbands—especially their second husbands, since by the time they had outlived their first husbands, many women had accumulated property and experience. Some women managed the family firm during their husband's business trips, traded in commodities, and bought

City Women The frequency with which women participated in urban commerce is illustrated in a fourteenth-century medical tract, showing a woman fishmonger selling saltwater fish to a man.

LORENZETTI'S *EFFECTS OF GOOD GOVERNMENT IN THE CITY AND IN THE COUNTRY*

Ambrogio Lorenzetti painted the *Effects of Good Government in the City and in the Country* (1338) in Siena's town hall to celebrate the Italian city's prosperity under its commune. Lorenzetti's fresco adorns the walls of the Room of the Nine, the private meeting place of the rotating nine leaders of the commune.

Among the effects of good government seen in this detail is work, commerce, a family ritual, and a public celebration, all occurring in a prosperous, peaceful cityscape. To the left we see what might be a wedding procession. A woman wearing a crown rides a white horse, followed by what might be her male relatives. In the near background we see men playing a board game, perhaps in a tavern, with children nearby. At the center are nine dancers celebrating Siena's harmonious republicanism. To their right, cobblers sell shoes, a lecturer teaches students, and a merchant displays his wares. All of this activity is set within the brilliantly colored lines of Siena itself, its balconies and battlements towering over the people.

QUESTIONS FOR ANALYSIS

1. In what sense is good government the foundation of the scene depicted here?
2. How does the fresco represent the social and economic changes taking place in European cities in the fourteenth century?
3. Does the fresco strike you as a more realistic or a more idealistic portrayal of the city? Why?

and sold properties. They became guild masters in industries that were growing so rapidly that there were too few men to rule all of the shops—for example, the cloth industry in thirteenth-century Barcelona. In the shops of the many master artisans who worked without journeymen or apprentices, wives and daughters provided expert assistance and served as sales staff.

In Paris, women worked as butchers and fishmongers, made rosaries, ground glass, and tailored clothing. In England, women played an especially prominent role as brewers of beer, but also worked as barber-surgeons, bakers, and candle-makers. Around 1300 the German city of Nuremberg enacted a statute that forbade women from selling fish, except when their husbands were absent—evidence that women had been working regularly at the fish stalls in the market. Though some moralists insisted that women should not learn to read and write unless they planned to become nuns, city governments acknowledged that women needed to be literate. Many cities opened schools for girls (Paris had more than twenty of them) and paid female schoolmasters to teach.

The women of wealthy families dressed in the expensive fabrics and jewelry that fit their rank. Even a pious woman, such as the wife of Jacopo dei Benedetti, a successful young lawyer in thirteenth-century Italy, wore expensive robes. But she wore a hair shirt under them, as he discovered when she died in an accident. Another wealthy and pious wife, the saintly Florentine Umiliata dei Cerchi, trimmed the excess fabric off the hemlines of her skirts and gave it to the poor. Rich women balanced the claims of social status and religious ideals in many ways.

THE CITY POOR For the majority of the population, urban life was harsh. The semiskilled workers who spun thread and wove cloth, the men and women who worked as unskilled laborers, and those whom injury, illness, or age deprived of the ability to work, lived not in comfortable houses, but in ancient tenements or the crude shacks that spread, unplanned and without services, as the population grew. In the countryside, the poor had ways to supplement their income. They could invade the forests that belonged to their lords and keep pigs, gather nuts, or trap game animals, and they could cultivate even small plots of ground intensively and effectively. In the cities, these ways of supplementing income and diet were largely out of reach. The wages of the poorer workers were inadequate to support themselves and their families. And cities did not provide safety nets to catch those who did not flourish. Crowds of the poor, sick, and maimed gathered in public places—in market squares, at church doors, by city gates—to ask for

The Urban Poor Beggars, vagabonds, and the sick were always part of the fabric of medieval city life. In this illustration from a mid-fourteenth-century French manuscript, a bishop displays a relic to an injured man and a group of pilgrims. The injured man's bandaged leg and crutches imply he would have trouble finding work.

alms. Food riots were rare—partly because the well-off saw it as a Christian duty to give to the poor who confronted them. But much of the population was undernourished and vulnerable to illness and injury.

A NEW INDEPENDENCE IN THE CITIES

In the eleventh and twelfth centuries, as we have seen, cities in the more economically developed parts of Europe—Flanders, northern France, Italy—often achieved independence after massive struggles with the bishops and other local lords who had previously ruled them. These struggles continued through the thirteenth century, even after guilds and other new economic structures took shape. To put an end to the violence, cities—especially the wealthier merchants and artisans—declared the powerful nobles "magnates" and excluded them from holding government offices. In Florence and many other cities, their towers—centers of noble resistance to city government—were torn down.

CAPTAINS OF THE PEOPLE The established city rulers also excluded newly arriving merchants and craftsmen from participation in government. But as many of the new arrivals rose to prosperity, they formed pressure groups. In Italy the members of these groups were often known, a little misleadingly, as "the people." Gradually they took over certain government responsibilities and chose their own professional administrators, the "captains of the people." Now housed in massive buildings designed to overawe potential criminals and rebels—especially the older, noble elites who still resorted to violence when challenged—these complex city governments grew to include professional specialists in law, finance, and military and police affairs.

Though small by the standards of later periods, these administrations enabled cities in Flanders, Italy, and elsewhere to emulate the legal, political, and military independence that Venice and Genoa had established for themselves centuries before. And though these cities normally offered obedience to a great lord—the pope, the Holy Roman Emperor, or a more local magnate—in practice they effectively were self-governing cities, as independent (and in some cases as inventive in maintaining their independence) as the cities of ancient Greece. Their counterparts in the monarchies of northern Europe were more closely controlled and taxed by their rulers, but cities such as London and Paris also created civic institutions, from city halls to prisons.

A NEW CITYSCAPE

Public buildings—along with the massive halls built by the stronger guilds for meetings and ceremonial feasts—dominated the thirteenth-century cityscape. Larger than any conceivable private building, the Palazzo Vecchio, built at the end of the thirteenth century to house the city's government, still looms over

Florence A fifteenth-century fresco documents the impressive skyline of medieval Florence, including its major public buildings: the octagonal Baptistery (1), the tower of the Badia abbey (2), and the Palazzo Vecchio (3).

the city of Florence. Public buildings were strategically placed at points where they would make the strongest possible impression on rulers and diplomats who visited the city or on citizens who might harbor rebellious thoughts. Roads were deliberately sunk and curved so that these buildings would seem to heave up like immense icebergs as visitors or citizens came in sight of them. In times of confrontation or rebellion, the government could defend its authority. These structures were the embodiment of a new civic world—one in which men of substance, but not of noble birth or chivalric skills, appeared as the rulers of a new society, mercantile in its foundations and, in Italy, republican in its form of government.

THE HANSA CITIES

Similar developments took place in northern Europe. In the later twelfth century, cities began to grow on the northern edge of the Holy Roman Empire. Hamburg, near the North Sea on the river Elbe, and Lübeck, on the river Trave near the Baltic Sea, developed trade with the eastern Baltic, a rich source of grain, amber, wax, and furs. German colonists moved into the area, led by a military order, the Teutonic Knights, and founded trading stations at Dorpat, Riga, and eventually at Novgorod, an old princely state on the Volkhov River that had become a republic in 1136. Traders also moved west. As early as 1157, merchants from Cologne won from Henry II the right to trade in England without paying tolls.

By 1241 Hamburg and Lübeck had formed an alliance, which won further privileges. As Cologne and other cities joined, it grew into the **Hanseatic League** (from *Hansa*, "convoy of ships"), a loose but powerful association of trading cities. As free imperial cities ruled directly by the weak Holy Roman emperors, the Hansa cities became centers of manufacture, making silk and linen cloth, armor, and religious art, and moving cloth from England to the east and salt fish and other products from the Baltic to the west. By 1356, when representatives of the cities assembled in their first formal meeting, or diet, in Lübeck, the league was a far-flung and powerful group of cities that made war and signed treaties with other powers.

LIFE ON THE LAND: THE PEASANTS' WORLD

Agrarian life in thirteenth- and early-fourteenth-century Europe was still immensely varied. It included everything from the country—flat, open lands that could be intensively tilled by heavy plows pulled by eight oxen—to the remaining forest with its small communities of peasants who produced charcoal. The constantly burning fires and black-smudged faces of these peasants reminded aristocratic hunters of the devils in hell. Yet, as urban economies grew, they also transformed the countryside.

Even in small villages, legal and financial arrangements became more complex. Landlords employed workers in two ways: as tenants bound to the land and legally required to do manual work, and as free workers who were paid wages. By the thirteenth century, many well-established peasants held some of their lands as serfs—some rich serfs even had serfs of their own—and worked others' land as free laborers, for pay. Two families that worked similar amounts of land might live in very different conditions, with one required by law to pay for permission to marry and to provide labor services for its lord, the other able to bargain for the highest price for its work and for its produce. Many serfs fought to escape, or at least to evade, legal restrictions. In England, many bought land and passed it on to their heirs, even though the law forbade them to do so. In France, as inflation bit into the incomes of landlords, many of them freed their serfs: these peasants escaped their degraded status, and the landlords could exploit their estates more efficiently than with forced, unwilling labor.

Village life was hard, and the work that went into sustaining it could be as complicated and demanding, in its own way, as artisanal work in the cities. Shepherds, cowherds, and swineherds all had to learn how to care for their animals, which were harder to replace, in normal circumstances, than human children. Shepherds had to master the long trails on which their flocks moved seasonally. Special knowledge was needed for beekeeping, which produced wax for candles and honey for use in food and drink—especially mead, made from fermented honey. Millers, carpenters, and leatherworkers had to master the tools of their trade and to bargain with clients.

In the countryside, most women married young, to somewhat older men. Before and after marrying, they took part in every form of rural work. Women goaded the animals that pulled the plows steered by men, sowed grain and pulled weeds, gathered crops and separated grain from chaff. They were normally responsible for poultry and dairy products—some of which, like cheese, also demanded specialized expertise. They also brewed ale. In at least one English village, a woman was even appointed to the honorable office of Taster of the Ale, though many more were indicted for trying to evade the regulations that governed brewing.

Peasant diets were varied. In addition to bread and vegetables, they ate rabbits and pigeons, large quantities of pork, and the fish and eels with which millponds and other bodies of fresh water were often stocked. The sophisticated, literate world of the cities was distant: few peasant men, and almost no women, received even the elementary education that was becoming more common there. But more and more they became part of a cash economy, selling what they produced to middlemen to feed the hungry cities, and if they lived close enough to them, spinning or doing other jobs for the urban manufacturers in addition to their work in the fields and tending livestock.

TRANSFORMING THE STATE

In diverse ways, the monarchs of the thirteenth and fourteenth centuries set their authority on new foundations. For the first time since the Roman Empire—but in forms that varied from place to place—the state once again became a major factor in the lives of people who had long lived without much interference from central authority.

FRANCE: ROYAL AUTHORITY AND ADMINISTRATION

The French monarchy flourished as never before in this expansive era. Energetic rulers innovated in multiple ways, extending their own powers and the state apparatus that supported them.

PHILIP AUGUSTUS During the reign of Philip Augustus (r. 1180–1223), it seemed that the French monarchy

Peasant Work Peasants perform farm labor in this illustration from an English manuscript (ca. 1300). One worker wields a sickle for cutting grain, while another—wearing a white cloth, perhaps for protection—shoos bees away from their hive.

REGULATING PROSTITUTION IN MARSEILLES

Many medieval secular and religious authorities demonstrated a distinctly ambivalent attitude toward prostitution. Though they often condemned prostitution's sinfulness and potential for social disturbance, they also tolerated or even accepted it as a practical way to channel the sexual urges of unmarried men. The French king Louis IX issued an edict in 1254 that condemned prostitution as a threat to public morality and ordered prostitutes to be expelled from the towns. However, based on later municipal legislation on prostitution and Louis IX's decision to repeal his edict in 1256, we can infer that such actions were unsuccessful. The statutes of Marseilles, revised between 1253 and 1257, provide the following restrictions on what prostitutes could wear and where they could work, as well as some general principles for the regulation of prostitution.

With the present statute we ordain that no public prostitute shall dare or be able to wear any clothing dyed with grana,[1] or furs of vair,[2] either grey squirrel or ermine, nor any mantle except one made of striped cloth, or with bars of another cloth; however, she may wear a shoulder cape dyed with grana if she wishes. And if any prostitute should rashly dare to go against this statute in any way, then the court is held to take away from her 60 sous royaux coronats for every time that she crosses it. And if she cannot provide this, she should be publicly beaten through the city of Marseille; for we judge that infamous and notorious women ought to be separated from chaste ones. A public prostitute is understood to be a woman who has intercourse publicly in a brothel or whorehouse, or who offers herself publicly to make a profit, or to whose house two or more men come publicly as if to a public woman, either by day or by night, with the intention or for the sake or reason of gratifying their lust or passion with her.

We decree accordingly that henceforth no prostitutes should dare or ought to make a house or residence, even a modest one, anywhere near the monastery of St. Sauveur of Marseille…nor around the church of Notre Dame des Accoules, from the hills of the mill-houses and the meat-market of the Towers, as far as it extends through the butchers' quarter up to the house of Bernard Bonaffossi. …And within one month after the proclamation of this Chapter all the said prostitutes shall be completely removed and expelled from the said places by the judgment of the honest men of the neighbourhoods, with whom it ought to rest [to judge] whether the said women who will have been accused of this are prostitutes or not, or also whether they should be expelled.

Moreover, we decree that the Court of Marseille should be held to expel all prostitutes who linger among the honest and respectable men of Marseille at the request of those honest men who are henceforth aggrieved.

[1]grana: an insect-based red dye
[2]vair: bluish-gray fur used to trim garments

Source: Translation by Kirsten Schut.

QUESTIONS FOR ANALYSIS

1. How would you characterize the basic attitude of civic authorities in Marseilles toward prostitution?
2. Why was prostitution prohibited in specific areas of the city?
3. What responsibilities does the statute assign to men and women in the regulation of prostitution?

would carry all before it. After losing the kingdom's official account books, which the court normally carried with it, on the field of battle, Philip Augustus decided that he needed a permanent base, and established Paris as the capital of his realm. He also defeated King John of England (r. 1199–1216) and won back the Norman lands that the kings of England had governed, by dynastic right, since the conquest of 1066. Working with the existing apparatus of officials, especially the regionally based judicial officers called bailiffs, he and his successors did much to unify the many powerful principalities of the French kingdom. The tradition of crusading, which Philip Augustus continued, also strengthened the position of France as the leading monarchy of Europe.

LOUIS IX Philip Augustus's successors—above all Louis IX (r. 1226–1270)—maintained the traditions Philip founded, and elaborated on them. They also went on crusade, even though the costs were enormous and the successes limited: Louis IX saw his army crushed by the Egyptians on his first effort at crusading in 1250, and he died in Tunis on his last one. Yet as the French monarchs organized expedition after expedition, they became increasingly skillful at a wide range of challenging practical tasks. French rulers and their counselors learned how to create and fortify ports, amass provisions for soldiers, and collect as much revenue as possible to support these ventures. Although many groups in France claimed exemption from taxation, the monarchy's jurists used the principles of Roman law to argue that "absolute necessity" and the common good could override these privileges.

ROYAL JUSTICE AND THE PARLEMENT In the realm of justice, in particular, Louis IX advanced beyond any of his predecessors or rivals. The bailiffs, originally jurists sent out to the provinces but now professional administrators appointed by the king, had strengthened the monarchy's ability to claim and defend its rights. In some cases, though, they proved as tenacious in defending the local privileges and customs of their fellow noblemen as in fighting for the prerogatives of the crown. Louis IX—a man so pious that he became a saint after his death—was determined to collect everything that was due the state and willingly entered into conflict with nobles or clerics to do so. But he also had a passion for providing justice to his subjects. He appointed men he could trust—often members of the new orders of mendicant friars, discussed later, who would not be tempted by personal ambition—to make formal inquiries into royal administration in the provinces. He also made himself available—sitting, as legend has it, outdoors, under a great oak at Vincennes, a few miles outside Paris—to hear the appeals of his subjects.

Over time, the French crown developed its own highly professional central law court comprised of jurists who laid down the theoretical basis of royal authority in treatises and imposed it in legal practice. The **Parlement**, as this sovereign court came to be called, became the apex of the French judicial system. It made clear to all that justice, everywhere in France, emanated from royal authority. Though Louis's successors differed from him in many important respects, they continued to assert, as he had, that royal authority was absolute. The king, as they and their jurists insisted, was emperor within his own kingdom: the leader of what French churchmen and writers

described as the most holy nation of France—a unique community, divinely chosen.

ENGLAND: ORIGINS OF REPRESENTATIVE INSTITUTIONS

Although England had developed strong central institutions during the long reign of Henry II in the twelfth century, it began the thirteenth century in a weaker position. Richard the Lionhearted (r. 1189–1199), great fighter that he was, had spent much of his life crusading. John, his brother, who remained in Europe, lost his family's Norman territories to the French.

THE KING AND THE BARONS Worse still, Richard and John had angered the barons of England by infringing on their privileges and by repeatedly imposing the tax known as scutage ("shield duty")—a tax paid by noble vassals in lieu of the forty days of military service that they owed their lord each year—only to spend this revenue on fruitless wars on the Continent. Inspired by rumors of threats to their rights and the precedent of an earlier charter issued by Henry I, the barons rose against John. Henry I had issued formal promises on his accession in 1100 that he would rule by ancient custom, which meant that he would cease charging his barons immense sums when they inherited their estates, and would stop collecting the revenues of churches between the death of a bishop or abbot and the installation of a successor. This charter was basically a dead letter, which Henry had no intention of following. But the barons took it as a model when in 1215, at Runnymede, an area of meadows and ponds by the river Thames twenty miles from London, they forced John to sign the document later known as **Magna Carta**.

MAGNA CARTA The new charter offered several guarantees. The king, in council with his barons, proclaimed that he would maintain the traditional liberties of the Church and the city of London. More important still, he promised to maintain justice throughout his realm, guaranteeing that no one would be deprived of land or goods except by a jury from his county of origin. Magna Carta also stated that "[n]o freeman shall be captured or imprisoned or disseised [unlawfully deprived of real property] or outlawed or exiled or in any way destroyed, nor will we go against him or send against him, except by the lawful judgment of his peers or by the law of the land," and that "[t]o no one will we sell, to no one will we deny or delay right or justice." The king thus bound himself to guarantee justice—not solely, or mainly, as a source of revenue for himself and the crown, but as a duty that he owed his subjects.

These guarantees were originally seen as applying to the nobility: to the barons, who held their estates from the king; and to the knights, who held their estates from the barons. But the English courts gradually applied them more and more widely. Magna Carta made no revolutionary claims. But it specified that if the king needed to ask for an "aid" (a subsidy) for his expenses, he would do so after obtaining "the common counsel of the realm" by summoning the great clerics and barons to meet him. This suggested a new view of the king's rule in England: not as an expression of the ruler's absolute will, but as carried on with the consent and in the interests of his subjects.

Henry III, whose long rule in England (r. 1216–1272) paralleled that of Louis IX in France, struggled endlessly for precedence with his barons. He provoked them into staging a (polite and very English) revolt: they did not depose him but attempted to limit his autonomy by imposing their own controls. Disputes continued, and efforts at mediation by the French king, to whom both sides appealed, failed to prevent civil war. Eventually, in 1265, the forces of Henry's eldest son, Edward, defeated the barons at Evesham in Worcestershire and killed their leader, Simon de Montfort, leaving the kings of England firmly in command.

PARLIAMENTS Yet during and after the decades of debate over privileges, new customs developed in England, some of them inspired by Magna Carta. These defined and strengthened the position of the monarchy by solidifying its connection to the rest of the English people. It became the custom, for example, for the king to make his laws and decisions in the presence of the barons, whom he summoned for that purpose, as he was supposed to do when asking for aids. As time passed, representatives of the knights of the shires (counties) and of the burgesses—free citizens of the boroughs (towns)—were also summoned to these meetings, which came to be called **parliaments** ("talkings together"). Gradually a principle was established: decisions made by this assembly represented the will of the realm as a whole. Whatever the Magna Carta authors had meant, they now seemed to state that when the king spoke in this council, he spoke for all of his subjects.

THE COMMON LAW A remarkable consensus developed also on English law. For all the struggles of the thirteenth century, by the end of it the English king could offer justice in all the counties of England. His justices

King's Council This miniature of a king sitting in council with his bishops and nobles comes from a fourteenth-century English manuscript that outlines the ideal form of parliamentary procedure.

traveled regular circuits to hold court in major towns, and followed the principles of England's distinctive law, which had been developed less by formal legislation than by the decisions of generations of judges. English jurists proudly proclaimed that the **common law** of England was not, and could not be, written down. Like the French, the English saw themselves, by the end of the thirteenth century, as members of a single community—one that stretched across the borders of individual counties, had its own distinctive laws and customs, and supported, served, and claimed justice from a single ruler. Even the sacred monarchy of France did not rest on more solid foundations than the realm of England.

SPAIN: CONSOLIDATING AUTHORITY

Monarchies elsewhere in Europe developed on similar lines. Alfonso IX (r. 1188–1230) of León and Galicia began his reign by summoning representatives of towns to formal meetings. Similar developments took place in

The Reconquista, ca. 1200–1400 In the thirteenth and fourteenth centuries, strong Spanish monarchs consolidated territory and conquered lands previously in Muslim hands. In the first half of the thirteenth century, Ferdinand III of the unified kingdoms of Castile and León led an army southward, winning major battles at Córdoba and Seville and reducing Muslim-controlled territory to a small portion of the southern coast.

Castile, in the north-central region of Spain, and on a larger scale. Ferdinand III (r. 1217–1252) unified the kingdoms of Castile and León and pushed hard against the Muslims, whose Almohad Caliphate was in political crisis. He took city after city, finally conquering Seville, the greatest city in Andalusia, in 1248. The Nazirid dynasty succeeded in founding a new Islamic state, the Emirate of Granada, in 1238. It became an important center of the arts and scholarship, and survived until 1492, but only at the price of accepting the Christian kings of Castile as overlords.

THE CORTES To pay for his military campaigns, Ferdinand needed regular financial help from his subjects. In the Spanish kingdoms, as in England, it became normal for the king to summon high-ranking clerics, noblemen, and representatives of the towns to meetings, known as *cortes* ("courts"), which took place every two to four years. The king would typically ask for a subsidy, and the members of the Cortes would reply by asking for

redress of their grievances (the Catalans refused to grant subsidies until the king had replied to their demands). Gradually, the Cortes developed a sense of responsibility not only for taxation, but also for the general welfare of their realm.

ALFONSO X The Castilian king Alfonso X (r. 1252–1284), long known as Alfonso the Wise, was a descendant of the German Hohenstaufen family that had fought for generations to enlarge and strengthen the Holy Roman Empire. Alfonso himself had aspired to become Holy Roman emperor, but at home he concentrated on Spanish matters. At first, Alfonso enlisted Jews and Muslims, as well as Christians, in his service; later he turned against the Jews. But he worked consistently to make the crown of Castile the center of a unified community. Like Louis IX and Henry III, he emphasized the importance of providing justice to his subjects. At his command, jurists compiled a massive legal code in Spanish, the Siete Partidas. Far earlier than in other parts of Europe, it became normal in Castile and elsewhere in Spain to formulate legal documents in Spanish rather than Latin. Alfonso also encouraged the formation of the Mesta, a large association of sheepherders who began to compete against producers of wool elsewhere. He also placed special importance—more than any of his royal rivals—on having up-to-date Islamic scientific work translated from Arabic into both Latin and Spanish.

Alfonso's Translators The Spanish king Alfonso X formally supported efforts to translate Arabic texts into Latin and Spanish, as conveyed by this illustration from a thirteenth-century manuscript showing the king flanked by his translators at court.

THE HOLY ROMAN EMPIRE: THE RULE OF FREDERICK II

In at least one case—that of the Holy Roman Empire—efforts to centralize authority proved less successful. Emperor Frederick II (r. 1220–1250), the last truly powerful member of the Hohenstaufen dynasty, proved to be a brilliant military leader. He regrouped the forces of the empire and asserted his power against the papacy and all other opponents. But his advances for the empire were not lasting.

A CAPABLE RULER Despite papal denunciations of his impiety and disobedience, Frederick II crusaded more successfully than most of his rivals, and in 1229 he managed to negotiate a return of Jerusalem to Christendom. (However, the city proved indefensible, so this restoration was temporary.) In the early part of Frederick's reign he also defeated a coalition of the most powerful northern Italian states, and sank the vessels of many of the church officials traveling to Rome to attend a council called against him. His court at Palermo became a center of poetry, classicizing art (his mint issued gold coins that represented him as a new Augustus), and intellectual inquiry: legend held that in order to find out if the soul really existed, Frederick ordered men to be nailed into barrels, which were opened after they died to see if they contained anything besides the corpses.

In fact, Frederick was not a freethinker but a deeply curious individual schooled in the philosophy of Aristotle. Documents show that he sent philosophical inquiries about the structure of the universe to Muslim thinkers around the Mediterranean as well as to his own court astrologer. He also showed an open mind—as well as an acute sense of his own advantage—in his response to an accusation that Jews in one imperial state had carried out the ritual murder of a Christian child. Frederick asked kings elsewhere in Christendom to send him Jewish converts who could explain whether the accusation was justified. He learned from two English converts that Jews not only did not practice but also abhorred human sacrifice. In 1236 he declared the accusations false, but also asserted the special status of the Jews as "serfs of our chamber." Frederick offered the Jews protection, but also insisted on his own rights as their exclusive lord—including the right to draw on them for financial help.

THE CONSTITUTIONS OF MELFI Frederick concentrated much of his effort on building a state in Sicily,

outside the traditional territories of the empire, but even there much of what he did followed precedents established elsewhere. He insisted on his absolute right as monarch to frame the laws. Yet the legal code that he issued in 1231, the Constitutions of Melfi, included innovations. Frederick insisted, for example, that no judge should hold office in a territory in which he held estates—a new principle, and one that suggests Frederick hoped to rely on professional officials. In the end, though, his university in Palermo developed too slowly, and he had to rely on local nobles to fill positions in the state. When he promised his subjects rapid justice and prohibited Christians from moneylending, he followed the same paths as contemporaries such as King John of England.

EMPIRE IN DECLINE To retain the loyalty of as many of the German princes as possible, Frederick gave them so much freedom that they dominated the core imperial territories in Germany. His own successes terrified neighboring powers in Italy and strengthened the hand of the papacy. After he died, it did not take long for his enemies to overcome his family. With the death of Conradin of Hohenstaufen in 1268, the power of the Holy Roman emperors was decisively broken, as their long contest with the papacy ended in victory for the Church.

TRANSFORMING THE CHURCH

Paradoxically, the greatest monarchy of all—and the one that played a crucial role in inducing subjects to look to their secular rulers for justice—was the Church. By the end of the twelfth century, as we have seen, the papacy had established itself as the center of a vast web of institutions—cathedrals and monasteries, schools and local churches. Although the heads of these institutions were often appointed by monarchs or lords, in theory the vast realm of the Church was ruled from Rome by the popes, with the help of the College of Cardinals. The popes claimed the right to appoint bishops to govern the dioceses from their cathedrals, and to appoint the heads of the great monastic houses. The popes also asserted their rights to payments from the bishops' dioceses and from monasteries, in return for appointing new heads. By the beginning of the thirteenth century, the canon law of the Church had become so well established that it was taught together with Roman law in university faculties of law. Many students became "doctors of both laws" so that they could practice in state and clerical courts. Universal in reach, wealthy in influence as well as money, and with social strength based on a carefully woven web of legal principles, the Church saw itself as rivaling the monarchies of France and England in power.

POPE INNOCENT AND THE FOURTH LATERAN COUNCIL

In one crucial element of practice, the Church deliberately refused to rival those monarchies. The hierarchy was now staffed, in its upper ranks, with men who had studied theology and canon law, many of whom looked back to the enthusiastic years of the Gregorian Reform movement of the eleventh century. With the accession to the papacy in 1198 of Lothario Segni, who became **Pope Innocent III** (d. 1216), a great scholar and thinker inspired by the Gregorian reformers occupied the summit of the system.

An Italian nobleman who had studied theology in Paris, Innocent saw humankind as the children of Adam and Eve, conceived in sin and in desperate need of the salvation that only the Church could extend: "Man has been formed of dust, clay, ashes, and, a thing far more vile, of the filthy sperm. Man has been conceived in the desire of the flesh, in the heat of sensual lust, in the foul stench of wantonness. He was born to labor, to fear, to suffering, and, most miserable of all, to death." Only the Church could draw on its treasury of grace to save such vile creatures from themselves. Innocent fought to reform the Church so that it could reach these goals throughout his reign, which climaxed in the **Fourth Lateran Council** of 1215. The assembled clerics laid down strong principles

Pope Innocent III A striking fresco from a church in Italy, painted shortly after Innocent's death in 1216, gives some indication of the pope's authority. Innocent used his power to reform the Church, suppress heresy, and call for new crusades.

regarding the lives of the clergy, their relation to laypeople, and the Church's role in the world.

THE ORDEAL AND THE CHURCH Pope Innocent believed that to achieve its sacred task, the Church must assert its sovereign independence from the world. For centuries, European monarchs considered themselves, in terms that went back to antiquity, divinely anointed rulers. This meant not only that they often claimed the right to appoint Church officials but also that they saw their own function as givers of justice in divine terms. In the eleventh and twelfth centuries, royal judges often faced problems that they could not resolve: how to fix responsibility for crimes that had no reliable witnesses, or how to settle civil complaints in which each side claimed to be in the right. Like the Carolingians before them, the royal judges settled such problems by offering the accused, or both parties in a dispute, the chance to swear an oath to their veracity and undertake an ordeal to prove it. (The parties could also appoint champions to undertake ordeals in their place.) Trial by ordeal continued to be a widespread practice throughout the twelfth century, although in England the rise of the jury system in criminal and civil law had already challenged and, to some extent, replaced it.

Ordeals ran from "taking the cross" (holding one's arms out in the form of a cross until it became impossible to hold them up; the party who collapsed first would be seen to be in the wrong) to the more notorious ordeals by fire and water. In the first, the person accused or demanding rights, or the appointed champion, would reach into a cauldron of boiling water to extract a ring or another object, carry hot iron for several paces, or walk across red-hot iron plates. The singed hand or foot would be bandaged for three days. If there was no sign of infection when the limb was unwrapped, the accusation was refuted or the oath confirmed. In the other, those who sank when immersed in a pool of water were held to be telling the truth, since the water accepted them.

These ordeals belonged to secular government, but priests had always taken part, and were paid fees for doing so. Before the accused grasped the hot iron, for example, the priest addressed God, asking that he "bless and sanctify this fiery iron, which is used in the just examination of doubtful issues." In the twelfth century—that great age of distinctions and law codes—more than one thinker had raised doubts about ordeals. The French theologian Peter the Chanter, for example, worried that the ordeal by hot iron tested not guilt or innocence but the thickness of the calluses on the hand and the heat of the metal.

Trial by Ordeal This page from a mid-fourteenth-century German law book illustrates the concept of the ordeal. One man stirs a cauldron of boiling water for an ordeal by fire, while another looks on, either participating in the preparations or getting ready to plunge his hand into the water. At left a man bears a sword and shield, perhaps readying for a trial by combat.

Pope Innocent finally transformed these scattered criticisms into firm legislation—not because he, or anyone else, suddenly decided that God never intervened in everyday life, but because he thought it vital to distinguish clergy from laity, and Church authority from secular. Secular authorities shed blood. Clerics, the Fourth Lateran Council decreed, must not do so. They were forbidden not only to do violence to others themselves, or to be present when blood was shed, but also to take part in ordeals. The decree established as a principle that the Church should not involve itself in purely worldly matters. For all its wealth and influence, the Church now also stood for a powerful distinction: the firm dividing line between that which belonged to Caesar and that which belonged to God.

TORTURE AND PROOF

One consequence of the Fourth Lateran Council's decree was to reinforce—even more than royal action had already done—the power of the secular state. The withdrawal of clerical participation, accompanied by the creation of courts and the provision of judges, made it clear that justice, in this world, was a secular matter, and that subjects must look to the state for it.

Sadly, though, this did not make trials more humane. For centuries in Continental Europe it became standard, following the precedents in Roman law, to employ a formal system of "inquisition" (inquiry by torture) to determine the accused's guilt or innocence when a confession or eyewitness testimony was lacking. The wisest rulers, from Frederick II to Alfonso X, agreed that this was the best method. In England, however, only those suspected of treason could be legally tortured. Suspects who refused to plead and accept the judgment of a jury could be subjected to the application of weights until they died or confessed. Even now, centuries after torture was abolished, Continental jurisprudence does not make the same presumption of innocence that the Anglo-American tradition does, and, especially in France, it relies on formal inquiry led by officials—a long-term consequence of the decisions made in the thirteenth century by a powerful pope and his contemporaries.

REFORMING CHRISTIANITY

The ordeal was not the only practice that Pope Innocent set out to transform. The Fourth Lateran Council's decrees applied broadly to the organization of the Church and deeply to the intimate lives of clergy and laypeople. To ensure that the Church administered the true Christian message to its flock, the council held every bishop responsible for holding synods ("gatherings") of his clergy, visiting religious houses, and combating **heresy**. Bishops who could not preach effectively must appoint preachers who would regularly address their congregations. Monastic orders and provinces of the Church (groups of diocese) were instructed to hold regular meetings and follow orthodox doctrines and proper procedures.

In keeping with Innocent's beliefs about the sinfulness of the flesh, the council insisted that clerics must be celibate. This principle, rooted in decrees from councils of the Roman period, had fallen away after the collapse of the Carolingian Empire. The Gregorian reformers had tried to restore celibacy, demanding that married priests separate from their wives. They encountered widespread, fierce resistance. Those who refused to divest themselves of families were excommunicated. The council of 1215 condemned priests, monks, and nuns who broke their vows—who failed to wear their proper habits, engaged in gluttony or sexual intercourse, watched mimes and entertainers, or went to taverns (except when on long journeys). In 1239, the council's decree on celibacy was reconfirmed on papal authority—strong evidence that resistance continued.

Faced with individuals such as Abelard and Héloïse, who asserted their passions even when laws or rules condemned them, the council took aim at the full-scale transformation of every Christian's life through the relationship between ordinary priests and their congregations. As we have seen, the Church had developed the practice of private confession in the early Middle Ages, when the first manuals were written to guide confessors. Now the practice was made mandatory. Every adult Christian must

Life in the Church In three of the panels from a late-thirteenth-century French manuscript, a nun prays before an altar with an image of Christ or one of the saints. At top left, a nun kneels to make confession—a mandatory practice after the Fourth Lateran Council of 1215—to a Dominican friar, who makes the sign of the cross over her in absolution.

confess his or her sins at least once a year, and receive the Eucharist at least annually (at Easter), or face excommunication and denial of Christian burial. And every priest must be able to perform the Mass, administer the sacraments, and serve as a sensitive, sympathetic, and discreet spiritual adviser who could treat spiritual wounds just as a skilled doctor would treat physical ones. Priests could seek advice in difficult cases, but they must never reveal the identities of those they served. In theory, at least, the confessional had been sealed and made private, though it would take centuries to realize a high level of consistency in clerical practice.

REVIVING THE CRUSADES

Pope Innocent passionately believed that Christians should hold and guard the places where Jesus had lived and suffered. In 1187, as we have seen, Saladin (Salah al-Din Yusuf ibn Ayyub) had defeated the Christians in the battle of Hattin, opening the way for the Muslim reconquest of Palestine. Innocent was horrified. More dramatically—and more systematically—than any of his predecessors, he made crusading a central priority of the Church. And as he did so, he reinserted the Church into political and military life with a vengeance by insisting that the Church, as the superior entity, should direct the policies of secular states, wherever necessary. At the very start of his papacy in 1198, Innocent issued a public statement calling for a new crusade. He claimed that Christ himself called for war against the Muslims, whose capture of faithful Christians reenacted the injury that the Jews had inflicted on the Savior when they crucified him.

The early crusades had suffered from the disunity of the Christian powers and from a lack of funds. So Innocent mobilized the enormous wealth of the Church to support a holy war. Every cleric in Christendom, he pronounced, must contribute one-fortieth of his income to a special tax to support the new crusade. His example had long-lasting impact. The Fourth Lateran Council promulgated a new crusading tax in 1215. Soon a comprehensive system of clerical taxation was built into the structure of the Catholic Church. In 1274, Pope Gregory X would divide all of Christendom into twenty-six "collectorates," or tax districts. Though the Church had washed its hands of Christian blood, it had also become a state in a new sense. If it could not wage war on its own, it could declare war and finance it.

THE LATER CRUSADES (1202–1272)

The first result of Pope Innocent's decision—the Fourth Crusade of 1202–4—was a debacle. To cross the Mediterranean, the crusaders made an arrangement with Venice, which promised to build, crew, and provision enough ships to carry 35,000 men, in return for a substantial payment and a half share in booty from any conquests that the crusade accomplished. Enrico Dandolo (ca. 1107–1205), the aged but sharp-witted Venetian doge, bargained with the crusaders to start by attacking Egypt as the more strategic target, rather than Palestine. The crusaders' envoys agreed.

But the necessary compromises went much further. The crusaders appeared in smaller numbers and with less cash than had been promised. Led by Dandolo, the Venetians conveyed them, in the first instance, to Zara, a Christian city on the Adriatic coast of what is now Croatia, which had recently rebelled against Venetian control, ironically placing itself under the lordship of the pope. Despite papal condemnations and protests from some of the crusaders themselves, the Christian army began its efforts in November 1202 by besieging and taking a

Routes of the Crusades
→ Fourth Crusade, 1202–1204
→ Fifth Crusade, 1217–1221, and
   Sixth Crusade, 1228–1229
→ Seventh Crusade, 1248–1254, and
   Eighth Crusade, 1270–1272
→ Albigensian Crusade, 1209–1229
✕ Battle

Catholic territory
Orthodox territory
Other Christian
Albigensian sect
Muslim territory
Other religion or pagan areas
Boundaries, ca. 1270

The Later Crusades, 1202–1272 Pope Innocent III renewed calls for holy war, though the ventures that followed were largely unsuccessful. The crusaders who crossed the Mediterranean and invaded Constantinople and Jerusalem did not make any lasting territorial gains, though they fought several battles in the eastern Mediterranean. Of greater consequence, however, was the crusade against the Albigensian Cathars in southern France, which established a precedent of war against heretics.

Christian city. Innocent denounced them, hurling all his metaphors into one basket: "Behold, your gold has turned into base metal and your silver has almost completely rusted since, departing from the purity of your plan and turning aside from the path onto the impassable road, you have, so to speak, withdrawn your hand from the plough." Innocent's words here had no immediate practical effect. In fact, the Venetians took the crusaders not to Egypt or Jerusalem but to Constantinople, capital of the Byzantine Empire and still the richest city in the Christian world. Amid riots by the Byzantine inhabitants, in 1204 the crusaders attacked the ancient city, managed to break through the walls, and pillaged Constantinople with terrible brutality. A quarter of the booty went to the treasury

of the great Venetian basilica of San Marco. No effort was made to invade Muslim lands or to recover Jerusalem.

Furious, but helpless to intervene, Pope Innocent eventually absolved the crusaders and accepted what they had done. Nonetheless, he continued to see holy war as a central purpose of the Church. At the end of his pontificate, the Fourth Lateran Council issued another call for a crusade. The opponent was the Ayyubid dynasty founded by Saladin, who had divided his territories among his sons after his death in 1193. This Fifth Crusade, chiefly made up of armies from the Holy Roman Empire, Flanders, and Hungary, took a Nile Delta port, Damietta, in 1219, but two years later the crusaders accepted a peace offer and left Egypt in Muslim hands.

In 1228 Holy Roman Emperor Frederick II led another crusade (the sixth), first to Cyprus and then to Palestine. He bargained with the Muslims, promising to give them freedom of worship, and regained Christian control over Jerusalem, Bethlehem, and Nazareth. Energetic diplomacy on the part of the crusader Theobald, Count of Champagne (1201–1253), reestablished the kingdom of Jerusalem after years of struggle.

After Muslim forces retook Jerusalem in 1244, the French monarch, Louis IX, mounted the Seventh Crusade. His preparations were systematic and effective. He gathered a massive army, built a special port near Marseilles, and gathered provisions and men before embarking. After spending time in Cyprus, where he negotiated with other powers, he sailed to Egypt and recaptured Damietta in 1249. But the Egyptians rallied to defeat Louis's main army, and a new sultan, Turanshah, captured Louis in 1250. His release cost an enormous ransom. Twenty years later, when Louis gathered a second massive force for the Eighth Crusade, he set out to establish a base in Tunis. But disease ravaged his army, and he himself died of "flux." The crusade was abandoned. When Prince Edward of England (son of Henry III) abandoned a campaign to shore up Christian rule in Palestine and returned to Europe in 1272 to be crowned Edward I (r. 1272–1307), it put an end to the crusading efforts of the thirteenth century. Acre, the last major Christian base in Palestine, fell to the Mamluk Sultan Kahlil (r. 1290–1293) in 1291.

During the course of the thirteenth and fourteenth centuries, the crusade would become a normal part of papal policy. Long before, Augustine had argued that a truly Christian ruler would use force to make heretics convert to Christianity. Now, orthodox doctrine became even harder. Christ, a great canon lawyer explained, had come into the world to bring sinners to repentance. The war against heretics—and any others whose resistance to the Church put the salvation of others at risk—was Christ's cause. Popes declared crusades against Frederick II; against a Roman noble family, the Colonna, that politically opposed the family of Pope Boniface VIII; and even against a company of German mercenaries, who were welcomed back to papal service as soon as conditions changed. Holy war had become a standard—if not a central—part of the Church's portfolio of activities.

THE CHURCH AND THE URBAN POOR

When Pope Innocent III and his successors trimmed the sails of the great ship of the papacy and tried to control its speed and direction more precisely, they found that they confronted a vast range of new problems for which war could be, at most, part of the solution.

ECONOMIC PROBLEMS AND SOCIAL UNREST

Growing populations and fluctuations in commercial activity posed problems that even the newly professional city governments could not keep up with. Shifts in patterns of trade and manufacture could devastate an industry and the communities that depended on it, and suffering, in turn, led to civil violence. When the textile entrepreneurs of Flanders pressed their workers to accept lower wages, strikes broke out. The first one on record took place in Douai in 1245. A quarter century later, the weavers and fullers of Ghent left their city en masse, moving to Brabant, a neighboring duchy of the Holy Roman Empire. Sometimes, as in this case, workers could take their skills and move to cities that still offered opportunity. In 1271, Henry III of England officially welcomed any textile workers who wished to come to England. Often, though, violence broke out between the craftsmen who made cloth and cut stone and their masters.

More generally, too, living conditions in the biggest cities worsened. Coal fires, chemical waste from the treatment of metal, cloth, and leather, and the vast quantities of body parts and ordure created by the thousands of animals needed to feed an urban population polluted the environment. So did the layers of excrement dropped by animals on dirt streets—and the further quantities of human excrement produced in each house, often from outside privies. Abandoned babies needed to be looked after or face immediate death. Thousands of city dwellers were undernourished.

On the land, an ever-growing rural population divided farms until the small plots could no longer support a family. In parts of Italy in the later thirteenth and early fourteenth centuries, farmers pushed cultivation to altitudes where agriculture could not be sustained. Landlords, themselves squeezed by inflation, demanded more money and work from tenants who had paid to free themselves. Peasant revolts like that of the *pastoureaux* (shepherds), which broke out in 1253 in France, may not have threatened the existing order, but they resulted in the deaths of officials and in frightening if temporary disorder.

NEW RELIGIOUS ORDERS: DOMINICANS AND FRANCISCANS As hunger and diseases spread—especially leprosy, the disfiguring, disabling illness that became endemic in medieval Europe—the orderly sermons offered in the cathedrals provided little practical help. Nor

Saint Francis Francis's poverty and humility infuse these scenes from an Italian church fresco, probably painted soon after his death. At top, barefoot and clad in a simple robe, he washes the feet of the poor in imitation of Jesus. The bottom image shows him founding a monastery.

Both men sought a new model of the religious life. Dominic, worried by the spread of heresy, found the Church's efforts to combat it counterproductive. He insisted that clerics show true dedication and constant self-discipline. As he explained in a letter to a community of nuns in Madrid, "From now on I want silence to be kept in the forbidden places, the refectory, the dormitory, and the oratory, and your law to be observed in all other matters. . . . Avoid talking idly to one another. Let not your time be wasted in conversation." Francis, a gentle soul whose belief in the kinship of all creatures emerges clearly from his hymns to Brother Sun and Sister Moon, was horrified by the suffering of the poor in cities like his own Assisi, a center of cloth manufacture in central Italy.

Both men gathered followers. And despite papal reluctance to see new orders founded, both received permission to create what rapidly became the most successful religious orders of the time. Like the members of existing orders, Dominicans and Franciscans felt a profound vocation for the religious life, and after spending time as novices, took vows of poverty, chastity, and obedience. Unlike monks, however, the friars, as they were called, did not pursue their salvation in the remote and quiet places of the world. Instead, they confronted the worst problems head on. **Dominicans**, who specialized in preaching orthodox

did the prayers offered up for all Christian souls in the aristocratic monasteries do much to console the urban poor. As in the past, the Church proved capable of responding to these challenges. Individuals appeared with the insight and energy to create institutions and offer solutions.

The religious innovators of the early thirteenth century were a Spaniard and an Italian: Dominic de Guzmán (1170–1221), who became Saint Dominic, and Giovanni Francesco di Bernardone (ca. 1182–1226), who became Saint Francis. Both devoted themselves to the Church, Dominic from early youth and Francis after long, bitter struggles with his merchant father, who wanted him to pursue profit. Both were ascetics: as a student, Dominic sold his books and clothes to help the victims of a plague. Francis insisted that his followers accept Jesus's words literally and not prepare at all for the next day. When he found himself locked out in a storm with nothing to eat, Francis rejoiced.

Saint Dominic Illustrations from a fifteenth-century French history display Dominic's piety. Above, the poor receive charity; below, Dominic leads a group of people in the burning of heretical texts. Dominic's own book does not burn in the flames, proving that it alone is true.

Catholic doctrine, traveled the roads of Europe looking for people who needed instruction and heretics who had to be defeated in debate. Franciscans, hoping to care for those whom the rest of society rejected, preached and built hospitals in the cities. Turning away from the models of Christian life that had been most popular in recent times, Francis instructed his followers to imitate Christ and Mary—to be as poor as the first Christians depicted in the Gospels. Both orders grew, as the Cistercians had a century before, with startling speed. Saint Clare (1194–1253), an Italian noblewoman inspired by Francis's teaching, created a new order for women. She drew up their rule, the first composed by a woman, and they became the second **Franciscan Order**.

THE LEARNING OF THE FRIARS

Originally, Francis had planned that he and his followers would live on whatever Christians happened to give them. One of the terms for the new friars, *mendicants*, literally means "those who beg." Over time, Franciscans as well as Dominicans found themselves in need of stable bases where they could carry out their tasks, train their novices, and receive gifts and legacies from grateful Christians. As preachers, moreover, members of both orders needed to devote years to the study of formal theology. Soon Dominican and Franciscan study houses came into being in Paris, Oxford, and other centers of theological study. They built up libraries of theological textbooks and collections of examples for use in preaching.

In their commitment to serving the practical needs of their fellow Christians, the mendicants adopted innovative positions: they saw that money was vital to the urban economy and allowed the charging of interest. They also developed their own highly practical style of book production, in which tables of contents and indexes allowed rapid consultation. These thirteenth-century friars invented the modern reference book.

HERETICS: ENEMIES OF THE CHURCH

European society—at least as viewed from the Roman citadel of the Church—seemed to be not only creating new wealth and perpetrating new injustices but also spawning new commercial values and new ideas even about basic Christian doctrines. Since the Schism of 1054, the formal opponents of Catholic teaching had been the theologians of Byzantium—or so the Catholic theologians held. Now, eloquent teachers within the walls of Latin Europe were devising new understandings of Christ's message, seducing the faithful away from orthodoxy, and leading them into religious error. Over the centuries, clerics and rulers had stumbled, repeatedly, on individuals and small groups who dissented from standard teachings. Often these dissenters claimed to follow Christ in rejecting the wealth and power of the institutional Church. Most of them were treated fairly gently, unless—like Arnold of Brescia (ca. 1090–1155), who led a rebellion against the popes at Rome in the middle of the twelfth century—they were clearly dangerous. But by the late twelfth and thirteenth centuries, heretics were becoming more numerous, more aggressive, and in some cases more powerful than ever before.

WALDENSIANS Heresy could begin inconspicuously, and even unintentionally. Around 1173 a merchant named Waldes in the French city of Lyon heard a minstrel sing about a saint who gave away his wealth and became a

Waldensians This anti-Waldensian tract (ca. 1460) depicts members of the group engaged in the alleged rite of kissing the rear of a goat during a meeting—a heretical act of idolatry. Demons and witches fly above the scene, cementing the Waldensians' link to Satan.

beggar. Stunned, he consulted a theologian, who told him what Jesus had said to a rich man in the Gospel of Matthew: "If you wish to be perfect, go and sell what you have, and give it to the poor . . . and follow me." Waldes decided to become a beggar himself, but he also paid priests to translate more of the Bible from Latin, and to preach. Soon he found followers, male and female, who begged their way through the world. The Waldensians' ostentatious poverty irritated traditional clerics, who denied them permission to teach. Like the ancient Donatists, the Waldensians came to feel contempt for ordinary priests, who, they thought, betrayed their own callings. Soon they challenged central Roman doctrines—for example, the existence of purgatory and the need for prayers for the dead. Waldensians held that women as well as men could serve as priests. And they developed their own hierarchy of priests and bishops.

The new church spread from southern France and the Piedmont region of Italy to Bohemia. Savage persecution wiped out Waldensians in most cities, though they survived in mountain valleys and isolated farming communities. As their case makes clear, even brief exposure to the raw text of the Gospels, with their vision of a religion that refused wealth and power, could start Christians on a path that led to radical dissidence. In the literate, mobile world of the late twelfth and thirteenth centuries, such exposure was common, and the results frightened the authorities.

CATHARS One group in particular, the **Cathars**, posed a danger that alarmed Church authorities, including Pope Innocent III. Unlike the Waldensians, they may have been inspired by missionaries from outside western Europe—from the Eastern Orthodox world, where dualist heretics had begun to develop their own theology and liturgy in the tenth century in Bulgaria, and carried their views to Constantinople and beyond. The numbers of Cathars never approached those of orthodox Catholics, and their theology was never so firmly and fully developed. Yet by the second half of the twelfth century, groups of Cathars were spreading in economically advanced areas such as Flanders, Champagne, and northern Italy, while others were moving into the Languedoc, an area in southern France where royal control was hard to exercise. Fiercely ascetic, they appealed to Christians from all levels of society, from nobles and wealthy merchants to peasants and poor laborers. The contrast between their poverty and purity and the wealth of the clerical establishment probably lay at the core of their appeal.

Cathar doctrines were not uniform, but they were

Albigensian Crusade This illustration from a French history (ca. 1335) depicts Pope Innocent III excommunicating the Albigensians, and crusading knights attacking them.

definitely unorthodox. Catholics who followed standard teachings believed in one omnipotent God and the Trinity. Cathars—who also saw themselves as Christians—embraced dualism. They envisioned the universe as a battlefield on which a good and an evil power, evenly matched, fought for supremacy. Whereas Catholics admitted that the material world was the domain of sin, Cathars denounced it as wholly evil, the creation of Satan. And whereas Catholics who decided to pursue holiness renounced marriage, Cathars renounced it entirely. They rejected the world of matter as evil and saw it as a sin to bring more souls into its contamination.

Pope Innocent III, the great defender of the Church, set out in the 1190s to attack the Cathars. But his efforts were largely unsuccessful, and his senior representative, who excommunicated the Cathar count of Toulouse in 1207, was murdered. In 1209, Innocent declared a crusade against the Cathars, also called Albigensians after their place of origin, the wealthy city of Albi in southern France. (See the map on page 307.) A massive army—with 500 knights from France alone—took the cross and marched south to besiege Cathar strongholds. At the small hilltop city of Béziers, crusaders asked the pope's representative how they could tell Cathars from Catholics. "Kill them all," he answered. "God will know his own." The crusaders massacred everyone they found, and those who had taken refuge in the cathedral died when it burned and collapsed on them. The war was waged with great cruelty, and even after it ended, continued inquisitions traced networks of Cathar believers and stamped out their safe houses and hiding places. Royal power and orthodox Catholic teaching were thus firmly established throughout southern France.

THOMAS AQUINAS: FRAMING ORTHODOXY

Confronted by heretics at home; by the Jews, who still inhabited most parts of Christian Europe; and by the Muslims, who threatened Christian pilgrims and traders throughout the Mediterranean, the mendicant orders raised intellectual bulwarks to protect the Church. **Thomas Aquinas** (1225–1274), an Italian Dominican who studied and taught theology at Paris, was a passionate believer in the order of the universe and the power of reason to master it. He used the best tools of the ancients—such as Aristotle's logic—to show that even they had been wrong on vital points where Christian teaching was right.

Thomas Aquinas A fourteenth-century fresco from an Italian church portrays Thomas, dressed in his Dominican habit, as a teacher of high stature. He holds open a book while the young monks sitting at his feet copy his teachings.

Aquinas's enterprise built on precedents set in previous centuries, but also went far beyond them. Whereas Abelard had collected opinions and raised questions, Aquinas developed a coherent structure of doctrines, argued point by point—and thus gave the definitive form to what has since been known as scholastic theology. In every case, he ensured that his arguments were free of errors and omissions by first assuming the negative of what he planned to prove and then disproving it. His proofs of the existence of God, for example, began with the statement that there is no God, followed by a cogent refutation of it. Only after Aquinas had stated and refuted the relevant errors did he set out to prove what he meant to prove. He worked with beautiful lucidity from assumptions that he and his pupils considered as solid as the structure of the Notre-Dame Cathedral. Many of these assumptions came from Aristotle and his commentators: for example, that all beings in the universe are ordered in a hierarchy, each at its own distinctive level, and that all things remain at rest unless they are set in motion by an outside cause. Yet Aquinas used these materials to support Christian arguments that Aristotle would have rejected: for example, the thesis that the universe had not existed forever.

Scholastic theology, which Aquinas and other university teachers developed to an extraordinary pitch of elegance and sophistication, became a specialty of the mendicants, and a natural candidate for their favorite style of book production. Not everyone in authority accepted Aquinas's conviction that reason, at its ancient best, could be relied on to support revelation: in 1277, the archbishop of Paris actually prohibited the study of Aristotle in the schools. Over time, however, formal argument based on Aristotelian logic—and on later elaborations of it, crafted by brilliant logicians—established itself as the core of Christian theology.

INQUISITIONS: ROOTING OUT HERESY

A coherent theology was necessary if the heretics were to be defeated, but it was certainly not sufficient. Dominicans and Franciscans did not confine themselves to formal debates in universities. Once trained, they went out into the field. They accompanied the crusaders into Languedoc to defeat the Cathars, and as their expertise in the detection and refutation of heresies won recognition, they moved into other areas as well. From the 1230s on, Gregory IX and later popes began to appoint Dominicans as inquisitors. They were not members of a single permanent office, for no permanent Inquisition existed in the

Middle Ages, but specialists given authority to hold an **inquisition**—that is, to inquire into the spread of heresy in a given diocese, acting independently of the local bishop if necessary.

There were never many Dominican inquisitors, and they did not cast the chilling shadow across high medieval society that later commentators have suggested. But they did become experts at finding, interrogating, and forcing confessions from those suspected of heresy. They even drew up handbooks for their colleagues. These works assumed that those interrogated were guilty, offered useful hints on how to confuse them and trip them up, and held—as those who persecute others so often do—that the imprisoned heretics were the true criminals.

Systematic, tireless interrogation broke many suspected Cathars. But in more difficult cases, torture—the standard tool of inquiry in the world of civil crime, once the ordeal was abolished—offered vital help. The inquisitors worked more carefully, and with more respect for procedure and the spiritual needs of those they investigated, than any secular court. But at times—as in Toulouse in 1247–48, when inquisitors interrogated almost 5,500 suspects—they tore to shreds the fabric of the societies that they meant to save. Most problematic of all was the vision of heresy that they created. Inquisitors treated heretics as if they were their fellow mendicants—methodical theologians who drew their ideas from authoritative texts—rather than a cross section of a complex society influenced by sermons and rumors, friends and lovers.

THE SPREAD OF PERSECUTION: ATTACKS ON THE JEWS

The drive against heretics and other enemies of Christian belief and society hardened attitudes against non-Christians as well. From the period of the First Crusade on, many Christians had come to view Jews with distaste, and sometimes charged them with the ritual murder of Christian children. In the late twelfth and thirteenth centuries, the pressures that Christians exerted on Jews grew heavier. Rulers sometimes protected Jews, partly or wholly to assess taxes on them, but such benevolence was not reliable. Philip Augustus expelled the Jews from France in 1182, and even though they were allowed to return somewhat later, the general expulsion was renewed in 1306 by Philip IV (r. 1285–1314). As Richard I prepared to join the Third Crusade in 1189, anti-Jewish riots broke out across England and Jews were massacred in London. Not long before Passover of the following year, the Jewish

Persecution of Jews An illumination from a mid-thirteenth-century French Bible shows lords or monarchs executing two Jews (kneeling at right). In the top left corner, Jesus looks down from heaven in approval.

community of York, alarmed by threats, took refuge in a tower of the royal castle. Besieged by crusaders, the Jews committed mass suicide. By 1218 England's remaining Jews were legally required to wear badges, and in 1290 King Edward I, who had made laws exacting special taxes from the Jews, expelled all of them from England.

FORCED SEPARATION Theologians—many of them Dominicans—urged Jews to convert, demanding that they defend their doctrines and practices in formal public disputations, the first of which took place in Paris in 1240. Copies of the Talmud, the massive code of Jewish law and belief, were confiscated and publicly burned there in 1242. In many communities, those who refused to convert were forcibly separated from the Christians among whom they had lived, in steady tension but also in productive coexistence, for centuries. Forbidden to own or farm land, Jews were required to wear yellow patches and other distinctive forms of dress, and to live in certain districts. The Jew was transformed, by force of law, preaching, and public pressure, into a greedy creature who lived by lending money—a vision that found expression in this period, for the first time in Western history, in caricatures of Jews portrayed with hooked noses and other features to identify them and express their evil characters. Lepers and prostitutes—though not representatives of a forbidden religion—were singled out as well for comparable treatment: a mixture of exploitation by rulers and cities, in the case of prostitutes, and confinement to houses specially built to keep them from spreading their contagion into the Christian world.

PERSECUTION AND SCHOLARSHIP

From the heartless standpoint of the historian, persecution yields one unique benefit. Inquisitors and other specialists genuinely wanted to know as much they could about their enemies. As professional scholars and ordinary people grew increasingly hostile to their Jewish neighbors, they came to see Jews—reasonably, from their own theological standpoint—as caught in a web of superstition that had first trapped them when they refused to acknowledge Jesus. This refusal to convert when the Messiah came meant that Jews could not change, and those who claimed they had converted were suspect: their conduct was regularly scrutinized for signs of nostalgia for their birth religion. The French Dominican Bernard Gui explained that Jews resembled dogs and liked to return to their own vomit. Accordingly, Gui offered inquisitors substantive information about Jewish prayer books and rituals—notably those in which, as he saw it, they denounced Christians and other Gentiles.

Some of Gui's colleagues went much further. A fellow Dominican, Ramon Martí, became Europe's greatest expert, in his own time and for centuries to come, on the Jewish tradition. After scrutinizing Jewish biblical commentaries and the Talmud, Martí compiled a spectacularly learned book, *The Dagger of the Faith* (ca. 1280), in which he argued that the canonical Jewish texts, rightly interpreted, showed that Jesus was in fact the Messiah whom the Jews had expected. Only their obstinacy had led them to reject him and to falsify some of their own texts in order to pretend that he was not the Son of God.

THE CONFESSIONS OF BEATRICE DE PLANISSOLES

The same combination of fascination and fury that motivated Martí's feats of scholarship impelled another inquisitor—Jacques Fournier, who would become Pope Benedict XII (d. 1342)—to interrogate the last Cathars in the Pyrenees, early in the fourteenth century. As the manuals of inquisitors recommended, Fournier interrogated each suspect systematically, pressing for revelations of doctrine and fact. Their depositions reveal worlds that would otherwise have been wholly lost. The testimony shows that shepherd boys gossiped about God and the angels while tending their sheep in high mountain passes, and that ordinary peasant women might discuss theology in their little houses while delousing one another. One of the most extraordinary characters who come to life in these inquisition transcripts is the noblewoman Beatrice de Planissoles.

One man recalled her vividly, sitting by the fire with "two of her daughters of whom one must have been six or seven years old and the other 4 or 5, and several other persons," and musing critically about the Eucharist: "We began to speak of priests and the sacrament of the altar, which is the concern of the priests. Beatrice said . . . that she wondered how, if God was present in the sacrament of the altar, he could permit himself to be eaten by priests (or even by a single priest). Hearing this, I left that house very upset." Pressed by the inquisitor, a witness revealed the names of "the persons very intimate with this Beatrice, who would have known her secrets." After others testified, Beatrice finally confessed to heresy.

In her confession Beatrice claimed that Raimond Roussel, the bursar of her husband's estates and an adherent to Cathar belief, had urged her to leave her family and accompany him to the "good Christians." Only they, he explained, would be saved. Always a critical listener, Beatrice demanded that he explain "how can it be that God has created such a quantity of men and women if so many among them will not be saved?" Raimond told her of the charisma of the Cathar "perfect ones": "He said he himself had seen and met several of these good Christians. They were such people that when one had heard them speak, one could not ever leave them, and if I myself heard them just one time, I would be theirs forever." Fascinated, Beatrice rejected his approaches only when he hid under her bed and tried to seduce her.

Years later, however, Beatrice succumbed to another Cathar: the local priest, Pierre Clergue, who not only seduced her but "also knew me carnally one year on the night of Christmas and he nevertheless said mass the next day, even though there were other priests present." Clergue, she recalled, instructed her in the history of the cosmos and the souls within it, explaining as he did so why the Cathars ate no flesh. She laid out a full account of the Creation and the Fall, as Clergue had narrated them. He had told her that the spirits of the fallen angels inhabited animals as well as humans: "This is why it is a sin to kill such a brute beast or a man, because each one as well as the other has a spirit endowed with reason and understanding." After a period of imprisonment, she was condemned to wear crosses on her garments.

Beatrice's story—and those of the others condemned with her—come from sources that cannot reveal everything we would like to know. But they show that the lively world of religious speculation the Dominicans sought to fix in a single, absolutely valid set of arguments was not the sole province of professional theologians. Up and down the social scale, by the fires in village houses as well as in the faculties of theology, men and women actively debated the structures of doctrine that everyone recognized as one of the characteristic achievements of the day. They mingled intellectual speculation with personal lives of astonishing passion and complexity.

THE MEDIEVAL WORLD IN CRISIS (1238–1382)

The extraordinary society of the High Middle Ages—aggressive and argumentative, expansive and self-destructive—would soon meet the limits of its resources and energy. Encounters with a world outside Europe—from confrontations with nomadic warriors to invasion by plague bacilli—were only the most dramatic of the events that shattered many of the formative structures reared in the late twelfth and thirteenth centuries. Famine prepared the way for plague, and plague in turn for bitter new kinds of conflict.

MONGOL INVASION AND THE ROAD TO ASIA

The first clear sign of crisis appeared as early as the middle of the thirteenth century, when the **Mongols**, nomadic horsemen from Central Asia, streamed into the Christian world. Skilled archers, they used compound bows built up from layers of birch wood, horn, and bark, which could fire arrows through the strongest armor. Led by the brilliant tactician Genghis Khan (c. 1156–1227), the Mongols carved out an empire in the early thirteenth century that ran all the way from northern China in the east to the Caspian Sea in the west. In 1238, led by Genghis Khan's grandsons, the Mongols burst into Muscovy, a new Christian state that had taken shape in the thirteenth century. They conquered it in short order. The Mongols inflicted

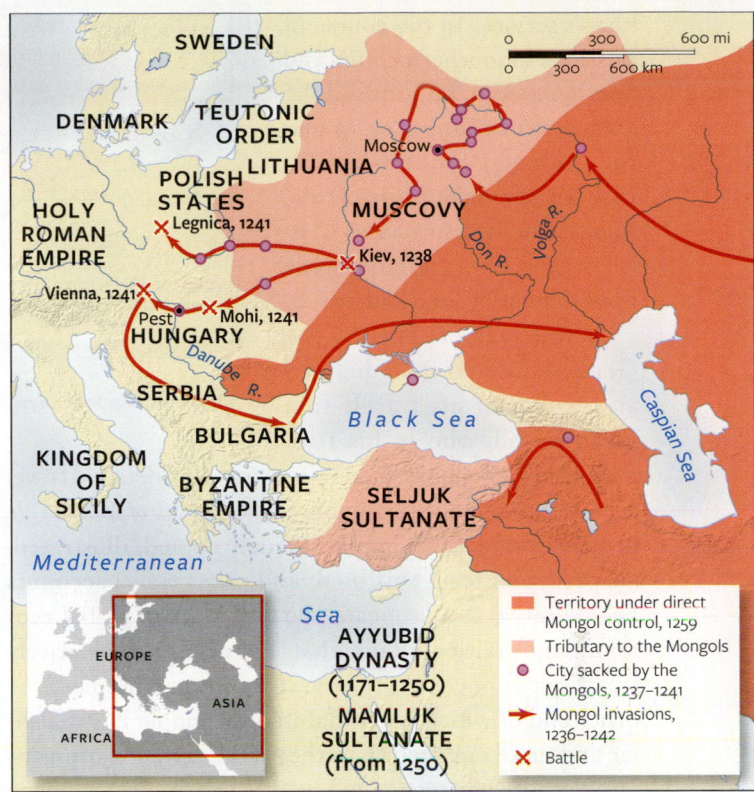

Mongol Incursions into Europe, 1206–1295 Genghis Khan's violent strategy of conquest quickly won the Mongols a vast empire, which within the span of only twenty years stretched from the Pacific in the east to the Caspian Sea. After Genghis's death in 1227, his successors pushed farther into Europe, conquering much of Muscovy and reaching as far as Vienna.

terrible damage on the Christian kingdoms of Hungary and Poland, and their forces reached as far as the gates of Vienna. No Christian army had been able to stop—much less defeat—them. Though the Mongols eventually turned back to Asia in the late 1240s, Europeans knew that they might have lost their autonomy almost overnight—as the Chinese actually did.

THE TRAVELS OF MARCO POLO The irruption of the Mongols opened Christian eyes to the vast, rich societies to the east, which they had never explored, much less tried to conquer, as they had tried to conquer the Islamic world. In 1271, Marco Polo (1254–1324), a member of a Venetian merchant family, set out with his father and uncle on a journey to the East—a journey that would take them along the Silk Road and, in the end, all the way to China. There, north of the Great Wall, they met the Mongol Kublai Khan (r. 1260–1294), emperor of China. Marco's father and uncle continued to trade, but Marco joined the khan's service. In the course of missions to southern China and Southeast Asia, he admired the greatness of Chinese cities and the calm and security of Chinese society under Mongol rule. Marco finally returned to Venice in 1295, after traveling some 15,000 miles by land and by sea.

While held prisoner by the Genoese, Marco Polo dictated an account of his travels to a Pisan friend, who in his turn produced a complex text, at once a granular, detailed travel account and a fantastic romance. *The Travels of Marco Polo* became immensely popular. Widely copied, illustrated, adapted, and read, this book and other travel accounts helped reveal to Europeans the true state of global economic and political affairs: that they occupied a relatively small spit at one end of the vast Eurasian landmass, the other end of which was inhabited by people far wealthier and more cultured than they were. The Dominicans and Franciscans responded to this enormous challenge by training missionaries and sending them along the merchant routes to try to convert the khan and his nation, a transformation that never took place. But they realized, for the first time that, as two Dominicans reflected during a five-year journey to the Arabian Sea and Ethiopia, "we who are the true Christians, are not the tenth, no not the twentieth of all men."

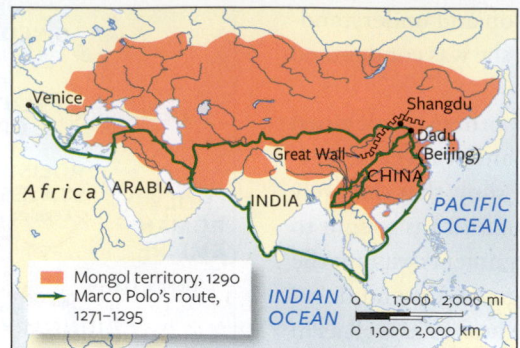

Marco Polo's Journeys, 1271–1295

SHAKING THE FOUNDATIONS OF CHURCH AND STATE

Yet even as the larger world opened up, some of the structures that had supported Europe's medieval revival and expansion crumbled. At the very end of the thirteenth century, Philip IV—the aggressive and brilliant French king who saw himself, in the old way, as a holy leader of a holy people—came into conflict with an equally aggressive and passionate pope, Boniface VIII (r. 1294–1303). Mobilizing for a crusade, Philip insisted on taxing his clergy aggressively. Eventually he arrested and tried a bishop, clearly violating the Church's canon law. The pope denounced Philip, and French jurists fought back. In April 1302, emboldened by a French defeat, Boniface revived and exceeded the most radical claims of his predecessors. In a bull—an official papal proclamation that took its name from the lead *bulla* ("seal") attached to it—Boniface declared the pope master of the entire world, lord over all kings. Philip refuted this claim in the most direct way: he sent an army to storm the papal palace at Anagni in central Italy and briefly imprisoned Boniface, who died soon after. Accusations flew against both sides.

Marco Polo This Spanish map from 1375 records the journey of Marco Polo and his caravan, including camels bearing supplies, shown here crossing a desert on their route through Asia.

Avignon Papacy A French chronicle from around 1370 illustrates the 1342 coronation of Pope Clement VI in Avignon. King Philip IV looks on at left, signaling the French crown's support.

TRAVELS OF MARCO POLO AND RABBAN BAR SAUMA

The networks of long-distance trade that developed in the thirteenth and fourteenth centuries brought Europeans new perspectives on their place in the world. The Venetian merchant Marco Polo (1254–1324) is probably the most famous traveler of the period. Though not everyone fully accepts the authenticity of the account of his travels (as dictated to Rustichello of Pisa, a popular writer of romances), the book is incontestably important because of its influence on European ideas of exploration and the East. Rabban Bar Sauma (ca. 1220–1294) was a Christian monk who traveled west from China to Europe at about the same time that Marco Polo was heading east. Bar Sauma's account of his journey, lost for hundreds of years and only rediscovered in the late nineteenth century, suggests how a Christian traveler from the East saw Europe in the thirteenth century.

From Marco Polo and Rustichello of Pisa, *The Travels of Marco Polo*

This excerpt from *The Travels of Marco Polo* (ca. 1298) describes lively commerce in the eastern Chinese city of Kinsay (modern Hangzhou).

[T]he city [Kinsay] is wholly on the water, and surrounded by it like Venice. It contains twelve arts or trades, and each trade has 12,000 stations or houses; and in each station there are of masters and labourers at least ten, in some fifteen, thirty and even forty, because this town supplies many others round it. The merchants are so numerous and so rich, that their wealth can neither be told nor believed….

There are within the city ten principal squares or market-places….Each of these, on three days in every week, contains an assemblage of from 40,000 to 50,000 persons, who bring for sale every desirable article of provision. There appears abundance of all kinds of game, such as roebuck, fallow-deer, hares, and rabbits, with partridges, pheasants …quails, common fowls…ducks and geese almost innumerable; these last being so easily bred on the lake, that for a Venetian silver grosso you may buy a couple of geese and two pairs of ducks. In the same place are also the shambles, where cattle, as oxen, calves, kids, and lambs, are killed for the tables of the rich and of magistrates. These markets afford at all seasons a great variety of herbs and fruits; in particular, uncommonly large pears, weighing each ten pounds, white in the inside like paste, and very fragrant….

To give some idea of the quantity of meat, wine, spices, and other articles brought for the consumption of the people of [Kinsay], I shall instance the single article of pepper. Marco Polo was informed by an officer employed in the customs, that the daily amount was forty-three loads, each weighing 243 pounds.

From Rabban Bar Sauma, *The Monks of Kublai Khan, Emperor of China*

With the permission of Kublai Khan, the monk Rabban Bar Sauma (also known as Rabban Sawma) visited many cities in Asia and Europe, including Paris, where he met the French king Philip IV and viewed Christian relics.

Rabban Sawma and his companions remained for a month of days in this great city of Paris, and they saw everything that was in it. There were in it thirty thousand scholars [i.e. pupils] who were engaged in the study of ecclesiastical books of instruction, that is to say of commentaries and exegesis of all the Holy Scriptures, and also of profane learning,…and all these pupils received money for subsistence from the king. And they also saw one Great Church wherein were the funerary coffers of dead kings, and statues of them in gold and in silver were upon their tombs. And five hundred monks were engaged in performing commemoration services in the burial-place [i.e. mausoleum] of the kings, and they all ate and drank at the expense of the king….In short Rabban Sawma and his companions saw everything which was splendid and renowned.

And after this the king sent and summoned them, and they went to him in the church, and they saw him standing by the side of the altar, and they saluted him. And he asked Rabban Sawma saying, "Have you seen what we have? And doth there not remain anything else for you to see?" Then Rabban Sawma thanked him [and said "There is not"]. Forthwith he went up with the king into an upper chamber of gold, which the king opened, and he brought forth from it a coffer of beryl wherein was laid the Crown of Thorns which the Jews placed upon the head of our Lord when they crucified Him. Now the Crown was visible in the coffer, which, thanks to the transparency of the beryl, remained unopened. And there was also in the coffer a piece of the wood of the Cross.

QUESTIONS FOR ANALYSIS

1. Which aspects of Kinsay's economy are most remarkable to Marco Polo?
2. What does Rabban Bar Sauma find most impressive about Paris?
3. How do these descriptions reflect the travelers' values as merchant (Polo) and monk (Bar Sauma)?

Sources: Hugh Murray, ed., *The Travels of Marco Polo* (New York: 1855), pp. 166, 169–71; E. A. Wallis Budge, trans., *The Monks of Kublai Khan, Emperor of China* (London: 1928), pp. 183–5.

THE AVIGNON PAPACY By 1309, the papacy itself had moved, under Philip's auspices, from Rome to the southern French city of Avignon. The **Avignon papacy** would remain there for almost seventy years, a period known as its Babylonian Captivity, during which it was constantly criticized for being overly wealthy, dominated by the French, and generally corrupt. Philip, for his part, also denounced another prominent Church institution, the Templars—one of the military orders that had formed to support the Crusades—as heretics and sodomites. Tortured, condemned, and expelled from France, the Templars also lost their property to expropriation by the French king. The immunity of the clerical estate would never seem absolutely safe again.

THE HUNDRED YEARS' WAR Neither, however, would royal authority. In the 1330s, after a long series of

minor hostilities, England and France engaged in what would eventually come to be known as the **Hundred Years' War**. This exhausting conflict was rooted to some extent in the ancient claims of the king of England to the duchies of Aquitaine and Normandy and much other territory in France. But it had no single cause, and its nature and purpose changed from decade to decade. What is clear is that the war left both monarchies shattered and their countries devastated.

In the early years of the war, the English scored major successes. Edward III (r. 1327–1377) demolished French armies at Crécy in 1346 and Poitiers in 1356, and took the port of Calais in 1347. As always, war proved more expensive than anyone had expected. Edward had to renege on his debts, helping to send the Florentine banks that had backed him, the Bardi and the Peruzzi, into bankruptcy. In a second phase of the conflict, from 1360 to 1413, the British failed to repeat their early successes, and Charles V (r. 1364–1380), who modernized the French forces, sharply reduced the territory that the English held. Henry V of England (r. 1413–1422) started the third phase with a brilliant victory at Agincourt in 1415, where a smaller English force of dismounted men-at-arms and archers surprised the world by defeating a larger French army. Henry reconquered Normandy in 1415–20, but by the war's final battle, at Castillon in 1453, the French had permanently regained Aquitaine and Normandy from the English.

FAMINE AND PLAGUE

Even more devastating than the damage done by rebellious humans were the blows dealt by nature in the fourteenth century. In the spring of 1315 the seasonal rains went on far longer than usual. In 1316 rain fell steadily across northern Europe. Unusual extremes in summer weather—alternating between droughts and deluges—and terribly cold winters followed until 1322. Both dry and wet weather drastically hindered plowing. Crop yields fell sharply—so much so that in some regions peasants harvested less than they had originally sown. Fruit rotted on vines and trees. Sheep and cows died off, as the wet weather brought infestations. Droughts dried out the millponds and killed off vast numbers of fish. Horses and pigs survived better than other animals, but the horses were overworked and underfed, and pig herds fell in size as pork was substituted for other kinds of meat that were no longer available.

The poor weather made it difficult to transport food from more prosperous regions to those harder hit.

The Hundred Years' War, 1330–1453 Early in England's long war with France, it achieved several key victories, and by 1360 controlled more than half of present-day France. In later phases of the war, France regained control. Despite Henry V's famous victory at Agincourt in 1415, by the end of the war in 1453, England had lost almost all its territory on the Continent.

Famine In this illustration of the 1335 famine from a fourteenth-century manuscript, townspeople receive rations of grain in the street outside a church in Florence. The angel at the top declares, "I will make you ache with hunger and high prices," casting the famine as a divine judgment.

Warfare and piracy also hindered distribution. And efforts to impose price controls were more likely to encourage hoarding than to help the poor. The biggest cities—London, Paris, and the large textile-producing centers in Flanders and Italy—could import and distribute grain, and the wealthy could feed themselves. But the poor starved while collective prayers were offered across Europe until the seven terrible years of famine finally came to an end in 1322.

THE BLACK DEATH
Then the plague struck. The travel and trade that was opening the Eurasian world also carried microorganisms to vulnerable populations. Rodents carrying fleas infected with plague were spreading the highly contagious disease in Asia in the 1330s, and by 1345–46 it had reached Muscovy. Borne, it seems, on the ships of Genoese merchants fleeing the Mongols, bubonic plague struck. This outbreak—known as the **Black Death**—was devastating. Bubonic plague caused painful swellings and hemorrhages. Europe's population dropped by 40 to 50 percent in the four years of the outbreak, from 1347 to 1350. Religious communities and other closed groups suffered even higher death rates than the general population. Historians once thought that contemporaries exaggerated the effects of the Black Death, but excavations have revealed urban graveyards with bodies piled five or more deep, as contemporary chroniclers claimed.

IMPACT OF THE PLAGUE
The plague moved quickly enough that it could not be escaped, but slowly enough that most cities knew it was approaching them for weeks before it struck. Inhabitants could only wait, "frantic with terror," in the words of a contemporary. Nothing authorities or medical practitioners could do could cure or even alleviate the plague. Many thought that it signaled the beginning of the biblical Apocalypse. Fraternities of flagellants marched in public, whipping one another to demonstrate penitence. Across Europe, many blamed Jews for causing the disease by poisoning wells. Though Pope Clement VI (d. 1362) formally denied these accusations and the authorities tried to protect them, Jews in the Holy Roman Empire, Switzerland, and southern France were tortured until they confessed to their imaginary crimes, and entire Jewish communities were massacred.

The plague never seemed to end. Periodic recurrences,

Black Death A 1352 Flemish medical text shows townspeople burying scores of victims of the 1349 plague.

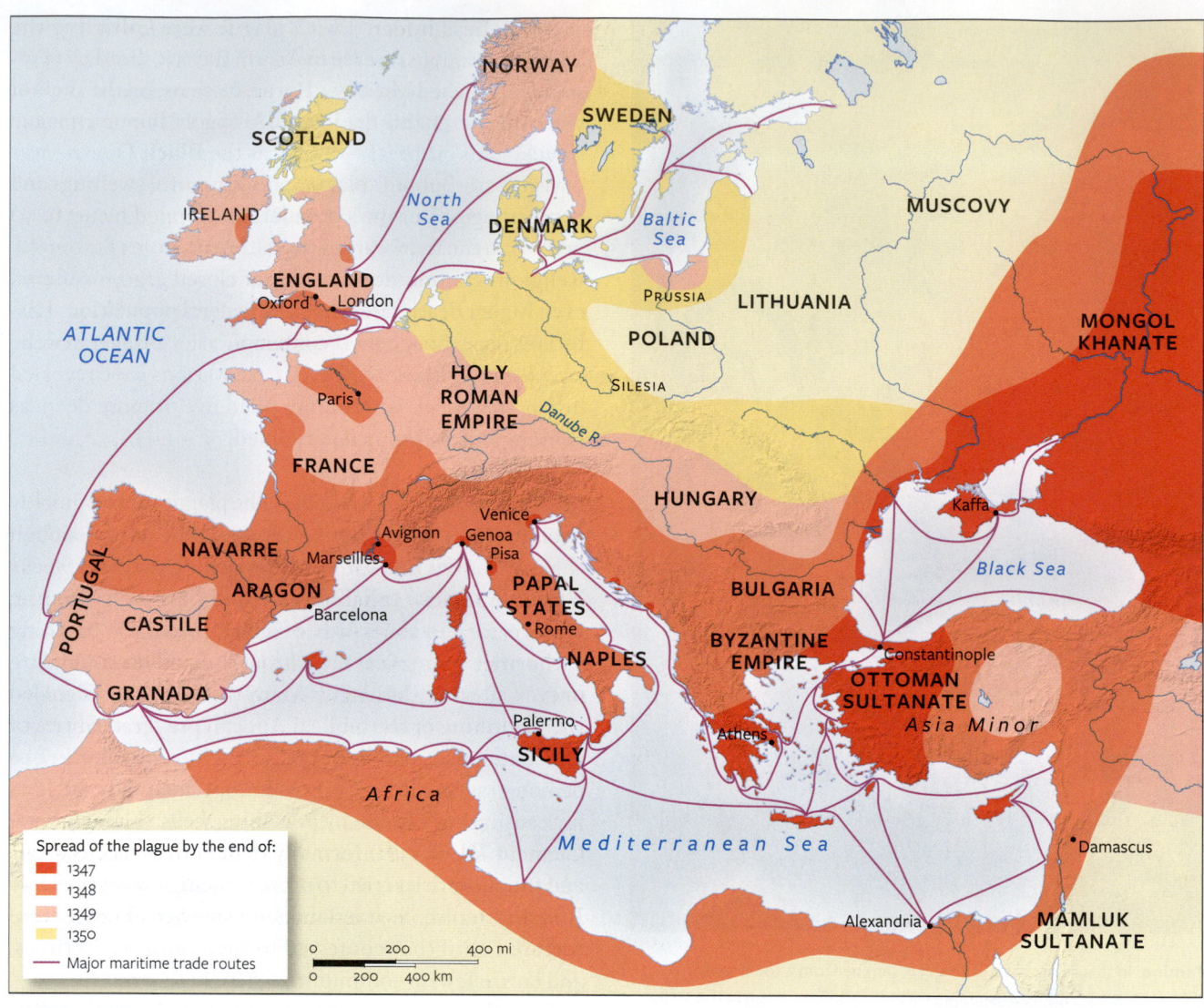

The Black Death, 1347–1350 The plague originated in Mongol-controlled Asia, but infected rats quickly spread it throughout the extensive network of maritime trade routes crisscrossing Europe. Within four years, the pandemic had spread from the eastern Mediterranean to areas as far north and west as Scotland and Scandinavia.

Map legend:

Spread of the plague by the end of:
- 1347
- 1348
- 1349
- 1350
— Major maritime trade routes

some of which caused very high mortality rates, continued through the fifteenth, sixteenth, and seventeenth centuries. Its last major outbreak in western Europe was the Great Plague of London, which struck in 1665–66 and killed an estimated 100,000 people.

SOCIAL UPHEAVAL

Massive outbreaks of human disease can, in some circumstances, benefit survivors, economically if not emotionally. Livestock, equipment, and capital generally remain, leaving some survivors better off. In the wake of the Black Death, however, the positive was difficult to

discern. Modern photography, archaeological surveys, and studies of the written record have made it possible to trace large networks of twelfth- and thirteenth-century farming settlements in the German lands and Britain that were abandoned forever after the plague devastated these communities.

ECONOMIC DISLOCATIONS The population collapse caused by the plague massively lowered demand for inexpensive products made on a large scale, such as the traditional products of the Florentine woolen cloth industry. Production in many other crafts fell as well, actually raising prices for goods even though fewer people remained to buy them. In the cities, masters responded to

The Jacquerie This chronicle (1475) illustrates a scene of mounted troops brutally suppressing the Jacquerie in the town of Meaux. The rebels' corpses are thrown into the river Marne below the town.

the dislocations of the mid-fourteenth century by making it much harder for journeymen to join their ranks, and by pushing wages lower. In the countryside, landlords fought to regain control of common areas and goods. In much of eastern Europe—especially Poland, Silesia, and Prussia—serfdom was reimposed on the rural laboring population that had so dramatically shrunk.

THE JACQUERIE

Violent responses followed in some areas. In 1358, shortly after the English defeated the French at Poitiers, the town's peasants, clerics, townsmen, and even some minor royal officials savagely attacked local nobles, furious at the defeat and the lack of protection from roving bands of soldiers and brigands. Called the Jacquerie, from "Jacques," the name that nobles applied indiscriminately to the poor, the movement was put down with brutal force.

WAT TYLER

In this same period, the English Parliament caused deep resentment by trying to use statutes to control the mobility of laborers and limit their wages.

between 1377 and 1380 to support the wars against France turned angry peasants into rebels. In 1381, enraged villagers in Essex, a relatively prosperous area northeast of London, attacked government officials sent to investigate tax evasion. Peasants in nearby Kent, just southeast of London, followed an able but otherwise unknown leader, Wat Tyler, to join their Essex comrades in a march on the city.

Another local leader, John Ball, a former Lollard priest, denounced the power and wealth of the Church. Sympathetic London artisans allowed the peasants to enter the city gates. When Tyler confronted King Richard II (r. 1377–1399) with demands for the abolition of serfdom and the redistribution of Church property, a scuffle broke out and Tyler was killed. Richard, only fourteen but thinking on his feet, told the peasants he would be their captain, and they followed him out of London. The king's professional soldiers then surrounded the rebels and sent them home, suppressing the Peasants' Revolt of 1381 with relatively little violence.

OLIGARCHY IN FLORENCE

In Florence, unskilled cloth workers had long resented their pay and working conditions. In 1345, shortly before the plague struck, a wool carder named Ciuto Brandini tried to organize them so that they could "more strongly resist" their masters. He was executed. After the disruptions caused by the plague, efforts to limit wages again brought crowds of laborers and poorer artisans into the streets. In June and July 1378, palaces were burned and city records destroyed. The brokers and subcontractors of the wool industry sided with the workers, and a new regime came into power. The laborers were allowed to form a guild of their own, but the cloth manufacturers closed their shops to put pressure on the workers. At the end of August, when the laborers again rose in revolt, the manufacturers and more established artisans joined to put them down in a short, sharp

Wat Tyler and the Peasants' Revolt In a French chronicle (ca. 1460–80), Wat Tyler, on horseback, leads a large army of armored men toward the king's forces. Both sides carry the royal standard and the English national flag.

outbreak of street fighting. By 1382, an oligarchical republic tightly controlled by rich bankers and wool merchants had taken power in Florence.

Short-lived though they were, these movements, like the heretical religious movements that sometimes intersected with and amplified them, spread fear and uncertainty, especially among those who ruled Europe's states and the Church, even as these elites put a stop to efforts by the urban and rural poor to improve their conditions by direct political action.

CONCLUSION

Fertile in innovations of every kind—from new ways of building and administering states to new ways of leading a Christian life, from new forms of economic activity to new kinds of literary creativity—the civilization of the High Middle Ages in many ways reached its own natural limits: its populations surpassed the ability of its agriculture to feed everyone; its cities surpassed the ability of its institutions to govern effectively; and even the Church encountered limits to its expansive authority. It collided repeatedly with those it considered heretics, and with the refusal of ordinary Christians to accept clerical leadership in all aspects of life. The great institutions of the High Middle Ages wore one another down in endless wars and confrontations, and their collapse might have taken place even if the plague had not arrived. Yet these institutions also laid foundations, as we will see, on which Europe would build again, as it began to move towards political and cultural expansion across the earth.

CHAPTER REVIEW

KEY TERMS

Dante Alighieri (p. 293)

Hanseatic League (p. 297)

Parlement (p. 300)

Magna Carta (p. 300)

parliament (p. 301)

common law (p. 301)

Pope Innocent III (p. 304)

Fourth Lateran Council
  (p. 304)

heresy (p. 305)

Dominican Order (p. 309)

Franciscan Order (p. 310)

Cathars (p. 311)

Thomas Aquinas (p. 312)

inquisition (p. 313)

Mongols (p. 315)

Avignon papacy (p. 318)

Hundred Years' War
  (p. 318)

Black Death (p. 319)

REVIEW QUESTIONS

1. How did the expansion of commerce help connect different regions in Europe, and link Europe and Asia?

2. How did the new urban economy change the way people worked?

3. What steps did cities take to break free from noble and clerical control?

4. How did European monarchies work to reestablish central authority in the High Middle Ages?

5. What were the most important legal and political principles set forth in Magna Carta?

6. What consequential reforms were made to Christian doctrine and practice by the Fourth Lateran Council?

7. In what ways did the papacy become more like a secular monarchy in the medieval period?

8. What were the most pressing problems facing urban residents in thirteenth-century Europe?

9. What methods did the Church employ to repress heresy and promote orthodoxy and uniformity?

10. How did famine and the Black Death affect European society?

CORE OBJECTIVES

After reading this chapter, you should have a solid understanding of the following core objectives. To strengthen your grasp of the core objectives, use the resources on the Student Site for The West.

- Analyze the growth of economic specialization and the cash economy of Europe in the High Middle Ages.

- Describe the culture and politics of urban life in the High Middle Ages.

- Describe the evolution of the medieval state in western Europe.

- Evaluate the institutional and doctrinal changes in the Church in the high medieval period.

- Assess the perceived threats to Church authority and the Church's response to them.

- Describe the crises that struck European society starting in the thirteenth century.

 GO TO inQuizitive TO SEE WHAT YOU'VE LEARNED—AND LEARN WHAT YOU'VE MISSED—WITH PERSONALIZED FEEDBACK ALONG THE WAY.

1378–1417
Great Schism

1415
Jan Hus burned at
the stake for heresy

1440s–1450s
Gutenberg invents
printing press

1454
Treaty of
Lodi

1469
Isabella and Ferdinand
unite Castile and Aragon

1482
Treaty of Arras

1414–1418
Council of Constance

1434
Medici family takes
power in Florence

1453
Mehmed II conquers
Constantinople

1455–1487
Wars of
the Roses

1478
Spanish
Inquisition
begins

Renaissance Europe

A WORLD TRANSFORMED

1400–1500

In June 1502, a Florentine civil servant named Niccolò Machiavelli (1469–1527) reached the military camp of Cesare Borgia (1475/6–1507); Cesare was the son of Rodrigo Borgia, now Pope Alexander VI. Cesare had been campaigning successfully in central Italy, where he was working, with his father's support, to build a state for himself. Having taken Bologna and massacred a group of mercenaries who had plotted against him, Cesare was now contemplating a campaign against Florence. The city seemed vulnerable in the wake of a political crisis brought on by invading French forces and the actions of a charismatic Dominican preacher, Girolamo Savonarola, whom the Florentines, acting under papal pressure, had arrested, tortured, and executed a few years earlier.

Machiavelli spent several months with Cesare, reporting back to the Florentine government on the twists and turns of Cesare's policies, doing his best to sniff out the military leader's secrets and to reveal none of his own. He saw that Cesare's rule, dependent on his father's support, was much more vulnerable than it seemed. On this basis Machiavelli correctly predicted that Cesare would not be able to attack, much less conquer, Florence.

Renaissance: Art and War Around 1438–40, Paolo Uccello created this ten-foot-long painting of the battle of San Romano (1432) between Florence and Siena, a Florentine victory in the wars between Italian city-states that dominated the early fifteenth century. With Uccello's use of brilliant colors and linear perspective, the work is an early example of the characteristics that would later define the achievements of Italian Renaissance painting.

- How were states changing the ways they organized themselves and competed?
- What were the dynamics of change in religious life?
- How did new technologies and skills enable Europeans to expand their reach?
- What were the major effects of first contact between Europe and the Americas?
- How did Renaissance humanism encourage new ambitions in European culture and society?

Machiavelli was playing a new game: professional diplomacy, as conducted by ambassadors sent abroad by their states to live with and report on foreign rulers. Both this position and the skills that Machiavelli brought to it were the products of a transformation in European politics.

The period in which Machiavelli lived, now known as the Renaissance, witnessed spectacular creativity in many areas of life. Europeans devised more effective ways of organizing and governing states, waging war, and making peace. They found their way by sea to Asia and the Americas, altering patterns of trade that had existed for hundreds or even thousands of years, and opening the Old and New Worlds to a transforming exchange of goods, ideas, beliefs, practices, and pathogens. They began to study the ancients in new ways that also reshaped their understanding of the world. They turned painting and sculpture into learned arts, and invented a way to print books instead of copying them by hand. Across Europe, borders and barriers fell as institutions and disciplines took on radically different forms.

Machiavelli himself helped to create both a new kind of state and a new way of writing and thinking about politics. His most famous and influential work, *The Prince*, rested on his own experience of states, including his own, undergoing revolutionary change, and on his study of the Greek and Roman classics. In this chapter, we will watch Machiavelli and his contemporaries begin to create what we can recognize as modern Europe.

RENAISSANCE STATES

In the fifteenth century, states of a new kind took shape across Europe. They developed permanent powers for raising revenue and waging war. They built civil services that could handle the large amounts of documentation, verbal and numerical, required to exercise these powers. Thinkers—many of them directly involved as civil servants—developed political theories that described, and made sense of, the changing political world.

ITALY: TERRITORIAL STATES (1454–1494)

In Italy, the centuries-long political decline of the empire and the papacy had left individual cities effectively independent. Through the late thirteenth and fourteenth centuries, trade rivalry and warfare had raged. Many Italian cities had been republics during the Middle Ages: independent communes inefficiently governed by local merchants and bankers, who appointed outside officials to preside over them. In the fourteenth and fifteenth centuries, most of these republican states came under princely rule. Noble families supported by mercenaries built their own tiny courts, which imitated the French and Burgundian ones. In some cases—as in Naples—these families claimed ancient dynastic rights. In others, they simply took power.

As city-states struggled against one another, weaker territories could not maintain their independence and consolidation followed. By the early fifteenth century, most of Italy belonged to one of five major powers: Venice, still rich and still a fiercely independent republic, ruled by a well-defined group of patricians; Milan, the center of a vast territory ruled by the Visconti family; the Papal States, ruled by the pope, who relied on them for his economic and military power; Naples, where a Spanish court dominated the large capital city and the vast agricultural estates around it; and Florence, which transformed itself gradually from a republic into a territorial state under the **Medici family**. Locked in competition for territory and power, all of them found their governments under pressure and developed new ways of coping with it.

FLORENCE In the late fourteenth and early fifteenth centuries, Florence was a republic in reality as well as in name—even if participation in government was limited to a small group of wealthy citizens. Day-to-day governance was handled by the Signoria, the group of nine officials chosen by lot for two-month terms, who moved into the government palace and made the vital decisions. Other citizens served rotating terms on committees that made the major political decisions, such as whether to go to war, and if so, whether to raise taxes. A small group of families that belonged to the city's most powerful guilds, dominated by the Albizzi, held enough of these offices to shape most decisions. Paid officials—especially the chancellors and their assistants—drafted the city's official correspondence with other powers, maintained the archives, and wrote histories and propaganda pamphlets.

Warfare tested this system to its limits. To pay its professional soldiers, the state had traditionally relied on taxes assessed on the basis of neighbors' testimony and informers' accounts—an inefficient system, to say the least. In the 1420s, Florence faced a vast public debt, the result of a war with Milan. To deal with it, the government created a wealth tax based on a systematic census of the city's entire population, carried out household by household. The records of the *catasto,* as this census was called, provided the Florentine government with a detailed understanding of the city's resources. Today, they offer historians a vivid record of family structures. They show, for example, that relatively few Florentines lived for very long in a patriarchal family dominated by an elderly male. Since men married late, they often died before their children were independent, leaving the children in families headed by mothers. In these circumstances, widows often steered their families' economic and political enterprises, achieving considerable authority.

Despite these reforms, Florence's republic proved unstable. Cosimo de' Medici (1389–1464), head of his family's bank, was a prominent member of the city's oligarchy. Exiled in 1433 for his part in a disastrous war against a neighboring city, he returned to take power a year later. Working largely behind the scenes as a power broker, Cosimo retained the committees that had traditionally ruled the city but manipulated the selection of their members in order to dominate them. During his twenty-year rule, it was still possible to believe that Florence was a republic in the traditional sense. Those who praised Cosimo in public wrote with deliberate vagueness that he had brought peace to the city, without discussing how. When Cosimo died, his son Piero (1416–1469) borrowed troops from his fellow ruler in Milan, lined the central square—the Piazza della Signoria—with them, and only then called in the citizens to hear a public announcement of his succession to power.

Cosimo de' Medici The Florentine painter Agnolo Bronzino created this portrait of Cosimo de' Medici, probably in the mid-fifteenth century.

Using the influence and resources of the Medici bank, as Cosimo had, Piero ruled the city effectively and defeated Venice in 1467—thanks to his alliance with Milan and the Papal States.

Cosimo's grandson Lorenzo (1449–1492) continued the Medici rule of Florence through surrogates who held the traditional offices. He behaved in some ways like a prince, holding tournaments and encouraging the prominent families of the city to build enormous palaces. When under his direction the Medici bank began to encounter serious difficulties, Lorenzo and his friends exploited state finances to maintain their incomes. Though officially still a republic, Florence looked more and more like such princely states as Milan, and Lorenzo himself like a ruler. Still, as he noted with pride, he and his predecessors had given a great deal to their city, spending 663,000 florins (a brand new palace might cost 11,000 florins) on taxes, charity, and building projects between 1434 and 1471.

One major enterprise continued uninterrupted

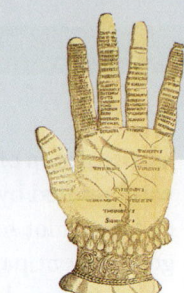

LORENZO GHIBERTI'S DECLARATION IN THE *CATASTO* OF 1427

The *catasto*, a census of the population and wealth of Florence, enabled the government to collect precise records of all households in the city, from the poor to the rich. The first survey was conducted in 1427 by ten officials and their staff, who interviewed the heads of almost 10,000 households. Each household's record lists property held, including land, payments received, and investments; other business interests; deductions for dependents; and debts owed, which reduced the taxable amount.

This record lists the possessions and debts of the sculptor Lorenzo Ghiberti as declared in the catasto of 1427, when he was forty-nine. His assets include balances owed to him for the sale of works, including one purchased by Cosimo de' Medici. His debts offer insight into the diverse trades in Florence's bustling economy. Ghiberti's taxable assets, valued at 999 florins[1]—worth about $42,000 today—assured his family a comfortable lifestyle, but his wealth was far from that of the top 1 percent of Florentines, who were assessed at upward of 10,000 florins.

[Assets]

A house located in the parish of S. Ambrogio in Florence in the Via Borgo Allegri…with household furnishings for the use of myself and my family…   0

A piece of land in the parish of S. Donato in Franzano…   100-0-0

In my shop are two pieces of bronze sculpture which I have made for a baptismal font in Siena.…I estimate that they are worth 400 florins or thereabouts, of which sum I have received 290 florins; so the balance is 110 florins.   110-0-0

Also in my shop is a bronze casket which I made for Cosimo de' Medici; I value it at approximately 200 florins, of which I have received 135 florins. The balance owed to me is 65 florins.   65-0-0

I have investments in the *Monte*[2] of 714 florins.   714-0-0

I am still owed 10 florins by the Friars of S. Maria Novella the tomb of the General [of the Dominican Order, Lionardo Dati].

Obligations

Personal exemptions:

Lorenzo di Bartolo, aged 46   200-0-0
Marsilia, my wife, aged 26   200-0-0
Tommaso, my son, aged 10 or thereabouts   200-0-0
Vettorio, my son, aged 7 or thereabouts   200-0-0

I owe money to the following persons:

Antonio di Piero del Vaglente and company, goldsmiths   33-0-0
Nicola di Vieri de' Medici   10-0-0
Domenico di Tano, cutler   9-0-0
Niccolò Carducci and company, retail cloth merchants   7-0-0
Papi d'Andrea, cabinet-maker   16-0-0
Mariano da Gambassi, mason   7-0-0
Papero di Mea of Settignano ⎫
Simone di Nanni of Fiesole ⎬
Cipriano di Bartolo of Pistoia ⎭
  (my apprentices in the shop)   48-0-0
Antonio, called El Maestro, tailor   15-0-0
Domenico di Lippi, culter   2-0-0
Alessandro Allesandri and company   4-0-0
Duccio Adimari and company, retail cloth merchants   8-0-0

Antonio di Giovanni, stationer   3-0-0
Isau d'Agnolo and company, bankers   50-0-0
Commissioners in charge of maintenance and rebuilding of the church of S. Croce   6-0-0
Lorenzo di Bruciane, kiln operator   3-0-0
Meo of S. Apollinare   45-0-0
Pippo, stocking maker   8-0-0
[Total of Lorenzo's taxable assets]   999-0-0
[Total obligations and exemptions]   1074-0-0

QUESTIONS FOR ANALYSIS

1. What does this declaration tell you about Ghiberti's personal life?
2. What do Ghiberti's debts and the balances owed to him suggest about the importance of banks and credit in Renaissance Florence?
3. What does the catasto suggest about Ghiberti's work as a sculptor and as a craftsman?

[1] **florin:** a skilled craftsman made slightly less than 1 florin for four days of work; a house in the upscale city center would rent for 20–50 florins per year
[2] **Monte:** a public fund

Source: Gene Brucker, ed., *The Society of Renaissance Florence: A Documentary Study* (Toronto: 1998), pp. 10–12.

throughout this period of institutional change: the city of Florence made itself the capital of a substantial state. Florentines proudly traced their city's origins back to republican Rome, and claimed that when they fought fiercely against the papacy in the late fourteenth century and against Milan and Naples in the early fifteenth, they were defending "Florentine liberty." Rather like the ancient Romans, the Florentines showed no reluctance to subject other states that had also been independent republics, such as Pisa, to their rule. Indeed, after the conquest of Pisa in 1406, the Florentines used it as a base for a state fleet of ten galleys. These ships made regular voyages between Florence and ports in the eastern Mediterranean, North Africa, and the North Sea, carrying Florentine wool and silk cloth to exchange for wool from England and spices from the East.

MILAN Although Florence offered the smaller states it conquered relatively little compensation, other Renaissance states offered their new subjects significant advantages. The Visconti, who ruled Milan in the late fourteenth and early fifteenth centuries, sponsored canal-building projects that eased travel and transport. They also subsidized the introduction of mulberry bushes and silkworms. By the later fifteenth century, rich merchants, mostly from Florence, created an independent silk industry. The Milanese government encouraged these foreign entrepreneurs to settle, and allowed them to import skilled artisans. In the middle of the sixteenth century, silk manufacturing was Milan's major industry, along with the production of other luxury goods such as tapestries.

VENICE Venice was also a self-governing republic ruled by an oligarchy: a small set of patrician families whose male members were eligible to sit in the representative assembly, or Great Council. Members of this body selected the doge, or chief of state, and elected the members of the smaller Senate and the Council of Ten, which did much of the work of governing the city. By the sixteenth century, more than 2,000 males had the right to take part in the meetings of the Great Council, ruling a city whose population was well over 100,000. Members of the Venetian oligarchy were expected to serve the city in multiple ways: representing Venice to foreign powers, governing cities that Venice had conquered on the mainland, or supervising communities of Venetians overseas. Few willingly left the city to serve. But those who did acquired knowledge about the world outside Venice, which they put to use in their commercial enterprises and in making laws and policies.

THE RISE OF DIPLOMACY: THE TREATY OF LODI

All of these Italian states, finally, developed a new way of conducting foreign affairs—one based on professional diplomacy, which would become a central institution in the rise of modern states. After a long series of wars and a transfer of power in Milan from the Visconti to the Sforza family had almost destroyed the Italian political system, Milan, Naples, and Florence made peace at Lodi, a city in Lombardy, in 1454. The Treaty of Lodi set permanent boundaries between Milanese and Venetian territory. Soon Venice and the Papal States also signed agreements with the other states. They pledged to maintain a balance of power, promising that they would all join in making war on any signatory that decided to attack another.

The Italian states devised a diplomatic system that they hoped could sustain this balance. They assigned resident **ambassadors** to one another's capitals: officials who

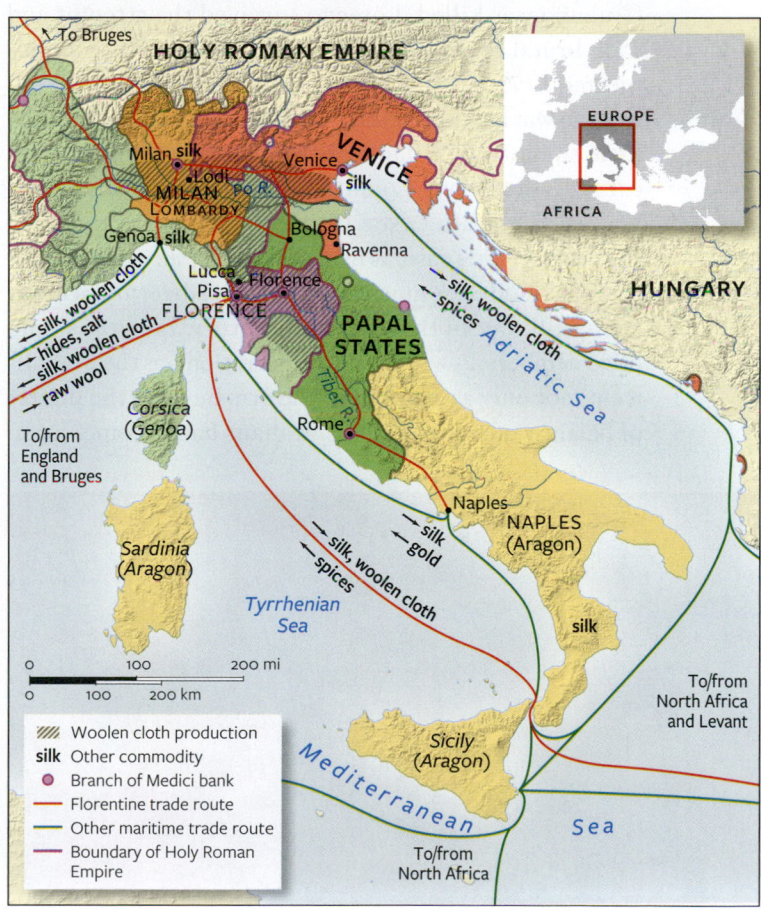

Italian States at the Treaty of Lodi, 1454 Despite their rivalries, the city-states that controlled the Italian Peninsula were tied together through mercantile relationships, with Florence at the center. The Medici bank had branches in Milan, Venice, Rome, and other cities, while Florentine trade routes conveyed luxury commodities such as silk from Milan, Venice, Genoa, and Naples to distant lands.

could represent their state's interests, gather information, and convey official communications. Governments developed systems for encoding dispatches to keep their communications safe and secret, and formulated rules for the treatment of ambassadors by hostile powers and during wartime. Diplomacy had existed for centuries, carried on by heralds and, often, through encounters between rulers. Now the Italian system of rapid interstate communication, run by political experts, gradually became a model for the rest of Europe.

Peace nevertheless remained precarious as limited wars broke out again and again. In 1478, when the Florentine Pazzi family conspired to assassinate Lorenzo de' Medici and his brother Giuliano and take over the state, the Pazzi had promises of help from the papacy and Naples. A mercenary captain in the papal service, Federigo da Montefeltro, was waiting outside Florence with his army, ready to move in and help the Pazzi consolidate their power. Though Giuliano was killed, Lorenzo survived the attempt and took brutal revenge on the Pazzi. The pope excommunicated Lorenzo, put Florence under the interdict, and went to war against the city with his ally, Naples. Offered little support by Milan, which was undergoing a political crisis of its own, Lorenzo eventually made his way to Naples, where, after a stay of months, he ultimately ended the crisis. In this case, as in many others, successful negotiations resulted as much from luck and determination as from skill. But in the sixteenth century, Lorenzo would be remembered—with some exaggeration—as the Magnificent, not only as a patron of the arts but also the master of balance-of-power politics. Italians had become—or so

many of them believed—the professional masters of politics, proud of the skill with which they manipulated powers both large and small to do their will.

MONARCHICAL STATES (1450–1494)

The Italians did not realize, however, that in the very decades in which they had been making politics into an art of feints and alliances, plots and proxy wars, the states of northern and western Europe had not only recovered from the crises of the fourteenth century but had developed stronger political and military resources. Improved military technology and large-scale forms of state organization gave them powers that dwarfed those available to the Italian states.

BURGUNDY During the wars that dominated the first half of the fifteenth century, as we have seen, the French royal house was challenged, for the last time, by the English, as well as by rivals of royal descent. These struggles left the French state weaker at times —and in control of less territory—than the rulers of some of its regions. The most important of these was Burgundy, a duchy in central and eastern France that was united by marriage, early in the fifteenth century, with Flanders and Brabant. These were the rich provinces of the **Low Countries**, the coastal region to the north and west whose cities, such as Bruges and Ghent, still ranked among Europe's most productive centers of industry and commerce. The Burgundians' French lands produced great wines. Their capital, Dijon, well located in eastern France, became a major trading center and the base of important commercial fairs.

For centuries, Burgundy had been ruled by branches of the same dynasties that ruled France—the Capetians and now the Valois. The last Valois dukes—especially Philip the Good (1396–1467) and Charles the Bold (1433–1477)—built Burgundy into a state that was, at its height, wealthier and more powerful than the kingdom of France itself, ruled by their Valois cousins. The Burgundian dukes pushed for independence, claiming prerogatives appropriate for a king. In 1423, for example, Philip the Good created a chivalric order—a small group of specially chosen noblemen, with their own meetings and rituals. Eventually Charles the Bold convinced the Holy Roman emperor to recognize him as the monarch of a separate kingdom, and had himself crowned. In 1465 he organized the League of the Public Weal—a group of powerful nobles, including the dukes of Brittany, Berry, and Lorraine, who demanded that the French king restore their ancient feudal prerogatives.

Federigo da Montefeltro In 1465, the artist Piero della Francesca painted this double portrait of Federigo and his wife, Battista Sforza.

European Monarchies, 1492 By the end of the fifteenth century, European monarchs ruled powerful and stable states. Louis XI achieved sovereignty over most of modern-day France; in England, Henry VII unified the country after defeating his rival Richard III at Bosworth. Maximilian I expanded the territory of the Holy Roman Empire and established new Habsburg claims, while Ferdinand and Isabella unified the Spanish kingdoms in 1469 and completed the Reconquista in 1492. Meanwhile, the Ottoman Empire under Mehmed I and II expanded dramatically.

FRANCE Yet the French monarchy had great residual strengths. Through the hard years of the fifteenth century, as fragmentation threatened, meetings of the **Estates General**—representatives of the Church, the nobility, and the Third Estate of urban merchants and traders—helped to preserve and enlarge the sense that France was a single nation. Although this assembly sometimes resisted individual kings, it also offered the monarchy essential help. As early as 1439, the Estates General conferred on King Charles VII (r. 1422–1461) the right to collect a permanent tax, the **taille**, from all those who were neither clerics nor nobles, and use it to support a permanent military formation, the Company of Ordinance. The taille rarely brought in enough to support all of the crown's military needs, especially as mercenaries played an increasingly

prominent role in warfare. The French kings supplemented their revenues with such problematic expedients as selling offices in the government, and the right to pass them on by inheritance. Still, the French monarchy had established its right to develop a standing army and to use the power of the royal purse to support it.

Louis XI (r. 1421–1483), known to his enemies as "the universal spider" for his skill at weaving webs of intrigue, managed to rebuild and extend the power of the monarchy. He made truces with most of his opponents, and when Charles the Bold, who unwisely invaded Switzerland, was defeated and killed, Louis dismembered much of Burgundy. In 1482, the Treaty of Arras gave him sovereignty over the historical duchy of Burgundy as well as Picardy, Artois, and Franche-Comté. An active ruler,

POVERTY AND THE STATE

Even as manufacturing and trade expanded in Renaissance Europe, poverty continued to afflict rural areas and cities alike. Farmers struggled against poor harvests, high taxes, and marauding bands of soldiers. In cities, abandoned children, the unemployed, and the sick begged on the streets. It had traditionally been the responsibility of the Church to ameliorate poverty, but as Renaissance states grew in scope and competence, people began to call on the state to harness its power to help the poor. The documents here address the problem of poverty in France and in Flanders.

Cahier of the Estates General, "The Plight of the French Poor"

This cahier, a catalog of grievances submitted to the king following the 1494 meeting of the Estates General, includes a plea for the relief of poor farmers from the demands of the taille and nobles' pensions.

When the poor labouring man has paid with great difficulty the quota he owes as tallage,[1] for the hire of the men of arms, and when he takes comfort in what is left to him, hoping it will be enough to live on for the year, or to sow, there suddenly come men of arms who eat up or waste this little reserve which the poor man has saved to live on….

While in the time of King Charles VII the quotas of the tallage imposed by the parish officials were counted only in the twenties, such as twenty, forty, sixty pounds, after his death they began to be levied by hundreds, and since, they have grown from hundreds to thousands….

Some have fled…others in great numbers have died of hunger, others in despair have killed their wives and children and themselves, seeing they had nothing left to live on. And many men, women, and children, having no animals, are forced to work yoked to the plough, and others labour at night out of fear that in daylight they will be seized and apprehended for the said tallage….

These things considered, it seems to the said estates that the king should take pity on his poor people, and relieve them of the said tallage and taxes….And this they beg of him very humbly….

And may it please my lords who take pensions to content themselves with income from their own lords, without taking any extraordinary pensions or sums of money. Or at least if some receive them, let the pensions be reasonable, moderate, and bearable, out of regard for the afflictions and miseries of the poor people….It is only the poor labourer who contributes to paying the said pensions.

Juan Luis Vives, "Concerning the Relief of the Poor"

In response to a request from the government of Bruges, longtime resident Juan Luis Vives proposed in 1526 a detailed plan for the state's improvement of living conditions in the city. This passage argues for the necessity of reducing poverty and teaching trades to the poor.

Surely it is a shame and disgrace to us Christians, to whom nothing has been more explicitly commanded than charity—and I am inclined to think that is the one injunction—that we meet everywhere in our cities so many poor men and beggars. Whithersoever you turn you encounter poverty and distress and those who are compelled to hold out their hands for alms. Why is it not true that, just as everything in the state is restored which is subject to the ravages of time and fortune—such as walls, ditches, ramparts, streams, institutions, customs, and the laws themselves—so it would be suitable to aid in meeting that primary obligation of giving, which has suffered damage in various ways?…

Some of the poor live in those institutions commonly called hospitals…; others beg publicly;…I call "hospitals" those places where the sick are fed and cared for, where a certain number of paupers is supported, where boys and girls are reared, where abandoned infants are nourished, where the insane are confined, and where the blind dwell. Let the governors of the state realize that all these institutions are a part of their responsibility….

Should the native poor be asked whether they have learned a trade? Yes; and those who have not, if they are of suitable age, should be taught the one to which they say they are most strongly inclined, provided it is feasible. If it is not feasible, let them be taught some similar trade….But if this trade is too difficult, or he is too slow in learning, let an easier one be assigned to him, all the way down to those which anyone can learn thoroughly in a few days: such as digging, drawing water, bearing loads, pushing a wheelbarrow, attending on magistrates, running errands, bearing letters or packets, driving horses.

QUESTIONS FOR ANALYSIS

1. What are some of the sources of poverty for French farmers?
2. How does Vives recommend reducing poverty in Bruges?
3. According to these sources, what responsibilities do governments have for the poor?

---

[1]**tallage:** the taille

Source: "The Plight of the French Poor," *Journal des états généraux de France tenus à Tours en 1484*, ed. A. Bernier (Paris: 1835), quoted in J. B. Ross and M. Martin, eds., *The Portable Renaissance Reader*, trans. J. B. Ross (New York: 1953), pp. 215–18; Juan-Luis Vivès, "Concerning the Relief of the Poor," trans. M. M. Sherwood, *Studies in Social Work* 11 (New York: 1917), pp. 10–11, 14–15.

Louis traveled constantly. He rebuilt the king's traditional council of advisers, adding professional jurists who extended the jurisdiction of the royal courts, and developed a system of post roads so that news and messages could be transmitted rapidly across his kingdom. He promoted trade fairs, supported the silk industry, and saw the potential of the Mediterranean port of Marseilles, which belonged to Provence and was united with France in 1481. Above all, Louis was good at outliving other nobles of royal blood and inheriting their lands. By the end of his reign, he ruled most of what is now France.

ENGLAND In the second half of the fifteenth century, England was divided by the **Wars of the Roses** (1455–87), a protracted local appendix to the Hundred Years' War named for the white and red roses that symbolized the two warring parties. England's ruling family, the Plantagenets, was divided into two separate houses, both descended from Edward III and thus both with a claim to the throne. The Lancastrians were led by the ruling king, Henry VI (r. 1422–1461, 1470–1471), who suffered from bouts of insanity; the Yorkists by Richard, Duke of York. After war broke out in 1455, control passed repeatedly from house to house. The Yorkist victory in the bloody battle of Towton in 1461 made Richard's first son king. Edward IV (r. 1461–1470, 1471–1483) suppressed Lancastrian resistance and captured Henry, but eventually lost the support of his chief adviser, the powerful and wealthy earl of Warwick. Known as "the Kingmaker," Warwick decided to replace Edward by restoring Henry to the throne, but Edward defeated his opponents, killed Warwick in 1471, and had Henry murdered in the Tower of London. In this period of warfare, Warwick the Kingmaker was only one of many lords who hired retainers and built up their own military forces—sometimes, as in Warwick's case, to the point where they were able to challenge the crown itself.

When Edward IV died suddenly in 1483, his brother, Richard of Gloucester, seized the throne. As King Richard III (r. 1482–1485), he was an effective ruler with close ties to the city of London. He began to build new institutions—such as the Council of the North, an administrative body centered in the northern city of York—and to offer rapid and inexpensive justice through the Court of Requests. He also saw to it that the laws of England were translated, at long last, from Latin and French into English. But Richard was defeated and killed at the battle of Bosworth Field, in central England, by Henry Tudor, a Lancastrian claimant to the throne who founded the new dynasty of the Tudors.

Henry VII (r. 1485–1509), in his own way, introduced a

Wars of the Roses An illustration from the French historian Jean de Wavrin's 1471 chronicle of England shows a battle of the Wars of the Roses. Wavrin was from Burgundy, an ally of the House of York, which may explain the royal standards and white roses (representing York) that appear in the manuscript's margin.

model of kingship as novel as Louis XI's in France. Some of his policies were borrowed from the talented Richard III, whom he denounced as a usurper; others were created by his chief minister, John Morton, the archbishop of Canterbury. Henry relied heavily on the system of **justices of the peace**, unpaid local officials recruited from the ranks of local notables. They served for a year at a time, making them dependent on him for reappointment. Henry tasked them with overseeing the juries that decided cases, keeping public order, and ensuring that legislation was enforced. At the same time, he adopted new laws against "livery and maintenance"—the tradition by which powerful nobles had amassed armed retinues that amounted to private armies. These laws and the Court of Star Chamber, which Henry used to break the power of aristocrats suspected of plotting against him, established the monarchy as far more powerful than any potential rival.

In 1494 Henry engineered a boycott of the Flemish cloth industry that led, two years later, to an agreement favorable to British merchants trading in Antwerp—one of the industrial and financial centers of Europe. Over time, Henry became notorious for his demands for taxes and personal income. He went over financial records himself and annotated them in his own hand. And he used his gains not only to enrich the monarchy but also to begin the creation of a royal navy, with its own harbor, dockyard, and dry dock at Portsmouth. So in England, as in France, policies and institutions that would play essential roles in the creation of a modern state had their origins in the consolidation of monarchical power at the end of the fifteenth century.

HOLY ROMAN EMPIRE The Holy Roman Empire, which had undergone a sharp decline in power during the crises of the fourteenth and early fifteenth centuries, also began to recover. In 1440 Frederick of Habsburg, a member of the **Habsburg dynasty** that had long ruled Austria, was elected Holy Roman Emperor Frederick III, and in 1452 he was finally crowned by the pope. He married Eleanor of Portugal, establishing connections with other royal dynasties, and consolidated his power over the other members of the Habsburg family. Frederick's son and successor, **Maximilian I** (r. 1508–1519), was a true believer in the traditional codes of chivalry. He loved falconry and hunting, tournaments and chivalry—he famously took only 97 shots to bring down 100 birds—and nourished a special passion for splendidly decorated suits of armor.

Maximilian not only practiced the courtly arts of a medieval monarch; in some ways, he acted like one in politics as well. He saw himself not as creating a single, unified realm, but as pulling together multiple territories that he and his Habsburg successors could rule. Through advantageous marriages, both his own and that of his son Philip, he established Habsburg claims over much of Burgundy, the kingdoms of Aragon and Castile, and Milan. Like the Italian rulers of his time, Maximilian believed in the powers of astrology and magic, and dispensed patronage to professors at Vienna whose predictions, he thought, could give him accurate information about the shifting fields of politics and war.

Yet Maximilian was also a modern prince. Lacking a single capital city and many of the other trappings of royalty found elsewhere, he wielded the powers of art and print—especially those of artists such as the brilliant Nuremberg painter and printmaker Albrecht Dürer (1471–1528)—to create images that emphasized the venerable antiquity of the Habsburg house and his own accomplishments. In an effort to create warmer support within the empire, Maximilian placed special emphasis on his German roots. In 1495, at a meeting of the Reichstag (the imperial general assembly) in Worms, he led an ambitious effort to reshape the empire, which was reorganized into a set of administrative districts and equipped, for the first time, with a supreme court. Imperial reform had only limited success, and Maximilian's early efforts to maintain authority over the Swiss and intervene in wars with the French elsewhere were unsuccessful. Nonetheless, he laid the foundations for what would remain, for centuries to come, the great power of the Habsburg family. The policy of creating alliances by marriage, at which he proved so successful, would continue to work well for his successors, and even gave rise to a famous proverb: "Let others wage war. You, happy Austria, need only marry."

SPAIN More dramatic still was the political transformation taking place on the Iberian Peninsula. In the fifteenth century, Spain had been divided into a number of states: chiefly the kingdoms of Castile, Aragon, and Portugal. From 1475 to 1479, Castile was torn by a war over succession, as France and England were. But the 1469 marriage of Isabella and Ferdinand, the so-called Catholic kings, connected Isabella's Castile, with its crusading traditions and military nobility, with Ferdinand's Aragon, the most economically advanced part of Spain. Valencia, a port city on the east coast of Aragon, had become wealthy in the fourteenth and fifteenth centuries as a center of banking, trade, and textile production. Politically, Aragon was oriented to the Mediterranean, and its rulers also claimed vast, productive agrarian lands in Sicily and southern Italy.

The energetic partnership of Aragon and Castile led to a renewal of the Reconquista, the effort, which began

Maximilian's Power Artwork such as this 1526 woodcut by the printmaker Albrecht Dürer symbolizes Maximilian I's power and authority. The Holy Roman emperor and his wife, Mary, Duchess of Burgundy, ride a richly decorated chariot bearing a crest that represents the unification of their families. They are surrounded by admiring courtiers and mythological figures.

Ferdinand and Isabella An anonymous fifteenth-century portrait depicts the Catholic monarchs of Castile and Aragon who united the Spanish kingdoms. They are dressed austerely, but wear jewelry that signifies their royal status.

as early as the eighth century, to restore all of the peninsula to Christian rule. The Reconquista culminated in 1492 when the last Muslim state—Granada, ruled from the magnificent eleventh-century Alhambra palace at the center of its splendid capital city—fell. The year 1492 also marked an end point for the Jews of Spain, who had long been pressured to convert to Christianity, and sometimes forced to do so. Now the **Alhambra Decree**, issued by Catholic monarchs Ferdinand and Isabella, gave Jews four months to convert or leave. Thousands fled, many of them to the rising empire of the Ottoman Turks. Tens of thousands of Jews converted to Christianity, but remained under suspicion of backsliding for decades to come.

Under Isabella and Ferdinand, each Spanish region retained its own name and individuality, and dealt with the crown through its own representatives, who met, as they had for centuries, in each region's Cortes. Still, a new system of government through royally appointed officers, the *corregidores* ("magistrates"), spread from Castile to the rest of the lands of the Catholic kings. Noble families cast their fate with the monarchy, serving—often for generations—as military officers and governors of settlements abroad.

The Spanish also developed their own formidable infantry, many of them professionals and veterans. They were organized in units called *tercios,* each with 1,500 to 3,000 soldiers armed with pikes, swords, and arquebuses, a new firearm. Their mastery of tactics and disciplined ability to dig in and repel attacks by formidable, numerically superior opponents enabled them to fight the Swiss and the German mercenaries on equal terms. Under the

leadership of Isabella's "Great Captain," the Castilian general Gonzalo Fernández de Córdoba (1453–1515), the Spanish became the most formidable army in Europe.

THE OTTOMAN EMPIRE

Even as the great monarchies of Europe were attaining new levels of political unity, a new empire in the eastern Mediterranean, that of the **Ottomans**, could muster even more resources than any of these Christian states. In 1261 the independent Greek state of Nicea, a remnant of the former Byzantine Empire, reconquered Constantinople from the so-called Latin empire established by the Fourth Crusade in 1204. The new Byzantine emperor, Michael VIII (r. 1261–1282), founded the Palaeologan dynasty and worked hard to repair the damage that had been done when the crusaders sacked the city. Michael also tried to restore parts of the ancient Byzantine Empire, but full restoration proved impossible.

Gradually, one of the small Muslim states near Constantinople, led by Osman I (1258–1326), began to expand. By the end of the fourteenth century, his Ottoman successors controlled most of Asia Minor. They had taken the ancient Greek city of Thessalonica from the Venetians in 1387, defeated the rival, rapidly growing Serbian empire, at the battle of Kosovo in 1389, and in 1396 routed a crusading army sent against them at the battle of Nicopolis in Bulgaria. They besieged Constantinople but were prevented from conquering the city itself when the Mongol leader Timur, who had already conquered vast amounts of territory in India, Persia, and Syria, invaded Asia Minor. Timur defeated the Ottoman sultan Bayezid I in 1402 at the battle of Ankara and imprisoned him. But Timur died only three years later, and his state collapsed.

Mehmed I (r. 1413–1421) restored the Ottoman lands and conquered new territory in Albania and the Crimea. Murad II (r. 1422–1451) and his son Mehmed II (r. 1451–1481) returned to the offense. The Byzantines appealed for help to the pope and the Latin powers. But the price of substantial aid was accepting papal primacy, and though the Byzantine emperor John VIII (r. 1425–1448) negotiated a union of the two churches, most of the Eastern Orthodox clergy rejected it. In 1453, Mehmed II conquered Constantinople. His soldiers killed the last Byzantine emperor, and after transforming the city into his capital, he went on to conquer the Morea peninsula (the Peloponnesus), Serbia, Albania, and Wallachia. In 1480, the Ottomans raided Italy itself. When Mehmed died in the next year,

Mehmed II This fifteenth-century Turkish portrait of the Ottoman sultan owes much to Italian artistic influence, particularly in the colors used and the subject's slightly turned pose. Yet his clothes and accoutrements—from the archer's ring on his right thumb to the scholar's turban—identify him as a Central Asian warrior and intellectual. The roses he holds in his right hand allude to his aesthetic and intellectual refinement.

as well as Muslim, to transform Christian Constantinople into the Muslim capital, which the Ottomans called Istanbul. Minarets were added to Justinian's church of Hagia Sophia, turning it into a spectacular mosque, and massive palaces and other public buildings went up rapidly. The Ottoman Empire was, in many ways, the most formidable of Europe's new states.

THE TRANSFORMATION OF WARFARE

Christian or Muslim, these new states acquired new kinds of military power. As early as the fourteenth century, the classic missile weapon of the Middle Ages, the British longbow, had proved its ability to decimate large armies of heavily armored knights. In the same period, European records begin to show the appearance of "fire-pots"— primitive metal cannon that used gunpowder to fire stone projectiles. The Chinese had invented gunpowder in the ninth century, and by the thirteenth they were using it in firearms. Knowledge of these devices reached Europe by unknown means—perhaps along the ancient routes of the Silk Road.

Between 1350 and 1450, guns developed in Europe with astonishing speed. Cannon—forged first of bronze, and then of iron—took multiple forms. Huge siege guns were made by expert iron founders such as Orban, the Hungarian Christian who built the cannon that Mehmed II used to breach Constantinople's legendarily impregnable walls. Smaller guns that could be pulled by horses or pivoted by their gunners also came into use, with devastating effect, on the battlefield and aboard ships. Projectiles themselves became more varied and effective, as metal balls replaced stones, and explosive shells came into use.

Poor regions—the cantons of Switzerland, the mountains of central Italy, some of the German states of the Holy Roman Empire—and areas torn by war such as England and France during the Hundred Years' War spawned professional soldiers, as landless young men left the homes that could not support them. Some mercenary units, such as the well-disciplined White Company led by the Englishman John Hawkwood (1320–1394), specialized in terrorizing civilian populations, burning villages, and destroying crops. Others—especially the Swiss—were skilled in fighting with long spears called pikes, with which they defeated the Burgundians in 1477.

Gunpowder gave these professional soldiers new possibilities. The arquebus—a muzzle-loading gun with a stock—became a standard infantry weapon. Aimed from

still campaigning, the Ottoman Empire sprawled across much of Europe as well as Asia Minor.

Latin Europe knew that the Ottoman Empire was not only large but well administered. The sultans' special guard of Janissaries—boys taken from Christian families and trained to be professional soldiers—impressed observers with their loyalty to the ruler, their military skills, and their ferocity. The millet system—which allowed Christians and Jews to live in their own semiautonomous communities, with leaders approved by the state—kept the peace in the empire's massive European domains. Mehmed hired the best architects and artisans, Christian

Arquebuses In an illustration from a 1517 German epic, opposing armies aim arquebuses at each other. In the foreground, a single soldier has wounded two enemy knights, indicating the new weapon's power.

the shoulder and fired with a new matchlock mechanism, the arquebus could penetrate the hardest armor at close range. Rulers soon realized that paid soldiers who could handle firearms could concentrate great force on their enemies. The king of Hungary built and trained a professional military force, the Black Army, from the 1450s on. Every fifth member of the force had an arquebus. Hungary and the German states became early centers of production, and during the course of the fifteenth century, the use of the arquebus spread from Portugal to Muscovy, a Russian monarchy that had taken shape in the late thirteenth century. Upholders of tradition hated these new weapons. Even more effectively than the longbow, they enabled men of low social position to kill their betters from a safe distance. Yet artisans such as Orban who built guns and cannon rose in stature—especially as illustrated texts about the new military devices began to circulate, and states competed for the services of the military engineers who wrote them.

The immediate impact of cannon, in particular, was dramatic. In Italy—where warfare was almost continuous in the fifteenth century—gunnery soon transformed the waging of war. The high stone walls that had traditionally protected cities and bastions against sieges proved too thin to withstand cannon fire. Within fifty years, Italian architects and their patrons had learned to replace the old style of fortification with a new one: low, thick walls of earth and stone designed to absorb the force of projectiles. These walls made it possible to resist a besieging army equipped with artillery. Projecting bastions served as gun platforms for defenders and enabled them to fire on attacks from the side. Ships equipped with cannon could engage in battle without having to draw alongside their opponents and engage in hand-to-hand combat. The European vessels that began to move outward into the Atlantic Ocean carried small crews, but they were far more formidably armed than any opposition they were likely to encounter, even in East Asia.

THE CAULDRON OF THE EARLY ITALIAN WARS (1494–1517)

The first to recognize how the political and military world had changed were the Italians—especially the Italian political classes—in the years around 1490. In 1492, Piero, the heir of Lorenzo de' Medici, succeeded his father as de facto ruler of Florence. Clumsier than the uniquely deft Lorenzo, Piero lost support in the city and failed to emulate his father in keeping a firm hand on foreign affairs. In 1494, Ludovico Sforza, Duke of Milan, worried that the Spanish forces in Naples threatened his rule, offered the French king Charles VIII (r. 1483–1498) free passage if he wished to take up the Valois family's ancient dynastic claim to the rule of Naples. Charles promptly invaded Italy. His massive army terrified the Italian rulers, who had honed their skills fighting on a far smaller scale and in less destructive and ruthless ways. Piero immediately surrendered Florence's fortresses to the French—only to find himself ejected from office and from the city. Girolamo Savonarola (1452–1498), a popular Dominican preacher, had reported visions in his recent sermons: he saw a sword over Italy, threatening divine vengeance, and Florence in triumph as the city of lilies—then as now the symbol of France. The invasion seemed to bear out his visions, and his prestige was enhanced when he helped to persuade Charles to move on from Florence without disturbing its inhabitants.

A believer in republican government, Savonarola used his influence to persuade the Florentines—split between wealthy patricians, many of whom still supported the Medici, and members of the craft guilds, who had been

Early Italian Wars, 1494–1517 The Italian Wars transformed the great powers of Europe and helped forge new, modern features of politics and war.

Christopher Columbus's sailors, broke out among them after they reached Naples. In 1498 the French invaded again, led by Charles VIII's successor Louis XII (r. 1498–1515). Though Sforza arrived with a Swiss army of his own, the French dispatched him easily. In 1501 Louis joined with the Spanish to conquer Naples. But they fell out, and the Spanish commander, "The Great Captain," Gonzalo Fernández de Córdoba, rapidly defeated the French. The Treaty of Lyon, signed in 1504, left the Spanish in Naples and the French in Milan. But the situation was highly unstable, and for more than five decades, the peninsula would be the site of what came to be called the Italian wars. This long series of conflicts established the modern form of warfare as a contest of professional soldiers armed with gunpowder weapons. Florence's republic, first put down in 1512, would revive for a last period of defiance from 1527 to 1530. In the end, the Spanish would control most of Italy, directly (in Milan, Naples, and Sicily) or indirectly.

The great powers transformed Italy, but they also were transformed by their experiences there. They learned to employ architects and build modern fortifications; to form and train a diplomatic corps and use it in the making of treaties and, even more important, the weaving of secret alliances; and to exploit propaganda of many kinds as a basic instrument of policy. By the 1530s, England, France, Spain, and the Holy Roman Empire all had chancellors and ambassadors who matched the Italians in craft and policy, but served their own, far more powerful states.

excluded from power and profit—to build a more open set of institutions than had been in place before the Medici took power. They preserved the traditional committee structure, but created a sovereign Great Council, in which more than 3,000 Florentines were eligible to serve—far more than had ever served actively in government before. Savonarola himself came into sharp conflict with Pope Alexander VI (r. 1492–1503). The threat of a papal interdict, which could have brought about the confiscation of Florentine goods everywhere, led to Savonarola's arrest and torture in 1498. He confessed that he had invented his visions, and was executed. But the republic he helped to bring into being survived him. Led by Piero Soderini, whom Machiavelli served as ambassador to Cesare Borgia, Rome, and France, the Republic lasted for another eighteen sharply contested years.

In 1494 French forces had moved down the Italian peninsula virtually unopposed—only to be driven back when syphilis, introduced by the Genoese mariner

Savonarola's Execution An unknown artist painted this picture of Girolamo Savonarola's 1498 execution by fire in the Piazza della Signoria in Florence. The cityscape includes the Palazzo Vecchio at right.

A new political and military world—one with distinctively modern features—was forged when Europe's revived territorial states were transmuted in the cauldron of the Italian Wars.

CHRISTIANITY: CRISIS AND REFORM

The papacy, once the most universal of European organizations, had lost power, resources, and spiritual authority during the thirteenth and fourteenth centuries. After seventy years of French domination in Avignon, the papacy returned to Rome in the 1370s. While in Avignon, the papacy had reorganized its central institutions, such as the supreme court of canon law, or Rota, and developed more efficient systems for collecting revenues. But its concentration on these practical matters had earned it a reputation for greed and corruption—one reinforced by its endless assertions of power over appointments to church offices (benefices), which were given out only in return for fees.

Antipope An illumination from a late-fourteenth-century French chronicle shows cardinals crowning the antipope Clement VII in Avignon.

THE GREAT SCHISM (1378–1417)

The return to Rome from Avignon was desired by many, from Italian members of the Curia itself to the influential writer Petrarch, who called Avignon "Babylon" and described the papal residence there as an exile like the Babylonian Captivity of the ancient Jews. Still, the return proved rough, even violent: the papacy waged war with Florence, traditionally a pro-papal city, over conflicting territorial claims in central Italy. And when the French pope Gregory XI (r. 1370–1378), who had brought the papacy back to Rome, died in 1378, the cardinals, pressed by the Roman populace, elected an Italian successor, Urban VI (r. 1378–1389). His conduct soon filled the cardinals with buyers' remorse. Urban insisted on the sole authority of the pope and demanded that the cardinals abandon their claims to a share of papal revenues. He called on them to live more simply and humbly, and continually abused them, exploding in fury at unpredictable intervals.

At the invitation of the French king Charles VI (r. 1380–1422), the French cardinals reconvened, deposed Urban, and elected Cardinal Robert of Geneva, who took the title of Pope Clement VII (r. 1378–1394) and set up his court in Avignon. Suddenly the universal church had two leaders, both apparently elected in the same way and by the same officials. Almost all of the Italian cardinals remained loyal to Urban. They declared Clement an antipope. Then the two popes excommunicated one another. For the next forty years, a period known as the **Great Schism**, Christians' allegiance was split, not between conflicting theologies but between two—and at one point among three—popes.

Much of Europe's business went on untroubled through this period. Bankers continued to transfer money and merchants to trade. Many Christians, having come to see the papacy as a purely administrative institution, paid little attention to which pope claimed ultimate authority over their sector of the Church, so long as masses were performed and the dead were buried. By the end of the 1380s, however, the Avignon church had increased its fiscal demands to even higher levels, while the Roman one campaigned to take control of Naples and southern Italy. The new Roman pope, Boniface IX (r. 1389–1404), became notorious for the financial pressures he exerted to maintain his political position. In 1390 alone, he excommunicated thirty bishops and sixty-five abbots for having fallen behind on the payments they owed the papacy for their offices. Savage attacks on the Roman papacy began to circulate, especially in northern Europe. More important, French clerics and theologians began to argue for other ways of defining the church. They identified it not with the pope but with the body of the faithful, represented by the bishops.

French kings and Burgundian dukes began to demand that both popes resign. A council held in Pisa from March through August 1409 declared both popes deposed for their grave sins. The popes struck back: they held councils of their own and eventually found successors. In 1417, at the **Council of Constance** (1414–18) in southern Germany, a Roman from the Colonna family, one of the noble clans that dominated the city of Rome, was elected Pope Martin V (r. 1417–1431). His international and financial positions were very weak. To gain the recognition of rulers and clerics across Europe, he had to give up many of his rights to bestow benefices and charge fees for doing so. His income amounted to a third of what his predecessors before the Great Schism had received. Accordingly, Martin used his local connections to begin the long process of reestablishing papal rule in Rome. From now on, there would be only one pope, and he would rule the Church from its ancient center, acting more and more like an Italian prince and drawing his chief power and revenues from Italy.

REFORM MOVEMENTS

Yet the Avignon Captivity and the subsequent Schism, together lasting from 1309 to 1417, had scratched and dented the aura of sanctity on which, in the end, papal authority rested. Signs of external resistance to papal authority accompanied these internal challenges. The English Parliament adopted the Statute of Provisors (1351), which prohibited papal interference in appointments to English benefices, and the Statute of Praemunire (1353), which forbade legal appeals outside the realm (i.e. to Rome). The latter also prohibited English subjects from obtaining bulls or other legal documents from the courts of the Roman Church, under penalty of expulsion from the king's protection and the forfeiture of property.

In England and Bohemia (now part of the Czech Republic), two vital centers of Christian culture, radical critics of the existing Church demanded that the Bible be translated from Latin and made available to all, and that religious services be held in the languages of ordinary men and women. Two theologians did much to form these movements. The Oxford theologian John Wycliffe (ca. 1330–1384) insisted on testing the institutions and practices of the Church against scripture. He found no support there for the idea that some Christians should lead a holier life than others as members of religious orders,

or for many of the Church's practices, which he insisted were superstitious. Jan Hus (ca. 1372–1415), trained in theology at Prague, was inspired by Wycliffe as well as by his own study of the Bible. He denounced the immorality of the clergy and the wrong doctrines they taught. Both men found followers.

LOLLARDS John Wycliffe's message spread rapidly, at first primarily in England. His followers, who came to be known as Lollards, included a few men and women of high birth and a much larger number of small merchants, artisans, and peasants. Lollard beliefs spread mostly through personal ties: spouses converted spouses, parents instructed children, masters and mistresses taught servants. Lollards believed that every Christian, women as well as men, should read and interpret scripture—and in many cases spent long hours teaching basic literacy to members of their families. On the basis of their reading of the Bible, they rejected the whole hierarchy of the Church, from the pope on down, and demanded radical changes in religious services. They held their own religious meetings.

An initial period during which Lollards found some support at the universities gave way by 1400 to intense persecution by the Church and the English state. When a rebellion in England led by the Lollard Sir John Oldcastle failed in 1414 and another effort was repressed in 1439, Wycliffe's followers ceased to be an active force for a time. Still, they made their own editions of the Bible in English, copying them in secret scriptoria, and around 1,500 groups of them began to emerge from the shadows.

HUSSITES Dissent traveled with surprising speed and found more fertile ground on the Continent than it had in Britain. The kingdom of Bohemia was the richest part of central Europe in the fourteenth century. Its ruler, Charles IV (r. 1346–1378), who would later become Holy Roman emperor, built Prague, its capital, into a metropolis with some 40,000 inhabitants. He spanned the Vltava River with a magnificent stone bridge, began a cathedral, and founded a university. The countryside was relatively rich, cultivated by free peasants. Under his patronage, the Church became extraordinarily wealthy, controlling a third of the Bohemian lands. Reformers began to denounce the clergy for their wealth and worldliness. Czech scholars who studied in England brought back Wycliffe's new message.

Jan Hus, a young theologian who copied Wycliffe's works, developed his own reforming program, which he expounded in eloquent sermons. He believed that all lay Christians should join clerics in partaking of the wine

Jan Hus's Heresy In this fifteenth century manuscript illustration, a priest looks on as men—some stern, others celebratory—stoke the flames burning Hus at the stake. Hus wears the robe of a dissident cleric, while the sign on his hat condemns him as a heretic.

and bread during Communion, and that the Church must reform itself by giving up most of its wealth and power. At first, he found support from every level of the population, from nobles to artisans and peasants. Although a relative moderate who hoped to persuade the authorities to carry out necessary changes, Hus was imprisoned and condemned by the Council of Constance. In 1415 he was burned at the stake for heresy.

Hus's death turned his movement into a revolution. Hussites in Prague, most of them craftsmen, threw German nobles from the windows of the city hall in the Czech part of the city, and destroyed religious images and relics. Artisans and peasants in southern Bohemia, frightened by outbreaks of the Black Death, saw this movement as the beginning of the end of the world. They took up residence in a fortress south of Prague, to which they gave the biblical name Mount Tabor. Traveling when necessary in wagon trains that could be chained together in fortified camps, they abandoned all distinctions of clothing between priests and laypeople, demanded the abolition of courts and oaths, and fought off the crusades that the papacy sent against them. In 1434 the Taborites were defeated by more moderate Hussites, who negotiated a compromise treaty with the Latin Church, which allowed them to read their scriptures and practice their rites so long as they formally acknowledged papal supremacy. The wealth and power of the Church in Bohemia remained greatly diminished, and the Hussites were allowed to use their own liturgy and give Communion with both bread and wine: a powerful exception to the long-established unity of the Latin Church.

CONCILIARISTS (1409–1449) Through the first decades of the fifteenth century, reforming cardinals and theologians, concerned about these threats to the Church as well as the problems of papal governance, continued to call councils. As early as the thirteenth century, some theologians—worried by increasing papal power and the possibility that its holder might become a heretic—theorized that although the pope was the steward of God, those who had elected him on behalf of the Christian people could also depose him when necessary. During the Great Schism, advocates of the councils—in later years they came to be called Conciliarists—argued that a representative body composed of cardinals, bishops, and others should hold supreme authority in the Church. The Council of Constance decreed that the authority of the council, since it came directly from God, was binding on all Christians, even the pope. Further councils met in Basel, Switzerland; Florence; and Ferrara, Italy, in the 1430s. All of these efforts, though attended with much powerful rhetoric and supported by some sincere believers, ran into the sand. Pope Pius II (r. 1458–1464), an Italian scholar and onetime Conciliarist, gained firm control of the Church in 1458 after he turned back a conspiracy of cardinals who hatched a plot against him in the Vatican lavatory, where they had gathered in the hope of electing a weaker Frenchman. Yet the papacy had lost much ground.

ORTHODOXY IN OTTOMAN LANDS Long before Pius became pope, he insisted that the whole Christian church was really one, and that Catholics had a duty to help the Orthodox Christians of Byzantium defend themselves against the Ottomans. Serious efforts were made to reunite the Greek and Russian Orthodox Churches with the Roman Church. At the Council of Florence in 1439, prelates from both eastern churches signed an act of union with Rome. But Vasily II (r. 1425–1462), the Grand Prince of Moscow, rejected the agreement. And though the Byzantine emperor John VIII Palaeologus accepted the union, the clergy and monks of the Greek Orthodox Church never did.

After Constantinople fell to the Ottomans in 1453, Pius proclaimed a crusade to retake the city. A brilliant writer of Latin, he did his best to appeal to all of the mixed groups of Europeans who held power and might take part, from feudal lords in northern Europe to merchants in Italy.

But only a small crusading force arrived in the port of Ancona on the eastern coast of Italy, most of which dissipated when the promised transport was slow to arrive. Pius himself died of fever, but the crusading ideal lived on, revived again and again, especially as Christian propaganda against the Ottomans.

A measure of coexistence developed in the Ottoman lands, where the Orthodox Church adapted to surviving under Muslim rule. Granted authority over all its churches and their property, the patriarchate of Constantinople was reestablished by Mehmed II in 1454 and conferred on a reliably anti-Catholic cleric. For centuries to come, the Greek Orthodox Church survived within the larger Ottoman framework. The Orthodox clergy were left in charge of powerful institutions, such as their many wealthy and massive monasteries. Gradually the Church was charged with legal as well as religious power over all of the sultan's Christian subjects. The patriarch collected taxes from Christians for the sultan, and handled all legal cases connected with marriage, divorce, or commercial relations between Christians and Muslims in the Ottoman lands.

"APPETITE FOR THE DIVINE"

The vast majority of western Europeans continued to be faithful Catholics, as their ancestors had been. If anything, in fact, they were more faithful than the generations that immediately preceded them. Most Christians made their yearly confession, attended their church each week, and followed the rituals of the Christian year, relatively austere in summer and fall but crammed with feast days in winter and spring. They attended the Latin Mass that was sung for them by cathedral or parish clergy, and viewed the stories of the Old and New Testaments rendered in sculpture, tapestry, or stained glass.

People who were neither rich nor saintly still showed— as the great French historian Lucien Febvre once remarked—a "boundless appetite for the divine." Plays and rituals based on the Bible continued to be staged before broad audiences. **Confraternities** (lay religious organizations) promoted active pursuit of Christian virtue in many ways. Hundreds of them flourished across Europe, especially in cities. Counting women as well as men as members, their activities ran the gamut, from doing penance together by flagellation, to visiting the sick, accompanying the condemned to execution, and writing letters to Saint Peter recommending fellow members, with whom they were buried.

A few saints continued to walk the streets, their

Christian Confraternities Members of the Florentine Compagnia dei Buonomini confraternity distribute clothes to the poor in this late-fifteenth-century fresco by the artist Domenico Ghirlandaio.

sanctity recognized by all. In the mid-fifteenth century, Rome was still largely vacant, with no more than 40,000 inhabitants wandering its streets and squares. Courtesans and merchants selling pilgrims' badges and other mementoes from small shops and outdoor tables crowded around the great Roman churches. Mingling among them was Saint Francesca Romana (1384–1440), the mystic who followed the course charted by her medieval predecessors as she made the ascent to spiritual union with God. Francesca had vivid visions and revelations, and worked, with the efficiency that only mystics and other supremely single-minded individuals enjoy, to create a hospital and a confraternity. She enjoyed such prestige that her very presence on the dark, violent streets of Rome could bring an end to feuds and, supposedly, heal mortal wounds.

NEW DIRECTIONS IN RELIGIOUS LIFE

Impresarios of the sacred created new ways of living a Christian life as deftly as Francis and Dominic had in the thirteenth century, when they called the mendicant orders into being. The Dutch cleric Geert Groot (1340–1384) founded houses for men and women who called themselves the Brothers and Sisters of the Common Life. They lived together, not taking vows. All of them—aristocrats and artisans, rich women and poor—worked for their living with their hands, in order to pursue poverty in a simpler, more literal way than that practiced by the powerful religious orders. Some members of this movement worked at first as scribes, then became printers when the new technology reached their city, using it to provide prayers and meditations for readers who shared their desire for a simple piety.

BEGUINES   Across Europe, women experimented with new ways of life, inspired by religion. In the thirteenth century, beguines appeared in French and Netherlandish cities: women who lived in their own houses or in communities without taking vows, dressed simply, and did not marry. In the fourteenth and fifteenth centuries, beguine residences in Bruges and other cities in the Low Countries grew as women from poorer families joined, expanding into large courtyards lined by tiny houses in which the women lived. In the same period, religious houses of women living communally, but without a rule or, in some cases, male supervision, appeared in every Italian city. A new literature took shape: lives of the sisters who had created the houses and treatises on contemplation, written by and for women.

DEPARTURES FROM SCHOLASTICISM   The energies of the Church went in other directions as well. In the twelfth and thirteenth centuries, scholastic theology had been a specialty of the universities of northern and western Europe. From the middle of the fourteenth century on, however, the effort to arrive at fundamental truths about God and the universe by formal argument spread into new parts of Europe. From Spain to Bohemia to Scotland, new universities popped up. And theologians were beginning to challenge the beautiful, coherent structures of doctrine that scholastics such as Thomas Aquinas had reared.

The Franciscan Roger Bacon (ca. 1214–ca. 1292), originally trained at Oxford, became an influential teacher at Paris in the mid-thirteenth century. He revised the scholastic program in multiple ways. It was wrong, he argued, to content oneself with word-for-word Latin translations from Aristotle, often hard to understand and sometimes inaccurate. Theologians must study Greek and other languages in which important forms of knowledge were preserved, and learn to read texts critically and correct them—or declare them spurious—when necessary. A believer in astrology, which he thought explained the course of world history, Bacon was also an engaged empiricist who devised experiments with lenses and argued that the university scholar needed to study the practical men who had learned to steer ships using a magnetic compass. In some ways, Bacon called for a return to the world of Aristotle and the Alexandrian scholars who had combined the study of texts with practical investigation of nature,

or that of the earlier House of Wisdom. But he believed that even more could be done. Someday, he claimed, magnificent technologies unknown in his day would make it possible for men to fly and transmute metals.

More radical, in some ways, than Bacon—and more influential in their time—was another Franciscan, William of Occam (ca. 1287–1347). Thomas Aquinas had believed, in a tradition going back to Plato, that general terms such as *beauty* and *goodness* referred to ideal forms that actually existed somewhere in the universe. Occam denied the existence of such abstract entities, and insisted that human language and argument could never prove the existence and justice of God. Fifteenth-century theologians took up and continued the debate between Occam and Aquinas; some shared Bacon's interest in astrology. And as the weighty issues about the structure of the Church and the location of its authority became the subjects of long, impassioned debates in the era of schism and councils, the French Conciliarist Jean Gerson and others began to devise ways of treating theological questions in shorter, more accessible forms such as pamphlets, which could be read by anyone literate, even if he or she did not have formal training in theology.

WITCHCRAFT: THEORY AND PRACTICE   The most fertile of all the late-medieval approaches to the scholastic form of argument, tragically, was taken by German Dominicans. Since antiquity, Christians had determined that the devil not only existed but also regularly intervened in everyday life, hoping to lure Christians to their damnation and drawing on the help of lower devils. They had also accepted that some humans were witches—magicians who invoked the help of the devil to cast spells. But the theologians of the fifteenth century applied their full methods—for the first time—to the scattered anecdotes and sometimes-contradictory laws about witchcraft. They developed a coherent theory, which they laid out in systematic, cogently presented treatises. Devils, they argued, really walked the earth. They were replicas of human beings, which could take either male or female form and could speak and act. In their male form, they seduced human women, whom they persuaded to join the legions of the evil and to conjure harm by killing babies, drawing down hailstorms to destroy crops, and rendering men impotent. Worst of all, they produced diabolic offspring by injecting women with corrupted sperm that, in their female form, they had drawn from men they seduced. Every time a wife failed to conceive, a baby died in childbirth, crops failed, or livestock died, a witch might be to blame—and the devil with her.

Dominican theologians believed that only subtle, trained interrogators—backed, as always, by the threat and application of torture—could wring the truth from these enemies of the human race, avert their efforts to seduce their accusers, and combat the terrifying threat they represented. By the end of the fifteenth century, the first large witch trials were being held in Germany, Switzerland, and Italy. True, the real rage for holding them did not catch on until after 1560 or so, when a series of trials began that would eventually take some 30,000 to 70,000 lives across Europe, the majority of them female. But the belief in a conspiracy to destroy mankind—as neat and logical in its own way as the universe that Aquinas had built—made sense in a precarious world where plague endlessly returned and death threatened humans and animals alike. Every Christian baby, after all, was exorcized to remove the corruption of the devil before being baptized—a practice not abandoned until a Church council ended it in the 1960s. It made sense—the specialty of the scholastic theologian—to take seriously the idea of diabolic intervention in the world, and to draw out all of the ramifications it might have, one by one.

PERSECUTION OF NON-CHRISTIANS

If witches did not materialize immediately on cue, however, other enemies did. In Trent, on the border between Italy and the Holy Roman Empire, Jews were accused in 1475, as they had been for centuries, of murdering Christian boys to use their blood for ritual purposes; several were condemned and executed. Further ritual-murder trials spread across the German world, and Jews were ejected from cities such as Regensburg, where they had lived since Roman times. The Jews of Spain, as we have seen, were forced in 1492 to convert or leave the country. In Italy, Jews were forced, far more systematically than ever before, to wear yellow patches—and in the case of women, earrings—to set them apart from Christians. Gradually they were confined to small, closed neighborhoods known as ghettos. Small groups of Ashkenazi Jews from western Europe and much larger communities of Sephardic Jews expelled from Spain and Portugal settled in cities across the Ottoman Empire, from Istanbul and Salonika in northern Greece to Jerusalem and Safed in Palestine. Like Orthodox Christians, the Jews lived as a protected nation in the Ottoman Empire, and many flourished in trade and banking.

Meanwhile, officials in Spain became increasingly expert in working out which supposed Christians not only had Jewish ancestors but continued to observe certain Jewish rituals, and which Moriscos, as Muslim converts were called, did the same with their traditions.

The Spanish Inquisition After ferreting out heretics, the Inquisition tribunal would pronounce judgment in a ceremony called the *auto da fé* (Portuguese for "act of faith") that would often include a procession, a mass, and a reading of the sentence in the town's piazza. Secular authorities would then carry out the sentence. In 1499, the tribunal asked painter Pedro Berruguete to depict Saint Dominic, the founder of the Dominican order, presiding over an *auto da fé*, as proof that the practice was a holy one.

From 1478, moreover, an official tribunal, the Spanish Inquisition, made the detection of crypto-Jews and, to a lesser extent, Moriscos its central business. Close inspection of genealogies and behavior, from eating to praying, enabled the inquisitors to detect the enemies of humanity. Modernity—as the history of the twentieth century shows—has brought with it both horrors and enlightenment. Both were amply present at the birth of the modern world, from the European settlements in the Iberian Peninsula to the heartlands of Catholic culture.

EUROPE EXPANDS: NEW TECHNOLOGIES AND THEIR CONSEQUENCES

Renaissance Europe was born under the signs of contraction and despair. The Black Death had devastated Europe in the mid-fourteenth century, and recurrences of the plague kept population levels low into the fifteenth century. And yet, beneath the turbulence, as we have seen in the areas of state formation and religion, Europeans were laying the foundations for recovery and transformation. The paired discoveries of a new world and an ancient past brought changes more startling than anything Europe—or the world—had previously experienced.

MARITIME ADVANCES

Even after 1453, when the Venetians lost the immense foothold in the eastern Mediterranean that Constantinople had provided, they and the Genoese continued to expand their mercantile empires. Venetian fleets, developed by state action, and Genoese ones, normally financed by private partnerships, ranged the Mediterranean. Venetians, Genoese, and other European mariners, moreover, continued to develop new techniques.

Although no one knows who invented the maps known as **portolan charts**, which came into widespread use in the fourteenth and fifteenth centuries, they were practical in a way that the scholars' schematic maps never had been. Portolan charts detailed the coastlines where European merchants mingled with the Asian and North African merchants with whom they could bargain for gold, spices, and silks. The new maps largely ignored the mainland interiors that Ptolemy and his Greek copyists had filled with rivers, mountains, and cities. Instead the maps traced, with ever-increasing precision, the primary routes that led from port to port. Equipped with portolans—and with magnetic compasses, the floating lodestones that also came into widespread use in the fourteenth and fifteenth centuries—European merchants could explore more widely than ever before.

The ships themselves, moreover, became capable of undertaking longer journeys. Alongside the low galleys, powered by oars and a single square sail, that had plied the Mediterranean since ancient times, new types of ships were developed with three or four masts. Equipped with complex rigging, they could both sail into the wind and tack before it, and could carry larger cargoes.

Portolan Charts New cartographic technology allowed navigators to follow the routes between ports. This fifteenth-century portolan chart of Italian trade routes includes illustrations of Venice and Genoa.

Caravels—small, slender, and maneuverable—navigated shallow coastal waters and explored rivers. Carracks—larger, with high, rounded sterns—were more stable and could carry more goods. The Europeans who sailed these ships mastered new navigation techniques. They learned, for example, that the Atlantic winds blew steadily back to the east. To return to Europe, ships entering the Atlantic from the Mediterranean or the western coastlines of Europe had to keep sailing west until they caught the wind, which brought them home.

EARLY ATLANTIC EXPEDITIONS

Support for these expeditions into the unknown came from more than one source. Henry the Navigator (1394–1460), fifth son of the king of Portugal, joined his father and brothers in 1415 in an attack on the Spanish city of Ceuta on the Moroccan coast, a convenient base for raids on Portugal across the narrow Strait of Gibraltar. Their success in taking the city encouraged Henry to organize

Henry the Navigator The Portuguese prince appears in a detail from a 1465 painting that shows the most important members of Portuguese society venerating Saint Vincent—hence Henry's pious posture and expression.

a series of further expeditions, which gradually pushed down the western coast of Africa and westward into the Atlantic. He was impelled by the hope of joining forces with a Christian ally in Africa, the king of Ethiopia, whose wealth and power were exaggerated by European reports. But possibilities of profit were also attractive.

The spice trade brought Europeans not only the sharp flavorings they demanded for their food but also a wider range of products, including such substances as opium, mummy (an aromatic exuded by embalmed bodies), and tutty (dried chimney scrapings), which were used in medicine. It yielded immense profits to the Muslim merchants who brought products to India and then across the Persian Gulf and Red Sea, where land routes continued to Europe. Venice had dominated the western end of these routes in the Mediterranean, but once Constantinople fell in 1453, the Ottomans controlled the trade and could raise taxes at will. Was it possible, the Portuguese and others now began to ask, to sail around Africa to reach the sources of spice directly?

By the beginning of the fifteenth century, the new techniques and vessels carried Spanish and Portuguese sailors and traders farther and farther from the known Mediterranean routes. Both groups found and settled massive island chains in the Atlantic: the Portuguese took the Azores, and the Spanish—after struggles with the Portuguese that ended only in 1479—the Canary Islands. These islands offered timber and land for cultivation. When the Madeira archipelago proved poor territory for grain production, Henry ordered the planting of sugarcane and sugar beets, both successful crops on the Mediterranean island of Cyprus. In the Mediterranean, Venice held a monopoly on the shipping of sugar. Genoese investors supported the building of sugar plantations on Madeira, which eventually surpassed Cyprus as a producer of sugar and brought great profits to Portugal.

TO THE INDIAN OCEAN

Gold, and ornaments made out of it, had always filtered north to Europe from Guinea, carried by Arab caravans across the Sahara to the ports of the North African region known as the Maghreb. But after the Portuguese established an African base in 1415, sailors made their way down Africa's west coast, where they came into direct contact with the kingdoms of Guinea. Their progress was often violent, combining trading with raiding. Slowly the Portuguese built forts, established trading posts, and staged a long series of expeditions that gradually charted the entire western coast of Africa.

Finally, the Portuguese navigator Vasco da Gama (ca. 1460–1524) rounded the Cape of Good Hope in an epic ocean journey that lasted from 1497 to 1499 and covered a greater distance than any previous European voyage. He touched down in eastern Africa, stunned by the quality and quantity of goods traded in the Indian Ocean. Da Gama was turned away, however, by the Muslim ruler of Mozambique, who found his gifts insultingly poor. With the help of an experienced Indian Ocean pilot, da Gama negotiated the monsoon winds and reached India in twenty-three days. He made land in Calicut, on the Malabar Coast, the center of the spice trade. Da Gama possessed only modest trading goods and found opposition at the hands of Muslim merchants, but he and his crew obtained some spices by bartering on the docks. Only a gift of meat and oranges from the ruler of Malindi enabled da Gama and his crew to make the voyage home, and fewer than a third of the crew survived. But when da Gama returned to Portugal in July 1499, it was clear that eastward voyages could yield extraordinary returns.

Further Portuguese voyages to Indian Ocean ports carried more extensive trading goods and were better prepared for the journey. The first was led by Pedro Álvares Cabral (1467/8–1520), who became the first European explorer to reach Brazil before he turned east to follow da Gama's route. But the Portuguese also came into sharp conflict with Muslim merchants, who killed fifty of Cabral's men. He retaliated by burning ten Muslim cargo vessels and killing almost 600 men, then moved on to establish a trading post at Cochin, also on the Malabar Coast. His return to Portugal, with seven of his original thirteen ships, showed that the old monopoly of Muslim traders on the spice trade was broken. Da Gama's next

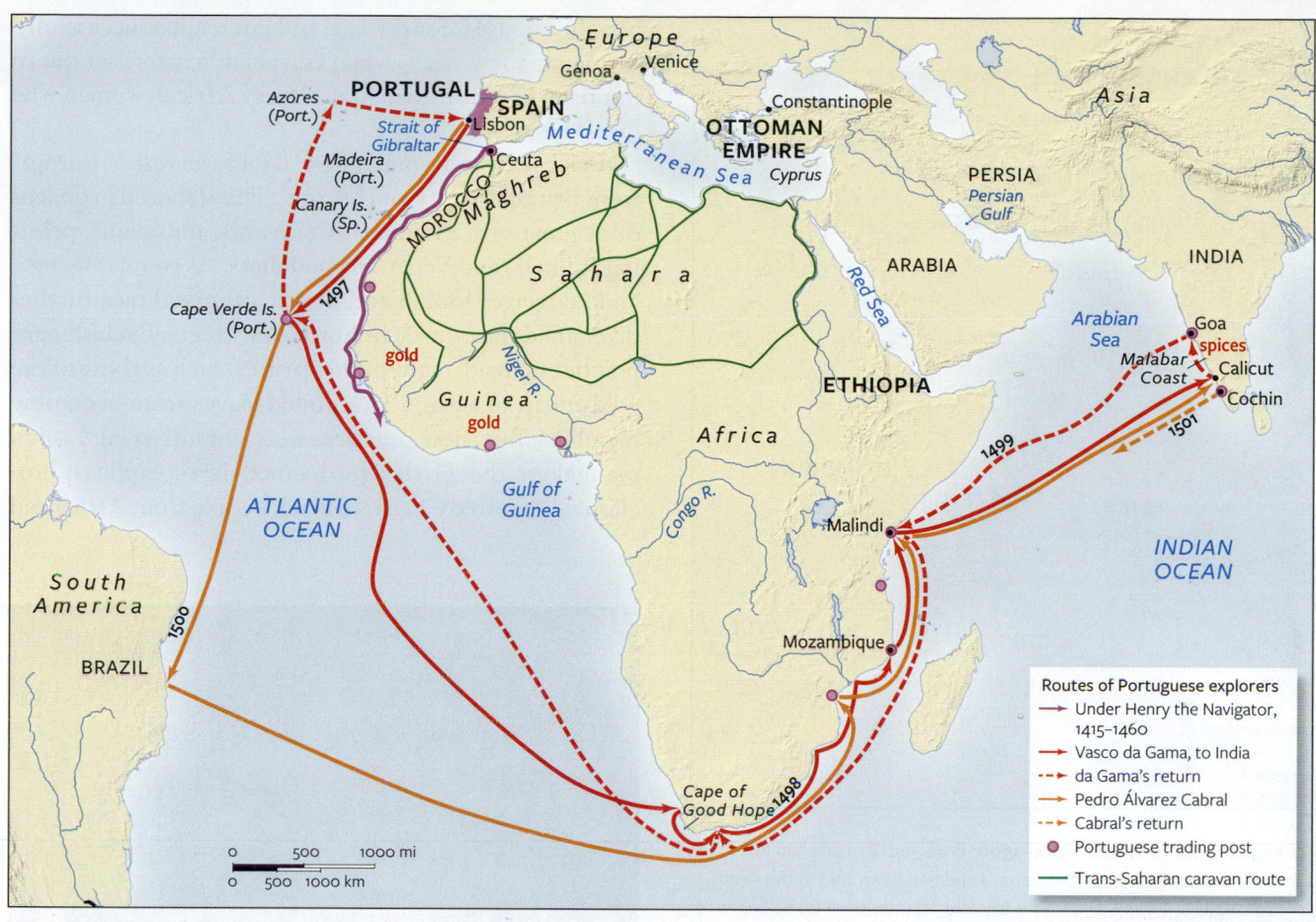

Portuguese Expeditions, 1415–1500 Following Henry the Navigator's voyage to western Africa in 1415, the Portuguese established trading posts along the coast and claimed the Azores and the Madeira archipelago. In 1497–99, Vasco da Gama's first voyage to western India opened up access to the spice trade, leading to expedition and Portuguese naval dominance in the Indian Ocean.

expedition amounted to a terror campaign against Muslim shipping, and he left a Portuguese naval force in Indian waters. Thanks to their superior military power, the Portuguese were soon able to establish a network of colonies that stretched from Mozambique to Goa, and to create a vastly profitable trade.

SLAVERY AND THE SLAVE TRADE

Europeans, Arabs, Africans, and others had traded for slaves for centuries. From the second half of the thirteenth century, Venetian and Genoese merchants bought slaves in markets around the Aegean and Black Seas. The high mortality induced by the Black Death helped to expand the market for this trade—most of whose victims were Mongols, Slavs, or Circassians, with a small number of Greeks and Christians from the Balkans. Practices differed according to local conditions. In Genoa, the number

of slaves doubled to 4,000 or 5,000—almost 10 percent of the population—during the fifteenth century. In Florence, by contrast, there were only 360 slaves in a population of 37,000 in 1427. These northern Italian slaves were mostly young women bought to serve as domestic workers. In the agricultural lands of southern Italy, by contrast, Muslim slaves were also sold, and men as well as women were bought to work in the fields.

Africa, like other parts of the world, had long been the scene of multiple forms of slavery: slaves included people captured in raids or in war, those who could not pay their debts, and people required for sacrifice in religious rituals. Slave women and children worked in the fields and households, men in the salt mines of the Sahara. Slaves were sold by Nubian, Ethiopian, and Funj masters, and brought by Arab merchants from the kingdoms of eastern and western Africa across the Sahara to markets in Algiers, Tripoli, and Cairo. The trans-Saharan slave trade supplied labor for the sugar plantations developed

by Moroccan entrepreneurs. In 1444, however, the Portuguese began to transport slaves by ship directly from western Africa to their homeland, eliminating the Arab middlemen of the Maghreb. Portuguese shipments of slave labor to the sugar plantations of Madeira, the Canary Islands, and the Cape Verde Islands formed the beginning of what would become the vast transatlantic slave trade, which the Portuguese extended to their colony in Brazil in the 1530s.

In Europe, more and more Africans, male and female, were brought to do every sort of work. Peoples and cultures mixed. Guinean artisans began to craft small sculptures of gold and ivory that included European objects (such as ships) and people, represented in styles that reflected European tastes. Enslaved and free black people entered Portugal—where, in some cities, they lived by the thousands, forming their own Christian congregations. In Valencia, a wealthy city on the Mediterranean coast of Spain, African slaves formed a religious confraternity,

Portuguese Slave Trade, 1444–1500 Enslaved Africans had long worked in the salt mines of the Sahara and had been sold in the Arab ports of Algiers, Tripoli, and Cairo. But the Atlantic slave trade began in 1444 when Portuguese traders brought slaves from western Africa to work on the sugar plantations on Madeira, the Canary Islands, and the Cape Verde Islands.

bought a house for meetings, and interceded successfully, in at least a few cases, when Christian masters set out to imprison or send into distant slavery African women who displeased them.

Black men and women moved into the rest of Europe, from Britain to Italy and beyond. They labored in dozens of occupations, as domestic servants, musicians, printing workers, and Venetian gondoliers. As couples formed and marriages took place, people of mixed race further diversified the crowds in European streets. Exclusionary practices spread: many guild statutes, such as those of the goldsmiths of Lisbon, prohibited slaves from becoming members. But these practices were not universal: Lisbon pie-makers, though they too banned slaves, explicitly proclaimed that free Christian black people from Africa and

Africans in Europe A portrait from the late sixteenth century, attributed to Italian painter Annibale Carracci (1560–1609), depicts an African woman in European clothing holding a clock of European manufacture, evidence of the presence of Africans in European society.

people of mixed European and African descent could be considered. The population on the streets of Europe was now, in part, nonwhite.

PRINTING: THE BOOK TRANSFORMED (1450–1517)

As transformative as the new ships and navigational techniques were, in some ways the most powerful—and potentially the most explosive—of all the new technologies that Europeans adopted in the fifteenth century was the printing press. For centuries, Asians had carved wood blocks and used them to print texts and illustrations. By the thirteenth century, Chinese printers were using wood blocks and moveable wooden type, which for the tens of thousands of Chinese characters were easier to produce and cheaper to replace than the cast metal type developed by the Koreans around the same time. Korea even developed a form of moveable type with a simplified alphabet rather than characters—though it was kept a royal monopoly and used only for official publications. Still, in the fifteenth and sixteenth centuries, bookshops in China and elsewhere in Asia brimmed with offerings of every kind, from official texts to pamphlets and gazetteers.

Europeans came later to the field, as the products needed for printing gradually reached the Continent. From the thirteenth century on, another Asian invention, paper made with cloth fibers from rags, came into wider use. It did not entirely replace parchment, made from the skin of calves and sheep, which had been the standard medium for centuries and continued to be used, especially for many types of legal documents. But paper sharply lowered the cost of writing materials and books. Through the first half of the fifteenth century, Europeans carried out experiments with printing single sheets from wood blocks and metal plates. These revolutionized the visual arts and yielded a fair number of illustrated books, printed page by page. They were narratives of biblical history and saints' lives, for the most part, reproduced in outline and then colored by hand, like graphic novels that combined a traditional faith in the old sacred narratives with an interest in new stories about the monsters that dwelled at the ends of the earth.

GUTENBERG In the 1450s, however, **Johannes Gutenberg** (1398–1468) created something that Europeans had not seen before. A craftsman—he seems to have been both a goldsmith and a blacksmith—Gutenberg came from a well-off merchant family in the German city of

Mainz. His ancestors had worked in the mint of the local bishop, and Gutenberg may have learned about presses and molds from them. He spent the 1430s and 1440s tinkering with various projects, including a device for polishing metal mirrors. At least one of these efforts ended in bankruptcy. By the late 1440s he was borrowing money and working on something new. By bringing together old and new technologies, Gutenberg made it possible to produce books mechanically, rather than by hand.

Gutenberg himself may have devised one of the vital components: an oil-based ink that would stick to the metal type and then transfer neatly onto paper. He also crafted type for the Latin alphabet, molding the individual characters in sand. And he worked out how to set lines of type into a frame and lock them in place. This frame could be set into the existing technology of the hand press, long used for producing olive oil and metal badges. Simply

Gutenberg Bible Early printed books were often decorated with elaborate illustrations in the style of handwritten illuminated manuscripts, as on this page from a Gutenberg Bible. The large initial letter "P" surrounds a miniature portrait of King Solomon, and marks the beginning of the book of Proverbs.

by turning a large metal screw that pressed the frame down onto paper, Gutenberg's workers could print a whole series of pages at one time. Each sheet of paper would then be extracted from the press, dried, and folded so that its component pages appeared in the correct order.

In some ways, Gutenberg—like other early modern revolutionaries—was conservative. The first book that he printed—the enormous and beautiful book known as the Gutenberg Bible—faithfully reproduced, in larger format, what had been a standard form for manuscript Bibles since the early thirteenth century: a Latin Bible laid out in two columns of text per page. An observer who saw the book as it went through the press was struck by the neatness and legibility of its type, not by the novelty of its production. Manuscripts were not only written but illuminated (illustrated): decorated with very large initial letters, for example, that incorporated exquisite miniature paintings. Many copies of the Gutenberg Bible were also illustrated by hand, giving them the look of traditional manuscripts. Some were purchased for use in monasteries, probably for reading aloud, since their large, clear type would have been helpful for that purpose.

THE IMMEDIATE IMPACT OF BOOK PRINTING

Gutenberg's breakthrough did not so much revolutionize literacy in Europe as accelerate a revolution that was already under way. Medieval European society was already highly literate. Cities swarmed with notaries, accountants, and government clerks, all of them skilled in writing and computation. Religious dissidents copied their own Bibles, prayer books, and commentaries. More conservative Christians did the same. Many of the most popular books—the ones that printers immediately began to reproduce—were highly traditional: for example, the books of hours, which developed from the breviaries used by priests to recite the daily service in the mid-thirteenth century. Some of these, beautifully illuminated by such artists as Jan Van Eyck (ca. 1395–ca. 1441), were spectacular works of art reserved for the wealthiest patrons. But stationers in France and the Netherlands also mass-produced less-expensive versions without full-page illustrations. By 1500, a British female pauper was indicted for stealing a book of hours from a female servant—evidence that these functional books were available not only to the rich.

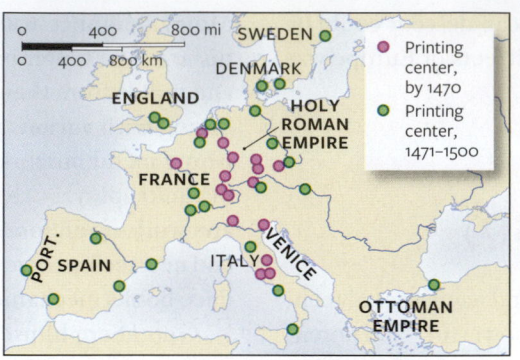

The Spread of Printing, 1455–1500

Printers rapidly transformed the existing networks of the book trade. Master printers found bankers to lend them capital so that they could obtain a house, type, a press, ink, and paper. Some printers formed partnerships with colleagues in other cities to exchange their products, so that each had a wider range of books to sell. Large and costly books, which required a great deal of paper, were produced by two or more printers working together in a syndicate. Universities, with their large student markets, proved especially welcoming. Two professors at the Sorbonne in Paris created a press in 1470, and then moved it to what became the center of the trade, the Rue Saint-Jacques. Other presses nested inside the colleges of the University of Paris, printing textbooks in small runs when the teaching staff needed them. Printing reached the University of Oxford by 1478.

Over time, printing proved to be, if anything, even more adaptable than the scribe's trade. Gutenberg printed not only his famous Bible, but also an almanac with instructions for bloodletting (a popular form of therapy) and a papal bull against the Turks in both German and Latin. Soon printers were turning out everything from editions of the Latin and Greek classics designed to please the educated elite, to theological and legal texts for the universities, to tiny pamphlets. Large books were designed to rest on wooden stands in university halls and scholars' studies. Books in the small octavo format—more or less the size of a modern mass-market paperback—could be carried in a bag or purse and dipped into at leisure. Broadsides—single sheets with vivid woodcut illustrations that described strange happenings and major battles—could be rapidly produced and peddled in city squares and village marketplaces. For the first time, people began to expect news to arrive regularly, in printed form.

Books multiplied faster than ever before, and as we well know, the speed with which messages travel can vastly increase their impact. By the end of the fifteenth century, some 27,000 distinct works had been printed—a flood of texts and images of every kind, ancient and medieval, Christian and Muslim, genuine and forged. One early media event makes clear their impact. At the beginning of the sixteenth century, almanac makers noticed that a conjunction of the planets would take place in 1524 in the zodiacal sign of Pisces, the Fish. They predicted that this

The Book Trade A French woodcut from around 1500 illustrates a Parisian street vendor hawking cheap books of hours and alphabet books for children, which the printing press made readily available to the public.

would cause a terrible flood, and the prediction went viral in almanacs and other small, inexpensive books. When 1524 came, the rains did not prove especially heavy. But thousands of Italians and Germans took to the hills, propelled by the rumors spread by the printing press. They and the astrologers became laughingstocks, mocked for years to come in another form of popular media, the comic plays performed in market squares.

It is difficult to assess the impact of printing in more general terms. It made books cheaper, though not cheap: prices for classical texts dropped by about half in Rome after a press was established there in 1470. The circulation of alphabet books, primers, and broadsides put literacy within the reach of more people across society than manuscript culture had. Print was provocative. Texts that had never been edited to ensure that they were factually accurate or theologically orthodox could now circulate in thousands of copies. Printing also gave publicity to figures whom the political and religious authorities would have liked to suppress. Thus small, elegant Italian editions of the works and doings of Savonarola, the rebellious

Dominican friar, helped to preserve his legacy and inspire his followers. Yet the traditional books of hours went through many more editions. Some of the first witnesses of presses in action praised the speed with which books could be produced. Others denounced printing as an invention of the devil. Even today, the effects of the first modern media revolution evade simple judgments.

DISCOVERY: A NEW WORLD

It was the products of the press—as well as the navigational skills and maritime technology that Europeans had amassed—that impelled the Spanish to undertake their extraordinary expansion to the New World and beyond. **Christopher Columbus** (1457–1506) was a skilled mariner from Genoa, who served in the 1470s and 1480s as a business representative for influential local families and helped to man armed convoys. By the late 1470s, he was sailing on a Portuguese ship and trading for Genoese backers at the Portuguese stations in western Africa. A passionate reader, he came across Latin texts by medieval and contemporary theologians that led him to believe that the world was approaching its end. All peoples, he thought, might soon be reunited as Christians. More important still, he read Ptolemy's *Geography*, the most detailed and technically precise ancient description of the surface of the earth, composed in second-century Alexandria. Ptolemy greatly overestimated the length of the continent of Asia and believed that only water separated it from Europe. Inspired by this ancient authority and filled with enthusiasm by his reading of theologians and prophets, Columbus became convinced that it must be possible to reach Asia relatively quickly by sailing due west.

COLUMBUS'S VOYAGES

Columbus persuaded the rulers of Spain, Ferdinand and Isabella, to support his enterprise by arguing—on the basis of Ptolemy—that the distance to Asia was far shorter than it actually is. On August 3, 1492, he set off with three ships. After stopping in the Canary Islands, he landed at a still unidentified island in the Bahamas. His mind stuffed with ancient reports of the strange races and gleaming treasures to be found in India, at the far eastern edge of the inhabited world, Columbus never worked out exactly what he had discovered. He described the natives he met as poor, naked, and generous, willing to swap treasures for

Columbus's Journeys This 1493 woodcut, from one of the earliest accounts of Columbus's first voyage to the Caribbean, shows King Ferdinand directing Columbus's ships to sail across the ocean. In the top half, the Spanish ships land in the New World, whose native inhabitants flee at the sight of them.

continent, but he believed then and for the rest of his life that the continent he had reached was Asia.

By the end of his third voyage, weakened by age and disease, Columbus found himself under attack by the colonists he had brought to the Americas. A fourth expedition launched in 1502 took him to Panama but ended with his ships beached in Jamaica, where he was stranded for a year. Beleaguered, criticized, and under heavy financial pressure, Columbus became convinced in the course of his later expeditions that he had actually discovered the Earthly Paradise, and believed that his discoveries were harbingers of the return of the Messiah. Bookishness could imprison as well as inspire readers.

EUROPEAN EXPLORATION AFTER COLUMBUS (1497–1522)

For all his illusions, however, Columbus was certain of one thing: the shores on which he landed offered resources of every kind for exploitation, from sheltered harbors to treasures of silver and gold to timber and spices. Expeditions set out from Europe in every direction. John Cabot (ca. 1450–ca. 1499), an Italian backed by King Henry VII of England, sailed straight west from Bristol in 1497 and made landfall in what was probably Newfoundland. By 1500 another Spanish fleet, led by the Florentine Amerigo Vespucci (ca. 1454–1512), had reached the mouth of the Amazon River. Portuguese expeditions, including a second one by Vespucci in 1501–2, found and explored the bulge of South America's eastern coast, and a French fleet landed in southern Brazil in 1504. In 1519, the Portuguese navigator Ferdinand Magellan (1480–1521) led a Spanish fleet of five ships on a voyage to circumnavigate the world. They sailed from Spain to South America and crossed through what is now called the Strait of Magellan into the Pacific Ocean, which they crossed on the way to the Spice Islands (now the Indonesian archipelago called the Moluccas). Though Magellan himself died in the Philippines, one ship returned to Seville in 1522.

Printing spread the news—often in the attractive if unreliable form of pamphlets, such as the short letters attributed to Vespucci that described both the Southern Cross and the cannibalism of American natives. Land expeditions began to fill in the vast blank spaces on the maps, as when Vasco Núñez de Balboa (1475–1519) crossed Panama in 1513 and became the first European to see the Pacific from the land side. Soldiers of fortune and missionary priests followed the first explorers. They spread

trinkets. But he also noted that some of them were "very fierce and eat human flesh," though he never explained how he had managed to learn this without knowing their languages.

This first trip took him to Cuba and Hispaniola, where one of his ships ran aground and had to be abandoned, and he left a small settlement behind. Using his mastery of the Atlantic winds, he sailed back to Europe, reaching Lisbon in March 1493 and Spain a week later. The news of his voyage spread rapidly, and the monarchs of Portugal and Spain both laid claim to the new discoveries. The dispute was eventually settled in 1494 by the **Treaty of Tordesillas**, which drew a boundary line 370 leagues (1,185 miles) west of the Cape Verde Islands, with Portugal controlling lands east of the line and Spain west.

Columbus set out again in September 1494, this time with seventeen ships and 1,200 men, planning to create settlements in the New World. Though his explorations were mostly confined to the Caribbean Islands—Guadeloupe, the Greater and Lesser Antilles and Hispaniola—on his third voyage in 1498 he reached the Orinoco delta at the northern edge of South America. Columbus correctly argued, from the vast amount of fresh water that the river sent out into the ocean, that he must have found an entire

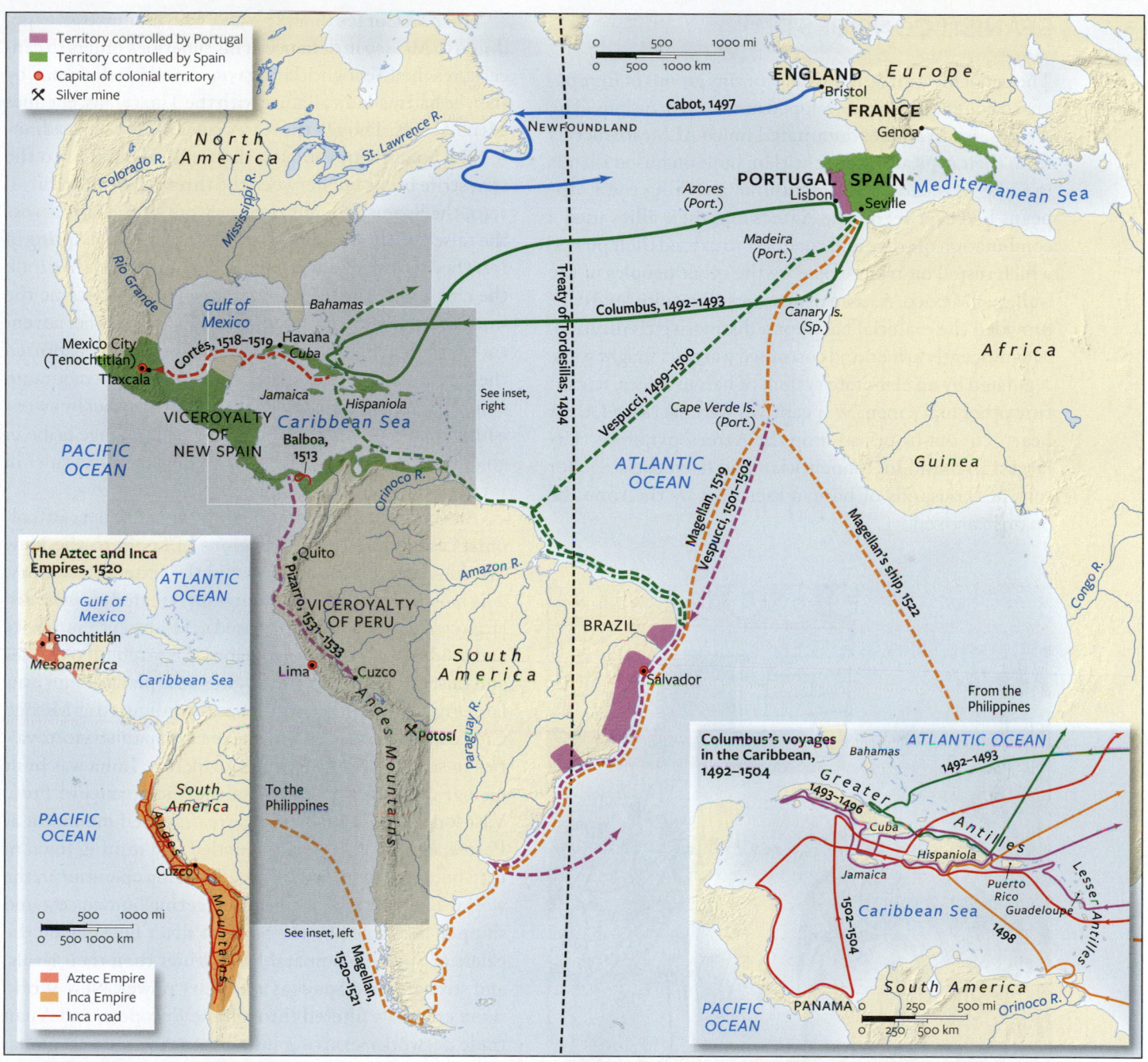

European Expeditions to the Western Hemisphere, 1492–1550 By the mid-sixteenth century, exploration and colonization linked Portugal and Spain to an expanse of new territory in the Americas and beyond. Christopher Columbus's voyages to the Caribbean first made Europeans aware of the resources of the Americas. Soon after, Amerigo Vespucci discovered the mouth of the Amazon River. Magellan crossed below the southern tip of South America into the Pacific, and one of his ships completed the first circumnavigation of the world. Later, Cortés travelled as far as central Mexico and conquered the Aztecs, and Pizarro pushed down into the Andes, where he overthrew the Inca. Once these ancient civilizations were defeated, the Spanish established control over much of the New World.

smallpox and other European diseases among the inhabitants of the New World, who had never been exposed to these pathogens and had no immunity. Millions died in the pandemics, radically weakening their states.

Exact statistics are impossible to provide, but many specialists believe that the population of the Americas fell from some 50 million in 1492 to as low as 6 million by 1650.

SPANISH CONQUEST

The pandemics made it possible for tiny groups of Europeans to conquer highly developed native civilizations. The Aztecs, for example, dominated much of Mesoamerica from their capital at Tenochtitlán, built on raised islands in Lake Texcoco—a setting unlike anything the Europeans had ever seen. The Aztecs and their allies used a combination of trade and conquest to extend their power, which rested on tribute paid by the other peoples of the Valley of Mexico. A caste of peasants who cultivated corn provided the material basis for a distinctive civilization. Magnificently armed and costumed warriors fought wars, regulated by an elaborate system of heroic values, to capture other brave men. War captives were sacrificed, their hearts cut out by priests atop the Aztecs' pyramids. The largest pyramid in Tenochtitlán had been the stage for tens of thousands of human sacrifices by the time the Spanish arrived.

Cortés and the Aztecs An illustration from a late-sixteenth-century Spanish history of the New World shows a tense meeting of Spanish and Aztec forces. The Aztec king Montezuma waves his finger angrily at Cortés and his soldiers, while an Aztec interpreter stands between the two parties.

Hernán Cortés (b. 1485–1547), who mounted an expedition to Mexico in defiance of his superior's orders to cancel it, reached Tenochtitlán by 1519. An adroit diplomat, by then he had made an alliance with the Tlaxcalans, enemies of the Aztecs. Though the Aztec ruler Montezuma admitted the Spanish and about a thousand Tlaxcalans to the city, strife broke out between the three parties. On July 1, 1520, the Spanish fought their way out of the city, across the raised causeways that gave access to it. In the spring of 1521 they returned to lay siege, and on August 13 they took the city, destroying it in the process. Cortés became the first governor of what was now New Spain. Another adventurous soldier, Francisco Pizarro (ca. 1475–1541), captured the emperor of the Incas, the people whose rich mountain empire stretched across the Andes, held together by astonishing roads and bridges. Though offered a huge bribe in gold, Pizarro found a pretext to execute the Inca ruler in 1533, making him master of another vast territory.

As the native kingdoms fell, great numbers of colonists emigrated from all regions of Spain to the New World—some 300,000 of them in the sixteenth century. The most successful of these migrants created *encomiendas*, large estates where they exercised near-absolute authority and used enserfed natives for labor. They rebuilt old cities and raised new ones on neat, systematic plans: Tenochtitlan, originally built on a grid, was reconfigured as Mexico City, capital of New Spain, one of two Spanish viceroyalties in sixteenth-century Latin America; Lima was built on a grid plan as the capital of the Viceroyalty of Peru. Vast lodes of silver in the sugarloaf-shaped mountain at Potosí, in modern Bolivia, founded as a mining town in 1545, became the site of the largest mining operation in the world. The treasure dug up at staggering human cost and shipped to Europe by the Spanish silver fleets made the rulers of Spain incomparably wealthier than their rivals, and strengthened Spain as a military power. New World silver gradually filtered through the European and Asian trade networks, exerting inflationary pressure on global prices and wages, and transforming China's economy.

Meanwhile, a historical struggle took shape in the Americas. Initially at Cortés's request, Franciscan and Dominican missionaries—many of them idealists—arrived in the New World nourishing high hopes for the American Indians, whom they saw as innocent and virtuous. They did their best to teach Christian doctrine and practice, and—as they became aware of the oppression many natives suffered as serfs of the colonists—tried to protect them against brutal exploitation. Bartolomé de Las Casas (1484–1566), a Dominican who became the first bishop of

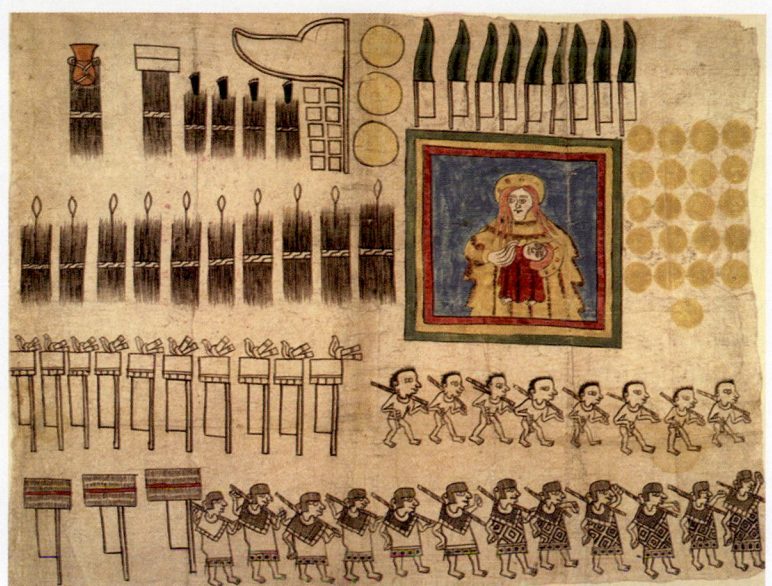

Christianity in the New World In a set of 1531 legal documents drawn up by the Huexotzinco people, from an area near Mexico City, a pictographic rendering lists the taxes the Spanish colonial authorities demanded of them. The inclusion of a banner of the Virgin Mary and Baby Jesus indicates the influence of Spanish religion on indigenous perceptions only ten years after conquest.

Chiapas, in southern Mexico, actually to live and work in his diocese, pleaded with the Spanish crown to end the system of forced labor. He argued that the Indians were highly intelligent, as the complexity of their preconquest societies proved, and should enjoy decent living conditions and a chance to become believing Christians. Largely due to Las Casas's efforts, in 1542 the Spanish king promulgated the New Laws, which forbade the *encomenderos* to force Indians to work for them or to bequeath their estates to their children. Although the encomiendas were made heritable again in 1545, and *encomenderos* resisted the New Laws, the number of serfs fell. But the population decline continued, indicating that the majority of American natives who survived the Spanish conquest suffered in many ways for having done so.

COLUMBIAN EXCHANGES

The encounter between European and New World peoples was one of the great dramas of human history—a drama that continued long after the initial, catastrophic population loss unleashed by conquest and disease. Europeans brought with them all the elements of their civilization, from their domesticated dogs and horses and their

technical devices to their Christian religion and romance literature, which helped to inspire the conquistadores as they rode out to battle. In Latin America a new society took shape—one whose elite was often created by intermarriage between the conquerors and the descendants of native princes. Intermarriage was common at all levels: by the eighteenth century, the majority of Mexicans and Central and South Americans were so-called mestizos, people of mixed blood. They were served by a distinctive form of Christianity. Church architecture and religious images blended traditional Christian stories and teachings with native imagery. Indians took part with special enthusiasm, as the best-informed missionaries realized, in those Christian rites and festivals that fell on significant days in their own ancient calendars. Meanwhile, the horse—unknown in the New World before the conquerors arrived—spread throughout the Americas, transforming the lives of the Plains Indians, who had relatively little direct contact with either the Spanish or the inhabitants of Latin America.

In return, the New World had far more to offer the Old. Transported east across the Atlantic, staple agricultural products found acceptance in Europe at differing rates. Tomatoes and potatoes had little impact in the sixteenth century, but eventually they transformed Old World agriculture and diet. By contrast, tobacco and chocolate—both far stronger than their modern versions, and both central to American Indian religious rituals that fascinated Western observers and taught them how to consume these powerful stimulants—reshaped European social customs. In 1500, Europeans did not use tobacco or anything like it. A hundred years later, Europeans of all social ranks smoked or inhaled it. Taverns and other gathering places reeked of tobacco, as they would for centuries to come. Meanwhile, hot chocolate became a beloved luxury of elites, served at festive meals and sipped elegantly from tiny cups.

European sailors and soldiers also returned home with an unwelcome import: syphilis, a sexually transmitted disease that seems not have existed in Europe before 1492. It spread across the European continent, where it soon became an epidemic, with results that horrified sufferers and observers. The standard treatment involved drinking or applying a medicine made from the bark of the guaiacum tree, which—like the disease—came from the New World. The Fuggers, a prominent German banking family, soon established a monopoly on the sale of this bark, as they did with mercury, another treatment that could be effective but caused horrific side effects.

At the same time, the feather headdresses, jewels, and

illuminated codices of New World rulers were exhibited in the court museums of Europe. The skill of their makers won the admiration of such great artists as Albrecht Dürer, who saw what he described as a sun of gold and a moon of silver, along with other treasures and weapons from Mexico, in Brussels in 1520. "All the days of my life," he reflected, "I have seen nothing that rejoiced my heart so much as these things, for I saw among them wonderful works of art, and I marveled at the subtle intellects of people in distant lands."

REDISCOVERY: RENAISSANCE CULTURE

Like Dürer, the Florentine philosopher Marsilio Ficino (1433–1499) marveled at the cultural splendors of a world in discovery, this one located not across the ocean but in the ancient past. Ficino had these rediscovered riches in mind when he declared, "This century, like a golden age, has restored to light the liberal arts, which were almost extinct: grammar, poetry, rhetoric, painting, sculpture, architecture, music." Explorers claimed to have found a new world, but European thinkers came to believe that they had brought about a rebirth—a renaissance—of ancient Greece and Rome. The Italian cities had always supported communities of notaries and lawyers—practical men who used ancient texts and medieval contract forms with equal dexterity to meet the practical needs of merchants and bankers. In the fourteenth century, some of them developed new cultural ambitions. They began to study the classics of Latin literature: the prose of Cicero and Seneca, the epic poetry of Virgil, and even the love poetry of Catullus.

PETRARCH

The fourteenth-century Florentine writer Francesco Petrarca, or **Petrarch** (1304–1374), pulled these threads together and wove a new intellectual program from them. Pushed by his father to study law, Petrarch found himself repelled by the way in which contemporary jurists read the ancient texts. To make Roman laws fit modern cases, they assumed that every reference to a pagan temple must apply to Christian churches as well. Petrarch, by contrast, was thrilled by what he described as the "history" concealed in the legal texts. He saw them not as a set of timeless codes but as the revelation of a lost world, at once unfamiliar and

more powerful and attractive than his own. Leaving the law, he pursued literature. Petrarch's Italian lyric poems—in which he described, at meticulous length, the sufferings of lovers and the beauty of the women who refused their pleas—made him famous. He created the language used by writers of sonnets down to the time of William Shakespeare and John Donne.

Petrarch's Latin scholarship and writing made him the standard-bearer of a new intellectual movement. Networking with learned men in the papal offices in France and Rome, he collected, and corrected, as many classical texts as he could. He annotated everything he read, both responding to the texts and entering personal remarks: for example, we know from a note in his massive copy of Virgil's works that Laura, the woman who inspired Petrarch's sonnets, died during the Black Death in 1348. And he carved out a career as the most expert and eloquent Latinist of his day.

As he discovered new texts—such as the highly political letters that Cicero addressed to his friend Atticus—Petrarch responded to them with verve and passion, showing just how serious a matter reading was for him. In the Middle Ages, clerical readers had thought of Cicero above all as the author of his late, Stoical works on philosophy. Now it became clear that he had been an active participant in the final drama of the Roman Republic. Horrified, Petrarch dashed off a letter to Cicero in which he denounced the Roman for betraying the ideals of philosophy—only to soften his judgment in a second, follow-up note.

A pious Christian who often criticized the Church but never questioned basic doctrines, Petrarch knew that his love of ancient literature might seem questionable or worse—as it had to Saint Jerome, whose work he knew

Petrarch In Andrea del Castagno's early-fifteenth-century rendering, the poet holds a book—the symbol of his craft—and extends his right hand in a delicate, artistic gesture.

intimately. At times he reproached himself for loving the beauty of the ancients' books too much. But challenged by friends, he devised a powerful justification for studying the literary classics—one partly based on the thought of Augustine, whose books he loved even more than those of the Romans. Contemporary philosophers and theologians, Petrarch argued, tried to learn the truth, a quest that often led them into blind alleys. They wasted their energy seeking goals no human could reach, and ended up fiercely debating questions of no relevance to the ordinary person. The ancients, by contrast, thanks to their mastery of rhetoric, had known how to make their readers want to change their lives, to be better men and women. And in the end, he argued, for Christians in his own day as for pagans in antiquity, "it is more important to will the good than to know the truth." The study of the classics had an eminently practical goal: it was the best way to make oneself a moral agent and to persuade others to do so as well.

SALUTATI'S BREAKTHROUGH

Petrarch's fame, and the power of his work, persuaded many younger scholars to follow him in the middle of the fourteenth century and after. His fellow Florentine, Giovanni Boccaccio (1313–1375), emulated him in many ways. Boccaccio developed a cultivated Italian prose, comparable in purity to Petrarch's verse, in which he composed his *Decameron*, a magnificent set of 100 tales in Italian about sex and love, marriage and deception. But he also searched for manuscripts of ancient books that had remained hidden in monasteries, and compiled a massive Latin book in which he sorted out the complex genealogies of the pagan gods. Even more influential was Coluccio Salutati (1331–1406), a younger notary who became chancellor of Florence in 1375. A systematic scholar in the new manner, Salutati also wrote about ancient myths, revealing a clear sense that the ancient world had been very different from his own. Confronting the many loves of Hercules, he explained both simply and radically that pagans, unlike Christians, had not been bound to monogamy.

Many younger men came under Salutati's influence—notably two deft Latinists, Leonardo Bruni (ca. 1370–1444) and Gian Francesco Poggio Bracciolini (1380–1459), both of whom would serve after him as chancellor of Florence. Poggio, who wrote in an open, highly legible script, worked with Salutati to define a layout for books more appropriate to the classics than the spiky, highly abbreviated books used in the universities. The model they chose—a clear minuscule script, written with few abbreviations

Poggio Bracciolini An illuminated initial letter "C" on the first page of one of Poggio's translations gives an indication of what the Latinist might have looked like as a young man.

and presented on its own, rather than immersed in a sea of minute commentary—was actually Carolingian, not ancient. Adopted by the efficient stationers of Florence, it became, first in manuscripts and then in print, the basic form of the modern book: a book designed not to serve as a source of information but to be read for its own sake, whether chained to a library table or carried on a journey.

Most important, in 1397 Salutati persuaded an eloquent and learned Byzantine, Manuel Chrysoloras, (d. 1415) to teach Greek in Florence. Bruni and others who studied with him began to read the Greek historians and philosophers, and to translate their works into Latin. For the first time in a thousand years, Latin intellectuals could read the works of Plato and his followers as well as Aristotle, whom they had known for centuries in the Latin translations used in universities. Chrysoloras—who, like many Byzantine scholars, took as strong an interest in the sciences as in literature—explicated Ptolemy's *Geography*, which was soon translated into Latin, and thus provided part of the inspiration that would send Columbus on his voyage west. The encounter with these alien works from another world could be shocking: the first Latin translation of Plato's *Symposium* discreetly eliminated the references to same-sex love. Soon, however, it became clear that, as Petrarch had already suspected, Plato offered a vision of the universe and a method of writing philosophy that seemed closer to Christianity in substance and better fitted to the needs of ordinary readers than the more technical books of Aristotle.

When Marsilio Ficino spoke of a great revival of the arts in his own day, he referred partly to his own project to translate and comment on the complete works of Plato—a project that came to fruition in 1484, when his work was printed in Florence. In the larger sense, what he saw himself as living through was nothing less than a revolution—one that looked not forward, as revolutions have in the nineteenth and twentieth centuries, but backward, and that sought to rebuild culture on a basis of ancient texts properly established and understood.

HUMANISM

The scholars who set out on this new road to the ancient past—from Petrarch to Ficino—took a special interest in the arts of language, grammar, and rhetoric; in poetry; and in the further studies that would help to inform and improve the characters of men and women who played important roles in society. These studies came to be known as "the studies of humanity," and those who pursued them as "humanists"—not in the modern secular sense, since almost all of them were faithful Christians, but in a larger one. All of them recognizably adopted the same general intellectual program, called **humanism**.

POLITICS Becoming a humanist did not imply a commitment to a particular view of society or the state. Petrarch, and many humanists after him, saw monarchy, when carried out by just and virtuous rulers, as a laudable form of government. Drawing on Seneca, who had offered an idealistic version of Roman imperial government as created by Augustus (until he was forced by Nero to commit suicide), Petrarch praised the rulers of Milan for their justice, their clemency, and their own commitment to urban planning, which had made their city cleaner and more beautiful than any other. Many later humanists would write similar "mirrors of princes." Bruni and his successors in the Florentine chancery took the opposite course. They learned from Thucydides, Aristotle, and Polybius how to analyze Florence as a classical republic, and effusively praised the city's balanced government, tradition of defending liberty, and splendid architecture.

Humanism also found a niche, and a large one, in the papal court. The fifteenth-century popes who rebuilt the Roman Curia (the papal administration) as a going concern established that the papacy was as committed to classical learning as any secular monarchy, and surrounded themselves with bright young scholars of the sort Salutati had recruited. Humanists in papal employ translated many of the Greek classics, wrote new lives of the ancient saints in an up-to-date style, and made the liturgy classical. By the beginning of the sixteenth century, they drew up official documents for the popes that referred to God as Jupiter Optimus Maximus and avoided using the special vocabulary of Christian Latin. In 1475 the popes created a great library for these humanists to work in: not a religious collection, as is often wrongly thought, but a systematic assembly of Greek and Latin texts meant to be used by the members of the Curia when they too turned to the ancients for practical advice. The Vatican Library remains one of the world's great centers of scholarly research.

SOCIETY Studying the classics was eminently practical. The subjects that the humanists cultivated proved useful in the new states and societies that had taken shape in fifteenth-century Italy. Ambassadors, for example, needed to give speeches, write forceful memoranda, and use history to shed light on the difficult moments of the present—all humanist skills. The families that ruled the most powerful cities embraced them. Many appointed humanist teachers, opened schools that offered instruction to princes and aristocrats, and built libraries designed, as the Vatican's was, for quiet reflection.

Humanism also created new possibilities for women, even within the social traditions of Renaissance cities and courts. For the most part, marriage among members of the elite continued to be arranged by parents to promote family strategies, and women in the Renaissance married much younger than men in the expectation that they would produce as many children as possible. They and the dowries they brought with them in marriage were in their husband's power, and even when they were widowed, they were normally put under the guardianship of a male relative of their late husband. Yet as we saw in the catasto records of Florence, many widows achieved considerable authority as heads of families.

CHRISTINE DE PIZAN Christine de Pizan (1364–1430) was a humanist who, writing in French rather than Latin, posed new questions about women and their social position. Married at the age of fifteen and widowed with three children a decade later, Christine found support in the courts of Burgundy and France for her poetry. She created a circle of scribes and miniaturists who produced beautifully illuminated copies of her works; she took charge

GHIRLANDAIO'S *PORTRAIT OF A LADY*

In Renaissance Italy, portraits served as tokens of friendship, political alliance, and marital exchange between courts or powerful families. Domenico Ghirlandaio (1449–1494) was a successful painter who operated a workshop in Florence with his family; Michelangelo apprenticed in the workshop. Ghirlandaio most likely created his *Portrait of a Lady* (ca. 1490) to commemorate the sitter's marriage.

Italian portraits of the second half of the fifteenth century, especially those featuring women, expressed both the subjects' personal characteristics and the broad cultural values of the time. In this portrait, the young woman's golden hair, fair skin, and formal posture conform to a standard of female beauty present in many other portraits of the period, inspired by the medieval poetry of Dante Alighieri (1265–1321) and Petrarch (1304–1374). The orange blossom in the woman's hand, representing chastity, and the pearls on her necklace, symbolizing purity and associated with the Virgin Mary, also convey the subject's moral integrity. Her pearls and elegant dress communicate the wealth of the woman's family, always of importance in marriage negotiations. Ghirlandaio combined these elements to create an image of femininity that aligned closely with Florentine values.

QUESTIONS FOR ANALYSIS

1. What does this portrait suggest about the woman's social status?
2. How would you describe the image of femininity conveyed in the portrait?
3. Why would Ghirlandaio include Florence and the surrounding countryside in this portrait?

Christine de Pizan The frontispiece of a 1411 manuscript of her writings shows Christine de Pizan hard at work at her desk. She closely supervised the creation of this manuscript, which she presented to the queen of France in 1414.

of every detail, including the scripts that her scribes employed.

In her allegorical history of women, *The Book of the City of Ladies* (1405), Christine conjured up Lady Reason, who gave her a powerful lesson. Christine had believed, in a traditional way, in the evil character of women, which male authors such as Boccaccio had repeatedly confirmed. Lady Reason urged her to forget the slanders that had been heaped on women, and carry them away like "hods of earth" on her shoulders—a brilliant image of the woman writer as workmanlike scholar. "If it were customary to send little girls to school," Christine now argued, "and teach them the same subjects as are taught to boys, they would learn just as fully and would understand the subtleties of all arts and sciences." Marriage, she wrote, when unaccompanied by a spiritual connection, was no better than slavery.

UNDERSTANDING THE PAST Like the scholastics, the humanists developed a new and powerful set of technical skills—one based less on formal argument (though some did cultivate that) than on the knowledge that language, forms of writing, laws, customs, art, and religion all changed over time. Whereas scholastics enjoyed finding contradictions in arguments, humanists hunted anachronisms—errors and inconsistencies that showed that a given work could not have been written or painted by its supposed author or in its supposed period. The last thousand years, during which ancient books survived only when fallible individuals copied them in full, had left the canon in some confusion—a state rendered worse by the habit of many medieval writers and librarians of ascribing works they admired, whatever their origins, to particular ancient authors.

The most dramatic exposure of a medieval forgery involved the so-called Donation of Constantine. Old documents, produced by the papal chancery in the age of Charlemagne, purported to show that Pope Sylvester I (r. 314–335) had cured Constantine, the first Christian emperor of Rome, of leprosy, and that the emperor had given the popes the western empire in gratitude. Lawyers and theologians debated for centuries about whether this grant was legitimate. In 1440, Lorenzo Valla (1407–1457) a humanist who worked for the king of Naples, used the new scholarly tools to show that the documents in question were fakes that could not have been written at the time claimed. It did not matter whether Constantine's gift had been just or unjust—it had never taken place.

Humanists even created a new kind of history—one based on the material remains of the ancient world. Cyriac, a merchant from the Italian port of Ancona, revealed the ancient world vividly to his contemporaries. He traveled the Mediterranean for decades in the fifteenth century, sketchbook in hand, hopping from one Venetian or Genoese ship to another. Cyriac brought western Europeans their first news—and their first images—of the ancient temples of Greece, including the Parthenon, and of the obelisks and sphinxes of Egypt.

During the fifteenth century, humanists also revived every form of philosophy that the ancient world had known. Not only Aristotelianism and Platonism but Stoicism, Skepticism, and Epicureanism were reconstructed by scholars and exhaustively debated in Latin. New and varied syntheses took shape. Ficino, the translator of Plato, found connections between the works of Plato, a wide range of later Neoplatonic texts, and the learned tradition of natural magic and astrology that had taken shape in the medieval Islamic world. Ficino's younger friend Giovanni Pico della Mirandola, by contrast, believed that all serious schools of thought—Islamic as well as Christian, modern as well as ancient, scholastic as well as humanist—possessed distinctive elements of the truth. Humanism, which began as the discovery of the otherness of ancient Rome, gradually opened eyes and minds to the richness of a wide range of ancient traditions.

INNOVATIONS IN THE ARTS

Marsilio Ficino celebrated the revival of the visual arts as well as classical learning. Painting, sculpture, and architecture had flourished in the late thirteenth and fourteenth centuries in the most economically advanced parts of Europe—Italy and the Low Countries. But they had been seen as crafts. Those who practiced them learned their techniques as apprentices in masters' workshops and became journeymen once fully trained. They did not even have guilds of their own in most cities: sculptors joined and were regulated by the masons' guild, and painters by that of physicians and apothecaries. In the later fourteenth and

fifteenth centuries, however, what we now call the fine arts began to pull away from other crafts. Architects insisted that their work required knowledge not only of traditional building crafts, but also of mathematics and physical science. They found support in the ancient Roman handbook on architecture by Vitruvius (d. after 15 CE), who made the case that an architect needed to have encyclopedic knowledge of nature as well as building techniques in order to build healthy houses and cities.

FLORENCE In 1418 Filippo Brunelleschi (1377–1446), a stunningly innovative Florentine sculptor and architect, told the committee responsible for finishing the city's Cathedral of Santa Maria del Fiore that he could build its enormous dome without any pillars to support it—as if deliberately mocking his predecessors, who had relied upon small forests of buttresses to support their cathedrals. The committee members treated him as insane at first, but eventually he convinced them. Brunelleschi worked with highly skilled craftsmen, but emphasized that he was responsible for their innovations. He designed the lifts, hoists, and scaffolds that enabled his crew to complete the dome in 1436—the biggest one built since the creation of the church of Hagia Sophia some

Brunelleschi and the Cathedral of Santa Maria del Fiore A 1427 fresco depicts Filippo Brunelleschi (right) alongside several contemporaries, including the painter Masaccio (left) and the writer and architect Leon Battista Alberti (center). Brunelleschi designed and built the magnificent dome of Florence's Cathedral of Santa Maria del Fiore using numerous architectural innovations, such as the rib-like support structure and an inner and outer dome.

Giotto's Frescoes In a vivid panel from Giotto di Bondone's frescoes narrating the Passion of Christ (1303–5), Jesus kisses Judas, who has betrayed him. The artist draws out the anger and tension of the scene through the facial expressions and gestures of the guards, disciples, and bystanders.

900 years earlier by the Roman emperor Justinian. As brilliant an engineer as he was an artist, Brunelleschi also devised war machines and transportation devices for the Florentines. He took out what amounted to the first modern patent to protect a piece of his intellectual property. He also created a new style of building that seemed classical, although, like the style of Renaissance books, it was medieval—in this case derived from churches of the twelfth century. He used it for the hospital built by the Florentines to accommodate foundlings.

Painters and sculptors also began to innovate. Giotto di Bondone (d. 1337), the most famous painter of the fourteenth century, used the large frescoes and mosaics that he was commissioned to create to find new ways of representing people, vividly and powerfully, as dominated by their emotions. Brunelleschi carried out experiments in linear perspective from the steps of the Florentine cathedral. He showed that by using a geometrical system of one-point perspective, he could produce an image of the octagonal Baptistery (the twelfth-century building across from the cathedral) that seemed genuinely three-dimensional.

Soon Florence became a center of artistic experiment. Brunelleschi's rival, the sculptor Lorenzo Ghiberti (ca. 1378–1455), experimented with foreshortening and perspective as he cast biblical scenes for the bronze doors of the Baptistery. Artists of the next generation—men such as Masaccio and Paolo Uccello, born around the year 1400—covered the walls of Florentine churches with vivid paintings: from a shrine, painted flat on the wall, that seemed to recede from the onlooker as if it were in three dimensions, to crowds and buildings that looked startlingly like their real-life counterparts. Uccello and other painters began to make systematic sketches, starting with nude figures and only later imagining them clothed. They depicted graceful men and women standing with their bodies curved symmetrically around vertical lines—figures as idealized, but also as apparently real, as the exquisite works of ancient Greeks like Phidias, whose sculptures filled the Parthenon.

NORTHERN EUROPE Innovation was just as rapid in the Low Countries, which produced a flood of illuminated manuscripts and tapestries as well as sculptures and paintings. Since the twelfth century, northern European artists had occasionally used oil as a painting medium, rather than the tempera (a mixture of pigment and a water-soluble binder such as egg yolk) that southern artists used when creating panels. In the fifteenth century, northern painters such as Jan van Eyck, who served his Burgundian master, Philip the Good, as diplomat as well as painter, learned how to apply oil paint in multiple thin layers. This technique enabled them to create rich, glowing colors and to produce microscopically faithful renditions of every sort of surface material, from stone to cloth, fur, and skin. They created many devotional pictures, but also specialized in painting portraits from life of prominent men and women. Works of art and techniques crossed the Alps and the Pyrenees. By the middle of the fifteenth century, Italian painters such as the Venetian Giovanni Bellini (ca. 1430–1516) were using oil as a medium, and the portrait was becoming a standard feature of Italian art.

PATRONAGE Support for the arts came from many sources. Committees of local notables oversaw the building and decoration of churches, such as the Florentine cathedral. Guilds also took part. The Florentine church of Orsanmichele, originally a grain market, was converted between 1380 and 1404 into the chapel of the Florentine craft and merchant guilds. Popes, princes, and patricians did their best to transform the built world. Merchant families and cardinals constructed huge palaces, drawing features from ancient structures like the Colosseum, in

RENAISSANCE FLORENCE

> **WHO COULD EVER BE HARD OR ENVIOUS ENOUGH TO FAIL TO PRAISE PIPPO THE ARCHITECT ON SEEING HERE SUCH A LARGE STRUCTURE, RISING ABOVE THE SKIES, AMPLE TO COVER WITH ITS SHADOW ALL THE TUSCAN PEOPLE?**
>
> LEON BATTISTA ALBERTI, *DE PICTURA*, ON FILIPPO BRUNELLESCHI'S DOME OF THE CATHEDRAL OF SANTA MARIA DEL FIORE

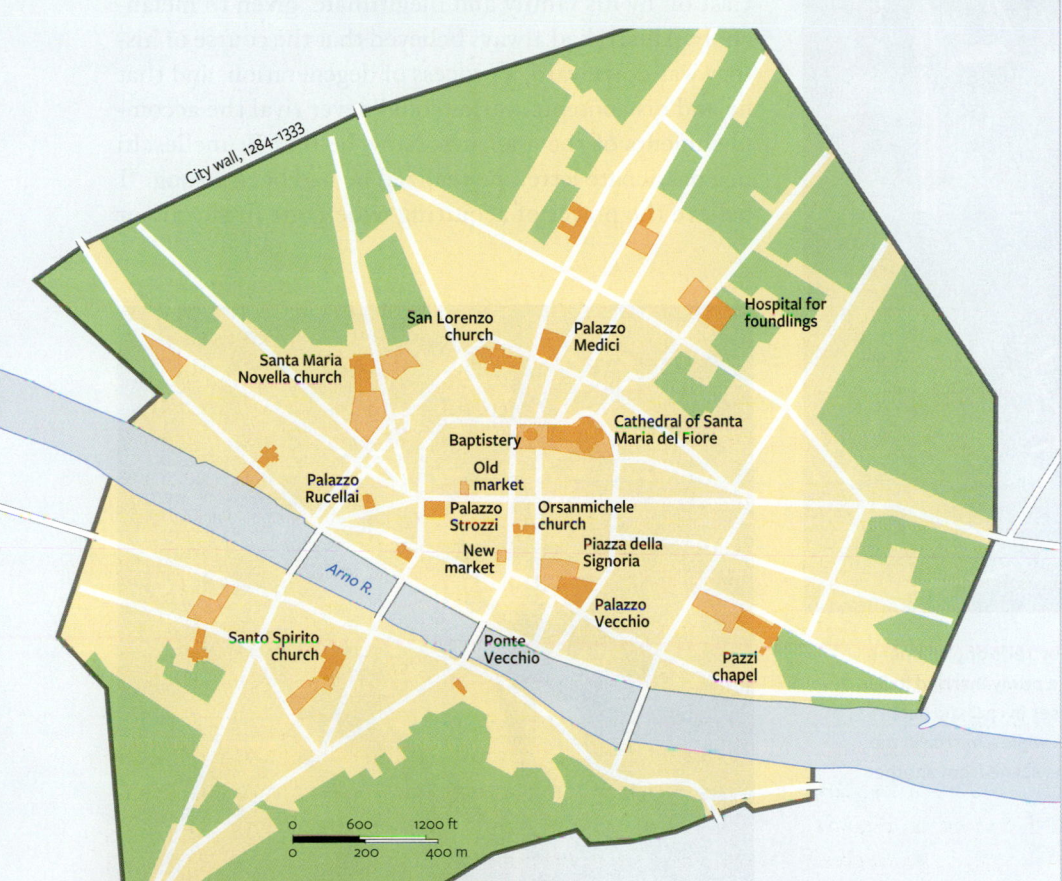

City wall, 1284–1333

Santa Maria Novella church

San Lorenzo church

Palazzo Medici

Hospital for foundlings

Cathedral of Santa Maria del Fiore

Baptistery

Old market

Palazzo Rucellai

Palazzo Strozzi

Orsanmichele church

New market

Piazza della Signoria

Palazzo Vecchio

Santo Spirito church

Arno R.

Ponte Vecchio

Pazzi chapel

0   600   1200 ft
0   200   400 m

Through much of the fifteenth century, a painting's materials, selected by its patron, determined its value. In this work (ca. 1483) by Florentine painter Filippino Lippi, the ultramarine pigment of the Virgin Mary's mantle would have been many times more expensive than gold. But by the end of the century, many patrons valued artists' skills more than the materials they used.

This bronze relief panel (1425–1452) from the doors of the Baptistery, depicting a Biblical scene, displays Lorenzo Ghiberti's ingenious use of perspective. He took great pride in his ability to set himself demanding technical problems and solve them with virtuosity.

WORKSHOPS, 1472

54 marble workers and stonecutters
44 master gold- and silversmiths
at least 30 master painters

NOTABLE PATRONS & WORKS THEY COMMISSIONED

MEDICI FAMILY
Brunelleschi's church of San Lorenzo and various works by Michelangelo

FILIPPO STROZZI (BANKER)
Benedetto da Maiano's Palazzo Strozzi and Lippi's frescoes in the Strozzi Chapel at Santa Maria Novella

GIOVANNI RUCELLAI (MERCHANT)
Alberti's façade of Santa Maria Novella and his design of the Palazzo Rucellai

> **THIS CENTURY, LIKE A GOLDEN AGE, HAS RESTORED TO LIGHT THE LIBERAL ARTS, WHICH WERE ALMOST EXTINCT: GRAMMAR, POETRY, RHETORIC, PAINTING, SCULPTURE, ARCHITECTURE, MUSIC... AND ALL THIS IN FLORENCE.**
>
> MARSILIO FICINO, "THE GOLDEN AGE IN FLORENCE"

QUESTIONS FOR ANALYSIS

1. What innovations in the arts and learning appeared in Renaissance Florence?
2. In what ways did artists and their patrons embellish the city?
3. How did the city's artists resemble and also distinguish themselves from craftsmen?

Jan van Eyck One of van Eyck's notable portraits of prominent members of society is this 1434 painting of a newly married Italian merchant and his wife. The picture showcases in realistic detail the luxurious interior of the couple's house, while a mirror in the background allows the viewer to glimpse the scene from another perspective.

work of the best masters. Some 16,000 letters record her requests to the greatest artists of the time.

ALBERTI: A NEW VISION As artists' practices changed, so did their position in society. In the 1430s, a Florentine exile named **Leon Battista Alberti** (1404–1472), a humanist who worked in the service of the papacy, returned to his native city. What he saw astonished him. Cast off by his family and illegitimate, given to melancholy, Alberti had always believed that the course of history was downward, a process of degeneration, and that he and his contemporaries could never rival the accomplishments of the ancients. Now, he told Brunelleschi in a passionate letter, he realized he had been wrong: "I believe the power of acquiring wide fame in any art or

Isabella d'Este The Venetian painter Titian created this 1534–36 portrait of the influential art connoisseur and collector Isabella d'Este. She was in her early sixties at the time, but Titian portrayed her as she might have appeared in her youth.

which they walled themselves off from the turmoil of the streets and created private worlds of great splendor, decorated according to their owners' distinctive tastes.

Wealthy individuals also presented paintings and chapels to the churches they favored, and bought painted chests, tapestries, and other expensive items for their homes. These consumers of luxury goods became more discriminating in the fifteenth and sixteenth centuries: not only in choosing beautiful things but also in selecting the artists they employed. A few women forged careers that would have only been possible in this new world. At the highest social levels, noble and royal women became as expert as any man in the new skills of connoisseurship and collection. Isabella d'Este (1474–1539), Marchesa of Mantua, spent her large income on art objects and became renowned for her determination to pay for only the best

Alberti's Emblem This mid-fifteenth-century medallion bears Leon Battista Alberti's emblem, a winged eye, an allusion, perhaps, to the eye of the artist, as well as the precision to which new forms of art and learning aspired. The motto below the eye, "Quid tum," is more mysterious, possibly meaning "What then?" or "So what?"—a hopeful anticipation of future developments in human knowledge.

science lies in our industry and diligence more than in the times or in the gifts of nature." Brunelleschi's dome ("ample to cover with its shadow all the Tuscan people, and constructed without the aid of centering or great quantity of wood"), Ghiberti's bronze doors for the Baptistery, and other achievements of Florentine art showed that progress was still possible.

Recognizing these dramatic changes when they had only just begun, Alberti set out to give painting—and by extension the other arts—a new theoretical foundation. He argued that painters really resembled scholars. As the humanist wrote in order to move readers, the painter depicted dramatic scenes—such as the Annunciation and the Crucifixion—in order to achieve the same end. And as the humanist's mastery of a classical vocabulary proved his worthiness to take part in public discussion, so the painter's mastery of techniques—anatomy, perspective, foreshortening—proved his worthiness to tell great stories in visual form. Traditionally, the painter had needed to know where to find the best pigments. Now he needed to master the geometry of the picture plane and the bony and muscular structures of the body, especially if he wanted to challenge the great ancient artists, whose feats of creating illusion Alberti described at length.

Most painters continued to work as guild members (though Brunelleschi refused to do so, even when he was imprisoned for refusing to pay his dues). But the new vision of the painter that Alberti described—someone who crossed what had previously been rugged intellectual borders, combining skilled hands with the sort of knowledge that had once been the province of scholars—proved infectious to painters and convincing to patrons. Even at lower levels, contracts for paintings now specified that the master must execute all hands and faces. Some of what we now call the fine arts were being identified as different from other crafts, and their products were coming to be seen not as the collaborative work of many craftsmen but as that of especially brilliant individuals.

LEONARDO, MICHELANGELO, RAPHAEL Three of these individuals have seemed—in their own time and since—to epitomize the new intellectual and cultural standing of the artist: Leonardo da Vinci (1452–1519), Raphael Santi (1483–1530), and Michelangelo Buonarotti (1475–1564). Leonardo and Michelangelo both came from Tuscany, near the centers of artistic innovation; Raphael came from the hilltop court town of Urbino, where his father was a painter. All three learned their arts in the traditional way, as apprentices. All three established their fame by creating ambitious and spectacular paintings: Leonardo's *Last Supper*, his *Mona Lisa*, and *The Virgin of the Rocks*; Raphael's frescoes in the papal palace that depicted the School of Athens (a panorama

Michelangelo's Sistine Chapel Ceiling The famous frescoes Michelangelo painted on the Sistine Chapel's ceiling in 1508–12 illustrate scenes from the Old Testament, including Adam and Eve eating the forbidden fruit and being banished from Eden (top) and God's creation of Eve (center) and Adam (bottom).

The School of Athens This fresco by Raphael Santi in the Vatican palace conveys the Renaissance's reverence for the famous figures of classical philosophy and science: Plato and Aristotle converse (center), Pythagoras reads (bottom left), and Euclid points at a writing slate (bottom right). The seemingly receding arches in the background demonstrate Raphael's command of one-point perspective.

These men embodied—and still embody—a distinctive vision of the artist. Far grander figures than the humanists, the great artists of the years around 1500 fought for their independence even as they were fought over by the patrons whose tastes were most refined. Michelangelo waged endless battles with his chief patron, Pope Julius II (r. 1503–1513), even as he decorated the ceiling of the Sistine Chapel. Their quarrels became legendary, as did the bill the painter presented, in which he asked thousands of ducats for his work but only a small amount for pigments.

Traditionally, in European society, people trained for specialized occupations: craftsmen did the work that they had mastered as apprentices, and scholars wrote about the

of the great classical philosophers in disputation) and the Parnassus; Michelangelo's Sistine Chapel ceiling, with its panorama of the Old Testament, and his *Last Judgment* on the altar wall of the same chapel. And all three knew and responded to one another—especially in 1500 and just after, when Leonardo and Michelangelo were both creating masterpieces in the council chamber of Florence's town hall, the Palazzo Vecchio.

Yet they were much more than brilliant practitioners of a single art form. Leonardo and Michelangelo were as much sculptors as painters. Although Leonardo's enormous equestrian monument for Milan was never cast in bronze (and the clay original was destroyed when the city fell to the French), Michelangelo's figure of David dominated the Piazza della Signoria, Florence's central square. Both were also military engineers: Leonardo in the service of the Sforza family in Milan and then of Cesare Borgia; Michelangelo in that of the Florentine Republic. And all three were architects: Both Raphael and Michelangelo served as the official architect for St. Peter's Basilica in Rome, which was begun by Donato Bramante (1444–1514). Michelangelo finished the design for the church's dome, though he died before it was completed. Leonardo pursued the study of nature, reading and drawing with fantastic energy and compiling his results in enormous, fascinating notebooks. Michelangelo wrote brilliant Italian poetry.

The Virgin of the Rocks Leonardo da Vinci included this painting as part of an altarpiece for the church of San Francesco Grande in Milan in 1506–8. The Virgin Mary sits with the infant John the Baptist and Jesus, while an angel wearing a red cape watches over them.

subjects they had studied at universities. In the Renaissance, as Alberti noted, such barriers began to come down. These powerful artists seemed able to cross the boundaries between the worlds of craft and high learning, and between the crafts themselves. Leonardo challenged the learned physicians of his time in his notebooks. He argued that his knowledge of anatomy and his accurate drawings, with their minutely skillful perspective and foreshortening, enabled him to observe and describe the human body more precisely than they could. He and his two rivals came to be seen as geniuses—unique talents not subject to the rules or limitations that restricted others.

MACHIAVELLI: THE NEW POLITICS

And yet, even as Italian society seemed to reach its zenith of development during the Renaissance, and even as the monarchs and noblemen of France and Germany whose armies ravaged the Italian Peninsula were captivated by the new classical culture of scholarship and art—it seemed that all might be a dream. One of the most loyal servants of the Florentine Republic in the years from 1498 to 1512 was **Niccolò Machiavelli**, whom we met at the beginning of this chapter. Trained in the classics, he worked in the city's chancery and eventually became the right-hand man of Pietro Soderini, chief executive of the republic. Machiavelli went on diplomatic missions and wrote detailed reports about Florence's allies and enemies. He came to see, through the eyes of the other states he visited, just how weak the Italian ones were. Always a believer in the exemplary character of Rome, he organized a civic militia, with uniforms and systematic drill sessions, in the hope that it might provide Florence more protection than mercenary armies. After the republic fell once again to the Medici in 1512, Machiavelli came under suspicion of treason. He was tortured and then exiled from Florence. Settled on his farm outside the city, he pursued an understanding of the events he had been forced to witness: the easy destruction of the Italian states, including his own, by the powerful armies from the north.

Like a good humanist, Machiavelli went back to the ancients—above all to the historians—in the hope of understanding the crisis of his state. In a letter to a trusted member of the Medici regime that had replaced the republic, he described his life—one in which casual reading mingled with lower pursuits such as gambling. But after passing the day in trivialities, Machiavelli explained, he returned home and engaged in reading of a different kind: "I enter

Machiavelli The Florentine artist Rosso Fiorentino painted this early sixteenth-century portrait of the politician and diplomat Niccolò Machiavelli writing in a book.

the ancient courts of ancient men. . . . I am not ashamed to speak with them and to ask them the reason for their actions, and they in their kindness answer me."

The book Machiavelli was writing as he spoke with the ancients was *The Prince*—perhaps the most famous book written during the Renaissance. It represented a radical departure from convention. Earlier humanists from Petrarch on, following ancient precedent, had advised princes to practice virtue at all times and to show mercy and generosity whenever possible. But Machiavelli had watched real princes and other powerful men behave, and he had seen, with fury and contempt, how the princes of Italy and their humanist counselors collapsed before the foreign onslaught. Now he recorded what he saw as the savage truth: safety, for a prince like Ludovico Sforza of Milan, had to come not from his subjects' love, but from their fear; violence, rationally and economically dealt out, was the monarch's chief tool for dealing with both his subjects and his enemies. Machiavelli insisted that "how one lives is so far distant from how one ought to live, that he who neglects what is done for what ought to be done, sooner effects his ruin than his preservation. . . . Hence it is necessary for a prince wishing to hold his own to know how to do wrong, and to make use of it or not according to necessity." Seneca had warned monarchs to be human, not to imitate the cruel lion or the vicious fox. Machiavelli advised the monarch to imitate both, as circumstances demanded.

Machiavelli went even further. He demanded, more eloquently than any previous writer, that people shake themselves free of the comforting belief that God might help them, and create the only order they could. Unlike many other humanists, Machiavelli clearly saw that the ancient Romans had not been pious in the Christian way. He even praised their warlike religion, which he considered better than Christianity for the health of the state. Yet even Machiavelli, clear-eyed radical that he was, did not foresee the greater tensions and contradictions that would soon tear the fabric, not only of Italy, but of Europe as a whole.

CONCLUSION

The Renaissance was a transformative period. The balance of power in society began to tip away from the powerful noblemen who still played such important roles in later medieval society, and toward central governments, with their new revenue systems, fortifications, and professional soldiers. Merchants and navigators, soldiers and sailors began to turn outward, to explore and conquer parts of the world that had been unfathomably remote or entirely unknown. Scholars discovered in the ancient world new models for understanding the cosmos and human society. Christians experimented with new ways of gaining contact with the divine and some assurance of salvation. And artists devised brilliant and unexpected forms of painting, sculpture, and architecture, transforming the public spaces in cities across Europe. Machiavelli was more pessimistic than the other innovators who were his contemporaries, but he shared with many of them the capacity for seeing the world as it is, and the belief that central governments must prevail.

[CHAPTER REVIEW]

KEY TERMS

Medici family (p. 326)
ambassador (p. 329)
Low Countries (p. 330)
Estates General (p. 331)
taille (p. 331)
Wars of the Roses (p. 333)
justices of the peace
  (p. 333)

Habsburg dynasty (p. 334)
Maximilian I (p. 334)
Alhambra Decree (p. 335)
Ottomans (p. 335)
Mehmed I (p. 335)
Great Schism (p. 339)
Council of Constance
  (p. 340)

confraternity (p. 342)
portolan chart (p. 345)
Johannes Gutenberg
  (p. 349)
Christopher Columbus
  (p. 351)
Treaty of Tordesillas
  (p. 352)

Hernán Cortés (p. 354)
Petrarch (p. 356)
humanism (p. 358)
Leon Battista Alberti
  (p. 364)
Niccolò Machiavelli
  (p. 367)

REVIEW QUESTIONS

1. What were the primary models or structures of government in the city-states of Renaissance Italy?

2. How did the French, Spanish, and English monarchs of the fifteenth century consolidate their power and authority?

3. What were the most important innovations in warfare during the Renaissance?

4. Who were the leading religious reformers of the fourteenth and fifteenth centuries, and what changes did they champion?

5. Why did the European states intensify their efforts in maritime exploration?

6. How did the slave trade change Europe both economically and demographically?

7. How did the arrival of the printing press transform European society?

8. What are the some of the most significant elements of the Columbian Exchange?

9. In what ways was the humanism of the Renaissance revolutionary for its time?

10. What are some of the most important innovations of Renaissance art and architecture?

CORE OBJECTIVES

After reading this chapter, you should have a solid understanding of the following core objectives. To strengthen your grasp of the core objectives, use the resources on the Student Site for The West.

- Describe the political changes that took place in Renaissance Europe.

- Evaluate the crises and reforms that transformed the Church during the Renaissance.

- Trace the emergence of new technologies and areas of knowledge in the fourteenth and fifteenth centuries.

- Analyze the encounter between the Old and New Worlds that began with Columbus's voyages.

- Assess the intellectual and artistic breakthroughs of the Renaissance.

 GO TO inQuizitive TO SEE WHAT YOU'VE LEARNED—AND LEARN WHAT YOU'VE MISSED—WITH PERSONALIZED FEEDBACK ALONG THE WAY.

1511
Erasmus publishes
In Praise of Folly

October 31, 1517
Luther presents his
Ninety-Five Theses
for formal debate

1524–1525
Peasants' War

October 1529
Luther and Zwingli
divide over Eucharist

1536
Calvin publishes *Institutes
of the Christian Religion*

1543
Copernicus argues
universe is heliocentric

1516
More publishes
Utopia

April 1521
Diet of Worms

1527
Holy Roman Emperor
Charles V's troops
sack Rome

1534
Henry VIII declares
himself head of
independent
Church of England

1540
Pope permits
Loyola to found
Jesuit order

1545–1563
Council of Trent

1555
Peace of Augsburg

Reformations

PROTESTANT AND CATHOLIC

1500–1600

O n October 31, 1517, an obscure professor of biblical theology at Wittenberg, the capital of Saxony, changed the world. Martin Luther (1483–1546) published a series of ninety-five theses about indulgences (remissions of penalties for sins, granted by the Catholic Church) and presented them to his superior, the bishop of Brandenburg, and to the archbishop of Mainz. Luther intended to preside over a formal debate of the theses among theologians, a type of public discussion that had been a normal part of academic life for centuries.

But Luther's theses were more radical than most. He denied that Christians should confess to priests, that the pope could remit guilt, and that indulgences could help a dead sinner or a living one who was not repentant. Luther's first concern—confession—was one of the standard practices of the medieval church. To cleanse themselves of sin, Christians had to confess their actions to a priest, feel genuine contrition, and make satisfaction for what they had done by, for example, saying particular prayers or going on pilgrimage to a shrine. Indulgences—certificates that drew on the Treasury of Merit that Christ's sacrifice and the virtues of the saints had created for the church—could remit the actual penalties that the priest imposed. They worked, in theory, only if the sinner had confessed and was repentant. In practice, however, as Luther objected, pardoners sold indulgences not

Reformed Worship In 1564, in a Calvinist church in Lyon, France, attendees practice a new style of worship. Sitting on benches that line the round room, they listen as a preacher delivers a sermon, the central feature of services in many of the reformist movements that spread across Europe in the sixteenth century.

- Why were Luther's criticisms of the Church so influential?
- How did the Reformation movement spread and then splinter?
- How did political and religious allegiance become entangled?
- In what ways did Catholicism renew itself in the sixteenth century?
- What new understandings of the natural world were emerging at this time?
- Why were the religious wars so devastating?
- How did observers make sense of the disruptions of this period?

only to those who wanted to benefit from them after death but also to those who wanted to shorten the time that a dead relative might have to spend in the fires of purgatory to be cleansed of their sin. Some pardoners promised that "so soon as the penny jingles into the money-box, the soul flies out [of purgatory]." But Luther insisted that no human cleric could legitimately make such a promise: "It is certain that when the penny jingles into the money-box, gain and avarice can be increased, but the result of the intercession of the Church is in the power of God alone."

The particular indulgence to which Luther objected was intended to raise money for the construction of the greatest of Renaissance churches, Saint Peter's Basilica in Rome. Pope Leo X (r. 1513–1521) commissioned a Dominican, Johann Tetzel, to sell indulgences in the Holy Roman Empire. Student reports of Tetzel's abuses of the system aroused Luther to action. But it was not only the pardoners' excessive zeal and absurd promises that bothered Luther. The whole enterprise seemed wrong to him. It had made many laypeople worry about the pope and his concern for ordinary Christians. "Why does not the pope empty purgatory," so Luther paraphrased them, "for the sake of holy love and of the dire need of the souls that are there, if he redeems an infinite number of souls for the sake of miserable money with which to build a Church? The former reasons would be most just; the latter is most trivial."

In the end, what mattered most to Luther was not the purpose for which the indulgence was offered but the very idea of it. Christian repentance took place inside the soul. Anyone who preached that Christians could ease their consciences and reconcile themselves with God by paying money failed to understand that all Christians were called to suffer. Their optimistic message, which Luther summed up as "Peace, peace," could not simply be corrected; it must be replaced with the true teaching that Christians must follow Christ, "their Head, through penalties, deaths, and hell."

By early 1518, Luther's theses were being printed in Latin and translated into German so that ordinary people could understand them. Copies flew through the Holy Roman Empire and beyond. Luther himself became a celebrity, a bold German hero who had stood up for his fellow countrymen against the greedy Church of Rome. More important, he became the leader of a movement, one that put an end to the unified Catholic Church that had survived all challenges to its authority in the West for more than a thousand years, and did so not only in the Holy Roman Empire but also across the European world. The movement took its name—Protestantism—from the protest in 1529 of German princes against the Imperial Diet (assembly) in Speyer, which prohibited further religious reforms in the Holy Roman Empire. How did Luther's small act of defiance in a corner of northern Germany have such seismic consequences?

MARTIN LUTHER AND THE CULTURE OF CHURCH REFORM

Part of the explanation of Luther's influence lies in his character. The son of a hard man, a mining entrepreneur, **Martin Luther** joined a religious order at age twenty-two in gratitude to Saint Anne, who, he thought, had saved him from a lightning bolt that struck near him during a thunderstorm. He observed the rule of his order with absolute, almost fanatical devotion. He fasted, prayed, and made himself an expert on the Bible. Luther learned Greek and Hebrew so that he would be able to read the Old and New Testaments in their original languages. He printed special editions of the Psalms for his students, stripping them of commentaries to force the students to confront the original texts, but leaving wide margins so that they could enter their own reflections as they read.

Martin Luther The German artist Lucas Cranach the Elder, a friend of Luther's, painted his portrait in 1529, when Luther was forty-five.

LUTHER'S BREAKTHROUGH

From 1513 to 1517 Luther taught courses on the Psalms, on the apostle Paul, and on the works of Augustine. Meanwhile, he himself suffered from fear and at times paralysis. He worried that God's law, as stated in the Old Testament, was too harsh and demanding for anyone to follow. He continually reproached himself for failing to accomplish one religious duty or another, or for having done it only incompletely or halfheartedly. And then suddenly, one day, he found all his questions answered, all of his problems solved. By reading the Bible in a new way, he discovered, he could absolve himself of the need to follow a massive, arbitrary code of conduct without abandoning his search for grace.

Luther realized that Paul, the author of many of the New Testament epistles, had the answer to his problem. In Romans 1:17, Paul had written: "For therein is the righteousness of God revealed from faith to faith: as it is written, 'The just shall live by faith.'" Here, Luther thought, Paul's message was that the righteousness of God was not something that Christians had to seek endlessly, in a futile effort to curb their own bodies and cure their own vices, but something that Christ had earned for them by his sacrifice. They could share his righteousness if they wanted to: not by buying **indulgences**, not by endless pursuit of perfect obedience to a monastic rule, but simply by having faith in him. Because the New Testament verse contained an internal quotation from an Old Testament prophet, Luther argued, it encapsulated the meaning of the Bible as a whole. The Old Testament taught righteousness, the evil nature of mankind after the Fall, and the demands of God's law. But the New Testament taught faith: that Jesus, by sacrificing himself, had made it possible for all who believed in him to become just as well.

Luther's mastery of theology and his command of the Bible enabled him to view the basic problems of sin and damnation from a new perspective. As we will see, his

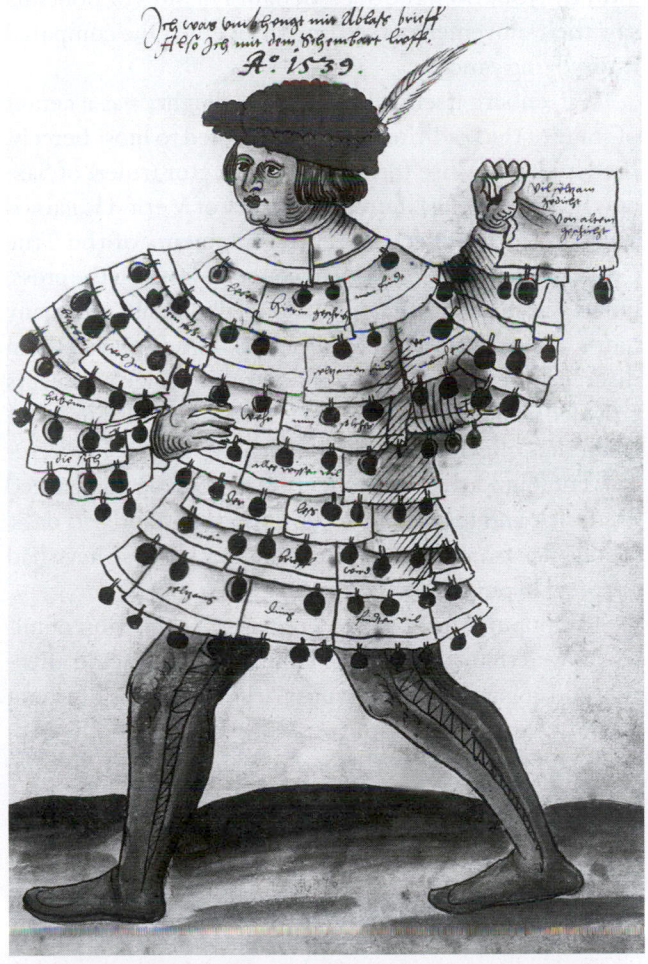

Sale of Indulgences A 1539 cartoon from Nuremberg mocks the proliferation of indulgences. The man is dressed in a costume made from letters of indulgences, and the caption explains that the letters are so ridiculous that the man had no choice but to join in the festivities of the Nuremberg carnival.

determination and abilities as a speaker and writer enabled him to bring his message to multiple audiences. Yet it was by no means obvious in 1517 and 1518 that Luther would create anything permanent, much less the first of many new versions of the Christian Church.

CHRISTIANITY IN 1517

In the first place, the world in which Luther lived—the world of late-medieval Christianity—seemed extremely solid. Serious, principled opposition to papal power in the Church had mostly come to an end with the conciliar movement by the middle of the fifteenth century. Girolamo Savonarola's defiance of papal authority in the 1490s had ended with his disgrace and death. The heretical movements of the decades around 1400 were fading slowly away by 1500. Even the once-defiant Hussites of Bohemia saw their movement as coming to an end. One compared it to a dying candle.

Wittenberg itself, where Luther taught, was a center of some of the traditions that he objected to most fiercely. Frederick the Wise (r. 1486–1525), Elector (ruler) of Saxony, believed in the Church's Treasury of Merit. He gained access to it by collecting relics—fragments of the True Cross and the Holy Spear that wounded Jesus on the cross, bones and garments that had belonged to saints, and many more, all encased in splendid vessels that displayed them discreetly through small windows. Frederick's subjects crowded into the local church every year on All Saint's Eve when the collection was put on display. In 1520, his secretary computed that the collection as a whole had earned Frederick and his subjects 1,902,202 years' and 270 days' indulgence from the time they would otherwise have had to spend in purgatory.

The popular response to Frederick's collection of relics showed that the Catholic Church still attracted affection and engagement from most believers, many of whom warmly valued the traditions that Luther challenged. Ordinary Christians crowded parish churches, finding deep rewards in hearing their priests perform the Mass. They embraced the rituals that celebrated the seasons of the agricultural year, such as the Harvest Home festival in the fall, and the yearly reliving of Christ's Passion in the Easter season. In cities, laypeople banded together in confraternities, religious organizations that among other benefits guaranteed their members proper burial.

Christians had always prayed. But the later Middle Ages saw the development of new, engaged forms of prayer. The

Thomas More's Family This 1593 copy of a painting originally by Hans Holbein shows Thomas More (far left) surrounded by his family, all holding books of hours.

rosary, for example—a devotion to the Virgin Mary that consisted of repetitions of the Lord's Prayer and ten Hail Marys—had been created in the thirteenth century. During the fifteenth century, it became normal to repeat the sequence fifteen times, with meditations on the mysteries of the Virgin added. Christians still saw the society of heaven as a hierarchical mirror of society on earth, and sought the help of the members of God's family and the larger community of saints. At the same time, though, worship became more intense and individual, as is clear from the spread of printed books of hours. A famous portrait of the family of Thomas More—English scholar, lawyer, and statesman—shows parents and children with their books of hours in hand, making their household a place of regular and intense devotion. Prayer seemed so precious that wealthy men and women endowed chantries—altars or chapels where masses would be said in perpetuity for their souls.

Serious efforts at reform continued to be made in the monastic and mendicant orders, some of which had become aristocratic preserves. The German Benedictine houses of the Bursfeld congregation, for example, came together for meetings at which the brilliant scholar Johannes Trithemius (1462–1516) called for a revival of the early monastic spirit. He laid out sensible rules for restoring discipline in houses for monks and nuns, and brought the rich spiritual writings of Hildegard of Bingen back into circulation. Franciscans and Dominicans, similarly, made serious efforts to restore their orders to the form that their founders had envisioned.

HUMANIST CRITICS OF THE CHURCH

Others found the Church, and the textures of Christian life, seriously problematic, and they helped to give Luther both the intellectual tools with which he set to work and a receptive audience. Some critics of the Church were rooted in the culture of humanism, which spread through northern Europe in the fifteenth century. As Italian humanists such as Aeneas Silvius Piccolomini (who became Pope Pius II) visited northern lands, and northern scholars such as the Englishman John Free visited Italy, the new methods of Italian humanism provoked increasing interest in the north. The scholarship of the humanists took on new forms, and showed new potentials, in the very different societies of England, France, and the Holy Roman Empire.

DESIDERIUS ERASMUS No one championed the humanism of the north more exuberantly or developed it more effectively than **Desiderius Erasmus** (1466–1536), and no one had a deeper impact on Luther. Born the

Erasmus Albrecht Dürer's 1526 engraving of Erasmus depicts the humanist priest in his element, surrounded by books and with pen in hand.

illegitimate son of a priest in the Netherlandish port city of Rotterdam, Erasmus studied in a school of the Brothers of the Common Life, whose members did not take vows but lived in community houses and earned their living as teachers, scribes, and early adopters of the new technology of printing. After joining a religious order, the Augustinian Canons, Erasmus became a priest. He found monastic life stifling, but never lost the taste he developed there for the meditative, gentle piety of the Brothers' and Canons' movement for religious reform known as Modern Devotion. Soon it became clear, to him and others, that he had unusual talents, especially for writing Latin. A French bishop employed him as a secretary and then gave him a stipend to study in Paris. Erasmus loathed the terrible food and squalid conditions of the Paris colleges, as well as what he considered the sterile pedantry of scholastic theology.

Gradually, however, he made the contacts that would determine the course of his intellectual life. Always a passionate classicist who hated what he called the "barbarians" of the university faculties with their inelegant Latin jargon, he turned out to have a wonderful knack for drawing up textbooks that could help aspiring Latinists become fluent and eventually find careers, as Erasmus had, in the employment of high-ranking clerics and government officials. In London in 1499, he met and was deeply impressed by John Colet (1467–1519), an austere senior scholar who loved the Platonist philosophy of Marsilio Ficino but insisted, at the same time, that Christians must study the New Testament directly. It was in the life, teachings, and death of Jesus, Colet insisted, not in formal theology and philosophy, that Christians would find the central principles of their faith. In 1504, Erasmus discovered a copy of the Italian humanist Lorenzo Valla's commentary on the New Testament. Valla taught him that just as the classics should be read in their original languages, so should the Christian scriptures. Erasmus, who had mastered Greek to support his secular scholarship, was delighted to apply his skills to the Bible.

From 1506 to 1509 Erasmus lived in Italy, where he earned a doctorate in theology from Turin. In Venice he found a home for several months in the printing shop of Aldus Manutius (1449–1515), whose handsome typefaces he admired. Manutius and the Byzantine exiles who corrected Greek texts for him made a wealth of Greek books available to this brilliant visitor. Even as Erasmus established himself as the first northern scholar who knew Greek and wrote Latin as well as any Italian, he continued to look for ways to connect his pursuit of learning with Christian piety.

As Erasmus steeped himself in the New Testament—especially the Gospels, with their vivid depiction of the life and teachings of Jesus—he found himself more and more at odds with society and the Church. The policies of the popes, with their pursuit of worldly power, seemed to contradict the message of Jesus, who had preached poverty and charity. So did the policies of most secular rulers. City burghers pursued wealth as passionately as kings, and nobles pursued power and glory. Their lives did not exemplify Christian principles in action—especially when they refused aid to the many poor people who lived in the streets outside their palaces.

Returning from Italy, Erasmus spent the years 1511 to 1514 in England, where he was professor of theology at the University of Cambridge and worked on the text of the New Testament. But he found other ways to try to reach and change public opinion. Imitating one of his favorite ancient writers, the second-century Greek satirist Lucian, Erasmus wrote a mock oration, *In Praise of Folly*, in which he ridiculed every order of Christian society—but reserved especially sharp mockery for the powerful. He couched criticisms of central features of Church practice in humorous form. Instead of denouncing the scholastic treatises on witches, for example, he made fun of a scholastic who defended them. He heaped ridicule on what he portrayed as the lifeless abstraction of scholastic theology. His book, which first appeared in Strasbourg in 1511, became a best-seller. It provoked furious protests from more traditional theologians.

THOMAS MORE'S *UTOPIA*

Erasmus's wit made him friends, as well as enemies, across Europe. A brilliant young English lawyer named **Thomas More** (1478–1535), for example, learned from both Colet and Erasmus and applied their principles in his own highly original way. The Church of the first Christians, as the Gospels portrayed it, had been very different from its contemporary counterpart: not a wealthy, established institution with stiff hierarchies of officials, monks, and mendicants competing for recruits and bequests, but a frail, countercultural movement that had stood against war and tried to help the poor. A gifted student of Greek, More took inspiration from Plato's *Republic* and from contemporary reports of newly discovered lands. In his own book, More imagined a society that he called Utopia (Greek for "no place") and a brilliant, worldly traveler, Raphael Hythloday, who described it to More and other friends. On this pagan island, far from Europe, everyone worked, no one went hungry, and a rigorous system of

More's *Utopia* An illustration from the original 1516 edition of Thomas More's book shows a ship sailing to the island of Utopia.

discipline ensured that no one desired money, the root of all evil.

More's book did not confine itself to portraying an ideal society. In its opening sections More has Hythloday apply the lessons of Utopia and the other imaginary countries he has visited to contemporary England. More, who served in the Parliament and was an expert in international trade, made clear that he thought the society of his day deeply unchristian in Erasmus's sense. It was unfair to the soldiers who were cast off after being injured in its service, and to the peasants whom landlords were allowed to evict so their land could be used more profitably for raising sheep. The sheep, More's narrator complained, were eating the people of England. He was equally critical of Christian kings who wasted their subjects' money on wars meant to pursue their own narrow dynastic aims.

More's *Utopia* was published in 1516 and soon reprinted with approving prefaces by European scholars and enthusiastic marginal notes by Erasmus himself. Although More's narrator claims that work in a royal council would corrupt him rather than improve matters, More himself agreed to serve as a counselor to his young, dynamic king, Henry VIII. In the meantime, though, many readers saw *Utopia* and the *Praise of Folly* as the works not of isolated thinkers but of a more or less united European avant-garde, who were finding sharp new ways to show that classical scholarship and authentic Christian piety complemented one another.

REFORMING THE BIBLE
Erasmus did more than remind European readers that Christ had told his followers to give all they had to the poor and turn the other cheek when violence was done to them. As a boy he had learned that true piety was not a matter of observances, of relics collected and indulgences bought, but of repentance and faith. Reading the New Testament in Greek, he found this central message in the words of Jesus and John the Baptist. In the Vulgate, the Latin translation of the Bible carried out in the late fourth century and used in all Catholic churches, Jesus tells Christians that they should "do penance." His command provided the foundation on which the complex system of confession, absolution, and remission of sin rested. In the Greek, however, Jesus instructs his hearers to "repent," meaning to come back to their right minds. Here and in many other passages, Erasmus held, the Latin Bible of the Church was clearly wrong.

Erasmus set out, accordingly, to reform the Vulgate itself. He prepared a revised Latin translation of the New Testament that made his new interpretations clear, and printed it with the Greek text to support it. Erasmus urged readers to refound theology, substituting direct study of the Bible for the logical arguments about doctrine that had traditionally formed the core of the field. His bold undertaking was flanked by even grander enterprises: an edition of the Psalms in Hebrew, Greek, and Arabic, as well as Latin; and a vast edition of the entire Bible, with the Old Testament in Hebrew, Greek, Aramaic, and Latin, and the New Testament in Greek and Latin. This polyglot Bible was sponsored by the Spanish cardinal and statesman Francisco Jiménez de Cisneros. A conservative, he compared the Vulgate text of the Old Testament, which his scholars printed between the Hebrew and the Greek, to Christ crucified between two thieves. But he still supported the study and publication of the originals. A massive controversy flared up in Germany over whether it was legitimate for Christians to learn from Jews and draw on their traditions of scholarship. The very identity of the Bible seemed debatable—just when Erasmus had placed its study at the center of theological inquiry.

LUTHER AND ERASMUS
Luther came to maturity in the years when Erasmus and his friends attained the peak of their prestige. He followed Erasmus's teachings and example in making the New Testament the source for all Christian truths, and he used Erasmus's New Testament edition. His critique of indulgences began from the same point that Erasmus had made: that Jesus commanded not the doing of penance but repentance. Many of those who read Luther's theses and sent them on to colleagues and printers were clerics and officials who had read Erasmus's textbooks in their youth and shared his belief that Christians needed to return to their original principles. Like Erasmus himself, they saw Luther at first as an ally—as someone who continued the Christian humanist critique of the Church and offered the Bible as a template for its reform.

LUTHER'S MESSAGE

In fact, however, as Luther's message began to spread—and to encounter challenges—it became clear that his vision differed sharply from that of Erasmus: Luther represented not a movement to reform the existing Church but a challenge to its very existence. Between 1517 and 1521, he definitively stated most of his central doctrines in short, accessible books in Latin and German. Only scripture, Luther argued, contained the truths a Christian needed. Only divine grace made it possible to read scripture properly. And only faith in Jesus could win salvation. Everything else the Church did and believed, Luther now argued, was superfluous, and much of it harmful. The Church must be rebuilt on a solid foundation of scripture, correctly interpreted.

Traditional Catholic doctrine held that priests occupied a special spiritual as well as social position: they could intervene for other Christians, releasing them from the consequences of their sins. Luther argued that all Christians were priests who could pray for one another. Whereas Catholic priests offered seven distinct sacraments, Luther recognized only two: infant baptism and the Eucharist. And whereas the Catholic Church presented itself as a spiritual body that transcended mere political and linguistic borders and owed obedience only to the pope, Luther demanded that Christian rulers emulate Constantine, the emperor who had established Christianity as the religion of the Roman Empire and convoked the Council of Nicea to settle disputed points of doctrine. Secular rulers, Luther insisted, must take responsibility for the local churches that were under their political jurisdiction.

THE DIET OF WORMS AND ITS AFTERMATH (1521)

Luther's ideas now circulated in high official circles, especially after Albert of Brandenburg, Cardinal and Elector of Mainz, forwarded the **Ninety-Five Theses** to Rome. In July 1519, the eminent Catholic theologian Johann Eck (1486–1543) engaged Luther in a debate at Leipzig. Eck forced Luther to admit that he believed popes and even Church councils could err: only scripture was infallible. Eck pushed for a response from the Church, and in June 1520 Pope Leo X issued a bull condemning Luther.

Called to the **Diet of Worms**, a formal meeting of the Imperial Estates in April 1521, Luther accepted the invitation and stood before Holy Roman Emperor Charles V (r. 1519–1556) himself. Eck showed Luther a display of his writings and asked if he acknowledged them as his own. Luther requested time to reflect, but the next day he gave his opponents a sharp answer that expressed his conviction that he was acting as grace dictated:

> Unless I am convinced by the testimony of the Scriptures or by clear reason (for I do not trust either in the pope or in councils alone, since it is well known that they have often erred and contradicted themselves), I am bound by the Scriptures I have quoted and my conscience is captive to the Word of God. I cannot and will not recant anything, since it is neither safe nor right to go against conscience. May God help me. Amen.

Of Luther's extraordinary courage there can be no doubt. But his unflinching stance did not impress the emperor, who soon afterward delivered an impressive reply. He insisted on his duty, inherited from his ancestors, to defend the Catholic faith. On May 25, 1521, the emperor made Luther an outlaw. He forbade all subjects of the empire to give Luther food or water and permitted anyone to kill him without fear of consequences.

When Luther left the Diet, he was arrested by servants of Frederick the Wise, Elector of Saxony. They took him to the Wartburg castle in Eisenach, almost in the center of Germany, where he remained for several months under a loose form of house arrest. He used the time to translate the New Testament into German, realizing Erasmus's program to make the Bible available to all Christians. He poured out a series of pamphlets and treatises in which he began to draw the full consequences of his new theology. He argued, for example, that monks and nuns need not follow their vows of chastity, since marriage was a holy state, or of obedience, since obeying a superior would not bring them farther along the path to salvation.

By the end of 1521, Luther was hearing worrying messages from Wittenberg. Another minister who wished to reform the Church, Andreas Karlstadt (1486–1541), had taken over Luther's pulpit there. A radical by temperament, Karlstadt was inspired not only by Luther but also by miners from a nearby city, uneducated men who had visions and prophesied. Together they set out to transform the Church in Wittenberg beyond recognition. Whereas Luther argued that Christians should be able to understand the Bible for themselves, Karlstadt replaced the Latin Mass with a German-language service. And whereas Luther argued that Christians should not set too much store on images of saints, Karlstadt gained consent from the city council in 1522 to remove them from Wittenberg's churches.

Allowed to return to Wittenberg in March 1522, Luther appeared on his pulpit in the robes of his Augustinian Canons order. In a brilliant series of sermons, he convinced his fellow inhabitants of Wittenberg that it was wrong to move too quickly or to change things too radically, since by doing so they threatened the consciences of Christians who were not yet certain of the truth. Taking command of the situation, Luther began to create a new Church order. Soon cities across the Holy Roman Empire and beyond,

Diet of Worms A sixteenth-century history of Germany illustrates the dramatic scene of Luther's defense of his ideas to Holy Roman Emperor Charles V. The Catholic theologian Johann Eck (holding a book at center left) interrogates Luther as courtiers look on.

especially in Switzerland, were publicly joining the cause of reform. Luther himself was certain of what made his views—some of them highly abstract and difficult—take wing as they did. He and his dear friend and helper Philip Melanchthon simply sat in Wittenberg, he told his students much later, and drank the local dark beer. The Holy Spirit did the rest.

THE REFORMATION MOVEMENT

Between 1521 and 1529, Luther's challenge to the authority of the Church became a movement—the movement that became known, after the Diet of Speyer in 1529, as the **Protestant Reformation**. Princes and cities across the Holy Roman Empire and Switzerland, and individuals across a far wider area, found inspiration in Luther's writings to transform local churches. But they also encountered resistance—sometimes from Catholics faithful to the established order of things, sometimes from fellow Protestants who disagreed with them on basic questions of theology or Church discipline. By 1529, it was clear that the Protestant challenge would not soon disappear. But it was also clear that Protestantism would not take a single form or remain a unified movement. Luther's success was extraordinary—and partial.

THE MOVEMENT'S APPEAL

Many clearly identifiable features of Luther's world, beyond Wittenberg's dark beer, made his success possible. The power of print and the structures of authority in cities and states played vital roles in transforming a message into a movement.

THE ROLE OF PRINT
Most important, the printing press gave Luther a megaphone that previous critics of the established Church lacked until the late fifteenth century, when the followers of Savonarola in Florence printed multiple editions of the Dominican's sermons. Luther used it with determination and brilliance. He became the master of the theological pamphlet, in both Latin and German. As a writer and translator, he developed a flexible German idiom that he could use both to render the word of God and to make his own arguments. He printed much of what he wrote—so much that, by the end of 1521, more than 100 editions of his works had already appeared. If each edition was produced in the period's standard quantity of 500 to 1,000 copies, then tens of thousands of copies of Luther's

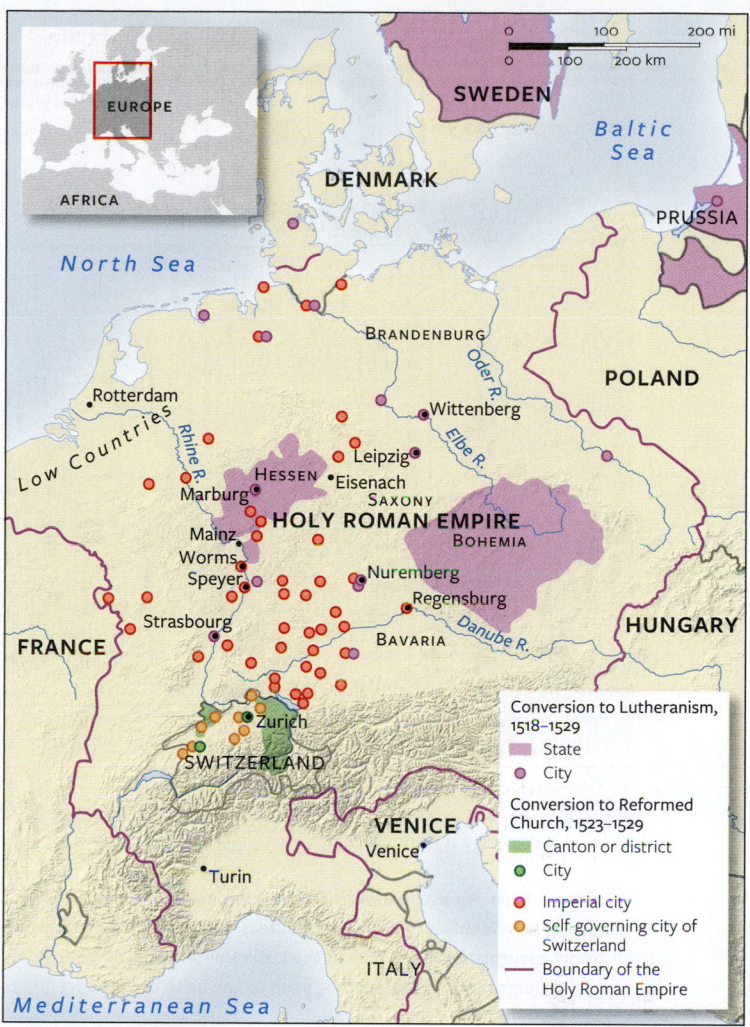

The Reformation Movement, 1521–1529 By 1529, Lutheranism had spread from the central German cities where Luther's message first took hold to large states like Bohemia, Hessen, Prussia, and Sweden. In the area around Zurich, meanwhile, Zwingli's Reformed movement gained converts.

texts must have been in circulation four years after the outbreak of his movement. Luther and his printers developed a uniform format that became closely associated with him—some historians call this the first media brand.

Luther and his followers used illustrations as well as texts to appeal to their fellow Christians. Even before printing with moveable type was introduced in the West, collections of woodcut illustrations with some text, known as block books, brought graphic versions of the biblical narratives to readers of modest means and education. When printers learned to reproduce substantial texts with moveable type, they continued to adorn them with woodcut illustrations. Illustrated texts were far more accessible than unbroken blocks of type. A single

Printing Bibles A 1465 "pauper's Bible" demonstrates how printing technology could make the stories and ideas of the Bible accessible to all. Short excerpts from the text of the Latin Vulgate are set alongside woodcut illustrations of key stories, such as the birth of Jesus (center).

literate person could read them aloud to a circle of illiterate hearers, who could still appreciate the illustrations. And illustrations lent themselves to polemic. They could be used to contrast the poverty and humility of the Jesus of the New Testament to the arrogant, overstuffed clerics in Rome. They could also be used to spread news of portents, such as the fall of meteors or the birth of strangely deformed animals, which suggested that God was warning his people of important changes soon to occur. The artists who followed Luther—above all Lucas Cranach the Elder (1472–1553), the Wittenberg court artist—became expert at composing religious comic books and illustrating the Bible with polemical woodcuts that presented a bold challenge to the established Church.

SOCIAL BASES OF REFORM
Luther's message would never have found the reception it did if he had not been speaking to the passions and interests of Christians, powerful and not, across the social spectrum. When Luther appealed to secular authorities to take control over the churches in their domains, he addressed princes and kings eager to enlarge their power and revenues, and city magistrates who believed that they were more qualified than any outsiders to see to the moral and spiritual health of their fellow citizens. When he addressed social and economic questions—such as bankers' practice of charging excess interest, which he denounced, or landlords' exploitation of their tenants—he seemed to offer hope to many that the message of the Gospel, as he defined it, would also change their position in life for the better. And when he told Christians that in so far as any of them were priests, all of them were, and all of them could intercede for one another, he seemed to offer women a religious position and role very different from anything that traditional Christianity in the West had provided. Support for Luther also came from master artisans and journeymen, printers and (in Saxony) miners—practitioners of new and expanding crafts.

REFORM IN THE CITIES
Luther's message held special appeal in the imperial cities of the Holy Roman Empire—some sixty-nine cities such as Nuremberg, most in southern Germany, that acknowledged no authority below the Holy Roman emperor himself—and in the self-governing cities of Switzerland. City magistrates had long taken responsibility for settling disputes between such Catholic institutions as religious orders in their territory. Many cities had traditional shrines to which pilgrims came, bringing income; but many resented the need to pay ecclesiastical dues to the Roman Church every time a new bishop or abbot was inaugurated. Each city played out its own complex drama, following its own pace; in many, members of established elites—wealthy merchants, for example, and university professors—acted as a brake on both popular pressure and government action.

The case of Regensburg, an imperial city in Bavaria, illustrates the complexity of these processes. In 1519, the city expelled its Jewish community, which had been there since Roman times, and destroyed their synagogue. During the destruction a workman fell from a roof or was struck by a beam (accounts vary), but escaped harm. He claimed that the Virgin Mary had held his hand. Others ascribed his salvation to a medieval image of the Virgin in Regensburg. A wooden chapel was built on the site to hold it, with a statue of the Virgin outside. Crowds began to visit it. "'All sorts of people came,' one witness noted: 'some with musical instruments, some with pitchforks and rakes; women came with their milk cans, spindles, and cooking pots. Artisans came with their tools: a weaver with his shuttle, a carpenter with his square, a cooper with his measuring tape.'" More than 100,000 pilgrims visited within a year, buying

The Virgin of Regensburg Printed at the height of enthusiasm for the Virgin at Regensburg, this woodcut image shows the statue in front of the wooden chapel, which is decorated with the arms of the city. Pilgrims line up to view the statue, with the most fervent collapsing in adoration.

badges to stick in their caps to show that they had done so. But by 1524, enthusiasm for the miracle-working image had ebbed. The city council busied itself trying to reform the local church while expelling Lutherans—clear evidence that Luther's message was being preached. By 1542, however, the council officially made the city Lutheran. A stone structure begun in 1525 to replace the wooden chapel was completed in 1542 and became the city's first Protestant church. Many cities experienced religious changes as rapid and unexpected as these in the 1520s.

LUTHER'S CRITICS

Yet Luther's success was anything but complete. In the first place, the radicalism of his challenge to the Church posed the question of authority in a new way. If the pope

and his theologians had no right to determine the correct interpretation of the Bible or the theological doctrines that rested on it, then who did? Luther claimed that this power rested with the individual Christian. But even many of the humanists who had agreed that traditional Church structures and doctrines needed reform were shocked by the clean sweep that Luther proposed to make. Thomas More, for example, persisted in believing that the prayers of the living were needed by the souls who suffered in purgatory—a place whose very existence Luther denied. More lampooned Luther as an "infallible donkey" who proposed to replace the infallible pope of tradition with his own equally unquestionable authority.

ERASMUS'S HUMANIST CRITIQUE Erasmus, on the whole, agreed. As the contours of Luther's doctrines became clearer, Erasmus realized that the reformer really saw human nature as devoid of any value or virtue except what came to it through faith. By definition, men and women could play no active part in their own salvation. Ever the humanist, Erasmus believed that the best of the pagans had lived and thought in a virtuous way—so virtuous that they were almost Christians. And he could not accept the idea that God simply reached down and saved certain individuals. In a treatise against Luther published in 1524, Erasmus attacked him for claiming certainty on issues too difficult for human understanding. True Christians, he explained, preferred to avoid the sort of furious debates with colleagues that Luther's brand of theology required.

More important, Erasmus claimed, Luther was simply wrong about the relationship between humankind and God. A little child, Erasmus explained, cannot walk without the help of an adult—or be made to walk by that adult if he or she refuses to cooperate. This was also the situation of the Christian soul: too weak to save itself, but a vital participant in the drama of its own salvation. Luther—a far more rigorous theologian than Erasmus—devastated the humanist in his reply, but by the same token he made clear that he was now going down a road where some of those who had supported him would not follow.

ULRICH ZWINGLI Even those who dedicated themselves to reform in Luther's sense, moreover, did not always agree with him on vital details. What was the sacrament of the Eucharist, for example? Catholics believed that though the bread and wine of the Mass still looked like the original substances, the priest's words transformed them into the body and blood of Christ (the doctrine of transubstantiation). Luther argued that the Eucharist contained both sets of substances at once: bread and body,

Ulrich Zwingli An uncompromising reformer, Zwingli founded the Reformed church and transformed public conduct in Zurich and beyond.

wine and blood (a doctrine called consubstantiation). But **Ulrich Zwingli** (1484–1531), a former priest who led the transformation of the church in the Swiss city of Zurich, took a different view. Zwingli and others argued that the bread and wine remained themselves, rather than changing into a new substance, and represented the body and blood of Christ only as symbols. Luther denounced these views. After some polemical exchanges, the disagreeing parties met at Marburg Castle, in Hessen, in October 1529. When Luther chalked "This is my body" on a table, laid a cloth over the words, and defended his views forcefully, Zwingli insisted that "is," in this context, meant "stands for," as it did when Jesus said "I am the true vine" or "I am the road." Discussion soon broke down as the theologians traded insults. What had started out as a single movement began to fragment into multiple reformations.

FISSURES IN THE MOVEMENT: ZURICH AND THE REFORMED TRADITION

In Zurich, Ulrich Zwingli built a distinctive church. He was inspired not only by Luther, who taught him to insist that all believers were priests and to eliminate the old clerical estate, but also by Erasmus and other Christian humanists who had hoped to see Christianity transform society. Uncompromising in his reforms, Zwingli found support in the radical journeymen and women who, in Zurich, wielded a measure of political influence and power. Through two public disputations and a long series of sermons, he and his colleagues won over the Zurich population and their magistrates, who accepted the Reformation in 1523.

Zwingli's church—the first of the Protestant churches, based in Switzerland, that came to be called Reformed rather than Lutheran—differed from Luther's in both style and substance. Whereas Luther refused to eliminate all Catholic observances at once, Zwingli fought to reduce Christian ritual as soon as possible to the minimum clearly prescribed by the New Testament. Whereas Luther retained, and reformed, church music, Zwingli banned both instrumental music and singing. When Zwingli denounced religious images as a violation of divine law, the authorities had the great triptychs in Zurich's main churches closed. But their action inspired Zwingli's followers to tear down other shrines and images. In June 1524 the local authorities made Zwingli's position official, ordering that all churches be "cleansed" of their religious images and stained glass. Zwingli was delighted by the "white" and "luminous" look of the undecorated churches.

Zwingli also set out to impose Christian discipline on the citizens of Zurich. Here too differing from Luther, who held that what mattered to Christians was the condition of their souls, Zwingli argued that the Christian magistrate must reform public behavior as well as worship. Zurich adopted laws that regulated Sabbath observance and other forms of public conduct, while a new Marriage Court oversaw the making of marriages and the conduct of married life. By the mid-1520s, the church of Reformed Zurich looked very different from the one that Luther had built in Wittenberg.

TRANSFORMING SOCIETY: THE PEASANTS' WAR (1524–1525)

In the same decade, moreover, the messages of Luther and his rivals rippled through German society, sometimes joined to social and political grievances held by people across the social order. Early in the 1520s, for example, the German knights—a group of minor aristocrats who, like the governments of the imperial cities, recognized only

MARTIN LUTHER AND THE PEASANTS' WAR

The rebels who took part in the Peasants' War of 1524–25 were influenced by radical religious ideas as well as long-standing social grievances. Their demands are well stated in their manifesto, the Twelve Articles of the Peasants (1525), largely the work of the preacher Christoph Schappeler and a journeyman furrier, Sebastian Lotzer. Several Reformation theologians published responses to the Twelve Articles, notably Martin Luther, who in his *Admonition to Peace Concerning the Twelve Articles of the Peasants* (1525) urged lords and peasants to reach an understanding. Luther's position hardened into strong opposition to the peasants, however, as the uprising intensified.

Twelve Articles of the Peasants

The First Article. First, it is our humble petition and desire, indeed our will and resolution, that in the future we shall have power and authority so that the entire community should choose and appoint a minister, and that we should have the right to depose him should he conduct himself improperly. The minister thus chosen should teach us the holy gospel pure and simple, without any human addition, doctrine or ordinance….

The Second Article. Since the right tithe is established in the Old Testament and fulfilled in the New, we are ready and willing to pay the fair tithe of grain. Nonetheless, it should be done properly. The Word of God plainly provides that it should be given to God and passed on to his own. If it is to be given to a minister, we will in the future collect the tithe through our church elders, appointed by the congregation, according to the judgment of the whole congregation. The remainder shall be given to the poor of the place, as the circumstances and the general opinion demand….

The Third Article. It has been the custom hitherto for men to hold us as their own property, which is pitiable enough considering that Christ has redeemed and purchased us without exception, by the shedding of his precious blood, the lowly as well as the great. Accordingly, it is consistent with Scripture that we should be free and we wish to be so. Not that we want to be absolutely free and under no authority. God does not teach us that we should lead a disorderly life according to the lusts of the flesh, but that we should live by the commandments, love the Lord our God and our neighbor….

Conclusion…If any one or more of these articles should not be in agreement with the Word of God, which we do not think, we will willingly recede from such article when it is proved to be against the Word of God by a clear explanation of the Scripture.

Martin Luther, *Admonition to Peace Concerning the Twelve Articles of the Peasants*

To the Princes and Lords

We have no one on earth to thank for this disastrous rebellion, except you princes and lords, and especially you blind bishops and mad priests and monks, whose hearts are hardened, even to the present day…. You do nothing but cheat and rob the people so that you may lead a life of luxury and extravagance. The poor common people cannot bear it any longer…. If it is still possible to give you advice, my lords, give way a little to the will and wrath of God…. Try kindness first, for you do not know what God will do to prevent the spark that will kindle all Germany and start a fire that no one can extinguish….

To the Peasants

In the first place, dear brethren, you bear the name of God and call yourselves a "Christian association" or union, and you allege that you want to live and act according to divine law. Now you know that the name, word, and cities of God are not to be assumed idly or in vain….

I say this, dear friends, as a faithful warning. In this case you should stop calling yourselves Christians and stop claiming that you have the Christian law on your side…. So again I say, however good and just your cause may be, nevertheless, because you would defend yourselves and are unwilling to suffer either violence or injustice, you may do anything that God does not prevent. However, leave the name Christian out of it….

If…you will…keep the name of Christian, then I must accept the fact that I am also involved in this struggle and consider you as enemies who, under the name of the gospel, act contrary to it, and want to do more to suppress my gospel than anything the pope and emperor have done to suppress it….

Admonition to Both Rulers and Peasants

Now, dear sirs, there is nothing Christian on either side and nothing Christian is at issue between you; both lords and peasants are discussing questions of justice and injustice in heathen, or worldly, terms…. For God's sake, then, take my advice! Take a hold of these matters properly, with justice and not with force or violence and do not start endless bloodshed in Germany….

QUESTIONS FOR ANALYSIS

1. How do the Twelve Articles interpret grievances according to religious principles?
2. What are Luther's greatest objections to the Twelve Articles?
3. Compare the ideals of the peasants and Martin Luther as articulated in these sources.

Sources: From "The Twelve Articles of the Peasants," in *Christianity and Revolution*, ed. Lowell Zuck (Philadelphia: 1975), pp. 14–16; from *Admonition to Peace Concerning the Twelve Articles of the Peasants*, in *Luther's Works*, vol. 46, eds. Robert C. Schultz and Helmut T. Lehmann (Philadelphia: 1967), pp. 19, 23–24, 32, 40.

the emperor as their superior—rebelled, claiming among other things that they meant to restore the true Church. They were soon put down. But during the **Peasants' War** of 1524–25, hundreds of thousands of peasants and craftsmen rebelled against their lords across central and southern Germany. This was not the first time, by any means, that peasants in these areas had risen. In 1476, thousands of them had converged on a town in southern Germany to hear the dramatic speeches of a former drummer turned prophet, Hans Böhm, who denounced the corruption of the clergy and demanded that all forests and waters be held in common. Others had followed a banner in the form of a peasant's rough shoe to denounce unjust taxes. In these earlier uprisings, peasants aimed generally for the restoration of traditional rights that had been taken from them.

The peasants who rose in 1524–25 also denounced

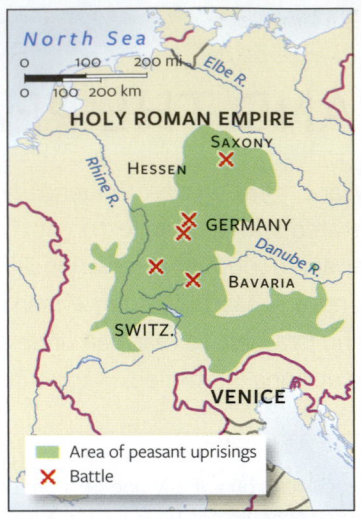

The Peasants' War, 1524–1525
Peasants' rebellions spread throughout a wide area of central and southern Germany, drawing thousands into pitched battles with royal forces from Bavaria, Hessen, and Saxony.

their landlords for depriving them of such traditional rights as gathering fallen firewood in the forests. Many of them were aggrieved by governments' and landlords' increasing use of written law and legal documents. But in the collections of articles drafted for them, they demanded much more. For the first time, peasants appealed to a fixed, printed text—that of the Gospels—to define their rights. As Christians, they claimed, they should be allowed to hear the true Gospel preached. As believers, moreover, they were free men and women, as Luther himself had written in a tract of 1521. Therefore, their lords had no right to make them serfs and bind them to the land.

The wave of peasant unrest and demands began in the countryside outside Zurich. Inspired by the transformation of the city, peasants and others called for a transformation of German society. The preacher Christoph Schappeler imagined that they might form a peasant republic, directly subject, as the imperial cities were, to the Holy Roman emperor. Schappeler defended their right, founded on the need to create a society of "brotherly love," to depose tyrants who opposed them. For a time, the princes and prelates seemed paralyzed as bands of peasants sacked castles and monasteries unopposed.

From Luther's standpoint, the peasant rebels were remaking his message of spiritual liberty into a charter for fundamental social change. Horrified by what he saw as a diabolic perversion of his enterprise, Luther called on the authorities to massacre the peasants. In May 1525, the princes of Bavaria, Hessen, and Saxony destroyed armed peasant bands in a series of pitched battles: in one encounter, 5,000 of the 6,000 peasants who took part were massacred in a single day.

The defeat of the peasants seemed total. Yet lords in much of the Holy Roman Empire came away from the uprising determined never to provoke another movement of the same kind. They changed the legal status of peasants to give them freedom of movement and of marriage, and peasants were accorded the clear right to long-term possession of their dwellings. Especially in the western parts of the Holy Roman Empire and in Switzerland, the successors of the massacred peasants enjoyed, from the sixteenth to the eighteenth centuries, many of the rights that they had demanded. By contrast, in eastern Germany,

Peasant Preaching Inspired by the writings of Martin Luther, peasants began to frame their sufferings and demands within the context of the Gospels. In this 1525 woodcut, a peasant preacher and follower of Luther gives a sermon to an attentive crowd.

Poland, and Russia during the same period, landlords succeeded in enserfing their peasants, building large estates, and tying their workforces to the land.

RADICAL REFORMATION: THE ANABAPTISTS

Even as the heaped corpses of the peasants were being buried, small groups, mostly in cities, were moving in what ultimately became an even more frightening direction for Luther, Zwingli, and other founders of reform. This movement began, like the Peasants' War, in Zurich, where Conrad Grebel (ca. 1498–1526) and other radical reformers were both inspired and infuriated by Zwingli. They agreed with him that the reform of religion meant the reform of society, and that scripture should serve as the rule for all changes. But they rejected Zwingli's defense of the tradition of infant baptism even though the New Testament always depicted baptism as for adults. When their ideas met resistance in Zurich, the radicals moved into the countryside. Peasants who found the city's rule oppressive were impressed by the denunciation of the tithes that they had to pay and the heavy hand of the city's government on areas outside the city walls. Others who heard these radicals preach, including merchants, craftsmen, and women, turned back to their own Bibles and found there a literal pattern for Christian life. They came to be known as **Anabaptists** ("re-baptizers"), because they believed that one could not properly join a church until one was an adult, like the adult converts of John the Baptist and Jesus.

Luther, in the tradition of Augustine, envisioned the Church as a universal community of the saved and the damned in this world. By contrast, the Anabaptists—like Augustine's ancient opponents, the Donatists—saw the Church as a small community of the saved, who had committed themselves to lead a Christian life. Luther accepted the need for private property, law, warfare, and all the other appurtenances of civil life in the world. The first Anabaptists refused to take oaths or fight, and they tried to live a literal version of the precepts of Jesus in the Gospels.

Luther was slow to turn against fellow reformers. Though he had helped to expel Andreas Karlstadt from the pulpit in Wittenberg and viewed him as a dangerous radical, he sheltered Karlstadt in his own house during the Peasants' War. But in the course of that conflict, as we saw, Luther had sided with the German princes—even Catholic princes—against the rebels. He and the secular

Persecution of Anabaptists A sixteenth-century engraving shows a crowd surrounding the cage containing the body of the Anabaptist leader John of Leiden, who was tortured and executed in Münster.

authorities responded to what they saw as the subversive program of the Anabaptists with special savagery. They made practicing or praising adult baptism and pacifism capital offenses. A number of the Anabaptists were executed for their beliefs. The ex-Benedictine monk Michael Sattler, who wrote the Anabaptist articles of faith known as the Schleitheim Confession and served as a roving missionary for his causes, was tortured and executed in 1527 while on a mission in southern Germany.

Many Anabaptists began to believe—as Luther himself did—that they were living through the last days of the world and that they were the holy martyrs whose lives and suffering were the central drama of the biblical book of Revelation. Divisions began to appear among them, and some of their leading figures, such as the one-time furrier-turned-preacher Melchior Hoffmann, predicted that the new era was about to start. Hoffmann was imprisoned in Strasbourg, the city where he had expected the

New Jerusalem to rise, and died in captivity in 1543. In Münster, in western Germany, groups of Anabaptists took up arms in 1534, expelled the bishop who ruled the city, and created a polygamous commune loosely modeled on the Israel of the Old Testament. After months of fierce resistance, they were crushed in June 1535, and their prophet, John of Leiden, was brutally executed some months later.

Surviving Anabaptists responded to this disaster in different ways. Pilgram Marpeck, a successful businessman from the Tirol, became an Anabaptist in 1527 and settled in Strasbourg in 1528. He became city engineer, first there and then in Augsburg, and his usefulness to governments protected him from violence. Weaving networks to bring his coreligionists together, he urged them to take oaths and pay taxes when the law required. Other Anabaptists, above all the Dutch ex-priest Menno Simons, insisted on the central importance of maintaining a communal life and the authority of the church. His followers, called Mennonites, became known for their commitment to pacifism. Thousands of Anabaptists took refuge in Moravia, now part of the Czech Republic, where they were eagerly sought as tenants by lords looking for reliable farmers. Some of the Moravian Anabaptists accepted the need of states to use force to defend themselves, while others rejected the use of arms on principle. The members of this latter group, which came to be known as Hutterites after their leader, Jacob Hutter (d. 1536), also decided to share all their property. Though the Anabaptists soon ceased to pose a serious challenge to the larger churches, they continued to be seen as a threat and were regularly persecuted. Their presence did much to make Luther and other reformers emphasize the need for central authority in church and state.

Lutheran Schools A 1516 painting illustrates the access to literacy that Lutheran Sunday schools provided. A schoolmaster directs a student in writing the alphabet, while other students read bound books.

RELIGIOUS EDUCATION

Luther and his allies saw education in the true principles of Christianity as one way to prevent further divisions, and did their best to ensure that all Lutherans knew the fundamentals of their faith. This view brought Philip Melanchthon, Luther's friend and a brilliant Greek scholar, to Wittenberg, where he created the curricula for what became Protestant secondary schools and universities. Luther's followers also established Sunday schools, where children learned the elements of literacy and the fundamentals of doctrine, which they memorized from catechisms. Bishops undertook regular visitations to ensure that ministers preached true doctrine and to oversee the quality of the schools. Luther loved music, and he and others wrote hymns that would become a cornerstone of Protestant religious practice. This was not complex music performed by professionals, as in the Catholic Church, but participatory singing in which the congregation could take part. In some Lutheran countries—especially in Denmark—male and female literacy seems to have become almost universal, and knowledge of religious doctrines with it. In Luther's own Germany, however, efforts at Protestant education met with varied levels of success. Some visitations reported orderly classes and knowledgeable parishioners; others described drunken mockers who scorned the Lord's Day. Building a new church was not easy.

WOMEN AND THE REFORMATION

Luther followed Paul in arguing that all Christians—women as well as men—were priests and could pray for one another. He himself married a former nun to show his rejection of celibacy as a human tradition. But he may have been surprised when he saw that some women were not only listening to and reading him but also imitating him. When a young man was imprisoned for Protestant heresy at Ingolstadt, a stronghold of traditional Catholicism, a Bavarian noblewoman, **Argula von Grumbach** (1492–ca. 1554), denounced what she considered to be the effort of Church authorities to attack the true Gospel.

A pious woman who had learned in her youth to pray to the Virgin Mary and to imagine herself conversing with angels, von Grumbach had also read the Bible—especially the Prophets and the New Testament. When she read the pamphlets that the Wittenberg presses were shipping in barrels across the Bavarian border, she was immediately convinced of the truth of Luther's message. She set out to defend the young man under accusation with all her strength. In a long letter to the theologians at Ingolstadt, she cited verse after verse from the Bible in support of Luther's new theology: "What do Luther and Melanchthon teach you but the word of God?" She used both the powerful language of the prophets and her own sharp idioms to tell the theologians that they were in the wrong: "The pot burns: and truly you and your university will never extinguish it."

Von Grumbach's letter to the Ingolstadt theologians circulated first in manuscript and then as a pamphlet, which was reprinted fourteen times. By the time she stopped writing, as many as 29,000 copies of that and other pamphlets by her may have been in circulation. She became a Protestant celebrity, who had the chance to share a meal with the legendarily busy Luther. She even gave him advice, for his wife, on how to wean her children. Von Grumbach and others—such as the former abbess Marie Dentière—rejected Paul's principle that women should not teach, arguing that Jesus had commanded all to preach his message. The British Protestant Anne Askew, who courted arrest by preaching, was tortured and then executed by burning at Smithfield in June 1546. She became one of the most famous Protestant martyrs; contemporary Protestant historians compared her to the early Christians who had died for their faith. Yet most of the women who set out to preach and write in public were silenced without winning fame.

Queens and noblewomen commanded the respectful attention of reformers—and were sometimes rewarded in special ways for doing so. Anna von Stolberg, abbess of Quedlinburg in the Black Forest, governed nine churches and two male monasteries. In the 1540s, when she converted to Protestantism, she ordered her priests to swear loyalty to Luther and turned her Franciscan monastery into an elementary school for boys and girls. Under her rule, Quedlinburg remained a convent even as it turned Protestant—as did many others.

Protestant women could leave convents and marry—as Katharina von Bora (1499–1552) did: after leaving her Cistercian monastery, she married Luther. Like earlier women we have encountered, von Bora participated actively in economic life even after finding a husband. The elector of Saxony gave her and Luther the property of the Augustinian cloister in Wittenberg. Teaching, preaching, and writing kept Martin busy. Accordingly, von Bora managed the estate, rising every day at 4:00 a.m. In addition to bearing Luther six children, she bred and sold cattle, brewed beer, and operated a hospital when epidemics struck. Yet von Bora always recognized Luther's supremacy in their

Katharina von Bora In 1528, Lucas Cranach the Elder painted this portrait of Katharina von Bora, the former nun who married Martin Luther.

marriage, calling him "Sir Doctor" and insisting that his calling was higher than hers.

As this case suggests, the larger position of women was not clearly transformed by the Reformation. The guildsmen who dominated cities that reformed their churches, such as Nuremberg, believed in the central importance of the patriarchal family. New legislation limited the roles that women could play—especially when, as happened in most Protestant cities, the convents were abolished and women could no longer live celibate lives as nuns. Sexual crimes were redefined: rape, for example, came to be treated less as a violent crime perpetrated by men than as evidence of licentious behavior by women. Male supremacy was reinforced in many ways: even Argula von Grumbach wrote with sorrow of the violence that she had suffered at the hands of her husband. Equality in the realm of the spirit did not bring with it the leveling of gender hierarchies.

THE MESSAGE SPREADS

By the later 1520s, Luther's period as the most influential spokesman of reform was coming to an end. But the messages of reform were spreading farther across Europe through efficient networks of exchange. Merchants and artisans—especially journeymen printers—carried the call for reform south to the Mediterranean and west and north to France, Britain, and Scandinavia. Hans Tauler, a former monk, preached the Reformation in Denmark and Norway. Though the king of Denmark and Norway, Frederick I (r. 1523–1533), claimed to oppose the Protestants, he protected Tauler and encouraged others to translate the Bible into the vernacular. Frederick was succeeded by Christian III (r. 1534–1559), who formally abolished the Mass, removed Catholic bishops, and installed Lutheran ones. Even in Spain, followers of Erasmus challenged and criticized traditional practices and beliefs. Some Italians—such as Bernardino Ochino, general of the Capuchin order, a branch of the Franciscans—realized that they agreed with the Protestants, and fled into exile in the north. Others continued to attend Catholic services but worshipped a Protestant God in secret. Germans in London made the Steelyard—the residence of merchants from the northern German trading cities that belonged to the Hanseatic League—a center of Protestant propaganda, to the fury of the British government. Even in France, traditionally "the most Christian nation" and loyal to the papacy, radical teachings spread. In 1534, in the Affair of the Placards, posters denouncing the Mass appeared all over Paris and other important cities—one of them on the king's bedroom door. These developments unleashed a vigorous effort to extirpate the new religion.

CALVINISM: THE CHURCH OF GENEVA

Many of the French Protestants who fled the campaign against them headed for Geneva, a small city in French-speaking Switzerland known chiefly for manufacturing kettles. One of the refugees, **John Calvin** (1509–1564), became the leading minister of Geneva and the second great intellectual leader of the Protestant movement. Trained as a humanist and Roman lawyer, Calvin initially encountered resistance in Geneva but overcame it by a combination of brilliant tactics and absolute commitment to his mission. By the early 1540s, Calvin and his allies dominated the city.

What Calvin devised there was, in the first place, the most rigorous version of Protestant theology, which he

John Calvin In this anonymous sixteenth-century portrait, Calvin appears as a determined young man, dressed somberly in black.

laid out in systematic form in his *Institutes of the Christian Religion*, a formal textbook of theology first published in 1536. In it he argued, more forcefully and consequentially than Luther, for the doctrine of predestination. Salvation was only God's affair, not man's. Human nature, Calvin explained, was vile, "a teeming horde of infamies." Only God could save humanity, and he did so by his own absolutely free choice, determining the fate of all—the damned as well as the saved. Evil as they were, human beings could not presume to question God's decision: "man falls by God's decree, but by his own fault." The rigor of this doctrine, which clarified points that Luther had not made clear, attracted many highly educated followers.

But Calvin did more than create a citadel of ideas. In Geneva, he also built up a church of a new kind—a Reformed church that went even further than Zwingli's in the imposition of discipline on all areas of life. He opened an academy to train ministers in Hebrew and Greek so that they could master the Bible in the original languages and learn its true doctrines as he had. Regular meetings and synods (formal meetings of all the clerics in a large district) oversaw the clergy once they were in the field, ensuring that they remained on message doctrinally

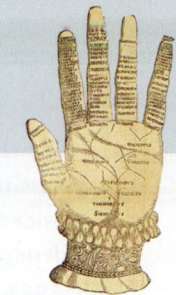

CHRISTMAS IN ST. ANDREWS

Kirk ("church") sessions were church courts in Scotland that, like the consistory in John Calvin's Geneva, enforced social discipline. They began to be established in Scottish towns during the Reformation, led in Scotland by John Knox, and within a generation had spread throughout much of the country. Ministers moderated weekly meetings of the courts, which focused largely on the morality of parishioners. Common charges ranged from fornication and adultery to popular but illegal Christmas customs such as singing carols. This excerpt is from the kirk session of St. Andrews in the winter of 1573/74.

The which day…upon Sunday the 24 day of January…Waltir Ramsay Iorimer,[1] Waltir Lathangye cutler,[2] and Johne Smyth blacksmith in Ergail, being accused and convicted before for observing of superstitious days and especially of Yule Day,[3] became penitent and made open satisfaction therefore in the presence of the whole congregation then being present. And therefore the minister, at command of the assembly, publicly [an]nounced that all persons, within this parish, that observe superstitiously the said Yule Day or any other days, should be punished in like manner; and such like should be punished in like manner if they abstain from their work and labour that day more than any other day except Sunday, which only should be kept holiday. And hereupon the session interposed their decision.

The said day, James Clwny cutler and Waltir Zownger being accused for violating the Sabbath day by superstitious keeping of Yule Day holiday, and abstaining from their work and labour that day, James Clwny promised to desist and cease from keeping of Yule Day in time coming, under pain contained in the act immediately preceding. And Waltir Zownger…being accused…that [he] made his neighbors disobedient to the kirk, saying, in the Gallowlaik[4] that it does not become honest men to sit upon the penitent stool[5] which words he confessed: and also said that he is a young man and saw Yule Day kept as a holiday, and that the time may come that he may see the like yet; and therefore would not become obliged or restricted in time coming to abstain from work that day, but at his own pleasure. In respect of the aforesaid, the session decides and orders that him to be admonished by public admonition to make satisfaction upon the penitent stool under pain of excommunication, and also [because] he being required would give no other answer nor yet submit himself to the voice of the kirk.

QUESTIONS FOR ANALYSIS

1. What were the people in this record accused and convicted of having done?
2. What evidence does this record provide about how people marked Christmas in sixteenth-century Scotland?
3. These cases came before the kirk session more than ten years after the Reformation was accomplished in Scotland. Is their appearance evidence of the success or failure of the reformers' agenda?

[1]**lorimer:** maker of bits, spurs, and other small metal objects
[2]**cutler:** maker or seller of knives and other utensils
[3]**Yule Day:** Christmas Day
[4]**Gallowlaik:** a meeting place for craftsmen
[5]**penitent stool:** a seat used for public shaming rituals

Source: *Register of the Minister, Elders, and Deacons of the Christian Congregation of St. Andrews*, pt. 1, ed. David Hay Fleming (Edinburgh: 1889), pp. 387–89; text modernized by Mairi Cowan.

and that they dealt vigorously and honorably with their parishioners. Every Calvinist cleric had to take his turn presenting a sermon in French and then waiting for comments from his hearers on both style and content. The consistory—an institution, based on the model of the Zurich marriage court, which brought together elders and ministers—oversaw the behavior of Genevans. It summoned and punished individuals for everything from quarreling with spouses and failing to attend or listen to the sermons given by Geneva's ministers to adultery and gluttony. Some patricians resisted, but Calvin defeated them in 1555, after a long struggle, thanks to the support of French immigrants who became Genevan citizens and elected a city council that supported him.

By the time Calvin died in 1564, Geneva had become a startlingly disciplined town, where heads of households presided over family prayers. The city became a symbol of independent Protestantism, and many of the young intellectuals who went there emerged as effective clergymen, brilliant missionaries for the cause of reform. In France and the Low Countries, and to a considerable extent in England and the Holy Roman Empire, Protestantism was Calvinism—even if the Zwinglian citizens of Zurich would not have agreed.

CHURCHES AND MONARCHS: A CHANGING BALANCE

Rulers watched as city councils accepted the Reformation movement, abolished the Mass, and set their clergy to preaching the Gospel in the vernacular. Some rulers, such as the brilliant soldier Philip of Hesse (1504–1567), took action themselves. There were, after all, many advantages to be had. On becoming a Protestant, Philip abolished the rich monasteries in his territory, which no longer had any function. He used 41 percent of their wealth to found schools and the University of Marburg, and to provide dowries for the noble nuns whose world he had shattered. But he kept 59 percent of it for his own use.

HENRY VIII AND THE CHURCH OF ENGLAND

Henry VIII of England (r. 1509–1547), the king whom Thomas More served as a counselor, also broke with the Catholic Church. Henry, who feared and hated disorder, at first saw no reason to transform the practice of Christianity in England. For years, he and his ministers—above all Thomas More, who became his lord chancellor from 1529 to 1532—hunted British Protestants such as William Tyndale, who translated the Bible into English and was strangled and burned by Catholic authorities in Flanders. Henry himself published a treatise that defended the sacraments against Luther. Thomas More engaged in literary duels with heretics. He defended the souls in purgatory against Protestants who claimed that purgatory did not exist and that prayers for the dead were wasted.

But Henry wanted desperately to have his marriage to his brother's widow, Catherine of Aragon, annulled on religious grounds, and marry Anne Boleyn, a noble at

Henry VIII This painting shows Henry flanked by his only legitimate son to survive him, the future Edward VI, and his third wife, Jane Seymour.

court. Though Henry failed to convince the papacy that his cause was just, he married Boleyn in 1533. He then declared himself head of an independent national church in 1534. More and the others who retained a passionate commitment to the universal church, and who refused to acknowledge Henry's supremacy, found themselves in danger. In 1535 More was executed, as were the members of the London Charterhouse, the most rigorous of the old monastic orders. Boleyn herself was executed for adultery, incest, and treason in 1536.

Henry, like most other kings, was always in need of money. He also showed sympathy, as a young man, for humanists like Erasmus and their criticisms of the wealth of the Church. His chief minister, Thomas Cromwell (ca. 1485–1540), convinced him to disestablish the monastic orders and confiscate their property. Cromwell made serious efforts to ensure that the monasteries could never be reestablished. His men used explosives to demolish them, and looted the sites of everything of value. Efforts to restore the old religion—such as the 1536 Pilgrimage of Grace, a rebellious movement based in Yorkshire and sparked in part by high grain prices—were put down with remorseless violence. Protestant doctrines spread in the universities, and the tutors who brought up Henry's son Edward, a superbly educated young man, saw to it that he was grounded in what they took as the true doctrines.

Despite the passive resistance of parishioners and priests who loved their ancient rituals, England slowly became a Protestant land. In 1539 Myles Coverdale, a

Protestant trained originally in the Augustinian order, produced the Great Bible, which was for the most part a revision of Tyndale's translation of the Bible into English, and was approved for use in church services. Thomas Cranmer, the archbishop of Canterbury, changed Communion so that the laity as well as the priest received both wine and bread. And he oversaw the translation of one element after another of the liturgy until, in 1549, the entire service was in English. Clerics with reformed sympathies complained that too much of the tradition had been retained. John Hooper, a Calvinist, refused to be made a bishop if he had to wear the traditional vestments, which, he thought, derived from the practice of Jewish priests. Through the 1540s, the English church was taking shape as a great compromise between tradition and innovation.

FRANCIS I AND CHARLES V (1521–1546)

Religious reform spread through Europe at a time when states were rapidly developing their powers. The brilliant young monarchs who controlled England (Henry VIII), France (Francis I), and the Holy Roman Empire (Charles V) benefited from vast personal resources; so did the princes of smaller territories, such as the Wittelsbachs, who ruled Bavaria. The French monarchy, which had revived during the course of the fifteenth century, worked effectively with its Estates General. The French state also devised increasingly efficient systems of tax collection and continually looked for other forms of revenue. One of these—the sale of offices in the state administration—ultimately proved counterproductive, since state officers held their positions by right, as private property, and could resist royal orders. Nonetheless, French state revenues were large enough to enable Francis I (r. 1515–1547) to wage a long and exhausting series of wars in Italy, where he tried to make good on the French claim to rule over Naples and Milan.

Charles, son of the Habsburg king of Spain Philip I, became Holy Roman Emperor **Charles V** and the lord of a vast series of domains before he was twenty. Born in Flanders in 1500, at age six he inherited his paternal grandfather Maximilian's Burgundian territories in the Low Countries. His aunt, Margaret of Austria, acted as regent until Charles was fifteen, and went to war with France to establish that Flanders was not a French fief. At sixteen, when his maternal grandfather, Ferdinand II, died, he became King Charles I of Spain, though he had

little knowledge of it. Three years later, when Maximilian died, he inherited the Habsburg monarchy and became the natural candidate to become Holy Roman emperor. The vast expense of bribing the German electors to make him emperor and maintaining his costly Flemish court placed him under financial pressure.

FOUNDATIONS OF STATE POWER State power was sustained not only by taxation and conquest. In the decades around 1500, European economic life entered a new phase. Entrepreneurs, such as the banker **Jacob Fugger** of Augsburg, worked with the Habsburgs and other monarchs to which they lent money. For each loan he issued, Fugger extracted something more important in return—for example, the right to exploit minerals that belonged to the sovereign. At a time when mining technology was rapidly improving, Fugger secured permission to dig for silver in the Tirol, copper in Hungary, mercury in Spain, and even gold and silver in the New World. The metals he extracted were vital for everything from making bronze cannon to coining money, and Fugger made money from each use, which he then employed to seek out new business opportunities, such as the trade in pepper from Asia.

Charles V borrowed enormous amounts from Fugger, which he tried to repay by raising taxes. The Spanish kingdoms of Castile and Aragon were already in financial difficulties, having spent vast amounts on the destruction of the last Islamic emirate, in Granada, in 1492, and on maintaining their armies. Agitation against Charles began in Toledo and Segovia in 1520, and soon other cities joined. The *comuneros*, an unstable coalition of lesser nobles, urban artisans, and others who saw Charles as an outsider, rebelled against him. They formed a new government, recognizing Charles's mother as queen, and raised armies. But Charles's representative in Spain raised more effective armies of his own, in alliance with much of the landed aristocracy, and defeated the comuneros.

HABSBURG CONTROL OF ITALY Even as the Spanish authorities crushed the comuneros, the old war between France and the Habsburgs in Italy was revived by Charles V and Francis I. Charles mustered an enormous force, including German mercenaries as well as his Spanish armies. Employing superior tactics, Charles's forces pulled the French army apart at Pavia in 1525, and Francis himself was taken prisoner. Frightened by Charles's power, Pope Clement VII, a member of the Medici family, formed a coalition against the emperor, the League

Habsburg Lands, ca. 1556 At the height of his power, Charles V controlled much of Europe, including inherited kingdoms in the Low Countries and Spain, the Holy Roman Empire, and conquests in Italy. He sustained his power with military might, putting down rebellions in Spain and defeating the Protestant Schmalkaldic League and several Italian uprisings. But rebellions in Protestant central Europe and pressure from the French and the Ottomans at the borders limited Charles's total control of the continent.

of Cognac, allying himself with Venice, Florence, and other powers. But the Venetians refused to take an active part, and Charles, after defeating Florence, found himself unable to pay his troops. In 1527 his soldiers shocked the world by sacking Rome, including the Vatican. The pope was imprisoned, and Charles now commanded the Italian Peninsula.

The Florentines rose up in one last attempt to defend their republican tradition—a magnificent, doomed effort that won the warm support of Michelangelo. But after furious resistance, they were defeated in 1530. Though Venice remained independent—and though Francis would launch more Italian wars—Italy would remain under the

control of the Habsburgs for centuries, as the Spanish transformed the south and Sicily into the agrarian province of the Iberian kingdom.

STALEMATE: PEACE OF AUGSBURG

Charles V never managed to win the one decisive victory that would have enabled him to pacify all of his territories and defeat the Protestant princes of the empire definitively—a goal that he thought it his religious duty to pursue as Holy Roman emperor. The French challenged him again in 1536 and 1542—both times in league with the Ottomans, whose empire, under Sultan Suleiman the Magnificent (r. 1520–1566), reached from North Africa to Asia Minor and deep into Hungary—but both wars ended in stalemates. In 1547 Charles did manage to defeat the Schmalkaldic League of Protestant powers, created in 1531 by Philip of Hesse and John Frederick I, Elector of Saxony, and gradually enlarged to include other German states and imperial cities. Charles imprisoned Philip, the league's most formidable commander. But the overwhelming power Charles thus achieved terrified many, and in 1552 a Protestant rebellion, supported by the new French king, Henry II (r. 1547–1559), drove Charles out of the German

lands. Dogged by ill health, he gave his Spanish crown to his son Philip in 1555, while his brother Ferdinand succeeded him as Holy Roman emperor in 1556.

In 1555 the **Peace of Augsburg**, a formal treaty agreed by Charles and the members of the Schmalkaldic League, officially recognized that the empire no longer followed one religion. The principle *cuius regio, eius religio* ("his realm, his religion") acknowledged that each prince could decide which religion, Catholic or Protestant, to establish in his domain. Those who refused to go along had the right to leave—itself a major innovation. At the Diet of Worms long before, Charles had stated that he had an inherited

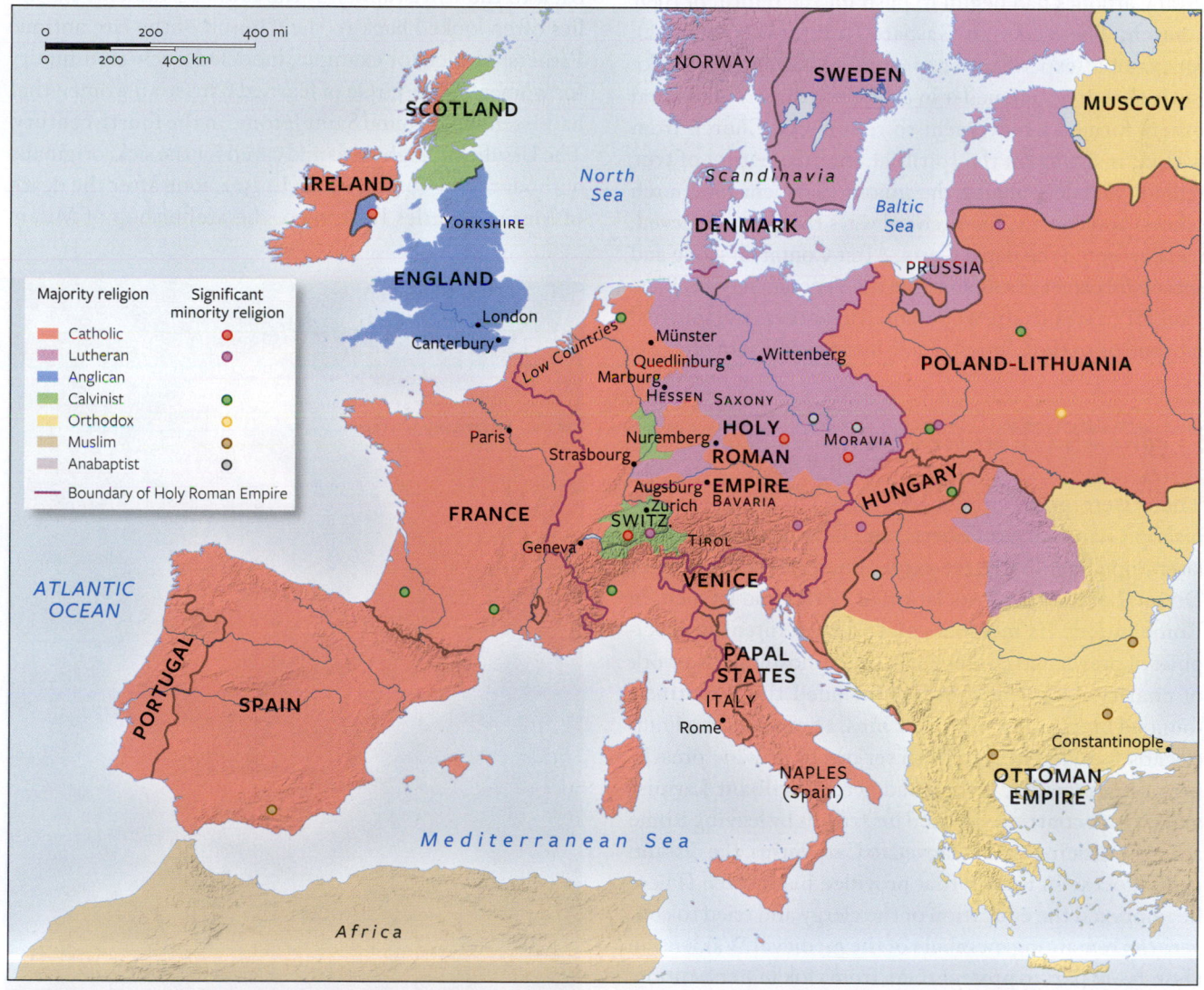

Europe after the Peace of Augsburg A complicated religious and political landscape followed the treaty: for the most part, northern Germany, Scandinavia, and Prussia were Lutheran, Scotland and Switzerland were Calvinist, England had its own state church, Muscovy and the European portion of the Ottoman Empire were Orthodox, and the rest of Europe remained Catholic. But religious minorities now had a foothold in many regions as well, from Catholics in northern Germany to Calvinists in France and Poland and Anabaptists in Germany and Hungary.

duty to defend the Catholic Church against innovators and rebels. Now it was clear that he had failed. Yet this religious and political settlement was highly provisional. The Anabaptists and vigorous Calvinists did not win acceptance from the rulers of Protestant and Catholic states, and they resented their precarious position. Meanwhile, the Catholic Church was beginning to regroup and even to go on the offensive against its critics and enemies.

RENEWING CATHOLICISM

Well before the sack of Rome by Charles V's forces in 1527, loyal Catholics had begun to push for the reform of their Church. The Venetian Gasparo Contarini (1483–1542), for example, experienced a spiritual awakening not unlike Luther's, but he pursued it in a different direction. He and others formed a movement to reform the Church from within, insisting on the spiritual, internal nature of true religion and denouncing the simony (payment for church offices) and courtly, hierarchical ways that, they believed, had corrupted the papal Curia. After Contarini's long and successful career as a diplomat in the Venetian service, Pope Paul III (r. 1534–1549), who wanted to harness the spiritual movement to the Church, made him a cardinal in 1535.

SOURCES OF RENEWAL

There were many others like him. The diplomat and bishop Gian Matteo Giberti, and Gian Pietro Carafa—later Pope Paul IV (r. 1555–1559)—founded the Oratory of Divine Love, a free association of clerics and laymen, in Rome in 1517. Its members practiced an intensive discipline of prayer and confession, visiting hospitals as a work of charity. Other new orders included the Theatines, founded in 1524, and the Capuchins, a branch of the Franciscans founded in 1525; both set out to provide preaching of high quality. Jacopo Sadoleto, a brilliant Latinist and elegant courtier, shocked his friends by leaving Rome after the sack in 1527. He moved to Carpentras, the distant, rural diocese in France that provided his income. There he improved the education of the clergy and tried to convert the remaining members of the medieval Waldensian church—in part to protect them from violent persecution.

HOLY WOMEN Women played a central role in the renewal of Catholicism. Many women did so through highly practical religious activities: Catherine of Genoa, for example, who later became a saint, moved with her husband into a hospital, where she dedicated herself to the care of incurable victims of syphilis. Other women became known—as Hildegard of Bingen had in the Middle Ages—as living exemplars of holiness. Known for their deep penitence for their sins and their pursuit of mystical union with God, some also developed renown as prophetesses and reformers. Holy women inspired and mentored the founders of the new Theatine order.

THE URSULINES Other new orders—such as the Ursulines, founded by Angela Merici in 1535—forged new paths for the Church. Whereas Protestants looked back to the Christianity of the New Testament, Catholics often looked back to the Church of the late antique Fathers: Merici, for example, modeled a new community for women on the circle of learned Christian women that had assembled around Saint Jerome in the fourth century. The Ursulines taught girls and cared for the sick, originally without taking formal vows. In 1572, long after the death of Merici, Charles Borromeo, the archbishop of Milan,

Angela Merici An anonymous 1550 painting depicts an elderly Angela Merici, the founder of the Ursuline order.

insisted that the Ursulines become a religious order and live an "enclosed" life. Their houses spread through the New World as well as the Old.

TERESA OF ÁVILA As in the Middle Ages, mystics of the sixteenth century showed that their union with God gave them an energy and efficiency that others lacked. Teresa of Ávila (1515–1582), who came from a Spanish family partly made up of Jewish converts, wrote dazzlingly of her religious experiences, vividly evoking the pains and torments she suffered, as well as the ecstasy of her final union with God. She created a new model of female monasticism for the Carmelite order, to which she belonged, eliminating outside visits and insisting that members remain strictly confined and pursue sanctity. John of the Cross, another mystic who, like Teresa, later became a saint, collaborated with her to found new houses. In the later sixteenth century, the Catholic religious authorities would turn a more critical eye on many holy women, looking for possible cases of diabolic possession that mimicked true sanctity, and cutting down the areas of free action that religious women had found in the early period of Catholic renewal. But the movement for renewal itself was shaped in considerable part by female hands.

The Society of Jesus In a 1540 French engraving, Ignatius Loyola and a group of his fellow Jesuits kneel before Pope Paul III to offer him a copy of their rule. The pope raises his right hand in a gesture of benediction.

THE SOCIETY OF JESUS

Though different in many respects, all of these Catholics believed that their church was the true one, and remained ardently faithful to it. One of them in particular—Ignatius Loyola (1491–1556), a Spanish nobleman who was badly wounded in the Italian wars—showed as vividly as Luther how an individual with a spiritual vocation could change the world, especially a world divided over questions of belief. After a long period of preparation, which included years of meditation as a hermit and intensive study in Paris, Loyola went to Rome in 1535 with a few ragged followers, and gained papal permission to create a new order, the Society of Jesus, in 1540.

What made the **Jesuits** special was not their numbers, for there were never many of them, but the training on which Loyola insisted and the intense commitment that it both demanded and generated. To join the order, one had to go through a long preparation of studying, doing humble tasks as a novice, and—most important—making the Spiritual Exercises (a set of meditative exercises that Loyola designed) under the supervision of a Jesuit spiritual director. By undergoing these rigors, Loyola argued,

Jesuits would establish for certain that they possessed a religious vocation, a question that earlier orders had too often ignored. Equally important, they and their superiors would learn exactly which tasks they were best equipped to carry out for the order: teaching in schools, working in cities with the poor, or going on missions to Asia and other lands.

Although the rigorous Jesuit training resembled that of Calvinist ministers in some ways, its texture and content were completely different. Full members of the Jesuit order not only swore the traditional vows of poverty, chastity, and obedience but also pledged to go at once to the Holy Land if ordered to do so and preach the word of God. The Jesuits saw themselves as committed to everything that Calvin hated. They would obey the pope absolutely, "like a stick in the hand." They would defend the church fathers and the scholastic theologians of the Middle Ages against Protestant insistence that only scripture mattered. They would serve wherever the order or the pope sent them.

Many Jesuits went on missions to preach and find converts. Some missions took them into perils of every kind, especially in lands that had turned Protestant. In other cases, they followed the Catholic empires of Spain, Portugal, and France into the New World and Asia. As teachers, they founded schools across the globe and often induced the children of Protestant nobles, sent to them solely for an education, to convert back to their ancestral faith. As priests, they built shrines—including countless replicas of the house of the Virgin Mary at Loreto, which had supposedly been brought there from the Holy Land by angels. As spiritual directors, they counseled rulers and nobles, scholars and merchants through spiritual crises. And as historians, they documented every step they took, from recruiting novices to dying as martyrs in Japan. By the 1540s and 1550s, Jesuits were crossing Europe, ready to engage Protestants in a war for Christian souls.

THE COUNCIL OF TRENT

The reformers were never wholly isolated within the Church, and soon they found powerful allies. From 1545 to 1563, a broad, ecumenical council of the Church met at Trent, on the border between the Holy Roman Empire and northern Italy. After long deliberations, the **Council of Trent** settled disputed questions of doctrine: for example, it decreed that the true text of the Bible was "the old and Vulgate edition," by which it meant the Latin text on which the Catholic Church had long relied. It affirmed such traditional practices as the sacraments and the veneration of saints. It laid out a set of tasks for the popes, including revision of the Mass and new editions of the Bible. And it filled participants with a new energy.

As clerics left the council to return to their dioceses, they felt a new responsibility to the Christian laity and

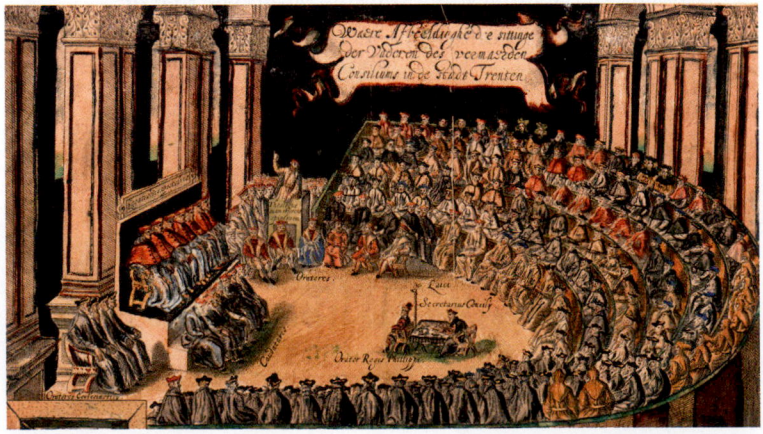

Council of Trent A Dutch watercolor from 1560 illustrates a meeting of the Council of Trent. Cardinals, monks, priests, ambassadors, generals, and other laymen pack the galleries of a church in Trent, while speakers from these groups discuss matters of doctrine.

devised new ways to raise the standard of the clergy and improve the religious lives of laypeople. In Italy, determined archbishops imposed order on religious services and created seminaries to ensure that clerics were literate and able to do their jobs. They also reformed monastic orders and adopted new ways of instilling Catholicism with the vitality that Luther and so many others had missed. The archbishop of Milan, for example, devised the confessional: an enclosed, private space in which the Christian would confess to a priest and receive instructions for amendment. Confession, long a public, external ritual, as Erasmus and other Christian reformers had complained, became a private, internal matter: a frightening leap into the spiritual darkness, made safe only by the presence of the confessor.

Meanwhile, the papacy restructured its administrative apparatus, the Roman Curia. Cardinals remained courtiers, as they had long been: aristocratic clerics who lived in palaces. But they also found themselves assigned to committees tasked to oversee particular areas of Church life. One of these committees took charge of the censorship of the printing press, which—if it had been institutionalized more effectively in earlier years—might have made it possible to suppress the Reformation entirely. By the 1550s, the Church was issuing indexes of forbidden books: detailed lists of books that Catholics could not read at all, or that they could read only after designated passages had been removed.

A system of censorship took shape. Catholic authors had to submit their works before publication to Church censors, whose approbations must be included in the published books. Protestant librarians soon found these indices useful instruments for creating libraries of past heretical works, the products of movements that they saw as ancestors of their own. Catholic thinkers, however, found themselves subject to a partial but serious effort at thought control. In Spain, the Inquisition was repurposed as a mechanism for examining and punishing suspected critics of Church doctrine.

RETHINKING THE NATURAL WORLD

The bite of censorship was all the more painful to thoughtful Catholics because, in the middle decades of the sixteenth century, Europe experienced widespread intellectual ferment. For centuries, the universities, with their canonical texts and elaborate curricula, had dominated the study of the natural world and much more. Humanists and reformers challenged them. But so, even more, did the simple facts that now came to light. The existence of a sea route to Asia and the New World proved that ancient maps of the earth and the sky were erroneous and incomplete. Not until the seventeenth century would Europeans carry out something like intellectual iconoclasm, arguing that moderns knew far more than the ancients had. But the roots of that development lie in the Reformation period.

OBSERVATION AND COLLABORATION

One intellectual who embraced the new knowledge was the brilliant, irascible German doctor Theophrastus Bombastus Paracelsus (1493–1541). By the late 1520s, he had decided that the traditional medical textbooks were useless. Like Luther, who burned the bull of excommunication against him, Paracelsus publicly burned the standard textbook, *The Canon of Medicine* by Avicenna (Ibn Sina; d. 1037). Paracelsus told his readers that they should rely instead on the empirical knowledge of ordinary men and women, which was worth far more than the nonsense of "the high colleges," and he elaborated his own alchemical version of medical theory and practice.

Nicolaus Copernicus (1473–1543), a cathedral canon whose career unfolded in Poland, devised an even more radical theory. Though he observed the heavens himself and used observations made by others, he was looking not for greater accuracy but for greater simplicity. The universe, he argued in 1543, was not geocentric (centered on the earth), as practically every thinker since Aristotle had believed, but heliocentric (centered on the sun). The earth, moreover, was not at rest: it rotated on its axis once a day and revolved around the sun once a year. Copernicus's theory revolutionized the understanding not only of the cosmos but also of the earth, since it could no longer be assumed that when objects fell they were seeking the center of the universe. By accepting these views, Copernicus argued, astronomers could simplify their models for the motion of the planets—but to do so they had to imagine a universe much larger than they had traditionally believed.

Andreas Vesalius (1514–1564), who studied and taught medicine at the university in Padua, took a lesson from artists such as Leonardo da Vinci. Vesalius argued that the study of the human organism must rest on actual

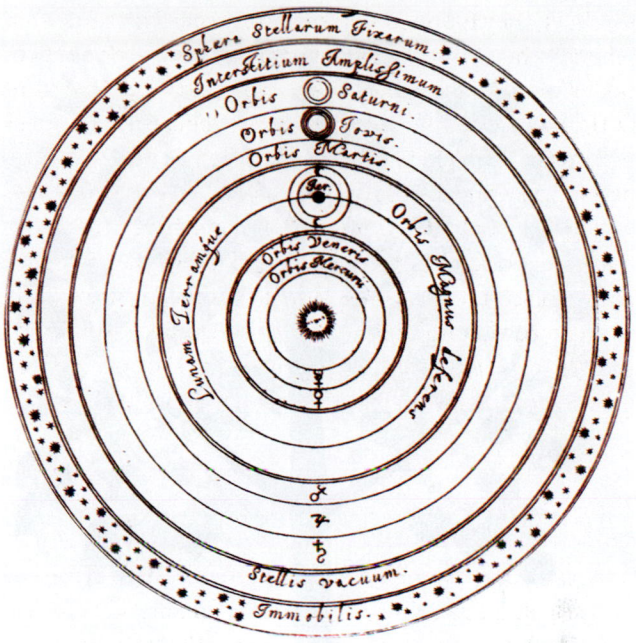

The Copernican Universe A 1647 scientific text includes this diagram of Copernicus's heliocentric theory of the cosmos. It shows the planets and Earth's moon orbiting the sun, surrounded by an immobile sphere of stars.

dissection of human bodies, as he thought it had in the ancient days of Greek physician and writer Galen, and the results recorded not only in writing but in detailed drawings. As Vesalius dissected the bodies of criminals, he discovered that Galen had committed many errors, some of them serious, because he had actually dissected apes rather than humans. In 1543, Vesalius brought out a magnificent study of the human body, illustrated by a Venetian artist. His work transformed medical study and laid the foundations for the further series of discoveries that would culminate, with William Harvey in 1628, in the demonstration that human blood circulated through the body, like the earth in the heavens.

Another sign of the radicalism of much—though not all—of the innovative thinking done in the sixteenth century is its collaborative character. Like Vesalius, many intellectuals found themselves changing the established body of knowledge by working with colleagues who were not learned at all. When the German botanist Leonhart Fuchs printed his illustrated guide to plants and their uses in 1542, he included portraits of the artists who had drawn the images and made and colored the printed woodcuts. It was a clear indication that knowledge was no longer, if it had ever been, the property of an elite trained to read canonical texts, but something to be discovered and

Fuchs's Botany One of the many painted woodcuts from Leonhart Fuchs's *De Historia Stirpium* (1542), this lime tree is labeled in Latin and German.

recorded by teams whose members crossed the boundaries of social orders and occupations to work together. In another example, Europeans learned from dozens of Native American informants, male and female, about the properties of New World plants and the products derived from them. Some of these products, such as chocolate and tobacco, were powerful stimulants whose use would transform Western society.

THE PERILS OF NEW THINKING

In a time of fear and censorship, ideas as radical as these could lead those who framed them into grave danger. Sometimes compromises were made: Andreas Osiander (1498–1552), the Lutheran cleric who oversaw the printing of Copernicus's work as the author was dying, added an anonymous preface in which he declared—contradicting the text that followed—that the author had meant only to advance a hypothesis, not to tell the truth about the universe. Though Copernicus's work was placed on the Church's indexes of forbidden books, this preface helped it survive, and annotated copies in libraries across Europe show that many were able to read it.

Not every book or author was so lucky. Michael Servetus (ca. 1511–1553), a Spanish theologian and medical specialist who speculated about the circulation of the blood, denied the doctrine of the Trinity. He managed to escape both Catholic and Protestant authorities for a time by using pseudonyms and moving frequently. In 1553, however, he made the fatal mistake of traveling to Geneva, even though Calvin was one of his harshest critics. Arrested and condemned, he was burned to death outside the city—a rare fate even for a heretic in the Protestant world—by Calvinists determined to show that they were no more lenient, when deadly heresies were concerned, than the Catholics.

WAR ACROSS THE CONTINENT

The peace established in the Holy Roman Empire by the Treaty of Augsburg (1555) did not extend to the rest of Europe. In England, Queen Mary I (r. 1553–1558), daughter of Henry VIII and his first wife, Catherine of Aragon, succeeded her half brother, Edward VI. A committed Catholic, Mary did her best to reestablish the Church. Hundreds of Protestants were forced to flee England; many sought refuge in Swiss cities. Almost 300 were burned, including the archbishop of Canterbury, Thomas Cranmer. In Italy, war had flared again in 1551, when a new French king, Henry II, declared war on Holy Roman Emperor Charles V, seeking to supplant Spanish control over the Italian Peninsula. After Charles abdicated, his son became King Philip II of Spain (r. 1556–1598) and opposed Henry.

Warfare was now completely professional, and both France and Spain had to borrow massive amounts to pay their troops. The capital came from banks and monarchs across Europe and beyond, including officials of the Ottoman Empire. Much of the capital flowed through Antwerp, the trading center of Europe. Its bourse, or financial exchange, founded in 1531, could broker enormous financial transactions. By late in the 1550s, neither country could maintain interest payments on the loans. First Spain and then France reneged on these debts, bankrupting thousands of investors. Forced to negotiate an end to the conflict, Henry and Philip signed the Peace of Cateau-Cambrésis in 1559. Henry II died after a joust held to celebrate the treaty, when a splinter of the lance belonging to one of his guards penetrated his eye.

GOVERNMENT AND WAR IN A NEW KEY: PHILIP II OF SPAIN

Bankruptcy did not deter Philip II from his systematic effort to make Spain the dominant European power. Neither did the death of Queen Mary I of England, whom he had married, and whose efforts to bring England back into the Catholic fold he had encouraged. In 1559 Philip took the reins of power in Spain, assuming direct charge of the councils that dealt with finance, war, and the colonies. In his search for information about all his domains, he read and annotated thousands of documents every year. His habit of bringing memoranda to every meeting with his counselors won him the title "the paper king." Though he had to deal with separate assemblies, or estates, in Castile, Aragon, and Navarre, he established himself as a uniquely powerful monarch. He compensated for the debts that his father had left him with the immense wealth generated by the trade and industry of the Habsburg-controlled Low Countries, and the gold, silver, spices, tobacco, and sugar carried by Spanish convoys from its empire in the New World. These convoys, connecting Spain to its colonies in the Philippines, Mexico, Cuba, and elsewhere, began in 1565 and soon reached fifty or more ships at a time.

A passionate believer, Philip devoted himself to what he saw as the cause of Christendom—the defeat of the Ottoman Empire in the Mediterranean, the defeat of Protestantism in western Europe, and the final purification of Spain. No expense seemed to him too great, no effort too arduous, where this cause was concerned. When his efforts to suppress the Islamic customs still observed by some Moriscos (former Muslims) provoked a revolt in Granada in 1569, he had them expelled from the city and scattered throughout Spain. And when an Ottoman fleet took the Balearic Islands off Spain's eastern coast, he organized a Holy League of the Popes, the Venetians, the grand dukes of Tuscany, and others to oppose Sultan Selim II (r. 1566–1574). They eventually demolished the Ottoman navy at Lepanto, off the western coast of Greece,

in 1571. And when Mary's sister, Elizabeth, rejected his proposal of marriage, and Protestant leaders flocked back to England as it became clear that the new queen was one of them, Philip planned a gradual, massive campaign to defeat Protestantism, first in the Low Countries and then in England.

RELIGIOUS WAR, POLITICAL UPHEAVAL

In France and the Low Countries, the conflict between the Catholic Church and the Calvinists—known in French as **Huguenots**—soon blazed up in a new way. Reformed preachers and their congregations gathered at night, often in the fields outside towns and cities, with women and children protected by armed aristocrats. Calvinism had little appeal for peasants, but in the cities, workers, merchants, and members of the nobility all found its starkly clear message compelling. Catholic preachers, including many Jesuits, did their best to combat what they saw as this frightening development. After Henry II's death in 1559, his widow, Catherine de' Medici, served as regent, but she lacked the authority to impose order as violence broke out between Protestants—to whom, at first, she made concessions—and Catholics. Protestants destroyed religious images and interrupted Catholic processions, while Catholics preferred to massacre Protestants when they found them praying in groups. War erupted in France in 1562—followed, a few years later, by war in the Netherlands.

THE DUTCH REVOLT (1566–1648) Philip II's first representative as governor of the Netherlands was Margaret of Parma, the politically savvy and experienced illegitimate daughter of Philip's father, Charles V. She had tried to find some compromise that could preserve order, and when a group of noblemen formally requested that persecution of Protestantism come to an end, she agreed. But oppressive taxes, attempts to introduce the Inquisition, and a famine caused by poor harvests and rising wheat prices in 1565 led to increasing anger against the Spanish. Influential Dutch nobles withdrew from the government, and in 1566 religious statues, pictures, and stained glass windows were smashed across the Netherlands.

Philip's response in 1567 was to send his extremely effective general, the duke of Alba, with an army to quell the spreading revolt. But Alba's stern policies made matters worse—especially when two local noblemen who had remained loyal to Spain but opposed the introduction

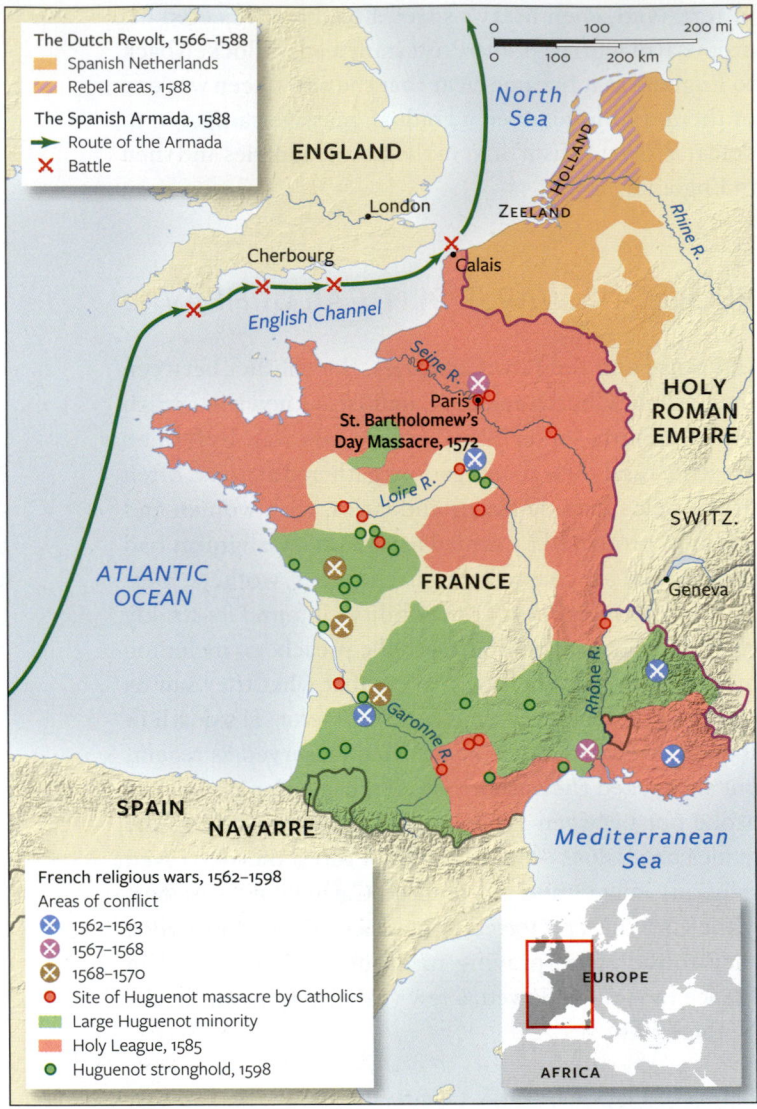

The Dutch Revolt, 1566–1588
- Spanish Netherlands
- Rebel areas, 1588

The Spanish Armada, 1588
- → Route of the Armada
- ✕ Battle

French religious wars, 1562–1598
Areas of conflict
- ⊗ 1562–1563
- ⊗ 1567–1568
- ⊗ 1568–1570
- ● Site of Huguenot massacre by Catholics
- Large Huguenot minority
- Holy League, 1585
- ● Huguenot stronghold, 1598

The Dutch Revolt and the French Religious Wars, 1562–1598
Violence between Protestants and Catholics flared throughout France in the 1560s and 1570s—particularly in southern areas with large Huguenot minorities—culminating in the St. Bartholomew's Day Massacre in Paris in 1572. In the Netherlands, Calvinists in the north rebelled against Catholic Spanish rule. Religious divisions also spurred Spain's naval conflict with England in 1588, ending with the English defeat of the Spanish Armada.

for more than eighty years, as we will see, and religious war spread across Europe.

ENGLAND: ANGLICANS AND PURITANS
Even in England, where Queen Elizabeth I (r. 1558–1603) refused "to make windows into men's souls," conflict spread. On the one hand, the archbishops and bishops of the Church of England set out to create an Anglican church that combined stern Protestant doctrine with a rich and appealing liturgy. Against them were arrayed the Puritans—reformed believers who wanted to rid the church of all traditions not supported explicitly by the Bible. Anglicans and Puritans clashed over proper priestly vestments and central theological doctrines. Thanks to the political astuteness of Elizabeth and her closest friends, the dispute between these two sides, though often bitter, never broke out in actual civil or religious war.

THE FRENCH WARS OF RELIGION (1562–1589)
On the Continent, however, savage wars erupted in 1562–63, 1567–68, and 1568–70. They were conflicts of a new kind, spawned by churches of a new kind. Both sides saw themselves as fighting for God against the devil. Violence became ritualized and almost normal as Catholics strove to cleanse the world of Protestant heretics, and Protestants sought to purify churches of the images, vessels, and incense that turned them into something like pagan temples.

The most famous atrocity of the French religious wars was the **Massacre of Saint Bartholomew's Day** in Paris on August 24, 1572. Catherine de' Medici, mother and regent of the young French king, Charles IX (r. 1560–1574), arranged a marriage between the Protestant Henry of Navarre and her daughter, the Catholic princess Margaret of Valois, and invited the Huguenot nobility to attend. This was provocative enough in a city that strongly favored the Catholic side. But on August 22, an assassin wounded the Protestant admiral Gaspard II de Coligny. Fearing reprisals from the Huguenots, the next day Charles ordered his own Swiss guards and other loyal troops to murder some 100 Protestant noblemen. The task was carried out, but instead of damping down violence, it ignited far more. Parisian civilians killed hundreds more Protestants—perhaps 2,000 in all. They mutilated the bodies of Coligny and others. Some were "tried" or "baptized" by being thrown into the Seine or soaked in the blood of their loved ones. These ritual parodies of the operations of courts and churches made clear that the Catholics saw themselves as carrying out an official act

of the Inquisition were arrested and executed. Another local nobleman, William the Silent (1533–1584), Prince of Orange, who had also served the Spanish state as a member of Margaret's council, fled and raised an army against Spain. Many of the Dutch—especially the Calvinists among them—renounced their loyalty to Philip II, whom they denounced as a tyrant. The **Dutch Revolt** continued of cleansing. Similar scenes took place in the provinces, where 3,000 more victims died—some of them, at Orléans, to the sound of serenades from musicians playing lutes and guitars.

The massacre put a stop to the expansion of the Huguenot church. Protestant numbers in northern and central French cities shrank. But in southern France, their stronghold, Protestants were, if anything, even more determined to resist what they saw as Catholic tyranny. Before the massacre, Protestant writers on politics had argued (following up a hint given by Calvin) that rebellion against a tyrannical monarchy might be legitimate if led by a lower official—since lower officials were appointed by God, just as higher ones were. Now they made open appeals for revolution, evoking a democratic French constitution. Soon the French Protestants had created their own, essentially independent kingdom in the south, close to Geneva, the capital city of Calvinism, and to Henry of Navarre's stronghold. The radical new temper of political thought—and politics—proved contagious. When Henry of Valois came to the French throne as Henry III (r. 1574–1589) and made concessions to the Protestants, a Catholic Holy League formed against him. Catholic political writers also claimed a right of resistance against tyranny, and in 1588 Henry fled Paris when the leader of the league, the duke of Guise, entered the city. Even political assassination became a tool of government. First, William the Silent, leader of the Dutch Revolt, was assassinated. Then Henry III, who had had the duke of Guise and his brother, a cardinal, murdered at the end of 1588, was himself killed in 1589 by a fanatical Dominican friar.

POLITICAL SETTLEMENTS

The Catholic forces of Spain, concentrated on the rebellious Netherlands, scored more successes at first. But for all their military superiority to the Dutch on land, the Spanish proved unable to suppress the Dutch Revolt, especially when many of its supporters took to the sea. Though Elizabeth infuriated some of her warlike subjects by her refusal to commit herself to a land war on the Continent in defense of European Protestantism, her privateers harried Spanish fleets and colonies. She gave modest but crucial assistance to the Dutch, and in 1588 the English fleet scattered and defeated the **Spanish Armada** that Philip II sent against her. Slowly it became clear on the larger European scale, as it had on the smaller German scale

Saint Bartholomew's Day Massacre The Huguenot painter François Dubois began this gory work shortly after the massacre took place in August 1572. Blood and corpses are strewn everywhere. Standing in front of the Louvre palace (in background at center) and dressed in black, Catherine de' Medici looks at a pile of bodies.

fifty years before, that neither party was strong enough to defeat the other definitively.

After witnessing the destruction caused by religious war, some influential French Catholics, including powerful lawyers and royal counselors, decided that it mattered more to have a unified state than a single religion. Known as *politiques*, these moderates often had valued Protestant as well as Catholic friends. They helped forge the brief alliance between Henry of Navarre—a Protestant but also a direct descendant of Louis IX—and the Catholic Henry III to fight the Spanish. After Henry III's assassination, Henry of Navarre renounced his Protestant faith (according to legend, he declared that "Paris is worth a mass"). Though his change of faith angered many Protestants, he was soon able to put an end to the resistance of the Holy League. In 1594 he was crowned King Henry IV, and in 1598, working from the principles of the politiques, he promulgated the **Edict of Nantes**, which gave Protestants limited religious freedom. Henry took up the tasks of restoring prosperity in France and rebuilding Paris, activities at which he proved very successful.

Though it took until 1609 for the Dutch to make a truce with the Spanish, the defeat of the Spanish Armada, repeated mutinies by Spanish troops, and the assumption of command by General Maurice of Nassau meant that the Dutch were able to conquer a number of major cities in the 1590s. Their independence secure, the counties of Holland and Zeeland, and the other states of Holland, reconfigured themselves as a Dutch republic, ruled by

DE WITTE'S *THE INTERIOR OF THE OUDE KERK*

John Calvin was even more rigorous than Martin Luther in his vision of reform. Whereas Luther expressed ambivalence toward religious images, which were sometimes retained in Lutheran churches, Calvin, like Zwingli, inspired Protestant reformers to shatter, burn, melt, or whitewash such images and decorations in their churches.

When Amsterdam's Oude Kerk (Old Church), built in the early fourteenth century, was transformed from a Roman Catholic to a Calvinist church in the late sixteenth century, Protestants destroyed its religious images. In this painting, *The Interior of the Oude Kerk* (ca.

1660), Emanuel de Witte portrays its clean columns, whitewashed walls, elegant arches, semicircular nave, and most important of all, its pulpit, where the word of God was preached.

The church was not only the community's religious center but also a popular meeting place where merchants conversed and sailors and their families prayed for the safe and successful conclusion of sea voyages. De Witte portrays scenes of everyday life in this unadorned setting: merchants discuss business (right), a mother nurses her child (far right), and a dog even urinates on a column (left). In the foreground, a burial is being prepared.

QUESTIONS FOR ANALYSIS

1. What does this depiction of a church's interior tell us about the influence of Calvinist theology in the Netherlands?
2. As indicated by this painting, what role did Reformed churches play in everyday life in the Netherlands?
3. How would you compare this scene to life in Calvin's Geneva as described earlier in the chapter?

their representative assemblies, or estates, and protected, but not ruled, by the House of Orange.

RUSSIA AND EASTERN EUROPE

More slowly than in the West, monarchs in Eastern Europe began to build up their states on modern lines. The power of Russian grand princes had been limited by the rival power of the boyars, or great noble families, and by their relatively old-fashioned armies, largely made up of mounted archers who offered their service in return for small grants of land. Ivan IV, known in Russian tradition as Ivan Grozny ("Ivan the Awesome"), was grand prince from 1533 to 1547, when he was crowned the first "Tsar of all the Russias," a title he held until he died in 1584. He thus claimed the status of an imperial ruler, like the early kings of Kiev and the emperors of Byzantium, and highlighted the existing claim that, after the fall of Constantinople, Moscow had become the third Rome.

Articulate and charismatic, Ivan rebuilt many Russian institutions. He established a council of advisers, forced the boyars to accept the duty of serving the tsar, regularized the system of taxation, and established a unified currency. He also gradually added well-trained musketeers and artillerymen to his armies. By conquering the Muslim Khanates of Kazan (1552) and Astrakhan (1556), he created a buffer against the Mongols and made Russia itself a multi-ethnic empire. Ivan celebrated these accomplishments by building a vast cathedral, St Basil's, in Moscow. In this and other ways he emulated the Renaissance rulers of Western Europe. Ivan built new fortresses, brought in foreign artists and craftsmen to improve Moscow, and engaged in elaborate diplomatic relations, especially with England. Though a formal alliance with Mary or Elizabeth eluded him, the Muscovy Company granted a monopoly, imported luxury goods and exported timber, tar, and other products needed to build English ships.

Like the western monarchies, Russia experienced crisis when Ivan's conduct became unpredictable. In 1564 he blackmailed his boyars into granting him absolute power, and used it to divide Russia. He established absolute control over a northern area, called the Oprichnina, in the former territory of Novgorod. A black-clad private army terrorized the inhabitants. On Ivan's orders they sacked Novgorod, already stricken by plague, in 1570. In 1572 he abolished the Oprichnina: his intentions in creating it remain unclear, though some historians believe he may have seen himself as creating a holy kingdom for the end of time. The Grand Duchy of Lithuania and the

Kingdom of Poland, both also expanding in resources and power, were joined in 1569 by the Union of Lublin, and in 1576 they joined the Ottomans in attacking Ivan's Empire. In 1581 he killed his son Ivan Ivanovich, apparently by accident. Expansion did not end. Toward the end of Ivan's reign, Cossacks —Slavic-speaking steppe dwellers, skilled in cavalry warfare, who served many lords— conquered Siberia and recognized him as Tsar. Famine, plague and war had exhausted Russia, which would fall into a crisis soon after Ivan's death. Yet he had established his country as the empire it would remain until the 20th century.

A TIME OF DARKNESS

The second half of the sixteenth century was—so many Europeans thought—a terrible age, perhaps uniquely terrible. The flow of silver and gold from the New World caused a slow but steady inflation of prices across the Continent. In a society that believed it possible to set fair prices and wages by statute, even a 2 percent rate of inflation was deeply unsettling. Harvest failures caused local spikes in the price of bread, which led to famines and often set off the most violent outbursts of religious rioting.

WITCH TRIALS

The famines also help to explain the outburst of witch trials across Europe during the period. The causes of

Burning Witches This woodcut illustration from a 1555 leaflet depicts witches being executed. Men stoke the flames, while a demon clings to one of the burning women. The women are shown again at right, descending into hell.

these trials varied, though they were always rooted in everyday events. Sometimes a woman who had difficulty giving birth, or whose baby was injured or died in the process, denounced her midwife; sometimes poor, older women who would have been objects of charity in traditional Catholic society provoked rage and denunciation from Protestants. In either case, the use of torture to interrogate those accused of witchcraft often led to further accusations. The largest witch hunts, sparked by famines, stopped only when members of the elite were accused.

The theory that witches conspired to attack Christian society took shape, as we have seen, in the fifteenth century. But it was in the age of religious war that the theory was applied in massive witch trials. By the time they came to an end in the late seventeenth century, some 30,000 to 70,000 people, 80 percent of them female, had been executed as witches. Thousands more were tried. The late sixteenth century genuinely was a time of darkness, and the fires that illuminated it too often consumed human beings.

TWO RESPONSES TO POLITICAL AND RELIGIOUS CRISIS: JEAN BODIN AND MICHEL DE MONTAIGNE

Jean Bodin (1530–1596) and Michel de Montaigne (1533–1592) both lived through the long series of religious wars unleashed in France by the Reformation; both were in their prime when the Massacre of Saint Bartholomew's Day took place. And both eagerly followed the intellectual revolutions of the mid-sixteenth century. Both realized that their world had changed, though they expressed their perceptions in different ways. Both were versed in the classics, trained in Roman law, and cosmopolitan in their interests and their reading. Bodin insisted that the only way to find the best constitution for one's country was to collect and compare laws from all over the world. He drew up one of the first guides to the study of history, which instructed the reader to pay as much attention to the East as to the West and as much to modern history as to ancient. Montaigne, who read Bodin's book, followed his instructions on how to read historians critically and fruitfully.

Both men took a deep interest in civilizations and religions other than their own, and regarded them with clear respect. Bodin wrote a provocative dialogue in which representatives of seven religions debate peacefully before parting from one another on terms of respect and affection. This work, with its suggestion that no religion could claim a monopoly on truth, could have endangered its author. It was not published, though manuscripts of it circulated widely. Montaigne, attending the circumcision of a Jewish baby in Rome, noted that Jewish babies cried "just as our babies do when they are baptized." Both Bodin and Montaigne, finally, were involved in trying to restore peace and stability to France.

BODIN But the solutions they arrived at differed radically. Bodin originally believed that constitutions could and should be mixed, as he thought the ancient Roman one, with its monarchical, aristocratic, and democratic elements, had been. He at first supported efforts by the French Estates General to limit the powers of the king, but in the late 1560s and 1570s he changed his mind. Only a ruler of absolute authority, he now insisted, could possibly maintain peace and order. Sovereignty—formal command over a state—could not be divided among contending parties but must rest with one of them: preferably the king, who should have the power of life and death over his subjects that the Roman head of household had held over his children. Bodin's doctrine, which came to be known as absolutism, proved highly attractive to monarchs and their ministers in the decades to come.

In the end, Bodin sided with the Catholic Holy League against the Huguenots and politiques, who included many of his former friends. More surprising still, he came to believe that witches, as well as heretics, threatened France. His treatise, *Of the Demonomania of Sorcerers*, made a powerful case for the prosecution of witches of both sexes. Its festering anecdotes of diabolic action in the world made it a reference book for two generations of witch-hunters.

MONTAIGNE Montaigne, by contrast, retired from public life as a lawyer in middle age to an estate outside Bordeaux. Reading and contemplating in his study, its rafters inscribed with classical proverbs, he tested the precepts of the ancients against his own experience. Although the Stoics, who had insisted that the wise must ignore pain and other distractions, had many followers in Montaigne's time, he found their precepts too demanding to be realistic. The ancient Skeptics, with their refusal to make dogmatic pronouncements, appealed to him more. Perhaps they offered a way out of the labyrinths of religious war. Gradually, Montaigne evolved a new literary form, the essay—literally, a trial or experiment. Whereas Bodin wrote formal treatises in Latin that propounded a single, absolute truth, Montaigne wrote short pieces in French that began from some supposed truth and subjected it to examination.

Dogmas of all kinds, Montaigne confessed, repelled and depressed him. He found it implausible that witches deserved to be burned for conspiring against humanity or that European culture, in its authoritarianism and violence, could claim ethical superiority to the so-called cannibals of the New World. Montaigne argued in a famous essay that New World natives practiced the arts with grace and subtlety, and had created an egalitarian society that put the supposed Christians of hierarchical, blood-thirsty Europe to shame. He expressed his horror at the Stoical hard men, Catholic and Protestant, who did not realize that knowing when to yield was a basic part of the moral life.

Montaigne's *Essays* (1580) spared few of the follies of his time. But Montaigne saw himself as a human brother, as much the prey of emotions and illusions as everyone else, and he made fun of his own tendency to draw radical conclusions. At the end of his essay on cannibals, for example, he told the story of how Brazilian natives brought to Europe to take part in royal ceremonies had exposed the un-Christian nature of Christian society to France's King Charles IX when he questioned them. Montaigne learned that they found two things odd: that grown men—strong, bearded, and armed—would obey a king who was still a child, and that the European poor did not kill the rich and take their goods. Montaigne's Indians sound like Thomas More's Raphael Hythloday denouncing the immorality of Europe. Unlike More, however, Montaigne immediately struck a comic note, conceding that he could not have understood everything he was told about the alien society he had tried to describe. He admitted that he had found it almost impossible to communicate with an Indian, even using an interpreter. And he summed up his elaborate, critical comparison of societies with rueful simplicity: "What's the use? They don't wear pants."

The first two books of the *Essays*, published in 1580, became best sellers. Now a celebrity, Montaigne traveled to Rome, examining the cities he passed through, their antiquities and customs. On his return to France, he continued writing essays, composing a third book in which he made himself, in all his own weaknesses and inconsistencies, his principal subject. But Montaigne also served as mayor of Bordeaux, political adviser to Henry of Navarre, and an intermediary in the negotiations between Catholics and Protestants that brought the French religious wars

Montaigne This portrait of a richly dressed Michel de Montaigne was painted during the writer's life by an anonymous artist.

to a close. The man who hated violence and intolerance did more than most to find a way to end what was, to that point, Europe's most violent and intolerant age. Neither Bodin nor Montaigne was an ordinary writer, typical of his time. But both shared their views with the thousands of readers who made their works so popular. And both, in their radically different ways, expressed the contradictions of a Europe torn by contending beliefs—and soon to be torn, in different ways, by new political, religious, and intellectual movements.

CONCLUSION

The Europeans of the sixteenth century lived through some of the most wracking changes in history. They became print professionals and skilled users of verbal and visual media, which could reproduce their ideas in hundreds, rather than dozens, of copies. They profited from the geographical discoveries of the late fifteenth century, and thought hard about what these discoveries implied about their traditional sense of Europe's central place in the universe. And they saw the unified Catholic Church, already more than one thousand years old, challenged by rivals that it could not defeat, even as its own powers revived.

Most Christians continued to believe that their own form of religion was the only true one. They saw it as reasonable—even virtuous—to persecute those who insisted on worshipping differently, or to rebel against political authorities that persecuted them. Only a few, such as Montaigne, shared the qualified belief in tolerance that had made Erasmus leery of persecuting heretics when the Reformation broke out. Eventually, however, the sheer human cost of religious conflict clearly outweighed any benefits, even in the eyes of many staunchly orthodox Catholics and Protestants. By the end of the sixteenth century, foundations had been laid for a development no one could have foreseen a century earlier: the creation not only of separate Catholic and Protestant churches but also of distinct Catholic and Protestant societies.

[CHAPTER REVIEW]

KEY TERMS

Martin Luther (p. 372)
indulgence (p. 373)
Desiderius Erasmus (p. 375)
Thomas More (p. 376)
Ninety-Five Theses (p. 378)
Diet of Worms (p. 378)

Protestant Reformation (p. 379)
Ulrich Zwingli (p. 382)
Peasants' War (p. 384)
Anabaptists (p. 385)
Argula von Grumbach (p. 386)
John Calvin (p. 388)

Henry VIII (p. 390)
Charles V (p. 391)
Jacob Fugger (p. 391)
Peace of Augsburg (p. 393)
Jesuits (p. 395)
Council of Trent (p. 396)
Nicolaus Copernicus (p. 397)

Huguenots (p. 399)
Dutch Revolt (p. 400)
Massacre of Saint Bartholomew's Day (p. 400)
Spanish Armada (p. 401)
Edict of Nantes (p. 401)

REVIEW QUESTIONS

1. What were Martin Luther's primary criticisms of the Catholic Church?

2. What factors spurred the expansion of the Reformation movement?

3. What were the most important differences in the thinking of Luther, Ulrich Zwingli, and John Calvin?

4. How did the Reformation inspire the Peasants' War in Germany?

5. How did the Reformation affect the lives of women?

6. What actions did Holy Roman Emperor Charles V take to expand and solidify his territories?

7. What were the most important outcomes of the Council of Trent?

8. What advances in scientific thinking took place during the Reformation?

9. Why did Europe's religious divisions lead to war in the sixteenth century?

10. What developments in the sixteenth century allowed for greater religious toleration?

CORE OBJECTIVES

After reading this chapter, you should have a solid understanding of the following core objectives. To strengthen your grasp of the core objectives, use the resources on the Student Site for The West.

- Analyze the intellectual and cultural context that influenced Martin Luther's ideas.
- Describe the major events of the Protestant Reformation.
- Compare the different Protestant movements inspired by Luther's message.

- Describe the social and political conditions that led to conflict between Protestants and Catholics.
- Explain the Catholic Reformation that arose in response to Protestantism.
- Identify the intellectual innovations and political conflicts that coincided with the Reformation.

 GO TO inQuizitive TO SEE WHAT YOU'VE LEARNED—AND LEARN WHAT YOU'VE MISSED—WITH PERSONALIZED FEEDBACK ALONG THE WAY.

CHRONOLOGY

12

Things Fall Apart

A CONTINENT IN CRISIS

1600–1640

1629–1640
Charles I of Britain
rules without Parliament
1629
Edict of Restitution

1633
Inquisition condemns
Galileo for defense
of heliocentrism

1637
Descartes publishes
Discourse on Method

O n December 26, 1606, a king watched a king go mad. As part of his annual Christmas festivities, King James I of England (r. 1603–1625) had invited his court to the first performance of a play by the fashionable author of the moment, William Shakespeare (1564–1616). The audience sat in crowded boxes in a sumptuously decorated London palace, watching a low stage on which the actors' company had erected a rudimentary set meant to evoke a wild, empty heath. The scent of hundreds of candles pervaded the drafty hall, and many of the courtiers wore heavy coats to protect against the cold and damp. With King James looking on, an actor portraying a much earlier English ruler, King Lear, raved and screamed. As men behind the makeshift stage rolled a metal ball on a metal sheet to simulate thunder and set off small firecrackers to mimic lightning, Lear tore off his clothes and howled:

> Blow, winds, and crack your cheeks! Rage! Blow!…
> Spit, fire! Spout, rain!…here I stand your slave,
> A poor, infirm, weak and despis'd old man
> …My wits begin to turn.

Velázquez and Domestic Life Early in his career, the Spanish painter Diego Velázquez (1599–1660), who would later be championed by the Spanish Count-Duke Olivares, was known for his paintings depicting domestic scenes. In his *Old Woman Cooking Eggs* (1618), the detailed portrayal of the titular subject and her kitchen seem to have been painted from life. A boy arrives with a melon and a flask of wine, luxuries amidst the widespread economic deprivation of the early seventeenth century.

FOCUS QUESTIONS

- Why did parts of Europe stagnate and others surge economically?

- What were the first footholds for Europe in North America?

- How did European states respond to the new financial challenges they faced?

- How did Catholicism and Protestantism attempt to reform the daily lives of Europeans?

- What political tensions were destabilizing Europe?

- What caused the many smaller conflicts in Europe to become one major war?

- Why did royal ministers become so powerful at this time?

- How did the growth of absolutism affect major developments in culture?

Lear was no longer king, no longer the father of a family, no longer sane.

The scene would not have been altogether shocking to James and his court. Madness had featured prominently in tragic drama since the earliest days of the theater. English stages had long developed something of a specialty in depicting the overthrow of kings, and Shakespeare had made his reputation through a series of "history plays" that touched on examples from the more recent past.

Even so, there was something sublimely powerful and troubling about Shakespeare's treatment of Lear's fall. In this, the playwright's greatest tragedy, it is not merely a king who is overthrown. Rather, the collapse of order in the kingdom is mirrored by the collapse of order in every other possible domain. Lear's daughters Goneril and Regan—played by teenage boys since it was considered immoral for women to act on stage—turn against their father. The order of the natural world itself seems to collapse with the storms that wrack the heath on which Lear raves. Most frightening, the order of the mind collapses as well, as the imperious monarch from the first act turns before the audience's eyes into a naked, shuddering, incoherently babbling wreck. And in the midst of it all arises a terrifying character who seems to delight in this lack of order, scorning attempts to shore it

up with custom and tradition, driven by nothing but his own ambition and resentment, proud and cruel—"the bastard Edmund," illegitimate son of Lear's counselor Gloucester. "Thou, nature, art my goddess;" Edmund declares, "to thy law my services are bound." Watching in the flickering darkness of the palace, King James might well have taken comfort from the play's defense of order and legitimate rule. But he could not have helped but shudder at what Shakespeare showed about its terrible fragility, and the terrible allure of characters like Edmund, who strove to destroy it.

Hundreds of years later, it is almost irresistible to see *King Lear* foreshadowing the following decades of European history. Of course, Europe was hardly ignorant of horrific violence and had experienced tragic bouts of it within recent memory. In France, the bloody sixteenth-century religious wars remained at the forefront of civic consciousness. "O desolate France! O bloody earth. Not earth, but ash," as a French Protestant poet had recently written. In England, just one year before *King Lear*'s premiere, Catholic conspirators in the Gun-powder Plot (1605) had nearly succeeded in blowing up the Houses of Parliament and assassinating the Protestant monarch. James—the king of Scotland who had succeeded his cousin Elizabeth I on the English throne in 1603, thereby bringing the two kingdoms under the same crown—could hardly take the stability of his new Stuart dynasty for granted. It is no accident that nearly all of Shakespeare's plays with historical subjects feature the threat or reality of civil war.

Even so, in the decades that followed *King Lear's* premiere, a particularly concentrated, intense series of real-life tragedies took place in Europe. These were set against a literal change in the natural order—a period of exceptional and destructive cooling known as the Little Ice Age. The greatest of the tragedies was the murderous Thirty Years' War (1618–1648), whose human toll, measured as a proportion of the European population, dwarfs even that of World War II. Civil strife affected every major European state, from the Ottoman Empire to England itself. Just over four decades after the Christmas performance of *King Lear*, English revolutionaries would erect a scaffold outside the palace where he had viewed it, and there behead his son and heir, Charles I.

No single cause lay behind these tragic events. The Little Ice Age was compounded by a series of plagues and harvest failures that contributed to economic distress and broad social and political turmoil. Other economic changes, particularly associated with Europe's burgeoning overseas trade, fostered dangerous new rivalries. Innovations in military technology that had begun well before 1600 continued to drive up the human and material cost of warfare. Political factors such as turmoil within the Habsburg dynasty played a key role in the Thirty Years' War. And the ongoing divisions of Western Europe between Catholics and Protestants—as well as those between different Protestant churches—sharpened the strife and drove it forward.

But these tragedies did have one great, common result: a pressure on governments everywhere to strengthen and reform themselves. Everywhere, they faced the challenge of mobilizing resources more efficiently, above all for the purposes of warfare. This was a period in which patterns of competition in Europe turned increasingly violent and desperate, while peaceful exchange suffered. In many parts of the Continent, monarchs and their chief ministers sought new ways to streamline, subvert, or cooperate with traditional institutions and elites, and often provoked angry protests or even revolts. Some countries—notably France—emerged strengthened from the process; others—notably Spain—did far less well. And some were shattered altogether. In 1600 Europe was largely a continent of empires and what historians call "**composite monarchies**" in which a single monarch ruled largely separate and distinct states. By mid-century, this form of government was beginning to give way to cohesive nation-states capable of raising large, well-disciplined armies.

ECONOMIC CHANGE

The beginning of the seventeenth century saw extremely uneven patterns of economic development. Some parts of Europe not only experienced growth but technological innovation that would pay very long-term dividends. Others experienced only misery. And everywhere, the rates of growth were affected by climate and war.

THE LITTLE ICE AGE

Just a year after the performance of *King Lear* for King James, the River Thames at London froze so deeply that for only the second time on record, the city held a "Frost Fair" on the ice for several weeks, with shops, sports, theaters, and taverns being built in the middle of the river. Londoners were able to hold these fairs roughly one year in ten during the seventeenth century, less frequently in the eighteenth,

and for the last time ever in 1814. In 1622 a large part of the Bosphorus (the strait separating Europe from Asia at Constantinople) froze solid, and there were years in the century when portions of the Baltic Sea froze as well. The **Little Ice Age** began well before 1600 and lasted for centuries, but the seventeenth century was its coldest point.

The effects of the Little Ice Age were intensified in the years immediately after 1600 by the massive eruption of a Peruvian volcano that spewed enough sulfur and other particulate matter into the atmosphere to dim the sunlight and lower global temperatures even further. These conditions depressed crop yields and increased the chance of harvest failures. The freezing temperatures also lowered people's resistance to epidemics. For populations that even in good times lived on the edge of disaster, the results were catastrophic. The worst famine in Russian history occurred in 1601–03. In Spain between 1598 and 1602, poor harvests combined with an outbreak of bubonic plague to kill as much as 10 percent of the population. Grain production fell across the Continent, particularly around the Mediterranean and in central Europe. In Hungary, tithes collected by the Catholic Church (in theory a fixed percentage of the harvest) fell by 72 percent between 1570 and 1670.

STAGNATION ON THE CONTINENT

Overall, across Europe, the turn of the seventeenth century marked an end to the price increases that had taken place, more-or-less steadily, since the aftermath of the Black Death, and that serve as a rough indicator of economic growth. Although exact figures are elusive, it also seems as if the new century saw stagnation in the overall European population. And it saw an exponential increase in the number of Europeans forced across the line from poverty into indigence—the point at which they had to resort to begging, crime, prostitution, or migration simply to survive. Some migrants went great distances indeed, with 30,000 Scots ending up in Poland by the 1620s, and 40,000 French heading across the border into Catalonia (in northeastern Spain). To help the tribes of the destitute, reforming states and churches on both sides of the Catholic-Protestant divide continued to found institutions that gave charity in return for hard labor.

DECLINING TRADE Further harming the European economy was a Continent-wide slump in trade, provoked by the collapse of what had driven commercial expansion for more than a century: the Atlantic traffic of the Spanish

BRUEGEL THE ELDER'S *HUNTERS IN THE SNOW*

In its clear, sharp depiction of landscape and everyday life, *Hunters in the Snow* (1565) by the Dutch artist Pieter Bruegel the Elder allows us to see how villagers responded to the harsh conditions of winter during the Little Ice Age. Peasant villages are engulfed in deep snow and surrounded by frozen rivers and ponds, bare trees, and heavy skies. In the foreground, tired hunters and their hungry dogs return with a meager catch as women tend a fire and crows watch overhead. Beyond these necessities, a more joyful scene unfolds in the distance, as villagers and their children skate and play games on the ice. The painting captures both the power of nature and capacity of humans to cope with it.

QUESTIONS FOR ANALYSIS

1. What aspects of daily life does *Hunters in the Snow* depict?
2. How does the painting convey the challenges of the Little Ice Age?
3. What kind of relationships between humankind and nature does Bruegel show?

Peasants and Beggars The economic hardships experienced by many Europeans in the early seventeenth century are suggested by the French printer Jacques Callot's 1622 illustration of two beggar women. Dressed in ragged clothes and stooped over, bearing expressions of despair and exhaustion, they share a tiny bowl of food.

at the expense of peasant small-holders, many of whom were driven off their land and forced into serfdom. Central and eastern European states imposed particularly drastic restrictions on serfs to guarantee the labor supply, especially for profitable export crops. Between 1608 and 1653, seven major central and eastern European states, including Hungary and Muscovy (the grand duchy of which Moscow was the capital, a forerunner to modern Russia), took away serfs' freedom of movement and bound them to the land they farmed. Meanwhile, seigniorial lords—including the church and the state itself, which both had vast landownings—gained increased power to tax, judge, and discipline their serfs. Punishments could include lashes with the "knout," a powerful whip with wires or hooks woven into the leather to inflict maximum pain (100 lashes usually amounted to a death sentence).

By the late seventeenth century, particularly in Russian-speaking lands, this "second serfdom" (so called to distinguish it from the medieval variety) became effectively a form of slavery. Serfs in Muscovy lived in mostly miserable conditions, farming the hard soil in short summers with the most backward technology in Europe (metal plows, for instance, were almost unknown). These men and women, who amounted to nearly half the duchy's population, could be bought and sold at their lords' pleasure. To keep reproduction rates high, lords not only encouraged early marriage among serfs but sometimes paired them off by force. Serfs not working on the land had to pay their lords for the privilege of doing so.

Empire. As Spain's New World colonies developed more complex economies of their own, they grew less dependent on trade with the mother country. At the same time, Spanish fleets increasingly fell prey to pirates and privateers (ships chartered to engage in piracy against a country's enemies). Spain's annual transatlantic trade dropped from 30,000 tons in the 1610s to 13,000 tons in the 1640s. In 1627/28, the Spanish government was forced to declare bankruptcy and devalue its currency by 50 percent. Soon after, Dutch privateers captured the entire Spanish silver fleet at sea. This combination of events created chaos in the international money markets and virtually destroyed the great banks of Genoa, which had financed the Spanish Empire's debt.

A SECOND SERFDOM In central and eastern Europe, falling harvest yields put pressure on large landowners to expand their farm holdings. With most fertile land already under cultivation by 1600, they could do so only

GROWTH IN MARITIME EUROPE

The economic decline had harsh effects in southern and eastern Europe, but it was by no means uniform across the Continent. Even as southern and eastern Europe suffered and much of France and central Europe stagnated, the maritime regions of northwestern Europe grew strongly, as shown above all by the expansion of cities. The populations of 30 cities situated on an arc from Bordeaux in France to Copenhagen in Denmark increased at an average rate of close to 60 percent in the first half of the seventeenth century. Capital cities benefitting from the growth of state bureaucracies also grew rapidly, with newly-founded Madrid more than quadrupling in size between 1561 and 1630—from 30,000 to 130,000, despite the stagnation of the Spanish economy as a whole.

THE DUTCH REPUBLIC The greatest economic success story in the early seventeenth century belonged to the Dutch Republic. This new state, still fighting for independence from Spain in 1600, was the most urbanized in Europe, with more than a third of the population living in cities. Amsterdam, the capital, grew from 50,000 to 150,000 people between 1600 and 1650. In 1609 the Dutch took a large step toward creating a stable currency and strong national finance with the establishment of the Bank of Amsterdam. Chartered by the city's government, it was the precursor of today's national banks, which manage currencies and interest rates, and put the faith and credit of a national institution behind the value of a currency.

One other important measure of a modern economy is its overall energy usage, for manufacturing, agriculture, heating and lighting. Per capita, the Dutch in this period used more energy than any other people in Europe. Sources included the burning of peat and coal, horse- and water-powered mills, and of course, the country's iconic windmills—3,000 of them, each doing the work of forty or more horses. The Dutch also led the way in rural development. Between 1600 and 1639, they reclaimed more than 300 square miles of arable land from lakes and marshes. This land largely lay below sea level, so they built a complex series of dikes to protect it against flooding. During what one historian has called the "industrious revolution," rural workers processed raw materials delivered to them by urban merchants to produce textiles and other manufactures.

MIDDLE-CLASS HOUSEHOLDS

The new wealth generated by these changes took on a striking physical expression in Dutch homes. More and more households—including among those we would now call the middle class—owned elaborately carved beds, cupboards, and other furniture. The cupboards were filled not only with local ceramics but with porcelain and china imported from Asia. Lottery prizes, which give a good idea of what aspiring families most desired, included engraved goblets, tankards, and ewers; mirrors; silver breadbaskets; candlesticks; and even sets of petticoats. Houses acquired sumptuously carved moldings, tapestries, and paintings on the inside, and elaborate gables on the outside. Pendulum-driven clocks made their appearance in middle-class homes, so that families of merchants and artisans no longer needed to depend on church bells or crude sundials to tell the time.

These economic changes also affected gender roles. The "industrious revolution" above all involved a form of labor—textile spinning—traditionally associated with women. But as it grew more important in northern European economies, men were increasingly seen behind the spinning wheel as well. They earned more money at it than

Domestic Luxuries A Dutch oil painting from the 1660s indicates the lavish interiors to which the newly wealthy could aspire. The light streams in through glass windows, which are covered, like the bed, in sumptuous textiles. While a servant sweeps in the background, the lady of the house plays a harpsichord in front of an extravagantly framed mirror.

their female counterparts, even as they were mocked for taking on women's work. Meanwhile, the growth of cities and of an urban middle class fueled an expansion in domestic service, one of the occupations most closely associated with women. Nearly all households with a modicum of disposable income—including those of merchants, clergymen, lawyers, doctors, and even moderately well-off artisans—kept servants. In the Netherlands, as throughout Europe, domestic service especially attracted young peasant women hoping to save money for a dowry or to purchase land.

OCEANIC TRADE

Even as the Dutch laid the groundwork for a more modern economy, they also increasingly came to dominate European trade. In the 1630s, the Dutch Republic's 2,500 merchant ships represented half of all European shipping. Each year 150 Dutch vessels sailed to the Caribbean. Hundreds more traded with Africa, Brazil, India, and the Far East. In 1599 a fleet of eight Dutch ships explored the Spice Islands in what is now Indonesia and returned with cargo that generated a 400 percent profit. Spices such as nutmeg and clove—which not only added diversity to the European diet but were believed to have health-giving properties—offered potentially huge wealth for Europeans. Nutmeg in particular sold in Europe for more than 100 times what it cost in Asia.

THE EARLY TRANSATLANTIC SLAVE TRADE

Another hugely profitable form of cargo, transported by all of the major maritime powers, was human beings. As we have seen, by the mid-fifteenth century the Portuguese had begun shipping African slaves to their overseas colonies. They and the Spanish enslaved Native Americans as well throughout the European colonies in the Americas in the seventeenth century, contributing to the decimation of native populations. But the Europeans rapidly discovered that Africans were better suited to the grueling regime required for labor-intensive crops such as sugar. (The first sugar refinery in the New World opened in the Portuguese colony of Brazil in 1601.) Under what is now called the transatlantic "**triangle trade,**" Europeans transported cheap trade goods such as tools, cloth, weapons, and alcohol to Africa, where they exchanged them for slaves provided by local rulers and coastal Arab slave traders. From there the slaves were shipped across the Atlantic and sold in colonial port towns in the Americas, such as Port Royal in Jamaica, where the proceeds were used to purchase colonial goods such as tobacco for European markets. Between 1600 and 1640, Europeans—principally the Spanish and Portuguese—caused more than half a million Africans to be enslaved in this manner, more than two and a half times the number taken in the previous forty years.

Overseas trade remained a dangerous business. "Ships are but boards, sailors but men; there be land-rats and water-rats, water-thieves and land-thieves, I mean pirates, and then there is the peril of waters, winds and rocks," to quote Shakespeare's *The Merchant of Venice* (1598). In 1600, to spread out the risk, a large group of English merchants came together to form the East India Company, and won a charter from Queen Elizabeth I giving them a monopoly over trade with India and the Far East. The Dutch followed with their own East India Company two years later. In the early seventeenth century, these two competing enterprises engaged in frequent skirmishes on the high seas. Their representatives also meted out brutal treatment to indigenous populations, especially in the Spice Islands, where Dutch East India Company officials established plantations and hoped to found a large colony.

MERCANTILISM The approach to trade taken by the English, the Dutch, and most other European states followed from the conviction that the world's economic resources were finite and that one country's commerce could grow only at the expense of another's. States therefore generally insisted on rigid control of trade, putting as much as possible in the hands of officially chartered monopoly companies and insisting that goods come to their home shores only in their own ships.

These policies, which have come to be known as **mercantilism**, were based on faulty evidence. Even in the crisis years of the seventeenth century, Europeans showed a remarkable ability to exploit ever-greater quantities of natural resources. Coal production on the Continent, for instance, increased from scarcely 200 tons a year in the early sixteenth century to nearly 3 million tons annually by the 1680s, an indication that the growing European population was using steadily more energy per capita for manufactures and heating. The first half of the seventeenth century also saw the opening up of new sources for another lucrative commodity, furs. The great sources of fur, namely Siberia and the French and English colonies in North America, provided some 200,000 pelts a year, principally for hats and coats. Even so, in the context of general economic decline, it seemed obvious to most Europeans that the growth of the Netherlands and England had come at the expense of other European countries, especially those on the Mediterranean.

EUROPEAN EXPANSION IN THE ATLANTIC

By 1600, the European powers had a massive overseas presence. They had established trading routes around the coasts of Africa to India and Southeast Asia, complete with networks of forts and trading posts. They were spreading east across Siberia toward China. Spanish conquistadores had overthrown the Aztec and Inca Empires in Mexico and Peru, and Spain and Portugal claimed sovereignty over nearly all of present-day Latin America. In the seventeenth century, the Spanish and Portuguese presence in Central and South America continued to grow, with changes that transformed even the physical environment. For example, at the start of the century, Spain's colonial authorities in Mexico City began one of the largest engineering projects of the early modern period: a series of canals that drained the lakes around the city and prevented its periodic flooding. The project would continue for centuries, and ultimately harm the indigenous population by depriving farmers of necessary irrigation water.

EARLY EUROPEAN SETTLEMENTS IN NORTH AMERICA

Yet one continent remained largely untouched by Europeans at the start of the seventeenth century: North America—or, rather, the portion of it north of Mexico. Several European powers had explored its coasts and attempted to establish small settlements in the late 1500s. The first English colony, on Roanoke Island in what is now North Carolina, vanished without a trace. The Spanish did succeed in establishing a small colony at St. Augustine, on the Atlantic coast of Florida, in 1565. Although nearly destroyed by French and British attacks, it remains the oldest continuously occupied European settlement in the continental United States. But it was not until three key events took place between 1607 and 1609 that permanent European colonization of the rest of North America began.

JAMESTOWN The first of these events involved three English ships that sailed into Chesapeake Bay in 1607 and

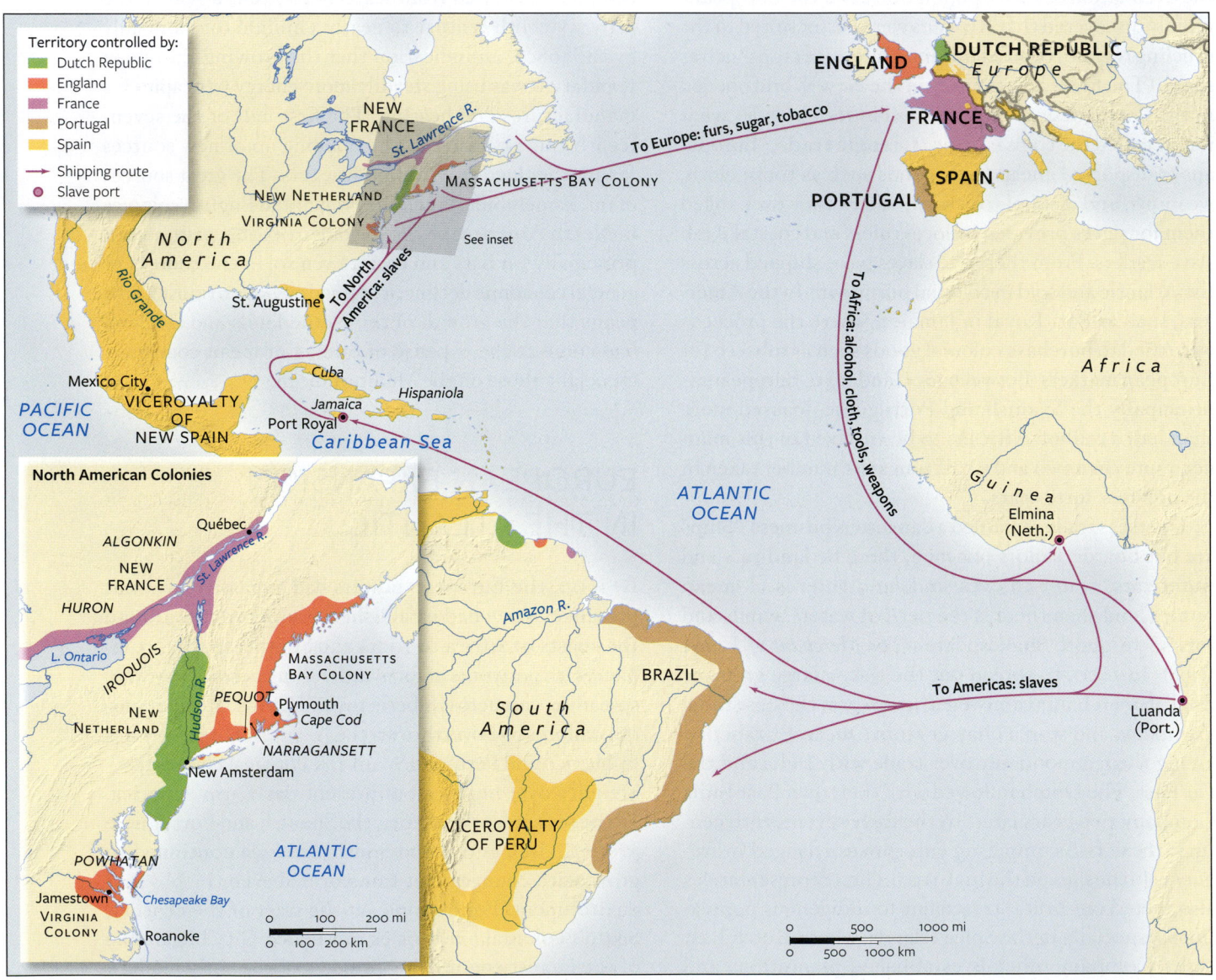

The Americas and the Triangle Trade, c. 1640 In the transatlantic "triangle trade," traders brought goods such as alcohol, cloth, tools, and weapons from Europe to the west coast of Africa and exchanged them for slaves bound for the plantations of the Americas. In destinations such as the Spanish West Indies, the ships picked up sugar and tobacco, which they transported to North America and back to Europe. New Dutch, French, and English colonies in northeastern North America also provided Europe with raw materials, such as furs.

established a fort called Jamestown. Although not the idle gentlemen of legend, the 240-odd colonists on board arrived with far too much optimism about the prospects for quick enrichment, and far too little knowledge of the region's climate, soil, resources (which included far fewer precious metals than they hoped), and native inhabitants. Disease, starvation, and hostilities with Algonquian Indians of the Powhatan tribe quickly killed off a majority of the colonists, and only the arrival of supply ships from England in 1610 saved Jamestown from Roanoke's fate.

Over the next few years, however, the surviving settlers discovered that they could grow a profitable cash crop: tobacco. King James I himself had railed against tobacco smoking in a 1604 essay, calling it a dangerous, addictive, "stinking suffumigation" that was particularly disgusting at the dinner table. But his condemnation did little to prevent the crop from finding a ready market in England and the rest of Europe. As a result, what soon became known as the Virginia Colony prospered. In 1619, following the example of the Spanish and Portuguese, the English colonists began to import African laborers to work the tobacco fields, and over the following decades the institution of North American slavery gradually took shape.

QUÉBEC   One year after the founding of Jamestown, the second key event took place when the French explorer Samuel de Champlain (1567–1635) founded a fort and trading post at Québec, on the Saint Lawrence River, which became the capital of New France. Champlain traveled long distances around the region's river systems. In the course of establishing a flourishing trade in furs, he made contact both with tribes of Algonquian hunter-gatherers and with the more settled Huron. To cement his alliance with the Huron, Champlain took part in an expedition against their Iroquois enemies, and dispersed a 200-strong war party by killing two of its chiefs with firearms. New France also became the base for missionary efforts by French Franciscan and Jesuit clergy, with several Jesuits traveling hundreds of miles into the North American interior to preach the Gospel to Native Americans. The Jesuit Jean de Brébeuf (1593–1649) mastered the Huron language and impressed the Indians with his oratory, physical strength, and courage. But the Jesuits' efforts were undercut by European diseases, which, as so often in the past, decimated the native populations from the moment of sustained contact. The Huron, badly weakened by smallpox, were conquered and dispersed in the 1640s by the Iroquois, who tortured and killed Brébeuf along with several other missionaries.

The Tobacco Trade In a 1620 engraving, African slaves pack tobacco leaves, grown in the fields beyond, into barrels to be exported from Jamestown. English plantation owners watch from the shade.

NEW AMSTERDAM   Meanwhile, in 1609, the third key event took place when a Dutch East India Company ship called the *Half Moon*, under the command of the Englishman Henry Hudson (ca. 1565–1611), explored the area now known as New York Harbor, and proceeded up the river that now bears his name as far as present-day Albany. The Dutch soon laid claim to the entire region. In 1624 they dispatched a group of settlers there in hopes of developing the fur trade. Soon after they purchased Manhattan Island from the local Indians and founded New Amsterdam, the future capital of New Netherland, at its southern tip. They paid with trade goods worth 60 Dutch guilders—perhaps $1,000 today.

Virginia Colony, New France, and New Netherland all had their origins in profit-seeking commercial enterprises and initially attracted colonists who, for the most part, intended to make money and return home, rather than settle permanently in North America. As a result, their populations grew only slowly. The French and Dutch colonies, dedicated to the fur trade and dependent on Native American trappers, remained particularly small and vulnerable. In each case, the population barely reached 2,000 in 1650. Virginia, with the rapid expansion of tobacco farming, attracted more settlers, numbering between 15,000 and 20,000 by mid-century. In all three colonies, European men greatly outnumbered European women. And unlike in the Spanish and Portuguese colonies, which tended to have much larger indigenous populations and where intermarriage quickly produced large communities of *mestizos*, relatively few of the European colonists in North America married native women.

NEW ENGLAND

The next English colony to be founded set a different pattern from its predecessors. In December 1620, a ship named the *Mayflower* sailed into Plymouth Harbor, in present-day Massachusetts. Its 102 passengers came, like the French and Dutch colonists, with financial backing from merchants back home hoping to develop the fur trade, but they themselves mostly had different goals in mind. Religious dissenters from Nottinghamshire, in east-central England, they favored a rigidly Calvinist variety of Protestantism that wanted to abolish priests, bishops, and liturgical practices not explicitly sanctioned by scripture. Persecuted by the English authorities, who practiced the Anglican variety of Protestantism that remained closer to Catholic beliefs, these men and women had initially fled to the Dutch Republic. Then, in 1619, the English authorities gave them permission to found a farming colony south of the Hudson River, which they envisaged as a model religious community "for the Glory of God and advancement of the Christian Faith," to quote their initial instrument of government, the Mayflower Compact. Having unexpectedly made initial landfall on Cape Cod, they settled in nearby Plymouth and eventually became known as the Pilgrims. Nearly half of them died in the first winter, including most of the adult women, but Plymouth survived with the help of local Indians. Their shared feast of thanksgiving is now celebrated as an American holiday.

A CITY UPON A HILL Other English dissenters followed, hoping, in the words of one of their leaders, to establish an exemplary "city upon a hill" in the New World. From 1630 on, they established colonies in Massachusetts Bay, Connecticut, and other areas of present-day New England. Like the Pilgrims, these settlers practiced a demanding form of Calvinism in which the community enforced rigorous moral norms and forbade many "worldly" pleasures, including dancing. Along with closely related Protestant communities in England, they would come to be known as "Puritans." They also came above all to farm, and despite the immense difficulty of clearing trees and rocks from the land, their new settlements quickly expanded. The Massachusetts Bay Colony alone saw the foundation of some fifty separate towns between 1630 and 1650. The population of what is now known as New England quickly dwarfed that of Virginia Colony, New France, and New Netherland combined, with more than 30,000 inhabitants by 1650. This number almost certainly exceeded that of the region's native populations, whose numbers fell rapidly from exposure to European diseases. By contrast, the Indian inhabitants of Latin America continued to outnumber the European settlers in those colonies.

SETTLERS AND NATIVE AMERICANS In New England, as in so many areas of the Americas previously, the European settlers quickly fell into violent conflict with the indigenous peoples. In the late 1630s, a dispute over the fur trade led to a brief but vicious war between the English colonies and the Pequot tribe, who were allied with the Dutch. In May 1637, an armed force of English and Narragansett Indian allies stormed a large Pequot village on the Mystic River (in present-day Connecticut) and massacred several hundred inhabitants. English Protestants, like the French Jesuits, did profess a desire to evangelize among the Indian tribes. The seal of the Massachusetts Bay Colony even included a Native American figure and

Massachusetts Bay Colony The 1630 seal of the colony shows a Native American wearing only leaves, an indication of the settlers' perception of the indigenous population as primitive. The Biblical quotation "Come over and help us" expresses the colonists' missionary intent.

the words "Come over and help us," a quotation from the biblical book of Acts. Several ministers struggled to learn the native languages. But they expected far more radical changes from their converts than the Jesuits in the French and Spanish colonies, insisting that Indians adopt European customs and learn to read scripture. As a result, the Protestants initially had far less success. The colonists also enslaved Native Americans, and brought African slaves to New England as well.

Overall, the colonies of New England and Virginia remained relatively small and vulnerable. Trade and settlement took place almost entirely along waterways, mostly near the Atlantic coast (it took enormous labor to clear roads through the thick eastern woodlands). European settlers remained highly vulnerable to disease, Native American raids, and attacks by other European powers. The same vulnerability and instability characterized other parts of Europe's overseas empires before 1650, even in the more well-established Spanish and Portuguese colonies. Throughout the New World, Europeans remained dependent on native allies. In 1623 and again in 1643, the Dutch sent fleets to the Pacific coast of South America in the hope of forging an alliance with the Indians there and fomenting a rebellion against their common enemy, Spain. But this idea came to naught, and the Spanish Empire continued to expand throughout the early seventeenth century. Its representatives explored the Pacific coast of North America and consolidated their authority in the Philippines, where they established a university in 1611.

STATES UNDER PRESSURE

Despite the relatively small scale of seventeenth-century imperialism, European overseas ventures were still expensive propositions. The Dutch fleet sent to South America in 1623 comprised eleven ships, 300 cannon, and 1,600 crew members, and took six years to prepare. When King Charles I of England (r. 1625–1649) decided to build a new fleet in the 1630s, it cost the equivalent of nearly a full year's state revenues. Looking for quick ways of raising money without having to ask Parliament for it, Charles hit on a medieval custom that obliged coastal towns to provide the crown with ships, or the money to build them. Charles was soon levying **"ship money"** on the entire kingdom, including areas far from any coast. It became one of the most important sources of royal income, as well as of grievances against him.

THE "MILITARY REVOLUTION"

But overseas ventures were just one source of financial pressure on European governments in the early seventeenth century. Others arose from the period's general economic and demographic crises, as shrinking and increasingly impoverished populations provided less tax revenue than they had in the past. Another factor was the impact of what some historians have misleadingly called the "military revolution," which refers to the changes in military technology and practice that took place in mostly evolutionary fashion over a long period.

We have already seen how the development of large-caliber gunpowder weapons affected warfare in the sixteenth century: it forced European powers to build much larger, stronger, and more elaborate fortifications, and put a new premium on siege warfare. It also transformed naval combat, as ship captains came to rely on broadsides from massed ranks of cannon to disable or sink opposing vessels. The trend toward bigger ships equipped with more cannon continued throughout the early seventeenth century. Whereas the vessels of the Spanish Armada in 1588 had roughly nineteen cannon each, the ships of the Dutch navy in 1665 averaged sixty-two.

One crucial set of innovations did come to fruition in a relatively short period in the early seventeenth century, thanks above all to the Dutch prince Maurice of Nassau (1567–1625). A keen student of ancient Roman military authors, Maurice placed new stress on intensive training and drill for common infantry, so that soldiers could maneuver in orderly fashion under fire. In combat, all the men in a line would fire their weapons in a single salvo and then march backward to reload, exposing a new line of soldiers who would fire in turn. In this way, despite the cumbersome procedures needed to load and discharge the muskets of the day (it took even a well-trained soldier up to a minute for each shot), a relatively rapid rate of fire could be maintained. Compared with the large, unwieldy square formations of infantry that had marched across typical sixteenth-century battlefields, these new, highly-trained units were far more expensive. Furthermore, the new requirements of training and constant drill effectively turned

Military Innovations A 1607 engraving from a Dutch manual of Maurice of Nassau's military drills shows a soldier lifting a smoking musket as well as the proper posture for balancing the formidable weapon. He also carries a sword, still necessary for fighting at close range.

the soldiers into full-time professionals, which pushed European states toward permanent standing armies. This development, in turn, only reinforced the long-term growth in army size.

STATE BUILDING

European states responded to the financial and administrative pressures by trying to wring as much revenue as possible from existing sources, as Charles I did with ship money. Another vivid example is the practice, developed most fully in France, called "**venality of office.**" Starting in the late fifteenth century, the French state had begun literally to sell some of the highest offices in the country—notably, judgeships in the high courts, or *parlements*. In return for the purchase price, the buyer (who needed a law degree, but few other qualifications) gained higher social status as well as the income from the office. By the sixteenth century, such "venal" offices were formally recognized as conferring nobility on their holders—and nobility, among other things, could provide exemptions from some of the heaviest forms of French taxation. This privilege made the offices highly desirable, and as their prices rose, the crown became increasingly dependent on their sale. By 1620, a special fee that allowed the owners of venal offices to pass them on to their heirs accounted for no less than 10 percent of the French state's total revenues. Law courts presided over by venal officeholders introduced new restrictions on women's property rights to ensure that the offices would pass to male heirs in perpetuity.

UNIFICATION OF FRANCE The French state was able to exploit the practice of venality so effectively because of a crucial postmedieval development: the administrative unification of the French nation. To be sure, early-seventeenth-century France remained, in some ways, a patchwork kingdom. In a number of provinces, the local representative bodies and powerful noble families still possessed considerable autonomy. Law codes still varied from province to province, and the spoken language often varied from village to village, although by 1600 Parisian French had become the dominant written language almost everywhere. Under the Edict of Nantes issued by King Henry IV in 1598, French Protestants retained considerable rights, and even a number of military strongholds. Nevertheless, France formed a single political unit. The entire country acknowledged the king's word as law, even if the king himself was bound to respect tradition, religion, and the so-called fundamental laws (which forbade

him, for instance, from selling off parts of the kingdom or from passing on the throne to whomever he pleased). The number of judges, tax collectors, and other agents of the French crown rose from just 12,000 in the early sixteenth century to 80,000 by 1664.

DIVISIONS IN WESTERN AND CENTRAL EUROPE
In 1600 few other European monarchs could count on presiding over this degree of unity. Most of their domains remained composite monarchies, with each separate territory possessing its own government, laws, and customs. James I, who became king of both England and Ireland (r. 1603–1625), for instance, continued to rule the separate kingdom of Scotland as James VI (r. 1567–1625). The Spanish king Philip III (r. 1598–1621) was also Philip II of Portugal and held sovereignty over the Spanish Netherlands (modern Belgium). Even within Spain, several of the provinces retained greater autonomy than any in France.

The central European territories of the House of Habsburg existed in a particular state of confusion.

Habsburg Possessions in the Holy Roman Empire, c. 1600 The Habsburg dynasty controlled vast lands in western and central Europe, yet its territory was far from unified. The Spanish Habsburg king Philip III controlled the Spanish Netherlands, Milan, and part of present-day France, while independent Habsburg archdukes ruled over Lower Austria, Upper Austria, Inner Austria, and the Tirol. Hungary and the lands around Prague were under the jurisdiction of the Habsburg Holy Roman emperor Rudolf II, but were administered separately.

Separate governments and royal courts—under different, largely independent archdukes—existed in Lower Austria, Upper Austria, Inner Austria, and the Tirol. Holy Roman Emperor Rudolf II (r. 1576–1612) ruled directly over the rest, but the Hungarian lands answered to his government in Bratislava (today the capital of Slovakia), and the others to his capital in Prague. Rudolf also held ultimate sovereignty over the entire Holy Roman Empire, which remained divided into more than a thousand separate units, including several large, effectively independent German states, such as Saxony, Brandenburg, and Bavaria. In comparison with these composite monarchies, France held a definite advantage when it came to state building.

REBELLIONS

Yet in France, as in virtually all European states, rulers seeking to increase revenues faced multiple forms of resistance. Institutions from the kingdom's estates to village councils protested any supposed violations of their traditional rights and liberties. Under certain circumstances, moreover, protest could turn into revolt and violence directed against tax collectors and other agents of the central state. In 1593–95, as many as 50,000 peasants in southwestern France joined a rebellion that forced King Henry IV to lighten their tax burden. Similar revolts erupted in France through the first half of the seventeenth century.

In short, Europe at the beginning of the 1600s suffered from a sort of positive feedback loop in which the steadily rising costs of war and overseas ventures put governments under increasing financial strain, which the ongoing economic crisis only worsened. All of this drove them to take increasingly aggressive measures against their neighbors and competitors, which increased the cost of wars and overseas ventures further. Looking at Europe in the first decade of the century, it was all too easy to predict that this pattern might soon lead to a continental conflagration. In 1618 such a conflagration would arrive. But for it to do so, one other crucial factor was required: religious strife.

A NEW SOCIAL DYNAMIC IN RELIGION

The Thirty Years' War of 1618–48, which opposed largely Catholic forces to largely Protestant ones, has frequently been depicted as a direct offshoot of the large-scale, violent fragmentation of Western Christianity that followed the Protestant Reformation. Certainly, both sides had frequent recourse to religious language and imagery. Preaching to Catholic troops before the pivotal battle of White Mountain outside Prague in 1620, a Spanish friar denounced the Protestant forces as heretics, and started a frenzy by displaying an image of the Virgin and Child that the Protestants had supposedly desecrated. The Swedish king Gustavus Adolphus (r. 1611–1632), the great champion of the Protestant cause, wrote to the wavering ruler of Brandenburg: "This is a fight between God and the Devil. If His Grace is with God, he must join me. If he is for the Devil, he must fight me. There is no third way."

Yet it is simply wrong to imagine the war as a direct consequence of religious passions that had burned unchecked since the days of Martin Luther. The initial wars of the Reformation period in Germany ended with the Peace of Augsburg in 1555, which established the principle that all subjects should observe the religion of their ruler. The treaty ushered in a long period of relative tranquility in central Europe—one of the longest in the region's history. Although religious warfare ravaged France between 1562 and 1598, well before it ended the "Politique" party had emerged, which explicitly prized national unity and peace over confessional victory. Throughout the later sixteenth century, despite the principle established at Augsburg, many parts of Europe tolerated both Catholic and Protestant worship. Ordinary people of both faiths often managed to coexist in peace.

RELIGION AND THE DISCIPLINE OF DAILY LIFE

The faiths themselves continued to evolve during the first decades of the century, with effects that stretched well beyond the walls of churches. After the initial conflicts of the Reformation, nearly every church in western and central Europe undertook ambitious missionary efforts aimed at improving the religious knowledge and practices of ordinary men and women. Alarmist reports by clergy to their superiors depicted common people as in danger of falling victim to heresy through ignorance of the church's basic teachings. As an English Calvinist evocatively put it in the 1630s, "You meet with hundreds that had need be taught their very ABC in matters of religion." Both Protestant and Catholic clergy frequently compared European peasants to the "savages" of the Americas and Asia.

ELITES AND COMMONERS One important effect of these new attitudes was to deepen the cultural gulf between social elites and commoners, with elites now abandoning to the "barbaric" lower classes many traditional cultural practices they had previously engaged in themselves such as raucous local festivals. In the course of these shifts, churches on both sides of the confessional divide undertook what amounted to the most intensive educational effort ever aimed at ordinary Europeans. In the western French province of Brittany in the late sixteenth and early seventeenth centuries, the Jesuits conducted hundreds of month-long "missions," each involving a score of priests who spent as many as 8,000 hours instructing the laity in the basic elements of their religion. By 1650, the Jesuit order was teaching 150,000 students every year in 520 separate schools throughout Europe.

Everywhere, the religious authorities sought to impose new forms of social discipline by "reforming" and censoring the cultural practices of ordinary people. These practices ranged from ritual hazing and humiliations, to superstitious or magical beliefs, to bawdy festivals and songs. One favored strategy of the reformers was to write pious new verses for salacious songs. In the Scottish book *Gude and Godlie Ballatis*, published repeatedly between 1567 and 1621, the authors rewrote the main verses of a popular ballad but left the traditional chorus: "Johne, cum kis me now."

Folk Culture Flemish peasants take part in a *charivari*—a ritual intended to shame and humiliate members of the community who engaged in antisocial behavior, such as having an affair—in this seventeenth-century oil painting.

An unexpected effect of these missions was to foster the development of Europe's many minority languages, some of which had never existed in written form. The first important printed texts in Slovene were Protestant religious tracts from the 1580s. The Protestant emphasis on the believer's encounter with scripture led to the publication of the first New Testament in Welsh in 1567. On the Catholic side, where religious education remained mostly oral, the late sixteenth and early seventeenth centuries saw the publication of the first printed dictionaries and grammars in languages such as Breton and Basque, to serve clergy who wanted to preach in the native language of their flocks. A 1641 catechism from the French city of Toulouse, written in the local Occitan language, put the matter eloquently: "The poor of this country should be able to say, like the poor of other nations . . . : 'we dare to speak in our own language of the grandeurs of God and of the articles of our Faith.'"

THE CHURCH AND EVANGELIZATION These missionary activities had mixed results. Reports from clergy continued to lament the extent of ignorance and superstition throughout the early seventeenth century. Yet it was also the case that the Catholic Church, overall, tended to have greater success than either the Lutherans or the Calvinists. One reason was that for Protestants, true religious knowledge required literacy and the reading of scripture, and most of Protestant Europe, particularly in rural areas, simply lacked the necessary educational infrastructure. There were exceptions. In Sweden, by the later seventeenth century, literacy rates (at least measured by catechism-reading tests) had reached 50 percent, although some of the "literate" may simply have memorized the answers. Urban areas also did well, with adults in Amsterdam, for instance, having a 57 percent literacy rate by 1630.

The Catholic Church, by contrast, attached little importance to literacy, actively discouraged the reading of scripture by ordinary people, and was far more ready to simplify the beliefs and practices it demanded of them. In the southern Netherlands, the religious authorities specifically instructed local priests on the need for an "uncomplicated faith." Instructions to the clergy in the French city of Lyon urged priests to demand nothing more of their flocks than a knowledge of basic prayers, the Ten Commandments, and a short catechism. The Jesuit order, and many others in the Church, promoted a theology that tried to smooth over the complexities of Christian doctrine on the subject of salvation. Saint Augustine had taught that God predestines certain people for salvation and others for damnation, a doctrine that Luther and Calvin had

Expulsion of Moriscos A seventeenth-century Spanish painting shows Moriscos boarding ships bound for North Africa at the port of Vinaros, on the eastern coast of Spain.

developed further. In place of this teaching, Jesuit theologians insisted that men and women have the free will to choose between the paths of sin and salvation.

THE INQUISITION In much of Europe, the Church also backed up its evangelizing efforts with the threat of correction by its tried-and-true instrument for enforcing religious conformity and rooting out heresy: the Inquisition. The Spanish Empire counted no fewer than twenty-two separate Inquisition courts, which together handled 150,000 cases between 1550 and 1700. Some 75 percent of them concerned religious deviance; the remainder dealt with moral offenses such as adultery. Surviving documents suggest that at least 4,000 cases resulted in death sentences, with perhaps 2,000 actual executions. In another sign of increasing intolerance of anything that deviated from orthodox Catholic worship, in 1609 King Philip III of Spain ordered the expulsion of the Moriscos to North Africa. These Christian descendants of Spanish Muslims, now dispersed throughout the kingdom, were suspected of practicing the Islamic faith in secret, or of preserving vestiges of it.

RELIGION AND GENDER On both sides of western Europe's confessional divide, these changes in the religious sphere had important implications for women and their relations with men. Among Protestants, the need for all believers to read and understand scripture continued to drive efforts to provide primary education for both sexes, and the number of girls attending school in the Dutch Republic and Protestant Germany rose significantly. But the reform of popular cultural practices often involved more stringent control over sexuality, and particularly female sexuality. Typical of the new spirit was a 1615 pamphlet by an English fencing master entitled *The Arraignment of Lewd, Idle, Forward, and Unconstant Women*. "Betwixt their breasts is the vale of destruction, and in their beds there is hell, sorrow, and repentance," the author warned his readers. Yet such outbursts were met with responses from women. including one named Rachel Speght, a well-educated Calvinist from London, who attacked this particular pamphlet and its author. She recalled Protestantism's promise that a man and a woman could find terrestrial happiness in a companionate marriage based on mutual respect. "Marriage," she put it eloquently, "is this world's Paradise, where there is mutual love."

WITCH TRIALS Such attempts to control sexuality helped feed a continuation of the European "witch craze" that had begun in the sixteenth century. The persecutions reached a height in the decades around 1600, above

Girls' Education At the Maison de St. Cyr, the first formal girls' school in France, girls were taught domestic arts as well as scripture. The students are learning to spin yarn in this seventeenth-century illustration, while the nuns, who ran the establishment, supervise.

all in Germany. In southwestern Germany alone, more than 300 witch trials took place between 1570 and 1630, leading to some 2,500 executions. Roughly four-fifths of those accused of witchcraft in the seventeenth century, and an even higher proportion of those put to death, were women. The persecutions often occurred in areas where one church or another had just established full control, and they tended to accompany precisely the sorts of intensive missionary enterprises that both Catholic and Protestant churches conducted. The torture and trials of suspected female witches were often highly sexualized, with investigators publicly stripping the accused to search their bodies for the devil's mark. The accused French witch Catherine Boyraionne was poked with needles to expose her mark, and died after her torturer poured burning lard into places it could be hidden.

THE CONTINUING CATHOLIC RECONQUEST

Although both Protestant and Catholic Europe experienced similar attempts at evangelization and social control in the early seventeenth century, the period also saw the continuation of the Catholic Reformation begun fifty years before. In 1590, Protestantism had commanded allegiance in roughly half of Europe west of Muscovy and the Ottoman Empire. In addition to Scandinavia, Britain, and northern Germany, it was a significant presence in France and the Habsburg German lands. Poland had hundreds of Protestant churches.

Two decades later, Protestant numbers across Europe had shrunk considerably. True, the highly disciplined Calvinists tended to be more resilient than the Lutherans, especially in Germany. In the Palatinate, a state in western Germany, Elector Frederick III (r. 1559–1576) had already converted to Calvinism from Lutheranism, and in the years around 1600 several other small Lutheran states followed suit. The numbers of Calvinist believers probably rose during this period. But in general, Protestants were increasingly on the defensive, which would quickly help to destabilize international politics.

CIVIL STRIFE

The fact that both the Protestant and Catholic populations had at least somewhat deeper religious knowledge and greater religious discipline than in earlier periods would prove highly conducive to religious militancy and even fanaticism. But many other factors could threaten the stability of states in these decades of crisis. Even as Catholicism and Protestantism continued to compete for authority in western Europe, large-scale civil strife shook the eastern part of the continent.

INSTABILITY IN MUSCOVY AND THE OTTOMAN EMPIRE

As seen in Chapter 11, soon after the death of Tsar Ivan IV (Ivan the Terrible) in 1584, effective power passed to his son-in-law, Boris Godunov (r. 1598–1605). Tsar Boris fought off attacks by Muslim Tatars from the southeast and continued Ivan's policy of imperial expansion into Siberia. But during the great famine of 1601–3, his authority weakened. He defeated a challenge from the powerful boyar (high-ranking noble) Fedor Romanov, whom he forced to become a monk. But in 1604 a Polish-backed army invaded, led by a man claiming to be Ivan the Terrible's younger son, Dmitri (who had actually died in 1591). In the ensuing turmoil, Boris himself died of illness, and Muscovy descended into a decade of chaos, featuring the tragicomic appearance of no fewer than nineteen further "false Dmitris" claiming the throne. A degree of order returned only when Michael Romanov, son of Fedor, became tsar in 1613, beginning a dynasty that would last three centuries. But Muscovy—now becoming known as Russia—lost considerable territory in what is now Belarus and Ukraine to Poland-Lithuania and along the Baltic

Wars in Muscovy   In an episode characteristic of the instability in Muscovy in the early seventeenth century, Polish forces captured Vasili Shuisky, one of the many claimants to the Muscovite throne, and forced him to pay allegiance to the Polish king. In 1611, an Italian engraver imagined the scene of Vasili before the *Sejm*.

coast to Sweden, and its population declined by as much as a quarter between 1600 and 1620.

Although Muscovy set a high standard when it came to internal instability, the other great eastern power, the Ottoman Empire, offered some worthy competition. At its height in the mid-sixteenth century, the Ottoman sultans ruled some 15 million people across three continents. It won repeated victories over Christian powers, including a major victory over Poland-Lithuania in 1620–21. But the impressive Ottoman achievements in developing an efficient system of government administration—a crucial factor in their continuing military successes—coexisted periodically with brutal struggles for power at the highest level. Sultan Murad III (r. 1574–1595) had at least forty-nine children, and when his son Mehmet III (r. 1595–1603) succeeded to the throne, he followed Ottoman tradition by murdering all possible competitors, including many of his half brothers and at least twenty of his half sisters. He did so, in all likelihood, at the instigation of his Venetian mother, Sophia, who remained the power behind the throne until Mehmet's own death eight years later, in 1603. Over the next twenty years, the Ottoman Empire also descended into large-scale civil conflict, with one sultan deposed two separate times and another murdered. Famine and plague struck, and one chronicler wrote that "such hardship and misery appeared that it was thought the Day of Judgment had arrived or that it meant death for the entire people." Over the decades after 1620, Ottoman rulers would attempt again to reform the state, with considerable success, but uprisings and assassinations continued.

POLAND AND SWEDEN

The lands that bordered the Baltic Sea were not spared from civil strife either. Here, the dominant states were Poland and Sweden. The former, as we have seen, had expanded successfully towards the east and formally entered into a union with Lithuania in 1569. The latter, over the course of the sixteenth century, had emerged from under the shadow of Danish monarchs and German trading leagues to become a significant regional power. Then, in 1592, Poland's King Sigismund III (r. 1587–1632) inherited the Swedish throne, apparently putting the two states on the road to political union. But this brooding, artistically minded Catholic monarch failed to gain much support in Protestant Sweden, and his uncle and regent there, Charles, took advantage of the situation to seize real power, leading to decades of warfare between the two countries. Meanwhile, Sigismund's attempts to raise

Polish taxes and limit the authority of the representative body, the *Sejm,* led to a major noble revolt that lasted from 1605 to 1607. The revolt failed to overthrow the King, but nonetheless weakened the power of the monarchy to the advantage of the noble class. Since the late sixteenth century, this class had enjoyed the so-called "Golden Freedoms" that allowed it to elect the king and conferred large powers on the *Sejm,* in which individual nobles could veto legislation, including on taxation. Over the course of the following decades—indeed, into the eighteenth century—these freedoms would make it difficult for the Polish state to build up its military and administrative capacities, and to compete effectively with its principal rivals.

FRANCE

Western Europe as well was not spared from violence, even before the Thirty Years' War that began in 1618. France, which had just emerged from the worst civil war in its history, soon faced the prospect of renewed internal conflict. Under Henry IV (r. 1589–1610), a popular and effective king who worked with his chief minister, the duke of Sully, to improve the country's finances, France did enjoy a period of prosperity. In Paris, Henry sponsored several large projects that aimed to let light and air into the dark, narrow, foul-smelling medieval streets. Among them was the wide Pont Neuf (New Bridge) across the river Seine, the first bridge in the city not lined with houses. But in May 1610, a Catholic zealot stabbed the king to death, leaving his sickly eight-year-old son Louis XIII as the new king, and royal power in the hands of his Italian widow, Marie de' Medici. Over the next four years, Marie governed in her

Urban Improvements An architect's rendering of the Pont Neuf from 1577—shortly before construction began on the bridge—shows its stone arches standing out against the backdrop of the city.

son's name as regent and asserted his absolute authority in uncompromising terms, provoking a revolt by resentful grandees in 1615. Just when Marie seemed about to vanquish them, Louis demonstrated his independence by having her favorite counselor, a fellow Italian, murdered. Louis himself was an easily-influenced and indecisive man, but powerful ministers managed to introduce far-reaching changes to French government during his reign.

TENSIONS IN THE GERMAN LANDS

It was in the lands of the Holy Roman Empire, where early-seventeenth-century tensions had the most tragic and long-lasting ramifications. Before 1618 these lands saw much less actual violence, but they experienced a dangerous increase in religious conflict. This conflict challenged the stability of the Habsburg dynasty, which ruled its own collection of smaller territories while also providing the Holy Roman Empire with a long string of emperors. Back in 1599, Ferdinand of Styria, the young archduke of Inner Austria (1578–1637) and student of the Jesuits, expelled all Protestants from his lands. Holy Roman Emperor Rudolf II generally took a more conciliatory line, but found himself dragged into religious conflict against his will, time after time. A man subject to deep depressions, Rudolf had a deep fascination for the occult, for alchemy, and for esoteric wisdom. He dreamed of helping to forge a humanist "third way" that would move beyond both Catholicism and Protestantism. Yet in 1607 and 1609 he allowed the Catholics to retake several Protestant territories, provoking the formation of a defensive Protestant Union, which in time spurred the creation of a rival Catholic League.

Even as the religious conflict developed, the Habsburg dynasty itself was hobbled by vicious feuding, particularly between the childless Rudolf and his aggressive younger brother Matthias, Archduke of Upper Austria (1557–1612). Despite Rudolf's opposition, in 1606 the other Habsburg archdukes recognized Matthias as the heir to the Holy Roman throne. Over the next five years Matthias, who shared his brother's lack of religious enthusiasm, allied himself with powerful Protestant aristocrats, who helped him successfully claim the crowns of both Hungary and Bohemia. In return, he made significant political and religious concessions to these Protestants. A resurgent Catholicism therefore found itself facing off, throughout the empire, against a newly emboldened Protestant nobility, without being able to count on support from the supposed leaders of German Catholicism. Rudolf, driven further into insanity by his brother's successes, died a gibbering wreck in early 1612, but Matthias himself was already aging and ill.

Matters soon came to a head. Holy Roman emperors were elected, but sons generally succeeded fathers. Matthias, like Rudolf, was childless, so the question of succession again presented itself acutely. In 1617 the fervently Catholic Archduke Ferdinand came to a secret agreement with the Spanish Habsburgs to sponsor his candidacy for the imperial throne. He took the first step by winning election as king of Bohemia. With his support, the Catholic Bohemian government took aggressive measures against Protestants in the kingdom, provoking widespread protests and fear.

THE THIRTY YEARS' WAR

On the morning of May 23, 1618, some 200 Protestant deputies from the Estates of Bohemia burst into Prague's royal palace and rushed to a high floor where four Catholic members of Ferdinand's "regency council" were working. The Protestants angrily accused them of attacking Bohemian liberties and Protestant rights. They then opened the windows and threw two of the counselors out of the tower, followed by a secretary who very unwisely protested. All three men luckily fell into piles of garbage and survived, and the secretary was later rewarded with the noble title of Freiherr von Hohenfall (Lord of the High Fall). News of the event, known as the **Defenestration of Prague**, rapidly spread across Europe. Fighting broke out almost immediately in Bohemia itself, with the Protestant estates and their allies scoring several quick victories.

The Defenestration of Prague A 1640 engraving captures the chaotic scene of Bohemian Protestants throwing Ferdinand's deputies out of the windows of Prague's royal palace.

The Thirty Years' War, 1618–1648 When war broke out, fighting was confined to the Bohemian lands around Prague, but within a few years, it had spread across the entirety of central Europe. At first, Catholic Habsburg forces were successful, winning the Battle of White Mountain, invading the Palatinate, and reaching as far north as mainland Denmark. But when France and Sweden joined the war in the 1630s, it intensified and escalated—bringing particular devastation to the German states, which saw the bulk of the fighting.

OUTBREAK OF WAR

It was not clear at the start that a general war would follow. The Bohemian Protestants' most obvious allies, the English and Dutch, failed to provide significant aid. England's king, James I, was reluctant to challenge the authority of other rulers. The Dutch were distracted by simmering civil unrest between Calvinist factions. Moreover, they had little desire to break the peace treaty with Spain that they had signed in 1609, which had effectively recognized the Dutch Republic's independence.

Even in Germany, the largely Lutheran Protestant Union attempted to remain neutral.

The Bohemian nobles, however, soon took two decisive steps that made a general war more likely. In July 1619 they began to confiscate Catholic property in the kingdom. And in August they formally voted to depose King Ferdinand just as he was about to become Holy Roman Emperor Ferdinand II (r. 1619–1637), Matthias having died in March. In Ferdinand's place, they elected Frederick V—the twenty-three-year-old Calvinist elector of the Palatinate, and the son-in-law of England's James I—as King Frederick

I of Bohemia. This was a revolutionary and provocative step, as a Palatine official clearly recognized: "Let everyone prepare at once for a war lasting twenty, thirty or forty years. The Spaniards and the House of Austria will deploy all their worldly goods to recover Bohemia."

The Spanish did come to the aid of their Austrian cousins, and in August 1620 an army marched from the Spanish Netherlands deep into the Palatinate. The first battle of the Thirty Years' War took place just a few months later, at the White Mountain outside of Prague. Spanish and Catholic German forces, 27,000 men strong, attacked and destroyed a much smaller Protestant army while losing only 800 soldiers of their own. Soon most of Bohemia had fallen to the Catholics.

As the king of Sweden commented several years later, "All the wars that are afoot in Europe have become one war." Indeed, in the decade after the battle of White Mountain, the whirlpool of conflict centered on Bohemia dragged in one major power after another. The Thirty Years' War had begun.

HABSBURG VICTORIES

In 1621, with the Spanish Habsburgs already deeply involved in the war, the twelve-year truce between Spain and the Dutch Republic expired, and the Dutch came into the war as well on the side of the Protestant powers. The Spanish, by this point, recognized that it would be "seeking the impossible," in the words of Philip III's chief minister, to reconquer the powerful, prosperous Netherlands. But they also feared that a continuation of the truce would allow the Dutch further to develop their Atlantic trade to Spain's detriment, and to aid Spain's enemies in Italy.

The Habsburgs followed up their victory at the White Mountain with other successes. They occupied most of Bohemia and dealt harshly with its Protestant population. The Austrians and Spanish overran the Palatinate and forced Frederick into exile. Denmark, still a major Lutheran power, tried to stem the Catholic tide but failed. In 1628 a Catholic army led by the Bohemian noble Albrecht von Wallenstein (1583–1634) marched all the way to the Baltic, ultimately occupying all of mainland Denmark and forcing the Danes to sign a humiliating peace treaty. Wallenstein, who proved to be a superb organizer and military entrepreneur, was rewarded with a rich northern German duchy and briefly became one of the dominant and ambitious figures in central Europe before being assassinated by Habsburg officers after he came under suspicion of treason to the Habsburg cause.

But the more victories the Habsburgs won, the more they overreached. In March 1629 Emperor Ferdinand II signed the **Edict of Restitution**, which returned to the Catholic Church all the church property in the Holy Roman Empire that had come into Protestant hands since 1552. Over a hundred convents were forcibly "restituted" in this way, along with many large tracts of land. Nothing could have been better calculated to inflame Protestant fears across Europe. Wallenstein himself warned that the edict would "turn the entire Empire against us."

Within two years, the war had sucked in two additional major powers. France had remained relatively aloof during the 1620s, distracted by peasant revolts, murderous feuding between noble factions, and a major rebellion by French Calvinists that Louis XIII's government managed to contain only with great difficulty. But by 1631 the French crown had gone a long way toward reestablishing its authority, thanks in large part to Louis's brilliant chief minister, Cardinal Richelieu (1585–1642), who, when it came to the larger European war, placed French dynastic interest above confessional loyalty. Richelieu—though a prelate of the Catholic Church—was anxious to keep the Habsburgs from achieving total dominance over central Europe, and soon began to intervene more actively in the war on the Protestant side. As part of his strategy, he offered Lutheran Sweden large subsidies to join the fight against the Catholic Habsburgs.

SWEDISH AND SPANISH INTERVENTION

Sweden was the other major power whose intervention now changed the face of the conflict. King Gustavus Adolphus (r. 1611–1632) had forged a renewed partnership with the Swedish nobility, and in collaboration with his own brilliant chief minister, Axel Oxenstierna (1583–1664), rapidly built up state finances and the military. Sweden (which now also controlled most of the modern states of Finland, Estonia, and Latvia) gained from the travails of the other major Baltic powers: Russia was still recovering from its civil wars; Poland-Lithuania had recently been defeated by the Ottomans, and Denmark by the Habsburgs.

Despite the legends that cast Gustavus Adolphus as the great champion of the Protestant cause, the king's religious beliefs were not as passionate as those of Frederick of the Palatinate, or Emperor Ferdinand II. But he saw in the war a great opportunity to secure Sweden's new position. In 1630 he seized part of the southern Baltic coast, then pushed deep into Germany. In September 1631 he prevailed in the desperate battle of Breitenfeld, in Saxony, which decisively checked the Catholic "reconquest." A year later he died at the battle of Lützen, leaving the throne to his infant daughter, Christina. The Swedes remained in the war, albeit with less enthusiasm.

In response to these Swedish successes, Spain stepped up its role in the war. In 1621 the Spanish throne had passed to Philip IV (r. 1621–1665), a competent ruler who, unlike his French counterparts, placed the interests of religion above most secular matters. ("There is no affair of state for which the smallest danger to Religion should be adventured," he wrote in 1627.) He relied on the services of yet another enormously ambitious, energetic minister, Gaspar de Gúzman, Count-Duke Olivares (1587–1645), the great rival of Richelieu. Olivares originally focused his efforts on the Netherlands, where Spain's forces retook the key town of Breda in 1624. Then, in 1634, he managed to send a powerful army to Germany that crushed the Swedes, pushing them out of the war altogether. This defeat also forced many of the northern German Protestant states to sue for peace.

Yet, once again, Habsburg victories led to a strong reaction, pushing France to commit its own forces fully to the conflict on the Protestant side, beginning hostilities with Spain that would last for more than a decade beyond the general European conflict of the Thirty Years' War. French finances squealed under the strain, forcing Richelieu to double the principal French tax, the *taille*, between 1635 and 1643, which provoked violent resistance throughout the country. Spanish finances suffered even more, and Spain met with several important defeats. The Dutch briefly captured much of Brazil from the Spanish Empire in the early 1630s, and then won a major naval victory in 1639. By 1640, when revolts broke out against Philip IV in both Portugal and Catalonia, Spain—despite the expansion of its holdings in North America and Asia—was at the breaking point. While the war would last another eight years, the Habsburgs would never again come close to true victory, let alone regaining the dominant European position they had enjoyed under Charles V a century earlier.

ATROCITIES AND MASS DEATH

As the fighting escalated, it took an increasingly hideous toll on civilian populations. Even by the bloody standards of early modern European warfare, the Thirty Years' War quickly gained a reputation for atrocity. In 1637, to take an example almost at random, the Estates of Niederhessen, in central Germany, accused imperial Bavarian troops of raping women, throwing children into hot ovens, cutting

Horrors of the Thirty Years' War Jacques Callot's 1633 series of prints "The Miseries and Misfortunes of War" includes this famous image of soldiers hanging dozens of people.

off noses, ears, tongues, and breasts, and pouring molten lead or tin into mouths. Massacres were a regular occurrence. One of the worst occurred in May 1631 when the German city of Magdeburg was sacked by imperial forces. As many as 30,000 people—three-quarters of the city's population—died. The French printmaker Jacques Callot recorded the horrors allegedly committed by his country's troops in his 1633 series of etchings, "The Miseries and Misfortunes of War"—most famously a "hanging tree" with a score of corpses dangling from its branches.

In most cases, it is impossible to tell which atrocities actually happened and which were exaggerated or even invented by propagandists and fiction-writers. But it is clear that the Thirty Years' War led to a breakdown of order on an unprecedented scale, not simply exposing civilians to violence but destroying homes, disrupting harvests, and facilitating the spread of famine and plague, even as average temperatures probably dropped to their lowest point in the Little Ice Age. The overall demographic consequences were catastrophic. Between 1618 and 1648, the population of the Holy Roman Empire seems to have fallen at least 30 percent, from 15 million people to fewer than 11 million. Some areas suffered even more, including Pomerania on the Baltic coast, Württemberg in the southwest, and Bohemia, where losses exceeded 40 percent.

This astonishing loss of life resulted in part from the nature of early-seventeenth-century armed forces. These were no longer the relatively small, long-serving, largely mercenary groups that characterized so much of warfare in the Renaissance, before the revolution in military discipline and tactics described above. They were often of unprecedented size—Gustavus Adolphus's invasion force of the early 1630s numbered roughly 175,000 soldiers—and contained an uneasy mix of mercenaries, professional recruits, and (especially in the Swedish army) conscripts.

THE SACK OF MAGDEBURG

A mostly Protestant trade center in the central German state of Saxony, the city of Magdeburg declared for the Swedish emperor Gustavus Adolphus when he invaded northern Germany to support the Protestant cause. In 1631, the army of the Catholic League general Count von Tilly—some 20,000 unpaid and hungry soldiers dependent on plunder for survival—sacked the city. With neither wealth to bribe soldiers nor rank to command protection, Magdeburg's common citizens faced slaughter by the conquering soldiers. Otto von Guericke, a scholar and later mayor of Magdeburg, survived the invasion and recorded the chaos and violence.

[When] the city was lost…[there was] nothing but murder, burning, plundering, torment, and beatings. In particular, each of the enemies sought more and greater booty. When such a party of looters entered a house and the head of the household had something he could give them, then he could use this to save and preserve himself and his family until another soldier, who also wanted something, came along. Finally there was nothing left to give, then the misery really began.

For then the soldiers began to beat and threaten to shoot, skewer, hang, etc., the people, so that even if something had been buried under the earth or locked away behind a thousand locks, the citizens would still have been forced to seek it out and hand it over. Through such enduring fury…many thousands of innocent men, women and children were, with horrid, fearful screams of pain and alarm, miserably murdered and wretchedly executed in manifold ways, so that no words can sufficiently describe it. As to the common craftspeople, day laborers, servants, and apprentices, as well as soldiers who had served on the side of the Swedes and the city and could give nothing, they had to carry the booty and bundles of the enemy for a while, to do all kinds of service for them, or even to join the enemy's service, and so be supported by them. However, things went very badly for many of those women, girls, daughters, and maids who either had no men, parents, or relatives who could pay a ransom on their behalf, or could not appeal to high officers for help or advice; some were defiled and disgraced, and some were kept as concubines.

However, there were also many who similarly had no friends or no means, but who still, amazingly, kept their honor—partially due to honorable soldiers who, by dint of the decency of those they had taken prisoner, simply let them free or even married them.

QUESTIONS FOR ANALYSIS

1. How did wealth and influence help some inhabitants of Magdeburg survive the slaughter?
2. How might the besieging troops' need for plunder have driven some of the violence in Magdeburg?
3. Why were women especially vulnerable to violence in the sack of the city?

Source: Tryntje Helfferich, ed. and trans., *The Essential Thirty Years War: a Documentary History* (Indianapolis: 2015), pp. 47–49.

But they had not yet become the uniformed, tightly disciplined, professionally commanded, and relatively well-supplied armies of the eighteenth century. And they certainly did not receive regular pay. Simply to stay alive—and to provide for the wives, children, prostitutes, servants, and laborers who followed in their baggage trains, sometimes numbering in the tens of thousands—soldiers often had no choice but to plunder. As one historian has concisely put it, "Abuse did not simply undermine the system; abuse *was* the system." These conditions guaranteed that soldiers and civilians would see each other as enemies, even when they were supposedly on the same side.

WAR AND ABSOLUTISM

A war that caused this degree of devastation, lasted so long, and involved such huge armies and expenditures, forced all the states that participated to seek new ways of mobilizing their resources. We have already seen that throughout Europe rulers faced severe constraints—especially in this period of economic decline—in their ability to raise all-important tax revenues. They depended on the cooperation of their most powerful subjects to carry out most of the business of government, including tax collection. These subjects in turn enjoyed well-established privileges, including (for nobles and clergy) exemptions from many forms of taxation. Rulers could only challenge them at the risk of upsetting a delicate political balance and provoking revolts. Moreover, in most cases rulers had little desire to undermine such practices because they shared the culture and outlook of the aristocrats and prelates, participated in court life with them, and often considered themselves the "first gentlemen" of their realms. As a result, before the 1630s, when European rulers sought fiscal innovations, they generally tried to disguise them as mere expansions of supposedly "traditional" practices such as venality of office or England's "ship money."

BREAKS WITH PRECEDENT

Yet such were the pressures of the Thirty Years' War that many monarchs now attempted to bypass institutions such as estates and parliaments altogether, overrule the complaints of powerful nobles, and funnel revenue directly to the central state. These moves did not involve crushing nobilities in favor of the rising middle classes, as historians once assumed. They did not imply the wholesale elimination of traditional political institutions or the assumption of tyrannical, arbitrary powers by sovereigns. But they did imply the recognition of a monarch's absolute and indivisible sovereignty, and therefore reflect the political trend generally referred to as **absolutism**.

These breaks with precedent were not seen to the same extent everywhere. In Poland, where, as we have seen, King Sigismund Vasa (r. 1587–1632) had failed to limit the powers of the Sejm in the early seventeenth century, the king remained heavily dependent on his most powerful nobles. The Austrian Habsburg lands, meanwhile, were so fragmented and war-torn that the dynasty had to rely on military entrepreneurs to undertake the mobilization of resources that absolutist governments accomplished in other states. The most significant moves toward absolutism in the smaller German and Italian states tended to come after the middle of the seventeenth century.

POWERFUL MINISTRIES

In the major states of western Europe, however, important changes were already under way. Those driving the changes were most often not the rulers themselves, but powerful ministers: Oxenstierna in Sweden, Olivares in Spain, and above all Richelieu in France. They tended to have better educations than the monarchs they served, and also more energy to attend to administrative tasks. Olivares famously worked from five in the morning until eleven at night, while the French poet François de Malherbe said of Richelieu, "I swear there is something supernatural about that man." They were all zealous advocates of unquestioned royal authority, and cultivated intimate, intensely emotional relationships with the monarchs they served. They all recognized as well that royal power was something constructed not just through force but through magnificent display, including architecture and works of art. And they all sought ways of clearing out and simplifying the tangle of privileges and institutions that constituted early modern governments.

RICHELIEU Richelieu had the greatest success. Well before he came to power in the 1620s, the French monarchy had begun to send agents known as **intendants** to the provinces with powers to advise, judge, and act as representatives of the king. But in 1635 Richelieu made

Cardinal Richelieu This "Triple Portrait" of Richelieu, painted in 1642, was a sketch for a sculptor who intended to make a bust of the cardinal.

the intendants permanent fixtures in each of France's thirty-odd administrative districts. Over the next few years he granted them extensive powers, particularly over the collection of the principal land tax, the taille. They frequently clashed with local estates and high courts, and made a point of establishing their symbolic preeminence in local processions and church services. The new demands they made for revenue contributed directly to the ongoing peasant revolts, and to a wave of urban protests. But Richelieu did succeed in raising large sums for the central treasury. Gaunt, cunning, and enormously vain, he planned an entire new city (to be named after him) and built a magnificent palace in Paris, where a gallery of paintings of "Great Frenchmen" started with figures from the early Middle Ages and concluded with his own portrait.

OLIVARES Olivares was a more tragic figure. Fat, red-faced, and given to dramatic outbursts, he too understood the importance of magnificent display, notably promoting the career of the painter Diego Velázquez (1599–1660), whose brilliant *Surrender of Breda* (1634–35) depicted the valor and magnanimity of the Spanish in one of their great victories over the Dutch. Despite the vast extent and wealth of the Spanish Empire, Olivares felt that it was hobbled by its patchwork division into different political units, each with its own customs and laws, and he pushed throughout his career for what he called "union and equality in the laws, customs, and forms of government." But while Olivares hoped to establish a more regular, uniform, rational administration, he did not have agents or financial resources adequate to the task. Even the Spanish government's basic knowledge of the kingdom was faulty: for example, it grossly overestimated the population of Catalonia, leading Olivares to demand more in taxes than the province could bear. In 1640 Catalonia revolted, as did Portugal, which had been ruled by the Spanish crown since 1580. Sick and exhausted, Olivares fell from power in 1642, sank into madness, and died three years later.

OXENSTIERNA In northern Europe, fiscal innovations in government took different forms. Oxenstierna in Sweden promoted cooperation between the highest-ranking nobles and the crown, notably in fixing the composition of the Swedish estates (which were henceforth divided among nobles, prelates, commoners, and peasants). His success allowed Sweden to introduce a more intensive system of conscription than any other European power of the time, with some 55,000 men drafted between 1621 and 1632. But Sweden too found it impossible to sustain the necessary level of mobilization, particularly because roughly half of all conscripts could expect to be killed, wounded, or taken prisoner during their military service.

THE DUTCH AND BRITISH EXCEPTIONS

The Dutch Republic was an exception to the continental pattern of government. Each of its seven provinces exercised considerable autonomy and sent deputies to the powerful representative body known as the States General. Although the "stadholders" (essentially, executive officials of the republic) from the House of Orange did manage to extend their powers, they never came close to achieving absolute authority equivalent to that of the French king. But the republic did not need to copy Richelieu to raise the funds necessary for war, thanks to the profits of trade and its innovative new Bank of Amsterdam, which stabilized the currency and national debt. By the end of the century the Dutch had become the chief exporters of guns and other military supplies to the rest of Europe, further adding to the positive side of their balance sheets.

Britain was yet another distinct case. James I, an unusually cultivated monarch, not only believed in the divine right of kings but wrote extensively on the subject. "Kings," he pronounced, "are justly called gods, for that they exercise a manner or resemblance of divine power upon earth." James respected the limited rights of the English Parliament, which sat at his pleasure and could not countermand his decisions. He did depend on the gentry who sat in Parliament to collect his taxes and appropriate funds for military expeditions. But particularly after 1620 they frequently provoked his anger by failing to vote him the money he requested. The most remarkable legacy of this strife was the **Petition of Right** of 1628, in which Parliament declared that only it had the right to levy taxes, that the king could not declare martial law in peacetime, and that prisoners had the right to appeal their detention before a judge or court. These principles remain in the bedrock of Anglo-American government and law to this day.

James's son, the shy and hesitant **Charles I**, inherited his father's quarrels with Parliament and was increasingly attracted to the continental absolutist model. He dissolved three Parliaments in five years when they failed to vote him open-ended funds for the war. From 1629 to 1640, Charles tried to rule without Parliament altogether, raising money through expedients such as ship money. The conflicts raised the possibility of a civil war throughout the British Isles, even as Portuguese and Catalan revolts flared against Spain, the French stumbled toward their own civil war, and the Thirty Years' War approached its climax. While monarchs put on ever more grandiose displays of power, the disorder presaged in *King Lear* was sweeping over Europe in a torrent.

ROYAL POWER AND CULTURE

One way in which Charles's reign in England resembled that of Louis XIII in France and Philip IV in Spain involved his use of architecture and the other arts as an instrument of royal power. Once again, European rulers were reaching back to the example of the Roman emperors who used the arts to glorify themselves and solidify their power. The sheer quantity, size, and expense of the paintings, sculpture, and architecture produced to celebrate the early-seventeenth-century absolutist monarchs dwarfed the commissions of earlier periods. Figures such as Cardinal Richelieu used projects like his portrait gallery and planned city to shape the spaces of artistic display in minute detail, so as to control exactly how onlookers would see and interpret them.

BAROQUE ART

Peter Paul Rubens (1577–1640), a favorite of Charles I, was a brilliant and prolific Flemish painter whose sensual canvases, filled with bright color and movement, conveyed the splendor of monarchs and their courts. Rubens employed easily deciphered allegories to endow his subjects with mythical or divine characteristics. In 1621 the French queen, Marie de' Medici, hired Rubens to paint a grandiose series depicting her life, including the death and ascension to heaven of her husband Henry IV, and her tumultuous relationship with her son, Louis XIII. Fourteen years later, after a spell in Madrid, Rubens went to London, where Charles commissioned him to paint the ceiling of Whitehall Palace's new Banqueting House. The mural centered on the ascension to heaven of the king's father, James I. Rubens received knighthoods from both Spain and England.

Some of the period's best artists kept their distance from the style that Rubens's work exemplified. Notable among them was the French painter Nicolas Poussin (1594–1665), who developed a subdued, precise style. Nevertheless, **Baroque** art, with its dramatic, visceral appeal to the senses, perfectly suited the needs of the rulers who were its patrons. It also suited the needs of the aggressive, post-Reformation Catholic Church. Baroque

Rubens and Marie de' Medici The fourth painting in Rubens' 21-painting cycle about Marie de' Medici, made in 1621–25, shows angels presenting the future queen of France's portrait to King Henri IV. The couple did not meet before their marriage, but exchanged portraits. In this telling, the king reportedly fell in love with Marie at first sight.

works of religious art and architecture, like their secular counterparts, sought to overwhelm viewers—for instance in the grand, undulating church facades constructed by the Swiss-Italian Francesco Borromini (1599–1667). The Jesuits, with their mission of "propagating the faith" by all possible means, eagerly adopted the baroque style for their churches.

The Baroque especially contributed to the development of European sculpture, notably in the work of Gian Lorenzo Bernini (1598–1680). An excellent example is a piece he created for Santa Maria della Vittoria in Rome, a church rededicated to the Virgin Mary after the Catholic triumph at the battle of White Mountain in 1620. The sculpture, which recalls some of the masterpieces of Greek and Roman antiquity, illustrates an episode from the autobiography of Saint Teresa of Avila in which she imagines an angel piercing her heart with a spear, filling her with divine ecstasy. Bernini depicted the saint in a seated position, covered in flowing robes, her mouth open in rapture.

Ecstasy of Saint Teresa Bernini's dramatic sculpture of an angel piercing Saint Theresa's heart displays all the characteristics of the Baroque style: neoclassical forms, flowing fabrics, and expressive figures.

The angel is almost astride her as beams of golden sunlight shower down on them, and the whole composition is set amid lavish expanses of marble and polished stone.

LANGUAGE AND LITERARY CULTURE

Language and literature were just as important as the fine arts for the purposes of political and religious glorification. In 1635 Cardinal Richelieu presided over the foundation of the French Academy to serve as the official authority on the French language. Aiming to create a pure, stable French that could aspire to equality with classical Latin (still the language of scholarship and philosophy), its forty members worked to banish vulgar, mechanical, technical, and foreign terms and phrases from elite usage. When the playwright Pierre Corneille (1606-1684) had a massive success in 1637 with *Le Cid*, a story of medieval Spain whose hero is torn between love and honor, the Academy condemned him for not respecting the "classical unities" of space, time, and action, according to which stage dramas should take place within a single 24-hour period, in a single

place, with one single plot. In his later work, Corneille paid greater heed to the Academy's strictures: a good example of how the state managed to exercise authority over French literature, and to use it as an instrument of its glory.

DON QUIXOTE *Le Cid* itself was based on a Spanish original, and in the early seventeenth century the center of innovation in European literature and art remained very much in the Mediterranean region. In Spain, the period saw the production of some of the country's greatest works—above all the publication (starting in 1605) of Miguel de Cervantes' (1547–1616) *Don Quixote*, widely regarded as the first modern novel. Meandering, playful, full of puns and digressions and switches of perspective, it tells the story of an aging rural gentleman whose mind has been addled by the chivalric romances associated with aristocratic medieval knights. Don Quixote decides to go off on quests, but meets with all manner of pitfalls and humiliations, including a famous scene in which he charges with his lance at windmills that he mistakes for giants.

Don Quixote and the novels that followed it had much the same effect in Spain as Martin Luther's popular theological pamphlets had in Germany: they gave a permanent stamp to the written vernacular language and helped it achieve a more stable form. The genre quickly spread across Europe and was actively promoted for a time by the post-Reformation Catholic Church, which preferred the novel's realism (and the punishments it depicted befalling the wicked) to the sort of romances that had entranced Don Quixote. The only European literature to equal Spain's before 1640 was that of England, where Shakespeare kept writing until his death in 1616 and poets such as John Donne, George Herbert, and the young John Milton found receptive audiences.

POPULAR CULTURE The development of standard vernacular languages that we have seen promoted by both states and churches (above all, Protestant churches), and the flourishing of new genres such as the novel, helped to transform European literary culture more broadly. Although literacy rates remained low, most peasants could find neighbors to read to them, especially in evening village gatherings at which one neighbor might read aloud while others repaired tools, sewed clothing, and took care of children. Only a limited range of printed matter reached rural villages: mostly poorly-bound and poorly-printed religious tracts, almanacs, and small books known as "chapbooks" that consisted in great part of ballads, medieval romances (including, in England, tales of

Arthur and Robin Hood), and medicinal tracts. But while their appearance might be delayed by years or decades, novels and lyric poetry also arrived in chapbook form.

City-dwellers, however, had access to a larger range of printed material, especially in the economically expanding societies of Protestant northern Europe. There, the combination of prosperity and the religious imperative of literacy spurred the development of thriving book markets. In the Netherlands, books took their place alongside housewares as signs of increasing prosperity for merchants, professionals, and well-to-do artisans. It became increasingly popular for portrait painters to depict their subjects—men and women alike—holding books.

Meanwhile, in Italy, another new genre took shape, as attempts to revive classical Greek mixtures of instrumental and vocal music and drama coalesced into what we now know as opera. Based on popular and familiar stories, both sacred and profane, but using a combination of extravagant scenery, dance, and music to provide an impressive sensory experience in keeping with the century's Baroque style, opera quickly gained a popular as well as elite audience, with public opera theaters opening in Venice as early as the 1630s.

PATRONAGE AND ITS LIMITS

The demands of monarchs and patrons continued to influence powerfully the worlds of philosophy, natural philosophy (the origins of what we today call science), and scholarship. The Dutchman Hugo Grotius (1583–1645), one of the greatest political thinkers of the period, began his career writing works that justified the actions of the Dutch Republic in the international realm: a history of its struggle against Spain, a treatise insisting on the freedom of the seas and international trade, and a justification of privateering. Francis Bacon (1561–1626), one of the creators of the modern scientific method, served in a succession of high offices in the English state. The astronomer Galileo Galilei (1564–1642) avidly sought the patronage of Florence's House of Medici, to the point of naming the four moons of Jupiter he discovered after members of the Medici family (the moons ultimately became known by different names).

Yet it would be a mistake to assume that this influence was the determining factor in the period's intellectual developments. The lines of patronage did not always run smooth, as suggested by the fact that Grotius, Bacon, and Galileo all spent time in prison, although for different reasons. Grotius was an ally of the moderate Protestant party in the Dutch Republic and shared in its fall. Bacon was charged by enemies in Parliament with taking bribes in his official government position. As we will see, Galileo was put on trial by the Inquisition because of his defense of the Copernican view of the solar system.

But together, these cases show that important works could be written without direct patronage, or in defiance of powerful interests. It was during a ten-year exile in France that Grotius wrote his most important work, *On the Law of War and Peace* (1625), in which he tried to lay out rules, grounded in natural law, by which states could legitimately go to war, and propose rules for the legitimate conduct of hostilities. The book constituted an obvious, critical commentary on the Thirty Years' War then in progress. "Throughout the Christian world," Grotius commented, "I have observed a lack of restraint in war that even barbarous races should be ashamed of." And although it had little immediate impact, the book built on medieval and Renaissance precedents to become one of the founding works of modern international law.

THE REPUBLIC OF LETTERS

As in the late sixteenth century, the leading intellectual figures of the period, even in the midst of war, engaged in impressively voluminous correspondence with each other, in the still-universal language of scholarship and philosophy that was Latin. In this correspondence, some of it written for eventual publication, they not only exchanged information, engaged in criticism, and provided practical advice and recommendations. Together they built an international community—the so-called **Republic of Letters**—whose judgments were crucial to the success and esteem of individual members. Like any republic, this one had its share of quarrels and corruption. But at its best it defended principles of open, rational inquiry and held it a moral duty to defend and publicize the results, even when they ran contrary to the dictates of established authorities.

The Republic of Letters even proved open to contributions from women, who were excluded from universities and most other formal scholarly venues. For instance, in 1638 the learned Dutch

Anna Maria van Schurman
This 1657 portrait of the Dutch scholar and artist speaks to her accomplishments and involvement in the Republic of Letters. The tower in the background is perhaps a church or university, while a globe, books, paintbrushes, and other scholarly objects surround the portrait.

scholar Anna Maria van Schurman (1607–1678) published a Latin treatise on whether scholarly study befitted a Christian woman. As in the sixteenth century, some women worked as translators, while wealthy women influenced the direction of scholarship through the patronage they provided. Many members of the Republic hoped their researches would ultimately serve the greater glory of God or their royal patrons. As Bacon strikingly put it, "human knowledge and human power meet as one." But these ambitions did not diminish the importance of the standards they established and the subjects of inquiry they undertook.

EARLY STAGES OF THE SCIENTIFIC REVOLUTION

It was in large part under the aegis of the Republic of Letters that, between 1600 and 1640, there took place the crucial early developments in what historians now call the Scientific Revolution.

GALILEO Galileo and Bacon were the most important figures in this revolution. Galileo, born to a wealthy family in Pisa, was a professor at the University of Padua, teaching mathematics, geometry, mechanics, and astronomy. In 1609 he built a telescope, an instrument recently invented in the Netherlands, and began systematic astronomical observations. His discoveries challenged ancient ideas as to the perfect, unchanging nature of the heavens. Notably, he identified sunspots, which not only marred the supposedly pure surface of the sun, but changed over time, and moved in such a way as to suggest that the sun rotated around an axis. Galileo also discovered moons orbiting Jupiter, mapped the surface of the earth's moon, and showed that the sky contained a far greater number of stars than the ancients had suspected, opening the possibility that the universe was infinite in extent.

Galileo's observations of planetary motion also, crucially, confirmed Copernicus's theory that the earth and other planets revolved around the sun. He demonstrated empirically, in other words, that the earth was not the center of the universe, as scientific and religious thinkers had maintained since the time of Ptolemy and Aristotle. Galileo made a host of other observations and experiments, notably proving that all objects, no matter what their weight, fall to earth at the same rate. "Philosophy," he wrote beautifully in 1623,

> is written in this grand book—I mean the universe— which stands continually open to our gaze, but it

Galileo's Telescope The telescope and lens Galileo built in 1609, with which he made his revolutionary observations.

cannot be understood unless one first learns to comprehend the language in which it is written. It is written in the language of mathematics, and its characters are triangles, circles, and other geometric figures, without which it is humanly impossible to understand a single word of it; without these, one is wandering about in a dark labyrinth.

In 1633 the Inquisition condemned Galileo as a heretic for defending the "heliocentric" or sun-centered, vision of the universe, and Galileo reluctantly renounced it.

KEPLER Galileo received crucial support from his correspondent in the Republic of Letters, the German astronomer Johannes Kepler (1571–1630), whose careful calculations revealed that the planets moved around the sun in elliptical orbits. These findings were crucial for suggesting not only that the heavens shared the imperfections of the terrestrial sphere (otherwise the planets should have moved in perfect circles, as Copernicus thought), but obeyed the same basic laws that were found on earth. Kepler himself expressed the point clearly, and with deliberately loaded language: "The machine of the universe is not similar to a divine animated being, but similar to a clock." From the very beginning, then, the scientific revolution revolved around the idea of the machine—both as a metaphor for the universe and as a real-life means of probing its secrets.

GALILEO AND THE INQUISITION

Galileo issued an early defense of his theories in a 1615 letter to the Grand Duchess Christina of Tuscany—the mother of his patron, Cosimo II de' Medici. Christina had expressed misgivings about the Copernican view that the planets orbit a stationary sun, a seeming contradiction of Biblical passages in which the sun moves. Copies of Galileo's letter were widely distributed, but despite his argument that his findings could be reconciled with Catholicism, he was forbidden by the Church in 1616 to continue his heliocentric studies. Galileo initially obeyed this injunction, but the Inquisition placed him on trial for heresy in 1633 following the publication of his *Dialogue Concerning the Two Chief World Systems*, which delved further into Copernican views of the universe.

Galileo, from letter to the Grand Duchess Christina

In this passage, Galileo argues against critics in the Church that it is better to rely on sensory experience than the Bible to reveal the workings of the natural world.

The reason they advance to condemn the opinion of the earth's mobility and sun's stability is this: since in many places in Holy Scripture one reads that the sun moves and the earth stands still, and that Scripture can never lie or err, it follows as a necessary consequence that the opinion of those who want to assert the sun to be motionless and the earth moving is erroneous and damnable....

I think that in disputes about natural phenomena one must begin not with the authority of scriptural passages but with sensory experience and necessary demonstrations. For the Holy Scripture and nature derive equally from the Godhead, the former as the dictation of the Holy Spirit and the latter as the most obedient executrix of God's orders; moreover, to accommodate the understanding of the common people it is appropriate for Scripture to say many things that are different (in appearance and in regard to the literal meaning of the words) from the absolute truth; on the other hand, nature is inexorable and immutable, never violates the terms of the laws imposed upon her, and does not care whether or not her recondite reasons and ways of operating are disclosed to human understanding...and so it seems that a natural phenomenon which is placed before our eyes by sensory experience or proved by necessary demonstrations should not be called into question, let alone condemned, on account of scriptural passages whose words appear to have a different meaning.

The Inquisition, sentence against Galileo

This source details the Inquisition's charge of heresy against Galileo. Faced with the threat of torture and execution, Galileo agreed to disavow his theories.

We say, pronounce, sentence, and declare that you, the above-mentioned Galileo, because of the things deduced in the trial and confessed by you as above, have rendered yourself according to this Holy Office [Inquisition] vehemently suspected of heresy, namely of having held and believed a doctrine which is false and contrary to the divine and Holy Scripture: that the sun is the center of the world and does not move from east to west, and the earth moves and is not the center of the world, and that one may hold and defend as probable an opinion after it has been declared and defined contrary to Holy Scripture. Consequently you have incurred all the censures and penalties imposed and promulgated by the second canons and all particular and general laws against such delinquents. We are willing to absolve you from them provided that first, with a sincere heart and unfeigned faith, in front of us you abjure, curse, and detest the above mentioned errors and heresies, and every other error and heresy contrary to the Catholic and Apostolic Church, in the manner and form we will prescribe to you.

Furthermore, so that this serious and pernicious error and transgression of yours does not remain completely unpunished, and so that you will be more cautious in the future and an example for others to abstain from similar crimes, we order that the book *Dialogue* by Galileo Galilei be prohibited by public edict.

QUESTIONS FOR ANALYSIS

1. According to Galileo, why are sensory experience and demonstrations better tools for observing natural phenomena than scripture?
2. Why does the Inquisition view Galileo's theories as heresy?
3. How do Galileo and the Church differ in their perceptions of the relationship between religion and science?

Sources: *The Galileo Affair*, ed. and trans. Maurice A. Finocchiaro (Berkeley, CA: 1989), pp. 92–3 and 291.

BACON **Francis Bacon** did not share Galileo's readiness to tinker with telescopes and mechanical devices, but in his works—above all, the *Novum Organum* (*New Instrument*) of 1620—he justified the sorts of approaches Galileo employed, using both philosophical rigor and rhetorical skill. Bacon insisted on the importance of empirical research—to go to the facts themselves. One cannot accept ideas simply on the basis of ancient authority, no matter how exalted, he insisted. Investigation should start not with citations from Aristotle or Galen, but with skepticism: "If a man will begin with certainties, he will end in doubts; but if he will be content to begin with doubts, he will end in certainties." These certainties would emerge through a process of induction—finding a general rule that would fit the observed facts. Furthermore, Bacon defended experimentation as the best means to discover the necessary facts. In his wonderful description: "The nature of things betrays itself more readily under the vexations of art than in its natural freedom." It is in Bacon's work that we find the origins of the modern experimental scientific method.

DESCARTES

It was left to a Frenchman, the prolific **René Descartes** (1596–1650), to make scientific skepticism—the systematic questioning of received truths and values—the basis of a radically new philosophical system. In his *Discourse on Method* (1637), Descartes proposed that thinkers had to apply doubt as rigorously as possible, until they reached principles they could not doubt—in the first place, their own existence. In Descartes's famous formulation: *cogito ergo sum*. I think, therefore I am. Then, from first principles, one could deduce more complex ideas, on the model of mathematicians constructing logical proofs. It was a method at odds with Bacon's project of starting with the observation of facts and then inducing principles from them.

Descartes made the "dualist" argument that the entire universe was composed of two basic substances, mind and matter, and that all visible phenomena, in keeping with Kepler's earlier observations, fell into the latter category. He believed that the visible universe necessarily obeyed universal, knowable laws that human beings could discover by proper observation and reasoning. Descartes in no way denied the existence of God. But his work proposed that if God created the universe and set it in motion—like a giant, infinitely complex machine—then he did not need to involve himself to keep it functioning thereafter. Not surprisingly, Descartes feared persecution from the Christian churches, particularly after the condemnation of Galileo. He lived much of his life as a wandering scholar, spending twenty years in a succession of Dutch towns and eventually serving as tutor to Queen Christina of Sweden, Gustavus Adolphus's daughter.

Even before Descartes, the consequences of the so-called New Philosophy were becoming evident to many observers. In 1611, the poet John Donne wrote:

> And New Philosophy calls all in doubt . . .
> 'Tis all in pieces, all coherence gone;
> All just supply, and all Relation.

It was just five years since Shakespeare had the bastard Edmund proclaim, "Thou, nature, art my goddess." But the proponents of the New Philosophy could not have differed more from Shakespeare's villain in *King Lear*. For where Edmund delighted in the collapse of a traditional order into chaos, they looked to the apparent chaos of the universe and found order in universal laws that could be discovered through observation and experimentation.

CONCLUSION

Although, in the early seventeenth century, the "New Philosophy" mattered principally to what we would now call "intellectuals," it had implications that stretched far beyond the intellectual realm. In the following decades, its proponents would explore the way that laws of nature could be applied to change the face of the world, while beginning to think that the same process of discovery they had initiated in the physical world might have a counterpart in human society as well. In principal, therefore, it might be possible to develop forms of political and social engineering to overcome the uncontrolled, violent forms of competition that had seemed, at so many points between 1600 and 1640, on the point of entirely engulfing the continent.

In this sense, the proponents of the New Philosophy had much in common with the architects of Europe's emerging absolutist monarchies, who also sought to rein in unbridled competition and channel social and political activity into more rational, harmonious forms. Yet the forces of disorder were still far from being vanquished. In the mid-seventeenth century they would prompt additional explosions of civil strife across Europe. Indeed, the combination of new and continuing conflicts between 1640 and 1680 would seem, to some, to herald nothing less than the end of the world. Would the new political and intellectual techniques for ordering the world allow Europeans to overcome these challenges?

KEY TERMS

composite monarchies (p. 411)

Little Ice Age (p. 411)

triangle trade (p. 415)

mercantilism (p. 415)

ship money (p. 419)

venality of office (p. 420)

Defenestration of Prague (p. 426)

Edict of Restitution (p. 428)

absolutism (p. 431)

intendants (p. 431)

Petition of Right (p. 432)

Charles I (p. 432)

Baroque (p. 433)

Republic of Letters (p. 435)

Francis Bacon (p. 438)

René Descartes (p. 438)

REVIEW QUESTIONS

1. What were the causes of the economic hardships in some areas of Europe and progress in others?

2. What obstacles did early European settlements in North America face?

3. How did new technologies and tactics change the nature of western warfare in the 1600s?

4. What changes in Catholicism and Protestantism led to an increasing control of women?

5. What developments led to the outbreak of the Thirty Years' War?

6. Why did the Thirty Years' War expand beyond Bohemia to involve Protestant and Catholic forces across Europe?

7. How did the Thirty Years' War promote the growth of royal absolutism?

8. Why did royal ministers emerge as such strong figures in this period?

9. How did developments in art and literature relate to political changes?

10. What were the key breakthroughs during the early Scientific Revolution?

CORE OBJECTIVES

After reading this chapter, you should have a solid understanding of the following core objectives. To strengthen your grasp of the core objectives, use the resources on the Student Site for The West.

- Analyze the environmental and economic changes that affected European society in the early seventeenth century.

- Describe the evolution of European states in the first half of the seventeenth century.

- Trace the changes in religious education and practices before the Thirty Years' War.

- Assess the political instability across Europe leading up to the Thirty Years' War.

- Evaluate the events, patterns, and consequences of the Thirty Years' War.

- Describe the artistic, intellectual, and scientific innovations of the early seventeenth century.

 GO TO **inQuizitive** TO SEE WHAT YOU'VE LEARNED—AND LEARN WHAT YOU'VE MISSED—WITH PERSONALIZED FEEDBACK ALONG THE WAY.

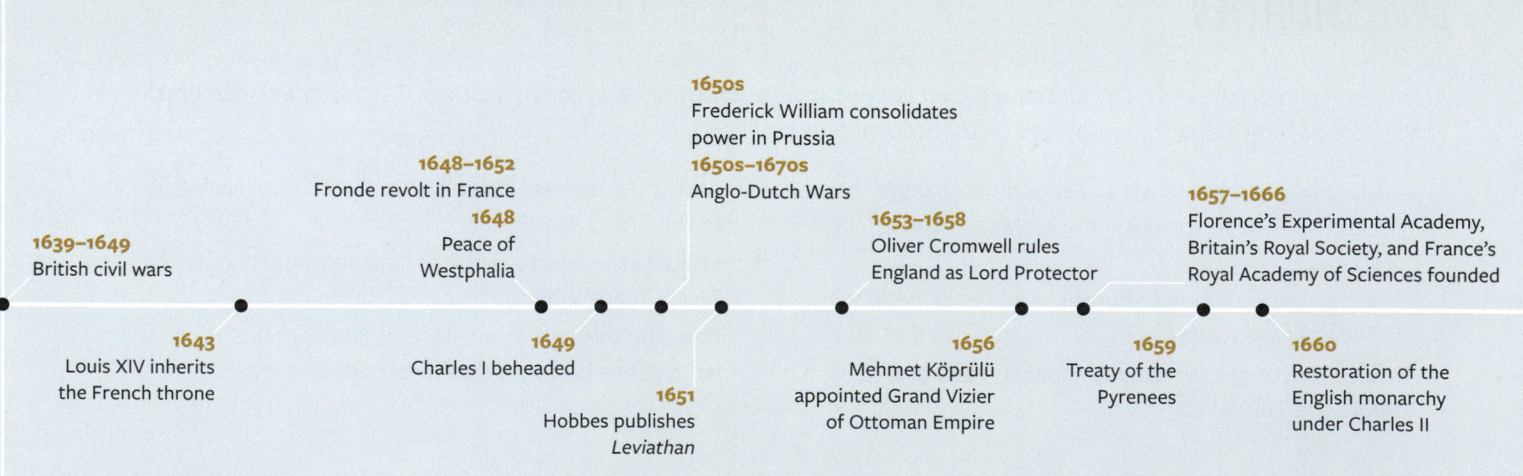

CHRONOLOGY

1650s
Frederick William consolidates
power in Prussia

1648–1652
Fronde revolt in France
1648
Peace of
Westphalia

1650s–1670s
Anglo-Dutch Wars

1653–1658
Oliver Cromwell rules
England as Lord Protector

1657–1666
Florence's Experimental Academy,
Britain's Royal Society, and France's
Royal Academy of Sciences founded

1639–1649
British civil wars

1643
Louis XIV inherits
the French throne

1649
Charles I beheaded

1651
Hobbes publishes
Leviathan

1656
Mehmet Köprülü
appointed Grand Vizier
of Ottoman Empire

1659
Treaty of the
Pyrenees

1660
Restoration of the
English monarchy
under Charles II

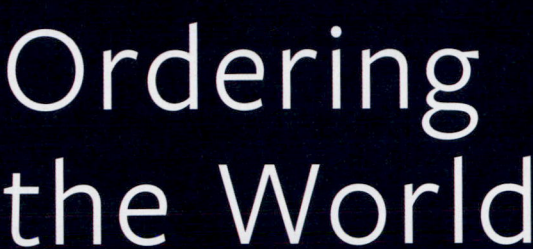

Ordering the World

NEW FORMS OF AUTHORITY AND KNOWLEDGE

1640–1680

1666
Great Fire destroys much of London

1672
Dutch "disaster year" leads to civil war
1672–1678
Louis XIV's Dutch War

The painting shows a scene so unexceptional as to be almost banal: two children playing cards, the gap-toothed girl grinning as she displays her winning ace. True, the Dutch artist Dirck Hals (1591–1656) probably intended the picture to bear some moral weight. Dutch Protestant culture frowned on gambling, and the children's apparently innocent merriness can be seen as dramatically heightening the contrast with the cards themselves, suggesting the unnerving ease with which such tempting instruments of perdition can ensnare even the least likely victims. Yet at the same time, the artist's skill in capturing childhood as a distinct stage of life—from the happily disheveled clothing and hair, to the relaxed poses, to the detail, taken entirely for granted, of a chair suitable only for a young child—tells against this dark interpretation. Only the most hard-hearted of observers could look at the painting and see nothing but the devil at work.

Such depictions of ordinary life—executed in brilliant detail, from the buttons on a dress to the sheen on the scales of a dead fish—pervade Dutch painting of the seventeenth century. More than any previous school of art, Dutch painters of the country's so-called Golden Age—from talented journeymen such as Dirck Hals to masters such as Rembrandt and Vermeer—devoted themselves to meticulous renderings of the world around them. The streets, canals, marketplaces, and taverns of Amsterdam and other Dutch cities; the rooms where women spun and cooked, and children played; the places of government

---

Children Playing Cards Dirck Hals's detailed picture of a mundane scene is a characteristically Dutch view into daily life in the mid-seventeenth century.

- What lasting changes were brought about by the British civil wars?
- What was the significance of civil strife in the continental states of western and eastern Europe?
- What new religious movements proved important in this period?
- How were Europeans beginning to rethink the foundations of political authority?
- How did the Peace of Westphalia represent a new direction for Europe?
- How did absolutism seek to establish order in state and society?
- How did Britain and the Netherlands foster new forms of political and economic organization?

and business and work—these are the settings Dutch painters preferred. Conventional artistic subjects such as biblical stories and classical mythology, while hardly absent, were pushed somewhat to the side.

In one sense, this attention to ordinary life owed a great deal to the Protestant Reformation. Whereas pre-Reformation Catholics had detected visible marks of the divine throughout the world—in miracles, relics, saints, and the Church, supposedly founded by Jesus himself—Protestants tended to imagine a starker division between the realm of fallen humanity and that of the all-powerful Creator. And seeing the latter as forbiddingly distant, they turned their attention back to the human realm, seeing it as their mission to *create* holiness around them in their daily lives. As an English preacher wrote, "Whatsoever our callings be, we serve the Lord Christ in them."

By the middle years of the seventeenth century, however, such attention to the ordinary functioning of the world had moved well beyond the bounds of any particular Christian confession. Increasingly, not just in art, but in everything from political philosophy and the continuing developments of the scientific revolution to the construction of new forms of monarchy, Europeans devoted remarkable new energy to describing and understanding the natural and social realms, and the ways they functioned, without reference to divine

intervention. They sought to uncover the laws that governed these realms and to discover how those laws could be manipulated. This project constituted, in a sense, the great theme of mid-seventeenth-century European culture and politics.

It was a project undertaken against considerable odds, for in the 1640s and 1650s much of Europe remained sunk in disorder. As in the earlier years of the century, it was the wasteful, destructive side of competition that seemed to have gained the upper hand. Civil wars flared in all areas of the continent, the Thirty Years' War sputtered to its conclusion, and the hopes of the despairing fed widespread belief in the imminent arrival of the Messiah. But the 1660s and 1670s saw, if not an era of peace and stability, nonetheless a definite retreat from the brink of continental anarchy. Wars continued—indeed, in some areas, intensified—and yet the very size and disciplined structures of the period's armies testified to the new power of European states to contain and monopolize violence, and to direct it to specific, limited targets. And Europeans grew increasingly confident that if they could come to understand and manipulate the laws of nature and society, then they could also, in the future, prevent the spasms of bloodshed they had all witnessed far too often. These are the themes of this chapter.

THE CIVIL WARS IN THE BRITISH ISLES (1639–1649)

The 1640s plausibly deserve the title of Europe's most disorderly decade. Among the areas that experienced civil conflict were the British Isles, France, the Iberian Peninsula, several Italian states, Ukraine, and the Ottoman Empire. In many of these areas, there was not one war but several, fought in different theaters and different periods. Meanwhile, nearly every major European power took part in international conflict. In some parts of the continent, the strife had relatively few long-term consequences, despite all the sound and fury it generated. But in other areas, it brought about truly radical change, and nowhere more than in the British Isles.

ORIGINS

Although the civil wars in the British Isles were not the costliest of these conflicts in lives lost, their long-term impact on European affairs was unparalleled. Only in Britain did the form of government change fundamentally, with the temporary replacement of the monarchy by a republic that claimed to derive its legitimacy from the will of the sovereign people. Only in Britain did successful rebels dare to put a monarch on trial and execute him. And only in Britain did political groups emerge—and briefly gain prominence—that not only imagined a millennial transformation of the world—one that would bring it closer to a state of holiness, and, perhaps to the end times—but sought to bring about this new phase of human history themselves through drastic political and social reforms that would inspire revolutionary movements for centuries thereafter.

In the 1620s and 1630s, events had given relatively little indication that Britain stood on the brink of such a remarkable upheaval. As we have seen, King Charles I frequently came into conflict with his parliaments. Yet the strife was no worse than what many other European monarchies of the period were experiencing. During the eleven-year period known as Charles's "personal rule," in which he governed without calling Parliament into session, he did not try to impose new taxes but resorted to the manipulation of older practices such as ship money to raise funds. Here again the British story resembled that of the other European states of the period. In France, for instance, the kings did without the representative body known as the Estates General for some 175 years after 1614. In keeping with the concepts of Jean Bodin, European monarchs increasingly saw their rule in terms of absolute "sovereignty," which, Bodin believed, belonged to the prince alone and could not be shared with the people's representatives. Such ideas suited Charles I, a man convinced of his divine right to rule and his superiority to other mortals. An elegantly mannered and cultivated king, Charles fit an emerging European model of "absolutist" monarchy. "Remember," he remarked on one occasion, "that Parliaments are altogether in my power."

By itself, Charles's move toward absolutism would probably not have caused a civil war, and might well have transformed Britain into a monarchy on the continental model. But in the 1630s, two other factors turned a bad situation disastrous: religion and conflict among the different kingdoms ruled by Charles. The king, whose French queen was a devout Catholic, rejected the more austere elements of Protestantism. He liked neither the doctrine of predestination of souls beloved of the Calvinists nor militant Protestant attempts to forge a more holy society by banning traditional forms of entertainment such as dancing and card-playing. His handpicked archbishop of Canterbury, William Laud, reintroduced sumptuous religious

services that often included the use of incense and music ("smells and bells"), ornately decorated altars, and priests in elaborate costumes. Laud and Charles also gave permission for popular entertainments to take place on Sundays, including archery, dancing, vaulting, and the setting up of Maypoles. To the rigidly Calvinist English Protestants who were now going by the name of Puritans these moves signaled dangerous backsliding toward Catholicism. But far from trying to placate the Puritans, Charles and Laud persecuted them mercilessly. In response, the Puritans began to develop arguments for religious toleration.

INITIAL CONFLICTS (1637–1641)

The final factor contributing to civil war was conflict among the kingdoms that Charles ruled. In 1637, Charles demanded that the Church of Scotland adopt the Church of England's *Book of Common Prayer*. It was a dangerously provocative step in light of Scotland's long tendency toward Calvinist beliefs and a system of ecclesiastical government by councils of elders, known as Presbyterianism, which stood in contrast to the more sharply hierarchical structure of the Anglican Church, with its bishops and archbishops. The king's move provoked riots in Scotland, mass adherence to a proclamation of resistance called the Scottish "National Covenant," and, in 1639, the formation of a rebel army, which a year later invaded northern England. Therefore, 1639 marks the start of the British civil wars.

To rally support and money for defense against the rebel invasion, Charles had no choice but to call two new parliaments in quick succession. The second of them, the so-called Long Parliament, elected in the autumn of 1640, would remain assembled in one form or another for thirteen years (and reassemble briefly in 1660). This new Parliament was more radical than any of its predecessors. From the start, it was dominated by a group of fervent Puritans who dreamed of remaking both the English Church and English society in line with Calvinist ideals, and defending them from the machinations of the king and his principal advisers, Archbishop Laud and Thomas Wentworth, the earl of Strafford (1593–1641). They envisaged a simplified church structure, shorn of bishops, a liturgy purified of what they considered Catholic corruptions, and the introduction of strict controls over public morality.

Initially led by the talented country squire and financier John Pym (1584–1643), the Long Parliament quickly took steps to counteract what it considered the abuses of Charles's reign. It banned the use of ship money and other such expedients, and abolished the widely hated

Court of Star Chamber, a long-established body subservient to the King which met in secret and had passed harsh and arbitrary sentences against Puritans and others accused of defying royal authority. The parliament passed a Triennial Act, demanding that parliaments meet at least every three years instead of at the monarch's pleasure. It tried to move the Church of England in a Puritan direction by proposing the elimination of bishops. And it voted a bill of attainder condemning Wentworth to death without trial, which it defiantly passed on to the king for his signature. Remarkably, the earl himself urged Charles to sign it "for the preventing of such massacres as may happen by your refusal." After two days of agonized indecision, Charles agreed. Wentworth was beheaded. The king also agreed to the other measures Parliament had passed in hopes of preventing further conflict and convincing the parliament to raise funds for him.

Events, however, quickly overwhelmed Charles's hopes. Wentworth had served as governor of largely Catholic Ireland, and although he had not been popular there, his execution led to Irish fears that the militant Protestants now ascendant in Britain might try to impose their religion on their neighboring island by force. The result was a revolt by Irish Catholics in 1641 and the massacre of at least 2,000 Irish Protestants, beginning a series of conflicts that would tear Ireland apart through the rest of the decade. The Irish revolt in turn strengthened English Puritan fears of Catholicism and so contributed to further radicalization in Parliament and among its supporters. In late 1641, Parliament narrowly passed a list of grievances known as the Grand Remonstrance accusing the king of hundreds of further offenses. Puritans gained control of the government of the City of London (the capital's commercial and financial district) and its powerful paramilitary forces.

PARLIAMENTARY VICTORY (1642–1645)

In January 1642, Charles finally broke with the Long Parliament. In a dramatic scene, he personally led eighty soldiers into the House of Commons to arrest its leaders. But, forewarned, they had escaped down the Thames River. "I see the birds have flown," the king snapped. But less than a week later, having failed to secure London, Charles himself fled the city, eventually joined by some two-fifths of the members of Parliament. The remaining members began to raise an army, which clashed with royal forces in September 1642. Civil war within England had begun.

Over the next four and a half years, the British Isles fell prey to some of the worst violence they have ever known. The civil wars were not a modern conflict with unbroken fighting between uniformed armies along well-defined front lines. Nor did they resemble the indiscriminate slaughter of the Thirty Years' War. Large pitched battles were rare, and no towns suffered the merciless sacking that took place so often in seventeenth-century Germany. But the death toll among the combatants was still high, and the civilian population suffered greatly from hunger and disease.

The Parliamentarians (also known as Roundheads because of the short haircuts some of them favored) ultimately prevailed in the first phase of the conflict. They controlled London, which had vast commercial wealth, a tenth of the English population, and the apparatus of government (including the navy). They had an advantage in manpower, outnumbering the Royalists (who were often called Cavaliers) by three to two in several key encounters. They had, at crucial moments, the support of the Scots. And although the Parliamentarians suffered both from internal divisions and from the death of their leader, Pym, in 1643, Charles's forces were even more fragmented and hard to control.

Irish Revolt A contemporary illustration accused Irish rebels of the brutal tactics against English Protestant settlers. Above, the rebels force the Protestants to jump off a bridge to their deaths; below, they massacre women.

In the winter of 1644–45, Parliament reorganized its own armed forces into the disciplined New Model Army, whose cavalry was commanded by a forceful Puritan member of Parliament from a gentry background, **Oliver Cromwell** (1599–1658). It was a radically new sort of armed force for Europe—one created to advance an ideological agenda rather than a social or national one. It had a more centralized organization than most European armed forces of the period, accepted only soldiers and officers committed to the Puritan cause, and promised that talent, not social standing, would determine promotion (its leaders included a brewer and a butcher). It made particularly effective use of light cavalry and practiced strict discipline within the ranks. In June 1645, at the battle of Naseby some 115 miles northwest of London, the New Model Army crushed the Royalists, and the next spring King Charles surrendered.

Area held by Parliament, early 1645
Area gained by Parliament, late 1645
Area held by Royalists, late 1645
✕ Battle

The British Civil Wars, 1641–1645

THE RADICAL TURN (1646–1649)

As yet, very few people in England had any thought of doing away with the monarchy. But over the next two years, the situation remained dangerously unstable. The leading voices in Parliament wanted to transform the Church of England into a Presbyterian Church close to the Scottish model. However, an increasingly powerful group within the parliamentary forces, known as the Independents, which enjoyed particular support from the radical New Model Army and Cromwell, favored a much looser structure for religious life. Building on earlier Puritan arguments, the Independents demanded religious toleration for all Christian groups, even Catholics. The Army proved fertile soil for the emergence of other sorts of radicalism as well. Demands emerged for the reform of Parliament along egalitarian lines, with an extension of the vote from wealthy social elites to the male middle classes. A particularly vocal group of soldiers, frustrated by the social conservatism of Cromwell and the parliamentary leaders, went even further. Known as the **Levellers**, they suggested, for the first time in European history, that class privileges be "leveled" and that *all* adult men have the right to vote. In an extraordinary series of debates at Army headquarters in Putney during the fall of 1647, the

Levellers pressed their case eloquently. One Army officer declared:

> For really I think that the poorest he that is in England hath a life to live, as the greatest he; and therefore truly, Sir, I think it clear, that every Man that is to live under a Government ought first by his own Consent to put himself under that Government; and I do think that the poorest man in England is not at all bound in a strict sense to that Government that he hath not had a voice to put Himself under.

The Levellers drew their ideas from the English parliamentary tradition stretching back to Magna Carta, not from any engagement with classical democracy. Their example would have lasting importance in English politics, providing inspiration for many later generations of reformers. At the time, though, they never gained more than minority support.

These tensions within the victorious parliamentary camp eventually triggered what amounted to a second civil war. The Scots and the English Presbyterian opponents of Cromwell now made common cause with Charles, who, though held prisoner by the New Model Army, pledged that he would accept a Presbyterian Church if restored to power. Much of the navy went over to him, and several regional insurgencies in his favor began. But once again the New Model Army proved a superior fighting force and prevailed over its opponents. In 1648, it forcibly expelled 270 of 470 members of Parliament from the House of Commons, including most of the English Presbyterians. The remaining members, known derisively as the Rump Parliament, convened a High Court of Justice that put Charles on trial and sentenced him to death.

On January 30, 1649, on a scaffold erected just outside the Banqueting House in London, where his father had watched *King Lear*, Charles was beheaded. Like another Shakespearean character, *Macbeth*'s Thane of Cawdor, "nothing in his life became him like the leaving it." In his last hours, Charles showed supreme cool and courage, and was hailed by his supporters as a martyr. Soon after the execution, the Rump Parliament abolished the House of Lords and the monarchy, and in May declared England a Commonwealth—the English translation of *res publica*, a reference to the ancient Roman republic. The exhausted population greeted this momentous change without enthusiasm, hoping mostly for an end to the bloodshed.

THE CONTINENTAL CIVIL WARS

After these dramatic events, many in England feared that the continental European powers might unite and launch an invasion force across the Channel to address this threat to the institution of monarchy. They particularly feared France, whose recently deceased king, Louis XIII, had been Charles's brother-in-law. But no such invasion took place, in large part because so much of the European continent was itself in the grip of civil wars.

THE FRONDE IN FRANCE (1648–1653)

France itself briefly seemed as if it might imitate the British example. By the early 1640s, the costs of participating in the Thirty Years' War had again put the country's finances under terrible strain. Following the deaths of Cardinal Richelieu and Louis XIII, the throne passed in 1643 to a child king, Louis XIV (r. 1643–1715), with the regency held by his unpopular mother, Anne of Austria. Advised by her lover and chief minister, Cardinal Jules Mazarin (1602–1661), Anne increased the level of direct taxes and resorted to a series of stopgap revenue-raising measures that took a particular toll on the city of Paris. These included fines on building houses in certain zones where construction was prohibited, and the suspension of salaries for judges in the Paris high court (*parlement*), whose jurisdiction covered one-third of the kingdom.

In response, the high court judges, who owned their offices as a form of property, began to act as leaders of a national opposition. "The country has been ruined these past ten years," one judge daringly declared in the presence of Mazarin and the queen regent in January 1648, referring to the widespread misery that the Thirty Years' War had inflicted on France. "Millions of innocent souls are obliged to live on black and oat bread . . . the glory of conquered provinces cannot nourish those who have no bread." Four months later, the levying of yet another new tax led the magistrates from the capital's various courts to join together into a new, self-appointed assembly, which demanded the lowering of taxes, the abolition of the royal agents known as *intendants* (who were increasingly taking on the role of provincial governors), and, most important, veto power for themselves over all new royal taxes. When after several months Mazarin attempted to arrest the

The Fronde In this mid-seventeenth century engraving, a crowd is gathered in a field on the outskirts of Paris to listen to a speech from a leader of the Fronde. He urges his audience to revolt against the tyranny of Cardinal Mazarin.

movement's leaders, in August 1648 the city of Paris rose in revolt, with commoners building barricades that blocked streets throughout the city. The royal family eventually fled from Paris in what became known as the revolt of the **Fronde**, after the French word for the slingshots used as weapons by the Parisian crowd.

If the revolt began with a bang, it soon faded to a confused whimper. A French army led by the king's cousin, the prince of Condé (1621–1686), besieged Paris and forced the leaders of the Fronde to sign a truce in 1649. There followed four years of intermittent conflict as the magistrates, the supporters of Anne and Mazarin, and an independent-minded Condé schemed and fought against each other. Mazarin and the queen became the objects of a ferocious pamphlet campaign waged by a variety of opponents, including "Frondeurs" hoping to rekindle the spirit of the initial revolt and weaken the monarchy. The works cast the Italian-born cardinal as a corrupt sexual deviant plotting to enslave the people. But Mazarin and the queen outlasted their opponents. The fourteen-year-old Louis XIV returned to Paris in October 1652, followed by Mazarin four months later, while Condé fled into exile.

At no moment in the revolt of the Fronde did a coherent challenge to the social and political order emerge. Unlike the English rebels, the leaders of the movement's various factions continued throughout to protest their undying loyalty to the divinely ordained monarch. In Bordeaux, on the Atlantic Coast, Condé helped spur a popular movement against the city's high court. It tried to enforce limits on food prices and rent, and to expand participation in the municipal government. But when the English Commonwealth sent envoys to the city, armed with French translations of Leveller pamphlets, in the hope of securing a military alliance against the French monarchy, they were met with puzzlement.

IBERIA AND ITALY (1640–1659)

The germ of civil war not only touched France but spread to the Habsburg lands as well, with some of the worst strife coming in the northeast Spanish region of Catalonia. It began in the 1630s with attempts by the central government in Madrid to extract additional revenues from the region in defiance of its traditional constitutional privileges. "Better that the Catalans should complain, than that we should all weep," chief minister Olivares sneered in 1639. But the complaints soon turned violent as peasants and laborers began to attack royal troops, leading to savage reprisals. In June 1640, a popular Catalan insurgent force took the Catalonian capital of Barcelona, murdered the viceroy and several other royal officials, and sacked the homes of wealthy citizens. But as in France, the uprising did not lead in the direction of permanent social or political change. The Catalan ruling elites quickly moved to reinforce their privileges. They also sought French aid, with the result that the province became a battlefield in the ongoing Franco-Spanish War. Peace only returned in 1659, at which point France permanently annexed a slice of Catalonia and the rest returned to Habsburg rule.

The Catalans did not do as well as the Portuguese, whose revolt against Spain in 1640 remained firmly under the control of the country's nobility. The new king of Portugal, John IV (r. 1640–1656), quickly established his authority, leading to full Portuguese independence. Revolts against the Spanish Habsburgs also took place in southern Italy. A popular movement briefly seized control of Naples in 1647 and proclaimed the city a republic before the Spanish suppressed the uprising.

UKRAINE AND POLAND-LITHUANIA (1648–1668)

The bloodiest civil war of the period occurred in the east, in the lands now known as Ukraine, between Poland-Lithuania and Russia. Throughout the early seventeenth century, Catholic Poland had been expanding its territory to the east and south, challenging the Orthodox Church (which had separated from Roman Catholicism

in the eleventh century) in these regions. Opposition to this expansion grew, especially among the Orthodox clans known as Cossacks, who had strong martial traditions. In early 1648, the charismatic **Bogdan Chmielnicki** (1595–1657) emerged as overall Cossack leader, forged an alliance with the Muslims from the Ottoman province of the Crimea (on the north shore of the Black Sea), and began a massive uprising against the Poles, whom he accused of betraying his people. The rebels particularly targeted Jews, who often managed estates for the Polish nobility. As many as 100,000 of them, a high percentage of the Jewish population of the region, were slaughtered in the greatest tragedy for European Jewry between the massacres of the late medieval period and the twentieth-century Nazi Holocaust. Tens or even hundreds of thousands of Polish Christians also perished. (Historians continue to dispute the numbers.)

Ukraine, 1648–1667

For a time, it seemed as if an independent Cossack state might take shape in Ukraine. Chmielnicki marched into Kiev in triumph in 1648 and proclaimed himself the ruler of "Rus," the medieval name for the state centered in the region. The Poles initially had no choice but to acknowledge his authority there and allowed him to impose Orthodox Christianity. But the war resumed in 1651 and ultimately forced Chmielnicki to seek protective overlords. After first threatening to sign an agreement with the Ottoman Empire, he found a Christian protector in the Russian tsar, who agreed to an alliance that guaranteed Cossack liberties in return for accepting Russian sovereignty and the right to impose taxes.

The entire episode hugely weakened Polish-Lithuania, which faced further challenges in the following decades. In a costly war with Russia between 1654 and 1667 the Poles were unable to exploit their military victories, and ended up ceding territory in Ukraine. And only a year after this war broke out, another contender for supremacy in northeastern Europe—Sweden—invaded Poland-Lithuania and rapidly conquered much of the western part of the country (the Poles referred to the invasion as the "Swedish Deluge"). Only the fact that Sweden was soon drawn into fighting with Russia and Denmark allowed the Poles to regain most of the lost ground.

THE OTTOMAN EMPIRE (1640–1656)

The Ottoman Empire also remained prey to instability in the 1640s and 1650s. It still claimed authority over vast territories: not just southeastern Europe, but much of the Middle East and North Africa as well. It was wealthy, with a capital city, Constantinople, larger than any other European city of the age. It had a relatively effective and flexible system of government, but it was still dangerously weak at the center. The reign of Sultan Ibrahim I ("the Mad") from 1640 to 1648 was marked by a costly failure to seize the Mediterranean island of Crete from the declining Venetian Republic, and by rampant corruption. Faced with demands for massive new bribes by the sultan, the empire's religious leadership made common cause with the powerful military order known as the Janissaries—elite household guards staffed mostly at this period by European Christians taken as slaves, converted to Islam, and subject to strict discipline. With their help, the sultan was deposed and soon strangled to death.

Ibrahim's six-year-old son took his place as Sultan Mehmet IV (r. 1648–1693). But political chaos continued, with thirteen grand viziers (prime ministers) in just eight years and a religious revolt in Anatolia (today, Asian Turkey) that nearly toppled the government. Finally, in 1656, the capable Albanian official Mehmet Köprülü (1575–1661) was appointed grand vizier. He quickly consolidated his own power, convinced the young sultan to devote himself principally to hunting, and won a series of decisive victories at sea against Venice and on land in Transylvania (in modern Romania) against the Austrian Empire. For a brief moment, the Ottoman Empire enjoyed stability and again emerged as a potent threat to the western powers. But here, too, the mid-seventeenth-century crisis brought about little permanent political change.

RELIGIOUS QUESTIONING

Against this background of continent-wide unrest and civil strife, messianic voices were heard. In widely separated areas of the continent, figures arose who claimed to know the will of God and promised that God would soon intervene to bring solace to the suffering. Some promised that the disorder of human affairs would be swept away entirely and replaced with a new, divine order.

MESSIANISM

In 1648, as the horrific news of Chmielnicki's massacres of Jews spread through Europe, a twenty-two-year-old Greek Jew named **Shabbetai Sevi** (1626–1676) heard the voice of God and decided he was the Messiah—the divinely appointed Savior of the world. Sevi was soon excommunicated by the Jewish community in Smyrna, but during the 1650s and early 1660s, he traveled throughout the Ottoman-ruled eastern Mediterranean to proclaim the coming of God's kingdom. When, in 1665, Sevi announced that the biblical prophecies would be fulfilled the following year, thousands of Jews throughout Europe began fasting and selling their possessions in preparation for the Messiah's reign and their return to their ancestral homeland of Israel, or Zion.

Eventually, Sevi made the mistake of challenging the authority of the sultan. On a visit to Constantinople, he was arrested and given the choice of death or conversion to Islam. He chose the latter and as news of the apostasy spread, his movement quickly collapsed. During his lifetime, though, Christian commentators tried to incorporate Sevi into their own millenarian prophecies, on the grounds that the return of Jesus would be preceded by the Jews' return to Zion.

Janissaries This Janissary's elite status as the sultan's guard is signaled by his rich attire and horse's equipment, both decorated with large feather plumes.

Britain itself saw more than its share of millennial activity during the turmoil of its civil wars. The Puritans believed firmly that the end of the world would come, but generally saw it as blasphemous to assert that it would do so in their own lifetimes. A small sect called the Fifth Monarchy Men, however, rose to the challenge. They claimed that the eternal monarchy of Jesus Christ would imminently be established, and that they themselves, as God's elect, should hold sovereign political power. Another even smaller group, called the Diggers, claimed that by abolishing private property and all forms of human dependence, they would lift the curse of Adam and bring human beings back to God. The Diggers set up a communal settlement in southern England, which the Puritan government forcibly closed. Meanwhile, the so-called Ranters declared that the millennium had actually arrived, releasing them from all morality, especially sexual morality. These groups were all tiny (for instance, in comparison with the Levellers), and drew their supporters from a variety of social backgrounds. But later generations of British radicals would find considerable inspiration in their actions and writings.

PROTESTANT AND CATHOLIC DISSENTERS

These small millenarian groups did not, for the most part, outlast the period of the civil wars. But the middle of the seventeenth century also saw, both in Britain and the European continent, the emergence of several non-millenarian currents of belief that would have a larger effect on the future of Christianity.

THE QUAKERS In Britain the most important of these were the **Quakers**. George Fox (1624–1691), the son of a weaver, began during the Civil Wars to preach the message that a piece of the divine—the "inner light"—dwells within all souls. The idea drew on tensions in Christianity that went all the way back to Jesus's raising of the spirit over the letter of Old Testament law. Fox also drew on the radical challenges to spiritual authority formulated in the Reformation, rooted in Luther's insistence that Christians should read the Scriptures themselves. But Fox's ideas had unprecedented social and institutional consequences. He and his followers rejected the very idea of a clergy, preferring to come together as equals in "meetings" of "friends" that included women. They refused to engage in traditional forms of social deference or to take oaths, dressed in plain, drab clothes, and, most controversially, renounced armed force under any circumstances, refusing to fight

for their country. (Quakers have numbered among the most prominent "conscientious objectors" to military service in Britain and the United States down to the present day.) Despite persecution by successive English governments, the Quakers survived. Later in the century one of their leaders, William Penn (1644–1718), would found the Pennsylvania colony in America, ensuring the spread of Quakerism beyond the British Isles. Their egalitarianism and aversion to violence and persecution in all its forms led many Quakers to oppose slavery. Some of the earliest, most prominent leaders of anti-slavery movements of Britain and the United States were Quakers.

THE JANSENISTS Catholic Europe did not experience the same sort of messianism as the Jewish and Protestant worlds. Yet neither did it avoid turmoil, despite all the efforts the Church had made over the century since the Council of Trent to assert stronger control over its clergy and their congregations. In fact, in the middle of the seventeenth century, the Church's stance on the differences between Catholic and Protestant belief provoked such a strong reaction that some observers feared a new schism, similar to the Reformation. Whereas, Luther, and particularly Calvin, had stressed the utter sinfulness of mankind, and therefore the inability of any person to achieve salvation by good works, Jesuit theologians claimed that humans enjoyed a much larger degree of free will in the matter. But in doing so, they seemed to many to contradict the writings of Saint Augustine which sought to reconcile free will with God's infinite power and foresight, and even to challenge long-agreed interpretations of scripture.

The reaction to these developments occurred above all in France and the Low Countries, among a group of Catholics known as the **Jansenists** (for Cornelius Jansen, an influential Catholic bishop in the Spanish Netherlands). They criticized many aspects of the Catholic Reformation: the overly lavish, sensual decoration of Baroque churches; the "laxity" with which the Jesuits sought converts overseas; and the practice of "frequent communion" that allowed the faithful to shuffle off the burdens of sin on a weekly basis. Like the Calvinists, the Jansenists stressed both the depravity of humanity and its inability to know the plans of a distant and disapproving deity. But unlike the Calvinists, they counseled that where possible people should withdraw from the world to lives of ascetic deprivation and penance, similar to what monastic movements in Catholicism had long advocated for members of their orders. The Jansenists' writings appealed mostly to clerics and a small set of literate noble and middle-class laypeople. But their very existence terrified powerful interests in the

Jansenists In 1662, a French painter made this portrait of his daughter (right), a Jansenist nun, with the mother superior of her community. The sparse scene and somber, reverent attitude of the nuns speak to the ascetic and devoted values the Jansenists sought to uphold.

Catholic Church, who knew all too well the dangers of religious disputes and strove to suppress Jansenism.

These examples of religious fracturing throughout Europe, despite the obvious differences between them, did have some tendencies in common. They all involved attempts to undermine established religious authorities—whether the rabbinic ones of the eastern Mediterranean attacked by Sabbatai Sevi, the Anglican ones deemed unnecessary by the Quakers, or the Catholic hierarchy criticized by the Jansenists. Each sought to promote a more direct relationship between individual believers and God. And each stressed, in different ways, the difficulty of knowing God's will, whether because of his distance from a sinful humanity or because of his fundamentally mysterious nature. And so this moment in religious history, despite provoking fears of fanaticism and schism, did not lead to religious divides like those of the Reformation.

CATHOLIC DISCIPLINE AND RELIGIOUS WOMEN

Despite these new challenges, the established churches remained powerful—particularly the resurgent Catholic Church, which had recovered considerable territory in Germany despite the setbacks of the Thirty Years' War.

The attempts to strengthen Catholic religious institutions continued apace in the mid-seventeenth century and had particular implications for the roles of women in the Church.

THE URSULINE ORDER The Catholic Reformation had contradictory effects on women. On the one hand, it had spurred the creation of new women's religious orders such as the Ursulines, dedicated to work among the poor. Yet over time, suspicion grew in the male Church hierarchy over allowing the female members of such orders to live and work freely in the midst of secular society. To better control them, the Church transformed most of the orders into cloistered orders of nuns. By the mid-seventeenth century, Ursuline nuns mostly lived behind convent walls and could not even speak with nonreligious men except under strictly supervised conditions, generally from behind the bars of a grille.

Yet a few groups of religious women managed to escape these disciplinary strictures. The Daughters of Charity, founded by Saint Vincent de Paul (1581–1660) and Saint Louise de Marillac (1591–1660), the illegitimate daughter of a French nobleman, lived in small, non-cloistered urban communities that sustained themselves by taking in sewing, spinning, and laundry. Their members ministered to the sick and ran schools for poor girls. Formally recognized by the papacy as a confraternity, or lay religious organization, in 1668, the Daughters expanded significantly over the next half century, eventually establishing more than 250 separate communities throughout Europe.

Religious Women In this seventeenth-century engraving, nuns serve hot food to the patients of the Hôtel-Dieu hospital in Paris, an example of the vast array of charitable work undertaken by religious women of the period.

MARIE GUYART The spiritual satisfaction that such work could bring to ordinary women shows through in the life of Marie Guyart, better known as Marie of the Incarnation (1599–1672). Born in western France to a wealthy baker, she married at age seventeen and was widowed two years later. Over the following decade, she grew more and more fervent in her religious devotion. To scourge herself of sin, she whipped herself with nettles, wore chains and a hairshirt under her clothing, and slept on a plank. She prayed intensely, did charitable work, and found release and joy in confession and absolution.

Marie had visions of Jesus Christ and dreamed of

becoming a nun. To this end, she even tried to deny her young son tenderness, so he would not miss her when she finally entered a convent. She did so when he was just twelve, joining the Ursuline Order and effectively abandoning him. Yet even this step was not enough for her. Like many notable Catholic figures before her, she longed for Christian martyrdom, and courted it by traveling to the newly founded, precarious French colony in Canada and helping to instruct the Indians there:

> I saw, in inner certainty, demons triumphing over those poor souls, ravishing them from the domain of Jesus Christ … I could not bear it. I embraced all these poor souls, I held them in my breast … And the Holy Spirit, which possessed me, led me to say to the Eternal father, "… I am learned enough to teach of [Christ] to all the nations. Give me a voice powerful enough to be heard at the ends of the earth."

In 1639, Marie and several other religious women founded an Ursuline monastery in Quebec, and schools for Indian girls. She spent the next thirty-three years there, until her death.

ORDER THROUGH REASON

In the twenty-first century, "faith" is often opposed to "reason" and "science." Seventeenth-century Europeans, however, did not think in these terms. The religious ferment of the times in no way precluded the continuous development of rationalist, skeptical, scientific thought. Many thinkers we now remember as "scientific" were also fervent believers in the literal word of scripture. Christian churches did not condemn rationalist philosophy per se, but rather ideas that they believed contradicted their teachings, as we have seen in the case of Galileo. Yet even if the century's most advanced thought did not necessarily challenge traditional religious authority, it ultimately provided those who would mount such challenges with powerful intellectual tools.

HOBBES'S *LEVIATHAN*

In 1651, two years after the execution of Charles I, a book appeared in London with the curious title *Leviathan: Or the Matter, Forme and Power of a Commonwealth Ecclesiastical and Civill.* Long and difficult, it began with a detailed consideration of how the mind works and concluded with a long section entitled "The Kingdom of Darkness." But

Hobbes's Leviathan The original 1651 frontispiece of *Leviathan* provides a powerful visual representation of Hobbes's characterization of the state. The body of the sovereign is comprised of all the people of the state, while his twin authorities—the military sword and the ecclesiastical bishop's crook—loom over the land spread before him.

what immediately drew the attention of readers was the new theory of political authority that the book presented.

According to the author, the sixty-three-year-old **Thomas Hobbes** (1588–1679), humans living in a "natural condition," without the order imposed by a state and its laws, inevitably fall into bloody competition for limited resources— "a warre … of every man against every man." Such violence made any sort of human social development impossible and, in Hobbes's memorable phrase, rendered "the life of man, solitary, poore, nasty, brutish and short." These words reflected Hobbes's horror at the period's civil strife, and in particular the near dissolution of the English state. (He himself spent the years from 1640 to 1651 in self-imposed exile in Paris.) But Hobbes then took a crucial step forward by suggesting that political authority initially arose as a solution to this state of affairs. People living in a state of nature entered into a "covenant," or contract, with each other, by which they surrendered their natural rights to a sovereign. In return, they received his protection and agreement to act on their behalf. The frontispiece of the book showed the members of a state coming together to form a single sovereign body.

Leviathan offered something to shock nearly all readers. Despite Hobbes's long sections on religion and earnest professions of faith, devout Christians recoiled from his secular account of the origins of sovereign political power. They also criticized him for limiting political obedience to subjects' actions, rather than insisting on conformity of beliefs, thus providing a rationale for toleration of dissent. And Hobbes's insistence that sovereign power depended on the initial consent of the governed shocked defenders of monarchy. More radical political voices, meanwhile, called him an apologist for royal tyranny. They rejected his claim that the transfer of rights from individuals to a sovereign was irrevocable and nearly total, leaving the governed no right to overturn an unjust ruler. In 1666, the House of Commons denounced *Leviathan* as a book that "tend[ed] to atheism, blasphemy and profaneness."

Despite the condemnation it aroused at the time, Hobbes's idea of a "social contract" would become one of the most important themes in the history of political philosophy, and *Leviathan* has become recognized as a founding text of modern political science. Its comprehensive theory largely provided the basic framework in which generations of later thinkers would try to understand political life. Many later secular thinkers discussed Hobbes and tried to refute him. Christian authors offered their own competing theories of politics in the mid-seventeenth century, but none of them had anything like Hobbes's enduring influence.

The power of Hobbes's work came above all from the fact that he approached politics in much the way the figures of the scientific revolution approached the physical universe. Just like them, he broke with classical and medieval theories of a preexisting, transcendent order in the universe. He too saw politics as a realm that obeyed fundamental, regular laws that could be observed or deduced from first principles. It was no accident that he began the work with an account of the operations of the mind and body that read like a work of anatomy, for *Leviathan* was a work of anatomy—the anatomy of the body politic. And it therefore offered the hope that the body politic's disorders could find a scientific cure, just like medical disorders. In the political context of the mid-seventeenth century, this was a powerful message. Could Europe finally escape from its seemingly endless cycles of turmoil and violence? To answer this question in the affirmative, as Hobbes did, meant abandoning traditional, religiously based theories of authority in favor of new theories based on reason—a leap into the unknown that few Europeans, as yet, were willing to make.

BARUCH SPINOZA

Hobbes had the most direct and immediate influence, but he was not the only author of the period to formulate ideas that defied prevailing Christian notions of politics and society. Another was his younger contemporary **Baruch Spinoza** (1632–1677), who, like him, read deeply in the scientific works of the time and studied the new scientific methods described above. Born in Amsterdam to a Jewish family descended from Portuguese exiles, Spinoza worked much of his adult life as a lens grinder, but eventually devoted himself full time to philosophy. His work, mostly written in Latin, was dense and difficult, but nonetheless aroused enough controversy to earn condemnations from Catholic, Protestant, and Jewish authorities alike.

Baruch Spinoza A mid-seventeenth-century portrait of the radical thinker.

Central to Spinoza's work is the idea that the universe is not divided between matter and spirit but consists of a single basic substance. This idea challenged Descartes's dualist philosophy and the basic Christian distinction between body and spirit. Furthermore, Spinoza maintained, everything in the universe is determined by an infinite chain of cause and effect. The true relations between things can be discovered only by reason, employing scientific observation, precise mathematical measurement, and logic. Spinoza wrote of a God, but his identification of God with the operations of the universe as a whole, and his refusal of the matter/spirit distinction, led his contemporaries to charge that he was really an atheist—at a time when atheism remained, in all European states, a crime.

Although Spinoza wrote extensively on ethics, he did not develop an explicit, formal system of politics in the manner of Hobbes. What he did write on politics, however, had even more corrosive implications than *Leviathan*. Spinoza advocated a political system in which most of the adult male population could vote for their rulers, calling it the "most natural form of state, approaching most closely to that freedom which Nature grants to every man." And while, like Hobbes, he defended the individual conscience, proclaiming that "everyone is by absolute natural right master of his own thoughts," he then went further and asserted a limited freedom of expression: "Utter failure will attend any attempt in a state to force men to speak only as prescribed by the sovereign despite their different and opposing opinions." Yet he also supported the right of states to impose forms of outward religious conformity on its subjects if this was necessary to ensure civil peace.

Spinoza was read in many different, often contradictory ways, and critics frequently used "Spinozism" as a blanket term for unorthodox beliefs. His works nonetheless helped inspire a current of radical thinking, particularly about the nature of the divine, that would later flow into the eighteenth-century Enlightenment.

BLAISE PASCAL

Another author of the period illustrated even more sharply how the confluence of the scientific revolution and new religious thought could contribute to fresh ways of thinking about society. **Blaise Pascal** (1623–1662), the son of a French tax collector, gained a reputation in his youth as a mathematician and made important contributions to probability theory and the study of fluids, pressure, and vacuum. In his twenties,

he became an enthusiastic devotee of Jansenism, writing bitingly witty attacks on the Jesuits that the royal administration suppressed. Pascal died young but left an extraordinary, incomplete work called *Pensées* (*Thoughts*), which he intended as a defense of the Christian faith. It included a famous declaration that humans had nothing to lose by betting on the existence of God ("Pascal's Wager") and poetic meditations on the universe. "The eternal silence of these infinite spaces terrifies me," Pascal wrote, in an astonishing vision of a universe without end.

Blaise Pascal Pascal's willingness to challenge conventional belief is hinted at in this mid-seventeenth-century portrait.

Pascal also wrote many passages that applied withering skepticism to conventional beliefs about society and the limits of human knowledge. For instance, he skewered the supposedly natural differences between national cultures, writing "We see neither justice nor injustice which does not change its nature with change in climate....Three degrees of latitude reverse all jurisprudence; a meridian decides the truth. Fundamental laws change after a few years of possession;...A strange justice that is bounded by a river! Truth on this side of the Pyrenees, error on the other side." Passages like this could have the effect of a

revelation, showing readers the essentially arbitrary and contingent character of arrangements they took as "natural" and even God-given.

POULAIN DE LA BARRE AND EARLY FEMINISM

In the 1670s, another French scholar—who remained largely unknown until the twentieth century—showed how such systematic, scientific skepticism could challenge even apparently fixed features of the social order. François Poulain de la Barre (1647–1725), a follower of Descartes, applied this skepticism to what we now think of as gender roles and produced a trio of works that asserted the equality of women to men. In a Pascalian vein of casting familiar subjects in new light, Poulain claimed that when it came to men and women's intellectual capacities, past philosophers had "attributed to nature a distinction that originates in custom." Grounding his arguments historically, he pointed out that customs changed over time and that "civil society," at present "governed and ordered by the male sex...has not always and everywhere been organized in the same way."

Bringing in what we would now call anthropological evidence from outside Europe, Poulain insisted that despite European conventional wisdom, pregnancy and childbirth did not necessarily bar women from useful employment. At times in his work, Poulain even extended his arguments from gender to questions of race and social class. Were "Turks, Barbarians and Savages" less capable of learning than Europeans? In fact, "these peoples are human beings like us, with the same abilities, and...if educated, they could equal us in any respect." Poulain's work—and a handful of other texts from the period that also deserve the label "proto-feminist"—had no immediate effect on European social practices, which continued to limit women's options for education and work. But they indicated clearly that new, skeptical, egalitarian forms of thinking about society had become possible and might eventually lead to real change.

A woman, who offered contemporaries a good illustration of Poulain's arguments for equality was Margaret Cavendish (1623–1673). An English aristocrat, she wrote plays, an

Margaret Cavendish In a 1650 portrait, Margaret Cavendish wears the elegant ermine robe and coronet to which she was entitled as the Duchess of Newcastle, her gaze boldly meeting the viewer's.

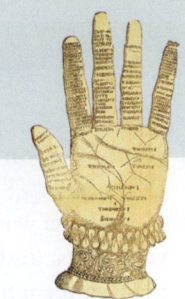

GENDER ROLES IN SEVENTEENTH-CENTURY ENGLAND

Opportunities for women remained limited in the seventeenth century. However, the growing interest in philosophy and science meant that the daughters of the elite often received a thorough education in all branches of human knowledge. A few continued on to careers as writers and scientists, corresponding with men of letters and writing their own poems, novels, and even scientific treatises.

Margaret Cavendish, the Duchess of Newcastle-upon-Tyne in northeastern England, was one of the better-known female intellects of the seventeenth century. She corresponded with Hobbes, Descartes, and other notable thinkers, and she was the author of a number of works of poetry, speculative fiction, philosophy, science, and drama. In *The World's Olio* (1655), Cavendish reflects on the differences between the genders and on women's capacity for knowledge.

And though it seem to be natural, that generally all Women are weaker than Men, both in Body and Understanding, and that the wisest Woman is not so wise as the wisest Man, wherefore not so fit to Rule; yet some are far wiser than some men, like Earth; for some Ground, though it be Barren by Nature, yet, being well mucked and well manured, may bear plentifull Crops, and sprout forth diverse sorts of Flowers, when the fertiller and richer Ground shall grow rank and corrupt, bringing nothing but gross and stinking Weeds, for want of Tillage; So Women by Education may come to be far more knowing and learned, than some Rustick and Rude-bred men. Besides, it is to be observed, that Nature hath Degrees in all her Mixtures and Temperaments, not only to her servile works, but in one and the same Matter and Form of Creatures, throughout all her Creations.

Again, it is to be observed, that although Nature hath not made Women so strong of Body, and so clear of understanding, as the ablest of Men, yet she hath made them fairer, softer, slenderer, and more delicate than they, separating as it were the finer parts from the grosser, which seems as if Nature had made Women as pure white Manchet,[1] for her own Table, and Palat, where Men are like coarse household Bread which the servants feed on; and if she hath not tempered Womens Brains to that height of understanding, nor hath put in such strong Species of Imaginations, yet she hath mixed them with Sugar of sweet conceits; and if she hath not planted in their Dispositions such firm Resolutions, yet she hath sowed gentle and willing Obedience, and though she hath not filled the mind with such Heroick Gallantry, yet she hath laid in tender Affections, as Love, Piety, Charity, Clemency, Patience, Humility, and the like; which makes them neerest to resemble Angells, which are the perfectest of all her Works; where men by their Ambitions, Extortion, Fury, and Cruelty, resemble the Devill.

QUESTIONS FOR ANALYSIS

1. How does Cavendish compare women to men?
2. According to Cavendish, what can women contribute to human knowledge?
3. What can we learn about seventeenth-century conventions regarding gender, femininity, and women's roles from this excerpt?

[1]**manchet:** the highest-quality bread

Source: *Paper Bodies: A Margaret Cavendish Reader,* eds. Sylvia Bowerbank and Sara Mendelson (Peterborough: 2000), 141–42.

autobiography, and also six books on science, grounded in her own research in alchemy. She frequently defended the right of women to write, insisted they could do so as well as men, and pleaded for them to be judged on their merit: "Many of our Sex may have as much wit, and be capable of Learning as well as men, but since they want Instructions, it is not possible they should attain to it." Indeed, most women lacked the advantages that enabled Cavendish to contribute to the arts and sciences in this period.

SCIENCE, EXPERIMENTALISM, AND THE STATE

This flowering of skeptical thought took place against the background of the scientific revolution that had begun in the early years of the seventeenth century. In the middle of the century this revolution deepened, mainly through the use of special instruments that natural philosophers continued to develop in close partnership with skilled artisans. Blaise Pascal, for instance, had a primitive barometer carried up a mountain in 1648 to show that the weight of air varied at different elevations. A few years later, the Anglo-Irish aristocrat Robert Boyle (1627–1691) devised a special air pump that created a near-vacuum, and used it to demonstrate both the phenomenon of air pressure and the mathematical relationship between the pressure and volume of a gas at constant temperature (Boyle's Law). The Dutch tradesman Antonie van Leeuwenhoek (1632–1723) invented the microscope (or at least made crucial improvements in its design), and in the 1670s made the first observations of bacteria and other organisms invisible to the naked eye.

Just as important, the middle of the century marked the moment at which western European governments and social elites fully grasped the practical implications of the new science and created institutions to support and control it. Florence led the way with its Experimental Academy in 1657, followed by Britain's Royal Society in 1660 and France's Royal Academy of Sciences in 1666. These new bodies provided alternatives to the universities as sites of learning. While most European universities still concentrated on training theologians, lawyers, and doctors, these new societies emphasized the production of new knowledge. They not only hosted lectures and demonstrations but also—starting with the Royal Society in 1665—published journals to make the results of scientific research known as widely as possible. The societies immediately came to play a key role in the validation of scientific research. Leeuwenhoek, for instance, leaped to prominence when the Royal Society's journal published his account of his observations of micro-organisms in 1673. And when his claims about bacteria met with disbelief (could an ordinary drop of water really swarm with animals too small for the eye to see?), the Society sent observers to evaluate his work in person, declared it valid, and offered him a membership in its ranks. Over the next fifty

Scientific Academies In 1666, Louis XIV's adviser Jean-Baptiste Colbert suggested that the king create a Royal Academy of Sciences. In this grand painting of the following year, Colbert presents the members of the new academy to the king. They are surrounded by tools of their trade—globes, maps, and books.

years, Leeuwenhoek sent more than 500 letters recounting his observations to Europe's leading scientific societies. The new societies and publications also strengthened ties among scholars in the "republic of letters."

Although the societies promoted the new science, they would never have approved of the radical speculations of a Spinoza or a Poulain. After all, they were chartered—and, in some cases, lavishly supported—by national governments. Their memberships were dominated by social elites, as exemplified by Boyle, the son of one of Ireland's largest noble landowners. The bylaws of the French Academy of Sciences stated that "in the meetings there will never be a discussion of the mysteries of religion or the affairs of state," and the other national bodies observed similar caution. They helped enforce "gentlemanly" forms of behavior among their members and in the Republic of Letters at large. For all their efforts, they could not prevent the scientific method, and the systematic skepticism they promoted, from being applied in ways that they themselves disapproved of and to subjects that they considered off limits. Still, whatever their radical potential, in the mid-seventeenth century itself, they mostly helped promote order and stability.

MAKING PEACE: CONSTRUCTING A NEW INTERNATIONAL ORDER AFTER THE THIRTY YEARS' WAR

Order and stability were also the goals of most European political action in the middle of the century. Monarchs and ministers, whether inspired by Hobbesian social contract theory or by more traditional Christian concerns for peace, had as their most important goal ending the anarchic bloodshed that had convulsed the continent since the start of the Thirty Years' War in 1618. To a remarkable extent, they met with success. By the early 1650s the sheer level of violence in Europe had begun to diminish significantly.

THE PEACE OF WESTPHALIA (1645–1648)

In diplomacy, the great event was the end of the massively destructive Thirty Years' War and the foundation of a new international order to prevent anything like it from happening again. As we have seen, the 1630s had been marked by titanic struggles between the armies of the Catholic Habsburg dynasty on the one side, and, on the other, a coalition that included Protestant Sweden and Catholic France. In the early 1640s the course of the war, which remained enormously destructive, turned decisively against the Habsburgs. The Swedes again sent their armies deep into Germany and won a pivotal victory at Breitenfeld in 1642, the site of their earlier victory in 1631. A brief war with Denmark then distracted them, but by 1644 Danish strength collapsed entirely. The Swedes then pushed south again, all the way to Bohemia, while allies from Transylvania invaded Hungary. Meanwhile, French forces secured the right bank of the Rhine River while also defeating Catholic Bavaria. By 1645, the Habsburgs had been pushed far enough onto the defensive to enter into serious peace negotiations.

These negotiations took place in the German state of Westphalia between 1645 and 1648 and marked a turn in the history of European diplomacy. Thousands of delegates came from no fewer than sixty-six states belonging to the Holy Roman Empire and sixteen other independent European states. (Roughly 200 German states had participated in the war.) Many of the negotiators had little diplomatic experience and relied on guidance from seasoned Venetian and papal professionals. They spent months simply establishing the ground rules for their talks, including particularly the ceremonial honors they would pay one another.

Nonetheless, the treaties that emerged from the peace talks in 1648—the **Peace of Westphalia**—were carefully written and elaborate: the treaty between France and the Holy Roman Empire contained 128 separate articles. And they had ambitious aims. In theory, they meant to establish a "Christian, general, and permanent peace," and although few negotiators believed they could really do so, they did at least hope to set up a durable structure for containing future conflict and managing international affairs. This structure would be based on the principle of respect for the sovereignty of individual states. With Westphalia, in short, the parties to the Thirty Years' War rejected the ancient dream of a united Europe and a united Christendom. In its place came a vision of a continent of independent, secular states existing in a balanced constellation of power.

These "Westphalian" principles would help guide European international relations until the mid-twentieth century. They did not, of course, prevent new wars. They did not even end the war between France and Spain, which dragged on for another eleven years. But the idea of peace

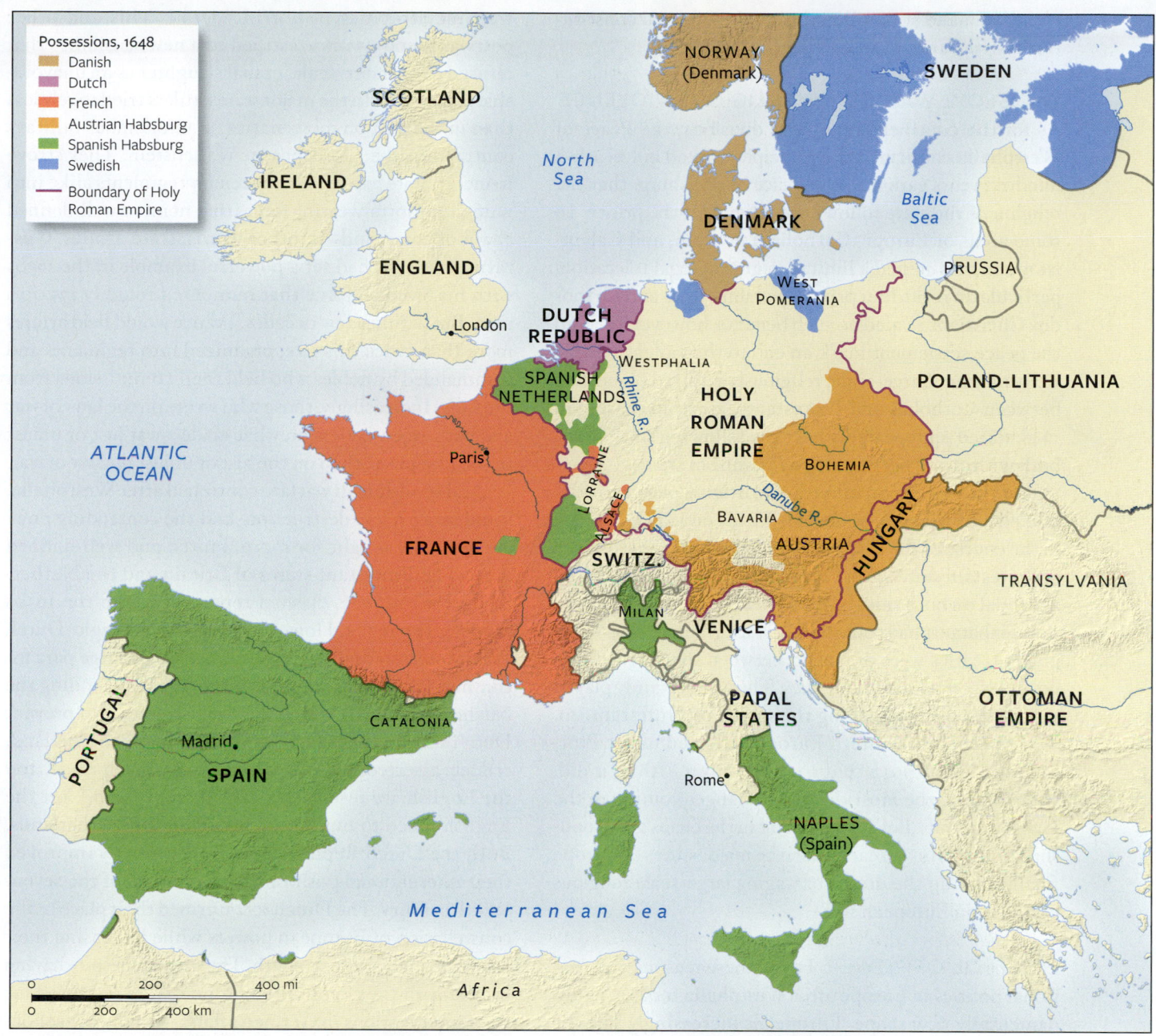

Possessions, 1648
- Danish
- Dutch
- French
- Austrian Habsburg
- Spanish Habsburg
- Swedish
- Boundary of Holy Roman Empire

The Peace of Westphalia, 1648 The peace settled many of the territorial disputes of the Thirty Years' War: France now controlled areas of Alsace and Lorraine; Sweden acquired West Pomerania on the Baltic; and the Netherlands gained independence from the Habsburg territories in the Low Countries. The Spanish Habsburgs still controlled territory across Europe, but the war and its outcome had reduced their power.

conferences that would settle major existing disputes, and reestablish a balance of power, provided the precedent for a series of conferences that only ended with the one at Versailles in 1919, following World War I.

The Westphalia treaties also confirmed the major territorial and political changes of the war. France received formal control over new German-speaking territories in Lorraine and Alsace, which had previously belonged to the Holy Roman Empire, and solidified its position on the Rhine. Sweden gained Western Pomerania, giving it a foothold on the southern shore of the Baltic Sea. Borders changed for many German states. The peace also confirmed the independence of the Netherlands from the Habsburg Empire, thereby ending the eighty years' struggle of the Dutch for self-determination, and reducing the empire's size. The treaties helped, overall, to strengthen and streamline the empire's formal constitutional structure.

THE SLOW WANING OF RELIGIOUS VIOLENCE

As for the continent's religious divisions, the Peace of Westphalia confirmed the principle worked out nearly a hundred years earlier in the Peace of Augsburg: that the religion of the state follows the religion of the prince. In some areas of Europe, Catholic, Lutheran, and Calvinist minorities gained a limited degree of legal toleration, particularly regarding private worship. Jews and Orthodox Christians reaped no such benefits, however. Nor did the peace settlement mark an end to the violence of the Reformation. Large-scale, religiously inspired bloodshed between Catholics and Protestants, far from ceasing in 1648, flared up repeatedly over the following sixty years, both within and between many European states.

Yet the expression of intra-Christian violence in warfare on a continental scale had already ended *before* 1648, in the course of the Thirty Years' War itself. The alliance of Protestant states with Catholic France may have caused a scandal on both sides in the 1630s; but by the late 1640s, the combatants had come to take it for granted. The Westphalia treaties were drawn up between sovereign states, not between religious alliances. The war certainly played a decisive role in checking the spread of Protestantism. Whereas half of western Europe had lived under Protestant rule in 1590, a century later only a fifth of it did, with some of the most dramatic changes coming in the Habsburg lands. But at some point in the chaos and bloodshed of the Thirty Years' War, the major states of Europe finally gave up the dream of waging large-scale religious crusades on European soil.

CONTROL OF POWER   For all these reasons, international politics in Europe after Westphalia took on a fundamentally new shape. Europeans increasingly saw the greatest threat to peace and stability as coming not from religious fervor, but from two other sources. First, there were those states whose excessive ambitions threatened the continent's overall balance of power. International alliances in the late seventeenth and eighteenth centuries would most often form not to protect coreligionists, or even to promote dynasties (although dynastic alliances remained important), but to restrain these ambitious states, France above all.

Second, there were the uncontrolled rampages of marauding soldiery that had caused so much of the war's devastation. *Simplicissimus*, a novel published in 1668 by Hans von Grimmelshausen (1621–1676), recounted these wartime atrocities in horrific detail. This and other postwar literary works testified to a new sensibility that refused to see large-scale, casual slaughter as an unavoidable part of war. In the major states, rulers tried to rely less than in the past on mercenaries or autonomous military contractors like Albrecht von Wallenstein. They strove to incorporate native and mercenary regiments alike into unified, uniform-wearing forces that fit into a well-defined chain of command—in other words, state armies. Gustavus Adolphus had set a powerful example in the 1630s with his Swedish force that numbered roughly 175,000 men. But within a few decades, France would field armies more than twice this size, organized into regiments and commanded by nobles who held their commissions from the king. Increasingly, those who wrote on the laws of war and peace focused less on what made a war just or unjust in the first place, than on the just or unjust *conduct* of war.

And so, although warfare continued after Westphalia, it did so with less destruction, and the contending powers generally fought for more limited and well-defined aims. The Protestant states of Britain and the Netherlands, for instance, clashed repeatedly from the 1650s through the 1670s. However, each of the Anglo-Dutch Wars was short and waged mostly at sea, in large part for commercial stakes. An English general, in defending the Navigation Acts by which the English sought to prevent Dutch ships from carrying goods to and from England, crudely asserted: "The Dutch have too much trade, and the English are resolved to take it from them." Yet the English failed to impose their will on the Netherlands. Both the Dutch Republic and France greatly improved their international positions in the middle of the seventeenth century. The Dutch reconfirmed their place in the constellation of European powers while increasing their naval and mercantile strength. The French, despite having to deal with the chaos of the Fronde, were rewarded for their interventions in German affairs with the consolidation of their eastern frontier.

But the period also had significant losers. Denmark, defeated once by the Habsburgs and once by Sweden, never again played a major international role in European affairs. Poland, torn apart by the Chmielnicki rebellion, lost territory to Russia and sank into political paralysis. Most important, Spain proved unable to regain its dominant position in Europe following the revolts in Catalonia and Italy, and the loss of Portugal. Instead, during the continuing warfare of the 1650s, it lost territory to France both in Catalonia and the Spanish Netherlands. The Treaty of the Pyrenees in 1659 marked Spain's eclipse as a major power on the continent. Its overseas empire, however, which still included vast territories in the Americas and stretched all the way to the Philippines, remained of crucial international importance.

THE ABSOLUTIST STATES

The search for political stability took European states in two broadly different directions. On the continent, the major monarchies for the most part followed the absolutist pattern set earlier in the century by ministers like Richelieu and Olivares. They pursued four major objectives: the further consolidation of royal authority, the weakening or elimination of independent political institutions, an assertion of greater state control over broad areas of social and economic life, and the transformation of the nobility from autonomous political actors to partners in a greater royal enterprise. The two great maritime powers of Britain and the Netherlands moved in a different direction. They experienced continuing political turmoil and a much less powerful role for the state. Commercial wealth in both countries helped shape new sorts of social relations and social institutions independent of the state. Overseas empire and trade had far greater importance in their cultures and politics than was the case in "absolutist" Europe, at least outside of Iberia.

DENMARK AND BRANDENBURG

The model absolutist power was not any of the larger monarchies, but tiny Denmark. The country had not only emerged badly battered from the Thirty Years' War, but also struggled with the exceptionally harsh winters of the Little Ice Age, in which the Baltic Sea itself sometimes froze over in part. Two unsuccessful campaigns against Sweden in 1657–60, as part of a larger northern alliance, only increased the pressures on the Danish government. King Frederick III (r. 1648–1670), a modest and reserved man, did not seem the sort to exploit these disasters to bring about major political change. But in 1660, advised by his brother-in-law Hannibal Sehestad (1609–1666), he managed to forge an alliance with the municipal elites of Copenhagen and the leaders of the Lutheran Church against the powerful

nobles of the Council of State. In a formal ceremony that autumn, the three Estates of the Kingdom recognized Frederick as the supreme sovereign power in Denmark and then dissolved, never to meet again. Sehestad brought non-nobles into a new Council of State, created a corps of official tax collectors in the provinces, and paid off the state's huge debt with grants of poor-quality royal land. New taxes and tariffs were imposed, including direct taxes on noble wealth. Frederick had gone a long way toward eliminating any independent authorities capable of challenging the monarchy.

Frederick III of Denmark
The Danish king's modesty is suggested in this mid-seventeenth-century portrait. He is dressed simply, with little of the pomp and grandeur associated with other European rulers of the time.

To the south of Denmark, the German state of Brandenburg followed a somewhat different absolutist path. A small agricultural state situated in a particularly defenseless part of the north German plains, Brandenburg had survived in large part because its rulers had the privilege of helping elect the Holy Roman emperor. In 1618, it acquired the large Baltic duchy of Prussia, but took another forty years to gain full authority there. A large and powerful noble class, the Junkers, resisted any encroachment on their authority. But in the aftermath of the Thirty Years' War, during which Habsburg and Swedish armies had both treated Brandenburg as a parade ground, the canny "Great Elector" Frederick William (r. 1640–1688) convinced the Junkers to grant him the funds necessary to create a standing army that could protect the territory. In return, he agreed to consult with them regularly and to confirm their considerable feudal privileges over the peasantry, including, as we have seen, the imposition of serfdom. Frederick William also created a civil service modeled on the army, in which officials with military titles took charge both of maintaining troops and collecting taxes in particular districts, in collaboration with local nobles. The cooperation among monarchy, aristocracy, and militarized bureaucracy proved a sturdy basis on which to build the state that would, in the future, be known simply as Prussia.

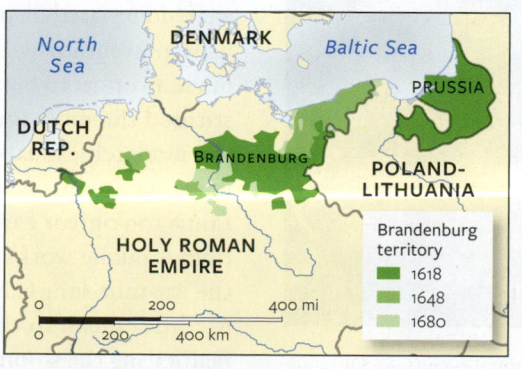

Brandenburg-Prussia, 1618–1680

LOUIS XIV OF FRANCE (1643–1715)

The absolutism of France's King **Louis XIV**, while often held up as the model followed by the rest of the continent, was actually unique in many respects. But because France reached the height of its power under Louis's reign, dominating the continent both politically and culturally, his story still deserves close attention.

Louis had an eventful childhood, to say the least. After losing his father and becoming king at age four in 1643, he had to flee his capital five years later during the popular turmoil of the Fronde. For five years after that he could do little more than watch as his mother, Anne of Austria, and her lover, Cardinal Mazarin, struggled to impose royal authority on the country's rebellious princes and high courts, only succeeding after all the sides were too exhausted to continue. For the rest of his life, Louis would have a visceral dislike for the common people of Paris who had rebelled against his mother.

Louis XIV This 1701 portrait captures Louis XIV's grandiosity, showing him draped in ermine and the royal *fleur de lys* symbol.

Upon Mazarin's death in 1661, Louis decided to rule without a chief minister. And he quickly demonstrated, in an extraordinarily dramatic act, that he would never again let any mere functionary upstage him. Since the end of the Fronde, an experienced civil servant named Nicolas Fouquet (1615–1680) had acquired a huge fortune while serving as France's superintendent of finances. He built a magnificent Baroque château near Paris called Vaux-le-Vicomte, and in August 1661 entertained the king and thousands of other guests there, serving delicacies on plates of gold. A new comedy by the great playwright Molière was staged in the open air, amid elaborate fireworks and fountains. Had the minister upstaged the king himself? Three weeks later, Louis had Fouquet arrested, subjected to a long trial on corruption charges, and imprisoned for the rest of his life. Louis henceforth relied for advice and assistance upon Mazarin's talented protégé Jean-Baptiste Colbert (1619–1683). Even while amassing his own fortune, Colbert never forgot that he owed everything to the monarch who had raised him up from a merchant background to the highest rank of the French nobility.

COLBERT'S REFORMS Some critics complained that in promoting men like Colbert, and in shutting great aristocratic families out of the royal council, Louis was favoring the urban bourgeoisie, or middle class, over the nobility. But if anything, the reverse was true. Throughout his long reign, Louis sought to placate, co-opt, and cooperate with his nobles. He saw himself as the "first gentleman" of his realm. Though he continued and regularized Richelieu's policy of sending royal intendants to act as effective royal governors in the country's major provinces, he instructed them to work alongside the local elites to ensure smooth and reliable collection of taxes. Nobles in the 1680s kept for themselves a higher proportion of the taxes collected in their provinces than had been the case fifty years before. In short, they did well out of Louis's absolutism. The provincial estates, local assemblies that were dominated by nobles, actually gained influence and fiscal power during Louis's reign. And although the king made an effort to muzzle the noble magistrates, who constituted the most important institutional opposition to the monarchy, he also reaffirmed their judicial role and made sure to involve them in his administration. Finally, Louis took great care to associate nobles with the prestigious public works projects that he undertook, such as the 150-mile-long Canal du Midi waterway that joined the Mediterranean to the Garonne River and the Atlantic, facilitating the shipment of goods.

By contrast, Louis showed little consideration for

the urban middle classes and trades. In a series of major reforms, he stripped French cities of municipal independence and subjected them to the rule of the intendants. He and Colbert promoted French manufactures, particularly luxury goods such as tapestries, high-end textiles, and porcelain. They also extended the guild system that had been developing since the middle ages, organizing nearly all the French trades into closed "corporations" chartered by the monarchy, removing much of the autonomy they had previously enjoyed. In many professions and trades, ranging from wig making to the practice of law, would-be members of the corporation now had to buy the right to practice from the state—making them part of the system analogous to the selling of venal offices that also included high-court judgeships. Louis and Colbert repeatedly manipulated this structure of "offices" to extort even more money from the hapless practitioners. The practice became an alternate form of state finance at a time when the French state, thanks to repeated defaults on its debt caused by the steep rise in military spending, could borrow from the international credit markets only at very high rates.

Colbert, the well-educated descendant of merchants and accountants, had the ambition of turning absolutism into a systematic, even scientific form of government, collecting data about population and resources, and experimenting with new, more rational ways of managing them. Colbert's ambitions shine through in the advice he gave to his son in 1671, just before the latter left on a trip to Italy. In each state, Colbert instructed:

> look at . . . its situation, its military forces, the number of its peoples, the greatness of the state, the number and size of cities, towns, and villages, the quantity of the peoples that compose the whole; . . . Visit the public works, maritime and on the ground, all the palaces, public houses, and generally all that is remarkable.

Although Colbert's specific system of information gathering did not survive beyond his death, the principle that states needed to collect and organize as much information as possible about their subjects and territory would become broadly accepted by all modern European governments. This sort of information-gathering had been pioneered by Italian city-states in the Renaissance, but only now, in the seventeenth century, did large territorial states begin to employ the same methods in a systematic manner.

THE "SUN KING"

At the heart of Louis's absolutist program—and what distinguished it from the models developed in Denmark or Brandenburg—was an intense

The "Sun King" The monarch was a master of style, using fashion and imagery to represent himself as the Sun King, radiating his grace throughout France. A ballet enthusiast, Louis even danced the role of the sun in an elaborate gold costume before his court in 1653.

and costly effort to glorify the monarch himself as a demigod. The sovereign's beneficence was seen as radiating outward from the royal person to embrace and ennoble his entire kingdom. As one philosopher wrote after Louis's death, "The prince stamps the character of his mind on the court, the court on the city, the city on the provinces. The sovereign's soul is a mould which gives its form to all the others."

In previous centuries, French royal ceremony had tended to stress the bonds between king and kingdom. Louis's predecessors had traveled extensively throughout the country, staging ceremonial "entries" into towns, in which they took part in elaborate processions with the local elites. Louis abandoned these practices in favor of distributing images that most often likened him to the sun. During his reign, the royal treasury paid for at least 700 engravings and some 300 statues of the "Sun King."

The equestrian statue of Louis in the Place Louis-le-Grand (Louis the Great) in central Paris was so large that during its installation, twenty workers could sit down for lunch inside of it. Dozens of French cities were adorned with Roman-style triumphal arches and churches dedicated to Louis's military victories.

POWER AND CULTURE AT VERSAILLES   The centerpiece of this enterprise of glorification was the vast palace Louis built on the site of a small hunting lodge in **Versailles**, twelve miles west of Paris. Work began in the 1660s and continued for more than four decades. The finished palace—designed by the same architects who had worked on Fouquet's lavish château—had some 725,000 square feet of usable space and 2,000 sumptuously furnished rooms. Together with its adjoining buildings, it could house some 10,000 people. The vast, meticulously tended gardens covered an additional thirty square miles. They boasted fifty ornate fountains and a "Grand Canal" on which the king staged mock naval combats with specially designed flat-bottomed boats. Louis shifted his residence and much of the government to Versailles, removing them from the dangers of Parisian rebellion. Once there, he hardly ever returned to the capital city he hated.

Louis's ultimate ambition was for his reign to match in splendor and glory the greatest days of Greece and Rome; and to this end, he zealously promoted the arts. Versailles itself put grand, impressive examples of French Baroque art and architecture on display for the world. An accomplished dancer, Louis participated in the elaborate ballets of Jean-Baptiste Lully (1632–1687), his Italian-born court composer.

Through his patronage, Louis encouraged the replacement of Latin with French in scholarship and supported the efforts of the French Academy to raise the French language to a level of purity and beauty that could, in theory, outshine the classical languages. The crown promoted the French theater, and during Louis's reign it marked its greatest triumphs with the works of the supremely witty playwright Jean-Baptiste Poquelin, known as Molière (1622–1673), and the tragedian Jean Racine (1639–1699). In *The Bourgeois Gentleman* and other plays, Molière skewered social pretentiousness and hypocrisy while subtly reinforcing norms of "sociable" and courtly behavior. Racine's verse tragedies, using material from ancient history, myth, and the Bible, focused on heroes and heroines driven by their passions into agonizing dilemmas.

FRENCH COURT LIFE   At Versailles, an elaborate system of royal etiquette and ceremony developed, based on many different European precedents but going well beyond them. In the morning, for instance, specially designated courtiers were allowed to witness and participate in the royal *lever* (arising). As Louis got out of bed, his clothes would be ceremonially passed from one noble to another, with the role of actually assisting the king into them bestowed as a mark of special favor. Others would stand by, watching. In the evening, the king would eat in front of an audience, with the most important courtiers standing closest to the royal table. The courtiers themselves had to maintain high standards of self-control, using a rigorously defined repertory of acceptable movements, gestures, language, and even facial expressions, not to mention clothes. Reputation depended on always displaying proper behavior, and a single mistake could, in extreme cases, invite a lifetime of ridicule. Aristocratic hostesses, such as the marquise of Rambouillet (1588–1655), played a crucial role in this court society by performing in the rituals of etiquette and instructing men and women alike in their intricacies at social gatherings devoted to witty and sophisticated conversation. These gatherings, later known as "salons," became fertile ground for the sort of early feminist thought that Poulain de la Barre had developed.

The construction of Versailles dramatically changed the relationship between the monarchy and the aristocracy in France. Increasingly, the most powerful families in the kingdom spent much of the year at court, living in the palace and participating in its rituals, associating

Versailles Inside the palace, magnificent rooms like the Hall of Mirrors displayed treasures and also reflected the opulence of the king and his courtiers back at them.

themselves with the Sun King's glory. Through his distribution of symbolic favors, Louis could manipulate aristocratic factions and thereby help ensure their obedience. The prince of Condé, the great rebel of the Fronde, was eventually pardoned by the king and spent his last days rowing on the Grand Canal at Versailles. But at the same time, the development of this new type of court bound the king himself more tightly than ever to the aristocracy, with whom he lived in such intimate contact. He also grew more isolated from the rest of his subjects, to whom he was no more than a name, an image, and a source of often unwelcome demands.

FRANCE AT WAR The single most important arena in which Louis both depended on and performed for his aristocracy was warfare. His twin goals throughout his reign were to secure France's international position—including especially its eastern and northern frontiers—and also to gain glory for himself. War was the means to both ends, and for the first part of his reign he had considerable success in it. Thanks in large part to Colbert's talent for raising revenue, he built up an army that numbered well over 100,000 in the 1670s and would eventually come to number some 400,000. Louis also employed brilliant military engineers who designed a series of massive fortifications for the French borders. Such demonstrations of military might not only enhanced the monarch's personal power and prestige, but bound him more closely to the aristocracy that commanded the expanded military.

Almost immediately, Louis put his forces to use. From 1667 to 1668, France attacked the Spanish Netherlands in the hope of annexing them. Very quickly, the new "balance of power" dynamic in European politics made itself felt. As France won dramatic victories, a broad coalition formed against it that included Sweden, Britain, and the Dutch Republic (the latter ending a war of its own to ally against France). Nonetheless, the French kept considerable territorial gains in the Spanish Netherlands. Louis then turned his attention to the Dutch Republic, which Colbert had long identified as a principal rival for France because of its growing commercial strength and large navy. From 1672 to 1678, Louis fought his "Dutch War," this time in alliance with the British, and sometimes leading his forces in person. To halt the French advance, the Dutch deliberately opened the dikes they had built over the previous century to reclaim land from the sea. The action flooded part of their country, literally bogging down Louis's troops.

Although France failed to conquer the Netherlands, it made gains on its eastern frontier at the expense of

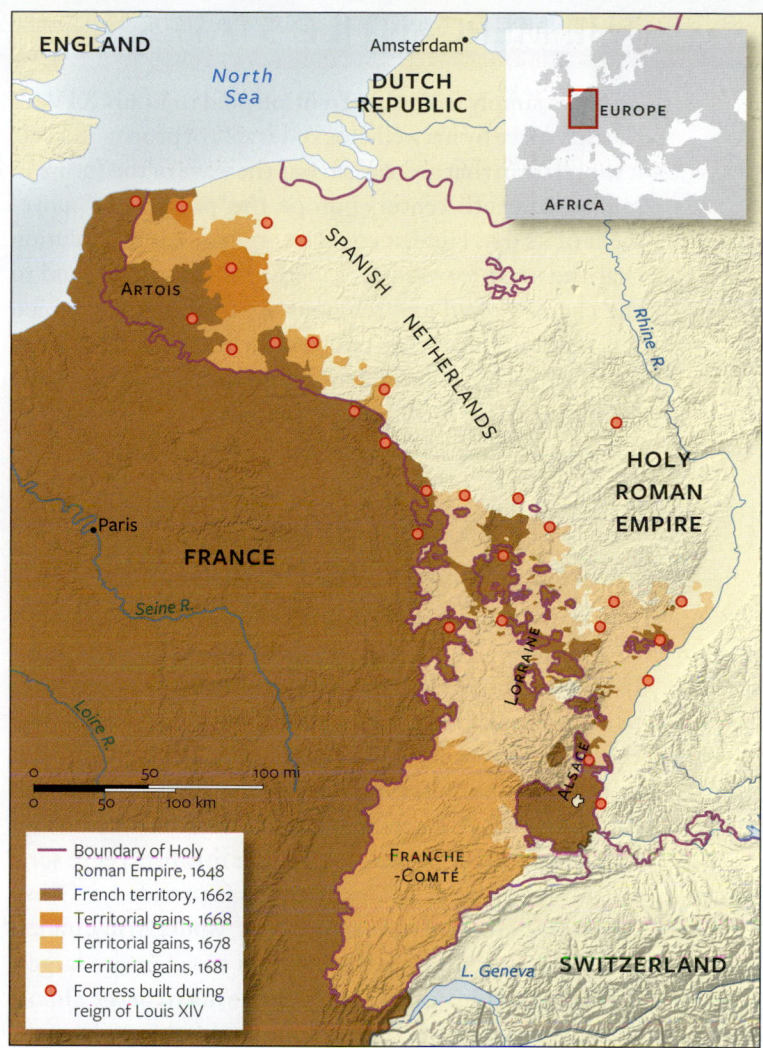

Louis XIV's Territorial Claims, 1662–1681 Louis's commitment to warfare led to territorial expansion along France's northeastern border, bolstered by a series of new fortifications. After twenty years of war, his armies enlarged the French-controlled territory in the east, including in Alsace and Lorraine, but such gains came at the cost of huge debt.

German states. In a brilliant campaign, Louis's army occupied most of the German-speaking province of Alsace, along the Rhine. These limited successes came at a vast cost, however. In addition to burdening France with a hugely increased state debt, they practically guaranteed that any further wars would quickly cause large new alliances to form against Louis XIV. But all of this mattered little to the king, who grandly commemorated his victories by building the largest and most ornate gallery in Versailles: the 220-foot-long Hall of Mirrors, filled with paintings depicting the Dutch War and Louis's personal rule.

THE MERCANTILE STATES

To judge simply from the attention paid to Louis XIV (in the first place by his well-stocked stable of propagandists), it would seem that absolutism was the wave of the future in mid-seventeenth-century Europe, the "progressive" movement of its day. Here, it could be argued, was the solution that the most forward-looking Europeans had found to the chaos of civil and religious strife and unrestrained international war. Yet two countries in northwestern Europe, Great Britain and the Netherlands, offered a powerful alternative to absolute monarchy.

BRITAIN: COMMONWEALTH, PROTECTORATE, RESTORATION (1648–1688)

Britain remained for decades the weaker of the two, thanks to the effects of its brutal civil war, which had ended with the execution of King Charles I and the establishment of the Commonwealth. Though the fighting ended in England by 1648, it continued in Scotland and Ireland for much of the next decade, even if the royalists there soon lost any real hope of victory. Between 1649 and 1652, Oliver Cromwell, as commander of the New Model Army, undertook a savage, large-scale campaign to subjugate largely Catholic Ireland. His victory there resulted in the almost total dispossession of the Catholic land-holding elites and the establishment of large new Protestant "plantations" on the island.

Meanwhile, political turmoil continued in London. Cromwell and his Army could not find ways of cooperating with the Rump Parliament, and in 1653, Cromwell himself led soldiers into the House of Commons to dissolve it. After a new, handpicked parliament also proved uncooperative, Cromwell formally seized power as Lord Protector of England, Wales, Scotland, and Ireland—a king in all but name, although he refused an actual crown. A written constitution—the only one in English history—theoretically guaranteed religious toleration and triennial parliaments. In practice, however, Cromwell's Protectorate soon turned effectively into a dictatorship. He ruled without parliament and divided England into twelve military zones, each headed by a major general. He then tried to impose a Puritan social order on the country, banning alehouses, Maypoles, swearing, Sabbath-breaking, and the observance of Christmas as a holiday.

Oliver Cromwell A 1653 portrait offers a heroic depiction of Cromwell. He wears armor and the plain white collar typically adopted by Puritans.

Upon Cromwell's death in 1658, his son Richard (1626–1712) briefly succeeded him, but by this point the Puritan revolution had grown both exhausted and hugely unpopular in the country. In May 1659, Richard Cromwell abdicated. Soon afterward the commander of British forces in Scotland, General George Monck, came south and staged a coup that led to the restoration of the Stuart dynasty in 1660. Charles I's son had lived in exile in France and the Low Countries after an attempt to reconquer England from his ancestral Scotland had failed in 1651. Now he returned to London and took the throne as Charles II (r. 1660–1685).

The poet John Dryden would later comment, acidly, on this period of British history that "thy wars brought nothing about." The conflicts that had toppled and killed one king ended with his son on the throne. Anglicanism was reestablished as the official state religion, and the country reverted to its traditional, unwritten constitution. A series of laws imposed penalties and loyalty oaths on Catholics and dissenting Protestants, and hundreds of Quakers who refused to swear oaths on principle were left to rot in prison. The bold experiments in parliamentary rule and religious toleration, and the calls for democracy and social equality, had all seemingly failed.

THE GROWTH OF POLITICAL PARTIES Yet the civil wars did prevent Britain from following the absolutist path of the continental monarchies. Charles II, a notoriously pleasure-loving monarch, did not imitate his father's repeated confrontations with Parliament. And although he secretly converted to Catholicism, and even pledged to Louis XIV that he would restore the religion in Britain, the new king did not dare make any serious moves in this direction. Parliament remained the active center of politics, and within it, two distinct factions emerged that in time would evolve into the world's first political parties. The Tories (originally an insult, from the Irish word for outlaw) generally supported the king. The Whigs (also originally an insult, meaning "cattle drivers") supported parliamentary supremacy and had greater sympathy for Protestant dissent. The Whigs, as we will see in the next chapter, failed to prevent Charles's Catholic brother and heir, James II, from succeeding to the throne in 1685 and reigning for three turbulent years. But in 1679 they passed the Habeas Corpus Act, which confirmed the

POLITICAL EQUALITY AFTER THE BRITISH CIVIL WARS

The British civil wars (1639–1649) ultimately became a dispute about the source of legitimate political power. For Royalists, the king was sovereign and his political authority derived from God. The Parliamentary view was more shifting and complicated. Some argued that men of property collectively held the right to rule, through their representatives in parliament. Radicals insisted that the right to vote be extended to all men. Oliver Cromwell's rise and the emergence of groups, such as the Levellers and the Diggers, clashed with the tradition of royal political authority. Despite the reestablishment of the monarchy in 1660, the questions the civil wars posed about power, equality, and the rights of Englishmen would persist through the eighteenth and nineteenth centuries.

Gerrard Winstanley, from *The True Levellers Standard Advanced*

Gerrard Winstanley, a former cloth merchant, led the Diggers—originally called the True Levellers for their adoption of a radical version of the Levellers' ideology. In this excerpt from his Digger manifesto, *The True Levellers Standard Advanced* (1649), Winstanley explores the origins of inequality and describes his plan to occupy and cultivate fallow land to provide for the poor and landless.

In the beginning of time, the great Creator Reason, made the Earth to be a Common Treasury, to preserve Beasts, Birds, Fishes, and Man, the lord that was to govern this Creation; for Man had Domination given to him, over the Beasts, Birds, and Fishes; but not one word was spoken in the beginning, That one branch of mankind should rule over another…Then he [man] fell into blindness of mind and weakness of heart, and runs abroad for a Teacher and Ruler: And so selfish imaginations taking possession of the Five Sences, and ruling as King in the room of Reason therein, and working with Covetousnesse, did set up one man to teach and rule over another; and thereby the Spirit was killed, and man was brought into bondage, and became a greater Slave to such of his own kind, then the Beasts of the field were to him…

The Work we are going about is this, To dig up Georges-Hill and the waste Ground thereabouts, and to Sow Corn, and to eat our bread together by the sweat of our brows.

And the First Reason is this, That we may work in righteousness, and lay the Foundation of making the Earth a Common Treasury for All, both Rich and Poor, That every one that is born in the land, may be fed by the Earth his Mother that brought him forth, according to the Reason that rules in the Creation…

Take notice, That England is not a Free People, till the Poor that have no Land, have a free allowance to dig and labour the Commons,[1] and so live as Comfortably as the Landlords that live in their Inclosures.

Anonymous, "The Protecting Brewer"

This Royalist ballad (1662) lampoons the rise of Oliver Cromwell from brewer's son to Lord Protector and leader of the Commonwealth. The song questions whether commoners are capable and worthy of political rule.

A brewer may be a burgess grave, and carry
   the matter so fine and so brave,
That he the better may play the knave, Which
   nobody can deny.
A brewer may be a Parliament man, for there
   the knavery first began—
And brew most cunning plots he can, Which
   nobody can deny.
…
A brewer may make his foes to flee, and raise
   his Fortunes so, that he

Lieutenant-General may be, Which nobody
   can deny.
A brewer may be all in all, and raise his
   powers both great and small,
That he may be a Lord General, Which
   nobody can deny.
…
Methinks I hear one say to me, pray, why may
   not a brewer be,
Lord Chancellor o' th' University? Which
   nobody can deny.
A brewer may be as bold as *Hector*,[2] when as
   he had drunk off his cup of nectar,
A brewer may be a Lord Protector, Which
   nobody can deny.
Now here remains the strangest thing, how
   this brewer about his liquor did bring,
To be an Emperor, or a King, Which nobody
   can deny.
A brewer may do what he will, and rob the
   Church and State, to sell,
His soul unto the Devil in Hell, Which nobody
   can deny.

QUESTIONS FOR ANALYSIS

1. According to Winstanley, why are all men fundamentally equal and free?
2. How does the "Protecting Brewer" suggest that Cromwell is unworthy of political power?
3. How do *The True Levellers Standard Advanced* and "The Protecting Brewer" differ in their views of political equality?

[1] **commons:** shared public land
[2] **Hector:** a hero of the Trojan War

Sources: *The True Levellers Standard Advanced: Or, The State of Commonly opened, and Presented to the Sons of Men*, Gerrard Winstanley (London: 1649), pp. 6–7; 12; 15; *Constable's Miscellany of Original and Selected Publications in the Various Departments of Literature, Science, & the Arts*, Vol. 47, ed. Archibald Constable (Edinburgh, 1829), pp. 312–3.

1628 Petition of Right by guaranteeing speedy trials for those under arrest.

TRADE AND THE CITY During the Stuart Restoration (1660–88), trade and the overseas empire grew ever more important to Britain, as reflected in the bustling capital city of London. (Neither Charles II nor his successors ever tried to build a British equivalent to Versailles.) The population of the British colonies in North America grew roughly fourfold over the period of 1640 to 1680, to reach more than 200,000. As a result of the Anglo-Dutch Wars, Britain captured the New Netherland colony and transformed its strategically located capital, New Amsterdam, into New York. Henceforth, the British enjoyed unbroken possession of the Eastern Seaboard of North America from South Carolina to present-day Maine.

London, meanwhile, grew from a population of roughly 350,000 in 1640 to as many as 575,000 by the end of the century. It did so despite suffering two horrendous blows in the 1660s. First, the Great Plague of 1665—an episode of bubonic plague similar to the Black Death of 1348—caused widespread panic and a death toll that topped 7,000 a week in September. As in previous plague outbreaks, households touched by the disease had their doors and windows boarded up to prevent the infection from spreading. Then in 1666, the Great Fire destroyed some 13,200 buildings in the capital, leaving up to 70,000 people homeless. Yet by the 1670s, London had recovered from both disasters, with buildings rapidly reconstructed and new residents arriving to take advantage of the capital's commercial wealth.

THE DUTCH "GOLDEN AGE"

For all of Britain's economic dynamism, in the middle of the seventeenth century it still trailed behind its great mercantile rival, the Netherlands. The Dutch had a greater per capita income than the British until the 1670s, and Dutch artisans earned roughly two-thirds more than their counterparts in southern England. Dutch fishing and textile manufacturing (mostly from domestic wool) continued to prosper, while international trade in wine and other commodities boomed. Dutch traders shipped French Bordeaux wine to Germany and Sweden, French Burgundy to the Baltic countries, German Rhine wines to Russia and Spain, and Spanish Malaga and Italian Marsala to England. The Dutch were not only major importers of American tobacco and furs, but turned the former into a true consumer product, offering varieties flavored with

citron, aniseed, thyme, lavender, nutmeg, beer, rosemary, prunes, and much else. When the English diarist Samuel Pepys (1633–1703) boarded a Dutch ship docked in London in November 1665, he was astonished at the value of the cargo: "As noble a sight as ever I saw in my life, the greatest wealth in confusion that a man can see in the world. Pepper scattered through every chink. You trod upon it and in cloves and nutmeg I walked above the knees, whole rooms full. And silk in bales and boxes of copper plate." Much of this wealth, especially the spices, came from another burgeoning area of Dutch trade, East Asia, and especially what is now Indonesia, where the Dutch East India Company was establishing a series of forts and trading posts that would eventually evolve into full-fledged colonial rule.

DUTCH WEALTH Dutch mercantile wealth was not, for the most part, channeled into grand building projects like Versailles. It went into banks, which reinvested it in further commercial ventures. Following the example of the great Italian merchant banks of the late Middle Ages, these institutions built grandiose headquarters and exercised considerable social and political power. The wealth funded the building of solid homes in Amsterdam and the Hague; it bought the well-tailored clothes worn by Dutch burghers, and a great deal of it ended up as food. Even Dutch common sailors ate extraordinarily well by

Stock Exchange Emmanuel de Witte captured the Netherlands' financial prosperity in this 1653 painting of the Amsterdam stock exchange's lofty cloisters and the hustle and bustle of businessmen performing transactions.

GOLDEN AGE AMSTERDAM

> **WHAT IS THERE THAT'S NOT FOUND HERE / OF CORN; FRENCH OR SPANISH WINE / ANY INDIES GOODS THAT ARE SOUGHT / IN AMSTERDAM MAY ALL BE BOUGHT / HERE'S NO FAMINE...THE LAND IS FAT.**
>
> CONSTANTIJN HUYGENS (DUTCH COMPOSER AND POET), *CORN-FLOWERS*, 1672

Map legend

- City wall
- Road
- Dike
- Weigh house (for weighing goods)
- × Windmill
- Garden

BUILDINGS
1. Old Church
2. Meat market
3. Lombard Bank
4. Stock exchange
5. City Hall and Bank of Amsterdam
6. New Church

Scale: 0 — 1000 — 2000 ft / 0 — 400 — 800 m

Map labels:
Salt warehouse · Area for drying herring · Wharves · The Ij · Grain exchange · Crane · Wharves · Dutch East India Company · Market · Dam Square · St. Anthony's market · Naval shipyard · Shipyards · Shipyards · Shipyard · National warehouse · Headquarters of Dutch East India Company · Fish market · New Canal · Warehouse · Hospital and almshouse · JEWISH QUARTER · Garden of medicinal plants · Rope warehouse · Grain warehouse · Market · Synagogues · Amstel R. · City-wall ca. 1663 · City stockyard · Cattle and pig markets

Jan Steen's *The Fat Kitchen* (ca. 1650–1655) may be an exaggerated representation of the Dutch appetite, but it is an exaggeration rooted in reality—feasts could stretch to twenty-five or thirty courses. Here a joyous family shares a meal, surrounded by kitchenware and hanging meats.

IMPORTS, JUNE 27, 1634

326,733 pounds of *Malaccan pepper*

297,446 pounds of *cloves*

292,623 pounds of *saltpeter*

141,278 pounds of *indigo*

75 pots of *spiced ginger* and other confections

3,989 rough *diamonds*

93 boxes of *pearls* and *rubies*

1,155 pounds of *Chinese silk*

199,800 pounds of unrefined *Sri Lankan sugar*

SOURCE: JOHAN DE BRUNE, *EMBLEMATA* (MIDDLEBURG: 1624), P. 9.

> **SWEETNESS AND EXCESS IS TODAY GROWN SO GREAT...THE MEN OF TODAY WOULD DEARLY LIKE TO HAIL COOKS AND OTHER SERVANTS OF THEIR GLUTTONY WITH TRUMPETS OF HONOR AND CROWNS OF LAUREL.**
>
> OTTO BELCAMPIUS, *THE LAST HOUR*, 1661

An intricate canal system supplied Amsterdam's vegetable markets with an abundance of fresh produce from farms. In Hendrick Martenszoon Sorgh's painting *The Vegetable Market* (1662), a woman working at her stall extends a gourd to the viewer. Her wares include cabbages, carrots, turnips, artichokes, squash, beets, and pumpkins.

POPULATION

1600: 60,000

1647: 140,000

QUESTIONS FOR ANALYSIS

1. How did the city life of Amsterdam revolve around food and its many dimensions?

2. What economic developments enabled the Dutch to enjoy such a rich selection of food?

3. How did food connect Amsterdam to the rest of Europe and the world?

Girl with a Pearl Earring This masterpiece from around 1665 conveys Vermeer's great genius for realistic depictions of people.

European standards of the period. One Dutch ship with a crew of a hundred carried, for each month at sea, no less than 450 pounds of cheese, 5 tons of cured meat, 400 pounds of cured fish, several tons of pickled herring, and 8,960 gallons of ale. It all came to nearly 5,000 calories a day per sailor. All of this was made possible by the development of sophisticated new financial instruments that allowed credit to flow quickly to profitable enterprises. Building on the example of the Renaissance Italians who had invented modern methods of accounting, the Dutch kept reliable track of larger and more complex financial transactions than any previous society had done.

TOLERATION AND CREATIVITY As Amsterdam became the great warehouse of world trade, thronged with merchants and sailors from every continent, Dutch culture and politics changed. The severe, intolerant Calvinism that had still prevailed at the start of the century ceased to set the tone, and the Dutch Republic welcomed Protestant dissenters of many different stripes, as well as Jews from Germany and Portugal. By 1672, the flourishing Jewish community of Amsterdam, which had produced

and then rejected Spinoza, numbered some 7,500 out of the city's population of 200,000. The British poet Andrew Marvell (1621–1678), in an anti-Dutch poem written on the eve of the First Anglo-Dutch War, condemned this "watery Babel," but could not help remarking on the spectacle. He likened the city's commerce in religious ideas to the other sort of commerce at which the Dutch excelled:

> Hence Amsterdam, Turk-Christian-Pagan-Jew,
> Staple of sects and mint of schism grew;
> That bank of conscience, where not one so strange
> Opinion but finds credit, and exchange.

The Netherlands also allowed an unprecedented degree of press freedom. Some of the first newspapers in the French and English languages were published there to avoid the state censorship imposed in France and Britain. Between 1650 and 1672, the Netherlands also enjoyed a tumultuous, relatively open, republican political system in which the elected representatives in the country's different provinces, gathered into legislative bodies called "states," were powerful political forces. And the Netherlands had a States General (in Dutch, Staaten Generaal, after which they named Staten Island in New Amsterdam), which dominated national political life.

It was in this wealthy, tolerant mercantile setting that the Dutch gave new attention to the contours and texture of ordinary life. Their artists increasingly found as much pleasure and beauty in everyday events and relationships as in the extraordinary, the mythical, and the world beyond. Dutch literature of the period celebrated companionate marriage and the joys of parenthood. Dutch Baroque architects devoted their most enduring efforts to intricately decorated town halls, marketplaces, and storehouses—not churches. And Dutch painters found their great subjects all around them: sober aldermen in their meeting halls, servants at work, children at play. Still-life and landscape painting flourished, even as religious and mythical themes faded. The painter Jan Vermeer (1632–1675) is known for his luminous depictions of such ordinary subjects as a girl wearing a pearl earring, and a simple street scene showing women at work. In Vermeer's hands, the sober, solid wealth of Dutch cities, fed by its trade and manufacturing, was vibrantly and memorably recorded. As for Rembrandt Harmenszoon van Rijn (1606–1669), perhaps the greatest painter of the age, he turned his mastery of color and brushwork to portraits of a militia company and to close studies of faces, as well as to biblical scenes. In many ways, Rembrandt, who came from a wealthy artisanal background in Leiden and became an apprentice painter at age sixteen, found his

REMBRANDT'S *ANATOMY LESSON OF DR. NICOLAES TULP*

Rembrandt's *The Anatomy Lesson of Dr. Nicolaes Tulp* (1632) conveys both his particular gifts as a painter and the intellectual curiosity developing in Amsterdam. The painting, commissioned by the city's guild of surgeons, captures a lesson during which a recently executed criminal's body was dissected. With the help of an anatomical textbook (bottom right), a group of surgeons observes Tulp's demonstration of the intricate workings of arm and hand muscles. Despite the seeming spontaneity of the figures, Rembrandt constructs a precisely arranged group portrait. His dramatic use of light and shadow emphasizes the surgeons' faces and the body's pale skin, and his careful rendering of the exposed muscles and tendons shows an interest in anatomic detail. As a whole, the painting serves as an example of the increasingly common realism of scenes in art and the new fascination with the pursuit of scientific knowledge.

QUESTIONS FOR ANALYSIS

1. How is this painting characteristic of Dutch Golden Age art?
2. What aspects of the painting contribute to its realism?
3. What attitudes toward science does this painting convey?

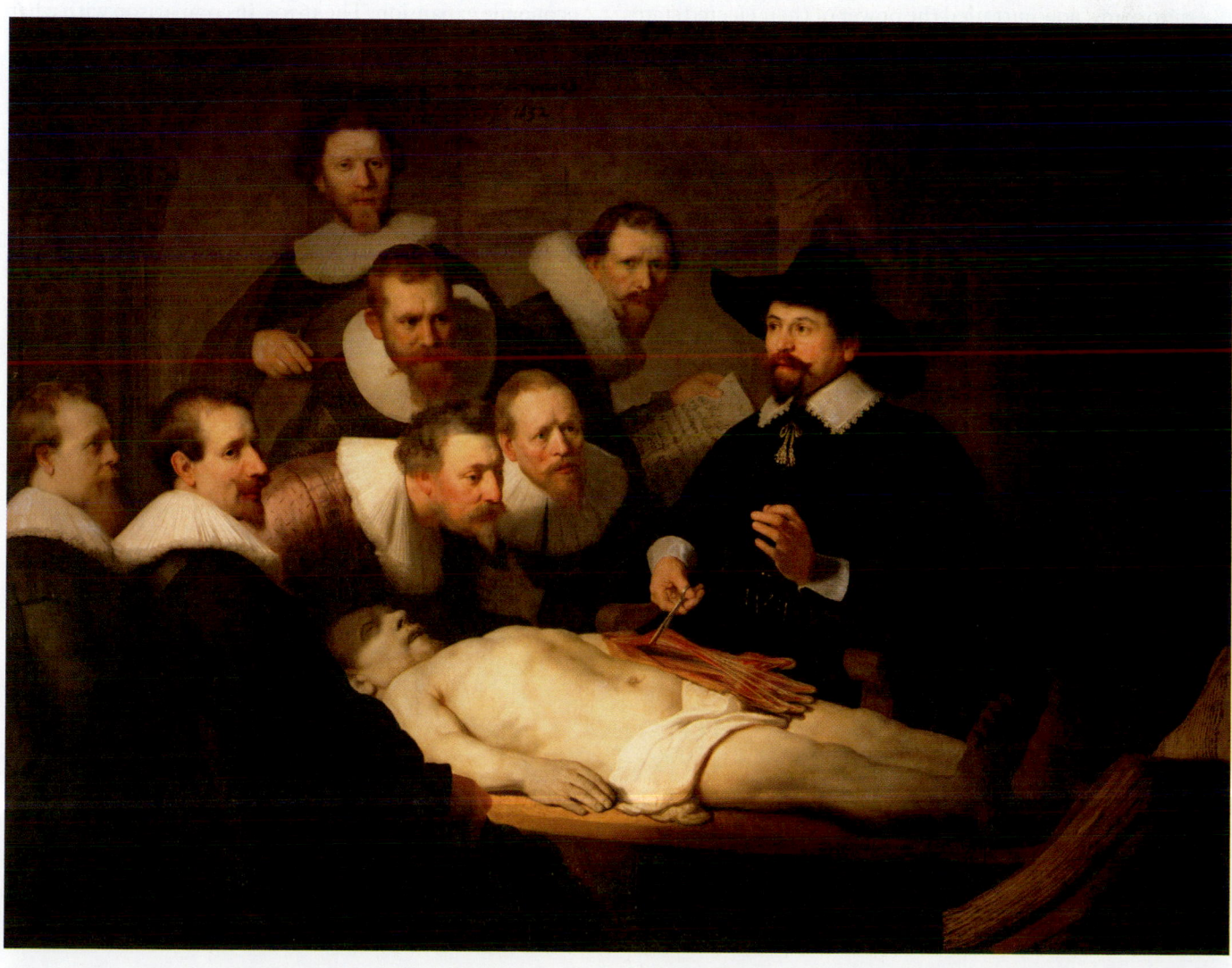

greatest subject in the mirror: he executed nearly ninety self-portraits over the course of his adult life, and never did a painter show greater fascination with wrinkles and the other ordinary marks of the aging, mortal self.

DECLINE The middle of the seventeenth century was the **Dutch "Golden Age,"** but by 1680 clear signs of decline were visible. The Anglo-Dutch Wars had hurt Dutch commerce and took away the promising New Netherland colony. Louis XIV's Dutch War, which lasted from 1672 to 1678, put the country under further pressure. Despite its naval and mercantile strength, the Netherlands was small (its population was less than 40 percent of England's) and its flat territory was difficult to defend. Internal political turmoil also took its toll. In the "disaster year" of 1672, the population again reached out to the country's leading noble dynasty, the House of Orange. The various Dutch provinces, which enjoyed considerable autonomy, now curtailed the power of their elected states general, the highest Dutch poitical authority, and chose the young Prince William III (r. 1672–1702) as executive "stadholder." "Orangist" mobs attacked members of the patrician elites who dominated in the states. There ensued a civil war lasting six years, from which the Dutch

Republic emerged in a weakened state. For all the glories of the Golden Age, the next century would belong to the absolutist powers and to the Netherlands' great maritime rival, Great Britain.

CONCLUSION

At the end of the 1670s, despite continuing international rivalries that promised an indefinite future of warfare, something fundamental had changed in Europe. The wave of chaotic civil wars, which had swept over nearly every European country in the middle of the century, had receded. Throughout most of the continent, states were asserting more control over the use of force, both within their own territories and when directed at enemy states. These trends, in combination with a slowly improving climate and rapidly expanding overseas trade, were driving economic expansion. The 1670s, in comparison with what had come before in the century, were a decade of relative order and prosperity. The following decades would fall largely into the same pattern. As time passed, these changing conditions would open new political, social, and intellectual horizons for Europeans.

[CHAPTER REVIEW]

KEY TERMS

Court of Star Chamber
(p. 444)
Oliver Cromwell (p. 445)
Levellers (p. 445)
Fronde (p. 446)

Bogdan Chmielnicki
(p. 447)
Shabbetai Sevi (p. 448)
Quakers (p. 449)
Jansenism (p. 449)

Thomas Hobbes (p. 451)
Baruch Spinoza (p. 452)
Blaise Pascal (p. 453)
Peace of Westphalia
(p. 456)

Louis XIV (p. 460)
Versailles (p. 462)
Dutch "Golden Age"
(p. 470)

REVIEW QUESTIONS

1. What political and religious issues contributed to the outbreak of the British civil wars?

2. What were the causes of the civil wars on the Continent in the mid-seventeenth century?

3. What common tendencies linked the millenarian and other radical religious movements that emerged in the mid-seventeenth century?

4. During the 1600s, how did women contribute to efforts to re-energize the Catholic Church?

5. How did Thomas Hobbes's ideas on the origin of government challenge older assumptions about politics and religion?

6. How do the writings of Spinoza, Pascal, and Poulain de la Barre reveal the emergence of a more skeptical, egalitarian approach to society?

7. How did the Peace of Westphalia mark a new approach to international relations in Europe?

8. In what ways did Louis XIV expand the power of the French monarchy?

9. What were the effects of the dissolution of Oliver Cromwell's Protectorate?

10. What contributed to the commercial wealth and high standard of living of the Dutch Republic in the mid-1600s?

CORE OBJECTIVES

After reading this chapter, you should have a solid understanding of the following core objectives. To strengthen your grasp of the core objectives, use the resources on the Student Site for The West.

- Analyze the causes and effects of the civil wars that disrupted European politics and society in the mid-seventeenth century.

- Trace the rise in messianism and other radical religious movements that arose during the civil wars.

- Examine the evolution of new forms of political analysis and philosophy inspired by the emerging scientific worldview of the seventeenth century.

- Explain the new political order that emerged in Europe at the end of the Thirty Years' War.

- Describe the practices of absolutist states such as Prussia and France.

- Identify the key characteristics of the mercantile states of Great Britain and the Netherlands.

 GO TO inQuizitive TO SEE WHAT YOU'VE LEARNED—AND LEARN WHAT YOU'VE MISSED—WITH PERSONALIZED FEEDBACK ALONG THE WAY.

1682
Peter the Great ascends
to the Russian throne

1683
Ottoman siege
of Vienna

1684
Pierre Bayle begins
editing *News from
the Republic of Letters*

1685
France institutes
"Black Code"
in its overseas
colonies

October 22, 1685
Louis XIV revokes
Edict of Nantes

1687
Isaac Newton publishes
Principia Mathematica

1688–1697
War of the
League of Augsburg

1688–9
Glorious Revolution
in England

1689
John Locke publishes *Second Treatise of
Government* and *Essay Concerning
Human Understanding*

July 12, 1690
Battle of
the Boyne

1700–21
Great Northern War

1701
Kingdom
of Prussia
established

1702–14
War of the
Spanish Succession

May 1703
Peter the Great founds
Saint Petersburg

1707
Act of Union
between England
and Scotland

From Court to City

EMERGING CULTURES, 1680–1740

I n 1697 Antonio de Vieira (1682–1745) experienced an unlikely twist of fate. Born into the same community of Amsterdam Sephardic Jews that had produced Baruch Spinoza, he was a fifteen-year-old cabin boy on a Dutch ship when Peter I, the young Tsar of Russia, came aboard for a sail during a tour of Western Europe. Peter, who spoke some Dutch, took a liking to Antonio and offered him a position as a page in his court. Over the next twenty years, the young Jew rose on the tide of the Tsar's favor, returning with him to Russia, converting to Russian Orthodoxy, winning the position of Adjutant-General of Police in the new capital city of Saint Petersburg, and even marrying into a princely family. In 1726 he became a Count of the Russian Empire.

The story is a revealing one for several reasons. First, it shows something about the occasionally spectacular opportunities for social advancement in a Europe that was growing more prosperous and settled. In an even more spectacular example, a Latvian serving maid named Marta Skawronska, who captured Tsar Peter's affections, ended up his empress and successor. As Tsarina Catherine I, she ruled the largest empire on earth, stretching from the Baltic Sea to the Pacific Ocean. The De Vieira story also points toward the growing cosmopolitanism of European elites, who over the next century would become increasingly

1714
Peace of Utrecht

1720
Financial bubbles cause crises in Britain and France

1719
Daniel Defoe publishes *Robinson Crusoe*

1721
Montesquieu publishes *Persian Letters*

Sugar Cultivation A 1667 engraving from a French history of the Antilles depicts the industrial process that was sugar cultivation. Turning cane into products such as molasses, treacle, and refined sugar entailed vast quantities of slave labor as well as sophisticated machinery. The slaves of Europe's overseas colonies suffered from terribly cruel working and living conditions.

- Why did levels of religious intolerance increase in the late seventeenth century?
- What was the significance of the Glorious Revolution of 1689?
- In what ways did absolutism reach its height in this period?
- What major changes in the conduct of war occurred at this time?
- Why was war such a regular occurrence in this period?
- How did the Atlantic world affect Europe's trade and economy?
- Why did cities replace some courts as centers of culture in the early eighteenth century?
- How did skepticism influence European thought?

comfortable crossing borders and even living for years in foreign countries. And it hints at the growing possibilities for toleration in a Europe grown weary of religious conflict. Here, Peter led the way, allowing Catholics and Protestants to worship freely in his empire at a time when religious minorities in much of Western Europe remained ferociously persecuted.

De Vieira's story also matters because of what he did in Saint Petersburg. As late as 1700, the city did not yet exist. In the swamplands where the Neva River emptied into the Baltic Sea stood nothing but a small Swedish fort. But in May 1703, Tsar Peter captured the area, used lessons he had learned from the Dutch to drain the swamps, and laid the foundations for a new capital city that he saw both as a strategic port and a "window on the West." Entranced with Amsterdam, the Tsar planned Saint Petersburg as a city of broad canals and sober, sturdy stone buildings very different from the extravagant domes and towers (and rotting wood) of the old Russian capital, Moscow. He also vowed to make it a "well-policed" city in the broad, eighteenth-century sense of the word: not just a crime-free place, but an orderly, clean, and healthy one.

This is where de Vieira came in. Modeling his office after the General Lieutenancy of Police created by French King Louis XIV for Paris in 1667, de Vieira issued regulations on everything from the freshness of the meat sold in Saint Petersburg markets to the moss used to fill cracks in wooden walls (he ordered that it be boiled to prevent cockroaches from feeding on it). He organized a trash collection service and a system of street lighting using candles. And he developed a force of policemen, night watchmen, barriers, and checkpoints to fight crime and keep tabs on the city's growing population. De Vieira's actions illustrated the social ideal of European absolutism: the well-ordered state, rationally managed by a single, central authority. To the European elites of Tsar Peter's day, a continent-wide system of such states seemed the best solution to the problem of managing competition among and within states, and preventing it from spinning out of control as it had done in the earlier years of the century.

Between 1680 and 1740, Europe seemed to belong more than ever to cultured, cosmopolitan servants of absolute monarchies like de Vieira. With the continuing exceptions of a few small republics including Venice, Switzerland, and the Netherlands, it remained a continent of monarchies. And while England took a strong move toward limiting its monarchy with its "Glorious Revolution" of 1688, no other country followed its trajectory. Indeed, during these years, as the destructiveness of European warfare waned and religious conflict, after briefly flaring anew, turned less strident, it seemed that absolute monarchs were more secure on their thrones than ever. When France's leading theologian wrote, around 1700, that monarchy was "the most common, oldest, and also the most natural form of government," it seemed to most of his readers that he was stating a self-evident truth.

Yet even as the placid, well-disciplined order envisaged by Tsar Peter seemed to be spreading, an intellectual revolution was beginning which would soon shake this order to its core. This revolution took place above all in Western Europe—particularly Britain, France, and Antonio de Vieira's home country of the Netherlands. And ironically, it was grounded in a principle also promoted by the advocates of the well-ordered police state, namely that reason should govern human affairs. The continuing spectacular progress of science—which served as a reference point for the absolutists as well—helped inspire this revolution, which took from it a vision of a universe that operated according to invariable, knowable laws. For the moment, the revolution remained largely limited to elite, learned circles, but it nonetheless marked a decisive break in European history: the beginning of the Enlightenment. This chapter will explore the conditions under which the Enlightenment was born, while also tracing the development of European politics, society, and culture in the late seventeenth and early eighteenth centuries.

INTOLERANCE INTENSIFIED

The road to the Enlightenment did not run smoothly, and the last decades of the seventeenth century actually brought heightened fears of renewed intolerance and religious strife. The intolerance did not, however, stem, as in earlier decades, from increased religious fervor. Now, it more often came from *fear of* religious fervor and the civil strife it could provoke. As European states continued to recover from the disruptions of the earlier decades, rulers felt that the best means of avoiding religious discord would be the strict enforcement of religious uniformity throughout their realms.

THE EDICT OF NANTES REVOKED

France offered the most spectacular example. Since 1598, King Henry IV's Edict of Nantes had offered French Protestants—known as Huguenots—limited toleration. It did not defend toleration as a principle: most French Catholics still saw Protestantism as a dangerous heresy, and tolerated it for the same reason the chronically ill tolerate the diseases they suffer from—because they felt they had no choice. The Edict did not grant even this limited toleration to Jews, who remained banished from most French territory. During the seventeenth century, Protestant privileges became increasingly restricted in France, and Louis XIV in particular undertook strong steps to encourage conversions to Catholicism (including forcing Protestant families to house unruly Catholic soldiers). Nonetheless, in practice the Edict allowed the Protestant community of some 850,000 to survive, and in many regions of France peaceful coexistence remained the norm.

On October 22, 1685, King Louis XIV finally felt the monarchy was strong enough to act against the so-called heretics, and formally revoked the Edict of Nantes. With the exception of recently annexed Lutheran territories

Flight of the Huguenots A Dutch engraving shows the Protestant families of La Rochelle, France hastily packing their belongings onto carts and leaving the city in 1661.

along the Rhine, Protestantism now became illegal on French soil. This action immediately posed French Protestants with the stark choice religious intolerance has always posed to its victims: conversion, exile, or death. A small number of Huguenots were executed for their beliefs. A large majority converted to Catholicism, although often with little or no sincerity. But approximately 200,000 fled France, joining others who had left earlier in the century. More than half of the refugees went to England and the Netherlands, but significant numbers settled in Germany and even farther afield. In 1700, London counted some 23,000 Huguenots among its population, and in Berlin they made up some 20 percent of the city's residents. In England's North American colonies, traces of Huguenot immigration still survive in towns like New Rochelle, New York (named for the Huguenot stronghold of La Rochelle), and in monuments to figures like Paul Revere (descended from Huguenots called De La Rivière).

INTOLERANCE ACROSS EUROPE

There were other examples of intensifying intolerance as well. Scarcely two months after Louis's action, the Catholic Duke of Savoy in northwest Italy revoked the toleration he had previously extended to 14,000 "Waldensian" Christians—spiritual descendants of a radical medieval reform movement that had embraced the Reformation. A joint French-Savoyard army massacred more than 1,000 of them, and imprisoned some 8,500 others in wretched prison camps. Even in the Netherlands, which had a reputation as the most tolerant state in Europe, only members of the Protestant Dutch Reformed Church could hold office or count on full freedom of worship. In England, the early 1680s marked a high point in the persecution of roughly 200,000 Protestants who "dissented" from the Church of England—predominantly Baptists, Quakers, and various sorts of Calvinists. If convicted of holding unsanctioned religious services, they ran the risk of heavy fines or imprisonment. The restored King Charles II, who flirted with Catholicism and converted secretly to it before his death, associated these denominations with the radicals who had cheered his father's execution during the civil wars.

THE GLORIOUS REVOLUTION AND ITS CONSEQUENCES

In England, these heightened religious tensions helped bring about one of the most consequential upheavals in the country's history. Although it did not make the country anything like a democracy in the modern meaning of the word, it established the supremacy of parliamentary representation, and guaranteed certain political rights more firmly than ever before.

A CHANGE IN RULE

In February 1685, just months before revocation of the Edict of Nantes would provoke outrage and fear across Protestant Europe, Charles II died and his brother, an open Catholic, took the English throne as King James II. Protestant preachers immediately labeled James another Queen Mary I in the making, and reminded their listeners (who needed no such reminders, so often had they heard the stories) of the Protestant martyrs who had bled and burned during her sixteenth-century reign. They predicted that James would abolish parliament and rule like an English Louis XIV—if, indeed, he did not actually surrender England to that autocratic monarch. James in fact initially tried to curry favor with dissenting Protestants (including Baptists, Quakers and Presbyterians) by relaxing the legal restrictions on them. But he also persisted in his advocacy of Catholicism, and in attempts to weaken Parliament. The dissenters' fear of "popery" quickly overwhelmed their hopes of toleration.

William and Mary This 1689 engraving emphasizes William and Mary's legitimacy as rulers of England. William carries the orb and scepter, symbols of the monarchy. At the bottom, the royal arms and pictures of other kings emphasize the monarchs' connections to the English royal lineage.

Almost as soon as James became king, the threat of a new civil war arose. In June 1685, Charles II's illegitimate Protestant son, the Duke of Monmouth, landed in western England and raised the flag of rebellion. James defeated him, had him beheaded, and meted out harsh justice to his supporters. These measures further alienated many Protestants. Three years later, James's Catholic queen gave birth to a son, who took precedence as the male heir over James's older Protestant daughters from an earlier marriage. Protestant opponents claimed that the birth had been fraudulent, with the real baby born dead and a substitute smuggled into the birthing chamber in a warming pan. Calls grew for James to be removed from the throne, and replaced by his adult Protestant daughter Mary (1662–1694).

Soon enough the calls were answered. Mary was married to William III of Orange (1650–1702), the Dutch Stadholder. Concerned above all to keep his country safe from another French invasion, William had initially resisted requests that he challenge James for the English throne. But when James signed a naval agreement with Louis XIV in 1688, posing a threat to the Netherlands, William changed his mind. On November 5, he successfully landed on the west coast of England, and issued a declaration in which he disingenuously claimed to be doing nothing other than ensuring the assembly of "a free and lawful Parliament . . . as soon as possible." The bulk of the English population quickly rallied to him, and within weeks, James II found his position untenable. The King fled to France, where he set up a court in exile. In the summer of 1689, a new Parliament declared King William III and Queen Mary II joint rulers, in what observers quickly dubbed the "**Glorious Revolution**."

THE ENGLISH BILL OF RIGHTS

This change of throne, which took place with almost no bloodshed in England itself, paved the way for important political reforms. In early 1689, the new Parliament, with overwhelming support from the population and from the grateful new monarchs, issued a "Bill of Rights." Through this act the Parliament effectively claimed sovereignty over the Kingdom, with the authority to approve taxes and laws and correct royal abuses up to and including removing unjust kings from office. In an effort to contain the scope of change, the revolutionaries themselves tried to play down what they had accomplished. They framed their reforms as a minimal, incremental set of changes that did little but correct King James's abuses, and introduce new constitutional safeguards in the spirit of an "ancient constitution" that supposedly traced its origins back to before the Norman Conquest of 1066. There could be no question, in other words, of confusing the events of 1688–1689 with the radical ones of 1649, which had toppled the monarchy and opened the door to religious millenarianism and radical theories of social equality. And in fact, the England of 1690 was no less dominated by large landowners and the Church of England than the England of 1685 had been.

The Glorious Revolution was not a social revolution. It was most definitely, however, a political one. While the Bill of Rights made few claims that Parliament had not made in the 1640s, this time they quickly became accepted as bedrock principles of the English constitution. After 1688, no English monarch ever dared imitate James II's absolutist ambitions or his insistence on a divine right to rule. Parliamentary rule had been established for good.

LOCKE'S *SECOND TREATISE*

This new political order also rested upon powerful, new intellectual bases. Just before the Revolution, the leading European political thinker of the age, **John Locke** (1632–1704), composed a powerful treatise that defended

just such action as Parliament would soon take. Locke, the brilliant son of Puritans, had read deeply in the political philosophy of the day, and especially in the work of Thomas Hobbes. But he broke with Hobbes in a significant way.

John Locke A late-seventeenth-century portrait made toward the end of the philosopher's life.

We have seen that Hobbes, writing during the turmoil of the mid-seventeenth century, had described mankind's natural state as a harsh one that amounted to the "war of all against all." For Hobbes, establishing social peace required the complete subjection of individuals to the sovereign power of the state, however tyrannical it might prove. Locke, by contrast, saw the "state of nature" as a relatively mild condition, which humanity evolved away from mostly out of the need to protect and preserve property. From this perspective, tyranny could not be justified so easily. In Locke's so-called *Second Treatise of Government* (1689), he offered a powerful theory of the people's right to oppose and even depose tyrannical rulers. Against unjust authority, he wrote, "the people are not [. . .] bound to obey; by which means they come again to be out of subjection, and may constitute themselves a new legislative [power]."

CHANGES IN RELIGION

The Glorious Revolution also marked a decisive change for England in matters of religion. Charles II and James II had favored the so-called "High Church" elements of the Church of England that most closely approached Catholicism, notably in its elaborate ritual and bishop-heavy church hierarchy. By contrast, William and Mary and the new Parliament favored the simpler, more egalitarian "Low Church" elements that were closer to Puritanism. The Toleration Act of 1689 instituted freedom of worship for all Protestants, including the "dissenting" groups marked by the radical spirit of the 1640s (although they could not hold office). The Act of Settlement of 1701 formally banned Catholics from inheriting the throne. Never again would British rulers flirt with the Church of Rome. After the 1690s, moreover, Catholics under British rule in Ireland (well over three quarters of the Irish population) suffered under some of the harshest restrictions of any religious community in Europe. They could not join the clergy, sit in parliament, teach, send their children overseas to university, purchase land, inherit from Protestants, or own a horse worth more than £5. Jews in Britain would not be able to vote or hold office until the nineteenth century.

A NEW ECONOMIC DIRECTION

Charles II and James II had also favored "mercantilist" economic policies similar to those of their patron and ally, Louis XIV of France. Taking land as the sole source of wealth, they promoted the interests of large landowners and sought to exploit the agricultural and mineral wealth of England's overseas colonies by means of state-chartered monopolies, such as the East India Company. They discouraged homegrown manufacturing—especially the textile industry—which depended on free trade with other countries to flourish. By contrast, the new regime followed the example of William of Orange's native Netherlands in favoring trade and manufacturing interests, lowering tariffs, and restricting the power of the great trading companies. The year 1694 saw the chartering by Parliament of an independent national bank, the Bank of England, on the model of the earlier Dutch Bank of Amsterdam. By providing stable, dependable credit to both the government and the manufacturing sector, the Bank supported a vast expansion of British trade in the following century.

A PROTESTANT BASE IN IRELAND

The final important effect of the Glorious Revolution came in foreign policy. After 1688–89, England quickly abandoned its alliance with France. War became inevitable when Louis XIV refused to acknowledge the change of government in London, and welcomed to Versailles the exiled James II as the legitimate king of England and Scotland. With French support, James sought to raise Ireland, with its large Catholic majority, against the Dutch "usurper" William. A year of brutal fighting in Ireland followed, ending the "bloodless" phase of the Glorious Revolution. On July 12, 1690, King William crushed a largely Irish and French force at the Boyne River. And by late 1691, his armies had driven James II's forces out of Ireland altogether. The victory guaranteed that the Protestant settlements initially implanted in northern Ireland by James I would remain in place. Indeed, these settlements established such deep roots that when the Catholic Irish finally achieved independence from Britain in the 1920s, their new state would be limited to the southern three-quarters of the island. The northern, Protestant-majority province of Ulster remains to this day part of the United Kingdom of Great Britain and Northern Ireland. Northern Irish Protestants continue to call themselves "Orangemen" in homage to William of Orange, and march in a triumphal parade every 12th of July, on the anniversary of the Battle of the Boyne.

PARLIAMENT AND POLITICS

In Britain, the changes wrought by the Glorious Revolution were cemented in the following decades. The principal change—parliamentary supremacy itself—owed at least something to the luck of monarchical succession. King William III was first and foremost a Dutchman, whose concern for domestic English politics centered on maintaining England as a powerful ally for the Netherlands. Queen Mary's sister, Anne (1655–1714), who succeeded to the throne after William's death in 1702, was a relatively weak monarch. When she died without heirs twelve years later, the new rules of Protestant-only succession meant that the crown again passed to a foreigner whose principal interests lay elsewhere. King George I (1660–1727), a descendant of James I, had previously been ruler of the north German state of Hanover. Even after becoming king, George spent as much time as possible in Germany and never learned more than rudimentary English. Under monarchs with little domestic interest or ambition, Parliament was able to consolidate the gains of the Glorious Revolution.

In Britain, this was also the period in which the first political parties in European history developed. The so-called Whigs supported the changes brought by the Revolution, while the Tories resisted them, remaining hostile to religious toleration, attached to High Church Anglicanism, and suspicious of England's new, commercially-oriented foreign policy. It took many decades for British observers to see party competition as legitimate rather than as selfish factionalism that detracted from the public good. The very words "Whig" and "Tory" were originally terms of abuse ("Whig," possibly drawn from Scottish Gaelic, originally meant "horse thief"). But over time, party organizations took shape, parliamentary elections became party contests, and the houses of parliament divided along party lines. The early eighteenth century became known as the period of Whig Ascendancy after the political party that dominated Parliament.

ABSOLUTISM AT ITS HEIGHT

Britain's mixed constitution and party system, however, represented an exception to the European rule. On the continent, the years 1680–1740 marked the high point of absolutism. The absolutist states did not, for the most part, engage in major reforms of the sort seen in France and Spain under Richelieu and Olivares. But monarchies consolidated their authority in important ways.

THE LAST YEARS OF LOUIS XIV

In France, despite the heavy financial burden imposed by warfare, the highly centralized system of rule developed by Louis XIV continued to unfold. The "intendants," who were appointed by the king and functioned as governors in France's provinces, steadily took on more responsibility, until by 1715 they and their cadre of bureaucrats had the final say over a large range of matters of public importance. Like Antonio de Vieira in Russia, they worked to regulate commerce and public hygiene, and to repress crime and corruption, without answering to any representative body. In 1715, when Louis died, the Estates General of France had not met for a full century. It would not meet again until 1789.

Louis did have to deal with some opposition to his rule. From abroad, French Protestants denounced him as a devil after the revocation of the Edict of Nantes. In France itself, during the last years of his reign, a circle of aristocrats around the duke of Saint-Simon (1675–1755) and the count of Boulainvilliers (1658–1722) discussed plans for government by a series of councils staffed by highborn men like themselves under a titular king. Meanwhile, several important religious figures deplored the human suffering, including epidemics and starvation, which followed upon Louis's wars. Archbishop François de Fénelon (1651–1715) condemned the King for living his "entire life apart from the paths of truth and justice [...] All France is nothing but a great, starving sick ward, and it is you yourself, Sire, who have brought all these troubles to pass." Such was Louis's stature, however, that nearly all these criticisms remained unpublished during the king's lifetime, circulating only in manuscript form among small numbers of like-minded critics.

So strong had Louis's system become that it even survived the near-extinction of the ruling Bourbon dynasty. In 1711–1712, Louis's son and grandson both died of infectious disease, leaving only a small, sickly great-grandson as heir to the French throne. On Louis's own death in 1715 a cousin, Philip of Orléans (1674–1723), became Regent. He brought the court back from Versailles to Paris, experimented with a series of aristocratic ruling councils of the sort that Saint-Simon and Boulainvilliers had proposed, and restored a measure of political autonomy to France's high courts (*parlements*). It seemed for a time that he might overturn Louis XIV's principal legacies. But he squandered any chances of serious reform with his support for his rakish financial advisor John Law, who, as we will see, nearly wrecked the French economy with a series of ambitious schemes. In the years after Philip died in 1723, power passed to Cardinal André-Hercule Fleury (1653–1743), the elderly tutor of King Louis XV (1710–1774). A cautious, intelligent minister who unexpectedly lived another twenty years, he reinforced Louis XIV's methods of rule.

Cardinal Fleury
This eighteenth-century portrait of Louis XV's tutor, adviser, and regent depicts him as a sagacious, elegantly-dressed older man.

The great weakness of French government, under Louis XIV and Fleury alike, remained its finances. In the 1690s, under the pressure of war, Louis introduced a head tax and an income tax that were payable by all his subjects, including the clergy and nobility. But to ward off opposition, he presented these as emergency wartime measures only. The principal tax on land, the *taille*, continued to be collected by a cumbersome bureaucracy. Excise taxes on goods—including heavy duties on salt in many parts of the country—were collected by private contractors known as tax farmers who pocketed a large share of the take as their commission. Louis and Fleury kept the treasury afloat through a series of familiar expedients, including devaluing the currency and borrowing on the international credit markets at ruinous rates of interest. These measures did raise additional revenue, but not nearly as much as the government needed. The situation contrasted strongly to the one in England, where the government also relied heavily on excise taxes (out of fear of alienating the great landed interests), but developed an efficient government service based on so-called "excisemen" to collect them.

PETER THE GREAT OF RUSSIA

In most other parts of Europe, the absolutist model continued to prevail. In Russia, **Peter I ("the Great,"** 1672–1725) had enormous admiration for Dutch technology (particularly ship-building and land drainage), but little desire to emulate Dutch republican form of government. Imposingly tall, Peter, the younger son of Tsar Alexei I, came to the throne in 1682, but the first ten years of his reign passed in bloody rivalry between him and various family members, including his own mother.

After emerging the victor of these feuds, Peter set about an ambitious program of reform aimed at reinforcing and streamlining his own rule. He eliminated the *boyar duma*, or council of nobles that had previously exercised considerable power, and also replaced semi-autonomous local authorities with a series of governorships controlled from the center. He created the first real Russian navy, and founded the new capital of Saint Petersburg. There, with the help of men like Antonio de Vieira—one of nearly a thousand Western European advisers whom he brought to Russia in the service of his Westernization projects—Peter aimed to realize the ideal of a well-ordered absolutist state on Russian soil.

As a crucial part of the program, he insisted on transforming his often recalcitrant nobility, the boyars, into a true Western-style service elite. Russia's noble families had traditionally possessed high state offices as a hereditary right, and used them for their own self-interest. Peter introduced a "Table of Ranks" that opened these offices to all—including ambitious commoners. Peter further demanded that all aristocrats serve in the army or civil service, shave their traditional beards, and adopt Western clothing. Peter himself personally shaved the beards of several boyars. He did not, however, cure his own family of their tendency toward murderous feuding. He ended up executing his own son Alexei for treason, and at least two of his eighteenth-century successors died violent deaths. But Peter did permanently change the structures of Russian government and society, greatly curtailing the social influence of the high aristocracy while orienting Russian elites far more toward the West.

ABSOLUTISM IN PRUSSIA

The same notions of the well-ordered state and the aristocracy as a service elite took hold in the northern German state of Brandenburg, whose increasing strength and influence led to its transformation in 1701 into the Kingdom of Prussia. By the time the ruler of Brandenburg, Elector Frederick William, died in 1688, he had already done a great deal to make his scattered and largely indefensible territories a successful proposition—notably by inviting 20,000 industrious French Protestant exiles to settle there, and by building up its manufactures. His son, Elector Frederick III (1657–1713, known as King Frederick I after 1701) continued these pragmatic policies. Exhibiting a frugality that contrasted with French absolutist custom, he paid for his civil government entirely from the proceeds of his own lands, and could therefore use tax revenues almost exclusively for the army. In some regions of what was now Prussia, virtually every able-bodied nobleman served as a military officer. Officers, in turn, largely staffed the state bureaucracy. A famous eighteenth-century witticism held that while most states had armies, Prussia was an army that had a state. Frederick also granted the great landowning nobles known as Junkers greater authority over their serfs and nearly-total exemption from taxes, in return for their obedience and personal service. Soon after receiving his royal title, with very little opposition, he simply abolished Prussia's Estates General.

Frederick's son, King Frederick William I, who ruled from 1713 to 1740, faithfully continued these state-building policies. His frugality, in fact, became something of a European joke, as he cut the already-minimal expenses

Peter the Great This eighteenth-century painting of Peter the Great winning the decisive battle of Poltava against Sweden in 1709 shows the monarch dressed in western European style. An angel descends from heaven to crown Peter with laurels, implying that his victory, like his rule, was divinely ordained.

The Russian Empire, 1689–1725 Peter the Great's early-eighteenth-century territorial acquisitions added little in landmass to the already vast Russian empire, but included key coastlines with access to the Caspian and Baltic Seas and the Pacific. The 1703 founding of his magnificent capital, Saint Petersburg, in newly conquered lands linked Russia much more closely to the rest of Europe.

of the royal household by 75 percent, dressed habitually in an old military uniform, and subjected his own family to strict military discipline. When his son rebelled against this harsh regime and tried to flee with a close male friend (possibly a lover), the king forced the future King Frederick the Great to watch as the man was executed. Frederick William lavished love and resources on one thing above all: the Prussian army, which he doubled in size. His pet project was a unit of exceptionally tall soldiers, many of whom were close to seven feet tall.

PEASANT MISERIES

The well-ordered absolutist state in theory promised a better life to all its inhabitants. It would crack down on internal violence, subject potentially rampaging soldiers to better discipline, and limit the ways in which feudal lords exploited their peasant tenants and serfs. In France, for instance, in the early eighteenth century, the royal government frequently stepped in to help peasant villages sue their feudal overlords in court to protect their rights to common land, and to limit rents, fees for the use of mills, and other feudal charges.

RUSSIA AND UKRAINE In practice, however, whatever European peasants gained from these protections, they lost more through the increased taxes they paid to the central states and the stronger limits the state itself placed on their liberty. Russia's Peter the Great, for example, created a new class of "state peasants" who had more freedom to acquire property and move from place to place than ordinary serfs. In return, however, they had to pay heavy dues directly to the state. Peter also drafted thousands of serfs to work on state construction projects under horrific conditions, such as the swamp-draining necessary for the building of the new capital on the shores of the Baltic, in which many died from infectious disease. During Peter's rule, it became increasingly common for serfs to be bought and sold as near-slaves. Serfs who fled their masters faced the death penalty, as did any lords who harbored the fugitives.

In 1739, Russia imposed its version of serfdom on Ukraine as well. There most serfs belonged to great noble houses, such as the Potocki family, which had some 130,000 working on its estates. But nearly a million belonged to the Russian Orthodox Church, with the monastery of St. Sergei alone owning some 92,000. Ukraine's noble landowners, who themselves owed heavy duties to the state, demanded more and more compulsory labor from their serfs and reduced the amount of land that serfs could farm for their own benefit.

Even in Western Europe, where serfdom had largely disappeared by 1700, states increasingly drew on forced peasant labor for large-scale construction projects. In eighteenth-century France, peasants worked as much as a month a year building an ambitious new system of state roads.

FAMINE IN FRANCE Conditions generally grew worse for the peasantry in these last decades of the "Little Ice Age" as harvest failures and plagues continued to occur regularly. In France, the worst hit country in this period, crises in 1693–1694 and 1709–1710 each killed as much as 5 percent of the population. Famine did not strike because of a complete absence of food, but because shortages drove up bread prices to unaffordable levels. The story of a typical family of five in the northern French village of Saint-Étienne brutally illustrates the point. In the early modern period, such a family relied on bread as its principal source of nutrition and energy, consuming together around 70 pounds a week. At the start of 1693, this peasant family needed to spend only a quarter of its income to purchase the needed amount of bread. But by the end of 1693, the price had more than doubled, forcing them to scrimp on all other expenses. And by mid-1694, the price had gone up another three-fold, so that the typical family of five could buy only 38 pounds of bread per week, even if they spent every penny on it. Starvation followed.

And there was worse to come. In the winter of 1709, one of the worst of the Little Ice Age, temperatures in northern France fell to as low as 40 degrees below zero. The Seine and Rhine Rivers froze, and as many as half a million people died of cold, disease, and starvation. No disasters of anywhere near this magnitude occurred after 1710, as the climate finally began to ease, and war moved largely away from French territory. Yet infectious disease remained a persistent threat. In 1720–1722, in one of the last great outbreaks of bubonic plague in Europe, over half of the 90,000 inhabitants of the great French port city of Marseilles died.

THE CONDUCT OF WAR

The absolutist states used most of the additional revenue they extracted from their populations for the familiar purpose of fighting wars. Warfare of the late 1600s and early 1700s did not match the Thirty Years' War in ferocity and destruction, but it remained a common feature of European life. Religion drove some of this conflict. Yet even more than during the Thirty Years' War, European powers proved willing to forge alliances across religious lines when it suited their dynastic interests and helped offset French power. And while religious intolerance within states continued to cause considerable misery, it became much less frequent for states to go to war to protect religious minorities elsewhere. This was also a period in which Europe's increasingly powerful absolutist states continued to transform their armed forces into highly disciplined, professional organizations.

French Famine The French government was not adequately able to stem the grain shortage, as suggested by this contemporary image, in which crowds of peasants press against a bread distribution center in Paris.

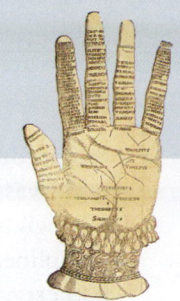

CHILDHOOD IN RURAL FRANCE

Despite new crops and advancements in agricultural techniques, the vast majority of France's population—some 90%—remained subsistence farmers in the early eighteenth century. Life was still hard: half of all children died before reaching adulthood, life expectancy was barely over 40 years, and hunger, even starvation, was a regular feature of rural life. Most peasants would never venture more than twenty miles from their place of birth.

One who did, however, was Valentin Jamerey-Duval. Born in 1695 in a poor rural commune, he eventually obtained an education and served the Holy Roman Emperor Francis I as a librarian. But despite his dramatic rise, his memoirs, published posthumously in 1784, make clear that he never forgot his humble origins. The following passage recounts the difficult conditions of his childhood in the French countryside.

I was born in France in a place that had once resembled a market town, but which the government's severity had in little time reduced to a poor village, thanks to the frequent storms of taxes. The house where I first saw the light of day had formerly been covered with tiles, but a heavy tax was raised, the tiles were sold to the benefit of the royal coffers, and soon the splendid roof was replaced by a modest covering of straw that could barely protect those it sheltered from the tempestuous weather of the seasons.

My upbringing hardly extended beyond my nourishment; I was raised in the way one cultivates plants, that is to say in a completely vegetative manner. My education consisted of learning the Lord's Prayer, in Latin and in poor French, along with a few other prayers that were explained to me in several elegant versions in dialect. About the same consideration was given to the catechism, and as a result of having fragments repeated to me, I arrived at a vague understanding that that there were a God, a Church, and some sacraments. I learned that there were a pope, the visible head of this Church, priests, and monks; I was taught to respect and even to fear them, and I do so still, although with some reservation.

Finding myself one day at a dinner held by our parish priest, I saw with astonishment that he was eating bread of a different color than that which I had lived on until then; this novelty struck me. I didn't dare ask for some, but the numerous circles I was making around the table and my watchful gaze made my wishes known, and my curious greed was satisfied; I had the pleasure, at the age of eight or nine, of eating white bread for the first time.

QUESTIONS FOR ANALYSIS

1. What challenges did Jamerey-Duval face as a child?
2. In this passage, what roles do the state and the Church play in peasant life?
3. Why do you think the memory of eating white bread for the first time is so vivid to Jamerey-Duval?

Source: Andrew Daily, trans., *Le XVIIIe siècle français au quotidien*, Roland Mortier, ed., (Brussels: 2002), p. 493.

DISCIPLINE AND VIOLENCE

As one example of the declining ferocity of warfare, consider an action widely denounced as one of the great atrocities of the age. In 1688–1689, Louis XIV, hoping to expand the borders of France eastward, invaded the western German region known as the Palatinate. When the Holy Roman Empire refused to yield to his demands, the French king coldly approved a plan that he hoped would intimidate the enemy and prevent it from undertaking offensive operations. In December, his armies began deliberately to destroy towns, villages, and manors throughout the Palatinate with fire and explosives, turning the inhabitants into refugees. A chorus of indignation rose up among France's enemies, and over the next century the scourging of the Palatinate remained a symbol of the Sun King's arrogance, and a permanent, ugly stain on his reputation.

The destruction was indeed severe. Yet in comparison to the vast slaughter of the Thirty Years' War, it was surprisingly mild. French troops remained largely under strict discipline, and concentrated their destructive activities on property, not humans. The fact that the episode became notorious speaks to the broadly lower levels of military violence against which it was measured.

Even when fighting one another, uniformed armies tended to maintain discipline far better than in the earlier part of the century. Commanders invested ever more time in drilling their troops and in maintaining discipline even in the most confusing moments of a battle, when thick clouds of greasy gunpowder smoke choked the soldiers and obscured their sight, and the overpowering roar of muskets and cannons made it difficult to hear orders. In most European states, common soldiers—drawn from the peasantry and urban poor—came to see the military as a long-term career.

Along with the disciplined men came a disciplined weapon, for the period 1660–1700 saw the perfection of the musket. Loaded with pre-packed cartridges, these long-barreled firearms could now be fired two or even three times per minute, allowing more controlled, continual fire than in the past. And a crucial late seventeenth-century addition to the musket—the removable bayonet—allowed infantrymen quickly to turn their guns into murderous edged weapons for use in hand-to-hand combat, eliminating the need for pikemen on the battlefield. But with a weapon of this sort, each of which cost the equivalent of an agricultural laborer's annual wages and demanded lengthy training, it became a priority for generals to preserve both the guns and the men who wielded them. Whereas the 1634 battle of Nördlingen, at the height of the Thirty Years' War, had cost the lives of one-third of the troops involved, a battle of similar importance six decades later—Malplaquet, during the War of the League of Augsburg—resulted in the deaths of only one-seventh of the combatants.

The end of the seventeenth century also saw a notable decrease in military violence against civilians. In siege warfare, commanders slowly evolved a code whereby a city or town would hold out until the first breaching of its defenses, but could then surrender honorably with the expectation of decent treatment. The initial siege could still bring widespread destruction—particularly if the besiegers shot red-hot cannonballs to start fires—but the wild sacking of towns and cities became far less frequent. Similarly, fewer and fewer armies allowed their soldiers to steal wantonly from civilians in their path. The armies of William and Mary developed a particular reputation

for discipline, and paying for the food and supplies they consumed.

ARISTOCRATS AT WAR

We have already seen some of the principal causes of the diminishing intensity of warfare: the logic of the "balance of power" that emerged after the 1648 Peace of Westphalia, the agonizing memory of the horrors of the Thirty Years' War, and a growing acceptance of religious differences among states, if not within states. Louis XIV, whatever his insistence on making France a wholly Catholic country, had little evangelical desire to make Europe a wholly Catholic continent. All of these trends, which first took shape in the mid-seventeenth century, continued in subsequent decades.

But the most important reason for the decreasing violence only made itself fully felt at the height of absolutism: the influence of the aristocracy in European societies in general, and in military leadership in particular. Louis XIV's Court of Versailles, with its complex etiquette and rigid attention to the smallest differences in rank, set the tone for the highest ranks of society, not only in France but also across much of the continent. Here, as we have seen, the ideal of the courtier saw its fullest flowering. This ideal described a man of splendid appearance, exquisite

The Versailles Court Courtiers kneel before Louis XIV to be inducted into the military Order of St Louis—one of the new institutions of court life—in a 1693 painting.

manners and speech, unblemished honor, perfect grace, and unquestioned devotion to the monarch, all undergirded by impeccable courage and self-discipline.

But at Versailles and its competitor courts, far more than in Renaissance Italy, the courtier was also a military officer, and a servant of the monarch. Noblemen, in fact, made little or no distinction between their social identity as nobles and their social identity as officers. And as a result, the twin theaters of the aristocracy that were the royal court and the military campaign were both governed by the courtly ideals that found their most intense expression at Versailles. War, like court life, ideally had to be conducted with self-control, restraint, and honor. Louis XIV's destruction of the Palatinate, which he barely even tried to justify, seemed shocking because it represented a violation of the aristocratic code of honor by the monarch who embodied that code. These ideals were widespread in absolutist continental Europe by 1700, and aligned with the insistence of monarchs from Versailles to Saint Petersburg that nobles become loyal servants of the state. Actual warfare, however, with its massive human and financial costs, never lived up to these ideals more than partially.

WAR AND THE BALANCE OF POWER (1680–1721)

Aristocratic officers wanted to limit the damage caused by war, but they did not want war itself to end. Since they saw war as their principal purpose, the source of their honor, prestige, and position within the state service, limiting its destruction above all offered them a means of engaging in it more often. For this reason, Europe did not see a single year of real peace between 1680 and 1721. France, the continent's most powerful nation, was at war for all but ten of these thirty-five years. France's ambitious king continued to drive the wars.

FRENCH AGGRESSION

In the mid-1680s, Louis XIV stood at the height of his power and glory. His palace of Versailles, now completed, awed and intimidated visitors from across Europe. As we have seen, he had restored internal order to France and presided over an unprecedented flourishing of the arts. Already by 1685, he had ruled far longer, and arguably more successfully, than any French king since Louis IX in the thirteenth century. On the international scene,

his immediate ambition was to expand France's frontier toward the Rhine in the north and east—the borders of the Roman province of Gaul—annexing the Dutch and German territories on the river's western bank. More generally, he hoped to establish France as the predominant power in Europe, and even to gain for himself and his heirs the crown of the Holy Roman Empire, making him the successor to the Roman Caesars.

In keeping with these ambitions, the period began with France trying to build on its territorial successes from the 1670s, annexing several Lutheran, German-speaking areas along the Rhine, including, in 1681, the city of Strasbourg. The Habsburg Holy Roman Emperor Leopold I (1640–1705), who ruled Austria and its Central European possessions, saw these moves as a direct threat. Despite Leopold's sickly appearance and cold, shy manner (until the death of his elder brother he had prepared for a career in the church), he had now ruled capably for a quarter of a century and saw himself as a serious rival to the French king.

THE LAST GREAT OTTOMAN OFFENSIVE (1683)

Leopold was distracted from this rivalry, however, in 1683, when his Austrian monarchy nearly fell to a renewed attack from the Ottoman Turks. Although the Ottomans no longer commanded the sort of military strength they had at the time of Suleiman the Magnificent in the sixteenth century, they still controlled the Balkans and much of present day Hungary. Leopold had unwisely renewed Austrian

Siege of Vienna This painting of the Ottoman siege of Vienna in July, 1683 shows the colorful tents and busy cavalry of the Ottoman army stationed in the hills above the city.

persecution of those Hungarian Protestants remaining under his rule, leading to a revolt by the largely Protestant Hungarian nobility, who called on the Turks for support. The Turks could not resist the temptation, and in 1683, Vizier Kara Mustafa (1635–1683) marched a 100,000-man army through Hungarian territory to besiege the capital of Vienna, raising fears that the Ottoman Empire might finally achieve its old ambitions and extend their rule into the heart of the European continent.

But Austria did not fall, for the threat prompted the quick formation of a Holy League financed by Pope Innocent XI and commanded by the dashing king of Poland, Jan III Sobieski (1629–1696), who routed the Ottoman army at Vienna in September 1683. Mustafa himself, after being stripped of his position by the sultan, was executed by strangulation with a silk cord. His defeat marked the last time the Turks would threaten Central Europe, and within a few years, nearly all Hungarian territory had again come under Habsburg rule. Even so, the war had shaken Austria, which remained in danger from revolt by the Hungarians and other subject peoples.

THE WARS OF LOUIS XIV

With Austria distracted by the Turks and England ruled by France's Catholic ally James II, Louis XIV felt all the more emboldened to push French expansion. But in 1688, when England's Glorious Revolution turned Louis's English ally into an enemy, the balance of power in Europe finally began to shift against him.

WAR OF THE LEAGUE OF AUGSBURG (1688–1697)
In the **War of the League of Augsburg**, France faced an alliance that drew other Catholic states (Austria, Spain, and Bavaria) and Protestant ones (Sweden, England, and the Netherlands) into a powerful coalition. The need to fight yet another European alliance pushed French resources to the breaking point. By 1693, the French armies had reached a strength of 400,000, the largest France had ever seen, but they still could not win a decisive victory. The catastrophic French harvest failures of 1693–1694 did not help. Finally, in 1697, the French and their enemies reached a compromise peace. It gave the combatants breathing time, but settled little, and everyone recognized that it had set the scene for another war to come.

WAR OF THE SPANISH SUCCESSION (1702–1714)
The most important issue left unsettled by the War of the League of Augsburg involved Spain. During the late seventeenth century, its titular ruler was the Habsburg Charles II (1661–1700), who was physically and mentally disabled. Charles had no heirs, but his two sisters had married Louis XIV and the Emperor Leopold I, and both the French and Austrian monarchs claimed the Spanish succession for their families. As the seventeenth century drew to an end, the three rulers seemed close to reaching an agreement to split the Spanish empire between them, but Charles's ministers objected. Spain was no longer the great power it had been in the sixteenth century, but it still controlled vast territories, including more than half of South America, Central America stretching through California and Florida, islands in the Caribbean, the southern Netherlands (present-day Belgium), southern Italy, and various other Italian territories. Any hopes for a Spanish revival depended on keeping these far-flung territories together.

In November, 1700, Charles died, and it was discovered to everyone's surprise that he had left a will bequeathing this entire vast empire to Louis XIV's younger grandson, who was soon crowned Philip V (1683–1746). Philip renounced all claims to the French throne, thereby in theory ruling out any unification of the French and Spanish empires. But just the prospect of all Spanish domains coming under the control of the Bourbon dynasty was bad enough for both the Austrian Habsburgs and the British. It led almost immediately to the formation of yet another alliance against France, and the outbreak of the **War of the Spanish Succession**. The fighting lasted until 1713 and involved the Americas as well as Europe. Despite Louis XIV's best efforts to establish French supremacy on the seas, the French navy proved no match for its Anglo-Dutch rivals, while on the continent, French commanders were defeated in a series of major battles. These reverses again pushed the French state to the breaking point. Between 1683 and 1708, its budget deficit rose by a factor of 45.

And then, at the worst possible moment, the climate itself seemed to turn against France, with the terrible cold and famine of 1709–1710. King Louis XIV, now in his late sixties, suffered from a variety of painful, chronic conditions, and these events pushed him to despair. In an astonishing move for an absolute monarch, he wrote a letter, to be read from every pulpit in the kingdom, stressing the need for the people to support the nation in its hour of need. Over the next two years, the French managed to stave off military disaster, but the days of French aggression and expansion had come to an end.

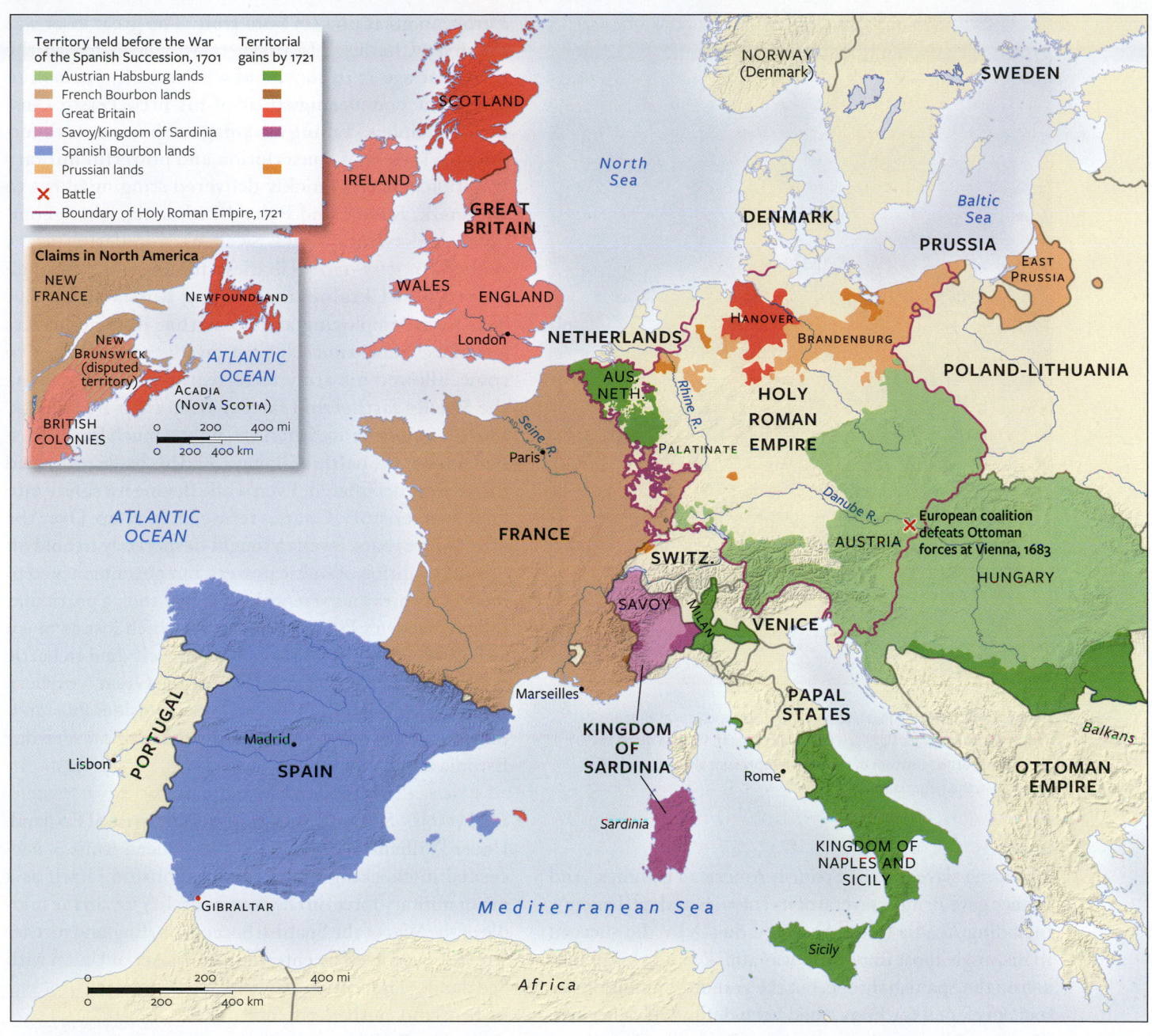

Territory held before the War of the Spanish Succession, 1701
- Austrian Habsburg lands
- French Bourbon lands
- Great Britain
- Savoy/Kingdom of Sardinia
- Spanish Bourbon lands
- Prussian lands

Territorial gains by 1721

✕ Battle
— Boundary of Holy Roman Empire, 1721

Europe, 1683–1721 Defeat of Ottoman forces in 1683 allowed Austria to cement its claim to the Hungarian lands, including new possessions on the Ottoman border. In 1707, the English and Scottish crowns were formally joined, creating the new Kingdom of Great Britain. The Peace of Utrecht in 1713–14 inaugurated the greatest changes of the early eighteenth century: control of the Southern Netherlands and Sicily passed from the Spanish Habsburgs to the Austrian Habsburgs, the independent kingdom of Sardinia came to rule the French duchy of Savoy, and Britain acquired several French territories in North America.

THE PEACE OF UTRECHT (1713–1714) The war ended with the compromise **Peace of Utrecht**, a series of treaties negotiated in 1713–1714 that aimed to update and supplant the earlier Peace of Westphalia. Under its terms, France recognized the Protestant succession in England, pulled its remaining forces out of the southern Netherlands and Italy, and allowed the southern Netherlands and Naples to pass from Spain to Austria, thereby keeping them under the House of Habsburg. France also conceded to Britain the enormously profitable monopoly

Peace of Utrecht An illustration from the French royal almanac of 1714 shows diplomats signing a treaty at Utrecht. Images along the border and at the bottom of the image represent the royal families involved in the negotiations.

European great powers bore fruit. The great loser was Sweden's Charles XII (1682–1718), who came to the throne at age 15 in 1697, and who initially seemed to revive the conquering spirit of his predecessor Gustavus Adolphus. Taking advantage of his country's formidable system of conscription and powerful military tradition, Charles quickly delivered stinging blows to Denmark, Russia, and Poland-Lithuania, which combined had twenty times Sweden's population of 1.5 million. In 1707–1708, Charles's forces struck through Poland into Ukraine, threatening Russia again. But Tsar Peter, employing a strategy that Russian leaders would use many times against invaders in centuries to come, allowed his army to retreat unbeaten, drawing the Swedes farther and farther from their home base. Finally, in June 1709, Charles fought a much larger Russian force at the battle of Poltava, and his badly weakened forces were decimated. Even while fleeing for safety into Ottoman territory, Charles refused to give up. Over the next twelve years, Sweden fought desperately to hold off a broad coalition of Baltic powers, but never managed to recover its previous strength. The war took a particular toll on Sweden's Finnish provinces, which lost as much as half their population. Charles himself died in battle in Norway in 1718, and at the end of the Great Northern War in 1721, Sweden had to surrender considerable territory, above all to Russia, including much of present-day Estonia and Latvia.

ENGLAND Second came the astonishing rise of England. Under William and Mary, and then Queen Anne, it succeeded in checking France and establishing itself as a major military force on the continent. In 1707, in the middle of the War of the Spanish Succession, England further strengthened itself by entering into an Act of Union with Scotland. The court party in Scotland pushed the act through its Parliament despite widespread opposition in the population at large. While the two kingdoms had obeyed the same monarch since 1603, and the term "British" was already widespread, now a single government would formally rule the entire island as the Kingdom of Great Britain. (Ireland remained a separate kingdom, and only joined the union a century later.)

on selling slaves to the Spanish American colonies. And France gave Britain several of its colonies and settlements, including Acadia (Nova Scotia). Louis XIV did succeed in his single most important war aim, keeping his grandson on the Spanish throne, but the grandiose ambitions he had developed for France had been definitively checked. They would not revive again until the time of Napoleon, a century later.

NEW GREAT POWERS

The period from 1680 to 1715 saw two other major developments on the international scene. First, the Great Northern War of 1700–1721 marked the rise of a new great power—Russia—and the eclipse of Sweden.

RUSSIA In this conflict, Peter the Great's efforts to reform the Russian state and join the company of

The Great Northern War, 1700–1721

AN ATLANTIC WORLD

Britain's success derived not only from its gains in Europe, but also from the development of its colonial empire, especially in North America and the Caribbean. Between 1680 and 1740, the New World continued to grow in importance as a source of European wealth and a site of competition among the European powers. During this period, Britain emerged as by far the most dynamic colonial power, aided by its unsurpassed navy.

BRITAIN'S MAINLAND COLONIES

Britain's North American colonies grew almost five-fold in population between 1680 and 1740, to a total of over 900,000 inhabitants. Much of the growth was driven by immigration. As in earlier decades, both the British and French North American colonies were integrated into patterns of migration within Europe. The same routes that took Britons from the Midlands to London, and French migrants from the countryside to cities like Rouen or Paris, also extended across the Atlantic. Britain's colonies varied greatly in economy, social structure, and population. In New England, immigration came mostly from England itself, especially the dissenting Protestant groups related to the early Puritan settlers. Coastal fishing and inland farming communities predominated.

The mid-Atlantic British colonies had a much more diverse population. Settlers of the early Dutch and Swedish colonies, all taken over by England by 1670, lived alongside English migrants and a large number of Germans in what English observers routinely referred to as a "Babel" of cultures. Pennsylvania, a prosperous colony founded in 1682 by the Quaker William Penn (1644–1718), who offered religious liberty to all settlers, quickly drew particularly large numbers of migrants from Germany. In 1740, close to a third of the colony was German-speaking. In the Chesapeake and southern colonies, the plantation economy continued to expand, attracting poorer English settlers who initially came as indentured servants. Slavery, of both Africans and their descendants born in America, existed in all the colonies, and in the eighteenth century slaves largely supplanted indentured servants in plantation labor.

SUGAR AND SLAVERY

By 1740, the European colonies in the Caribbean were eclipsing those in mainland North America as sites of colonization and imperial competition. The huge profitability of Caribbean cash crops drove this change. Whereas Virginia relied on a single crop, tobacco, for its economic growth, the Caribbean islands provided different consumer products: coffee, indigo, and, especially, cane sugar. In the seventeenth century, Europeans who had previously relied on honey and fruit for sweets increasingly grew addicted to cane sugar from the tropics. The Portuguese began large-scale cultivation in Brazil, but by late in the century the center of sugar cultivation was moving north into the Caribbean. By 1700, Britain's island colonies, most importantly Barbados and Jamaica, had together outstripped Brazil, producing roughly 25,000 tons of sugar per year. By 1730, their capitals of Bridgetown and Port Royal had grown larger than any other city in British America except Boston. France began to catch up with Britain after the treaty ending the War of the League of Augsburg divided the large Caribbean island of Hispaniola (today, Haiti and the Dominican Republic) between France and Spain. The Spanish colony of Cuba was also an important source of European sugar.

The rise of sugar as a consumer product, and also, to a lesser extent, coffee, led to major changes in patterns of colonization. Both crops were hugely labor-intensive. The harvesting and processing of sugar cane into a form suitable for export could push work forces to the limit and beyond. During the harvest, the back-breaking labor of grinding and boiling cane went on day and night without cease. Colonial landowners quickly found it far more profitable to do this work with African slaves than with white indentured servants. In the 1640s, Barbados's population of 30,000 had included only a few slaves, and large numbers of European indentured servants. By 1700, however, the indentured servants had largely departed, and 15,000 free whites shared the island with 50,000 black slaves. Later in the eighteenth century, in some Caribbean colonies, black slaves would outnumber free whites by as much as twenty to one. Among the consequences of this demographic shift was that white colonists, fearful of slave rebellion, became tightly dependent on military force supplied by the imperial home country.

THE ATLANTIC SLAVE TRADE
This shift also provided an enormous impetus to the Atlantic slave trade. As we have already seen, this trade developed in the sixteenth and early seventeenth century as a "triangle trade" in which Europeans used various goods, including textiles, metal tools, and guns, to purchase slaves in Africa, shipped the slaves across the Atlantic to the Americas, and then brought cash crops back to Europe. This pattern did not fundamentally change in the late seventeenth century, but

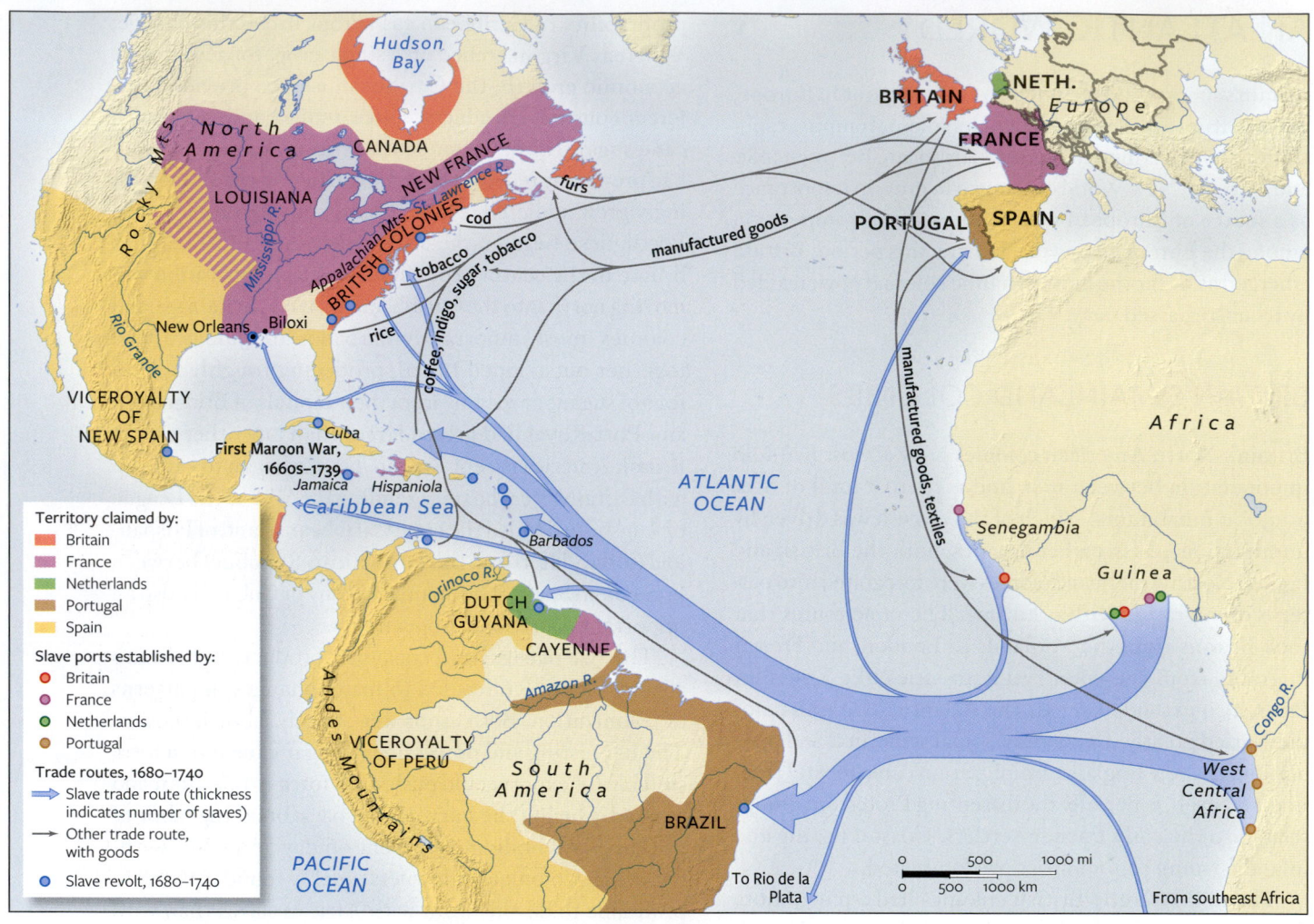

The Atlantic World, 1680–1740 A vast trading economy—particularly in enslaved people—linked European powers with their rapidly expanding colonies overseas. The slave trade moved staggering numbers of human cargo from Portuguese slave ports in west-central Africa to Brazil, and from Dutch, British, and French ports in Guinea and Senegambia to Dutch Guyana, the British colonies on the eastern coast of North America, and French colonies in North America and the Caribbean. There enslaved people produced huge quantities of trading goods such as sugar and tobacco to be sent back to Europe—although slave revolts in response to this violent economic system occurred frequently throughout the colonies.

it expanded enormously in scale. Between 1625 and 1650, Europeans transported roughly 7,000 Africans a year through the "middle passage." By 1700, this number had nearly quadrupled, and the growth continued through the following decades. Over its entire history, the slave trade shipped more than 11,000,000 Africans to the Americas, with 90 percent going to the Caribbean and South America. The **middle passage** across the Atlantic took place under horrific conditions for the slaves, who were shackled and crammed into filthy hulls, shaved of hair to reduce disease, and abused by the European crews (women, in particular, were routinely raped). Slave traders coldly calculated how many slaves they could cram into a single ship before the conditions led too many of them to die en route.

In the colonies, especially in the Caribbean, the slaves' condition could be equally cruel. In Jamaica and Saint-Domingue, the French territory of present-day Haiti, at some periods, newly arrived slaves could expect to live no more than ten years thanks to the terrible labor required of them. The death rates rose so high that the slave populations could not naturally reproduce, and the plantation owners needed to import more slaves just to keep up the numbers. There is some evidence that slave women deliberately avoided pregnancy by any means possible (including using their knowledge of plants to induce abortions) so as not to bring children into lives of slavery. Attempts to mitigate the horrors, such as a "Black Code" introduced in the French colonies in 1685 to prevent abuses

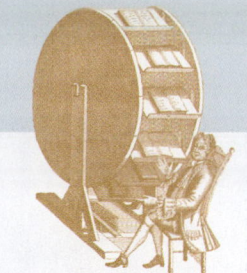

THE LIMITS OF LIBERTY

Though European governments granted greater rights and protections to the people, the expansion of liberty was limited: certain rights, like the right to property, reinforced European ownership of slaves. The differences between the English Bill of Rights and the Black Code of the French colonies demonstrate the contradiction between this increased liberty at home and slavery abroad. As the Bill of Rights extended the rights of white Europeans, the Code systematized the strict control of slaves' lives. These documents capture the ambiguous nature of liberty and equality in the late seventeenth century.

English Bill of Rights

The Bill of Rights (1689) made clear that while Parliament accepted the rule of William III and Mary II, their authority was limited by the rights of the English people.

And thereupon the said lords spiritual and temporal[1] and commons[2]…declare:

- That the pretended power of suspending the laws, or the execution of laws, by regal authority, without consent of parliament, is illegal…

- That the pretended power of dispensing with laws, or the execution of laws, by regal authority, as it hath been assumed and exercised of late, is illegal…

- That levying money for or to the use of the Crown by pretence of prerogative, without grant of parliament, for longer time, or in other manner than the same is or shall be granted, is illegal…

- That it is the right of the subjects to petition the king, and all commitments and prosecutions for such petitioning are illegal…

- That the raising or keeping a standing army within the kingdom in time of peace unless it be with consent of parliament, is against law…

- That the subjects which are Protestants, may have arms for their defence suitable to their conditions and as allowed by law…

- That election of members of parliament ought to be free…

- That the freedom of speech and debates or proceedings in parliament, ought not to be impeached or questioned in any court or place out of parliament;

- That excessive bail ought not to be required, nor excessive fines imposed; nor cruel and unusual punishments inflicted…

- That all grants and promises of fines and forfeitures of particular persons before conviction, are illegal and void;

- And that for redress of all grievances, and for the amending, strengthening, and preserving of the laws, parliaments ought to be held frequently.

The Black Code

While the following sections of the Code allow for rights for freed slaves, they also legalize harsh punishments.

XII. The children born of marriages between slaves will be slaves and will belong to the master of the female slaves, and not to those of their husbands, if the husband and the wife have different masters.

XIII. We wish that if a slave husband has married a free woman, the children, both male and girls, will follow the condition of their mother and be free like her, in spite of the servitude of their father; and that if the father is free and the mother enslaved, the children will be slaves for the same reason.…

XVI. In the same way we forbid slaves belonging to different masters to gather in the day or night…on pain of corporal punishment …frequent violations and other aggravating circumstances can be punished with death…

XXXI. Slaves cannot be party to either judgments or civil proceedings, nor can they be plaintiffs or defendants in civil or criminal proceedings…

XXXIII. The slave who will have struck his master or the wife of his master, his mistress, or their children and drawn to bring blood, or in the face, will be punished with death.…

LVIII. We command manumitted slaves to retain a particular respect for their former masters, their widows, and their children; and any insult that they make against them will be punished more severely than if it had been done to another person. However, we declare them free and absolved of any other burdens, services, and rights that their former masters would like to claim, as much on their persons as on their possessions and estates as patrons.

LIX. We grant to manumitted slaves the same rights, privileges, and liberties enjoyed by persons born free; desiring that they merit this acquired liberty and that it produce in them, both for their persons and for their property, the same effects that the good fortune of natural liberty causes in our other subjects.

QUESTIONS FOR ANALYSIS

1. In what ways does the Bill of Rights extend the rights of the English people?
2. How does the Black Code restrict the rights of slaves?
3. Do you see any similarities in the ways these documents approach the subject of rights?

---

[1] **lords spiritual and temporal:** bishops of the Church of England and secular members, respectively, in Parliament's House of Lords
[2] **commons:** Members of Parliament's lower House of Commons

Sources: *The Parliamentary History of England, from the Earliest Period to the Year 1803*, Vol. 5 (London: 1809), pp. 484–485; *Slave Revolution in the Caribbean, 1789–1804*, Laurent Dubois and John D. Garrigus, eds. (New York: 2006, pp. 51–54).

The First Maroon War An eighteenth-century oil painting shows British troops ending the Maroon revolt in Jamaica. Escaped slaves—depicted in exotic "native" dress—lay down their weapons, while a British officer reads the terms of surrender.

and encourage the slaves' conversion to Catholicism, were widely ignored.

SLAVE RESISTANCE The slaves themselves offered resistance to their condition. Slave revolts were common in the Caribbean, and brutally suppressed. In other cases, slaves fled and established fugitive communities in inaccessible regions of mountain or swamp. Known in English as "Maroons" (from an Indian word meaning "flight of an arrow"), these escaped slaves established some successful communities. During the "First Maroon War" in Jamaica, which lasted from the 1660s until 1739, the British authorities could not manage to suppress or capture the fugitives. In the end, they negotiated an agreement that allowed the Maroons to remain in their settlements under British supervision, provided that they not provide shelter to any other escaped slaves.

FRENCH EXPANSION IN NORTH AMERICA

The new wealth intensified imperial competition in the Americas, especially between France and Britain. The French, however, unwittingly sabotaged their own efforts, particularly on the North American mainland. While the English continued to allow religious dissidents to populate

their colonies, the French maintained their policy of banning all Protestants from New France (in 1685 they banned Jews as well). As a result, the French Protestant emigration strengthened Massachusetts, New York, and South Carolina rather than French possessions. In Canada, Louis XIV's minister Colbert also limited growth by trying to rein in the French settlers who often travelled for months into the "Upper Country" of Canada to take part in the lucrative fur trade with the Indians. While tolerant of continuing Catholic efforts aimed at converting the Indians, Colbert insisted that all French subjects other than missionaries remain in a narrow, well-defined belt of territory along the Saint Lawrence River. There he tried to impose an idealized version of French absolutist society in which settlers were forced to pay heavy dues to feudal lords. As a result, relatively few French subjects opted to emigrate to Canada. Those who did mostly hoped to make money and return to France.

Nonetheless, the period 1680–1740 saw France expand its American colonies in new directions. In 1681–1682 the French explorer René-Robert Cavelier de La Salle (1643–1687) travelled from Montreal through the Great Lakes system into what is now Illinois, from where he followed the Mississippi River all the way to the Gulf of Mexico. Although encountering many Indian settlements along the way, La Salle followed the standard procedure of European explorers and claimed the entire vast Mississippi basin—from the Appalachians to the Rocky Mountains, roughly one-third of the present-day continental United States—for France, and named it Louisiana after Louis XIV.

FRENCH LOUISIANA In 1699, other French explorers established a settlement at Biloxi, near the mouth of the Mississippi (New Orleans followed in 1718). A large majority of the initial settlers died within months of infectious disease. Still, the French government was determined to colonize the Mississippi basin, so as to keep the major river system of North America out of British hands and fence off Britain's thirteen colonies with a thin ribbon of French settlement to the north and west. France deported prisoners to Louisiana (including roughly 1,000 female prostitutes), which pushed the colony's population to 3,000 by the 1740s. These settlers imported African slaves, who brought with them farming techniques well suited to the climate, particularly for rice. But while Louisiana developed into a slave colony, the food crops cultivated there did not require the sort of massive slave labor seen in the Caribbean, and did not generate the same profits.

THE FRENCH AND NATIVE PEOPLES Although the French could not compete in population with the British in America, they were adept at forging strategic alliances with the native peoples who lived across the British and French territories. Through these alliances, they managed to keep steady military pressure on the British colonies—often by raiding unprotected British towns. In early 1704, for instance, a force of French Canadians and Indians attacked the Massachusetts town of Deerfield, killing over fifty of its residents. French Jesuit missionaries continued their close study of the Indians and began to develop the elements of what we now know as anthropology. In his pioneering 1724 book *The Customs of American Savages Compared to the Customs of Early Times*, Joseph-François Lafitau (1681–1746) argued that American Indians resembled no one so much as the ancient Greeks. His work would follow the idea that *all* human societies evolve from similar "primitive" stages to more "advanced" ones. As we will see in later chapters, imperialists have often employed this idea to justify the subjugation of "primitive" peoples. Yet it also presupposes the essential similarity of all humans, whatever their social condition—a notion that would continue to resonate in Western social and political thought.

AMERICAN TRADE AND EUROPEAN ECONOMIES

The French and British both continued to govern their colonies according to strict mercantilist principles. They gave the monopoly of trade to government-chartered companies, and tried to forbid free exchange with Europe. When Spain passed to Bourbon rule under Philip V in 1700, its empire started to emulate the French, with more and more activity controlled by a series of new trading companies. Throughout the American colonies, overall economic growth rates remained surprisingly modest in the eighteenth century—as little as 1 percent per year per capita. The profits generated by the colonies did not stay in the colonies, but largely traveled back across the Atlantic to enrich European investors.

At the same time, European economies became increasingly powered by American trade, as twin financial crises in France and England illustrated in the years around 1720. Both crises derived from attempts to link state finances to the chartered companies that had monopolies over trade with the colonies. These "joint stock" companies sold shares to the public to raise money and spread the risk in their ventures. In France, the Scottish economist John Law (1671–1729), a gambling companion of the Regent Philippe d'Orléans, became effective finance minister in 1716, with unprecedented control over the country's economy. He founded a national bank, took over management of the huge national debt, and linked both to a new overseas trading corporation, the **Mississippi Company**. Convinced of Law's genius, the French public quickly bid up the price of shares in the company nearly twenty-fold. They did not recognize that their investments depended on reliable profits from the colonies, including especially Louisiana, where a few hundred disease-ridden colonists were at this point barely surviving. In 1720 the bubble burst, destroying the bank and company and sending Law fleeing from the country. In Britain, a similar situation developed with the South Sea Company, which had the right to supply Spanish South America with slaves. The company attempted to purchase the British national debt with its own shares, driving up their price. The bubble created by these inflated share prices burst in 1720 and precipitated a collapse in the English stock market as a whole.

Understanding Native Culture Lafitau's 1724 account of American Indians included these etchings depicting Native Canadian religious rituals, emphasizing the customs' exoticism and also their connection to the natural world.

MIGNARD'S *PORTRAIT OF LOUISE DE KÉROUAILLE, DUCHESS OF PORTSMOUTH*

Louise de Kérouaille, one of Charles II's favorite mistresses, used her position and influence to become the Duchess of Portsmouth in 1673. Located to the southwest of London, Portsmouth was a major port with strong ties to the burgeoning colonial trade of the seventeenth century.

The French painter Pierre Mignard's 1682 portrait of the Duchess emphasizes her legendary beauty, enhanced by delicate makeup, pearl earrings, and extravagant fabrics. But it also speaks to the importance of transatlantic trade to her wealth and standing: a black slave child kneels at her side, holding out a branch of red coral and a shell overflowing with pearls, expensive commodities from Britain's overseas colonies. The glimpse of the sea in the background alludes to the source of these luxuries. The Duchess—and Portsmouth—were increasingly dependent on the colonial trade represented by these symbols.

QUESTIONS FOR ANALYSIS

1. What impressions of the Duchess does Mignard convey?
2. Why do you think Mignard included a slave child in the portrait?
3. In what ways is the Duchess's physical beauty tied to colonial trade in this painting?

The story of these twin bubbles illustrates the increasing complexity and international character of the European economy in this period. The patterns of commercial development seen in the Netherlands earlier in the seventeenth century were spreading to neighboring states. Already in England by the time of the Glorious Revolution, only half the population was working directly in agriculture. Manufacturing, above all of textiles, increasingly drove the economies of England and northern France. Meanwhile, as colonial populations grew, they became not only a source of cash crops like tobacco, coffee, and sugar, but also a market for goods from the home country. In this world of increasingly sophisticated patterns of trade, merchants developed ever more intricate instruments of credit, and depended ever more on a stable currency. The founding of the Bank of England in 1694 proved an enormous boon to English merchants in this regard, preventing the South Sea bubble from doing long-term damage. In France, by contrast, the collapse of Law's system acted to delay the country's financial modernization—it would not acquire a true national bank until the nineteenth century.

CITY LIFE AND CULTURE

If the patterns set in the mid-seventeenth century had continued, the expanding economy would have fueled ever more opulent displays of courtly luxury by Europe's crowned heads. But after the 1680s, the drive for ostentation embodied in the construction of Versailles became less popular. In France, an increasingly influential Jansenist Catholicism, with its emphasis on simplicity and repentance, criticized the sensuality of court life as an invitation to sin. Louis XIV himself grew less fond of ostentation as he grew older, and started spending more time away from Versailles and its rigorous etiquette. After his death, the Regent moved the court to Paris, and while it later returned to Versailles, King Louis XV did not have his great-grandfather's taste for pageantry. In Russia, although Peter the Great built himself a magnificent palace on the Baltic in the style of Versailles, called Peterhof, he reserved his principal architectural energies for

the new city of Saint Petersburg. In Prussia, as we have seen, Kings Frederick and Frederick William rejected the example of Versailles altogether in favor of a simpler, more frugal style of rule.

But as the courts declined in importance, cities rose. The decades around 1700 mark the period when cities—above all London and Paris—supplanted courts as the centers of gravity of European cultures. London, its port brimming with ships and products from around the world, had a particular attraction. Its population, probably around 575,000 in 1700, would grow to 750,000 over the next fifty years. More importantly, one in six inhabitants of England and Wales lived in the metropolis at some point in their lives. The ranks of middle-class merchants, professionals, and state officials all swelled.

NEW CULTURAL INSTITUTIONS IN THE CITIES

In keeping with these shifts, in the decades around 1700 new urban institutions began to draw people of different social backgrounds together.

THE COFFEEHOUSES The first Western European coffeehouses, copying Turkish models, had been founded in mid-seventeenth-century London. Their numbers then jumped from less than a thousand in 1675 to three thousand by 1710. Ranging from poorly furnished ground-floor rooms to large buildings decorated in a self-consciously

Saint Petersburg The towers of the new fortress Peter the Great built in his capital city rise out of the snow in this colored engraving of people promenading along the Neva River, made shortly after the fortress was completed in 1740.

London Coffeehouses Inside an early-eighteenth-century London coffeehouse, a landlady and boy serve coffee and other drinks and food to the male patrons, who gather around tables to read newspapers and discuss the issues of the day. Numerous pots of coffee boil on the fire.

"oriental" style with Turkish carpets and tapestries, these institutions attracted a broad, although mostly male social clientele, ranging from aristocrats to merchants, professionals, and well-off artisans.

SALONS In France, a key urban institution was what has come to be known as the **salon**: gatherings at aristocratic homes where writers read their works aloud or participated in discussions of literature and current events. As we have seen, the early salons had functioned principally as means of instructing newcomers in the customs and traditions of the court. However, particularly after the death of Louis XIV, they turned increasingly urban and literary in their focus.

Salons proved especially receptive to elite women, who not only attended them but frequently served as hostesses presiding over the discussions. For these women they offered new opportunities for self-expression. Consider, for instance, the remarkable case of Claudine Guérin de Tencin (1682–1749). Her father, a magistrate in Grenoble, destined her for the clergy, but before taking her vows, she secretly signed an affidavit stating that she was entering the convent against her will. When her father died, she used the affidavit to sue for release from her vows, and in 1712, was able to leave the convent. She joined her sister, already a notable hostess, in Paris, and within a few years had founded a salon of her own that welcomed some of the greatest writers of the day, including Montesquieu and Fontenelle. She herself became a published novelist. Her illegitimate son Jean Le Rond d'Alembert became a great philosopher and mathematician.

PERIODICALS These urban institutions flourished not just because of the period's economic development, but also thanks to important changes in western European printing and bookselling. In 1662, soon after the restoration of the Stuarts, the conservative Parliament passed the Licensing Act, which banned "heretical, schismatical, blasphemous, seditious, and treasonable books, pamphlets, and papers," and stipulated that all printed matter needed a government license. Just thirty-three years later, however, the post–Glorious Revolution parliament allowed the Act to lapse, and did not replace it. As a result, something approaching freedom of the press appeared for the first time in England, and printers found it far easier to disseminate works of all sorts. By 1700, London had several newspapers, and in 1702, a daily. Provincial newspapers quickly followed, as did a thrice-weekly satirical magazine called the *Tatler*. All these printed works stimulated the flow of coffee shop conversation as surely as caffeine did (and many coffee shops provided newspapers free for their customers to read). While much harsher licensing rules remained in effect on most of the continent, periodicals began to appear there as well. By 1710, France had journals devoted to literary and scholarly matters as well as the formal, court-centered *Gazette de France*.

URBAN POVERTY, CRIME, AND REFORM

To be sure, most city dwellers did not patronize coffeehouses, visit salons, or read periodicals. The centers of most leading cities remained broadly similar to what they had been throughout the previous century and more: crowded warrens of narrow, unhealthy, dark streets, where many lived in poverty. In London, perhaps one in ten men, women, and children suffered from serious malnutrition. In moments of economic crisis, when servants, day laborers, and journeymen were turned out of work, the percentage could rise steeply. These men and women only survived thanks to what historians call an economy of makeshifts, which could include pawning possessions, hiring themselves out for whatever small jobs they could find, but also theft and prostitution. And despite Christian teachings on the subject of poverty, members of social elites often showed little sympathy for the poor in their midst. A member of the British parliament warned in 1741, speaking of London: "The filth, sir, of some parts of the town, and the inequality and ruggedness of others, cannot but in the eyes of foreigners disgrace our nation, and incline them to imagine a people, not only without decency, but without government, a herd of barbarians."

The report was not only exaggerated and unsympathetic, but an indication that the British government found it difficult to keep control over its capital, where crime was rampant. There the legendary Jonathan Wild, while supposedly acting as a "thief-taker" (catcher) on behalf of the government, actually ran one of the largest criminal enterprises in Europe. Contemporaries claimed that Wild had thousands of thieves reporting to him. Among the urban poor, Wild was a folk hero, and when finally put on trial and executed in 1725, he went to his death cheered by crowds of thousands.

The London poor themselves had a striking capacity for violence, especially when it came to reinforcing solidarity against a system of justice they saw, with some justification, as oppressive. In June of 1732, a crowd grabbed a man named John Waller, whom they resented for serving as a police informer and witness against a series of highway robbers. They stripped him naked, beat him to death, and abused the corpse. "My Son had neither Eyes, nor Ears, nor Nose to be seen," his mother piteously recounted. "They had squeezed his head flat."

British suspicions of over-powerful central government made effective policing more difficult. In the cities of absolutist continental states, however, the reforms introduced by officials like Antonio de Vieira achieved an unprecedented degree of social control. In Paris, as the office of the Lieutenant General of Police expanded its power, squads of watchmen reporting to neighborhood police "commissioners" sought to repress criminality and defend the moral and political order. They kept a particularly keen watch out for "bad speech" directed against the King or the Church, while also arresting men accused of homosexuality. City dwellers reacted with suspicion to these changes, and on occasions when order broke down—notably at times of bread shortages—the police watchmen found themselves the first target of rioters. To prevent such riots, which were often led by women, posing as guardians of the family breadbasket—they were also less likely to be attacked by soldiers or mounted police—the French crown and the Lieutenant General attempted to guarantee a supply of reasonably priced bread to Paris and other large cities. They did so by putting the entire process of bread production under greater government control. By the middle of the eighteenth century, a complex system controlled to whom farmers in the Parisian countryside could sell their grain and at what price; how millers would mill it into flour; how bakers would sell it to consumers and at what final price.

A NEW CULTURAL CLIMATE

In keeping with the general retreat from ostentation and the broadening consumption of culture, the fine arts and literature experienced a turn away from vast, epic productions in this period. Ambitious literary authors increasingly eschewed the epic poetic ambitions of Milton and Racine, and embraced forms of extended prose fiction that connected more directly with the experience of ordinary readers—including especially middle-class readers.

DEFOE Novels of a sort had existed in European culture since antiquity, and the sixteenth and early seventeenth centuries had seen the publication of such classic examples as *The Life of Gargantua and Pantagruel* by the French satirist François Rabelais (1494–1553) and especially *Don Quixote* by the Spanish writer Miguel de Cervantes (1547–1616). But in London in April, 1719, a new sort of novel appeared.

London Crime Eighteenth-century illustrations depict the violent world of crime and punishment in London. Pickpockets or highway robbers (left) might meet their comeuppance in a rowdy public hanging (right) attended by hundreds: robbery was punishable by death.

The preface to *Robinson Crusoe* proclaims that it is "a Just History of Fact; neither is there any appearance of Fiction in it." The narrative begins with the words "I was born in the Year 1632, in the city of *York*," and proceeds to tell the life story of a man from northern England who had gone to sea, nearly perished in a shipwreck, and washed up, alone, on a desert island: "I am divided from Mankind, a Solitaire." There Robinson Crusoe forges clothing, tools, and habitation for himself, and enlists in his service a pliable native he dubs his "man Friday."

In this book, Daniel Defoe (1660–1731)—the son of a wealthy candle-maker with a checkered career in business and a long record of political agitation—managed something remarkable. He presented a fictional tale of extraordinary individual initiative both as a "true" story and as something with which readers from many different backgrounds could identify. And they did. The 364-page novel sold some 20,000 copies in its first eight months, bringing its publisher unprecedented earnings. Still read today with pleasure, *Robinson Crusoe* arguably represents the first modern realist novel, and as we will see, in the later eighteenth century, it and its successors would have a decisive influence on European culture, society, and politics.

SWIFT The same literary climate also favored lighter works of fantasy, satire, and wit. In Britain, this was the age of the great Irish satirist Jonathan Swift (1667–1745), best remembered today for *Gulliver's Travels*, whose visions of lands inhabited by talking horses and humans both tiny and immense make it one of the earliest examples of science fiction. Among Swift's most brilliant satirical productions was his 1729 essay "A Modest Proposal," which drew attention to the miserable condition of Ireland's peasantry, and mocked overly ambitious projects for social improvement. It did all this by suggesting a simple solution to the problem of Irish food shortages: reducing the population by eating Irish children. "I have been assured by a very knowing American of my acquaintance in London," Swift wrote, "that a young healthy child well nursed is at a year old a most delicious, nourishing, and wholesome food, whether stewed, roasted, baked, or boiled . . . ."

LEARNED PERIODICALS AND THE REPUBLIC OF LETTERS

In the period 1680–1740, one other important new form of printed work appeared as well: the learned periodical. In 1684, in the Netherlands, an apparently modest French-language journal began publishing, with the unremarkable title *News from the Republic of Letters*. Edited and largely written by **Pierre Bayle**, a young Protestant exile from the France of Louis XIV, it contained book reviews, correspondence from different cities, the occasional letter to the editor, obituaries, and other literary tidbits, all bound together in a form that modern readers of a certain age will find remarkably familiar. It was soon joined by other, similar journals, but still had a very low circulation by modern standards (in the hundreds). Unlike *Robinson Crusoe*, it did not make anyone rich. But it and its successors had a critical effect on the community referred to in its title: the Republic of Letters.

The Republic of Letters had a long history. Networks of scholars who exchanged correspondence and manuscripts, engaged in reasoned criticism of each other's work, and provided assistance to each other, had existed at least since the days of Erasmus in the late fifteenth and early sixteenth centuries. By allowing authors to compare texts and identify where copyists had made mistakes or alterations, the emergence of the "republic" had spurred the development of modern standards of critical scholarship. By establishing standards of civil discussion by which scholars could admit mistakes or change their minds without shame, it laid the foundations for modern forms of scholarly debate. The Republic of Letters created a community of scholars and writers that could feel more real to its participants than the actual physical communities in which they lived. As John Locke eloquently put it to a correspondent, "I draw breath everywhere but I live with my friends."

But in the late seventeenth century, periodicals like Bayle's changed the Republic of Letters in several ways. They gave it more visibility, a better-defined structure, and they associated it with a cause: religious toleration. The principal journals all came from the same place: the French Protestant refugee population in the Netherlands, which exploded in numbers after the revocation of the Edict of Nantes in 1685. In their reviews and discussions, the journals provided a forum for the strongest and most sustained arguments yet seen for religious toleration. *News from the Republic of Letters* and other French-language journals soon spawned English and Dutch imitators, but as French remained the most widely spoken vernacular language of the continent, it was the French Protestants who found the greatest audience.

THE CAMPAIGN FOR TOLERATION

The campaign for toleration came at precisely the moment that the need seemed greatest. Against Louis XIV's position that religious uniformity ensured civil peace, these writers insisted that such uniformity had driven civil strife and even civil war throughout history: thousands of years of "quarrels, blood and butchery," as John Locke put it. The Dutch theologian Philipp van Limborch wrote a magisterial *History of the Inquisition*, which cast that institution's

Religious Toleration European interest in learning about non-western religions is suggested by a 1724 illustration from an encyclopedia called *Religious Customs and Ceremonies of All the Peoples of the World*. At left a Hindu Brahmin wears an iron collar to raise money for a hospital; at right, another has suspended himself over a fire to show his faith.

campaigns against heresy as one of the great crimes of human history. The **tolerationists**, who remained, for the most part, believing Christians, ridiculed the idea that all subjects should follow the religion of their prince. Should the Christian subjects of the Ottoman sultan then mutely accept Islam, they asked? They also argued, most potently, that since heresy and other forms of religious deviance constituted crimes against God, not mankind, they should be punished by God alone. The tolerationists did not generally extend their good will to atheists, for they feared that without some sort of belief in the divine, humans would lose all conscience and turn completely amoral. But for everyone else, sometimes including even Jews, Muslims, and pagans, they defended a principle they called "liberty of conscience."

In adopting the cause of toleration, the Republic of Letters took on a political identity that it had previously lacked, and emerged as a potent critic of many of Europe's absolutist regimes. Still, absolute monarchy and toleration did not necessarily contradict each other. As we have seen, Peter the Great extended considerable toleration to Catholics and Protestants in Russia. Later in the eighteenth century, King Frederick II of Prussia would similarly embrace toleration. These monarchs were happy enough to let subjects follow their individual consciences in religious matters, so long as they remained unquestioningly obedient in others. It was particularly in France and Spain, where kings had retained a quasi-religious status, that monarchies remained wedded to an official ideal of religious uniformity, and were therefore most vulnerable to tolerationist critiques.

A REVOLUTION IN THOUGHT

But in a broader sense, the spread of tolerationist ideas in the Republic of Letters formed part of an intellectual upheaval that would ultimately shake all European regimes to the core. Centered in the Netherlands, France, and England, it would lead to a radical questioning, not just of religious intolerance, but also of Christianity itself, and the entire European social and political order.

This revolution in thought had many sides. Most generally, however, it involved the systematic application of a deep philosophical skepticism to all forms of authority, spiritual and secular alike. This skepticism owed a great deal to philosophical predecessors from the mid-century, especially Descartes and Spinoza, but it applied their inflammatory insights to particularly combustible timber.

PIERRE BAYLE AND SKEPTICISM

Although often presented as antireligious, this revolution also owed an enormous amount to the evolution of Christianity itself in the late 1600s and early 1700s. We have seen how Jansenism, with its search for a pure, uncompromising Catholicism, ended up casting doubt on the idea that sinful humans could really know anything of the mind of God and his influence on the world. As a result, some Jansenists started looking for ways to understand the world on its own terms, and to discover the regular natural laws by which it worked, thereby bringing them close to the natural philosophers of the day.

Similar tendencies were at work in the Calvinist churches. Pierre Bayle (1647–1706), the French Protestant founder of the *News from the Republic of Letters*, so strongly accepted the idea of the incomprehensibility of God, and so sharply attacked the idea that religion could be defended by reason, that some historians have taken him for an atheist. In fact, Bayle, an enormously influential figure in his time, remained religious all his life, but in an increasingly unorthodox manner. The son of a Calvinist minister, he fled from his native France to the Netherlands in 1681. His first major work, *Diverse Thoughts on the Comet of 1680* (published in 1682) debunked the idea that comets were a supernatural phenomenon, or harbingers of disaster. A few years later, he began his most famous project, an encyclopedic *Historical and Critical Dictionary,* which applied the same sharp skepticism, and a sly wit, to a wide range of historical figures and topics, including religious ones. To take just one example, the *Dictionary* called King David "a sun of holiness" only to add that "that sun had its spots," and then listed every one of David's crimes. And it concluded, mischievously, that "crowned heads" could take solace from the story of David, because it proved that even the worst kings could achieve salvation.

CHALLENGING CHRISTIAN DOCTRINE

While Bayle's *Dictionary* accepted the literal word of the Bible, some deeply observant Christian contemporaries did not. In 1685, the French priest Richard Simon (1638–1712) published, in Rotterdam, his *Critical History of the Old Testament,* which for the first time applied the techniques of textual criticism developed since the Renaissance to scripture itself. Through a careful analysis of the Hebrew texts, Simon argued that Moses could not have been the author of the many pieces of scripture attributed to him. The book aroused fierce opposition among both Catholics and Protestants. In the 1690s, Simon then dared apply the techniques to the New Testament, although insisting he was only trying to rescue the pure, original text of the Gospels from later corruption.

Other Christians went even further. In Britain, some radical dissenting Protestants rejected the Christian trinity (God, Jesus, and the Holy Ghost), insisting on God's fundamental unity. John Locke, in opposition to Bayle, attempted to reconcile Christianity with reason, but his efforts had unexpected consequences. In a 1695 essay, Locke argued that examples of divine revelation could only be accepted if they were fully supported by historical evidence, and accorded with reason and with principles of ethics derived directly from nature. Building on this work, Locke's compatriot Anthony Collins (1676–1729), one of the first self-proclaimed "free-thinkers," rejected prophecy and miracles altogether, and denied the proposition that the Jews had prophesied the coming of Christ. And from there, it was a short step for "deists" like Matthew Tindal (1657–1733) to dispense with Christianity altogether. Tindal did not dispute the existence of God, but presented the deity as a largely unknowable creator who had set the universe in motion, established a natural harmony, but thereafter had ceased to interfere with the world or manifest himself in it. The stories of the Bible were fiction, he maintained, and insights into the true "natural religion" could be found in many places, including Confucianism.

The figure of Baruch Spinoza, whom we met earlier, lurked behind many of these radical thoughts, and in the decades around 1700, Spinoza's work itself continued to gain readers and adherents. In the Netherlands, small circles of devoted followers circulated clandestine editions of his writings, along with biographical studies and commentaries. One of the most notorious, entitled *Treatise on the Three Impostors*—Moses, Jesus, and Mohammed—frankly made the case for atheism: "There are no such things in Nature as God or Devil or Soul or Heaven or Hell." Theologians, the anonymous treatise continued, were mostly "people of villainous principles who maliciously abuse and impose on the credulous populace." To be sure, views of this sort remained horrifying to the large majority of the European population, who continued to embrace the truths of Christianity.

SKEPTICISM AND POLITICAL AUTHORITY

The spirit of skepticism that pervaded all of these works corroded more than just religious authority. Pierre Bayle distrusted the claims of princes as much as those of prophets, and wrote scathingly about abuses of political authority, above all, those of Louis XIV. The Republic of Letters, by its emphasis on civil, rational interchange among its members, naturally encouraged a certain degree of egalitarian thinking. Its leading English representative, John Locke, exemplified this thinking with his insistence that government derives its legitimacy from the consent of the governed. Religious and political critiques tended to go hand in hand. When Prime Minister Fleury continued Louis XIV's persecution of the Jansenists in the name of religious uniformity, radical Jansenist lawyers began to circulate clandestine pamphlets that claimed for France's high courts (*parlements*), as heirs to the ancient councils of the kingdom, a position above the King himself. In the 1730s, the French crown perceived the greatest threat to its authority as coming from Jansenists who claimed to have experienced miraculous cures and revelations at the gravesite of a particularly pious Jansenist deacon (King Louis XV ordered the gravesite closed, thereby prompting one of history's great pieces of graffiti: "By the King's command God is forbidden to make miracles here.")

Compared to the Jansenist works, which enjoyed large audiences, the still more radical works of Bayle and Locke had limited influence at the time. Their readers largely belonged to the Republic of Letters, and numbered in the low thousands, perhaps even only in the hundreds. The number of true atheists in Europe in 1700 was also probably very low. Nonetheless, versions of these ideas did circulate more widely, often in the form of works of satirical fiction, which allowed more timid readers to encounter them without feeling required to fully accept or reject them.

MONTESQUIEU One of the greatest works of European fiction, first published (clandestinely, in the Netherlands) in 1721, exemplifies the use of fiction to convey such radical ideas. Its young author, **Baron Montesquieu** (1689–1755), regularly attended the Parisian salons of Madame de Tencin and others. His novel *Persian Letters* conveys the spirit of that institution, with its gentle stabs of wit, risqué allusions to sex, and short, easily digestible digressions. But despite this form, Montesquieu's work was no parlor tale. Cast as a series of letters between Persians traveling in Europe and correspondents back home, it initially provoked audiences by suggesting what Europe might look like to a Muslim visitor:

> The king of France . . . is a great magician . . . if there are only a million *écus* in his treasury and he needs two million, he simply tells his subjects that one is worth

two, and they believe him.... But there is another magician even stronger than him.... This magician is called the pope: he makes people believe that three equals one, or that bread is not bread, and wine is not wine, and a thousand other things of this sort.

This was bad enough. But underneath these jokes lay a profoundly seditious message. The bulk of *Persian Letters* followed the deteriorating relations between the leading traveler and his harem back in Persia, over which he ruled with despotic authority, but which he could not ultimately control. By the end of the book, it became clear to attentive readers that Montesquieu was using the harem as an allegory for despotic political authority in general. One short fable included in the novel presented a primitive republic of shepherds as the ideal political form, albeit one that was almost impossible to sustain over long periods. Another gave voice to the sort of women's longings that appeared in the early feminist literature discussed in Chapter 13—and not just for liberty and respect. In a daring reversal of the paradise reserved for male martyrs in Islam, it presented a female paradise where virtuous women would receive their reward in the form of sexual satiation from young, virile lovers. Not surprisingly, Montesquieu's novel was both immensely popular and immediately banned by authorities across Europe.

ISAAC NEWTON'S UNIVERSE

This revolution in European thought of around 1700 was greatly aided by the progress of natural science, and above all by the work of a toweringly important English physicist and mathematician, **Isaac Newton** (1642–1727). His scientific work ranged from seminal studies of optics to an obsession with the alchemists' Philosopher's Stone, which could supposedly turn base metals into gold. A devout Christian, Newton also spent many years trying to unravel the chronology of the ancient kingdoms of biblical times. But in all of his work Newton applied the principles of skepticism and systematic reasoning as elaborated by Francis Bacon and developed through the seventeenth century. He achieved undying fame with his stunning book on the motion of terrestrial and celestial bodies, *Principia Mathematica* (1687).

As we have seen, in the early seventeenth century, Galileo had demonstrated that objects moved along a straight line unless affected by a force, and that the earth exerted an identical pull on all objects. Meanwhile, the astronomer Kepler had perplexed learned Europeans with his discovery, based on careful observation through a telescope,

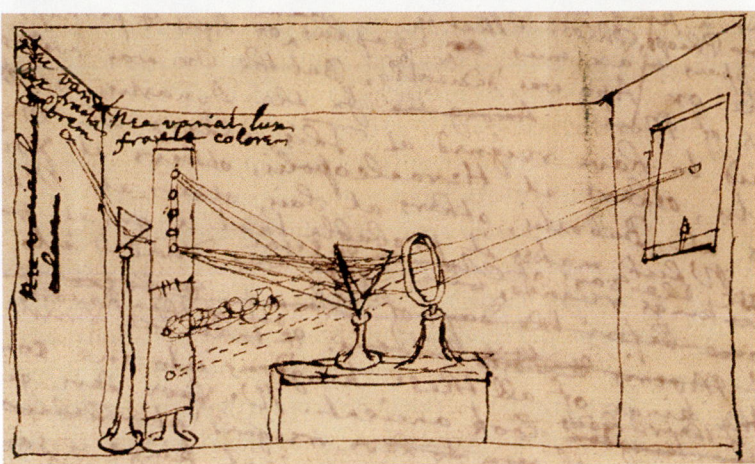

Isaac Newton The scientist made this sketch of one of his most important experiments about optics. It shows light from the sun being refracted through a series of prisms, which allowed Newton to understand that visible light is made up of many colors.

that the planets did not orbit the sun in perfect circular orbits, but in elliptical ones. Newton brought these works together, and resolved the puzzle that Kepler had raised, by proposing a law of universal gravitation: all bodies are attracted to other bodies by a force that is proportionate to the product of their mass and inversely proportionate to the square of their distance. In order to accomplish this crucial insight Newton had to invent a new sort of mathematics, differential calculus, which he did more or less simultaneously with the German philosopher Gottfried Wilhelm Leibniz (1646–1716). The resulting equations predicted precisely the orbits Kepler had observed for the planets. Newton's conclusions stood unchallenged until the twentieth century, and remain the basis for much of the science of physics today.

In the late seventeenth and early eighteenth centuries, Newton's work had a double significance. First, it seemed to restore to the physical universe the simplicity and perfection attributed to it by the ancient astronomical science of Ptolemy. We have seen that one early achievement of the "scientific revolution" was to challenge Ptolemaic conceptions of the perfection of the heavenly spheres, but as astronomers of the period peered more deeply into the skies, what they found proved difficult to account for. The systems they devised to explain the motion of celestial bodies were difficult to follow. Newton's theory of universal gravitation swept away the complexities, and restored perfection in the form of simple, easily understood equations that explained all the complex celestial motions the astronomers had observed. But this perfection seemed to derive directly from nature itself. Newton himself remained a devout Christian, but the only God needed in his scheme was a "watchmaker God" who built the machine, set it in motion, but thereafter let it run on its own. His physics was entirely compatible with this religious belief.

Secondly, Newton showed Europeans of the time the potential of the human mind to penetrate nature's mysteries. The idea was not simply that nature was governed by a set of clear, infallible laws, but also that these laws could be uncovered by humans of sufficient genius, given the proper conditions of observation. The national academies of science founded in the mid-1600s had already begun the public celebration of particularly talented natural philosophers, as those who studied the natural world were still called, but Newton, with his immense stature, raised this process to an entirely new level. As the English poet Alexander Pope wrote: "Nature and Nature's laws lay hid in night: / God said, Let Newton be! And all was light." It was in this period that the modern figure of the "genius" emerged. Previously, people were said to have genius—that is, innate talent—for various things, but not to *be* geniuses. Newton, with his immense prestige and seemingly superhuman intellect, exemplified for the eighteenth century what it meant to "be" a genius.

LOCKE ON THE HUMAN MIND

Just two years after Newton's *Principia*, John Locke published a massive book, *Essay Concerning Human Understanding*, which many contemporaries saw as a counterpart. Focused on the human mind, this work represented a decisive break with the philosophy of Descartes and his followers—especially with the notion that humans are imprinted from birth with certain innate ideas having to do with the nature of God or the physical properties of the universe. To the contrary, Locke presented the mind, in a famous formulation, as a "blank slate." Sense impressions struck this slate, and combined in various ways to form ideas and patterns of thought. All human thinking ultimately derived from the raw sense impressions received by particular minds. In short, the *Essay* seemed to offer what we would call natural laws of human thought, parallel to Newton's natural laws of physics. It was an approach that would dominate European philosophy for the next century.

THE INVENTION OF "SOCIETY"

The power and success of these ideas prompted Europeans of the day to look for yet another set of natural laws—the ones that governed society and politics. Did human society obey the same sort of fixed rules as the motions of the planets? Here, too, the ongoing transformations in the religious sphere made it easier to imagine a social world that existed apart from the heavenly one—a world in which God had no direct, on-going presence. It is around the year 1700 that large numbers of learned Europeans started to use the word "society" as we do today—that is, in the sense of a human formation that exists independently of and prior to political life. Only when Europeans stopped seeing God's presence constantly at work in the world—ordaining monarchs, rewarding the just and punishing the wicked—could such a notion of "society" emerge, and only then could it be thought of as possessing its own laws, equivalent to the laws of motion and gravitation elaborated by Newton. Only then could observers begin to contemplate the rational reform of society to put it in conformity with these natural laws.

CONCLUSION

Even when popularized by writers like Montesquieu, the skeptical ideas discussed in this chapter had little if any immediate impact on the lives of most Europeans. Most people encountered rational projects of social reform only through servants of the absolutist state like Antonio de Vieira, with his pragmatic plans for improving public hygiene, reducing crime, and keeping the population of Saint Petersburg under surveillance. De Vieira and other reformers were under no illusions that they were working in accordance with natural social laws. They were serving divinely ordained monarchs, and everything else faded before the priority of ensuring those monarchs' survival and success. And through the period 1680–1740, the absolutist ideal flourished, even amidst the financial challenges of war and the emergence of a counter-model represented by the supremacy of parliament in Great Britain after the Glorious Revolution.

But in the decades after 1740, the ideas circulating in the Republic of Letters would resonate far beyond the world of scholarship. The goal of reforming society in accordance with the dictates of reason would gain many thousands of adherents. And increasingly, in this age that historians now call the Enlightenment, Europeans would come to see the social and political structures that they had inherited from the past in a very different, more critical light.

[CHAPTER REVIEW]

KEY TERMS

Glorious Revolution
(p. 477)
John Locke (p. 477)
Peter the Great (p. 479)

War of the League of Augsburg (p. 486)
War of the Spanish Succession (p. 486)
Peace of Utrecht (p. 487)

middle passage (p. 490)
Mississippi Company
(p. 493)
salons (p. 496)
Robinson Crusoe (p. 497)

Pierre Bayle (p. 498)
tolerationists (p. 499)
Baron Montesquieu
(p. 500)
Isaac Newton (p. 501)

REVIEW QUESTIONS

1. What new forms of religious persecution arose within some European states during the 1680s?

2. How did the Glorious Revolution reshape English government?

3. Under Peter the Great, how did Russia become more westernized?

4. How did military discipline and the conduct of war change in the late seventeenth century?

5. What forces contributed to the end of French expansion in the early eighteenth century?

6. How did the European balance of power change as a result of conflicts such as the War of the League of Augsburg and the War of the Spanish Succession?

7. How did imperial competition affect European colonies in North America and the Caribbean?

8. What cultural developments took place in cities during the early 1700s?

9. How did periodical journals and the Republic of Letters change the nature of scholarly exchange in Europe?

10. What is the evidence for the emergence of a greater skepticism regarding religious and political authority starting in the late 1600s?

CORE OBJECTIVES

After reading this chapter, you should have a solid understanding of the following core objectives. To strengthen your grasp of the core objectives, use the resources on the Student Site for The West.

- Consider the Glorious Revolution and its aftermath.

- Analyze absolutist monarchy at its height in France, Russia, and Prussia.

- Evaluate both the wars and the conduct of warfare in the absolutist period.

- Trace the development of the Atlantic World in the eighteenth century.

- Assess urban life and the emergence of new forms of culture.

- Compare the major themes of skepticism and reason in the thought of the period.

 GO TO **inQuizitive** TO SEE WHAT YOU'VE LEARNED—AND LEARN WHAT YOU'VE MISSED—WITH PERSONALIZED FEEDBACK ALONG THE WAY.

CHRONOLOGY

1730s
John Wesley founds
Methodism

1740–1748
War of the Austrian
Succession

1745
Charles Edward
Stuart invades
Scotland

1748
Montesquieu publishes
The Spirit of the Laws

1749
Handel's *Music for the
Royal Fireworks* performed
at Vauxhall Gardens

1751–1772
Diderot and d'Alembert
publish their *Encyclopedia*

1756–1763
Seven Years' War

1758–1779
Cook's three
expeditions

1759
Voltaire publishes
Candide

1760s
John Wilkes challenges
British government

1760s
Physiocrats advocate
economic reform in France

1762
Rousseau publishes
The Social Contract
and *Emile*

1771
Arkwright
develops
water frame

Enlightenment

CHALLENGING THE PREVAILING ORDER

1740–1780

O n a hot day in October 1749, a thirty-seven-year-old aspiring man of letters set out to walk the four miles from Paris to the nearby town of Vincennes. The largely self-educated son of a watchmaker from Geneva, he had knocked about France and northern Italy for years without much to show for it. Brilliant, and abrasive, he had a reputation as an eccentric.

As he walked, the man glanced through a magazine, his attention drawn to an advertisement announcing an essay competition. The theme was whether the revival of the sciences and the arts had contributed to the purification of public morals. As the man later described it, "The moment I read this, I seemed to behold another world, and became a different man." In his telling, he immediately saw that the answer to the question was "no," and feverishly composed an essay explaining why. Others would tell the story differently, claiming that the man had chosen to answer the question in the negative for cynical reasons, to distinguish himself from other contestants.

In any case, the final essay was a stunning piece of work. Thundering and impassioned, it denounced the arts and sciences for distracting men from their civic duties, weakening their character, and leading them into lives of constant pretense. It took the judges

Vauxhall Gardens Londoners gather among the elaborate stone buildings, gazebos, and formal gardens at Vauxhall, near the river Thames, in this mid-eighteenth-century engraving. An orchestra plays from above. Events at the garden, such as the 1749 preview of Handel's *Music for the Royal Fireworks*, provided new venues for social classes to mix in public.

1775–1783
American Revolution

1775
"Flour war" in France

1778
French enter American Revolution

1781
Watt perfects steam engine

1772
First partition of Poland

1776
Adam Smith publishes *The Wealth of Nations*

FOCUS QUESTIONS

- What was driving economic change in the period?
- How was warfare becoming more global?
- How was cultural change expanding in the period?
- How did religion reflect broader cultural and political change?
- What were the distinctive features of the Enlightenment at its height?
- What were the major political effects of the Enlightenment?

the Republic of Letters. Writers increasingly made their livings and their reputations by appealing to that diffuse body known as the "public," rather than to a tiny number of wealthy and influential patrons. The public in turn became recognized as an increasingly significant force—and, by the end of the period, a revolutionary one.

The Enlightenment in its heyday broke from earlier European intellectual movements in another way as well. It involved a more sustained and well-informed curiosity about the non-European world. Its most important works—including Rousseau's—drew extensively on travel literature, early forms of anthropological observation, and historical works about Asia, the Americas, and Africa. The authors often offered wildly distorted pictures of non-European societies to suit their own purposes: using supposed, often imaginary, Polynesian sexual practices to criticize priestly celibacy, for instance, or casting Buddhism as an Eastern version of intolerant European churches. But increasingly the work made European readers more deeply aware of human diversity, and by the later part of the century some European authors were offering provocative critiques of slavery and imperialism.

aback, but also impressed them deeply with its force and eloquence. After some heated debate, they awarded it the top prize, and it was soon published. The man, whose name was Jean-Jacques Rousseau, suddenly found himself an intellectual celebrity. A former king of Poland was just one of the many well-known Europeans who published replies to him. Over the next twenty-nine years, Rousseau (1712–1778) would build on this success to become one of the most famous writers in Europe, and a figure widely credited with inspiring the French Revolution.

This story reveals a great deal about the phenomenon now referred to as the European "Enlightenment," whose origins we have seen in the previous chapter. Its full flowering was the most significant European development of the years 1740–80. The Enlightenment followed naturally from the intellectual ruptures of the years around 1700, but it occurred in a rapidly changing social and cultural context that gave it a new sort of importance. The earlier great debates about science, the arts, and religion had taken place largely among a narrow, well-to-do, well-educated elite, many of whom participated in the scholarly networks of the Republic of Letters. If these controversies had powerful consequences, it was because powerful figures had paid attention to them. By contrast, during the mid- and later eighteenth century, a much wider spectrum of individuals not only read about but actively took part in intellectual debate. Through a variety of new and transformed institutions—newspapers, coffeehouses, learned academies, debating societies, libraries, public lecture series—serious intellectual conversation spilled out far beyond the bounds of

ECONOMIC CHANGE

The development of this new, more wide-ranging Enlightenment could take place in large part because of favorable economic, social, and political circumstances. Most critically, the period 1740–80 saw a continuing improvement in the European climate and relatively few destructive epidemics. The most famous European natural disaster of the mid-eighteenth century was a great earthquake that destroyed 85 percent of the buildings in Lisbon in 1755 and may have killed as many as 90,000 people there. In the broader Western world this seismic shock had cultural repercussions, leading some intellectuals to question their faith in a beneficent nature. But overall a natural disaster on this scale was an exception in the period.

AGRICULTURAL EXPANSION

Under these largely favorable conditions, the European population and economy continued to experience impressive growth. Over the course of the eighteenth century, the population of the Continent rose by nearly 60 percent, to 190 million, with the most sustained growth between 1740 and 1780. Agricultural production rose as well. In most countries, the growth in output did not come as the result of any revolutionary change in farming techniques. Landowners expanded the areas under cultivation, notably through draining wetlands and consolidating small, inefficient strips of land into larger, more easily plowed ones. Yet in the northwestern corner of Europe, in a rough circle that included the Low Countries, southern England, and northern France, more striking improvements took place. In this "charmed circle," as we have seen, a culture of innovation and tinkering had already begun to spur economic growth in the seventeenth century, followed by dramatic agricultural improvements in the eighteenth. Where landowners and their tenants had once let fields lie fallow to restore their fertility, now many of them introduced into their agricultural cycle the planting of legumes that actively replenished the soil with nutrients.

In Britain, some wealthy landlords began "enclosing"—and taking for themselves—common lands that farmers had traditionally used to pasture animals, in a movement that would pick up speed toward the end of the eighteenth century. They farmed this land with tenants and applied the new innovations aggressively, earning significant profits. By the 1750s, farmers in some areas of Britain were more than twice as productive as their counterparts outside northwestern Europe, and Britain was exporting 15 percent of its agricultural product to the Continent. The potato, imported from the Americas in the sixteenth century, was rapidly gaining adherents throughout Europe as an efficient source of nutrition and caloric energy—and while it was consumed above all by laborers, social elites fully recognized its importance. One French queen even attached a small bouquet of potato flowers to her headdress at a royal ball.

INDUSTRIAL EXPANSION

In this charmed geographical circle of northwest Europe, increased productivity also led to changes that we now associate with the development of modern capitalism—notably an increased flow of private capital (money and credit) into non-agricultural investments, such as textiles manufacturing and mining of metals and coal, in the expectation that such investments would yield steadily stronger returns. Heightened agricultural productivity

also allowed more and more poor country-dwellers (principally tenants and landless laborers) to diversify their activities. Foreign trade, notably with Asia, had increased the supply of finished textiles, resulting in cheaper prices, just as demand for these products rose. But finished textiles could be produced even more cheaply domestically, in country cottages where peasants devoted part of their time to handicrafts and part to farming. Thus there continued to develop what historians now call the **"putting out" system**, in which city-based merchants purchased wool and delivered it to these peasant producers, who processed and spun it into coarse cloth in their homes, receiving payment in cash or credit.

THE "PUTTING OUT" SYSTEM The roots of the putting out system go back to well before the eighteenth century, but it was only after 1740 that it took on its full economic importance. By 1780, half of all the inhabitants of certain rural areas in northern France abutting the Low Countries had abandoned full-time subsistence agriculture for part-time or full-time textile work. Most of these peasant men, women, and children remained in the countryside, in their own farmhouses. Yet the change profoundly affected the texture of their daily lives. Whereas earlier generations of peasants had spent winters in relative idleness, or left home to make money as laborers or servants elsewhere, now a cycle of work continued unbroken throughout much of the year. "Putting out" brought cash into the hands of peasants whose economies had previously consisted largely of barter and credit, although generally not enough cash to lessen significantly their dependence on large landowners. The system also put them in routine contact with city-dwellers who spoke and dressed differently, and brought news of the outside world more regularly than at any time in the past. In Britain, the changes were even more dramatic. By 1750, less than half the British population was employed full-time in agriculture, as opposed to 80 to 90 percent in most of eastern and central Europe.

NEW TECHNOLOGIES New technologies, and the accompanying flows of capital, brought other significant changes to rural life. In 1771, the British inventor Richard Arkwright (1732–1792) perfected a "water frame" technology that allowed large spinning wheels to be powered by flowing water. The invention quickly spread to river towns throughout Britain, increasing productivity and textile production, particularly of cloth made from cotton, imported increasingly from slave societies in the

Steam Engine An eighteenth-century watercolor offers a technical rendering of Watt's steam engine, which used a system of gears and shafts to harness the energy from burning coal to power machines.

Americas. And in the same period James Watt (1736–1819) perfected his steam engine, which allowed looms and wheels to be powered by burning wood or coal, and not just by flowing water, thereby freeing production from river-based locations. Throughout western Europe, large landowners, belonging mostly to the nobility, began to exploit the riches in coal and ore that lay beneath the surface of their estates. In the nineteenth century, these new technologies would make a full-scale Industrial Revolution possible.

NEW INFRASTRUCTURE This technological and economic change in turn helped drive the development of what we would now call "infrastructure," especially in western Europe. The French and British states invested large sums in road building, allowing for the development of far more rapid and reliable commercial coach service. To reach the port city of Bordeaux from Paris by horse-drawn coach in the mid-seventeenth century—a distance of some 360 miles—had taken over two weeks. By the 1780s, the same journey took less than six days. Travel time from London to Edinburgh (400 miles) fell even more dramatically, from nearly eleven days to under three. Schedules for coaches became more precise, forcing travelers to pay attention to minutes, not just hours; the London–Glasgow mail coach, for instance, gave passengers precisely thirty-five minutes for a dinner stop. The same improvements allowed for more rapid and reliable mail service than ever before, making it possible for readers to subscribe to periodicals published hundreds of miles away.

RISING INEQUALITY Most of Europe, however, remained largely untouched by these developments. In southern Europe, and throughout most of France and Germany, the majority of peasants continued to farm the land in much the same way they had done two hundred years previously, and probably did not produce much more per acre than their distant predecessors at the time of the Roman Empire. In eastern Europe and the Russian Empire, as we have seen, great landowners were forcing more peasants than ever into conditions of serfdom that hardly differed from slavery. France was widely accounted a prosperous country and had rates of economic growth comparable to Britain's. Nonetheless, when the British agriculturalist Arthur Young (1741–1820) visited France in the late 1780s, he was shocked by the misery of the rural population, which he attributed to the small size of individual farms. At one stop in southern France, he wrote: "The poor people seem poor indeed; the children terribly ragged,—if possible, worse clad than if with no clothes at all; as to shoes and stockings, they are luxuries. A beautiful girl of six or seven years playing with a stick, and smiling under such a bundle of rags as made my heart ache to see her." In 1775 a rise in grain prices in France, caused in part by bad harvests, led to a massive series of rural riots called the "flour war." As in earlier riots, women often took the lead. The threat of famine remained very real. Meanwhile, outside of northwestern Europe travel remained almost as difficult and dangerous as a hundred years before. Crossing the relatively small but mountainous island of Sicily on land, for instance, could take nearly three weeks—longer than it took to traverse all of France.

Even in the most prosperous areas, the gap between rich and poor was vast. The city of London, among its rapidly expanding population, counted at least 15,000 full-time beggars, the large majority of them women and children. A woman named Elizabeth Evans, arrested for infanticide in 1740, insisted that her child had been stillborn and defended herself with the heartbreaking argument that she would never kill a child she could use as a prop while begging. Eighteenth-century Britons fretted that poverty was generating an overpowering tide of crime. Smuggling gangs terrorized parts of the southern coasts, while in London pickpockets, thieves, and muggers gained a fearsome reputation. In response, Parliament quadrupled the number of offenses against property carrying the death penalty, although the courts exercised considerable discretion and actually sent fewer convicts to the gallows than in the previous century. One reason, though, is that they increasingly had the option of deporting convicts and debtors to overseas colonies. By the early 1770s, England and Wales were deporting over a thousand convicts and debtors a year just to the thirteen North American colonies. In 1795, local magistrates meeting in the town of Speenhamland, Berkshire, introduced a system of welfare payments for the rural poor that was widely adopted throughout England. In this "Speenhamland system," local landowners financed payments to the poor to ensure that they could buy bread.

COLONIAL WEALTH AND SLAVERY

Colonies, however, were far more than a dumping ground for convicts: they were probably the single most important source of the European economy's mid-eighteenth-century expansion. British trade, for instance, more than doubled between 1740 and 1780, mostly thanks to commerce with the colonies. British ports like Bristol saw over a hundred ships depart each year for destinations across the Atlantic, carrying manufactures and returning with tobacco, coffee, indigo, cotton, furs, molasses, and much else, all aimed at the developing mass market in Europe. Continuing a pattern begun earlier in the century, these ships plied a route that took them through the Caribbean and Latin America, where European plantation owners were making vast fortunes from sugarcane. By the 1780s the French territory of Saint-Domingue was the wealthiest colony in the world, by itself producing 40 percent of the globe's sugar. Its principal city, Le Cap François, had a population of 20,000—more than any North American city except Philadelphia or New York. The French port of Bordeaux saw 20 million pounds of sugar a year pass through its harbor in the 1730s; fifty years later the figure had grown fivefold.

But this wealth depended on the most brutal system of slave labor ever seen on the planet. Building on the "triangle trade" begun in the previous century, ships bound for the Americas would often make the slave markets of West Africa their first stop. Sugar production demanded tremendous physical effort in a hot, unhealthy climate—to plant and weed the cane, to chop down and transport it, and then to crush, mill, and boil it. All of this had to be done on the plantation, as the first stage of producing raw sugar. Without new arrivals, the slave populations of Saint-Domingue and Jamaica, the chief sugar colony of Britain, would have fallen between 2 and 5 percent

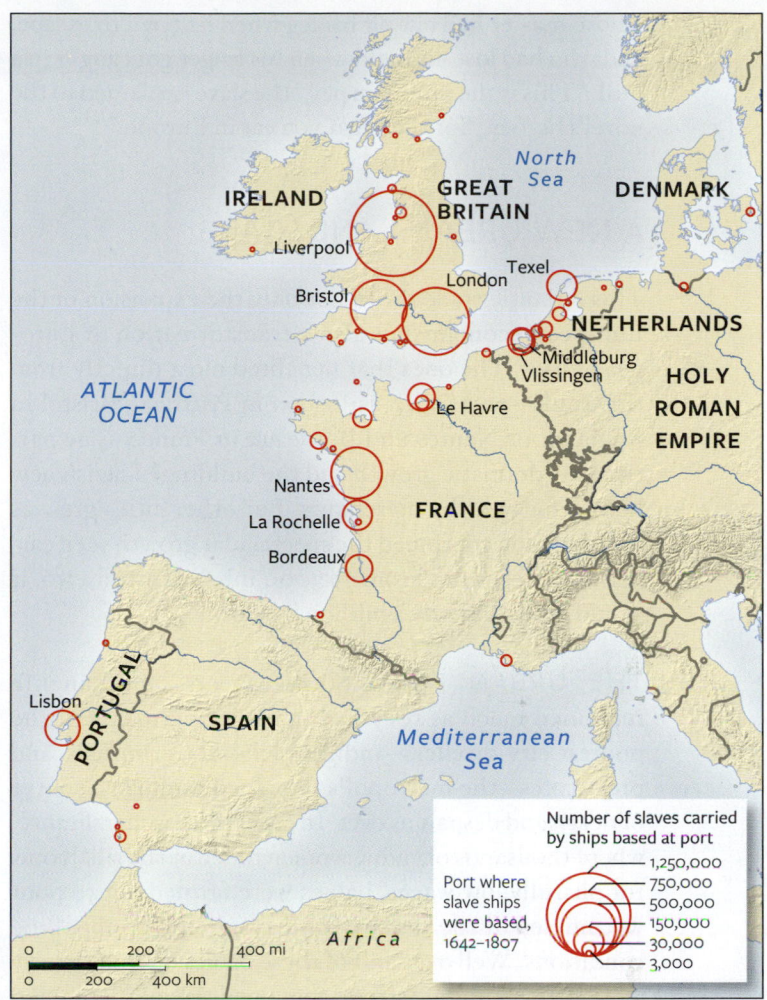

European Ports of Origin of the Atlantic Slave Trade, 1642–1807
Slave ships from over fifty coastal cities throughout Europe transported hundreds of thousands of slaves from Africa to the Americas, thoroughly transforming the fortunes of some of their ports of origin, such as Lisbon, Bordeaux, La Rochelle, Nantes, Texel, and above all, Bristol, Liverpool, and London.

every year because of premature death and the inability or unwillingness of the exhausted, traumatized, and largely male slave population to reproduce itself. But new slaves did come: traders brought well over 3 million from West Africa to the Caribbean during the years 1701–1810—far more than went to any other region. By 1789 Saint-Domingue alone had a population of 500,000 slaves, mostly African-born, who outnumbered whites and a growing population of free blacks and mulattoes (persons of mixed race) by roughly ten to one. The United States at the time had only 40 percent more slaves.

Europeans knew perfectly well of the horrors of the sugar industry. In 1759, in a scene of his masterpiece, *Candide*, the French writer Voltaire described a black slave whose master had cut off his leg when he tried to escape, and who had lost his hand when his finger got caught in a mill. "This is the price you pay," the slave explained to the novel's heroes, "for the sugar you eat in Europe."

A NEW URBAN LANDSCAPE

This Atlantic trade drove not only the expansion of the European economy but also a transformation of European cities. The ones that benefited most directly from this trade—ports such as Lisbon in Portugal, Bristol in England, or Nantes and Bordeaux in France—saw particularly dramatic growth and the building of lavish new homes for wealthy merchants. But other cities grew as well. London continued the spectacular growth seen earlier in the century. From 750,000 inhabitants in 1750, it would grow to nearly a million by 1800.

THE URBAN POOR
Some aspects of urban life remained much as they had in earlier periods. For the poorest city-dwellers—indigent laborers, criminals, and prostitutes—the metropolis remained as much a source of death and despair as ever. In cities like Lyon in France, where thousands of young women toiled at the silk looms for pitifully low wages, babies were farmed out to poor wet-nurses in the nearby countryside under appalling conditions. Well over half of these babies did not survive to adulthood. Public streets remained the most common receptacle for trash and sewage, so that most city-dwellers lived in a world of powerful odors that we find hard to imagine today. (It did not help that most physicians continued to insist that bathing was dangerous to health.)

The traditional structure of the urban trades, with apprentices, journeymen, masters, and merchants organized into tight-knit "corporate bodies," continued to prevail throughout most of Europe. Organizations of artisans called "confraternities," which had elaborate initiation rituals, would offer raucous if ritual protests against the injustice of masters, and their rough brand of humor dominated popular urban culture. The Paris print worker Nicolas Contat recalled in his memoirs that by meowing loudly during the night next to a hated master's window, one of his fellow apprentices tricked the master into ordering all the cats in the neighborhood killed. The apprentices went about the task with glee, venting their frustrations over their work by trapping dozens of cats, smashing their spines with iron bars, and stringing them up on mock gallows, all the while convulsing with laughter. They took particular delight when the master's hated wife saw the spectacle and feared—correctly—that her own beloved gray cat was among the victims.

THE GROWING MIDDLE CLASSES
Yet overall, the tenor of urban life underwent some important changes in the period 1740–80. Writers in England frequently commented on the growing significance of what they called the "middling sorts" or "middle classes." They generally meant men and women who did not work with their hands and had moderate wealth, but who could not be considered wealthy or noble. Not all "middle-class" people lived in the cities, but most did. The group included merchants, low-ranking government officials, men and women living off investment income, and professionals such as lawyers, architects, and doctors. It could also include well-off master artisans. Such groups had existed since the Middle Ages but had rarely been seen as forming a discrete group and a fundamental element of the social order. Now their increasing numbers and prominence forced observers to start conceiving of the social order itself in different, and more complex, ways.

Already by the earlier years of the century, the urban middle classes in western Europe had established a distinct style of life, defined in large part by their education and by what they did with their money. This lifestyle resembled that of the urban elites of the seventeenth-century Netherlands, but now it spread much more widely. The middle classes generally had at least a primary education (men almost entirely, and women far more than in the past) and displayed recognizably modern patterns of consumer behavior. They tended to possess well-crafted furniture, mirrors, coffeepots, pocket watches, and china, along with wallpaper and framed prints. It also became common for even relatively modest families to accumulate savings and to make modest investments, usually not in risky business ventures such as the outfitting of ships or the building of mills, but in land or relatively safe annuities—financial instruments that guaranteed a regular stream of income, often paid by the state. In Britain, more and more companies offered life insurance, which in turn stimulated the development of actuarial science (how many years was a given individual likely to live?). Those lucky enough to enjoy a middle-class lifestyle—still a minority in Europe's largely rural societies—enjoyed a degree of social stability and physical comfort that their ancestors could not have counted on. In England, politicians increasingly argued that the well-being of the middle classes was crucial to the well-being of the nation as a whole.

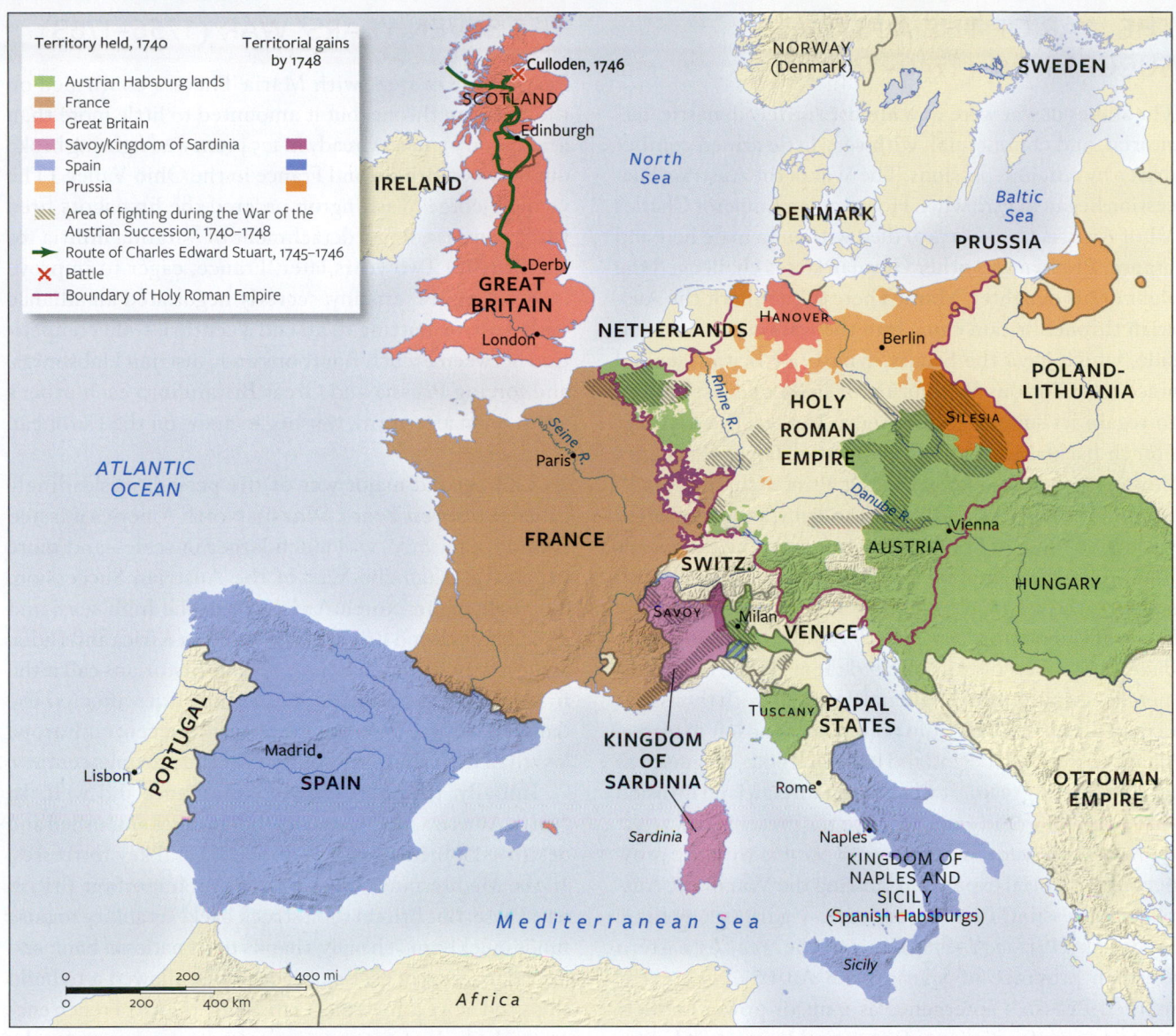

Legend:

Territory held, 1740

- Austrian Habsburg lands
- France
- Great Britain
- Savoy/Kingdom of Sardinia
- Spain
- Prussia

Territorial gains by 1748

- (magenta)
- (blue)

- Area of fighting during the War of the Austrian Succession, 1740–1748
- Route of Charles Edward Stuart, 1745–1746
- X Battle
- Boundary of Holy Roman Empire

The War of the Austrian Succession, 1740–1748 During the war, in which fighting ranged across the Austrian Habsburg lands, Prussia gained the formerly Austrian province of Silesia. Meanwhile, Prince Charles Edward Stuart took advantage of the conflict to march his Scottish army as far south in Great Britain as Derby, before a retreat and final defeat at Culloden.

WARFARE TURNED GLOBAL

Europe's increasing prosperity in this period was not threatened by warfare. The major powers continued to fight as often as before, and pitched battles remained devastating affairs in which one-quarter or more of the participants were left dead or wounded. But such battles took place relatively rarely, with most commanders preferring wars of attrition and maneuver. As one of France's most decorated mid-century commanders and best strategists wrote, "I am not at all for battles . . . and am convinced that a skillful general can go all his life without being forced to fight one." Some observers associated the slackening intensity of war with the rise of international trade. A Scottish author noted in 1769, "Commerce tends to wear off those prejudices which maintain distinction and animosity between nations." However, as overseas colonies and world trade became increasingly important to western European states, warfare itself turned increasingly global—requiring ever larger expenditures on navies and overseas armies.

THE WAR OF THE AUSTRIAN SUCCESSION (1740–1748)

The stakes of war were now almost entirely dynastic, territorial, and commercial, with very little armed conflict driven by religious passions. The War of the Austrian Succession began in 1740 when Holy Roman Emperor Charles VI of Austria (r. 1711–1740) died without a male heir and France, Prussia, and other German states challenged the right of his daughter, Maria Theresa, to inherit the Austrian throne. Britain came into the war on the Austrian side, which gave the Stuart dynasty of Britain (exiled since the Glorious Revolution of 1688) one last chance to regain its supposed birthright. In 1745, the dashing, French-backed grandson of the deposed James II, Charles Edward Stuart (known as "Bonnie Prince Charlie," 1720–1788), landed in Scotland, rallied an army, and marched to within 120 miles of London. For a moment the Protestant king George II feared for his throne. But lacking English support, the rebels retreated to Scotland, where, at the battle of Culloden, in April 1746, a British army under the duke of Cumberland annihilated them. There followed a merciless scourging of Highland Scotland, with thousands of poor farmers driven from their homes and left to starve. Charlie himself fled Scotland in a small boat, disguised as an Irish serving maid. It was the last foreign land invasion that England would experience to the present day.

As always, war tempted several powers with the prospect of territorial expansion. During the War of the Austrian Succession, Prussia, under its vigorous new king, Frederick II (r. 1740–1786), seized the wealthy eastern German province of Silesia from Austria. The event marked Prussia's emergence as a major power and left Austria eager for revenge. France and Britain dueled for territory across the globe. In North America, Britain's colonies were quickly expanding, their population doubling every twenty-five years through immigration and natural growth to reach over 1 million by the end of the 1750s. By contrast, the French colonies in Canada and "Louisiana" (a much larger area than the present state, stretching across the continent from present-day New Orleans to Montana) numbered well under 100,000, most of them concentrated along the shores of the Saint Lawrence River in Quebec. The French sought to hem in the British along the Atlantic seaboard by building chains of fortresses to the west of the thirteen colonies, and by forging a series of strategic alliances with Indian peoples. The North American war ended with the two sides still facing each other across the line of the Allegheny Mountains.

THE SEVEN YEARS' WAR (1756–1763)

Peace came in 1748, with Maria Theresa confirmed on the Austrian throne, but it amounted to little more than a temporary truce. Already in 1754 renewed fighting broke out between Britain and France in the Ohio Valley. (The young George Washington ordered the first shots fired while commanding a detachment of Virginia militia for the British.) Two years later, France, eager to improve its position in Germany, secretly negotiated an alliance with Austria, putting to an end a centuries-old competition between French Bourbons and Austrian Habsburgs, and forcing Prussia and Great Britain into each other's arms. Soon afterward, war began anew on the European continent.

This second major war of the period, misleadingly called the **Seven Years' War** (in North America it lasted from 1754 to 1763), was much larger in scale—and more expensive—than the War of the Austrian Succession. The fighting in North America, on the high seas, and also in French and British possessions in Africa and India, achieved such proportions that some historians call it the first true world war. Even so, the hostilities affected the daily lives of most people in western and central Europe less than the mammoth conflicts of the previous century.

Initially, the Franco-Austrian alliance did well. In North America, France and its Indian allies ambushed and destroyed a British army and took several key fortresses. In the Mediterranean, France took an important British naval base. But Britain soon struck back. Its ability to raise funds quickly and cheaply, thanks to its national bank and legendary army of excise tax collectors, allowed it to build ships and move armies more efficiently than its French enemies, who had to borrow money at high interest rates on the international markets. The well-equipped British navy in turn made it difficult for the French to resupply their forces in the Americas. In 1759, the British succeeded in capturing the French Canadian capital of Quebec City, putting an end to France's hopes of retaining colonies on the North American mainland. At the peace table in 1763, France ceded Canada to Britain and Louisiana to Spain in order to keep its valuable Caribbean sugar colonies—the French regime little understood the potential of Louisiana's millions of acres of forest and plain, which in another century would become the heartland of the United States. Meanwhile, halfway around the world, the British East India Company defeated French forces in India, reducing France's areas of influence to a small area and confirming Britain as the dominant European power on the Indian subcontinent.

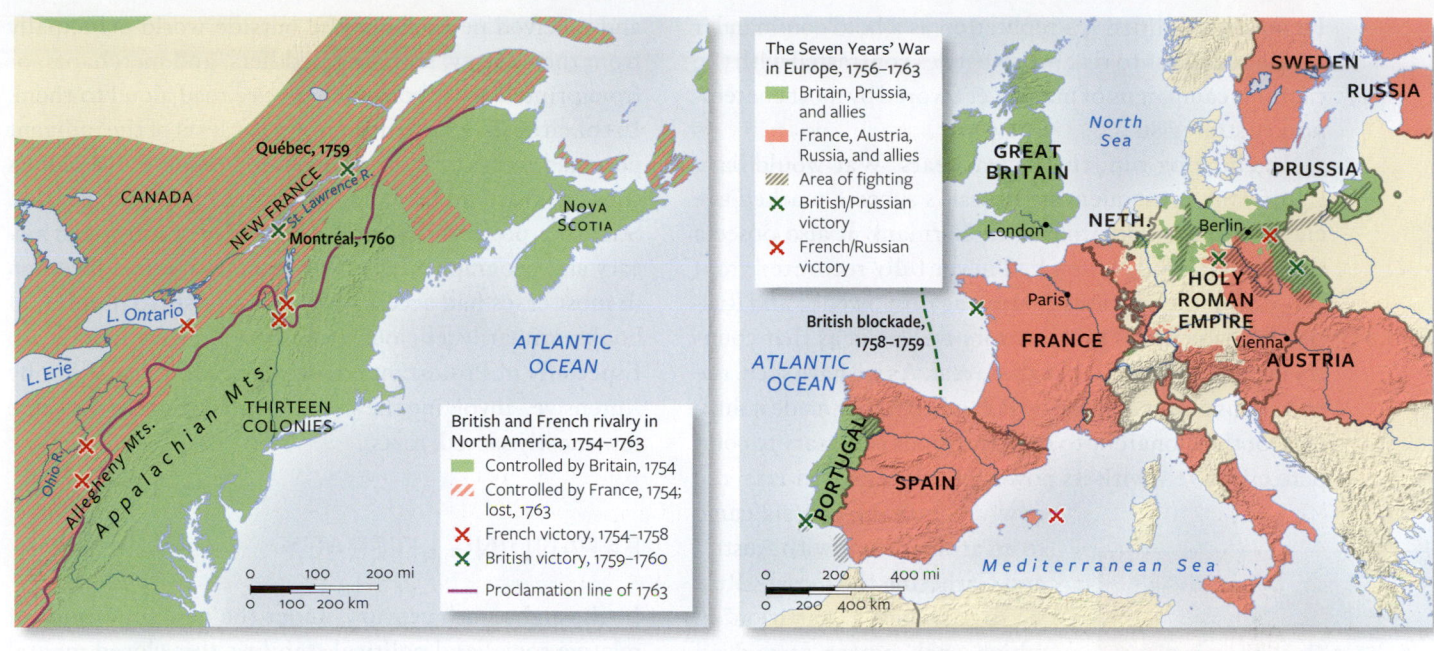

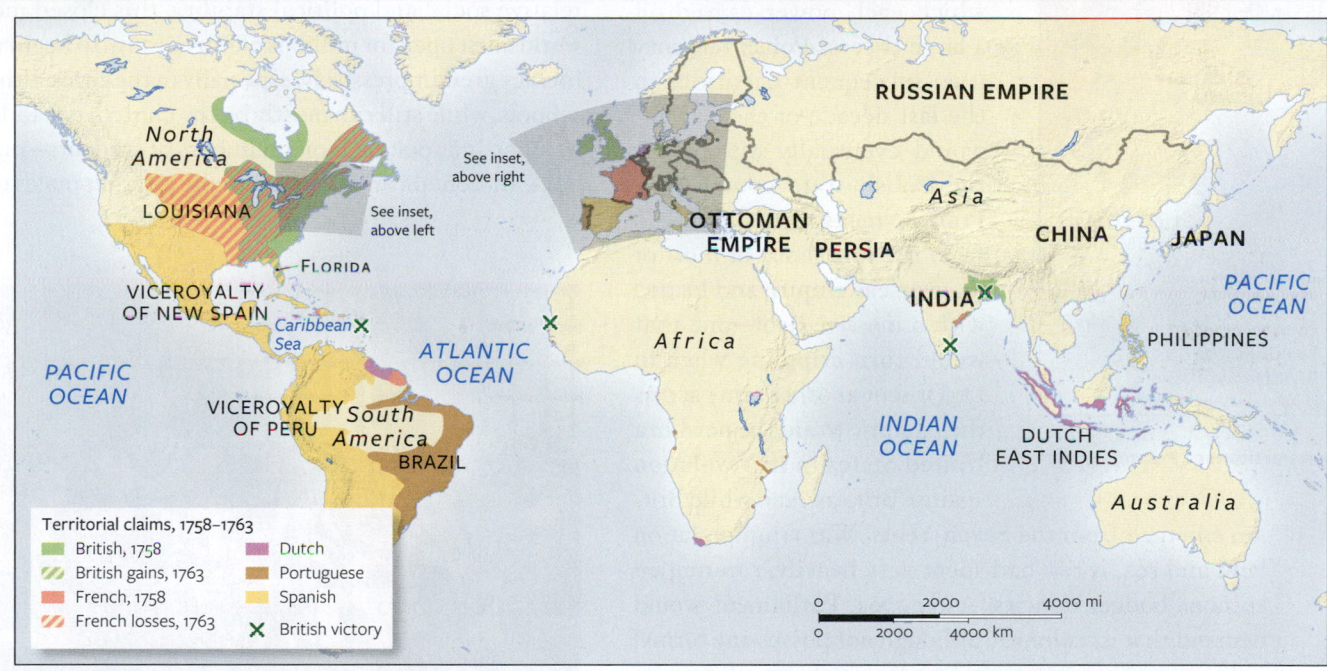

The Seven Years' War and Associated Hostilities, 1754–1763 The Seven Years' War was concentrated in Europe, where Prussia achieved key victories and Britain blockaded France's access to the Atlantic, and also in North America, where despite early French victories, Britain and Spain gained control of enormous French territory. But the conflict was global in scope, with British victories around the world—most notably in India, beginning a century and a half of British dominance in the region.

In Europe, France and its allies did no better, with Frederick II (now known as Frederick the Great) crushing French forces in Germany. Prussia's fortunes did waver when Russia entered the war and routed Frederick's men in 1759 ("I believe everything is lost," the Prussian king wrote melodramatically after the defeat. "Farewell forever!"). But just when the Russians seemed poised to strike at Berlin, Russia's tsarina Elizabeth (r. 1741–1762) died unexpectedly and was replaced by the preening, unstable, German-born Peter III (r. Jan. 1762–July 1762), a great admirer of Frederick who promptly withdrew from the war. So Prussia, like Britain, emerged from the Seven Years' War a victor, and

Frederick solidified his reputation as a bold commander whose readiness to risk major battles contrasted with the cautious campaigns of maneuver favored by most contemporary strategists.

In the long run, the Seven Years' War would have significant consequences. Prussia's success marked the end of Austrian dominance in Germany. It also posed a threat to Poland, which had never fully recovered from the wars of the previous century against Sweden and Russia, and which had lost territory to Russia as that country expanded under Peter the Great. As we have seen, the enormous power enjoyed by Poland's nobility made it difficult for the monarchy to raise the funds necessary to compete effectively with its powerful neighbors. In 1772, the newly dominant Prussia came to an arrangement with Austria and Catherine the Great's Russia to carry out a "partition" in which each power carved off a large slice of Polish territory (two subsequent partitions in the last decade of the century would eventually dismember the Polish state completely). France, meanwhile, emerged from the war shorn of most of its overseas empire and loaded with a massive debt—one that would turn crippling when in 1778 it sent another army across the Atlantic to aid the newborn United States in its revolution against Britain. And while Britain emerged from the Seven Years' War triumphant on land and sea, it too had spent very heavily, running up ruinous budget deficits. After 1763, Parliament would demand that its colonies, although not possessing formal political representation in London, make much heavier contributions to their own defense, mostly in the form of new, stringently enforced taxes.

The First Partition of Poland, 1772

A CULTURAL TRANSFORMATION

In the shadow of this limited but still continuous and increasingly global war, major cultural changes were under way. Before the eighteenth century, as we have seen, only a tiny minority of Europeans had had real access to a broad spectrum of information. Most peasants were illiterate and received news about the outside world principally from their clergy, traveling peddlers, and merchants, or from printed "chapbooks" that were read aloud to them. In the cities, by 1700, those above the level of the indigent poor had access to some primary education, and as adults they could attend theaters, official pageants and parades. Still, they probably had only a hazy idea of European history and geography. Even fully literate men and women in most cases had access only to a very small number of books, primarily religious in character, and no periodicals. Especially in Protestant countries, reading tended to be "intensive," involving the slow, repeated study of the same few, mostly sacred, texts.

EXPANDING LITERACY

In the eighteenth century, under the new conditions of relative social and political stability, this closed mental world burst open for millions of Europeans. To begin with, literacy grew impressively, especially in the cities. Primary schools, while still run mostly by the church, expanded in number and took on larger numbers of students—mainly boys. In London and Paris, virtually all adult males could

Schooling and Literacy Boys and girls sit on separate benches but are educated together in this eighteenth-century German engraving of a Berlin community primary school. Students learned by rote, with the schoolmaster reading aloud to them.

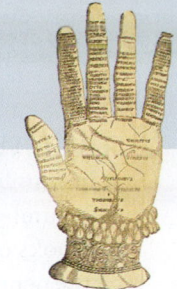

COFFEEHOUSES AND NEWSPAPERS IN THE AGE OF ENLIGHTENMENT

The Swiss writer César de Saussure traveled to London in the 1720s and was particularly struck by coffeehouses and their unique role in the city's daily life. He recorded in his letters many visits to London coffeehouses, noting the diverse clientele, the lively discussions, and the many kinds of business conducted in this new institution.

For Saussure, much of the appeal of the coffeehouses stemmed from the availability of the many newspapers, journals, and magazines that disseminated not only the new ideas of the era—which ranged from scientific discoveries to new theories about politics—but also local advertisements and gossip. Coffeehouses provided spaces in which patrons could read about and debate controversial ideas, open to all classes and trades—as long as you could afford the price of a cup.

In London there are a great number of coffee-houses, most of which, to tell the truth, are not over clean or well furnished, owing to the quantity of people who resort to these places and because of the smoke, which would quickly destroy good furniture. Englishmen are great drinkers. In these coffee-houses you can partake of chocolate, tea, or coffee, and of all sorts of liquors, served hot; also in many places you can have wine, punch, or ale.

What attracts enormously in these coffee-houses are the gazettes and other public papers. All Englishmen are great newsmongers.... About a dozen different papers appear in London—some every day, others twice a week or only once.... The article dated from London is always the most important.

In it you read of marriages and deaths, of the doings of distinguished personages, of the advancement of others in civil, military, and ecclesiastical employments, and in fact of everything interesting, comical and tragical, that has occurred in this big city. You can easily imagine of what amusing adventures you occasionally read, and the remaining part is filled up with advertisements. A lady will offer five guineas reward for a little lost dog worth five-pence. A husband will warn the public not to lend or sell his wife anything on credit.... Entertainments and spectacles are advertised; also offers of houses, domains, furniture, carriages, horses for sale or on hire, books, pamphlets, etc., and by reading these papers you know of all the gossip and

of everything that has been said and done in this big town....

Some coffee-houses are a resort for learned scholars and for wits; others are the resort of dandies or of politicians, or again of professional newsmongers.

QUESTIONS FOR ANALYSIS

1. According to Saussure, who patronized coffeehouses, and why?
2. What could coffeehouse customers learn from the newspapers and magazines they read?
3. How did coffeehouses represent a new type of social interaction?

Source: Madame Van Muyden, ed. and trans., *A Foreign View of England in the Reigns of George I. and George II.: The Letters of Monsieur Cesar de Saussure to His Family* (London: 1902), pp. 161–64.

read by the end of the century. The countryside lagged far behind, and even in England, one of the most literate of European countries, male literacy for the country as a whole barely reached 60 percent by 1800, and female literacy 40 percent.

Relatively open publishing climates permitted several dozen newspapers and magazines to circulate in Britain by the 1740s, and a similar number in the Netherlands. In France and most other continental states, the government continued to keep a much tighter watch on printed material, requiring works to pass a formal review by state censors before publication. But French-language newspapers printed in the Netherlands circulated widely in France, as did several illicit newspapers.

THE RISE OF THE MAGAZINE AND THE NOVEL

The number of books in print expanded even faster than the number of readers. But just as important, the nature of books changed as more people became literate, and as those people acquired more disposable income. In place of large, heavy, expensive tomes suitable for intensive, repetitive study, publishers found they could make a profit selling books in smaller, cheaper formats of just a few inches on a side, which could be carried around easily—even in a pocket—and read more casually. Magazines like the one Rousseau read while he was walking to Vincennes in 1749 were often specifically designed for portability. The most popular magazines provided a lively mixture of short, humorous essays, longer more serious essays, verse, and, increasingly, illustrations. The great prototype was the British magazine *The Spectator*, founded in 1711, which promised "to enliven morality with wit, and to temper wit with morality . . . to bring philosophy out of the closets and libraries, schools and colleges, to dwell in clubs and assemblies, at tea-tables and coffeehouses."

The subject matter of books changed as well over the eighteenth century. Religious works, while still an important part of publishers' catalogues, were challenged in popularity by histories, popular discussions of scientific topics, philosophical essays, travel narratives, and especially that most important literary genre of the period, the novel. Eighteenth-century novelists such as Daniel Defoe (1660–1731) presented their fictional worlds as slices of reality—as memoirs or letters that had fallen into their hands. Just as Defoe's *Robinson Crusoe* of 1719 purported to be the true story of a castaway, so *Pamela* (1740) and *Clarissa* (1748) by **Samuel Richardson** (1689–1761) adopted the form of letters written by young heroines trying to preserve their virtue from predatory men.

The new novel had a powerful impact on European culture. The brilliant French philosopher **Denis Diderot** (1713–1784) found Richardson's novels as realistic and absorbing as live acting. He said they drew him in so deeply that he continually wanted to shout warnings to the characters as he read. Novels offered an immersive experience in a form that readers could appreciate alone, at their leisure, rather than in a crowded, raucous theater. Thousands of men and women, moved as Diderot was by the compelling characters they encountered in these novels, wrote impassioned letters to their authors, sometimes with praise but often out of dismay that a cherished character had died. In the late 1760s Rousseau applied the psychological techniques and insights of the novel to his own life, and produced the first, and perhaps greatest, example of modern autobiography: the *Confessions*.

WOMEN AS READERS

Women provided not only some of the most memorable characters in early novels but also the genre's most enthusiastic readers. Male critics soon came to complain that novels were distracting women from their domestic chores and filling their heads with dangerous fantasies. But novels opened new psychological horizons for middle-class and aristocratic women who, in many parts of Europe, did not work, could scarcely leave their homes without male escorts, and could only attend a fraction of the entertainments available to their husbands and fathers. Even if women's literacy rates remained far behind men's, and even if their formal educations remained far less developed, novels helped bring unprecedented numbers of them into the realm of literature. And by the end of the century, hundreds of women were becoming novelists themselves—and writing novels that explored the limits of women's freedom more explicitly than any previous works of art. The French writer Françoise de Graffigny (1695–1785) became one of the best known novelists of the century thanks to her 1747 *Letters from a Peruvian Woman*, which tells the story of an Inca

Women Readers A young woman reads attentively in a 1770 oil painting by the French artist Jean-Honoré Fragonard (1732–1806). The size of the book suggests that it is one of the novels that had recently become popular among women readers and writers alike.

princess kidnapped by Europeans, and which offers satirical observations on French society.

PUBLIC CULTURE

Beyond the novel, Europeans with sufficient education, leisure, and income could also sample a variety of other new or transformed cultural forms, at least in the larger cities. They could attend exhibitions of new paintings at the Royal Academy in London and the public displays of art held at the Louvre palace in Paris after 1737. And if they wanted paintings to decorate their own homes, they could find enterprising artists ready to supply them. One artist in London cleverly painted a continuous landscape on a long canvas and then sold off sections by the foot. Even more common in homes were cheaply produced engravings, predominantly depicting contemporary figures, including famous actors and writers as well as kings and queens. In Paris, dozens of new engravings appeared each year, and over half of all households possessed at least one. Great actors like London's David Garrick became celebrities on a level previously reached only by monarchs. He had his portrait painted or engraved at least 450 times.

Music played a particularly important role in the changing public culture. In addition to hearing it performed in public, at concerts, and at the opera, Europeans of the upper and middle classes played it more than ever before at home, thanks especially to a new instrument that had evolved out of the harpsichord in the early 1700s: the piano. Musical training became an especially important part of the education of middle- and upper-class women. Germany, Austria, and England particularly shone as sites of musical innovation, thanks to such figures as George Frideric Handel (1685–1759), Joseph Haydn (1732–1809), and the transcendently talented Wolfgang Amadeus Mozart (1756–1791). Mozart, who became known from early childhood as a musical prodigy (he composed his earliest keyboard pieces at the age of five), enjoyed a greater celebrity than any previous musician.

But there were also more academic entertainments, such as public scientific lectures and demonstrations, and exhibitions of curiosities brought from America and Asia. Constituting another window on the world were the subscription libraries that proliferated throughout Europe, modeled on the Library Company of Philadelphia that Benjamin Franklin founded in 1731. These quasi-public libraries allowed unlimited borrowing privileges to members, whose dues paid for the purchase of books. As all these cultural offerings multiplied, a new type of cultural

Musical Culture In a 1759 watercolor, an elegantly dressed woman identified as the wife of a war commissioner plays the piano—an example of the instrument's association with upper-class refinement.

figure emerged to help make sense of it all: the critic who reviewed new books, plays, music, and art exhibitions.

NEW SOCIAL SETTINGS In this expanded cultural world, the new venues for public socializing that had emerged in the late seventeenth century took on even greater importance. Coffee shops featured even more prominently in the daily life of middle-class and noble elites in major cities, and now could offer their patrons an expanded selection of periodicals to read (in Italy, one influential periodical even called itself *Il Caffè*). Paris and London each had well over a thousand of these institutions. In France and Germany, the aristocratic "salons," originally founded to encourage polite conversation and instruct nobles in the customs of royal courts, opened themselves ever more to serious intellectual pursuits. Often presided by women like Françoise de Graffigny, salons gave many key Enlightenment authors access to noble patrons and contributed to the circulation of their ideas in high society.

The number of scholarly academies multiplied too, with dozens in France by the mid-eighteenth century

LEMONNIER'S *AN EVENING WITH MADAME GEOFFRIN*

In this 1812 painting, Anicet-Charles-Gabriel Lemmonier depicts the celebrated salon of Madame Marie Thérèse Geoffrin, an important patron of the arts and learning in eighteenth-century Paris, as it might have looked in 1755. Despite encouraging discussion and including women, salons like Madame Geoffrin's nonetheless remained elite social gatherings, and as such were highly structured and mannered. While topics ranged across discoveries in the natural sciences to new techniques of manufacture, participants were expected to follow aristocratic norms of decorum and propriety, and wit and eloquence were highly prized.

Lemmonier's painting depicts the dual nature of the salon as intellectual gathering and as elite social event. Madame Geoffrin (in blue) sits at right, flanked by nobles and others of high rank, while many of the artists and intellectuals in attendance stand. A bust of Voltaire looks on as one of his works is read aloud. Though most of the attendees are men, women sit among them and speak freely.

QUESTIONS FOR ANALYSIS

1. How does Lemmonier's painting depict the social hierarchies that governed Madame Geoffrin's salon?
2. What opportunities did salons extend to women as shown in this painting?
3. How does Madame Geoffrin's salon reflect the tension between the Enlightenment ideals of inquiry and free thought and the aristocratic order of eighteenth-century Europe?

and an expanding number in Germany as well. They gave ordinary people the chance to participate actively in intellectual life by submitting responses to essay contests of the sort Rousseau won in 1749. Since entries were judged anonymously, hundreds of women felt free to submit entries, with several of them winning. The society of the **Freemasons**, which had its origins in seventeenth-century British confraternities of artisans, grew into a vast network of "lodges" throughout Europe and extended its social reach to the highest rank of society. The Freemasons developed complex rituals supposedly derived from ancient Egypt and Greece, and devoted themselves to a vision of the public good that descended from the radical ideas of the English Civil War, although it expressed itself publicly chiefly in charity. Salons, academies, and Masonic lodges all respected existing social hierarchies, but nonetheless facilitated new, loose forms of interactions between members from different social backgrounds.

THE GARDEN AT VAUXHALL

A good example of the broad changes in European society and culture could be seen in 1749, when the British monarchy commissioned the composer Handel to write *Music for the Royal Fireworks* to commemorate the recent treaty that ended the War of the Austrian Succession. An ambitious entrepreneur named Jonathan Tyers secured the right to hold a public "rehearsal" of the work in his pleasure garden at Vauxhall, on the south bank of the river Thames. Since entrance was free, some 12,000 Londoners of all classes flocked to this popular amusement park to hear concerts, see exhibitions of art, eat, drink, and walk along carefully landscaped and illuminated pathways. For the performance of Handel's work, Tyers made full use of the garden to stage an extravagant spectacle for a socially mixed crowd that earned him gross receipts of over £1,500—a huge amount at a time when many urban laborers earned less than £20 per year. The event also caused a three-hour traffic jam on London Bridge, prompting many complaints. Such entertainments would soon become common throughout Europe.

A BROADENING GLOBAL VIEW

More than ever before, these new cultural venues exposed Europeans to the larger world. Earlier generations of Europeans had wondered at the "marvels" and "curiosities" brought back by explorers and colonizers in the sixteenth and seventeenth centuries. But the Europeans of the mid-eighteenth century looked at the rest of the world with more sustained attention, and with a greater sense that humanity was a single unit that stretched across national and religious borders. Travel literature enjoyed great popularity—and not just the religious, evangelizing varieties that highlighted the conversion of heathen "savages." As we will see, many of the Enlightenment's great works made serious use of this travel literature, comparative histories, and early works of anthropology.

COOK'S VOYAGES

Voyages of scientific exploration, often large in scale and sponsored by national scientific academies, were particularly important in stimulating this new global view. The earliest of these dated back to the seventeenth century, but the mid-eighteenth again saw a significant increase in their scale, ambition, and prominence. The most important of these voyages were the three undertaken by Britain's Captain **James Cook** (1728–1779). Initially engaged by the Royal Society in 1766 to make astronomical observations in the South Pacific, Cook explored vast stretches of ocean over the next thirteen years. He ranged from the Nootka Sound in present-day British Columbia to just off the coast of Antarctica, and to Australia, where he made the first detailed observations of the indigenous population. Cook and his collaborator, the botanist Joseph Banks (1743–1820), brought back a trove of previously unknown flora and fauna, and sketches of the lands explored.

Cook's second expedition brought back a young Pacific Islander named Omai, who became a sensation in London and was introduced to King George III. Cook and explorers such as the French officer Louis-Antoine de Bougainville (1729–1811), whose scientific expedition sailed around the world in the late 1760s, reported a lack of sexual taboos or restrictions in Pacific islands such as Tahiti. These stories inflamed European imaginations and contributed to the idea that "noble savages"—men and women who lived in mankind's original, innocent state of nature—actually existed. Denis Diderot wrote a satirical *Supplement* to Bougainville's relation of his voyage that, among other things, contrasted the free-loving Tahitians to Catholic priests who unnaturally repressed their sexual urges. Having already spent time in prison for seditious writings, however, Diderot declined to publish the work.

European readers reacted more ambivalently to evidence that the sailors on the voyages were "going native"—marrying indigenous women, taking ritual oaths of friendship, and getting elaborate tattoos. And they were horrified when cultural misunderstandings turned violent, leading to the deaths of Europeans and sometimes

Views of Native Peoples A 1773 British travel narrative included this illustration of natives of Tahiti. The individual on the left is shown with a traditional facial tattoo; the one on the right is described as making an expression used to frighten enemies in battle.

even to ritual cannibalism. James Cook himself was killed by Hawaiians in 1779. Even as his killers, who continued to respect Cook, carefully cleaned and preserved his bones, the British reading public made him into a martyr and hailed him as a model of sensitive, enlightened masculinity.

COSMOPOLITANISM The sense of a common European identity fostered by this new global view, and by social interactions in spaces such as coffeehouses and Masonic lodges, contributed to another remarkable eighteenth-century phenomenon: growing homogeneity among social elites. In the age of Louis XIV, nobles and the wealthiest commoners might have taken on the speech and manners of royal courts, and read fashionable poetry and plays. Yet outside the courts, on the Continent, nearly all the population continued to speak local dialects and take part in traditional local entertainments, even if the elites increasingly condemned the excessive violence and obscenity they perceived in these entertainments. The middle classes continued to dress in traditional local fashion. Festivals and holidays also followed local custom.

But by the middle of the eighteenth century, a broad social elite—nobles, but also professionals (especially doctors and lawyers), the upper clergy, wealthy merchants and tradesmen, and their families—no longer participated in local cultural life in the same way. Now these men and

women increasingly took their cues from a small number of urban centers, which themselves were intensely aware of one another—London, Paris, Berlin, Milan, Naples, Vienna, Saint Petersburg. They read the same books and periodicals as their counterparts in the other cities, discussed the same plays and music—and performed this music themselves at home—and increasingly dressed and spoke in the same manner. This common high culture even extended to far-flung colonial locales: by the 1770s, in towns such as Philadelphia, and Le Cap François in Saint-Domingue, theaters and booksellers boasted the latest productions from Europe, while elegant men and women paraded in the latest European fashions. In Saint-Domingue, wealthy male planters ordered the same fashions for favored slave concubines, whose children they sometimes recognized as legitimate. Indeed, some of these mixed-race children became slave owners themselves.

Overall, then, Europe and its empires were becoming more cosmopolitan places, with the purveyors and products of culture alike readily crossing borders. Between 1675 and 1750, nearly 100 Italian composers took up residence in London. Between the 1720s and the 1770s, the British purchased from Italy, France, and Holland some 50,000 paintings and half a million etchings and engravings. Thousands of wealthy young Britons undertook "grand tours" of the Continent every year. There they visited public buildings and ancient ruins, studied modern languages, and developed social ties with continental Europeans of their own class.

But if the new high culture was international, it nonetheless had a clear focal point: France and the French language. Works in French were circulated and translated more widely than any others. Diplomats spoke French, and so did the nobles of Berlin and Saint Petersburg. King Frederick the Great of Prussia wrote in French and dismissed his mother tongue, German, as suitable only for addressing servants and dogs. In Russia, the tsars encouraged the use of French as well, in keeping with the "Westernization" policies first developed by Peter the Great. Noble Russian families hired French servants and tutors.

ANTI-COSMOPOLITANISM Some writers, however, began to lament the supposed disappearance of national differences. Jean-Jacques Rousseau, a Genevan-born French-speaker, wrote in 1772 that "today...there are no longer any Frenchmen, Germans, Spaniards, or even Englishmen: there are only Europeans. They all have the same tastes, the same passions, and the same customs." In England, by the 1750s a full-fledged cultural reaction was beginning, with influential critics decrying the supremacy of the French language and calling for a return to national, ethnic traditions. The years 1750–70 saw the foundation of a Society of Antiquaries devoted solely to the English past, and the publication of the first major English dictionary, biographical dictionary, and encyclopedia (the *Encyclopedia Britannica*). Aided by celebrities like the actor Garrick, a specifically English literary and dramatic canon was established, centering, of course, on Shakespeare. This cultural reaction was not politically conservative, however. In fact, in the appeal to a mythical national past, critics often sketched out a vision of a more egalitarian future.

Similarly, in Germany, a cohort of young writers challenged the dominance of French culture and urged Germans to rediscover the sources of their own literature by seeking out the supposedly unsullied speech and stories of the peasantry. The writer Johann Wolfgang von Goethe (1749–1832) rhapsodized about the peculiarly German splendors of Strasbourg Cathedral. The philosopher and critic Johann Gottfried Herder (1744–1803) developed the theory that each language and literature had its own particular character, which demanded protection from foreign influences. "Spew out the slime of the Seine," he urged his readers. "Speak German, O German."

These critiques would take on great importance in the early years of the nineteenth century, when they would help drive the emergence of nationalism as a major force in European politics and culture. But even in the cosmopolitan 1750s, Europeans frequently displayed remarkable intolerance toward foreigners. The British had the worst reputation, to the extent that one French visitor thought the English phrase for "foreigner" was "French dog." The Seven Years' War saw the French and British, for the first time, condemn entire enemy peoples for supposed war crimes. Yet even taking this intolerance into account, the mid-eighteenth century still stands, in most respects, as the period in history when European elites, including wealthy members of the middle class as well as nobles, had the most in common with each other. An educated traveler, assuming he or she spoke French, could find familiar institutions, and men and women who knew the same works of art, literature, and philosophy, in any major European city.

RELIGIOUS CHANGE

An additional element contributing to the emergence of a common European culture among elites was the declining public importance of religion. By the middle of the eighteenth century, the intense feelings that had led Louis XIV of France to declare Protestantism illegal in 1685 had ceased to shape policy in most European states. True, Protestantism did remain illegal in many Catholic countries, while Catholics continued to suffer under a host of "penal laws" in Britain and other Protestant states. But just as religion had largely faded as a motive for international warfare, so the brutal religious violence that had claimed so many lives in previous times largely subsided. The place of religion in European public life was changing in important ways.

THE DECLINE OF FORMAL OBSERVANCE

For one thing, throughout much of western Europe, overt forms of Christian observance were declining. In France, dying men and women left less money to pay for masses for their souls in purgatory, while local elites abandoned religious confraternities in favor of secular Masonic lodges. The number of men choosing to enter the priesthood fell. Most strikingly, the birthrate declined measurably, pointing to the widespread adoption of primitive contraception (coitus interruptus and condoms made from linen or animal entrails) in defiance of religious teachings. But these changes remained uneven across Europe. Just across the French border in the northern Italian kingdom of Piedmont, bequests for masses, religious vocations, and the birthrate remained at the same rates as at the beginning of the century.

Where religious observance did decline, one reason was the growing influence of the skepticism and other new philosophical perspectives of the late seventeenth and early eighteenth centuries. Yet paradoxically, the churches themselves also helped drive the change. By the middle of the eighteenth century, the large-scale reform programs undertaken by both Protestant and Catholic churches since the late sixteenth century had reached fruition. Clergy had far better educations and lived under a greater degree of supervision than their predecessors. (Catholic clergy, in particular, observed much higher rates of celibacy.) They tended to participate in the cosmopolitan high culture and saw their parishioners' customs, and even language, as primitive. Throughout much of Catholic Europe, some clergy sought to impose a rigid, uncompromising form of Catholic practice that denied men and women many of the spiritual comforts they expected from religion. They decreased the frequency with which parishioners received absolution from their sins and took Communion. And so, especially in rural areas, a gap developed between the clergy and their own church members. "Let us regard ourselves," a French priest wrote to a colleague in 1731, "you and I, in these cantons, as if we were in China or in Turkey, even though we are in the middle of Christianity, where one sees practically naught but pagans." Not surprisingly, perhaps, the "pagans" in question reacted badly to such condescension.

NEW "ENTHUSIASMS"

The increasing distance from formal religious observance did not necessarily testify to a decline in religious belief itself. True atheists remained scarce, even in the most advanced intellectual circles. Many men and women seeking a more rational form of religion purged of what they saw as Christian "superstition" turned to some version of **deism**—a set of beliefs that envisioned a single, non-Christian God figure who was held to have created the universe and then left it to its own devices. Among those who embraced deism were prominent Enlightenment-era figures such as Rousseau and Voltaire.

Religious Revival A 1750 illustration of the Methodist leader George Whitefield (1714–1770) preaching on the outskirts of London is captioned "Enthusiasm Displayed," an indication of the kind of emotion that accompanied new religious movements in the period.

Many others, faced with what they saw as the cold, stultifying practices of the established churches, sought new, more vibrant forms of Christianity. In Protestant Germany, **pietism**, which had begun in the seventeenth century, flourished in the mid-eighteenth. Pietists insisted on the need for an enthusiastic religion of the heart, fed by intense Bible study and fervent "revival" meetings. In England, Pietism helped inspire the charismatic preacher John Wesley (1703–1791), who insisted on the redemptive power of ecstatic faith and founded the confession that has become known as Methodism. By the 1740s Wesley's followers had emerged as a mass movement, using every means at their disposal to excite and galvanize congregations, including a virtual obsession with the imagery of Christ's sacrificial blood:

> We thirst to drink Thy precious blood,
> We languish in Thy wounds to rest,
> And hunger for immortal food
> And long on all Thy love to feast.

In Britain's North American colonies, Methodism contributed to the Great Awakening of the 1730s and 1740s, in which preachers challenged their listeners to embrace a personal, passionate relationship with Christ to save them from hellfire. But Methodism remained frowned on by the established churches, with the result that Methodists often became advocates for religious toleration.

The mood of religious revivalism even reached the different setting of eastern European Judaism. In Poland and Lithuania in the 1740s and 1750s, a charismatic rabbi named Israel ben Eliezer (1698–1760) helped to found the movement known as Hasidism, which emphasized loud, joyful singing and prayer to stimulate ecstatic states in which believers would feel God's presence. Even as wealthier and better-educated Jews were embracing secular learning and the Haskalah (Jewish Enlightenment), the Hasids gained hundreds of thousands of followers among the poorer village Jews who remained the large majority of the European Jewish population.

In short, established religions across the Continent found themselves increasingly boxed in between the spread of radical freethinking or deism, on the one hand, and the new religious revival movements, on the other. But they retained their official status, their secular power stood undiminished, and despite the overall decline in religious violence, they could still strike out against supposed heretics in ways that recalled the persecutions of earlier years. Indeed, as examples of brutal intolerance became more rare, the ones that did occur seemed all the

Death of Calas An illustration from a late-eighteenth-century British pamphlet critical of the cruel punishment meted out to Jean Calas shows him being broken on the wheel. Armed guards keep a large crowd at bay in the background, and a priest triumphantly raises his arms.

more shocking. The most notorious example took place in 1761, in the southern French city of Toulouse, after a young Protestant named Marc-Antoine Calas was found dead in his home, a probable suicide. Rumors quickly spread that his father Jean had killed him to prevent him from converting to Catholicism, and on this flimsy basis the father was arrested. In March 1762 the high court of Toulouse, acting in concert with the Catholic authorities, found him guilty and condemned him to death by the gruesome traditional method known as "breaking on the wheel," in which the executioner tied the victim to a cart wheel, systematically broke his bones with an iron rod, inflicted other tortures on him, and left him to die. Episodes of religious rioting continued to occur as well, most notably in London in 1780. When Parliament considered an act to relieve Roman Catholics of some legal burdens, over 40,000 protesters ran amok in central London, forcing the government to call out the army to restore order in what became known, after one of the protest leaders, as the "Gordon riots." Nearly 300 died.

THE ENLIGHTENMENT AT ITS HEIGHT

It was against this broad backdrop of cultural and religious change that the great transformation of European thought

and society known as the "**Enlightenment**" intensified. Unlike the Reformation, which Martin Luther had launched so spectacularly in 1517, the Enlightenment did not have a clear starting date. Nor did it take the shape of an organized movement. It spread through existing institutions and practices, including sites of sociability such as coffeehouses, salons and libraries, masonic lodges, printed periodicals, and the network of scholars known as "the Republic of Letters." But it had an enormous impact nonetheless, and also generated enormous opposition.

THE CULT OF REASON

Historians still have lively debates about how to judge the Enlightenment. Was it fundamentally a single phenomenon? Or can we talk about multiple "Enlightenments"— radical, moderate, conservative, even religious? How much do the national contexts matter? Did it arise out of the radical philosophical speculations of the seventeenth century, or did the mid-eighteenth century represent a new departure? Did the Enlightenment mark a step toward the liberation of humanity from the weight of tradition and superstition, or its imprisonment in a new mental straitjacket?

It is worth noting that the term "the Enlightenment" itself did not come into widespread use until the end of the eighteenth century, when Europeans looked back at the period and tried to make sense of it. Earlier attempts to define a single, great movement of thought in the mid-eighteenth century came largely from its self-declared enemies—from clergy, and from scandalized defenders of traditional political authority. Although the great German philosopher Immanuel Kant (1724–1804) wrote a path-breaking essay entitled "What Is Enlightenment?" in 1784, which did much to popularize the term, he omitted the definite article. He also largely avoided defining its specific intellectual content, focusing instead on the issue of how to allow the most profitable exchange of ideas, especially in print, which could in turn encourage "man's emergence from his self-imposed immaturity."

Overall, historians generally concede that "the Enlightenment" did not agree on any particular political program, any form of social organization, or any single view of aesthetics, economics, or metaphysics. Rather than defining the Enlightenment as a single current of thought, it makes most sense to associate it with a loose collection of characteristics shared by figures from a remarkable variety of political, social, and cultural backgrounds. Arguably the most important of these characteristics was inherited directly from radical thinkers of the late seventeenth century such as Baruch Spinoza and Pierre Bayle: this was a supreme confidence in the powers of reason.

REASON AND RELIGION

Intellectual leaders such as Denis Diderot of the mid-eighteenth century sought to remove divine revelation almost entirely from the discussion of things human. Consider the most emblematic work of the Enlightenment: the mammoth, innovative *Encyclopedia* that Diderot published between 1751 and 1772 with Jean le Rond d'Alembert (1717–1783), the son of the salonnière Madame de Tencin. The "tree of knowledge" that appears in this work—an attempt to map how all the branches of knowledge relate to one another—shows revealed religion banished from the central place it had possessed in earlier such exercises. Diderot and d'Alembert placed it instead on an upper branch, under the label "Superstition," next to the category "Black Magic." Some of the most radical thinkers of the mid-eighteenth century went beyond their predecessor Spinoza to offer a purely materialist view of human nature. Julien de La Mettrie (1709–1751) gained notoriety with a book entitled *Man: A Machine*.

Also in keeping with their radical seventeenth-century predecessors, Enlightenment thinkers generally downplayed or eliminated the idea of original sin that had weighed so heavily on the souls of previous generations of European Christians. Particularly important in this regard was **Jean-Jacques Rousseau**. He began his *Discourse on the Origins of Inequality* (1754) with a description of the characteristics humanity might have possessed in the "state of nature" that supposedly existed before civilization. According to Rousseau, primitive humans had two fundamental impulses: self-preservation, but also compassion for their fellows. This second impulse ensured that primitive humans had not existed in a state of permanent competition with one another, to say nothing of Thomas Hobbes's "warre . . . of every man against every man." They lived largely in isolation from one another, and when they first came together into families and societies, they dwelt in a condition of idyllic harmony—what contemporaries often called "noble savagery." In short, humans were fundamentally good, or at least benign, and only developed a capacity for evil as they grew corrupt, invented property rights, and started to exploit one another. While many contemporary thinkers challenged Rousseau's vision of human history, they largely shared his rejection of original sin and the deep pessimism about human nature that had informed European thought since the triumph of Christianity.

SCIENCE AND PRACTICAL VALUE

A broad faith in the scientific method marked one final major continuity with seventeenth-century thought. Enlightenment thinkers generally embraced John Locke's vision of the mind as a blank slate shaped by sense impressions. Their greatest heroes were Locke and especially Isaac Newton, whose work was translated and popularized by the French writer and philosopher **Voltaire** (1694–1778), who considered it a model of how human reason could penetrate nature's mysteries. In Voltaire's comic masterpiece *Candide* (1759), the characters discover a paradise called El Dorado in a remote South American mountain range. It lacks prisons and an established church, but does possess a massive Palace of Sciences full of ingenious instruments and machines.

Diderot and d'Alembert's *Encyclopedia* rejected the venerable notion that manual labor and machines belonged to a lesser order of nature than pure thought, a staple of European thinking since the ancient Greeks. The project devoted a large percentage of its 70,000-odd articles to careful expositions of technical disciplines, from watch-making to weaving to artillery, illustrated by meticulous diagrams and sketches. In keeping with this broad practical perspective, Enlightenment thinkers tended to measure value on the basis of what produced the greatest benefit for the greatest number of people—a concept soon to be known as "utilitarianism." As Rousseau remarked, "it is not a question of knowing what *is*, but only what is useful." Contrary to their opponents' vision of them as idle thinkers lost in the clouds, Enlightenment-era reformers devoted considerable effort to such practical matters as urban street lighting, improved sewage, the draining of marshes to reduce rates of malaria, and the use of street numbers on houses to help travelers navigate strange cities. In this way, their efforts echoed those of absolutist reformers such as Peter the Great and his servant Antonio de Vieira.

Jean-Jacques Rousseau
A portrait from 1753, when the philosopher was forty-one years old.

THE SPREAD OF ENLIGHTENED THOUGHT

The continuities of the Enlightenment with seventeenth- and early eighteenth-century thought are striking. Yet as the story of Rousseau's victory in the essay contest illustrates, these continuities were most important on the level of formal intellectual content. For a full understanding of the Enlightenment and the break it represented in European cultural history, we must consider how ideas were transmitted and their effects within the broad cultural and political context.

WRITING FOR THE PUBLIC

To begin with, there was the question of audience. Spinoza and Newton had written in Latin for a small number of learned readers, mostly in the Republic of Letters. Locke's *Essay on Human Understanding* was a dry, technical piece of philosophical exposition that still defeats most readers. By contrast, when the French writer Montesquieu first attracted attention in 1721, it was with a scandalous, witty French-language novel called *Persian Letters*. As he himself commented in the book, "there are certain truths that you cannot simply persuade people of, but which you must make them feel." This sentence marked a clear shift to a new sort of intellectual enterprise, which came to fruition in the mid-century. Montesquieu was not writing for scholars or princely patrons, but for the emerging new public that attended salons and coffee houses and academies, read newspapers and novels, joined Masonic lodges, and even entered essay competitions. And to appeal to them—indeed, just to get their attention—he needed to do more than simply reason well. He needed to shock, titillate, and entertain.

Many of the most famous works of the Enlightenment similarly took the form of provocative entertainments, often set outside Europe. Voltaire's fable *Candide* presents a character named Dr. Pangloss (a spoof of the rationalist philosopher Leibniz), who hangs on to his belief in the pre-established harmony of the universe even after catching syphilis, losing an eye and an ear, nearly dying in an earthquake, barely escaping a hanging, and having been cut open by a surgeon, flogged almost to death, and forced to row in the Turkish galleys. The German intellectual Gotthold Lessing (1729–1781) made many of his most serious arguments for religious tolerance in the form of stage dramas like *Nathan the Wise*, set at the time of the Crusades. Even the deeply serious *Encyclopedia* was enlivened with constant small stabs of wit. For instance, under the heading "Cannibalism," readers could find a learned discussion of the subject followed by a mischievous cross-reference to the article on Holy Communion.

UNDERGROUND ENLIGHTENMENT

Not surprisingly, such deliberate provocations frequently ran afoul of the authorities—particularly in the absolute monarchy of France. Voltaire first achieved notoriety in 1734 with a series of *English Letters* that praised, and deliberately exaggerated, the political freedom and religious toleration found in Britain. The high court of Paris condemned the work, and Voltaire fled to Switzerland rather than face imprisonment. Montesquieu and Rousseau both had trouble with the French authorities as well, and the *Encyclopedia* was banned in 1759 for its irreligion, although the sympathetic director of the French book trade arranged for publication quietly to resume a few years later.

Few of the important works of the French Enlightenment actually appeared with the official permission in theory required of all books. Many were published clandestinely, sold "under the cloak" by booksellers willing to take the risk of imprisonment. Large publishing operations grew in Switzerland, the Netherlands, and Britain to feed the insatiable French appetite for illegal "philosophical" books—a genre that mixed true philosophy with provocative fiction, scurrilous gossip about figures at court, and explicit pornography. Smugglers carried them over remote mountain passes like any other sort of contraband. The authorities strove to suppress this booming trade, but their attempts proved counterproductive, for nothing spurred a book's sale like an official persecution. And authors gained heroic reputations for their defiance of censorship.

VOLTAIRE THE PHILOSOPHE

Partly for this reason, the most successful Enlightenment authors enjoyed a public status unlike anything their seventeenth-century predecessors had known. They joined figures like the actor Garrick in the ranks of that new eighteenth-century phenomenon, the celebrity. Voltaire, the son of a Paris notary, had by the 1730s become the first of these—a true literary celebrity. Every educated person in Europe knew his name, and most had probably read something he had written. Even the public executioner charged with burning the *English Letters* on the steps

Voltaire A portrait of the philosophe in his study, at work on a piece of writing, shows him wearing his luxurious velvet housecoat.

ENLIGHTENMENT THINKERS AND PROGRESS

Many Enlightenment thinkers argued that properly directed, rational societies would liberate human genius and lead to the steady improvement of human life—or, in other words, to progress. Progress was a powerful idea, and it animated scientific and technological research and political and social reforms. Some thinkers, such as the French philosophe the marquis de Condorcet, believed that the gradual improvement of human life was inevitable, as one generation built on the work of the preceding generations. The idea of progress also had a utopian dimension, as in the French writer Louis-Sébastien Mercier's novel *L'An 2440* (*The Year 2440*, 1771), which suggested that progress would lead to the perfection of human society.

Marquis de Condorcet, *Sketch for a Historical Picture of the Progress of the Human Mind*

In this passage from his *Sketch* (1795), Condorcet foresees the gradual advancement of humanity through the progress of industry, science, and education.

As the progress of industry and welfare leads to a more advantageous ratio between human capacities and needs, each generation will be brought to greater enjoyments, as a result either of this progress or of the conservation of goods produced earlier…

The most enlightened peoples, reclaiming the right to expend their blood and their wealth, will gradually learn to see war as the deadliest scourge and the greatest of crimes. …Peoples will know that they cannot become conquerors without losing their own liberty; that permanent confederations are the sole means of maintaining their independence; that they must seek security, not power. Commercial prejudices will gradually dissipate; false mercantile interests will lose their dreadful power to cover the earth with blood, ruining nations under the pretext of enriching them.…

The progress of the sciences guarantees that of the art of instruction, which in turn accelerates scientific advance. The constant action of this reciprocal influence must be counted among the most dynamic and powerful causes of the amelioration of the human species. A young man leaving school today knows more mathematics than Newton acquired by profound study or discovered through his genius;…

Finally, can these same hopes be extended to intellectual and moral faculties? Our parents pass on to us the advantages and defects of their physical constitution, from which we derive distinctive bodily characteristics and dispositions to particular physical states. Can they not also pass on to us that part of physical organization governing intelligence, strength of mind, emotional energy, and moral sensibility? Is it not plausible that in improving these qualities education could affect this same physical organization, modifying and improving it? Analogy, analysis of the development of human faculties, and even some observed facts seem to prove the reality of these conjectures…

And how welcome to the philosopher is this picture of the human race freed from all its chains, released from the domination of chance and of the enemies of its progress, advancing with a firm and sure step in the path of truth, virtue, and happiness!

Louis-Sébastien Mercier, from *L'An 2440*

Mercier's popular utopian novel imagined an idealized Paris of the distant future. Here the narrator visits the ruins of Versailles.

I arrived at Versailles, and looked around for that superb palace, from whence issued the destiny of many nations. What was my surprise! I could perceive nothing but ruins, gaping walls, and mutilated statues; some porticos, half demolished, afforded a confused idea of its ancient magnificence. As I walked over these ruins, I saw an old man sitting upon the capital of a column. Alas! I said to him, what is become of this vast palace? "It is fallen."—How?—"It was crushed by its own weight. A man in his impatient pride would have here forced nature. He hastily heaped buildings upon buildings; greedy of gratifying his capricious will, he harassed his subjects; all the wealth of the nation was here swallowed up; here flowed a stream of tears to compose those reservoirs of which there are no traces. Behold all that remains of that colossus which a million of hands erected with so much painful labor.…O, may these ruins cry aloud to all sovereigns; that they who abuse a momentary power, only discover their weakness to future generations." At these words he shed a flood of tears, and turned his eyes to heaven with a mournful, repenting look. Why do you weep? I said. These ruins by no means declare any public calamity. He raised his voice and said: "Oh, how wretched is my fate! Know that I am Louis XIV who built this rueful palace. The Divine Justice has again illumined the torch of my days, to make me contemplate more nearly my deplorable enterprise. How transient are the moments of pride!…"

QUESTIONS FOR ANALYSIS

1. In Condorcet's essay, how does education contribute to the progress of humankind?
2. What do you think Mercier hopes to achieve by imagining the ruination of Louis XIV and Versailles?
3. What do Condorcet and Mercier see as obstacles to progress?

Sources: Marquis de Condorcet, *Sketch for a Historical Picture of the Progress of the Human Mind,* trans. Keith Michael Baker, *Daedalus* 133, no. 3 (Cambridge, MA: 2004), pp. 74, 77–78, 81; Louis-Sébastien Mercier, *Memoirs of the Year Two Thousand Five Hundred,* trans. W. Hooper (Dublin: 1772), pp. 198–99.

of the Palace of Justice in Paris secretly substituted a Spanish history book at the last minute, because he wanted Voltaire's work to read for himself. Voltaire's stories, plays, poetry, and histories sold well enough to equip the chalet where he lived in exile just across the border from France with six horses, four carriages, two footmen, a valet, two cooks, a secretary, and other servants. Voltaire himself wore a velvet housecoat that cost a year's wages for the average worker. Even before his death, biographers compared him to the greatest figures in French history. In fact, he was not just a celebrity but also the most successful of a new type of public intellectual—in the French term that will remain forever associated with the Enlightenment, a *philosophe*.

Yet despite this new status, Voltaire did not achieve a position of true independence. Operating in what was still a hierarchical, noble-dominated society, he continued to cultivate noble patrons and spent several years in Berlin as a sort of official philosophe at the court of the philosophically minded King Frederick the Great. Similarly, Diderot, the son of a cutler, paid visits to his own financial patron Catherine the Great of Russia. Even Rousseau, who enjoyed a degree of celebrity second only to Voltaire's, and who loudly deplored his colleagues' thirst for noble patronage as a sign of corruption, throughout his career accepted housing and financial support from a succession of bedazzled aristocrats.

Even as they received this support, the philosophes managed to remain at odds with the existing order. They continued to see their role as defending certain basic principles, most importantly those of religious toleration that nearly every European state continued to deny. When the Protestant Jean Calas was broken on the wheel in Toulouse in 1762, Voltaire quickly found out about the case. Soon convinced of Calas's innocence, he not only condemned what had happened but led a large-scale public campaign to have the verdict posthumously reversed and the family compensated, making use of pamphlets, newspaper articles, and a massive letter-writing campaign. He took to signing his letters "Crush that which is Infamous!"—meaning intolerance in general and the Catholic Church in particular. His efforts in the Calas case succeeded, showing the power inherent in the transformed, enlightened public sphere.

Opposition to the philosophes eventually crumbled in the face of their growing popularity. In 1772, just thirteen years after the condemnation of the *Encyclopedia* for irreligion, its co-editor d'Alembert became permanent secretary of the powerful French Academy. Six years after that, Voltaire, now eighty-four years old, returned to Paris for the first time in decades to attend a performance of his newest play. Admirers camped outside the house he was staying in to catch a glimpse of the great man, and crowds lined the street as he passed. At the theater, the author watched as the players solemnly crowned his bust with laurel leaves.

Critics in the Church still raged against the rising tide of irreligion in France, but they seemed to reach fewer and fewer listeners. Indeed, the Church itself was increasingly dominated by figures like Étienne Charles de Loménie de Brienne (1727–1794), archbishop of Toulouse from 1776, who eagerly corresponded with Voltaire and other philosophes. He was said to have every quality necessary for a prelate, with one small exception: he did not believe in God.

THE SCIENCE OF SOCIETY

The Enlightenment, then, was defined in large part by the changed relationship between its leading thinkers and the societies in which they lived. But this relationship was not limited simply to the new or transformed institutions and media through which Enlightenment ideas spread. The leading thinkers also came to see society itself in a new way—as an entity in its own right, which functioned according to its own complex laws and was susceptible to change through political action. The Enlightenment saw the emergence of a true, practical science of society, and it is in this respect that it moved beyond the thought of earlier periods.

MONTESQUIEU The key figure in this re-envisioning of society was Baron Montesquieu, who in 1748 published a massive, disorganized book entitled *The Spirit of the Laws*. Based on Montesquieu's extensive reading in the classics, French history, and especially travel literature from across the globe, *The Spirit of the Laws* offers a classification of governments, in much the way Aristotle had analyzed monarchy, aristocracy, and democracy in his *Politics*. But unlike Aristotle, Montesquieu grounded his analysis of governments in a classification of societies, which he saw as shaped above all by climate and history.

Montesquieu In an anonymous portrait of Montesquieu dated 1728, the thinker is portrayed in profile with a classical hairstyle and cloak—perhaps an allusion to the classical influences on his writing.

Here the new global perspective characteristic of the mature Enlightenment assumed crucial importance. Montesquieu drew a contrast between the supposedly despotic empires that arose in the lush, torpid climates of the South and East (such as China, in his view) and the small republics that flourished in allegedly hardier regions (such as Switzerland). He speculated on the "driving principles" that lay behind different forms of government, linking republics to the practice of virtue, monarchies to the idea of honor, and despotism to naked fear. He praised Great Britain's limited monarchy for its system of checks and balances, but also suggested that an absolute monarchy tempered by justice and restraint might prove best suited to France. The book remains the foundation stone of political sociology, and indeed of modern social science in general.

THE SCOTTISH ENLIGHTENMENT Montesquieu found readers not only in France but across the European world. In the American colonies, his theory of checks and balances helped inspire the authors of the United States Constitution of 1787. And he also had keen readers in a place far removed from the contentious atmosphere of Paris: Scotland, where a group of talented professors, lawyers, clergymen, and other professionals were developing their own version of the Enlightenment in the middle of the eighteenth century. These men, like their French counterparts, shared the radical inheritance of late-seventeenth-century thought. The most profound thinker among them, **David Hume** (1711–1776), a champion of rigorous philosophical skepticism, argued in his 1755 book *The Natural History of Religion* that belief in God had its origin in superstition and fear.

But unlike their French counterparts, these Scots mostly did not come into open conflict with the authorities, and many of them gained prominent positions at the universities of Glasgow and Edinburgh. There they developed sophisticated new approaches to history, deeply informed by readings in non-European history, tracing how "primitive" societies ruled by warrior classes and practicing subsistence agriculture evolved over the centuries into complex modern social organisms. They placed particular emphasis on the development of commerce, showing how it softened and moderated social relations, stimulating the development of politeness and the art of conversation, and also bringing women into public life.

Another great figure of the Scottish Enlightenment took the science of society in a new direction by pioneering the discipline that we now call economics. **Adam Smith** (1723–1790), a philosopher and professor, in 1776 published his great work *The Wealth of Nations*, which fundamentally broke with the mercantilist idea that a country's wealth was limited by its supply of precious metals and agricultural production. Smith proposed instead that countries could increase their economic productivity by adopting the division of labor, which organized the production process into particular tasks in which workers specialized. In making this recommendation, Smith was drawing on his own observations of the economic changes taking place in his lifetime, but also advocating their further spread and systematization. Smith also proposed abolishing barriers to trade, including across international borders. He believed firmly that each individual's drive to accumulate wealth would contribute to social harmony by a process that he dubbed the "invisible hand" of the free market. Prices would be set by the free interactions of producers who supplied goods, and the men and women who wielded a demand for them. If allowed to proceed without the interference of religious or secular authorities, the market itself would set prices and profits efficiently. In this system, which we refer to now as **laissez-faire** or free-market capitalism, private individuals and privately owned corporations control most economic activity.

Smith was not the first to make such arguments. Earlier in the century the British satirical writer Bernard Mandeville (1670–1733) had stressed the connection between "private vices" such as greed and "public benefits," while a variety of continental writers had challenged the conventional wisdom that luxury always had a corrupting effect. But Smith developed the ideas more systematically and with a greater understanding of how economic systems actually work. He also warned that unfettered freedom to pursue wealth would increase social inequities. Nonetheless, to the extent that modern free-market capitalism has a founding father, it is Adam Smith.

SENTIMENT AND CITIZENSHIP

Critics of the Enlightenment, from the eighteenth century to the present day, have often charged that its leading thinkers promoted a mechanistic view of human nature, coldly treating men and women like cogs in one of the machines so lovingly illustrated in the *Encyclopedia*. The Enlightenment's science of society put the lie to this claim. Although many eighteenth-century authors, including Voltaire, failed to recognize the degree of comfort people find in tradition, irrational belief, and even prejudice, others such as Montesquieu and the Scottish thinkers never insisted on managing human affairs by cold reason alone. They held a nuanced, careful view of human nature, grounded in empirical observation, and gave full scope to emotion and sentiment.

SOCIAL EXCHANGE The hallmark of modern civilization, from the perspective of these thinkers, was not that emotion had given way to reason, but that violent passion had given way to tender, gentle feeling that encouraged peaceful social intercourse. Women were key to this view of society. Not only was tender sentiment associated with femininity, but women were held to have a "civilizing" influence on men, calming their passions and teaching them how to be properly social. The role that women played in continental salons, and as patrons of Enlightenment writers, reinforced this argument. Many of the philosophes believed women could participate fully in Enlightenment culture. Emilie du Châtelet (1706–1749), a lover of Voltaire's who had studied and published on advanced physics and mathematics, collaborated with him on a translation of and commentary on Isaac Newton's *Principia Mathematica*.

An attention to sentiment runs through most Enlightenment writings. Readers often spoke of the tears they had shed on reading Voltaire's tragedy *Zaïre*—a combination love story and denunciation of intolerance, set in the time of the Crusades—or Rousseau's novel *The New Eloise*. Diderot and other critics openly praised the genre of melodrama, with its exaggerated sentimentality, for the tears it elicited, and tried their hand at writing such works themselves. The French painter Jean-Baptiste Greuze (1725–1805) made his name painting melodramatic scenes of family reconciliation and of tender rural virtue. Rousseau stressed the need to allow emotions and passions to develop naturally. He particularly praised the bond between mother and child and, in his popular educational treatise *Emile*, urged Europeans to return to the practice of breastfeeding. Such was the popularity of the book that thousands of them did, and continued to do so even after the eccentric Rousseau confessed to having unsentimentally abandoned five of his own children to orphanages.

ROUSSEAU'S *SOCIAL CONTRACT* While Rousseau championed sentiment in many works, in others he remained enthralled by the lure of the ancient Greek city of Sparta, whose citizens supposedly suppressed emotion the better to serve the common good. He himself recognized the dilemma. To cultivate the sort of stern patriotic

Sentiment in Art In this 1763 painting by Jean-Baptiste Greuze, a faithful family cares for a paralyzed man. Denis Diderot, who described Greuze's work as "morality in paint," appreciatively named this painting *The Benefits of a Good Education* and admired its expressive emotion.

loyalties expected of a Spartan, one had to suppress one's natural inclinations. Cultivating "tender" natural sentiments to the fullest made a person incapable of the bellicosity and self-sacrifice shown by Spartan citizens. Or, as he himself put it in *Emile*: "Forced to fight nature or social institutions, we must choose between making a man or making a citizen; we cannot do both." As the century wore on, figures associated with the Enlightenment increasingly opted for the latter course.

Rousseau himself did more than anyone to define the meaning of citizenship for the eighteenth century in *The Social Contract*, a powerful and enormously influential book he published almost simultaneously with *Emile* in 1762. Compared to *The Spirit of the Laws* or the works of the Scottish historians, this political treatise stood out for its relatively abstract language and frequent invocation of mathematics and geometry rather than history to describe forms of government. In its pages, Rousseau addressed the question that Hobbes had posed a century before in *Leviathan*: How could citizens live together in society without descending into civil war or tyranny? Like Hobbes, Rousseau argued that individuals must cede their rights to the sovereign power as part of a "social contract." But unlike Hobbes, he associated this sovereign power with the entire citizenry and insisted that true freedom could only be enjoyed collectively, by submission to what he called the "general will." Rousseau held out the enticing prospect that such submission would produce "a remarkable change in man, substituting justice for instinct in his behavior and endowing his actions with the morality they previously lacked." But he added, chillingly, that "anyone who refuses to obey the general will must be obliged to do so by the body [of citizens], which means nothing other than that he will be forced to be free."

The Social Contract represented a clear rejection of the science of society explored by Montesquieu and the writers of the Scottish Enlightenment. Whereas they had sought to explain political systems by reference to social conditions, and to find ways to harmonize society and politics, Rousseau insisted that "everything depended on politics," by which he meant that the nature of customs and social relations were fundamentally shaped by the form of a people's government. *The Social Contract* formulated a high standard of political virtue against which all existing political systems could only come up short. Rousseau himself believed that the principles set forth in his book could be implemented only in small city-states such as those of ancient Greece, and that in any case Europe's nations had nearly all grown too corrupt to establish the sort of democratic government he advocated. Nonetheless, by the 1780s many readers saw *The Social Contract* not as an intellectual exercise, but as a blueprint for political action.

REPUBLICANISM Even in the 1760s, the core theme of patriotic sacrifice for the common good that Rousseau helped to develop was already finding eager audiences. Because of the inspiration Rousseau and other authors took from the ancient republics, this current of thought is often called "**republican**," even if its adherents did not literally advocate the creation of republics in the place of the monarchies under which they lived. During the Seven Years' War, French and British propagandists alike presented their nations as the reincarnation of the virtuous Roman republic at war with its corrupt enemy, Carthage. After the war, many French writers blamed their defeat on their country's allegedly loose morals, and demanded a return to the strict standards of ancient Rome. The embrace of austerity even extended to painting, where

Neoclassical Art The French painter Jacques-Louis David's (1748–1825) *Oath of the Horatii* (1784) embodies the enthusiasm for antiquity and precise technique shared by neoclassical artists beginning in the late eighteenth century. The painting depicts three Roman brothers willing to sacrifice themselves in battle for their city.

the 1770s saw the flourishing of a neoclassicism that favored subjects of patriotic sacrifice rather than domestic tenderness.

Republican thinkers and artists signaled their critical stance toward their culture most clearly in their strict attitude toward women, whom they deemed unfit for public life on account of their supposed inability to overcome their emotions. In contrast to Montesquieu and the Scottish historians, who saw a prominent role for women in society as a sign of social progress, the classical republicans condemned it as a symptom of social collapse and corruption. Rousseau himself demanded a strict separation of the sexes, with women restricted to the domestic roles of wife and mother.

Expulsion of the Jesuits Clerics bemoan their fate—one even collapsing on the ground—as soldiers herd them toward waiting boats, in an engraving depicting the expulsion of the Jesuits from Spain in 1767.

THE POLITICS OF ENLIGHTENMENT

It should be clear that the major thinkers of mid-eighteenth-century Europe had widely varying political philosophies. The systems they advocated included both the collectivist republican democracy of Rousseau's *Social Contract* and the moderate, British-style representative politics advocated by Montesquieu and the young Voltaire. And especially in the 1760s and 1770s, the Enlightenment also appeared compatible with absolute monarchy, in a pattern that held remarkably steady across Europe. This period, indeed, might be called the brief golden age of "**enlightened absolutism**."

ENLIGHTENED ABSOLUTISM

It should not be surprising that Europe's absolute monarchs found much to appreciate in the Enlightenment. In the growing support for religious toleration and skepticism about revealed religion, they discovered an end to the doctrinal quarrels that had shaken their ancestors' thrones in the Reformation, and an excuse for curtailing the power and independence of established churches. In the growing embrace of utility ("the greatest good for the greatest number"), they saw the justification for the rational management of their societies by a single, controlling authority—their own. In the new concepts of economic productivity and free trade, later absolute monarchs saw a chance to increase their nations' wealth and their own tax revenues. While they continued to find individual

philosophes dangerously independent, they increasingly took the cause of Enlightened reform for their own. In Catholic Europe, they sought to exercise greater authority over the Church and to take greater control of education. This led, in several countries, to their expulsion of the Jesuit Order, which had previously dominated secondary education and which owed direct allegiance to the pope. Following these expulsions, the Order itself was dissolved, and only re-created in the nineteenth century.

THE CASE OF PORTUGAL Portugal offers one good example of the way monarchs could make use of Enlightenment ideas. In 1755 King José I (r. 1750–1777) appointed as prime minister the reform-minded Sebastião José de Carvalho e Melo, later known as the marquis of Pombal (1699–1782). During his twenty-four years in office, Pombal reduced the power of the Catholic Church, expelled the Jesuit Order from the country, instituted a degree of religious toleration for non-Catholic Christians, overhauled the tax system, and laid the basis for public primary and secondary education. He also did a great deal to limit the power of the high aristocracy, which hated him. Pombal governed ruthlessly, tolerated no dissent, and took every opportunity to increase the power of the central government. Neighboring Spain also saw considerable reform under King Charles III (r. 1759–1788), including the creation of a national bank, the streamlining of the central bureaucracy, an overhaul of the educational system, and a reduction of tariffs and price controls on basic commodities. These so-called Bourbon reforms also introduced efficiencies into the sprawling Spanish Empire.

GERMANY AND AUSTRIA The German states saw similar developments. As early as 1727, Prussia created the first university chairs in "cameralism"—the science of public administration—and other German states soon followed. Frederick the Great of Prussia cast himself as an enlightened ruler who reigned only for his subjects' happiness. He lightened the financial burdens of Prussian serfs, introduced greater religious toleration, and abolished torture and corporal punishment in the Prussian lands. Voltaire came to reside briefly at his court, under the mistaken impression that the king would treat him as something other than a servant. In fact, Frederick betrayed his true opinion of Voltaire when he wrote, "I shall have need of him for another year at most, no longer. One squeezes the orange and one throws away the peel." Yet unlike Pombal, Frederick identified thoroughly with the nobility. He promoted their interests and dedicated himself above all to the aristocratic vocation of war.

For a more thoroughgoing reform program, German-speakers had to look to Habsburg Austria, where Queen Maria Theresa (r. 1740–1780) and her son, Joseph II (r. 1780–1790), ruled in succession between 1740 and 1790. Joseph especially gained a reputation as a model of enlightened absolutism. He granted a degree of religious toleration to Protestants, Orthodox Christians, and Jews; banished the Jesuit order; and reorganized the Catholic Church in Austrian territories, confiscating much of its property in the process. Like Frederick, he lessened the financial and labor burden on the serfs, with the ultimate goal of turning them into rent-paying tenants. He also founded a public education system and relaxed censorship. But Joseph, too, saw reforms as a means of allowing the state to function more efficiently under the guidance of an unchecked, although impartial, monarchy. One of his advisers compared the state to a machine in which the ruler acted as the "mainspring," setting everything else in motion.

CATHERINE THE GREAT Even in Russia, the monarchy made some moves toward enlightened reform. Upon becoming tsar in 1762, the German-born Peter III alienated most of the Russian high aristocracy. After just six months a group of disaffected nobles killed him in a coup d'état and the throne passed to his German-born wife, who ruled as Catherine II ("the Great") until 1796. Catherine (r. 1762–1796) proved a very strong ruler. She fought and won two costly wars against the Ottoman Turks

Catherine the Great A portrait of the queen, dressed in the regal finery of a western European monarch, in 1770.

and annexed large territories in the south, including the Crimea, giving Russia warm-water ports on the Black Sea. She corresponded with Voltaire and Diderot, and even invited the latter to visit her court in Saint Petersburg. She convened a commission to produce a general statement of legal principles that included equality before the law for non-serfs, religious toleration, and an end to cruel punishments. But believing Russia not yet ready for such radical change, she did not try to put the principles into practice. Much of the Russian population remained in the virtual slavery that was Russian serfdom.

ENLIGHTENED REFORM IN FRANCE In France, despite the frequent conflicts between the philosophes and the monarchy, proponents of enlightened reform had some success as well. Although intelligent and energetic, King Louis XV had few of Frederick II's or Joseph II's ambitions. He spent much of his reign embroiled in disputes with the kingdom's high courts (*parlements*), which exercised their traditional right to protest royal decisions in order to protect Jansenist Catholics and block new forms of taxation. The high courts even forced the king to expel the Jesuit Order from France, a decision that helped persuade the pope—after similar expulsions in Portugal,

Spain, and Austria—to dissolve the order. In response to such obstructions, in 1770, in a hugely unpopular move, the king stripped the high courts of the right to protest and replaced the magistrates with pliant nominees of his own.

In the 1760s, however, a new school of philosophes arose in France who called themselves physiocrats, or "economists." They supported free markets, opposed mercantilist ideas, and argued for a streamlined, efficient monarchy in much the way Joseph II did. After Louis XV's death, his young grandson, Louis XVI (r. 1774–1792), named one of them, an ambitious official named **Anne-Robert Turgot** (1727–1781), to head his ministry. Turgot favored an innovative plan for a series of elected assemblies to advise the monarch, although not to legislate on their own. He freed price controls on grains and then moved to abolish the guilds, which still claimed a monopoly on virtually all trades. He also ended the conscription of peasants as road-builders. The edicts led to loud protests from leaders of guilds and the *parlements*, who feared the expansion of royal power. The edicts also spurred bread riots as prices began to rise. In the midst of this turmoil, enemies at court engineered Turgot's dismissal, but his efforts still amounted to the most ambitious reforms attempted by the French crown before the Revolution of 1789.

BRITAIN AND THE WILKES AFFAIR

Great Britain, while hailed by many on the Continent as a model of enlightened government, yet again stood out as an exception to the European pattern. Until 1760 and the death of King George II, British politics remained dominated by the Whig Party (descended from the victors of the Glorious Revolution of 1688) and a vast patronage system created by the party's leading figure, Robert Walpole. Until the 1760s, the Whigs controlled the principal government ministries. Thanks to the Bank of England and the well-organized tax-collection system, the British crown enjoyed a financial stability that its continental rivals could only envy. As a result, Britain could continue to build its navy into the force that ensured its triumph in the Seven Years' War. The king and his ministers saw little need for the sorts of reforms adopted by their continental counterparts.

The accession of George III (r. 1760–1820) in 1760 briefly seemed to alter the political equation, as the new monarch showed favor to the Whigs' opponents, the Tories, raising the fear that he might prove another would-be absolutist, like James II. Yet in fact, the major political conflicts of the 1760s and 1770s turned less around the monarchy than around Parliament, which still represented only a small, wealthy minority of adult British males. In 1763, Parliament refused to allow a radical critic of the government, John Wilkes, to take his seat. In the ensuing controversies, which dragged on over several years, there coalesced a movement for parliamentary reform (especially an end to the handpicking of some members by powerful aristocrats), an expansion of the franchise, and freedom of speech. This movement, while not seeking to create a fundamentally new political order, as had been the case with the Levellers and other mid-seventeenth-century radicals, nonetheless echoed some of the democratic aspirations of these earlier movements.

The **Wilkes affair** offered some of the most powerful evidence, before 1780, that the Enlightenment might ultimately have different political implications from what the absolute monarchs hoped. Wilkes himself had direct ties to the most daring thinkers of the Parisian Enlightenment. In the movement to seat him in Parliament, a newly assertive "public opinion," born out of the social and cultural transformations described above, especially the expansion of the press, claimed a formal voice in politics. Wilkes himself emerged as one of the first political celebrities, with followers delightedly following his escapades in the press. Engravings of him outsold those of famous actors, and the slogan "Wilkes and Liberty" appeared on many consumer products, including crockery and linens.

The Wilkesite movement had no direct counterpart on the Continent, where representative bodies had largely ceased to function. Still, the European public found other

"Wilkes and Liberty" This 1763 cream-colored ceramic teapot bearing the "Wilkes and Liberty" slogan exemplifies the types of consumer products that were popular with Wilkes's supporters.

venues to express itself. In a series of spectacular trials in France in the 1760s and 1770s, lawyers used the plight of persecuted Protestants, unjustly condemned prisoners, and children imprisoned at their parents' request, to highlight the flaws in the existing legal and political systems, and to call for enlightened reform.

THE RIGHTS OF MAN

More generally, the period 1740–80 saw the emergence of a broad new concept in European political life: "the rights of man," a phrase that dates to this period. The idea of natural rights had roots in the seventeenth-century political philosophies of Hobbes and Locke. But natural rights by definition arose out of the state of nature and did not necessarily apply to people once they had entered society. Indeed, the entry into society had implied, for many philosophers, the *surrender* of "natural rights" to the state. The rights of man (what we now call "human rights"), by contrast, belonged to people regardless of their social condition. They were unalienable.

The idea of the rights of man arose when it did because of the social and cultural changes we have seen. By the mid-eighteenth century, the men and women of

The Anti-Slavery Movement A 1780 French engraving from *The History of the Two Indies* pictures an Englishman selling a weeping African into slavery. Antislavery activists often highlighted such personal cruelties to bolster support for their cause.

cosmopolitan Europe and its colonial extensions had learned to feel a degree of sympathetic identification with people of different social ranks, whom they did not even know. This large, educated public mixed as equals in coffeehouses and other new settings, and learned through cultural forms like the novel to identify with servants, peasants—even criminals. The idea of human rights also received a boost from the enormous popularity of Rousseau's thought: his biting condemnations of inequality, his stirring evocations of the ancient republics (even if "the rights of man" had no place in such regimented societies), and the unforgettable opening words of *The Social Contract*: "Man is born free, but is everywhere in chains."

Although through 1780 the cause of the rights of man in continental Europe mostly stopped well short of calls for revolt against the monarchies, it had important political effects. In the 1760s, it helped inspire a movement for an end to official torture and horrific punishments such as breaking on the wheel. Voltaire had given little thought to the manner of Jean Calas's death when he started writing about the case in 1762, but within a few years he had come to denounce breaking on the wheel as a "barbaric" punishment. In his 1764 book *On Crimes and Punishments*, the Milanese reformer Cesare Beccaria (1738–1794) argued for swift, humane punishments, made the first sustained case in European history against the death penalty, and pointed the way toward imprisonment as the sole legitimate punishment for criminal offenses. Legal reform of this sort was compatible with enlightened absolutism because it tended to reduce the power of the noble magistrates who were defying the crown's power in France.

The cause of human rights also prompted some key thinkers to see the issue of slavery in a new light. In 1770 a group of philosophes led by Guillaume-Thomas-François Raynal (1713–1796) and including Diderot published a massive compendium entitled *The History of the Two Indies*, which took the long-standing Enlightenment interest in non-European societies to a new level. It surveyed the history of European imperialism, denounced the exploitation of indigenous peoples in scorching terms, protested slavery as one of the greatest human evils, and, invoking the leader of a great slave revolt in ancient Rome, called for a "Black Spartacus" to rise up and free the slaves in the Americas. The book went through some seventy printings before the French Revolution and helped inspire French societies promoting the abolition of slavery. Antislavery societies were also appearing in England, organized largely by the Quakers and other devout Christian opponents of the slave trade. The antislavery cause potentially threatened the economic well-being of Europe's American empires, but it did not yet represent a direct challenge to existing regimes.

THE AMERICAN REVOLUTION (1776–1783)

It was in the English-speaking world where the idea of "the rights of man" first posed a real threat to the ruling political order. The Wilkes affair, with its linking of human rights to parliamentary reform, set off tremors. But the first real earthquake occurred across the Atlantic Ocean, in Britain's colonies on the eastern seaboard of North America. There, in the 1760s, opposition to the British government swelled as Britain imposed new taxes to pay the enormous costs of defending the colonies in the Seven Years' War. But Britain did not give the colonists, who had no representation in Parliament, any say in the matter and furiously dismissed colonial protests on the issue.

These developments seemed to threaten the broad autonomy long enjoyed by the colonies. In addition, a strong strand of radical republicanism, especially in the northern colonies, had taught the American colonists to see government in general as prone to corruption and tyranny. The American cities had developed a public culture as vigorous and diverse as that in any European country—with higher literacy rates, more newspapers and books per capita, and an assortment of institutions in which people could gather to discuss politics and plan their actions. This provided the perfect setting for "public opinion" to be transformed into the "will of the people." Protests against the mother country swelled, and some of them turned violent. Patriotic societies, some of them taking the name "Sons of Liberty," organized boycotts of goods imported from Britain.

In the 1770s, these protests built into revolution. The unrest had led the British to send the army to Boston, and on March 5, 1770, troops opened fire on a hostile crowd there, killing five men and greatly increasing animosity toward the British government. In 1773, a new tax on imported tea led Sons of Liberty masquerading as Indians to storm a ship in Boston harbor and dump tea into the water (the original "Tea Party"). The British government responded with a series of punitive actions, including closing the city's port. In spring 1775, a Continental Congress drawn from all thirteen colonies raised a joint army and began moving toward independence.

Battle of Yorktown A French engraving shows the British surrendering to the large combined American and French force at the battle of Yorktown in 1781, ending the war.

From the very start, the **American Revolution** (1775–1783) justified itself in the new language of the rights of man. An enormously influential pamphlet written by Thomas Paine (1737–1809), a recent British arrival, helped establish a bedrock principle of modern democracies: *Common Sense* proclaimed in its very title that ordinary people, rather than kings, were the ultimate source of political authority. Thanks in large part to Paine's influence, colonial anger that had originally directed itself largely against the British Parliament, and had looked to King George III as a potential ally, turned republican and antimonarchical.

In July 1776, Thomas Jefferson (1743–1826)—a slave-holding lawyer and legislator from Virginia who was deeply influenced by Enlightenment thought—placed the concept of the rights of man at the heart of the American Declaration of Independence: "We hold these truths to be self-evident, that all men are created equal, that they are endowed by their Creator with certain unalienable Rights, that among these are Life, Liberty and the pursuit of Happiness. — That to secure these rights, Governments are instituted among Men, deriving their just powers from the consent of the governed."

In fact, securing the rights of Americans—or, at least, white Americans—also required a painful, grinding military conflict that lasted until 1781. The new United States faced heavy odds, fighting against a well-trained British military and also against many of their own number who remained loyal to Britain. But it benefited from steady, cautious leadership by George Washington, who quickly emerged as the greatest political hero of the age. And in

1778, a French government eager for revenge on Britain for the Seven Years' War came into the conflict on the American side, providing much-needed support. Finally, the United States defeated the British army on the ground. The new nation adopted a constitution that borrowed heavily from Montesquieu's theory of a mixed constitution, and enshrined human rights in its first ten amendments, known as the Bill of Rights.

CONCLUSION

These revolutionary events generated immense interest in Europe, especially for what they seemed to reveal about the liberationist potential of the Enlightenment. Documents such as the United States Constitution and especially the Declaration of Independence were quickly reprinted and translated, along with Paine's *Common Sense*. In the American Revolution, Europeans saw that the ideas they had been discussing for the past half century, in the transformed public culture of the Enlightenment, could have consequences far different from, and greater than, strengthening the hand of absolute monarchs against traditional opponents. They saw new outcomes to the trends of the previous four decades: increasing prosperity, increasing global communications and trade, a transformed cultural environment, and an intellectual movement committed to toleration and even to the "rights of man." And they grasped that Enlightenment—what the British thinker and politician Edmund Burke would soon castigate as "this new conquering empire of light and reason"—might soon strike at the very foundations of their own politics and societies.

[CHAPTER REVIEW]

KEY TERMS

enclosure (p. 507)

"putting out" system
   (p. 507)

Seven Years' War (p. 512)

Samuel Richardson (p. 516)

Denis Diderot (p. 516)

Freemasons (p. 519)

James Cook (p. 519)

deism (p. 522)

pietism (p. 522)

Enlightenment (p. 523)

Jean-Jacques Rousseau
   (p. 524)

Voltaire (p. 524)

philosophe (p. 527)

David Hume (p. 528)

Adam Smith (p. 528)

laissez-faire (p. 528)

republican (p. 530)

enlightened absolutism
   (p. 531)

Anne-Robert Turgot
   (p. 533)

Wilkes affair (p. 533)

American Revolution
   (p. 535)

REVIEW QUESTIONS

1. What important developments lay behind the economic expansion and improved standards of living in eighteenth-century Europe?

2. Why did warfare reach a global scale during the mid-eighteenth century?

3. What new venues made the arts and intellectual pursuits more widely available to the public?

4. What evidence shows the emergence of a more cosmopolitan culture in eighteenth-century Europe and its colonies?

5. What religious movements developed in the eighteenth century?

6. What set the Enlightenment apart from earlier intellectual movements?

7. What roles did the philosophes play in the culture and society of the eighteenth century?

8. How did the philosophes change the meaning of citizenship?

9. What appeal did Enlightenment ideas hold for some of Europe's absolute monarchs? With what results?

10. In the later eighteenth century, how did the new concept of the rights of man lead to proposals for political reform?

CORE OBJECTIVES

After reading this chapter, you should have a solid understanding of the following core objectives. To strengthen your grasp of the core objectives, use the resources on the Student Site for The West.

- Analyze the economic, political, and social context of the Enlightenment.

- Describe the emergence of new cultural patterns contributing to the Enlightenment.

- Trace the development of a newly cosmopolitan worldview in the second half of the eighteenth century.

- Identify the essential intellectual elements of the Enlightenment.

- Assess the social and political themes of Enlightenment thought.

- Evaluate the political changes that were influenced by the Enlightenment.

 GO TO inQuizitive TO SEE WHAT YOU'VE LEARNED—AND LEARN WHAT YOU'VE MISSED—WITH PERSONALIZED FEEDBACK ALONG THE WAY.

CHRONOLOGY

1787
Prussians quell
Dutch Patriot Revolt

May 1789
French Estates
General convene

August 1789
National Assembly issues
Declaration of the Rights
of Man and Citizen

1790–1791
National Assembly
writes new constitution

January 21, 1793
Execution of
Louis XVI

1793
Second partition
of Poland

October 1793
Execution of
Marie Antoinette

**Summer 1793–
Summer 1794**
Reign of Terror

1795
Thermidorians
create Directory

1795
Third and last
partition of Poland

June 17, 1789
Formation
of National
Assembly

October 5, 1789
Bread rioters march
on Versailles

July 14, 1789
Storming of
the Bastille

1791
Slave revolt in
Saint-Domingue
(Haiti)

September 2–7, 1792
September Massacres in Paris

September 20, 1792
French defeat
Prussians at Valmy

April 1793
Committee of Public
Safety is formed

Summer 1794
Massacres in
the Vendée

July 27–28, 1794
Ninth Thermidor revolt;
Robespierre is executed

16

Revolution

LIBERTY AND TERROR

1780–1799

High over the eastern edge of Paris, at the end of the eighteenth century, there loomed a bleak, eight-towered stone fortress known as the Bastille. The French monarchy had long used its jail cells to incarcerate notorious prisoners, and by the 1780s it had acquired a reputation as a place of horrid punishments. In fact, little torture or abuse had taken place for years, and as the French monarchy grew more concerned about its public image, the number of prisoners had declined. By July 14, 1789, only seven were actually in residence, including two suffering from mental illness.

The crowds who approached the Bastille that morning still mostly believed the fearsome legends. They had not, however, come to free the prisoners, but to take control of the large stocks of gunpowder kept at the fortress, so as to defend Paris against an expected attack. By mid-morning, around a thousand people had gathered outside the walls, many armed with guns or long, sharp pikes. They demanded that the Bastille's governor, Bernard-René de Launay, turn over all the powder and weapons at his disposal.

These ordinary Parisians—mostly artisans, shopkeepers, and laborers—were in a state of wild excitement and anxiety. Two months before, France's traditional representative body, the Estates General, had assembled for the first time since 1614–15 and had

---

Storming the Bastille The Bastille fortress rises high above a confrontation between revolutionaries and soldiers in this late-eighteenth-century painting, in which Parisian protesters have captured the prison and set fire to the surrounding buildings. From its outset, popular uprisings played a vital part in the Revolution's overthrow of authority and accelerating radicalism.

[FOCUS QUESTIONS]

- What were the long-term and short-term causes of the crisis in France?
- How did the question of the Third Estate help bring on the Revolution?
- What drove the Revolution to become more radical, international, and violent?
- What pressures fractured the First French Republic?
- What was the significance of the Reign of Terror?
- How did the Directory channel the Revolution into war?

immediately fallen into paralyzing squabbles over organizational issues. Finally, in June 1789, the representatives of the Third Estate—that is, the common people and middle classes—had broken the deadlock by declaring themselves a "National Assembly" and announcing their intention to write a new constitution. The representatives of the other estates—the clergy and nobility—had eventually gone along, and the weak-willed, thirty-four-year-old king, Louis XVI, had apparently accepted the change. But even as the new Assembly set to work, rumors spread that the king and his advisers were preparing a military coup to restore full royal authority. On July 11, these rumors gained credibility when Louis abruptly dismissed a popular reforming minister and troops began to concentrate around the capital. On July 13, anxious crowds had gathered at various points in the city, then stormed a government arsenal and seized thousands of firearms. Now, on July 14, they had come to the Bastille in search of ammunition.

For a time, Governor de Launay tried to negotiate with them, but in the early afternoon the crowds, restless and frustrated, swarmed into the Bastille's undefended outer courtyard. Shots rang out (which side fired first remains a mystery), and soon a full-fledged battle was raging. Mutinous members of the French military soon joined the crowds, bringing guns and cannon along with them. At 5:00 p.m., de Launay surrendered, but he received no mercy. The crowds dragged him into the street outside and hacked him to death, after which an apprentice sawed off his head with a knife and stuck it on the end of a pike, to be paraded around Paris. The enraged crowd also killed several other officials, including the city's top municipal official. The Bastille had fallen, and its gunpowder was in the hands of the insurgents. In Versailles the king, intimidated by this stunning expression of the popular will, quickly recalled the popular minister and dispersed the troops that had threatened Paris.

The fall of the Bastille did not mark the beginning of the French Revolution, which is usually dated to the meeting of the Estates General. But what happened on July 14, 1789, had an enormous and immediate effect on public opinion, not just in France but throughout the world. It was seen, rightly, as the moment when ordinary people forced their way into a political process hitherto dominated by well-educated elites. It was seen, also rightly, as the death knell of a royal power that had proclaimed itself "absolute." And it was seen, rightly once again, as the harbinger of spectacular and sometimes horrifying violence. Ever since, the date of July 14—now a French national holiday corresponding to the Fourth of July in the United States—has symbolized both the promise and the peril of modern politics. It stands not only for the revolutionary triumph of the people over undeserved social privilege and arbitrary rule, but also for the possible slide of revolutionary energy into bloodshed and terror.

In the last years of the eighteenth century, events in Europe as a whole took their lead from these tumultuous changes, which marked a more decisive break in the Continent's history than any since the Reformation. Prevailing patterns of thought, social interaction, and competition among and within states did not vanish, but they were now forever marked as belonging to the past, to tradition, to something that Europeans would soon call by the telling phrase "the Old Regime."

THE ORIGINS OF THE FRENCH REVOLUTION

How and why did the French nation come to this crossroads? To answer this question, we must first recognize that the rising up of the people symbolized by the storming of the **Bastille** is by no means the whole story. An event as complex as the French Revolution simply did not have one single, dominant cause. Rather, it arose out of the confluence of a great many events and trends—some ranging over many years and involving millions of men and women, others almost absurdly small and arbitrary;

some involving the loftiest matters of philosophy, others turning on pressing questions of brute physical survival; some limited to France itself, and others involving large stretches of the globe. Taken individually, none of these factors would have led to revolution. But taken together, they triggered the great upheaval.

SOCIAL TRANSFORMATIONS

Many of these broader developments had affected other countries as well as France. As we have seen, most of northern Europe, including Britain and the Low Countries, had experienced a century of strong, if often stressful, economic growth, which in turn helped cause social disruption. "Middling" groups, which in France belonged to the Third Estate, had expanded enormously in wealth and prominence. Lawyers, for instance, more than tripled their numbers in France between 1700 and 1789. And in France, the boundaries between these middling groups and traditional social elites had grown more porous than ever, as the state sold noble titles by the thousands to wealthy commoners. Indeed, many historians argue that wealthy commoners and the nobility were consolidating into a single social class of "notables." Meanwhile, France, like the other major powers, also faced the challenge of financing warfare on a global scale. Its participation in victory over Britain in the American War of Independence, in particular, had come at a terrific price, for the cost of sending land and sea forces across the Atlantic to aid the American revolutionaries came close to doubling French public expenditures.

The French state, however, was much less well prepared to confront new social and economic challenges than some of its neighbors—Britain, in particular. France, it will be remembered, had no central bank to help finance its wars, and its baroque system of tax collection was much less efficient than that of the legendary "excisemen" who collected Britain's excise taxes. Nor did France possess a government capable of successfully implementing serious financial reforms, despite many attempts to do so. Before 1789, its closest equivalent to a national parliament, the Estates General, had not met for nearly 175 years (the so-called *parlements*, as we have seen, were not legislative bodies but courts of law). In theory, the king—as "absolute" executive, legislator, and judge all at once—had broad power to introduce change. But in practice, he had much more limited room for maneuver, depending as he did for much of his revenue on a massive system of social privilege that could not easily be dismantled. Indeed, tens of thousands of Frenchmen owned

their jobs or positions as a privileged form of property, and many of the wealthiest people in the kingdom enjoyed exemptions from key taxes. Any reform that sufficiently threatened social privileges might undermine confidence in the entire system. Desperate for new revenues, Louis XIV and Louis XV (who between them reigned from 1643 to 1774) had managed to introduce some new taxes on the privileged orders, but in the process they stirred up large-scale opposition, which contributed to the formation of a critical public opinion. In short, any piecemeal, gradual reform of the regime seemed practically impossible, raising the odds that problems would build up until explosive, radical change became the only course to follow.

THE IMPACT OF CULTURAL AND INTELLECTUAL CHANGE

The broad currents of cultural and intellectual change that now go by the name of the Enlightenment had, as we have seen, swept through nearly all of Europe in one form or another, but they had touched France most intensely. Religious belief and observance in France suffered more than elsewhere from "enlightened" criticism, and as it did the almost sacred respect long given to the king, supposedly anointed by God himself, began to ebb away. Still, taken together, the most popular works of Enlightenment thought did not offer anything like a coherent political philosophy. And while the American Revolution inspired great excitement in France, with its soaring promises of liberty and equality and its commitment to a republic that seemed to recall the days of ancient Greece and Rome, most French observers did not believe that the experiences of a "new people" across the Atlantic could be transplanted to Europe.

Before the summer of 1789, almost no one imagined that the calling of the Estates General might trigger anything other than moderate reforms—to say nothing of the replacement of the monarchy by a democratic republic. One elite observer, the future revolutionary Guy Target, sputtered that the very idea was ridiculous: "One hears tell, that . . . the kingdom (truthfully, I have heard this said) will degenerate into a democracy. Nothing of the sort is to be feared. . . . Democracy in a nation of twenty-five million . . . ! I confess in good faith that I have no idea what this means." French elites, with their impeccable classical educations, still associated "democracy" solely with the tumultuous city-states of ancient Greece.

Yet the Enlightenment's principal political effects did not take the form of constitutional blueprints implemented by politicians. Particularly in France, its most popular works were intensely moralizing: what some scholars have called the "age of reason" actually longed to be the "age of virtue." Authors like Rousseau held up ideal images of virtuous behavior, mostly inspired by accounts of ancient Greece and Rome, and with soaring eloquence contrasted them to the corruption that supposedly prevailed throughout Europe. In particular, they dismissed the difference between private and public morality. For them, a country where wives and husbands deceived each other, or where fathers oppressed sons, was a degenerate one in need of radical change. Public figures were to be judged by their private conduct.

From this perspective, the court of Versailles, with its intrigues, lavish displays of wealth, elaborate rituals, and biting cynicism, looked like the pinnacle of corruption and degeneracy. The eighteenth century's legions of newly minted authors and journalists liked nothing more than reporting on the lives and misdeeds, real and alleged, of courtly aristocrats. And what legal publications said with sly indirection and euphemism, illegal publications, sold "under the cloak" to avoid the formidable system of censorship then in place, said directly and with much use of obscenity. In both cases, they fastened on to the "unnatural" role played at court by powerful, pleasure-loving women, who should instead, according to the authors, have retired from public view to tend virtuously to their hearths and children.

AN APPROACHING FISCAL CRISIS

In 1774, these authors had received a stroke of good luck—and the French monarchy a bad one. In that year, when King Louis XV succumbed to smallpox, the vagaries of genetics and dynastic marriage brought to the French throne a couple perfectly suited to preside over catastrophe. **Louis XVI** (r. 1774–1792) was a well-meaning, timid, physically unimpressive young man who preferred tinkering in his workshop to deciding matters of policy. His queen, Marie-Antoinette (1755–1793), was a beautiful, naïve young woman who had been sent to France from her native Austria to seal the alliance the two countries had contracted at the time of the Seven Years' War. Louis, it appears, suffered from a genital condition that made sexual intercourse impossible, and for several years after his marriage he refused to undergo the minor operation needed to correct it. Rumors spread not only of his impotence but also of Marie-Antoinette's willingness to satisfy her lusts elsewhere. In short, not only did the monarchy

no longer enjoy quasi-sacral status, but the royal couple were now the butt of ridicule. In the queen's case, visceral hatred would soon follow.

Taken together, all of these circumstances differentiated France from its neighbors in a way that made a revolutionary explosion there possible. Still, it took a particular sequence of events to bring that explosion about. It started with the new king's hesitant attempts at reform. Upon taking the throne, in a show of reconciliation he restored the traditional position of the *parlements*, which Louis XV had largely stripped of their ability to obstruct royal legislation, and brought back

Louis XVI In a portrait painted shortly after his coronation in 1774, King Louis XVI appears wearing his gold and ermine coronation robes, symbols of the lavish grandeur of the monarchy.

the magistrates dismissed by the old king. This decision quickly brought him trouble when his ambitious minister Anne-Robert Turgot, a brilliant disciple of the *philosophes*, attempted a radical liberalization of the French economy. The *parlements* became the powerful voices of the entrenched interests threatened by Turgot, and in 1777 his opponents at court forced his departure. The episode set a pattern for the reign in which ambitious changes were proposed, criticized, and then withdrawn, leaving behind little but increased resentment.

Meanwhile, in 1778 Louis decided to send French forces to aid the American revolutionaries. Their joint victory in 1783 weakened the British, but it did not restore France's lost colonies in the Americas, and the cost for France was the vast sum of over 1 billion French pounds, or roughly four times the state's entire annual peacetime budget. Instead of raising the necessary funds through taxation, the new finance minister, Jacques Necker (1732–1804), resorted to high-interest borrowing on international capital markets. He also published a self-serving account of the budgetary situation that disguised the enormous size of the debt. Necker, a brilliant and energetic Swiss banker, did try to simplify France's financial system and created the first of a projected series of provincial assemblies during his tenure as minister. But these reforms, like Turgot's, threatened entrenched interests, and Necker's opponents forced him out of office before he could achieve significant results.

THE THREAT OF BANKRUPTCY By 1786, France's fiscal situation had turned catastrophic, and government bankruptcy loomed. That year, yet another new finance

minister, Charles-Alexandre de Calonne (1734–1802), proposed a complete overhaul of the tax system. Although nobles had paid a considerable amount since the start of the century, they still benefited disproportionately from France's complex system of fiscal privilege. In particular, they mostly enjoyed exemption from the hated land tax, the *taille*, which fell principally on rural commoners. Calonne's plan involved the abolition of the *taille* and the institution of a new tax that all landowners—nobles and clergy as well as commoners—would pay. He also suggested a show of national confidence by submitting the plan to a special Assembly of Notables comprising a small number of high-ranking nobles and prelates. But this body unexpectedly balked at undertaking such radical reform, leading the frustrated king to replace Calonne with the freethinking archbishop of Toulouse, Étienne Charles Loménie de Brienne.

Loménie tried to enact Calonne's plan by fiat, only to find himself challenged by the *parlements*, which deliberately paralyzed the French judicial system in protest and helped instigate riots in Paris and other major cities. In the spring of 1788, the king and his ministers raised the stakes even higher by trying to dissolve the *parlements* altogether, but this high-handed act of authority only led to even larger-scale violent disorders—above all, from the many people who depended financially upon the *parlements*. Finally, in August, the king gave in, dismissed Brienne, recalled the popular Necker (who would be dismissed and recalled once again in 1789), and agreed to assemble the Estates General in the hope that this older body might be able to introduce real financial reforms.

DUTCH PATRIOT REVOLT (1781–1787)

The burgeoning French crisis caused powerful ripple effects throughout Europe, particularly in the Netherlands. In 1781, some eight years before the fall of the Bastille, the Dutch had begun a relatively moderate revolutionary movement of their own. A so-called Patriot Party had taken a stand against the country's aristocratic "Stadholder" chief executive, demanding an end to corruption and the enactment of democratic reforms inspired in part by the American revolutionary example. Conflict between the Patriots and the Stadholder's Orangist Party swelled over the next several years, with the Orangists backed by the new Prussian king, Frederick William II (r. 1786–1797), who was the Stadholder's brother-in-law. Finally, after a series of armed Patriot victories over the Orangists, a Prussian army invaded the Netherlands in September 1787, smashed the Patriots, and firmly cemented the Stadholder's authority. France had every interest in helping the

Dutch Patriot Revolt A 1787 satirical cartoon shows a disorganized band of Dutch rebels using a drawing of a Prussian soldier for target practice. It mocks the rebels as country bumpkins: their party even includes the armed frogs at their feet (bottom left).

Patriots and preventing the Netherlands from becoming a satellite of Prussia, its enemy since the Seven Years' War. But because of the crisis it could not intervene, and so suffered an international humiliation.

THE REVOLUTION BEGINS (1788–1789)

With Louis XVI's rapidly taken and somewhat desperate decision in August 1788 to convoke the Estates General, the entire French nation took a giant leap into the unknown. The Estates were a national representative body—but what did it mean, exactly, to "represent" the nation?

THE QUESTION OF REFORMING THE ESTATES GENERAL

Through their last meeting in 1614–15, the Estates had followed a classic medieval model of representation, which likened the different estates to different organs of a single body. In this way of thinking, it made sense for each estate to elect members to a chamber of its own, with each chamber having equal weight in deliberations. This arrangement, however, gave the first two estates—which, together, amounted to less than 2 percent of the population—an automatic majority. Yet in 1788 the French could look abroad and see other representative systems that gave equal voting rights to most white male adults (as in the United States) or that privileged wealth as much as inherited status (as in Great Britain). Well-to-do French commoners also knew that their Third Estate had increased tremendously in wealth and education since the Renaissance, and felt they should have a correspondingly greater say in national government. Yet the *parlements* feared that a larger Third Estate might join forces with the king to erode traditional privileges and long-standing barriers against royal "despotism." So in September 1788, the *parlement* of Paris declared that the Estates General would meet "according to the forms of 1614"—that is, one chamber per estate, with each chamber voting separately.

The result was a storm of protest, much of it in printed form. The king, in calling for elections to the Estates, had invited the people to express their views of what the Estates should discuss, and printers throughout the kingdom had taken these words as a de facto declaration of press freedom. Journalists and pamphleteers loudly denounced the nobility and demanded an Estates General in which half the deputies would come from the Third Estate and all deputies would vote "in common." The most powerful expression of the argument came from a clergyman named Emmanuel Sieyès (1748–1836) in a pamphlet he entitled **What Is the Third Estate?** Drawing not only on Enlightenment social science that placed new value on the economic productivity of commoners, but also on the political theory of Jean-Jacques Rousseau, he answered his title question in a single deafening word: "Everything." As the crushing majority, the Third Estate could stand in for the whole. Anyone who refused to join them effectively became an outsider to the nation.

The debate dragged on all through the winter of 1788–89. King Louis eventually decided to double the number of Third Estate deputies but did not allow deliberation or voting in common, which made the decision meaningless. As a result, the elections to the Estates took place in an atmosphere of bitterness and confusion, and produced an assembly doomed to fall into conflict. The Third Estate numbered many heroes of the protests of 1787–88, along with a host of lawyers, judges, and civil servants. Its chamber also included radical members of other estates, such as the clergyman Sieyès and the noble Honoré Riqueti de Mirabeau (1749–1791), who had made a reputation crusading against the laws that had allowed his own father, a notable political economist, to have him thrown in prison for filial disobedience. They chose to stand for election as commoners.

Among the clergy, a surprising number of poor parish

The Three Estates An eighteenth-century political cartoon provides a visual representation of Sieyès's argument. A farm laborer carries a clergyman and a nobleman on his back, just as the Third Estate holds up the two privileged orders.

priests emerged alongside the prelates. But in the ranks of the noble deputies, grand, wealthy old military families dominated. As part of the election process, local electors (themselves chosen in primary elections in which all adult male taxpayers could participate) also prepared petitions to redress "grievances," to present to the Estates General. These documents make for remarkable reading—the closest thing to a modern opinion survey produced anywhere in the eighteenth century. The most common demands included tax reform, judicial reform, religious toleration, and an end to fiscal privileges such as tax exemption for nobles. Collectively, the "grievances" called into question so many aspects of French government and society that the great nineteenth-century French thinker Alexis de Tocqueville would later claim that they amounted to a demand for the abolition of the entire Old Regime.

The Estates General faced almost insurmountable challenges. First came the unanswered question of its own organization, given the claims of the Third Estate to a greater share of representation. Second, there was the looming bankruptcy of the French state. And as if all this were not enough, national economic disaster and famine threatened as well. In the late summer of 1788, freakish cold, accompanied by hailstorms, had ruined much of the harvest. The price of bread—still the principal source of nourishment for most of the population—rose through the winter until it was devouring more than two-thirds of the income of even well-off artisans and workers. This inflation in turn choked off spending on everything else, leading to distress and unemployment throughout the economy. In late April 1789, just before the Estates met, unfounded rumors that a Paris wallpaper manufacturer was lowering wages led angry crowds to sack his house and factory, shouting "Down with the rich!" The riots were suppressed at the cost of twenty-five dead and hundreds wounded—the worst violence the capital had seen in many decades.

THE THIRD ESTATE TAKES POWER

The Estates General finally convened on May 5, 1789, with all the considerable pomp, ritual, and class prejudice that the Old Regime could muster. Gaudily attired lords and prelates paraded through the streets of Versailles, followed by the 600-odd deputies of the Third Estate, clad in basic black. Grandiose opening ceremonies took place, with the Third Estate confined to standing room at the back of the palace's Hall of Small Pleasures. But afterward, the three estates could not even agree on how to verify the members' credentials, let alone get down to business. The stalemate dragged on for a month. Angry emotions simmered.

Finally, in mid-June, a group of deputies decided to take action. They were led by the cold, precise Sieyès and by Mirabeau, a squat, ugly man (his face had been scarred by smallpox) whose natural talent for oratory was fortified by an extraordinary bass voice. Together, they convinced the Third Estate deputies that they could achieve their aims only by following Sieyès's argument to its logical conclusion. If the Third Estate was "everything"—that is, the entire nation—then logically its deputies constituted a **National Assembly** and should declare themselves such. On June 17, with considerable trepidation, the deputies did exactly that. And then they waited to see how the other estates and the king would react.

They did not have to wait long. As early as June 13, a number of parish priests who belonged to the First Estate by vocation but had been born into humble, commoner families had moved to join the Third Estate. Several liberal-minded nobles followed their example, and the number of defectors swelled after the proclamation of the National Assembly. Then on June 20 came a particularly dramatic moment. The defiant deputies arrived at their meeting hall to find the doors barred. It was an accident, but the men, fearing a royal coup, immediately rushed to a large, nearby indoor tennis court, where they pledged—in what was later known as the **Tennis Court Oath**—not to disperse until they had provided France with a new, written constitution. Fully appreciating the historical significance of the moment, they chose to swear the oath with arms extended, like reborn versions of Roman heroes.

Louis XVI was not in fact ready to use force, even if a powerful faction at court (led by his brothers and Marie-Antoinette) already saw the Third Estate deputies as dangerous rebels. On June 23, he made an attempt at conciliation, addressing all three estates together in a "royal session" and proposing a broad reform program. A month earlier the speech might have won enthusiastic support from the Third Estate, but now it came too late. The deputies from all three estates would now settle for nothing short of truly fundamental changes in the political system. When the king had finished, most of the deputies stayed in place, refusing to disperse. The king sent an official to order them to leave. "We are here by the will of the people, and will only leave by the force of bayonets," declaimed Mirabeau. Unnerved by the defiance, and acutely conscious of the deputies' popular following, the king again retreated and ordered the deputies from all three estates to join together. The National Assembly had been born, and the French Revolution had begun.

THE INTERVENTION OF THE PEOPLE

There remained, however, the Revolution's baptism in blood and fire. Over the next few weeks, even as the Assembly began to deliberate over the form of a future constitution, the king dithered and doubted. The queen and his brothers tried to persuade him that he needed to reassert his authority by force. On July 11, 1789, Louis again dismissed Necker, replacing him with conservative aristocrats, and the new government began to concentrate troops around Paris. When the news reached Paris, thousands of people gathered in wild agitation in the center of the city, cheering orators who demanded immediate action. There followed the seizure of weapons and the fall of the Bastille on July 14.

In the wake of this extraordinary and symbolic event, royal authority throughout France seemed to evaporate.

DAVID'S *THE TENNIS COURT OATH*

Jacques-Louis David (1748–1825) was one of eighteenth-century France's greatest painters, a master of neoclassicism and also an enthusiastic participant in the French Revolution. Recognizing that the arts had long served to simultaneously represent the world and project rulers' authority and legitimacy, David turned his extensive talents to creating images that celebrated and mythologized the new revolutionary order.

His unfinished study *The Tennis Court Oath* (1789–91) emphasizes the passion, idealism, and egalitarianism of the oath that helped mark the start of the 1789 revolution. The emptiness of the upper half of the drawing draws the eye to the three deputies—a cleric, an aristocrat, and a member of the Third Estate—who have joined hands in the foreground. At the center, Jean-Sylvain Bailly, the soon-to-be mayor of Paris, leads the deputies in their oath to remain assembled until the ratification of a new constitution. The outstretched arms of the oath takers—many of them actual participants—echoes the pose of the patriotic, self-sacrificing Romans of David's earlier masterpiece *Oath of the Horatii* (page 530). In this new image, David sought to invest France's revolutionary birth with the dignity and grandeur of the world's great historical events.

QUESTIONS FOR ANALYSIS

1. What does the embrace of the three deputies at the center of David's drawing represent?
2. Why would David want to depict the participants in the Tennis Court Oath similarly to subjects from antiquity, such as the Romans of *Oath of the Horatii*?
3. How does David's image illustrate and celebrate the values of the Revolution?

In Paris and other major towns, the leaders of the Third Estate asserted their control over municipal governments. Middle-class men took up arms and began to form paramilitary units that would soon coalesce into a large new armed force controlled by the National Assembly: the National Guard. The king then reversed himself yet again, recalling Necker to office for a second time and visiting Paris on July 27. There the new mayor presented him with a cockade, a badge of ribbons in which the colors of Paris—blue and red—surrounded the white of the Bourbon dynasty. Reminiscent of the American and British national colors, this "tricolor" pattern would soon be used in the new French flag.

But the country remained deeply unsettled. On July 22, two royal officials were lynched in Paris. Anticipating many later endorsements of violence by leading revolutionaries, a young leader of the Third Estate remarked: "What, was their blood so pure?" In the countryside, the prevailing uncertainty and food shortages fueled wild rumors that spread at breakneck pace. In what became known as the "**Great Fear**," peasants throughout France became convinced that hordes of lawless brigands would soon descend on their villages. In response, they too took up arms and often ended up attacking noble property and destroying records of the heavy feudal obligations (including forms of rent and restrictions on movement and trade) that they owed their seigneurial overlords (the lords of the manor were called "*seigneurs*" in French). The movement forever altered the social structure of the French countryside, helping to end its domination by a tiny minority of wealthy landowners and thereby laying the foundation of a new, more democratic social order.

In the face of the continuing unrest, on the night of August 4, 1789, the new National Assembly took an unplanned, astonishing step. Prompted by a group of progressive deputies from Brittany, various noble members of the Assembly proposed the abolition of certain onerous seigneurial dues. As if on cue, other deputies then demanded that other forms of social privilege—hunting rights, private tolls, private courts of law—also be thrown onto the scrapheap. Deputy after deputy, swept up in the fervor, clamored to propose yet more abolitions of privilege. The tumultuous session dragged on through the night, and by the end virtually the entire "feudal regime" had been swept away. "There vanished that night," the great French historian Jules Michelet later wrote, romantically but not without a measure of truth, "the vast and toilsome dream of a thousand years of the Middle Ages. The dawn that would soon break was the dawn of liberty." Within days, the deputies would backtrack, insisting that the peasants reimburse their overlords for many of the abolished privileges. Nonetheless, the Assembly had swept aside the principles of hierarchy that had governed French society for centuries, and replaced them with a new, revolutionary ideal: civic equality, the principle that all are equal in law.

The summer of 1789 concluded with the publication of the French Revolution's most enduring and influential statement of principles: the Assembly's **Declaration of the Rights of Man and Citizen**. In its seventeen articles, it guaranteed the principles of freedom and civil equality, and the sovereignty of the entire nation. It established rights for criminal suspects and the presumption of innocence, and proclaimed freedom of the press, religion, and property. Strikingly, unlike the American Bill of Rights, it did not speak of one country alone but of "men" in general—women were nowhere mentioned, and the question of just which rights applied to them was left unposed. "Men are born free and equal in rights," it proclaimed. The Declaration was not simply a statement of principle, however. Through the very act of promulgating it, and particularly the statement that "no individual can exercise authority that does not expressly emanate from the Nation," the Assembly deliberately asserted its own role as the embodiment of national sovereignty, superior even to the king.

RADICALIZATION (1789–1792)

With the abolitions of privilege on the night of August 4 and the promulgation of the Declaration of the Rights of Man and Citizen a few weeks later, many observers, both inside and outside the Assembly, assumed that the "revolution" had now come to an end. They were using the word in the older, limited sense of a sudden, unpredictable whirling-about of human affairs. But as events would soon show, the French Revolution was a dramatically unprecedented sort of political phenomenon: again and again it would defy all attempts to bring it to an end, and lurch forward, often in an outburst of violence. Even the American Revolution had been relatively moderate in comparison, because while it led to vast changes in the political order, it always remained far more under the control of its original political leadership and the changes it prompted in the social order were more gradual and consensual. It was in France that the word "revolution" itself soon took on its modern meaning: as a deliberate, open-ended, and explosive expression of a people's collective will. A revolution was a process of continuous radicalization.

THE OCTOBER DAYS

In the fall of 1789, the immediate impetus for radical change again came from the common people of Paris. Despite the great symbolic victory of the Bastille, little had followed to relieve their difficulties. The price of bread remained dangerously high, and work dangerously scarce. The resulting popular anger was further stoked by fears that the king or his advisers might still try a military strike to restore royal authority. In early October, these fears seemingly received confirmation when news spread that at a banquet in Versailles military officers had pledged unlimited support to the embattled king and trampled tricolor cockades, the symbol of the revolution, underfoot.

On October 5, a huge crowd assembled spontaneously in front of the Paris City Hall, demanding food and action against enemies of the Revolution. Women, traditional defenders of the family breadbox, had often taken a leading role in bread riots in the seventeenth and eighteenth centuries, and now the market women of Paris, swept up in the same revolutionary fervor as their male relatives, led the greatest bread riot in history. The cry went up "To Versailles!" and thousands of women and men, without much obvious organization, set off on foot for the royal palace twelve miles away. The new revolutionary municipal government in Paris, unable to stop them, instead sent armed National Guards to attempt to keep the crowd in line. In the evening, drenched by rain and mud-spattered, the crowds reached Versailles, where a small delegation met with the king, who promised immediate shipments of grain to the capital.

But as the hungry, wet, and cold Parisians camped outdoors throughout the night, their mood again darkened. At dawn, a group found the main gate of the palace unguarded and charged inside, killing guards, smashing their way through the ornate Hall of Mirrors, and shouting threats against the hated Marie-Antoinette (one woman declared she would cut out and cook the queen's liver). The queen barely escaped, shrieking and running barefoot to the king's apartments, her children in tow, and then pounding on the door for nearly ten minutes before someone heard and let her in. Finally, National Guards moved in to restore order, but the Parisians, by now as many as 60,000 strong, demanded that the royal family return with them to Paris, where it could be kept under permanent popular surveillance.

Fearing further violence, the king again gave in. On the afternoon of October 6, he and his family left Versailles in a hastily packed carriage, accompanied by the National Guard, listening to the crowd's wild songs and shouts. The magnificent palace of Versailles that Louis XIV had built as a refuge from Parisian turmoil stood abandoned, never again to have a king in residence. What had started as a crowd action closely related to many similar events under the Old Regime had turned into something very different: perhaps the most tangible and dramatic display of popular sovereignty in history.

FORGING A NEW REGIME

With the weakened king now removed to Paris, the Assembly set up shop there as well and began its work of drafting a written constitution—a task that would take the better part of two years. Unlike the American Constitutional Convention, which had concerned itself with the single task of constitution-writing and had only 55 active members, the National Assembly did its constitutional work while also attempting to govern the country, and numbered no less than 1,200 men. So not surprisingly, its debates—which took place in a long, narrow, foul-smelling, hastily converted indoor riding arena with abominable acoustics—were chaotic and often turned vituperative as well. Distinct liberal and conservative factions emerged, seated on the left and right sides, respectively, of the long, narrow meeting hall (thus giving rise to the modern political terms "left-wing" and "right-wing"). Indeed, it is at this moment in European history that we can begin, without anachronism, to distinguish between political "liberals" who favored individual rights and civic reforms such as the

Women's March on Versailles A dramatic contemporary engraving shows women—mostly poor—bearing weapons as they shout, "To Versailles!" In what may be creative license, several women pull a cannon; one also drags along a wealthy, well-dressed woman (left).

expansion of the suffrage, and "conservative" defenders of the traditional social order.

But despite the chaos and conflict, the Assembly was engaged in an unprecedented enterprise: dismantling a massively complex, inefficient, discriminatory system of government, and rebuilding it according to principles of reason and justice. Helen Maria Williams, a young British poet who attended in the spring of 1790, wrote of having seen history in the making with an enthusiasm that well conveys the emotions that the Revolution generated: "Those men now before my eyes are the men who engross the attention, the astonishment of Europe . . . and whose fame has already extended through every civilized region of the globe."

This momentous project was remarkably multifaceted. In less than two years, among other things, the National Assembly dissolved the guilds, implemented free trade, and replaced the uneven patchwork of French provinces with eighty-odd "departments" of equal size. It also offered membership in the national community to groups whose exclusion had previously been taken for granted. In the final days of the Old Regime, Louis XVI had already restored civil rights to Protestants. Then, in a series of measures adopted in 1790–91, the Assembly extended toleration, and full citizenship, to French Jews as well. In 1791, free men of color in France's Caribbean colonies were granted citizenship, while an influential Society of Friends of the Blacks campaigned for an end to slavery. The largest group of second-class citizens in the French population—women—made some tangible gains, notably with the legalization of divorce. An actress and playwright named Olympe de Gouges (1748–1793) even, optimistically, published a "Declaration of the Rights of Woman." Her demands mostly fell on deaf ears. Still, more voices were raised on behalf of women's rights than had been the case in previous Western upheavals. One prominent philosopher and political writer dismissed the argument that the burdens of menstration and pregnancy should bar women from voting, noting mischievously that no one would impose such an exclusion on men suffering from gout.

THE REVOLUTION'S INTERNATIONAL IMPACT

Helen Maria Williams's prediction that the influence of the French Revolution would quickly spread through the globe was correct. In the Southern Netherlands—modern

Patriotic Women's Club In a 1793 illustration, women supporters of the Revolution discuss politics as one of their number reads aloud from a newspaper. Another woman (center) contributes coins to a charitable fund. This range of activities suggests the roles envisioned by some women themselves in the new republican France.

Belgium—events in France helped trigger revolutionary uprisings in the summer and fall of 1789. In one area, the independent principality of Liège, a popular movement overthrew the absolutist prince-bishop and issued a Declaration of the Rights of Man and Citizen on the French model. Elsewhere in the Southern Netherlands, the so-called revolution mostly took the form of relatively conservative protests against the territory's current overlords, the Austrian Habsburgs. In both cases, however, the movements were eventually crushed by troops from Austria and the Holy Roman Empire.

THWARTED REFORMS IN POLAND-LITHUANIA

The Polish-Lithuanian Commonwealth underwent a similarly abortive revolutionary experience. By the last decades of the eighteenth century, it had lost much of the influence it had possessed a century before and was increasingly vulnerable to the depredations of its powerful neighbors, Russia, Austria, and Prussia. As we have seen, in 1772 these neighbors carried out the so-called First Partition, each stripping away a slice of Polish territory. King Stanisław August Poniatowski (r. 1764–95) believed, along with many supporters, that the traditional Polish constitution was no longer workable. The so-called Golden Freedoms, which gave the nobility a dominant role in government, allowed it to block reforms while frequently causing political paralysis.

In 1791, even as excitement grew in Poland-Lithuania over the French Revolution, Stanisław August believed he had a chance to break the logjam. Russia had been weakened and distracted by wars against the Ottoman Empire and Sweden, and Austria had participated in the first of these. In May 1791, the king issued a new constitution that established a mixed government on the British model, but with a more powerful executive. It drew heavily on Enlightenment thinking, especially Montesquieu's theory of the separation of powers. But the events provoked the anger of the increasingly reactionary tsarina of Russia, Catherine the Great (r. 1762–1796). In 1792, after her army defeated the Turks, she invaded Poland-Lithuania and forced Stanisław August to abandon the reforms. The kingdom was now entirely at the mercy of the predatory great powers that surrounded it.

POLITICAL AND IDEOLOGICAL RESPONSES

Elsewhere in Europe, the news of the French Revolution prompted monarchs to fear for their own authority, while also driving hopes that they might profit from the turmoil in France. In 1790, Austria and Prussia signed an alliance and encouraged French nobles who had fled France to assemble a counterrevolutionary army in the hopes of restoring Louis XVI to his full powers. Austria, ruled by French queen Marie-Antoinette's brother, encouraged the French royal family to resist revolutionary change.

In Britain, opinions about the French Revolution were split. The *Times* of London spoke for many British observers when it praised the National Assembly as a collection of "Statesmen and Philosophers" and claimed to see in their actions nothing less than the "renovation of the golden age of society." The poet William Wordsworth, looking back on his youthful enthusiasm for the Revolution, memorably wrote: "Bliss was it in that dawn to be alive / But to be young was very heaven."

But in 1790, well before the outbreak of large-scale violence in France, the Whig parliamentarian **Edmund Burke** (1729–1797) delivered a blistering response to such views in a book that became the founding text of modern conservatism. His *Reflections on the Revolution in France* argued that political reform could succeed only if it was gradual, cautious, and built carefully upon existing tradition. The French revolutionaries, he charged, were instead trying to squeeze human beings into jarringly new, rigid shapes. Burke added that if the French, guided by their "barbarous philosophy," persisted in their blind enthusiasm for change, they would end up drowning in their own blood: "In the groves of their academy, at the end of every vista, you see nothing but the gallows."

In response to Burke's polemic, the great radical publicist Thomas Paine delivered a counterblast under the title *The Rights of Man* in which he argued that to defend their natural rights it was legitimate for a people to replace a tyrannical government. Paine, who was himself now living in France, treated Burke's eloquent praise of tradition with deadly scorn: "He pities the plumage, but forgets the dying bird." By 1791, the French Revolution had become a source of civil violence in Britain. That year, supporters of the Revolution, including the noted chemist Joseph Priestley, planned a banquet in Birmingham to commemorate the fall of the Bastille. A riot ensued, and Priestley's home was burned, along with two churches where many of the supporters had worshipped. Another English admirer of the Revolution, the writer Mary Wollstonecraft (1759–1797), followed her own response to Burke with the powerful *Vindication of the Rights of Women* (1792). Like Olympe de Gouges in France, she defended women's intellectual capacities and insisted that they enjoyed the same natural rights God had given to men.

SLAVE REVOLT IN SAINT-DOMINGUE The French Revolution had even more direct effects in the Caribbean. It will be remembered that in the French colony of Saint-Domingue—modern Haiti—nearly 500,000 African slaves working under inhuman conditions drove highly profitable sugar and coffee production. In 1790–91, wealthy white planters persuaded the new French revolutionary government to give them their own assembly, with considerable control over colonial affairs. At the same time, free people of color demanded full citizenship rights,

Slave Revolt in Saint-Domingue A late-eighteenth-century engraving vividly depicts the unrest in Saint-Domingue, as enslaved people rise up against their masters and destroy property.

HOPES AND FEARS OF THE FRENCH REVOLUTION

The French Revolution profoundly divided Europe. Imbued with a new sense of political possibility, many observers looked to the upheaval in France with enthusiasm and pride, publishing pamphlets and newspapers in support of the ongoing changes. Opponents of the Revolution, however, including Edmund Burke, perceived this new order as harmful to civilization. They argued that Revolution threatened not just social and political structures but also the values and achievements that European culture had accumulated over the centuries. While some welcomed the promise and progress of the Revolution, others worried that such a break with the past would destroy all that they held dear.

The People of Marseilles, "Farewell to the Year 1790"

Issued by a group of citizens of Marseilles, this pamphlet was one of many that commemorated the revolutionary events of the year 1790. In this excerpt, the authors celebrate in particular the involvement of the citizenry.

Incomparable year! Never will any resemble you! Your older sister brought liberty and patriotism from her breast. (It was a child who had only just been born;) but you nourished him, weaned him, & he's beginning to walk unaided. What hopes don't we have, at the rate he's growing? His youth gives us the hidden premonition that he'll make rapid progress in the system of the revolution....

But you, dear year! You have triumphed over their weakness. It wasn't reasonable that ordinary Citizens were the victims of so many injustices; they [certain officials] have finally deserted the walls of this charming city, & their flight makes the Citizens' courage & patriotism bloom. Your older sister saw the demolition of the Bastille of the Capital...This is not enough; a new order must return authority to the people....

Fanaticism has contributed much to our fear, the rest arising from despotism as well; but despite the efforts of both, you triumph. Besides, you were almost assured of your glory; do you not remember the past fourteenth of July when you saw three million bayonets hurry to your defense, & close to eighteen million free Citizens, swearing to preserve the right of all men? Well! that suffices to crown your victory.

Edmund Burke, from *Reflections on the Revolution in France*

In this passage from his famous book (1790), Burke bemoans the Revolution's destruction of European tradition and warns of the dangers ahead.

The age of chivalry is gone. That of sophisters, economists, and calculators, has succeeded; and the glory of Europe is extinguished forever....Never, never more, shall we behold that generous loyalty to rank and sex, that proud submission, that dignified obedience, that subordination of the heart, which kept alive, even in servitude itself, the spirit of an exalted freedom....

But now all is to be changed. All the pleasing illusions, which made power gentle, and obedience liberal, which harmonized the different shades of life, and which, by a bland assimilation, incorporated into politics the sentiments which beautify and soften private society, are to be dissolved by this new conquering empire of light and reason....

On the scheme of this barbarous philosophy, which is the offspring of cold hearts and muddy understandings, and which is as void of solid wisdom, as it is destitute of all taste and elegance, laws are to be supported only by their own terrors, and by the concern which each individual may find in them from his own private speculations, or can spare to them from his own private interests. In the groves of their academy, at the end of every visto, you see nothing but the gallows. Nothing is left which engages the affections on the part of the commonwealth....

To make a government requires no great prudence....But to form a *free government*; that is, to temper together these opposite elements of liberty and restraint in one consistent work, requires much thought; deep reflection; a sagacious, powerful, and combining mind....But when the leaders choose to make themselves bidders at an auction of popularity, their talents, in the construction of the state, will be of no service. They will become flatterers instead of legislators; the instruments, not the guides of the people....

Moderation will be stigmatized as the virtue of cowards, and compromise as the prudence of traitors; until, in hopes of preserving the credit which may enable him to temper and moderate on some occasions, the popular leader is obliged to become active in propagating doctrines, and establishing powers, that will afterwards defeat any sober purpose at which he ultimately might have aimed.

QUESTIONS FOR ANALYSIS

1. What made 1790 an "incomparable year" for the citizens of Marseilles?
2. What possible consequences of the Revolution does Burke fear?
3. What do the writers of these documents understand to be the political role of "the people"?

Sources: Andrew Daily, trans., *Les Adieux à l'année 1790*, le peuple Marseillais, (Marseille: 1790), pp. 5–7; Edmund Burke, *Reflections on the Revolution in France* (London: 1790), pp. 113–15, 352–53.

and some of them took to arms in pursuit of this goal. By August 1791, the colony had become the scene of a complex struggle between these different groups. And then, against this backdrop, the black slaves who made up the great majority of the population staged the largest and most successful slave revolt in history, burning rich plantations on the northern plain and threatening the colony's principal towns. Within two years the French commissioners on the island, desperate to retain control of events, issued an emancipation proclamation, which the revolutionary French government endorsed several months later and expanded upon by abolishing slavery throughout all French possessions. Another ten years of confused and vicious fighting followed, during which the former slave Toussaint Louverture took an increasingly important role. By 1798, with French support, he had become the de facto ruler of Saint-Domingue. Eventually, Haiti would join the United States as the second new independent state in the Americas—and would also be the first black republic in the world.

FAILURE TO REACH CONSENSUS

Back in France, violence remained more limited through 1791, but a national consensus over the Revolution stubbornly refused to take shape. Instead, as the National Assembly struggled to finish writing the constitution, the country split over fundamental issues of sovereignty. Where did ultimate political authority lie? With the people as a whole, as proclaimed in the Declaration of the Rights of Man and Citizen? With the people's representatives in the Assembly? Or with its traditional embodiment, the king? Few people in this long-standing European monarchy could yet imagine the country without a king, but it was unclear what role he should now play. His supporters demanded that the new constitution give him an absolute veto over legislative decisions, but the Assembly granted him only the power to suspend legislation temporarily.

The advocates of popular sovereignty demanded that all adult males receive the right to vote, but the Assembly's constitution of 1791 instead divided the citizenry into "active" and "passive" citizens, with only the former—those who possessed substantial property and income—enjoying the suffrage. Most divisively, the Assembly undertook a massive reform of the Catholic Church in France. In 1789 it had already confiscated the Church's vast landholdings and sold them off to ease the state's fiscal problems. The next year it attempted to subject the Church itself to state authority and to transform priests and bishops into elected officials on the public payroll. This act challenged both the king, in his role as the Church's protector, and the spiritual sovereignty claimed by the pope over all Catholics. Fully half the French priesthood refused to swear an oath of loyalty to the new Civil Constitution of the Clergy, leading to their dismissal from office, often over the indignant protests of their parishioners.

As these disputes dragged on, much of the country remained in an unsettled state, with frequent riots and clashes between revolutionary crowds and units of the royal army. On the first anniversary of the fall of the Bastille, the Assembly ordered a nationwide Festival of Federation, in which the army and the National Guard swore oaths of loyalty, accompanied by parading, fireworks, and revolutionary songs. But the grand and impressive symbolism did little to calm fears of civil war.

DEMOCRACY AND VIOLENCE From this point, the Revolution entered a new phase marked by increasing violence. It was a shift that still casts a forbidding shadow over the origins of modern democratic politics and poses an urgent question: Why did it happen? As with the origins of the Revolution itself, the reasons are not reducible to any single factor. Much of the reason, certainly, lies in what historians call the "political culture" bequeathed to the Revolution by the Old Regime. Unlike the American revolutionaries, with their long experience of various forms

The Jacobin Club A minister of the revolutionary government speaks to the crowded meeting room of the Jacobin Club in January 1792. Women crowd behind him (right) and soldiers stand guard (left), while club members shout back and one man even exposes his buttocks (center), leaving no doubt as to the club's lively political culture.

of self-government, the French revolutionaries had little familiarity with practical politics before 1789—especially the need to forge coalitions, negotiate compromises, and abide by the will of the majority. France's history of absolute, indivisible royal sovereignty made the prospect of parties competing for power, and one branch of the state checking another, seem unbearably discordant and disruptive. Political parties, or even independent popular movements of the sort that took shape in the American Revolution, seemed wholly illegitimate and dangerously anarchic.

In France, then, it was all too easy to perceive opposition as treason, and indeed, cries of treason resounded incessantly from right and left alike after 1789. They did so in the Assembly, in the streets, and in hundreds of political clubs and societies, the most important of which were the **Jacobins**, the name of the religious order in whose building they originally met. In the pages of a new, raucous newspaper press, writers competed to denounce their enemies in as eloquently vicious terms as possible. None did so more successfully than a Swiss doctor named Jean-Paul Marat (1743–1793), who published a wildly popular left-wing newspaper in Paris. "Your enemies need only to triumph for a moment," he warned in a typical outburst, "for blood to flow in torrents. . . . They will rip open the bellies of your wives, and their bloody hands will search the entrails of your children to find their hearts." Kill those enemies first, he demanded. "Sacrifice 200,000 heads, and you will save a million." Royalist, counterrevolutionary demagogues issued blood-curdling threats of their own. Meanwhile, in the major cities, and especially in Paris, independent popular movements developed, demanding that the revolutionary leadership take the demands of ordinary people into account—especially for food at a fair price.

COUNTERREVOLUTIONARY FORCES But it was not just these factors that drove the Revolution toward violent conflict. The very nature of revolutionary politics contributed powerfully as well. As different groups competed to pose as the true representatives of the people, the moderates who initially attracted the most support found themselves pushed to the side by others willing not just to oppose but also to demonize the aristocracy, recalcitrant priests, and counterrevolutionaries. In the Assembly, one of the most important of these was a deputy from the northern town of Arras named **Maximilien Robespierre** (1758–1794). Fussily dressed and a poor speaker, this former lawyer initially failed to impress his colleagues but gradually built up a reputation for coldly precise logic and compellingly absolute, unswerving dedication to the

Revolution. A British observer rightly saw in him "a character to be contemplated" who would shortly "be the man of sway . . . and govern the million." Between men like Robespierre and the supporters of the king, it soon became impossible to find common ground.

Maximilien Robespierre
An eighteenth-century portrait of the radical leader depicts him in the formal clothing he preferred.

Still, if Marat and Robespierre built up a terrifying, nightmarish image of the counterrevolution, the better to advance their own program, the fact remains that the counterrevolution itself was no myth and its activities too drove the Revolution into violent conflict. In the Assembly, political clubs, and the press, a determined right-wing faction called for the reversal of the Revolution and the restoration of the king and nobility to their former powers and privileges. Thousands of nobles—including a large majority of France's army officers—fled the country to join the émigré army taking shape in Germany. And while the king and queen publicly professed support of the Revolution, privately they corresponded with the émigrés and hoped for their victory.

THE KING'S FLIGHT AND ITS IMPACT

And then, in June 1791, Louis XVI showed his cards in an extraordinary—but, typically enough, botched—fashion. He and Marie-Antoinette plotted a dramatic escape from their quasi-captivity in Paris: in the dead of night they would sneak out of the Tuileries Palace in disguise and embark in a carriage for the eastern border. There troops were waiting, backed by the armed might of the Austrian Empire, now ruled by Marie-Antoinette's brother, Leopold II. The royal couple then planned to dissolve the Assembly and repeal most of its decisions. But they were undone by their genius for blundering. The bulky carriage, laden with baggage that the couple refused to do without, moved at a leaden pace, missing the rendezvous with loyal troops and arousing suspicions from local authorities, who detained them in the small eastern town of Varennes. Representatives of the Assembly who hoped to preserve a constitutional monarchy escorted the royal family back to Paris, claiming unpersuasively that the king had been "kidnapped." But their excuses could not prevent a wave of indignation from sweeping the country, as millions of

Capture of Louis XVI and Marie-Antoinette A colored etching dramatizes the moment at which revolutionaries apprehend the fleeing royal family in Varennes, as troops rush into an inn where the family are having dinner.

citizens realized that the fevered left-wing allegations of royal treason might actually be true.

The most virulent outcries against the monarchy came not only from left-wing journalists and deputies but also from revolutionary crowds in Paris and other cities. The same groups who had taken the Bastille and stormed Versailles had remained active participants in the Revolution. In Paris, they dominated many of the forty-eight "sections" into which the new municipal authorities had divided the city, each of which possessed its own, small, tumultuous "sectional assembly." With supplies of affordable bread still being in question and rumors of counterrevolutionary plots circulating feverishly (in part thanks to newspapers like Marat's), new, potentially violent crowd actions were a constant possibility.

By late 1791, the most active urban militants had started to be known as "*sans-culottes*"—those who wore full-length trousers instead of the calf-length breeches (*culottes*) of the upper classes. Although their leaders consisted largely of educated professionals and successful artisans, the rank-and-file came in large part from the urban working classes, and they preached hatred not only of aristocrats but of the wealthy in general. Their watchwords were bread for the people and death to counterrevolutionaries. In July 1791, less than a month after the king's flight, tens of thousands of *sans-culottes* flooded into Mars Field, a large open space in central Paris, to sign a petition demanding the replacement of the king by an executive

council. When a group of them killed two suspected spies, the mayor and Lafayette, a former hero of the American War of Independence now heading the National Guard, together ordered armed Guards into the field to restore order. A massacre of up to fifty crowd members ensued, further incensing radical opinion. The *sans-culottes* movement would continue to evolve, acquiring an effective organization and a hugely popular newspaper.

Despite these tumultuous events, for another year a delicate balance held. Louis remained king, and in the fall of 1791 the long-prepared new constitution finally came into effect. The Legislative Assembly that took office consisted entirely of new faces, for their predecessors had declared themselves ineligible for reelection. The deputies also came almost entirely from the former Third Estate, as the clergy and nobility had lost their old privileges. In fact, the nobility itself had legally ceased to exist, along with the system of estates—all French men were now equal.

THE RUSH TO WAR Although overt counterrevolutionaries were largely absent from the deputies' ranks, the new Legislative Assembly remained as prone to conflict as its predecessor, with radical Jacobins and more moderate deputies continuing heatedly to dispute the course of the Revolution. And almost immediately, the body found itself confronting the most divisive issue of all: war. The émigré counterrevolutionary army in Germany had continued to grow, while Austria and Prussia showed increasing hostility toward the revolutionary regime. In response, a group of French deputies known as the **"Girondins"** (who mostly belonged to the Jacobin Club) began agitating for an attack on Austria. Their leader was an ambitious deputy from Paris named Jacques-Pierre Brissot (1754–1793), who had struggled to establish himself as a *philosophe* under the Old Regime. As a journalist in the early Revolution, he gained a reputation for eloquent radicalism in the service of oppressed people. But once elected to the Legislative Assembly, he fastened on war as the issue that would bring him to power, presenting it as necessary both for quelling the threat of counterrevolution and for reinvigorating France itself. His allies eagerly echoed the message. As one wrote: "It is a cruel thing to think, but . . . peace is taking us backwards. We will only be regenerated by blood."

Not all members of the left agreed with the Girondins, but in the winter of 1791–92 they found it impossible to stop the rush to war. Robespierre, notably, distrusted Brissot's ambitions and considered war a distraction from the need to root out counterrevolution at home. Nor did he believe Brissot's promise that the revolutionary armies would bring liberation to oppressed peoples across Europe. "No one loves armed missionaries," Robespierre insisted in a speech at the Jacobin Club (to which he also belonged). Yet few of his colleagues listened, especially after the king and queen cynically threw their own weight behind Brissot's campaign, in the hope that a war would bring them back to full power ("these imbeciles don't see that they are helping us," Marie-Antoinette privately remarked). In April 1792, France declared war on Austria, and two months later Prussia joined the fight on the Austrian side.

INSURRECTION But far from strengthening the monarchy, the war helped ensure its final collapse. The French army, undermined by the emigration of much of the officer corps and heavily staffed by raw volunteers, fought poorly. Some troops fled at the first contact with Austrian regulars, and a few even massacred their own commanders. By early summer 1792, not only had the early French forays into the Austrian Netherlands been repulsed but France itself seemed dangerously open to invasion. At the same time, the Austrians and Prussians made the ideological stakes of the war perfectly clear. On July 25, the Prussian commander, the duke of Brunswick (1735–1806), issued a manifesto stating his intention to end the "anarchy" in France and to restore full powers to the king. And if the people of Paris offered violence to the royal family, he promised to take "ever memorable vengeance," including the "complete destruction" of the French capital. From this moment on, the Revolution's success depended on French military victory.

In this climate, the new French constitutional regime had no chance of solidifying itself. By now, a significant number of deputies, and radical journalists, were demanding the establishment of a republic, and they were backed by the increasingly assertive *sans-culotte* movement. On August 10, 1792, strengthened by detachments of radical National Guards from around the country, the *sans-culottes* attacked the royal palace in Paris. For the first time in the history of the Revolution, Paris itself witnessed a large-scale battle, as the king's loyal Swiss guards vainly tried to protect their master and were shot down. Finally, the royal family took refuge in the hall of the Assembly, whose members, faced with a popular fait accompli, took yet another leap into the unknown. Within days, they had abolished the monarchy and ordered the election of a **National Convention** to write a new, republican constitution. For the first time in European history, all of a nation's adult men would vote.

THE BIRTH OF THE FIRST FRENCH REPUBLIC (1792–1793)

If the first French revolutionary government had started its work in an atmosphere of crisis and violence in 1789, this second one—the First French Republic—came into being amid full-scale war and large-scale massacre. On August 19, 1792, the Prussian army crossed the eastern frontier into France, and two weeks later it took the key eastern fortress of Verdun. In Paris, a mood of panic soon found violent expression.

THE SEPTEMBER MASSACRES AND THE BATTLE OF VALMY

Between September 2 and 7, 1792, armed *sans-culottes* stormed prisons in the capital, where hundreds of suspected counterrevolutionaries had been detained. Setting up improvised courts, they dragged each prisoner in turn forward for a brief hearing, followed immediately by a pronouncement of innocence or guilt. In the latter case, the *sans-culottes* delivered the death sentence then and there, usually with clubs or knives to spare ammunition for the army. Lurid tales spread of tortures committed and bodies mutilated after death, most of which were likely invented. But between 1,100 and 1,400 men and women did die, mostly common criminals but including some 200 priests and many prominent nobles. The so-called

September Massacres Blood stains the revolutionaries' axes as they slaughter supposed counterrevolutionaries emerging from a prison. This 1790s engraving seeks to emphasize the carnage associated with the increasingly radical revolution.

September Massacres deeply shocked public opinion outside of France, with many observers renouncing their former approval of the Revolution to denounce the "monsters" in Paris.

Yet the same moment of extreme danger also saw the birth of a new, fervent revolutionary patriotism. In the dark, narrow streets of Paris, baking in the summer heat, bells rang constantly while soldiers marched to the sound of drums and cannon, calling for volunteers to defend the fatherland from the Prussians. Some 15,000 responded in a single week and were sent eastward in a disorganized mob, without training or even weapons. In the Convention, a new leader came to the fore—a former lawyer named Georges Danton (1759–1794) with a great mane of hair, prominent brows, a deep, bellowing voice, and an instinctive talent for rousing a crowd. On September 2, he gave his greatest speech, roaring that "To defeat our enemies, *Messieurs*, we need boldness, again boldness, forever boldness, and France is saved."

The volunteers, bold as they were, by themselves could not do much against well-drilled Prussian infantry. But the Prussians had problems of their own, their ranks having been decimated by an outbreak of dysentery that turned their line of march into one long, foul-smelling latrine. The French army confronted them on September 20 near the eastern town of Valmy, and the battle quickly turned into an artillery duel. Among the officers on the French side was a member of the royal family, Louis-Philippe (1773–1850), who had embraced the Revolution along with his father, the Duke of Orléans. The French artillery, which was staffed—unlike the infantry—by long-serving professionals, carried the day, and the weakened Prussians, commanded by the elderly, cautious duke of Brunswick, quickly withdrew. The revolutionaries hailed Valmy as a momentous victory that had saved France from invasion and that left the newly elected National Convention free to begin its work.

THE TRIAL AND EXECUTION OF THE KING

The Convention, though, was no freer from discord than its predecessors. The same dynamic of radicalization that had destabilized revolutionary politics from the start continued in this newest assembly, with different factions competing to pose as the purest, most determined representatives of the popular will. Now the principal division would come between two groups of Jacobins: Brissot and the Girondins, on the one hand, and a group that came to be known as the "Mountain" because it occupied the upper seats in the Assembly hall. It included Danton, the wild journalist Marat, and Robespierre, now making his return to elected office. And Robespierre had a new ally: a pale, thin, intense man just twenty-five years of age named Louis-Antoine Saint-Just (1767–1794). Meanwhile, the restive, well-organized *sans-culottes* continued to put pressure on the Convention from the left.

The Convention also had no shortage of crises to deal with, of which the first and greatest was the question of the king. After the fall of the monarchy in the summer of 1792, the Convention had placed Louis under arrest. Should he be expelled from the country? Placed on trial? Killed? Saint-Just argued in his maiden speech that the people of France had already found Louis guilty by overthrowing him, but the deputies, who included a heavy proportion of lawyers, hesitated to condemn the king without due process of law. Finally, in December a trial took place before the Convention itself. The deputies found the king guilty of betraying the people by a wide margin and then, by a smaller one, sentenced him to die.

On January 21, 1793, Louis XVI was led to the large square in Paris that is today called the "Place de la Concorde." There awaited him one of the Revolution's most

Execution of Louis XVI Troops maintain order among massed spectators as a soldier displays the king's severed head to the crowd in this 1792 painting.

infamous inventions: the guillotine, whose heavy blade delivered the bloody but rapid punishment of decapitation. His hands bound behind him and his hair cut so as not to impede the blade, Louis was strapped to a board and thrust into the machine while continuous drumrolls drowned out the last words he tried to shout to the crowds. The blade fell, and the king of France perished. (Grotesquely, the guillotine did not cut cleanly through his pudgy neck, and the executioner had to pull the blade back up into position and drop it again.)

TOWARD CIVIL WAR

The king's trial and execution horrified social elites across Europe and ended any chance of the revolutionary regime conciliating with its enemies. Coupled as it was with revolutionary attacks on religion and promises of radical social equality not just for the French but for all humankind, Louis's death inspired even stronger opposition than the execution of England's Charles I had done in 1649. Britain and Spain soon opened hostilities against France, turning the war into a general European conflict—the first in nearly thirty years. In Britain, the government of Prime Minister William Pitt the younger undertook increasingly repressive actions. By the mid-1790s it had suspended the right of habeas corpus (which protects those arrested from indefinite, unlawful detention), put several dissidents on trial for treason, and passed laws banning "seditious" publications and meetings. British caricatures, especially those by the talented printmaker James Gillray, portrayed the French revolutionaries as cannibals.

The French, following their victory at Valmy, did well on the battlefield for a time, again invading the Austrian Netherlands and capturing Brussels. But the strains of war quickly took their toll on the new regime, which faced severe shortages of weapons, ammunition, and soldiers. In February 1793, the Convention decreed the conscription of 300,000 men, but the move met with massive resistance. Indeed, across western France, particularly in isolated rural areas where loyalty to the old Catholic priesthood ran strong, widespread resistance developed, and in several places crowds of peasants murdered revolutionary officials. The Convention managed to suppress most of these uprisings, but in the department of the **Vendée** peasant rebels put an ill-trained and badly led column of revolutionary soldiers to flight, and with the help of local nobles announced the formation of a "Catholic and Royal Army" pledged to fight for Louis XVI's young son, whom the Convention was

Anti-Revolutionary Cartoons Captioned "A Family of Sans Culotts [sic] refreshing after the fatigues of the day," Gillray's cartoon mocks the movement's name by portraying its members naked from the waist down as they eat a nobleman and sit on his riches. A woman roasts a child over the fire, and even the *sans-culottes* children feast on entrails.

holding prisoner in Paris. A true civil war had now begun, although it remained limited to the west.

RENEWED ECONOMIC CRISIS
Meanwhile, the quality of life for ordinary French people, which had improved somewhat after 1789, again fell into a tailspin. A British blockade, coming hard on the heels of the slave revolt in Saint-Domingue, decimated French overseas trade, while internal conflict played havoc with the supply of bread to French cities. And the French had to face another, largely unprecedented economic crisis: a steep rise in the prices of goods, known today as "hyperinflation." The National Assembly of 1789 had temporarily eased the problem of the national debt by selling off the lands of the French clergy. But they did so by issuing paper notes called *assignats*, which could be redeemed for Church land. By 1791, the *assignats* had effectively become a paper currency, and within two years their value was in free fall, with prices rising out of control. In February 1793, *sans-culottes* rioted in Paris, calling for a "maximum" price on bread, and perhaps on other necessities as well, violating the principles of free trade declared after 1789.

Brissot and the Girondin faction in the Convention considered the *sans-culottes* a threat. They opposed the "maximum," called for an end to the popular movement's assemblies in the "sections" of Paris, and toyed with the idea of moving the government out of the capital

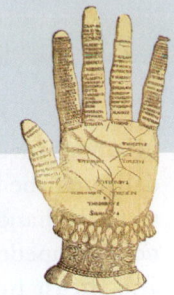

BREAD RIOTS IN PARIS

While the French revolutionary government debated the contours of the new legal and constitutional order, the common people challenged the state to ameliorate endemic poverty. The Parisian masses in particular, notably women, pressured successive revolutionary governments to cap food prices and even to distribute bread to the hungry. Bread riots and other civil disturbances were common throughout the revolutionary period, and merchants suspected of "hoarding" were beaten and even killed by angry crowds.

In February 1793, the Paris prefecture of police issued this report on the tense situation in the capital as the revolutionary government worked to maintain peace among its hungry and restive masses. For the poor, questions of liberty and equality were not simply abstract debates, but issues of real and pressing material needs.

The following day, the twenty-fifth of the same month, same year, at 7 A.M., we went, still assisted by the citizen-secretary-registrar, to the doors of the bakers in our Section to see whether bread deliveries were being made without incident and to take remedial action, if possible. We had the satisfaction of seeing that the measures we had taken the night before, in joint action with the Committee, had produced the full effect we were hoping for. Consequently, we returned to the Committee to find out whether there wasn't some new order, and finding none, we returned to our arrondissement.

There wasn't what you would call a tumult, but [rather] small groupings of citizens and *citoyennes*[1] at intervals. In some [of these groups] it was being said, "The bakers were rascals and deserved to be worked over." In others, "The grocers deserved the same, because they were hoarders," and finally, in others, "The majority of those who were directing the Republic were also rascals." And among others [there was] a drunk citizen who made himself conspicuous by saying, "We used to have only one king, and now there are thirty or forty of them." We did everything we could to restore calm in these groups. We succeeded in some; it was impossible in others; and lastly, it was folly in still others. All this [was happening] without our being able to arrest any of the leaders, who were absolutely unknown to us and not from this Section.

QUESTIONS FOR ANALYSIS

1. Why was the revolutionary government so concerned with the distributions of bread and other staples?
2. What complaints did the citizens of Paris direct toward the commissioners who were dispatched to monitor the situation?
3. What does this source show about the Revolution's effect on France's poorest citizens?

[1] *citoyennes:* female citizens

Source: *Commissaire's* report on events of February 24, 25, 26, 1793, Section de l'Arsenal, in Archives de la Préfecture de Police de Paris, AA 69, nos. 296–97, in *Women in Revolutionary Paris*, eds. and trans. Darline Gay Levy, Harriet Branson Applewhite, and Mary Durham Johnson (Urbana: 1979), pp. 137–38.

altogether. One of their deputies threatened that if the Parisian movement were not curbed, one day passers-by would wander the banks of the Seine river "and ask where once Paris had stood." **The Mountain**, however, largely supported the *sans-culottes*, and on May 4 the Convention instituted a maximum on bread prices over Girondin protests. On May 30, in the major industrial city of Lyons, the conflict turned violent, as forces sympathetic to the Girondins overthrew the municipal government.

THE FALL OF THE GIRONDINS By the spring of 1793, the politics of the Revolution had once again reached an impasse, and yet again the impasse was broken by popular action. On May 31, alarm bells rang in Paris as the *sans-culottes* mobilized. On June 2, with tens of thousands of them surrounding the Convention's assembly hall, they demanded the expulsion and arrest of the principal Girondin deputies. The *sans-culotte* commander of the Paris National Guard aimed a cannon at the door and demanded that the Girondins be sent out—or else. Even some of the "Mountaineers" quailed at this direct assault on the Convention's democratic authority, but others argued that they had no choice if they were to save the infant republic from an even worse fate. Brissot and twenty-eight others were expelled and arrested.

The Convention would eventually restore its authority, but in the late spring and summer of 1793 both it and the Revolution seemed poised at the edge of disaster. In the west, the Vendéan revolt accelerated, as the Catholic and Royal Army captured one major town after another. Following the example of Lyon, several major cities sympathetic to the Girondins broke into open revolt against Paris. A young woman from Normandy, hoping to silence the loudest advocate of revolutionary violence, calmly walked into the Paris apartment of Jean-Paul Marat and stabbed him to death in his bathtub. The murder (for which the woman was quickly executed) led to bizarre scenes of mourning in which Marat's admirers hailed him as the Jesus of the *sans-culottes* and, at his funeral, placed his bathtub on an altar in place of Christ's crucifix. Meanwhile, French armies were driven back in the Austrian Netherlands and Germany, and the frontiers seemed open to invasion. In August, out of desperation, the Convention decreed a "mass levy"—a mobilization of the entire French population for the war effort, including the conscription of all unmarried young men. But thrusting yet more untrained and ill-equipped draftees into the firing line, for all its symbolic appeal, did not seem likely to save the Revolution from defeat.

THE COMMITTEE OF PUBLIC SAFETY It was at this moment, however, that the Revolution entered its most extraordinary phase—one that blended the most extravagantly utopian hopes with terrible violence, and whose events devoured almost everyone who tried to master them. It presented yet again, in the starkest terms, some of the promise and a great deal of the peril of modern revolutionary politics. Its dazed survivors would later compare it to an earthquake, or a volcanic eruption, or some other overpowering natural disaster.

Key to this phase of the Revolution, which lasted from the summer of 1793 through the summer of 1794, was a group of twelve men from the Convention, most famously Robespierre and Saint-Just, who made up the **Committee of Public Safety**. Originally created in April 1793, the committee had by late summer become the central organ of French government. The Convention itself retained ultimate authority, having first written and then almost immediately suspended a new constitution for the

Death of Marat Jacques-Louis David memorialized Marat in 1793 by depicting the journalist in his tub shortly after his stabbing. In David's vision, Marat was at work on his next article at the time of his death.

duration of the emergency. But its 700-odd members were far too unwieldy a body to govern, particularly in the midst of the numerous crises besetting the country. Effective authority quickly devolved upon the Committee, which used it to act as a collective executive in the emergency. Together, the Convention and the Committee set out to save the Revolution from destruction.

THE REIGN OF TERROR (1793–1794)

The leading revolutionaries of this period—Robespierre in particular—now operated according to ideas very different from what had prevailed in 1789. They were no longer concerned with devising constitutional means for translating the great abstraction of "popular sovereignty" into concrete forms of governance. Increasingly, they invoked the authority, not of the people or the nation, but of the Revolution itself—a form of irresistible historical progress that demanded total commitment from its followers. And increasingly, these revolutionaries placed their faith less in the institutions they governed through, and more in the moral strength and purity of their followers. It is not for nothing that so many commentators have compared the French Revolution to a religious movement, for in its fervent emphasis on the beliefs and righteousness of its adherents, it did indeed have this quality during its most radical moment. At the same time, alleged counterrevolutionaries became a species of heretic, damned as moral monsters—"enemies of the human race" who deserved nothing but extermination. And thus France entered into what historians now call the "**Reign of Terror.**"

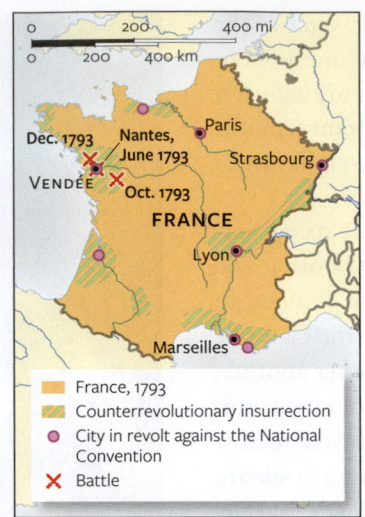

Counterrevolutionary Rebellion in France, 1793

THE MECHANISMS OF REPRESSION

The Terror, properly speaking, dates from the late summer of 1793. On September 5, Parisian crowds dramatically demanded that the Convention declare that "Terror is the order of the day." The deputies refrained from taking this step, but on September 17 they passed a Law of Suspects empowering revolutionary watch committees to arrest almost anyone suspected of counterrevolutionary sympathies. They followed that up on September 29 with a General Maximum law setting price controls on a wide range of necessities including wood, clothing, and tobacco. All these moves responded to the *sans-culotte* agenda, but at the same time the Mountain worked craftily to undercut *sans-culotte* influence. The Mountaineers ended the raucous "permanent sessions" of the *sans-culotte*–controlled district assemblies and also created several "revolutionary armies," drawn in large part from *sans-culotte* ranks, and sent them out into the countryside to maintain order.

To end the revolts against its authority and strengthen the armed forces, the Convention also sent its own members out into the country as "representatives on mission," entrusted with virtual dictatorial authority. Saint-Just, for instance, went to Strasbourg on France's eastern border. He extracted a huge forced loan from the city and demanded that the terrified citizenry supply the army with clothing from their own wardrobes. Some 17,000 pairs of shoes and 21,000 shirts quickly materialized. He also supervised a military tribunal as it handed down 27

death sentences against local officers and soldiers, mostly for the unforgivable crime of losing battles. During the Terror, no fewer than 84 generals went to the guillotine. In Lyons, meanwhile, another member of the Committee of Public Safety brought destruction on a terrible scale after the city finally fell to revolutionary forces in mid-October 1793.

By far the worst repression, however, came in the Vendée, in the west, where in June 1793 the Catholic and Royal Army finally met with competent revolutionary opposition and was soundly defeated outside the port city of Nantes. The revolutionaries pursued their new advantage through the summer and finally, in October, crushed the Vendéans in a pitched battle on their home territory. In December, the revolutionary forces wiped out what remained of the Vendéan army. "Following the orders you gave me," one commander wrote back to Paris, "I have crushed children under the hooves of horses, and massacred women who, these at least, will give birth to no more brigands. I do not have a single prisoner with which to reproach myself."

There then began slaughter on a scale unimagined in Europe since the wars of religion of the seventeenth century—far greater, for instance, than the September Massacres of 1792 in Paris. With the politicians in Paris feverishly demanding the "extermination" of the Vendée,

Nantes Drownings The Terror reached far outside Paris, as indicated by this 1793 lithograph, which depicts revolutionaries in the city of Nantes drowning suspected counter-revolutionaries, including Catholic priests and nuns, in the Loire estuary. As many as four thousand people, including women and children, were killed in this way.

the forces on the ground devised a plan to crisscross the territory with a series of armed columns, with orders to kill all suspected rebels and burn their villages. "We are going to be bearing iron and fire, a gun in one hand and a torch in the other," wrote one soldier to his family. "Men and women, all will be put to the sword. All must die, except the small children." In nearby Nantes, the revolutionaries lashed prisoners into barges, which were towed out into the Loire estuary and sunk. The killing in the region lasted for several months, and the total death toll probably ranged well over 100,000—most likely as high as 250,000.

THE ACHIEVEMENTS OF THE RADICAL REVOLUTION

Yet in a horrifying sense, the Terror worked. Although the western rebellion continued to smolder in places, it ceased to pose a mortal threat to the Revolution. The cities that had revolted against the Convention fell, one by one. And in the larger war as well, French forces recovered from the crisis of the summer of 1793. The Committee of Public Safety worked frantically to ensure adequate supplies for the army and to provide it with competent commanders. Volunteer units were molded together with the remnants of the old royal army and acquired proper training and weaponry. They were also taught new tactics: "The general rules are always to act *en masse* and offensively," stated a directive of the Committee of Public Safety. In key battles in the fall of 1793, French leaders concentrated the great mass of their troops against small weak spots in the Austrian lines and won narrow but significant victories in the Netherlands. By the beginning of 1794, the worst threats to France had been removed.

The military successes were extraordinary. But still more extraordinary was the ability of the deputies, in the midst of these terrible crises, to elaborate some of the most far-reaching plans in history for the betterment of society and the creation of a truly cohesive national community. In a new Declaration of Rights, issued in 1793, they proclaimed the rights of all citizens to primary education, subsistence, and work, and began to devise systems to guarantee these rights. They formulated an ambitious scheme for teaching the French language to all the citizens of what was still a typically European multilingual country, where only a minority of the citizens spoke standard French fluently. They designed a new calendar, numbering the years from the foundation of the First Republic in 1792 and dividing them into newly named months of

Cult of the Supreme Being A painting from around 1794 shows colorfully dressed citizens gathering at the foot of Robespierre's column in Mars Field to celebrate the Festival of the Supreme Being. The architecture of the column and the rings of laurel branches around the hill evoke the classical associations that Robespierre imagined for the new deist religion.

thirty days and weeks of ten. In these reforms they looked back, as their idol Jean-Jacques Rousseau had done, to the ancient world, seeing the Greek city-states and especially the Roman Republic as models of civic virtue.

In their most radical initiative the deputies, having already broken with the Catholic Church through the suppression of its privileges, the seizure of its land, and the attempt to make clergy into public functionaries, now attempted to suppress Christianity entirely. One group of deputies attempted to institute official atheism, with churches and cathedrals, including the Cathedral of Notre Dame in Paris, converted into "temples of reason" and signs posted over cemeteries reading "death is an eternal sleep." Robespierre, however, advocated the formation of a new religion: the "cult of the supreme being," which worshipped a God who had created the universe but did not personalize him or claim that he intervened in human affairs. In a grandiose festival in June 1794, Robespierre inaugurated it personally. Men and women paraded in white robes and sang hymns. In the center of Mars Field in Paris, an enormous plaster-and-cardboard mountain was erected, with a fifty-foot column near its summit bearing a tree and a statue of Hercules. Robespierre, dressed in a sky-blue coat, descended from the mountain in the manner of Moses, bearing a torch. In an ecstatic report drafted for the occasion, he hailed the event as a new beginning for the French people, whom the Revolution had advanced so

THERMIDOR AND THE END OF THE TERROR

Yet neither these moments of extravagant hope, nor the Convention's real success in reasserting its authority, did anything to halt the Terror. Instead, the pace of executions redoubled. In mid-October 1793, Marie-Antoinette followed her husband to the guillotine after a grotesque trial in which prosecutors accused her of sexually molesting her young son. The Revolution was turning misogynistic, with the Jacobins associating public virtue with masculinity and insisting with new fervor that women remain outside the public eye, tending to the hearth, raising children, and certainly not claiming political rights. Pro-revolutionary women's political clubs were dissolved. Two weeks after the queen, the arrested Girondins died in their turn.

In the winter and spring of 1793–94, Robespierre and the Committee of Public Safety moved to purge both "ultra-revolutionaries" on the left and a party of supposedly over-moderate revolutionaries on the right. Here the increasingly erratic and allegedly corrupt orator Danton became the chief scapegoat, and after yet another show trial in April 1794 he and a number of others were also executed. In his trial, Danton bravely defied the Committee and denounced its "dictatorship," and in his last moments showed genuine bravura. "Show my head to the crowd," he instructed the executioner. "It deserves it. It is a fine head." In June, the Convention passed a law further streamlining the procedure for trying suspected traitors, and despite a decisive military victory over the Austrians, the executions continued. In June and July alone, fully 1,515 men and women were condemned to death in Paris, bringing the total for revolutionary courts to over 20,000. Many were convicted for the bad luck of having been born into the nobility or as the result of anonymous denunciations.

It was becoming clear that Robespierre and his allies had lost control of the Terror that they had set in motion. Robespierre himself seemed, to those around him, in the grip of paranoid suspicion. The Committee of Public Safety justified the executions with the argument that France's very success in defeating foreign enemies had given it the freedom to eliminate future internal threats and conspiracies. But in the Convention, many deputies

Thermidorian Reaction In this engraving from around 1794, chaos erupts at the National Convention as delegates fight one another and a group rushes to the podium to seize Robespierre.

feared for their lives, especially after Robespierre, on July 26, denounced a "conspiracy against public liberty" involving deputies yet to be named.

The very next day—9 Thermidor under the new calendar—numerous deputies, including several members of the Committee, finally attacked Robespierre on the floor of the Convention. Scores of others, seeing a chance for safety, joined in and managed to pass a motion calling for the arrest of Robespierre, Saint-Just, and their allies. The leaders of the *sans-culotte* movement tried to organize a new insurrection against the Convention in support of Robespierre, but the events of the previous year had weakened them, and their efforts succeeded only in giving the Convention a pretext to declare the Robespierrist deputies "outlaws," subject to immediate execution. Robespierre attempted to commit suicide but managed only to shoot himself in the jaw. The next day—July 28, 1794, by the Christian calendar—he and his allies went to the guillotine in their turn. The Terror was over, and with it the most radical phase of the French Revolution. The next phase of the Revolution would be known as the **"Thermidorian Reaction."**

THE MEANING OF THE TERROR

Ever since the Ninth of Thermidor, the Terror has appalled and amazed even sympathetic observers. Some have echoed Edmund Burke, seeing in it proof that the

French Revolution contained the seeds of tyranny and slaughter within it from the start—and that, perhaps, all radical revolutions do. Others view the Terror as an unfortunate deviation from the true spirit of the Revolution, as embodied, for instance, in the Declaration of Rights of 1789. And still others defend it as a necessary measure of self-defense by a revolution besieged on all sides by deadly enemies. Looking back in 1819, the great Swiss writer Benjamin Constant blamed the Terror on the revolutionaries' romantic but misguided desire to recover the "liberty of the ancients"—the practices of direct democracy and public austerity that they had read about in Greek and Roman authors, and that they saw as the key to "regenerating" a supposedly corrupt, effeminate, and weak society, even at the cost of individual rights. Such practices, Constant lectured, made no sense in modern commercial civilizations, in which individuals were far less willing to give up their individual rights and possessions in the name of the common good. Attempting to squeeze modern citizens into ancient molds could only cause frustration, resistance, and, if pushed too far, bloodshed.

Constant's interpretation of the Revolution remains one of the most powerful ever devised. Yet at the same time, he underplayed the Revolution's most important modern aspect, namely, the role of the French common people—urban artisans and shopkeepers, peasants and villagers—who had done as much as any learned deputy to drive events forward. In this, they did not resemble earlier generations of European lower-class rebels, who had generally fought either for a religious cause or to protest excessive rents or taxes. The French of 1789, like the Americans of 1776, fought for explicitly modern political goals—above all, those expressed by the two transcendent words "liberty" and "equality." In doing so, ordinary French people forced the wealthier and better-educated members of the Assemblies to adopt policies more radical than anyone had dreamed of before the Revolution. So in the end, the Terror stemmed not only from the dynamic of radicalization discussed above but also from the failure of successive revolutionary governments to contain the awesome political forces unleashed by the people of France themselves.

THE INTERNATIONAL SYSTEM DISRUPTED

The radical Revolution and the Terror had effects that spread far beyond France. It permanently disrupted the international system, which had been based on balance-of-power politics and restrained warfare since the reign of Louis XIV (r. 1643–1715). From as early as 1790, leading revolutionaries in France such as Brissot had extended the principle of popular sovereignty to international affairs, insisting that the will of the people trumped existing treaty law, even in determining international boundaries. They were proclaiming what would become known as the principle of "self-determination," and they implemented it by allowing the populations of various conquered territories to vote on whether they wanted to become part of France. Following the former papal territory of Avignon in southeastern France and the Piedmontese coastal city of Nice, a "Rhenish-German National Convention," governing western German territories conquered by French troops, also successfully appealed for annexation to France in March 1793.

The political initiative in the Rhineland came from groups—mostly middle-class journalists, lawyers, and clerics—who enthusiastically founded political clubs on the French Jacobin model. Scores of similar clubs sprung up throughout Germany, as well as in Italy, and as far afield as Poland, Greece, and Spain. In Britain and the United States, radical political societies "affiliated" themselves with the Jacobins, and even in India, French mercenaries in the service of the sultan of Mysore, an opponent of British expansion in the subcontinent, founded a Jacobin club. An international revolutionary movement, the first of its kind, was taking shape, and many of its members flocked to Paris, fervently proclaiming their belief in universal brotherhood and the coming end of all international divisions.

Yet these radical actions provoked equally radical reactions on the part of the states aligned against France. Now there was to be no question of limited warfare and balance-of-power politics. Each side was committing itself to the destruction of the enemies' political regimes. The French proclaimed as their slogan "peace to the cottages, war on the palaces." Now there would be no toleration of domestic opponents—"enemies within"— and when Prussia reoccupied the Rhineland capital of Mainz in the summer of 1793, it ferociously persecuted the local Jacobins in what amounted to a

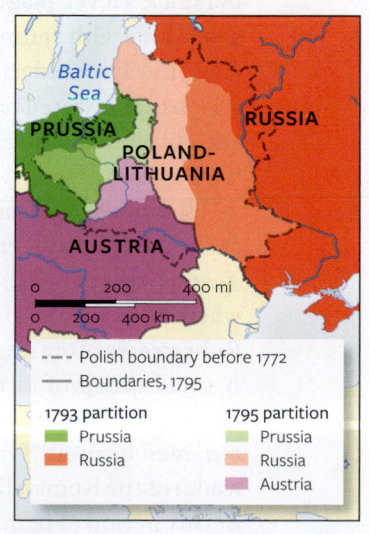

Second and Third Partitions of Poland, 1793–1795

reverse Terror, although with a much smaller body count. And far from respecting national "self-determination," the central European powers took advantage of the war and disruption to gobble up new territory. Following Russia's defeat of Poland-Lithuania in 1792 and the dismantling of its liberal reforms, Prussia joined with Catherine the Great in carrying out a second, drastic partition of the Polish state. Afterward, only a third of the pre-1772 Polish population still lived under Polish sovereignty. And two years later, in a third and final partition, independent Poland-Lithuania would cease to exist altogether, only to be reborn more than a century later, after World War I.

THE DIRECTORY AND RISE OF NAPOLEON BONAPARTE (1795–1799)

Even before the fall of Robespierre on the Ninth of Thermidor (July 27, 1794), the popular forces that had done so much to spur revolutionary radicalization had suffered significant setbacks. But the men who took power on that date were even less tolerant than the Mountain of what they saw as dangerously anarchic and uncontrollable crowds. Their hostility quickly provoked an uprising by the remnants of the *sans-culottes*, who were also angered by a new bout of hyperinflation and food shortages in the spring of 1795. The so-called Thermidorians responded with a brutal military crackdown, breaking the movement forever, with hundreds sent to the guillotine or into exile in France's fever-plagued South American colony of Guyana. Along with ending the Terror and closing the Jacobin Club, the Thermidorians drew up yet another new constitution that restored property qualifications for voters and thereby ended France's brief experiment with universal manhood suffrage.

Hundreds of former Jacobin activists fell victim to an anarchic "White Terror" (as opposed to the radical "Red Terror" of 1793–94), particularly in southern France, where the settling of political scores from the period of Robespierre often degenerated into pure revenge-killing. A small group of ultra-revolutionaries, led by a former clerk named François-Noël Babeuf (1760–1797), who had renamed himself "Gracchus" Babeuf after the plebeian leader of the Roman Republic, also plotted to seize power in this period. Their plans called for communal ownership of all property. But the plotters were discovered and arrested. Babeuf died on the guillotine, and the last echoes of the radical revolution died with him.

THE DIRECTORY

The Thermidorians did not break with the revolutionary tradition altogether. When resurgent royalists tried to seize power in the fall of 1795, the Thermidorians responded every bit as brutally as they had done to the *sans-culottes*. A young army officer named Napoleon Bonaparte (1769–1821) made a reputation for ruthlessness by confronting an unruly crowd in central Paris and, so it was later claimed, ordering them dispersed with grapeshot (bullets and scrap metal fired from cannon at point-blank range). The regime the Thermidorians created in late 1795, called the "**Directory**" after its new five-man executive, remained very much a republic. When royalists who wanted to put Louis XVI's younger brother on the throne gained a majority in parliamentary elections in 1797, republican "directors" staged a coup with military backing, purging their enemies from all branches of the government.

The leading politicians and intellectuals associated with the Directory remained committed to republican ideas and did much to foster their development in France. But it was in war that the Directory showed its greatest commitment to continuing the Revolution, and also where revolutionary popular energy now expressed itself most strikingly. Many of the hundreds of thousands of young men drafted into the army in 1793 remained in uniform through the late 1790s, and with seasoning they became the most fearsome military force in Europe. Having eliminated threats to French territory in the spring of 1794, this revolutionary army conquered present-day Belgium and then pressed northward. In January 1795, the ruler of the Netherlands fled to Britain, and the French armies established a new regime there, with a constitution and institutions partly copied from France. In April, Prussia bowed out of the war in order to concentrate on its expansion to the east. Spain, which had lost a series of bloody encounters in the Pyrenees, made peace with France in July. Only Britain and Austria, of the major powers, were left in what we now call the "Revolutionary Wars."

THE RISE OF NAPOLEON BONAPARTE

In the spring of 1796, the Directory launched a triple thrust at Austria through central Germany, southern Germany, and northern Italy. The last of these attacks, involving only 38,000 French soldiers, was meant mostly as a diversion. No one in Paris expected much of the ill-fed and ill-equipped troops or of their commander, the inexperienced, twenty-seven-year-old **Napoleon Bonaparte**. It was not merely his youth that made him an unlikely French general. He had been born on the island of Corsica, to a minor noble family, just a year after France annexed it in 1768. He was slender and poorly dressed, had long greasy hair, and spoke with a thick Corsican accent. But he quickly proved a tremendous surprise to both his sponsors and his enemies.

After making heroic efforts to provide his tattered army with proper food and supplies, he invaded Italy in April and in a series of brilliant small battles crushed Austria's minor ally, Piedmont. He then carried out an ingenious campaign of maneuvers against the Austrians themselves, occupying the heart of northern Italy. In January 1797 the French won the crucial battle of Rivoli, forcing the Austrians to abandon the strategic citadel of Mantua, and by April Napoleon's men had crossed into the Austrian Alps and come within seventy-five miles of Vienna itself. Forced to the peace table, the Austrians allowed the French to set up dependent "sister republics" in northern Italy and to annex new territories to France itself. In scarcely more than a year, Napoleon had established the sort of dominance over the Italian peninsula that French rulers had been longing for, without success, since the fifteenth century. In doing so, he immediately established himself not merely as the most popular of French generals but as the most popular political figure in France itself.

A MODERN CAESAR In the politics of the revolutionary era, Napoleon represented something very new. Unlike Robespierre or Saint-Just, with their cold, high abstractions about national regeneration, he was a true populist who mixed easily with common soldiers and delighted in the nickname given him after he had allegedly helped aim artillery pieces himself during one of his Italian battles: "the little corporal." Unlike earlier revolutionary populists such as Mirabeau and Danton, he managed to present himself as above and removed from petty political squabbling—as a soldier who had risked his life for the Republic and cared solely about the common good. But unlike other French generals who had ventured into revolutionary politics, he also recognized the importance of not basing his appeal entirely on his military record. Since the earliest days of the French Revolution, astute observers—with the example of Rome very much in their minds—had expressed concerns that a new Caesar might arise to build a tyrannical empire on the ruins of the Republic. Napoleon cannily defused such fears by joining the civilian National Institute (a center for scholarship)

Revolutionary Wars, 1791–1799 After the battle of Valmy in 1792, France's wars with its European neighbors turned in its favor. Despite British naval blockades and Prussian and Austrian military opposition, France conquered several territories in the Rhineland, the Low Countries, and the Alps, and helped to install a republic in the Netherlands. Napoleon's brilliant campaigns later in the 1790s drove the Austrians from Italy. In addition to occupying Piedmont and Tuscany in 1799, the French established dependent "sister republics" throughout the Italian Peninsula.

and appearing at its public lectures in civilian clothes. In politics, he carefully navigated the treacherous politics of the Revolution, mostly by siding with the moderate republicans who had carried out the antiroyalist coup in 1797.

Napoleon also amounted to the world's first "media general." He sponsored newspapers to report on his and his army's exploits—including one called *Journal of Bonaparte and Virtuous Men*. He encouraged poets and playwrights to celebrate his victories. Several popular biographies embroidered his already-spectacular career by adding such feats as strategic victories in schoolboy snowball fights and

The Young Napoleon An 1801 portrait by Antoine-Jean Gros depicts Napoleon as a romanticized military hero, with flowing unkempt hair and wielding a banner and a sword, during a 1796 battle against Austrian forces.

an epic balloon flight over Paris at age fifteen. As early as 1797, Napoleon appeared in scores of widely circulated popular engravings and the greatest painters of the day painted him as a glorious leader, his face shining with confidence as he led exultant troops into battle. "He flies like lightning, and strikes like thunder," wrote one over-excited journalist. "He is everywhere. He sees everything. Like a comet cleaving the clouds, he appears at the same moment on the astonished banks of two separate rivers." Police spies in Paris regularly reported on the "flood of praise" that the young general received from the common people of the

capital. In his conquest of public opinion, he was aided by his glamorous wife, the aristocratic Joséphine de Beauharnais (1763–1814) whose first husband had died during the Terror.

THE EGYPTIAN CAMPAIGN For a time, Napoleon resisted temptations to put himself forth as a political leader. He judged the time not ripe. Instead, he decided to start a military campaign that might even eclipse his Italian victories. For some time, French strategists had dreamed of establishing a colony in Egypt to threaten Britain's supply routes to India and to start building a new colonial empire to replace the one they had lost to Britain in the 1760s. Napoleon easily gained the support of the Directory for the campaign, as the politicians in Paris already feared he might try to exploit his popularity by making a bid for power and were happy to see him leave the country.

In the summer of 1798, Napoleon landed with 25,000 men near the Egyptian city of Alexandria. The Mameluke military caste that ruled Egypt in the name of the decaying Ottoman Empire posed little serious resistance to him, and after a gruesome forced march of 120 miles through the North African heat, his men smashed the Mameluke army in a battle carried out within sight of the ancient pyramids. Napoleon, who became head of the new colony, made an effort to create enlightened Egyptian political institutions on the European model, while also founding hospitals and redistributing land to the peasantry. He also set to work 160 artists, scientists, and scholars he had brought with him from France. Among their achievements was the discovery of the Rosetta Stone, the ancient stele inscribed with a royal decree from 196 BCE that first enabled scholars to decipher the ancient Egyptian writing system known as hieroglyphs. The Egyptian campaign marked a new French commitment to overseas empire that would have important consequences

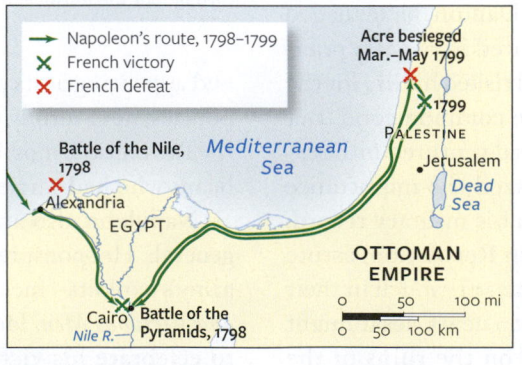

Napoleon's Egyptian Campaign, 1798–1799

for the nineteenth-century age of imperialism.

In the end, the Egyptian campaign turned into a fiasco. In a crucial naval battle on August 1, 1798, the British destroyed much of the French fleet, cutting off the newly born French colony from its supply base. Napoleon launched a campaign along the coast of Palestine to forestall an Ottoman attempt to retake their former possession, but failed to capture the crucial fortress of Acre (near present-day Haifa in Israel) and lost thousands of his troops to plague. Although he beat a Turkish army (and murdered hundreds of Turkish prisoners whom he had no means of caring for), he soon retreated to Cairo.

News of these failures took time to arrive in France, however, and the Napoleonic legend remained powerful. Indeed, in the winter and spring of 1798–99 it grew ever greater, as the French Republic seemed once again to totter on the edge of collapse. Not only did the unstable Directory experience two more coups by beleaguered directors against their own colleagues and legislature, but they could not even maintain basic law and order. In desperation, the Directory gave significant power to the military in close to 40 percent of French territory.

FURTHER FRENCH REVERSES

Meanwhile, across the territories conquered in Italy, Germany, and the Low Countries, revolts broke out against French rule. A new allied coalition, with Russia adding its forces to those of Austria and Britain, drove the French back in Switzerland and the Netherlands. French territory itself seemed in danger, leading to calls for a renewal of the Terror. A law enacted by the Directory in 1798 created the first regular system of conscription in French history, institutionalizing the revolutionary concept of the people's army.

The French also failed in an attempt to cripple Great Britain by gaining a foothold in Ireland. There the hopeful echoes of the French Revolution had combined with resentment on the part of the disenfranchised Catholic majority to foster the emergence of a revolutionary society known as the United Irishmen, who wished to "break the connection with England." By 1797, it counted some 200,000 members. The British government carried out a very effective campaign of repression, spying upon and imprisoning suspected rebels, and the Royal Navy prevented a French fleet from landing in southern Ireland in 1796. But in 1798 a rebellion broke out, aided by a contingent of 1,000 French soldiers who landed in the northwest of the island. The Navy again prevented a larger contingent of French troops from arriving, and within months the rebellion had failed. The leader of the United Irishmen, Theobald Wolfe Tone (1763–1798), committed suicide in prison before his scheduled execution. Following the rebellion, in an attempt to bind Ireland more firmly to Great Britain, the British and Irish parliaments would pass Acts of Union in 1800, creating the United Kingdom of Great Britain and Ireland. The French had lost their best chance of undermining the British war effort.

A MILITARY COUP

It was in the context of the French failures across Europe that Bonaparte left Egypt in the late summer of 1799, slipped past the British blockade, and landed back on the southern coast of France. As he headed north to Paris, crowds cheered him at every stop, and at Lyons the local theater celebrated him with a play entitled *The Return of the Hero*. Once in Paris in mid-October 1799, he quickly entered into a conspiracy with Emmanuel Sieyès, the early hero of the Revolution, who had survived the Terror and reemerged as a cynical and unscrupulous Director. The Directory, they agreed, should be terminated. Its assemblies should be prompted to dissolve themselves and place power in the hands of three interim "consuls": Napoleon, Sieyès, and a nonentity named Roger Ducos. Although several capable generals had driven back the new enemy coalition without any help from Napoleon, the plotters still judged the national crisis severe enough that the public—and especially wealthy property-owners—would support leaders committed to stability and security above all else. And Napoleon could also count on the support of the army, whose long-serving soldiers had grown increasingly disgusted with the Republic's endemic bickering and corruption.

The coup began on November 9, 1799—18 Brumaire under the new calendar. In the event, it did not take place with the smoothness Napoleon and Sieyès had hoped for. The lower house of the parliament refused to dissolve itself, and Napoleon, for once, found himself able to do little but bluster: "Don't forget, I walk with the God of war and the God of victory!" Instead of cheering, the deputies protested loudly, forcing him to flee the assembly and send soldiers in to clear out the hall ("Citizens," his subordinate Joachim Murat bellowed to them, "you are dissolved!"). The remaining handful cooperated with Napoleon's demands, but this did not change the fact that the coup had taken on a military character. For the first time in French history, the army had acted to put a general in power.

CONCLUSION

Napoleon himself continued to pose as a civilian leader and quickly gained the support of a large part of the population, especially as he acted effectively to restore law and order. Nonetheless, his coming to power marked the final extinguishing of the democratic flame that had burst out so brightly with the calling of the Estates General and the storming of the Bastille in 1789. Other aspects of the French Revolution would endure under his rule. These included civic equality, the end of the seigneurial system in the countryside, the confiscation of Church lands, the institution of religious toleration, and the administrative reforms that accompanied the breaking up of the old provinces. But many of the rights so proudly accorded to "man and citizen" in 1789 would now disappear, including

freedom of the press and the right of the people to choose their own rulers. And from now on, what was left of the popular enthusiasm that had expressed itself so forcefully at the taking of the Bastille would be channeled above all in one direction: military conquest. As the year 1799 came to an end, the French Revolution did as well. The chapter of European history now beginning would be one of total war.

[CHAPTER REVIEW]

KEY TERMS

Bastille (p. 540)
Louis XVI (p. 542)
What Is the Third Estate?
    (p. 544)
National Assembly (p. 545)
Tennis Court Oath (p. 545)
"Great Fear" (p. 547)

Declaration of the Rights
    of Man and Citizen
    (p. 547)
Edmund Burke (p. 550)
Jacobins (p. 553)
Maximilien Robespierre
    (p. 553)
sans-culottes (p. 554)

Girondins (p. 554)
National Convention
    (p. 555)
September Massacres
    (p. 556)
Vendée (p. 557)
The Mountain (p. 558)

Committee of Public
    Safety (p. 559)
Reign of Terror (p. 560)
Thermidorian Reaction
    (p. 562)
Directory (p. 564)
Napoleon Bonaparte
    (p. 565)

REVIEW QUESTIONS

1. How did long-term changes in French society and culture, combined with a shorter-term fiscal crisis, bring France to the point of revolution in 1789?

2. How did the meeting of the French Estates General in 1789 result in the formation of a National Assembly?

3. How did the National Assembly transform the nature of the Revolution?

4. From 1789 to 1791, in what ways did the French Revolution prove to be an event of international significance?

5. In what ways did the political culture of pre-revolutionary France, as well as the very nature of revolutionary politics, lead to violence?

6. What movements within the Revolution and the counterrevolution developed beginning in 1791?

7. How did the *sans-culottes* shape the Revolution?

8. What atrocities took place during the Reign of Terror, and in what ways did it succeed in preserving the Revolution?

9. How did the Revolution transform the model of warfare and diplomacy that had prevailed in Europe over most of the eighteenth century?

10. In the later 1790s, how did Napoleon Bonaparte establish himself as a popular political figure as well as a military leader?

CORE OBJECTIVES

After reading this chapter, you should have a solid understanding of the following core objectives. To strengthen your grasp of the core objectives, use the resources on the Student Site for The West.

- Analyze the origins of the French Revolution.
- Explain the radicalization of the French Revolution during its first few years.
- Evaluate the crises that shook the First French Republic.

- Describe the Reign of Terror and its consequences.
- Trace the establishment of the Directory and Napoleon Bonaparte's rise to power.

GO TO inQuizitive TO SEE WHAT YOU'VE LEARNED—AND LEARN WHAT YOU'VE MISSED—WITH PERSONALIZED FEEDBACK ALONG THE WAY.

1800
Napoleon creates first
French National Bank

1800
Napoleon's second
Italian Campaign

1804
Napoleon proclaimed
emperor of France

1804
Civil (Napoleonic)
Code established

1804
Republic of Haiti
gains independence

1806
Napoleon devises
Continental System

1806
End of Holy
Roman Empire

1808–1814
Peninsular War
in Iberia

1813
"Battle of the
Nations" at Leipzig

1814–1815
Congress of Vienna;
Napoleon exiled
to Elba

1814
Bourbon Restoration
in France

1803
Louisiana Purchase

1805
Battle of Trafalgar

1805
Austria, Russia, Britain
form coalition against France

1805
Battle of Austerlitz

1807
Battle of Eylau

1807
Treaties of Tilsit

1812
Napoleon's
Russian campaign

1812–1815
War of 1812 between
Great Britain and
United States

1815
The Hundred Days;
battle of Waterloo

1815
Napoleon exiled
to Saint Helena

The Age of Napoleon

EMPIRE AND RESISTANCE

1799–1820

I n December 1812, a twenty-four-year-old soldier from southern Germany named Jakob Walter stumbled in retreat westward across the border of the Russian Empire. Soon afterward, he caught sight of himself in a mirror and could not recognize the person who stared back at him. "The crusts on my hands, ears and nose had grown like fir-bark, with cracks and coal black scales," he recalled much later in life. "My face resembled that of a heavily bearded Russian peasant." Yet as Walter, a former stonemason, knew well, he was lucky to be alive. Just six months earlier, he had marched into Russia as one of over 650,000 soldiers whom Napoleon Bonaparte, emperor of France, had gathered into the Grand Army—the largest yet seen in European history. Less than a third were French; some 160,000 were Germans like Walter, from states allied to France. They marched hundreds of miles, in oppressive heat, through country stripped bare by their retreating Russian foes and the fleeing Russian peasantry. Walter would later recall that the desperately hungry soldiers did not even stop to cook a hog when they caught it, but ate the flesh raw, while drinking slimy, worm-infested water that they filtered as best they could through their handkerchiefs.

Napoleon himself did not want to occupy Russia, but to destroy its army and make it a pliable ally. But the Russian army retreated ahead of him. When the French finally

The Emperor Napoleon In this 1808 painting by Antoine-Jean Gros, Napoleon surveys the battlefield upon his narrow victory against the Russians and Prussians at Eylau in 1807. Despite the dead and maimed piled in the foreground, the work seems to glorify the emperor: a ray of sunlight shines on him, and wounded enemy soldiers reach out to him for mercy.

- What were the most important reforms enacted by Napoleon?
- How did Napoleon's conquests remake the map of Europe?
- What were the sources of resistance to Napoleon's empire?
- What were the main effects of the Napoleonic era?
- What were the pivotal events in Napoleon's downfall?
- How did the Concert of Europe attempt to bring the Napoleonic era to a close?
- What major political and social changes were reflected in the Europe of 1815?

At the start of his Russian campaign in 1812, Napoleon Bonaparte had been at the apex of his power. In the almost uninterrupted series of wars he had fought since coming to power in 1799, he had vastly increased the territory of France, crowned himself its emperor, and defeated his major continental rivals. He had become arguably the greatest European conqueror since Alexander the Great in the fourth century BCE, outdoing even Julius Caesar and Charlemagne. But he could not defeat Great Britain, which had decimated his navy and tried to strangle French trade. In fact, it was Napoleon's vain attempt to close the European continent to British trade that ultimately led him toward the disastrous invasion of Russia.

The Russian catastrophe did not by itself spell the end of Napoleon's empire. His remarkable military talent, the institutions he had forged, and the wealth he had accumulated allowed him to survive as emperor for another two years and to come close to defeating his enemies yet again. But ultimately he fell from power (twice, as we will see). France lost its conquests, and the Bourbon dynasty toppled by the French Revolution returned to the throne.

Although historians often downplay the story of Napoleon's epic rise and fall, in fact the Napoleonic adventure led to many important changes and deserves close attention. The wars that reached their climax in the Russian campaign can be considered an early example of "total war"—one that drives entire nations, including their civilian populations, toward ever-greater mobilization, with the goal of utterly destroying an enemy. Indeed, the year 1812 marked a highpoint in the occurrence of organized violence throughout the Western world that would not be matched again for a century. The Napoleonic Wars not only exacted a massive human toll but also forced the victors—above all, Britain, Russia, and Austria—to realize that competition among states could no longer be trusted to remain within the bounds of eighteenth-century "balance of power" politics. From now on, maintaining peace would depend on continuous management of international disputes by a "concert"—a formal system of close cooperation—among great powers.

notched up a major victory outside Moscow in early September, the bulk of the Russian force escaped. The French occupied Moscow, but as they did much of the city burned to the ground—most likely an act of Russian arson that went out of control. Napoleon himself would later recall: "It was the spectacle of a sea and billows of fire, a sky and clouds of flame—mountains of red rolling flames,…" It left the city largely uninhabitable, and after several weeks of dithering Napoleon decided to march back west.

There followed one of the most epic disasters in the history of warfare. Winter had come early. Snow, wind, and sub-zero temperatures assaulted soldiers who lacked proper coats and boots, and often had no tents to shelter in. Frostbite, disease, and starvation took ferocious tolls. Men went to sleep next to their comrades and woke up to find a field of snow-covered corpses. When horses died—and Napoleon lost some 200,000 of them during the campaign—they were immediately stripped for meat, after which the wounded took shelter in the still-steaming carcasses. On November 23, 1812, the Russians caught up to Napoleon's weakened force at the Berezina River, in modern Belarus. As panicked crowds of Grand Army soldiers and supporters rushed onto makeshift bridges, one bridge collapsed, sending hundreds into the freezing water. By the time Jakob Walter saw his transformed face in the mirror a month later, more than half the 650,000 men of the original force had died.

The wars also spurred the development of national independence movements that would flourish over the following decades, challenging the great multinational empires that had dominated the map of Europe before the French Revolution. By 1820, the revolutionary idea that Europeans should live in national states, whose governments' legitimacy derived at least in part from the consent of their citizens, had become widespread. The wars also shook the Spanish and Portuguese empires to the core and helped spread the national idea beyond Europe, notably to Latin America. They confirmed the supremacy of one great power—Great Britain—that would dominate the Continent in the nineteenth century while carving out for itself an unprecedented, worldwide empire. Finally, the wars marked the period in which a powerful new cultural movement, now known as romanticism, began to emerge.

This chapter will concentrate on Napoleon's rise and fall, and the immediate aftermath. It will also track the changes that continued in the shadow of the wars, particularly in the lives of ordinary men and women. And it will suggest that by 1820, these ordinary lives were becoming caught up in powerful new social, economic, and political forces that European elites were desperate to bring under control.

NAPOLEON BONAPARTE IN POWER (1799–1804)

The upheavals of this period, like those of the earlier revolutionary decade, had their center in France. They were tightly bound up with the continuing warfare that, by 1799, had raged over the Continent for seven years. And, to a degree unequaled in European history before or since, they revolved around a single man. Napoleon's formal rule began with the coup d'état that brought him to power in 1799 and ended with his abdication in 1815, but it took at least until 1820 for a post-Napoleonic order to stabilize.

EFFORTS TO RESTORE FRANCE'S INTERNATIONAL POSITION

Although other generals had removed the immediate threats to French territory even before Napoleon took power, he realized quite well that he would not remain long in power unless he restored France to the commanding position it had held before the military debacles of 1798–99.

ITALY In the spring of 1800, Napoleon decided to lead an invasion of northern Italy to gain back the territories he had first won in his electric campaign of 1796–97. In a

daring move, he decided to cross the Alps over the high, treacherous St. Bernard Pass, putting his army at risk in the hope of surprising the Austrians who had reoccupied the northern Italian plain. The French made it through, despite bitter cold, with Napoleon himself crossing on a mule, swathed in heavy blankets. Months went by without news of any obvious success, and in the French capital ambitious politicians and generals started to speculate on who might seize power next, if Napoleon failed.

But he did not fail. His army made it into Italy intact, surprising the Austrians and defeating them decisively at the Battle of Marengo. And Napoleon knew well how to exploit such a victory, organizing writers and artists to hail him as the hero of the new century and the savior of the French Republic. In Jacques-Louis David's great painting of him crossing the Alps, the heavy blankets are nowhere to be seen and a magnificent, rearing horse has taken the place of the mule. Napoleon himself, astride the horse, seems to command the very wind. By 1801, Austria had limped out of the war altogether, allowing France to

Crossing the Alps Painted in 1800–1801, Jacques-Louis David's portrait shows Napoleon—atop a horse, not a mule—leading his army across the Alps on his daring invasion of Italy. At bottom left, a stone engraved with "Bonaparte" lies ahead of rocks inscribed with the names of Hannibal and Charlemagne, casting Napoleon as the greatest conqueror of all.

establish a new satellite state in northern Italy and leaving Napoleon securely in power.

HAITI Outside of Italy, Napoleon did not immediately do so well. He had dreamed of retaking the wealthy Caribbean sugar colony of Saint-Domingue (modern-day Haiti), which had experienced the massive slave revolt of 1791. By 1801, the charismatic Haitian general Toussaint Louverture (1743–1803), while theoretically loyal to France, had established an autonomous regime there with its own constitution. To reassert firmer French control, in 1801 Napoleon dispatched an expeditionary force that succeeded in taking Louverture prisoner and deporting him to France, where he died in captivity. But yellow fever decimated the French army, forcing Napoleon to abandon his plans and to acquiesce, in 1804, in the colony's independence. The new nation took the name of the Republic of Haiti—the second independent state in the Americas after the United States, and the first independent black state.

As a result of the defeat, Napoleon also gave up on the idea of developing the Louisiana Territory of North America, which he had reacquired from Spain in 1800 and had hoped to use in large part as a supply base for Saint-Domingue. When representatives from the United States approached him with proposals to purchase New Orleans, he surprised them by offering the entire 530 million acres—nearly a third of the present-day continental United States—and eventually parted with it all for the sum of $15 million. France did retain the smaller Caribbean islands of Guadeloupe and Martinique. There, in 1802, Napoleon reversed the French Revolution's 1794 emancipation decree and forced free blacks back into slavery.

THE CONSULATE OF 1799–1804

Napoleon accomplished a great deal domestically during his first years in power. Shunting aside his partners in the 1799 coup, he asserted strong executive power as first consul and built upon emergency legislation of the previous Directory government to impose law and order with a heavy hand. He increased police powers and surveillance and dispensed harsh punishments, but dealt magnanimously with those former rebels who were willing to cooperate. The tactics proved effective at quelling the low-level revolts, brigandage, and simple disobedience that had plagued the country before his coup. In keeping with this increased social control, he imposed the strictest censorship in French history and reduced the number of Parisian newspapers to four, from the hundreds that had appeared during the Revolution.

Drawing liberally on precedents from the Old Regime monarchy and eighteenth-century theories of "enlightened despotism," he developed a streamlined and centralized state administration. It placed government firmly in the hands of highly trained bureaucrats drawn from France's social elites, including "prefects" who would now govern each of France's "departments." Napoleon also worked to stabilize French finances, notably by creating the country's first permanent National Bank in 1800. He introduced a new constitution that confirmed his own executive role, although it also allowed for a three-chamber legislature. This body was theoretically elected by universal manhood suffrage, but the choice of representatives in practice lay largely in the hands of men loyal to Napoleon.

NAPOLEON'S CIVIL CODE Napoleon and his collaborators also began to prepare a revised, efficient national legal code to replace the patchwork quilt of laws inherited from the Old Regime. The new **Civil Code** (also known as the Napoleonic Code) reaffirmed the Revolution's abolition of formal social privilege and confirmed its large-scale transfer of property (especially Church lands) to new owners, including many peasants. In other respects, however, it was socially conservative. It greatly restricted the rights of women within marriage—for instance, by requiring that women receive their husbands' permission to work or to travel abroad. (The Code did not, however, repeal the revolutionary legislation that had introduced divorce.) In the same conservative vein, Napoleon negotiated a new agreement with the Vatican that recognized Catholicism as the dominant religion in France, although it stopped short of reestablishing it as an official religion. In short, Napoleon preserved some important features of the revolutionary heritage—especially formal legal equality of adult males—while also bringing back important aspects of the Old Regime. "I am the French Revolution," he boasted at one point. But he would also remark: "I picked the crown of France out of the gutter, and placed it on my head."

EMPEROR OF THE FRENCH In accomplishing all these tasks within less than five years, Napoleon impressed all who met him with his apparently boundless energy and intelligence. Rising at dawn, he would generally work straight through until eight or nine in the evening, sleep until midnight, wake up, and work an additional three or four hours. He could keep details of hundreds of military units, or provisions of laws, in his head and may indeed have had a photographic memory. As one of his subordinates remarked many years later, after he had led the French to disaster: "What a pity the man wasn't lazy."

The reforms Napoleon introduced quickly earned him real popularity among a French people left exhausted by political and social disorder. In fact, he was so popular that he did not even need to cheat to win several plebiscites (referendums) designed to legitimize his rule between 1800 and 1804. He did so anyway, and in one of them he supposedly received 3,000,000 "yes" votes and only 1,500 "noes." In 1802, he changed his title from "first consul" to "consul for life," and asserted the right to appoint a successor—a monarch in all but name. Two years later his tame Senate, one chamber of the new legislature, added the name by proclaiming him emperor. In the Paris cathedral of Notre Dame, now restored as a church from the godless "Temple of Reason" established there by the revolutionaries less than ten years before, the pope himself took part in an elaborate ceremony crowning Napoleon emperor of the French. Turning to his brother at one point in the festivities, Napoleon whispered, in his native Italian: "If only Papa could see us now."

FAILED ATTEMPTS AT PEACE

In all these early reforms, Napoleon seemed intent on demonstrating that despite his military origins, he did not want to establish a military regime. His prefects and other top officials came mostly from civilian life, and he actually reduced the role of the army in maintaining law and order. He also attempted, between 1800 and 1803, to bring about a permanent European peace settlement. During this short period, he not only made peace with Austria but also negotiated treaties with the United States, Spain, Austria, Naples, Bavaria, Portugal, Russia, and the Ottoman Empire. And on March 25, 1802, he signed the Peace of Amiens with Great Britain, France's strongest and most determined opponent. For the first time in nearly a decade, Europe's guns fell silent.

But the peace did not last, and Napoleon's principal legacy remains one of bloodshed. True, his new administrative system forms the basis of French government to this day and has been widely imitated around the world. The same is true for his Napoleonic Code, which serves as the foundation for law codes in dozens of countries. The Code represents a rationalized, simplified version of Roman law and has particularly appealed to societies seeking to combine a strong centralized power with a recognition of equality before the law. But despite these achievements, Napoleon knew that staying in power would require more

The Corsican Spider In 1808, a British cartoonist satirized Napoleon's imperial ambitions by depicting him as a spider who has subdued most of the states of continental Europe like flies in his web. The Russian Fly and Turkish Fly (bottom) are afraid they will be dragged in as well, but the British Fly (top left) proudly insists, "I am not to be caught in your web."

than just thoroughgoing and popular domestic reform. "My power is dependent on my glory, and my glory on my victories," he once keenly remarked. "My power would fail if I did not base it on still more glory and still more victories."

But it was not just Napoleon's own thirst for glory that ensured the continuation of the European wars. Despite his coronation, relatively few Europeans outside of France perceived him as a legitimate ruler. In Britain in particular, he was still seen as "a stranger, a foreigner, and an usurper," to quote Prime Minister William Pitt (1759–1806) in 1800. The British remembered with fury that France had aided the rebellion against British rule in Ireland in 1798, which led Pitt two years later to dissolve Ireland's parliament and pass Acts of Union in 1800 to merge the country entirely into the "United Kingdom." The threat of French Jacobinism remained a strong presence in British politics, spurring both a powerful conservative turn and an upsurge of patriotism. The British press, meanwhile, railed with such vitriol against the "Corsican Ogre" that Napoleon protested to the British government and demanded the suppression of the offending articles.

The resumption of peace in 1802 therefore failed to end the tremendous hostility and suspicion that had characterized European international relations since 1789. While wealthy Britons flocked to Paris to catch up on a decade of French fashion, Napoleon continued to seethe against British plots. Meanwhile, the British protested France's continued military presence in the Netherlands, Napoleon's actions in the Caribbean, and his annexation of additional territories in Italy beyond the "natural frontier" of the Alps. Such disputes were inevitable, given how greatly the French Revolution had altered European borders after more than a century of slow, incremental change. And Napoleon continued to push for territorial reorganization, especially along his eastern frontier in Germany. Between 1800 and 1803, he eliminated most of the tiny statelets that had survived for centuries under the loose umbrella of the Holy Roman Empire, grouping them into larger entities. Not surprisingly, while Napoleon saw this move as a simple consolidation of what was already France's dominant position in Germany, his adversaries, in the prevailing atmosphere of hostility, perceived it as naked aggression.

THE CONQUEST OF EUROPE (1804–1807)

Given all these potential flashpoints, the peace could not hold. In 1803, scarcely a year after the agreement at Amiens, Napoleon decided that a resumption of hostilities was on the horizon. And so he declared war.

THE WHALE AND THE ELEPHANT

As soon as the war started, Britain seized all French ships in British ports, while Napoleon ordered the arrest and internment of all Britons on French soil. He also began to prepare for a full-fledged invasion of the British Isles. In French ports on the English Channel, he ordered the construction of a flotilla of small boats, while in the nearby countryside he assembled and trained an army filled with long-serving, seasoned professionals. With the French economy recovered from its earlier difficulties, and with the government newly streamlined and efficient thanks to Napoleon's reforms, France could make full use of its abundant natural resources and large population—well in excess of 30 million, thanks to the recent annexations.

Napoleon's "Army of England" quickly emerged as the most formidable fighting force seen in Europe in centuries. And yet this great army could not reach its intended target. Great Britain remained under the protection of its own formidable military force, the Royal Navy, which kept the French fleet and its Spanish allies bottled up in port. Without cover from warships, Napoleon's invasion flotilla would have been blasted into so many floating splinters by the British navy. When Napoleon finally ordered the combined French and Spanish navies back to sea in 1805, the British annihilated them off Cape Trafalgar on the Spanish coast. The battle of Trafalgar ensured that Britain would remain safe from invasion and committed to France's defeat: the "whale" facing France's "elephant," as British wits put it.

VICTORY IN CENTRAL EUROPE

But the elephant soon found other enemies it could trample. Even as Napoleon planned his invasion of Britain, tensions had been rising once again with Austria and Russia, thanks above all to the changes Napoleon had engineered in Germany. Napoleon made matters worse in 1804 by sending French agents across the Rhine into the German state of Baden to capture a member of the old French royal family who had been plotting against him. The man's execution horrified public opinion across Europe and led one of Napoleon's counselors to remark famously that the event "was worse than a crime—it was a blunder."

Most horrified of all was the tsar of Russia, Alexander I (r. 1801–1825), who had come to the throne three years previously after the murder of his erratic father by disaffected officers and courtiers (Alexander himself had encouraged the plotters). Just twenty-five years old in 1804, Alexander was an ambitious, reform-minded, but mystically inclined man who believed he had a divine mission to redeem Europe. And although initially an admirer of Napoleon, by 1805 his mistrust of the "Corsican usurper" led him to join with Austria and Britain in a new anti-French coalition.

It was a disastrous decision. On August 23, Napoleon took what had been his Army of England out of its Channel-coast camps and headed toward Germany, marching over 200,000 men as much as thirty-five miles a day. Five weeks later they crossed the Rhine, and by

Invasion of Prussia An 1810 painting propagandistically shows townspeople cheering as Napoleon and his army march under the Brandenburg Gate into the center of Berlin.

mid-October they had reached the Danube. Napoleon was now at the height of his abilities and commanded the best army he was ever to have under his orders. In a complex campaign of brilliant, nimble maneuvers, he succeeded in crushing the Austrian army and occupying Vienna. Then, on the anniversary of his coronation, December 2, 1805, he confronted a combined Austro-Russian force near the small village of **Austerlitz**, in what is now the Czech Republic. Tsar Alexander and Austrian emperor Francis II (r. 1804–1835) were there in person, and Alexander rashly insisted on battle despite the advice of his experienced commander. Napoleon notched up another decisive victory, which left the tsar literally weeping under a tree.

THE REMAKING OF GERMANY After their previous defeats at Napoleon's hands, Austria's Habsburg rulers had survived relatively unscathed, but this time Napoleon showed little mercy. He stripped Austria of its remaining Italian possessions and undertook another round of

territorial organization, forging the midsized western German states into a new organization called the "Confederation of the Rhine," dominated by France. And in the wake of these changes, he insisted on a further, heavily symbolic change. On August 6, 1806, the Holy Roman Empire formally came to an end. Although it had long since ceased to function as a real political unit, it remained, in many eyes, the legitimate heir to the throne of Charlemagne, and beyond that to the Roman Empire itself. Now, for the first time since Augustus, no European sovereign claimed the mantle of universal emperor. More important, in an immediate political sense, the Habsburg emperor lost the influence he had once wielded over Germany through the old institutions of the Holy Roman Empire. Germany had spun out of the orbit of Vienna and fallen into that of Paris.

Napoleon was soaring close to the zenith of his astonishing career but had still not quite reached it, for there remained one last German enemy to defeat. Prussia had remained out of the wars with France since making its separate peace in 1795. Its young and unsteady king, Frederick

William III (r. 1797–1840), had preferred to turn his attention toward Poland, whose heartland (including Warsaw) had fallen under Prussian rule in the successive partitions of 1772, 1793 and 1795, which, as we have seen, had wiped Poland from the map of Europe.

In 1806, with disastrous timing, Frederick William entered into a new coalition with Britain and Russia, which was still hoping to avenge its defeat at Austerlitz. In response, Napoleon took 180,000 superbly trained soldiers into the heart of Germany. He quickly won a pair of battles with overwhelming force and proceeded swiftly to capture one Prussian stronghold after another, finally marching triumphantly into Berlin in early November. Of the 171,000 soldiers that King Frederick William had sent against Napoleon, he lost 25,000 dead or wounded and 140,000 taken prisoner. The campaign had taken less time than Hitler's "Blitzkrieg" against France would take in 1940, and it eventually resulted in Prussia's losing half its territory and subjects, paying massive reparations to France, and seeing its army reduced to a token force. Even before the key battle, one of its witnesses, the German philosopher Georg Friedrich Hegel, wrote in amazement that the entire history of the world had been changed: "The connecting bonds of the world are dissolved and have collapsed like images in a dream."

And yet it took time to bring the Prussians to surrender, and the end of the campaign brought a hint that Napoleon's great streak of fortune might not last forever. The emperor chased the remaining Prussians north into East Prussia, where they had joined forces with the Russians. In the battle of Eylau, in February 1807, fought in the midst of a massive snowstorm, at least 30,000 men from the two sides fell dead and wounded. At the end, Napoleon controlled the battlefield. But he had failed to destroy the enemy armies and was left with little more than heaps of snow-covered corpses. "What a massacre—and with no result," commented a French field marshal. Although Napoleon finally overcame the last Prussian resistance, the days of his greatest victories were past.

THE EMPIRE CONTESTED (1807–1814)

In July 1807, Napoleon and Tsar Alexander met in person on a raft symbolically towed out into the middle of the Neman River, Russia's western frontier, near the town of Tilsit. Prussia's Frederick William was in attendance but was forced to wait on the shore, a poor supplicant. Napoleon concentrated on seducing the young tsar, whom he called his "brother monarch," and by showing a generosity that the dazzled Alexander did not expect, he at least partly succeeded. Together, he promised, the empires of France and Russia would henceforth dominate the Continent. Two **treaties of Tilsit** arranged a Franco-Russian alliance, drastically reduced Prussian territory, and established new French satellite states in Westphalia (in western Germany) and Poland. The latter, known as the "duchy of Warsaw," occupied only a portion of the former kingdom of Poland but did represent at least a partial rebirth of the Polish state.

Napoleon was already moving quickly to ensure French dominance of virtually all of continental Europe west of Russia. Having defeated the Bourbon kingdom of Naples (which included all of southern Italy and Sicily), he placed on its throne his older brother, Joseph Bonaparte (1768–1844), a dreamy man, far less ambitious than his brother, who before the Revolution had studied for the priesthood. Napoleon gave the new kingdom of Westphalia to his younger brother Jerome (1784–1860). He transformed the Netherlands into yet another kingdom under the rule of his younger brother Louis (1778–1846). And throughout Europe, he turned smaller areas into fiefdoms for his generals and ministers, who now became dukes and princes. From the list of titles now on display at the glittering French court—Duke of Ragusa, Duke of Otranto, Prince of Neuchâtel, Prince of Benevento—it might almost seem as if the French Revolution had never happened.

THE SPREAD OF THE REVOLUTIONARY LEGACY

Still, like Napoleon's Consulate and its administrative reforms, his French Empire remained true to the revolutionary tradition in several crucial ways. Napoleon himself did not abandon his commitment to the principles of civil equality and meritocracy: allocating offices to people on the basis of their talents and achievements. Although he welcomed Old Regime nobles to his court, he still did not move to undo the Revolution's redistribution of land and wealth, which had included the confiscation of émigré nobles' estates. He kept numerous former Jacobins among the ranks of his top advisers and ministers; and despite having made peace with the Catholic Church, he remained opposed to the influence of the clergy in secular affairs. Pope Pius VII, who had come to Paris to crown him in 1804, eventually excommunicated him, and Napoleon retaliated by keeping the pope prisoner in French territory for over six years. The French armies remained largely without chaplains.

REFORM IN THE EMPIRE Napoleon also helped spread the Revolution's legacy beyond France's old frontiers. Newly annexed imperial territories, notably in Italy and Germany, were transformed into French "departments." They were subjected to a full program of revolutionary reform, and their inhabitants received full French citizenship. These areas constituted the inner core of Napoleon's empire. The outer core of satellite kingdoms (including the former "sister republics" now ruled by members of the Bonaparte family) generally underwent a lesser but still important degree of revolutionary change, including the introduction of the Napoleonic Code and religious toleration. Jews in central and eastern Europe often remembered Napoleon as a liberator for granting them full civil rights. Notably, he eliminated the restrictions of ghetto life, allowing Jews to live and work where they wished. Thanks to these processes, which had the effect of reducing regional differences throughout the Continent, Napoleon was moving in the direction of founding a true European superstate. He told one subordinate: "I must make all the peoples of Europe one people, and Paris the capital of the world."

REFORMS IN PRUSSIA Even outside the areas of direct French influence, the Napoleonic upheavals led to rapid reform. In Prussia, after the humiliating defeat of 1806, two ministers in Frederick William's government—the pragmatic Karl von Hardenberg (1750–1822) and the aristocratic reformer Karl vom Stein (1757–1831)—began what has been called a "revolution from above." Their reforms imitated the French Revolution's assault on inefficient privilege but not its moves toward democracy; nor did the Prussians adopt the Revolution's emphasis on civil equality, which Napoleon defended. They abolished the last vestiges of rural serfdom in Prussia, instituted a more egalitarian tax system, introduced a measure of religious toleration, and pushed to make advancement in government service dependent on merit rather than favor. They promoted primary education and worked to transform the army into a more efficient, supple force. The upgrades to the Prussian military enraged Napoleon, who accused vom Stein of plotting a new war and put pressure on King Frederick William to restrain his minister. Fearful for his life, vom Stein fled to Russia.

RESISTANCE

Despite Napoleon's meeting with Tsar Alexander at Tilsit, a lasting peace settlement remained out of reach. Above all, Great Britain remained at war with France, its navy effectively blockading the Continent and strangling its foreign trade. In retaliation, in 1806 Napoleon began to devise what he would eventually call the "**Continental System**"—a Europe-wide boycott of British manufactures and British markets. Without European trade, he promised, the British would eventually be driven to economic collapse and would accept French dominance. But for the system to work, it would be necessary to impose it on literally tens of thousands of miles of European coastline. Napoleon had set himself an impossible task.

And then there was the specter of revolt. In France itself, the extension of the principles of the Revolution had provoked violent resistance, leading to the hideous guerrilla war in the Vendée. In the late 1790s, the imposition of the same principles on large areas of Italy, Germany, and the Low Countries had produced similar, if less bloody, results. The greatest source of resistance was the revolutionary practice of conscription (compulsory military service for all), which was imposed not only in territories that had become formally French but in the satellite republics and kingdoms as well. But there was also opposition to the huge new tax burdens imposed by the French and the new law codes that disrupted traditional patterns of social life by, for instance, legalizing divorce and imposing new rules for inheritance. Not surprisingly, where French authority seemed weak or uncertain, the population often seized the chance to revolt. Napoleon himself told his brother Joseph, on sending him to Naples in 1806: "Include in your calculations the fact that within a fortnight, more or less, you will have an insurrection. It is an event that constantly occurs in occupied countries."

REVOLT IN SOUTHERN ITALY The kingdom of Naples—the largest of the many independent states in Italy, covering the southern half of the peninsula and the island of Sicily—provided the first example of serious revolt against the empire. Although Napoleon's men had easily conquered the mainland portion of the kingdom, they could not overcome Sicily, which was protected by the British navy and where the Neapolitan royal family fled to rally resistance to the Bonapartes. Within months of Joseph Bonaparte's taking the throne in Naples, scores of towns rose up against him, especially in the remote, rocky region known as Calabria, at the tip of the Italian

Revolt in Calabria In 1806, a British force came to the aid of the rebels in Calabria against Joseph Bonaparte's rule. An English engraving shows the British (in red) victory over the French (in blue) at the battle of Maida, a small town in the region.

boot. The French had scarcely 9,000 soldiers there, many of them sick, and when it became clear that they could not restore order, dozens of bands of armed rebels sprang up under commanders known by such nicknames as "the Executioner," "the Monk," and "Brother Devil." Cutting French supply lines, swooping down on small detachments of French soldiers, and murdering supporters of the new regime, they quickly made it nearly impossible for the French to maintain control.

The insurrection never seriously threatened overall French control of Italy, and Joseph's regime eventually managed to suppress it, in part through sheer brutality. In July 1807, Joseph Bonaparte's Cabinet Council declared Calabria in a state of rebellion and warned that rebel villages would be sacked and burned. A month later, a town that continued to resist was burned to the ground, with at least 734 people killed. The French applied the same tactics—which strongly resembled the way French revolutionary forces had dealt with the Vendée in 1793–94—to many other villages in the rebel region, if not on so large a scale.

THE IBERIAN TRAP

The French managed to suppress rebellions elsewhere in Europe as well. But in one key location of southern Europe, the Iberian Peninsula (comprising Spain and Portugal), they failed. Here continuous resistance against Napoleon became what contemporaries called "the Spanish ulcer," which ate away at the vitals of the French Empire and ultimately proved a key factor in its collapse.

Napoleon did not originally want to invade Iberia. Spain had made peace with revolutionary France in 1795, and later became Napoleon's ally. It shared in the naval debacle of Trafalgar in 1805. But the Spanish government seemed paralyzed by the unseemly and erratic behavior of its royal family. The unstable Bourbon king, Carlos IV (r. 1788–1808), had handed over much of his authority to his favorite, Manuel Godoy, who was also the lover of the queen. Carlos also squabbled incessantly with his vain twenty-three-year-old son and heir, Fernando (1784–1833). In October 1807, Carlos placed Fernando under arrest for plotting a coup against him. Still, Spain posed France no immediate danger.

Portugal was a different matter, at least in Napoleon's view. Long linked to Great Britain by strong trade ties and a naval alliance, Portugal quickly emerged after 1806 as the principal weak point in Napoleon's continental blockade—an entry point for British manufactures and an outlet for continental goods. Enraged, Napoleon invaded in the fall of 1807, with the Spanish allowing him to send an army through their territory. The French quickly defeated Portugal's small military and sent its royal family fleeing across the Atlantic to their colony of Brazil, although a British expeditionary force soon recaptured the capital of Lisbon. But Spain's continuing instability raised anxieties about supply lines to Portugal, while Napoleon's disgust at the Spanish royals' antics soon led him to think that the country might be a more effective ally if it had a Bonaparte rather than a Bourbon as king. The obvious candidate was Joseph, who was already ruling Naples but was eager to move to this larger and more prestigious throne.

In March 1808, the opportunity presented itself when riots against Godoy forced his dismissal and King Carlos's abdication. Napoleon refused to recognize Fernando as the new king, but instead ordered both father and son to meet him in the French-Spanish border town of Bayonne. There he overwhelmed them with threats until they *both* agreed to abdicate. With the Bourbons out of the way, he then summoned Joseph Bonaparte to Madrid, replacing him in Naples with their brother-in-law, Marshal Joachim Murat, a former greengrocer and army sergeant.

THE PENINSULAR WAR (1808–1814) Even before this game of musical thrones, the French had already moved 120,000 troops into Spain on a series of pretexts and taken control of strategic Spanish fortresses. They were hoping for a smooth transition of power. A large number of Spaniards, especially from the urban middle classes and nobility, admired Napoleon and the French Revolution, believing that they embodied the ideas of the Enlightenment. These Spaniards were ready to support a new regime with enthusiasm. But soon after Napoleon browbeat the Bourbons into submission, an uprising took place in Madrid in May 1808, led by supporters of the old dynasty and backed by most of the common people. The French suppressed it with brutal force, executing hundreds of prisoners. The great Spanish painter Francisco de Goya (1746–1828) left an indelible, dreamlike image of the event in *The Third of May*, whose central figure—an illuminated, Christ-like victim, arms askew—draws the eye irresistibly.

Following this event, scores more Spanish cities and towns rose in open revolt against the new Bonapartist regime. The **Peninsular War** lasted for more than five years and badly drained French resources. In response to early Spanish victories, Napoleon himself took personal charge of the war, crushing the Spanish army, and by the fall of 1809 Joseph Bonaparte seemed secure on the Spanish throne. He imposed a revolutionary constitution that struck at long-entrenched feudal rights and also at the enormous power of the Catholic Church in the country. But the French still could not stamp out resistance. A legitimist government, loyal to Fernando, remained in operation, mostly in the southern port city of Cádiz. For a brief time there, Spanish liberals came to power and promulgated a constitution in 1812 that provided for a powerful parliament and a limited monarchy. The British, meanwhile, retained their base in Portugal, protected by massive fortifications around Lisbon and led by the brilliant, efficient Arthur Wellesley (later known as Lord Wellington and then the Duke of Wellington, 1769–1852). And throughout the peninsula, popular resistance remained powerful. In some areas, it was led by elements of the old Spanish and Portuguese armies. In others, it took the form of bands of insurgents fighting what was called "the little war"—or, in Spanish, *la guerrilla*, giving rise to the concept of **guerrilla warfare**.

TOTAL WAR IN SPAIN

In places, the horrific fighting in Spain anticipated the massively destructive wars of the twentieth century. In June 1808, for instance, the city of Saragossa declared itself in revolt against the "intruder king" Joseph Bonaparte. To subdue it, the French fired thousands of explosive shells and then advanced street by street—often house by house—in some of the worst urban combat seen to date in Europe. Macabre scenes played out in the city's many religious establishments, where

The Third of May, 1808 Francisco de Goya's arresting, dark painting (1814) shows French soldiers executing defenseless Spanish prisoners, including a monk (left) and a laborer (in the white shirt).

explosions blew ancient skeletons out of their tombs and shattered containers holding thousands of gallons of sacramental oil and wine. It took until February 1809 for Saragossa to surrender, and at least 50,000 Spaniards died in its defense.

Elsewhere in Spain, the "guerrilla war" played itself out in a way quite similar to that of the rebellion in Calabria—but on a much larger scale. Bands led by charismatic leaders made it impossible for the French forces to operate in large areas. Contingents of French soldiers risked attack from groups of hundreds or even thousands of guerrillas, who would rely on sheer surprise and shock to overwhelm their enemies and then quickly melt back into the countryside. French soldiers themselves came to see every Spaniard as a potential guerrilla. They resorted to increasingly brutal counterinsurgency tactics, burning villages, taking and executing hostages, and generating ever-greater hatred on the part of the Spanish population.

EFFECTS OF THE PENINSULAR WAR

In addition to showing how uncontrollable warfare had become—very different from the far more limited wars of the eighteenth century—the Peninsular War had another crucial consequence. Because of the conflict in Spain, its far-flung imperial territories—from the Philippines in Asia to all of Spanish-speaking South and Central America—found themselves cut off from the mother country. Colonial elites, often frustrated with Spanish restrictions on their economic and political actions, took advantage of the circumstances to assert greater rights. In some parts of the

THE COLOSSUS

In the Peninsular War (1808–1814), the Spanish army proved no match for Napoleon, but guerrillas constantly harassed French troops and supply lines. Their attacks in turn were met with violent reprisals that exacted a terrible toll on the Spanish population.

The violence and suffering of the war years influenced a dark turn in Spanish art, leading to works such as *The Colossus* (1808–12), previously attributed to Goya and possibly painted by one of his collaborators (the controversy is ongoing). In this painting, an imposing, nightmarish figure looms over a valley filled with a scattered caravan of fleeing people and their cattle. Against a tempestuous sky, the giant assumes a fighting stance, its left fist raised. The artist's technique is defined by dark tones and rough, thick paint-strokes, a style that perhaps reflected a visceral reaction to the agony and the uncertainty of the French occupation.

QUESTIONS FOR ANALYSIS

1. What do you think the colossus represents in this painting?
2. Who might the people in the valley represent?
3. What insight does this work provide into the horrors of the Peninsular War?

Spanish Empire, such as the future Argentina, these "creole" (that is, colonial-born) elites declared that they would function independently until the Bourbon king returned to the throne in Madrid. The liberal Cádiz constitution of 1812, which some creole representatives helped to draft, further encouraged these movements by giving the overseas possessions equal rights within the empire. In a stunning move, the constitution granted Spanish citizenship, if not voting rights, to indigenous peoples and more limited civil rights to free blacks and mulattoes. The Latin American revolutions of the 1810s and 1820s had their roots in the turmoil of this war.

The festering sore of the Peninsular War, and continuing British hostility, left Napoleon unable to turn the peace agreements reached at Tilsit into a permanent settlement for the Continent. Indeed, the Peninsular War provoked another conflict in central Europe when the Austrian Empire, trying to take advantage of the redeployment of French forces from central Europe to Spain, declared war on France yet again in 1809. At the same time, another major insurrection broke out in the Alpine region of the Tyrol, which had been annexed by France's ally, Bavaria. While it did not turn into a second Spain, the French were forced to come to Bavaria's aid. To deal with these emergencies, Napoleon drew on his efficient conscription system and managed an unprecedented mobilization of French strength. He soon defeated the Tyroleans and, after a decisive victory in the 1809 Battle of Wagram, forced Austria to sue for peace. But seasoned observers understood that continental conflict would continue.

EUROPE IN THE ERA OF NAPOLEON

Despite this turmoil, during the years 1809–12 Napoleon seemed more secure on his throne. Following the 1809 war with Austria, he not only reaffirmed his control over central Europe but also took the Austrian emperor's daughter, Maria-Louise (1791–1847), as his bride and empress. (Josephine continued her hold over Napoleon's affections, but her failure to produce an heir had led him to divorce her.) Brought to Paris in 1810, the new empress dutifully gave birth to a son the next year, apparently securing the future of the Bonaparte dynasty. Napoleon also continued apace with his annexations, even taking over territories he had previously delegated to members of his own family, such as the Netherlands. By 1812, France's borders extended over a greater territory than at any time since the reign of Charlemagne in the early Middle Ages. Indeed, when taking into account that France also maintained full control over the satellite regimes in Italy, Germany, and the Duchy of Warsaw, its empire dwarfed anything seen since Rome.

A NEW ROMAN EMPIRE?

Rome, indeed, served as the inspiration for Napoleon's grandiose dreams and plans. He imagined that just as Rome had supposedly melted the diverse peoples it ruled into a single, homogeneous polity, so Paris could now do the same. The French language would prevail as the language of government, trade, and scholarship from Gibraltar to the Baltic Sea. Europeans would use the same currency and the same weights and measures. A new system of broad, well-paved roads would improve

communications and transportation. And this new, united Europe would in turn fulfill its destiny by conquering the whole world. "Europe is nothing but an anthill," Napoleon remarked to his secretary. "You have to go to the Orient— all the great glories come from there." He even proposed to Tsar Alexander that France and Russia combine forces to invade British India. The tsar prudently declined.

IMPERIAL CULTURE   In Paris, to which he returned after each campaign, Napoleon began to sketch out plans for a capital city worthy of such a world empire. He imagined broad boulevards sweeping through the congested, dark, and filthy streets of the medieval city center (a plan eventually implemented by his nephew, Napoleon III, in the mid-nineteenth century). He commissioned grand buildings and monuments in the Roman style, including a Temple of Glory (today the Church of the Madeleine), a grand column cast from melted Russian cannon, and a huge triumphal arch at the city's western edge (the present-day Arc de Triomphe). In the empty space where the great fortress of the Bastille had stood before the French Revolution, he planned a grand statue of an elephant to embody "the Orient" and his planned conquests there. His regime did not get further than erecting a giant papier-mâché model of it, which quickly was dilapidated by rain and eaten from within by hordes of rats.

Like his Roman and French predecessors, Napoleon tried to harness the arts and literature to glorify himself and his regime. The works produced mostly belonged to the same neoclassical school that had flourished during

Napoleon's Paris   Napoleon's vision for grand, neoclassical Paris included the Arc de Triomphe, which the emperor commissioned after his victory at Austerlitz. Though it was not completed until 1836, it memorializes the soldiers killed in the revolutionary and Napoleonic wars.

Napoleon's Empire, 1812 Despite some defeats—against the British at Trafalgar, in guerrilla war in Spain—by 1812 Napoleon had brought much of Europe under his control. French territory extended into the Pyrenees to the west and the Italian Alps and the Low Countries in the east and north. The Iberian and Italian Peninsulas, many of the German states, and much of Poland also fell under his control, and he reorganized them into new satellite states. This was Napoleon's empire at its height, before his retreat from Russia in 1812.

the late eighteenth century. Indeed, Napoleon had as his chief court painter Jacques-Louis David (1748–1825), who had previously inspired the French revolutionaries with his depictions of stern Roman virtue and the supposed martyrdom of the radical demagogue Marat. Now David and his students turned their talents to immortalizing the emperor of France. The contrast could not be greater between the sober, muted style of David's *Coronation of Napoleon* and the wild flourishes of color with which Goya rendered the suppression of the revolt in Madrid. Many other artists and writers turned away from Napoleon, accusing him of having betrayed the ideals of the Revolution. These included the French novelist Germaine de Staël, whose initial flirtations with Napoleon quickly gave way to mutual loathing.

IMPERIAL SOCIETY Napoleon also imagined a new imperial society. It would be genuinely multinational: by 1813, nearly a third of the emperor's senate (the highest chamber of his new legislature) came from territories annexed to France since 1792. The empire would be rational and progressive, with the role of the Church reduced to a symbolic presence and far greater resources given over to research and education. Indeed, Napoleon laid the basis for the modern French university system. The society would be highly centralized under the rational management of the emperor and the experts gathered in his various councils. Orders would pass from them down through the various ministries to the prefects who ruled the individual "departments" into which the imperial territory was divided; thence to subprefects, town mayors, and eventually to ordinary citizens. Government would definitely *not* be democratic. Although there would be elected legislative bodies, in practice they would do little more than endorse the emperor's decisions.

Despite its supposedly progressive cast, the empire would also be distinctly patriarchal and hierarchical. Women would have no public role at all, but instead remain at home, dutifully bearing and raising children and managing the domestic sphere. The peasants who still made up the vast majority of the population would raise their crops, offer their sons to the armies, and otherwise remain distinctly in the background. Real power in French society would rest with the wealthy, property-owning men called "notables": members of the old nobility; contractors who had enriched themselves during the endless wars; other well-off financiers, merchants, and professionals; and above all the generals who had led France's armies to victory. The lives of ordinary people would be far more regimented, and placed under far greater surveillance, than in the past, especially in cities. In Paris, Napoleon's ambitious interior minister organized a system whereby the caretakers of apartment buildings regularly spied on the tenants and reported on their activities to the police.

Napoleon did not set out to militarize his new imperial society, but a good deal of militarization took place nonetheless, in keeping with the overall ethos of regimentation and control. Military uniforms proliferated far away from the battlefield, becoming required dress in many government ministries. Schools took on a military cast as well, as students in new elite *lycées* (high schools) were formed into battalions of cadets and trained for the wars. Napoleon created a new "Legion of Honor" to reward citizens who had shown particular merit, and he promised at the outset that it would be open to men (not women) from all walks of life. But over 95 percent of those named to it during his reign came from the armies.

Indeed, of all the emperor's grand plans and hopes, the ones that came closest to fulfillment were his military ones. The most efficient arm of his new state administration was the gigantic system of conscription established to feed the endless hunger of the armies for men. All young men in the empire and most of the satellite kingdoms had to register at age eighteen for military service. Each year, the government decided what percentage of them actually to put into uniform, and sometimes took them all. An efficient

Napoleon's Coronation As depicted in David's grand commemorative painting (1806–7), Napoleon invited Pope Pius VII to his coronation but personally crowned Josephine and himself, showing that he did not recognize the Church's ultimate authority.

bureaucratic system ensured that few slipped out of the net. Still, wealthy young men had the option of paying someone else to serve in their place. Others sought to exploit loopholes in the law. Since married men enjoyed exemptions, the last years of the empire saw a rise in the marriage rate, including a suspicious number of unions between boys of age eighteen and widows in their sixties and seventies. The army was also plagued by large-scale desertion.

SOCIAL AND ECONOMIC EFFECTS OF THE NAPOLEONIC WARS

Events as destructive as the Napoleonic Wars could hardly fail to have massive economic and social consequences. The disruption of shipping caused by the wars, and the attempts by France and Britain to destroy each other's commerce, represented a major potential blow to European prosperity. But the blow was felt very unevenly.

FRANCE In France, the combination of the wars and the slave revolt in Saint-Domingue had already badly damaged trade in the 1790s. By 1807, French exports had finally come back to their 1787 levels. But thereafter, as the battle over Napoleon's Continental System took hold, they fell by half. French imports, meanwhile, remained well below the 1787 levels in 1807, and thereafter fell by two-thirds. Activity in the great French Atlantic ports such as Bordeaux, where slaves and sugar had generated dazzling wealth in the eighteenth century, now shriveled. The French economy turned inward. French textile centers such as Lyon did well for much of the period, but even here by 1810 shortages of imported raw material, such as cotton from India, caused a major downturn. Elsewhere on the European continent, effects were more mixed, but the fighting still caused major disruptions. In the Netherlands, the prices of imported goods such as sugar and coffee came close to tripling, while in Sweden imported textiles became almost impossibly expensive.

GREAT BRITAIN Great Britain also suffered disruptions during the Napoleonic Wars, but overall its economy performed far better. Despite Napoleon's attempt to blockade the Continent to British commerce, British merchants still found many European ports they could enter. The supple and sophisticated system of banking and credit in Britain handled the stresses of the wars better than its continental counterparts. The French national bank created by Napoleon did not entirely alter his reliance, in the manner of his Old Regime predecessors, on private financiers to manage state revenues, and they did so inefficiently.

And while the price of imported goods rose substantially in Britain, levels of imports and exports did not fall anywhere near as drastically as they did across the Channel. The price of grain rose, prompting many more landlords to enclose with fences, and farm for their own profit, fields that had previously been left for common use. Indeed, the acreage enclosed between 1800 and 1810 was nearly double that of the previous decade. The enclosure process, which had begun in the eighteenth century, hurt many agricultural workers but generated considerable profits for landowners. Capital remained available for investment. And while British wages were high compared to those on the Continent (and elsewhere in the world), the price of energy there remained far lower, the result of the abundance of coal. The price of transportation was also low, thanks in part to over 4,000 miles of serviceable canals, most of them built since 1750.

As a result, the wars did not materially slow the development of business and industry in Britain. Although the most dramatic developments would take place after 1820, in the years between 1800 and 1820 Britain continued to lay the groundwork for modern industry. The construction of steam engines continued apace. Already in 1800 there were more than 2,000 in operation—a quarter of them built by James Watt, the Scottish engineer who had developed the technology in the 1770s. Their numbers would increase steadily in the first two decades of the new century, while further technological advances resulted in the production of steam engines that could generate eight times the horsepower of earlier models. The number of steam-powered looms in operation went up by a factor of more than six in this period.

The spread of industrialization was uneven across Britain, with textile mills concentrated in the north of England around the city of Manchester, and in the south around London. And industrialization also brought disruption and opposition. Many observers were shocked by the noise and smoke that the textile mills generated, and found their functional architecture ugly. Already in 1804, the poet and artist William Blake decried the phenomenon in a poem about a supposed appearance of Jesus in England: "And was Jerusalem builded here, / Among these dark Satanic Mills?" A few years later, as textile manufacturers in the north introduced power looms in the mills, they began to dismiss large numbers of skilled, high-paid textile workers. Some of these workers—known as **Luddites** after Ned Ludd, a semi-mythical "captain" or "general" said to have smashed looms thirty years earlier—protested the use of

Ned Ludd An 1812 political cartoon depicts the semi-mythical figure of Ned Ludd—clad in rags and the kind of smock worn by pre-industrial agricultural laborers—encouraging his followers to rebellion.

such labor-saving machines by attacking workshops and destroying equipment. The British government, primed by twenty years of repressing radical activity associated with the French Revolution, responded harshly. In 1812, "machine breaking" was made a capital crime. Hundreds of Luddites were arrested, seventeen died on the scaffold, and many others were imprisoned or sentenced to penal transportation to Australia. In this sense, much like militarized France, Britain in this period saw moves toward a more disciplined, regimented society.

NAPOLEON'S DOWNFALL (1812–1815)

The wave of organized violence that had been building in the Western world since the French Revolution came to a climax in 1812. Following Napoleon's disruption of the Spanish Empire, independence movements and peasant revolts battled authorities in Latin America. Britain's attempts to keep the United States from trading with France, and to force American sailors into its overstretched navy (a practice known as "impressment"), helped provoke a declaration of war on Britain by the United States,

which also had designs on British Canada. The War of 1812 dragged on for two and a half years, with fighting in the Great Lakes region and on the eastern American seaboard, and ended in an unsatisfying draw. And in Europe itself, the cycle of violence spun completely out of control.

THE RUSSIAN CAMPAIGN

Despite Napoleon's stated desire for peace, France and its enemies could still not manage to acknowledge one another's legitimacy. Napoleon's men still tended to see the allied powers as the decrepit remains of Old Regime Europe, hobbled by religious superstition, unjust privilege, and blind obedience to tradition. The allies still tended to see Napoleon as a usurper, an ogre, and even the Antichrist, in a judgment formally pronounced by the Russian Orthodox Church. Together with the emperor's ambition and the inherent instability of the Continental System, these factors not only kept the wars going but led them to escalate. In 1800, at the battle of Marengo, roughly 60,000 soldiers had taken part in the fighting. Five years later, at Austerlitz, the number had grown to nearly 165,000. Four years after that, at Wagram, the largest battle yet seen in the gunpowder age since its start in the fifteenth century, some 300,000 men took part, with 80,000 of them dead and wounded. But such escalation could not continue indefinitely without pushing one side

Burning of Moscow In 1812, a German engraver made this dramatic image of smoke and flames lighting up the sky as the entire city of Moscow burns. A scattered band of French soldiers watches from the road.

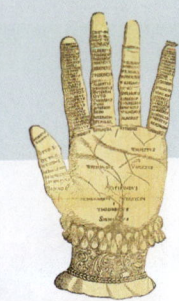

THE RETREAT FROM RUSSIA

Napoleon's 1812 invasion of Russia was a massive undertaking, drawing soldiers from across his vast empire. One such soldier was Adrien Bourgogne, a sergeant in the elite Imperial Guard. Born into a merchant family in northern France, by the time of the invasion of Russia he was already a battle-hardened veteran who had served in Austria, Spain, and Portugal. Bourgogne's memoirs (ca. 1840s) of the retreat from Moscow captured both the wretched suffering and the fierce dedication of the Grand Army. In this excerpt, he recounts how under constant Russian harassment, soldiers starved and froze to death. Yet despite the brutal conditions, he also conveys the common soldier's proud sense of loyalty to Napoleon.

We were just then packed very closely together near a wood, and had a long time to wait before we could resume our march, as the road was narrow. As several of us sat together beating with our feet to keep warm, and talking of the fearful hunger we felt, all at once I became aware of the smell of warm bread. I turned round and behind me saw a man wrapped in a great fur cape, from which came the smell I had noticed. I spoke to him at once, saying, "Sir, you have some bread; you must sell it to me."…With one hand I seized the cake, while with the other I gave him five francs. But hardly had I the cake in my hand, when my companions threw themselves on it like madmen, and tore it from me. I only had the little bit I held between my thumb and two first fingers….

During this half-hour several men had lain down and died; many more had fallen in the column while marching. Our ranks were getting thinned already, and this was only the very beginning of our troubles. Whenever we stopped to eat hastily, the horses left behind were bled. The blood was caught in a saucepan, cooked, and eaten. But often we were forced to eat it before there was time to cook it. Either the order for departure was given, or the Russians were upon us. In the latter case we did not take much notice. I have sometimes seen men eating calmly, while others fired at the Russians to keep them off. But when the order was imperative and we were obliged to go, the saucepan was carried with us, and each man, as he marched, dipped his hands in and took what

he wanted; his face in consequence became smeared with blood.…

Those who went through this lamentable but glorious campaign proved, as the Emperor said, that they must have been made of iron to bear so many privations and so much misery; this was surely the very greatest test to which men were ever exposed.

QUESTIONS FOR ANALYSIS

1. What were conditions like for solders during Napoleon's retreat from Russia?
2. What does the excerpt reveal about the relationships among the soldiers?
3. Why does Bourgogne, despite the hardships he suffered, describe the Russian campaign as "glorious"?

Source: Adrien Bourgogne, *Memoirs of Sergeant Bourgogne, 1812–1813*, ed. Paul Cottin (New York: 1899), pp. 67–68, 351.

or another to collapse. In 1812, the collapse began with Napoleon's decision to invade Russia.

For Napoleon, there seemed to be good reasons to take this step. To begin with, Tsar Alexander had become a highly unreliable ally, resisting the Continental System and trying to assert new influence over central Europe. In 1809 he also seized Finland from Sweden—it would remain under Russian rule for more than a century. More broadly, Russia remained the only power with a sufficiently large army to challenge French domination over continental Europe. And Napoleon had already shown, in 1805–7, that

he could beat the Russians. Therefore, in June 1812 the French army of 650,000 men—including the young Jakob Walter, whom we met earlier—assembled on Russia's western frontier. Moscow lay some 600 miles to the east. There followed the epic disaster captured by the great Russian novelist Leo Tolstoy (1828–1910), who would later write in *War and Peace*, set in Russia during the Napoleonic era: "Assuming that Napoleon's object was to destroy his own army, the most expert strategist could hardly conceive of any other series of actions which would so completely and infallibly have accomplished that purpose."

In France, the rapidly rising human costs of the war strengthened discontent with Napoleon and his military adventures. Desertion and draft avoidance rose precipitously. During the Russian campaign, a general attempted a coup against Napoleon, which was quickly crushed. The liberal French writer Benjamin Constant offered a searching evaluation of Napoleon. Constant insisted that the emperor's "spirit of conquest," reminiscent of Alexander the Great and Julius Caesar, had no place in a modern, commercial world:

> In some ages of history, war was in the nature of man.... But the modern world is, in this regard, the opposite of the ancient world.... We have reached the age of commerce, which must necessarily replace the age of war...war has lost both its utility and its charm.

Constant's anger, however, did not keep him from succumbing to Napoleon's charm and bribery a few years later and becoming one of the emperor's advisers.

Despite the scale of the Russian disaster, Napoleon's efficient conscription machine replenished his armies with appalling speed, quickly putting over 200,000 new French soldiers in uniform, although many were nearly past fighting age. It could not so easily replace the thousands of artillery pieces his men left behind in the Russian snows, or the horses—which remained key to any military operation in the period. Nor did fresh, ill-trained conscripts compare with the seasoned, capable soldiers who had died during the campaign. And at the other end of Europe, the "Spanish ulcer" continued to pin down hundreds of thousands of men who might have otherwise served Napoleon elsewhere. Still, by the spring of 1813 Napoleon again commanded a formidable fighting force and seemed poised, if not to reverse his recent losses, at least to force the allied powers to a draw. But could he keep his own coalition together? Before invading Russia, he had been able to count on the support of Austria, which he had defeated time after time, and Prussia, which he had crushed in 1806. Now both wavered.

GERMAN NATIONAL RESISTANCE

Even as Austria and Prussia hesitated, an influential group of German intellectuals were actively pushing for a break with France in the name of a powerful new idea: the unification of the multiple German-speaking states of central Europe.

THE ORIGINS OF ROMANTICISM
As early as the 1770s, German writers like Johann Wolfgang von Goethe and Johann Gottfried Herder had begun to challenge the powerful Enlightenment idea that human societies differed from one another principally in the progress they had made along a scale that led from "savagery" to "civilization," with all savage peoples, and all civilized peoples—that is, those of western Europe—essentially alike. To the contrary, Goethe and Herder argued, peoples such as the Germans and the French had different spirits, which found expression in everything from the folktales told around their peasant hearths to the architecture of their greatest buildings. These writers advocated a return to nature, to the simplicity of the common people, and, as many of the Enlightenment authors had also urged, to sentiment. Out of these ideas would come the artistic, musical, and literary movement known as **romanticism**. Out of them would also come powerful new ways of inspiring devotion to that great abstraction that the French Revolution had already placed at the heart of European politics: the "nation." Napoleon himself broke with French revolutionary nationalism in his attempt to forge a multinational European empire. The same project, however, provoked the rise of explicitly nationalist feeling elsewhere, against him.

True, many of the German romantics initially swooned over Napoleon himself, seeing in him an elemental force of nature. Ludwig van Beethoven (1770–1827), greatest of romantic composers and an admirer of the French Revolution, initially wrote his Third Symphony to praise Napoleon, but he angrily changed his mind after the first consul crowned himself emperor. In 1808, Goethe and Napoleon met and exchanged fulsome compliments. But by 1812, to many onlookers Napoleon seemed less a force than a freak of nature: bloated, rapacious, and deadly. And the German intellectuals increasingly condemned him, while calling for all Germans to unite and forge a national spirit in opposition to him. The playwright Heinrich von Kleist (1777–1811), a veteran of the Prussian army, caused a sensation with a play in honor of the Germanic tribesmen who had risen up against the Roman emperor Augustus—its contemporary message was clear. The poet and historian Ernst Moritz Arndt (1769–1860) called for a single German fatherland, united by its common language, while preaching "hatred against the French forever.... This hatred glows as the religion of the German people."

PRUSSIA AND AUSTRIA SWITCH SIDES
These ideas, it should be emphasized, had very limited resonance in German society as a whole. They did not spur peasants

Klemens von Metternich
A nineteenth-century portrait of Metternich shows the statesman richly adorned with medals and honors.

to rise from the plow in the name of the Fatherland. Nor did they prompt German princes to lay aside their thrones so as to forge a larger German nation. But they did have a great influence among well-educated young men, including a large portion of the Prussian officer corps. Emblematic in this regard was the young officer Carl von Clausewitz (1780–1831), the grandson of a theologian who began his military service in 1792, at age twelve, and spent two years as a prisoner of war in France following the terrible Prussian defeat of 1806. An enthusiastic supporter of the Prussian reforms introduced after this defeat, he could not bear serving in a diminished Prussian army subservient to France, and instead offered his services to Russia. In the last days of 1812, he helped negotiate an agreement under which a Prussian general commanding 30,000 men formally switched sides from France to Russia. Although Frederick William angrily denounced them as traitors, more and more officers followed their example, and pressure steadily built. Finally, in March 1813, Prussia renounced its alliance with Napoleon and entered the growing allied coalition against him.

Austria did not initially follow suit. After having sent a token force to join in the Russian campaign, it had subsequently taken its distance from France, but not so far as to enter the coalition against it. The key figure directing its diplomacy at this point was the Austrian foreign minister, Klemens Lothar von Metternich (1773–1859). A brilliant, vain man, he was also an incomparably skillful negotiator. Through early 1813, he still hoped for a peaceful settlement of the Napoleonic Wars. His hopes rose when Napoleon narrowly beat combined Russian-Prussian forces in two battles in Germany in May and then agreed to an armistice. Napoleon himself met with Metternich in June and agreed to a peace conference the next month. But the resulting discussions never came close to succeeding. Napoleon still hoped to divide the allies, while they—particularly the British—distrusted him too much to offer serious terms. Furthermore, they used the armistice to build up their own forces. In August the negotiations collapsed, and Austria, seeing itself with no choice, declared war on France in its turn.

THE BATTLE FOR GERMANY With this large coalition in place, Germany quickly became the theater of the largest-scale warfare it had seen since the Thirty Years'

War of the seventeenth century. Austria, and to a greater extent Prussia, made serious attempts to imitate French conscription methods and draft all available young men. In April 1813, Frederick William ordered all adult males under age sixty to serve in a Prussian Home Army and, taking inspiration from the Spanish guerrillas, encouraged "every citizen . . . to harm the enemy using all available means." In fact, Germany saw very little guerrilla activity, nor did the draftees add significantly to Prussia's military capacity. Nonetheless, the coalition forces were now benefiting from the spirit of patriotic enthusiasm that previously had mainly bolstered the French revolutionaries. And in October 1813, it helped carry them to victory in the mammoth "Battle of the Nations" at Leipzig, in central Germany. More than 500,000 soldiers took part, with 150,000 of them killed or wounded. And despite Napoleon's best efforts, it ended in a decisive French defeat.

THE BATTLE FOR FRANCE AND NAPOLEON'S FALL

Scenting victory, the coalition decided that it would settle for nothing less than the complete defeat of Napoleon's regime. As French forces fell back westward across the Rhine, a combined force of Russians, Prussians, and Austrians pushed the fighting onto French soil for the first time since the early 1790s. Meanwhile, as Napoleon desperately pulled men out of Spain, his brother's regime there collapsed. On June 21, 1813, Lord Wellington crushed the French at the battle of Vitoria in Spain. Joseph Bonaparte himself barely escaped back to France, while his carriages, loaded with Spanish gold, silver, and jewelry, were abandoned to whooping British redcoats. Seeing their rapacious behavior, Wellington denounced his own men in a letter as "the scum of the earth." By 1814, a combined British, Spanish and Portuguese army had pushed over the Pyrenees to invade France from the south, while the Bourbon king Fernando reclaimed his father's throne in Madrid. In the spring of 1814, Napoleon fought a brilliant campaign in eastern France, recapturing something of his old élan, with the help of soldiers desperate to protect their own homeland. But the combined forces of Russia, Prussia, Austria, and Britain simply proved too powerful for him. The fall of the empire appeared certain. But what would follow it?

TALLEYRAND At this point, a figure emerged who, along with Metternich, would prove crucial in determining the

EUROPEAN ATTITUDES TOWARD NAPOLEON

Napoleon's consolidation of many aspects of the French Revolution, along with his extensive military conquests, reshaped European society so profoundly that his influence became a matter of contentious debate among his contemporaries. For many observers, his Napoleonic Code, which established that all men were subject to a single legal order (women were subject to a plethora of civil disabilities), was an important step toward civil liberty and equality. Some saw his continued presence on the battlefield as a sign of bravery and self-sacrifice that brought glory to all who followed him. Yet others reviled Napoleon as a conqueror, usurper, and tyrant who had destroyed centuries-old traditions and practices. Napoleon would remain a polarizing figure throughout the nineteenth century: a tireless, courageous leader to some, and an iron-fisted, dangerous egoist to others.

William Cobbett, from the *Political Register*, January 16, 1814

A radical British journalist, Cobbett argued in this edition of his weekly newspaper for Napoleon's suitability as ruler for France.

Napoleon has many qualities…calculated to make him an object of respect with the people. Upon all occasions he shares the toils and the dangers of his armies. His attention to public business is almost incessant. He is sober. His associates…are men famed for their talents…for their wisdom, for their application to business. His hours of recreation are not spent at the gaming table, but in the manly exercises of the field. And yet this is the man whom our news-writers denominate a *monster*, though he is the son-in-law of our august ally, the Emperor of Austria!…

If indeed, Napoleon were a half-mad tyrant; if he were a sort of malignant idiot, who, while he kept his own worthless carcass safe…made it his sport to send forth armies to butcher or to be butchered; if he were a drunkard, a sot, a gambler, a swindler, a man, who, if in common life, would be kicked out of every hotel in Paris; if he were an emaciated creature, incapable of any sort of exertion bodily or mental…*then* might we *justly* accuse the people of France of *baseness* in patiently submitting to his sway.… But, if Napoleon be none of this; if he be *precisely the contrary* of the imaginary character that I have drawn, with what justice do we, or some of us, revile the people of France…for submitting to be ruled by him?

Madame de Rémusat, from *Memoirs*

Madame de Rémusat was a member of Napoleon's imperial court, a lady in waiting to Empress Josephine, and a noted diarist. In her memoirs (1802–8), she weighed Napoleon's capacity as a leader and criticized what she perceived as his self-centered ambition.

His [Napoleon's] reception by the troops was nothing short of rapturous. It was well worth seeing how he talked to the soldiers—how he questioned them one after the other respecting their campaigns or their wounds; taking particular interest in men who had accompanied him to Egypt.…He spoke to the subalterns in a tone of good fellowship, which delighted them all, as he reminded them of their common feats of arms.…Afterward… when he addressed his soldiers before leading them into battle, it was as a perpetually renewed posterity, to which the preceding and destroyed army had bequeathed its glory. But even this somber style of encouragement availed for a long time with a nation which believed itself to be fulfilling its destiny while sending its sons year after year to die for Bonaparte.…

If Bonaparte, who was so successful in conciliating individuals, had but gone a step further, and, instead of governing by force alone, had yielded to the reaction which longed for repose; if, now, that he had conquered the present moment, he had made himself master of the future, by creating durable institutions independent of his own caprice—there is little doubt but that his victory over our recollections, our prejudices, and our regrets would have been as lasting as it was remarkable. But it must be confessed that liberty, true liberty, was wanting everywhere; and the fault of the nation consisted in not perceiving this in time. As I have said before, the Emperor improved finances and encouraged trade, science and art; merit was rewarded in every class; but all this was spoiled by the stamp of slavery. Being resolved on ruling everything himself, and for his own advantage, he always put himself forwards as the ultimate aim. It is said that on starting for the first campaign in Italy, he told a friend who was editor of a newspaper: "Recollect in your accounts of our victories to speak of *me*, and always of *me*. Do you understand?" This "*me*" was the ceaseless cry of purely egotistical ambition.

QUESTIONS FOR ANALYSIS

1. Why does Cobbett support Napoleon's rule?
2. In Madame de Rémusat's estimation, what was Napoleon's great strength and his principal flaw?
3. What do Cobbett and Rémusat see as the French people's role in determining the nation's government?

Sources: William Cobbett, *Political Register*, Vol. XXV, from January to June (London: 1814), pp. 94–96; Madame de Rémusat, *Memoirs of Madame de Rémusat*, trans. Cashel Hoey and John Lillie (New York: 1880), pp. 86–87, 363–64.

Charles-Maurice de Talleyrand An early nineteenth-century engraving of Talleyrand as foreign minister, wearing splendid robes of state and imperial insignia.

shape of post-Napoleonic Europe. **Charles-Maurice de Talleyrand** (1754–1838) was a man whose subtlety, irony, and world-weary cynicism made him a perfect contrast to Napoleon Bonaparte. Born to great wealth and high rank before the Revolution, he had a club foot that kept him from his family's usual career of military service. Instead, he headed into the priesthood, where his connections, charm, and raw intelligence brought him to a key position—representative of the entire French clergy to the crown—by age twenty-six and earned him a bishopric at thirty-five. Siding with the Revolution, he first abandoned the Church and then abandoned France itself in 1792 when failure to keep up with the pace of political radicalization put his life in danger. He traveled in the United States, speculated on land in Pennsylvania and Ohio, and then returned home under the less radical Directorial regime of 1795–99, where his skills earned him the position of foreign minister. He quickly attached himself to Napoleon, who kept him in office after his 1799 coup.

Crafty and sophisticated, Talleyrand managed French diplomacy ably and was rewarded with huge wealth and an Italian principality. But even as Napoleon grew more ambitious, Talleyrand turned more cautious and warned that permanent expansion would lead France to disaster. He began private discussions with Tsar Alexander and with Metternich on how to control Napoleon, and these gradually developed into a conspiracy to ease the French emperor off his throne. When Napoleon discovered the plot in 1808, he banished Talleyrand, whom he cursed to his face as excrement "in a silk stocking"; but he could not bring himself to have the man executed, and allowed Talleyrand to return to Paris a few years later as a private citizen.

With the allied armies approaching Paris in 1814, Talleyrand, who had retained the trust of the allies, again began to scheme. For weeks, the situation remained chaotic as the allies explored different plans, including the abdication of Napoleon in favor of his young son, the king of Rome. But Talleyrand urged a different outcome. Ever since the heir to Louis XVI had died in prison in 1795, the executed king's younger brother had claimed the French throne as Louis XVIII. Although the British had given

him refuge and token support, most of the world had forgotten him. But as Napoleon's regime crumbled, the idea of a Bourbon restoration gained support in France. After all, it would be far more difficult for the allies to impose harsh terms on a Bourbon government that they recognized as legitimate, and an ally, than on a Bonapartist one that they considered the work of a dictatorial usurper. In southwestern France, a pro-Bourbon group called the "Knights of the Faith" engineered demonstrations in favor of Louis XVIII that impressed the advancing British. Talleyrand, meanwhile, worked to convince Metternich and Tsar Alexander of the Bourbons' merits, presenting their return to the throne as the beginning of a new age of stability in European politics.

THE BOURBON RESTORATION In the spring of 1814, the end appeared to come. Napoleon made a half-hearted attempt at suicide, taking a poison that had lost its potency. He survived and had to endure the humiliation of defeat, formally agreeing to abdicate. The Senate that had once done his bidding declared his reign at an end and welcomed the portly, faintly comical figure of Louis XVIII (1755–1824), who proceeded to "grant" a new constitution to the country that had rejected his family twenty-two years before. It seemed that French history had turned full circle—but in fact the new constitution represented anything but a return to the Old Regime. The new king knew perfectly well that the French would never accord the Church, the nobility, and the monarchy their old powers and privileges. As a result, France under the Bourbon Restoration looked very much like a compromise that retained many of the features of the Republic and Empire. The authority of the monarch was restrained by a legislature, although one elected by a tiny minority of wealthy male property-holders. The new regime also maintained the division of the country into departments, Napoleon's system of centralization, and his law code. It preserved the treaty with the Vatican that acknowledged Catholicism as the country's leading religion and gave the state a broad degree of control over religious life.

THE CONGRESS OF VIENNA (1814–1815)

Meanwhile, the allies prepared a peace settlement that, as Talleyrand had hoped, was relatively favorable to the loser. By the spring of 1814, the four major allied

Napoleon in Exile An 1814 British cartoon represents Elba as a tiny rock outcropping within sight of a European coast guarded against Napoleon's return. The former emperor sobs as crows and bats fly over his head, presumably waiting for his death.

powers—Britain, Austria, Russia, and Prussia—had agreed on the central points. France would have to surrender the major territorial conquests of the previous two decades, including Belgium (which would be joined to Holland in a new kingdom of the United Netherlands) and its annexations in northern and central Italy. Napoleon's satellite kingdoms such as Naples would revert to their original rulers, except for the quasi-independent duchy of Warsaw, most of which would become the autonomous "Congress Kingdom of Poland" under Russian rule. Although the allies did not want to restore the old Holy Roman Empire, they did plan for a loose German Confederation to take its place. But France would keep defensible borders and would not have to pay large reparations.

As for Napoleon himself, the allies agreed not to put him on trial. Instead, they gave him the tiny Italian island of Elba, within sight of his native Corsica, for a place of exile. He would even keep the title of emperor. To be sure, sending the man who had ruled most of Europe to reign over a flyspeck of territory had a measure of cruelty to it, and the English newspapers mercilessly quipped that in his new home Napoleon would not have much "Elba room." But all in all, it seemed that after the torrent of blood spilled over the previous twenty-two years, the Napoleonic empire was coming to a surprisingly peaceful end.

THE CONCERT OF EUROPE

In the fall of 1814, the major powers gathered for a peace conference in the Austrian capital that would become known as the **Congress of Vienna**. In several ways, the Congress marked a break from earlier peace conferences, such as the one held in Westphalia in 1648. Rather than sending ambassadors, the major powers' foreign ministers came themselves, accompanied by large retinues of assistants. It was a dazzling social occasion for the city. Metternich and Wellington took part, and Tsar Alexander himself represented Russia. The participants had as their ambition not simply to finalize their earlier agreements but to settle *all* outstanding European conflicts, put in place a permanent peace settlement for the Continent, and prevent anything like the slaughter of the previous twenty years from ever repeating itself. The young tsar in particular dreamed of putting an end to warfare forever—much the same dream that had beguiled so many men and women of the Enlightenment—and joining all European states together into a grand Christian coalition. Metternich and Viscount Castlereagh (1769–1822), the British

Congress of Vienna An Austrian illustration from the early nineteenth century shows representatives of the major European powers poring over a map and globe as they establish new borders and seek to maintain the balance of power.

Congress of Vienna, 1815 The allied powers attempted to restore pre-French Revolution borders, seeking a balance of power that would maintain peace and stability. France's territorial conquests were either made into new kingdoms, like the United Netherlands, or given to other powers—like the parts of northern Italy ceded to Austria, or the Congress Kingdom of Poland, placed under Russian rule.

foreign secretary, had considerably less lofty visions but still hoped to devise a workable, long-lasting peace.

Recognizing that such a settlement could not succeed without active French support, the four allied powers quickly allowed France, in the person of Talleyrand, to join them at the Congress. (A grateful Louis XVIII had yet again appointed Talleyrand as foreign minister.) Many other rulers and foreign ministers from across Europe came to Vienna as well. Most important, the powers quickly came to realize that a durable settlement required the establishment of enforcement mechanisms. Although they did not specify exact mechanisms, they did agree to consult on disputes that might arise in the future and impose solutions, by force if necessary, before crises could spin out of control. This system would soon come to

be known as the "**Concert of Europe**." During meetings that lasted for some nine months, the powers arbitrated disputes over borders throughout Europe, notably in the former territory of Poland-Lithuania, Italy, and Scandinavia. Russia was confirmed in its possession of Finland, which it had seized from Sweden in 1809.

The Congress of Vienna did succeed in laying the groundwork for the longest period of relative peace in European history before 1945. For forty years, although numerous small conflicts did arise, the major powers did not fight one another. And in the Crimean War of 1854–56, the operations would remain on a far more limited scale than during the Napoleonic Wars and were confined to a small region of the Russian Empire. Not until the Franco-Prussian War of 1870–71 would major European armies collide, in the western European heartland, with anything like the fury of the wars of 1792–1815, and even then the conflict was over in a matter of months. Only in 1914 would total war return to Europe.

THE HUNDRED DAYS

But the story of Napoleon Bonaparte did not come to an end without one great, last, surprising twist. At the end of February 1815, with the Congress of Vienna still in session, the emperor escaped from Elba and landed on France's Mediterranean coast with a handful of loyal supporters. The inhabitants of the villages where he first stopped found it almost impossible to believe that this balding, paunchy man in a bedraggled uniform was truly the emperor who had led France's armies across Europe. But once convinced of Napoleon's true identity, crowds quickly came to cheer him on. Disaffection with the new regime of Louis XVIII already ran high. The new Bourbon king not only lacked charisma but also seemed incapable of repairing the massive economic woes caused by the wars. Units of the French army disobeyed orders to capture Napoleon and, instead, joined him. On one occasion whose drama Napoleon savored, he stepped out in front of his men, opened his coat to the Royalist soldiers confronting them, and dared the soldiers to shoot (he had already received strong hints that they would not). Rather than do so, they promised to follow him. One field marshal who had declared his loyalty to the new regime initially promised to bring Napoleon back to Paris in a cage but then switched sides yet again. Louis XVIII pledged to die rather than leave Paris but quickly thought better of the idea and fled to Belgium.

Within three weeks of his escape, to the shock and consternation of the allies, Napoleon had returned to Paris amid scenes of frenzied enthusiasm. But could he, this time, remain in power? Although his feat excited admiration in the population, genuine support for Napoleon was fragile and thin. Very few people in France wanted a resumption of the wars, while the remnants of the revolutionary left sought a new Republic, not the return of Empire. In an attempt to gain their support, Napoleon quickly issued an amended constitution, with firm guarantees for freedom

The Hundred Days, 1815

of speech and real power for his previously rubber-stamp legislature. He also insisted that he had no desire to resume his program of conquest. But the allied powers quickly ruled out any idea of compromise, instead declaring Napoleon an outlaw. They began to reassemble their armies, even while continuing with the negotiations at Vienna for a general peace settlement.

This time, Napoleon's fate was decided in little more than three months, giving the bizarre episode the title of "**the Hundred Days.**" Frantically, Napoleon tried to raise a new army and to convert factories to the production of munitions. In June 1815, he marched north into Belgium to meet the allied armies, hoping against hope that a quick, decisive victory might bring them to the negotiating table, or at least divide them sufficiently to increase the chances of his political survival. On June 18, near the small Belgian village of Waterloo, he found himself pitted against a general he had never previously faced: Britain's Wellington, who had led the efforts to defeat him in Spain. Wellington deployed his red-coated infantry in a long firing line at the crucial moment to blast Napoleon's elite Imperial Guard. The timely appearance of Prussian forces helped win the day for the allies. The defeated French streamed back toward Paris, and after another brief period of confusion, Napoleon surrendered.

The allies did not prove as lenient in 1815 as in 1814. They quickly dispatched the emperor into exile on the tiny island of Saint Helena, in the South Atlantic, as a prisoner under the guard of the British army, with only a handful of loyal retainers by his side. There, in 1821 he died, probably of stomach cancer. In the hastily revised peace settlement, France lost additional small slices of territory and had additional reparations imposed upon it. Louis XVIII returned for a second time to Paris, where the exhausted population greeted him with muted acceptance. But because the episode had taken so little time, the Vienna peace settlement survived the shock.

POST-NAPOLEONIC EUROPE

At first glance, it might seem as if the new Europe of 1815 resembled nothing so much as the old Europe of 1788.

Nearly every European state remained a monarchy, and in most cases the same family sat on the throne as thirty years before. The most important exception was Sweden, where in 1809 the parliament had tried to placate Napoleon by appointing his marshal Jean-Baptiste Bernadotte to the throne (Bernadotte's descendants sit on the Swedish throne to this day). The overall apparent continuity, however, masked a break with the past that was almost as radical as the one that had occurred in 1789.

ABSORBING THE CHANGES

The French author François-René de Chateaubriand (1768–1848) did not exaggerate much when he commented, soon after 1815, about the period just ended, that "this quarter of a century contained many centuries." Just as Napoleon's glittery coronation as emperor in 1804 had concealed the continuing effects of the French Revolution, so too did the apparent restoration of the old order after his defeat. In fact, the Revolution had wrought immense changes even on those states that explicitly defined their policies *against* it. Most important, in the Europe of 1815 few European sovereigns still seriously claimed to rule by divine right. To one extent or another, they now mostly admitted the principle of the sovereignty of the nation. Even France's Louis XVIII, who claimed that he had only "granted" a constitution to the country, did not challenge the idea that an elected legislature would henceforth express the national will and make laws. The most important exception to this broad European rule was Russia, where Tsar Alexander had largely abandoned his earlier inclination toward reform. After 1815, he not only continued to claim absolute authority on the basis of divine ordination but also refused to allow for the possibility of an elected parliament. He also defended the system of serfdom that continued to keep the majority of the peasantry in a condition of effective slavery. Yet even in Russia, as we will see, a liberal opposition was beginning to take shape.

A NEW POLITICS

The very notion of a "**liberal**" opposition signified that throughout Europe political life as a whole was taking on a new shape, centered on the division between liberal and conservative movements. Before 1789, the very terms "liberal" and "**conservative**" had been largely unknown and would have poorly described the politics of most European countries. But after 1815, starting in Britain and France, "liberal" became a common term, used to signify a desire for extending democratic representation to as large a swathe of the population as possible; defending the revolutionary principle of human rights; and breaking down the cumbersome systems of state-chartered corporate bodies that had previously characterized most European economies. At the same time, the term "conservative" came to signify an opposition to liberal and revolutionary politics. Some conservatives, following the great British political thinker Edmund Burke, venerated tradition for the stability and purpose it supposedly brought to society. Others did so in the name of Christian faith. In Britain, the pro-monarchical Tory Party of William Pitt would soon become known as the Conservative Party, a name it holds to this day.

Although the "liberal" agenda remained very far from fulfilled, a much greater degree of actual liberty prevailed in Europe in 1815 than in 1789. Throughout Germany and Italy, the French and their local allies had largely abolished the old guild systems that controlled artisanal work and trade. In most cases, these systems did not return in anything like their previous form. The French had also instituted religious freedom, and while several states (notably Spain) in 1815 moved to reestablish the hegemony of their traditional churches, most members of religious minorities faced fewer restrictions than before. In Germany and Italy, where the French tore down the walls of Jewish ghettos, anti-Semitism was restrained, at least for the time being. (By contrast, the Jews in the expanded Russian Empire faced continuing legal hardships.) In most European states, freedom of speech after 1815 was still highly restricted by modern standards, with Britain and the Netherlands being the main exceptions. But vigorous newspaper cultures were taking hold throughout nearly all of western and central Europe. In France, where Napoleon had shut down all but four national newspapers, a lively and combative press sprang back into operation upon his defeat.

THE SURVIVAL OF REVOLUTIONARY RADICALISM

As Alexis de Tocqueville astutely observed of the French Revolution, nothing stimulates demands for change like the beginnings of change, especially when governments then act to frustrate it. The years immediately after 1815, even while seeing both the triumph of a revitalized monarchical order in Europe and the subtle penetration of many French revolutionary values, also saw the birth of new, radical, and often nationalist revolutionary movements.

In Italy, these movements took the form of secret societies known as the **Carbonari** ("charcoal-burners"), organized into lodges with elaborate initiation rituals on the model of the freemasons, and originally formed to resist Napoleonic rule. After 1815, however, they quickly began to conspire against the restored regimes, particularly of the Austrian Empire in northern Italy and the Bourbon kingdom of the Two Sicilies (the name now taken by the kingdom of Naples) in the south. The Carbonari sought the establishment of a revolutionary democracy and a unified Italy. In France as well, pro-revolutionary sentiment remained strong, although mixed in with nostalgia for Napoleon. It deeply frightened the police, who diligently recorded even its smallest and most bizarre manifestations (including the appearance of Napoleon's

Carbonari Members of a Carbonari group crowd into a windowless room lit by a single lamp to listen to a speaker in this 1820 illustration. Some of the men read books in the low light, emphasizing the clandestine intellectual culture that accompanied the movement.

image in packs of cards, and a family who claimed to have seen his face on the surface of a flattened egg). In 1820, a radical artisan hoping for the overthrow of the monarchy fatally stabbed the duke of Berry, second in line to the throne. In Greece, where the Ottoman Turks had ruled since the fifteenth century, a radical nationalist movement began to take shape, led by a secret society of exiled Greeks founded in 1814 on the model of the Carbonari.

REFORM AND REPRESSION IN BRITAIN

Vigorous radical movements also took shape in Britain. During the French Revolutionary and Napoleonic wars, a surge of popular patriotism curtailed much of the agitation for reform that had been developing in the 1760s and 1770s around such figures as John Wilkes. Some half a million men volunteered for military service in the event of a French invasion and underwent military training. Yet a number of notable radicals continued to press for an extension of the vote to all adult males and for a reform of the election system, which excluded millions of Britons from the suffrage and which, in many cases, left the choice of members of parliaments up to a handful of powerful local grandees. In 1815 a leading radical, the journalist William Cobbett, who had once been known for his anti-Jacobinism, even praised the hated Napoleon, saying: "Thy fame still lives in every Freeman's heart." Enough Britons shared Cobbett's views that when the ship bearing Napoleon to Saint Helena briefly stopped in Plymouth, the government rushed to move it out of British territorial waters, lest a sympathetic magistrate attempt to order the former emperor's release. Although in 1799 the government had outlawed the so-called corresponding societies—which had formed seven years earlier to press for parliamentary reform—their point of view was still regularly heard in the robust radical press.

On August 16, 1819, radical agitation and government repression collided violently in the northern English city of Manchester, which was then just beginning to change under the impact of industrialization. A crowd of some 60,000 to 80,000, mostly working people but well dressed and peaceful, gathered in St. Peter's Fields to demonstrate for parliamentary reform and the repeal of the so-called corn laws, which kept the price of cereals artificially high by restricting foreign imports. Local magistrates, fearing a riot, ordered out hundreds of police, infantry, and cavalrymen. When the crowd apparently resisted orders to disperse, the cavalrymen attacked, injuring hundreds and killing eleven. The episode immediately became known as

Peterloo Massacre The great British illustrator George Cruikshank (1792–1878) made this etching of cavalry, with swords drawn, trampling demonstrators at St. Peter's Fields. The illustration was addressed to a radical member of Parliament, urging him to condemn the attack.

the "**Peterloo Massacre**" and further galvanized British reformers, as we will soon see.

CONCLUSION

In a poem of savage beauty titled "England in 1819," inspired by the tragedy in Manchester, Percy Bysshe Shelley (1792–1822) memorialized "a people starved and stabbed in the untilled field" at the behest of

> Rulers who neither see nor feel nor know,
> But leechlike to their fainting country cling
> Till they drop, blind in blood, without a blow. . . .

But Shelley also offered hope that from the graves of Peterloo and the desperate attempts of Britain's elites to hold on to their privileges, a "glorious Phantom" of hope might yet "burst, to illumine our tempestuous day."

The years that would follow 1819 indeed saw many such phantoms bursting forth in Europe. These movements inherited the passions of the Napoleonic years but did not equal the wars in their ferocity. The massive tide of organized violence that had reached its height in 1812 steadily receded. Napoleon Bonaparte himself, for all the enormous disruption he had caused, quickly faded into a faintly comic figure, mocked for his pretentious poses and allegedly small stature (actually, he was of average height). He became known as the man whose identity was most often claimed by the inmates of insane asylums. Yet his enormous impact on virtually every aspect of European society, politics, and culture could not be denied—it was greater than that of any other single individual of the eighteenth or nineteenth centuries. As his enemies attempted to impose newer, stricter forms of order on the Continent, new forms of resistance were germinating, thanks in large part to stunningly rapid economic change. It is to those that we now turn.

[CHAPTER REVIEW]

KEY TERMS

Civil Code (p. 574)
Austerlitz (p. 577)
treaties of Tilsit (p. 578)
Continental System (p. 579)

Peninsular War (p. 581)
guerrilla warfare (p. 581)
Luddites (p. 586)
romanticism (p. 589)

Charles-Maurice de Talleyrand (p. 592)
Congress of Vienna (p. 593)
Concert of Europe (p. 594)
the Hundred Days (p. 595)

liberalism (p. 596)
conservatism (p. 596)
Carbonari (p. 597)
Peterloo Massacre (p. 598)

REVIEW QUESTIONS

1. During his first five years in power, how did Napoleon restore French influence and prestige in Europe?

2. What were Napoleon's principal domestic accomplishments from 1799 to 1804?

3. What provoked resistance to French rule in Italy and Spain?

4. How did Napoleon design his capital and use the arts to reflect his ambition of creating a world empire?

5. In what ways did European society become more militarized during the Napoleonic age?

6. Why did Britain's economy outperform other European countries' economies during the Napoleonic age?

7. How did the Russian campaign contribute to Napoleon's downfall?

8. What led Prussia and Austria to break their alliance with France?

9. What were the principal elements of the agreement reached at the Congress of Vienna?

10. What major changes had taken place in European society and politics by 1815?

CORE OBJECTIVES

After reading this chapter, you should have a solid understanding of the following core objectives. To strengthen your grasp of the core objectives, use the resources on the Student Site for The West.

- Explain how Napoleon created his European empire.
- Evaluate the factors that undermined the stability of the Napoleonic order.
- Analyze the Napoleonic empire at its height.

- Assess the downfall of Napoleon and his empire.
- Describe the political order that emerged from Napoleon's defeat.

 GO TO **inQuizitive** TO SEE WHAT YOU'VE LEARNED—AND LEARN WHAT YOU'VE MISSED—WITH PERSONALIZED FEEDBACK ALONG THE WAY.

1810s–1820s
Latin American colonies
seek independence

1819
First transatlantic
steamship crossing

September 27, 1825
First commercial
railroad opens in England

December 1825
Decembrist revolt
against Nikolai I

1828–1829
Russo-Turkish War

1830
France begins
colonization of Algeria

1830–1832
Polish revolt against Russia

Early 1830s
Cholera epidemic
across Europe

July 1830
July Revolution
in France

1831
Mazzini founds
Young Italy movement

1832
Greece gains
independence

1832
Reform Bill
in Britain

1833
Unrest in Spain
following
Fernando VII's
death

1833
Abolition of
slavery in
British Empire

1835, 1840
Tocqueville publishes
Democracy in America

Acceleration

THE AGE OF INDUSTRY

1820–1845

1838–1848
Chartist movement
in Britain

1839–1842
First Opium War

1844
Morse invents telegraph

Early on the morning of September 27, 1825, several thousand men and women converged on the small town of Brusselton, in northern England, to see an unusual spectacle. The starring role was played by a large, ungainly metal cylinder, resting on four hefty wheels and sporting a thick black funnel on one end. The whole contraption, including a coal-burning furnace, weighed eight tons. As the spectators watched, engineers lit the furnace, which powered a steam engine that turned the wheels. Slowly, the entire machine began to roll along two parallel metal tracks. It pulled thirty-six small wagons loaded with flour, coal, and six hundred passengers, everything together weighing over fifty tons. The spectators later went home, but the engine and wagons continued to roll, reaching a speed of over six miles per hour. On some downhill sections of the track, the speed increased to as much as fifteen miles an hour, panicking passengers, at least one of whom jumped off and badly injured himself. Four hours after leaving Brusselton, the train arrived safely at the port town of Stockton, twenty-four miles down the tracks. The world's first commercial railway had just staged its inaugural trip.

Despite the shock felt by some at the train's occasional high speed, there was nothing particularly new about the technology on view that September morning. Primitive steam

Industrial Innovations A lithograph celebrates the opening of the first railway in Italy, which ran from Naples to Portici, five miles to the south, in 1839. People of all classes watch from a distance, while a crowd on the platform rushes to board the train. The speed and accessibility of train travel completely transformed the lives of people across Europe.

FOCUS QUESTIONS

- What were the most significant causes and effects of the Industrial Revolution?
- What were the key elements of middle-class life in this period?
- How was the industrial working class changing in this period?
- What were the major themes of the Romantic movement?
- What broad changes occurred in the politics of the period?
- In what ways was this a period of repression and reform?
- How did the rise of nationalism affect the international order?

engines dated back to more than a century earlier, and James Watt's commercially successful models had come into wide use by the 1770s. As early as 1801, the inventor Richard Trevithick (1771–1833) used a steam engine to power a moving coach he called the Puffing Devil. But Trevithick's invention did not immediately lead to commercial railroads. Despite the popular image of inventors changing the world and striking it rich simply by tinkering at workbenches, technological progress required a great deal more than just individual genius, even in the early nineteenth century. It also required capital—to develop and test prototypes, pay employees, purchase property and material, and build infrastructure. At a time when the average British agricultural laborer earned just £30 per year, the Brusselton–Stockton railway cost some £125,000 to build—tens of millions of today's dollars. The railway's promoters raised the money from wealthy investors who hoped to make a profit by moving coal efficiently from the mines around Brusselton to ships that would deliver it to port cities in Britain and around the world. And technological progress involved politics as well—just to build this first line required two separate acts of the British Parliament, to appropriate land for the train tracks and to charter the company.

The same factors also slowed the initial spread of railways, even after this first line proved successful. Investors were not always easy to find, especially since prominent British engineers were still dismissing as "ridiculous expectations" the idea that trains could ever reach the frighteningly high speed of even twelve miles per hour on an even grade. In 1830, a 35-mile-long railway opened between the emerging British industrial centers of Liverpool and Manchester. But proposals to connect London to the commercial city of Birmingham, some 112 miles away, met with ferocious opposition from landowners who did not want their property taken for tracks, and from road- and canal-builders who saw in the proposed railway a threat to their interests. It took Parliament three years to approve the project. The line itself cost £5,000,000, with construction lasting five years and involving 20,000 workers.

Still, the early experiments eventually spurred an explosion of railway building in Britain. Although in 1835 the country still had only 293 miles of railroad, by 1840 this number had risen to 1,435, and by 1850 to over 6,600. Other countries followed the British example. Russia opened its first passenger railroad in 1837 and had 3,000 miles of track by the mid-1860s. Rail transport became routine for cargo and passengers alike, with millions of people and millions of tons of goods traveling each year on journeys of tens or even hundreds of miles on regular schedules. And they did so at speeds that, as early as 1840, could reach as high as fifty miles per hour.

Historians today tend to dislike the term **Industrial Revolution**. It implies a sudden, violent break in patterns of economic and social activity, as if agricultural societies gave way in just a few years to systems of large-scale industrial production. Instead, historians stress that economic change in the nineteenth century occurred gradually, with a full-fledged industrial system first taking hold only in a few specialized zones. The system required many decades to become a major presence even in the most economically advanced European countries.

Yet we should not discount the immensity of the changes that did follow upon industrialization. The spectators who descended on Brusselton in 1825 knew that they were witnessing a historic event. And by the early 1840s, when it became clear that all corners of the Continent would soon be joined in one gigantic rail network, some farsighted observers already grasped the profound implications for the way human beings understood and experienced the world. Heinrich Heine (1797–1856), a German poet living in France, wrote in 1843: "Even the elementary concepts of time and space have begun to vacillate. Space is killed by the railways. …I feel as if the mountains and forests of all countries are advancing on Paris. Even now, I can smell the German linden trees, the North Sea's breakers are rolling against my door." And even as this transportation revolution disrupted concepts of space, the broader process of industrialization altered patterns of everyday life for people throughout Europe and the conduct of everything from warfare to novel-writing.

And industrialization represented only one form of the radical disorientation and sense of acceleration that Europeans experienced during the years 1820–45. In literature and the arts, the period saw the heyday of the romantic movement, which sought to overturn long-established stylistic practices and unsettle its audiences. In politics, it saw a revival of democratic, even revolutionary, energies that were often met by fierce, violent reaction. It saw the development of new forms of social thought. For the first time, writers and politicians, some radical but some conservative, began to define the most important forms of competition within European states as *social* competition that pitted different parts of society against one another. Meanwhile, with France's conquest of Algeria in 1830, the period saw the start of a new and unsettling phase in the history of European empire, involving the way European states both competed with one another abroad and dealt with non-European peoples.

Historians often isolate these different forms of disorienting change from one another. But the experience of what we now call "modernity" in fact derived in large part from the way they reinforced and interacted with one another. This chapter, therefore, will examine the period 1820–45 as a whole, exploring the parallels between these different, but connected, realms of human existence.

THE INDUSTRIAL REVOLUTION

Of the many disrupting and disorienting changes that occurred in Europe between 1820 and 1845, the most significant, in long-term perspective, were those connected with industrial development. As we have already seen, what historians now call the Industrial Revolution had begun well before 1820. But in these decades it accelerated dramatically, forever changing daily life for a large proportion of Europeans, and setting in motion a process that would eventually do the same for nearly all of the human race.

FIVE FACTORS PROMOTING INDUSTRIAL DEVELOPMENT

The revolution was driven by the same factors we have already seen at work in the eighteenth century. First came coal, whose combustion releases energy initially absorbed from the sun hundreds of millions of years ago by vegetation, and stored in what eventually hardened under pressure into sedimentary rock. When the steam engine made possible the conversion of this energy into mechanical power, humans gained the ability to do far more work, more efficiently, than with muscles alone (whether human or animal) and far more conveniently than with wind or water mills. To take just one example, a textile worker in the 1820s using a steam-driven spindle could produce a hundred times more thread per hour than his or her pre-industrial counterpart had managed. The only alternate fuel at this stage of technological development—charcoal from wood—simply did not exist in sufficient quantities. As a British writer put it in mid-century: "Coal in truth stands not beside, but entirely above, all other commodities. It is the material source of the energy of the country—the universal aid—the factor in everything we do. With coal almost any feat is possible; without it we are thrown back into the laborious poverty of early times."

Second, an engineering culture of constant, competitive innovation not only rewarded inventions but also quickly multiplied their efficiency. The spinning mule, for instance, was invented in 1779 and made possible mechanized cotton production. Then in 1825, the inventor Richard Roberts developed an automatic mule that did not require skilled workers to operate it. By 1837, some 500,000 mules based on this design were in operation in the British Isles. The steam engine itself underwent constant improvement. Richard Trevithick could only create his "Puffing Devil" because he had invented a high-pressure engine that operated with greater efficiency than James Watt's engine of the 1780s.

Financial innovations that made capital easily available for industrial expansion were also crucial. The early nineteenth century saw a rapid expansion of banks that provided loans to companies and helped them sell bonds, and of stock exchanges where shares of ownership could be offered up for sale. The driving force here was so-called railway mania, especially in Britain. By 1847, the total value of British railway shares had risen to some £126,000,000, far outstripping the level of investment in cotton or iron.

A fourth factor, agricultural productivity, also mattered greatly. The eighteenth century, as we have seen, brought a milder climate to Europe, while the destructive effects of war were limited in comparison to previous centuries. Meanwhile, farmers in northwestern Europe developed sophisticated crop rotation techniques, a better use of fertilizer, and the reclamation of marshland and heath previously deemed unsuitable for cultivation. The widespread adoption of potato cultivation helped the rural poor to raise their caloric intake significantly. Overall "yields" of wheat and other cereal crops (the amount produced for a given amount of seed) increased as well. All these trends continued in the decades after 1800, spurring greater agricultural profits, a rapidly rising population, and a larger overall food supply. The profits from these innovations produced capital that could be invested in industry, the rising population made available an industrial workforce, and the food supply ensured that this workforce had enough to eat.

Finally, while industrial capitalism is usually associated with the concept of free markets, the importance of state support must be acknowledged. States protected the rights of inventors with patent systems and helped provide a transportation and communications infrastructure. They projected diplomatic and military power abroad to open up export markets and to protect merchant shipping. The Industrial Revolution proceeded hand in hand with global trade, and it was European states and their armed forces that ensured this trade would be conducted to the advantage of Europeans.

WHY GREAT BRITAIN?

These five factors not only made the Industrial Revolution possible but also determined the place where it would begin: Great Britain. Rich seams of coal were more easily exploitable in Britain than almost anywhere else on earth. Britain's culture of innovation had flourished for centuries—thanks in part to the Protestant minority groups who valued gainful activity but were barred by law from government positions. Britain led the way in financial innovation as well. Between 1836 and 1845, stock exchanges were founded in most major British provincial cities, including Manchester, Liverpool, Birmingham, and

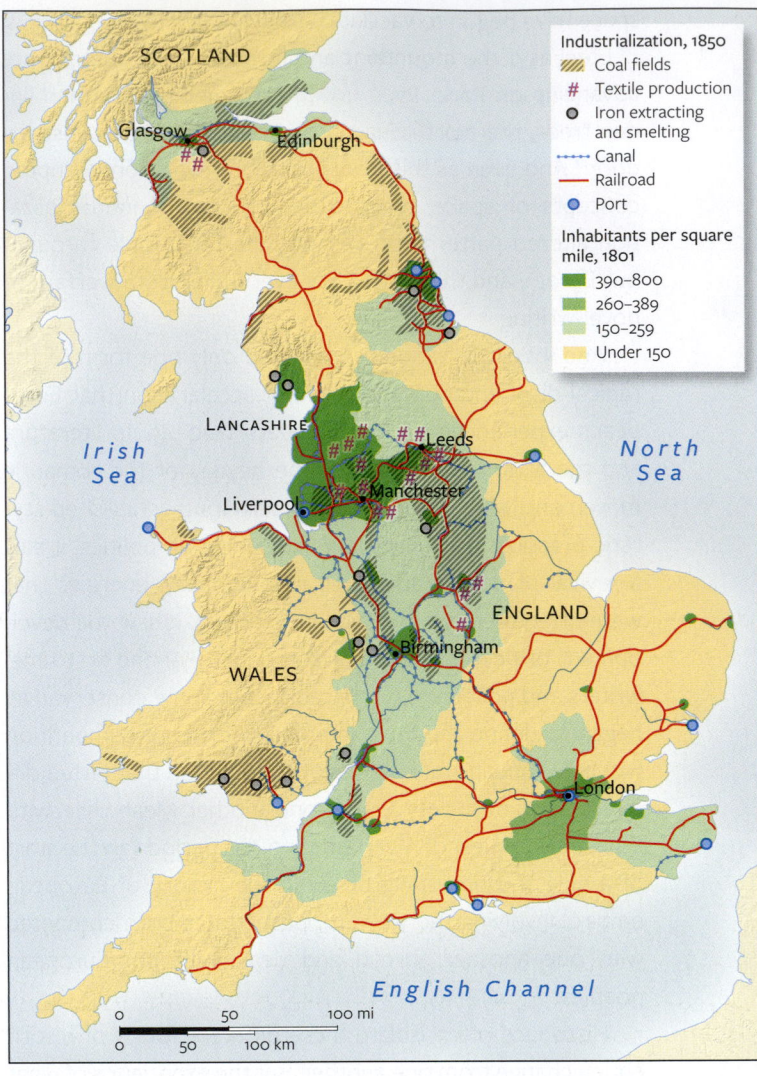

Industrialization in Britain, 1800–1850 By 1850, industrialization had changed the geography of Britain. Coal had been discovered in Wales, Scotland, and central northeast England. Though London remained a population center, workers also flocked to the factories in the booming industrial cities of Manchester, Leeds, and Birmingham, and dockworkers to the port of Liverpool. Railways increasingly linked far-flung parts of the country together, facilitating migration to the cities.

Edinburgh. The enclosure movement in Britain—which continued into the nineteenth century—favored the creation of large, market-oriented farms over small-scale subsistence farming. Already by the 1830s, England was producing three times as much grain as it had in the mid-eighteenth century. And the British state fully recognized the importance of commercial and industrial wealth to the nation's political fortunes, and acted accordingly. British merchant ships could bring raw materials to

Britain, and ship manufactured goods to the rest of the world, because they enjoyed the protection of the world's most formidable navy.

From its earliest years, the Industrial Revolution impacted many different sectors of the European economy. Given the centrality of coal, mining developed rapidly. Between 1800 and 1850, Great Britain's annual coal output increased fivefold. But soon Britain was not alone. By 1850, the Ruhr region of Germany had 300 coal mines, and the industry was expanding rapidly as well in Belgium. Iron had enormous importance as well, being necessary for engines, locomotives, railroad tracks, and bridges strong enough to bear the weight of trains. A series of technological innovations in the last decades of the eighteenth century in Britain allowed for the production of stronger steel at lower cost than in previous times, and production boomed. Annual production, which had stood at only 12,000 metric tons in Britain in 1700, reached 250,000 metric tons soon after 1800, and 2,000,000 by 1850.

COTTON: THE THREAD OF GLOBAL EXCHANGE

But the most important industry, overall, was textiles, and more specifically, cotton. A fabric lighter and more comfortable than wool, sturdier than linen, and easily dyed with bright colors, cotton grew in tropical climates and had long been imported into Europe. But its production had been time consuming and expensive, because of the need to separate seeds from the raw cotton by hand. Then in 1793 a young American inventor named Eli Whitney built a machine—the "cotton gin"—that could do the job faster and more efficiently than human hands could. Once regular Atlantic trade resumed in 1815 with the end of the Napoleonic Wars, cotton production expanded at a dizzying rate. British imports of raw cotton grew fortyfold between 1785 and 1850, by which date cotton goods accounted for two-thirds of British textile exports and a full 40 percent of British exports overall. The number of power looms in use in England rose nearly one hundredfold between 1813 and 1850.

Like sugar in the eighteenth century, cotton was a commodity that tied together European consumer capitalism and global trade. The production of cheap cotton did more than any other single factor to put fashion within the reach of non-elite social groups. Even poor people could now purchase outfits for pleasure as well as for practical use and change them before they wore out. As a moralizing

contributor to a British magazine warned sternly in 1828: "The present low price of articles of dress naturally tempts persons to an improper fondness for show." Textile manufacturers eagerly took advantage of the trend, encouraging regular changes in women's fashions in particular, in the hope of stimulating consumption.

Cotton thread bound Europe more tightly than ever into global patterns of exchange. The need to import ever-greater quantities of raw cotton made Britain even more dependent on the slave economies of the Americas. Most of these slave economies no longer formed part of European empires, thanks to the independence of the United States followed by most of Latin America by the mid-1820s. Slavery in the remaining European colonies, particularly in the Caribbean, was overwhelmingly dedicated to sugar production, and while slave-produced sugar did not lose its profitability, it represented a shrinking proportion of European trade overall. But the expansion of cotton textile production strengthened the slave plantation system elsewhere, especially in the southern United States and Brazil. Fully 80 percent of all cotton spun in British mills was picked by slaves.

At the same time, the cotton boom had devastating consequences for other parts of the globe. Originally, Indians had manufactured most of the cotton fabric consumed in Europe. But competition with Britain, which colonial officials made harsher by imposing new financial burdens on indigenous production, turned the tables. Imports of manufactured cotton by south Asia from Europe increased

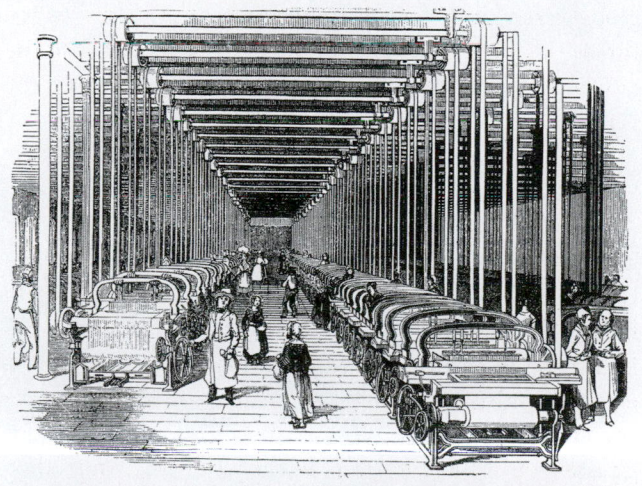

Textile Mills The scale of the new methods of textile production is evident in this 1830 illustration of a Lancashire cotton mill. Workers attend to rows and rows of power looms, which are attached to the shafts and belts that supply them with steam power.

TURNER'S *RAIN, STEAM AND SPEED—THE GREAT WESTERN RAILWAY*

J. M. W. Turner (1775–1851) was one of nineteenth-century Britain's leading painters. His work from the 1830s and 1840s reflected the effects of industrialization on Britain. In the course of a few decades, Britain was overlaid with a network of railways linking together the nation at speeds from 30 to 50 miles per hour, much faster than previous modes of transportation. Reflecting Turner's predisposition to experimenting on his canvases, his 1844 painting *Rain, Steam and Speed—The Great Western Railway* invented a new visual and painterly repertoire to capture the speed of rail transport and its transformation of the landscape. A train from London starts as a blurry dark streak against a pale white and blue background of steam and rain, with only the locomotive's chimney attaining a clear shape and form as it hurtles across a bridge over the Thames and toward the viewer. Turner's work illustrates how the industrial era both awed observers and stretched the bounds of human perception.

QUESTIONS FOR ANALYSIS

1. How does Turner attempt to represent the speed and movement of the train?
2. What effects of industrialization do you see in this painting?
3. How does Turner's painting capture the ways in which industrialization transformed humans' relationship to the natural world?

fifteenfold between 1820 and 1840, leading to an effective deindustrialization of this sector of the Indian economy.

NEW MEANS OF TRANSPORTATION AND COMMUNICATION

The new industrial technology did a great deal to facilitate faster and denser patterns of transportation and communication. Within Europe, railroads made it possible to transport coal, steel, and manufactured goods far more quickly and efficiently than in previous centuries. And nearly as important as the railroads was the introduction of steamships into maritime transport. The first steamships had come into commercial use in the 1810s, starting in the United States. In 1819, the first ship using steam to supplement sail power crossed the Atlantic from Savannah, Georgia, to Liverpool, England, and it was followed within a decade by ships that made the crossing on steam alone. By 1840, the Canadian Samuel Cunard (1787–1865) had a line of four steamships making trips across the Atlantic on a weekly schedule, carrying both passengers and cargo. In the same year, some eighty steamships were being used full-time to bring Irish cattle and dairy products to England.

In 1844, news came to Europe of a particularly astonishing invention. A dozen years before, a fashionable American painter, traveling in France, had come across a system first developed under Napoleon Bonaparte for quickly transmitting messages over long distances: a network of towers, spaced six miles apart, with mechanical arms or flags that could be seen through a telescope from the next tower down the line. The painter—his name was Samuel Morse (1791–1872)—became convinced that electric wires could transmit messages more quickly and efficiently using a simple binary code, and in 1844 he successfully demonstrated a prototype connecting Washington and Baltimore. An English-language newspaper in Paris quickly relayed an American journalist's verdict on Morse's "telegraph," which uncannily echoed Heine's comment on the railroads: "This is indeed the annihilation of space."

THE SURGING GROWTH OF CITIES

In Europe, the most visible effect of the Industrial Revolution was the spectacular and uncontrolled growth of cities—especially in Britain. The textile-manufacturing city of Manchester, whose population had barely exceeded

Steamships In this 1838 painting by the British artist J. M. W. Turner (1775–1851), an iron steamship belching smoke tows an old sailing ship to the dock where it will be demolished. The setting sun bathes the scene in a nostalgic glow, despite what a great many people would have viewed as progress.

15,000 in 1750, grew to over 70,000 inhabitants by 1800, and 185,000 by 1850. Cities involved in shipping and finance as well as textiles grew rapidly as well: in the same period, London's population more than doubled to 2.3 million, and Liverpool's more than quadrupled to 400,000. In 1850, for the first time in world history, fully half the population of a major territorial state—Great Britain—lived in large cities. And the very layout and appearance of these cities was undergoing drastic alteration. Rapidly built industrial housing in Britain most often used dark brick, each house virtually identical to the next. And now the largest and tallest buildings, visible from afar, were increasingly not cathedrals but factories with huge chimneys belching smoke. In 1842, a chemical manufacturer in Glasgow named Charles Tennant erected a chimney 435 feet tall—the highest in the world at the time, and higher than all but nine cathedral spires in Europe.

DAILY LIFE AND WORKING CONDITIONS

Daily life in this new industrial landscape differed from anything previously seen in world history. For the first time, most people no longer worked where they lived. Charles Tennant's chemical plant, for example, covered over a hundred acres, had 250,000 square feet of work space, and employed over a thousand people. Work itself became divorced from natural rhythms, with factories sometimes operating twenty-four hours a day to achieve greater efficiency. And the work was more intensive and repetitive than anything seen in pre-industrial workshops.

CHILD LABOR

And it was not just adult men doing this work. In one survey of Lancashire cotton mills from 1833, 35 percent of all workers were under the age of sixteen, and 5 percent under eleven. In the 1840s, close to half of all workers in the British textile industry were female, and many now brought their children to work with them in factories. Factory owners insisted, in testimony to Parliament, that it was better to have small children usefully employed than running wild—the owners did not consider school as an alternative. They even claimed that the children's smaller fingers were necessary for some of the more delicate work on the great mechanical looms used to make cloth. But repeated investigations showed children working exhausting hours (as many as sixteen per day) in dangerous and unsanitary conditions. In response, Parliament passed a series of Factory Acts, starting in 1819, that put increasingly strict limits on working hours for children, banned those under age nine from the workplace, and mandated some degree of schooling. The same legislation prescribed limited working hours for women as well. Yet critics saw the acts as inadequate to the problem and complained that their provisions were frequently ignored.

Industrial Labor The new system of industrial labor affected people of all ages, who might previously have worked together on farms. This illustration of a London glassworks from 1842 shows small boys laboring alongside men in a hot and dangerous workshop.

THE RESPONSE TO INDUSTRY

The rise of these new industrial landscapes horrified many observers. Consider, for instance, the reformer Ernest Jones's savage 1847 poem "The Factory Town." Whereas Jones's more famous predecessor William Blake had used the memorable phrase "dark satanic mills" to describe factories arising in supposedly pastoral settings, Jones sketched out an entire infernal landscape. In his description, "lurid fires" spring everywhere from chimneys so that the industrial town "like a cauldron bubbled"—and with "poison," no less. Within the factories' "reeking walls," amid "heavy, choking air" full of whirling dust, workers with "white, cracked, fevered lips" toiled day after day, alongside "half-naked infants" and spectral women. Even as the "bloated" factory owner boasted of his productivity to foreign visitors, his "crushed" masses, longing for the "dewy grasses" of their childhoods, cried out their misery:

> Hark! Amid the bloodless slaughter
> Comes the wailing of despair:
> "Oh! For but one drop of water!
> "Oh! For but one breath of air!"

A constant theme in the literature of the day was the contrast between the beauties of the British countryside, where men and women could lead "natural" lives, and the ugliness, artificiality, and filth of factory towns, along with the inhuman forms of exploitation, scarcely better than slavery, that prevailed there.

INDUSTRIAL EVOLUTION: THE PACE OF CHANGE

Nearly two centuries later, these criticisms retain their power to shock; but in some important ways they are also misleading. For all its importance, the Industrial Revolution did not transform all of European society at once. It affected different parts of the Continent at different times and at different rates. Even in the areas that were first and most sharply affected, not everyone experienced the changes in the same way. And despite factories like Charles Tennant's, the overall movement of the workforce into large factories took place more slowly than these spectacular examples might suggest. The "Industrial Revolution" was in many ways more of an "Industrial Evolution."

VARIATIONS ACROSS THE CONTINENT

Before 1845, the new forces associated with industrialism barely touched large portions of the Continent. During this

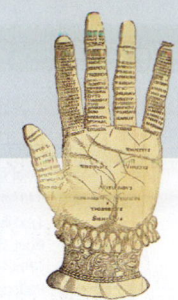

A GIRL'S LIFE IN THE MINES

In the early nineteenth century, cotton mills, factories, and coal mines were only too happy to take on workers who would command a lower wage than adult male workers, and families desperate for income sent children to work. The sight of young girls and boys working in brutal conditions in the mines scandalized some—in particular, Lord Ashley, the earl of Shaftesbury, who introduced legislation in Parliament to regulate children's work. In 1841–42, he invited young workers to testify before his Parliamentary Commission. Their testimony painted a grim portrait of industrial labor.

Patience Kershaw was a coal "hurrier"—a worker who hauled coal from the pits to the surface—and she testified before Lord Ashley's Commission about the hard work in the mines. Testimony like Kershaw's helped spur Parliament to approve the Mines and Collieries Act of 1842, an early example of British workplace legislation.

My father has been dead about a year; my mother is living and has ten children, five lads and five lasses; the oldest is about thirty, the youngest is four; three lasses go to mill; all the lads are colliers,[1] two getters[2] and three hurriers; one lives at home and does nothing; mother does nought but look after home.

All my sisters have been hurriers, but three went to the mill. Alice went because her legs swelled from hurrying in cold water when she was hot. I never went to day-school; I go to Sunday-school, but I cannot read or write; I go to pit at five o'clock in the morning and come out at five in the evening; I get my breakfast of porridge and milk first; I take my dinner with me, a cake, and eat it as I go; I do not stop or rest any time for the purpose; I get nothing else until I get home, and then have potatoes and meat, not every day meat. I hurry in the clothes I have now got on, trousers and ragged jacket; the bald place upon my head is made by thrusting the corves[3]; my legs have never swelled, but sisters' did when they went to mill; I hurry the corves a mile and more under ground and back; they weigh three hundred pounds; I hurry 11 a-day; I wear a belt and chain at the workings, to get the corves out; the getters that I work for are naked except their caps; they pull off all their clothes; I see them at work when I go up; sometimes they beat me, if I am not quick enough, with their hands; they strike me upon my back; the boys take liberties with me; sometimes they pull me about; I am the only girl in the pit; there are about 20 boys and 15 men; all the men are naked; I would rather work in mill than in coal-pit.

QUESTIONS FOR ANALYSIS

1. According to Patience Kershaw's testimony, what kinds of work did children do in the coal mines?
2. What were conditions like in the mines, both for children and for adults?
3. What abuses did Kershaw suffer in the mines?

[1] **colliers:** coal miners
[2] **getters:** coal cutters
[3] **corves:** wagons

Source: Patience Kershaw, *Testimony before the Parliamentary Committee on Mines, Parliamentary Papers*, 1842, XV–XVII, Appendix 1; Appendix 2.

---

period, fully 70 percent of all the growth in European urban populations took place in a single country: Great Britain. Some "**factory towns**" sprang up in France, the Low Countries, and Catalonia, and by 1850 the Ruhr region of Germany counted hundreds of mills and foundries producing textiles, lumber, and iron. But most of eastern and southern Germany, along with most of southern France, remained heavily agricultural; and further east the Russian economy did not differ all that greatly from what it had been in the previous century, with over a third of the population living in the virtual slavery of serfdom. The Italian economy would likewise only see substantial increases in industrial production later in the century. Even in Britain, the rise of "factory towns" took place above all in a single rough geographical triangle, 100 miles or so on a side, between the cities of Birmingham,

Industrialization in Europe, 1800–1850 Industrialization was slower to take hold on the Continent than in Britain. Coal- and iron-producing regions were spread more sparsely, and along with railroads were concentrated in northern Europe. Though many areas, including in the south, retained historic strengths as ports or textile-producing regions, nowhere came close to Britain's concentration of large industrial cities.

Liverpool, and Leeds (and bulging up to the north over the county of Lancashire). This area had large coal deposits and, even before the railroads began, a robust transportation system in the form of canals.

A MIX OF TECHNOLOGIES Even in the industrial centers, factories did not simply replace older forms of home-based hand labor—instead, they complemented it. In the textile industry, for instance, weaving long remained the province of predominantly female and predominantly rural "piece workers," who now worked with factory-produced fibers. And even in 1850, even in Britain,

only a minority of industrial workers spent their days in factories. The massive installations employing thousands of workers in Manchester and Birmingham existed alongside hundreds of smaller workshops employing a few dozen workers each. And in many industries, older, artisanal forms of labor survived well into the industrial age, including wood- and metal-workers, clothes-makers, glaziers, barrel-makers, and many others. The London Census of 1841 listed no fewer than 840 separate crafts occupations in the city.

Still, industrialization produced significant effects even in areas hundreds of miles from the nearest factory.

Cheap industrial products made their way into the marketplace, often undercutting local production, while farmers now had large new urban markets to produce for. Most significant, overall western European economic growth increased from a rate of around 1 percent a year in 1820 to just under 2 percent by 1845, allowing for the fastest rise in per capita income in the Continent's history.

SOCIAL CHANGE AND THE MIDDLE CLASSES

It was long believed that the Industrial Revolution took place as part of a fundamental upheaval in social structure. It supposedly marked the rise of the capitalist **bourgeoisie**, or middle classes, at the expense of the old aristocracy, and the birth of a new class, the industrial **proletariat** (working class). The founders of socialism, Karl Marx and Friedrich Engels, put it this way in 1848: "The bourgeoisie has subjected the country to the rule of the towns. It has created enormous cities, has greatly increased the urban population as compared with the rural.... Modern Industry has converted the little workshop of the patriarchal master into the great factory of the industrial capitalist." Yet in fact, just as the Industrial Revolution itself took place in a slower and more uneven manner than the term "revolution" might suggest, the changes in social structure were also more gradual and complex than Marx and Engels believed.

To begin with, there was no simple correlation between a person's social class and economic role. Even in the most "middle-class" country of all, Great Britain, a high proportion of the investment capital crucial to industrialization actually came from the landed aristocracy, which had long been more open to entrepreneurial activity than its continental counterparts. Indeed, traditional landed interests literally fueled the process, for industry could not have developed without a massive increase in the supply of coal to power steam engines and looms—and British coal came mostly from land owned by the gentry. As we have seen with the railroads, industrialization also required the support of a Parliament that was still elected by a tiny sliver of male landowners—just 200,000 men in the 1820s. In the early nineteenth century, this Parliament commanded a British state that spent more, borrowed more, and employed more people than any other institution in the country.

In France, meanwhile, not only did the nobility still possess much of the country's wealth, despite the attacks on them during the French Revolution; it now provided one of the major sources of investment capital. And under the Bourbon monarchy restored to power in 1815, nobles and wealthy landed bourgeois dominated a state that had even more influence on economic development than its British counterpart. Despite incessant political turmoil, successive French governments carried on the industrial policies sketched out by Napoleon's interior minister, Jean-Antoine Chaptal (1756–1832). He believed in free markets but sought to stimulate them through close supervision and to temper their inegalitarian excesses. Elsewhere in the industrializing portions of the Continent, traditional elites generally stood in even more favorable positions, leading one historian to describe the history of nineteenth-century Europe with the phrase "the persistence of the Old Regime."

DEFINING THE MIDDLE

The "middle classes" themselves were a particularly tricky phenomenon to define. Even in Britain, supposedly the country with the strongest middle class in the nineteenth century, not all observers perceived society as divided neatly into upper, middle, and lower classes. Some saw it as a more complex social hierarchy, while others believed it really consisted mostly of poor workers and farmers pitted against a handful of wealthy aristocrats, with little of significance in between. In France, the word "bourgeois"—which had originally designated non-noble town-dwellers—most often functioned as a term of abuse, designating a grasping individual who put self-interest above the public good.

Yet even with these qualifications, it is clear that the "middle class," which had existed as a social phenomenon for centuries, did take on extraordinary new importance in the first half of the nineteenth century. In a rough, common-sense definition, the middle class had always been composed of people who on the one hand did not possess noble titles or extraordinary wealth, and on the other did not work with their hands but lived comfortably (something that generally required, even for a small household, at least one or two servants). In this period, the middle class expanded greatly in numbers and wealth. Although exact numbers are impossible to come by, somewhere between 15 and 20 percent of the British population could be classified as "middle class" by 1845—considerably more than in previous periods. In most of southern and eastern Europe, by contrast, the figure was closer to 5 percent. Beyond their numbers, the middle class was becoming more of a social force: in a world where aristocratic courts set fashions less and less, noble rank no longer conferred automatic legal privilege, and nobles now paid taxes like anyone else, the middle class no longer existed in a state of subservience to its social superiors.

ROUTES TO THE MIDDLE CLASS: PROFESSIONS AND EDUCATION

Much of the expansion of the middle class was driven by their participation in trade and industry, but it would be a mistake to associate the middle class only with these economic sectors. Even in an industrial city like Leeds, in England, fewer than half of all middle-class families in the 1840s derived their incomes from employment in trade and industry. More often, heads of middle-class families worked as professionals in fields that experienced expansion as they served the growing industrial sector: lawyers, doctors, architects, teachers, and clergymen. Teaching proved particularly accessible to women, with an almost three-to-one ratio of female to male teachers in London by the 1850s. Where states were expanding, more middle-class civil servants were recruited to work in them. French state expenditures, for instance, rose some 50 percent between 1822 and 1842, and as they did, the middle class expanded.

Because of the importance of the professions and state bureaucracies, entry into which generally demanded formal training, the most reliable route into the middle class was not wealth but education. Of course, education itself generally required some wealth, but well-to-do artisans, farmers, clerks, and (in Protestant Europe) clergymen gladly subsidized their children's schooling in the hope of securing their social advancement. Few European states in this period provided free public schooling, even at the primary level. France began to introduce such a system in 1833 but did not make schooling compulsory, and many poorer families withdrew their children from school as soon as they became old enough to work. In the early nineteenth century, only one out of two hundred French boys, and far fewer girls, completed secondary school. In the German states, the number of secondary-school graduates doubled from 1820 to 1830 but still only reached 2,000 per year and comprised nearly all men. Outside of northwestern Europe, the numbers were even smaller. In 1848, Russia, with a population of roughly 70 million, had only 5,000 students, all male, enrolled in higher education. However, unlike today, one did not need a university degree, or even to have completed secondary school,

to enter many middle-class professions. Across Europe, literacy rates for the peasants who still made up the large majority of the population remained low—with the exception of highly evangelized Protestant areas such as Prussia, where by the mid-nineteenth century illiteracy had fallen to just 5 percent for both sexes.

School curricula, after the primary years, remained heavily classical. In much of Europe, secondary students spent 50 percent of their time on Latin and Greek and less than 20 percent on math and science. Yet most educators still took the utility of classical instruction for granted. Britons saw in the study of ancient texts a source of mental rigor and the knowledge of people and institutions necessary to govern a steadily expanding empire. Still, especially in Britain the period 1820–45 also saw the creation of new educational institutes with a more practical focus. In 1826, the first unit of London University opened, along with its Department of Economics—the first in the world, for economics itself was emerging as a distinct area of study during this period. It was also the first British university to admit non-Anglicans, including Jews.

MIDDLE-CLASS CULTURE

Just as entry to the middle class depended heavily on education, so participation in middle-class life was in large part a matter of culture. There was no such thing as a "typical" middle-class family, but middle-class people did increasingly share a distinct set of cultural practices. At home, the young—especially young women—were expected to learn music (Paris had 60,000 pianos by the 1830s) and to perform at regular gatherings of families and friends. With most middle-class people in Europe literate by 1820, middle-class culture also involved reading newspapers, poetry, and especially novels. Here a technological innovation—the development of machines that produced paper cheaply in long rolls rather than expensive single sheets—played a significant part, allowing books and periodicals to sell at much lower prices. The price of printed material would plunge further when inventors discovered how to manufacture paper from cheap wood pulp in the 1840s. Novelists commonly serialized their work in newspapers, developing the technique of the cliffhanger to keep readers interested from one issue to the next. Charles Dickens (1812–1870) in Britain and Honoré de Balzac (1799–1850) in France proved particularly popular in Europe and America. In 1841, New Yorkers waited anxiously at the docks for an arriving ship to hear if one of the characters in Dickens's *The Old Curiosity Shop* was

MIDDLE-CLASS LONDON, ca. 1850

" THE MIDDLE CLASSES ARE THE REAL TYRANTS OF SOCIETY... THEY SURPASS THE ARISTOCRACY IN ARROGANCE TOWARDS THE POOR, AND THE POOR THEMSELVES, IN OBSEQUIOUSNESS TOWARDS THE ARISTOCRACY. "

THE POOR MAN'S GUARDIAN, AUGUST 17, 1833

Legend:
- Road
- Mixed residential and commercial
- Industrial
- Park
- Factory
- Governmental or cultural institution
- Prison or workhouse
- School

BUILDINGS
1. St. Paul's Cathedral
2. Post Office
3. Bank of England
4. East India House
5. Customs House
6. Parliament
7. Westminster Abbey
8. Buckingham Palace

The temperance movement targeted alcohol as a threat to the stable family, the middle-class ideal. In this etching by George Cruikshank, from a popular 1847 series of illustrations warning of the dangers of alcohol, a man offers his wife a drink for the first time, triggering their descent into homelessness, insanity, and death.

MIDDLE-CLASS OCCUPATIONS

TOTAL POPULATION		2,362,236
MALES		**FEMALES**
1,106,558		1,255,678
GOVERNMENT OFFICERS		
10,099		225
CLERGY AND CHURCH OFFICERS		
2,393		529
LAWYERS AND LAW CLERKS		
11,293		8
PHYSICIANS AND SURGEONS		
5,331		0
TEACHERS		
4,739		12,299
MERCHANTS AND SHOPKEEPERS		
11,344		2,018
COMMERCIAL CLERKS		
16,120		0

Source: *Census of England and Wales*, 1851, "Occupations of the People, London."

" [THE POOR WORKER] IS... FREE... WHEN HE TAKES THE TEMPERANCE PLEDGE... WE INVITE HIM TO EXCHANGE HIS BEER... FOR A COMFORTABLE AND RESPECTABLE HOME. "

SARAH STICKNEY ELLIS,
A VOICE FROM THE VINTAGE, 1843

QUESTIONS FOR ANALYSIS

1. How did the professions of middle-class Londoners reflect the social and economic changes of the period?
2. In what ways did the family represent the ideal of middle-class life?
3. How did the middle class seek to establish its values throughout London society?

Leisure Activities Well-dressed middle-class families gather to admire exotic animals at the Regent's Park Zoo in London in this 1835 illustration.

still alive. Across Europe, middle-class people tended to belong to churches and to attend services regularly. Indeed, thanks in large part to the middle classes, in the late 1840s churchgoing rates reached their highest point of the century throughout western Europe.

ORGANIZED LEISURE Beyond religion, middle-class culture outside of the home centered on organized leisure: visits to public art museums (the Louvre in Paris had opened its doors during the French Revolution), concerts, lectures, holiday parades, and sporting events. The London Zoo, founded as a scientific institution, opened to the public in 1847. In the self-conscious linkage of leisure to "self-improvement" and cultivation, these pursuits stood in stark contrast to such traditional aristocratic entertainments as horse-racing and fox-hunting. Meanwhile, in part to control what was seen as the unruly behavior of the lower classes, middle-class British reformers worked to replace traditional popular entertainments like bear-baiting and cock-fighting with public soccer and cricket matches; they also closely regulated boxing. Rules for boxing published in 1838 formally forbade biting and hitting below the belt.

The early nineteenth century also saw the development of another modern form of leisure: the organized vacation. Already by the 1820s, an enterprising bookstore owner in Paris had begun to publish a guidebook for the city in English ("The English traveler must not expect to find on the continent all the cleanliness and comfort to which he has been accustomed..."). A decade later, the Englishman Thomas Cook (1808–1892) founded the first tourist agency, arranging excursions for hundreds of vacationers at a time and, increasingly, entire families traveling together, generally by railroad. The seashore became

a popular destination. Before the mid-eighteenth century, northern Europeans in particular tended to regard beaches as unattractive wasteland and the sea beyond as threatening and wild. But in the 1750s, doctors began to extol the health benefits of bathing in seawater, spurring the development of coastal resorts. The 1820s saw the construction of elaborate wooden pavilions in beach towns on both sides of the English Channel, as well as hotels and inns to house vacationers.

THE CULT OF DOMESTICITY Central to middle-class identity was the burgeoning **cult of domesticity**, centered on the idea of radically different roles for the sexes. Since the late eighteenth century, economic change in western Europe had brought steadily more rigid boundaries between workplaces and the "home." Male heads of household who had previously lived "above the shop" increasingly worked in offices, factories, and larger workshops,

Cult of Domesticity A profusion of advice manuals like *The Female Instructor or Young Woman's Companion* (1811) guided young women in the appropriate pastimes of a respectable wife and mother, such as sewing and educating children, as depicted on this title page.

away from their residences. Middle-class women were cut off from workplaces, and a growing body of "domestic" literature defined them as guardians of the home and hearth, subordinate to their husbands and devoted principally to the care of children. In Britain, a resurgent evangelical Christianity presented the middle-class home as the true source and model of morality, insisting on strict sexual continence for wives but paying much less attention to male infidelities.

At this point, little public support yet existed for what Queen Victoria (r. 1837–1901) would call the "mad, wicked folly of 'Woman's Rights.'" The brief upsurge in feminist demands by figures like Olympe de Gouges and Mary Wollstonecraft at the time of the French Revolution had not yet developed into a sustained movement. In France, and in other countries that had been swept into Napoleon's empire, the Napoleonic Code enacted strict limits on women's freedom, reversing much of the liberal legislation of the French Revolutionary period. It prohibited French wives from selling property or even publishing a book without their husband's written consent, and the latter law would remain in effect until the 1960s. The cult of domesticity was premised on an ideal of romantic love, and by the early nineteenth century the practice of arranged marriages had largely died out among the European middle classes. Yet middle-class families still expected their offspring to find socially acceptable partners and for the match to work to their economic benefit, with women providing dowries and men a regular income. The resulting tensions provided grist for some of the age's greatest fiction—particularly that of the British novelist Jane Austen (1775–1817).

THE MIDDLE CLASS AS MODEL Together, these middle-class ideals—of the home as a citadel of domestic bliss; of leisure activity as orderly and self-improving; and of work as meritorious—provided a model of behavior that reformers could also attempt to impose on the lower classes. During the 1820s and 1830s, as cities seemed to expand uncontrollably, fears had proliferated of the dangers supposedly posed by mobile, uprooted populations. Urban crime in the cities did increase during this period, and much middle-class fiction—Dickens's *Oliver Twist*, for example—depicted urban slums with some accuracy as lawless and threatening, to be avoided by unwary visitors. This fiction, in turn, helped spur reform movements aimed at transforming the lower classes into poorer copies of their social "superiors." In Britain, the single most powerful reform movement of this sort was temperance: the cause of restricting or even banning the consumption of alcohol. In 1829, a Belfast professor and minister, John Edgar, poured all of his whiskey out of his window and went on to form the Ulster Temperance Movement. A British Society for the Promotion of Temperance followed in 1835, and working-class movements would soon adopt the cause as well in the hope of improving their own image. In short, middle-class culture increasingly served as the pattern to which reformers hoped lower-class life could be shaped.

THE INDUSTRIAL LOWER CLASSES

Middle-class reformers often had a fearful, exaggerated image of workers as drunken and uncontrollable. But they did recognize, however distortedly, an important social fact: that a coherent new social entity, the urban working class, was coming into being. In fact, the very term *working class* came into common usage in this period to denote people who worked for wages in the new industrial economy. The gap between the realities of life for the working class and the ideal sketched out by the middle-class reformers was vast.

THE WORKING POOR

A legislative report from 1832 on the English industrial center of Manchester spoke of the "dense masses of houses" lacking in decent light and ventilation, and barely furnished: "A whole family is often accommodated on a single bed, and sometimes a heap of filthy straw and a covering of old sacking hide them in one undistinguished heap." Sewers and running water were largely absent: "Among 579 streets inspected, 243 were altogether unpaved, 46 partially paved, 93 ill ventilated, and 307 contained heaps of refuse, deep ruts, stagnant pools, ordure...." Diseases like typhoid, spread by poor sanitation, ran rampant. Similar conditions prevailed in even the wealthiest cities—including Paris, where fewer than one in five households had a connection to public sewers. Throughout western Europe, the death rate in large cities often ran twice as high as in rural areas.

Nothing could have been further from the middle-class cult of domesticity than the presence of small children and women laboring in factories in order to make ends meet for their families. But the pressures of industrialization led as well to many other dislocations in traditional patterns

INDUSTRIAL PROMISE AND SOCIAL MISERY

Industrialization unleashed tremendous productive and social forces, and transformed Europe's largely rural and agrarian society into an urban and industrial one. New machines and forms of work boosted production and efficiency. Many observers predicted that mechanization would liberate mankind from drudgery and labor. At the same time, the first industrial workers suffered incredible social dislocation and physical strain. Thousands poured into cities and settled in overcrowded districts where basic needs such as running water, heat, plumbing, and sanitation were scarce or nonexistent. Working hours were long, pay was poor, factories were often poorly heated and cooled, and accidents and injuries were commonplace. For many workers, these developments seemed less like the beginnings of a glorious new society than a different form of exploitation.

Andrew Ure, from *The Philosophy of Manufactures*

In his *Philosophy of Manufactures* (1835), the Scottish chemist and medical doctor Andrew Ure (1778–1857) pointed to machinery's capacity to make work less laborious.

The blessings which physico-mechanical science has bestowed on society, and the means it has still in store for ameliorating the lot of mankind, have been too little dwelt upon....

It has been said, for example, that the steam-engine now drives the power-looms with such velocity as to urge on their attendant weavers at the same rapid pace; but that the hand-weaver, not being subjected to this restless agent, can throw his shuttle and move his treddles at his convenience. There is, however, this difference in the two cases, that in the factory, every member of the loom is so adjusted, that the driving force leaves the attendant nearly nothing at all to do, certainly no muscular fatigue to sustain...whereas the non-factory weaver, having everything to execute by muscular exertion, finds the labour irksome, makes in consequence innumerable short pauses, separately of little account, but great when added together....

The constant aim and effect of scientific improvement in manufactures are philanthropic, as they tend to relieve the workmen either from niceties of adjustment which exhaust his mind and fatigue his eyes, or from painful repetition of effort which distort or wear out his frame. At every step of each manufacturing process described in this volume, the humanity of science will be manifest....

...The grand object therefore of the modern manufacturer is, through the union of capital and science, to reduce the task of his work-people to the exercise of vigilance and dexterity....

...It is, in fact, the constant aim and tendency of every improvement in machinery to supersede human labour altogether.

Friedrich Engels, from *The Condition of the Working Class in England*

The German philosopher Friedrich Engels (1820–1895) described the conditions of the industrial workplace as a system of oppression in this 1845 passage.

The consequences of improvement in machinery under our present social conditions are, for the working-man, solely injurious, and often in the highest degree oppressive. Every new advance brings with it loss of employment, want, and suffering, and in a country like England where, without that, there is usually a "surplus population," to be discharged from work is the worst that can befall the operative....

...We have seen, too, that this work affords the muscles no opportunity for physical activity. Thus it is, properly speaking, not work, but tedium, the most deadening, wearing process conceivable. The operative is condemned to let his physical and mental powers decay in this utter monotony, it is his mission to be bored every day and all day long from his eighth year. Moreover, he must not take a moment's rest; the engine moves unceasingly; the wheels, the straps, the spindles hum and rattle in his ears without a pause, and if he tries to snatch one instant, there is the overlooker at his back with the book of fines....

...Here ends all freedom in law and in fact. The operative must be in the mill at half-past five in the morning; if he comes a couple of minutes too late, he is fined; if he comes ten minutes too late, he is not let in until breakfast is over, and a quarter of the day's wages is withheld, though he loses only two and one-half hours' work out of twelve. He must eat, drink, and sleep at command....

...Here the employer is absolute law-giver.

QUESTIONS FOR ANALYSIS

1. In Ure's opinion, how will mechanization improve the lot of workers?
2. Why does Engels argue that the factory system represents a new form of exploitation of the working class?
3. What are the key differences between Ure's and Engels's arguments?

Sources: Andrew Ure, *The Philosophy of Manufactures* (London: 1835), pp. 7–8, 20–21, 23; Friedrich Engels, *The Condition of the Working-Class in England* (London: 1892), pp. 139, 177–79.

of lower-class social life. In the 1830s and 1840s, major western European cities saw illegitimacy rates rise to as much as one-half of all births, as compared to under 10 percent in most rural areas. In Paris, mothers unable to care for newborns abandoned as many as 33,000 of them per year. Women, who generally earned only a third to a half of what their male counterparts did, fared disproportionately badly in the process of industrialization. They also continued to have far worse access to education and higher rates of illiteracy. In general, despite middle-class gains in this area, overall illiteracy rates remained high for both men and women during this period.

Even so, it is wrong to describe the process of industrialization as an unremitting disaster for the men and women who toiled in its factories. In Britain, between the 1820s and the 1850s, the wages of non-agricultural workers rose 50 percent faster than those of agricultural ones. City-dwellers generally consumed more calories than their country cousins, even if a higher proportion of those calories came from sugar and alcohol. And city-dwellers did not live with the constant risk of famine or ruin from crop failures, such as the blights that struck Irish potato-growing with catastrophic results in the late 1840s, or the French silk industry a decade later. And as we will see, especially in Great Britain, workers in this period learned how to organize effectively to advocate for their collective interests.

URBAN DISEASE AND THE MEDICAL RESPONSE

Yet industrial cities were vulnerable to other natural threats, notably the **cholera** bacillus. This highly infectious water-borne disease struck cities across the Continent in the early 1830s with terrifying force, killing hundreds of thousands (50 percent of all afflicted persons died, usually within a day or two of infection). Parisians in 1832 reacted with macabre humor, one theater sponsoring a masquerade ball with a "cholera waltz" and an actor dressed up as the disease itself—in the words of a visiting American medical student, "with skeleton armor, bloodshot eyes, and other horrible appurtenances of a walking pestilence." Medical scientists did not yet associate disease with the bacteria they had been seeing in their microscopes since the seventeenth century, but they did notice that cholera outbreaks seemed to concentrate in areas of poor sanitation, and they called for the cleansing and purification of water systems and sewers.

These sanitary efforts themselves reflected a broader

Cholera Epidemic Patients suffering from cholera at the Hôtel-Dieu hospital in Paris beg a visiting nobleman for assistance in this artistic rendering (1832–1837) of the cholera epidemic of 1832.

turn in advanced European medical thought. Increasingly, progressive physicians were moving away from earlier models of diagnosis and treatment that concentrated on the physical and even moral constitution of individual patients. They were adopting more "epidemiological" approaches that looked for patterns of disease in large populations. In 1821, the French scientist Louis René Villermé (1782–1863) published a statistical study of the city of Paris demonstrating that contagious diseases flourished particularly in poor districts. French medical educators such as Pierre Louis (1787–1872) led the way in using aggregate data from hospitals to assess the effectiveness of medical treatments—a technique that led him to argue successfully in 1835 against the widespread (and counterproductive) practice of bleeding the sick. Foreign medical students flocked to Paris to hear his lectures.

SOCIAL REFORM: POVERTY AND CRIMINALITY

These new approaches in turn helped spur what could be called the growing medicalization of social thought in this period. Observers tended more and more to treat social problems such as poverty and criminality as medical in cause. Would the poor "always be with you," as was written in scripture (Matthew 26:11)? Was criminality too a permanent scourge of mankind? Or were these things social pathologies that might be treated in much the same way that doctors treated infectious disease? In keeping with this idea, and with the idea of the middle class as model, the period 1820–45 saw new efforts to "discipline" the poor and criminals alike.

For the former, the most spectacular example was England and Wales's **Poor Law Amendment of 1834**. Whereas the earlier Speenhamland system of poor relief had been based on individual parishes and involved income supplements for those in need, the new system operated on a national scale and centered on a network of residential "workhouses" for the indigent. Originally, the system's architects in Parliament had hoped to establish the workhouses as the sole source of poor relief and to make them such an unattractive, prison-like option that potential "inmates" would do almost anything to raise themselves out of poverty. In practice, the new law did not abolish all existing forms of poor relief, and while the workhouse environment usually proved grim and unhealthy—indeed, often brutal and dangerous—it still provided a welcome alternative to starvation. Although the total population of English and Welsh workhouses remained just under 200,000 in 1845, as many as ten times more had spent at least some time in the institution—roughly one out of

every eight people, and a considerably higher proportion of city-dwellers.

As for criminal justice, early nineteenth-century western European states continued trends, begun in the Enlightenment, away from corporal punishment and toward imprisonment as the most common penalty. Theorists increasingly portrayed prisons as a way to quarantine prisoners entirely from society and from normal forms of human interaction. London's Pentonville Prison, opened in 1842 on the model of earlier institutions in the United States, kept prisoners rigidly separated from one another in individual cells. Guards referred to them by number, not name, and walked the corridors on padded shoes so as not to be heard. Although the "Pentonville model" proved too expensive and cumbersome for the Continent as a whole to copy, it had great influence. Meanwhile, French theorists in the 1840s began to speculate that criminality derived from the physical "degeneration" of criminals, perhaps because of alcoholism or sexual deviance. Like the insane, the criminally "degenerate" had to be forcibly separated from society, for its good and their own.

THE "UTOPIAN" REFORMERS

Despite this trend toward increasingly strict measures of social control, grounded in medicalized visions of society, the period also saw considerably more hopeful schemes for improving social conditions. The authors of these proposals had inherited the Enlightenment idea that society functioned according to knowable principles and could be reshaped by the scientific application of policy, but they had greater ambitions than the *philosophes* for actually accomplishing this reshaping in their own lifetimes. In France, Henri, Count Saint-Simon (1760–1825), published several works arguing that the rise of industry required the development of an entirely new social system, centralized and imposed from above, dominated by intellectuals (principally scientists) and the leaders of the productive industrial class, all working for the general good. Although his ideas had relatively little influence before his death in 1825, a group of devoted followers popularized them in the following decades.

Saint-Simon's countryman François-Charles Fourier (1773–1837) believed that reform had to start on a smaller scale, in individual communities, but the communities he sketched out represented a particularly radical departure: Fourier envisaged self-sustaining groups of, ideally, 1,620 men and women, each couple representing one of

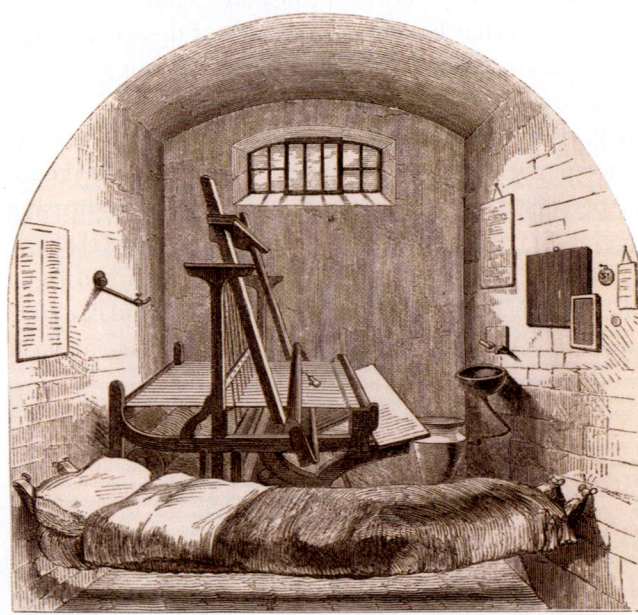

Penal Reform As this illustration from around 1860 shows, London's model Pentonville Prison featured individual cells, with hammocks for sleeping and looms so that prisoners could pass their days in productive labor. The signs on the walls are probably Bible passages and lists of prison rules.

what he saw as 810 distinct human personality types. All 1,620 would live together in a single vast building, called a phalanstery, working harmoniously with one another and with equality between the sexes. Eventually, Fourier hoped, all humans would live in such communities. Yet another Frenchman, Pierre-Joseph Proudhon (1809–1865), openly advocated "communist" principles of common ownership of property, declaring in an 1840 tract that "property is theft." Such calls for a complete overhauling of the social order inspired women who saw in them a chance to overturn the subjugation of their sex. Flora Tristan (1801–1844), an early French feminist horrified by the conditions of the working class, traveled around France giving speeches in which she eloquently argued that workers could only achieve true emancipation if men and women were treated equally. But despite her efforts, a large-scale feminist movement would not coalesce in France until much later.

Across the English Channel, the Welsh industrialist Robert Owen (1771–1858) offered more practical ideas for self-governing communities in which all would work for the common good without poverty or misery. He tried to create an example in the Scottish mill town of New Lanark, centered on his own cotton mill, in which he built spacious, comfortable, and clean homes for his workers and a model school. Owen, who first popularized the word *socialism* to describe a social system that guaranteed decent living conditions and employment for all people, inspired several other such utopian communities in Europe and America, although he was frequently reproached for governing his own workers with a heavy hand.

New Lanark Robert Owens's model mill town included provision for respectable leisure pursuits for workers. In this 1825 engraving, young girls are given dancing lessons while well-dressed adults look on.

RELIGIOUS REFORM AND ROMANTIC CULTURE

These movements for social reform did not just aim to improve the material welfare of European populations. Reformers like Fourier and Owen were also centrally concerned with questions of spiritual welfare. Overall, the period experienced an important upsurge in religious revival movements, and, as in previous decades, the most popular of these took place outside of or against the established churches. It also saw the continued flowering of the romantic movement in the arts—a movement that, more than any previous European artistic school, explicitly sought to address the spiritual condition of the Continent.

NEW RELIGIOUS MOVEMENTS

Among Protestants in Britain, Switzerland, Germany, and the Low Countries, the most important religious reform movements of the decades after 1820 drew on Pietist and Methodist precursors, with open-air meetings of tens of thousands at which preachers insisted that believers develop an individual relationship with God. These movements offered roles to ordinary worshippers, including women, that the more established churches generally closed off. Within the Church of England, members of the dissident Oxford movement sought a more vivid, sensual form of religion, ultimately leading some of their leaders all the way back to Roman Catholicism. Among Catholics themselves, new strains of liberal observance developed, typified by the French priest Hugues de Lamennais (1782–1854), who became an advocate of popular sovereignty and social welfare policies. In 1834, he broke openly with the conservative Church hierarchy in a book that the pope condemned as "small in size, but immense in perversity."

These dissident movements proved all the more popular because, during this period, the balance of power between established churches and states shifted decisively in favor of the latter, across virtually all the Continent. The churches came to look increasingly like weak branches of the ruling political elites, unable to preserve the independent political power they had once possessed. In Britain, conservative Anglicans could not prevent the government from abolishing legal restrictions on Catholics and Protestant dissenters. In France the Restoration government resisted attempts by Catholic missionaries to "rechristianize" the country in massive rallies and to ban or burn offending books. In Russia, as we will see, Tsar Nikolai I cemented the transformation of the Russian Orthodox Church into essentially an obedient arm of the imperial state.

During these decades, Germany became the center of a series of movements that sought to make religion compatible with the liberal, post-Enlightenment social and political order. One key figure was the Protestant theologian and philosopher Friedrich Schleiermacher (1768–1834), who saw religion as intuition, experience, and feeling rather than the literal truth of scripture. His liberal Protestantism had an even more striking counterpart in Reformed Judaism, which coalesced in Germany in the 1820s. Building on the so-called Haskalah, or Jewish Enlightenment, the Reform movement removed the Hebrew language from most of the liturgy, deleted prayers for the return of the Jews to Israel, shortened religious services, and introduced organ music. Its leaders presented this new form of Judaism—the first competitor to Orthodox Judaism to emerge in the modern period—as rational and modern. It would permit Jews to integrate into the existing social and political order, and to assume their rights and responsibilities as equal citizens. To their detractors, both liberal Protestantism and Reform Judaism were overly rational forms of religion that lacked spiritual depth and emotional resonance.

SPIRITUAL LONGING AND ROMANTICISM

But in the early nineteenth century, it was not just to religion that Europeans turned to satisfy their spiritual longings: they also turned to art, music, and literature. More directly than in the past, painters, composers, and writers presented their work as spiritual guides that would help their audiences find a more profound connection with nature and God. In turn, these artists and writers found themselves worshiped by audiences, further encouraging what would become the modern cult of celebrity. The Hungarian composer and pianist Franz Liszt (1811–1886) had a reputation akin to that of modern rock stars. In the 1840s, he performed over a thousand times, mostly to sold-out crowds. Newspapers reported eagerly on his personal life, and thanks to the improvements in printing technology, thousands of engravings of him and other "virtuosi" were sold for framing and display in middle-class homes. Sometimes the work of these artists and writers was of an explicitly religious nature, as in the mystical, Catholic writings of François-René de Chateaubriand (1768–1848),

Franz Liszt In a nineteenth-century cartoon, women are enraptured by Liszt's performance. One releases butterflies in his direction and another, overcome, faints; all crowd around him, applauding wildly.

starting with his *Genius of Christianity*, first published in 1802. Sometimes it was clearly secular. Almost always, it evoked a sense of movement and speed that echoed the disorientations that accompanied industrialization.

THE ROMANTIC MOVEMENT

Nearly all of these artists were associated with the romantic movement. As we have seen, this movement began in the late eighteenth century with the reaction of figures like Goethe against the formal rules and decorous symmetries of neoclassical art and literature. Artists and writers associated with **romanticism** took inspiration from Jean-Jacques Rousseau's exaltation of sentiment and instinct, his worship of nature, and his denunciations of artifice and hypocrisy. Like the *philosophes* of the Enlightenment, the romantics saw their goal as exploring, in Goethe's words, "what holds the world together most deeply." But the romantics saw the path to this knowledge as lying not through the rationalism of science, but through exploration of their own, subjective perceptions, thoughts, and emotions. As the German romantic writer Novalis (1772–1801) put it: "We dream of travel through the universe, but is not the universe in us? We do not know the depths of our own souls. It is inwardly that the secret path leads." They also recognized the spiritual peril that accompanied the journey—the hero of Goethe's great poetic epic, Faust, thirsted for knowledge of the eternal mysteries. Finally, to achieve the desired knowledge, he sold his soul to the devil.

The romantics put new emphasis on their audiences' emotional reactions and tried to connect with them on a visceral level through a succession of vivid images. They often ridiculed reason, preferring to celebrate life in all its glorious disorder. The romantic sensibility emerges clearly in the British poet William Wordsworth's (1770–1850) evocation of the way a beautiful landscape fired his sense of deep connection to the natural world:

> And I have felt
> A presence that disturbs me with the joy
> Of elevated thoughts; a sense sublime
> Of something far more deeply interfused,
> Whose dwelling is the light of setting suns,
> And the round ocean and the living air,
> And the blue sky, and in the mind of man . . .

BRITAIN AND EASTERN EUROPE The romantic movement took different shapes across Europe. In England, where poetry was perhaps most important, Wordsworth's work was joined by John Keats's (1795–1821) beautiful evocations of love and melancholy, cut tragically short by his death at age twenty-five in 1821. George Gordon, Lord Byron (1788–1824), achieved the sort of celebrity enjoyed on the Continent by Liszt thanks to his famously good looks (he used curlers to keep his hair properly coiled) and his notoriously dissolute lifestyle, as well as his entertaining and accessible poetry. Competing with Byron for an "immoral" reputation was the master lyricist Percy Bysshe Shelley (1792–1822), whose radical political views inspired melodious imaginings of a better future. Shelley married Mary Wollstonecraft's daughter Mary (1797–1851), who at age eighteen wrote one of the great modern fables about science and technology: *Frankenstein*, featuring the monster created in a laboratory who runs amok. All of these works appealed deeply to the new, "self-improving" middle-class audiences for art and literature.

Romantic poetry had a crucial importance in eastern Europe as well. In Poland and Russia, the towering figures of Adam Mickiewicz (1798–1855) and Alexander Pushkin (1799–1837) helped define their countries' respective national literatures to such an extent that even today their works and lives remain crucial to Polish and Russian national identity. Mickiewicz's poetry, much of it composed in exile (the Russian authorities banished him from Poland in 1824), had a melancholy, elegiac tone, even as it celebrated the delights of Polish rural life. In his poem "The Grave of Countess Potocki," Mickiewicz mused on the "faded rose" who had died in exile from Poland and was now prey to the "worms of memories." As for Pushkin—the descendant, on his mother's side, of an African page raised by Peter the Great—he had literary genius that spilled over different genres and schools. Much of his work displays a precision and elegance that would become characteristic of realist writers in the decades to come. But in Pushkin's exaltation of the Russian nation, exemplified in his great narrative poem "The Bronze Horseman" (1833), and in his flamboyant life, which ended tragically in a duel with his own brother-in-law, he closely resembled the other great romantic poets of the day.

GERMANY Germany also held a commanding place in the pantheon of romantic poetry, thanks above all to the prolific genius of Goethe. Widely considered the most important figure in German cultural history, Goethe made brilliant and voluminous contributions to genres ranging from the novel to epic poetry to travel writing, history, art criticism, botany, and much else. But it is for his poetic works, especially *Faust*, that he is above all remembered.

Wanderer above the Sea of Fog It is the scene of sublime natural beauty, not the man, that is the focus of Caspar David Friedrich's (1774–1840) 1818 painting. Even the titular wanderer, as a good romantic should, turns away to admire the view.

Germany made another, particularly important contribution in the realm of music. The works of Ludwig van Beethoven (1770–1827), especially in the last years of his life, exemplified romantic principles: they challenged the classical harmonies beloved of earlier generations of composers; assaulted audiences with crescendos (as in the booming four notes that open the Fifth Symphony of 1807–1808); but then soothed them with the most delicate piano compositions (as in the "Moonlight" Sonata of 1801)—all of which proved uncannily able to elicit emotional responses. Beethoven's Austrian contemporary Franz Schubert (1797–1828), born of Moravian peasant stock, looked for inspiration in folk music for the more than 600 lieder (songs) he composed. As in the late eighteenth century, romantic artists and writers tended to believe in the "genius" or "spirit" of nations that was best preserved among simple rural people.

FRANCE It was in France that romanticism prompted the most controversy. After the Restoration in 1815, the Comédie Française—the country's national theater and one of its most prestigious artistic institutions—remained in the hands of self-declared classicists who saw nothing in their own century to surpass the glories of an earlier age. But in early 1830, a group of young, self-declared partisans of the romantics finally managed to stage a contemporary play, *Hernani*, that deliberately challenged the strict canons of classical drama. Its author was a young writer of extravagant talent and ego: Victor Hugo (1802–1885),

the son of a Napoleonic general and a poet of extraordinary verbal facility (he claimed to compose verse in his dreams). At the first, hugely successful performances of *Hernani*, young supporters gleefully hurled insults at a bust of a seventeenth-century playwright in the theater's lobby. The same year, the French romantic composer Hector Berlioz (1803–1869) composed his masterpiece, the *Fantastic* Symphony, a "tone poem" that explored dream states in a fashion influenced by romantic verse. France also had great romantic painters such as Eugène Delacroix (1798–1863) and Théodore Géricault (1791–1824), who sought to stimulate the emotions of their viewers by using deep, vibrant, swirling colors to portray exotic subjects and extreme human experiences such as shipwrecks.

THE NOVEL In England and France, the novel was the one great artistic and literary form that resisted the influence of romanticism. Writers like Jane Austen (1775–1817), Honoré de Balzac (1799–1850), Charles Dickens (1812–1870), and Stendhal (the pen-name of Henri Beyle, 1783–1842) were notable above all for their meticulous social and psychological observation. Austen, as we have seen, found drama in middle-class marriage practices, which she described with penetrating wit. Balzac produced a massive, panoramic series of works called *The Human Comedy* (after Dante's *Divine Comedy*) that savagely exposed the greed, selfishness, and delusions he saw at work in post-Napoleonic France. Dickens blended broad comedy with heart-rending melodramatic accounts of social injustice.

It was in Scotland, with Sir Walter Scott (1771–1832), that the romantic novel flourished most spectacularly. Scott's many works, starting with *Waverly* (1814), often called the first historical novel, sold astonishingly well. They displayed the characteristic romantic attention to sentiment and spiritual journeys, and to the reader's emotional response. However, as their principal setting they did not employ the natural environment, in the manner of Wordsworth, but rather human history. Scott's novels, many of them set in the Middle Ages, implied that people in earlier historical periods had experienced life differently, more deeply and vividly, than people of his own time. These works made Scott, alongside Dickens, one of the best-known English-language writers in the world.

THE TURN TO HISTORY Scott's experiments with the historical novel illustrated another important shift in European thought taking place during the period. In many different realms of culture, Europeans were beginning to display a heightened sensitivity to the way

The Raft of the Medusa Contrasting light and shadows heighten the stark emotions conveyed by this 1818–1819 painting by Théodore Géricault. Survivors of a shipwreck reach out desperately for help, while dead bodies litter the foreground.

thought and behavior changed over the course of historical time, and an increasing attention to the historical roots of their own social and political practices and beliefs. We have already seen the way in which historical understanding developed during the Renaissance, but now an organized historical profession began to take shape. Specialized journals and institutions dedicated to history emerged, and universities, especially in Germany, added historians to their faculties. Scholars worked out systematic methods for organizing and analyzing archival documents. In Britain in 1838, Parliament passed the Public Record Office Act, which led to the establishment of formal government archives. European countries spent large sums to build museums displaying artifacts of the past, and the director of Denmark's national museum pioneered the division of "prehistory" into Stone, Bronze, and Iron Ages. By 1825, a Frenchman could write: "History is the Muse of our time; we are, I think, the first who have understood the past."

This "historical turn" had a particularly profound impact on European philosophy. The German philosopher Georg Wilhelm Friedrich Hegel wrote that in history the human spirit developed and became conscious of itself, and brought about human freedom. For him this "spirit," and human thought itself, did not exist in the abstract, outside of their historical context. Hegel saw the human spirit realizing itself above all within particular nation-states, with Germany as the most important and most advanced. Despite the difficult and abstract prose, educated Germans embraced Hegel's work with an almost religious enthusiasm.

The new philosophy of history joined hands with the religious and artistic movements of the period. Despite the differences among them, they all imparted to their followers a sense of participating in a process of revival and renewal. With the great political revolutions of the late eighteenth century now finished, and with socialist organizations still in their infancy, it was to these movements of inner, personal renewal that idealistic Europeans were now turning.

NEW POLITICAL PATTERNS

In the midst of these great economic, social, and cultural changes, and with the tumult of the revolutionary era still fresh in living memory, the 1820s saw political life across Europe take on new patterns. This was the first decade in European history in which we can accurately describe the principal political factions as "reactionary," "conservative,"

"liberal," or "radical." It was a period in which party systems, already well developed in Britain in the eighteenth century, began to spread to the Continent. And it was a period in which a great deal of political life began to turn around questions of what constituted a nation and where sovereign power within it lay.

LIBERALISM AND CONSERVATISM

Liberal politics in the period tended to center on claims to individual rights—especially the right to vote. Liberals inherited from older thinkers like Hobbes, Locke, and Rousseau the idea that sovereign authority derived from the consent of the governed and that citizens possessed certain inalienable, individual rights. From a later, predominantly British school known as **utilitarians** they developed a more insistent focus on the welfare of individuals as the ultimate measure of political good. The most famous of the utilitarians, Jeremy Bentham (1748–1832), held that governments should always pursue "the greatest good of the greatest number" and believed that this quality could be quantified through what he called a "felicific calculus." One basic assumption of liberalism was that people tended to act rationally, in their own economic self-interest, and that the market mediated these individual economic actions and desires to produce the best possible outcomes for society overall.

Liberals inspired by these principles campaigned for such goals as the expansion of the suffrage, legal protections for freedom of speech and religion, and promotion of free markets. They did not necessarily seek the vote for all adult men (still less women) and most had little quarrel with constitutional monarchy. Unlike modern American liberals, they generally distrusted strong government intervention in social and economic matters, even for the purpose of alleviating human misery. For this reason, they are now often referred to as classical liberals. They were poles apart from Saint-Simon, Fourier, and the other early utopian socialists, who were ready to curtail individual property rights and free markets in the name of the common good.

Liberals were particularly favorable to commercial and industrial interests. In Britain, the pioneering economic thinker David Ricardo (1772–1823) built upon the foundation established by Adam Smith in making a case for free trade, both within countries and between countries. His theory of "comparative advantage" held that countries should manufacture the products that they could produce most efficiently, and trade for the others. Elected to Parliament, Ricardo fought trade restrictions and supported industrial entrepreneurs.

Conservatives, in contrast, tended to stress the need for tradition and social order, and were prominent in support of monarchies across the Continent. The most important conservative ideas in the immediate post-Napoleonic period remained those of Edmund Burke. Like him, the later conservatives warned that too-rapid change, and too great an emphasis on individual desires and rights, could destroy the "organic" bonds that held nations together. Often hostile to commercial and industrial interests, they idealized monarchs, nobility, and rural society. Conservatives also insisted on the centrality of established, orthodox religion to the political and social order, praising the "union of throne and altar" despite the diminished power of the latter. They yearned for a mythical lost golden age when a pious peasantry dutifully followed the dictates of their religious leaders and social superiors.

One of the greatest thinkers in this period, the French noble Alexis de Tocqueville (1805–1859), combined aspects of liberal and conservative thought into one of the most profound bodies of work in European political thought. Descended from a grand noble family of the Old Regime, he openly lamented the passing of the aristocratic societies of the Old Regime. But having toured the United States in the early 1830s, he was impressed with the young nation's energy and returned to France to write a grand meditation entitled *Democracy in America*. While most of his contemporaries still saw America as an "infant" society that trailed behind Europe in civilization and sophistication, Tocqueville presented it as an incarnation of modernity, which he associated with democracy, pluralism, and social equality. But at the same time, he saw these phenomena as mixed blessings at best, warning darkly about the "tyranny of the majority" over individuals in the United States. And more generally, he warned that in modern times, individuals needed to fear not only open despotism but also more subtle and insidious mechanisms of repression by the state. Over the citizens, he wrote, there

Alexis de Tocqueville
Théodore Chassériau painted Tocqueville in 1850, when the latter was serving as foreign minister of France.

…is elevated an immense, tutelary power, which takes sole charge of assuring their enjoyment and of watching over their fate. It is absolute, attentive to detail, regular, provident, and gentle. It would resemble the paternal power if, like that power, it had as its object to prepare men for adulthood, but it seeks, to the contrary, to keep them irrevocably fixed in childhood [...] It works willingly for their happiness, but it wishes to be the only agent and the sole arbiter of that happiness.

It is a passage that remarkably anticipates later criticisms of excessive state power.

REACTION AND RADICALISM

Then there were the political extremes. At one end of the spectrum, reactionaries called for a full return to pre-Revolutionary social and political orders. French thinkers like Louis de Bonald (1754–1840) demanded the restoration of the old French Estates General, the abolition of press freedom, and the imposition of the death penalty for blasphemy. The Savoyard writer Joseph de Maistre (1753–1821) gained a wide influence with works that presented the French Revolution as fundamentally evil, but also part of God's plan for redeeming humanity. Monarchs like France's Charles X (r. 1824–1830) and Spain's Fernando VII (r. 1808; 1813–1833) eagerly subscribed to these ideas.

At the other end of the political spectrum, political radicals embraced a wide variety of goals. Some hoped above all for an expansion of the suffrage to all adult males; others advocated massive social and economic reforms, often taking inspiration from utopian socialists like Fourier and Owen. But not all of them limited themselves to Fourier's utopian fantasies of communal living or Owen's earnest blueprints for humane mill towns. As we will soon see, socialism took an important turn toward what its advocates considered a more scientific analysis of social forces and their direction. Other radicals formed secret societies to advance their goals through violence, of which the most famous, and strangest, was the Italian group known as the Carbonari ("charcoal-burners"), whom we met in the last chapter. One of their collaborators, Philippe Buonarotti, had worked with the French ultra-revolutionaries in the 1790s, and in an influential book he held them up as a model for a new generation to follow. The Carbonari themselves had imitators across the Continent.

REPRESSION AND REFORM

The competition among liberals, conservatives, reactionaries, and radicals played out differently from country to country in this period. In Spain this competition led to open civil war; in France, to successful revolution. Elsewhere, violence was mostly limited to riots, sometimes on a large scale, and police repression. Indeed, throughout much of the Continent, the years between 1820 and 1845 marked a period of repression and reaction. Yet this repression itself helped generate new political forces that would soon coalesce into organized movements calling for power to the working classes.

In 1843, Prussian censors shut down a newspaper in the city of Cologne called the *Rheinische Zeitung* ("The Rhine Newspaper"), whose contributors included a young student of philosophy named Karl Marx (1818–1883). The paper advocated greater freedom of the press and campaigned for the rights of peasants against powerful landowners. The suppression helped convince Marx and other young Germans that a strategy of incremental liberal reform could not work, making revolution, perhaps even violent revolution, necessary. Marx began to read more deeply in the work of the early French and British socialists, and in 1845 he would proclaim that "the philosophers have only interpreted the world, the point is to change it." Even as many German liberals began to place their hope in a program of national unity, Marx and others began to envisage an international movement to combat social oppression.

SPAIN

Germany managed to avoid open civil war. The same was not true in Spain, which had barely recovered from its long and bloody struggle against Napoleon Bonaparte, and the loss of most of its overseas empire. On returning to Madrid after Napoleon's initial defeat in 1814, King Fernando VII repealed the liberal constitution that the national legislature in Cádiz had promulgated in 1812 under the influence of Enlightenment ideas and the French Revolution. In 1820, mutinous liberal soldiers put the king under virtual house arrest and forced him to implement the constitution, but his own followers soon revolted in turn. Fernando appealed to the European powers for help, and the Quadruple Alliance of Britain, France, the Netherlands, and Austria authorized the intervention of a French military force. With the Spanish far more divided than under Napoleon, the French won an easy victory and restored Fernando to full power.

Yet after Fernando's death in 1833, a quarrel over the succession led to new hostilities. The king had left the throne to his three-year-old daughter, with his liberal

Italian queen as regent. But conservatives insisted that females could not inherit the throne and flocked to the standard of Fernando's brother Carlos, leading to the first of three nineteenth-century Carlist Wars that would last until 1876. Conservatives looked for their principal support in the countryside and in the northern Basque country, which feared for its traditional privileges under a liberal regime. But after six grinding years of conflict, and the death of as much as 3 percent of the entire Spanish population, in 1839 the liberals eked out a victory.

RUSSIA

Large-scale violence also broke out at the other end of Europe, in Russia. In 1825, Tsar Alexander I, the increasingly religious ruler who had led Russia in its defeat of Napoleon, died without legitimate offspring. Russia did not have much of a native liberal tradition, but since the French Revolution western European liberal ideas had found considerable support among intellectuals and in the army. These figures had watched with dismay as the tsar, increasingly fearful of revolution, had again ruled out any prospect of political reform. Now Russian liberals pinned their hopes on Alexander's brother Constantine. But unbeknown to them, Constantine had renounced his claim to the throne in favor of a third, far more autocratic brother, Nikolai. When Nikolai I (r. 1825–1855) took the throne in December 1825, the secret societies staged a massive protest in St. Petersburg aimed at sparking a popular revolution. But after a standoff lasting several hours,

Decembrist Revolt Crowds look on as a commander orders his troops to fire a cannon at protesters occupying a square in Saint Petersburg, in this watercolor depicting the suppression of the 1825 revolt.

Nikolai ordered his supporters to disperse the crowds with artillery, and the revolt crumbled. The leaders of the so-called **Decembrists** were hanged, and many of their followers banished to Siberia. Nikolai reigned for another thirty years as one of the most reactionary of European monarchs. The events drove idealistic young Russians to despair, and the romantic poet Mikhail Lermontov (1814–1841) made a grimly prescient prediction:

A year will come for Russia, a black year,
When its crowned head will fall into the mud,
When mobs will turn on all they once held dear
And Russians come to dine on death and blood.
…
Then shrouds will cover victims on the pyre
And famine will torment this wretched sphere,
While rivers glisten with reflected fire
—On this day will a mighty man appear.
And you will know him well, and understand
Why in his hand he holds a knife of steel.

FRANCE AND THE REVOLUTION OF 1830

In France, the twice-restored monarchy of Louis XVIII tried, much like Napoleon himself, to plot a centrist course between reaction and liberalism. It had a written constitution and parliament, but a very small, wealthy, conservative electorate. Louis initially found himself opposed principally by the so-called ultras—ultraroyalist reactionaries—whose slogan "Long live the king in spite of himself!" expressed their dilemma of idealizing the monarchy while objecting to the actual monarch. But France's liberal moment came to an abrupt end in 1820, when an admirer of Bonaparte stabbed to death the king's nephew and heir to the throne, and public opinion turned sharply rightward. When Louis died in 1824, the throne passed to his younger brother Charles, whose instincts lay solidly with the ultras. King Charles X raised the specter of a broader restoration of the Old Regime, flirting with the possibility of reimbursing noble émigrés for property confiscated during the Revolution. And he staged a full Old Regime coronation for himself in Rheims Cathedral, where the kings of France were traditionally crowned. He even revived, to much ridicule, the medieval rite of trying to cure sufferers of scrofula by laying his royal hands on them.

Tensions with the liberal opposition finally came to a head in the summer of 1830, when Charles's government

Liberty Leading the People Delacroix's allegorical painting of the July Revolution shows Liberty, wearing the red revolutionary cap of 1789 and waving a tricolor flag, as she leads revolutionaries over the barricades into battle.

issued a series of ordinances that drastically reduced press freedom, dissolved a newly elected assembly, and culled opponents from the electoral rolls. In response, on July 27 a revolt broke out in Paris that quickly turned to revolution. Barricades sprang up in the city, and within four days the king had fled to London, leaving insurgents in command of the French state. The painter Eugène Delacroix immortalized this brief **July Revolution** in his grand tableau *Liberty Leading the People*.

For a moment, the return of a revolutionary republic seemed a possibility, but the leaders of the insurrection instead offered the throne to one of Charles's cousins, the fifty-six-year-old Louis-Philippe, duke of Orléans, who had served in the revolutionary army. Louis-Philippe (r. 1830–1848), popularly known as the Citizen King, took many symbolic steps aimed at reconciling monarchy more thoroughly with revolution. He dispensed with court etiquette, surrounded himself with bourgeois financiers, and restored the revolutionary tricolor as the national flag. He took the title "King of the French" (rather than "King of France"), signaling his respect for the sovereignty of the nation with the king as its agent. He also took more substantial measures, including more than doubling the size of the electorate and restricting the role of the executive in what became known as the July Monarchy of 1830–48. Radical workers were nonetheless disappointed by the limited scope of Louis-Philippe's reforms, particularly in regard to the suffrage and support for the poor. In the early 1830s several further uprisings took place, but the government violently suppressed them, and by the end of the decade a centrist and seemingly stable parliamentary regime had emerged. The king's most famous minister, François Guizot (1787–1874), dismissed queries from disenfranchised men demanding the vote with the words: "Get rich."

GREAT BRITAIN AND THE PATH OF REFORM

At several moments, revolution also seemed possible in Great Britain. In the 1820s, food riots and machine breaking continued across much of the kingdom. So did radical agitation against an electoral system that not only barred fourteen out of fifteen adult males from voting, mostly because of property requirements, but also left many parliamentary seats entirely in the control of powerful individual landowners. A series of acts dating to the seventeenth century had banned Catholics, Jews, and Protestant dissenters from serving in Parliament as well, and this effectively disenfranchised Ireland's large Catholic majority. In the late 1820s, the flamboyant Irish Catholic leader Daniel O'Connell (1775–1847) won election to Parliament but was barred from taking his seat. Even conservatives warned of serious unrest in Ireland unless the law was changed.

THE REFORM BILL OF 1832 But in the years around 1830 Britain's rulers, unlike Charles X of France, revealed a talent for compromise. The Tory and Whig Parties were used to shifting their positions in order to win elections, and both were fearful of revolution. Thus in 1829, faced with a deteriorating political situation in Ireland, a conservative government headed by the now duke of Wellington, the hero of the Napoleonic wars, repealed the measures barring Catholics from Parliament and allowed O'Connell and others to be seated. Then in 1830, a general election fought against the background of popular unrest brought a Whig government to power with a mandate to enact electoral reform. The failure of an initial attempt in 1831 prompted large-scale public protests, especially in northern industrial areas that still had little or no parliamentary representation despite huge increases in population. Finally, under pressure from his own conservative party and the new king, William IV (r. 1830–1837), Wellington agreed not to oppose the **Reform Bill of 1832**. It provided for elections in most parliamentary districts, redrew the country's electoral map more fairly, and expanded the electorate to include a large swathe of the middle classes—although still only 20 percent of the adult male population.

THE CHARTISTS With the Reform Bill as a precedent, liberal and radical activity over the next sixteen years aimed at achieving a further, peaceful expansion of the franchise. In 1838, six liberal members of Parliament and six members of radical workingmen's associations published the "People's Charter," which called for universal adult male suffrage and annually elected parliaments. Although several of the so-called Chartists were arrested and jailed for sedition, they managed to organize a series of massive rallies, in London and other cities, and collected even more massive numbers of signatures on petitions calling for the Charter's enactment. In 1842, the National Chartist Association delivered to the House of Commons a giant scroll with no fewer than 3.3 million signatures, which Parliament summarily rejected as too threatening to its own rights. The **Chartist movement** was not entirely peaceful—a clash with authorities in Wales in 1839 left up to twenty-four people dead—but the movement never turned revolutionary, despite failing to achieve its goals. Full suffrage for men and women only arrived in Britain in the twentieth century.

REPEAL OF THE CORN LAWS Radicals had greater success in another cause: repealing the Corn Laws, which imposed heavy tariffs on imported wheat, keeping domestic wheat prices high to the advantage of large landowners. The Anti–Corn Law League, founded in 1839 by Richard Cobden (1804–1865) and John Bright (1811–1889), united radicals with free-market liberals and a large portion of the urban middle classes. Bright, an evangelical and talented orator, cast the issue squarely as a contest between "the class of the great proprietors of the soil" and "trade and manufactures," and insisted that the time had come for the latter to prevail. In 1846 it did, when the Conservative government of Robert Peel agreed to the Corn Laws' repeal.

TRADE UNIONISM A final area in which politics now turned increasingly around explicit questions of social class involved trade unionism. Prior to the 1830s, European industrial workers had engaged in relatively limited forms of collective action. On the Continent, journeymen's fraternities had sometimes tried to put pressure on masters and other employers—in Old Regime France, they had even initiated lawsuits for better wages and working conditions. In Britain, artisans had flocked to the radical corresponding societies of the 1790s, which agitated for

political reform. And "friendly societies" that provided mutual aid for workers proliferated in the early nineteenth century, with over 200 in London alone. But legislation in many countries forbade the most direct and effective forms of workers' collective action, including formal unionization and strikes.

In 1824, however, Parliament repealed the principal British legislation on the subject, the so-called Combination Acts, and **trade unions** quickly came into existence. Robert Owen helped organize unions of skilled builders, and then a rickety Grand National Consolidated Trades Union, which collapsed a few months after it began in 1834. Unions in the individual crafts, however, developed successfully in the following decades. Unionism among unskilled, manual workers would not take hold until later in the century. Unionism nonetheless helped drive the various attempts by Parliament to alleviate working conditions in factories and to regulate the use of child labor. And British union members contributed to many of the great political causes of the day—particularly the call to expand the suffrage to all adult males.

THE NEW INTERNATIONAL ORDER AND NATIONALISM

At first glance, the years 1820–45 seem as turbulent, even violent, as any in European history. In addition to the upheavals already described in Spain, France, Russia, and Britain, the period saw revolutions in Belgium and Poland (the first successful; the second brutally repressed), civil strife throughout Germany and Italy, a successful independence struggle in Greece, and a new war between Russia and the Ottoman Empire. Yet in comparison with the bloody turmoil of 1789–1815, these struggles were relatively minor. Overall, the period was actually one of comparative calm, at least on the European continent, if not in Europe's overseas empires. The developments with the greatest potential for sparking international conflict were the stirrings of nationalist sentiment in Europe, driven in part by the cultural changes discussed above and the continuing expansion of overseas empires.

THE PEACE KEEPERS

The arrangements worked out at the Congress of Vienna after Napoleon's defeat were largely responsible for keeping the peace inside Europe for four decades after the battle of Waterloo in 1815. For the first time, the great powers—Britain, France, Austria, Prussia, and Russia—saw their role as not only maintaining a competitive balance of power, its terms worked out at successive peace conferences, but also actively managing the international order to prevent war through diplomacy—indeed, through a sort of joint security policy. The powers did not create a formal body analogous to the United Nations. However, the flurry of consultations among London, Vienna, St. Petersburg, Paris, and Berlin made this period a golden age of modern European diplomacy. The powers often disagreed—in general, the British felt more comfortable with adjustments to the order than did Metternich's Austria, particularly when it came to allowing new states to come into being in southeastern Europe. The "Holy Alliance" signed in 1815 by Austria, Russia, and Prussia also saw its mission as repressing social revolution throughout the Continent. But the diplomats generally managed to come to agreement.

Together, the powers repeatedly took steps to preserve monarchical authority. Recall that they authorized the French intervention in the Spanish civil war in 1823. Then, in the early 1830s, they ensured that Tsar Nikolai had a free hand when the autonomous kingdom of "**Congress Poland**" tried to claim full independence from Russia. This Polish revolt occurred when young Polish officers, inspired by the July Revolution in France and resentful of increasingly heavy-handed Russian rule, took up arms, leading to the establishment of a new revolutionary government that declared independence in January 1831. Russian troops finally crushed the revolt when they stormed Warsaw in the fall of 1832, driving tens of thousands of Poles into exile. The tsar then abolished the autonomous Polish Congress kingdom, revoking its constitution and dissolving its legislature and army.

In the same years, the powers similarly allowed Austria to crush a series of disorganized risings by liberal nationalists and radical secret societies elsewhere in Europe. The most important exception to the pattern occurred in 1830, when the Southern Netherlands declared independence from the Dutch government, which had ruled them since 1815 without giving its elites much say in the running of the newly enlarged kingdom. When it became clear that both Flemish and French speakers in the south supported the rebellion, the powers—driven by Great Britain—agreed to act as midwife for the newborn country of Belgium and to provide a German nobleman to sit on its new throne.

TENSIONS IN THE OTTOMAN EMPIRE

The order established by the Congress of Vienna came under greatest immediate pressure in eastern Europe. There, emergent nationalist movements and the strain put on the increasingly fragile Ottoman Empire by Russia led to repeated international crises.

GREEK INDEPENDENCE In 1821, Greeks living in the area of present-day Romania, led by a Russian prince of Greek descent, revolted against an Ottoman Turkish government that was struggling to reform its military and to keep its provincial officials in line. Although the Turks, with the initial support of the Congress powers, overcame these early rebels, the movement soon spread to Turkish-controlled Greece itself and gained the support of writers and artists like Byron, whose imaginations were captured by the largely fantastical idea of a revival

The Massacre at Chios Western outrage at Turkey is evident in Delacroix's painting of a scene from the Greek revolt. Women with their clothes torn off are at the mercy of Turkish soldiers on horseback, while other Greeks lie on the ground—some dead, some destitute.

of ancient Greek glory (Byron himself died on the way to help the rebels). Western European sympathy turned to anti-Turkish rage after the Turks massacred thousands of Greeks on the Aegean island of Chios and executed the Greek Orthodox patriarch of Constantinople.

By 1827, France and Britain had come to the conclusion that the hostilities could only be ended by Greek independence, and Russia, which had its own designs on the European possessions of the Ottoman Empire, including Constantinople, eagerly supported them. The Turks resisted, leading the allies to send a naval force that destroyed a Turkish fleet at the battle of Navarino, off the western Greek coast, in 1827. Five years later the Ottomans finally agreed to Greek independence, and the allied powers again dipped into Germany's large supply of under-employed princelings to find Greece a suitable monarch.

RUSSIAN EXPANSION After Navarino, Russia took advantage of the Turks' weakness to launch the only major war of the period and to pursue a dream of establishing itself as the preeminent power on the European continent by expanding to the Mediterranean—a key factor in the diplomatic and military history of the nineteenth century. The Russian army penetrated deep into the Balkans, occupying much of present-day Romania and Bulgaria. At this point Britain, France, and Austria grew nervous that the entire Turkish Empire might dissolve, with Russia reaping the spoils and gaining direct access to the Aegean. Thanks to their pressure, Russia made peace with the Ottomans in 1829. But it still gained effective control over the Romanian provinces of Moldavia and Wallachia, while the small Slavic principality of Serbia confirmed its autonomy from the Turks.

The Ottoman Empire would remain one of the most important sources of instability in Europe for the rest of the nineteenth century. Just a decade after the Russo-Turkish War of 1828–1829, the ambitious ruler of Egypt, Mehmet Ali (r. 1805–1848), attempted to declare independence for that country and conquered large portions of present-day Israel, Lebanon, and Syria. Although he hoped for support from France, the other major powers sent a naval expedition and forced him to withdraw.

THE RISE OF NATIONAL INDEPENDENCE MOVEMENTS

As the Greek, Polish, and Belgian events suggest, another important long-term threat to the stability of the 1815 settlement came from the growth of national independence movements. National sentiment itself was hardly a new phenomenon in Europe—even many medieval Europeans had a clear sense of the division of the Continent into separate nations. And as we have seen, **nationalism**—which is best defined as an explicit political program aimed at constructing nation-states—dates back to the French Revolution. During the Napoleonic Wars, the nationalist rhetoric deployed by the Jacobins to mobilize the French in the 1790s proved equally successful in spurring resistance against France, especially in Spain and Germany.

THE EMERGENCE OF NATIONALISM

But in the 1820s, something changed: nationalism emerged for the first time as a potent, peacetime political force that posed particular dangers to Europe's multi-ethnic empires—the Austrian, Ottoman, and Russian. One reason for this emergence was that with the advent of liberalism and its priorities on individual rights, educated elites from Greece to Norway came to resent the denial of voting rights and constitutional protections by a regime controlled by another national group—and sought redress through their own national unity and independence. In addition, the romantic movement, with its emphasis on the individual character (or "genius") of different ethnic groups and its emotional appeal to national history, provided a powerful language for expressing nationalist aspirations and grievances.

The period 1820–45 saw only two large-scale nationalist revolts in Europe itself: the successful war for independence in Greece and the failed Polish uprising in 1830–32. But throughout the great European land empires, other nationalist movements started to take shape, as the case of the Czechs illustrates. Before 1800, most Czechs in the Austrian Empire lived in rural areas, often as serfs. The city of Prague was almost entirely German-speaking; the Czech language had largely disappeared from schools, the state administration, and print culture. But with the economic expansion of the early nineteenth century, Czechs began making their way back into the cities, and their levels of wealth and literacy rose. In 1809, the scholar and former Jesuit Josef Dobrovský (1753–1829) published a path-breaking grammar of the Czech language, and over the next twenty years lexicographers developed a modern Czech vocabulary. In the 1830s, large-scale Czech publishing began, and as it did, Czech politicians began pushing for greater autonomy within the Austrian Empire.

Similar developments occurred in Romania (still largely under Ottoman rule) and also Norway, which had passed from Danish to Swedish rule with the end of the Napoleonic Wars. In both Norway and Greece, scholars attempted to invent standard languages for the aspiring nation-states, combining different dialects and coining new words from traditional roots. In Hungary, which under Austrian rule had preserved many of its national institutions (including a parliament), as well as its literary language, nationalist leaders also began pushing for greater autonomy. Serbia continued its own gradual process of divorce from the Ottoman Empire, winning the right to hereditary rule by its own princes in 1833, and gaining its first constitution two years later.

NATIONALISM IN ITALY AND GERMANY

An even more visible nationalist movement within the Austrian Empire took shape in Italy. Under the 1815 settlement, Austria claimed most of northern Italy east of Piedmont, including Venice and Milan. The remainder of the peninsula continued to be divided among a number of states, principally Naples (now called the kingdom of the Two Sicilies), the Papal States, and Tuscany. In 1831, a liberal Genoese lawyer named Giuseppe Mazzini (1805–1872) founded a group called Young Italy, which rejected the conspiratorial tactics of the Carbonari and envisioned a unification of the peninsula as a step in the creation of a peaceful Europe of federated, cooperative nation-states. "The map of Europe has to be remade," Mazzini would declare in 1852 after leading several failed insurrections, punctuated by spells in Austrian jails. Italian artists, including the composer Gioacchino Rossini (1792–1868), began to dramatize the cause of the Italian nation in their works.

In Germany as well, liberal aspirations began to drive calls for national unity in the years after the Congress of Vienna. Under the **German Confederation**, the largely toothless successor to the Holy Roman Empire, student groups in the German universities issued calls for uniting the fragmented German states. They even made one abortive attempt to storm the meeting place of the Confederation's parliament in Frankfurt. The dominant states in the Confederation—Prussia and Austria—feared anything that smacked of revolution and relentlessly repressed democratic activism.

In the end, developments in the years after 1815 suggested that German unification would follow a different model. With the Vienna settlement, Prussia gained significant territories in the western German area of the Rhineland, thereby becoming the dominant state in the German lands outside the Austrian Empire. Hoping that economic unity under autocratic Prussian leadership might foreshadow political unity under Prussia, its government then pushed through the creation of a customs union to facilitate intra-German trade. By 1835, it included a majority of the Confederation's member states. The ideal of a united Germany, hailed by writers and artists during the Napoleonic period, now seemed closer to institutional realization.

THE CRISIS OF THE IBERIAN EMPIRES Even with the emergence of nationalist sentiments and the destabilizing crises in the Ottoman Empire, the Congress arrangements still helped maintain an unprecedented degree of stability and peace in Europe itself during the period 1820–45. European overseas empires were a different story, however. Here the period saw considerable instability and violence, with setbacks as well as significant gains for imperialist causes. Much of the imperial instability was stirred by the spread of liberal and nationalist ideas from Europe to the Americas.

The greatest setbacks to the imperial cause took place in the Spanish and Portuguese empires. Revolts by settlers born in the Americas ("creoles") had occurred against Spanish rule in Latin America since the late eighteenth century. Napoleon's conquest of Spain allowed these scattered brushfires to explode into a continental conflagration, driven in large part by the resentment of creoles against Iberian-born officials. King Fernando then destroyed any hope for reconciliation with the heavy-handed absolutist policies he pursued upon his restoration in 1814. Spanish authorities initially won some victories over South American insurgents, but by 1818 the tide had definitively turned, and Spain had no choice but to give up most of its American empire.

Inspired above all by the leadership of the Argentinian general José de San Martín (1778–1850) and the Venezuelan leader Simón Bolívar (1783–1830), a constellation of independent nations emerged that would eventually stretch from Panama to Cape Horn in South America. They were joined by Mexico and a collection of smaller Central American states. The Congress powers, again concerned above all to maintain stability, refused Spanish requests for aid and soon granted diplomatic recognition to the newly independent nations. Britain played a particularly important role here and soon moved to establish a significant sphere of influence in South America, despite attempts by the United States to limit the role of European powers through the Monroe Doctrine of 1823. Spain preserved only a few island fragments of empire: principally the Philippines, Cuba, Puerto Rico, and some scattered Pacific territories.

Latin American Nations, 1800–1830 By 1830, states including Argentina, Chile, Mexico, and Brazil achieved independence from the Spanish and Portuguese empires that had previously controlled the entirety of Central and South America. This map shows the initial borders of these new states. Spain only retained a few small colonies such as Cuba and Puerto Rico, while Britain, the Netherlands, and France also held small interests in Central and South America.

Meanwhile, in 1821, Brazil staged a successful, largely peaceful revolution against Portugal, which also found its empire reduced to a chain of trading posts and island territories, in this case stretching from Macao in China to India and southern Africa. In Latin America, the independence movements harkened back to the American Revolution. Many of the new nations quickly produced Declarations of Independence and Constitutions modeled on the American ones. Native Americans—a very large portion of the population in some of the new states—remained repressed and discriminated against, and in Brazil black slavery lasted until 1888.

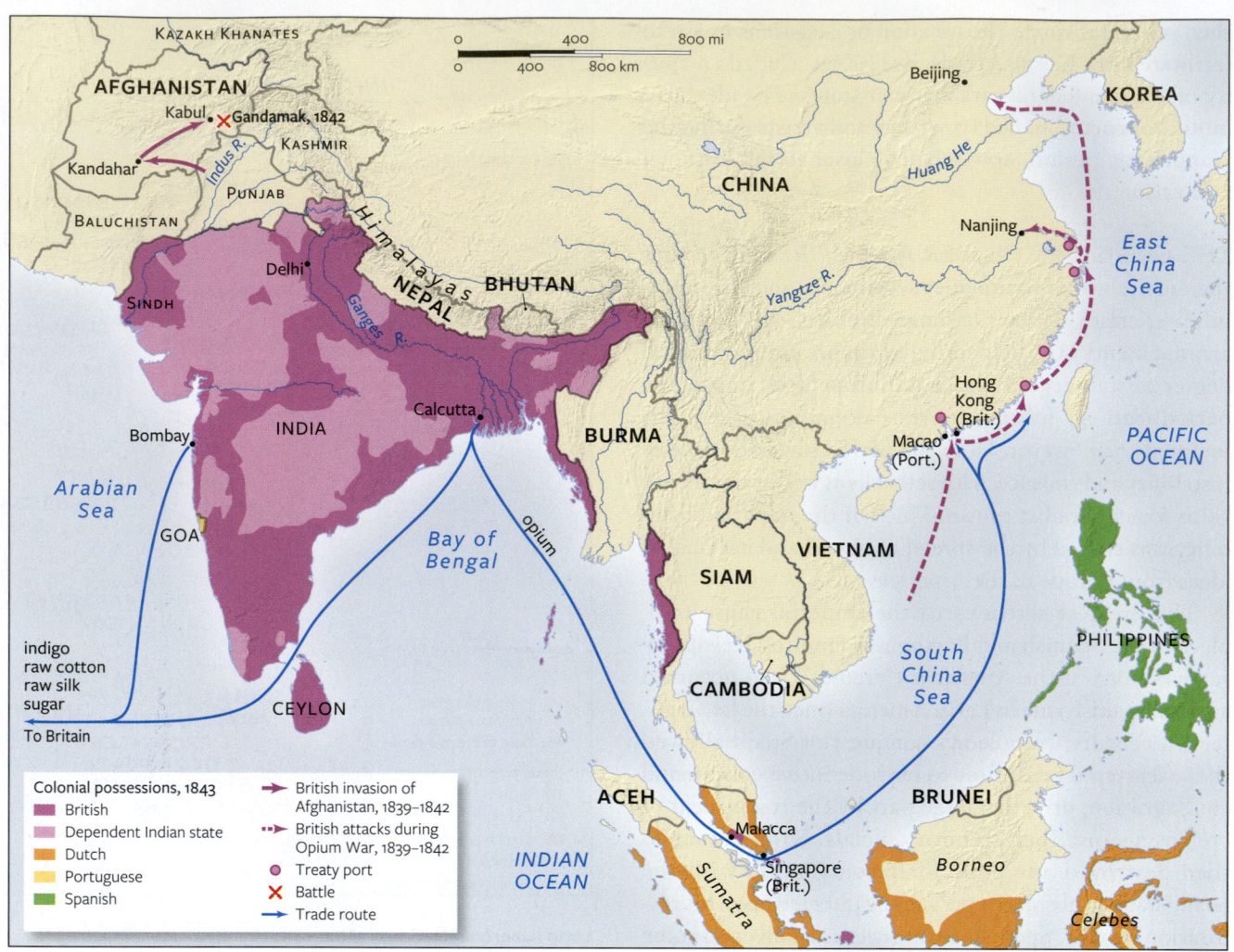

British Expansion in Asia, 1843 Despite Britain's failures in Afghanistan, the wars of the early 19th century made it an extremely powerful presence in Asia, eclipsing the other European empires in the region. Britain controlled the entire Indian subcontinent—either directly or through agreements with local rulers—as well as Hong Kong and parts of Burma and Siam. Also, it had established naval control over trade routes that brought Indian opium to China and Asian goods back to Britain.

IMPERIAL EXPANSION AND RESISTANCE

In these decades, European imperialism moved into a new phase. European empires shifted the principal theater of their activities from the Americas to Asia and Africa, and one empire in particular would far outstrip its rivals in establishing a worldwide colonial presence.

THE BRITISH EMPIRE ASCENDANT As the Iberian empires contracted, the British Empire expanded mightily. The British East India Company already ruled significant areas in India—partly on its own, and partly through dependent local princes. In the mid-1820s, a long and costly war against the kingdom of Burma allowed the British to annex several rich eastern Indian provinces. And between the 1830s and 1843, the predominantly Muslim province of Sindh, covering much of present-day Pakistan and Afghanistan, fell under Company rule as well. Between 1839 and 1842, Britain also fought the short, decisive **Opium War** against China, forcing the Chinese to open ports to British trade—particularly the profitable trade in highly addictive Indian opium. The 1842 Treaty of Nanking gave Britain the port city of Hong Kong as well. In addition to this trade, the empire in this period increasingly supplied British factories with raw materials, notably cotton from the expanding cotton fields of India.

But the limits to British expansionism in Asia became

apparent in that graveyard of empires, Afghanistan. Here the British had largely groundless strategic concerns—they worried that the expanding Russian Empire might eventually use the country as a base from which to threaten Britain's Indian possessions. British observers would come to refer to this competition between their country and Russia as the great game. Judging Afghanistan's king unreliable as an ally, they sent a 20,000-strong army north from India in 1839, which won a series of quick victories and set up camp in the capital of Kabul. But as the British presence in the city swelled, Afghans rallied to the king's son and carried out increasingly daring attacks on the British forces. The top British commander, after dithering for several months, finally decided to withdraw. But in the mountain passes leading back to India, Afghan tribesmen attacked the British, slaughtering all but a few of the soldiers and their family members. The news caused consternation in Britain, and dramatic images of the column's last stand at Gandamak proliferated. Afghanistan remained independent.

Last Stand at Gandamak This 1898 painting of the final moments of the British campaign in Afghanistan shows a small group of wounded soldiers, surrounded by dead comrades, preparing to face off against the enemy coming over the hill.

THE FRENCH CONQUEST OF ALGERIA

The most important new theater of European imperialism in this period was Muslim north Africa. The local regimes along the southern Mediterranean coast, nominally loyal to the Ottomans, had fought with European regimes for centuries and frequently seized European ships, enslaving Christian passengers. In the late 1820s, the Restoration government in France, in part to distract public attention from its domestic troubles, decided to subdue what are now the coastal provinces of Algeria, the principal source of this piracy, and to bring them under French rule. The successful campaign, involving some 600 French ships and 34,000 soldiers, took place in June 1830, just days before the July Revolution. But the new king, Louis-Philippe, endorsed the conquest and began the transformation of Algeria into a French possession.

Local rebels resisted until well into the 1840s, but the French army eventually overcame them. French officials quickly developed the ambition of making Algeria a part of France. They also encouraged settlement by European colonists—unlike the British in India—and by 1845 over 100,000 had come from France, mostly to the temperate coastal cities. They were in a distinct minority, however, compared to the two million Algerian Muslims to whom the French denied equal rights. For the moment, Algeria had principally a strategic role for France, giving it effective control over the western Mediterranean, although in the future Algeria would develop considerable economic importance.

BRITAIN'S ABOLITION OF SLAVERY

Overall, European imperialism in the period, from the conquests in Algeria and India to the Opium War in China, is often presented as an enterprise pursued without any moral checks whatsoever. But it is important to realize that from as early as Bartolomé de las Casas's condemnation of Spanish treatment of native Americans in the sixteenth century, moral critiques of imperialism had developed alongside imperialism itself. During the Enlightenment, influential works like the *History of the Two Indies*, composed by Parisian *philosophes*, had found large audiences with their arguments that supposedly "primitive" peoples had to be understood as social and cultural actors capable of developing their own path to modernity. Christian evangelical thought, Enlightenment conceptions of "the rights of man," and moralizing middle-class reform movements also spurred critiques of imperialism.

And in Britain, these critiques found important political expression. In 1807, Britain outlawed the slave trade throughout its possessions. Then in 1833 it proceeded to abolish slavery itself throughout most of the British Empire, with the notable exception of East India Company territories in South Asia and the Indian Ocean. Abolition was spurred by the strong opposition to slavery among dissenting Protestants, especially Quakers, who had a particularly strong presence in the middle-class electorate enfranchised by the Reform Bill. Still, slavery remained a profitable enterprise, especially on the sugar and coffee plantations of the French and Spanish Caribbean colonies, and the plantations of the United States. In the end, the spread of moralizing evangelical movements, and the rise of a liberal current of thought that was increasingly willing to attribute basic rights to all humans, won out over economic interests. Other than the abortive French Revolution emancipation decree of 1794, Britain's was the first major step to abolish slavery taken by a European power.

CONCLUSION

Some liberal British thinkers, including John Bright and Richard Cobden, wanted to go further than abolishing slavery. They proposed that Great Britain retreat from empire altogether, inviting opponents to brand them Little Englanders. But their efforts were unsuccessful. The heyday of European overseas empire was yet to come. In fact, between 1820 and 1845, and especially with the conquest of Algeria, Europe entered a second age of empire that differed in important ways from what had come before, even as it kept evolving through the rest of the nineteenth century.

The first age of European overseas empire, which had begun with the explorations of the fifteenth century, centered on the Americas and ended with the independence of most American territories during the half-century that followed 1776. The second age would above all involve Africa and Asia and would be shaped by the transformations Europe had undergone since the late eighteenth century. What the nineteenth century called imperialism would be powered by steam, plated with iron, and fed with a steady stream of raw materials awaiting their transformation into industrial manufactures and consumer goods. It would be a program carried out in large part by the new European middle classes. And it would be a program that inadvertently brought with it ideas of liberal democracy and national self-determination, which indigenous peoples would appropriate, adapt, combine with traditions of their own, and ultimately wield with destructive effect against the very countries that had sought to exploit them. In this way, the period 1820–45 set the stage both for the greatest global expansion of European power in history and for that expansion's ultimate end.

[CHAPTER REVIEW]

KEY TERMS

Industrial Revolution (p. 602)
factory towns (p. 609)
bourgeoisie (p. 611)
proletariat (p. 611)
cult of domesticity (p. 614)

cholera (p. 617)
Poor Law Amendment of 1834 (p. 618)
socialism (p. 619)
romanticism (p. 620)
utilitarianism (p. 623)

Democracy in America (p. 624)
Decembrists (p. 626)
July Revolution (p. 626)
Reform Bill of 1832 (p. 627)
Chartist movement (p. 627)

trade unions (p. 628)
Congress Poland (p. 628)
nationalism (p. 630)
German Confederation (p. 630)
Opium War (p. 632)

REVIEW QUESTIONS

1. What factors established Britain's lead in industrial growth?

2. How did early industrialization transform Europe?

3. Describe some of the distinctive features of the family life and culture of the European urban middle classes of the mid-nineteenth century.

4. What made living and working conditions in cities during this period so unhealthy?

5. What social and religious reforms occurred during the first half of the nineteenth century?

6. How did romanticism shape the literature and arts of the early nineteenth century?

7. What did reactionaries, conservatives, liberals, and radicals, respectively, identify as the chief political problems of their time, and what solutions did each group propose?

8. What were the effects of the violent revolutions and uprisings that spread throughout Europe and Latin America during the first half of the nineteenth century?

9. How did national independence movements challenge the existing order?

10. What were the goals of the European overseas expansion that began in the 1830s?

CORE OBJECTIVES

After reading this chapter, you should have a solid understanding of the following core objectives. To strengthen your grasp of the core objectives, use the resources on the Student Site for The West.

- Identify the factors that led to the Industrial Revolution in the nineteenth century.
- Analyze the roles of the middle and lower classes in nineteenth-century industrial societies.
- Describe the negative impacts of industrialization and the responses to them.

- Assess the emergence of new religious movements and romanticism.
- Evaluate the emergent political ideologies and civil conflicts of the period.
- Consider the impact of nationalism and imperialism on Europe and the world in the first half of the nineteenth century.

 GO TO **inQuizitive** TO SEE WHAT YOU'VE LEARNED—AND LEARN WHAT YOU'VE MISSED—WITH PERSONALIZED FEEDBACK ALONG THE WAY.

CHRONOLOGY

Growing Pains

SOCIAL AND POLITICAL UPHEAVALS

1845–1880

"The old Paris is no more. A city's shape changes more quickly, alas, than a human heart." When the author of these lines, the poet Charles Baudelaire, was born in 1821, the capital of France still had much the appearance of a medieval city. Although it had lost its medieval city walls, demolished well before the French Revolution, the city center remained a tangle of narrow streets and alleyways clustered tightly about the banks of the Seine River. Buildings seemed crammed into every available space: around the dozens of churches and convents that still dotted the urban landscape, right up against the walls of the old royal palace of the Louvre, now a museum, and even spilling into its massive courtyards. It was only in the late eighteenth century that the monarchy had cleared the last buildings off the city's bridges.

In the first decades of the 1800s, Paris had inadequate supplies of fresh water and a small, poorly maintained sewer system. Most inhabitants drew their drinking water from the filthy river, while human and animal waste collected in the streets. These conditions generated overpowering odors in warm weather and provided a fertile breeding ground for water-borne diseases like cholera. The city's narrow, winding streets also made it easy for insurgents to block off whole neighborhoods with impromptu but effective barricades, to the despair of successive governments. For centuries, reformers had dreamed

Haussmannization Gustave Caillebotte's 1877 painting *Paris Street; Rainy Day*, depicting elegantly dressed pedestrians walking along as if on display, as well as wide boulevards and gas lamps, perfectly illustrates the city's new character.

- What sparked the revolutions of 1848 across the continent?
- How did politics drive reform and imperial power in Britain?
- What drove national unification and international rivalry in this period?
- How did city life change over these years?
- What important challenges to bourgeois life emerged at this time?

of opening Paris up to light, air, fresh water—and to government authority—by constructing broad boulevards and leafy squares, aqueducts and proper sewers. Their efforts, however, had been limited.

But when Baudelaire reached his thirties, the old Paris, as he observed, was no more. The unlikely agent of change was a balding, portly civil servant with a passion for music who had spent his career avoiding the political storms of the century and steadily advanced up the ranks of the French national administration. Baron Georges-Eugène Haussmann (1809–1891) took office as prefect of Paris and the surrounding areas in 1853, with a mandate from Emperor Napoleon III to reshape the city of Paris. Napoleon, the nephew of Napoleon I, had originally come to power as an elected president of the French Republic, but in 1851 he staged a coup d'état against his own government, and a year later he proclaimed himself emperor. Now Napoleon III intended to use his power to achieve what the previous decades' constitutional monarchies and republics had not.

Under Haussmann's direction, the regime turned virtually the entire city into a dirt-clogged construction zone. Wide new boulevards were driven into Paris on north-south and east-west axes, facilitating, among other things, the movement of troops in case of rebellion. Napoleon I's Arc de Triomphe became the center of a spectacular intersection of twelve massive boulevards. To make room for these thoroughfares, and for imposing new government structures on the city's central island, thousands of old buildings were demolished. The process forced tens of thousands of Parisians to move out of their homes, in most cases to the city's gritty, expanding industrial suburbs.

Haussmann also took on the problem of sanitation. A new aqueduct system brought in plentiful fresh water from a source 80 miles to the east. Engineers added over 300 miles of sewer lines, including central "galleries" twelve feet high and twelve feet wide. As the most famous French writer of the century, Victor Hugo, would point out in the 1860s in *Les Misérables*: "Paris has another Paris under herself, a Paris of sewers; which has its streets, its crossings, its squares, its blind alleys, its arteries, and its circulation, which is slime, minus the human form." The organizers of the World Exposition of 1867, which aimed to show off the new Paris to the world, included guided tours of the sewer system.

The Paris that emerged from "Haussmannization," with its clean, broad streets flanked by stately apartment blocks, was now a middle-class showcase. A network of covered shopping arcades encouraged the conspicuous consumption of sophisticated pleasures. Horse-drawn taxis became a common sight, along with larger vehicles that carried passengers from both the middle and working classes along set routes. These vehicles took their name from the Latin word meaning "for all"—*omnibus*, or, in its more common abbreviation, *bus*.

More than a century and a half later, it is all too easy to look back on the transformation of Paris and imagine the middle years of the nineteenth century as ones of steady social and political progress. The middle classes became more prominent than ever before. Industrialization and urbanization continued apace, across more and more of Europe. Parliamentary democracy seemed ascendant as well, with western European countries mostly moving, by 1880, toward political systems in which all or most adult males voted for representative bodies with significant political power. Napoleon III himself left the scene for good in 1870, making way for the triumph of republicanism in France.

Nationalism seemed to be reshaping Europe into an orderly system of coherent nation-states. After centuries of division, both Italy and Germany unified, while the Austrian Empire devolved significant power to its largest ethnic minority, the Hungarians. Their partially autonomous kingdom took up more than half of the territory of what was now called the Austro-Hungarian Empire, extending well beyond the boundaries of the Hungarian ethnic group to include most of present-day Croatia and Slovakia, as well as parts of Poland, Serbia, Romania, and Ukraine. And the European powers flexed their muscles across the globe. Most telling, in October 1860, in the Second Opium War, a combined Anglo-French force crushed Chinese resistance and entered Beijing to force the Qing dynasty (1644–1912) to open more ports to Western trade—particularly the trade in opium.

Yet few of these developments were actually pointing in a clear, unambiguous direction. Industrialization provoked ever-sharper critiques and helped lead to the emergence of a coherent ideological movement committed to the wholesale transformation of European social structures—Marxist socialism. The period's greatest explosion of democratic and nationalist energies, in what came to be called the "springtime of nations" of 1848, was followed by a summer and autumn of reaction across much of the Continent, typified by Napoleon III. And Europe's expanding overseas empires remained fragile, capable not only of astonishing conquests but also of bloody reverses. British and French triumphs in China in 1860 nursed movements that would later emerge to oppose them. In short, even on the eve of Europe's greatest period of global power, the supposedly inevitable and irresistible advance of European civilization was anything but certain.

THE REVOLUTIONS OF 1848

At the end of the Napoleonic Wars in 1815, Europeans exhausted by carnage and instability had looked to politics principally for the maintenance of peace and order. Thirty years later, however, memories of the carnage had faded, and personalities and arrangements once praised as the height of rational security seemed crabbed and repressive. Once again, conditions were ripe for the outbreak of revolution across the Continent. The first sparks burst out in 1846, when Polish nationalists plotted simultaneous uprisings in the Polish regions of Prussia, Austria, and Russia, only to see them crushed by the police and, in Austria, by the army. In 1848, full-fledged revolutions again ignited, and as in the late eighteenth century, the flames burned brightest in France.

THE FRENCH SECOND REPUBLIC (1848–1852)

No person better illustrated the shift in political climate that brought about the revolutions than France's king,

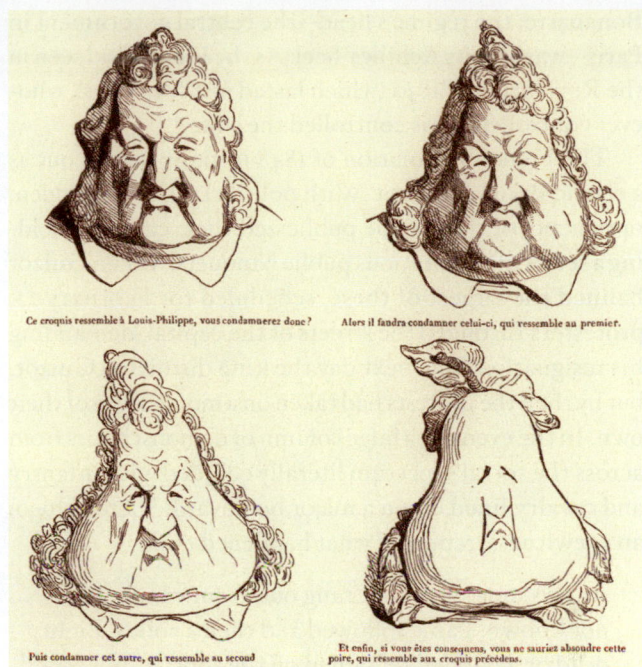

Louis-Philippe The caricaturist Charles Philipon made this illustration of Louis-Philippe turning into a pear, an enduring symbol of popular frustration with the monarch.

Louis-Philippe. At age eighteen, in 1792, he had been the dashing prince turned revolutionary who helped save the day for the newborn French Republic at the critical battle of Valmy. At age fifty-six, in 1830, he had been the reassuringly practical, unpretentious "citizen king" who seemed ideally suited for reuniting his country after the tumult and dissension of the Empire and the failed Restoration. But by age seventy-four, in early 1848, he seemed a corrupt curmudgeon whose jowly face lent itself all too easily to cruel caricature. Although Louis-Philippe's July Monarchy (named for the July Revolution that had brought it into being) had doubled the size of the electorate, the vote was still limited to just 200,000 men out of a total French population of 35,000,000, and real power lay with a small network of the king's cronies from the world of finance.

François Guizot, the talented Protestant historian and political writer who served as prime minister in the late 1840s, steadfastly resisted calls for universal suffrage and seemed for a time to command respect. But in 1846 and 1847, Louis-Philippe's regime came under new pressure from financial scandals, a severe industrial slump that started in the railroad sector, a banking panic, and an agricultural crisis that sent the price of grain soaring. Thanks to the radical centralization of the French state that had begun under the absolute monarchy and was completed by

Bonaparte, the regime's head—the central government in Paris—was also its Achilles' heel. As the French had seen in the Revolution of 1830 (which lasted just four days), whoever controlled Paris controlled the state.

The French Revolution of 1848 initially played out as a classic Parisian drama. With political rallies forbidden, opponents of the regime publicized their cause by holding a series of ostentatious public banquets. When Guizot banned the largest of these, scheduled for February 22, protesters thronged the streets of the capital, demanding his resignation. The next day the king dismissed Guizot, but by then the protests had taken on a momentum of their own. In the evening, a huge column of demonstrators from across the social spectrum literally collided with infantry and cavalry lined up on a major boulevard. Victor Hugo, an eyewitness, reported what happened next:

> At this moment a shot rang out, from which side is not known. Panic followed and then a volley. Eighty dead or wounded remained on the spot. A universal cry of horror and fury arose: "Vengeance!" The bodies of the victims were loaded on a cart lit with torches. The cortège moved back amidst curses at a funereal pace. And in a few hours Paris was covered with barricades.

The barricades, some built around the new "buses," blocked off scores of narrow, pre-Haussmann streets and proved effective. Louis-Philippe desperately sought to save the day, reshuffling his government and finally trying to abdicate in favor of his grandson. But by this point, insurgents—mostly skilled workers, students, and middle-class professionals—had captured key sites in central Paris and were proclaiming the Second Republic (the first was the regime that had lasted from 1792 to Napoleon's coronation in 1804). Rather than risk sharing the fate of his guillotined cousin Louis XVI, Louis-Philippe fled to London. A provisional government took power, on February 26, headed by nine republicans drawn from the liberal opposition to Louis-Philippe. At the insistence of the Parisian crowds, they then added two others to the list: the radical Louis Blanc and a worker by the name of Albert. Hopes were high that the new government would move toward extending the franchise to all adult men and institute social welfare policies to ease the lives of urban workers.

THE SPREAD OF REVOLUTION

Six decades before, the French Revolution of 1789 had not immediately provoked widespread imitations beyond the borders of France. It mostly took the arrival of aggressive, republican French armies to precipitate revolutionary action elsewhere. In 1848, things were different—in part because the telegraph now spread news instantaneously. Even before the 1848 Revolution in France, Sicilian nobles had revolted against the Bourbon government of the kingdom of the Two Sicilies (covering the southern half of the Italian peninsula). And afterward, revolutionary movements coalesced throughout the Continent, often led by university students inspired both by the news from Paris and by now-distant memories of the eighteenth-century revolutionary era.

The motivations of this new generation of revolutionaries were varied. In part, they reflected social tensions spurred by the disruptions of the Industrial Revolution. In many areas, they derived from nationalist sentiments and movements, with newly self-conscious national groups demanding greater sovereignty and independence. Partly they came from the spread of liberal political demands for greater freedom of expression and a wider suffrage, combined with frustration at what increasingly seemed an allergy to change on the part of stubborn ruling regimes. Examples of revolution in other countries both provided a model to follow and also provoked the anxiety that if the moment was not seized, the opportunity might disappear forever. All these factors combined to produce, in scarcely a month and a half, more sweeping political changes across Europe than at any time since 1815.

GERMANY AND AUSTRIA On March 3, scarcely a week after Louis-Philippe's abdication, protests and petitions began to proliferate in areas of western Germany that had belonged to Prussia since 1815. Demands from liberal groups included increased constitutional freedoms and the creation of new systems of social welfare to alleviate economic misery. On the same day, 650 miles to the east in Budapest, the nationalist lawyer Lajos Kossuth (1802–1894) established his leadership of Hungarian liberals with a fiery speech demanding representative government and additional rights for the Hungarians within the Austrian Empire, which remained a looser political entity than the hyper-centralized French state.

Ten days after that, in Vienna, it seemed as if the French events were repeating themselves. Students and radical artisans marched in the streets demanding expanded voting rights and the participation of the empire's German-speaking regions in a new pan-German federation. Troops opened fire, and the movement turned revolutionary. The dominant figure in Austrian political life had been the same man since early in the century: the

The Revolutions of 1848 Nationalist and liberal revolutions broke out in cities throughout Europe in the spring of 1848, from Paris to Budapest. But by 1849, conservatives had largely quashed the uprisings.

conservative diplomat and politician Klemens von Metternich, one of the guiding spirits of the Congress of Vienna. But he was the same age as Louis-Philippe, and deeply unpopular. Now the Habsburg family, headed by the often incoherent emperor Ferdinand I (r. 1835–1848), prevailed upon Metternich to resign his position as chancellor and hoped that sweeping concessions would preempt further upheaval. Most important, they announced that all adult males would be able to vote for a new imperial Austrian parliament. This put the empire's German-speakers, still its largest ethnic group, in a distinct minority, outnumbered collectively by the empire's Hungarians, Czechs, Slovaks, and others.

The wave of revolutions continued in the second half of March 1848, sweeping over every major German state. In conservative, Catholic Bavaria, the unrest had begun a few weeks earlier with outraged protests against the mistress of King Ludwig I (r. 1825–1848), a flamboyant Irish adventuress named Eliza Gilbert who had previously enthralled London music hall audiences under the stage name Lola

Montez. She fled the country, but soon afterward students took to the streets of Munich with liberal demands and forced Ludwig to abdicate in favor of his eldest son.

Elsewhere, princes remained on their thrones but only by promising substantial reforms. The most important events occurred in Prussia. Polish nationalists in the Polish-speaking region around Poznan revolted unsuccessfully in yet another attempt to unify their country and restore its sovereignty. Meanwhile, a revolution took place in Berlin itself, driven largely by urban artisans who feared both competition from outside the traditional guild structures and also the effects of mechanization. Violent crowds in the capital intimidated King Friedrich Wilhelm IV (r. 1840–1861) into conceding free elections, freedom of the press, and a new constitution. Like their counterparts in Vienna, the Berlin revolutionaries called for the creation of a united Germany.

In a proclamation to the Prussian nation on March 21, the king declared: "I have today...placed myself and my people under the venerable banner of the German Empire. Prussia is from now on part of Germany." It seemed as if the German states, after their long centuries of fragmentation, were about to perform a spontaneous act of unification. At the end of March, a group of liberal reformers, mostly from southwestern Germany, met in Frankfurt to propose elections for a **pan-German parliament**, chosen by universal manhood suffrage, which would draw up a constitution for the entire country. The Diet, or assembly, of the weak German Confederation—which had replaced

Revolution in Berlin In a lithograph from the period, imperial troops fire upon revolutionaries on a barricade in Berlin in March 1848. The revolutionaries wave a new tricolor flag—first widely seen in the 1848 Revolution—that signals their support for a unified Germany.

the old Holy Roman Empire at the end of the Napoleonic Wars—approved the plan, and elections to the new united parliament in Frankfurt began almost immediately.

ITALY At the same moment, it seemed as if a drive for unification might overtake Italy as well. In mid-March, nationalist crowds skirmished with troops in the streets of Austrian-ruled Lombardy and Venice, leading to open revolts and proclamations of independence. Further south, protests elicited promises of reform from the rulers of Tuscany and the kingdom of the Two Sicilies. Newspapers from across Italy called on the prosperous northwest Italian state of Piedmont-Sardinia to take a more active role in uniting the peninsula, despite the initial reluctance of King Carlo Alberto (r. 1831–1849). Anxious about the movement taking too radical a direction, the king finally sent his army into Lombardy, defeating the aged but canny Austrian general Josef Radetzky, a veteran of the wars against Napoleon. But Piedmont-Sardinia didn't follow up on the victory, and the Austrians retreated into a chain of well-defended Italian fortresses. Not until 1859 would the drive toward Italian unification regain its momentum.

RADICALISM AND *THE COMMUNIST MANIFESTO*

The question was now whether, in fulfillment of Carlo Alberto's fears and those of conservatives across the Continent, the revolutions of 1848 would follow the example of the original French Revolution and descend into an uncontrolled spiral of radicalization—perhaps even leading to their own Reigns of Terror. Would long-standing forms of privilege crumble and churches be overturned? Would the short-lived urban street violence of February and March beget more widespread bloodshed or full-fledged civil war? Indeed, given the progress of radical utopian ideas over the previous decades, would the new revolutions give rise to movements even *more* radical than Jacobinism?

Some revolutionaries certainly hoped so. In February 1848, two German writers issued a summary of their political program that began with these dramatic words: "A specter is haunting Europe: the specter of Communism." We have already met one of these men, the socialist writer and organizer **Karl Marx**. Marx's early work explored, among other things, the contradictions between the universal rights theoretically on offer in liberal bourgeois societies, and the economic forces that he claimed limited effective enjoyment of these rights to the wealthy and the middle class. Unlike the utopian thinkers we have seen such as Saint-Simon, Marx did not believe that the solution to social problems lay in new schemes of social organization imposed from above by well-meaning reformers. Instead, he was developing a powerful new philosophy of history, derived from German thinkers such as Hegel and early economists like David Ricardo, that predicted social change would take place largely on its own propelled by the operation of ineluctable economic forces.

In the early 1840s, Marx met the well-born German thinker and journalist **Friedrich Engels** (1820–1895), author of a scathing account of the condition of the working class in England under the industrial system. Now the two men distilled their thought into a short, accessible, enormously influential pamphlet known as ***The Communist Manifesto*** (1848). It laid out in stark terms an all-encompassing vision of history and politics: "All history is the history of class struggle." Just as the bourgeoisie had supposedly overcome the feudal order during the French Revolution, so, Marx and Engels argued, the industrial working class, which they called the **proletariat**, would eventually rise up and overcame the bourgeoisie. This upheaval would yield an egalitarian worker's paradise in which property would be owned communally and a truly representative government would equitably manage all resources: "from each according to his abilities, to each according to his needs." The revolution of the working class would also eliminate international competition, for the proletariat's interests were the same everywhere. To quote the most famous Marxist slogan, taken from the conclusion to the *Manifesto*: "Workers of the World, unite! You have nothing to lose but your chains."

THE CONSERVATIVE REACTION

In France, there were signs that the Second Republic was moving in radical directions. The provisional government quickly drew up plans for new elections based on universal manhood suffrage. It set up a series of National Workshops, proposed by the socialist Louis Blanc, to provide the unemployed with work and a minimum income. On April 27, 1848, declaring slavery an "offense against human dignity," the government abolished the practice

Karl Marx A portrait of the German socialist from around 1865. Marx's hugely influential writings on society, including his collaboration with Engels, *The Communist Manifesto,* foresaw a class struggle in which the proletariat would overthrow the bourgeoisie.

throughout France's overseas possessions, finally delivering on the promise originally made by the First French Republic and betrayed by Napoleon Bonaparte. Although coming fifteen years after the abolition of slavery in the British Empire, the measure anticipated abolition in the United States by over fifteen years. As in the early 1790s, calls were heard to extend the suffrage to women, and women's political clubs formed. In March, a group petitioned the government—in vain—to grant women equal political rights with men, and Eugénie Niboyet, a prolific author, founded the world's first feminist newspaper, a short-lived venture called *Womens' Voice*.

But if the fires of revolution spread far more quickly in 1848 than in 1789, they burned less hot, and in many cases soon blew out. The month of March turned out to be their high point, not their starting point. In most cases, the revolutionary movements, mainly comprising urban skilled artisans, professionals, and students, simply could not muster sufficient strength in their respective countries to cement their initial victories. The peasants who still made up the majority of the population in nearly every European state, and whose material interests often diverged considerably from those of urban workers, proved particularly resistant. So what followed these victories was not a new Terror, but months of frustration and confusion that could not resist, in most of the affected states, a well-organized and violent conservative reaction.

Even while radical hopes remained alive in France, the Austrian authorities in Vienna quickly discovered that the way to prevent liberal nationalism from threatening the empire was to play its different nationalities against one another. They began to exploit the resentment felt by Croats and Slovaks toward the Hungarians who claimed authority over their territories. As early as March 1848, the Austrian government appointed a Croat as governor of Croatia, knowing full well he would refuse to cooperate with the Hungarian authorities. Kossuth and the other Hungarian leaders, in no mood to compromise, passed a series of discriminatory measures against non-Hungarians, leading to an uprising in Slovakia and considerable tumult elsewhere. Meanwhile, the traditional Diet in Bohemia (now part of the Czech Republic) remained dominated by German-speakers who, with support from Vienna, resisted the calls by the region's Czech majority for greater autonomy within the empire. A Pan-Slav Congress made up of representatives from the empire's different Slav nationalities (including Czechs, Slovaks, Slovenes, Croats, and Ukrainians) convened in Prague in June but nearly fell apart as the delegations squabbled about how best to reorganize the imperial government.

THE JUNE TURNING POINT Just as March 1848 had been the crucial month for revolution, June proved the crucial one for counterrevolution. In Prague, even as the Pan-Slav Congress got under way, frustrated workers and artisans built barricades and tried to wrest control of the city away from the hated Austrian governor. He did not hesitate to bombard Prague with artillery, and managed to suppress the insurrection within four days.

Barely a week later, similar events occurred in Paris. In April, some 9 million newly enfranchised French men had gone to the polls and elected a Constituent Assembly charged with the task of writing a new constitution. But France was still a heavily rural country, and most peasant voters did not support a program of drastic social reforms. Few of the new deputies had much sympathy for the economic difficulties of Parisian workers. They saw the reforms implemented by February's provisional government as a dangerous drain on the national purse, even as the unemployed flooded to Paris to take advantage of the National Workshops there.

On June 23, the new government ordered the Workshops closed and called on General Eugène Cavaignac (1802–1857) to maintain order. In the so-called June Days, Cavaignac brutally suppressed a workers' insurgency, his forces killing over 1,500 and taking 12,000 prisoners.

June Days A supporter of the revolution, the painter Ernest Meissonier (1815–1891) depicted the outcome of the June Days as a bloodbath. The corpses of revolutionaries pile up in a narrow Paris street amid the rubble of a demolished barricade.

The government exiled more than 4,000 of the prisoners to French Algeria. Cavaignac became provisional chief executive, and the Assembly finalized plans for a new conservative republican regime that would give significant powers to an elected president. The elections took place in December 1848, and a surprising candidate emerged victorious: Louis-Napoleon Bonaparte (1808–1873), the nephew of Napoleon Bonaparte, who promised to restore stability and moderation to the shaken country.

Even as the barricades were being blasted apart by cannon fire in the streets of Paris and Prague, the new pan-German Parliament was meeting in Frankfurt to devise a constitution for a united German state. But while the deputies, largely representing the legal profession, indulged in high-flown rhetoric, they quickly found they had little ability to translate the rhetoric into reality. The two most powerful German states, Prussia and Austria, had no desire to surrender authority to a new national government; and, following the spring's shift in the European winds, they discovered new confidence that they could resist doing so. Nor did the Frankfurt deputies make a serious attempt to garner support among the urban and rural masses. In particular, they balked at endorsing measures to protect artisans against the twin threats to the traditional trades: industrial mechanization, and competition from outside the old guild structure. In September 1848, the Parliament had to call on Prussian and Hessian soldiers to protect them from workers who had stormed into their meeting hall to demand radical action.

THE END GAME

The final act of the 1848 revolutions was the longest and most tragic, stretching through 1849 and into the early years of the next decade. In country after country, the forces of "order" continued to reassert themselves, violently suppressed liberal and radical movements, and restored autocratic monarchy as the continental status quo.

AUSTRIA AND PRUSSIA In August and October 1848, the Austrian government quelled new rebellions in Vienna—the second time at a cost of more than 3,000 dead. Martial law was declared and censorship reestablished, even as the erratic emperor, Ferdinand, abdicated in favor of his pliable eighteen-year-old grandson Franz Josef (r. 1848–1916). In 1849, when the Austrian assembly elected the previous year completed work on a new

constitution, the new Austrian minister-president, Prince Felix von Schwarzenberg (1800–1852), paid little heed. He dissolved the body and imposed his own, more autocratic constitution which, among other things, made no concessions to non-German nationalities. These actions pushed the Hungarians under Kossuth into launching a full-scale war for independence. But in response, Schwarzenberg and Franz Josef appealed to Russia's reactionary tsar, Nikolai, who feared nationalist rumblings within his own multi-ethnic empire. With the help of a large detachment of Russian troops, the Austrians stamped out the Hungarian resistance and sent Kossuth fleeing for his life.

In Prussia as well, the tide quickly turned against the revolutionary movement. In May 1848, King Friedrich Wilhelm IV had acquiesced in the election, by universal male suffrage, of a liberal Berlin Assembly that was charged with writing a new Prussian constitution (this Prussian body was different from the Frankfurt pan-German Parliament). But after the failure of the June insurrection in Paris, the king dismissed the liberal cabinet that had been serving since March. In December, he proclaimed martial law and dissolved the Berlin Assembly, and then, like Schwarzenberg, promulgated a monarchist, conservative constitution of his own. In April of the next year, he imposed new restrictions on voting that would give conservatives the upper hand for decades.

Despite these events in Austria and Prussia, the men elected to the new pan-German parliament in Frankfurt were still hoping against hope to achieve the unification of Germany under a liberal constitution. In December 1848, they issued a grand document: the Fundamental Rights of the German People, which insisted on equality before the law and freedom of speech and religion. Four months later, they completed work on a constitution that would provide for a hereditary German emperor, an upper house composed of representatives from the individual German states, and a lower house elected by universal manhood suffrage. They limited membership in the new state to areas with German-speaking majorities, meaning that most of the Austrian Empire would be ineligible.

But the proposal won no support from ruling German sovereigns. The Habsburgs refused even to consider splitting their empire. And King Friedrich Wilhelm IV of Prussia rejected the constitution as well, even when the Frankfurt Parliament offered him the German crown— he scorned it as a "crown from the gutter" and dissolved his own Prussian assembly so its members would have no chance to defy him on the issue. In despair, the Frankfurt Parliament broke up, and in September 1849 the German states revived the German Confederation of 1815.

ITALY AND FRANCE The revolutionary movements also largely failed in Italy and France. In 1849, the war resumed between Austria and Piedmont-Sardinia, and this time Radeztky's forces took the upper hand. King Carlo Alberto of Piedmont-Sardinia abdicated in favor of his son Vittorio Emmanuele II (r. 1849–1861), and the Austrians returned to rule in Milan. In August 1849, after a long blockade and bombardment, they also reoccupied Venice.

In late 1848, one of the most radical and ambitious Italian revolutions had begun in Rome. It was launched against Pope Pius IX (r. 1846–1878), who ruled the extensive Papal States of central Italy, which had existed in one form or another since the eighth century. After making some initial concessions to the liberal rebels, Pius fled to Naples disguised as a simple parish priest. The new liberal government confiscated Church property and, in early 1849, held elections for an assembly that quickly proclaimed a Roman Republic. But a coalition of Catholic powers—including Louis-Napoleon's France—marched on Rome in support of the pope. A ragtag army of volunteers from across Italy briefly held them off, but eventually the Republic capitulated and the pope returned to reimpose autocratic rule. This Roman revolution brought to prominence one of the most important figures in modern Italian history: a former merchant-sailor named **Giuseppe Garibaldi** (1807–1882). Garibaldi's work for Mazzini's Young Italy had led to a prolonged exile in South America, where he gained military experience in Brazilian and

Napoleon III A painting from the late 1850s by Edouard Detaille shows Louis Napoleon at a French military camp flanked by his officers. He is dressed as a general, with metals and epaulets—and a meticulously waxed mustache.

Giuseppe Garibaldi The revolutionary (seated in the carriage with hat in hand) and his Red Shirts triumphantly enter Naples after capturing the city in September 1860 in this contemporary illustration.

Uruguayan civil wars. Returning to Italy, he led the Roman Republic's volunteer force and became a hero by himself leading them in bayonet charges against the French.

It was in France that history seemed to repeat itself most closely. Until 1848, Louis-Napoleon had been seen largely as a joke. Although nostalgia for his uncle remained surprisingly strong, few saw the pompous, grandstanding nephew as a worthy heir. His two attempts to imitate the adventure of the Hundred Days by invading France with a handful of supporters failed miserably, the second time landing him in a French prison, from which he escaped by exchanging clothes with a workman. But by late 1848, nearly every major political figure in France had been discredited by the year's tumultuous events, and Louis-Napoleon, now directly imitating his uncle, posed as a figure above politics, capable of uniting a bloodied country. After winning the presidential election in December, he initially governed as a moderate, positioning himself against a largely monarchist assembly but also reaching out to the Catholic Church by restoring the dominant role in the educational system that it had possessed before 1848.

In 1851, faced with an Assembly that refused to amend the constitution to allow him to run for a second presidential term, Louis-Napoleon staged his coup d'état. It met significant resistance, particularly from peasants who favored the so-called démoc-soc (that is, democratic-socialist) program of lowering rural taxation and increasing access to property ownership, which had gained some support in the Assembly. But Louis-Napoleon prevailed, and in December 1852 he completed the rewriting of his uncle's story by declaring himself **Napoleon III**, emperor of the French. From the Second Republic, France had moved to the Second Empire. Even before this action, Karl Marx delivered a devastating verdict on the history of France since 1848 in one of his most famous lines: "Hegel remarks somewhere that all great world-historical facts and personages appear, so to speak, twice. He forgot to add: the first time as tragedy, the second time as farce."

RUSSIA AND BRITAIN Only two of the major European powers did not see significant disruptions of their politics in 1848 and 1849. One was Russia, where Tsar Nikolai had constructed a powerful apparatus of police repression and dreamed of building a literal wall around the country to protect it from revolutionary "contagion." The other was Britain, where the parliamentary system and the extended franchise adopted in the Reform Act of 1832 proved sufficiently flexible to forestall moves toward revolution.

For a brief moment in early 1848, the last great gasp of the democratic Chartist movement did stir fears that Britain might yet follow the path of the Continent. In April, after one of the largest mass meetings in British history, in London, the Chartist leadership presented a petition with 6 million signatures to Parliament, which scornfully rejected it. But the Chartists disavowed any action that might lead to violence, while the government mobilized thousands of troops and volunteer "special constables" against possible threats. A British revolution failed to materialize. As the great Whig historian Thomas Macaulay (1800–1859) wrote, comparing Britain's stability to the Continent's tumult: "We have order in the midst of anarchy."

BRITAIN'S ASCENDANCE

Between 1815 and 1848, European politics had been shaped largely by the domestic and international frameworks constructed by the victors of the Napoleonic Wars to ensure peace and stability on the Continent. Between 1848 and 1852, they were shaped largely by the dynamics of revolution and counterrevolution. But between 1852 and 1880, with powerful states less constrained than before by the international system, European politics came to be influenced, to a remarkable degree, by strong personalities. These belonged both to sovereigns and to talented ministers who managed, even in parliamentary systems, to retain power for many years and to change the map of Europe. This pattern was especially true of Great Britain, which was now approaching the zenith of its power and influence. There, by the mid-nineteenth century, it was the prime minister who headed the government and set policy, while the monarch served largely as a figurehead. The office of prime minister now went, in most cases, to the leader of the largest party in Parliament.

THE VICTORIAN AGE (1837–1901)

Despite the weakness of her office, the single most famous British personality was undoubtedly **Queen Victoria** (r. 1837–1901). Born when the British monarchy's popularity was at an especially low ebb, she became queen at age eighteen in 1837. In 1840, she married the German prince Albert von Saxe-Coburg (1819–1861), whose personal stiffness and inexperience with British politics contributed to the royal couple's initial unpopularity. However, over the next two decades Victoria bore nine children and survived several assassination attempts, while Albert helped organize the hugely successful Great Exhibition of 1851, and their image was transformed.

Albert's death, at age forty-two in 1861, plunged the queen into an extended period of grief and despair, but by the 1870s she had nonetheless gained lasting support from the population. Victoria was legendarily rigid in matters sexual—she refused to believe in the possibility of lesbianism, frowned deeply on sex outside of marriage, and saw sex within marriage as a duty to be endured. The adjective *Victorian* is today often synonymous with a repressive Puritanism. But in 1851, the word referred rather to a country and an empire moving toward the height of confidence and power. That confidence was still tested, however, in the early decades of Victoria's exceptionally long reign, when Great Britain faced several large challenges, including a devastating famine in Ireland and a war of independence in India.

THE IRISH FAMINE In Ireland, a rural Catholic peasantry subsisting on tiny farms had become dangerously dependent on a single crop, the potato, originally imported from the Americas. Potatoes were easy to grow, had a high caloric and nutritional value, and did not require special preparation (such as milling into flour) before being cooked. The Irish population had expanded more than twice as fast as that of England or Scotland in the nineteenth century, reaching 8 million by 1845 and putting a strain on the food supply. In that year, a "wet rot" struck the potato crop and two successive harvests failed almost completely. Soon widespread starvation set in, which the British government proved miserably incapable of alleviating. It was the **Irish famine** that in 1846 finally helped liberal forces in the British Parliament to repeal the Corn Laws, which since 1815 had obstructed a free market in grains and corns, including imported ones. But lower prices for imported corn proved of only limited help to the starving Irish.

The Irish death toll, caused mostly by the diseases that struck the emaciated population, reached at least 800,000, one-tenth of the population. A further million Irish followed what was by now a longstanding pattern of dealing with hard times: they emigrated, principally to North American cities such as Boston and New York. This movement in turn marked the beginning of a massive overall increase in emigration from Europe that would involve tens of millions of people by the end of the nineteenth century. In the 1850s, for example, fully 1 million Germans emigrated to the United States, driven by economic turbulence, the promise of greater wealth on the other side of the Atlantic, cheaper and safer transoceanic travel, and the failure of the revolutions of 1848.

INDIAN WAR OF INDEPENDENCE (1857–1858)

In the 1850s, another crisis struck Britain, this time in what was becoming the crown jewel of the empire: India. Over the first half of the century, the officially chartered East India Company, through which Britain ruled in the subcontinent, had greatly increased its territory and influence, stirring resentment among supporters of native authorities. It long had its own army, staffed largely by native Indian troops known as sepoys. India served as a large and growing market for British goods, while exporting significant quantities of rice, spices, silks, tea, and raw cotton. But in April 1857, in the unlikely setting of a military exercise in the small city of Meerut, northeast of the capital Delhi, a revolt began. The exercise was meant to train some 4,500 Company troops, a large majority of them Indian, in the use of a new rifle. But when ordered to load the guns, all but five of the men refused. They protested that their cartridges were greased with beef and pork fat—the one considered unclean by Hindus, the other by Muslims.

British India, 1857–1880 The uprising that began in Meerut in 1857 soon spread throughout a wide area of northern India. But the British army successfully repressed the Mutiny and affirmed the influence of the British Empire, which by 1880 controlled the entire subcontinent and Afghanistan.

The British officers in charge insisted—truthfully—that the cartridges had no animal fat on them. But the soldiers remained defiant. Finally, the regiment's lieutenant colonel, who had spent his entire, undistinguished career in India, ordered the protesting soldiers placed under arrest. They were stripped of their ranks and almost all sentenced to ten years of hard labor after a ceremony of public humiliation. Soon afterward, members of the regiment turned on their British superiors, and soldiers from other Indian regiments in Meerut followed their example. They attacked officers' homes; tore through the city bazaar; killed roughly fifty British men, women and children, and a similar number of Indians; and called for a march on Delhi. Within weeks, Indian troops of the East India Company throughout northern India had revolted in what the British referred to simply as **the Mutiny**. For a time, it seemed Britain might lose its most important colonial territory.

As one of the more farseeing British politicians of the Victorian period, Benjamin Disraeli (1804–1881), insisted: "The decline and fall of great empires are not affairs of

The Indian Mutiny In an 1884 painting, British soldiers execute Indian rebels by tying them to cannons and firing through their bodies.

greased cartridges. Such results are occasioned by adequate causes." These causes included increasingly intrusive proselytism by British missionaries, which offended both Hindu and Muslim religious sensibilities. They also included increasingly aggressive attempts by the East India Company to annex Indian territory by dispossessing native ruling families. With Indian resentment of the British already so volatile, the affair of the cartridges was simply the spark that set off an almost inevitable explosion.

Indians now celebrate the events of 1857–58 as a war of independence, presaging their country's eventual twentieth-century achievement of independent sovereignty. In the shorter run, however, the events arguably strengthened not only British rule in India but also the British Empire as a whole. Throughout 1857, atrocities multiplied on both sides, with the British press giving sensationalist treatment to the deaths of British civilians. These accounts helped justify savage forms of retaliation, including executing rebels by tying them to the mouths of cannon and firing. Spurred to undertake a massive military effort aided by 35,000 additional troops brought in from Britain, imperial forces eventually retook all the cities captured by the "mutineers" and dispersed their forces. The conflict finally ended in June 1858, after which the British government dissolved the East India Company and took over direct rule of its Indian possessions. A new era of British imperialism, in which the London government made sure to back its ventures with large-scale military force, had begun. Great Britain did not face another colonial challenge on the scale of the Mutiny for many decades.

DISRAELI AND THE POLITICS OF REFORM

Disraeli (1804–1881) was the most eloquent exponent of British imperialism. A descendant of Jews who had migrated to Britain from Italy in the previous century, he made a very unlikely British leader. Although baptized at his father's request in 1817, he still had to contend with the anti-Semitism that pervaded British society. As a young man, moreover, he earned a reputation for flamboyant dress and risky behavior, including ruinous financial speculations. He also wrote a series of skillfully executed, popular novels. Elected to Parliament as a Conservative in 1837, he spent three decades, in his own words, "climbing the greasy pole," maneuvering against rivals until in 1868 he began the first of his terms as prime minister.

Britain at the time remained a deeply unequal society. A mere 1,200 people owned a quarter of all the land in England, and even after the Reform Act of 1832 a majority of adult men remained disenfranchised. The Conservative Party seemingly existed to protect this status quo. Indeed, this period in British politics is often seen as one of polarization between the Conservatives and the Liberals, who had gradually taken over from the Whigs. Formally founded in 1859, the Liberal Party carried on the Whig tradition of supporting free trade and parliamentary reform, although it was tied far more to middle-class and business interests than to the landed interests that had dominated the earlier party. It was shaped into a powerful political force by William Ewart Gladstone (1809–1898). But Disraeli was no reactionary. Like the Liberals, he, too, had reforming impulses, but he wanted to move reforms in a paternalistic direction.

In 1867, as party leader, Disraeli, fearing social unrest if the franchise did not expand, sponsored a second major Reform Act that for the first time gave the vote to every male householder. (The Liberals under Gladstone also supported the act.) As prime minister for a second time, between 1874 and 1880, Disraeli also pushed through a Health Act that mandated improved public sanitation and a Trade Union Act that removed most of the last restrictions on labor organizing. He and Gladstone competed for the new, working-class voters with increasingly modern electoral techniques, including Gladstone's novel campaigning by railroad in the election of 1879. And Disraeli competed effectively, even as many voters rejected the Liberals' often-rigid laissez-faire program, which aimed to limit poor relief. "It is not by the State that man can be regenerated," Gladstone famously proclaimed, to which one labor leader responded in 1879: "The Conservative party have done more for the working classes in five years than the Liberals have in fifty."

Disraeli's most important legacy, however, came in the imperial realm, which he saw not simply as a means of increasing his country's power and wealth but also as a source of unity for its often-divided population. In 1872, he declared that "the people of England . . . are proud of belonging to a great country, and wish to maintain its greatness—. . . they are proud of belonging to an Imperial country, and are resolved to maintain, if they can, the empire of England." As prime minister, Disraeli moved to protect Britain's valuable possessions in Asia by confronting Russia as it moved to expand its rule in Central Asia. He also avenged the previous British debacle in Afghanistan by defeating the Afghans in 1878–80 and securing the country in the British sphere of influence.

In India, Disraeli moved to consolidate Britain's possessions into a single vast colony. In 1876, he put the capstone on these policies by persuading Queen Victoria

"New Crowns for Old Ones!" This British cartoon from 1876 shows a caricatured Disraeli presenting the crown of empress of India to Queen Victoria, conveying suspicion of Disraeli's offer.

to take the title "empress of India"—it was with this act that the British state and its colonies formally became an empire. And Disraeli's Britain bought out Egypt's share of the Suez Canal. Constructed in the 1860s by a French company to connect the Mediterranean to the Red Sea, the canal greatly facilitated travel and trade with India. Although many Liberals also supported imperialist policies in this period, breaking in practice with their earlier "Little England" rhetoric, it was Disraeli's Conservatives who did the most to define the British imperialist mission for the rest of the century. British imperial power did continue to receive challenges—notably in 1879, by an uprising in what is now South Africa when a massive Zulu army overwhelmed a small British force at the battle of Isandlwana. Even so, by 1880 the British Empire had expanded enormously in influence and power.

POWER POLITICS

The rest of Europe also had more than its share of dominant political personalities. In an age where political success accrued increasingly to leaders who could appeal to mass audiences through the mass media of the day (above all, newspapers), the ability to craft a striking image for oneself mattered as never before. The most successful of these images were often those associated with strong nationalist or imperialist programs.

CAVOUR, GARIBALDI, AND ITALIAN UNIFICATION

One of the most unlikely of these personalities was Italian: a nearsighted, impulsive Piedmontese named **Camillo di Cavour**, who spoke French better than Italian but nonetheless ended up the architect of Italian unity. In the 1850s, Italy's unification movement was driven more by statesmen such as Cavour than by pressure from below. It drew support largely from intellectuals, middle-class professionals, and business figures, who had the most to gain from the creation of a single, Italian-speaking nation free of the internal borders and tariffs that blocked the movement of people and goods. In 1852, Cavour became the dominant political figure of Piedmont-Sardinia, which was still reeling from its defeat by Austria in the aftermath of the revolutions of 1848. A classical liberal, he opened up markets by working to abolish guilds and remove price controls, and as prime minister he oversaw a period of significant economic growth. Hostile to anything that smacked of radical revolution, he did not hesitate on one occasion to betray the leading Italian nationalist militant, Giuseppe Mazzini, to the Austrians to forestall a new revolution in Lombardy.

Cavour also maneuvered skillfully on the international scene, drawing close to Napoleon III of France. In 1859, France and Piedmont-Sardinia signed a formal alliance with the aim of forcing Austria out of northern Italy and increasing France's sphere of influence at Austria's expense. Soon afterward, war broke out. Austria was decisively defeated, while Cavour's agents provoked revolts in several northern Italian states, including Tuscany

Unification of Italy, 1859–1870 In 1860, with Italian unification seemingly unattainable, Garibaldi and the Red Shirts sailed to Sicily to wage their campaign against the Neapolitan army. Marching to Naples, they claimed much of the Italian peninsula for the Piedmontese king Vittorio Emanuele. Battles in 1859 had already joined Lombardy to Piedmont; when Venice and Rome joined the kingdom in 1866 and 1870, the unification of Italy was complete.

and Modena, with the goal of having them annexed to Piedmont-Sardinia. Napoleon III, suddenly anxious that a united Italy might be more a rival than an ally, moved quickly to sign a peace treaty with the Habsburgs that left Venice under Austrian control, and the Papal States and the kingdom of the Two Sicilies as separate, independent states. For the moment, the prospect of Italian unification seemed blocked.

But at this point yet another remarkable personality took a hand in Italian events: Giuseppe Garibaldi. After the defeat of his Roman volunteers in 1849, the former sailor had returned to the high seas, touching land everywhere from Nicaragua to Peru, the Philippines, and even Staten Island, New York, where he briefly worked in a candle factory. But in the mid-1850s he returned to Italy, and during the 1859–60 war with Austria he offered his services to Piedmont-Sardinia, seeing no path to Italian unity other than a monarchy headed by the Piedmontese Vittorio Emmanuele II. Cavour, although leery of Garibaldi's republican, revolutionary tendencies, accepted the offer.

In April 1860, seeing the movement toward Italian unity stalled, Garibaldi took the initiative. A rural revolt had broken out on the island of Sicily against the Bourbon government in Naples and the burdensome feudal regime it enforced. Garibaldi raised a legion of 1,000 volunteers from around the peninsula, known as the Red Shirts after the men's informal uniforms. Landing on the westernmost point of Sicily, it defeated the Neapolitan army in a dashing engagement (charging uphill with bayonets fixed) and then marched into the island's capital of Palermo, where Garibaldi announced he was taking power in the name of Vittorio Emmanuele. He then crossed the Strait of Messina and marched on Naples itself, capturing it with the help of a Piedmontese army. Garibaldi's forces also occupied most of the Papal States, although the pope retained control over the city of Rome itself until 1870. Cavour praised Garibaldi's extraordinary expedition as "the most poetic fact of the century," but at the same time he instructed the Piedmontese forces to keep a watchful eye on the Red Shirts.

In April 1861, with nearly all the peninsula under Piedmont-Sardinia's control, Vittorio Emmanuele declared himself king of Italy, with Cavour as his prime minister. The so-called Risorgimento, or rebirth of Italy, was nearly complete, at least as far as political boundaries were concerned. Venice would be added in 1866, while the last piece, Rome and its surrounding area, would join the new kingdom in 1870, leaving the pope sovereign only over the 109 acres of the Vatican in central Rome. Cavour himself, however, had little chance to savor his triumph, as he died of a stroke in June 1861.

BISMARCK AND THE FORMATION OF THE GERMAN NATION

Just as a single state, Piedmont-Sardinia, drove Italian unification, so Prussia did the same in Germany. But if the Italian process required, among its driving factors, the efforts of Mazzini, Cavour, and Garibaldi with his movement of volunteers, German unification is associated above all with one dominant personality: **Otto von Bismarck** (1815–1898). The descendant of Prussian military nobles (known as Junkers), Bismarck was described unforgettably by an English journalist in the 1880s: "strong-willed, choleric, utterly unscrupulous, pitiless towards such as cross his path, though ready enough to forgive a vanquished foe; in a word, a splendid heathen." But Bismarck was also superbly educated, speaking several languages and writing crisp, elegant German. He spent many years as a diplomat, representing Prussia in the German Confederation and then serving as ambassador to Russia. Wilhelm I (r. 1861–1888), who became king of Prussia in 1861, had little love for Bismarck but reluctantly appointed him minister-president (that is, prime minister) of Prussia in 1862.

Bismarck originally feared that German unification might destroy Prussian independence. By the early 1860s, however, he had become convinced that if Prussia could play the role of Piedmont-Sardinia, it could unify the nation on its own terms and make Germany a Prussia writ large. He took diplomatic steps toward this goal but insisted that the final process would depend on force, not negotiation. As he declared in his most famous speech, in 1862: "The great questions of the day will not be decided by speeches or majority votes—that was the great mistake of 1848 and 1849—but by iron and blood."

Bismarck took advantage of Prussia's strong industrial base, which by 1860, although far behind Britain's, could provide its soldiers with high-quality, machine-tooled weapons, especially rapid-firing rifles. And Prussia had a dense railroad network that enabled it to mobilize soldiers quickly. Throughout the 1860s, Bismarck played the game of European power politics with ruthless skill, focusing on Prussia's advantage to the exclusion of moral or ideological concerns, exemplifying what German writers were beginning to call **Realpolitik**. He helped the new tsar of Russia, Alexander II, defeat another Polish uprising in 1863, and

thereby gained Russian goodwill for his ambitions. The next year, Prussia fought a decisive war with Denmark and moved toward annexing the large border province of Schleswig-Holstein, ending a diplomatic tangle whose complexities had befuddled diplomats for a generation.

THE AUSTRO-PRUSSIAN WAR (1866) Then, in 1866, there came a confrontation with Prussia's major rival in Germany, the Austrian Empire, in which Prussia drew on long-standing military tradition and ethos as well as its newfound industrial advantages. The Austro-Prussian War lasted just seven weeks and ended with major changes to the European balance of power. Prussia emerged greatly strengthened and on a clear path to unifying a "small Germany," excluding the German-speaking regions of Austria, under its rule. It soon established a North German Confederation as one step toward this goal and, as another, expanded the Zollverein, the German customs union it had long been promoting. Austria itself emerged from the war badly weakened. It was forced to surrender Venice to the new Italian state, which had backed Prussia, and in 1867 had to confirm a much greater degree of autonomy for Hungary. Austria now acknowledged that the empire was a dual monarchy, the Austro-Hungarian Empire.

With hindsight, it can seem puzzling that the other major European powers—Britain, France, and Russia—did not work harder to prevent the rise of a united, aggressive, militarized Germany. But Britain in particular still saw Russia, not Germany, as its greatest potential enemy, in part because of what British officers called the "great game" that the two powers were playing against each other in central Asia (driven largely by British fears that Russian expansion might eventually threaten India). Furthermore, because of a bitter recent experience, Britain was reluctant to be dragged into another European conflict. That experience was to be the **Crimean War**, the first major conflict among the great powers since the battle of Waterloo in 1815, if also one of the least decisive of modern European history.

THE CRIMEAN WAR (1853–1856) The war had begun in 1853, when Tsar Nikolai fell into another of his country's long series of wars against the Turks. He wanted to protect the increasingly fragile interests of Orthodox Christians in the unstable Ottoman Empire, to assert Orthodox authority over Christian holy sites in Palestine (then still under Ottoman rule), and also to resume the Russian drive into the Balkans that the western powers had halted twenty years before. Russia hoped eventually to take control of the city of Constantinople, still the symbolic heart of Eastern Orthodox Christianity despite its centuries under Muslim rule, and to gain access to the Mediterranean Sea. Britain and France both decided to help Turkey, so as to block this threatened Russian expansion, and sent their armies to invade Russia's Crimean Peninsula in the Black Sea. After the capture of the Crimean town of Sebastopol in 1855, the war stuttered to a limited allied victory, which left British public opinion—at least as expressed in the newspaper press— deeply frustrated at the inability of the most powerful nation on earth to impose its will more forcefully.

The Crimean War, 1853–1856

Thanks to the telegraph and the development of the newspaper press, especially in Britain, the Crimean War was the first major conflict in which journalists filed regular reports from the front lines. These dispatches brimmed with patriotic fervor, but they also exposed the blundering and disorganization of the allied campaign, and the wretched condition of wounded and sick soldiers. "The worn-out pensioners who were brought out as an ambulance corps are totally useless," the London *Times* reported to its readers. "And not only are surgeons not to be had, but there are no dressers or nurses . . . to attend on the sick."

Partly as a result, the war saw the first concerted attempts at battlefield nursing, led by the famous British nurse and writer **Florence Nightingale** (1820–1910), who had defied her family by taking up a career that they deemed unsuitable for a woman. In calling additional attention to the abominable treatment given to sick and wounded soldiers, Nightingale helped to establish nursing as a profession and improve standards of healthcare on and off the battlefield. The war also led to the founding of the Red Cross in 1859. Falling military death rates, however, owed just as much to the British army's own improving sanitary practices, including a prefabricated hospital facility designed by the engineer Isambard Kingdom Brunel (1806–1859).

TURMOIL IN FRANCE

Despite its frustrations, the Crimean War did not dissuade Napoleon III's France from playing a steadily more aggressive role beyond its borders. In 1859, as we have seen, it sided with Piedmont-Sardinia against Austria and was rewarded with the Alpine province of Savoy and the city of Nice. During the same period, France also sent its troops

Battlefield Nursing Florence Nightingale, pictured at left in a photograph from around 1860, pioneered the nursing of soldiers on the battlefield. At right, a nurse cares for a wounded soldier during the Crimean War.

to help Britain in the Second Opium War in China. In the 1860s, Napoleon III committed his country to two further major overseas adventures. In the successful one, French forces defeated the kingdom of Vietnam in 1858, allegedly to protect Catholic missionaries but in reality to project French power abroad and to match Britain's efforts in India. It ultimately annexed several southern Vietnamese provinces as a French colony. In the other, disastrous adventure, aimed at establishing a French presence in the Americas, a French army installed an Austrian archduke, Maximilian, as emperor of Mexico in the early 1860s. The episode ended after several years with a humiliating French withdrawal and Maximilian's execution.

Yet even then Napoleon III still longed to play a more decisive role in world politics. By the late 1860s, he had ruled France for longer than any other figure since Louis XV a century before. He felt secure enough to bring some liberal reforms to his regime, including greater freedom of the press and a larger role for the legislature. But he still dreamed of equaling his famous uncle's reputation and establishing France firmly as the dominant power on the Continent. A confrontation with Bismarck's aggressive Prussia, which saw a confrontation with France as a way of completing its unification of Germany, therefore became all too likely.

THE FRANCO-PRUSSIAN WAR (1870–1871) This confrontation arrived quickly. Napoleon III hoped to annex the small country of Luxembourg, strategically located between France, Germany, and Belgium, but was blocked by Bismarck's shrewd diplomacy. Then in 1870, the emperor worked feverishly to ensure that the throne of Spain, which had become vacant, would not go to a member of Prussia's royal family, the Hohenzollerns. When a French ambassador pressed Prussia's King Wilhelm to renounce his family's claims to Spain in perpetuity, the king reported his annoyance to Bismarck in a telegram, which Bismarck himself edited to make it seem as if both parties to the conversation had grievously insulted each other—and then released to the press.

A week later, France declared war. It was a major blunder, for few wars in European history were as one-sided as the **Franco-Prussian War** of 1870–71. Prussia had its dense railroad network, its increasingly formidable steelworks, its long-standing military tradition, and a well-seasoned, superbly trained military that was managed far better than its French rival, owing to a General Staff headed by the brilliant strategist Helmuth von Moltke (1800–1891). It also had secret alliances with the southern German states, the momentum toward German unity that derived from the recent victory over Austria, and even the tacit support of Russia, which remained grateful for Bismarck's earlier support against the Poles.

France had a large but markedly less efficient and less mobile army, and its leader was, so to speak, no Napoleon. In early September 1870, the Prussians crushed the French at the battle of Sedan, in eastern France, and captured the emperor himself, who had tried to imitate his far more talented uncle by accompanying his troops into the field. In Paris, an uprising took place almost immediately, leading to the overthrow of Napoleon III and the proclamation of a Third Republic. But while its leaders continued the war, the Germans moved toward Paris and put it under siege. Further French defeats followed, while the capital ran dangerously short of food. With gastronomic flair, the Parisians butchered the animals in the city zoo and traded recipes for rat pâté (it was generally agreed that brewery rats tasted better than sewer rats). Finally, in the winter, France surrendered, agreeing to the loss of its wealthy eastern regions of Alsace and Lorraine, which to French public opinion seemed an almost unbearable humiliation.

GERMAN UNIFICATION In a ceremony designed to highlight France's humiliation, a united German Empire or Reich—a German nation-state—was proclaimed in the former French royal palace of Versailles on January 18, 1871. Prussia's King Wilhelm now became Emperor Wilhelm, reviving the German title *Kaiser*, derived from the

German Unification King Wilhelm is proclaimed kaiser of the German Reich at Versailles in this 1885 painting. At right, in white uniform, Bismarck looks on approvingly.

Unification of Germany, 1862–1871 Prussia achieved control over a united Germany both through military campaigns against Austria and clever diplomatic negotiations that joined Prussia economically and politically with states such as Saxony and Bavaria. Finally, the end of the Franco-Prussian War in 1871 marked the birth of a unified German Empire.

Roman *Caesar*. Bismarck's ambitions had been realized. The next ten years saw Germany peacefully consolidate its position as a major European power. Bismarck himself saw little need for further military adventures in Europe, commenting that the Balkans—where war threatened at the end of the 1870s—were not worth "the bones of a single Pomeranian grenadier." Bismarck became the first chancellor (prime minister) of the new, united Germany.

In this new Germany, which included every German-speaking state except Austria-Hungary, the monarchy and the Junker aristocracy held the predominance of power, with the latter controlling the high positions of the army and civil service. Although all adult males did gain the right to vote for the parliament, the Reichstag, it had limited legislative powers and could do little without the assent of the emperor and a Federal Council (Bundesrat) consisting of aristocratic representatives of the different German states. And while the former non-Prussian states, including Bavaria and Saxony, retained some autonomy, Prussia made up two-thirds of German territory.

But the Prussian elites could not control the new state as closely as they wanted. While Prussia had been very largely Lutheran, fully one-third of the united German population was Catholic and used to taking guidance in social issues from the Church. Bismarck saw these German Catholics as potentially seditious, since most of them had favored Catholic Austria over Prussia. In the 1870s, he waged a *Kulturkampf* ("culture struggle") aimed at banishing Catholics from positions of influence in German society and reducing the role of the Church in education. Hundreds of priests were imprisoned or dismissed from their positions. Eventually, though, Bismarck softened the campaign in order to win Catholic support against another perceived threat: socialism, which was gaining adherents among the rapidly growing German industrial working class, as well as among the educated middle classes. Bismarck strove to banish and imprison socialists but could not prevent the Social Democratic Party, founded in 1875 under the influence of Marx and Engels's writings, from steadily gaining adherents.

THE PARIS COMMUNE AND THIRD REPUBLIC

France, meanwhile, lurched directly from defeat into the horror of civil war. In early 1871, soon after the armistice, with a German occupation army still present on French soil, the provisional government of the new Third Republic organized elections for a National Assembly. But just as in 1848, a political gulf opened up between the new deputies—elected by a still heavily rural, relatively conservative country—and the city of Paris, where, despite Baron Haussmann's renovations, the working class still had a heavy presence outside the wealthy central districts. In fact, a majority of the Assembly favored the return (yet again) of the Bourbon monarchy. In mid-March, the radical Parisian National Guard violently resisted the new national government's attempts to confiscate its artillery, seized control of Paris, and organized elections for a municipal authority, or Commune, to govern in defiance of that government.

With a heavy representation of socialists, anarchists, and self-proclaimed Jacobin republicans, the **Paris Commune** passed measures to protect workers, decreed the total separation of church and state, encouraged participatory democracy, and even brought back the revolutionary calendar of the French Revolution (under which it was now Year 79). The national government, headed by the veteran politician and historian Adolphe Thiers (1797–1877), who had first been prime minister under Louis-Philippe, laid siege to the city and then in May 1871 carried out a full-scale assault. Even as the Commune

Execution of Communards In this 1871 engraving from an American newspaper, soldiers of the French army execute members of the Commune.

executed hostages, including the archbishop of Paris, the army swept bloodily through working-class neighborhoods, shooting thousands of "Communards" out of hand. After Thiers's forces had finally restored order, thousands more Parisians were imprisoned or exiled, including small French colonies in the South Pacific.

In the coming decades, the Commune, although not strictly Marxist in its politics and in many ways closer to the Jacobin tradition of the French Revolution, became a symbol around which socialist movements rallied. Karl Marx praised "the self-sacrificing heroism with which the population of Paris" had acted, while commenting bitterly about the Commune's defeat that "the civilization and justice of bourgeois order comes out in its lurid light whenever the slaves and drudges of that order rise against their masters." For its part, France slowly recovered from this debacle over the next decade. Its form of government remained uncertain for several years, with the return of the monarchy a real possibility. But the heir to the Bourbon dynasty, the count of Chambord, proved to be a most uninspiring potential king. Petulant and stiff-necked, he refused to reach out to moderate republicans, rejecting the tricolor flag of the French Revolution. Despite the best efforts of Marshal Patrice MacMahon (1808–1893), who served as head of state for much of the 1870s, a monarchist consensus never coalesced, and the republican Assembly, elected by universal manhood suffrage, ended up establishing itself as the dominant power. Léon Gambetta (1838–1882), a flamboyant, anti-clerical

lawyer and politician, emerged as its leading figure. The Third Republic would have frequent elections and a revolving-door series of unstable coalition governments but nonetheless became the longest-lived regime in modern French history, lasting until 1940.

RUSSIA UNDER ALEXANDER II

At the other end of Europe, Russia in the mid-nineteenth century did not have outsize political personalities like Cavour or Bismarck. When the harshly autocratic Tsar Nikolai died in 1855, during the Crimean War, power passed to his son, **Alexander II**, who was liberal in comparison. But Alexander (r. 1855–1881) proved almost as aggressive as his father when it came to the empire's territorial integrity and its international position.

POLAND In 1863, a move to conscript 30,000 Poles into Russian military service prompted another Polish nationalist revolt. Russian forces crushed it, publicly hanged ringleaders in Warsaw, exiled thousands of political prisoners to Siberia, closed Polish universities, and began a program of Russification. The Russian authorities removed the last traces of Poland's autonomous Congress kingdom, even renaming the territory Vistula Land after its principal river. In 1877, Alexander launched the fourth Russo-Turkish war of the century and forced the Ottoman Empire to grant full independence to the Balkan countries of Serbia, Montenegro, Romania, and Bulgaria. In reaction—in a move that recalled the Congress of Vienna—the other European powers convoked the Congress of 1878 and forced Russia to scale back the territorial gains for the new states.

SERFDOM ABOLISHED Although Alexander remained committed to this program of Russian expansionism and absolute monarchy, he did carry out the most important Russian social reform of the nineteenth century. In 1861, he abolished serfdom and freed over 23 million men, women, and children from virtual slavery. Various forms of resistance by the serfs themselves, including violent protests, had grown over the preceding decades. Between 1857 and 1861 alone, the army had to muster over 900 times to quell the disorder. Furthermore, Russia's defeat in the Crimean War exposed the poor condition of the serfs, who supplied a large percentage of the army's forces. By 1861, the Russian elites had broadly accepted that serious reform of the country required the institution's abolition. The measure therefore took place peacefully and with little resistance,

THE LIMITS OF EMANCIPATION

Alexander II's emancipation of the serfs in 1861 constituted a significant gain for the millions of Russians laboring in extreme poverty in rural areas. But although the tsar's decree granted land-ownership rights to the serfs, it also forced them to repay their former masters for land and their freedom, and it preserved the superiority of nobles, who retained ownership over the most valuable properties. As expressed in petitions such as the second document excerpted below, peasants who protested this arrangement were often brutally punished by government officials.

Alexander II's Decree Emancipating the Serfs

Here the tsar describes the "obligations" owed by the serfs in exchange for their freedom.

When word of the Government's plan to abolish the law of bondage [serfdom] reached peasants unprepared for it, there arose a partial misunderstanding. Some [peasants] thought about freedom and forgot about obligations. But the general good sense [of the people] was not disturbed in the conviction that anyone freely enjoying the goods of society correspondingly owes it to the common good to fulfill certain obligations, [a conviction held] both by natural reason and by Christian law, according to which "every soul must be subject to the governing authorities."…Rights legally acquired by the landlords cannot be taken from them without a decent return or [their] voluntary concession; and that it would be contrary to all justice to make use of the lords' land without bearing the corresponding obligation.

And now We hopefully expect that the bonded people, as a new future opens before them, will understand and accept with gratitude the important sacrifice made by the Well-born Nobility for the improvement of their lives.

Petition from Peasants in Podosinovka to Alexander II

This May 1863 petition from peasants in western Russia describes the flogging of hundreds of members of their community after they rejected unfair land allotment.

The most merciful manifesto of Your Imperial Majesty from 19 February 1861, with the published rules, put a limit to the enslavement of the people in blessed Russia. But some former serfowners—who desire not to improve the peasants' life, but to oppress and ruin them—apportion land contrary to the laws, choose the best land from all the fields for themselves, and give the poor peasants…the worst and least usable lands.

To this group of squires must be counted our own, Anna Mikhailovna Raevskaia.…Of our fields and resources, she chose the best places from amidst our strips.…But our community refused to accept so ruinous an allotment and requested that we be given an allotment in accordance with the local Statute.…The peace arbitrator…and the police chief…slandered us before the governor, alleging that we were rioting and that it is impossible for them to enter our village.

The provincial governor believed this lie and sent 1,200 soldiers of the penal command to our village.…Without any cause, our village priest Father Peter—rather than give an uplifting pastoral exhortation to stop the spilling of innocent blood—joined these reptiles, with the unanimous incitement of the authorities.…The provincial governor—without making any investigation and without interrogating a single person—ordered that the birch rods be brought and that the punishment commence, which was carried out with cruelty and mercilessness. They punished up to 200 men and women; 80 people were at four levels (with 500, 400, 300 and 200 blows); some received lesser punishment.…

We dare to implore you, Orthodox emperor and our merciful father, not to reject the petition of a community with 600 souls, including wives and children. Order with your tsarist word that our community be allotted land…as the law dictates (without selecting the best sections of fields and meadows, but in straight lines).

QUESTIONS FOR ANALYSIS

1. How does Alexander justify the limitations on the serfs' newly granted rights?
2. What injustices do the peasants of Podosinovka suffer?
3. In what ways do these sources demonstrate Alexander's consolidation of the Russian government's power?

Sources: James Cracraft, ed., Major Problems in the History of Imperial Russia (Lexington, MA: 1994), pp. 340–44; Gregory L. Freeze, ed., From Supplication to Revolution: A Documentary Social History of Imperial Russia (New York: 1988), pp. 170–73.

very much unlike the abolition of slavery at the same time during the American Civil War.

Yet Alexander II was no promoter of social equality. The emancipation measures required the serfs themselves to make redemption payments to their masters for the lost labor, over a period of no less than forty-nine years. To these masters, Alexander also cannily argued that it was better to free the serfs from above than wait for them to free themselves from below. Meanwhile, advocates of a more efficient, modernized state bureaucracy knew that the reform would diminish the political power of the landowners, to the benefit of the monarchy. Above all, they hoped to create a more flexible labor force that would accept agricultural innovations and help feed a still-nascent Russian industrial revolution. And while a few former serfs had managed to rise well above their station even before 1861, most remained mired in desperate poverty for the rest of the century.

Europe after 1870 Widely reprinted, this map, originally designed by a French cartoonist, took a humorous approach to the geopolitical changes of the mid-nineteenth century. Prussia stretches out its hands to grab more of Europe while France fends it off. In the meantime, Italy seems ready to leap into the fray. Russia waits expectantly for its chance, and Britain isolates itself.

ECONOMIC GROWTH AND SOCIAL CHANGE

"Italy is made. Now it remains to make Italians." When the Piedmontese statesman Massimo d'Azeglio wrote these words in the mid-1860s, he pointed to one of the most paradoxical features of nineteenth-century European social and political change. On maps, by the 1870s the Continent now seemed divided into a tidy collection of well-delineated nation-states—some mapmakers rendered them satirically as jostling men and animals. But in reality, the borderlines disguised tremendous cultural, social, political, and even linguistic diversity within states.

FORGING MORE UNIFIED NATIONS

In Italy, scarcely any of the population spoke standard, literary Italian at home, preferring native dialects that were often mutually unintelligible such as Piedmontese, Tuscan, Venetian, Roman, and Sicilian. A 70 percent illiteracy rate made these dialects all the more durable. Similar diversity prevailed in Germany and Spain. Even in France, with its long history of state centralization, a large number of Romance (derived from Latin) and non-Romance regional languages survived, including the Celtic Breton (a close cousin of Welsh) in the west and Basque (which has no linguistic relatives) in the southwest. Urban visitors

to remote rural areas of almost every European country reported with dismay that the population often had little knowledge of or loyalty to the larger nation. They casually referred to the peasants as "savages" or "our Indians."

In truth, these perceptions were often exaggerated. An illiterate Sicilian or Provençal peasant might not be able to carry on an extended conversation with a middle-class person from Rome or Paris, but he or she could probably engage in a basic business transaction and understand a simple sermon or speech in standard Italian. And while such peasants might well seem to be shirking the call of patriotic duty when it came to paying taxes or doing military service, on many other national issues they expressed themselves forcefully. When Louis-Napoleon Bonaparte staged his coup d'état against the French Second Republic in 1851, peasants across much of the country rose up in insurrection, despite their supposed disinterest in national issues. Yet the condescension of city-dwellers was itself a significant historical fact. In 1870, more than 70 percent of all Europeans still lived in the country. But the educated classes, increasingly, saw these men and women as irrelevant to the great currents of European history, which seemed now to turn on the social tensions in cities between the middle and working classes. Karl Marx, who believed in a great coming battle between the bourgeoisie and the proletariat, devoted little thought to the peasants of his own day and wrote scornfully of the "idiocy of rural life."

Europe in 1878 By the late nineteenth century, new borders divided Europe. The resulting states now included the newly unified Germany and Italy, the major eastern empires of Russia, Austria-Hungary, and the Ottomans, countries with significant overseas empires such as Britain and France, and smaller nation-states such as the Netherlands, Belgium, Denmark, and Switzerland.

INDUSTRIAL GROWTH AND ITS IMPACT

These perceptions were fueled by the progress of industrialization. In the 1850s, the English inventor Henry Bessemer (1813–1898) devised a radically cheaper method of producing high-quality steel. In 1867, German and English inventors produced the first dynamo capable of generating electricity in the quantities necessary for industrial usage. And levels of coal and iron production continued to leap upward. Iron output in Britain quintupled between 1840 and 1870, while in Germany it rose nearly eightfold in an even shorter period, from 1850 to 1871. European railway construction continued apace, reaching a high point around 1880 thanks in part to a huge expansion of the railroad network in Russia. These developments made

mobility within nations easier than ever before, while increasing the importance of major industrial centers to national economies.

THE RISE OF INVESTMENT BANKS But it was not just industrialization that continued to develop in this period. This degree of industrial growth also required the development of more sophisticated forms of capitalist finance. Investment banks with close links to national governments arose, with the highly centralized French state taking the lead. In 1852, Napoleon III's French government approved the founding of a private investment bank on a new scale. Called the Crédit Mobilier, it had an initial capital of 60 million francs, which quickly multiplied through investments from industrialists and the general public. It and other French banks established on its model provided huge loans to the French government during the Crimean War and helped finance major transportation and infrastructure projects throughout the country, including Baron Haussmann's rebuilding of Paris. The model rapidly spread, and by 1880 forty large investment banks had been created in Europe.

CONTINUING URBANIZATION Industrial growth helped drive the continuing urbanization of Europe. By 1870, despite the overall European rural majority, the most industrialized areas of England, Scotland, Belgium, and the Netherlands already had a population density of over 200 people per square kilometer—well more than could be supported by farming the land in question. Already by 1851, nearly 40 percent of the British population lived in towns of 20,000 or more people. London, which had long been the biggest city in Europe, tripled in population between 1815 and 1860 to reach a total of 3.2 million. Many other cities experienced tremendous growth, and not just in the most heavily industrialized northwestern

portion of the Continent. Budapest, for instance, went from a population of just 180,000 in 1848 to over 280,000 in 1867, and by 1914 would reach fully 900,000, fed by a movement from the countryside that included significant numbers of Jews.

The poorer portions of these expanding urban populations still endured the deplorable living conditions that early critics of industrial society had condemned in the 1830s and 1840s. Yet at the same time, the greater attention to public hygiene that also began in this earlier period started to pay dividends. Paris in the period of Haussmannization provides one of the clearest examples, with the building of the new aqueducts and sewer systems that we have already described. As a result of such measures, which had imitations across Europe, overall mortality rates finally began to drop steeply in the mid-nineteenth century. In the Netherlands, they fell from 26.6 per thousand per year in the 1840s to just 15.7 per thousand per year in 1900. And largely owing to this change (and also, by the 1870s, to higher levels of food consumption), the European population as a whole continued its steep nineteenth-century rise, from 274 million in 1850 to 423 million in 1900. The population of Russia doubled in the same period to nearly 120 million.

CITIES AS A STAGE FOR THE MIDDLE CLASS

Cities like Haussmann's Paris provided a new stage for the performance of middle-class life. Elegant shopping arcades that catered to the tastes of the urban bourgeoisie were constructed using the same techniques and materials that went into railroad stations and other grand public buildings. Middle-class men and women could attend the theater, museums, concerts, and the single most magnificent public entertainment of the century: the opera. The grandest new Parisian building of the mid-century was the new opera house built between 1861 and 1875. It was widely copied elsewhere in Europe.

Middle-class life in the later nineteenth century involved far more formality than it does today. Attending a performance at the Opéra required what we would now call formal dress—tuxedos and gowns. Novels and diaries of the period offer many examples of stern father figures who would rarely leave home without a top hat or appear in their own parlor except in jacket and tie. Indeed, the middle-class parlor, where family gathered and guests were received, was itself a stage of middle-class life, expensively furnished with elaborately designed furniture. By

Paris Opéra In this 1877 painting of the grand staircase of the Paris Opéra, gas-lit lamps flood the ornately decorated room with light. Fashionable men and women in evening dress promenade up and down the stairs, becoming part of the spectacle of the opera.

the 1870s, middle-class homes were lit by the brightest source of interior illumination yet developed, gas light, which had already been in use in streetlights and theaters for several decades. Middle-class furnishings also reflected Europe's increasing dominance in the world economy, often featuring decorative pieces of Asian porcelain and china, as well as vast new buffets and bookcases that were only affordable because of supplies of cheap wood from overseas.

As we have seen, according to many writers from earlier in the century, middle-class life also demanded a strict delineation between the "public" world of men and the "private," domestic sphere of women. The distinction was never fully followed in practice. By mid-century, middle-class life had in fact come to involve a great deal of public display for women as well as men. Although the wealthiest and highest-born European women remained relatively out of sight—transported in private carriages, having their shopping done for them by servants, and viewing operas and plays from the privacy of boxes— middle-class urban women were visible as never before on the boulevards, in stores, in theaters and museums. As we will see, however, the education of middle-class women still lagged far behind that of middle-class men, and the large-scale entry of middle-class women into the workforce would not take place until later in the nineteenth century.

DEPARTMENT STORES
One of the most prominent sites for middle-class display were the new temples of consumerism called department stores, where all manner of household goods, furniture, and clothing were laid out on vast surfaces for the largely female clientele to inspect and purchase. The Bon Marché department store, founded in Paris in 1869, had 15,000 customers a day by the late 1880s. It also provided free meals for its largely lower-middle-class, largely male staff, along with free language classes, lectures, a small library, medical services, and regular evening concerts. To attract customers, stores also began to develop the art of advertising, filling urban streets with massive printed posters hawking their wares and resorting to other, more theatrical ways of attracting attention. One London hat-maker had a custom-made, seven-foot-tall hat carried through the streets with his name prominently affixed to it.

THE CRYSTAL PALACE
The most conspicuous venue for middle-class display, as well as British power, may have been the great World Exhibition held in London in 1851.

Crystal Palace A contemporary lithograph shows how the engineering marvels of the Crystal Palace created a huge, light-filled open space, crammed with displays from lands as far away as Turkey and the British West Indies.

The Exhibition showcased technological and industrial progress—Britain's in the first instance, but more generally the Western world's. Its centerpiece was the so-called Crystal Palace, a massive structure built of steel (3,300 columns and 2,300 girders) and glass (nearly 1 million square feet, the most ever used in a single building). Six stories tall, 400 feet wide, and 1,850 feet long, it had 100,000 separate items on display and welcomed no fewer than 6 million visitors. Huge water towers designed by the engineer Isambard Kingdom Brunel held 1,200 tons of water and delivered a flow of 120,000 gallons per minute to some 12,000 water jets in the Palace's fountains.

Entrepreneurs constructed special rail lines and bus routes to bring visitors to the Crystal Palace, where organizers steered them past the displays in carefully designed pedestrian traffic patterns. What struck visitors above all was the sheer sense of abundance. The American editor and politician Horace Greeley described it in this way:

How magnificent the prospect! Far above is the sober sky of canvas-covered glass, through which the abundant light falls gently and mellowly. Spacious and richly decorated galleries, some sixty feet apart, overhang all the ground floor but the grand aisle, and are themselves the depositories of many of the richest and most tempting fabrics and lighter wares exhibited.

VALLOTTON'S *LE BON MARCHÉ*

The second half of the nineteenth century was a period of increasing material security for an expanding middle class of Europeans who could afford goods that a few decades earlier were only available to elites. The Bon Marché department store in Paris catered to this growing consumerism, gathering a wide variety of goods into a modern steel-and-glass retail space. The store also pioneered new business techniques—advertising, sales, and tea salons and dressing rooms—that retailers from London to Chicago soon copied.

Parisian urban life fascinated the artist Félix Vallotton (1865–1925), and his prints, engravings, and paintings often depict everyday scenes from the modern metropolis. This panel from an 1898 set of paintings of the Bon Marché casts the crowd of shoppers in dark shadow, in strong contrast to the bright gleam of the shop's lights, goods, and placards. Clerks wait attentively on the well-dressed customers, who carefully browse displays of jewelry, works of art, and fine fabrics. The painting captures the Bon Marché's bustle, glitter, and abundance.

QUESTIONS FOR ANALYSIS

1. What can you tell about the clientele of the Bon Marché from this painting?
2. What does the painting reveal about public life in Paris in the second half of the nineteenth century?
3. Why might Vallotton have decided to emphasize the shop's product displays, using light and color?

CULTURE AND CLASS WARS

Although middle-class culture had its origins well before the mid-nineteenth century, it reached extraordinary new prominence in this period, tied to the new political and economic power of people identified as *bourgeois*, a term that implied both membership in a class and also a well-defined set of cultural practices. An awareness of social class suffused European culture, shaping political, artistic, and even scientific debates and discussion. The brilliant British political theorist and philosopher John Stuart Mill (1806–1873) put the idea well: "Wherever there is an ascendant class, a large portion of the morality of the country emanates from its class interests, and its feelings of class superiority." It was generally believed that the middle class had finally and definitively supplanted the old aristocracy as the Continent's dominant social group.

CHALLENGES TO BOURGEOIS CULTURE

Not everyone born to the comforts of bourgeois, middle-class life willingly embraced it, however. Even as Haussmann's Paris became a stage for the top-hatted men and silk-draped women of Caillebotte's *Paris Street; Rainy Day*, it also gave birth to the rebellious stepchild of modern middle-class life: Bohemian life (the term *Bohemian* was often used in the nineteenth century for gypsies and had connotations of poverty and vagabondage). In the 1830s and 1840s, this word came to designate an ill-defined

Bohemians A nineteenth-century French illustration shows the proprietor of a cafe complaining to a Bohemian man about how little the man and his friends spend.

world of struggling writers and artists who deliberately defied middle-class conventions of dress, domesticity, sexual morality, and ambition. As the French novelist Amantine-Lucile-Aurore Dupin (1804–1876), who wrote under the pen name George Sand, proclaimed: "The artist's country is the whole world, the great Bohemia, as we say. . . . Let us mock the pride of the great, laugh at their foolishness, spend our wealth gaily when we have it, accept poverty without worry when it comes. Above all let us preserve our liberty, enjoy life whatever happens, and *vive la Bohème*!" Gathering in a constellation of clubs, artists' studios, cabarets, and cafes, criticized by more conventional observers as unsanitary, dangerous vagabonds, **Bohemians** loudly proclaimed their alienation from middle-class culture. In most of Europe, their challenge never coalesced into any sort of political program, but it did help to inspire the Paris Commune of 1871, whose somewhat diffuse rebel program consisted in part of simple hostility to bourgeois society.

MARXISM AND ANARCHISM Overlapping Bohemian critiques of the bourgeoisie, but far more serious in its radical ambitions, was the world of revolutionary political parties devoted to the overthrow of bourgeois power. During the decades of the mid-century, Karl Marx and Friedrich Engels remained its most important figures, organizing international meetings of representatives from working-class movements in different European countries. Persecuted by the police, especially in Germany, they and other socialist leaders often had to go into hiding, and Marx himself lived from 1849 onward in exile in London. There he wrote his massive masterwork, *Capital* (published between 1867 and 1894), which analyzed the economic contradictions that he believed were undermining the capitalist system and leading inevitably to a working-class revolution.

Marxian socialists had considerable company, however, on the revolutionary left. Although Marx's followers held that a "dictatorship of the proletariat" was necessary to advance working-class goals and believed that this historical stage would eventually enable the state itself to "wither away," anarchists disputed the need for states at all. They called for the immediate replacement of organized states by various forms of social cooperative. The Russian anarchist Mikhail Bakunin (1814–1876), one of Marx's principal rivals, argued both for revolutionary uprisings and for spectacular acts of violence to inspire them—this "propaganda of the deed" included political assassinations. Violent conspiratorial groups, composed heavily of students, had particular prominence in Russia, and in 1881 one of them succeeded in assassinating Tsar Alexander II.

TOCQUEVILLE AND MILL Not all the important political thinkers of the mid-century were radicals, however. The traditions of political thought that traced back to John Locke, Edmund Burke, and Jeremy Bentham in Britain, as well as Montesquieu and Rousseau in France, remained very much alive. In France, the great aristocratic liberal Alexis de Tocqueville, who had particular debts to Montesquieu and Burke, followed up his earlier *Democracy in America* with the brilliant historical study *The Old Regime and the French Revolution* (1856). In it, he blamed state centralization for weakening social bonds, thereby paving the way for revolution and Napoleonic tyranny. To Tocqueville, though, a free society—not anarchism—was the solution. He was little more sympathetic to the bourgeoisie than the radicals, however, and decried the increasing power of money in the social order.

In England, **John Stuart Mill** (1806–1873) published the incisive study *On Liberty* (1859), which argued for granting citizens the greatest possible freedom in all their actions. Unlike most modern libertarians, however, Mill did not advocate restricting the government's role to an absolute minimum. He did not have complete faith in capitalism and believed that the state should assist workers in forming cooperative enterprises to mitigate the harmful effects of the market. He shared with Tocqueville—and the radicals and Bohemians—a scorn for the middle classes. He warned against the social power of public opinion, which he associated above all with the middle classes and disdained as a "collective mediocrity."

RETHINKING GENDER AND SEXUALITY

Both radical and liberal thought in this period had long-term implications for the status of women. During the 1848 revolutions, feminists such as **Jeanne Deroin** (1805–1894) in France founded women's clubs and newspapers. Deroin even tried, without success, to present herself as a candidate for election to the Assembly in 1849, arguing that "an Assembly entirely composed of men is . . . incompetent to pass laws regulating our society, which is composed of men and women." Women (including Deroin) played a prominent role in the emerging socialist movements as well, hoping that under socialism women would obtain equal rights. An estimated 12 percent of the members of underground revolutionary groups in Russia in the 1870s were women—and the Russian government targeted them

Jeanne Deroin A French engraving from 1848 shows the feminist leader and socialist activist carried on women's shoulders. She bears a vase inscribed, "Universal suffrage for women."

disproportionately in arrests and show trials. John Stuart Mill was a prominent advocate for women's rights, owing in part to his long-term intellectual and romantic partnership with the feminist writer Harriet Taylor (1807–1858). Mill's 1869 essay *The Subjection of Women* argued the case with particular force: "The legal subordination of one sex to another . . . is wrong in itself, and now one of the chief hindrances to human improvement . . . it ought to be replaced by a system of perfect equality, admitting no power and privilege on the one side, nor disability on the other."

The questioning of sex roles in these works, along with the changing status of women in bourgeois society, contributed to a broad rethinking of human sexuality in the middle of the century. This rethinking was neither entirely repressive—despite popular modern images of Victorian culture—nor necessarily liberating. Rather, it provided new languages for both the regulation and the expression of sexuality. In Britain, for example, the 1860s saw the passage of harsh Contagious Diseases Acts, which gave police broad powers to intimately examine and imprison prostitutes suspected of carrying venereal diseases. But the same

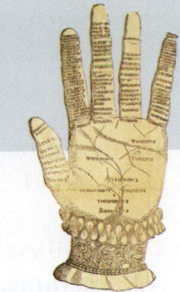

WOMEN OF THE PARIS COMMUNE

The Commune was a laboratory for many forms of political and cultural expression, including experiments in radical feminism. The women of Paris organized in their communities, establishing soup kitchens, orphanages, and other aid services, serving on local councils, and fighting in the streets and on the barricades. When the Commune was suppressed in May 1871, the ferocity of women activists in working-class neighborhoods led anti-Commune politicians to blame them for the fires that broke out across Paris as government forces stormed the city. Paris's women were not spared the reprisals that followed: hundreds were executed or exiled alongside their male counterparts.

Prominent women activists pressured the Commune government to grant female suffrage and support initiatives for gender equality. In the following excerpt, from April 14, 1871, a women's group argues for the necessity of women's participation in the defense of the Commune.

Address by the Female Citizens to the Executive Commission of the Commune of Paris:

Considering:

That since it is everyone's duty and right to fight for the great cause of the people, for the Revolution;

That since the peril is imminent and the enemy is at the gates of Paris;

That since strength comes from unity, in the hour of danger all individual efforts need to fuse together into the collective resistance of the entire population, which is itself irresistible;

That since the Commune represents the great principle of the annihilation of all privileges, and all inequality—and is therefore is pledged to take into account the just claims of the entire population, without distinctions of sex—distinctions that were created and maintained by the governing classes whose privileges depend on antagonism amidst the people they govern;

That since victory in the current struggle—which aims at an end to abuses, and in due course a complete social regeneration that will ensure the reign of labor and justice—is equally of interest to female and male citizens;

That since the massacre of the defenders of Paris by the assassins of Versailles has enormously inflamed the mass of female citizens and driven them to seek vengeance;

That since a great number of these female citizens have resolved, in the event that the enemy should breach the gates of Paris, to fight and conquer or die for the defense of our common rights;

That since a serious effort to organize this revolutionary element into a force capable of effectively and vigorously supporting the Commune of Paris can only succeed with the help and cooperation of the government of the Commune;

Consequently,

The delegates of the female citizens of Paris request that the executive commission of the Commune

1. Order each of the district governments in Paris to provide a meeting hall for the local committees, as well as for the Central committee formed by female citizens for the defense of the city; or, if this is impossible, a separate location where these committees can meet in permanent session;

2. For the same purpose to set aside a large location where the female citizens can hold public meetings;

3. To have printed, at the Commune's expense, whatever circulars, posters and notices that these committees judge necessary to send out.

QUESTIONS FOR ANALYSIS

1. What do the women citizens of Paris demand from the Commune government?
2. In what ways do you think that the requested assistance would enable women to defend the Commune?
3. How do the authors of this request link their fight for women's equality to the Commune's fight for economic freedom and equality?

Source: "Adresse Des Citoyennes," in *Réimpression du Journal officiel de la République française sous la Commune, du 19 mars au 24 mai 1871*, ed. V Brunel (Paris: 1871), p. 260. Translated by David A. Bell.

acts also prompted a spirited feminist reaction that called attention, among other things, to the sexual double standard under which society policed female sexuality while turning a blind eye to male infidelity. In the 1860s, doctors such as the German-Austrian Richard von Krafft-Ebing (1840–1902) began to diagnose sexual "pathologies" such as sadism and masochism, and to define sexual attraction to a member of the same sex as a form of identity rather than behavior—the origins of modern understandings of homosexuality. In 1861, Great Britain abolished the death penalty for sodomy, substituting a prison term of ten years.

SCIENCE AND RELIGION

Sexuality was hardly the only area in which the biological sciences gained new social and political prominence in this period. These decades also saw astonishing changes in the way that scientists understood the world of living things, and their work had immediate, powerful resonance far beyond the walls of laboratories and universities.

CHARLES DARWIN In the early 1830s, a young English naturalist named **Charles Darwin** (1809–1882) had spent several years on board the HMS *Beagle*, making geological and biological observations along the coast of South America. The species he saw in the remote Galápagos Islands—in particular, several varieties of finch—especially fascinated him, and after returning to Britain he began to formulate a theory that species might over time mutate or go extinct through a process of what he called natural selection. He worked on the theory over the next twenty years, and in 1859—prompted by the competing work of Alfred Russel Wallace (1823–1913), who had come to very similar conclusions—he published his book *On the Origin of Species*. Here Darwin made the case for biological evolution, presenting a "general law, leading to the advancement of all organic beings, namely multiply, vary, let the strongest live and the weakest die." Species that mutated in a way useful to their survival would thrive and displace others, and over the long history of the earth they would therefore mutate out of all recognition. The theory made sense of the fossil remains of extinct species—especially dinosaurs—that had long puzzled observers.

Darwin did not initially take the logical step of asserting the evolution of humans from other animals, but in 1871, in his book *The Descent of Man*, he made this case as well. The fossil evidence supported Darwin's claim: in 1856, bones from a primate ancestor of modern humans had been discovered in the Neander Valley of Germany (in

German, *Neanderthal*). Nonetheless, Darwin's books generated the greatest controversy around science seen since Galileo in the seventeenth century, if not before. Christians who took the book of Genesis as literal, sacred truth fulminated against Darwin's theory and the implication that humankind did not have a specially ordained role in the universe, but had evolved in a seemingly random process from creatures that resembled apes. This controversy remains alive today.

But in an imperialist, bourgeois Europe increasingly obsessed with race and class, Darwin's work had other effects as well. Almost immediately, social theorists began speculating on its possible application to human affairs: Did what Darwin called natural selection influence the competition among different human races the way it influenced the competition among different species? In 1855, the French writer Arthur de Gobineau (1816–1882) had published an *Essay on the Inequality of Human Races,* which insisted on the existence of rigid, biologically grounded differences among races and the innate superiority of Caucasians over Asians, Africans, and Native Americans. While Darwin's work did not support such conclusions, many thought it did. Other writers, known as social Darwinists, began to argue that human progress depended on a merciless competition in all spheres of life—including among social classes. Darwin's compatriot Herbert Spencer (1820–1903) memorably referred to this competition as "the survival of the fittest." Darwin himself speculated on whether the "civilized races" would eventually exterminate the "savage" ones.

LOUIS PASTEUR Even as the theory of evolution captured European imaginations, other advances in biology promised increased survival rates for all humans. Although microscopes had permitted observation of microorganisms since the late seventeenth century, scientists had so far reaped relatively little practical benefit from their use. Many continued to believe erroneously that bacteria were generated spontaneously in processes of decay, fermentation, and disease. But in the 1840s, German and Italian scientists had begun to speculate that microorganisms might actually *cause* disease.

In the 1850s, the great French biologist Louis Pasteur (1822–1895), working in the French university system, carried out experiments that demonstrated the role these organisms played in fermentation. By the 1870s, this work led to the isolation of the bacterium that caused anthrax, and soon of the tuberculosis bacterium as well. Pasteur was soon able to develop vaccines against several bacterial and viral diseases and also to develop techniques to kill bacteria in food products, giving them a much longer shelf-life (we now call it pasteurization). Combined with the discovery of crude forms of anesthesia in the 1840s, which significantly increased the survival rate from surgical operations, these biological discoveries began to contribute to Europe's declining mortality rates. Already in his lifetime, Pasteur was hailed by his contemporaries as one of the geniuses of the day and treated to the sort of public adulation usually reserved for great writers.

RELIGIOUS BACKLASH   In the face of these challenges from science, the Christian churches and particularly the Catholic Church strongly reasserted the claims of faith. In 1858, one opportunity arose when a young girl in the southern French town of Lourdes, Bernadette Soubirous, had visions of the Virgin Mary. The Church authorities, aided by Louis-Napoleon's Second Empire, soon confirmed the occurrence of miracles at the site, including miraculous cures for those treated with its spring water. Within a decade, a vast basilica had been built and Lourdes was attracting hundreds of thousands of visitors annually, including thousands of the desperately ill. A gushing account of the miracles by a Catholic journalist sold more than a million copies, becoming one of the greatest bestsellers of the century.

Priests insisted that Lourdes showed the superiority of faith to Pasteur's biology. Some even went so far as to drink water from the springs contaminated by the scabs, pus, and blood of sick pilgrims; one visitor commented that "the water of the good mother of Heaven is always delicious." In 1868, Pope Pius IX convened the first Church Council since the sixteenth century, specifically to combat the dangers of "rationalism." Among other things, the Council established the doctrine of papal infallibility in matters of dogma—a deliberate challenge to those who wished to reconcile the Church with ideas of scientific skepticism.

NEW ARTISTIC DIRECTIONS

Artists and writers responded to the cultural changes of the mid-century in different ways, with some building on the heritage of romanticism and others reacting against it. The criticism of middle-class society voiced so directly by political radicals and Bohemian critics found many sorts of artistic expression. In the theater, the Norwegian playwright Henrik Ibsen (1828–1906) wrote a series of dark, piercing dramas that sought to expose the hypocrisy and constraints that afflicted intimate relationships in small-town and middle-class Scandinavia. Britain's Mary Ann Evans, writing under the pen name George Eliot (1819–1880), brought piercing psychological insight and wit to her novels set in English towns buffeted by social change. The French novelist Gustave Flaubert (1821–1880) brought the art of the novel to perhaps the highest point yet reached in western Europe with several meticulously constructed, perfectly executed accounts of middle-class life. His *Madame Bovary* (1857) earned him a legal prosecution for immorality because of its surgical dissection of life in small-town Normandy, where the title character seeks relief from the tedium of her existence in extramarital affairs.

REALISM   Ibsen, Eliot, and Flaubert are often labeled leaders of realism in nineteenth-century literature, not only because of their attention to accuracy and detail but above all because of the probing psychological insight they brought to their characters. **Realism** marked a clear break with the romantic movement in the arts and literature, and it reflected a sense that modern times required from the arts a stern, unvarnished depiction of society and social problems. The term also describes much of the painting of the mid-century, with artists such as Jean-François Millet (1814–1875) and Gustave Courbet (1819–1877) giving pride of place to ordinary, imperfect, and sometimes visibly bored subjects, including peasants and workers, in grand canvases that some observers perceived as mocking classical traditions.

Realism developed in different directions in Russia, particularly in the sublime novels written by Fyodor Dostoyevsky (1821–1881) and Leo Tolstoy (1828–1910). The young Dostoyevsky's attraction to liberal politics earned him a terrifying mock execution and a prison sentence, during which he underwent something of a conversion to Slavophile positions that rejected the influence of the West on Russia. The Slavophile writer Nikolai Gogol famously boasted that "we are a backward people, and therein lies our salvation." Dostoyevsky's novels, especially *Crime and Punishment* (1866) and *The Brothers Karamazov* (1880), employed meticulous attention to detail and psychology, much like Flaubert's, but did so to explore alienation and evil in modern society. *The Demons* (1872) was a searingly critical portrait of Russian revolutionaries. Tolstoy, meanwhile, wrote massive, panoramic descriptions of Russian life—his *War and Peace* (1869), for instance, has some 580 characters and over a thousand pages in most editions. Set against the background of Napoleon's wars against Russia, this grand novel focuses on the quest for spiritual fulfillment of a young Russian aristocrat, who finally finds it in the simple, contented life of ordinary Russian peasants.

Realist Art Characteristic of Millet's realism, *The Gleaners* (1857) shows in detail women agricultural laborers during one of the everyday tasks of the harvest, gleaning—collecting small pieces of hay left behind in a reaped field.

NEW FORMS OF ROMANTICISM

Yet not all the art and fiction of this exceptionally brilliant period in European culture can be considered realist. In France, Victor Hugo continued to publish lush romantic poetry and intensely melodramatic novels such as *Les Misérables* (1862), which left readers across the West weeping at a series of tragic scenes designed to expose and condemn social injustice. Also in France, the immensely popular writer Jules Verne (1828–1905) became the king of European escapist fiction, with early ventures in science fiction such as *20,000 Leagues under the Sea* (1870) and *From the Earth to the Moon* (1865), which satisfied the reading public's growing fascination with the impact of technology on modern society. If novel-reading had once been associated with middle-class women, it was now—thanks to improving literacy rates, serialization in newspapers, and the availability of cheap editions—a universal practice among middle-class people of both sexes, and among an increasing proportion of the working class as well.

Finally, opera developed further in the long, lushly orchestrated, and dramatic works of composers such as the German Richard Wagner (1813–1883) and the Italian Giuseppe Verdi (1813–1901). Both composers were associated with the romantic nationalism that accompanied their countries' unifications. Wagner drew on traditional German mythology for his greatest works, especially the Ring cycle, a four-part epic that integrated music, drama, and stagecraft in an innovative "artwork of the future." Verdi, working in a more populist but still recognizably romantic style, became an icon of what the new Italian nation could accomplish. His very name was used as a nationalist acronym against the Austrians: "Viva VERDI" stood for "Viva Vittorio Emmanuele Re d'Italia," or "Long live Vittorio Emmanuele, king of Italy."

ANTIREALIST REACTION

As early as the 1850s and 1860s, some European artists and writers were explicitly revolting *against* realism. A group of young French painters that included Édouard Manet (1832–1883), Claude Monet (1840–1926), and Pierre-Auguste Renoir (1841–1919) began producing experimental works that included deliberately shocking juxtapositions (such as the nude woman next to two fully clothed men in Manet's *Le Déjeuner sur l'herbe* of 1863), and canvases that seemed to blur or obscure the persons and objects depicted so as to draw attention to the play of light and color. Derided as "**impressionists**," some of the group eventually adopted the label as their own and gloried, in language similar to that of the Bohemians, in their exclusion from the annual exhibition of officially approved French works in Paris. In an era in which photography could produce perfectly accurate images, these artists seemed to be saying, visual art needed to find new frontiers.

An important advocate of this revolt against realism was the French poet Baudelaire, who, like several of the impressionist painters, closely observed the changes that transformed Paris in his lifetime. Baudelaire's own works shockingly challenged the older conventions of European poetry in subject and form. Some read like opium-induced fantasies. Others evoked corpses or filthy beggars. Some rejected poetic meter and rhyme, presenting themselves as prose poems. Baudelaire could directly scold his audience ("hypocritical reader—my likeness—my brother!") or produce a whirlwind of fragmentary images to capture the hubbub of the Parisian boulevards. "Plunge into the Abyss," he wrote famously; "—heaven or hell, it makes no difference—to the depths of the unknown to find what is NEW!" This was Baudelaire's creed, and from it would burst forth the artistic modernism of the late nineteenth and early twentieth centuries.

CONCLUSION

This ferment in the world of the arts and letters testified to the disorientation that many Europeans felt at the rapid social and political change they were experiencing in the mid-nineteenth century. The progress of industrialism and the triumph of bourgeois culture were the most important of these changes. Many artists and writers also expressed the widespread conviction—shared in radically different ways by revolutionaries, Bohemians, and religious reactionaries—that these changes had come at a very high human price, destroying older forms of community and eroding many different forms of faith. Yet others saw these changes as dynamic and energetic, capable of begetting new forms of social organization and cultural expression. Despite the political legacy of failed revolutions between 1845 and 1880, and the continued existence of conservative monarchies, Baudelaire's thirst for the "new" remained widely shared, along with the belief that it was attainable. It was this belief that would help drive Europe to its greatest heights of power and worldwide influence in the decades that followed.

Antirealist Art Manet's *Le Déjeuner sur l'herbe* shocked viewers not only for its juxtaposition of the nude woman and two clothed men, but also because of the woman's bold stare out of the painting to meet the viewer's gaze.

[CHAPTER REVIEW]

KEY TERMS

pan-German parliament (p. 641)

Karl Marx (p. 642)

Friedrich Engels (p. 642)

The Communist Manifesto (p. 642)

proletariat (p. 642)

Giuseppe Garibaldi (p. 645)

Napoleon III (p. 646)

Queen Victoria (p. 646)

Irish famine (p. 647)

The Mutiny (p. 647)

Camillo di Cavour (p. 649)

Otto von Bismarck (p. 651)

Realpolitik (p. 651)

Crimean War (p. 651)

Florence Nightingale (p. 652)

Franco-Prussian War (p. 653)

Paris Commune (p. 654)

Alexander II (p. 655)

Bohemians (p. 662)

John Stuart Mill (p. 663)

Jeanne Deroin (p. 663)

Charles Darwin (p. 665)

realism (p. 666)

impressionism (p. 667)

REVIEW QUESTIONS

1. What events catalyzed the revolutions throughout Europe in 1848?

2. Why did the 1848 revolutions generally lose momentum by the summer?

3. What people and forces increased British power and influence in the second half of the nineteenth century?

4. How did Cavour and Garibaldi succeed in unifying Italy?

5. Under Otto von Bismarck, how did Prussia create and assume leadership over a unified German Empire?

6. From about 1840 to 1880, what lay behind a new wave of European economic and urban growth?

7. How did city life change during this period, especially for the middle class?

8. In what very different ways did Bohemians, socialists, and liberals such as Tocqueville and Mill challenge middle-class culture and values?

9. How did discoveries by Darwin and Pasteur affect society?

10. What new artistic movements developed in the second half of the nineteenth century?

CORE OBJECTIVES

After reading this chapter, you should have a solid understanding of the following core objectives. To strengthen your grasp of the core objectives, use the resources on the Student Site for The West.

- Trace the course of the revolutions of 1848 across Europe.

- Analyze the events that shaped British politics as the British Empire expanded.

- Describe the new power politics of the mid-nineteenth century, including the Crimean War and the unifications of Italy and Germany.

- Assess the social and cultural changes associated with middle-class life in the nineteenth century.

- Identify the political, scientific, and artistic achievements and controversies of the second half of the nineteenth century.

 GO TO **inQuizitive** TO SEE WHAT YOU'VE LEARNED—AND LEARN WHAT YOU'VE MISSED—WITH **PERSONALIZED FEEDBACK** ALONG THE WAY.

CHRONOLOGY

1881–1882
Officially tolerated
pogroms in Russia

1882
Germany, Austria-Hungary,
and Italy form Triple Alliance

1884–1885
Berlin Conference
partitions Africa

1883–1885
Nietzsche publishes
Thus Spoke Zarathustra

1889
Universal Exposition of 1889;
Eiffel Tower completed

1894–1906
Dreyfus Affair

1896
Marie and Pierre
Curie isolate radium

1898–1899
Spanish-American War

1899–1902
Boer War

1899
Freud publishes
*The Interpretation
of Dreams*

1900
Labour Party
founded
in Britain

1900–1901
Boxer Rebellion
in China

Apogee

IMPERIAL RIVALRY AND GLOBAL POWER

1880–1910

The first genocide of the twentieth century took place in 1904. In January of that year, around 7,000 well-armed Herero tribesmen in German Southwest Africa (present-day Namibia), which Germany had ruled since 1884, rose up in revolt against the colonial administration. Enraged by German confiscation of their land and a series of epidemics they blamed on German colonists, they killed around 125 Germans, almost all of them adult males. But in Germany itself, wild reports circulated of massacres of German women and children. Kaiser Wilhelm II ordered reinforcements and placed the campaign under the direct control of the General Staff in Berlin. When the colonial governor, Theodor Leutwein, began negotiations with the Herero, an outraged Berlin newspaper insisted that although "humanity" had its claims, "national honor and the future of the colony require punishment and suppression of the rebels via force of weapons and the superiority of the white man."

Leutwein's forces drove most of the nomadic Herero population of 80,000 onto an encampment on the Waterberg plateau, at the edge of the Omaheke desert. But after Leutwein began a strategic withdrawal, his superiors replaced him with an aggressive general

---

Modernism and City Life   The turn of the century saw the rise of modernism—new forms of art, literature, music, and thought that challenged tradition and captured the rapid changes taking place in urban life. Included in this movement were the German expressionists, who depicted abstracted, distorted street scenes in vivid color. In this 1912 painting, the German artist Ernst Ludwig Kirchner shows the frenetic convergence of city dwellers and streetcars in a busy Berlin intersection.

committed to a policy of total destruction. On August 11, 1904, the Germans attacked the Waterberg encampment and drove the Herero into the desert, where tens of thousands died of thirst. Survivors were forced into military prison camps, where the death rate reached 45 percent. In October, another ethnic group in the territory, the Nama (whom the Germans called Hottentots, after their clicking language), rose up in turn and were repressed with similarly ghastly casualties. At the start of 1904, there had been roughly 100,000 Herero and Nama living in southwestern Africa. Four years later, 75,000 of them were dead.

Germany's actions were all the more horrific because they seemed so utterly senseless. Just a quarter-century earlier, few if any Germans would have seen any need for their country to have a strategic presence, let alone a colony, in southern Africa. Even in 1904, the future Namibia provided only a tiny market for German goods, and, with its rich diamond mines yet to be discovered, it generated little wealth for the mother country. The German army caused the deaths of 75,000 Africans in order to protect just 4,500 German settlers.

But starting in the 1880s, all the major western European powers had entered a ferocious drive for colonial expansion that dwarfed anything they had attempted in previous centuries, even at the height of the slave trade. This expansion amounted to a new imperialism in which major European powers competed with one another for colonies meant not for settlement but for the plunder of material resources and for their use as markets for European goods. Focused on Asia and Africa, the new imperialism subjected indigenous populations to severe racial discrimination, reflecting ideas and practices that were also operative at home.

During the last two decades of the century the European powers carried out a massive land grab—the so-called scramble for Africa—while also expanding their overseas colonies elsewhere. Although Europe itself covers barely 7 percent of the world's land mass, by 1900 European countries and their former settler colonies ruled 84 percent of the globe. Great Britain itself claimed domination over a quarter of the world's population. Germany, a country without any tradition of overseas settlement to speak of, in the thirty years after its unification in 1871 increased the land area under its rule sixfold through imperial annexations, principally in Africa. German Southwest Africa alone was considerably larger than Germany itself. King Leopold II of Belgium (r. 1865–1909) had acquired, essentially as his personal fiefdom, a central African colony, the Congo, eighty times the size of Belgium.

This expansion had important effects on the European countries: on everything from the character and population of their major cities, to the products available in their markets, to the careers followed by men and women of every social class, to the themes explored in their art, literature, and philosophy. This **new imperialism** made for a crude but effective sign of the economic and technological superiority that Europe had gained over the rest of the world by the late nineteenth century. In fact, in the period 1880–1914, in terms of raw power, wealth, and cultural influence, Europe had reached its apogee. And the arrogance shown by the great powers abroad was matched by their apparent confidence and strength at home. Despite continuing social strife, wars, and one major revolution—in Russia in 1905—Europe nonetheless seemed in this period to have attained an unprecedented degree of social and economic integration.

The major European powers showed such self-satisfaction that in 1897 the poet most closely associated with the imperial enterprise—Britain's Rudyard Kipling—felt obliged to offer a stern warning against hubris, albeit in the accents of the period's pervasive racism:

> If drunk with sight of power we loose
> Wild tongues that hold not Thee in awe—
> Such boastings as the gentiles use
> Or lesser breeds without the Law—
> Lord God of Hosts be with us yet,
> Lest we forget, lest we forget!

In fact, anxieties about Europe's future and premonitions of a coming apocalypse rose strikingly in the decades around

1900, not least in the period's art and philosophy. Liberalism, with its promise of steady, benign progress toward ever-greater prosperity, faltered and found itself increasingly on the defensive from political forces prophesying titanic political struggles that would lead to the violent birth of a better world. Even so, liberal self-satisfaction remained strong.

The German campaign in southwest Africa, even while demonstrating Europe's crushing military superiority over "natives," showed why the premonitions of strife were all too accurate, and why the age of European dominance would soon be cut brutally short. For the most important factor driving the European powers into empire—and driving Germany into genocide—was dangerously unstable international competition. Like all the great powers, Germany hoped to exploit its new colonies' resources and to use them to expand the markets for its own goods. But above all, it plunged into Africa to keep abreast of its geopolitical rivals—for what the German newspaper quoted above called "national honor." And while sheer racism has its part in explaining the genocide of the Herero and the Nama, it was probably not the most important cause. Rather, the Germans' policies reflected German military practices, as worked out in the wars Prussia had fought for German unification and continuously refined thereafter in preparation for an eventual showdown with Russia, France, and Britain. The German military had the ability to operate with almost no civilian oversight. And the German General Staff put a strong emphasis on relentless offense, on rapid movement that did not allow for the taking of prisoners in large numbers, and on wagering everything on massive battles of annihilation. Above all, as Governor Leutwein put it: "In Germany what counts as a success is not a simple victory, but only the destruction of the enemy."

ACCELERATING SOCIAL CHANGE

The rise of Europe in the late nineteenth century took place with a speed and intensity that has few parallels in history. But unlike the cases of the Roman or imperial Chinese empires, this process did not see one power eventually vanquish its principal rivals. Instead, the competition continued even as all the powers participated in an increasingly intertwined global economy. And always, therefore, the danger lurked of this competition spinning out of control and becoming self-destructive, as the Continent had previously seen with such conflicts as the Thirty Years' War of the seventeenth century. In the age of European apogee, the danger was avoided. But soon enough, competition would break loose from its chains.

THE SECOND INDUSTRIAL REVOLUTION

The heightened international competition of the years after 1880 developed in the context of accelerating economic and social change. The years around 1900 marked the completion of what historians call the **Second Industrial Revolution**, which brought fundamental shifts in the structures of European economic life. Steel, because of its strength, durability, and flexibility, was the key industrial material in this expansion.

By 1914, nearly all of northern and central Europe possessed full-fledged industrial economies, with Germany making the most spectacularly rapid progress. German coal production rose sixfold between 1880 and 1910, almost up to the British level, and German steel production rose tenfold in the same period, surpassing Britain's own impressive eightfold increase. Russian industry also

The Factory System Workers at the Krupp Steel Works in Essen, Germany, run machines and stack piles of their finished product— wheels for railway locomotives—in a photograph taken around 1900.

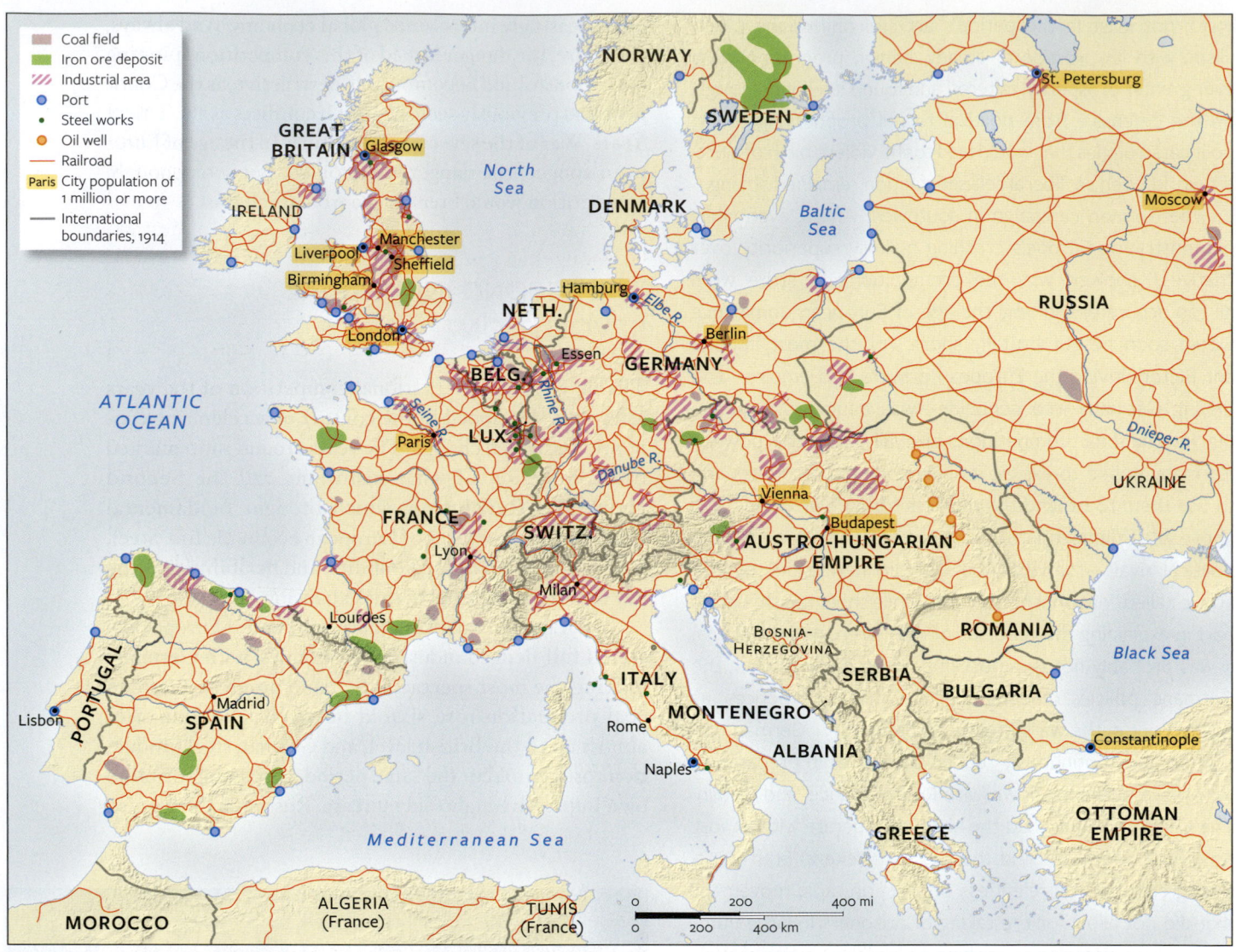

The Second Industrial Revolution, 1880–1914 By 1914, industrialization spread across Europe, drawing on new materials and technologies. Discovery of coal and oil transformed formerly rural areas such as eastern Europe and northern Italy. Railway networks knit together towns and cities from Lisbon to Moscow. Germany, in particular, was able to draw on its resources of coal and iron to rival Britain for industrial supremacy.

expanded furiously. Its steel production, minimal before the 1870s, shot up by a factor of 50 by the start of World War I. The Russian urban working class expanded by 50 percent, from 2 to 3 million, just in the years 1900–14, although its peasantry of 100 million still dwarfed that number. Among European cities, only Paris and London had had populations in excess of 1 million in the mid-nineteenth century; by 1914, they had been joined by Berlin, Vienna, Saint Petersburg, and Moscow, among others. For men and women in these and other cities, lit by electric light, resounding with the noise of heavy machinery, trains, and cars, and stinking of coal smoke, the world in 1910 seemed to have changed beyond recognition.

AN INCREASE IN SCALE With the vast expansion of industry in this period came a new scale of operation. By 1900, a majority of workers in the industrialized countries labored in a true factory system. Industrial firms now employed hundreds or thousands of people in plants whose complex infrastructure often resembled that of a small city. The greatest example in 1900 was the Krupp Steel Works, based in Essen, in northwest Germany, which employed over 25,000 people. Founded in 1816, it was run by a merchant dynasty that had been producing weapons since the seventeenth century. The company's property included 100 miles of private rail lines, 60 factory buildings, 7 electrical power stations, and 130 miles of electrical power lines. Its steelworks processed some 685,000 tons of iron ore per year and used as much water as the entire city of Frankfurt. Companies like Krupp increasingly tried to control all the different phases of the production process, from raw materials to finished goods. Critics, notably from the emerging socialist parties, charged these companies with amassing unhealthy degrees of power, but the firms certainly contributed to the vast increases in overall industrial capacity of European societies.

Illustrating this overall capacity was the gigantic scale on which Europeans now built things. Consider Paris's 1,000-foot-tall Eiffel Tower, the tallest structure in Europe at the time, completed in 1889. It used 18,000 separate pieces of steel, together weighing some 7,000 tons, and was held together by 2.5 million rivets. More important economically were the vast ships that, by 1900, carried passengers and cargo between Europe and the rest of the world. The *Lusitania* and the *Mauritania*, ships of the British Cunard Line launched in 1907, featured steel hulls and each displaced some 45,000 tons of water. Each one could carry some 2,400 passengers, including 500 who traveled in luxurious first class and a larger number of poor emigrants in the crowded, airless quarters at the bottom of the ship known as steerage. To feed the passengers on a single voyage across the Atlantic (usually requiring six days), a similar ship carried some 13,000 pounds of butter, 30,000 pounds of sugar, 240,000 eggs, and 80 tons of meat, including geese, turkeys, ducks, pheasants, pigeons, grouse, quail, and partridges. Over the sixty years from 1850 to 1910, the overall capacity of the world's merchant fleets nearly quadrupled.

TECHNICAL EXPERTISE The Second Industrial Revolution required considerably more scientific expertise than the first, and hence higher levels of education in the skilled workforce. Industries increasingly made use of complex processes that had to be managed by engineers with sophisticated knowledge of chemistry, mechanics, electricity, and metallurgy. Electricity was particularly important. As the Krupp example shows, while European manufacturing remained powered by coal, the coal increasingly was burned to generate electricity rather than to drive machines directly by steam power.

One reason for Germany's rapid advance in the late nineteenth century was its university system, which by mid-century had made engineering and scientific research central activities. While Britain saw the founding of several new universities and institutes devoted to engineering and science, the older, more prestigious universities of Oxford and Cambridge remained focused on providing a classical education to future civil servants, lawyers, and clergymen. In 1900, Germany spent 12 percent of its annual budget on education at all levels, as opposed to 10 percent in Britain, 8 percent in France, and just 1.5 percent in Spain. German universities served as a model around the world—notably in the United States, where Johns Hopkins University (founded in 1876) and the University of Chicago (1890) built German-style degree programs and filled their first faculties with German-trained professors. Germany also benefited from coming later to industrialization than other European countries. German factories such as the Krupp Works were designed to make use of the new industrial processes; there was no need to rebuild older, less suitable facilities.

The larger, more complex industries of the late nineteenth century required larger, more complex organizations to manage them. Rather than belonging exclusively to a single person or family, large firms became impersonal corporations owned by stockholders and run by trained executives chosen by boards of directors. These firms were organized into many different departments, from mail rooms to personnel offices, and required trained staffs of managers and accountants: among its 25,000 employees in 1900, Krupp counted some 2,207 such white-collar workers. All of them needed a high level of literacy, and across Europe firms like Krupp benefited from the steadily rising proportion of men and women receiving secondary education. The companies also needed messengers, telephone operators, deliverymen, and secretaries.

NEW ECONOMIC OPPORTUNITIES FOR WOMEN
In the 1870s, another new invention, the typewriter, became common in European offices, and schools arose to train young women in secretarial skills such as typewriting and shorthand. Between 1881 and 1901, the number of secretaries in Britain rose twelvefold. This increase in secretarial labor points to a broader shift in patterns of European work. As we have seen, in pre-industrial societies women and children had composed a large part of the labor force. Women could not generally become masters or journeymen in the early trades, but they made up a majority of domestic servants, worked in many capacities in shops and doing piece work at home, and filled early textile factories in cities like Lyon, in France. And of course they performed back-breaking labor on farms and spent countless hours maintaining their own families.

The first Industrial Revolution did not deviate greatly from this pattern. Women and children initially made up a large portion of the labor force in factory towns like Manchester. But over the course of the nineteenth century, progressive legislators, starting with Britain's 1833 Factory

Act, had succeeded in curtailing child labor. Meanwhile, in industries such as metalworking and munitions, the factory became increasingly a male preserve. But new positions opened up for women as clerical workers, both in private industry and in government. In Britain, women filled fewer than 10 percent of government and post office clerical jobs in 1861, but more than half of them by 1911. In Germany, a popular women's magazine published nineteen articles on business opportunities for women just in the years 1893–94. Among the possible professions recommended were honey cultivation, bookselling, gardening, interior decoration, and photography. Women's professional organizations were founded in major German cities such as Berlin and Hamburg.

This move by women into the labor force often met with considerable resistance from white-collar male workers, who felt their jobs threatened and sometimes used their professional unions to advocate discriminatory measures. In 1904, Austria's Conference of White-Collar Workers declared that "it has never been considered cultural progress but rather a product of necessity for women to earn their livelihood; it is a sign of disease in the social body." A year later, the Austrian union of postal employees unsuccessfully demanded the exclusion of all married women from employment, the exclusion of women in general from skilled jobs, and the separation of women and men in the workplace.

The same shifts caused widespread anxieties that women's work would destroy traditional family life. In Germany, newspapers and books lamented a supposed epidemic of "surplus women," especially in the so-called better classes. Some pamphlets alleged that as many as 50 percent of educated women never married, in part as a result of changes in patterns of work. But these allegations had little basis in fact. In one north German city closely studied by historians, the proportion of women who never married in fact actually dropped slightly between 1890 and 1910. Patterns of family life changed more slowly than the critics feared. Yet cultural panics about marriage and motherhood, then as now, could have a life of their own. The newspaper press gave inordinate attention to actresses and women writers whose "disruptive" lifestyles seemed to confirm fears about the breakdown of family life. The French actress and journalist Marguerite Durand (1864–1936), who founded a women's newspaper and campaigned for women's rights while divorcing her husband and raising an illegitimate son, exemplified figures of this sort.

GLOBALIZATION Expansion in the industrial economy was powered not only by these changes in the workforce but also by the rising flow of capital, facilitated by the kinds of free-trade policies introduced in Britain earlier in the century. By 1900, unprecedented amounts of capital were flowing within Europe, and between Europe and the rest of the world. From 1850 to 1910, the volume of world trade rose tenfold. Facilitating this increase, between 1880 and 1914 most Western countries adopted the gold standard, pegging the value of their currencies to a fixed amount of gold. The effect was to create fixed exchange rates between currencies and easily convertible prices throughout the world economy. **Globalization**, or the integration of world economies, accelerated remarkably in the wake of the economic slump in 1896. An increasingly sophisticated banking system, with London as its world center, facilitated loans and payments. The British pound sterling functioned as the international currency of choice.

European investors increasingly saw other continents as the source of their most profitable investments. British capital helped to finance the building of American railroads, and by 1914 Britain exported more than half of all its capital. These capital flows contributed to a growing European trade deficit with the rest of the world, but European control of shipping and the international insurance market helped make up for it. The capital flows also helped labor and goods cross international borders with unprecedented ease.

Telephone Exchange The rapid spread of the telephone created a need for skilled operators, many of whom were women. Here women operators at a telephone exchange in London in 1910 manually connect callers across the network.

CHANGING PATTERNS OF MIGRATION The economic developments of the period had very real effects on ordinary lives, mainly through the impetus they gave to

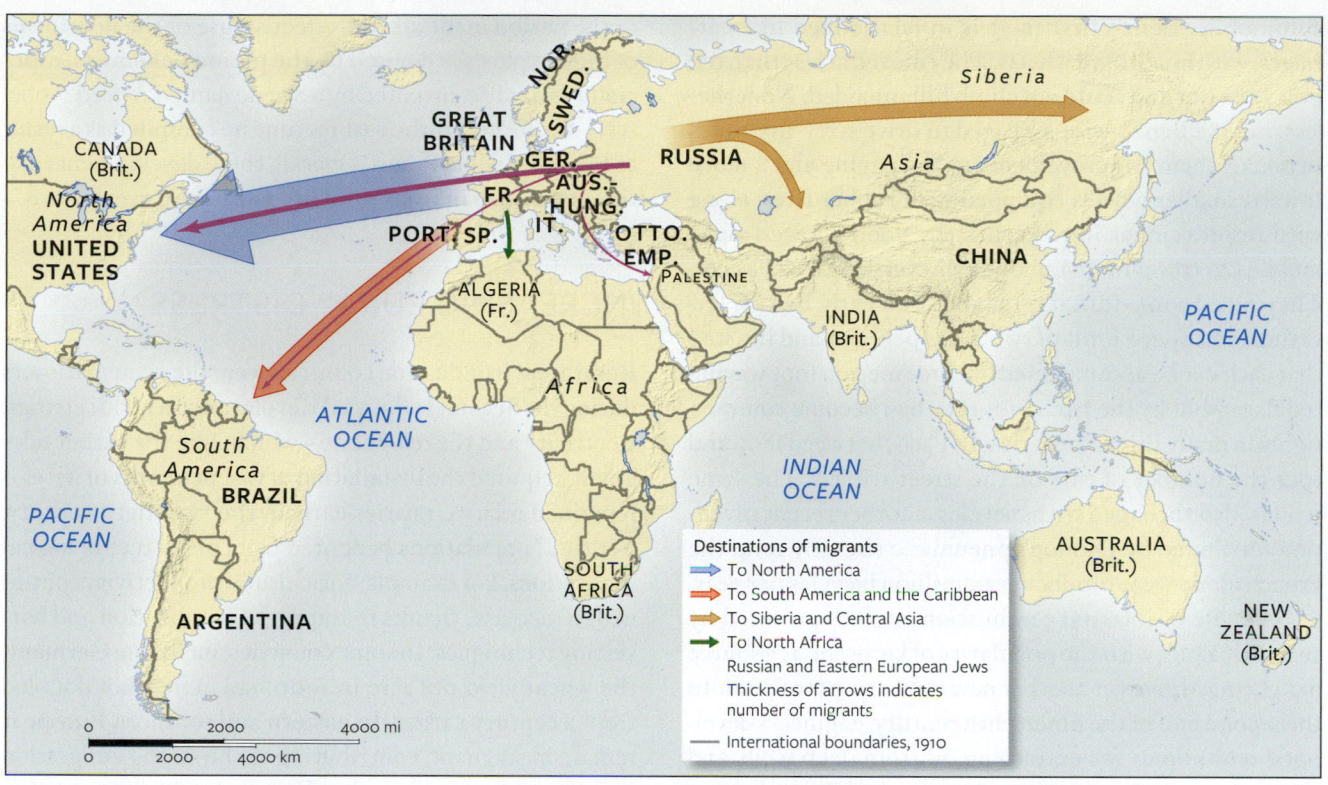

Emigration from Europe, 1880–1910 At the turn of the twentieth century, huge numbers of Europeans—including eastern European Jews fleeing persecution—emigrated to North America, but also to a wider range of destinations. Spanish and Portuguese speakers led migration to South America, Russians moved within the vast Russian Empire, Jews emigrated to Palestine, and French and southern European people settled in the French colonies in North Africa.

migration. With cheap steamship tickets and few formal barriers to movement, emigration from Europe accelerated dramatically at the end of the nineteenth century: to the British "settler" colonies (Australia, New Zealand, Canada, South Africa), to Latin America, and above all to the United States, with the emigrants coming increasingly from eastern and southern Europe. In the period 1880–1910, for instance, fully one-seventh of the Greek population emigrated, as did one-third of the Jews in the Russian Empire. As these Jews moved across the Atlantic, the Jewish population of New York City rose more than sevenfold. In one example that typified emigration patterns to the United States, Avrom-Meir Bolotsky, in 1904, left a small village in present-day Belarus to join three of his brothers already in New York. After finding work driving a cart, delivering coal in winter and ice in summer, he sent for his wife and seven children, one member of the family coming over each year until all were reunited in America. Another important form of European migration took place within a single country: the movement of between 7 and 10 million people from European Russia to Siberia, to work in mines, expanding cities, and to build

the Trans-Siberian Railroad linking Moscow and Saint Petersburg to the Pacific.

NEW INVENTIONS Other changes in ordinary life were a result of technological advances. Sometimes they had very humble beginnings. In 1887, for instance, an inventor in northern Ireland named John Boyd Dunlop (1840–1921) puzzled over how he might equip his son's tricycle with more comfortable wheels. He developed a process for shaping rubber into inflatable tires. Although Dunlop himself earned very little money from it, rubber tires were an immediate sensation and made the use of new sorts of wheeled vehicles practical. Within a few years, rubber consumption in the United States and Europe had jumped to hundreds of thousands of tons a year. As we will see, this change had disastrous implications for the inhabitants of the principal source of world rubber, the Belgian Congo.

Even more important, in the 1880s a German engineer named Karl Benz (1844–1929) made decisive steps in perfecting an internal combustion engine that could power a new wheeled vehicle: the "horseless carriage," or automobile. Benz's first models in fact looked like carriages, with huge, rigid wheels. They moved at less than ten miles an hour and could not climb hills unaided. Nonetheless, in 1888 Benz's wife managed to drive sixty-five miles in one of them. Improvements to the engine and a move toward smaller wheels equipped with rubber tires, along with improvement in road surfaces, soon allowed automobiles to travel more rapidly over ever-longer distances. They faced some initial resistance—an early British law mandated a speed limit of two miles per hour and insisted that each car be accompanied by three men on foot waving red flags—but by the late 1890s they had become common sights in many European cities. In Paris, between 1896 and 1914 the number of cars on the street tripled. The same streets also thronged with bicycles, another recent invention facilitated by Dunlop's pneumatic tires. By 1914, the French alone were producing 3.5 million bicycles per year.

The rise of internal combustion engines powered by gasoline, along with the popularity of kerosene as a source of lighting, drove yet another new industry: petroleum. In the second half of the nineteenth century, engineers developed techniques for extracting oil from deep wells and then refining it. Important early centers of oil production included Pennsylvania, Mexico, and Romania.

Daily life in the cities changed in other largely beneficial ways during the last two decades of the nineteenth century. The cities literally grew brighter as electricity began to replace gas lighting in urban homes and public places—although kerosene and other oils remained important until well into the twentieth century. At the same time, telephones, invented in the United States in the 1870s, spread rapidly, with owners in London, Paris, and Berlin placing millions of calls per year (telephone exchanges became another heavily female workplace). French inventors perfected "moving pictures," and between 1908 and 1914 the first European movie theaters opened. The Italian Guglielmo Marconi (1874–1937) invented long-distance radio transmission. And in London, the first true underground subway lines opened in 1890, marking the beginning of rapid transit systems in European cities. At surface level, slower-moving streetcars, also running on rails, supplemented the bus systems developed earlier in the century.

Improved water and sewer systems in cities helped to reduce the incidence of water-borne diseases. Between these changes and the invention of the first vaccines against the disease, the scourge of cholera began to vanish from European cities, with the last major outbreak in western Europe occurring in Hamburg in 1892. In eastern Europe, the disease remained a major killer into the early twentieth century. In a more sinister vein, the terrorists of the period made all-too-effective use of the new forms of high explosives devised by the period's chemists, especially dynamite, invented by a Swede named Alfred Nobel (1833–1896); he left the vast fortune he compiled as a result to fund the Nobel Prizes. Overall, these developments distinguished urban from rural life more than ever before.

INCREASING RURAL DISTRESS

Rural areas in industrial countries were the principal losers during the Second Industrial Revolution. In rural settings, electricity and the telephone—which, like the earlier telegraph, required the installation of vast networks of wires—remained relative rarities early in the twentieth century. Yet rural populations benefited from other technological innovations. For example, agricultural productivity continued to increase, thanks to improved fertilization and harvesting techniques. In some countries, including Germany, the wheat yield per acre in 1900 had more than doubled from a century earlier. In eastern and southern Europe it remained stagnant, contributing to the strong emigration rates from these regions, but European wheat production as a whole continued to rise impressively.

POPULATION PRESSURE AND AGRICULTURAL PRODUCTION Yet even so, the increase in agricultural productivity could not keep up with the rise in population, which led to increased demand for food and kept prices high. Robust rates of population growth continued in southern and eastern Europe during these decades, with the Russian population rising more than 36 percent. Furthermore, the integrated world economy meant that European agriculture increasingly faced competition from North America, Australia, and Argentina. By 1900, Britain was importing 80 percent of its grain, a development that enriched urban merchants and middlemen but contributed to an agricultural depression at home and diminished the power of the country's great landowners. By the early twentieth century, 80 of Britain's 100 greatest family fortunes came from manufacturing, not land. England, where less than 10 percent of the population now worked on the land, was an extreme case. But even Germany, with a much larger and healthier agricultural sector, was importing more than 10 percent of its grain by 1900. Russia exported grain on a large scale, and partly as a result its foreign trade tripled between 1885 and 1913, but the gain came from a relatively small number of efficiently managed farms. Overall, the precarious situation of European agriculture in this period contributed to a prolonged

business depression in the 1870s and 1880s. It also fed the accelerating stream of emigration.

LOWER BIRTHRATES IN THE WEST

The travails of agriculture, coupled with urbanization, in turn contributed to an ongoing change in demographic patterns in the western half of the Continent. Even as population growth remained strong in southern and eastern Europe, the birthrate was already falling in France early in the nineteenth century, leading Germany to move past it in population by 1870, followed by the British Isles twenty-five years later. The French feared that the trend pointed to national decline, which the government answered with largely unsuccessful economic incentives for bearing children. But a low birthrate, coupled with a low mortality rate, is typical of modern industrial societies. Between 1890 and 1910, the French population rose by only 3 percent, and by the end of the century other northern and central European countries were moving in this direction. So in addition to all the other changes they were experiencing, Europeans had to get used to smaller numbers of children in families less likely to have lost children and young adults to infectious disease.

INDUSTRIAL ARMAMENTS

Overall, the strong growth of European industry in these decades held the promise of a new age of prosperity and peaceful international exchange. And yet observers could hardly fail to notice that the industries benefiting most directly from Europe's remarkable economic developments were the armaments industries. The same shipyards that turned out the huge new commercial steamships also turned out battleships. The same manufacturing processes that produced textiles, bicycles, rubber tires, and electric lights also produced guns and cannon. Chemical factories could turn out the high explosives developed by Alfred Nobel. Europe's robust industrial capacity could easily be turned to purposes of destruction. And despite the developing networks of global economic integration and the growing numbers of newly founded international organizations (on which more below), the intense competition among the great powers made such a turn increasingly likely.

LIBERALISM AT BAY

The intensity of international competition at the century's end did not strike all observers as necessary. To the contrary, many liberals hoped that a new era of peace and international cooperation was arriving, and they failed to see that liberalism itself would increasingly come under pressure from across the political spectrum. Much like Enlightenment thinkers before them, they argued that commerce was binding the powers of Europe closer together. As the British politician Richard Cobden had written in 1843: "Commerce is the grand panacea, which ... will serve to inoculate with the health and saving taste for civilization all the nations of the world." His fellow liberal John Bright agreed, calling war sheer "madness" for commercial nations and insisting that "any peace is better than the most successful war." The fact that the European powers had not fought a truly large-scale, unlimited war since 1815 seemed to lend credence to these ideas.

Other Europeans felt that the progress of industry had made war so potentially destructive that no sane leader would ever again dare to begin one. And they seemingly had a point, for in the 1880s Britain's Sir Hiram Maxim (1840–1916) perfected a machine gun that could shoot more than 600 rounds a minute, while in 1900 the Krupp firm in Germany began to produce a howitzer cannon that could fire 800-pound shells over a distance of five miles.

Between 1890 and 1910, the threat of war led the major powers to sign a number of agreements meant to enhance international cooperation, of which the most important were the Hague Conventions of 1899 and 1907. These treaties aimed to regulate the conduct of war, including the treatment of prisoners of war, and to prohibit abuses such as the use of poison gas. They even set up a permanent court of arbitration to rule on international disputes and prevent the outbreak of violent conflict. The conventions were welcomed as a further sign that liberal cooperation would in the future take the place of war. In 1910, the Anglo-American journalist Norman Angell (1872–1967) made this case in *The Great Illusion,* a compellingly written book that sold 2 million copies, was translated into twenty-five languages, and earned its author a knighthood.

THE LIBERAL WORLDVIEW AND ITS CRITICS

But at the so-called fin de siècle ("end of the century"), the liberal worldview was increasingly on the defensive in Europe. On one side, a variety of socialist movements were gaining strength and advocating policies that ranged from expanded suffrage and a stronger social safety net to the wholesale expropriation and redistribution of property by revolutionary dictatorships. The socialist Second

International (an alliance of workers' organizations and political groups committed to the overthrow of capitalism), which succeeded the earlier International Workingmen's Association, held nine internationalist congresses between 1889 and 1912. On the other side, a variety of right-wing movements were condemning liberal society as soulless and decadent, and insisting on a return—often a violent one—to a more "organic," "spiritual" form of society. Very often these latter movements grounded their claims in theories of inevitable conflict between nations and races, in which only the "fittest" would survive. And increasingly, they defined their chief enemies as the supposedly rootless, money-obsessed, and God-hating "race" they associated with the worst evils of market liberalism: the Jews.

FRANCE UNDER THE THIRD REPUBLIC

The pattern showed through even in the countries that were apparently most hospitable to moderate liberalism, such as France. There the 1880s saw the consolidation of the Third Republic, a stable regime that had beaten back challenges both from the left-wing Paris Commune of 1871 and from right-wing monarchists. In 1881–82, the French minister for public instruction, Jules Ferry, instituted an ambitious system of free, universal, secular primary education. The Third Republic enforced religious toleration, allowing French Jews to attain high positions in the universities, business, and even the army well ahead

Trade Trade Unions A room of somber men, women, and children stage a peaceful strike in Limoges, France in 1910.

of their counterparts elsewhere in Europe. The economy expanded, with the French taking a lead in new industries such as automobiles. Railroads penetrated formerly isolated parts of the countryside. Soon the Republic celebrated itself in a massive world's fair—the Universal Exposition of 1889—marking the centenary of the French Revolution. The fairgrounds covered a portion of central Paris, their centerpiece being that preeminent symbol of industrial modernity, the Eiffel Tower.

NEW CHALLENGES FROM THE LEFT AND RIGHT

Yet despite this apparent success, the Third Republic remained embattled throughout the late nineteenth and early twentieth centuries. On the left, the fin de siècle saw a resurgence of trade union activity in industry. The movement culminated in 1895 with the foundation of the General Confederation of Labor, which was committed to the overthrow of capitalism by means of general strikes. While its membership initially included only a minority of industrial workers, the Confederation expanded rapidly and by 1912 boasted over 600,000 members. Its 1906 charter explained that "the working class . . . can expect nothing from men, powers and forces exterior to itself, but must create its own conditions for struggle and find in itself the means of acting." Militant political action by unions came to be known in France as **syndicalism**. Its chief exponent was the French philosopher Georges Sorel (1847–1922), who in 1908 dramatized the idea of the general strike in 1908 as an event that would lead to the violent cleansing and regeneration of society as a whole. Although the Confederation never managed to bring a general strike about, the principal French unions continued to pursue the ideal.

Meanwhile, in 1905, France's fractious socialist political parties united into the French Section of the Workers' International, referring to the Second International discussed above. Although it refused to participate in "bourgeois" governments, the socialist group nonetheless quickly became one of the most important players in French political life. Standing apart from the socialist movements, and excluded from the International, were anarchist groups, often inspired by Mikhail Bakunin. In the 1890s, anarchist groups increasingly reoriented their terrorist tactics toward random persons rather than prominent political figures, prefiguring contemporary forms of terrorism. They called the use of violence "propaganda of the deed." In 1894, an anarchist named Emile Henry threw a bomb in a crowded cafe in a Paris train station, killing one person and wounding many more.

An even more significant challenge to the French

Republic in this period came from the right. Despite the failure of conservatives to restore the monarchy in the 1870s, they never accepted the new regime's legitimacy. The religious fervor associated with sites like Lourdes was channeled into political directions through a host of popular associations and periodicals, reinforcing the message that a corrupt Republic was undermining the French nation. In the 1880s, an apparent right-wing savior came to the fore: a general named Georges Boulanger, who openly challenged the regime and came close to staging a coup d'état. But his career collapsed spectacularly amid charges he had embezzled from the war ministry, and in 1891, overcome with grief at the death of his mistress, Boulanger blew his brains out at her graveside. But even without him, anti-Republican activity continued apace. The novelist Maurice Barrès (1862–1923) dramatized the supposed decadence of the Third Republic in his hugely popular novel *The Uprooted* (1897), and soon afterward a powerful right-wing periodical and political movement committed to monarchism, Action Française ("French Action"), came into being.

FRENCH ANTI-SEMITISM

In the 1880s, anti-Republican sentiment became tightly bound up with a virulent wave of anti-Semitism. France was of course hardly alien territory for anti-Semitism, and it flourished on the left as well as the right. Despite the political emancipation of Jews in the French Revolution and their entry into the army, universities, and professions, the small French Jewish community (less than one-quarter of 1 percent of the population, concentrated in the eastern province of Alsace and large cities) remained the regular target of discrimination, and of caricatures and attacks in the press and popular culture. But through the mid-nineteenth century, anti-Semitism in France remained relatively low-key compared with Russia, which as we will see subjected its much larger Jewish population to heavy legal burdens and frequent, officially tolerated popular violence.

After the foundation of the Third Republic, however, this began to change. In 1886, a journalist named Édouard Drumont (1844–1917) published an anti-Semitic tract entitled *Jewish France*, which became one of the greatest bestsellers in French history, going through 140 editions in just two years and making the fortune of the Flammarion publishing house. Drumont and his followers spun out bizarre conspiracy theories about a Jewish plot for world domination and about a Jewish role in various French financial scandals. Drumont's message spread throughout the country, relayed especially by Catholic clergy: "We are being pillaged, dishonored, exploited, and emptied by the Jew," one Church newsletter declared. "Servile, slithering, artful, filthy, and vile when he is the weaker one, he becomes arrogant when he has the upper hand, as he does now. The Jew is our master."

THE DREYFUS AFFAIR

In this hateful climate, it is hardly surprising that when the French intelligence services found evidence of a highly placed German spy in the French army in 1894, suspicion immediately fell on a Jewish officer, Alfred Dreyfus (1859–1935). Army officials quickly conducted a perfunctory court martial, in which they failed to disclose evidence that supported Dreyfus's innocence. Dreyfus received a life sentence, to be served on Devil's Island off the coast of South America, where life sentences were usually short.

And then what had started as a simple albeit outrageous miscarriage of justice turned into a full-blown political crisis. As the extent of Dreyfus's innocence became clear, largely through the efforts of Dreyfus's family, desperate officers forged further evidence against him. They

The Dreyfus Affair This 1899 caricature uses anti-Semitic imagery to demonize Dreyfus, depicting him as a horrific, traitorous monster threatening the state.

even went so far as to protect the real spy when his guilt became apparent, so as to protect the honor of the army. The **Dreyfus Affair** dominated headlines and public discussion, divided families, and seemed to threaten the Republic's survival.

In 1898, the novelist Émile Zola published one of the great political polemics of all time in defense of Dreyfus: a lengthy newspaper article entitled simply "J'accuse" ("I accuse"). But on the other side there flowed a torrent of venom. Jews throughout France were vilified and threatened, and mobs paraded in the street calling for their deaths, while Dreyfus was caricatured as a treasonous monster. An Anti-Semitic League founded by Drumont flourished broadly, with hundreds of branches throughout France.

It took many years, a long series of trials, and an unprecedented campaign for public opinion before Dreyfus finally won exoneration in 1906. In theory, this exoneration meant a victory for the secular, liberal Third Republic. It was quickly followed by the removal of the Roman Catholic Church's privileged status in France, and the separation of church and state—although the government continued to fund many religious activities. But to most observers the Republic looked weaker, not stronger, after the Affair. And as many historians have suggested, simply based on the extent of public anti-Semitism, the European country that looked, in 1900, most likely someday to attempt a violent extermination of the Jews was not Germany or Russia, but France.

Already in the 1880s, a Jewish nationalist movement known as Zionism had begun to take shape in response to the rising threat of anti-Semitism in Europe. Most of its adherents hoped to found a new Jewish state in their ancestral homeland of Palestine, and in the 1880s and 1890s tens of thousands of Jews, mostly from the Russian Empire, migrated to Palestine, which still belonged to the Ottoman Empire. The horror aroused in European Jewry by the Dreyfus Affair enormously strengthened the movement and led to a second wave of emigration to Palestine. The Austrian Jewish journalist Theodor Herzl (1860–1904) saw Dreyfus's ordeal as confirmation that Jews could only live normal lives in a homeland of their own and went on to convene a worldwide Zionist conference and to found a formal Zionist organization.

Russia, 1910

THE PERSISTENCE OF AUTOCRACY IN RUSSIA

Liberalism was even more embattled in Russia. The assassination of Tsar Alexander II in 1881 by a revolutionary group called The People's Will led to the accession of his staunchly autocratic son, Alexander III (r. 1881–1894). In a country with no parliament of any sort, one of the new tsar's first actions was to retract a tentative move toward creating political assemblies that would have been dominated by large landowners and wealthy townspeople. And in a burgeoning Russian Empire that by 1905 would contain some 200 nationalities speaking 145 separate languages, Alexander III dreamed of a homogenous Russian nation-state. He pursued vigorous Russification policies that prompted the Russian language, the Russian Orthodox Church, and ethnic Russians. He also gave free rein to anti-Semitic elements who wanted to force on the Empire's Jews the stark choice between conversion, emigration, or death, so as to eliminate them entirely from Russian soil. In 1881–82, a series of officially tolerated anti-Jewish **pogroms** (riots) took place, leaving hundreds dead and thousands wounded, and spurring the massive Jewish emigration to America and Palestine.

Alexander III did preside over a rapid expansion of the Russian economy. Between the 1880s and 1910, foreign trade and railroad lines tripled in size (with the Trans-Siberian Railroad reaching all the way from Moscow to the Pacific by 1916), and coal and steel production grew exponentially. But even though the urban working class was some 2 million strong by 1900, mostly concentrated in the two great cities of Saint Petersburg and Moscow, the vast majority of the population of 100 million still lived as peasants. The Russian peasants were no longer tied to the land as serfs, and this new freedom spurred emigration abroad, particularly from Ukraine. Still, most of the peasantry continued to live near their places of birth.

Alexander died prematurely in 1894, and initially liberals—mostly professionals living in cities—placed great hopes in his son, Nikolai II (r. 1894–1917). The nephew, on his mother's side, of Britain's future queen Alexandra (r. 1901–1910), he had traveled to Britain and pronounced himself impressed with its institutions. But upon taking the throne he too quickly returned to a defense of autocracy. In 1903, his government sanctioned another series of bloody pogroms against Russia's Jews. The Russian state also renewed its persecution of socialists. When a united and largely urban Russian Social Democratic Workers' Party formed in 1898, the police quickly moved against it and its members had to continue their work in exile. In 1903, the party split into two factions: the more moderate **Mensheviks** ("minority") and the radical **Bolsheviks** ("majority"), who insisted on violent revolution leading to a dictatorship of the proletariat. The names of the factions were misleading as the Mensheviks were actually more numerous.

THE RUSSIAN REVOLUTION OF 1905

An opening for change in Russia only arrived with the disastrous Russo-Japanese War of 1904–1905 (see below), in which the Japanese largely destroyed two of the three Russian fleets and took considerable territory. The Russians had to face the humiliation of losing a conflict to a people they considered to be inferior non-Europeans.

In the midst of this crisis, Russian liberals—rather like their French predecessors in 1848—organized a series of public banquets to draw attention to their calls for political representation. The movement, launched in the fall of 1904, brought together opponents of the regime ranging from Marxist groups to liberal professionals who hoped above all for the creation of a Russian political democracy—but who were hampered by their lack of strong leadership. The local Moscow assembly issued a series of demands that included a national legislature, freedom of religion, and freedom of the press. Grudgingly, the tsar promised some limited reforms.

Then, on so-called Bloody Sunday, January 22, 1905, a huge crowd of workers led by a charismatic priest converged on the Winter Palace in Saint Petersburg, only to be met by gunfire from the army. Hundreds died, and again, as in the 1848 revolutions, the horrific spectacle led to a much larger groundswell of protest. The Marxists and the liberal Constitutional Democrats (called the Kadets) now competed to organize the opposition, with the former helping to form workers' councils, or soviets, in the major cities. In October, the Saint Petersburg soviet led a successful general strike. Tsar Nikolai desperately issued an October Manifesto promising a new constitution that would guarantee civil liberties and create a national parliament, or **Duma**.

But in the end, the revolutionaries could not preserve their momentum against relentless counterattacks from the tsarist state. The principal socialist parties, including the Bolsheviks and Mensheviks, refused to participate in

Bloody Sunday This oil painting from 1905 dramatizes the victims of Bloody Sunday at the Winter Palace in Saint Petersburg. Protestors look on in horror as some of them are hit by the army's gunfire, their blood staining the snow.

the initial elections for the Duma, while a complex system of proportional representation limited the influence of peasants and workers. The Kadets swept into the Duma by default but found their powers starkly limited. The tsar insisted on reserving control over the executive, the military, and foreign policy; retaining the right to legislate in the Duma's absence, and on placing it below a State Council that he controlled. Even so, the Duma proved insufficiently pliant, and he dissolved it in 1906. He did the same the next year with its successor, which this time included socialist deputies. And he followed the second dissolution with a campaign of savage repression against political opponents, with several thousand imprisoned or executed. A new electoral law ensured an even more conservative, compliant third Duma, and for the remaining few years of the Russian Empire political opposition was effectively stifled. The Bolsheviks and Mensheviks largely went underground or organized abroad.

FIN DE SIÈCLE GERMANY AND AUSTRIA-HUNGARY

Germany as well proved inhospitable territory for liberalism in the fin de siècle. Just as in Russia, liberals, especially in the universities and the professions, placed great hopes in a new ruler, Friedrich III (r. March–June 1888), who succeeded his father, Wilhelm I, as kaiser in 1888. Although a hero of the wars of German unification, Friedrich, like

Nikolai of Russia, had close ties to Britain—his wife was the eldest daughter of Queen Victoria. He supported an expansion of the franchise and a greater role for the Reichstag (the lower house of parliament) in state affairs. But his ambitions were thwarted by his father's longevity—Wilhelm I lived to age ninety, and just before Friedrich finally came to the throne a fatal throat cancer struck him. He ruled for just ninety-nine days.

Friedrich's own son, Wilhelm II (r. 1888–1918), had a very different character. Intelligent and well educated, Wilhelm was also temperamental and aggressive. He had a strong, paternalist sense of obligation to ordinary Germans, but was also deeply militarist, with a fetish for elaborate uniforms, and he despised democracy. "We Hohenzollerns," he declared once, "are answerable only to heaven." He was obsessed above all with surpassing Great Britain and did everything he could to expand Germany's armed forces—in particular, sponsoring aggressive expansion of the navy. Within a couple of years of his accession, anxious to rule without rivals, he dismissed the aging Bismarck from office and thereafter oversaw a series of much weaker chancellors.

During the decades around 1900, Germany, like other European countries, saw its political culture increasingly dominated by the language of racial conflict. German militarists insisted that the country's racial destiny was to dominate Europe through violent competition. Influential writers such as the historian Heinrich von Treitschke (1834–1896) rejected the liberal idea of perpetual peace among nations, calling it "not just impossible, but immoral as well." War, Treitschke declared, was something "sacred." Ardent nationalists such as the composer Richard Wagner, who had attacked "Jewishness in Music" in a notorious 1850 article, insisted that German culture had to be preserved from "alien" and "artificial" influences—above all, Jewish ones. In 1892, the German Conservative Party officially added anti-Semitic positions to its platform, calling for limiting the Jewish presence in broad areas of German public life.

At the same time, pressuring German liberals from the other side of the political spectrum, the Social Democratic Party experienced remarkable growth, drawing support from German workers to become the largest and best-organized socialist party in Europe. Although in 1891 it adopted a hard-line Marxist revolutionary program, calling for the nationalization of major industries, it thereafter moved in a more moderate direction, cooperating with other parliamentary forces. But in an authoritarian system dominated by the Kaiser, the socialists could exercise only limited influence.

Ethnic conflict was even more pronounced in the polyglot Habsburg Empire. Czechs agitated successfully for their language to be put on an equal footing with German, and when pressure from German-speakers forced a reversal of the policy in 1893, they protested so energetically that the government had to impose martial law on the Czech regions. In Bosnia-Herzegovina, which Austria-Hungary had acquired from the Ottoman Empire in 1878, the sizable Serbian Christian population there demanded union with the newly independent Serbian state. Croats and Slovenes bristled at the policies of Magyarization (imposition of the Hungarian language) that had followed the creation of the Austro-Hungarian dual monarchy in 1867. And in the empire's vibrant, multi-ethnic capitals of Vienna and Budapest, Austrian and Hungarian politicians increasingly strove to appeal to the workers and middle classes by inciting resentment against a group that supposedly exploited them and blocked their social advancement: the Jews. A self-professed admirer of the French anti-Semite Drumont, Karl Lueger (1844–1910) routinely denounced Jewish conspiracies and the unfair business practices that Jews supposedly used to compete with Christians. In 1895, he won election as mayor of Vienna. Anti-Semitism reached a fever pitch in Austria-Hungary at much the same time as it did in France with the Dreyfus Affair.

BRITAIN AND IRELAND

In Great Britain, ethnic and religious tensions put liberalism under pressure in a different way. Here these tensions involved above all the country's oldest and closest overseas possession: Ireland. As we have seen, the early nineteenth century witnessed significant political agitation in Ireland, as the Catholic majority pushed for full civil rights. But the end of legal discrimination only emboldened Catholic activists to demand the repeal of the 1801 Act of Union between Ireland and Britain. The push for **home rule**, or Irish self-government, was led by the Irish National League and its flamboyant chief, Charles Stewart Parnell (1846–1891), whose career was cut short when he died of a heart attack at age forty-five. But in the early 1880s, more radical forces tried to take matters into their own hands, with the violent Irish Republican Army murdering two British officials in Dublin. Home rule nonetheless won significant support in Britain, including that of Liberal Party leader William Ewart Gladstone. But it provoked white-hot opposition from many others in Britain, not to mention the Protestants who held the majority in several

Home Rule A 1912 political cartoon representing the perspective of the northern Irish province of Ulster, whose Protestant majority supported continued union with Great Britain. It shows England holding on to Ulster by a rope to prevent Ireland from floating off and running aground on the symbolic "Home Rule Rocks."

counties of northern Ireland and feared oppression from a future Catholic majority.

In 1886, Britain's Liberal Party split over the issue of Irish home rule, with the Birmingham politician Joseph Chamberlain (1836–1914) dominating a new Liberal Unionist Party (named for its support of continuing union with Ireland), which would soon ally with the Conservatives and eventually merge with them. The original Liberals remained strong enough to win one last election in 1906, and the party accomplished some major reforms—notably, forcing the House of Lords to give up its veto over legislation. This put far more power in the hands of the House of Commons, elected by nearly all adult males.

But the Liberal Party would soon be reduced to marginal status, and not just because of Ireland. In 1893, a group of socialists dissatisfied with them, and hoping to introduce social welfare policies and checks on the power of business, founded an Independent Labour Party, which successfully contested several parliamentary seats. In the new century, the British trade union movement then helped sponsor the creation of a larger Labour Party, which gradually overtook the Liberals as one of two major British parties, along with the Conservatives.

INCREASING SOCIAL PROTECTIONS

Liberalism's difficulties throughout Europe at the end of the century did not mean the end of social reform. To the contrary, continuing labor activism and right-wing paternalism both drove forward the extension of social protections for the working classes and the very poor. By 1914, fully 3 million British workers and 1.5 million German ones belonged to labor unions—although even in Britain the number still amounted to just 25 percent of the workforce, concentrated in industries such as metallurgy. In France, the year 1904 saw more than a thousand strikes. But the country that made the greatest progress on social reform was neither liberal Britain nor republican France, but the more authoritarian Germany whose government had paternalist plans to strengthen and modernize the state. Starting with a sickness insurance act passed in 1883, Germany went on, by 1900, to provide workers with national insurance programs for accidents and disability. It also enacted a pension system, although it required forty-eight years of contributions, and workers did not draw full pensions until age seventy. Britain did not match Germany's social policies, but between 1875 and 1910 a series of laws reduced the length of the workweek, put in new regulations against unsanitary housing, and provided limited pensions for the desperately poor who had no other sources of income. France also limited the workweek and began to regulate working conditions more thoroughly.

FIN DE SIÈCLE FEMINISM

In many ways, the most important liberal movements in Europe between 1880 and 1910 were those advocating women's rights. By 1910, Britain, France, and Germany all had something close to universal adult male suffrage; several other European countries, including Greece (1864) and Norway (1898), did as well. But only the Grand Principality of Finland, an autonomous area within the Russian Empire, gave the vote, in 1907, to women as well. Laws throughout Europe restricted women's control of property and many other rights. In France, husbands had the right to their wives' salaries. The calls for woman suffrage in the 1789 and 1848 revolutions had had little effect. Women in much of southern Europe still had no right to divorce, owing to the influence of the Catholic Church.

While women did move rapidly into some new economic sectors, the professions (for example, law, medicine, architecture) remained largely barred to them. Figures such as Marie Curie (see below), a French scientist who won two Nobel Prizes, were very much the exception. Male scientists in the period routinely argued that men innately possessed greater intelligence than women.

Nonetheless, during the fin de siècle, women's groups

Woman Suffrage A 1914 photograph shows Emmeline Pankhurst, leader of the militant wing of the British woman suffrage movement, being arrested outside Buckingham Palace in London while trying to present a petition to the king.

Like the Chartists of the previous generation, they gathered petitions with hundreds of thousands of signatures in favor of their cause. **Emmeline Pankhurst** (1858–1928), founder of the Women's Social and Political Union in 1903, urged civil disobedience in the hope of drawing attention to the cause of woman suffrage and ultimately persuading Parliament to enact it. She was a charismatic leader whose speaking style was memorably described by the writer Rebecca West: "Trembling like a reed, she lifted up her hoarse, sweet voice on the platform, but the reed was of steel and it was tremendous." She called herself a "soldier" engaged in a "civil war" and justified her "trouble-making" with eloquent language:

> You have two babies very hungry and wanting to be fed. One baby is a patient baby, and waits indefinitely until its mother is ready to feed it. The other baby is an impatient baby and cries lustily, screams and kicks and makes everybody unpleasant until it is fed. Well, we know perfectly well which baby is attended to first. That is the whole history of politics. You have to make more noise than anybody else, you have to make yourself more obtrusive than anybody else, you have to fill all the papers more than anybody else, in fact you have to be there all the time and see that they do not snow you under.

Some of her supporters took her martial language literally and resorted to bomb-throwing in their frustration at Parliament's failure to act in their favor. More of them engaged in forms of peaceful protest, such as chaining themselves to fences. Upon arrest, they demanded to be treated as political prisoners, and when denied the right, went on hunger strikes. In response, prison authorities had them violently force-fed. These tactics did have the effect of drawing enormous attention to the issue of suffrage, and sympathetic declarations from both Liberal and Labour politicians. In 1912, the Labour Party came out in favor of votes for women. But British women would not actually gain the right to vote until after World War I.

INTERNATIONAL RIVALRY AND THE NEW IMPERIALISM

The struggles of liberalism against both socialist and right-wing opponents throughout Europe, coupled with the growing nationalist passions that we have seen developing on the Continent, helped to foster a climate of ever-more-intense international competition at the end

throughout Europe gained in numbers and influence. In Germany, the Socialist leader August Bebel's 1879 book *Women under Socialism* became something of a feminist bible and helped foster a powerful feminist socialist movement led by Clara Zetkin (1857–1933). But many women's groups favored "spiritual motherhood" rather than political equality. Many French Catholic women's groups had a similar focus, engaging in charitable work (particularly in connection with the pilgrimage to Lourdes) rather than political organizing. In 1889, however, an International Congress on Women's Rights and Feminine Institutions convened in Paris. It would prove influential in forging ties among mostly middle-class feminist leaders and in developing common agendas among the different national movements.

British suffragists—whom male politicians patronizingly dubbed suffragettes—provided particularly forceful and eloquent voices in favor of women's right to vote.

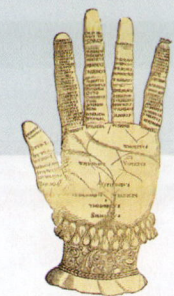

FEMINISM AND DOMESTIC LIFE

Feminism gained strength in the late nineteenth and early twentieth centuries as women used the language of liberalism to argue for equal rights. In Britain, the suffrage campaign united feminists, but the movement was remarkably diverse. While some feminists argued that men and women were essentially equal, others, like the English suffragist Millicent Garrett Fawcett, drew on the ideology that men belonged in the public sphere and women in the household. In the following passage from her speech "Home and Politics" (1894), Fawcett argues that women's experience with domestic life is crucial to effective governance.

With regard to the differences between men and women, those who advocate the enfranchisement of women have no wish to disregard them or make little of them. On the contrary, we base our claim to representation to a large extent on them. If men and women were exactly alike, the representation of men would represent us; but not being alike, that wherein we differ is unrepresented under the present system.

The motherhood of women, either actual or potential, is one of those great facts of everyday life which we must never lose sight of. To women as mothers, is given the charge of the home and the care of children. Women are, therefore, by nature as well as by occupation and training, more accustomed than men to concentrate their minds on the home and the domestic side of things. But this difference between men and women, instead of being a reason against their enfranchisement, seems to me the strongest possible reason in favour of it; we want the home and the domestic side of things to count for more in politics and in the administration of public affairs than they do at present. We want to know how various kinds of legislative enactments bear on the home and on domestic life. And we want to force our legislators to consider the domestic as well as the political results of any legislation which many of them are advocating....

Depend upon it, the most important institution in the country is the home.

QUESTIONS FOR ANALYSIS

1. What makes men and women different, according to Fawcett?
2. Why is the difference between men and women not an argument against, but in fact an argument for, women's suffrage?
3. How does women's command of the home contribute to the well-being of the nation?

Source: Millicent Garrett Fawcett, "Home and Politics," in *Before the Vote Was Won: Arguments for and against Women's Suffrage, 1864–1896*, ed. Jane Lewis (London: 1987), pp. 419–20.

of the nineteenth century. In France, rage and humiliation at the country's defeat in the Franco-Prussian War fed steady calls for revenge and for recovery of the "lost provinces" of Alsace and Lorraine. In Germany, rivalry with Britain was zealously stoked by Kaiser Wilhelm II and military leaders. A Navy League that they sponsored, to support the rapid expansion of German naval power, counted over 300,000 paying members by 1900. Russia chafed at the way the other great powers, particularly Germany, had tried to limit its influence in the Balkans at the 1878 Congress of Berlin. And Great Britain sought to retain its status as the preeminent imperial power. To strengthen their positions, the great powers squared off in alliances, with Germany, Austria-Hungary, and Italy forming the **Triple Alliance** in 1882. In response, France and Russia eventually negotiated an alliance of their own, and in 1907 Russia signed an accord with Britain as well, effectively creating the **Triple Entente**.

International competition was hardly a new phenomenon in Europe, but between 1880 and 1910 it assumed a new form. Once before, in the mid-eighteenth century, an important European rivalry, between Britain and France, had played out in large part overseas. But France's defeat in the Napoleonic Wars largely ended this phase of international relations. And particularly after most Latin American nations gained independence in the early

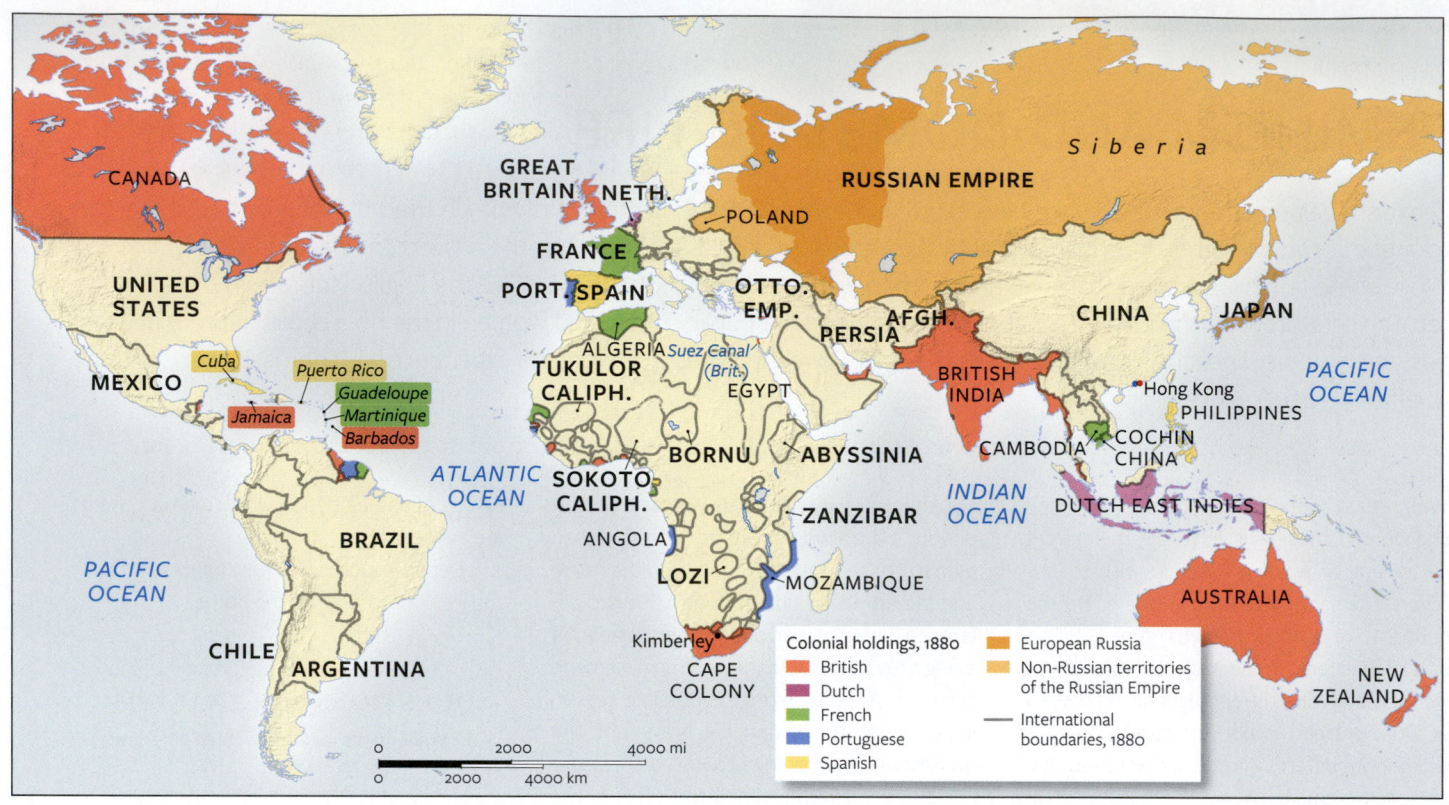

European Imperialism, ca. 1880 In the late nineteenth century, several older imperial powers—Spain, Portugal, the Netherlands—retained control of territories on the other side of the world. Other European empires were just beginning to expand, such as France in North Africa and Southeast Asia. Russia also controlled an extensive landmass across Europe and Asia. But the most powerful empire, Britain, controlled territories on five continents, ranging from the vast land expanses of Canada and Australia to the economically significant Egypt, Cape Colony, and India.

nineteenth century, Britain remained by far the most significant European imperial power. True, the Netherlands preserved its far-flung colonies in present-day Indonesia. Spain held on to Cuba, Puerto Rico, the Philippines, and a few other territories. Portugal had colonies in southern Africa and trading posts throughout Asia. And France by the mid-nineteenth century had established a significant presence in Algeria, kept some small island colonies in the Caribbean, and was moving to take over most of southeast Asia.

But these empires paled in comparison with Britain's, which by the 1880s included all of south Asia from present-day Pakistan to Burma; significant and strategic colonies at the southern tip of Africa; Jamaica, Barbados, and other island possessions in the Caribbean and elsewhere; and the large, autonomous British settler states of Canada, Australia, and New Zealand. Massive emigration from the British Isles (one million people just in the 1850s) led to stunning growth in these settler states.

In New Zealand in 1842, just 2,000 white settlers lived among some 80,000 native Maori. By 1896, disease and violent conflict had reduced Maori numbers by half, while the white population had exploded to 700,000. In China, Britain controlled the most important trading port, the city of Hong Kong, although other European powers also enjoyed trade concessions from the ruling Qing dynasty.

And the British Navy continued to exercise unquestioned dominance on the high seas. As a result, competition among European states overseas had remained limited for many decades. Until the late nineteenth century, Britain's most important competitor in areas outside of Europe had been Russia, whose land empire extended west from Poland to the Pacific Ocean. In the mid-nineteenth century, the tsarist regime extended its control from Russia and Siberia south into present day Turkmenistan, Uzbekistan, and Tajikistan, and threatened to proceed into Afghanistan and thence toward

British India. Russia was now the largest territorial state in the world.

THE SCRAMBLE FOR AFRICA

In the 1880s and 1890s, the so-called **scramble for Africa** upset the European states' previous calculations. As late as 1880, the European powers had a relatively minimal presence in Africa: the French colony of Algeria in the Arab north; the British at the Cape; the Portuguese in Angola, Mozambique, and a series of trading posts along the coasts. Altogether, Europeans claimed less than 10 percent of Africa and were relatively inactive in the areas they did claim. After the end of the slave trade in the early nineteenth century, the economic significance of the continent for Europeans had actually declined. Infectious disease—especially malaria—dissuaded Europeans from venturing into the African interior, and transportation away from the coast remained hugely expensive. It has been estimated that to move 50 tons of freight a distance of 20 miles in many parts of Africa, in the absence of water transport, required over 13,000 porters.

But as the nineteenth century unfolded, technological advances made African exploration and conquest far more practical. Europeans discovered how to extract quinine efficiently from tree bark and to use it to prevent malaria. Railroads and newly cheap shipping enabled the affordable extraction of natural resources from the continent's interior. And the new military technology—especially the deadly machine gun—dramatically increased Europeans' military advantages over indigenous Africans.

With these new tools of empire in hand, throughout the century Europeans explored and mapped vast areas of Africa that had been previously unknown to them. Sponsored by both Protestant and Catholic churches hoping to establish African missions, by governments interested in natural resources and colonial markets, and by newspapers hoping for good stories, a series of colorful explorers such as David Livingstone (1813–1873), Pierre Savorgnan de Brazza (1852–1905), and Henry Morton Stanley (1841–1904) captured European imaginations. In 1871, when Livingstone went missing in central Africa, the founder of the *New York Herald* hired the Welsh-born Stanley to venture into unknown territory to find him; Stanley succeeded, allegedly uttering the words "Dr. Livingstone, I presume," and went on to chart the course of the Congo River.

The expeditions helped make European rulers aware of the tremendous resources available in Africa: gold and other precious metals; crops like cotton and cocoa; and plant extracts such as rubber and palm oil for which the Second Industrial Revolution was finding increasingly profitable uses. Particularly spectacular was the discovery of diamonds at Kimberly in southern Africa in 1871—it led to a diamond rush in which tens of thousands of immigrant European miners transformed a small hillock into a vast hole a quarter of a mile across and up to 700 feet deep, producing some 6,000 pounds of diamonds between 1871 and 1914.

Such wealth also made Europeans aware of Africa's potential as a market for their own manufactured goods, such as textiles, at a time when shrinking domestic markets and overproduction were leading to dangerously lower prices. With the European powers already primed for competition, the realization of this potential set off the

Explorers in Africa An illustration from a late-nineteenth-century biography of David Livingstone shows his famous meeting with Henry Stanley in East Africa in 1871. The event was a publicity stunt devised by the *New York Herald*—hence the American flag carried by one of the expedition's native facilitators.

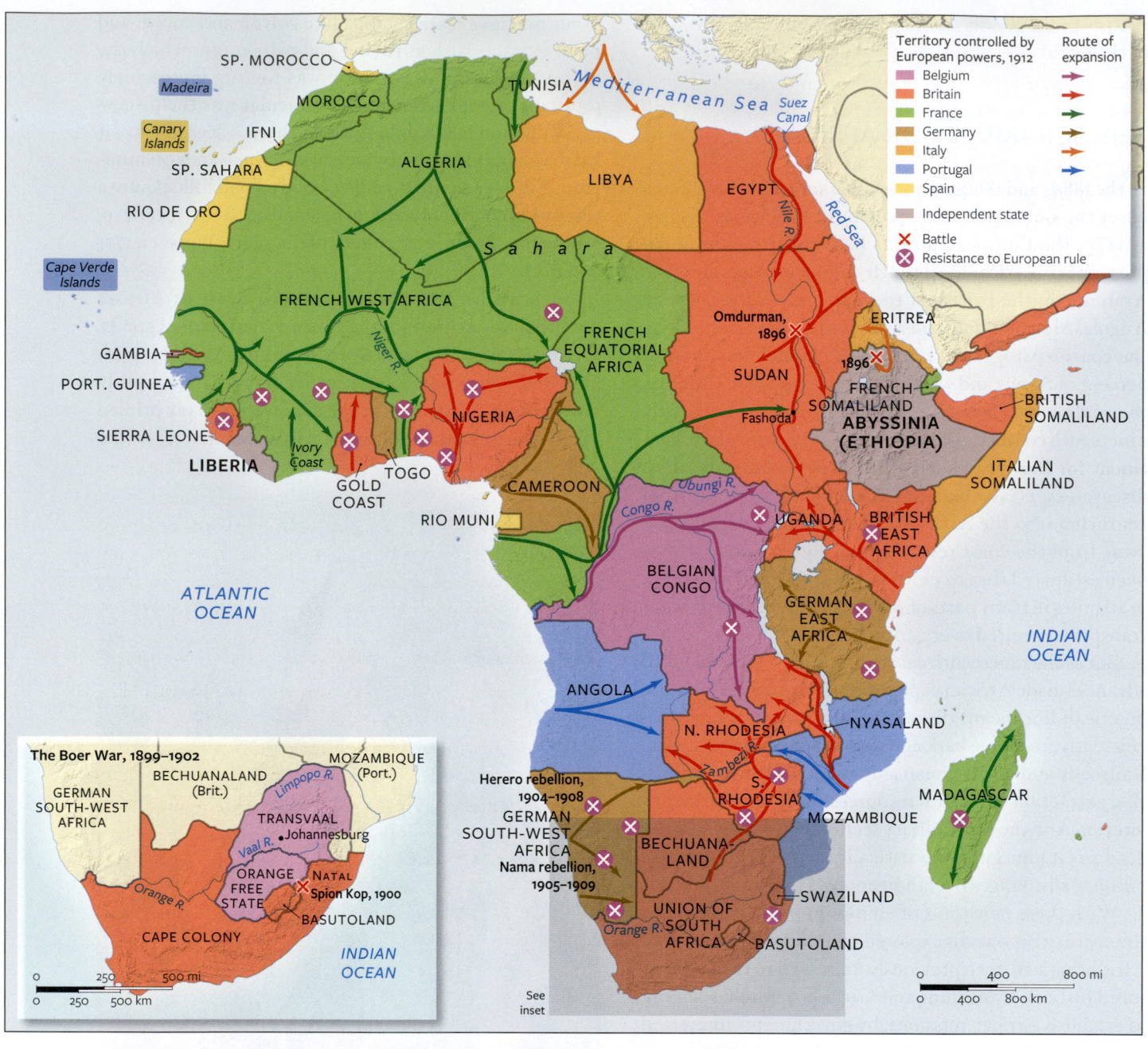

The Partition of Africa, 1880–1912 From 1880, European powers moved in from the African coast to claim large tracts of land in the interior. Resistance to colonization was fierce, leading to violence throughout the continent. But by 1912, major imperial possessions—such as the French in northwest Africa, the British claims that stretched "from Cape to Cairo," and the Belgian Congo—meant that Africa was a theater of European conflicts such as the Boer War (1899–1902). Only Abyssinia remained independent of European rule.

scramble, which developed quickly. The British statesman Lord Salisbury remarked in 1891: "When I left the Foreign Office in 1880, nobody thought about Africa. When I returned to it in 1885 the nations of Europe were almost quarreling with each other as to the various portions of Africa which they should obtain." He correctly called the event a "sudden revolution."

PARTITION OF THE CONTINENT In the early 1880s, a fear of being left behind overcame Britain, France, and Germany. Smaller powers such as Belgium and Italy also started to see an advantage in pursuing their own African empires through military force. In 1882, Britain, taking advantage of chaos in Egypt and acting to ensure that its Asia-bound ships could pass through the new Suez Canal, established a **protectorate** in Egypt. This was a form of imperial rule supposedly intended to protect the indigenous population but in fact designed to assert significant control for the imperial power. France established a similar protectorate over Tunisia and made claims in the Congo. Germany, initially reluctant to pursue an overseas expansion for which its history offered no precedent, became convinced that it had to join in or cede a crucial strategic and economic advantage to its rivals. It claimed German Southwest Africa and soon moved to establish protectorates in the future states of Togo, Cameroon, and Tanzania. Seeking to make their scramble more orderly, the European powers convened the **Berlin Conference of 1884–1885** to draw borders. Delegates divided the vast area of the Congo between France and Belgium, and gave free rein to France in much of West Africa, particularly the future Ivory Coast. Britain had its interests in Egypt recognized and received effective authority over large areas of East Africa as well.

By 1911, the European partition of the continent had been completed. The French consolidated their empire by seizing the vast western African territories between Algeria and the Ivory Coast, while also moving into central Africa, taking the large island of Madagascar, and establishing a protectorate over Morocco. Italy entered the race late, establishing the colony of Eritrea on the Red Sea and fighting a successful war against the Ottoman Empire for Libya in 1911. It failed, however, in an earlier, more ambitious war against the independent kingdom of Abyssinia (Ethiopia). In a campaign marked by remarkable incompetence, the Italians lost a crucial battle in 1896, leaving the Abyssinians in possession of one of two significant independent states in Africa. The other was the Republic of Liberia, which had been settled in the 1840s by former American slaves.

For the most part, the scramble for Africa took place without significant violence between Europeans. A crisis briefly developed between Britain and France over the Sudan in the mid-1890s, with British gunboats confronting a small French expedition at the remote river fort of Fashoda in 1898. But the French simply did not have the resources to challenge the British presence, and eventually backed down in return for British acknowledgment of their positions in West Africa and the hope of future British support against Germany.

THE BOER WAR (1899–1902) The largest exception to the pattern of peaceful competition came in South Africa, where, by the mid-nineteenth century, the descendants of the early Dutch colonists (with a fair

admixture of French Huguenots and other Protestants) had carved out two independent states: the Transvaal and the Orange Free State. In both, small white minorities dominated much larger populations of Africans and mixed-race "coloreds," who lacked the vote and any meaningful civil rights. These states resisted attempts at British annexation (with a Liberal government in London confirming the Transvaal's independence), but the discovery of rich deposits of gold and diamonds, particularly in the Transvaal town of Johannesburg, triggered an inrush of English-speaking immigrants from throughout the British Empire and put new pressure on the relationship. In 1895, the British-born South African politician and entrepreneur Cecil Rhodes (1853–1902) sponsored a botched attempt to take the Transvaal for Britain by force.

Four years later, open war broke out between Britain and the two **Boers** (from the Dutch word for "farmer") republics. The Boers shocked the British army with unexpectedly effective resistance by both regular troops and guerrillas. In response, the British shipped in hundreds of thousands of soldiers and adopted increasingly harsh tactics. They executed guerrillas and drove Boer families off their farms into dangerous, unsanitary compounds referred to—in a foreshadowing of the horror of the century to come—as concentration camps. The tactics caused enormous controversy in Britain, with a faction of pro-Boers defending the Boer cause against their own country, and the leader of the Liberal Party denouncing "methods of barbarism in South Africa." Finally, in 1902 the Boers sued for peace but soon afterward had their states admitted into a Union of South

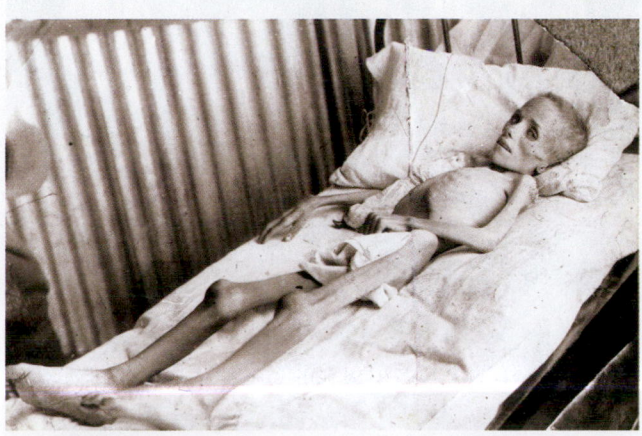

British Concentration Camps During the Boer War, social investigators visited South Africa to document what they argued were the atrocities of the British concentration camps. Their work included this 1900 photograph of a child who died of malnutrition in one such camp.

Africa, which quickly achieved self-governing dominion status similar to that of Canada within the British Empire. This arrangement also signified official British approval of South Africa's policies of racial inequality, inherited from the Boer republics, which subordinated the African population to whites, depriving them of the vote and civil rights.

VIOLENCE AGAINST AFRICANS The relative lack of violence between Europeans in Africa was more than offset by the massive violence inflicted on native African populations. When armed with European weapons, African forces could still sometimes defeat European armies. Abyssinia's triumph over Italy was one example; another was the victory in 1885 of Muslim Sudanese rebels over an Anglo-Egyptian force, and the killing of the British general Charles Gordon (1833–1885). But more typical was Britain's revenge on the Sudanese at the battle of Omdurman in 1898, when a larger Anglo-Egyptian force under Field Marshal Herbert Kitchener (1850–1916), armed with Maxim machine guns, killed 10,000 Sudanese and wounded 13,000, while losing only 47 dead and 382 wounded of their own. A popular verse of the period ended with the words "Whatever happens, we have the Maxim Gun and they do not."

The worst violence inflicted on Africans, however,

Belgian Congo A white overseer poses with his forced African laborers and their bountiful rubber harvest in this photograph from 1899.

happened off the battlefield. We have already seen how in 1904 the Germans deliberately slaughtered the Herero and Nama peoples in Southwest Africa. But even that example of mass killing was overshadowed by the horrifying exploitation of the Congo by Belgium after it became the private fiefdom of King Leopold II in 1885. The king's agents forced Congolese to work for little or no pay harvesting rubber, gathering ivory, and mining valuable ores. Many died as a result of the appalling work conditions; others perished in the epidemics that spread through the disrupted territory (as in Latin America three hundred years before, the indigenous population often had little immunity to European diseases); still others starved to death after Leopold's army had carted off the available foodstuffs for itself. And huge numbers were simply shot for disobeying orders.

In a particularly terrible turn of events, Belgian military leaders insisted that to save on ammunition, soldiers turn in a severed hand of a Congolese native for every bullet they fired. The Belgians took to hacking hands off defenseless women and children if a bullet missed the mark. All in all, as many as 8 million Congolese—half the population—lost their lives between 1885 and 1908, while King Leopold himself reaped over a billion dollars in today's money in profits. Finally, international protests led him to give up his fiefdom and in effect sell his private colony to the Belgian government. The Congo became the setting for the most powerful European novel about the horrors of imperialism in Africa, by the Polish-born British novelist Joseph Conrad (1857–1924): *Heart of Darkness*.

THE "CIVILIZING" MISSION Despite the naked power politics and economic impulses that prompted the new imperialism, the European powers nonetheless justified their conduct by stressing the beneficial effects of their rule for native peoples. Non-Europeans, it was explained, were in desperate need of "civilization"—in the words of Rudyard Kipling's 1897 poem "The White Man's Burden," they were "half-devil and half-child." The same Universal Exposition of 1889 that led to the construction of the Eiffel Tower in Paris also featured a so-called negro village—a literal human zoo featuring some 400 Africans in a re-creation of their "native" habitat, reinforcing the message that indigenous peoples needed European teaching to learn everything from proper hygiene and manners to civics and Christianity.

In practice, what became known as Europeans' civilizing mission in Africa came to focus on the building of schools, the teaching of European languages, and the provision of elementary medical services, as well as attempts

DISCRIMINATION AGAINST INDIANS IN SOUTH AFRICA

By the 1890s, tens of thousands of Indians had immigrated to South Africa, often to work as indentured servants—contracted for a fixed period, after which they could return to India or settle permanently—on sugar plantations, railways, or mines, or as independent merchants. Most lived in the southeastern British colony of Natal, others in the independent state of the Transvaal to the north. As the Indian presence in these regions continued to grow, settlers of European origin increasingly passed legislation to deny them rights. However, some merchants and lawyers, including the future Indian independence leader Mohandas Gandhi, fought to expose the injustice of these discriminatory measures.

Henry Campbell, *Re* British Indians in Transvaal

Although British subjects living in the Transvaal could own property and engage in commerce, an 1885 law severely restricted these rights for all Asians, including Indians. In response, a lawyer representing a group of Indian merchants, Henry Campbell, wrote the following letter in 1890 requesting intervention from Britain's Colonial Office.

The ordinary license to trade is now being refused to the Indian Merchants....

Owing to the refusals now notified to me the whole of the Indians are in fear that at the end of the year they will be refused licenses for 1891 in all districts simultaneously.

I fear such is the view held by officials and their intent likewise. As the law providing for the licenses sets out, any person trading without a license is liable to fine and imprisonment.

In all probability licenses will not be issued, their tender of money on January 1st 1891 will be refused, and they will be brought face to face with closed doors and a ruined business, or, opening their doors, being [hauled] to prison....

Some two hundred mercantile firms and businesses are thus threatened....

Their capital sum invested totals a quarter of a million sterling in the Transvaal alone. The paralysis of this quarter of a million sterling would react on the Head Offices in India amongst their commercial and financial banking in Bombay and the other Presidencies....

Capital invested by those people in the Transvaal on the security of their status as British subjects is made the sport of a local law which has given the power to compel them to leave the towns where alone business can be done, and go into a semi-leper isolation into a so-called "location, ward, or street" removed from the centres of traffic and from the towns, markets, bazaars, or marts.

This position is alike cruelly unjust and intolerable; either those people have the right of British subjects to "full liberty with their families to enter, travel, or reside in any part of the South African Republic; entitled to hire or possess houses, manufactories, warehouses, shops, and premises; to carry on their commerce either in person or by any agents whom they may think fit to employ or not." They either have the right to do all this or they have not.

Gandhi, Open Letter on Franchise Law

In 1894, the colony of Natal passed a law stripping Indians of the right to vote. Shortly thereafter, Gandhi wrote an open letter to the legislature in protest.

I suppose there can be no doubt that the Indian is a despised being in the Colony, and that every opposition to him proceeds directly from that hatred.

If that hatred is simply based upon his colour, then, of course, he has no hope. The sooner he leaves the Colony the better. No matter what he does, he will never have the white skin. If, however, it is based upon something else, if it is based upon an ignorance of his general character and attainments, he may hope to receive his due at the hands of the Europeans in the Colony.

The question what use the Colony will make of the 40,000 Indians is, I submit, worthy of the most serious consideration....

It is for you to say whether you will lower them or raise them in the scale of civilization, whether you will bring them down to a level lower than what they should occupy on account of heredity, whether you will alienate their hearts from you, or whether you will draw them closer to you—whether, in short, you would govern them despotically or sympathetically....

Withdraw the Indian from the sugar estate, and where would the main industry of the Colony be?

QUESTIONS FOR ANALYSIS

1. According to Campbell, what makes the treatment of Indians in the Transvaal unjust?
2. What does Gandhi see as the root cause of British discrimination against Indians in the Natal colony?
3. What economic arguments do both Campbell and Gandhi make for the fair treatment of Indians in South Africa?

Sources: Henry Campbell, letter, in *India: A Journal for the Discussion of Indian Affairs* (London: 1890), p. 281; Mahatma Gandhi, *The Collected Works of Mahatma Gandhi*, vol. 1 (New Delhi: 1958), pp. 171–72.

to limit the use of native law, reduce the influence of tribal chiefs, and eradicate slavery. In the British and German colonies, much of the educational mission was left up to Christian missionaries. In the French empire, and especially in the extensive territories that made up French West Africa, the republican state took the leading role, while proclaiming as its goal the assimilation of Africans to French values and customs. But the fundamental tension—indeed, the hypocrisy—of the civilizing mission showed through in the reluctance of the French administration to grant full citizenship to anyone outside a tiny indigenous elite.

THE GROWTH OF SETTLER COLONIES

The scramble for Africa was the most striking and visible aspect of European imperialism between 1880 and 1910, but it was not the whole story. Several European empires, particularly the British, expanded through Asia and other parts of the world during this period. The growing British presence in India can be measured in miles of track. British rail networks in the country grew from 300 miles in 1857 to 25,000 in 1900. Europeans continued to flow to settler colonies and dominions, which were former settler colonies that now had self-rule, such as Canada and Australia. By 1900, close to 500,000 white French citizens were living in Algeria and had direct representation in the French parliament. Large parts of the capital Algiers had become, in effect, a European city.

But it was not just Europeans who took part in new global migrations. Within the British Empire, Indian laborers migrated to Burma, to the future Malaysia, to South Africa, and to British colonies in the Caribbean. By 1914, there were 250,000 Indians in Guyana and 134,000 in Trinidad. The French facilitated the immigration of Chinese into French Southeast Asia. The French would also soon begin using black officials from their Caribbean territories of Martinique and Guadeloupe to help them administer their empire in Africa.

The one great exception to the story of imperial expansion in the period was Spain, which lost its principal remaining colonies—Cuba, Puerto Rico, and the Philippines—to the United States in the Spanish-American War of 1898. This war also marked the rising international power of the United States, which increasingly saw itself in competition with Europeans in the race for empire. U.S. senator Albert Beveridge, a promoter of the outright annexation of the Philippines, made a daring call for America to establish its own overseas empire: "We will not renounce our part

Colonial Cities A view of the Algiers railway station in 1894 shows the influence of French colonization. Besides the newly developed infrastructure, European-style buildings rise to the left, reminiscent of the apartment buildings of Paris.

in the mission of our race, trustee, under God, of the civilization of the world." The British poet Rudyard Kipling agreed, calling on the United States to "take up the white man's burden."

EUROPE AND EAST ASIA

As the European empires expanded across the globe, they came into conflict with the two most prominent East Asian nations, Japan and China, but with different results. Japan was making a concerted effort to Westernize in the Meiji Restoration that began in 1868. It modeled large parts of its government and law on that of the German Empire, and its military on the French army. By the end of the nineteenth century, it had increased its power sufficiently to deliver a decisive defeat to China in the Sino-Japanese War of 1894–1895 and then to Russia in the Russo-Japanese War of 1904–1905. Russia's humiliation contributed to the Revolution of 1905 and persuaded Russia to bring Britain into its alliance with France, for protection against the rising power of Germany.

The Chinese story was different. In the last decades of the nineteenth century, the Western powers continued to press China to open its markets to their goods and to allow them to establish trading ports, building on the

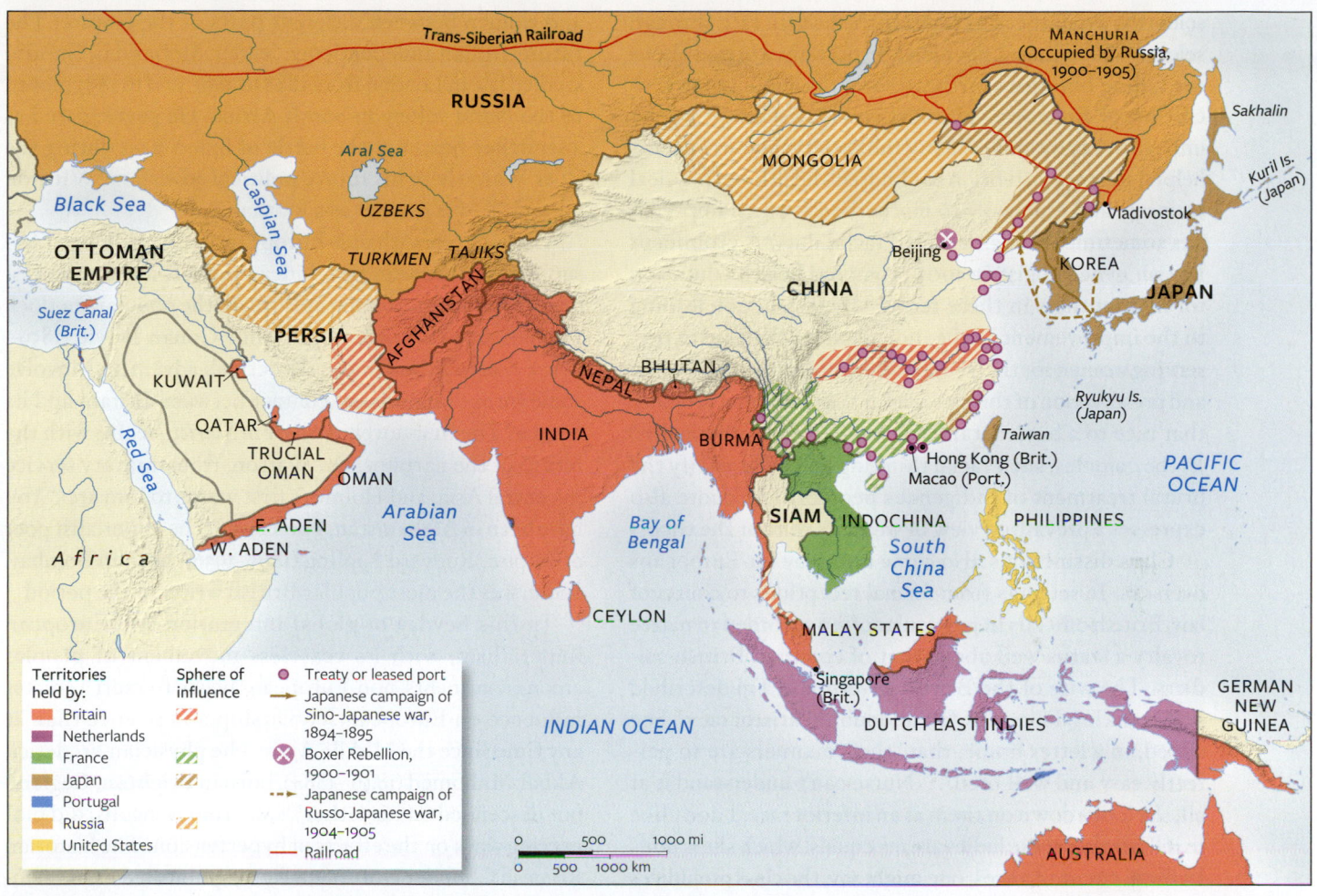

Imperialism in Asia, 1880–1910 By the end of the nineteenth century, Asia had become a key site for the negotiation of geopolitical power. Though Britain remained dominant, controlling South Asia, Malaysia, Australia, and key territories in the Persian Gulf (including the Suez Canal), France was becoming increasingly powerful in Southeast Asia, controlling key ports on the South China Sea. The Trans-Siberian Railroad enabled Russia to extend its reach eastward, but the Russian Empire reached its limit with defeat by the Japanese Empire in the Russo-Japanese War. China was surrounded on all sides by other empires, which exerted their power over it through punishing trade deals and the defeat of the Boxer Rebellion.

precedents established in the mid-century Opium Wars and the "unequal treaties" that the Chinese acquiesced in. Many Chinese felt outraged and humiliated by these events and by the proselytizing activities of Christian missionaries in China. In 1900, a secret Chinese nationalist society known as the Boxers carried out attacks on European missionaries, merchants, and soldiers, killing several hundred. In response, a combined force of British, French, German, Russian, Japanese, and American troops landed in China, put down the Boxer Rebellion, and forced the Chinese government to pay crushing reparations. The Europeans thereby preserved their commercial advantages in China, but at the cost of further destabilizing China's teetering Qing Empire and helping to bring about the country's first modern revolution, in 1911.

IMPERIALISM, RACE, AND CLASS

As they built their empires, Europeans were deeply influenced by what many at the time thought of as the "science" of race. Since mid-century, biologists and anthropologists had attempted to apply Charles Darwin's theory of evolution to human racial differences, and in the decades around 1900 these efforts multiplied. Scientists posited differences in brain types and intelligence not only between Europeans and non-Europeans, but also among Europeans themselves—usually to the advantage of northern (Teutonic or Aryan) Europeans, and to the disadvantage of Mediterraneans, especially Jews.

In Britain, Darwin's cousin Francis Galton (1822–1911) coined the term **eugenics** to describe a supposedly scientific program of improving the human race through selective breeding. Eugenicists especially worried about the falling European birthrates and the supposed degeneration of European physical stock as a result of the unhealthy conditions of industrial society. These concerns helped spur new attention to children's health and physical training, and especially to motherhood, which imperialists sometimes cast as a sacred racial duty. A prominent British gynecologist in 1903 promoted health education for new mothers in these terms: "By instruction leading to the improvement of the individual we shall aid in preserving women for their supreme purpose, the procreation and preservation of the race, and at the same time promote that race to a better standard, mentally and physically." In the colonies, such racial thinking helped to justify the brutal treatment of indigenous peoples. The quote also expresses a prevailing view of women's roles at the time.

Class distinctions also came into play for Europeans overseas. In settings from formal receptions to courts of law, British officials in particular often accorded to native royalty a status well above that of common British soldiers. The wife of the British governor of Fiji described high-ranking Fijians as "an undoubted aristocracy." She added, in a letter home, that "their manners are so perfectly easy and well bred.... Nurse can't understand it at all, she looks down on them as an inferior race. I don't like to tell her that these ladies are my equals, which she is not!" In these circumstances, one might say, the class prejudices of the British trumped their racial prejudices.

THE EFFECTS OF IMPERIALISM ON EUROPE

Overall, the imperialism of this period had powerful effects on the European countries themselves as well as on their colonial territories. Economically, it opened up new sources of raw materials for European industry and new markets for manufactured goods, including textiles and metals. By 1900, one-third of all Britain's exports were to its empire. Even by 1914, however, the equivalent figure for Germany, which had yet to develop the full economic potential of its new empire, was just 1 percent. Important new career paths also opened up. In 1900, for instance, fully one-quarter of the graduates of Oxford University's elite Balliol College had left Britain for positions somewhere in the empire, often as administrators of vast territories. Imperial trade and military service brought non-Europeans to Europe by the thousands, thronging the streets of port cities and capitals, while also moving men and women between different parts of the empire. The future Indian independence leader Mohandas Gandhi studied law in London from 1888 to 1891, and in 1893 moved to the Natal colony in South Africa. He participated as a stretcher-bearer at the battle of Spion Kop during the Boer War, where his future political adversary, Winston Churchill, was present as a journalist.

Interactions with non-Europeans both challenged and supported European racial ideas and left a deep impression on European popular culture. In the popular Sherlock Holmes stories written by Arthur Conan Doyle (1859–1930), most of the famous detective's adventures involve some form of significant contact between Britain and its empire. The first novel, *A Study in Scarlet*, begins with the return of the narrator, Dr. Watson, from military service in central Asia, and Holmes's first words to him are: "You have been in Afghanistan, I perceive." The imperialist poet of empire, Rudyard Kipling (1865–1936), born in Bombay, India, was the most popular British writer of the period.

In this heyday of global integration and European imperialism, with its ceaseless movement of peoples among continents, non-Europeans began to exert a greater influence on European scholarship and science than at any time since the Middle Ages. The physician Frederick Akbar Mahomed (1849–1884), born in Brighton, England but descended on his father's side from Bengalis, did pioneering work on the effects of hypertension. The historian Romesh Chunder Dutt (1848–1909) published fundamental works on Indian economic history—showing, among other things, how British colonialism had inhibited Indian economic development.

MODERNISM RISING

The newly intense engagement with overseas peoples also contributed to the astonishing developments in European art, literature, and thought that now go by the name of **modernism**, which represented a conscious break with earlier styles of art. To take one of the most prominent examples, in the 1880s the French painter Paul Gauguin (1848–1903), dazzled by the example of the impressionists such as Monet and Renoir, increasingly moved away from representational art toward the expressive use of brilliant color and coarse brushwork. In 1891, seeking inspiration, he traveled to the French colony of Tahiti in the South Pacific, where he was overcome by the vibrant native art. Its strong colors, shapes, and departures from realistic representation strongly influenced his development as a painter.

During the next two decades, one of the greatest

modernist artists, the Spaniard **Pablo Picasso** (1881–1973), discovered African sculpture, with its emphasis on simple shapes, dramatic angles and planes, and expressive treatment of the human form. It influenced many of his works, including his 1907 masterpiece *The Young Ladies of Avignon*. In 1913, the Russian composer Igor Stravinsky (1882–1971) shocked Parisian audiences with the jarring, unfamiliar harmonies and jagged rhythms of the music he wrote to accompany a ballet called *The Rite of Spring*. Although the ballet depicted pre-Christian Russia, the music, especially in its rhythms, bore the strong influence of non-European cultures, including West African ones.

THE ROOTS OF ARTISTIC MODERNISM

Modernism had many other, complex roots. Modernist artists, writers, and composers sought to capture something of the fractured, frantic, whirling existence they associated with urban life in the fin de siècle. They sought to give artistic expression to what was often perceived as the destruction of traditional certitudes by heady advances in science. With photography now enabling amateurs to make precise images of physical reality, artists increasingly turned toward exploring the pure play of color, light, and shape, without representing any recognizable object. And so-called avant-garde artists and writers deliberately sought to assert the value of their work by differentiating it from the unchallenging, sentimental compositions, artworks, and literature that were being churned out in ever greater numbers to satisfy the demands of burgeoning middle-class audiences. The French phrase *épater la bourgeoisie* ("shock the bourgeoisie") became the avant-garde's watchword, and the easiest way to do so was through art that was seen as morally questionable or simply alien and bizarre. Avant-garde artists challenged the standards of rationalism that they associated with middle-class culture and sought to unlock hidden depths of the human psyche.

LITERATURE Before World War I, the most important modernist innovations in literature took place in poetry. There, especially in France, a rapid evolution occurred from the hauntingly strange verse of Baudelaire (see Chapter 19) toward more difficult symbolist experiments with pure sound, with the vivid depiction of momentary, discontinuous sensations, and invocations of a mysterious realm of human transcendence that had distinct pagan accents. Symbols, the advocates of this school argued, represented the way to bridge the gap between the world of nature and the world of spiritual exploration. Symbolist poets such

The Young Ladies of Avignon Picasso's 1907 masterpiece bears the influence of African sculpture and is characteristic of the angular, abstract cubist style he pioneered.

as Stéphane Mallarmé (1842–1898) were criticized for the impenetrability of their work, but nonetheless emerged as dominant poetic voices. Outside of France, more popular poets such as the American-born Ezra Pound (1885–1972), the German Rainer Maria Rilke (1875–1926), and the Irish William Butler Yeats (1865–1939) were developing a distinctive modernist style that would flourish after 1914. Fiction-writing did not experience such dramatic changes, but the great novelists of the fin de siècle, such as Thomas Hardy (1840–1928) in England and Émile Zola (1840–1902) in France, often generated controversy with unsparing depictions of the underside of bourgeois society, including especially its sexual mores.

MUSIC Music saw, in some ways, the most radical break with earlier standards. Some composers, while seeking to create dreamscapes in sound, nonetheless remained tied to a melodic late-romantic tradition. But the French composers Erik Satie (1866–1925) and Claude Debussy (1862–1918) moved further away from traditional tonalities, harmonies, and rhythms with wildly playful, if sometimes remarkably gentle, pieces that involved unfamiliar chords, scales, and forms of modulation. Stravinsky's modernist experiments in *The Rite of Spring* caused the greatest public controversy; but even before they did, the Austrian composer Arnold Schoenberg (1874–1951) attracted criticism for experimental atonal music that avoided ordinary melodies and key signatures altogether.

Modernists like Schoenberg had an enormous influence on twentieth-century music, but their difficult pieces never attracted anything like the audiences for the music of Wagner, Verdi, and other late romantic composers. As a result, the modernist moment in music, more than in any other art form, opened up a stark divide between a relatively small, heavily academic realm of "serious" composition and a much larger sector of performance and instruction that remained tied mostly to the classical canon of eighteenth- and nineteenth-century composers.

PAINTING By contrast, modernism in painting—while also subject to fierce criticism—was wildly popular. Its most important figures, Pablo Picasso first and foremost, became wealthy, universally recognized celebrities.

The evolution of painting in the fin de siècle began with the innovations of the impressionists but soon moved beyond them. Painters of the 1880s and 1890s such as Gauguin, the Dutch Vincent Van Gogh (1853–1890), and Paul Cézanne (1839–1906) left far behind the goal of producing accurate reproductions and experimented with color combinations unseen in nature. "Instead of trying to render what I see before me," wrote Van Gogh, who cut off part of his own ear in a psychotic rage, "I use color in a completely arbitrary way to express myself powerfully." Van Gogh produced some of the most glorious and popular works of the period. These artists in turn inspired a younger group of painters, whom critics labeled the *fauves* ("wild beasts") for their spirited use of bright colors and simple, geometrical shapes (one opponent compared them to small children who had uncovered a paint box).

Most of these artists, whether French or not, soon gravitated to Paris, still the undisputed capital of Western art. Its principal competition as a center of modernist painting was Vienna, where the clash of cultures and politics from across the Austro-Hungarian Empire, along with the liberal cultural tradition associated with the city's large Jewish minority, created a whirling, intensely attractive milieu for artistic experimentation. There Gustav Klimt (1862–1918) experimented with deliberately shocking works that melded classically erotic imagery with abstract shapes and color combinations, as in his 1905 masterpiece *The Kiss*.

Soon painters began daring to move away from representational art altogether. Picasso, who first visited Paris in 1900, declared: "I paint objects as I think them, not as I see them." Works such as *The Young Ladies of Avignon* deliberately violated the traditional rules of perspective and plane, reduced its distorted figures to the essentials

The Kiss Klimt's groundbreaking painting (1905) depicts a man leaning down to kiss a woman in a field; the clothing of the two figures and the background are painted in abstract designs of shimmering gold.

of shape, and placed them at unconventional angles to one another. Critics blasted Picasso for painting as a child might, and Picasso's defenders retorted that he was trying precisely to recapture a child's view of the world and to move beyond the staid conventions of realism. But soon Picasso and his colleagues went even further, painting so-called cubist works that seemed to break up images and reassemble them into arbitrary, geometric patterns, as if seen through a series of prisms or kaleidoscopes. Russian artists even moved toward entirely abstract works. One of them, Cazimir Malevich (1879–1935), would take the process to its logical conclusion in 1915 with the painting *Black Square*, which was exactly that.

PHILOSOPHY, SOCIAL SCIENCE, AND PSYCHIATRY

The exploration of the unconscious, irrational, and "primitive" by modernist artists, writers, and composers had its counterpart in European thought between 1880 and 1910. The German philosopher **Friedrich Nietzsche** (1844–1900), himself chronically plagued by mental and physical illness, delivered one of the most powerful challenges to European rationalism. Nietzsche defined the human by reference not to reason or morality, but to a mysterious,

> " ... [T]HE NATURE OF OUR EPOCH IS MULTIPLICITY AND INDETERMINACY. "
>
> HUGO VON HOFMANNSTHAL, *THE POET AND THIS AGE, 1905*

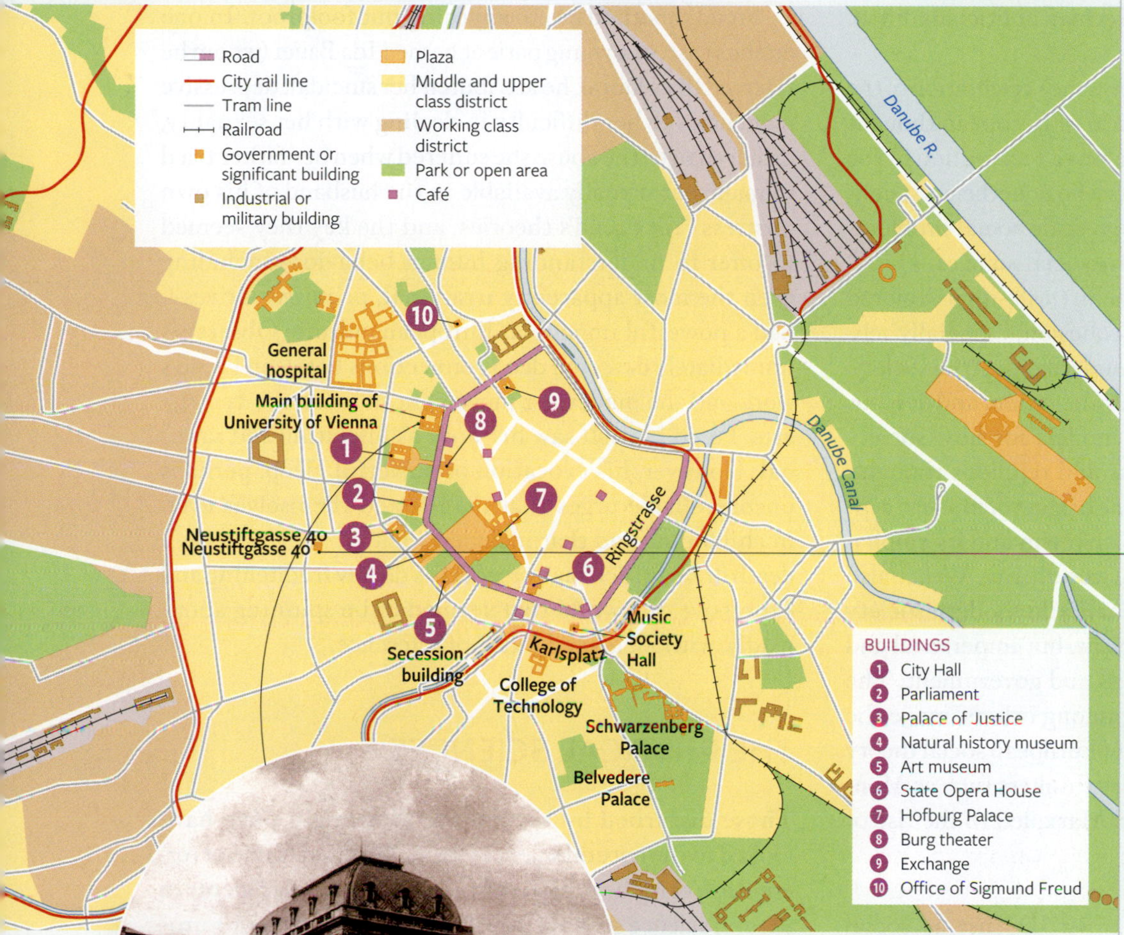

Map Legend

- Road
- City rail line
- Tram line
- Railroad
- Government or significant building
- Industrial or military building
- Plaza
- Middle and upper class district
- Working class district
- Park or open area
- Café

Map labels

General hospital
Main building of University of Vienna
Neustiftgasse 40
Neustiftgasse 40
Secession building
College of Technology
Karlsplatz
Music Society Hall
Schwarzenberg Palace
Belvedere Palace
Ringstrasse
Danube R.
Danube Canal

BUILDINGS

1. City Hall
2. Parliament
3. Palace of Justice
4. Natural history museum
5. Art museum
6. State Opera House
7. Hofburg Palace
8. Burg theater
9. Exchange
10. Office of Sigmund Freud

Otto Wagner's apartment building (Neustiftgasse 40, built in 1910) shows the unornamented, functional uniformity characteristic of modernist design. Stores occupy the ground floor, with residences in the floors above.

When liberal, constitutional rule came to Vienna, its leaders built a ring road lined with monumental public buildings in the center of the city. The University building shown here was Renaissance in style to proclaim its alignment with rational, secular culture.

POLITICS AND CULTURE

1859
Development of the Ringstrasse begins

1860s–1880s
Austria ruled by a liberal, constitutionalist regime

1880s–1900s
Liberal rule defeated by nationalist and socialist mass movements

1893
Otto Wagner's modernist plans win competition for new urban development

> " THE ONLY POSSIBLE POINT OF DEPARTURE FOR OUR ARTISTIC CREATION IS MODERN LIFE. "
>
> OTTO WAGNER, *MODERN ARCHITECTURE, 1895*

QUESTIONS FOR ANALYSIS

1. In what ways is the modernist style of Otto Wagner's apartment building a rejection of the Renaissance style embodied in the University building?

2. How was the apartment building a fitting reflection of modern life?

3. What connections can you draw between political and cultural change in Vienna at this time?

creative, irrational life force. As his work developed, he tried to show how rationalist philosophy and Christian morality had shackled that life force. He challenged Europeans, to cite the title of one of his best-known works, to think "beyond good and evil." In his most lyrical book, *Thus Spoke Zarathustra* (1883–1885), he prophesied a "superman" who could destroy the "slave morality" of the "herd" and release the life force. Nietzsche did not describe this superman in racial terms, but following his death many interpreters and opportunistic German politicians did so.

DURKHEIM AND WEBER Nietzsche's celebration of the irrational was not, however, typical of European thought in this period. Far more common was a recognition of the power of the irrational by thinkers who nonetheless sought to harness reason to analyze large-scale social problems and thereby develop more effective social policies. Thinkers such as France's Émile Durkheim (1858–1917) explored how traditional forms of social cohesion, especially religious ones, had broken down in modern industrial society, producing the isolated individual, alienation, and despair. Durkheim proposed powerful models for how society shaped individual consciousness and religious thought. Max Weber (1864–1920) traced the origins of modern capitalist society to Reformation Calvinism and its emphasis on living a productive, active, worldly life. Weber also argued that the growth of rationality in modern society led to the creation of large, efficient, but impersonal and soulless bureaucracies in business and government. The work of Durkheim and Weber, among others, made the period 1880–1910 the golden age of European social theory and, building on the work of older thinkers such as Montesquieu, Adam Smith, and Karl Marx, led to the rise of the discipline of sociology.

Sigmund Freud This 1921 photo shows the psychoanalyst posing with his trademark cigar.

SIGMUND FREUD Just as social scientists sought to analyze the problems of society, so the Austrian doctor **Sigmund Freud** (1856–1939) aspired to develop rational, scientific methods for understanding and treating mental disorders. After having studied in France with the great neurologist Jean Charcot (1825–1893), Freud adopted Charcot's technique of using hypnosis and also began exploring the way that dreams expressed unconscious desires. His 1899 book *The Interpretation of Dreams* marked a milestone in modern psychological understanding.

Then, six years later, Freud shocked the medical community with a book of essays arguing that even very young children were not innocent of sexuality and that childhood experience could have a deep influence on adult sexual desire. These ideas, and practical work with women suffering from hysteria, led Freud to develop methods of treatment based on sustained conversation with an analyst who could uncover the formative experiences at the root of a person's condition.

Freud's methods were anything but foolproof. In one famous case, of a young patient named Ida Bauer (whom he referred to as Dora), he attributed her suicidal, depressive tendencies to her difficulty in dealing with her sexuality, rather than to the abuse she suffered when her father tried to make her sexually available to the husband of his own mistress. Yet Freud's theories, and the key they seemed to offer to understanding human behavior—including even the most apparently irrational, primitive drives—had a powerful impact on European culture. Observers immediately detected deep connections between Freud's work and the modernist movement in literature and the arts. Freud himself saw his work as liberating and rational. However, his evocation of powerful, deep, perhaps uncontrollable urges that manifested themselves even in childhood, and that included what he referred to as a death drive, struck many readers as deeply frightening and expressive of a world that seemed to be spinning about madly, without a fixed frame of reference.

THE PHYSICAL SCIENCES

Those disturbed by Freud's theories might once have looked to the natural sciences for such a fixed frame of reference. Yet in the period 1880–1910 even developments in natural science seemed to be conspiring to unmoor Europeans from their certainties.

THE CURIES In Paris, in 1896, the Polish-born scientist Marie Curie (1867–1934), along with her French husband, Pierre Curie (1859–1906), isolated the element of radium and thereby discovered the phenomenon of radioactivity. Scientists built on this work to describe the structure of the atom and to prove what ancient alchemists had asserted and modern science had strongly denied—namely, that one element could transmute into another. The German scientist Max Planck (1858–1947) challenged earlier understanding of light and other forms of radiant energy, showing that it was not emitted as a single constant wave but in discrete tiny packages, or quanta.

BOCCIONI'S *THE CITY RISES*

Umberto Boccioni (1882–1916) was an Italian painter who believed that artistic form had to accord to the conditions of modern life. His career was short—he was killed during World War I—but his canvases and sculptures expressed the increasingly abstract modernist aesthetic that transformed European art and culture in the early twentieth century.

In his large painting *The City Rises* (1910), originally titled *Work*, Boccioni celebrates the dizzy activity of the construction of a new electric plant, visible in the background, in Milan. The moving lines, splashes of color, and blurring of figures combine to convey the chaotic dynamism of a city street, where workers struggle to control a horse. Boccioni emphasizes the collective nature of work, with the men and horses heaving together in an energetic mass. Just as life in a modern city never stood still, neither, the painter suggests, could an art that hoped to capture that life.

QUESTIONS FOR ANALYSIS

1. In what ways is this painting representative of modernism?
2. What attitudes toward work and the modern city does Boccioni convey?
3. How does this painting suggest the ways in which the modern city transformed people's experience of the world in the late nineteenth and early twentieth centuries?

ALBERT EINSTEIN Most unsettling, however, was the work of an obscure German physicist working as a patent clerk in Switzerland: **Albert Einstein** (1879–1955). Like other physicists of the period, Einstein had observed with dissatisfaction the results of a series of experiments involving light and electromagnetic radiation. But whereas other physicists tried to find where the experiments had gone wrong, Einstein accepted the experiments as valid and asked where the underlying theories had gone wrong. In 1905, he published a revolutionary paper with the modest title "On the Electrodynamics of Bodies in Motion." It postulated that time itself could flow at different rates for different bodies, depending on their relative motion; that the speed of light is always constant for all observers, regardless of their motion; and that there exists no absolute state of rest in the universe.

And then, after linking space and time in this manner, in another paper the same year Einstein also linked mass and energy, suggesting that as a body's relative speed increases, so does its mass. Einstein concisely expressed this connection in the formula $e = mc^2$ (energy equals mass times the speed of light squared). It asserted the essential equivalency of mass and energy, and also the potential for transforming small quantities of the former into massive quantities of the latter, thereby opening the door, theoretically, to nuclear fission and fusion. Einstein's theory of relativity arguably had a greater impact than the work of any scientist since Isaac Newton in the seventeenth century.

CONCLUSION

Of all the creative works of this period, one of the most eerie is a painting: the German artist Ludwig Meidner's 1913 work *Apocalyptic Landscape*. It belongs to the modernist school generally referred to as German expressionism, which favored violent, clashing colors and tortured images, and seemed to be reaching into the darkest corners of the human psyche. *Apocalyptic Landscape* is not the most distinguished work of the school, but it uncannily seems to predict the horrific destruction that would break out just a year after its composition, with the beginning of World War I.

To many Europeans, Meidner's premonitions must have seemed absurd. As we have seen in this chapter, in

Apocalyptic Landscape The thickly applied paint and jagged lines of Meidner's 1913 painting indicate a new departure for abstract art in the early twentieth century—and seem to suggest the approaching chaos of World War I.

1913 Europeans collectively enjoyed a greater degree of wealth, material comfort, health, leisure, and social security than ever before in history, and they dominated the globe as never before. Global commerce seemed to be binding humanity closer together than ever before, and the development of science and industry seemed to many to confirm the power of reason to better the human condition, even if voices had arisen protesting the ways industry had produced disruption and exploitation.

Yet at the same time, despite this "progress" (to use a word then much in vogue), national rivalries remained as strong as ever and were fueled more than ever before by poisonous ideologies of racial superiority. Scientific and industrial progress expressed itself not only in material comfort but also in massive new levels of destructive armaments. The developments in art, philosophy, and social science that we have just discussed highlighted the frightening power of the irrational. And with Einstein's work on relativity, science itself seemed to be breaking apart the comfortingly stable, predictable, Newtonian vision of the universe that had prevailed since the scientific revolution. From this perspective, it seemed all too likely that the vast energies Europeans were now capable of harnessing could be turned to purposes of destruction. In 1914, with stunning speed, Meidner's premonitions would come terrifyingly to life.

[CHAPTER REVIEW]

KEY TERMS

new imperialism (p. 672)
Second Industrial Revolution (p. 673)
globalization (p. 676)
syndicalism (p. 680)
Dreyfus Affair (p. 682)
pogroms (p. 682)

Mensheviks (p. 683)
Bolsheviks (p. 683)
Duma (p. 683)
home rule (p. 684)
Emmeline Pankhurst (p. 686)
Triple Alliance (p. 687)

Triple Entente (p. 687)
scramble for Africa (p. 689)
protectorate (p. 691)
Berlin Conference of 1884–1885 (p. 691)
Boers (p. 691)

eugenics (p. 695)
modernism (p. 696)
Pablo Picasso (p. 697)
Friedrich Nietzsche (p. 698)
Sigmund Freud (p. 700)
Albert Einstein (p. 702)

REVIEW QUESTIONS

1. How did the Second Industrial Revolution change European economies?

2. Why did emigration increase during this period?

3. During the period 1880–1910, how did technological advances widen the differences between rural and urban life?

4. What tensions between liberal and conservative movements developed in the late nineteenth century?

5. What factors led to the Russian Revolution of 1905, and what were the revolution's effects?

6. What feminist movements developed during the fin de siècle?

7. By the 1880s, what gave Britain the greatest global influence of any power?

8. What accounts for the tremendous expansion of European control of Africa between 1880 and 1914?

9. What effects did the new imperialism have on Europe?

10. What were the principal characteristics of modernist culture?

CORE OBJECTIVES

After reading this chapter, you should have a solid understanding of the following core objectives. To strengthen your grasp of the core objectives, use the resources on the Student Site for The West.

- Analyze the rapid technological and economic changes in European societies around the turn of the twentieth century.

- Describe the shifts in social roles, demographics, and emigration during the period.

- Trace the challenges to the liberal worldview in the major European countries.

- Identify the characteristics of the new imperialism in Africa and Asia.

- Assess the intellectual and artistic innovations of the period.

 GO TO **INQUIZITIVE** TO SEE WHAT YOU'VE LEARNED—AND LEARN WHAT YOU'VE MISSED—WITH PERSONALIZED FEEDBACK ALONG THE WAY.

CHRONOLOGY

21

Things Blow Up

Katikati, New Zealand, is a small agricultural town with a lively arts community and tourist business on the country's northern island. Settled by migrants from northern Ireland in 1875 on land confiscated from the native Maori, it is a quiet, peaceful, ordinary place. And with no less than 11,500 miles separating it from Belgium and northern France, it seems as remote as any spot on earth from the blood-soaked battlefields of 1914–18.

Yet at the center of Katikati stands a War Memorial Hall. A nearby bay is named for the Australian and New Zealand Army Corps (ANZAC) and its disastrous landing on Turkey's Gallipoli Peninsula in 1915. In a nature park a quarter-mile out of town, beneath a kauri tree, lies a plaque commemorating the armistice of 1918. And at the park's entrance stand memorial gates bearing the names of ten men who left Katikati between 1915 and 1918 and never returned home. Henry Pritt fell at Gallipoli in August 1915. Albert Squinobal, a twenty-six-year-old farmer, died at the Somme fifteen months later and was buried "in a grave known only to God." Otto Diggelmann, age twenty-two, also a farmer and of German ancestry, was shot in the head in October 1918 and died in England just two weeks before the war's end. There are seven more, including two grandsons of the town's founder. Fifty other men from Katikati went off to the war and survived, but nineteen of

No-Man's-Land The British war artist Paul Nash uses modernist forms and stark color to depict the unprecedented destruction of World War I in his 1919 painting *The Menin Road*. Soldiers trek across a barren battlefield littered with debris and shattered trees. Smoke rises from artillery fire in the background.

FOCUS QUESTIONS

- What were the major causes of World War I?
- How were the basic patterns of the war set in its early years?
- In what ways was World War I a total war?
- How did the strains of war make themselves felt in the later years?
- What were the basic causes of the Russian Revolution?
- How did World War I finally come to an end?

them were wounded, four more than once. And all this from a town that in 1915 had just 400 inhabitants. A war fought on the opposite side of the globe remains, by far, the most traumatic event in Katikati's history, and vividly illustrates why it deserves to be called the First World War. In its aftermath, many simply called it the Great War.

Katikati's experience was a tragically typical one. In New Zealand, fully 42 percent of men between the ages of nineteen and forty-five went to fight in Europe, and over half of these—58 percent—were killed or wounded. Katikati's war memorial is just one of 500 in the country. And although New Zealand, as a loyal dominion of the British Empire, sent an exceptionally large proportion of its young men to the European slaughterhouse, similar monuments appear throughout the Western world: in remote cattle towns on the Canadian plains; in Oxford colleges; in industrial city centers in Germany; in the villages of Serbia. The bodies of the fallen lie in cemeteries throughout Europe, under endless rows of white crosses or simple headstones, or crammed namelessly into ossuaries. The vaults of the ossuary of Douaumont, near the battlefields of Verdun in eastern France, contain the bones of 130,000 unidentified French and German soldiers.

If Europe between 1880 and 1910 had seemed to reach its apogee, dominating the globe and attaining unprecedented levels of wealth and comfort, one can say that between 1914 and 1918 it fell bloodily to earth. Historians generally dislike making large-scale generalizations about collective psychology, but they agree that what took place on the Continent in these years inflicted a brutal, collective trauma on

populations throughout the world, and especially in Europe. Most immediately, the war killed and maimed a higher proportion of that population than any other European catastrophe since the Thirty Years' War of the seventeenth century, and it did so more quickly than anything since the Black Death three hundred years before that. It left the survivors shocked, dispirited, and cynical—with a sense of living in what the future British leader Winston Churchill called "a crippled, broken world." It destroyed two empires, the Ottoman and the Habsburg, and toppled the regimes of two others, in Russia and Germany. It was a decisive factor behind the most significant—and, ultimately, the most violent—of modern European revolutions, in Russia. It helped give birth to the rise of fascist regimes, most immediately in Italy and later in Germany and elsewhere. Although defined by many of its participants as "the war to end all wars," it created the conditions under which the world would go to war again, even more horrifically, just two decades later.

The First World War was, quite simply, one of the greatest disasters in world history. And while Europeans on all sides justified their participation in grandiose terms, calling it a war for peace and for civilization, even at the time those justifications rang hollow. Today very few people think the war was worth the cost.

ORIGINS

The war's horrors have long overshadowed and distorted the search for its origins. How, it is asked agonizingly, could rational, responsible statesmen possibly have led their peoples into such a cataclysm? The question has obsessed generations of historians, who have pored over every scrap of paper pertaining to pre-war planning and every link in the chain of decisions that led to the outbreak of hostilities. But the question presumes that the statesmen had at least a premonition of the horrors to come. Not all of them did.

WAR PLANS

Upon the outbreak of the war in August 1914, the British foreign secretary, Sir Edward Grey (1862–1933), uttered a lament that has become famous: "The lamps are going out all over Europe. We shall not see them lit again in our time." Yet Grey was in a minority. Far more statesmen had the attitude of Germany's Kaiser Wilhelm II, who thought the conflict would take the form of a quick, invigorating adventure and who told troops departing for the front that they would be home again before the leaves fell. The German General Staff based its war strategy on the so-called **Schlieffen Plan**, finalized by Count Alfred von Schlieffen (1833–1913) in 1905, which laid out steps to achieve victory over France in just forty-two days, with a longer campaign against Russia to follow. All of the major countries involved based their military planning on the assumption that a war would move at industrial speed and be decided by a handful of monumental offensives. The recent history of the West seemed to support that assumption: with the exception of the American Civil War (1861–1865), it offered several compelling examples of quick and decisive wars, such as Prussia's victories over Austria in 1866 and France in 1870, or Japan's over Russia in 1904–5.

And while the outbreak of war in 1914 dismayed many, few found it mysterious. Most observers took it for granted that ambitious, aggressive nations will naturally come to blows. Nonetheless, the outbreak of war was not inevitable. If most statesmen anticipated a quick and decisive conflict, they knew they were taking large risks. The years, months, and days before the fighting were marked by incessant calculation and recalculation of these risks, and the final decisions to move ahead rested in part on the classic gambler's mixture of faith and hope that the odds had turned in the right direction. Other factors of course mattered too, including national pride, sheer chance, pure blundering, the structures of European diplomacy, and the codes of honor whose obligations ensnared elites across the Continent.

GERMAN AMBITIONS

The story starts with Germany. Its unification and emergence as a major power were the most important European geopolitical developments of the late nineteenth and early twentieth centuries. Germany's rapidly increasing economic and military strength, and its leaders' obvious ambitions, upset the European balance of power that had largely prevailed since the Congress of Vienna in 1815. Fearing that Germany, with its large population and industrial capacity, could come to dominate the Continent, Britain and France put aside their age-old rivalry for good. As we have seen, the two countries had nearly gone to war over competing ambitions in Sudan as late as 1898; now they became steadfast allies. The same dynamic also

eventually drove both these democracies into the arms of autocratic Russia, which the British had long seen as their principal rival on the international stage. By 1907, Europe had split into two antagonistic blocs: the Triple Alliance of Germany, Austria-Hungary, and Italy; and the Franco-British-Russian Triple Entente.

For the latter, a fear that Germany would continue to rise generated a willingness to go to war sooner rather than later. But the Germans themselves were anything but confident about their future, and continually worried that the odds against *them* were increasing. Thus came about the Moroccan Crises of 1905 and 1911, in which the Germans challenged France's right to establish a protectorate over the North African state in the hope of checking any further expansion of French power on the African continent. The Germans also hoped that casting France as an aggressor might isolate it diplomatically and put pressure on the Franco-British partnership. But in both episodes, the British stood by their allies and international mediation averted a conflict. By now, a thick web of diplomatic connections existed between the major powers, as well as close family relationships between the major royal houses (Germany's emperor Wilhelm II and Tsarina Alexandra of Russia were both grandchildren of Britain's Queen Victoria). Still, at both of these moments, war seemed more likely than it did to most observers in the spring of 1914.

NATIONALISM AND EMPIRE IN SOUTHEASTERN EUROPE

A second set of long-term causes of the war involved nationalism and the threat it posed to two empires that the war ultimately smashed to pieces: Austria-Hungary and Ottoman Turkey. Neither empire was as fragile as is sometimes thought, especially before 1900. The Austrian Habsburgs had developed a workable relationship with the empire's largest national minority, the Hungarians, and affection for the dynasty went beyond the German-speaking minority. As for the Ottomans, their long practice of providing a degree of autonomy and protection for different ethnic and religious communities, combined with opportunities for groups such as Albanians and Greeks in the Ottoman military, administration, and commerce, continued to keep the empire viable long after its military weakness had made it known as the Sick Man of Europe. But by 1908, tensions in both empires reached dangerous levels. And in both cases, the center of tension was the Balkan Peninsula.

IMPERIAL COMPETITION IN THE BALKANS The Balkan Peninsula had a long tradition of violence stemming partly from its volatile mix of religious and ethnic groups and partly from its strategic position in relation to the Austro-Hungarian, Ottoman, and Russian empires. As we have seen, Ottoman control over the Balkans had begun to crumble in the 1820s with the war for Greek independence. By 1900, Greece, Romania, Serbia, Montenegro, and Bulgaria were all independent, leaving Turkey with a narrow strip of territory cutting through the peninsula's heart to predominantly Muslim Albania on the Adriatic coast.

The triangular territory of Bosnia-Herzegovina, to the west of Serbia—divided then as now between Muslim Bosnians and Christian Orthodox Serbs, with a smaller admixture of Catholic Croats—had come under Austro-Hungarian occupation in 1878, although it remained theoretically still under Ottoman sovereignty. Its acquisition proved problematic for the Habsburgs, for it spurred the resentment of Serbian nationalists who hoped to join all the "Yugoslav" (southern Slav) territories into a single Serbian-led nation. The revolutionary Serb group the Black Hand resisted Austro-Hungarian rule in the name of this cause and wielded enormous influence in Serbia itself. In 1903, its members staged a coup there, assassinating the king and queen. Russia, meanwhile, lent support to Serbia in the name of pan-Slavism (the brotherhood of Slav peoples) and the hope that any new Yugoslav state would become its ally. In 1908, the Habsburgs decided formally to annex Bosnia-Herzegovina so as to integrate its population as swiftly as possible into the empire.

TURMOIL IN TURKEY In the Ottoman Empire, tensions came in large part from the capital, Constantinople. In the 1870s, a new sultan, Abdulhamid II (r. 1872–1909), had come to the throne and raised hopes in Europe that his regime would move toward Western democratic practices. A new constitution established parliamentary rule and equality before the law. But Abdulhamid reneged on his promises and, in a break with Ottoman precedent, initiated brutal persecution of non-Muslims, especially Armenian Christians living in what is now Armenia and eastern Turkey. In response, forward-looking opponents of the regime founded a Committee of Union and Progress in Paris. And in 1908 its members, known as the **Young Turks**, staged a coup, forcing the reintroduction of Abdulhamid's constitution but causing further disruption. Exploiting the situation, Italy undertook its successful conquest of Ottoman-ruled Libya in 1911. Soon afterward

The Balkans, 1913 By 1913, a number of Balkan states had established their independence, and in the Balkan wars of 1912–13 they almost entirely ejected the Ottoman Empire from the peninsula. But continued Ottoman and Austro-Hungarian interest in the Balkans—including the Austro-Hungarian annexation of Bosnia-Herzegovina—contributed to the volatile political situation that led to World War I.

Serbia, Bulgaria, Montenegro, and Greece formed a Balkan League and defeated Turkey in the short First Balkan War of 1912. After dividing up nearly all the rest of the Ottomans' European territory, however, the victors fell out, leading to a Second Balkan War (1913) in which Serbia and Greece took territory from Bulgaria, and Albania saw its independence (proclaimed the year before) confirmed.

ARMS RACES AND MILITARY MOBILIZATION

The two Moroccan crises, the Bosnian crisis, and the two Balkan wars, all driven by nationalist rivalries and occurring within just eight years, amplified anxieties about a general European war. These anxieties also drove a massive, unprecedented arms race. In just the five years from 1908 to 1913, the six countries that made up the Triple Alliance and Triple Entente collectively increased their military spending by 50 percent. Factories turned out guns and ammunition, armies stockpiled supplies, and shipyards rushed to build Dreadnoughts—a new class of battleship almost as long as two football fields, bristling with heavy artillery and protected by metal armor up to eleven inches thick. A single vessel cost the British the then-enormous sum of over 1.5 million pounds. But at this moment in history, warfare had not yet become entirely mechanized. The major powers also still relied heavily on a very longstanding auxiliary of Western armies—horses—to transport men and supplies where train tracks did not reach (although, as we will see, they did build tracks in some areas of the front).

Alongside these vast expenses, the process of mobilizing a country's military—calling up reserve soldiers from civilian life, getting them equipped, and transporting them to the right places, along with the necessary weaponry and supplies—was costly and time-consuming. Even before the war, the combatants realized they would need to put tens of millions of men into uniform (together, they ultimately deployed no fewer than 74 million). German mobilization plans involved a schedule of some 11,000 train trips, calculated down to the minute. So if one country mobilized, its adversaries faced enormous pressure to do the same or risk getting caught unprepared. The same factors put ever-greater pressure on the European alliances to coordinate their actions during a crisis, to ensure that if one country entered into war, its partners would be ready to support it.

MILITARISM AND THE MARCH TO WAR

The general population's attitudes toward a possible war remained distinctly mixed. Socialists and pacifists throughout Europe insisted that class solidarity should trump nationality. French and German Socialist leaders traveled to each other's countries to pledge that their members would not take up arms if a conflict broke out. Keir Hardie (1856–1915), a founder of Britain's radical Independent Labour Party, organized a massive peace demonstration in London shortly before Britain's declaration of war in 1914. Yet at the same time, the idea that a society might purge and cleanse itself through warfare remained frighteningly powerful. In 1909, the Italian

Dreadnoughts A postcard shows the British battleship HMS *Dreadnought*, in 1906, leaving the shipyard where it was built. Employing the very latest developments in steam power and weaponry, it was indicative of increases in military spending during the pre-war arms race.

writer Filippo Tommaso Marinetti (1876–1944) composed a manifesto for the so-called Futurist group of artists in which he called war "the only hygiene of the world ...we want to glorify war." Similarly, the London *Daily Mail* argued in 1912 that "peace may and has ruined many a nationality with its surfeit of everything except those tonics of privation and sacrifice." Modernist critiques of "decadent" bourgeois society all too easily fed the perception that only a purifying war could save the West from inevitable decline.

With many Europeans seeing war as inevitable, national leaders not surprisingly looked for the best moment to start it on their own terms. As early as 1911, the chief of the German General Staff, Helmuth von Moltke, openly expressed his belief that a war would come soon. During the Second Moroccan Crisis he pressed his government "to make an energetic demand which we are prepared to enforce with the sword." Many other statesmen and soldiers across the Continent shared von Moltke's point of view to some degree. "We shall have a war. I will make it, and I will win it," declared France's marshal, Joseph Joffre (1852–1931), in 1911. It only required the right combination of circumstances for these men's collective calculations to unleash an inferno.

THE SPARK In the summer of 1914, these circumstances materialized. On June 28, Archduke Franz Ferdinand (1863–1914), heir to the throne of the Austro-Hungarian Empire, paid a visit to Sarajevo, capital of Bosnia-Herzegovina. The city's appearance itself vividly expressed the tensions of the region, with traditional Ottoman market streets leading into broad new boulevards equipped with tramways in which the western Latin script had displaced the older Cyrillic. Franz Ferdinand, although a temperamental, unpopular figure, was more favorable to South Slav aspirations than most Austrian leaders. But his relatively liberal political views did not stop a motley group of Bosnian Serb terrorists from hatching a plot to kill him. These terrorists were not skilled commandos but young, half-trained, excitable men. Their initial attempt to bomb the archduke's motorcade on the morning of June 28 turned into something of a farce. Two assassins failed to throw their bombs, while a third bounced his bomb off the back of Franz Ferdinand's car, leaving it to detonate under the following vehicle.

But what the terrorists lacked in competence was made up for by the incompetence of their enemies and by sheer dumb luck. Following the failed bombing, Franz Ferdinand and his wife decided to visit wounded victims in the hospital. His car turned by mistake onto a side street, tried to reverse, and stalled. By chance, one of the terrorists, Gaurilo Princip (1894–1918), a twenty-year-old, was in the

Assassination of Franz Ferdinand In a contemporary illustration from an Italian newspaper, Gavrilo Princip emerges from a crowd with his pistol drawn. Soldiers lunge forward, but they are unable to stop him from shooting the archduke and his wife.

street having stopped at a nearby delicatessen for a bite to eat. He whipped out a pistol, pushed his way forward, and fired two shots into the car. One pierced Franz Ferdinand's jugular vein, and the other hit his wife in the stomach. Within an hour, both were dead.

THE MOVE TOWARD WAR The assassination of Archduke Franz Ferdinand caused a furor in Austria and led to calls for revenge on Serbia, whose secret police was immediately suspected of complicity. In fact, the Black Hand, which still wielded influence in Serbia, particularly in the secret police, had provided supplies and advice to the assassins. Germany's Kaiser Wilhelm shared in the outrage and urged Austria-Hungary to take forceful measures against the Serbs. The Germans and Austrians knew the risks involved. Russia might intervene to protect Serbia, and hostilities between Russia and Austria-Hungary might oblige their allies to fight as well, leading to a general war. But even while hoping that Russia would hesitate before taking sides with terrorists and assassins, the two German-speaking powers were prepared to fight. "If we must go under, we had better go under decently," the Austrian emperor Franz Josef reportedly remarked.

There followed weeks of tense diplomatic exchanges during which Austria-Hungary quietly recalled soldiers who had taken leave to work on their family farms. As usual in summer, European elites departed on vacation. General von Moltke enjoyed a few days at a Bohemian spa. But the appearance of normality was deceptive. Even as Austria prepared to present Serbia with harsh terms, the Russians made clear that they would not stand by and see their fellow Slavs overrun. Nonetheless, on July 23, Austria-Hungary demanded that Serbia take immediate action to suppress anti-Austrian activity, including censoring publications, banning independence organizations, and—most provocatively—giving Austrian officials free rein to interrogate and arrest Serbian citizens on Serbian soil. Even as the diplomatic exchanges reached a desperate crescendo, Serbia refused this last demand and ordered its forces to mobilize. Austria mobilized in turn, and Germany refused a last-minute offer of British mediation. On July 28, Austrian gunboats opened fire from the Danube River on the Serbian capital of Belgrade.

THE OUTBREAK OF WAR At this point, fears of being caught unprepared began to overwhelm all other considerations. The transformation of an Austro-Serbian skirmish into World War I took just one week. After two days of anxious vacillation, Tsar Nikolai II ordered a general mobilization on July 30 against both Austria-Hungary and Germany—a step that in practice would have been enormously difficult to reverse. Germany nonetheless demanded that Russia step down and, upon receiving no response, declared war against Russia on August 1. France now acted to fulfill its treaty of alliance with Russia, rejecting German requests that it remain neutral.

The Germans prepared to implement an updated version of the 1905 Schlieffen Plan, which called on the German army to make a great arc through neutral Belgium and sweep into France from the north. When the Germans demanded Belgium's permission to cross its territory, the Belgians refused and Germany invaded. Britain had so far hesitated to fulfill its own treaty promises to France and Russia. Prime Minister Herbert Asquith (1852–1928) wrote to a friend that the country might yet remain a "spectator," even while warning that "we are within measurable . . . distance of a real Armageddon." But German aggression against Belgium, a country the British had long regarded as belonging to its sphere of influence, smashed hopes for British neutrality. On August 4, Britain declared war on Germany. All the combatants now completed their mobilization, and as early as August 5 fighting had started along a long arc from southern Alsace to central Belgium.

The Schlieffen Plan

INTO THE ABYSS (1914–1915)

For nearly a hundred years, starting with the Congress of Vienna, Europe had avoided a war involving all of the major powers. Despite the many smaller wars that had occurred, the diplomatic safeguards set in place by the exhausted victors of the struggle against Napoleon had continued, more or less, to function. But in 1914, diplomatic considerations crumbled before fears that restraint—a delay in mobilization, a reluctance to strike first—might lead to quick defeat. And so Europe hurtled into the abyss.

PUBLIC ATTITUDES

Popular reactions to the outbreak of war were anything but uniform. The pacifists and socialists who dreamed of workers defying the call to arms met with bitter

disappointment. Only 1.5 percent of French reservists did not report when mobilized—far fewer than the government feared. The percentage was barely different in Austria-Hungary, despite the nationalist turmoil there. In Britain, 750,000 men, including over half the undergraduates at Oxford and Cambridge, voluntarily enlisted in the armed forces just in the months of August and September 1914, overwhelming recruiting offices. Emmeline Pankhurst, leader of the British woman suffrage movement, broke off contact with her pacifist daughter Sylvia and ordered members of the Women's Social and Political Union to suspend political protests in the name of national unity. The one antimilitarist leader in Europe who might have rallied significant numbers against the war was the charismatic French Socialist leader Jean Jaurès (1859–1914). And on July 31, 1914, just as France prepared to enter the war, a nationalist militant shot him dead in a Parisian cafe.

Many onlookers and participants in fact saw the war as a welcome release from peacetime frustrations. Adolf Hitler (1889–1945), an indigent and sometimes homeless Austrian artist, had failed to meet the physical requirements for Austrian military service in February 1914. In August, in Munich, he joined a crowd cheering Germany's declaration of war. "I sank to my knees and thanked heaven that it had given me the good fortune to live at such a time," the future dictator who would lead Germany into World War II wrote a decade later. (Hitler enlisted in the German army and spent the entire war at the front.) The young British poet Rupert Brooke (1887–1915) spoke for many when he compared his war-bound generation to "swimmers into cleanness leaping / Glad from a world grown old and cold and weary." (Less than a year later, he died of an infected mosquito bite while on service with the Royal Navy.)

Even so, true war fervor was most often brief and did not extend to entire populations. Especially outside of major urban centers, a sense of patriotic duty and grim determination predominated. Some writers, like Britain's H. G. Wells (1866–1944), hoped that the war would prove a last great spasm of violence before an age of perpetual peace: it was he who coined the phrase *the war to end all wars*. Politicians on both sides—the so-called Allies (France, Britain, and Russia, soon to be joined by Italy) and the Central powers (Germany, Austria-Hungary, Turkey, and, belatedly,

Bulgaria)—appealed for public support with lofty speeches about fighting for "civilization" against "barbarism" or (in the case of German rhetoric) "decadence." And many people looked upon the coming conflict with nothing but dread. The Russian poet Anna Akhmatova wrote that in the month of July 1914 "we grew a hundred years older." And she continued, describing the moment:

> Out of the mind, like a burden now fled,
> There vanished all traces of passion and song.
> And in their place the Almighty now read
> From a book of portents, horrific and long.

EARLY GERMAN SUCCESSES

Early in the war, the German army gave Allied propagandists altogether too much material to support the idea that Germans were a new barbarian horde threatening civilization. In order to have any hope of prevailing against enemies on both east and west, German strategy, as formulated in the Schlieffen Plan, called for a victory over France in just six weeks, before the vast but lumbering Russian military could fully mobilize. Furthermore, the German army was committed to carrying out what its tactical doctrine referred to as "absolute destruction" against civilian populations to reach its objectives. When in August 1914 the Belgians put up unexpectedly stiff resistance to German forces, the Germans shot over 5,000 Belgian hostages, burned whole sections of Belgian towns, and turned a blind eye to their troops raping women and despoiling civilian property. Lurid atrocity stories circulated in the French and British press and were relayed personally by Belgian refugees, of whom a quarter of a million fled across the English Channel.

Despite the Belgian resistance, the first weeks of the conflict went well for Germany and fit the pattern of rapid, mobile warfare, punctuated by massive battles, that its General Staff had expected. On August 23, the German First Army fought the British Expeditionary Force around the Belgian town of Mons, near the French border, and forced it into a two-week-long retreat. But the same day, more than eight hundred miles to the east, a Russian army over 400,000 strong, which had mobilized with unexpected speed, approached German East Prussia. In a week-long struggle that became known as the battle of Tannenberg, the well-organized and well-equipped Germans, commanded by Paul von Hindenburg (1847–1934), massacred the Russian force and a week later forced it back over the Russian border. The battle cost the Russians dear:

German Atrocities in Belgium An apelike German soldier clutching a smoking rifle menaces a defenseless Belgian woman in this French cartoon (1915). The illustration is representative of Allied perceptions of the German army's brutal treatment of Belgian civilians.

They lost close to 200,000 men killed and wounded in the battle, and over 100,000 prisoners. Russia would not again threaten German territory during the war. The despairing Russian commander committed suicide. But the battle also helped, at a crucial moment, to relieve pressure on the Western Allies in Belgium and France by diverting German troops east.

BEGINNINGS OF THE STALEMATE

German strategy dictated quick victory over France, but in 1914 this victory failed to materialize. The Germans closed to within thirty miles of Paris in the first week of September. But they had deployed crucial troops away from the western front to hold back the Russians, and more to defend Alsace against a French attack. They were plagued by hesitation and poor communications among their generals. French scorched-earth tactics disrupted their supply chain. And Italy, the supposed ally of Germany and Austria-Hungary, failed to enter the war, allowing the French to redeploy troops from its southern

World War I, 1914–1916 The war remained a stalemate on the western front in France and Belgium, with neither army advancing despite several protracted, bloody battles. Conflict in the Balkans saw an Austro-Hungarian invasion of Serbia and the failed invasion of Gallipoli by British imperial troops. Successive waves of invasion on the German-Russian border saw territory change hands frequently, as well as high casualty rates. Meanwhile, German use of submarines won victories of a different kind, cutting off Allied supply lines in the Atlantic Ocean and the North Sea.

Alpine border to the north. Finally, at a crucial moment, a twentieth-century innovation—aerial reconnaissance—enabled the French to identify a weak spot on the Germans' flank as they crossed the Marne River. French commanders rushed troops into the line, even commandeering

600 Parisian taxis to help carry them, and the Germans retreated.

YPRES In late October and early November, the Germans made one last attempt to sweep around the British and French toward the English Channel, in the so-called Race to the Sea. A desperate battle ensued around the town of Ypres in western Belgium (the British troops, not knowing how to pronounce the name, called it Wipers), where the Germans again found their way blocked. And this time, in the mud and rain, the combatants' great industrial war machines locked gears with one another and stalled. Over half the Germans' trucks broke down, while horses died for lack of adequate feed (they required 2 million pounds of it per day). Meanwhile, the use of high-powered machine guns and high-explosive shells against infantry in the open field—and even more against the brightly uniformed cavalry to which the generals on both sides remained stubbornly attached—was causing insupportable carnage. By the end of 1914, fully 300,000 French and German soldiers had died, along with one-third of the original British Expeditionary Force.

TRENCH WARFARE And so the front lines froze in place, and both sides began to fortify them with deep trenches, fronted with sandbags or walls of earth. Quickly

Trench Warfare In this photo from 1917, German troops stand shoulder-to-shoulder in narrow, neck-deep trenches during a break between battles.

they learned to build several rows of trenches and to lay impenetrable thickets of barbed wire, up to 100 feet wide and 5 feet high, in front of them. As 1915 began, such trench systems ran for hundreds of miles through Belgium and northern France. Sheltering in the trenches, troops were safe from gunfire and anything but a direct hit from artillery. And from the trenches, they could sweep the battlefield in front of them with machine gun fire, cutting down enemies floundering through barbed-wire barriers. So the fighting continued, but neither side could advance.

ATTEMPTS AT BREAKTHROUGH

At this point, the war took a tragic turn. Stabilization of the western front, and the beginnings of **trench warfare**, made it impossible for the armies to fight mobile, decisive campaigns. But neither the generals nor the civilian leaderships could accept the new circumstances. Commanders like Sir John French (1852–1925), who led the British Expeditionary Force, remained stubbornly attached to the old tactics. He insisted that the moment would soon come to release the British cavalry, which he imagined charging triumphantly past the trenches, across ranks of dazed Germans, as if in a replay of the battle of Waterloo. Faced with trench warfare, the generals became obsessed with the idea of a breakthrough that would allow a return to these older and supposedly more honorable forms of combat. And they assumed that only brute force would allow them to achieve it: first bombarding the enemy trenches with the greatest possible quantity of explosive shells, and then sending wave after wave of infantry to attack through the barbed wire until the enemy crumbled. But such was the advantage enjoyed by the defenders that these tactics accomplished little. Most of the shells burst harmlessly outside the trenches, and the infantry smashed against the enemy machine guns like so much human porcelain.

All too typical was the British attempt to break through German lines near the French village of Neuve Chapelle in mid-March 1915. The British commanders planned an early-morning artillery barrage, to be followed by an infantry assault by 40,000 British and Indian troops. They hoped that once the lead German trenches had fallen, the cavalry could follow. But the barrage accomplished little, and the infantry found themselves trapped in the open, caught on barbed wire, and easy prey. Just two German machine guns killed a thousand men, and by the time Sir John French suspended the attack two days later, the British had suffered 13,000 casualties (that is, killed, wounded, and missing) in exchange for less than a mile of ground. An offensive directed by Marshal Joffre in Champagne did scarcely better and cost 145,000 French killed and wounded. But the British, French, and Germans all continued to try variant after variant on the same plan, turning the front into a slaughterhouse. In the year 1915 alone, total casualties on the western front surpassed 2 million. And total Allied gains amounted to exactly 8 of the nearly 20,000 square miles of France and Belgium occupied by Germany.

TOWARD TOTAL WAR

The sheer scale of the war, and the ghastly tactics developed on the western front, imposed a brutal logic on the war efforts of both sides: strategic skill mattered less than sheer volume. Whoever managed to put the most men, weaponry, and ammunition into the field would have the advantage. And this logic put enormous pressure on what was being called the home front—the millions of civilian men and women who were not in uniform but who were nonetheless called on to sacrifice and contribute to the war effort.

THE HOME FRONT

From the earliest periods of European history, warfare had taken a ferocious toll on noncombatants, and by the time of Napoleon the notion of mobilizing an entire society for war had become firmly established. But in World War I, governments could exercise considerably more control over economies and societies than in previous centuries, and they did so with remarkable results. The goal of **total war**—the phrase itself first appeared toward the end of the conflict—was coming closer to realization.

MANPOWER The most pressing concern was military manpower. Most countries employed conscription at the start of the war, subjecting all young men to military service without possibility of substitution, and backed it up with intensive government recruitment drives. Britain only resorted to conscription in 1916 as its own need for manpower increased, but even before that an enormous stigma attached to young British men who did not volunteer. The British novelist Mary Ward (1851–1920) helped found the Order of the White Feather, whose female members presented this traditional symbol of cowardice to healthy young men they saw in civilian clothes. In every country, the numbers of people in military service

Women and Recruitment British women such as those who joined the Order of the White Feather played a significant role in promoting patriotism and commitment to the war effort. The government also capitalized on women's influence, as in this 1915 recruitment poster that shows both a wealthy woman and a working-class woman united in urging men to enlist.

set records, with Russia calling up an astonishing 14.6 million—over a quarter of all adult men. Sometimes overly intensive recruitment efforts could actually hurt the war effort—in 1915, France had to release half a million skilled workers from the army to aid in munitions production at home.

ECONOMIC PLANNING As in France, governments everywhere took larger and more direct roles in their economies. They worked with industrialists to optimize production for the war effort and spent overall far more than they had before 1914. In Britain, government spending as a percentage of gross domestic product (the total value of goods and services) rose nearly fivefold, from 8.1 percent in

1913 to 38.7 percent in 1917. In both France and Germany, by 1918 the figure topped 50 percent. The British government founded a Munitions Ministry in 1915, which took over management of much of the armaments industry and even built its own factories. The government also took control of the railroads and shipping, and restricted industrial output unrelated to the war effort. The huge increase in the proportion of munitions manufacturing caused the production of consumer goods and services to fall. In 1918, with supplies of food from the Americas threatened by German submarines, the British government imposed food rationing. Families were issued weekly ration cards with which the could buy limited quantities of meat, milk, sugar, flour, and other basic products—but no more. Even the king and queen received ration cards. Similar measures were taken by the other Allies.

Among the Central powers, the need for economic coordination was even greater. At the start of the war, their combined economic output stood at just one-quarter that of the Allies, making it even more necessary for them to direct every possible resource to the war effort. In Germany, coordination between the state and private industry (notably the Krupp firm) grew so tight that Russian Communists later took it as a model for their own central planning. With food imports largely cut off by a British blockade, Germany began a strict regime of food rationing in 1915.

WAR FINANCE Paying for the war also became a critical challenge for all of the combatants. Every country carried out strenuous propaganda campaigns urging its population to buy war bonds, which amounted to loans to the government. Taxes were increased. In Britain, the standard rate of income tax rose from 6 percent in 1914 to 30 percent in 1918. Governments also resorted to printing money, resulting in high inflation rates (up to 400 percent over the course of the war in the case of Italy). To do so, they had to abandon the gold standard to which they had pegged their currencies since the late nineteenth century. The three major Allied powers—Britain, France, and Russia—used their combined gold reserves as collateral on a massive series of loans from American banks, above all the firm of J. P. Morgan, which enabled them to purchase food and war materiel from American firms. Well before the entry of the United States into the war in 1917, these loans effectively tied America to the Allied side.

PROPAGANDA The propaganda campaigns launched by all the combatant nations made use of both literature and the visual arts. Garish war posters proliferated on city and

Wartime Propaganda Recruitment posters drew on the latest advertising techniques, including eye-catching, colorful illustrations and bold slogans, to encourage participation in the war. This German poster from the war reads: "Your Fatherland is in danger: Enlist!"

town walls urging citizens to purchase war bonds, to avoid "loose talk" that might reveal military secrets to enemy spies, and above all, if they were young men, to enlist. The Allies exploited accounts of rapes committed by Germans in occupied Belgium and France, depicting the enemy as horrific wild beasts. Germany's execution of a British nurse, Edith Cavell, for helping Allied soldiers escape from Belgium became central to British propaganda efforts. In Russia, propaganda activities were accompanied by government programs aimed at identifying and surveilling "suspect" ethnic groups, including the German-speakers who lived along the Volga River and also the Russian Jewish population. Civilian institutions added fervent voices to the bellicose chorus as well—including churches. In 1915, the bishop of London gave a sermon urging his listeners to "Kill Germans! Kill them!... Not for the sake of killing, but to save the world.... Kill the good as well as the bad."

WOMEN'S PARTICIPATION

Although only Russia of the belligerent nations permitted women to fight alongside men—and that only in 1917—the war brought major changes to women's lives. At the front, they served as nurses, ambulance drivers, and cooks. Back home, with virtually all able-bodied men away at war, women entered the labor force in vast numbers: over a million in Austria-Hungary by war's end, and 400,000 in Britain just in the war's first year. In Britain, the proportion of adult women earning wages rose from 24 percent to 37 percent over the course of the war. Governments encouraged this shift, as did most women's movements. Women particularly took on jobs in munitions factories. As we have seen, after constituting a considerable proportion of the industrial workforce early in the nineteenth century, women had gradually been driven from the factory floor. But in World War I, they came back in force, as well as taking up more of what now seemed "conventional" female jobs such as nursing and secretarial work.

The long-term implications of these shifts can be exaggerated. Once the war ended, the percentage of female participation in the workforce returned to pre-war levels in most countries. Yet the wartime experiences showed women capable of a wider range of work than most pre-war observers had allowed for, including jobs as mechanics and factory workers in sectors such as munitions production. Female membership in trade unions rose to record levels. In Russia, women entered the most stereotypically male profession of all when the government approved the creation of several battalions of women soldiers in 1917. One of them, the Women's Battalion of Death, led by a former laborer named Maria Bochkareva (1889–1920), briefly saw action in the summer of 1917 and made a lasting impression on European women's movements.

The wartime sacrifices and contributions made by women in Britain played a major role in leading Parliament to grant the vote to most women over age thirty (with all British adult women finally enfranchised in 1928). Germany, too, and several other European countries, including Russia, would give women the vote at the war's end. Woman suffrage occurred in the United States with ratification of the Nineteenth Amendment to the Constitution in 1920.

THE EXPANDING THEATER OF WAR

As the fighting dragged on, the Allies and the Central powers put ever-greater demands on their colonial empires, turning the European war into a global war. France extended conscription to men in some of its African colonies, while Britain urged its former white settler colonies, now autonomous dominions, to help the mother country. Young men from Katikati and the rest of New Zealand willingly volunteered, as did millions of others in Australia, Canada, and South Africa. Meanwhile, the fighting itself extended abroad. British, French, and Belgian troops attacked German colonies in East Africa, where German troops engaged in stubborn guerrilla resistance until 1918. The Union of South Africa overran German Southwest Africa, putting an end to that tragic chapter in German colonial history. In East Asia, Japan had already entered the war on the Allied side in 1914, fighting naval battles with the Germans and capturing German outposts in China.

The geographical scope of the war increased within Europe as well. Even as hostilities were breaking out in the summer of 1914, Ottoman Turkey, now ruled by the Young Turks, signed a treaty with Germany that promised

Women and the War A remarkable photo from the summer of 1917 shows Maria Bochkareva embracing the British suffragist leader Emmeline Pankhurst: two very different faces of European feminism. Pankhurst even wears a military decoration, suggestive of their common dedication to the war effort.

Turkey rich rewards in the Balkans and German economic help in return for its entry into the war. In response, the Allies began greedily to plot the partition of the Ottoman Empire, with France and Britain secretly promising Russia control of Constantinople and allotting themselves spheres of influence in the Arab world. In 1915, another ally joined the Central powers: Bulgaria, which hoped to regain territory taken by Serbia in the Second Balkan War. And the same year Italy, having abandoned the Central powers, entered the war on the Allied side, leading to long and costly battles with Austria-Hungary in difficult, mountainous terrain. So by 1915 the war had four separate European fronts: western, Italian, Balkan, and eastern.

THE EASTERN FRONT

Of these four fronts, the eastern and Balkan remained the most volatile and rarely bogged down into the sort of trench warfare seen in the west. While Russia's early assault on East Prussia failed spectacularly at Tannenberg, the country did better against Austria-Hungary in 1914, advancing into Galicia (a region straddling the border between modern Poland and Ukraine) and occupying the strategic city of Lvov. A Habsburg attempt to repel the Russians early in 1915 failed, costing Austria-Hungary some 350,000 dead and wounded. But then in May the Germans came to the aid of their allies. In a successful six-month offensive, they drove the Russians back 300 miles along a front that stretched for twice that distance. By autumn, all of present-day Poland, most of Lithuania, and large portions of Latvia, Belarus, and Ukraine had fallen under German and Austrian occupation. Meanwhile, in the fall of 1915 Austria-Hungary and Bulgaria managed to overrun most of Serbia.

These campaigns, like the ones we have seen in the west, took an enormous toll. Not only did Russia suffer a staggering 1.4 million casualties in the 1915 German offensive alone; it carried out a scorched-earth policy, destroying its own towns, farms, railroads, and food stockpiles to keep them from falling into German hands. The Russian army also forced local populations—especially non-Russians such as Ukrainians and Jews who the army feared might collaborate with the enemy—to flee east deeper into Russia: some 3 million people in 1915 alone became internal refugees. But Russia did not suffer as badly as Serbia, where a brutal Austrian occupation, widespread famine, and one of the worst typhus epidemics in history produced a human catastrophe. Estimates of the total loss of life in Serbia during the war vary from one-sixth to well over one-fifth of the entire population. Casualties among adult males ran over 50 percent.

THE GALLIPOLI CAMPAIGN

In 1915, the British tried to open up a front in Turkey. The initiative here belonged to the boisterous, forty-year-old Winston Churchill (1874–1965), who served as first lord of the Admiralty. A direct descendant of the duke of Marlborough and veteran of numerous adventures as a soldier and war correspondent, Churchill pressed for an Allied assault on the Dardanelles, the narrow strait west of Constantinople that, together with the Bosphorus, links the Black Sea to the Mediterranean and separates mainland Europe from Asia. He believed that such a campaign could knock Turkey out of the war, divert German forces from the western front, protect the Suez Canal (which Turkey, as the principal power in the eastern Mediterranean, could potentially threaten), and thereby preserve Britain's all-important passage to India.

But the **Gallipoli Campaign**, organized with excessive speed and insufficient care, turned disastrous. An initial naval attack failed when the British lost six out of nine battleships to Turkish mines. In April and May, the British managed to land on the Gallipoli Peninsula, but the Turkish army, while under strength and of mixed quality, had dug in well and used machine guns to the same frightening effect seen on the western front. Thousands of men died in the water and on the beaches, and the survivors remained pinned down. More than half the 400,000 soldiers under British command had become casualties before Britain decided to evacuate in early 1916. The 400,000 included a particularly large contingent of Australians and New Zealanders in the ANZAC corps, and their heavy losses spurred a resentment against Britain that has never quite faded in either nation.

THE WAR AT SEA

Britain put pressure on the Central powers more effectively through its use of naval power. Despite all of Kaiser Wilhelm's efforts to develop the German navy before the war, it was no match for the Royal Navy on the high seas—partly because British intelligence had broken the German navy's codes and knew its plans. In 1914, Britain won sea battles in the Indian Ocean and the South Atlantic, and effectively forced the German fleet back into harbor. The Germans attempted naval breakouts, but despite bloodying the British off the coast of Denmark in 1916 at the battle of Jutland, in which some 250 ships participated, they could not break the British blockade, which was slowly strangling the German economy.

German naval hopes increasingly focused not on massive battleships but on submarines, which had been under development since the 1860s. Both Britain and Germany had substantial numbers of submarines at the start of the war, but the Germans augmented their use against the merchant shipping that brought crucial supplies, including oil and food, to Britain. By the war's end, Germany had put some 375 of its torpedo-carrying U-boats (*Untersee*, or underwater boats) with crews of as many as 60 men, into service. The British had no means of detecting them while submerged, and they inflicted huge damage. U-boats sank over 5,000 merchant ships by the end of the war, killing tens of thousands of sailors and destroying massive quantities of foodstuffs and industrial goods. Initially, however, the Germans refrained from targeting the vessels of neutral countries. The most important of these countries was the United States, which had not formed part of any European alliance before 1914.

But the expanding German submarine campaign also raised the chance that the United States, already increasingly tied to the Allies because of the massive loans made to them, might join the war on the Allied side. On May 7, 1915, a U-boat torpedoed and sank the British ocean liner *Lusitania* off the coast of Ireland. The ship had been carrying munitions and therefore amounted to a legitimate military target. But the huge loss of life—1,195 out of 1,959 passengers, including 128 of 139 U.S. citizens—caused outrage in America. One magazine denounced "a deed for which a Hun would blush, a Turk be ashamed, and a Barbary pirate apologize." American president Woodrow Wilson (1856–1924) sent a series of protest notes to the German government, warning that the United States would see any further German attacks on merchant vessels carrying American citizens as "deliberately unfriendly." Wilson also ordered an increase in American military spending, although he continued to promise the American public that he would keep the country out of war.

NEW BATTLEFIELD WEAPONS AND OLD TACTICS

Submarines were not the only technological innovation as the combatants searched desperately to break the stalemate on the western front. As early as the fall of 1914, the British used airplanes to drop small bombs on German strongholds. In May 1915, a large German blimp appeared over London and released incendiary devices in a deliberate if ineffective attack on civilians. Airplanes provided crucial intelligence, and soon fighter planes took to the sky to shoot down other planes. Throughout the war

Fighting in the Air British (circular insignia) and German (cross insignia) planes engage in a dogfight, a form of airborne close combat.

the size, speed, range, and sophistication of warplanes all increased. By the war's end, the British, French, and Germans had produced over 150,000 planes, while "flying aces" became popular heroes.

And toward the end of the war, the Germans made another advance with striking implications for aeronautics. The Krupp steel and munitions works developed a railroad-mounted artillery piece with a 100-foot-long barrel that could fire a 210-pound shell a distance of over eighty miles. The shells took three minutes to reach their targets and rose to the greatest height yet attained by a man-made projectile: twenty-five miles above the ground. From a position in Champagne, in eastern France, the Germans managed to bombard the city of Paris for several weeks with the giant field cannon known as the Paris Gun. On Good Friday, 1918, one shell collapsed the roof of the Church of Saint-Gervais, killing eighty-eight members of the congregation.

Earlier in the war, the Germans had begun to use a much more sinister weapon. In April 1915, they released

Chemical Weapons British soldiers at the battle of Ypres wear gas masks for protection as they stand in a trench, awaiting a German advance.

suit. The British war poet Wilfred Owen (1893–1918) wrote unforgettably about the horrifying experience of a gas attack:

> Gas! GAS! Quick, boys!—An ecstasy of fumbling,
> Fitting the clumsy helmets just in time;
> But someone still was yelling out and stumbling
> And flound'ring like a man in fire or lime . . .
> Dim, through the misty panes and thick green light,
> As under a green sea, I saw him drowning.
>
> In all my dreams, before my helpless sight,
> He plunges at me, guttering, drowning.

Yet the cruel fact was that none of these technological innovations could relieve the terrible stalemate on the western front. Although poison gas was terrifying and frequently deadly, it remained far less effective than machine guns and artillery. One other new weapon did have the potential to change the nature of the war. A fast-moving, heavily armored tank could cross the no-man's-land between the trenches, roll over barbed wire, and use its heavy guns to destroy enemy machine-gun positions from close range. But while the British began to deploy primitive tanks in 1916, until the very end of the war they made little difference: they were as yet too slow, unreliable, poorly shielded, and not organized into the concentrated units that would have made the greatest difference. Lacking a technological solution, the generals on the western front therefore felt they had to stick with the same gruesome tactics they had deployed from the start of the stalemate. And millions of soldiers paid the price.

THE CONTINUING BLOODBATH The years 1915 and 1916 brought repeated Allied efforts to achieve the longed-for breakthrough via sheer force, but these efforts failed. The Germans meanwhile followed a different strategy. Faced with fighting on two fronts, and increasingly plagued by the British blockade, they doubted their ability to assemble the force necessary for a major offensive in the west. Much of their high command now believed that they could and should drive the Russians from the war first—a sort of Schlieffen Plan in reverse.

But the new German commander in chief, Erich von Falkenhayn (1861–1922), still believed the western Allies could be brought to sue for a negotiated peace. The method was to be a grisly campaign of attrition, aimed less at capturing territory than at inflicting the maximum number of casualties. In early 1916, he opened a major attack against a series of fortresses in eastern France, around the town of Verdun, making use of massive artillery and hoping to

thick chlorine gas from their trenches near Ypres, Belgium. It blew into French positions, choking the soldiers and sending them into convulsions. Heavier than air, the chlorine settled into the trenches, forcing men out into the unprotected open ground. It even killed the rats that infested nearly all the trenches. By September, British general Douglas Haig (1861–1928) was ordering chlorine containers as well for yet another failed attempt at a breakthrough on the western front. In some cases, the poison gas blew back over British positions.

Soon both sides were issuing gas masks as standard equipment, leading the Germans to yet another escalation. In 1916, they started using mustard gas, which was not only far more concentrated and easier to deploy than chlorine but also could enter the body through the skin, rendering gas masks ineffective. The international conventions signed at the Hague in 1899 and 1907 had prohibited these chemical weapons (along with aerial bombing), but once one country had violated them, the others followed inflict five casualties on the French defenders for every two of his own. The French held out and then, in the fall, counterattacked. But in the process they lost 540,000 men killed and wounded. The Germans, unable to stick to Falkenhayn's desired ratio, lost 430,000. The flood of corpses at the **battle of Verdun** overwhelmed attempts to bury them. As late as the 1930s, it was possible to stumble across bones of the dead in the hills near Verdun.

OPPOSITION TO THE WAR

It is remarkable that despite the relentless killing, popular opinion throughout Europe remained largely committed to the war effort, and few soldiers spoke out against their commanders. Propaganda helped nurture this support, but so did the genuine sense of patriotic duty felt in each of the countries, coupled with outrage at the enemy for the damage already inflicted. And of course characterizing the war as a pointless and obscene mistake was to suggest that millions of men were dying for nothing.

In Britain, a small antiwar movement did consistently express its opposition to the continuing hostilities, despite legislation that curtailed freedom of speech for the duration of the war emergency. One prominent member was the country's greatest living philosopher, Bertrand Russell (1872–1970), who lost his university position and briefly went to prison for his pacifist writings. Another was the leading suffragist and socialist Charlotte Despard (1844–1939), sister to none other than the British commander in chief Sir John French (the siblings remained close despite their totally opposed positions on the war). Britain did permit men to qualify as conscientious objectors, especially Quakers, whose pacifist convictions dated back to the beginning of their movement. In Germany, a handful of socialists publicly protested the war, and after two of their leaders were jailed in 1916, 50,000 munitions workers in Berlin staged a one-day strike. But overall, antiwar activity had tragically little effect.

LIFE IN THE TRENCHES For most front-line soldiers, the flames of patriotic zeal quickly sputtered out in the mud of the trenches. That mud was everywhere, along with pools of stagnant water, mice, rats, frogs, slugs, insects, human waste, and, worst of all, the dead. The British soldier George Coppard (1898–1984) recalled, in a memoir of the war:

> Every square yard of ground seemed to be layered with corpses, producing a sickening stench. We

would curtain off protruding parts with a sandbag, pinned to the side of the trench with cartridges. A swollen right arm, with a German eagle tattooed on it, used to stick out and brush us as we squeezed by; once a head appeared which wasn't there an hour before.

In the winter, food and water froze solid. In the fall and spring, the men could spend hours standing in the water, which often led to a dangerous, painful swelling called trench foot that sometimes destroyed the limb altogether. Post-traumatic stress disorder affected an unknown but very large number of soldiers. The British army alone diagnosed 80,000 men as suffering from what was called "shell shock," supposedly induced by artillery barrages.

Fortunately, battlefield medical care had improved markedly since the reforms of the Crimean War, when field hospitals and organized nursing care had been introduced. The field hospitals were now equipped with surgical theaters where soldiers could be operated on under anesthesia. The use of antiseptics to prevent the spread of infection (although true antibiotics only arrived after 1940) meant that serious wounds were no longer an almost-certain death sentence. Vaccinations now protected soldiers from many common illnesses, with the result that in the war, for the first time in European history, more soldiers died from battle wounds than from

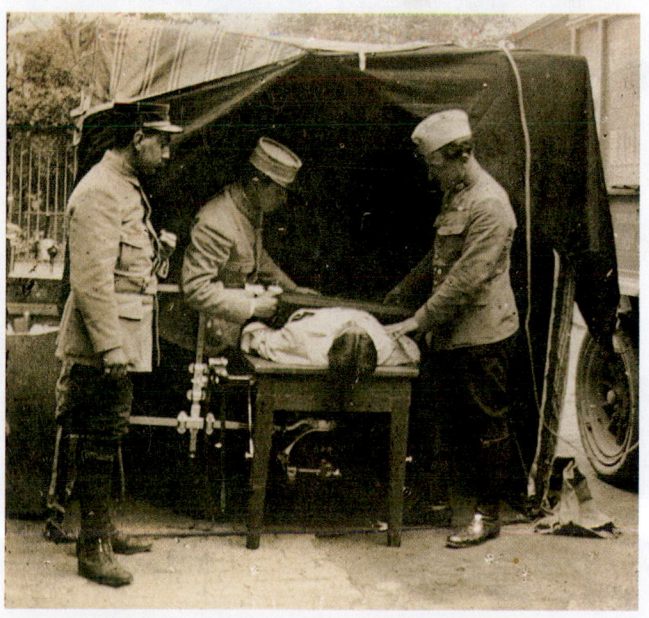

Field Hospitals New medical technology could increasingly save lives close to the front. In this photograph, doctors at a French field hospital use a brand-new X-ray machine to locate a bullet in a soldier's abdomen.

NASH'S *OVER THE TOP*

As soldiers tried to make sense of the violent and alienating experience of World War I, they produced a large body of visual art that expressed the horrors of life in the trenches. A successful painter before the war, the Englishman John Nash (1893–1977) was one such artist.

Nash was one of only twelve men from a regiment of eighty who avoided death or injury while participating in a British counterattack during the battle of Cambrai, in northern France, in late 1917. His painting *Over the Top* (1918) depicts the first minutes of the unit's tragic assault, capturing in bold forms and colors the carnage, confusion, tedium, and futility of the fighting. Against a backdrop of smoke and shellfire, the men of the regiment clamber out of their trench, past the bodies of their comrades, and trudge toward enemy lines and almost certain death.

QUESTIONS FOR ANALYSIS

1. What does Nash's painting reveal about conditions on the western front?
2. What do the expressions and postures of the men convey about their feelings regarding the war?
3. What does the painting suggest about interaction among soldiers in battle?

disease. Yet soldiers now had to deal with the psychological trauma of battles that lasted not for hours or even days but for months on end, keeping them at risk of death the entire time.

During attacks, battle police ensured that no one stayed behind in the trenches, and those who refused to go "over the top" risked arrest and even execution. As is frequent in wartime, the soldiers often felt the greatest loyalty not to their officers, or even to their country, but to their fellow soldiers. The common experience of the trenches could even, on occasion, create a form of camaraderie with the enemy. In a famous incident, on several parts of the western front on Christmas Day 1914, soldiers managed to organize informal truces, exchanging food and cigarettes and arranging impromptu soccer games in the no-man's-land. Commanders on both sides were horrified and worked hard to ensure that nothing of the sort would happen again.

Lochnagar Crater The explosions of the mines with which the Allies began the battle of the Somme left giant craters like this one on the battlefield. Today Lochnagar Crater—named after the type of British mine used—is a memorial site.

BREAKING POINTS (1916–1917)

At this point in the war, victory—to say nothing of planning for the postwar world—seemed further away than ever to nearly all the participants. But this was total war, in which each side attempted to mobilize every possible resource to achieve destruction of the enemy. As the losses on each side mounted into the millions, it became increasingly difficult for either the Allies or the Central powers to imagine any end to the war short of complete victory for their side.

THE BATTLE OF THE SOMME

In the summer of 1916, following the massive German offensive at Verdun, the Allies made the largest and most intensive effort yet to achieve a breakthrough on the western front. The so-called Big Push, planned for a sector of the front near the Somme River in northern France, did not differ greatly in form from earlier offensives. It was to start with an artillery bombardment to destroy the German defenses, to be followed by a massed infantry attack. Once the infantry had captured the German trenches, the Allies would begin a rapid, triumphant advance through the open country beyond.

What was new about the Big Push was above all the plan's scale, which dwarfed anything previously seen in this or any other war. The **battle of the Somme** was scheduled to last five full days and involve 21,000 tons of explosives—1.5 million shells—all directed at a strip of land 14 miles long and slightly more than 1 mile wide, or nearly 150 shells per acre. The infantry attack would begin with the detonation of enormous mines under or near German trenches, containing as much as 30 tons of high explosives each (one of them blew a crater that still measures 55 feet deep and 220 feet wide). The British infantry attacks alone would involve 120,000 men. Just to bring the necessary men and materiel to the front, the Allies set about building 55 miles of railroad track.

Yet the Allied commanders were deluding themselves in thinking that an increase in scale could make the difference, for nothing had changed in the implacable logic that gave such a tremendous advantage to the defense. Over long months, the Germans had dug themselves deep at the Somme, building a chain of reinforced, ventilated bunkers thirty feet or more below ground. For all the fury of the initial artillery barrage, two-thirds of the shells were shrapnel, which mostly spent itself in the earth or pinged harmlessly off steel and concrete fortifications. Of the remaining high-explosive shells, very few hit close enough to bunkers or machine-gun emplacements to destroy them. And a quarter of all the shells did not detonate at all.

At 7:28 on the morning of July 1, 1916, the Allies set off their massive mines. Two minutes later (the time it took for the mine debris to fall back to earth), officers blew whistles to send their first waves of infantry "over the top" and advance. Even as they climbed ladders to exit their trenches, Allied infantry heard the ominous sound of bugles from the German trenches, summoning the defenders into position. And as the troops started across no-man's-land, they found the German positions virtually unscathed, the barbed wire uncut, and machine-gun fire cutting through their ranks like giant scythes. The slaughter was almost unimaginable. One Newfoundland regiment suffered 90 percent casualties in the space of forty minutes. Every one of its twenty-six officers was killed or wounded. And yet the Allied commanders, having staked so much on the attack, could not bring themselves to call it off, and they continued to send wave after wave of soldiers to their deaths. On this single day, nearly as many British soldiers died as during the entire Crimean War—some 19,000 with another 2,000 mortally wounded. Total British casualties for this one day came close to 60,000, or nearly half the 120,000 men who took part in the attack. Nearly all of them fell onto territory the British had already held.

And still the offensive continued. All through the summer and early fall, the British and French battered on the Somme defenses with human hammers and succeeded in doing little but smashing those hammers to pieces. In only a few spots did the Allies manage to advance more than a mile or two. In mid-November, when they finally admitted failure, their casualties had risen to 620,000 for this campaign alone. General Haig, now the British commander in chief, began to adopt the viewpoint of his German counterpart Falkenhayn, coming to see the struggle as one of attrition. It led him to the perverse logic of treating massive British casualty figures as a sign of success in their own right, confident that the Germans must be suffering even more. "The total losses of this division are under a thousand!" he exclaimed with frustration in his diary after yet another failed advance. On January 1, 1917, King George V (r. 1910–1936) promoted him to field marshal, the highest rank in the army.

CENTRAL POWERS UNDER STRAIN

In 1917, the colossal strain the war had placed on all the combatants made itself felt more strongly. Germany had ceased to make headway against Russia, which in 1916 carried out another successful offensive against Austria-Hungary. It did not knock Austria-Hungary out of the war, as the Russian commanders had hoped, and it put further strain on the Russian army, which was suffering ever-higher rates of desertion. But it inflicted ghastly casualties (over 2 million total), severely damaged Austria-Hungary's military capacities, and helped relieve the pressure on the western front.

AMERICAN INTERVENTION Germany now faced the prospect of indefinite stalemate on both fronts and slow strangulation from the British blockade. The so-called turnip winter of 1916–17 (so named because Germans had little else to eat) was one of the coldest on record. Hundreds of thousands of Germans died of malnutrition and exposure. Paul von Hindenburg, who now succeeded Falkenhayn as commander in chief, and Hindenburg's powerful deputy Erich von Ludendorff (1865–1937), both realized the need for a drastic gamble. They convinced the government to allow unrestricted submarine warfare in the Atlantic, targeting neutral as well as British vessels carrying food and war materiel across the Atlantic, with the goal of starving Britain out of the war. They understood correctly that the move would probably provoke American intervention, but they hoped to overcome the British before the Americans could make a difference. They also hoped that political turmoil in Russia (discussed below) would weaken the Russian war effort and allow them to concentrate on the western front.

The gamble failed. The German submarine campaign initially succeeded, with hundreds of ships sunk—in March 1917 a quarter of all those bound for Britain, principally from the Americas. British food reserves dwindled. But by the summer, the Allies had begun organizing their transatlantic shipping into convoys, escorted by warships, and the losses fell back to manageable proportions. Meanwhile, the submarine campaign indeed stirred American outrage, as did the exposure of a farcical German attempt to distract America by provoking a war with Mexico. President Woodrow Wilson angrily cut off diplomatic relations with Germany. In April 1917, he convinced Congress to declare war.

It took the United States many months to mobilize, but its involvement promised the Allies a decisive advantage in the long run. The American economy had expanded enormously over the previous decades, and in 1916 it became the largest in the world, surpassing Great Britain's. The United States could also draw on a large population of military-age men.

TURMOIL IN THE MIDDLE EAST AND ARMENIA
Meanwhile, Turkey also stumbled toward the brink of collapse. Although the British attempt to knock it out of the war at Gallipoli had failed, the British succeeded at the other end of the Ottoman Empire, where by 1916 they had taken possession of Mesopotamia, the heart of the future state of Iraq. With oil, as we have seen, emerging as a steadily more crucial fuel for the Western world,

the Allies made it a priority to capture control of the rich Middle Eastern oil fields. The British also attacked the Turks in the Arabian Peninsula, with the aid of nationalists seeking an independent Arab state. In 1917, a British army fought its way from Egypt up the Mediterranean coast into Palestine, Syria, and Lebanon, and for the first time since the Crusades a European army took possession of Jerusalem. And in contradiction to earlier promises to Arab nationalist leaders, the British foreign secretary, Arthur Balfour (1848–1930), declared his government's support for the establishment of a Jewish national state in Palestine.

In eastern Turkey, where the Turks came into conflict with Russia, Turkish setbacks provided the immediate cause for a campaign of horrifying repression by the Turks against Christian minorities, above all Armenians. Already in the late nineteenth century, several Armenian nationalist groups in the empire had campaigned for the foundation of an independent Armenian state. The rise of the nationalist Young Turks, and the Ottoman's humiliating defeat in the Balkan Wars, had led to increasing resentment and suspicion of the Christian minorities by Muslim Turks (Balkan Christians were accused of treacherously siding with the Ottomans' enemies). In 1915, a crushing Russian victory of the Ottomans at the Battle of Sarıkamış in eastern Anatolia led to outright accusations of treason against Armenians. The government demobilized Armenian soldiers, many of whom it subsequently executed. Resistance by Armenians then provided a pretext for the Ottoman government to order the mass deportation of virtually the entire Armenian population under Ottoman rule to desert camps in present-day Syria. Without

Armenian Genocide A group of Armenian refugees fleeing the genocide in the winter of 1915 stands next to a house or shelter covered in snow, bundled up against the cold of the Caucasus Mountains.

food and water, Armenians died by the thousands during the forced march south, while Ottoman irregular forces carried out numerous massacres. The campaign ended up causing the deaths of at least 600,000 people, and possibly more than a million. Most scholars consider it a genocide: a deliberate, systematic attempt to exterminate an entire people. Like the German campaign of extermination against the Herero and Nama in Southwest Africa at the beginning of the century, but on a much larger scale, the **Armenian genocide** foreshadowed further such crimes in the twentieth century, eventually leading, after World War II, to international covenants recognizing genocide as the worst of all crimes against humanity.

RESISTANCE TO THE WAR

The increased strain of the war on all the combatants called forth unprecedented forms of resistance in 1916 and 1917. In the British Isles, resistance found its sharpest expression in Ireland, where nationalists felt outrage at the sacrifices demanded of them for a British war. Although conscription was never introduced in Ireland during World War I, some 200,000 Irishmen served in the military and some 30,000 died. Nationalists also saw an opportunity to achieve independence while British forces were pinned down in Europe. In Dublin at Easter 1916, some 1,000 nationalists led by Pádraig Pearse (1879–1916), a poet, lawyer, and teacher, staged a badly organized uprising that British forces quickly suppressed. The British executed the ringleaders, but in the long run they succeeded only in creating martyr-heroes and ensuring that if given the choice, the southern, Catholic provinces of Ireland would settle for nothing less than national independence. As the poet William Butler Yeats wrote in a haunting poem about the Easter Rising, the ringleaders—and by extension, all of Ireland—had been "changed, changed utterly. / A terrible beauty is born."

In France, the moment of crisis arrived in the spring of 1917, after commander in chief Robert Nivelle (1856–1924) led yet another failed attempt at a decisive breakthrough. The battle of the Chemin des Dames, along the Aisne River, repeated many elements of the previous summer's Somme offensive, and while in some areas the French forces succeeded in advancing several miles, they did not achieve their objective and casualties were again enormous. In early May, tens of thousands of French soldiers began refusing commands to attack, and mutinies spread through the French army. Desertion rates soared.

EXPERIENCING WORLD WAR I

Following the outbreak of war, many young men rushed to enlist in the British army, whether out of a sense of patriotic duty or in search of a glorious adventure. However, the realities of industrialized warfare—machine guns, high explosives, tanks, the trenches, poison gas—proved a bitter revelation. As the war ground on, the expectant and even enthusiastic mood that had driven many young men to enlist, energetically captured by the British poet Rupert Brooke—who never saw combat—in his War Sonnets (1914), gave way to resignation, fatalism, and anger. Many letters home penned later in the war, including the following message sent from Major Sidney Harold Baker to his brother, exposed the horrors of the war and the disenchantment of the young men who were sent to fight it.

Rupert Brooke, War Sonnets

In "Peace," the first of the two War Sonnets presented below, Brooke embraces the opportunity for action brought by the war. In "The Soldier," he finds comfort in patriotic self-sacrifice.

I. Peace

Now, God be thanked Who has matched us
　　with His hour,
　　　　And caught our youth, and wakened
　　　　　　us from sleeping,
With hand made sure, clear eye, and
　　sharpened power,
　　　　To turn, as swimmers into cleanness
　　　　　　leaping,
Glad from a world grown old and cold and
　　weary,
　　　　Leave the sick hearts that honour
　　　　　　could not move,
And half-men, and their dirty songs and
　　dreary,
　　　　And all the little emptiness of love!

Oh! we, who have known shame, we have
　　found release there,
　　　　Where there's no ill, no grief, but sleep
　　　　　　has mending,
　　　　　　　　Naught broken save this body,
　　　　　　　　　　lost but breath;
Nothing to shake the laughing heart's long
　　peace there
　　　　But only agony, and that has ending;
　　　　　　And the worst friend and
　　　　　　　　enemy is but Death.

V. The Soldier

If I should die, think only this of me:
　　　　That there's some corner of a foreign
　　　　　　field
That is for ever England. There shall be
　　　　In that rich earth a richer dust
　　　　　　concealed;
A dust whom England bore, shaped, made
　　aware,
　　　　Gave, once, her flowers to love, her
　　　　　　ways to roam,
A body of England's, breathing English air,
　　　　Washed by the rivers, blest by suns of
　　　　　　home.

And think, this heart, all evil shed away,
　　　　A pulse in the eternal mind, no less
　　　　　　Gives somewhere back the
　　　　　　　　thoughts by England given;
Her sights and sounds; dreams happy as
　　her day;
　　　　And laughter, learnt of friends; and
　　　　　　gentleness,
　　　　　　In hearts at peace, under an
　　　　　　　　English heaven.

Sidney Harold Baker, "Letter to his brother"

Baker was a frontline officer stationed in northern France who was killed in action in March 1918. In this November 1917 letter, he describes a night spent watching over a wounded fellow soldier.

I found myself trying to comfort a wretched wounded man till the stretcher-bearers should somehow scramble through the torn branches and cross the shell holes and get him back to the Aid Post. Poor fellow, I found him there by his cries; he had been calling, calling, calling, hour after hour, ever since a shell had knocked him out in the darkness, long before the dawn, and now it was night again. He had crept into a hole for shelter, alongside a ruined pill-box,[1] and was utterly helpless and numbed with cold. I could get no warmth into him at all, but a drink and a cigarette and yet another drink helped him a bit, till at last four stretcher-bearers stumbled and scrambled back with him. Poor chap, I doubt if he comes through....

'Tis a horrible business—enough to make a strong man weep. It seems to me just one long degradation; it is the enemy who has "willed it," and we have to go through with it.

QUESTIONS FOR ANALYSIS

1. Why does Brooke describe the war in such a poetic, even celebratory, tone?
2. Whom does Baker blame for the war, and why?
3. What do you think accounts for the dramatic differences between Brooke's poem and Baker's letter in their attitudes toward the war?

---

[1]**Pill-box:** bunker

Sources: Rupert Brooke, "Peace" and "The Soldier," in *New Numbers*, vol. t, no. 4 (Ryton, UK: 1914), pp. 165, 169; Sidney Harold Baker, letter, in *War Letters of Fallen Englishmen*, ed. Laurence Housman (New York: 1930), pp. 35–36.

For the most part, the rebellious soldiers had no desire to overthrow the French state or even to end the war. They wanted the war prosecuted in a more effective manner. Even so, French authorities held some 23,000 courts martial, which ended up condemning hundreds of mutineers to death, although only fifty or so were actually executed. But at least partly in reaction to the mutinies, in mid-May Nivelle was replaced by the more cautious Philippe Pétain (1856–1951), the general who had prevailed at Verdun and who had a reputation (even if, in World War I, these things were sadly relative) for keeping soldiers alive.

LOSS OF HOPE

Despite the strains, throughout 1917 the leaderships in the warring countries remained unable to break out of the gruesome pattern of combat in which the western front was still tragically locked. In July, General Haig launched another major offensive, in Belgium. The new campaign featured the first mass attacks by British tanks, which were slowly gaining in efficiency, and took place in such heavy mud that hundreds, perhaps thousands, of soldiers died by drowning far from the sea. But this latest offensive accomplished little more than earlier ones. Among the soldiers the mood turned ever more cynical, despairing, and numb. Already in January, an Indian soldier in British service had written to his family: "Now I write the truth. . . . Consider us as having died today or tomorrow. There is absolutely no hope of our ever returning. . . . None will survive." In October, the British poet Wilfred Owen, who would die on the western front a year later, wrote his poem about comrades dying from poison gas, and concluded:

> If you could hear, at every jolt, the blood
> Come gargling from the froth-corrupted lungs,
> Obscene as cancer, bitter as the cud
> Of vile, incurable sores on innocent tongues, —
> My friend, you would not tell with such high zest
> To children ardent for some desperate glory,
> The old lie: *Dulce et decorum est*
> *Pro patria mori.*

The last two lines translate to "How sweet and fitting it is to die for one's country," as Latin poet Horace had written in the first century BCE, lines familiar to every educated European of the period. By late 1917, the experience of World War I had come close to scorching such traditional notions of patriotism and glory out of Western culture altogether.

THE BEGINNING OF THE RUSSIAN REVOLUTION

The first of the combatants to break, and in the most spectacular fashion, was Russia. Of all the major powers, it had suffered most from the war. Some of its wealthiest western provinces, with a population of over 65 million, spent much of the war under German occupation. Six million refugees from these provinces overwhelmed the state's severely limited resources. Of over 14 million soldiers mobilized, nearly a quarter were killed or disappeared—a far larger number than in any previous Russian war. Unable to pay for the war with taxes and loans, the tsarist government ended up printing money, which started an inflationary spiral. Between 1914 and 1916, real wages in Russia fell by a third, as did overall gross domestic product. The fierce winter of 1916–17 intensified the misery beyond anything even the Germans were experiencing. Worst of all, the antiquated and autocratic Russian state was far less capable of dealing with such strains than its counterparts to the west.

RUSSIA'S FEBRUARY REVOLUTION

By 1914, Tsar Nikolai had rolled back nearly all the liberal gains made during the Revolution of 1905. As a result, Russia had nothing like an independent parliament or civil service. Corruption was rampant, and the Romanov court continued its displays of luxury. Critics charged that Tsarina Alexandra increasingly dominated the weak-willed tsar. Both she and her husband had fallen under the spell of an erratic Russian Orthodox holy man named Grigori Rasputin (1869–1916). In December 1916, a group of nobles at court attacked Rasputin. After a massive dose of cyanide failed to kill him, they shot him, clubbed him, and then tied him into a carpet and threw him into the freezing Neva River. Still, he nearly escaped before finally drowning. By the end of 1916, public loyalty to the tsarist government was collapsing, especially among the urban working classes. The secret police, the Okhranka, was warning the government that a revolutionary situation was brewing.

Despite the government's calls for patriotic unity and sacrifice, waves of strikes and protests broke out. In early March 1917 (February by the Julian calendar then followed in Russia), they intensified, leading to a general strike in the capital, now called Petrograd rather than the German-sounding Saint Petersburg. The tsar ordered troops to disperse the protests by force, and demonstrators were killed, including women. The soldiers reacted with dismay; thousands of them switched sides and stormed arsenals to obtain weapons. Rebels in Petrograd and elsewhere created their own **soviets** (councils), prominently including workers as members. Moscow fell into the hands of insurgents, and within days the army leadership abandoned the hapless ruler. On March 15, 1917, a panicked Nikolai abdicated, and his brother, whom he had named to succeed him, refused the throne. The centuries-old Russian monarchy had, in a matter of days, come to an inglorious end.

Over the following months, the political situation in Russia turned even more chaotic. A **Provisional Government** appointed by the old parliament, the State Duma, took power but had to compete for authority with the increasingly influential soviets. Owing partly to continuing close ties between urban workers and the peasant communities where many still had relatives, most of the peasants who dominated the army rank-and-file increasingly saw the prominent Petrograd soviet as the country's legitimate government. Through the early spring of 1917, the eastern front remained calm, with the Germans happy to look on as Russia fell apart. They contributed to the disorder by bringing leaders of the Bolsheviks, the most radical Russian revolutionary faction, back to Russia from Swiss exile in a special train across German territory.

Finally, in June the Russian Provisional Government, now effectively led by the moderate Socialist Alexander Kerensky (1881–1970), attempted another offensive against Austria-Hungary, hoping to rally the people patriotically behind the government. The offensive, which failed disastrously, had the opposite effect. The Provisional Government now lost even more credit with the population. The writer Maxim Gorky wrote: "Everybody agrees that the Russian state is splitting apart like an old barge in a flood." In August, a right-wing coup failed, and expectations mounted that the Bolsheviks would try to seize power.

RUSSIA AND MARXISM

In the fall of 1917, the Russian revolutionary turmoil reached a dramatic climax that brought greater long-term consequences for Europe than anything since the French Revolution of 1789. A radical Marxist regime came to power, led by a political party possessing dictatorial authority, committed to common ownership of the means of production and to the abolition of all or most private property. It was the world's first successful communist revolution.

According to orthodox Marxist thinking, communism, as the most advanced stage of human society, should have properly come first to the most economically advanced industrial countries: Great Britain, Germany, and the United States. Russia, whose 100-million-strong peasantry vastly outnumbered its fledgling urban working class, and where political and social power still lay largely in the hands of an aristocratic, quasi-feudal elite, seemed an unsuitable candidate. Even during the Russian Revolution itself, many Russian socialists continued to argue that the time for direct action had not yet arrived.

And yet, as we have seen, these theories had not stopped a small but hardy socialist revolutionary movement from emerging in Russia in the late nineteenth century, led by disaffected intellectuals who seethed with hatred of the tsarist regime. Some of them were committed to revolutionary change in Russia as part of a world revolution. Many endorsed the idea that in a "backward" country like Russia, the liberal bourgeoisie would never succeed in bringing about a sufficient level of industrialization for a spontaneous proletarian revolution, so historical progress depended on the efforts of a revolutionary party.

LENIN AND THE BOLSHEVIKS

Vladimir Ilich Ulyanov (1870–1924)—better known by his revolutionary alias, **Lenin**—was the son of a school inspector in the central Russian town of Simbirsk and was fairly typical of the revolutionary intelligentsia. Trained as a lawyer, short, balding, bearded, and unkempt, he was given to long, intense pronouncements on the fine points of revolutionary social theory. The American journalist John Reed (1887–1920) memorably described him as "a leader purely by virtue of intellect: colorless, humorless, uncompromising and detached...but with the power of explaining profound ideas in simple terms." He had turned to revolutionary activity after his adored older brother died on the gallows for participating in an assassination attempt on Tsar Alexander III. But at age thirty, after release from internal exile in Siberia, Ulyanov left Russia for Switzerland and spent the next seventeen years living in a succession of shabby apartments, spied on by the Russian secret services, writing for and speaking to tiny audiences, wrapped up in factional quarrels that often seemed of little interest to anyone outside his small circle of like-minded zealots. But he was anything but a fool. He was hardheaded, ruthless, relentless, and shrewd.

In his years abroad, as leader of the Bolshevik faction of Russian socialists, Lenin developed the theory of

Vladimir Lenin A photo from October, 1917, captures Lenin addressing a crowd of Bolsheviks in Red Square, Moscow, marking the collapse of the Russian government and the rise of Soviet rule.

revolution centered on the role of a secretive, highly centralized, tightly organized party. He strove to shape the Bolsheviks into such a party, both in Russia and abroad. To raise funds, its members sometimes resorted to armed robbery. Slowly, it gained influence in the Russian trade unions. After 1914, Lenin attacked socialists who supported the Russian war effort and also those calling for peace. Instead, he demanded immediate violent revolution and the establishment of a communist state.

In April 1917, when the Germans delivered him back to Russia, Lenin again called for an immediate uprising of workers and peasants to place power in the hands of the soviets, which had already established themselves as an alternate foundation of authority. He demanded an end to Russia's involvement in the war and to the massive privations Russians had suffered since 1914. Petrograd workers welcomed the message, and the Bolsheviks capitalized on their increasing popularity in the city to recruit volunteers for a militia. In July, the Provisional Government cracked down on them, and Lenin fled to nearby Finland. But Kerensky, now prime minister, needed Bolshevik support to resist the attempted right-wing coup in August, and by early fall the party was recovering its strength. In the fall, Kerensky attempted to form a new, more left-wing coalition to outflank the Bolsheviks, but it was too late. The Bolsheviks were ready to seize power.

THE OCTOBER REVOLUTION

The **Bolshevik Revolution** (or October Revolution), for all the violence it ultimately caused, was itself surprisingly rapid and relatively bloodless. Its success was owed above all to Lenin, who through sheer strength of argument persuaded doubtful Bolshevik colleagues that the time had come to act. In particular, he persuaded his brilliant and charismatic fellow party-member, Leon Trotsky (1879–1940)—as with Lenin, the surname was a revolutionary alias; he was born into a prosperous Ukrainian Jewish family named Bronstein. On October 24 and 25, 1917 (by the Julian calendar), the Bolsheviks seized key sites in Petrograd and surrounded the Provisional Government's headquarters in the tsar's Winter Palace. As the cruiser *Aurora* fired blank warning shots at the palace from the Neva River, the Bolsheviks prepared for a drawn-out conflict. But Kerensky had lost popular support, and his government collapsed without a struggle. By telegraph, the Bolsheviks sent word across Russia that power had passed to the soviets, which immediately cast an aura of legitimacy over what might otherwise have seemed a simple coup d'état. It seemed incredible to many that men with little experience of politics beyond revolutionary pamphleteering and conspiracy, and little popular support outside of Petrograd and Moscow, could assert control over the vast Russian Empire. But owing to the almost complete vacuum of power that had opened up following the tsar's abdication, and the failure of the Provisional Government and Kerensky to fill it, Lenin and his party had their chance.

Trotsky, in fact, cleverly timed the insurrection to take place on the eve of a national congress of soviets. Many of its moderate socialist deputies criticized the Bolsheviks for acting independently and walked out when it became

Bolshevik Revolution Bolshevik fighters take aim with rifles during the short-lived military confrontation at the Winter Palace in Petrograd in late October 1917.

clear the Bolsheviks had an effective majority. Trotsky, in one of his most famous lines, scornfully quipped that they had tossed themselves into the "dustbin of history." The Bolsheviks then brusquely sidestepped the soviets, announcing that control of the central government would not pass to the soviets' Central Committee, which had representatives from several parties, but to a new, all-Bolshevik Council of People's Commissars. Lenin himself was now the head of government, and Trotsky was responsible for foreign affairs. Russia was moving toward one-party rule.

During the winter of 1917–18, the Bolsheviks moved to establish a revolutionary communist dictatorship. They nationalized the banking system, suppressed hostile newspapers, banned the liberal Kadet Party, and unleashed a powerful new police apparatus known by its Russian acronym as the Cheka—the forerunner to the KGB. They allowed elections to take place for a Constituent Assembly that would in theory write a new constitution, but when they lost heavily to the more moderate Socialist Revolutionaries, they adjourned the new body after a single day. In February 1918, the government nationalized the great landed estates and church lands. Peasant support surged even as armed opposition crystallized, setting the stage for civil war.

A few weeks later, Soviet Russia agreed to the exceptionally harsh peace terms offered by Germany in the Treaty of Brest-Litovsk. Although Germany had facilitated Lenin's return to Russia in hopes of adding to the country's chaos, it had not controlled him or sponsored the Bolshevik coup. Germany reaped the benefit, however, because the Bolshevik leadership desperately wanted peace—in order to deliver on its promises to the Russian population and to concentrate fully on its domestic program. By the terms of Brest-Litovsk, the Russians gave up 1.3 million square miles of territory to Germany and to a new, German-dominated independent state of Ukraine. This territory included a quarter of Russia's population, a third of its grain fields, and a third of its heavy industry. The treaty also meant that for the first time in the war Germany did not have to fight on two fronts, but could concentrate all of its efforts against the western Allies.

THE WAR'S END

At the start of 1918, even with the Russian Revolution scrambling everyone's calculations, Europeans could be forgiven for thinking of the ongoing war as a nightmare that would never end. But finally in 1918 the stubborn balance of destruction that had prevailed since 1914 burst apart. The war did not end with the long-hoped-for breakthrough in the trenches. But it finally did end.

GERMANY'S SPRING OFFENSIVE

One key factor upsetting the balance was Russia's exit from the war. Not only did the armistice with the Bolsheviks allow the Germans to concentrate all their efforts in the west—it also provided them with crucial new resources to gamble everything on a final cataclysmic western offensive. Even before Germany and Soviet Russia signed the Treaty of Brest-Litovsk, the German army had marched far beyond the old eastern front lines and was busily shipping foodstuffs, manufactured goods, and even whole factories westward. At the same time, the German high command knew that with American soldiers steaming toward Europe, they had to act quickly. As General Ludendorff put it, they would either win or "go under."

In March 1918, the Germans launched a Spring Offensive along a forty-mile stretch of the western front extending south from the English Channel through Belgium and northern France. It was the most massive offensive of the entire war, involving some 1.6 million soldiers and 10,000 field guns. They began by firing an unprecedented 1 million shells in just five hours, many loaded with a mixture of explosives and poison gas (at the Somme in 1916, the British had taken almost a week to fire 1.5 million shells). The barrage was audible a hundred miles away in southern England. And after three years in which the Germans had mostly remained on the defensive, British forces in the sector were complacent and unprepared. They did not break altogether, but the offensive came closer than any other of the war to achieving true breakthrough.

In May, the Germans made another massive push, preceded by an even larger artillery barrage (2 million shells in less than five hours), and came within less than forty miles of Paris. But at this crucial moment, with Parisians fleeing south, the French government evacuating its offices, and the Allies contemplating defeat, two other factors came into play. First, the Germans reached the end of their resources, both materiel and human—they had taken half a million casualties in the offensive and simply had few fresh troops left. Second, the arrival of hundreds of thousands of soldiers from the United States gave critical support to the Allies. In June and July 1918, the Americans held their ground at the battles of Château-Thierry and

World War I, 1917–1918 Events in 1917–18 brought the war to a swift conclusion. The British invasion of the Arabian Peninsula meant that Allied powers surrounded the Ottoman Empire, while the Bolshevik Revolution led to Russia pulling out of the war, ceding large territories in eastern Europe to Germany. Finally, in 1918, American resistance to the German Spring Offensive broke the stalemate on the western front, leading to Germany's surrender.

Belleau Wood, and the great German push finally stalled. Ludendorff had lost his gamble.

THE COLLAPSE OF THE CENTRAL POWERS

In the summer and fall of 1918, the Central powers, bled white by four years of total war, fell to pieces. In July, the Allies opened a counteroffensive, pushing the Germans out of the territory they had gained in the spring. For the

first time, in a sign of wars to come, the Allies made effective use of tanks, manufactured primarily by automobile and tractor firms, which neither barbed wire nor machine guns could easily stop. Meanwhile, the Austrian armies were collapsing on the Italian front. In September, an exhausted Bulgaria sued for peace and was followed the next month by Turkey. Allied forces occupied Constantinople. Ludendorff, now the effective leader of the German armed forces, showed signs of incipient madness, sometimes falling to the floor in convulsions. In September, he declared that defeat was imminent. Soon afterward, the

Reichstag approved constitutional changes that stripped significant powers from the kaiser and the army, making Germany for the first time a true parliamentary monarchy. A new government tried to start peace negotiations with the Allies.

WILSON AND PLANS FOR PEACE

It was Wilson, more than any other individual, who shaped the end of the war and the subsequent peace settlement. He was both an idealist who believed that he could function as a peacemaker, not just as a combatant, and also a firm believer in American destiny who thought America should take the lead in determining the new world order. In keeping with both these ambitions, he outlined his goals for the post-war world more explicitly than any other wartime leader. In January 1918, he spoke to a joint session of the U.S. Congress and outlined the so-called **Fourteen Points** that he hoped would form the basis for a new European order. Among other things, he called for the creation of a League of Nations to settle international disputes. He also insisted on the redrawing of European borders according to the principle of national self-determination: individual nationalities, such as those within the Austro-Hungarian Empire, should have the right to decide what nation they should belong to. Only with the satisfying of legitimate national grievances, he claimed, could a lasting peace take hold.

Unfortunately, Wilson, who knew the western half of Europe far better than the eastern one, underestimated how difficult it would be in practice to respect this principle. What of the many areas, especially in eastern and southeastern Europe, whose demographic maps resembled a crazy quilt of different ethnic groups? And how narrowly should "national groups" be defined? Did the Croats constitute a nation of their own, or a branch of a larger Yugoslav one? Could Ukraine, the ancient heartland of the Russian monarchy, split off from Russia? None of these questions had obvious or uncontroversial answers.

RUSSIA, AUSTRIA-HUNGARY, AND THE THREAT OF NATIONALISM

Wilson's defense of national self-determination only encouraged national groups to push for independence from the great multi-ethnic empires; and as the war sputtered to an end, nationalist groups took matters into their own hands. In the winter of 1917–18, Ukraine, Lithuania, and Estonia all proclaimed independence from Russia, with Latvia soon to follow. In 1917, Croat and Slovene nationalists in Austria-Hungary had announced their intention to fulfill Serbia's pre-war dreams and merge into a larger state of Yugoslavia. Czechs and Slovaks pushed for their own joint independence.

Poles in Austria-Hungary, Russia, and Germany prepared to revive the independent Poland that had vanished at the end of the eighteenth century.

The Austrian emperor Karl I (r. 1916–1918) desperately tried to forestall the dissolution of his empire, promising to give his Polish territories independence and to reconstitute the rest as a loose federation of peoples. In mid-October 1918, he sued for peace on the basis of the Fourteen Points. But the Allies had already endorsed the idea of full Czechoslovak and Yugoslav independence, and the new states now formally declared their sovereignty. On October 31, the Hungarian government tried to follow suit by dissolving the dual monarchy. However, the Hungarians' success in gaining equal status in the empire in 1867 now told against them, for the Allies considered them enemies and made it clear that Hungary could not hope to preserve its pre-war borders. On November 3, Austria-Hungary laid down its weapons.

GERMANY: REVOLUTION AND SURRENDER

The war's last act played out in the country that had done the most to bring it about: Germany. After having accepted the inevitability of defeat in September, General Ludendorff suddenly changed his mind and, along with some civilian politicians, called explicitly for "total war." But the Germans had reached the limits of their resources. Desertion from the army had become rampant. Strikes spread throughout the country. In defiance of the army, the new government tried to open negotiations with the Allies on the basis of what Wilson had called "peace without victory"; but France and Britain, after so much sacrifice, refused to contemplate anything but a decisive victory.

On October 28, the German navy ordered its ships to sea for a final, suicidal battle against the British. In response, sailors in the northern port city of Kiel mutinied and prevented the departure. When the authorities imprisoned the ringleaders, a wider rebellion began, with workers' unions and the Social Democratic Party joining the struggle. The commander of the Baltic Fleet—none other than the kaiser's brother—snuck out of Kiel in disguise. Within days, the rebellion became a revolution. Troops in Berlin mutinied, and parliamentary liberals and socialists joined to proclaim a republic and sue for peace. Kaiser Wilhelm, informed that he had "abdicated," fled across the border to the Netherlands.

At 5:00 a.m. on November 11, 1918, the German commanders signed an armistice with the Allies in a railway car in eastern France. It went into effect six hours later. Not a long space of time, and yet, during those six hours, a further 8,000 soldiers were wounded and 2,738 killed. It was a cruel and pointless end to a war that had long lost its point for all but its most fervent participants.

THE RUSSIAN CIVIL WAR

Even as hostilities elsewhere in Europe sputtered to their dispiriting end, civil war raged as fiercely as ever in Russia. In 1918, several White armies emerged to oppose the "red" Bolsheviks, and in response Trotsky organized a new Red Army, partly commanded by former tsarist officers. The resulting conflict saw atrocities, terror, and mass murder on both sides. In the summer of 1918, after holding Nikolai II and his family prisoners, the Bolsheviks murdered them, probably on Lenin's orders, to prevent them from becoming a White rallying point. The Russian Civil War of 1918–1921 pushed the Bolsheviks toward the more radical position known as **war communism**, which involved nationalization of all heavy industry and the development of a centrally planned, largely money-free economy.

In addition to the Whites, the Reds had to fight against independence movements in Ukraine and the Caucasus, and against the newly independent state of Poland, which sought to exploit the chaos in Russia to expand its own territory. The Red Army managed to drive the Poles back to the outskirts of Warsaw but ultimately made peace when their final offensive failed. Meanwhile, the Allied powers sent supplies and small, largely ineffective armed contingents of their own to aid the Whites, in hopes of containing what they considered to be the communist threat to Western democracy and capitalism. Americans landed in Russia's far north, and also the far east, near Vladivostok. The presence of these foreign contingents made it easier for Lenin and the Communists to portray themselves as patriots fighting against hostile outsiders.

THE HOPE AND PROMISE OF COMMUNISM

Despite this violence, revolutionary Russia, like revolutionary France before it, was also producing extraordinary outbursts of utopian hope. The Bolsheviks did not just promise a more equitable society; they promised a transformation in human relations. Women would be liberated not just from domestic drudgery and political repression but from the confines of traditional gender roles. The Communist Party (as the Bolsheviks formally became known in 1918) supported legal divorce and legal abortion, and some leaders hinted that marriage itself could be abolished. The party also supported the vote for women, although suffrage would become mostly symbolic

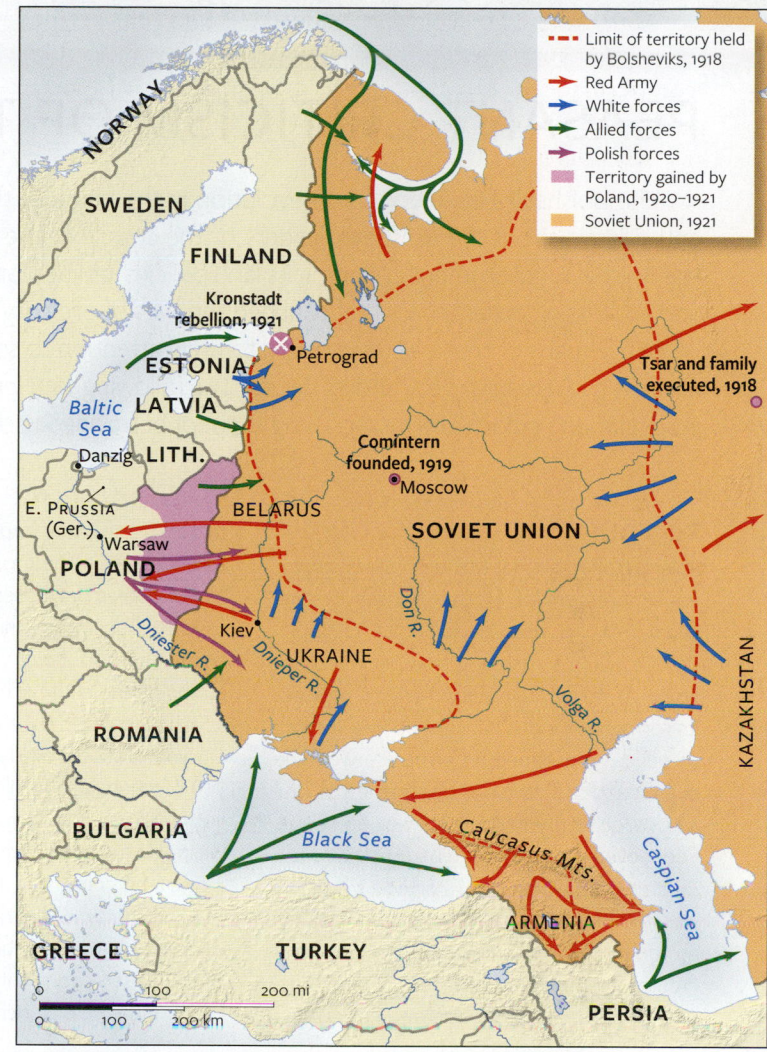

The Russian Civil War, 1918–1921 Fighting occurred at all the borders of the territory that the Bolsheviks controlled from Moscow. The Red Army fought White forces in the east and west and pushed back British, Japanese, and American forces in the north and south. It also engaged an independent Polish invasion, ultimately ceding territory to Poland. By 1921, though, the Red Army had established stable borders for an expansive USSR.

under the party dictatorship. The new regime would not only break the political power of the Russian Orthodox Church; it would also free men and women from their addiction to religion, which Karl Marx had famously called "the opium of the people."

Bolshevik agents in the countryside mocked Jesus and publicly dared God to strike them dead. Avant-garde, nonrepresentational art received official support and flourished more strongly than elsewhere in Europe. And in a utopian tract entitled *The ABC of Communism* (1919), two Bolshevik leaders promised that once the dictatorship of

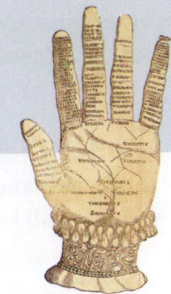

PEASANT CRITICISM OF THE BOLSHEVIKS

The Bolsheviks launched their revolution in the name of the Russian people, but the Russian people were not always enthusiastic about the Bolshevik leaders or the course of the Revolution. Hundreds of ordinary Russians wrote letters to the Bolshevik government criticizing its land policies, political program, and suppression of competing revolutionary groups, and addressing other topics that touched the lives of ordinary Russians.

While many of these letters sought to draw attention to specific injustices, others denounced the entire Revolution as a threat to Russian society and its values. The following 1918 letter, from a Russian peasant, attacks the Bolshevik leaders in indignant and colorful terms, accusing them of betraying Russia and overseeing myriad crimes against its people.

TO YOU!

Rulers, plunderers, rapists, destroyers, usurpers, oppressors of Mother Russia, citizens Lenin, Trotsky…and Co.

Allow me to ask you how long you are going to go on degrading Russia's millions, its tormented and exhausted people. Instead of peace, you signed an armistice with the enemy, and this gave our opponent a painful advantage, and you declared war on Russia. You moved the troops you had tricked to the Russian-Russian front and started a fratricidal war. Your mercenary Red Guards[1] are looting, murdering, and raping everywhere they go. A fire has consumed all our dear Mother Russia. Rail transport is idle, as are the plants and factories; the entire population has woken up to find itself in the most pathetic situation, without bread or kerosene or any of the other essentials, unclothed and unshod in unheated houses. In short: hungry and cold.…You have strangled the entire press, and freedom with it, you have wiped out the best freedom fighters, you have destroyed all Russia. Think it over, you butchers, you hirelings of the Kaiser. Isn't your turn about up, too? For all you are doing, we, politically aware Great Russians, are sending you butchers, you hirelings of the Kaiser, our curse. May you be damned, you accursed one, you bloodthirsty butchers, you hirelings of the Kaiser—don't think you're in the clear, because the Russian people will sober up and that will be the end of you. I'm writing in red ink to show that you are bloodthirsty.… I'm writing these curses, a Great Russian native of Orel Province.[2]

QUESTIONS FOR ANALYSIS

1. What crimes and abuses does the peasant accuse the Bolsheviks of perpetrating?
2. What does the letter writer mean when he calls the revolutionary leaders "hirelings of the Kaiser"?
3. What does this letter suggest about the political engagement of Russian peasants during the Russian Revolution?

[1] **Red Guards:** volunteer groups of armed workers
[2] **Orel Province:** province south of Moscow in western Russia

"Letter from a Peasant to the Bolshevik Leaders (1918)," in *Voices of Revolution, 1917,* ed. Mark D. Steinberg, trans. Marian Schwartz (New Haven: Yale University Press, 2001), pp. 302–303.

---

the proletariat had completed its work, the state would wither away, just as Marx had promised: "There will be no need for special ministers of State, for police or prisons, for laws and decrees—nothing of the sort. Just as in an orchestra all the performers watch the conductor's baton and act accordingly, so here all will consult the statistical reports and will direct their work accordingly."

These hopes extended well beyond the borders of Russia. Across the world, many socialists cheered the Bolsheviks' seizure of power and formed Communist Parties explicitly aligned with them. In 1919, the Soviet Union formally gathered these parties into a Communist International, or **Comintern**, on the model of the older Workers' Internationals, but largely under soviet control. European leaders waited nervously to see if the "plague bacillus" of communist revolution, as Churchill called it, would spread to their own countries. But it did not, thanks in part to effective resistance from national

Women and Communism A 1920 Russian propaganda poster shows the sun shining on a triumphant woman worker, who gestures to other women streaming into social or cultural institutions such as a day care center, library, and a social club. Celebrating the Revolution's gains for women, the caption reads: "What the October Revolution gave to the woman worker and the woman peasant."

BIRTH OF THE USSR

In 1919–21, Russia lurched through one of the most devastating phases of its history. Partly owing to the disruptions of the Civil War, a massive famine struck, killing as many as 7 million people. Reports circulated of cannibalism. Yet eventually, the Bolsheviks and the Red Army, which Trotsky, despite his lack of military experience, had forged into an effective fighting force, managed to eke out a victory and restore order. The Whites, suffering from disunity and poor communications, could only mobilize 300,000 men, counting the small western expeditionary forces. The Reds mobilized 800,000 and benefited from controlling the traditional power centers of the rigidly centralized Russian state: Petrograd and Moscow. They could also count on support from urban workers and a large portion of the peasantry.

The end of the Civil War in 1921 left little doubt about the sort of regime that would now rule the Union of Soviet Socialist Republics (USSR), as the former Russian Empire became known. In theory, a new federal structure gave considerable autonomy to the most important ethnic groups, such as Ukrainians, Belorussians, and Kazakhs, each now gathered into a separate Soviet Republic of their own. In practice, however, local authorities remained subordinate to the party bosses in Moscow.

Lenin proved willing to compromise, temporarily, on economic issues. To deal with the effects of the famine and wartime disruption, he proclaimed the New Economic

armies and right-wing paramilitary forces. Proclamation of a Soviet Republic in Berlin, in November 1918, by German Communist Party co-founder Karl Liebknecht (1871–1919), went nowhere, and Liebknecht and his charismatic colleague Rosa Luxemburg (1871–1919) were later assassinated by right-wing militants. In Bavaria, socialists actually did establish a short-lived Soviet Republic, but it was suppressed by German soldiers aided by right-wing paramilitary groups. A Hungarian Soviet Republic, which nationalized all private property in the country, lasted for several months in 1919 under the leadership of the communist Béla Kun (1886–1938). But it quickly found itself at war with Czechoslovakia and Romania, which had strong backing from the Allies, and within months Kun, too, had been overthrown.

Rosa Luxemburg Co-founder of the German Communist Party, Luxemburg is photographed here at a meeting of the Second International Social Democratic Congress in 1907. The highly educated Luxemburg argued for a party committed to revolution—though she later criticized Lenin's power-centralizing approach in the wake of the Bolshevik Revolution.

Kronstadt Mutiny Sailors salute the commander of the rebels who took control of a battleship during the 1921 mutiny of sailors at the Kronstadt naval base.

Policy, which retreated from the severe measures of war communism by allowing limited free trade in food and services, although it left the central state firmly in control of the economy's "commanding heights." But the Bolsheviks would not compromise on the issue of their own political power. They refused to allow free elections, a free press, or free trade unions. The Cheka quickly evolved into a much-feared secret police. And in March 1921, the regime demonstrated it would not even brook opposition from its most legendary supporters. After strikes broke out in Petrograd, sailors at the Kronstadt naval base near Petrograd, who had provided key support for the Bolsheviks in 1917, mutinied in support of the strikers. They demanded that Bolshevik commissars cede power and allow the creation of a truly popular soviet republic, controlled by peasants and workers. Trotsky sent Red Army and Cheka units to slaughter them. A wave of disillusionment spread across Russia and among its supporters in the West. But Lenin remained securely in power.

THE VERSAILLES PEACE SETTLEMENT

At the other end of Europe, the victorious western Allies were trying to resolve a host of questions that the war had left dangerously unsettled. How would Wilson's principle of national self-determination be put into practice? What would happen to the Central powers' colonial possessions? What about questions of responsibility for the war? Would some sort of international body come into being to prevent further outbreaks of war? To settle these questions, representatives from thirty-one countries gathered for six months in 1919 in the vast palace complex of Versailles outside of Paris. The meeting fell squarely into the tradition of peace conferences that stretched back to the 1648 Peace of Westphalia. It was by far the largest and most ambitious of these conferences. And it was also, by most measures, the least successful.

President Wilson, who attended, hoped that the **Versailles Peace Conference** would inaugurate an era of peaceful international cooperation, overseen by a new **League of Nations**. The League indeed came into being in 1919–20. But the American's idealism collided with the desire of France and Britain to exact revenge on the Germans. Both countries were just beginning to come to terms with their appalling losses in the war. France had buried nearly 1.4 million of its young men, and fewer than a quarter of the nearly 8 million it mobilized had come home unscathed. Britain had lost nearly a million men, and the grief touched every part of its vast empire and dominions. In both countries, social elites accounted for a disproportionate number of the dead. The two countries' prime ministers, the canny republican centrist Georges Clemenceau (1841–1929) and the Welsh Liberal David Lloyd George (1863–1945), came to Versailles convinced of the Germans' guilt for the war. They insisted that Germany accept full responsibility and pay mammoth reparations—equivalent to hundreds of billions of dollars today—while reducing its army to a token force of 100,000.

Guided in theory by the principle of self-determination, the participants at Versailles signed a series of treaties that radically redrew the map of Europe. The Austro-Hungarian Empire vanished, with Austria and Hungary reduced to small, ethnically homogenous republics. Its remaining territory was parceled out to the new states of Yugoslavia (initially called the Kingdom of Serbs, Croats, and Slovenes) and Czechoslovakia, to an expanded Romania, to Italy, and to the newly independent Poland. The four centuries in which Habsburgs had helped shape the fortunes of a continent had come to an abrupt end. Meanwhile, Germany lost significant territory to Poland, returned Alsace-Lorraine to France, and accepted the demilitarization of the German Rhineland. Although the situation within the former Russian Empire remained enormously unstable, the independence of Finland and the

Europe, the Middle East, and Africa after World War I, 1922 At the Versailles Peace Conference, Allied leaders divided up the territory of the defeated powers. Germany had to return Alsace-Lorraine to France, with the Rhineland established as a demilitarized zone; Poland regained its independence; other parts of eastern Europe and the Austro-Hungarian Empire were divided into independent states. The newly founded League of Nations designated former German colonies in Africa and parts of the Ottoman Empire as mandates to be administered by Britain, France, and other Allied powers.

three Baltic states was recognized. Turkey was reduced to the ethnically Turkish areas of Europe and Anatolia. The Young Turks now formally abolished the sultanate and proclaimed a republic. The Ottoman Empire was no more.

THE SEEDS OF FUTURE CONFLICT Yet at Versailles and a number of successor conferences, the Allies applied the principle of self-determination very unevenly. In some areas, they staged plebiscites (referenda) to determine the new borders. But they assigned the mountainous Sudetenland region of western Bohemia to the new Czechoslovak state, despite its heavily German population, and stranded large Hungarian populations within Romania and Yugoslavia. Large Greek and Turkish minorities remained within each other's countries. And the principle completely failed to apply to non-Europeans. The former German overseas colonies such as Southwest Africa (now Namibia) and Tanganyika (now Tanzania), and most of Turkey's Middle Eastern possessions (Lebanon, Syria, Palestine, Iraq), were given the status of "mandates" theoretically subject to the League of Nations. But their administration fell principally to Britain and France, which treated them largely as additions to their own colonial empires. Calls by national movements within those empires for representation at Versailles were ignored.

Even as the representatives returned home from Versailles, it was clear that the conference had done more to provoke future conflicts than to prevent them. In the early 1920s, Greece and Turkey carried out a massive, bloody population exchange to "resolve" the issue of their reciprocal minorities. Greeks were expelled from the new Turkish Republic, and Turks from Greece. Traditionally Greek cities in Asia Minor were transformed into almost entirely Turkish ones: Smyrna, for instance, became the Turkish Izmir. Along the new borders and existing ethnic divides, violence and political instability remained endemic. And the new League of Nations, while hardly toothless, proved tragically inadequate to the task of managing the peace, especially after an isolationist U.S. Senate rebuffed a broken-hearted and incapacitated President Wilson and rejected American membership. Worst of all, in Germany the same conservative, militarist forces that had done the most to bring the war about now blamed the new, left-leaning German Republic for the humiliating peace terms, even alleging that Germany had not been defeated but "stabbed in the back" by disloyal socialists, liberals, and Jews. (The point seemed superficially plausible, since Germany surrendered without having had its own territory invaded.) Already in 1919, the raucous German political sphere was filled with strident calls for revenge.

An exhausted continent suffered one additional body blow. In 1918–19, as soldiers returned home in crowded, unsanitary railroad cars and refugees streamed across newly erected borders, they carried with them deadly invisible passengers: a new and virulent flu virus. Within months, the so-called Spanish flu had killed 21 million Europeans and 40 million people world-wide, deepening the oceans of grief left by the war. It was a tragic end to what had been, arguably, the most tragic decade yet seen in European history.

CONCLUSION

Overall, a war fought in the name of civilization had produced unprecedented barbarism. The hopes for quick victory, and the claim that war would have a cleansing effect like swimmers leaping into pure water, died choking and screaming in the muck of the trenches. So did ancient ideals of military glory and honor. All the contending powers had discovered, to their horror and grief, what total war looked like when driven by the full force of modern industry. Since World War I, and in direct reaction to its horrors, the West has had a fundamentally different attitude toward war from what often prevailed before. While accepted as a grim necessity, it is no longer something to be glorified for its own sake. Since World War I, nearly all serious war literature has been antiwar literature.

A war fought to make the world "safe for democracy," in Woodrow Wilson's words, had left democracy somewhat more widespread than in 1914, but also deeply imperiled. Everywhere in the new regimes of central Europe, fragile democratic constitutions swayed under the attacks of angry nationalist and ideological militants. In Russia, the greatest European revolution since the eighteenth century had produced, after ghastly civil war, an increasingly repressive ideological dictatorship. And in one other country, soon after the war, democracy failed as well. In the fall of 1922, after a period of extended political and social turmoil, the Italian parliament granted its new prime minister the power to rule by decree for a year. His name was Benito Mussolini, the head of a party that had not only an expanding membership but also a dangerous paramilitary force: the Fascists. Many in Europe saw him as a role model. The stage was set for a battle of ideological extremes.

CHAPTER REVIEW

KEY TERMS

Schlieffen Plan (p. 707)
Young Turks (p. 708)
trench warfare (p. 714)
total war (p. 715)
Gallipoli Campaign (p. 718)

Lusitania (p. 719)
battle of Verdun (p. 721)
battle of the Somme
 (p. 723)
Armenian genocide
 (p. 725)

soviets (p. 728)
Provisional Government
 (p. 728)
Lenin (p. 728)
Bolshevik Revolution
 (p. 729)

Fourteen Points (p. 732)
war communism (p. 733)
Comintern (p. 734)
Versailles Peace
 Conference (p. 736)
League of Nations (p. 736)

REVIEW QUESTIONS

1. By the early 1900s, why was there an increased likelihood of war in Europe?

2. Why did the assassination of Franz Ferdinand spark World War I?

3. What factors contributed to the bloody stalemate that persisted on the western front?

4. In what ways did civilians become involved in the war effort?

5. How did governments mobilize their societies and economies for total war?

6. How did the war expand into a global conflict?

7. In what ways did new technologies change the conduct of war?

8. Following the collapse of the tsarist government in Russia, what led to the October Revolution in Russia?

9. How did the Bolsheviks change Russian government and society?

10. How did the peace settlements established at the Versailles Peace Conference reshape Europe and set in motion future conflicts?

CORE OBJECTIVES

After reading this chapter, you should have a solid understanding of the following core objectives. To strengthen your grasp of the core objectives, use the resources on the Student Site for The West.

- Identify the factors and events that led to the outbreak of World War I.
- Outline how and why the war developed into a horrific stalemate.
- Analyze the war's impact on the home front and on overseas colonies.

- Describe the major events of the late period of the war.
- Explain the causes and main events of the Russian Revolution of 1917.
- Evaluate the aftermath of the war around the world.

 GO TO **inQuizitive** TO SEE WHAT YOU'VE LEARNED—AND LEARN WHAT YOU'VE MISSED—WITH PERSONALIZED FEEDBACK ALONG THE WAY.

CHRONOLOGY

22

Ideologies

THE TRIUMPH OF POLITICAL EXTREMES

1922–1940

1936–1939
Spanish Civil War

1936–1938
Great Terror in
Soviet Union

1936
Nazi Germany
and Fascist Italy
sign alliance

Sept. 1, 1939
Germany invades
Poland

Aug. 23, 1939
Nazi-Soviet
non-aggression
pact

1935
Nazi regime passes
Nuremberg Laws

Nov. 9, 1938
Kristallnacht

1935
Italy invades Ethiopia

1938–1939
Germany gains control
of Czechoslovakia

March 1938
Germany annexes Austria

I n the late afternoon of May 18, 1933, four large barges anchored on the shores of the island of Nazino, in the Ob River in Siberia, some 1,500 miles east of Moscow. The island was desolate and uninhabited—a flat, wet expanse of swamp grass and poplar trees. A light snow was falling as the barges unloaded their cargo: some 5,000 human beings. A local official described them as "these injured and ill people, these poor wretches with deathly pale faces, most of them in rags, a few dressed in city clothes, with shoes and a coat, but all of them without even a bag. All these people got off the boat—if they could still stand up—with nothing, without any provisions at all, empty-handed." It had taken the barges four days to reach Nazino from the Siberian city of Tomsk, during which time the passengers had received little or nothing to eat. The barges also carried twenty tons of flour, most of which was dumped into wet sandbags on the riverbank.

Over the next several days, official reports described scenes of chaos as the men and women abandoned on the shore tried to make fires and primitive shelters, and fought for flour that they lacked the means to bake into bread. Those who ate raw flour mixed with river water developed dysentery. Hundreds died of hunger, exposure, or violence. Hundreds more drowned attempting to cross the frigid, swiftly flowing river in primitive

Political Upheaval The Surrealist artist Max Ernst (1891–1976) painted his *Fireside Angel* in 1937. The grotesque image is a protest against the successes of Fascist forces against leftist Republicans in the Spanish Civil War. The creature's hideousness and its rampage over the landscape are suggestive of the rise of totalitarian regimes and the threat of war that haunted Europe in the 1930s.

- Why was there so much instability across Europe in the early 1920s?
- What were the major characteristics of modernist culture in the period?
- What were the effects of the Great Depression in Europe?
- How did anti-imperial nationalism grow in this period?
- What led to the emergence of Hitler and Stalin?
- What were the major steps leading to the outbreak of World War II?

rafts, or were shot by guards. And the survivors resorted to the most desperate possible measures. One official wrote: "They told us that people had begun eating the dead bodies, that they were cooking human flesh." On May 27, more barges brought thousands more helpless men and women to the island. They suffered the same fate as their predecessors. Within two months, two-thirds of those delivered to Nazino—what historians have since dubbed Cannibal Island—in late May had died.

Who were these people? Most had been rounded up off the streets of Moscow and Leningrad (the former Saint Petersburg) because they lacked proper documentation, or were suspected of counterrevolutionary activity, or belonged to the class of kulaks (rich peasants) that the Soviet government was bent on eradicating. Soviet officials had no intention of actually killing these people and the others who died on Nazino. They were part of a planned deportation of nearly 500,000 "socially undesirable elements" whom the Soviet regime expelled from its cities in 1933.

But a high proportion of these 500,000 did die. They, in turn, represent only a small proportion of the total victims of the government of Joseph Stalin, who came to power in the 1920s and ruled until his death in 1953. The best estimates of the total number range as high as 10 to 15 million Soviet citizens.

In 1918, the victorious Allies of World War I had hoped that their success would bring a better world into being. Instead, for too many Europeans the 1920s and 1930s became an age of ideological dictatorship, totalitarianism, terror, and mass murder, of which the horrors on Nazino were just one extreme example. In the two largest European states, the Soviet Union and Germany, there came to power two of the most repressive regimes in the history of the world. Dictatorships spread across more than half of all European states, and in many of the rest, democracy seemed on the verge of extinction. It was an age of intrusive surveillance of civilian populations, of arrests and executions of innocent victims, of vast archipelagos of prison camps, and, ultimately, of genocide. And it led directly into the most murderous and horrific conflict in human history: World War II, which began in 1939.

Today, in the West, we tend to associate the word *totalitarianism* with the idea of a ruthlessly efficient government that controls every aspect of its citizens' lives. Yet as the Nazino example suggests, the reality of the USSR in these years was considerably more chaotic and disorganized, a bizarre mixture of frightening power and shocking weakness. The Soviet officials who brought the deportees to the island were cogs in a fatally dysfunctional system that could not handle the massive strains put upon it, and they feared disobeying orders lest they, too, become victims. Yet, as we will see, neither Stalin's regime, nor Adolf Hitler's in Germany, can be reduced to repression, brutality, and fear alone. Both regimes enjoyed, for a long time, the support of millions of people who participated willingly in what they considered to be experiments to create a new, superior sort of human society. The Soviet system remained dedicated, in theory, to socialist ideals that continued to inspire millions around the globe.

The story of Europe in the 1920s and 1930s is not just a story of ideological extremism. It is also a story of remarkable artistic energies in the heyday of modernism. It is a story of continued economic and technological development, even amid the worst economic slump of modern times. It is a story of western European countries struggling to retain their overseas empires in the face of a floodtide of nationalism that they themselves helped to inspire. And it is a story of the western democracies bending, almost breaking, but eventually being forced to confront the worst of the dictators, Adolf Hitler.

A BLIGHTED RECOVERY

The men and women who, in 1914, believed that war would have a cleansing, regenerative effect on European society were proven wrong, not merely by the war itself but by its chaotic aftermath. Recovery from the bloodletting and destruction of 1914–18 would be a difficult, painful process.

CONTINUING VIOLENCE AND INSTABILITY

Indeed, the end of the war did not even bring relief from mass violence. Hundreds of thousands—possibly millions—died in the aftermath of the Armenian genocide, the Russian Civil War and accompanying famine, and border conflicts between Poland and Russia. Hundreds of thousands more lost their lives in the expulsions of populations in Greece and Turkey; the suppression of the communist revolutions in Hungary and Germany; and the more small-scale violence that accompanied Mussolini's Fascist takeover in Italy.

The British Isles as well experienced a small civil war after a majority of Irish voters chose the pro-independence Sinn Féin Party in the 1918 general election, following the failed Easter Uprising of 1916. After a year and a half of sporadic fighting, the British recognized the southern, Catholic-majority provinces of the island as an independent Irish Free State. In northern Africa, Spain suffered a humiliating defeat by Moroccan Berber insurgents in the so-called Rif War, with half its army of 20,000 killed or wounded in a single battle in the summer of 1921. The defeat led to a military coup in Spain two years later.

Although less destructive than the massive battlefield clashes of the world war, these outbreaks were dangerously destabilizing. The battles between the Irish Republican Army and Protestant forces, the orchestrated street thuggery of Mussolini's Fascists, and the fighting in the former Russian Empire brought violence directly into the heart of European cities. They made a return to anything Europeans saw as normal life almost impossible, while creating a yearning in many places for strong executive power that could enforce civil peace—even at the cost of human rights. While most European countries—including the newly independent states of central and eastern Europe—began the 1920s as nominal democracies, in relatively few states did democratic practice have a firm anchor.

POST-WAR GERMANY AND THE ORIGINS OF NAZISM

This pattern held true particularly in the country whose stability mattered most to post-Versailles Europe:

Germany. In 1919, a convention in the town of Weimar produced a constitution for the Republic proclaimed the previous November. It gave the vote to all adult men and women, and it included provisions for a powerful elected president who had the ability to dissolve the Reichstag (parliament) and, in certain situations, rule by decree.

But despite the attempts to ground the new regime in popular sovereignty, many Germans considered it illegitimate. They associated the **Weimar Republic** with the malevolent conspirators—above all, socialists and Jews—who had supposedly stabbed the country in the back, precipitating the defeat and the 1918 revolution. German military leaders resisted the demilitarization demanded by the Versailles treaty, and supported the formation of paramilitary Freikorps ("free corps"). In Berlin and other major cities, these right-wing groups fought street battles with police and with Communists and Socialists throughout the early 1920s. And in early 1920, they supported army and navy officers who attempted an unsuccessful coup d'état in Berlin.

Among the radical groups that proliferated in Germany at this time was the tiny, Munich-based German Workers' Party. Its members were racist, nationalist, and generally hostile to capitalism, and some had occult beliefs related to traditional Nordic mythology. In September 1919, the German army sent a low-ranking soldier to observe and report on the party. The man duly showed up for a meeting at a beer hall and promptly fell into an argument with one of the members. Impressed with the soldier's debating skills, the party leader invited him to join, and he accepted, becoming member number 55. His name was **Adolf Hitler**.

At this point in his life, Hitler struck many people as a crank. Born in 1889 in the small Austrian town of Braunau-am-Inn, the son of a minor customs official, he was a poor and rebellious student who left school at age sixteen. Dreaming of a career as an artist, he applied to the Academy of Fine Arts in Vienna, but it rejected him. He spent most of the next nine years in the Austrian capital, making a poor living painting postcards and hanging wallpaper, living mostly in flophouses, and absorbing the venomous anti-Semitism that permeated so much of Viennese life at the time. Pale-skinned, with lank dark hair and poor teeth, badly dressed and given to obsessive ranting, he cut a strange, unimpressive figure. He found salvation of a sort in the war. Joining the German army in the summer of 1914, he beat considerable odds by surviving more than four years at the front.

In the German Workers' Party, Hitler found his true calling. To all who would listen, he expounded a political

Hyperinflation A banknote for 100 trillion ("billion" in German) marks, issued by Germany's national bank in February 1924, indicates the extent of inflation during the economic crisis of the early 1920s.

theory hammered together out of spare boards of socialism, tales of worldwide Jewish conspiracy, and an extreme racial nationalism. He also spoke with a mesmerizing intensity and conviction that led others to follow him. Soon he had risen to head the party, which he renamed the National Socialist German Workers' Party, nicknamed the **Nazis** (from the first two syllables of the German word for *national*). Under his leadership, membership quickly increased. By the fall of 1923, it had reached nearly 20,000 and acquired a paramilitary arm known as the brown shirts in echo of Italy's black shirts, the followers of the Fascist leader Mussolini. With a genius for effective symbolism, Hitler had also chosen a striking visual emblem for the party: the ancient Indian twisted cross known as the swastika.

WEIMAR IN CRISIS

Conditions in Germany seemed almost perfect for the rise of just such a fanatical, antidemocratic party. Resentment against the Weimar government for accepting Allied demands remained high. In particular, the massive reparations imposed on Germany at Versailles threatened to smother the economy before a recovery from the war could even start. To put some pressure back on the Allies, Foreign Minister Walter Rathenau negotiated a treaty of military and economic cooperation with the Soviet Union in 1922, the Rapallo Treaty. But the Allies remained rigid in their demands, and when an inflation-plagued Germany failed to meet its payment schedule in late 1922, the Belgian and French armies moved in to occupy the rich industrial territory of the Ruhr, enraging German public opinion. It was a climate in which political violence continued to fester—the Jewish Rathenau himself was shot

and killed by anti-Semitic assassins in 1922. The German government printed money to finance a strike of Ruhr miners against the occupation forces, thereby feeding a catastrophic inflationary spiral and economic collapse.

The great German inflation of 1923 was not the first incident of post-war hyperinflation: that honor belonged to Austria and Hungary, which had inherited the crushing war debt of the entire Austro-Hungarian Empire. But the German inflation remains emblematic of the phenomenon. The reichsmark, which had traded at a little over 4 to the dollar in 1914, and 400 to the dollar in the early summer of 1922, fell to a rate of some 4 trillion to the dollar by November 1923. On November 15, a 100-billion-mark bill bought just one loaf of bread. The national and local governments alike frantically issued new banknotes by the day or reprinted new values on old ones. Hapless shoppers carried their money to the shop in large baskets, returning home with their purchases in their purses and wallets. The inflation wiped out both savings and debt, and impoverished anyone living on a fixed income. Germany's economy had effectively collapsed.

At precisely this moment, the Nazi Party attempted to seize power. Hitler had managed to enlist the support of General Erich von Ludendorff, who had served under the aged Paul von Hindenburg as effective commander of German forces at the end of the war. On November 9, 1923, the Nazis assembled in a Munich beer hall with plans to seize the government of Bavaria and then march on Berlin. However, local police and military units remained loyal to the Republic and quickly squelched the so-called **Beer Hall Putsch**. Hitler and Ludendorff were put on trial, and Hitler received a five-year sentence, of which he served less

Beer Hall Putsch Hitler stands at the front of a crowd during the Beer Hall Putsch in Munich on November 9, 1923. He is flanked by Alfred Rosenberg (left), head of the Nazis during Hitler's stint in jail, and Friedrich Weber (right), one of the architects of the Putsch.

than a year in comfortable conditions. Despite the failure, the incident raised the party's profile and did not greatly damage Hitler's political credibility. He used his time in prison to write a ranting, rambling book called *Mein Kampf* ("My Struggle"), which was animated by a vicious anti-Semitism and insisted on the need for Germany to find "living space" (*Lebensraum*) to the east, at the expense of its Slavic neighbors.

POST-WAR BRITAIN AND FRANCE

Although other western European countries did not experience the same degree of political instability as Germany, the early 1920s were everywhere years of difficulty and disruption. In Britain, unemployment exceeding 10 percent belied Prime Minister David Lloyd George's campaign slogan about making a country "fit for heroes to live in." As returning soldiers swelled the labor force, industrial employers tried to lengthen the working day while reducing pay—especially in the key coal-mining sector. Working-class frustration swelled the ranks of the Labour Party, now led by the charismatic orator Ramsey MacDonald (1866–1937). In 1924, Labour won its first election. The party's platform called for public ownership of major industries and an expanded social welfare net, including subsidized low-income housing, unemployment insurance, and pensions for the elderly and war widows. But Labour also rejected the Soviet model, and the Communist Party itself only attracted a small minority of the British electorate.

Things were different in France, where the Communist Party had split off from the Socialists in 1920 and quickly outstripped their membership numbers. The Communists did well in the industrial, working-class suburbs that had sprung up around major French cities, taking over a large number of municipalities in the 1920s. There they worked to enact ambitious social programs on a local level, such as a series of free holiday camps for children—who were thereby exposed to both a healthier climate and a degree of ideological indoctrination. Conservatives feared with some justification that the French Communist Party was taking orders directly from Moscow and might place Soviet interests above their own national ones. In France, as in Britain, conservatives stayed in office throughout most of the 1920s, initially benefiting from nationalist enthusiasm at the military victory. But in 1924, France suffered a bout of destabilizing inflation (although nothing to compare with the German experience), which helped propel a Radical-Socialist "cartel of the left" into power, but only for a short time.

FRAGILE NEW STATES

The new European states created in the wake of World War I came into being amid waves of national pride and hopes that democracy might now take root in the heart of the Continent. And just like many countries to the west, the new states—Austria, Hungary, Czechoslovakia, Yugoslavia, Poland, Turkey, and the Baltic states Lithuania, Latvia, and Estonia—mostly embraced an expanded, "social" vision of democracy, which counted subsistence and even work as a basic right. In localities where socialist parties came to power, they tried to pursue ambitious social welfare policies. Social Democratic officials in Red Vienna, as the capital of the new, shrunken Austrian republic quickly became known, offered perhaps the best example. They built public housing to relieve a housing crisis, imposed stringent taxes on luxury goods, and gave generous assistance packages, including clothes, to all needy new parents. At the same time, the city supervised its residents more carefully than before, moving quickly, for instance, to remove children from families it deemed irresponsible.

Turkey emerged as a new state following the Versailles conference, when in 1920 the Treaty of Sèvres dismantled the Ottoman Empire, leaving it with only a small foothold in Europe and reducing its Asian possessions to Anatolia. A charismatic Ottoman general, Mustafa Kemal (1881–1938), successfully drove foreign forces out of this territory, and in 1923 he became the first president of the new Republic of Turkey. Taking the name of Atatürk ("Father of the Turks"), he pursued a radical policy of Westernization, secularization, and Turkish nationalism, seeking to transform the Republic into a modern, ethnically homogeneous nation-state. He abolished the Muslim caliphate that had been associated with the Ottoman sultanate and separated civil law from Islamic law. He advocated integrating women more fully into Turkish society through education, a greater degree of legal equality, and the adoption of Western dress. He also supported the replacement of the Arabic alphabet by a new Turkish alphabet derived from the Latin.

ETHNIC TENSIONS
All of the new states that emerged from the post-war conferences faced a thicket of challenges, with nationalism first among them. The Versailles agreement had given some 60 million inhabitants of the former Austro-Hungarian, Russian, and Ottoman Empires nation-states of their own. But at the same time it left 25 million more Europeans living as members of "national minorities" within these new states. The newly

minority groups, the Polish government repeatedly trod on minority rights. During the inter-war period, it shuttered almost all Ukrainian-language schools and violently repressed Ukrainian nationalist activity.

In Czechoslovakia, the dominant Czechs and Slovaks had to deal not only with each other but also with large, homogeneously German and Hungarian territories, whose populations felt little allegiance to the new state. And Yugoslavia (initially called the Kingdom of Serbs, Croats and Slovenes) was a wild ethnic and religious stew of Serbs, Croats, Bosnian Muslims, Slovenes, Germans, Hungarians, and Albanians, to name only the largest groups, and of Roman Catholics, Eastern Orthodox Christians, and Muslims. By contrast, the newly independent state of Hungary had a far more ethnically homogeneous population, but over 30 percent of Europe's Hungarians lived outside its newly shrunken borders, leading to resentments of a different sort.

The ethnic tensions in turn worsened the urban-rural divide in the new states. Most of them still had large peasant majorities who looked with suspicion on capital cities like Warsaw, Budapest, and Riga, where a large proportion of the businesses and visible wealth belonged to Jews, Germans, and other minority groups. Many of the new states, including Poland and the Baltic countries, immediately implemented land reform, breaking up large estates (especially those owned by Germans and Russians) and turning the descendants of serfs into property owners for the first time. But lingering disputes over land ownership led to the spread of "smallholder" political parties that had little loyalty to democratic institutions and were often virulently anti-Semitic.

CRUMBLING DEMOCRACIES Already by the mid-1920s, many of the frail new democracies were crumbling. In Poland and Lithuania, the armed forces carried out coups against elected governments in 1926. In Poland, they brought to power Marshal Józef Piłsudski (1867–1935), the leader of Polish forces in the recent war against the Soviet Union, who called for a "healing" of the Polish body politic. Although Poland never veered entirely into dictatorship, democratic rights remained starkly curtailed. In Yugoslavia, a Serbian member of parliament himself shot dead the leader of a major Croatian political party in 1928. A year later, King Alexander (r. 1921–1934) banned all political parties. Of all the new states, only Czechoslovakia managed to remain democratic throughout the inter-war period, and that with some difficulty.

In Italy, **Benito Mussolini** and his Fascist movement consolidated their hold on the country between 1922 and

National Minorities in Eastern Europe, 1920s The new countries of eastern Europe were far from the ethnically homogeneous nation-states that had been imagined by western diplomats. Poland and Hungary, for instance, contained significant German minorities; Czechoslovakia was split evenly between two ethnic groups; and Romania and Yugoslavia were a mix of many different groups. Many cities—especially in Poland and the Soviet Union—contained large Jewish populations. This would all have consequences for the nationalisms of the 1930s and the outbreak of World War II.

independent Poland, for instance, included 18 million ethnic Poles and nearly 9 million others, including some 4 million Ukrainians, 1 million Germans, and 3 million Jews. And despite an international treaty that made the new League of Nations the formal protector of Poland's

1925 with considerable help from the social and political elites. Mussolini, a former editor of the official Italian Socialist newspaper, had come to prominence because of his skill in using the press, and by developing a program that combined an insistence on social order with considerable promises to the working class and peasantry (including an eight-hour work day and free public education). His National Fascist Party grew, and in October 1922 he staged a "March on Rome" with 20,000 of his paramilitary black shirts. With the political system in a state of paralysis, King Vittorio Emmanuelle III (r. 1900–1946) named Mussolini Prime Minister. Mussolini presented himself to the social elites as the only possible bulwark against Russian-style revolution, and presented himself to the people (and particularly to embittered war veterans) as their advocate against the ruling oligarchy. He deployed his black shirts to intimidate or even kill his political opponents, and by 1925 he and the Fascists had a commanding majority in Parliament and were moving toward total control of the Italian state.

The only large European region where democracy survived without serious threats between the wars was Scandinavia. There, in contrast to the new central and eastern European states, urban social democrats managed to work out alliances with rural voters and introduced robust social welfare programs. Sweden, ruled by the Social Democratic Party after 1932, introduced particularly generous social insurance and pension programs, supported by high levels of income tax.

THE SOVIET UNION AND RISE OF JOSEPH STALIN

The newly founded Soviet Union, no more democratic than its tsarist predecessor, remained as dangerously unstable as central and eastern Europe. Although the Communists had won the Civil War, and the New Economic Policy had saved the economy from meltdown and preserved a partial market system, the regime's future direction remained uncertain. Leon Trotsky, the charismatic leader of the Red Army, argued that the USSR should continue to promote revolution abroad (using the Comintern to coordinate the actions of foreign Communist parties) and also begin a process of rapid, forced industrialization. Others in the party suspected Trotsky of Bonapartist tendencies—nearly all the party leaders had read deeply in the history of the French Revolution and feared that the Revolution of 1917 would degenerate into militarism along the lines of the Revolution of 1789. When

Stalin and Lenin Stalin (right) visited an ailing Lenin at his estate in 1922. This photo of their meeting was heavily doctored to conceal Lenin's illness. In later years, the photo was used to demonstrate Stalin's supposed closeness to the founder of the Soviet Union.

Lenin, who had already barely survived an assassination attempt, suffered a stroke in 1922, it became clear that he would not be able to retain control of the party for long.

The man who quickly emerged as Trotsky's most effective challenger for the succession was almost as unlikely a leader for this new version of the Russian Empire as Adolf Hitler would be for Germany. Josef Dzhugashvili (later changing his name to **Joseph Stalin**) had been born in 1879 in Georgia, in the Caucasus region. The son of a violently hard-drinking artisan and a devout mother, he had initially hoped to enter the priesthood, only to rebel against the conservatism of the Eastern Orthodox churches. Joining the Bolsheviks, he became known both for organizing ability and for violence; at one point, he personally took part in a bank robbery to raise funds. He then took on the Russian name Stalin ("steel"). Repeated spells in prison and in Siberian exile won him a high reputation and Lenin's favor. He even became editor of the Bolshevik newspaper *Pravda*, despite never speaking Russian with complete fluency.

Stalin served as one of Lenin's most important deputies in the Bolshevik takeover in 1917 and thereafter had a place in the highest circles of the party. In 1922, he became its general secretary—a position that gave him control over the all-important party bureaucracy. As general secretary, he argued against too heavy a focus on fomenting revolution elsewhere, suggesting instead that the Soviet government first build "socialism in a single country." And he opposed Trotsky's ambitious program of industrialization.

At the end of 1922, Lenin suffered a second, even more debilitating stroke. In a testament that circulated soon afterward and was attributed to Lenin (the authorship remains disputed), the Soviet leader warned of the "boundless power" Stalin was accumulating and suggested that the Georgian be removed from the position of general secretary. But by this point, Stalin had placed too many allies in key positions in the party. And when Lenin died in early 1924, Stalin had his followers ready to hail him as Lenin's hand-picked successor.

Trotsky tried to organize a so-called Left Opposition to Stalin. He even argued for allowing a degree of freedom to non-Communist organizations. But Stalin ruthlessly outmaneuvered him and by 1927 had won a decisive victory. Trotsky and his allies were expelled from the Communist Party. Understanding all too well the need for a cult of leadership in a country with such powerful autocratic traditions, Stalin's propagandists presented him as an almost superhuman genius, working tirelessly to promote the welfare of the Soviet people. Lenin, meanwhile, was virtually deified, his body carefully preserved and put on permanent display in a mausoleum in Red Square next to the Kremlin.

MODERNIST CULTURE AND SOCIETY

The highly unsettled political, social, and economic conditions of the 1920s gave new inspiration to the modernist movement in art and literature, and encouraged new ways of living in cities such as Paris and Berlin.

MODERNIST CULTURE

Many artists and writers in the 1920s, particularly those who had experienced the trenches, testified to the cultural impact of the war. The British painter and author Wyndham Lewis (1882–1957), a veteran of the western front, referred to the war as a "dividing wall in time, a thousand miles high and a thousand miles thick." Yet in many ways, the war simply gave further impetus to modernist tendencies clearly visible before 1914.

LITERATURE Much post-war poetry continued to experiment with the whirling, fragmentary, disorienting forms of verse that were already common in pre-war Paris and Vienna. Here one of the greatest examples was provided by the Anglo-American poet T. S. Eliot (1888–1965). The opening section of his 1922 masterpiece, "The Waste Land," consisted mostly of apparently disconnected shards of speech, the effect being rather like scanning rapidly through different radio stations. The poem mixed figures out of classical mythology, stray invocations of Shakespeare and Dante, and caustic images of passionless sex to create a tableau of a fragmented, sterile civilization, although the conclusion contained a faint promise of renewed fertility and hope amid the ruins. The Irish poet William Butler Yeats (1865–1939) evoked the horrifying image of a monstrous "second coming" in a 1919 poem that seemed to lament the continuing political turmoil of the post-war period:

> Things fall apart; the centre cannot hold;
> Mere anarchy is loosed upon the world,
> The blood-dimmed tide is loosed, and everywhere
> The ceremony of innocence is drowned;
> The best lack all conviction, while the worst
> Are full of passionate intensity.

The post-war period also saw the triumph of modernist prose fiction. The greatest single example (as well as one of the longest) was *In Search of Lost Time* by the French novelist Marcel Proust (1871–1922), whose publication in seven large volumes stretched from 1913 to 1927. Unlike the great novels of the nineteenth century, its plot, set in the aristocratic world where Proust himself had grown up, mattered much less than the narrator's delicate exploration of his own memories and emotions and ruminations on the nature of art. In 1922 the Irish writer James Joyce (1882–1941) published his monumental novel *Ulysses*, devoted to chronicling a single day seen through the eyes of a Dubliner named Leopold Bloom. The novel is fiercely difficult: a tangle of classical allusions, abrupt breaks in the narrative, long digressions, and numerous puns, and requiring intimate familiarity with the topography of early twentieth-century Dublin. Its use of obscenity led to several attempts to ban it. But its stream-of-consciousness technique was widely hailed for capturing something essential about the operations of the human mind, and Joyce was widely imitated. Further east, the Prague writer Franz Kafka (1883–1924) published stories and novels that

GROSZ'S *THE PILLARS OF SOCIETY*

The German painter George Grosz (1893–1959) was a major figure in German art circles and a prominent left-wing activist. During the 1920s, he produced scathing canvases, such as *The Pillars of Society* (1926), that blended satiric critiques of Weimar society with an absurdist black humor that he developed during his time in Berlin's Dada movement. Borrowing from the caricatures and cartoons of the popular press, *The Pillars of Society* expresses Grosz's view that the German elite was complicit with right-wing extremism and responsible for the nation's economic collapse.

In the foreground, a trio of bourgeois figures drink together: a businessman brandishing a sword and wearing a tie decorated with a swastika; an editor clutching bloodstained newspapers; and a politician bearing a German flag and a placard reading "Socialism is work," his head topped with a pile of excrement. Behind them, a smug priest delivers a blessing, seemingly blind to the burning building in the top-left corner, a symbol of the dire conditions in Germany. At top right, advancing soldiers suggest a renewed militarism. Together, these elements present a harsh condemnation of the elite's control of German society.

QUESTIONS FOR ANALYSIS

1. How does Grosz use symbolism to criticize German society?
2. What aspects of the painting refer to the rise of Nazism?
3. What do you think Grosz meant by titling this painting *The Pillars of Society*?

featured bizarrely surreal situations (most famously, a man waking up to find himself transformed into a giant insect) and highlighted the absurdity—and often, the hopelessness—of modern life.

Among them, Proust, Joyce, and Kafka greatly expanded what prose fiction was capable of—but at the price of reinforcing the separation between high art and popular art that we have already seen at work in the world of music. While these modernists found readers in all social classes, they did not attain the popularity of nineteenth-century writers like Charles Dickens or Victor Hugo. Modernist authors, like their Bohemian predecessors but in a much more influential manner, tended to disdain the mass societies produced by large-scale industrialization and urbanization. They considered these societies smotheringly conformist and often deliberately sought to produce works at odds with popular tastes.

VISUAL ARTS During this period of high modernism, the same attitudes were evident in visual art. Painters like the Dutch Piet Mondrian (1872–1944) experimented with wholly abstract compositions of lines and colors in a grid pattern. The so-called Dada group of artists, formed in Zurich in 1916, argued that the entire mental world of bourgeois Europe needed to be turned upside down, to eradicate the ideas that had brought about the war's destruction. To do so, they called for challenging supposed common sense by an explicit celebration of nonsense—which they tried to represent both visually and in prose. Marcel Duchamp (1887–1968), a French artist, memorably challenged the privileged status of art objects by submitting a urinal as his contribution to a 1917 art exhibit. More accessible were the so-called surrealists, who emerged as a distinct group, complete with manifestos, in the late 1920s. They also sought to challenge ordinary ideas of rationality and common sense, but did so in hauntingly strange, distorted images and verse seemingly drawn directly from the human unconscious analyzed by Sigmund Freud. The school also had an important influence on the Spaniard Pablo Picasso, the great pioneer of modernism who remained through the inter-war period probably the best-known visual artist in the world as well as the most highly paid.

NEW MEDIA Even as the modernists repeatedly challenged conventional standards of art and literature, the very boundaries of culture were shifting with the rise of new media. Just as the initial spread of print had led to new cultural forms such as the Republic of Letters in the sixteenth and seventeenth centuries, and the use of photography had changed everything from journalism to high art to family life in the nineteenth century, two equally powerful new technologies now had a significant cultural impact. By the 1920s, Britain, France, and Germany each possessed thousands of movie theaters, with a large proportion of the population seeing silent films on a regular basis. In the 1930s, the introduction of sound to film would change the landscape yet again. The importance of Hollywood imports, even at this early date, signaled a new role for American culture in Europe that would only grow through the century. However, European directors such as the Russian Sergei Eisenstein, the German Fritz Lang, and the French Abel Gance also directed major works that convinced Europeans to take cinema seriously as an art form. With Robert Wiene's 1920 German film *The Cabinet of Doctor Caligari*, which mostly took place in a surreal dreamscape, high modernism established its presence in the movies. Commercial radio stations opened in most of western Europe in the early 1920s, and by the 1930s most middle-class families owned a radio receiver—an innovation that enabled political leaders to speak directly into private homes. Magazines illustrated with photographs proliferated, and all these new media served as effective vehicles for commercial advertising.

ARCHITECTURE The 1920s also saw one of the most important shifts in the history of European architecture, one with major implications for the shape of European

The Bauhaus School The campus of the Bauhaus School in Dessau (in the east of Germany) itself exemplifies the use of straight lines, rows of grid-like windows, and application of reinforced concrete pioneered by Bauhaus architects.

Potsdamer Platz A 1929 photo of Berlin's famous square conveys its buzzing commercial activity. Storefronts and large, vivid advertisements face the streets, which are crisscrossed by trams, buses, automobiles, and pedestrians.

cities and the texture of urban life. The influential **Bauhaus School**, founded in 1919 and active until 1933 in Germany, advocated a strictly functional design for buildings. Bauhaus structures showed no ornamentation and emphasized clear, clean geometrical forms with muted colors. The architects—notably the school's founder, Walter Gropius (1883–1969), and Mies van der Rohe (1886–1969)—favored steel-reinforced concrete as a building material, while opening up whole sides of buildings to natural light through striking, floor-to-ceiling windows. It was the start of the modernist architecture that now dominates nearly all major cities around the world.

CITY LIFE

European cities of the inter-war period were transformed by Bauhaus-style buildings and cinemas and much else. The continuing spread of automobiles—which had now largely edged out horse-drawn carriages from the centers of major metropolises—along with expanding systems of public transportation, made it easier than ever for members of all social classes to live in distant suburbs and travel to city centers for both work and leisure. These now bustled with a newly intense sort of commercial urban life, lit not only by electrical lamps but—from the mid-1920s on—by neon signs.

Consider the Potsdamer Platz, the large square at the center of Berlin. By the 1920s, up to 60,000 cars a day were passing through it, along with hundreds of trams. To manage the traffic flow required the services of eleven policemen, and then, in 1924, the construction of a tower with traffic lights—one of Europe's first. Within easy walking distance were scores of cafes and beer halls, five major hotels, the mammoth Wertheim department store, and an establishment called Haus Vaterland ("Fatherland House"), opened in 1928, that included a dozen national-themed restaurants, one of them named the Wild West Bar. There was also space for half a dozen orchestras and a 1,400-seat movie theater. Nothing like it had ever been seen in Europe. All this was joined in 1932 by an ultra-modernist, nine-story office block called Columbushaus, one of the largest Bauhaus-style projects yet completed. Piccadilly Circus in London and the Champs-Élysées in Paris had similar roles as the gaudy centerpieces of inter-war commercial culture. But despite the growing popularity of modernist architecture, European cities did not follow the lead of New York and permit the large-scale construction of modern skyscrapers.

The new urban consumer culture did have its dangers. In most major European cities, a large majority of men and close to 40 percent of women smoked (mostly unfiltered) cigarettes, raising the levels of heart disease and cancer. And the automobile brought other dangers. In Britain in 1930, with only a million cars on the road, 7,000 people died in auto accidents. Today Britain has 33 million private cars, but only 3,000 annual road deaths.

PARIS AND BERLIN

Paris and Berlin served as joint capitals of modernist culture in the 1920s. Paris continued to draw the greatest artists and writers of the Western world—not only Spaniards like Picasso and Dalí, but American writers such as Ernest Hemingway, F. Scott Fitzgerald, the songwriter Cole Porter, and Gertrude Stein. Paris also teemed with immigrants and political refugees who gave it a renewed cosmopolitan atmosphere. The groups included White Russian exiles from the Soviet Union; Greeks and Turks fleeing the bloodshed in the eastern Mediterranean; and Italians, Poles, Belgians, Spaniards, and Portuguese in search of work. Between the wars, France welcomed a higher percentage of immigrants than any other Western country.

Berlin gained a reputation for its raucous and daring cabarets (immortalized in Christopher Isherwood's stories, the basis for the musical *Cabaret*) and for its wildly experimental music, painting, and film. The playwright Berthold Brecht (1898–1956) combined biting Marxist social commentary with surrealist motifs that aimed to defamiliarize their subjects. In *The Three-Penny Opera* (1928), Brecht's words were set to the jagged, modernist rhythms of the composer Kurt Weill to produce a masterpiece that appeared thousands of times on European stages before World War II. In an increasingly common pattern, popular plays and novels were also adapted for the cinema and the radio. In both Paris and Berlin, the whirl of modernist culture—with the new freedoms embraced by women and the open depictions of both straight and gay sexuality—was loudly condemned as "degenerate" by political and religious conservatives.

CULTURE OF COMMEMORATION

Modernism did not entirely dominate European culture in the inter-war period. Particularly in their intense efforts to commemorate the war dead of 1914–18, most of the former combatant nations also reached back to traditional—indeed, classical—cultural forms. Poets and novelists continued to condemn the war as a ghastly blunder, most famously in the shockingly explicit 1929 novel about the trenches, *All Quiet on the Western Front*, written by German novelist Erich Maria Remarque (1898–1970). But the designers of war memorials such as the sober Cenotaph in London struggled to find ways to endow the wartime sacrifices with meaning. Commemorations of the war, especially on the anniversary of the November 11 armistice, played a key role in public culture of all the major states with the exception of the Soviet Union. But in one sense, these regular outpourings of grief reinforced rather than contradicted the message of the modernist antiwar works. They

Memorializing the War A color photograph shows the Cenotaph war memorial in central London shortly after it was completed in 1920. Mourners who might not have been able to recover their own loved ones' bodies gather to pay their respects.

strengthened the widespread public conviction, particularly in Britain and France, that their countries must avoid future war at any cost.

WOMEN IN THE CITY In such new urban spaces, women could experiment with new roles. The end of the war had brought mixed results for women's rights, as demobilized soldiers flooding back into the job market displaced women from wartime employment. The large numbers of men killed at the front left many widows and single women whose lack of family attachment raised anxieties. But at the same time, women finally won the right to vote in Britain (although not fully until 1928) and in Germany, Austria, and most of the countries of northern Europe. As early as 1919, women took seats in the British House of Commons. In France and much of southern Europe, the battle for woman suffrage continued.

Relatively small-scale technological changes had a large impact on urban women's lives in this period. The spread of sewing machines, gas stoves, electric irons, and running hot water, even in the upper segment of working-class homes, reduced the time spent on domestic chores. Leisure time increased correspondingly, with women taking advantage of the sort of attractions now found in urban centers like Potsdamer Platz. The fashion industry rushed to supply them with clothing and cosmetics, and sales boomed, driven by a flood of new advertising aimed at women. So did the number of European beauty parlors. Women's clothing styles, especially in the cities, shifted toward shorter, less constraining dresses and skirts, and shorter, simpler hairstyles that bespoke a more liberated social role for women—and a more liberated sexuality.

In these years, birth control became more easily available in some European countries. In Britain, in 1920, the scientist and author Marie Stopes (1880–1958) founded the first public birth-control clinic in Europe, dispensing advice and contraceptives that included the cervical cap and spermicides. But like many early birth-control campaigners in both Europe and America, Stopes was motivated as much by the pseudo-science of eugenics as by concern for the quality of women's lives. In one pamphlet, she lamented "reckless breeding" as "the worst end of our community," which supposedly led to higher rates of mental disability. The German feminist Helene Stöcker (1869–1943) similarly touted birth control as a means "to prevent the incurably ill or degenerate from reproducing." In nearly all of Catholic Europe, birth control remained illegal.

All of these changes in women's lives reactivated familiar anxieties about gender and national health.

Changing Fashions A 1927 tabloid photograph of a French aristocrat gives an indication of the new women's fashions, including shorter skirts, silk stockings, and cropped hairstyles.

Conservative cultural critics condemned the opening up of new cultural and social roles for women, and, as in previous centuries, pointed to declining birthrates to support their claims. After a brief post-war jump, birthrates did in fact fall throughout most of Europe during the inter-war period, due above all to the increasing availability of birth control and the prevailing economic uncertainty. In countries as diverse as Norway, Italy, and France, birthrates fell by close to a third during the 1920s. Mussolini's relentless promotion of domesticity and motherhood ("Maternity," to quote one Fascist slogan, "is the patriotism of women") made little difference.

In the cinema and especially literature, sexuality itself was represented far more openly than before the war. In 1928, the British novelist D. H. Lawrence (1885–1930) published *Lady Chatterley's Lover*, about a high-born woman who finds sexual and emotional satisfaction with a gamekeeper, her husband having lost his sexual function as a result of war injuries. Because of its highly explicit language, the British government banned the book, and it did not appear in an unexpurgated British edition until

1960. The British modernist author Virginia Woolf (1882–1941) used such literary tools as stream of consciousness to explore the inner lives of female characters. In a landmark 1929 essay entitled "A Room of One's Own," she analyzed the barriers to women's ability to write. In France, the novelist Colette (1873–1954) explored female emotions and sexuality, and made no secret of her own lesbian relationships. Several novelists risked prosecution by openly describing male homosexuality, including Proust and the Frenchman André Gide (1869–1951).

A FRAGILE ORDER

In the mid-1920s, the chaos and disruptions of the immediate post-war period finally seemed to recede. Following the collapse of the German currency in 1923, a League of Nations commission negotiated a new, less severe schedule for German reparations. And a series of international conferences took place with the goal of ensuring that the vast bloodshed of the war would never repeat itself.

ARMS CONTROL

Following the first international arms control conference, in Washington, D.C., in 1921–22, a series of treaties effectively limited the size of the great powers' navies and ended the construction of new battleship fleets. The Locarno Treaty of 1925 stabilized relations between Germany and its western neighbors, and paved the way for the country's entry into the League of Nations a year later. In 1928, all the major European powers, including the Soviet Union, formally adhered to the Kellogg-Briand Pact (named for the U.S. secretary of state and the French foreign minister), which attempted to ban war as "an instrument of national policy" altogether. It seemed that a new comity had finally entered into international relations. Yet in Germany, resentment against the post-war settlement remained strong, as shown by the election of former military chief Paul von Hindenburg—the embodiment of the old Prussian military spirit—as president in 1925.

ECONOMIC PLANNING

The economies of most European countries also strengthened in the mid-1920s. Unemployment levels dropped, industry expanded, and by 1925 in most cases production

had returned to its pre-war levels. By 1927, many European countries had returned to the gold standard and its promise of economic stability.

Yet growth remained hampered by a number of factors. High tariffs, introduced to protect emerging industries, particularly in the new central and eastern European states, slowed trade. The war's disruption of foreign investment in European economies continued in the 1920s. France had lost nearly half its foreign investment, and Germany nearly all of it. Britain did better, but London still effectively surrendered the title of the world's financial center to New York, and the United States attracted much of Europe's available investment capital. Labour leader Ramsey MacDonald was just one of the prominent Europeans expressing fears that the United States had become a "super-national power." Meanwhile, reduced peacetime demand for certain commodities—particularly those related to the military—created painful dislocations. In Britain, in 1926, an attempt to cut wages and hours for miners led to the most ambitious attempt at a general strike in the country's history, spearheaded by the Trades Union Congress, but it achieved relatively little.

European governments responded to economic unpredictability by embracing concepts of scientific management and planning, and by relying more heavily on advice from university-trained economists. The theories of the American engineer Frederick Winslow Taylor (1856–1915), who sought to maximize productivity by applying various forms of standardization, labor discipline, and supposedly scientific rules to workflow, gained popularity. Even more important was the work of **John Maynard Keynes** (1883–1946), the most influential economist of the twentieth century. Keynes argued that free markets by themselves would not necessarily produce high economic growth and low unemployment. To combat economic slumps, he advocated government action to stimulate overall economic demand through public spending. Even industrialists generally agreed that governments needed to take a role in coordinating economic production. A similar message came to Europe from the United States, where even the chief executive of General Electric called for the formation of state-coordinated industrial cartels. In the Western world, the idea of an unrestricted market system had few champions in the 1920s and 1930s.

Although state planning went furthest in the Soviet Union, a form of it also developed in Fascist Italy, where Benito Mussolini promoted a type of social organization generally called **corporatism**. To coordinate the needs of business owners, industrial workers, peasants,

Communist and Fascist State Control

Amid the economic and social instability left in the wake of World War I, the new governments of Communist Russia and Fascist Italy claimed to offer political systems that could energetically and efficiently restore order. To many people, both communism and fascism seemed to represent a cathartic reinvigoration of society through strict state control. And leaders of both movements offered confident visions of how these new ideologies would transform their nations, as expressed in the following two sources.

Nikolai Bukharin and Evgenii Preobrazhensky, *The ABC of Communism*

Bukharin (1888–1938) and Preobrazhensky (1886–1937), notable Bolshevik leaders, originally wrote their *The ABC of Communism* (1919) to convince Russian citizens—particularly those with little education—to support the Communist Party. Though the book was written before Stalin's rise, this passage hints at the absolute control that he would come to have over the state in the name of the proletariat.

The basis of communist society must be the social ownership of the means of production and exchange. Machinery, locomotives, steamships, factory buildings, warehouses, grain elevators, mines, telegraphs and telephones, the land, sheep, horses, and cattle, must all be at the disposal of society. All these means of production must be under the control of society as a whole, and not as at present under the control of individual capitalists or capitalist combines.…

For the realisation of the communist system the proletariat must have all authority and all power in its hands. The proletariat cannot overthrow the old world unless it has power in its hands, unless for a time it becomes the ruling class. Manifestly the bourgeoisie will not abandon its position without a fight.… Precisely because the opposition will inevitably be so embittered, it is necessary that the workers' authority, the proletarian rule, shall take the form of a dictatorship. Now "dictatorship" signifies very strict methods of government and a resolute crushing of enemies.

It is obvious that in such a state of affairs there can be no talk of "freedom" for everyone. The dictatorship of the proletariat is incompatible with freedom for the bourgeoisie.… In extreme cases the workers' government must not hesitate to use the method of the terror. Only when the suppression of the exploiters is complete, when they have ceased to resist, when it is no longer in their power to injure the working class, will the proletarian dictatorship grow progressively milder.

Benito Mussolini and Giovanni Gentile, "The Doctrine of Fascism"

In 1932, Mussolini and the Italian philosopher Giovanni Gentile (1875–1944) published the essay "The Doctrine of Fascism," which in the following passage describes the central ideas of the all-controlling Fascist state.

Against individualism, the Fascist conception is for the State; and it is for the individual in so far as he coincides with the State, which is the conscience and universal will of man in his historical existence.… For the Fascist, everything is in the State, and nothing human or spiritual exists, much less has value, outside the State. In this sense Fascism is totalitarian, and the Fascist State, the synthesis and unity of all values, interprets, develops and gives strength to the whole life of the people.…

Therefore Fascism is opposed to Socialism, which confines the movement of history within the class struggle and ignores the unity of classes established in one economic and moral reality in the State.…

Fascism is opposed to Democracy, which equates the nation to the majority, lowering it to the level of that majority.…

The Fascist State, the highest and most powerful form of personality, is a force, but a spiritual force, which takes over all the forms of the moral and intellectual life of man.…

Fascism…thus repudiates the doctrine of Pacifism—born of a renunciation of the struggle and an act of cowardice in the face of sacrifice. War alone brings up to their highest tension all human energies and puts the stamp of nobility upon the peoples who have the courage to meet it.…

In the Fascist State the individual is not suppressed, but rather multiplied, just as in a regiment a soldier is not weakened but multiplied by the number of his comrades. The Fascist State organizes the nation, but it leaves sufficient scope to individuals; it has limited useless or harmful liberties and has preserved those that are essential. It cannot be the individual who decides in this matter, but only the State.

QUESTIONS FOR ANALYSIS

1. What are the methods of control that must be used by "dictatorship of the proletariat," as described by Bukharin and Preobrazhensky?
2. Why are Mussolini and Gentile opposed to socialism, democracy, and pacifism?
3. What are the key differences between communism and fascism as described in these sources, and how do they resemble each other?

Sources: Nikolai Bukharin and Evgenii Preobrazhensky, *The ABC of Communism*, trans. Eden and Cedar Paul (London: 1922), pp. 70, 80–81; Benito Mussolini and Giovanni Gentile, "The Doctrine of Fascism," in *The Social and Political Doctrines of Contemporary Europe*, ed. Michael Oakeshott (Cambridge: 1939), pp. 166–68, 170–71, 177–78.

shopkeepers, and others, the Fascist government divided the economy into sectors managed by corporations that bore a superficial relationship to medieval guilds. As Mussolini himself explained in 1932: "Fascism recognizes the real needs which gave rise to socialism and trade unionism, allowing them due weight in the guild or corporative system in which divergent interests are coordinated and harmonized in the unity of the State." The state would therefore intervene to set production targets in particular industries, and it would also determine wages and benefits.

In practice, the system replaced Adam Smith's "invisible hand" of free markets with the heavily visible hand of government, leading to the creation of huge government bureaucracies. It was typical of the contradictions of Italian **fascism**, which combined brutal repression of opposition (mostly political, but also including the infamous criminal organizations of southern Italy) with sporadic displays of efficiency (often referred to by the phrase "making the trains run on time") and considerable bombast. Mussolini contrasted fascism to democracy, which he blasted for its "spirit of collective irresponsibility, and the myth of happiness and indefinite progress."

THE GREAT DEPRESSION

Despite the economic growth of the late 1920s, the European economy remained fragile. Wartime disruptions, the huge war debts incurred to the U.S. government, and investments in the booming American economy had combined to yoke Europe's economic fate to that of the United States, which in 1916 had become the world's largest economy. During the later 1920s, a full-fledged financial bubble developed on Wall Street, with companies hugely overvalued in the stock market. When the United States fell into recession in 1929, a financial panic ensued and Wall Street crashed, destroying vast quantities of paper wealth and severely cutting demand for goods and services. The result was the **Great Depression** of the 1930s. American unemployment rates soared to nearly 25 percent, while industrial production plunged by nearly 50 percent in 1932.

FALTERING EUROPEAN ECONOMIES As the American economy sank, it dragged European ones down. The hardest-hit country was Germany, whose banks were tied to American ones through a thick web of loans linked to wartime reparations. There, too, unemployment quickly hit 20 percent, and industrial production fell sharply. Fears of a new bout of hyperinflation kept the German

government from trying to stimulate economic demand in line with Keynes's theories, making the situation even worse. Central European countries such as Austria and Hungary, whose economies were tied to Germany's, experienced similar conditions. The downward pressure in the international financial system led most major countries finally to go off the gold standard altogether in order to gain more control over their own currencies.

The British economy suffered badly as well, although not on the same scale. A new Labour government under MacDonald briefly tried to stimulate demand through public works and higher unemployment benefits, as Keynes urged. The writer George Orwell (1903–1950) brilliantly described the plight of the unemployed in a study of a northern English mining community, *The Road to Wigan Pier*, which addressed the filth, crowding, and general ugliness produced by poverty that eroded basic decency and hope. Commenting on what he believed capitalism had wrought, Orwell wrote: "We are living in a world in which nobody is free, in which hardly anybody is secure, in which it is almost impossible to be honest and to remain alive."

The Depression played out differently in the other industrial countries. France initially seemed more resistant, owing to an economic self-sufficiency rooted in the continuing importance of the rural sector and small businesses. But ultimately the downturn affected France as well, and the refusal of successive governments to devalue the franc hurt exports and made France one of the last countries to recover. The European country that best resisted the Depression was Sweden, where, in keeping with Keynesian economics, the government made up for investment shortfalls with its own spending and continued its ambitious central planning and social welfare programs. In Sweden, productivity grew by 20 percent between 1929 and 1935.

POLITICAL AND CULTURAL EFFECTS OF THE DEPRESSION In some ways, the Depression did not have worse social and economic effects than several nineteenth-century economic crises. Although many Europeans went hungry in the early 1930s or experienced crowded, unhealthy living conditions, very few starved or were forced to live on the streets. Europe had no real equivalent to the so-called Hoovervilles of shacks and tents that sprang up in American cities. But the Depression arrived in Europe at a moment of exceptional political and cultural instability. Democracies had begun to fail even before 1929, and the Depression hastened this process. In Portugal, General António de Oliveira Salazar

Economic Crisis Crowds line up outside a Berlin bank in July 1931 in order to withdraw their money. Such bank runs became common during the economic crisis that began in 1929.

(1889–1970) consolidated a conservative, corporatist dictatorship that would survive from the 1930s until the mid-1970s. And in the 1930s, the remaining democracies of central and eastern Europe succumbed to authoritarianism, one by one, until only Czechoslovakia was left.

Britain and France, with their much deeper democratic traditions, survived the Depression with their political systems intact, but not without significant bruising. In Britain, Oswald Mosley (1896–1980) founded the British Union of Fascists, modeled on Mussolini's party, although with a stronger anti-Semitic tinge. Membership for a time reached the tens of thousands, but Mosley never established a major electoral presence, and a string of Conservative Party governments remained comfortably in power. In 1936, Britain even survived a potential constitutional crisis when the government successfully pressured the new king, Edward VIII (r. Jan. 1936–Dec. 1936), to abdicate after he refused to break off a relationship with an American divorcée.

France came much closer to the brink of real political instability, enduring no fewer than eighteen separate governments in the 1930s. As the Depression worsened, so did attacks on the Republic from both the extreme left and the extreme right. On the night of February 6, 1934, a huge protest organized by right-wing leagues descended on the Place de la Concorde, in central Paris, and threatened the National Assembly just across the river. In the wake of the incident, the French Socialists and Communists partly reconciled and eventually formed a Popular Front that won elections in 1936. The Jewish Socialist Léon Blum (1872–1950) became prime minister, heightening right-wing and anti-Semitic outrage. But the Popular Front itself, despite passing important social reforms, could not stay in power for long. Caught between Communist allies who wanted to proceed with the nationalization of key industries, and a financial sector that threatened to undermine even much more mild steps toward socialism, Blum could not keep his fractious coalition intact.

THE COLONIAL EMPIRES

In some ways, both Britain and France emerged from World War I with their empires stronger than ever. Thanks to the addition of former German colonies and Ottoman territories in the form of League of Nations **mandates**, British officials now ruled in Palestine and Iraq, and French officials in Syria and Lebanon. Large new African territories such as Southwest Africa, Tanzania, and Cameroon also became British and French possessions.

MIDDLE EASTERN MANDATES

As oil became ever more important to run automobiles, ships, and planes, the Middle Eastern mandates, with their rich oil reserves, gained particular importance. The British somewhat cavalierly cobbled together several former Ottoman provinces, divided by religion and ethnicity (Shia Muslim Arabs, Sunni Muslim Arabs, and Sunni Muslim Kurds), into the new state of Iraq. According to one story, Winston Churchill first sketched out its borders on a napkin during a dinner party. They placed on its throne a member of a family that had contended unsuccessfully for control of independent Saudi Arabia, and they granted the new state independence in 1932. But they ensured that Iraq's policies continued to benefit British oil companies. Another member of the family installed to rule in Iraq

ended up as king of Transjordan (later changed to Jordan), which the British carved out of the original Palestine mandate. In the rest of that mandate, immigration from Europe swelled the Jewish population in the 1920s and 1930s, leading to conflict with Palestinian Arabs.

NATIONALIST RESISTANCE

By the 1920s, many British and French colonial and mandate territories had growing middle classes, some of whose members had studied in Europe, spoke English or French fluently, and—crucially—had appropriated European ideas of national self-determination for themselves. These ideas had fertile soil to grow and change in, given native traditions of patriotism and self-respect, plus resentment against a colonial system that obviously benefited the European powers at the colonies' expense, and a well-justified sense of entitlement deriving from the importance of colonial troops to the Allied war effort.

The result, across the globe, was the rise of potent independence movements in which European patterns of national competition now turned against Europe itself. Already during the Versailles Peace Conference, some nationalists from European colonies, such as Vietnam's Ho Chi Minh, had attempted, without success, to receive a hearing from the negotiators. Men and women in the mandate territories did somewhat better after the peace, when they could send petitions to the League of Nations. They thereby gained publicity and the possibility of League pressure to give indigenous peoples a greater role in their own government.

Subjects of the French Empire did not fare so well. In the 1920s and 1930s, France faced nationalist agitation—sometimes violent—in Southeast Asia, North Africa, and Madagascar. In response, the French government cracked down brutally on more moderate organizations seeking merely to obtain equal rights for colonial subjects, and it further restricted the rights these subjects already enjoyed. In a reversal of earlier, more liberal policies, it restricted the access to French citizenship once offered to certain African elites. This repression pushed moderates toward advocating full independence—and also, in France's Caribbean and African possessions, toward the development of a new literary and political movement of black pride that went by the name of Négritude. The movement included among its most prominent voices the Senegalese poet and future national leader Léopold Senghor (1906–2001) and the Martinique poet Aimé Césaire (1913–2008).

The British faced a variety of independence movements

Middle Eastern Mandates, 1920s Through the mandates system, Britain and France became dominant powers in the Middle East. The creation of the Iraq mandate allowed Britain control of key oil reserves in Iraq and on the Persian Gulf, in addition to numerous other territories throughout the region.

as well, some of which adopted violent means. In Palestine, it faced two such movements at once. One came from the Jews, seeking to make good on former foreign minister Arthur Balfour's promise that the country would become a Jewish national home. The other came from Palestinian Arabs desperate to prevent the establishment of a Jewish state in what they considered Arab land.

GANDHI AND INDIAN NATIONALISM

The most important anti-imperial resistance, however, came in India, where resentment at British rule predated the failed War of Independence of 1857. In 1919, the British abandoned the use of juries in Indian political trials, and when indignant protesters rallied in the city of Amritsar, British soldiers panicked and massacred over 400 men and women.

Over the next decade, a powerful independence movement developed under the leadership of **Mohandas Gandhi** (1869–1948), who had first become involved in civil rights agitation while working as a lawyer in South Africa. Abandoning his prim suits for traditional Hindu garb, adopting an ascetic lifestyle, and preaching a philosophy of nonviolent resistance that he drew from Indian sources and the writings of Christian authors such as Leo Tolstoy, Gandhi stood as a living rebuke to British imperialism. On being asked by a reporter what he thought of Western civilization, he famously replied: "It would be a good idea."

In 1930, Gandhi staged the most important symbolic protest yet against British rule, leading thousands of

Mahatma Gandhi The Indian nationalist leader, clad in minimalist clothing, spins cotton on a traditional spinning wheel in 1931. Reclaiming indigenous methods of production could be an important way of demonstrating independence from colonial rule and customs.

followers on a 240-mile march to the sea to gather salt, a commodity on which the British claimed a monopoly. Gandhi and tens of thousands of other Indians were arrested by the British authorities; and while he did not win concessions on the salt issue, he attracted massive attention and sympathy worldwide—including in Britain itself. But through the 1930s, India remained firmly under British control.

TOTALITARIAN DICTATORSHIPS

While democracy managed to survive the troubled years of the Depression in some of central Europe and much of western Europe, in Germany it did not. As unemployment worsened and industrial production plummeted, the parties of the extreme surged in public support.

THE NAZI SEIZURE OF POWER

Hitler and his deputy, Joseph Goebbels (1897–1945), proved geniuses in the use of propaganda: visual, oral, and in the form of well-orchestrated rallies. In September 1930, the Nazi party gained 18 percent of the vote in a national election. Two years later, the Nazis and Communists together won a majority of German votes, and the Nazis emerged as the largest party in the Reichstag. At the same time, some of the most powerful institutions in German life, notably the army and big business, lost what little commitment they had to the Weimar Republic. Under these conditions, the Social Democratic–led coalition that had governed through much of the 1920s collapsed, and no credible successor emerged. As early as 1930, many of the functions of government were being carried out by presidential decree. And unlike in France after 1934, in Germany the Communists and Socialists failed to join forces to defeat the right. Indeed, with encouragement from the USSR, the Communists in the early 1930s attacked the German Socialists as "Social Fascists," undercutting them just when they most desperately needed popular support.

Nonetheless, right up to the Nazi seizure of power in 1933, few Germans imagined that their country would follow Italy's path toward fascist dictatorship. Hitler's vicious anti-Semitic rhetoric, and the brutal tactics of the Nazi paramilitary forces, repelled many Germans who saw their country as a "land of poets and thinkers." Influential businessmen, soldiers, and politicians had little but contempt for a man and a movement they considered ignorant and vulgar. But fatally, some of them thought they could control him, particularly after Nazi support slipped in new parliamentary elections held in November 1932. In December, President von Hindenburg appointed as chancellor a general, Kurt von Schleicher, who tried to form a government that would include some Nazis, but not Hitler. When the attempt floundered, the political initiative passed to the previous chancellor, the conservative Franz von Papen, who proposed giving the top spot in government to Hitler but keeping him on a short leash by reserving most of the Cabinet posts for non-Nazis. Von Hindenburg agreed, boasting that he had put Hitler in a box.

In fact, all of Germany was about to become a Nazi prison. Von Papen and the men around the failing president had not counted on Hitler's ruthlessness and how he might abuse the state power now in his hands. At the end of February 1933, a mysterious fire destroyed much of the Reichstag building. It remains unclear who started it (the most recent research suggests it was the Nazis themselves), but Hitler blamed it on a Communist conspiracy to seize power. He convinced the deputies to suspend civil rights throughout Germany, allowing him to arrest the leadership of the Communist Party and other opponents. Less than a week later, with the voters cowed by increasing Nazi control of the police, a new election took place that made the Nazis by far the largest party in Germany, although they still won only 44 percent of the popular vote. Hitler then convinced conservative and Catholic parties to vote with him, the latter in return for guaranteeing the rights of the Catholic Church in Germany.

Hitler thereby had the two-thirds of the Reichstag necessary to pass the so-called Enabling Act of March 23, which gave him and his party unlimited "emergency" powers. By July, he had used these powers to ban all other political parties, arrest thousands of political opponents, impose strict censorship on the press, and allow his party's paramilitary forces to grow into an inviolable state-within-the-state. Germany had become a fascist dictatorship. A few figures inside the party retained enough of a power base to challenge Hitler—especially Ernst Röhm, the head of the powerful Nazi paramilitary. But in June 1934, Hitler had Röhm and eighty other potential opponents savagely murdered in the so-called Night of the Long Knives. Two months later, upon the death of von Hindenburg, Hitler assumed the title of Führer—supreme leader. Political opposition was entirely silenced, with dissidents arrested and imprisoned in special camps, such as Dachau on the outskirts of Munich.

THE NAZI REGIME

Over the next few years, Hitler and his allies created a regime that, while sharing some features with both Italian fascism and Stalinism, represented something new on the European scene. To begin with, it was grounded in an extreme racial science, loyally propagated by schools and government-controlled media. Nazi race theorists exalted the blond, northern ("Aryan") races, while alleging the physical and moral inferiority of other races, including especially Slavs and the supposedly subhuman, vermin-like Jews. It was the destiny of the Aryans to dominate other races, the Nazis argued, and they therefore required their new "living space" in the vast Slavic territories to the east. The British biologist Julian Huxley (1887–1975) was one of many European scientists who ridiculed the Nazis' racial ideas, invoking Hitler's portly deputy Hermann Goering and the 5′4″ propaganda chief Goebbels:

> Our German neighbors have ascribed to themselves a teutonic type that is fair ... tall and virile. Let us make a composite picture of a typical Teuton from the most prominent exponents of this view. Let him be as blond as Hitler ... as tall as Goebbels, as slender as Goering. ... How much would this resemble the German ideal?

However, the Nazi ideas in fact came all too close to those popularized since the late nineteenth century by influential racial theorists and eugenicists, and they enjoyed considerable legitimacy, even outside of Germany.

PENETRATING SOCIETY In Germany, the Nazis began organizing social life into new, highly ideological forms that challenged long-standing Western distinctions between public and private life. Boys were pressured into joining the Hitler Youth, which combined activities drawn from scouting with rudimentary military training and heavy ideological indoctrination. Although the Nazis favored the elimination of women from most public life, preferring to restrict them to the home, they also started women's organizations that provided ordinary housewives with new forms of social recognition. The Nazis staged food drives for the poor and encouraged young men to join the military or the paramilitary organizations called the SA and SS. Uniforms and parades became ubiquitous.

A massive propaganda apparatus, led by Goebbels, everywhere saluted the Nazi revival and hailed Hitler as the infallible genius saving Germany from ruin. The party staged mammoth rallies every year in the city of

Nazi Propaganda A 1938 propaganda poster shows a member of the girls' wing of the Hitler Youth holding a collecting tin. The caption reads, "Build youth hostels and homes," referring to the kinds of social welfare programs that the Nazi regime promised to the Germans.

Although foreign observers sometimes found it hard to believe, particularly in these early years, the Nazis enjoyed significant popularity. Despite its brutality, the party exuded a strength that the war and defeat otherwise seemed (in the eyes of many) to have scorched out of German life. It imposed a strict civil order that showed no mercy to criminals and enforced a new efficiency in public services. Middle-class Germans who were horrified by the open sexuality of the Weimar period and its experimental cultural life looked on with pleasure as the Nazis reimposed strict forms of sexual morality, imprisoned homosexuals, and staged bonfires of supposedly degenerate books and art. In the depths of the Depression, the Allies had already cancelled the remaining German reparations, but Hitler still repeatedly decried British and French "oppression" and won applause for doing so. Many Germans felt that he was making the country great again after the horrors of the war and the turbulence of Weimar and the Depression. In 1936, Hitler put his new Germany on display to an international audience by hosting the Olympic Games in Berlin. Germany won the most medals, but in a blow to the Nazis' racial theories, the African-American Jesse Owens was the single most successful athlete of the games, with four gold medals in track and field events.

NAZI ANTI-SEMITISM With their long-standing traditions of anti-Semitism now endorsed and strengthened by the Nazis' racial pseudo-science, many Germans also applauded the regime's implementation of an anti-Semitic program without precedent since the Middle Ages. In 1933, the Jews constituted well under 1 percent of the German population (barely 500,000 out of 67 million people) but enjoyed disproportionate prominence in many fields, including the universities, the arts, and retail business. They were also highly visible in the Socialist and Communist parties. With malign skill, the Nazi propaganda machine focused all the anger that had built up in Germany since the war—anger over the defeat and subsequent national humiliation, over the economic disasters and frustrations, over the corrupt spectacle of Weimar politics, over the supposed excesses of Weimar culture—on this one, vulnerable scapegoat.

The Nazi propaganda sheet *Der Stürmer* ("The Stormer," or "Attacker") exemplified the campaign, every week unleashing a new torrent of abuse, lies, and conspiracy theories about the Jewish threat to Germany, sometimes associating it with capitalism, sometimes with socialism. "Who Is the Enemy?" asked one typical issue

Nuremberg and filmed them so that the rest of the country could watch. The Nazis even required Germans to replace ordinary greetings with the words *Heil Hitler!* A remarkable number of prominent Germans—including the country's most prominent philosopher, Martin Heidegger (1889–1976)—gave the regime their enthusiastic support. This insistence on popular participation, the exaltation of the supreme leader, the suppression of civil liberties, and the unleashing of the Gestapo secret police are all considered hallmarks of **totalitarianism**. This concept, first invented by Italian Fascists to describe the state they saw Mussolini as building, generally denotes a system in which the state aims at a far greater, more deliberate, more ideologically driven control over all aspects of public and private life than any earlier state had achieved.

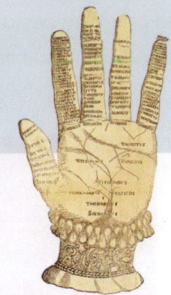

GERMAN RACIAL EDUCATION

Melita Maschmann (1918–2010) was born into a wealthy and conservative German family just after World War I. She joined the Hitler Youth over her family's objections and worked as a propagandist in a Nazi women's organization before taking part in the colonization of Poland following Germany's invasion of the country in 1939.

In this passage from her memoir, *Account Rendered* (1963), Maschmann recounts the racial propaganda and education that shaped her perceptions of the Poles. Well before the outbreak of World War II, racist beliefs were firmly entrenched in German society.

I must have been still at primary school the day I pulled a map out of our letter box which pleased me because of its gaiety. The countries of Europe stood out from one another in bright colours and on each country sat, crawled or stood a naked baby. I showed the map to my father because I wanted to know the significance of the babies. He explained to me that each of these children was a symbol of the birthrate of the country. The German families had on the average far less children than, say, Polish families. That was why only a frightened little girl sat on the patch of blue that meant Germany. On the yellow patch, just next door to the right, a sturdy little boy was crawling on all fours aggressively in the direction of the German frontier.

"Look at the boy," said my father. "He is bursting with health and strength. One day he will overrun the little girl."

The picture map stuck in my memory. It kept alive in me the feeling that the Poles were a menace to the German nation.

Later in "racial science" classes in the upper school the emotional lesson was "scientifically" reinforced. [Previously] we compared the birth rates of the Slavonic nations with those of the German nation and were instructed about the "average qualities of the east European races." Amongst them, so we heard, the intellectual and particularly the creative element came to the fore much more rarely. The noble, refined and intellectual qualities were everywhere in danger of being suppressed by the brutality of the primitive. That was why the Nordic nations were threatened with annihilation by…the Slavs. Primed with these views I came to the region which had been for generations a battlefield in the nationalist struggle between Poles and

Germans. What I saw and heard seemed to confirm the National Socialist theories: the foreign nation seemed to consist only of manual workers, poor peasants and lower middle class townspeople, and the few Polish families I had a chance to study had substantially more children than corresponding German families.

QUESTIONS FOR ANALYSIS

1. In what ways did propaganda expose Maschmann to racist thinking as a child?
2. What supposedly scientific evidence of the Slavs' inferiority was taught to Maschmann in school?
3. What does Maschmann's memoir tell us about the importance of race to Nazi ideology?

Source: Melita Maschmann, *Account Rendered: A Dossier on my Former Self*, trans. Geoffrey Strachan (London: 1964), p. 66.

from 1934, and answered the question with a grotesque caricature of a Jew. "The Jews Are Our Misfortune," ran the paper's weekly motto, quoting from Hitler's *Mein Kampf*. The Nazis called for the boycott of Jewish business as early as April 1933, and party members defaced storefronts with signs and graffiti reading "Don't Buy from Jews."

The anti-Semitic campaigns stunned German Jews themselves. Numbering among the most secular, integrated, and best-educated Jewish populations in all of

Europe, they generally took intense pride in their German culture. A high proportion of middle-aged Jewish men were war veterans. Although part of the Jewish community—especially those with strong ties abroad—emigrated soon after Hitler's seizure of power, many others did not. But conditions quickly grew worse.

In 1935, the Nazis passed the so-called **Nuremberg Laws**, which stripped Jews of citizenship and obliged them to wear large yellow stars of David on their clothing.

Nazi Anti-Semitism The headline of the Nazi newspaper *Der Stürmer* asks, "Who is the enemy?" The answer, as suggested by the grotesque cartoon, is the Jews, whom the article blames for World War I and the German defeat.

Jews were banned from most professions—often with the enthusiastic support of those professions' governing bodies. In November 1938, after an unbalanced, stateless Polish Jew shot and killed a German diplomat in Paris, the Nazis staged a massive pogrom, encouraging ordinary Germans and the paramilitaries to attack Jewish businesses and synagogues. Hundreds of synagogues were burned. The event came to be known as Kristallnacht—"Crystal Night"—after the shards of glass left in the street. At this point, another stampede for emigration began in the remaining Jewish population, but in some cases it was too late—Western governments, fearful of losing favor with their own populations by seeming too favorable to Jews, had started to close their doors.

And yet, despite the savage repression and anti-Semitism, the Nazi regime had not—at this point—made Germany into a land of mass murder. In some ways the Nazis were highly legalistic, passing no fewer than 4,000 laws during their first three years in power. Finding many enthusiastic collaborators in the conservative German judiciary, and purging other judges, they found it easy to twist the court system to their ends. Before 1939, Hitler's murder victims still numbered in the thousands, not the millions—and the large majority of them were political opponents. The same generalization holds for the other right-wing authoritarian states in Europe as well, including Mussolini's Italy. Stalin's USSR was different. There, already in the late 1920s, totalitarianism had taken a new, catastrophic turn.

STALINISM: THE FIVE-YEAR PLAN

After consolidating his power in the years around 1930, Stalin quickly adopted as his own the plan for rapid industrialization that he had previously opposed. The survival of the Soviet state, he declared, demanded that the Communists "put an end to backwardness in the shortest possible time." The party's central planners drew up a so-called **Five-Year Plan** (1928–32) to drag what was still largely a peasant country into the industrial age.

BUILDING A NEW SOCIETY Labor would be harnessed not just to build and staff factories, but also to construct entirely new industrial cities. The ambition of the plan was staggering. During these five years, Soviet officials put more people on the move (mostly, without their consent) than any other country in the world had seen for centuries, outside of wartime. The population of Moscow ballooned from 2 million in 1926 to 3.3 million just seven years later, causing severe housing shortages. In the same period, the Ural city of Sverdlovsk exploded by 346 percent after the Soviets designated it a center of heavy industry. In 1929, the Soviets set up a camp and railhead in the southern Ural Mountains, where hundreds of millions of tons of iron ore were easily accessible. Just three years later, Magnitogorsk ("Magnetic Mountain Town") had become a city of 250,000 people, most still housed in barracks and tents. Enduring temperatures that ranged from forty below zero Fahrenheit in winter to over a hundred in summer, these men and women struggled to build a massive steel works, completed in 1937.

Despite the harsh conditions, the workers in Magnitogorsk and other, similar industrial sites in some ways enjoyed a special, elite status in the Soviet Union. Stalin hailed them as the pioneers building socialism—indeed, building a new civilization—and elaborate propaganda campaigns treated them as heroes. The planners made every effort to ensure adequate supplies of food and fuel for Soviet proletarians. Workers who exceeded their production quotas won special rewards and recognition, including medals for "labor valor." In Moscow, the state built a lavish underground metro system, with many of the stations lined with marble. It was intended as a sign that under communism, beautiful things would be provided to the masses rather than restricted to the rich. In practice, the party elites themselves grew into a new upper class, enjoying access to the best apartments and special stores where they could purchase goods unavailable to ordinary citizens. Yet historians have found that in this early period, the Soviet industrialization project called forth a great deal of popular enthusiasm and willing participation. Ordinary citizens felt themselves engaged in constructing a new and better form of society.

COLLECTIVIZATION OF AGRICULTURE

But city-dwellers and industrial workers were not the only Soviet citizens on the move, and if they enjoyed relative privilege, others suffered grievously. The Five-Year Plan depended on reliable supplies of cheap grain to feed the swelling numbers of industrial workers. Yet Lenin's New Economic Policy had left over 95 percent of arable land in the hands of individual proprietors, who could choose how much grain to sell on the open market. Even as the new industrial cities were coming into being, Stalin therefore decreed, in 1928, a larger-scale transformation in the countryside: the forcible replacement of private agriculture with vast, state-run collective farms.

The decision immediately provoked peasant resistance,

Anti-Kulak Propaganda Stalin's government sought to generate resentment against kulaks with propaganda like this cartoon, which shows a fist descending to push an evidently well-fed farmer off land that is instead to be farmed collectively.

which Stalin blamed on wealthy peasants, called kulaks. But it was not just kulaks who objected to **collectivization**, particularly when it meant handing over what was often their principal form of wealth: farm animals. Across the Soviet Union, peasants sold or slaughtered their animals rather than give them up to the collective. In response, the government forcibly expelled nearly 2 million people from their homes, sending them into internal exile, often thousands of miles away to inhospitable conditions in Siberia, the Urals, and Soviet Kazakhstan.

FAMINE The campaign to collectivize agriculture quickly caused other forms of disruption. Grain production dropped, and the products of the collective farms themselves were diverted to the cities. By early 1930, famine spread through the countryside. Foreign travelers in Ukraine, formerly known as the breadbasket of the Russian Empire, were shocked to see children with distended bellies, the telltale sign of starvation, and even corpses lying unburied in fallow fields. In the towns and cities, endless lines outside bakeries from before dawn became a common sight.

In March 1930, Stalin signaled a reversal of course in an article in the official newspaper, *Pravda* ("Truth"), disingenuously titled "Dizzy with Success." The collectivization drive had succeeded brilliantly, he declared: "A radical turn of the countryside toward socialism may be considered as already achieved." But some lower-level functionaries, he continued, were committing excesses, and so it was time to slow the process down. But the famine did not end, and in at least some areas of the Soviet Union, the state prevented the starving peasants from fleeing to the cities, which were themselves facing food shortages, or across the border to neighboring provinces or countries. The death toll mounted. By 1937, the collectivization program had largely succeeded, with roughly 93 percent of all arable land now in collective farms. But at least 6 million people had died of hunger.

No area suffered more from collectivization than the western Soviet republic of Ukraine. After seeing its bid for independence crushed by the Red Army during the Revolution, the region had remained restive under Soviet rule. The Soviet state did in principle promote a degree of autonomy for its most important nationalities. Soviet Ukrainians, unlike Polish Ukrainians, could go to school in their own native language. But Stalin was determined to crush Ukrainian opposition to his policies, and many historians believe he made use of the famine to do so. Perhaps 50 percent of all Soviet deaths in the great famine occurred in this one region, mostly in 1932–33. Some desperate Ukrainian peasants managed to flee into neighboring Poland. Others took up arms in resistance and were quickly repressed. Even so, while anecdotal reports of the horrors filtered out of the region with them, neither the Soviet population itself nor foreign observers became aware of the famine's full, hideous dimensions until many years afterward.

The first Five-Year Plan came to an end six months early in 1932 with Stalin's planners already gearing up for a second one. Yet despite the considerable progress made toward the goals of industrialization and collectivization, it was clear that ultimate success would take far longer, and involve far greater costs, than the planners had expected. Sympathetic left-wing visitors from abroad, treated to tours of showcase factories and towns but kept far away from the regions of famine, went home convinced that the Soviets really had managed to create "a new civilization" (to quote the title of a long, laudatory book by two English socialists). But Soviet officials themselves felt increasingly frustrated and were prone to blame delays on counterrevolutionary sabotage.

THE GREAT TERROR   In the late 1930s, these frustrations, and Stalin's own increasing isolation and paranoia, led to what historians now refer to as the **Great Terror**. At every level of Soviet society, citizens were encouraged to look for signs of counterrevolutionary activity and denounce suspected traitors. In 1936, the secret police began to arrest hundreds of well-known Communists, including the leadership of the former Left Opposition (except for Trotsky, who left the country), and many other leading Old Bolsheviks—party members since before the Revolution. In a series of spectacular public trials, these men admitted that they had spied for Nazi Germany, engaged in industrial sabotage, and much else—the confessions were fantastical, the victims having been browbeaten, tortured, or threatened into making them. Death sentences followed, and quickly the purges widened out, with the head of the secret police himself falling victim.

In July 1937, Stalin issued his infamous secret order 00447, which called for the arrest and execution of 80,000 supposed traitors and the banishment of 193,000 others to the swelling system of labor and punishment camps known by their Russian acronym as the Gulag and located across the Soviet Union, but most notoriously in Siberia. By September, the new head of the secret police reported enthusiastically back to Stalin that 35,434 people had already been shot. But the Terror continued for more than another year and spun even further out of control. Official Soviet records themselves report the execution of a staggering 680,000 people. Millions more ended up in the Gulag, in horrific conditions under which as many as a million more died. It was during this period that the secret police began carrying out sweeps in the major cities, leading to the terrible events on Cannibal Island.

Before it was over, the Great Terror came close to decimating Soviet society. The intelligentsia paid a particularly high price, with a large proportion of leading artists and writers falling victim. The poet Osip Mandelstam (1891–1938), who dared satirize Stalin in a 1934 epigram ("Every killing is for him a delight"), was just one of the thousands to be arrested and die in prison. Even those professions most essential to the Soviet system were purged—in Stalin's paranoid viewpoint, they were also the professions in which treason and sabotage could do the worst damage. The ranks of leading engineers were devastated, as was the high command of the military, including 16 out of the 21 highest-ranking army generals and 8 out of 9 admirals. The Soviet Union would pay a massive price for these purges when facing a Nazi invasion in 1941. But it was the Communist Party itself that suffered the most. Of the 139 people chosen as members of its Central Committee in 1934, fully 98 were dead four years later.

By the end of the 1930s, then, both Nazi Germany and Stalin's Soviet Union had become totalitarian states. Both had power-drunk, unstable leaders possessed of unlimited power and supported by mammoth cults of personality. Both had secret police forces that had crushed all serious political opposition and orchestrated pervasive climates of fear and denunciation. Both had targeted vulnerable minorities for destruction. Both had undertaken vast transformations of public and private life. And both could still count, remarkably, on considerable popular enthusiasm for the regime and the leader. The Nazi revolution had so far occurred without massive damage to the country as a whole—though Jews, homosexuals and political opponents had of course suffered greatly. The damage and destruction in the USSR, however, was already reaching a massive scale. Even as the Five-Year Plans began to manage and mobilize the Soviet Union's vast human and material resources, the accompanying social disruptions, the famine, and the Great Terror had left it reeling from self-inflicted wounds. As the 1930s came to an end, it was in no condition whatsoever for a military showdown with its totalitarian competitor to the west. But it seemed clear to most observers in Europe that such a showdown was coming—and soon.

THE COMING OF WORLD WAR II

Historians have labored endlessly over the origins of the first world war, but there has been no need for comparable debates in regard to the second. Adolf Hitler built much of his political career on the idea that Germany, supposedly betrayed and victimized in 1918–19, should seek revenge on its tormentors and fulfill its destiny by carving out a new empire, by force, in the rich agricultural lands to its east. The point was there for all to read in *Mein Kampf*, published in 1925–26.

HITLER'S EARLY MOVES

Soon after taking power in 1933, Hitler informed his generals that his long-term foreign policy would in fact aim at these expansive goals. For a time, he played a double game, proclaiming his peaceful intentions even while working to prepare Germany for war. Some Allied statesmen, desperate to prevent another frightful cataclysm, grabbed at his words like a life raft in an ocean storm. But the actions

Mussolini and Hitler At a rally in Munich in 1937, Mussolini and Hitler appear together, indicating the close ties between the two totalitarian rulers following their alliance in 1936.

of Germany and its allies between 1933 and 1939 demonstrated all too clearly an accelerating pattern of aggression.

ALLIANCES From the very start of his rule, Hitler cultivated close relations with Mussolini, and he signed an initial alliance with Fascist Italy in 1936. As early as 1933–34, he took Germany out of the League of Nations and signed a nonaggression pact with Poland—a clear attempt to avoid another two-front war. He moved toward an alliance with authoritarian Japan, which was engaged in a brutal campaign of expansion on the Asian mainland. And while Hitler did not attempt to put Germany's still-weak military into action in his first years in power, he encouraged Mussolini to unleash Italy's forces. In 1935, Italy tried to wipe out the memory of its humiliating defeat in Ethiopia forty years before by invading the country again, this time with the help of an air force and armored vehicles. The capital, Addis Ababa, fell seven months later, after a campaign that caused the death of some half a million Ethiopians. The Allies and the League of Nations responded to the war with empty rebukes and ineffective, short-lived sanctions, which further encouraged both dictators. Italy soon began moving toward an absorption of Albania into its empire as well.

REARMAMENT In 1935, Hitler openly broke the terms of the Versailles treaty. He reinstated compulsory military service, re-created the German air force (which the treaty had prohibited), and announced his intention to increase the size of his army to half a million men, far above the Versailles-imposed limits. Then, in March 1936, Hitler sent the German army back into the Rhineland, which Versailles had established as a demilitarized zone. At every turn, he insisted to world public opinion that he was merely acting to address the injustices of Versailles and had no aggressive intentions. Had the Allies confronted him forcefully, he probably would have backed down, particularly in the Rhineland.

But Britain and France did not push back. For one thing, their elites had strong fears of another continental bloodbath—in one telltale sign, students at Oxford University's principal debating society had overwhelmingly voted, in 1933, for the proposition that "this House will under no circumstances fight for its King and Country." But they also saw a balanced competition between strong states as Europe's normal historical condition, and they hoped against hope that once Germany had reclaimed its "rightful" place, it would make no further demands. But with Germany's rearmament, the various agreements of the 1920s to limit the size of European militaries largely collapsed.

The Nationalists, led by General Francisco Franco (1892–1975) and supported by the Catholic Church, aimed to replace the Republic with an authoritarian regime. On the other side, a coalition of liberals, socialists, anarchists, and the rapidly growing Communist Party defended the Republic but largely failed to agree on their own ultimate goals. George Orwell, whose *Homage to Catalonia* offers a vivid account of his experiences fighting for the Republic (he barely survived a bullet wound to the neck), noted that the Communists often seemed more concerned with undercutting their own allies than with winning the struggle.

From the larger European perspective, the **Spanish Civil War** was important for the way it served as a proxy war and testing ground for the future combatants in World War II. The German and Italian air forces openly participated on the Nationalist side, transporting men and supplies, and bombing and strafing Republican positions. For the first time, Europe witnessed major cities under sustained aerial bombardment. The small Basque town of Guernica was virtually wiped out by one raid—Picasso illustrated the incident in one of his most famous paintings. Some 100,000 Italian soldiers participated, and both German and Italian advisers were prominent in the Nationalist ranks.

Stalin sent advisers and aid to the Republicans, funneling as much as possible through the Spanish Communist Party, but Britain and France largely adopted a position of non-intervention. Ragged International Brigades drawn from across the Western world, including the Abraham Lincoln Brigade from the United States, helped the Republicans as well; but poorly trained and equipped, they ultimately made little difference. The Nationalists besieged Madrid for much of the war and

The Spanish Civil War, 1936–1939 Nationalist forces based in northern Spain attacked the lines of the Republican-held southeast, and with the support of German and Italian forces besieged Madrid and bombed Republican towns such as Guernica. Despite the Soviet Union's support for the Republicans, by 1939 the Nationalists gained control of most of the country—including the key Republican stronghold of Barcelona—when they defeated the Republicans.

THE SPANISH CIVIL WAR

The leaders of Britain and France were terribly wrong, as events in Spain soon showed. Throughout most of the 1920s and early 1930s, the country had lurched from one crisis to another. General Primo de Rivera's erratic dictatorship ended in 1930, as the Depression hit Spain and he lost the confidence of the military and King Alfonso XIII (r. 1886–1931). A year later, after the election of a left-wing majority in the Cortes (parliament), the king abdicated and a new Republic came into being.

Between 1931 and 1936, the Republic's leaders struggled to reduce the power of the Church and wealthy landowners, but not quickly enough to satisfy radical labor unions and nationalists in the northeastern region of Catalonia, whose armed resistance to the central government was bloodily suppressed in 1933–35. A quasi-Fascist party called the Falange took shape; and after the government tried to ban it in the spring of 1936, a right-wing insurrection in the military began, leading to full-fledged civil war.

Guernica Picasso commemorated the devastating bombing of the Basque town of Guernica in his huge 1937 painting of the same name. The stark black-and-white canvas shows fragmented figures writhing in pain and shocked at the destruction, as if shattered by the attack.

advanced westward along a confused front that ran from the French border to the Mediterranean. After the fall of Barcelona in early 1939, remaining Republican resistance collapsed. The right-wing dictators marked another triumph.

GERMAN AGGRESSION: AUSTRIA AND CZECHOSLOVAKIA

Hitler now felt sufficiently encouraged to turn his sights to the east. The diminished Austrian state created by Versailles, like many of its central European neighbors, had experienced its share of turmoil in the Depression years, including a brief attempt to establish a fascist dictatorship. In the mid-1930s, it remained deeply unstable with a growing and aggressive Nazi Party calling for union with Germany and a weak government largely running the country by dictate. Hitler, Austrian by birth, pushed for union, accused the Austrians of persecuting

Nazis, and met every attempt to placate him with further demands.

In March 1938, when the Austrian president refused to make a Nazi the country's chancellor, German troops poured across the border, where in most cases enthusiastic crowds greeted them with German flags. In another clear violation of the Versailles treaty, but without significant French or British opposition, Austria was quickly absorbed into Hitler's Reich, with tens of thousands of socialists and liberals immediately arrested. Over 180,000 more Jews had also fallen under Nazi rule and found themselves subject to the Nuremberg Laws, as well as to forms of ritual humiliation—some were forced by crowds to scrub the streets of Vienna with their toothbrushes.

THE CZECH CRISIS On the map of Europe, greater Germany, engorged with new territory, now menacingly surrounded the western half of Czechoslovakia—the one remaining central European democracy, a major industrial state, and an ally of France and the USSR. The country's

Humiliation of Jews Nazi supporters (including members of the Hitler Youth in the foreground) force Jewish residents of Vienna to scrub a street following the German annexation of Austria in 1938.

mountainous western border regions, known as the Sudetenland, where the population was largely German speaking, had a growing Nazi Party led by a demagogue named Konrad Henlein. Having completed the annexation of Austria, in mid-1938 Hitler turned his attention here, denouncing Czech harassment of the Sudeten Germans and massing his army on the border.

The Allies had by now realized that Hitler's ambitions were unlikely to stop with redressing the supposed injustices of Versailles. Still, they remained reluctant to go to war less than twenty years since the end of the last war, especially since Hitler was claiming to act in favor of the principle of national self-determination and a majority of Sudeten Germans clearly wanted union with Germany. Even as Britain's Conservative prime minister, Neville Chamberlain, reluctantly began organizing civil defense during the Czechoslovak crisis in late September 1938, he gave a speech in which he lamented: "How horrible, fantastic, incredible it is that we should begin digging trenches and trying on gas masks here because of a quarrel in a faraway country between people of whom we know nothing."

MUNICH After several months of ineffective discussions and increasingly aggressive German demands, Hitler, Mussolini, Chamberlain, and French prime minister Édouard Daladier met in Munich, in September 1938, in an effort to settle the crisis. The Czechs were not invited. The resulting agreement gave Hitler virtually everything he wanted: above all, the immediate annexation of the Sudetenland, with its heavy industry and the very fortifications designed to protect the Czech heartland from Germany. Chamberlain returned home to Britain and declared at the airport, waving the agreement in the air, that he had secured "peace in our time." Scarcely half a year later, Hitler replied to Chamberlain with a gesture of undisguised contempt. He sent the German army across the new borders to occupy the now-defenseless western half of Czechoslovakia, turning it into a German protectorate. Slovaks friendly to the Nazis established an independent Slovakia in the eastern half.

PREPARING FOR WAR

The Czech crisis also had a profound effect on Joseph Stalin. Before the Munich meeting, he had pleaded with the British and French to discuss with him a joint stance to contain Hitler's aggression. He even began mobilizing part of his armed forces in the hope that the British and French would follow suit. But the British and French leaders, driven by their long-standing hatred of communism and their horror at the excesses of Stalin's rule, refused his request for a meeting. Stalin now came to believe that if Hitler attacked him, he could not count on support from the West.

ARMS RACE With war all but inevitable, the major powers began a frantic arms race, producing ships and planes, mobilizing draftees, and stockpiling supplies and munitions. Over the course of 1938, British production of new military aircraft more than doubled to over 330 per month. By June 1939, the figure had doubled again. The French also worked to reinforce a line of fortresses on their eastern frontier—the so-called Maginot Line—in which their military command put a dangerously absolute faith, believing it sufficiently strong to resist even a major armored offensive by the Germans. They did not, however, extend the line to their northern frontier with neutral Belgium, in part because they believed the densely forested frontier zones to be impassable by heavy armored vehicles (they were not, as they would learn to their enormous cost). They also ignored the recommendations of a mid-ranking officer, Charles de Gaulle, to increase their own reliance on tanks and other armored vehicles.

In the spring and summer of 1939, the scene of the developing pre-war tragedy moved to Poland. Hitler had already determined, in accordance with his long-standing plans for eastward expansion, to attack the vulnerable Polish state despite its alliance with Britain and France. Already in the spring, he had given orders to his high command to prepare for a start to hostilities on September 1. Hitler did not just want to recapture the German territories ceded to Poland in 1919 (including the so-called Polish Corridor that now divided East Prussia from the rest of Germany), but to annex sizable new territories, from which Slavic and Jewish "subhumans" would eventually be expelled to make way for Aryan settlers. To justify the attack, the German propaganda machine began to churn out stories about the abuse of ethnic Germans in Poland and the supposed desire of the "free city" of Danzig, in the Polish Corridor, to be reunited with the Reich. Should we "die for Danzig?" asked British and French appeasers.

THE NAZI-SOVIET PACT The major question, throughout the summer, was whether the Nazis would have to fight a war on two fronts. Despite the vast ideological differences between the Soviet Union and the western Allies, most onlookers assumed they would eventually conclude an alliance against the common fascist enemy whom the Soviets had spent the past six years denouncing.

Nazi-Soviet Pact A 1939 British cartoon mocks the shocking revelation of the agreement between Hitler and Stalin. The two meet over the body of a fallen soldier, greeting each other as "the scum of the earth" and "the bloody assassin of the workers."

The German high command of course desperately wanted to avoid a repetition of the two-front war that had proven fatal to them in 1914–18. But Stalin also wanted to avoid an immediate confrontation with the Nazis. The Soviet Union was facing Japanese encroachments into its eastern territory from Japan's new puppet state in Manchuria—the conflicts there even boiled up into a brief border war in 1939, in which the Soviets prevailed. But the USSR remained unprepared for a war in the west, especially after the disruptions of the Five-Year Plans and the Great Terror, and the decimation of the military command. A rapid Nazi offensive into Poland might quickly place them on the borders of Ukraine, whose devastated and resentful population had every reason to rise up against the Communists.

In these conditions, the two dictators had strong incentives to work out a deal of their own. During the summer of 1939, German foreign minister Joachim von Ribbentrop (1893–1946) and Soviet foreign minister Vyacheslav Molotov (1890–1986) came to an arrangement in secret. The Soviets agreed not to respond to a German attack on Poland, and in return the Germans promised them a sphere of influence in the regions the USSR had lost after World War I: eastern Poland and the Baltic states of Estonia, Latvia, and Lithuania.

Only the first part of the deal, the **Nazi-Soviet Pact**, was announced publicly, but the announcement on August 23 caused shock in the west. Never before had a diplomatic switch of such proportions and speed taken place, even in the reversal of alliances that had preceded the Seven Years' War in the eighteenth century. Western Communists who had spent the previous six years dutifully repeating the Soviet line about the demonic Nazis, and who genuinely saw Stalin as the architect of a new socialist society, reeled. Thousands left the party. Millions more westerners who had felt some sympathy for the Soviet experiment now expressed outrage at the Soviet leader's hypocrisy. Across Europe, another generation of young men now knew they would soon have to go off to war, but the realization led to none of the scenes of enthusiasm that had taken place in 1914, and none of the hopes that war might regenerate their societies. A mood of grim determination prevailed.

INVASION OF POLAND

Early in the morning of September 1, 1939, a mass of 1.5 million German troops, accompanied by tanks and supported by the powerful German air force—the Luftwaffe—began to cross the frontier into Poland. Britain and France reluctantly declared war but did not attempt to attack Germany themselves. Instead, they watched as the German troops advanced eastward and German planes subjected Warsaw to the largest aerial bombing Europe had yet seen, killing thousands. The Polish armed forces offered a gallant and determined resistance, but they were no match for the Nazi forces. Then, on September 17, Soviet troops marched into Poland from the east, as permitted by the secret terms of the Nazi-Soviet Pact. On September 27, Warsaw fell to the Germans, and the remnants of the Polish government fled to London. On October 6, the remaining Polish forces surrendered.

In the newly occupied Poland, the two totalitarian regimes showed all too brutally what Europe had to expect from the coming six years of total war. In both occupation zones, thousands of members of the Polish elites—top officials, academics, journalists, army officers—were arrested and sent to prison camps or simply executed outright. The Germans annexed large territories directly to the Reich, while a central area around Warsaw was transformed into a so-called General Government under German military rule. Harsh discipline prevailed, with the slightest resistance to the German occupation forces punishable by the arrest and execution of scores of hostages.

With their sudden conquest, the Germans also now found themselves ruling over a vast new population of Jews. Unlike in Germany, in Poland Jews made up close

Aggression in Europe, 1936–1939 In the years before war broke out, Hitler's Germany asserted its military power by occupying the previously demilitarized Rhineland, annexing Austria, and ultimately invading Czechoslovakia and Poland in 1938–39. Italy and the Soviet Union also rearmed and asserted their authority over new territories with the aid of non-aggression pacts with Germany.

in secular Polish life. But lower-class urban Jews, and the large majority of rural ones, remained marked off by their orthodox religion, their traditional dress, and their Yiddish language.

Now all these Jews were at the mercy of the Nazis, who quickly began to force them into crowded, walled ghettoes, while publicly humiliating them in the streets. Although the Nazis had not yet come to a formal decision to kill the Jews under their control, let alone attempt to implement such a decision, their ultimate goal was clear to those with eyes to see, that the coming war would not just be a total war, but a war of extermination.

JAPANESE AGGRESSION

And it would be another world war. Japan's violent occupation of Manchuria and invasion of north China had already produced millions of casualties. In 1937–38, Japanese forces committed atrocities against hundreds of thousands of Chinese civilians in the city of Nanjing. Japan had proclaimed the aims of freeing East Asia from Western colonialism and sharing resources among its peoples—what would become known as the East Asian Co-Prosperity Sphere. Its ambitions threatened not just China proper but also French Indochina, the Dutch Netherlands, British Malaysia, and Hong Kong—even the American-dominated Philippines. In the United States, a powerful isolationist movement, which had taken shape over the course of the inter-war period, insisted that the country keep out of the fighting, and for the time being President Franklin Roosevelt went along. But given the close political and economic ties between the United States and western Europe, and the potential for conflict between America and Hitler's ally Japan, eventual U.S. involvement seemed likely.

THE PHONY WAR

to 10 percent of the population—and roughly one-third in some major cities, including Warsaw. Assimilation of this population had taken place with relative speed over the previous twenty years as the Jews, freed from tsarist restrictions on their employment, were able to explore new economic opportunities. Particularly in the cities, middle-class Jews generally spoke Polish as a first language, dressed in modern fashion, and did their best, despite continuing discrimination and quotas on their presence in the universities and professions, to take part

But at the end of autumn 1939, not only did the war remain limited to Europe; it had fallen into a strange lull—what would soon be called the Phony War. The guns in Poland had gone silent, and the western front remained largely inactive. Across Europe, the powers continued frantically to arm. The world waited in dread. And the dread was all too justified. Despite the setbacks of the Great Depression, Europe's industrial capacity had reached new heights, which, as the Spanish Civil War had shown, could be deployed all too easily for purposes of mass destruction.

Paired with the ideological capacity of the totalitarian dictators to mobilize vast forces for the purpose of all-out conflict, and to demonize enemies as subhumans deserving of death, the peril had no precedent in world history.

CONCLUSION

At this moment, it had been barely twenty years since the end of World War I. And despite the best efforts of men and women across Europe, the Continent had not yet emerged from the dark shadow of the earlier war. In two of the empires that had collapsed at the end of World War I—Germany and Russia—the inter-war period had brought further violence and political chaos that facilitated the emergence of totalitarian dictatorships. In the wreckage of a third empire—Austria-Hungary—the emergence of new national states founded very imperfectly on the principle of national self-determination had not brought peace, but instead sowed the seeds of new conflicts. The economic cost of the war had left all parties depleted, vulnerable to the severe dislocations of the Great Depression, and increasingly dependent on the economy of the United States, an ocean away. Finally, the sense that the devastating death toll of the war had served little purpose fed resentment and cynicism among some, while leading others to embrace extreme ideologies that promised a rebirth of the human species—or at least their own part thereof. In all these ways, the first world war led to the second. Now, in the winter of 1939–40, a storm of blood was about to break.

[CHAPTER REVIEW]

KEY TERMS

Weimar Republic (p. 743)
Adolf Hitler (p. 743)
Nazis (p. 744)
Beer Hall Putsch (p. 744)
Benito Mussolini (p. 746)
Joseph Stalin (p. 747)

Bauhaus School (p. 751)
John Maynard Keynes (p. 754)
corporatism (p. 754)
fascism (p. 756)

Great Depression (p. 756)
mandates (p. 757)
Mohandas Gandhi (p. 759)
totalitarianism (p. 761)
Nuremberg Laws (p. 762)

Five-Year Plan (p. 763)
collectivization (p. 764)
Great Terror (p. 765)
Spanish Civil War (p. 767)
Nazi-Soviet Pact (p. 770)

REVIEW QUESTIONS

1. What conditions created openings for the rise of Nazism in the Weimar Republic?

2. During the 1920s, what were the causes of political instability in the new states of central and eastern Europe?

3. What were the major characteristics of modernist literature, art, film, and architecture during the 1920s and early 1930s?

4. During the 1920s and 1930s, what were the most significant shifts in life in European cities?

5. What impact did the Great Depression have on Europe?

6. How did colonial peoples challenge Britain and France's control of their newly expanded empires?

7. How did Hitler's Nazi regime establish control over Germany's government and society?

8. What were the successes and failures of Stalin's first Five-Year Plan?

9. In what ways did the Spanish Civil War presage World War II?

10. What methods did Germany use to expand its territory in the late 1930s?

CORE OBJECTIVES

After reading this chapter, you should have a solid understanding of the following core objectives. To strengthen your grasp of the core objectives, use the resources on the Student Site for The West.

- Analyze the causes of social and political instability in the aftermath of World War I.

- Assess the cultural changes associated with modernism, new technologies, and gender roles in the 1920s and 1930s.

- Describe the economic and political struggles in Europe and the European colonies during the inter-war period.

- Compare Germany under Hitler and the Soviet Union under Stalin in the period before World War II.

- Trace the events that led to the outbreak of World War II.

 GO TO **inQuizitive** TO SEE WHAT YOU'VE LEARNED—AND LEARN WHAT YOU'VE MISSED—WITH PERSONALIZED FEEDBACK ALONG THE WAY.

CHRONOLOGY

April–June 1940
German blitzkrieg in
Norway, Denmark,
Low Countries,
and France

June 21, 1940
France signs armistice
with Germany

Sept. 1940–May 1941
The Blitz in London

June 22, 1941
Germany invades
the Soviet Union

December 7, 1941
Japan attacks
Pearl Harbor

Spring 1943
Axis driven from
North Africa

July–October 1940
Battle of Britain

May 27–June 4, 1940
Evacuation
of Dunkirk

1941
U.S. Congress
approves Lend-Lease

1941–1944
Siege of Leningrad

January 1942
Wannsee
conference

Aug. 1942–Jan. 1943
Battle of Stalingrad

September 3, 1943
Italy attempts to
surrender to the Allies

The Abyss

WORLD WAR II AND THE HOLOCAUST

1940–1945

In Britain and France, the year 1940 began in a guarded but hopeful mood. In Paris, revelers packed the streets to celebrate the New Year's holiday and thronged to the horse races at Vincennes, which had just reopened after a four-month suspension. At Piccadilly Circus in the heart of London, young men and women obeyed "blackout" rules against fireworks and instead clicked flashlights on and off while singing the popular song of the moment, the "Beer Barrel Polka." British journalists calmly mused that the imminent introduction of food rationing (four ounces of butter and twelve ounces of sugar per week per person) would do wonders for the national waistline. Total war deaths on the western front to date were calculated at 9,604, giving credence to the idea that a Phony War was in progress—with no one sure if or when it would give way to a more intense conflict. The *New York Times* summarized the conventional wisdom as follows:

> No one can fail to notice how much less alarming the outlook seems at the beginning of the new year, after four months of war, than it seemed three or four months ago. In spite of the brilliant success of the *Blitzkrieg* in Poland, there has been no *Blitzkrieg* in the West. Hitler has not dared seriously to attack the Maginot Line…there has been no mass airplane bombing of London and Paris…the Nazi military machine is not as smoothly functioning and irresistible as the Polish campaign made it seem.

A Call to Attack An iconic photograph by the Soviet photojournalist Max Alpert captures a lieutenant of the Red Army on July 12, 1942, raising his pistol to the sky to rally his fellow soldiers to attack the Germans. The lieutenant is thought to be Aleksey Gordeyevich Yeremenko, who was stationed in eastern Ukraine and died shortly after the photograph was taken.

- How did France and Britain respond to the German offensives of 1940?
- What were the major patterns in the German occupation of the countries they conquered?
- Why did Germany invade the Soviet Union, and what was the immediate outcome of its attack?
- What were the turning points of war in Europe and the Pacific?
- What were the distinguishing characteristics of the Holocaust?
- How important were the economic advantages of the Allies?
- What changes did war bring behind the front lines?
- What events drove the war to its conclusion?
- What were the immediate consequences of World War II?

In fact, the Phony War would not last much longer. Within months, the apparent lull would break, and Europe and the world would be plunged fully into the most intense, destructive war that the planet has ever known.

FROM BLITZKRIEG TO THE BATTLE OF BRITAIN

Blitzkrieg—German for "lightning war"—was coming to the west. Now Germany would begin an assault against the full strength of the western Allies, Britain and France. Most observers expected a drawn-out series of titanic battles, but the reality was shockingly different.

THE GERMAN OFFENSIVES IN SCANDINAVIA AND WESTERN EUROPE

In early April 1940, German forces invaded Denmark and Norway, in order to exploit the latter's strategic position in the North Atlantic and to ensure continuing supplies

of Scandinavian iron ore. While Denmark was immediately overwhelmed, Norwegian resistance continued, with Allied help, through the spring, but the Wehrmacht—the German army—seized most of its strategic objectives quickly. By the late spring, Germany had occupied and fortified Norway and installed a puppet government under Norwegian fascist leader Vidkun Quisling (1887–1945), whose last name has become a synonym for treasonous collaboration with invaders.

Then, on May 10, the Germans launched a major offensive in the main theater of operations. Using tanks, infantry, paratroopers, and even gliders, they simultaneously attacked France and the three neutral countries of Belgium, Luxembourg, and the Netherlands. The Allies initially seemed in a strong position to push them back. They had more soldiers in the field than Germany, and more tanks as well. Had the Germans followed their initial plan of attacking through central Belgium, they would have run into heavy Allied concentrations. But instead they targeted their forces on the heavily forested Ardennes region, which the Allies had assumed was impassable. Some 1,800 German tanks proved them wrong, pushing through with ease, overwhelming Belgian resistance, and then driving toward the Channel coast. The Germans made full use of airpower, strafing Allied soldiers with Stuka dive-bombers mounted with guns and blaring sirens that panicked the infantry in their path. The French Ninth Army crumbled and surrendered. At one point, German general Erwin Rommel (1891–1944) took 10,000 French prisoners while losing only 41 of his own men. Adolf Hitler was ecstatic: "I could have wept for joy, they had fallen into the trap."

Events now moved with stunning speed. On May 10, 1940, Neville Chamberlain resigned and Winston Churchill became the British prime minister. The Germans completed their occupation of the Netherlands and began to close their "trap" on the Allied forces cut off in Belgium and northern France. Hitler did make one large mistake, however: German tanks stopped for a fateful two days in late May, giving the British time to organize a makeshift flotilla to evacuate its army. Some 337,000 soldiers escaped from the northern French port of **Dunkirk** in an operational success that gave a much-needed boost to British morale. In early June, the French desperately set up a new defensive line across northern France, but the Germans broke through easily. On June 10, the French government declared Paris an "open city" and fled south. Up to 10 million people from northern France fled as well in an exodus of indescribable chaos and fear. They clogged the roads with overloaded cars, carts, and bicycles, hindering the maneuvering of the Allied forces. The Germans deliberately heightened the chaos by strafing the refugees with their horrifying Stukas. Paris seemed empty as the first German soldiers entered on June 14, 1940.

THE FALL OF FRANCE

The Battle of France now came to an inglorious end. When French premier Paul Reynaud refused to surrender, he resigned and was replaced by eighty-four-year-old Marshal Philippe Pétain (1856–1951), a heroic World War I commander. Pétain immediately went on the radio to announce France's surrender: "I give myself to France to assuage her misfortune.... It is with a heavy heart that I say we must end the fight." On June 22, the French signed an armistice in the same railroad coach where German envoys had surrendered in 1918. With Hitler himself looking on exultantly, they agreed to severe terms: German occupation of northern France and the Atlantic coastline; the effective demilitarization of a large unoccupied zone; and the indefinite use of 2 million French soldiers as forced labor in Germany.

Early in the morning of June 23, Hitler landed at Le Bourget airport north of Paris and took a three-hour tour of the city. He loudly admired the ornate nineteenth-century Opera House and tried to tip the French attendant, who refused. At the military monument of the Invalides, he spent many minutes staring silently down at the tomb of Napoleon Bonaparte. In London, five days earlier, a little-known French general named Charles de Gaulle had gone on the radio to defy his own government and urge further resistance. But in France, his appeal was little heard or heeded. The vast majority of the French population rallied to Pétain as their savior.

The blitzkrieg was not quite the inevitable triumph that it appears in retrospect. The French high command had made a number of disastrous mistakes, including restoring normal leave to the army just three days before the start of the German offensive. Worst of all, when defeat stared the French in the face in early June, the conservative military and political leadership cared less about rallying the nation to resist than about ensuring that the German victory would not lead to a left-wing uprising in Paris, as had happened in 1871. When the French National Assembly voted in July to give dictatorial powers to Pétain, they acted not to provide a "shield" for the defeated and divided nation but to allow French ultra-conservatives to exploit the German victory for their own benefit and impose a conservative National Revolution. A new ultra-conservative regime, headquartered in the spa town of **Vichy** in the unoccupied zone, soon took shape.

Fall of Paris German soldiers march through the Arc de Triomphe down the Champs Élysées, in central Paris, following France's surrender to Germany in June 1940.

BRITAIN ISOLATED

In short, just six months after the hopeful New Year's celebrations of 1940, the war had changed beyond recognition. Germany, its allies, and the Soviet Union (which had signed the non-aggression pact with Hitler in 1939) now controlled virtually the entire European continent. After the fall of France, Stalin, taking advantage of the secret provisions of the Nazi-Soviet pact, invaded the three Baltic states of Lithuania, Latvia, and Estonia and annexed them to the USSR. On the Continent only the Balkans, Iberia, and neutral Sweden and Switzerland remained outside of Nazi or Soviet control. With the vast territories of the French Empire now under the uncertain control of France's Vichy regime (under the terms of the armistice, French colonies were bound to neutrality, but both sides tried to gain control of them), and with Japan occupying large stretches of China, the war had truly become a world war. Against the German juggernaut, Britain stood very much alone.

At this decisive moment, the British leadership lay in the hands of a man widely lampooned as a washed-up, unscrupulous, pigheaded drunk. **Winston Churchill**, then sixty-six years old, had led by any account a checkered career as soldier, journalist, adventurer, and maverick, party-switching politician. His reputation remained tarnished in part because of his role as architect of Britain's disastrous Gallipoli expedition in World War I.

Legend:
- Axis powers, 1939
- Co-belligerent, June 1941
- Axis controlled, May 1941
- Axis controlled, Nov. 1942
- Allies
- Neutral nation
- Axis offensive
- Allied offensive
- X Battle
- Boundaries, 1939

Battles
1. Mers-el-Kebir, July 3, 1940
2. Battle of Britain, Aug. 1–Oct. 12, 1940
3. Tobruk, June 21, 1942
4. El Alamein, June–Nov. 1942
5. Stalingrad, Aug. 21, 1942–Jan. 31, 1943
6. Kursk, July–Aug. 1943
7. D-Day, June 6, 1944
8. Battle of the Bulge, Dec. 16, 1944–Jan. 31, 1945

World War II in Europe and North Africa At the start of the war, Hitler's blitzkrieg saw numerous territorial gains: Poland in 1939; Scandinavia, the Low Countries, and France in 1940; and the Balkans by 1941. But when Hitler's invasion of Russia faltered in the winter of 1942–43, the Red Army pushed back across swathes of eastern Europe. The British-led Allied invasion from North Africa up through Italy, and then the famous D-Day landings at Normandy in June 1944, ultimately combined with the Red Army to bring down Berlin in 1945.

He had an astonishing ability to avoid seeing certain unpalatable truths, even though he saw others with piercing clarity. Probably no other leading British politician had retained such a romantic view of warfare undiminished by the trauma of World War I. And few other British politicians held as deep and uncomplicated a faith in the British Empire, which had led him resolutely to fight against Indian independence in the 1930s. Yet no other British politician had seen the Nazi threat so clearly.

But in the desperate spring and summer of 1940, Churchill's qualities proved to be exactly what Britain needed. A more "realistic," less stubborn politician would have been more tempted to seek terms with the German colossus, as some in Britain were urging. A more sensitive one, without Churchill's enormous stamina (fueled, as the legend rightly has it, by massive overindulgence in whisky and cigars), could never have borne the strain. And a less romantically minded one could not have so brilliantly

Winston Churchill Britain's new prime minister in 1940, just over two weeks after he became leader of the country and thus of the Allied war effort.

inspired the British to continue fighting. Churchill did inspire the British people in a series of unforgettable speeches—in most cases, broadcast on radio—that matched a sober assessment of the challenge with Shakespearean calls to arms. Upon taking office as prime minister in May, he declared: "I have nothing to offer but blood, toil, tears and sweat." On June 4, as the situation in France went from terrible to catastrophic, he concluded with defiance: "We shall not flag or fail. . . . We shall defend our Island, whatever the cost may be, we shall fight on the beaches, we shall fight on the landing grounds, we shall fight in the fields and in the streets, we shall fight in the hills; we shall never surrender." Two weeks later, with France surrendering, his eloquence reached new heights:

> The Battle of France is over. The Battle of Britain is about to begin. . . . The whole fury and might of the enemy must very soon be turned on us. . . . If we can stand up to him, all Europe may be freed and the life of the world may move forward into broad, sunlit uplands. But if we fail, then the whole world, including the United States, including all that we have known and cared for, will sink into the abyss of a new Dark Age made more sinister, and perhaps more protracted, by the lights of perverted science. Let us therefore brace ourselves to our duties, so bear ourselves that, if the British Empire and its Commonwealth last for a thousand years, men will still say, "This was their finest hour."

During the summer, Hitler made peace overtures to Britain and indicated that he would allow the British Empire to remain intact. Churchill spurned all notion of an agreement, and thanks in considerable part to the success of his oratory, few of his compatriots challenged him.

THE BATTLE OF BRITAIN

As Churchill proclaimed, there followed the Battle of Britain, a duel of aerial forces that Hitler meant as the prelude to a full-fledged invasion across the English Channel. After early attacks on coastal forces, the Luftwaffe attempted to destroy the Royal Air Force in battles that

sometimes involved over a thousand planes. It had some success, shooting down more fighter planes than the British did. But the British could turn out 500 fighter planes a month compared to Germany's 140. They employed a primitive version of radar that gave them early warning of German attacks. And they were fighting over friendly soil and waters from which they could rescue damaged planes and surviving crews. In August, Churchill saluted the Royal Air Force's fighter pilots with forgivable exaggeration as latter-day knights: "Never in the field of human conflict was so much owed by so many to so few."

With the arrival of stormy autumn weather, a frustrated Hitler gave up on the idea of a cross-Channel invasion and began deliberately targeting civilians in the hope of breaking the British population's morale. This bombing, known to the British as the **Blitz**, continued intensively for two months, and more sporadically thereafter, forcing Londoners to take shelter in deep subway tunnels and send their children into the countryside for safety. Between September 1940 and May 1941, the Germans killed 43,000 British civilians and destroyed or severely damaged more than a hundred thousand buildings in London alone. They did not, however, significantly damage British morale or industrial capacity. Initially, the Germans hit the grittier, industrial areas of east London, but their bombs eventually fell all over major cities. When one of them landed on Buckingham Palace, Queen Elizabeth (mother of Elizabeth II) remarked: "It makes me feel I can look the East End in the face."

Although the Nazis failed to break the British with their air war, Britain remained in deep peril from another source. Unlike Germany, which was largely self-sufficient in food and coal (if not in high-grade iron ore and oil),

The Blitz East London families shelter in the London subway during an air raid in September 1940.

Britain depended heavily on imports to keep its economy going: 55 million tons of food, fuel, and other raw materials in 1939, requiring a merchant fleet of some 4,000 vessels. In June 1940, when French Atlantic ports fell under German control, this fleet became vulnerable to German mine-laying and especially to German U-boats, or submarines. By mid-1942, the Germans had 300 in service and were sinking 7 million tons of British shipping per year.

Britain managed, for the moment, to stave off economic strangulation through a combination of American help, superlative intelligence work, and sheer good luck. President Franklin Roosevelt was not prepared to take America into the war, but he did use his considerable political capital to push through substantial aid to the Allies. In early 1941, the U.S. Congress approved the so-called **Lend-Lease** policy, which authorized the United States to supply the Allies with war materiel in return for leases on bases or a promise of eventual repayment. Meanwhile, British intelligence efforts paid off particularly in the cracking of the complex German Enigma ciphers by teams of mathematicians and cryptanalysts, based on work carried out by Polish intelligence in the 1930s. Overall, by the spring of 1941 it had become clear that Britain would survive the initial Nazi onslaught.

OCCUPIED EUROPE

Despite the failure of the Nazi attempt to defeat Britain in 1940–41, there would be no return to the Phony War—and no chance for peace. It was clear that the war would continue until the utter defeat of one side or the other, and that the conflict would require the utmost efforts of all the combatants. This was total war, and a truly global war. In September 1940, Germany, Italy, and Japan signed the Tripartite Pact creating an even closer military alliance among them. They would now be known as the Axis powers, and they seemed on the brink of worldwide domination.

WESTERN EUROPE UNDER NAZI OCCUPATION

In 1940–41, the Nazis consolidated their rule on the European continent. They found support from so-called collaborators whose perception of an inevitable German victory conveniently reinforced existing or newfound pro-fascist convictions. Following the blitzkrieg, it became fashionable to see Germany as a transcendent agent of History itself. "This collapse of a decrepit world," declared the prominent Belgian politician Hendrik de Man, "far from being a disaster, is a deliverance." In Norway, Denmark, and the Netherlands, collaborators proclaimed their nations' racial kindred to the Germans. In France, conservatives and anti-Semites who had denounced the fragile Third Republic before 1940 now rallied to the Vichy regime's National Revolution.

At this stage of the war, the Nazis preferred in most cases to rule through local authorities such as the Vichy regime. In Denmark, they allowed the king and Parliament to remain in place, and managed the country with a German staff of scarcely 100. In Norway, they tried to rule through their puppet Quisling, and in the rump state of Slovakia through a nationalist priest named Josef Tiso. In the Netherlands and Belgium, German officials supervised the native civil service. In France, Pétain's Vichy government had considerable authority in the occupied zone as well.

VICHY FRANCE Among the conquered western European countries, France mattered the most because of its expanse and population (41,510,000), its worldwide empire, and its powerful fleet. After the fall of France, some possessions (such as Chad and Congo) rallied to the Free French organized by General de Gaulle; some, especially in North Africa, came under the authority of Vichy; and some remained in uneasy limbo. As for the French fleet, in the summer of 1940 the British made it clear that they would not allow it to fall into German hands or be used in the German interest. The largest concentration of French warships lay in the Algerian port of Mers-el-Kébir, and on July 3, 1940, a British squadron sank or damaged most of them, killing 1,250 French sailors. The incident helped turn French public opinion against Britain and led Pétain and his advisers into more active collaboration with Germany.

Vichy's program, which took effect across the entire country and in several French possessions, was remarkably aggressive. It involved authoritarian rule by "the Marshal" and his deputies, an attempt to reorder the economy along corporatist lines similar to those of fascist Italy, and systematic hostility to foreigners and minorities, especially Jews. Within a few months of the 1940 defeat, Vichy, not waiting for German compulsion, banned all French Jews from the army, journalism, and the civil service. There would follow exclusions from the universities, law, and medicine, from commercial and industrial jobs; and confiscation of Jewish businesses. Jewish men and women were forced to sew yellow stars of David onto their clothing. In Indochina, Vichy's authoritarian nationalism helped spur indigenous nationalist resistance movements.

Throughout the war, civilian populations in occupied western Europe suffered considerable hardship. In the occupied zone of France, where conditions were worst, agricultural production fell, and much of what remained was confiscated by the Germans. A corrupt and inefficient rationing system permitted French adults only 1,180 calories a day of food over the course of the war, roughly half the amount needed to maintain their weight and health. Malnutrition caused the average height of French boys to decline by nearly three inches during the war, and that of girls by over four. Desperate Parisians raised an estimated 400,000 rabbits in their apartments as a source of meat. One and a half million French soldiers were transported to Germany as prisoners. Other western countries generally did somewhat better (Dutch civilians had an average of 1,900 calories a day) but still suffered considerably. Everywhere, black markets flourished, often with the enthusiastic collaboration of German occupation officials. With men absent and jobs scarce, women sometimes formed liaisons with German soldiers, producing, in France alone, an estimated 200,000 children during the war years.

OCCUPIED POLAND AND THE JEWS

From the beginning of the war, it was clear that Poland would suffer a cruel fate under occupation. After the German and Soviet invasions in 1939, Hitler and Stalin officially wiped the country off the map. Large chunks bordering Germany and along the Baltic, known as Warthegau and Danzig, were absorbed into the German Reich as part of its plans for racial expansion. The Soviet Union annexed Poland's eastern half, including the cities of Bialystok, Lvov, and Vilnius. The remainder, centered on Warsaw and Kraków, became known simply as the General Government under direct Nazi rule.

By the summer of 1941, the Germans had expelled upward of 1 million Poles and Jews from the annexed regions into the General Government. In this area, they began to establish labor camps for slave laborers, and concentration camps in which to imprison anyone they saw as a threat to their rule. Nazi officials, in keeping with their racial ideology, saw the Poles as subhumans who should be "spiritually sterilized"—that is, be deprived of any but the most rudimentary education and culture. Heinrich Himmler (1900–1945), head of the SS, wrote in May 1940 that Polish schools should teach nothing

Nazi Occupation of Poland In the winter of 1939–40, a man walks past the remains of the city of Lodz's synagogue, which the invading German army had destroyed.

more than "simple arithmetic up to 500 at most; writing of one's name; a doctrine that it is a divine law to obey the Germans." In the fall of 1939, the entire faculty of Kraków University was deported to a German concentration camp, and in the spring and summer of 1940 some 30,000 more Polish intellectuals and civic leaders were arrested, and 7,000 massacred. Food shortages quickly became endemic.

The Nazis reserved their cruelest treatment for the Jews, of whom 3 million (nearly one-third of the European Jewish population) lived within Poland's pre-war borders. Despite Hitler's dreams of extermination and the ferocious anti-Semitism he had cultivated in the German population, through the end of 1940 the German government did not pursue a deliberate policy of genocide. It aimed at expelling the Jews of German Europe to the General Government, and then possibly expelling all the Jews out of Europe altogether (for a time, it seriously considered a mass deportation to Madagascar). Perhaps 100,000 Jews died at Nazi hands during 1940—a horrifying figure, but one that would soon pale before the almost unimaginable totals of the **Holocaust**. But the Nazis engaged in every form of oppression short of genocide at this time. They banned Polish Jews from any but menial professions, stole wealth, and imprisoned entire populations behind the walls and barbed wires of hastily constructed ghettos. In Warsaw, where the Jews had made up one-third of the population in 1939, they were forced into just one-tenth of the city's surface area—400,000 people in 1.3 square miles, packed 7.2 persons per room. Similar patterns repeated themselves in every major Polish city.

OCCUPATION OF EASTERN AND SOUTHERN EUROPE

It was not only German rule that oppressed Europeans in the first years of the war. Soviet rule in eastern Poland and the Baltic states also brought serious disruptions. In these areas, local authorities were dismissed or arrested, and local institutions forcibly integrated into Soviet ones. The Soviet secret police also simply murdered some 22,000 Polish officers, policemen, and civic leaders in the spring of 1940, with the largest number of victims buried in mass graves in the forest of Katyń.

In the fall of 1939, Stalin also tried to return another former Russian province, Finland, to his sphere of influence by force. The Finns ended up surrendering considerable territory. But despite being vastly outnumbered, they fought against Stalin until March 1940 and inflicted a string of humiliating defeats on a Red Army that had been demoralized and stripped of leadership by Stalin's purges. Their successes encouraged Hitler to conclude that the Soviet Union would not stand up to a serious military challenge.

In the second half of 1940, more of Europe fell under hostile occupation. In October 1940, Benito Mussolini's Italy invaded Greece, hoping to add this prize to his expanding Italian empire in the Mediterranean—one he explicitly modeled on the Roman Empire. Instead, the Greeks forced the Italians back and made overtures to the British, raising the possibility that Britain could gain bases from which to bomb the Romanian oilfields on which Germany depended. To prevent this turn of events, and to secure the Balkans in case of war with the Soviet Union, Hitler decided to invade Greece himself and pressured the Balkan countries into giving him full military support. In Yugoslavia, the government's decision to accept this alliance provoked an anti-German coup d'état, whereupon Hitler added Yugoslavia to his invasion list. In the spring of 1940, he carried blitzkrieg into southeastern Europe and again won quick victories. Greece came under German occupation and Yugoslavia itself was dismembered, with large swathes of territory taken by Germany, Italy, Hungary, and Bulgaria. Hitler allowed Yugoslav collaborators to declare a newly independent state of Croatia.

BARBAROSSA

Even with all this fighting, through the spring of 1941 World War II could not yet stand comparison with World War I

as a sheer devourer of human life. The increasing mechanization of warfare—and particularly the dominance of tanks in land warfare, backed by aerial bombers—ensured that Europe would not see a repetition of the grinding slaughter of the trenches of 1914–18. So far, campaigns had moved quickly and ended quickly, limiting the death tolls. The German bombing of British cities, and particularly German and Soviet atrocities in Poland, amounted to crimes on a terrifying but not yet wholly unprecedented scale. In June 1941, most of Poland's pre-war population, Christian and Jewish alike, was still alive.

HITLER'S DECISION TO ATTACK THE SOVIET UNION

The war's real plunge into the abyss began on June 22, 1941, when Germany invaded the Soviet Union in what it called **Operation Barbarossa**, a reference to the Holy Roman emperor who had expanded German power in the twelfth century. From then on, the sheer scale of death would dwarf anything yet seen in human history. The fault lay above all with Adolf Hitler and those, German and otherwise, who turned executioner in his service. But the war led to a general barbarization of conduct that affected all the combatants.

At first glance, Hitler's decision to open a new front to the east seemed suicidal. The Soviet Union dwarfed Germany in population, land, and natural resources. Fighting it at the same time as Great Britain meant taking on both the world's greatest land and the greatest sea empires—and Britain could also increasingly draw on the resources of the United States through Lend-Lease. History offered vivid cautionary tales of conquerors whose ambitions shattered on the rock of Russia: notably, Charles XII of Sweden and Napoleon.

Yet from Hitler's perspective in 1941, attacking the Soviet Union had considerable logic to it. The USSR was Britain's one remaining potential ally on the Continent. Furthermore, Hitler considered an eastern war inevitable in the long run. Not only did the Nazi and Stalinist systems conflict radically in their models of how society and politics should be organized, but both—despite the Soviet slogan "Socialism in one country"—had aggressive agendas that threatened the other. Stalin continued to support Communist parties outside the Soviet Union, while Hitler still dreamed of "living space" (*Lebensraum*) for Germany in the east.

All of this meant that in Hitler's eyes the Nazi-Soviet Pact of 1939 could never be anything more than a

Operation Barbarossa The German army used tanks to move quickly through Russian territory, although they often eventually became bogged down in the snow and mud. This 1941 photograph shows a German tank and soldiers advancing on a village on the outskirts of Moscow.

temporary measure, allowing him to avoid a war on two fronts during the conquest of continental western Europe. A so-called General Plan for the East, worked out in 1941 by German strategists and revised as the war progressed, called for even more massive population transfers than seen in Poland, as well as large-scale German colonization of eastern territories. Hitler spoke of Russia's "immeasurable riches" and told his aides he planned to annex virtually all of Belarus, Ukraine, and European Russia. Finally, from Hitler's perspective, if the conflict was to come, it was better perhaps for it to come early, while the Soviet Union and the Red Army were still reeling from the purges of the 1930s, and before Stalin had the chance fully to rebuild and rearm. By the summer of 1940, Hitler had already made up his mind to attack, and throughout the winter and spring of 1941 the Nazis built up their forces. After many delays, they attacked on June 22 with the largest armed force ever seen in history: some 3 million men, 2,000 aircraft, and over 3,000 tanks.

SOVIET CATASTROPHE

The Soviets should have anticipated the invasion. During the spring of 1941, they received scores of credible warnings from their own intelligence services and from the British. But Stalin, having by now invested so much planning and personal prestige in the Nazi-Soviet Pact, did not want to face the possibility that Hitler would betray him. Nor could he believe that the Germans would undertake

such a costly and dangerous campaign. Instead of fortifying his existing defenses against attack, he ordered them abandoned and began the construction of a new defensive line farther west. It was in a vulnerable position hard up against the new frontier that cut through the middle of pre-1939 Poland. Only in March, as a safety measure, did he agree to the mobilization of reservists and an acceleration of arms production. But the Red Army remained poorly armed and supplied, and its officer ranks remained depleted, disorganized, and demoralized from the purges.

The result, for the Soviets, was catastrophe. Attacking along a front almost a thousand miles long, the Germans crushed initial resistance. Within hours, the Luftwaffe had destroyed a significant proportion of Stalin's aerial forces on the ground. Within five days, the German army was approaching the Belarussian capital of Minsk, some 300 miles east of the frontier. A panic gripped the Soviet population, prompting an exodus that dwarfed the one seen in France the year before: perhaps 25 million people fled east ahead of the advancing Germans.

Stalin himself seemed gripped by panic. At a meeting with his top generals on June 27, he stomped out of the room, allegedly growling: "Lenin founded our state, and we've f***ed it up." For several days, he remained incommunicado at his dacha outside of Moscow. He returned to the Kremlin on July 1 and two days later delivered a radio address in which he described the conflict as a "war of the entire Soviet people." Soviet propagandists appealed forcefully to Russian history and tradition, including frequent evocations of Napoleon's invasion of 1812. But for the moment, the words did nothing. Minsk fell on June 28, Smolensk on July 16, and Kiev, the Ukrainian capital, in mid-September. Also in September the Germans surrounded Leningrad—the former Saint Petersburg, capital of Peter the Great. In the Baltic states and Ukraine, some local populations were welcoming the Germans with flowers, denouncing local Soviet officials (and Jews), and volunteering their services to the new regime.

THE TURN TO MASS MURDER

An upsurge in German barbarity began practically the moment the Germans crossed the frontier, driven by the sheer scale of the hostilities and the Nazis' sense of having entered into a truly apocalyptic struggle. "The war against Russia," Hitler had told his generals in March, "will be such that it cannot be conducted in a chivalric fashion: the struggle is one of ideologies and racial differences and will have to be conducted with unprecedented, unmerciful and unrelenting harshness." His contempt for Slavs as "subhumans" reinforced his sense that Germany could only control their vast territories and populations with brutality. Following his lead, the German commanders made no attempt to treat the men and women who fell under their rule with even minimal humanity. In any case, they had few resources at their command to do so. Soviet prisoners of war became the largest group of victims yet to suffer Nazi mass murder. Frequently, the Germans made no attempt to keep alive the men who surrendered, but simply herded them into huge pens and left them to die of thirst, starvation, and disease. Of the 3 million Soviet prisoners taken by the end of 1941, as many as two-thirds died by the next summer.

With this mass murder already occurring, and with German forces seemingly on the way to yet another stunning victory, historians believe that Adolf Hitler lost any remaining hesitation about putting into practice his long-held dream of exterminating the Jews. He now believed Germany had a unique opportunity to cleanse the Continent of those he saw as dangerous parasites. Adolf Eichmann (1906–1962), one of the principal organizers of the Holocaust, later testified that it was in July 1941 that he heard, from the deputy head of the SS, that Hitler had decided upon "physical extermination." It would take more than another year for the Nazis to organize the system of transports and extermination camps that today symbolize the Holocaust. But the actual liquidation of the Jews and others began as German forces moved eastward in the summer of 1941. The work was carried out above all by special "task forces" (*Einsatzgruppen*) composed of SS members, ordinary police units from Germany, and local auxiliaries, all under SS command.

These forces had the murder of innocent men, women, and children as their principal purpose, and they received full support from the German army in doing so. In the newly occupied territories, they systematically hunted down and slaughtered the targets of Nazi ideology: Jews, Communists, the mentally handicapped, homosexuals, and Roma, a largely itinerant ethnic group with roots in India who numbered over 1 million in 1939. The Nazis forced the victims to dig mass graves, confiscated their valuables, and then machine-gunned them. At the end of September, the Germans took 33,771 of Kiev's Jews, who believed they were being resettled, to the ravine of Babi Yar at the edge of the city. Over the course of two days, nearly all were killed with the help of Ukrainian collaborators. The reports of the *Einsatzgruppen* themselves suggest that by the end of 1942 they had murdered well over

1.1 million Jews. In almost all cases, the killers took part willingly in the slaughter. In few cases were Germans who refused to participate punished, let alone killed.

TOTAL MOBILIZATION

The German actions quickly pushed the Soviets into seeing the conflict in apocalyptic terms as well, and into total mobilization. "These people without honor or conscience, these people with the morality of animals, have the effrontery to call for the extermination of the great Russian nation," Stalin thundered on November 6, 1941. "Very well, then! If they want a war of extermination, they shall have it!" The Germans found that despite the Soviet lack of arms and supplies, individual Soviet units fought with ferocity and often to the last recruit. Very quickly, the Soviet government conscripted most adult men and women under age forty-five for military service or other defense work. Following the example set by revolutionary Russia in 1917–18, but on a much larger scale, some 800,000 Soviet women served in the armed forces alongside the men. The Soviet air force assembled three regiments of bombers flown and serviced entirely by women, one of which became known as the Night Witches. In August 1941, the USSR declared that it was treason for an officer to become a German prisoner or to retreat under fire. To drive the point home, the Soviet government arrested the

"Night Witches" A group of Soviet women pilots receive orders from their commander—also a woman—for an upcoming bombing raid in 1944. These so-called Night Witches were among the roughly 800,000 women in the Soviet army.

wives of prisoners, including Stalin's own daughter-in-law (his son died in German captivity in 1943).

Under the threat of extinction, the communist command economy that had performed so unevenly in the 1930s finally began to function as its architects had intended. Drawing on the experience of the Five-Year Plans, the Soviets frantically dismantled thousands of factories—as much as 80 percent of the country's industrial capacity—and shipped the pieces eastward to the Ural Mountains, where workers put them back together and began turning out munitions, weapons, and vehicles within a few months. In addition, the United States quickly extended its Lend-Lease program to the USSR and began shipping millions of tons of goods. U.S. trucks, jeeps, high-grade steel, and foodstuffs all played an important role in the Soviet war effort.

THE STRUGGLES FOR LENINGRAD AND MOSCOW

These emergency measures came just in time. The Germans might well have captured Leningrad, but the city's new military commander, a talented peasant-born soldier named Georgi Zhukov, refused to contemplate surrender. Leningraders constructed seventeen miles of barricades and anti-tank ditches throughout the city, and set up 20,000 fortified posts. In late September 1941, the Germans abandoned the idea of a frontal attack on the city and instead began a siege. They still counted on eventual victory and the extermination of Leningrad's inhabitants. "In this war for existence we have no interest in keeping even part of this large city's population," commented Hitler.

The German army kept up merciless bombardments and waited for the Leningraders to starve. During the terrible winter of 1941–42, as many as 1 million of the 3.3 million people caught in the city did in fact die of starvation, cold, and disease. As the siege lengthened to 900 days, the city almost ceased functioning entirely, and the desperate citizenry ate pets, medicines, leather, and even, sometimes, one another. Yet somehow Leningrad did not give in, and during the winter months of the long siege the Soviets managed to open an "ice road" across a frozen lake from unoccupied territory and bring in enough supplies to keep the remaining population alive.

Even as Leningrad held, the Germans pushed hard toward the greater prize of Moscow, where the Soviet situation was also beyond desperate. In mid-October 1941, the Soviets had just 90,000 men standing between the German army and their capital. Once again, Stalin called on Zhukov, who strengthened a defensive line sixty miles from the capital and used hundreds of thousands of women and children to build a second one just ten miles from the Kremlin. For a time, the weather—early snow that melted and turned the Russian soil into an ocean of mud—slowed the German advance. But by early November, as the soil again hardened, the German vanguard stood just forty miles from Moscow; by the end of November, just twelve. Hitler held a ceremony to declare victory, and Stalin began evacuating the government 500 miles to the east.

But here, finally, before Moscow, the titanic scale of the war and the tremendous material resources of the Soviet Union began to tell on the seemingly invincible German army. The rough terrain led vehicles to succumb to mechanical failure. As early as September, two-thirds of all German tanks could no longer function, and by November one German army group had abandoned half its trucks in favor of horse-drawn wagons. The terrible cold of the Russian winter began to affect men and machines. The army suffered 133,000 cases of frostbite. All in all, by the end of November 1941 fully 25 percent of the German infantry had been killed, wounded, or incapacitated by disease.

The Soviet resistance remained as desperate as ever: soldiers fought tanks with rifles and Molotov cocktails—bottles filled with gasoline, named after Stalin's foreign minister. The Soviets held on to the key city of Tula, south of Moscow, preventing the capital's encirclement. In early December, with the Germans believing that the Soviets had no reserves left, the Soviets launched a surprise counteroffensive that broke the German pincers and drove the Wehrmacht back two hundred miles. It was the first major German defeat of the war. As the year 1941 came to an end, the German army remained in a powerful position, and an eventual victory in Russia still seemed possible. But the day of the blitzkrieg was clearly over.

CRUCIAL POINTS

Up until the end of 1941, the course of the war had depended in large part on the strategic choices made by the different combatants—particularly on the decisions Hitler made in the invasions of western Europe and then of the Soviet Union. But thereafter, increasingly, it would depend on the sheer ability of the contending powers to mobilize natural resources, industry, and soldiers, to organize them, and to deploy them against the enemy. And the number of contending powers expanded as the war turned truly global in scope.

PEARL HARBOR AND THE GLOBAL WAR

Even as Soviet forces were beginning to drive the Nazis back from Moscow, a stunning event took place 7,000 miles away in the middle of the Pacific Ocean. On December 7, 1941, the Japanese Empire launched a surprise attack on the American fleet at **Pearl Harbor** in Hawaii and declared war on both the United States and Great Britain. Hitler greeted the news with exultation. "Now it is impossible for us to lose the war," he burbled to top generals. "Now we have an ally who has never been vanquished in three thousand years." Four days later, over the objections of Foreign Minister Ribbentrop, he declared war on the United States.

Hitler's reaction hinted at a loss of touch with reality

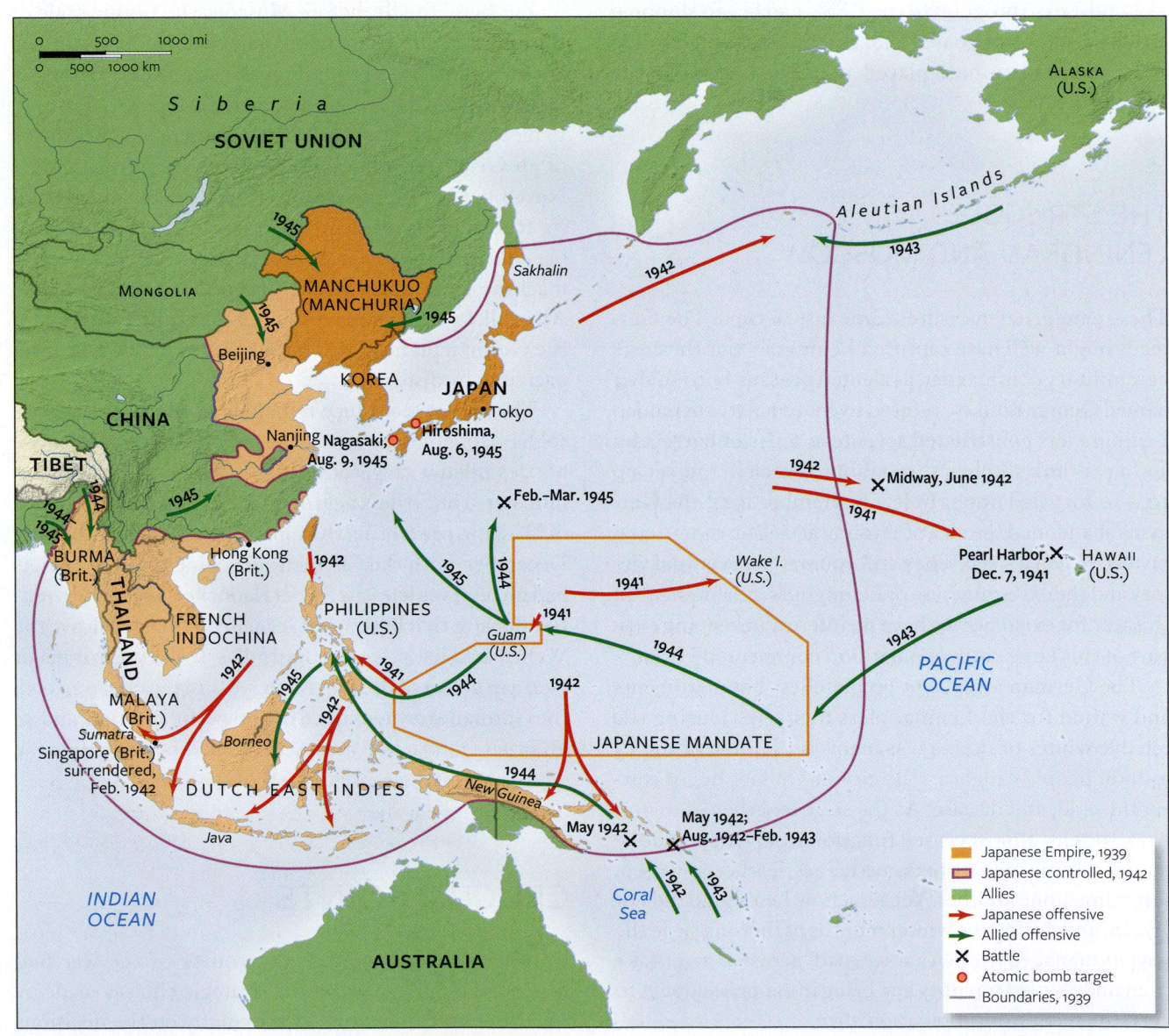

World War II in the Pacific The war in Asia began with the Japanese attack on Pearl Harbor in December 1941, quickly followed by Japanese offensives throughout the South Pacific: Malaya, the Dutch East Indies, the Philippines, New Guinea, and elsewhere. Major engagements between Japanese and U.S. forces took place at sea, such as at Midway in 1942. Despite U.S. offensives in 1944–45, the war dragged on in the South Pacific until the atomic bombs dropped in August 1945 forced Japan's surrender.

that would increasingly afflict him over the next three and a half years. There was little hope that Japan could help him beat the Soviet Union or Britain, even if it managed to expand its Pacific empire at U.S. and British expense. The Soviets had already beaten back Japanese forces during their short border war of 1938–39. And bringing the United States into the war threw its unmatched industrial capacity into the balance on the Allied side. Winston Churchill, on hearing the news of Pearl Harbor, correctly drew the opposite conclusion from Hitler's: "So we had won after all."

With Pearl Harbor, an alliance of the United States, the United Kingdom, and the Soviet Union quickly took shape. Churchill and U.S. president Franklin Roosevelt had already met in the summer of 1941 and signed an Atlantic Charter laying out a vision for a peaceful, postwar world in which the occupied countries would regain their freedom. As we have seen, the United States was already supplying considerable materiel to Britain and the USSR under its Lend-Lease program. During the war the so-called Big Three powers would hold a series of summit meetings to coordinate strategy, including personal meetings among Churchill, Roosevelt, and Stalin.

Colonial Troops All of the colonial empires participating in the war drew on their overseas holdings for soldiers; many non-Europeans, but not all, served willingly. A January 1941 photograph shows soldiers from Somaliland (in East Africa) serving in the Italian army in North Africa.

A WAR OF EMPIRES Even before Pearl Harbor, the war between the European powers had spilled into the far-flung reaches of Europe's colonial empires. The colonies mattered as sources of raw material and men, and also as bases from which to protect supply lines and to disrupt enemy supply lines. Soon after the fall of France, Italian forces in Ethiopia occupied the British colony in what is now Somalia, on the horn of eastern Africa. In 1941, the British counterattacked from their East African colonies, drove Italy out of Ethiopia, and restored to the throne Emperor Haile Selassie. Elsewhere in Africa, British and Free French forces loyal to Charles de Gaulle tried and failed to capture the strategic port of Dakar, in present-day Senegal, bringing them into direct combat with Vichy France.

In the Middle East, the pro-German general Rashid Ali revolted against Iraq's British overlords, with the complicity of the Vichy authorities in neighboring Syria. The British government responded with a costly but successful invasion of Syria from its own bases in Iraq and Palestine. Some of the most vicious fighting took place precisely where Israel and Syria now confront each other, on the Golan Heights. In these various conflicts, as in the sinking of the French fleet at Mers-el-Kébir in 1940, British forces fought the French for the last time in the two nations' long history of belligerency. With the British controlling Egypt

and Italy controlling Libya, fighting also broke out across the deserts of North Africa. And after the shah of Iran flirted with the Germans, Britain and the Soviet Union staged a successful joint invasion of that country in the summer of 1941 to secure its valuable oilfields.

The colonial empires in turn relied more heavily than ever on their subjects to prosecute the war. Britain's Indian holdings provided 2.5 million soldiers, who fought in all the principal theaters of operation, including Europe. The Free French army that formed after France's capitulation in 1940 drew heavily on the French Foreign Legion and on black African troops. The celebrated French Second Armored Division initially included thousands of black African and Muslim North African soldiers. Colonial soldiers felt that their service placed the empires in their debt, and they resented the increased exploitation of colonial resources for the war effort.

Pearl Harbor greatly expanded the global dimensions of the war. It connected the European fighting with the bloody conflict that had been occurring in East Asia since the 1930s as the Japanese Empire gobbled up large areas of China, and it tied events in Europe to a vast struggle for control of the Pacific Ocean. In the days after the attack on Hawaii, Japanese forces took the strategic American islands of Guam and Wake. They also launched devastating attacks on British-held Malaya (present-day Malaysia) and, crucially, the Dutch colonies in the East Indies (present-day Indonesia): a source of oil for the Japanese war machine. In one of the worst defeats for Britain in modern history, its colony of Singapore surrendered to Japan in February 1942, and some 130,000 British, Indian, Australian, and local troops went into Japanese captivity. In ensuing months, Japan conquered the American-held Philippines and moved into British-held Burma, on the doorstep of India.

NORTH AFRICA AND THE QUESTION OF A SECOND FRONT

In the first few months of 1942, the newly enlarged scale of the fighting did little to diminish Hitler's confidence. At the southern end of the eastern front, the Germans continued to score significant victories, occupying nearly all of Ukraine and the Crimean Peninsula. In North Africa, General Erwin Rommel was leading a second German-Italian offensive from Italian-held Libya against British and Allied forces in Egypt. On June 21, 1942, he took the key fortress of Tobruk, along with some 33,000 prisoners—the greatest British defeat of the war after Singapore. Within a month, Rommel's tanks had reached El Alamein, just fifty miles west of the ancient Egyptian port city of Alexandria. North Africa mattered particularly to the British, who controlled Egypt and with it the crucial Suez Canal that allowed for rapid transport to British India.

But at El Alamein, the British finally stopped the German advance, forcing a retreat that would take Rommel's forces all the way back to Vichy-held Tunisia. In November 1942, Churchill famously declared: "The Germans have received back again that measure of fire and steel which they have so often meted out to others. Now this is not the end. It is not even the beginning of the end. But it is, perhaps, the end of the beginning."

Even as Churchill was speaking, the North African campaign took a new turn. British and U.S. forces invaded Morocco, Algeria, and Tunisia, making use of new amphibious technology to land troops quickly on beaches. They easily overcame scattered and confused resistance by the Vichy French, and by the next spring the Allies had driven the Axis from North Africa altogether.

TENSIONS IN THE ALLIANCE This new British-American offensive, however, provoked some objections from the third major Allied power, the Soviet Union.

Stalin, fighting for his country's survival against Hitler, had pushed Roosevelt and Churchill to put all their efforts into an invasion of France that would open up a second, western front for the Germans and relieve some of the pressure on his own country. He made this case in his first meeting with Churchill, in Moscow, in August 1942. Churchill insisted that an invasion of France would require a massive concentration of force that the Allies were not yet capable of deploying. He also believed that the invasion of North Africa would help preserve the British colonial empire by ensuring Britain's connections with India and Africa. While Churchill developed a wary respect for Stalin's cunning, memory, and "crude wit" (Churchill's words), the two men remained suspicious of each other, with Stalin fearing that the British preferred to see the Soviet Union bled white to minimize the threat it might pose after the war. Stalin prompted Communist parties in the west and their sympathizers to adopt "Second Front Now!" as their slogan. The question of the second front would remain a major source of tension among the Allies for the next year and a half.

STALINGRAD

In the summer and fall of 1942, the Soviets felt even more pressure because Hitler's eastern forces were gaining new momentum. Rejecting his generals' desire for another major assault on Moscow, Hitler instead ordered an attack through Ukraine to the city of Stalingrad, some 1,500 miles east of Berlin, and then to follow the Volga River southeast to the Caspian Sea, cutting the Caucasus region and its crucial oilfields off from the Soviet heartland. By the late summer of 1942, the German Sixth Army established a fortification on the banks of the Volga north of Stalingrad.

But once again, the Soviet defenders resisted with unexpected tenacity. The Soviet command economy functioned best under emergency conditions, and by now it was producing war materiel at a stunning pace. In the summer of 1942, Germany was producing 500 tanks a month. A German general told Hitler that the Soviets were doing better, with 1,200 tanks a month. Hitler, pounding the table for effect, insisted the figure was exaggerated. But in fact the Soviets were actually producing 2,200 tanks a month, and 2,600 aircraft.

The Soviet government also demanded total mobilization and obedience from the population. On July 28, Stalin issued his infamous Order 227: "Not a Step Back!"

It commanded all Soviet troops to defend "every meter of Soviet territory to the last drop of blood." Anyone who disobeyed and retreated could be shot out of hand or condemned to serve in penal battalions charged with suicide missions on the front lines. By some estimates, as many as 158,000 Soviet soldiers were sentenced to death by their own side during the war. The formidable propaganda capacity of the Soviet state was also mobilized to inspire the Soviet population and demonize the enemy. Ilya Ehrenburg (1891–1967), one of the most acclaimed Soviet journalists of the war, wrote in the press in 1942: "Do not count days; do not count miles. Count only the number of Germans you have killed. Kill the German—this is your mother's prayer. Kill the German—this is the cry of your Russian earth. Do not waver. Do not let up. Kill."

In what became the most important battle of the entire war, the **battle of Stalingrad**, like Moscow, somehow did not fall. A hugely expansive city filled with factories, Stalingrad stretched for miles along the sandy western bank of the Volga. It was named for Stalin because of his role in securing it for the communists during the Civil War. In late August and early September, as the Germans advanced, Stalin sent his most competent commander, Zhukov, to investigate the situation. He and his colleagues soon devised a plan for a counteroffensive both north and south of the city. Yet even as the Soviets prepared, German divisions surrounded the city center. The fighting defied comprehension: every green leaf was burned off trees; every building was destroyed or heavily damaged, and covered in a thick layer of dust and ash. The Germans advanced over the rubble, capturing the central railroad station seven times, but each time they were driven back by the desperate defenders.

On November 19, a Soviet counteroffensive finally started. Thanks to the factories that had moved to the east in 1941, Lend-Lease aid from the United States, and conscription, the Soviets managed to bring an additional 1,350 aircraft, nearly a thousand tanks, 14,000 heavy guns, and a million more men into the battle. Within days, they broke the German flanks and encircled the German Sixth Army, along with other German and Axis units, numbering some 330,000 soldiers. The tables had been turned. Hitler ordered his forces to stand their ground despite the hopeless situation. Finally, at the end of January 1943, having lost nearly 150,000 dead, they surrendered. The Soviet toll was even higher.

Yet for the Allies overall, the cost was worth it. Stalingrad delivered an immense material blow to Nazi Germany, and an even more important moral one. "Losses

Soviet War Propaganda A bold 1943 propaganda poster shows a Soviet bayonet stabbing and killing a lion emblazoned with a swastika. The caption reads: "Beat the German beasts! Destroy the Hitlerian Army! Can and Must Be Done!"

can never be too high," Hitler raved in 1942. "They sow the seeds of future glory." But fewer and fewer Germans agreed with him. Stalingrad broke the myth of German military superiority and prevented the Germans from strangling the Soviet economy. It also won crucial time for the Allies—above all, the Soviet Union and the United States—fully to exploit their advantages in population and industrial capacity.

HUNGER ON THE EASTERN FRONT

On the eastern front, soldiers on both sides had to learn to survive with scarce rations. Heavy mud and thick snows choked the overextended German supply lines as the Wehrmacht pushed deeper into Russia, while Soviet resources were strained by the destruction wrought by the fighting, although Lend-Lease provided aid from the United States. Field kitchens could be located miles away from the fighting, and fuel for cooking was often scarce. Soldiers generally had to make do with small amounts of stale bread, watery soup, margarine, or horsemeat, with perhaps a small allowance of liquor. In this desperate state, troops seized any opportunities to scavenge, steal, or requisition fresh food to enrich their meager diet.

Willy Peter Reese, from *A Stranger to Myself*

A young German soldier, Reese kept a poetically worded diary of his struggles on the eastern front from 1941 until his death in combat in 1944. In this early passage, he describes staving off hunger by stealing food from Russian civilians.

We were hungry. The cooks slaughtered cattle and pigs on the way and requisitioned peas, beans, and cucumbers everywhere. But a little midday soup wasn't enough to get us through our exertions. So we started taking the last piece of bread from women and children, had chickens and geese prepared for us, pocketed their small supplies of butter and lard, weighed down our vehicles with flitches of bacon and flour from the larders, drank the overrich milk, and cooked and roasted on their stoves, stole honey from the collective farms, came upon stashes of eggs, and weren't bothered by tears, hand wringings, and curses. We were the victors. War excused our thefts, encouraged cruelty, and the need to survive didn't go around getting permission from conscience. Women and children were made to go to the wells for us, water our horses, watch our fires, and peel our potatoes. We used their straw for our horses or for bedding for ourselves, or else we drove them out of their beds and stretched out on their stoves....

…We suffered from diarrhea. Our bellies were a ferment of swamp. We were disgusted and appalled, but we couldn't fast. Hunger hurt too much.

We moved in semipermanently. We drove the women out of their homes and pushed them into the most wretched of the dwellings. Pregnant or blind, they all had to go. Crippled children we shooed out into the rain, and some were left with nothing better than a barn or shed, where they lay down with our horses.... [W]e lived as well as we could and didn't think about the deprivation that would come after us....

…I would give up God and my own humanity for a piece of bread. I had no comrades. Everyone fended for himself, hated anyone who found better booty than himself, wouldn't share, would only trade, and tried to get the better of the other.... The weaker was exploited, the helpless left in his misery.

Vasily Grossman, from *Life and Fate*

Grossman was a Russian war correspondent who drew on his observations at the battle of Stalingrad in writing the novel *Life and Fate* (1959). In this passage, a Major Byerozkin catches his men cooking a fish—a rare treat in the midst of the battle.

Byerozkin said: "So where's this five-kilo pike-perch, comrade Movshovich? The whole division's talking of nothing else."

With the same sad look, Movshovich ordered: "Cook, show him the fish please." The cook, the only man present to have been carrying out his duties, explained: "The comrade captain wanted it stuffed in the Jewish manner. I've got some pepper and bay-leaves, but I haven't any white bread or horse-radish...."

"I see," said Byerozkin. "I once had one done like that in Bobruysk, at the house of one Sara Aronovna—though, to be quite frank, I didn't think much of it."

Suddenly they all realized that it hadn't even occurred to Byerozkin to get angry. It was as though he knew that Podchufarov had fought off a German attack during the night; that he had been half-buried under falling earth during the small hours; that his orderly…had had to dig him out, shouting: "Don't worry, comrade Captain, I'll get you out of there." It was as though he knew that Movshovich and his sappers had crept along one particularly vulnerable street, scattering earth and crushed brick over a chessboard pattern of anti-tank mines.

They were all young and they were glad to be alive one more morning, to be able to lift up a tin mug and say, "Your good health!", to be able to eat cabbage and smoke cigarettes. …In any case, nothing had really happened—they had just stood up for a moment before a superior and then invited him to eat, watching with pleasure how he enjoyed his cabbage.

QUESTIONS FOR ANALYSIS

1. What reasons does Reese give for his thefts?
2. Why do you think the soldiers fear Major Byerozkin's anger?
3. What are the similarities and differences between the soldiers' interactions in both sources?

Sources: Willy Peter Reese, *A Stranger to Myself: The Inhumanity of War: Russia, 1914–1944*, trans. Michael Hofmann (New York: 2003), pp. 35–36; Vasily Grossman, *Life and Fate*, trans. Robert Chandler (New York: 1985), pp. 61–62.

MIDWAY AND THE TURN IN THE PACIFIC

Even as Stalingrad marked the turning of the war in Europe, the Allies were also managing to push back the Axis powers in the Pacific theater. In a series of critical battles waged largely by airplanes launched from aircraft carriers against enemy ships (in some cases, the opposing fleets did not even see each other), the United States halted the Japanese advance across the ocean. Breaking crucial Japanese codes, the U.S. navy was able successfully to concentrate its forces against a Japanese carrier group at the decisive battle of Midway in June 1942, destroying four Japanese carriers.

Now, even as the Soviets were beginning the long, difficult land campaign to push the Nazis toward Germany, the Americans began an extended naval campaign to push Japan back across strings of small Pacific islands toward Asia. The Americans also developed a submarine fleet to attack Japanese merchant shipping, because Japan had much the same basic vulnerability during the war as Great Britain: it was a small, resource-poor archipelago dependent on oil and food imports. Despite Japanese success in taking the Dutch East Indies and their oil reserves, by the end of 1943 the American submarine campaign had proven so successful that the Japanese did not have enough shipping to get the oil they needed to their military and their home islands.

HOLOCAUST

The turning of the tide in the war provided no immediate relief for most of the millions of men, women, and children under Nazi occupation. Even as the Axis powers reached the limits of their expansion and felt their militaries buckle under the strain, the Nazis fell upon their most helpless victims with hideous fury.

PLANNING GENOCIDE

In January 1942, well before the German thrust toward Stalingrad began, fifteen high-ranking Nazis gathered for a day-long conference at a luxurious villa on the Wannsee Lake west of Berlin. Convened by Reinhard Heydrich, the deputy head of the SS, they discussed in cold-blooded, bureaucratic terms the German government's plans,

already decided upon by Hitler, to exterminate the Jewish population of Europe. As the Nazis conquered new territories in the east after June 1941, they had continued the policy begun in Poland of forcing the Jews to live in densely populated, unsanitary ghettos. In September 1941, they started deporting German, Austrian, and Czech Jews to the eastern ghettos as well. Disease and starvation took their toll in these city-sized prisons, with 83,000 Jews dying prematurely in Warsaw alone between 1940 and mid-1942. At the same time, the *Einsatzgruppen* carried out their grisly mass executions.

The **Wannsee conference** marked the moment at which the Nazis moved toward a more efficient, industrialized process of mass murder. Under the control of Heydrich's Reich Main Security Office, a vast system of

The Holocaust Hitler's plan for the extermination of the Jews included concentration camps and ghettos across Europe, the many sites in eastern Europe where "task forces" perpetrated mass executions, and ultimately the extermination camps in Poland.

transport was designed to move Jews and other populations destined for slaughter to a series of vast concentration camps being built largely in Poland. The most important groups targeted for the camps, other than Jews, were homosexuals, political opponents of the Reich, and the Poles, Soviets, and Roma.

In the camps, the able-bodied would be allowed to live and work as slave laborers for the German war effort. Everyone else was to be killed on arrival. Initially, these killings were done with machine guns. But in the fall of 1941, after members of the *Einsatzgruppen* had complained about the costs of mass shootings—both the psychological toll taken on the executioners and the simple price of ammunition—the Nazis began experimenting with gas as an alternative. At first, they killed with truck exhaust that was modified to empty into sealed containers holding the prisoners. Later, they built stationary gas chambers that they flooded, first with diesel exhaust and then with a poison gas called Zyklon B originally invented for fumigation.

THE DEATH CAMPS

The worst of the killings occurred between mid-March 1942 and mid-February 1943. At the start of this period, over three-quarters of all victims of the Holocaust were still alive. At the end, more than three-quarters were dead.

In the summer of 1942, the Nazis began carrying out mass deportations from Warsaw and other ghettos to the killing centers. The victims were told they were being "resettled" in the east, but those who resisted or fled were shot out of hand, as were hospital patients, the elderly, the insane, and others who could not walk to the designated departure sites. Some Jews cooperated with the Nazis in the vain hope of mollifying them, lowering the death toll, or perhaps just saving their own lives. On arrival at the camps, the victims had to hand over their valuables and present themselves for "selection," during which doctors would choose those fit for slave labor. Those condemned to death were made to undress and were herded into gas chambers disguised as showers. Afterward, prisoners themselves disposed of the bodies, initially in mass graves but later in a sophisticated system of crematoria.

The largest and most infamous concentration and extermination camp was **Auschwitz-Birkenau**, some thirty-seven miles west of Kraków near the old German-Polish border. At its peak in early to mid-1944, it contained more than 100,000 prisoners engaged in slave labor producing synthetic rubber, fuel, and other war materiel.

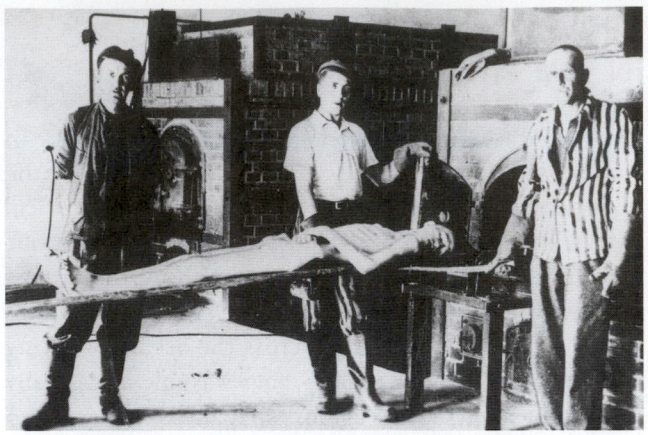

Death Camps Imprisoned laborers at the Auschwitz death camp were made to pose with an emaciated corpse in front of a furnace that was used to cremate the bodies of the dead.

Its gas chambers and crematoria could dispose of up to 15,000 men, women, and children per day. Between 1940 and 1945, approximately 1.1 million European Jews were deported there, of whom some 960,000 were killed, along with hundreds of thousands of others, especially Poles, Roma, and Soviet prisoners of war.

Auschwitz-Birkenau, however, was only one part of a network of death camps in occupied Poland that included Majdanek, Sobibór, and Treblinka. In the Greek city of Salonika, where Jews had long formed a large percentage of the population, the Germans deported nearly the entire Jewish community to their deaths in Auschwitz. In July 1942, the Vichy police arrested nearly 13,000 Parisian Jews, including more than 4,000 children, and shut them up for days in stifling heat before sending them on to the extermination camps. Some 60,000 more Jews from France would eventually follow.

All in all, at least 5.4 million Jews perished during the Holocaust, along with an estimated 250,000 Roma, tens of thousands of homosexuals and political prisoners, and millions of Soviet prisoners of war. In country after country, a long Jewish history was brutally cut off. Nearly all the 3 million Jews of Poland died. Throughout Europe, the Germans relied not only on their own military forces but also on German police units, prisoners of war (especially Ukrainians, Lithuanians, and Latvians), and local populations that, while suffering from constraint and fear, were also driven by their own anti-Semitic traditions. In one of the most well-documented episodes, Polish Christians in the town of Jedwabne turned on their Jewish neighbors, torturing them and raping women before herding

DEPORTATION FROM THE LODZ GHETTO

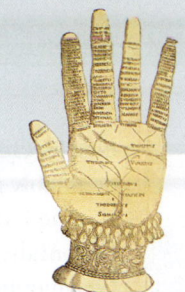

The city of Lodz in central Poland was the site of the second-largest Jewish ghetto, with over 200,000 Jews passing through over the course of World War II. In 1942, the Germans began to deport Jews to a nearby extermination camp. When the ghetto was liberated at the end of the war, fewer than 900 Jewish survivors remained.

An inhabitant and archivist of the Lodz ghetto, Josef Zelkowicz (1897–1944) kept a detailed diary of daily life there before he was deported to Auschwitz, where he died in 1944. In this excerpt from September 4, 1942, he describes the ghetto's reaction to the news of the impending deportation of children and the elderly.

The ghetto was dealt a horrific blow this morning. What only yesterday was considered impossible and inconceivable became, tragically, a fact. Children up to age ten are being torn from their parents and siblings and are doomed to deportation....

If it were only a "deportation." If only there were the slightest surety that the deportees would be allowed to continue living—even under the harshest conditions—the tragedy would not be so horrific.... But in this case, no one has even a vestige of doubt that the deportees from the ghetto are not being taken to any other location. They are being led to perdition, at least the elderly.... They are being thrown on the garbage heap....

No house, no apartment, no family is unaffected by this terrible edict. Every-one has a son, an elderly father or an aged mother....

Hearts have turned into ice. Hands pound each other in agony. Facial features are twisted, eyes are lowered to the ground, and all eyes are crying....

The wretched children still know nothing. Infants, incapable of perceiving the sword... suspended over their guileless heads, unwittingly sense the great danger that lurks in their midst and they clutch their fathers' and mothers' skinny, emaciated necks with all the strength in their two little hands....

Mothers race about in the streets, one shoe on and the other off, half of their hair combed and the rest unkempt, kerchiefs half draped over their shoulders and half dragging on the ground. They still have their children. They can still clutch them fiercely to their shriveled bosoms. They can still kiss their clear eyes. But what will happen afterwards, in another hour, tomorrow? Rumor has it that the children will be removed from their parents and sent away on Monday. Sent away—where?

QUESTIONS FOR ANALYSIS

1. How do the inhabitants of the Lodz ghetto respond to the deportation announcement?

2. What do the Jews of Lodz know about the fate that awaits the deportees?

3. What does this excerpt from Zelkowicz's diary reveal about the everyday experience of the victims of the Holocaust?

Source: Josef Zelkowicz, *In Those Terrible Days: Writings from the Lodz Ghetto*, ed. Michal Ungar (Jerusalem: 2002), pp. 261–64.

a thousand or more (the numbers remain disputed) into a barn, dousing it with kerosene, and burning it to the ground. In the extermination camps, the Germans made widespread use of Polish and Ukrainian auxiliaries, and also of prisoners, including Jews, willing to serve as *kapos* (low-level guards). In many individual cases, however, Polish Christians sheltered Jews from the Nazis and aided them in the camps.

"Never shall I forget the little faces of the children, whose bodies I saw turned into wreaths of smoke beneath a silent blue sky. Never shall I forget those flames which consumed my faith." The Holocaust survivor Elie Wiesel (1928–2016) wrote these lines in his novel *Night*, about his experiences at Auschwitz. Other former Auschwitz inmates such as the Italian Jew Primo Levi (*The Saved and the Damned*) and the Polish Catholic Tadeusz Borowski (*This Way to the Gas, Ladies and Gentlemen*) also left astonishing literary portraits of the Holocaust, as did the German-Jewish poet Paul Celan. (All three, irredeemably scarred by their experiences, later committed suicide.) Thousands of other victims left memoirs, testimonials, and diaries—notably, the diary of the young German Jew Anne Frank, who went into hiding with her family in Amsterdam, was arrested by the Germans in the summer of 1944, and died at age fifteen in the camp of Bergen-Belsen.

The Holocaust is distinguished from other episodes of genocide in history by the cold-minded, bureaucratic planning that went into the process through which the Nazis rounded up entire Jewish populations, transported them hundreds or even thousands of miles, and then systematically murdered them. Of all the physical evidence from the Holocaust, which includes vast storehouses of possessions taken from the victims—jewelry, suitcases, clothes, shoes, eyeglasses, and toothbrushes—as well as the actual remains of the camps, nothing is quite so chilling as the paperwork. In millions of daily memoranda, invoices, account books, and minutes of meetings, one sees that hallmark modern phenomenon—a large-scale industrial bureaucracy—turned to the purpose of destroying innocent life.

Evidence of the Holocaust Those murdered in the camps had their belongings confiscated and stored in huge warehouses. A modern-day display at the Auschwitz Museum consists of a colossal pile of victims' shoes, a sobering reminder of the scale of the death toll.

TOTAL WAR

Even as Hitler was waging this merciless campaign against millions of innocent victims, the war continued on a worldwide scale. An Allied victory now looked likely, but to achieve it would require enormous expenditures of material resources and blood.

THE ALLIED ADVANTAGE

Historians have often claimed that after the Allied victories in North Africa and Stalingrad, the final defeat of the Axis powers was inevitable. This idea rests particularly on the Allied economic superiority attained once the United States came into the war. After all, in 1942 the combined gross domestic product (GDP) of the Allied countries dwarfed that of the Axis by more than two to one. By 1944, the ratio had reached almost three to one. While the GDP of Germany rose by 13 percent from 1939 to 1944, that of the United States grew by an astonishing 72 percent. The leviathan that was American industry, after having engaged in relatively little military manufacturing before the war, ramped up to produce 141 aircraft carriers, 88,410 armored vehicles, 324,750 aircraft, and 41 billion rounds of ammunition during the war. Even Britain's GDP went up by 20 percent, while the Soviet Union, despite the German invasion and occupation of much of its industrial heartland, had returned by 1944 to its 1939 economic level.

But economics does not explain everything. As the American general Dwight David Eisenhower wrote in his diary in 1942 after meeting with politicians in Washington: "Not one man in twenty in the government realizes what a grisly, dirty, tough business we are in. They think we can buy victory." Economic strength did not translate directly into military effectiveness. The Allies had to learn, often at a steep price, how best to deploy their resources. They had to learn to cooperate with one another—a difficult task given the differences between Soviet communism and western democracy, and the differences in war aims and strategies. The most important of these was Stalin's insistence on the quick opening of a second front in western Europe, and Churchill's reluctance to comply. They also had to learn, within their own militaries, how best to coordinate land, air, and sea power. For their part, the highly militarized societies of Germany and Japan assigned little prestige to the unglamorous but vital tasks of supply and maintenance, and therefore often handled them badly. The German army in the east lost two-thirds of its tanks and half its trucks in the winter of 1941–42, and it never entirely recovered from this loss. As the war went on, it relied increasingly on horses for transport, in what some historians call a demodernization.

THE BOMBING CAMPAIGN

The Allies made particularly deadly use of their superior aircraft production. As early as the summer of 1940, Churchill declared that victory required "an absolutely devastating, exterminating attack by very heavy bombers upon the Nazi homeland." He hoped such attacks would devastate German industry and cripple the Nazi war effort. But through 1942, Allied bombing of German cities achieved relatively little. Daylight raids saw high losses for the attackers—during the war, the British and Americans combined lost 21,000 bombers and 140,000 airmen. Night raids, while safer, were woefully inaccurate. But bombing gradually became more effective as a result of technical innovations designed in consultation with British and American industry.

In July 1943, over a thousand Allied planes attacked the northern German port city of Hamburg, suffering only a 2.8 percent loss rate. Over two days, they dropped high-explosive and incendiary bombs that set off an unstoppable firestorm. Some 40,000 people were killed, and 1 million left homeless. Yet even with destruction on this scale, the bombing did not always achieve the desired results. Although the Allies above all targeted Germany's industrial base, not civilians, as the war progressed they also came to hope that the civilian deaths would break Germany's morale and discipline. There is little evidence that this occurred. Five months after the Hamburg raid, industrial production in the city had returned to 80 percent of the pre-raid level. Germany did see its weapons production and industrial capacity severely damaged by the bombing, but mainly in the last year of the war.

The case of Dresden, capital of the German state of Saxony, has achieved special notoriety because the beautiful baroque city, called Venice on the Elbe, had little strategic or industrial importance. In February 1945, it was crammed with refugees. The attack on the city that month involved 1,300 Allied bombers dropping nearly 4 million tons of explosives that killed between 24,000 and 40,000 civilians and wiped out the baroque center almost entirely. Altogether, bombing raids probably killed somewhere on the order of 600,000 German civilians during the war, including over 100,000 children.

The United States inflicted massive civilian casualties on Japan once it started sustained strategic bombing of

Allied Bombing A solitary statue of an angel looks out over the city of Dresden, largely destroyed by the Allied bombing campaign of February 1945.

the Japanese home islands in mid-1944. Even before the atomic bombing of Hiroshima and Nagasaki in August 1945, the firebombing of Tokyo in March killed over 80,000 people. Debates continue about the Allies' moral responsibility for the deaths of innocents on this scale, and the ways in which the "barbarization" of warfare initiated by the Axis ended up affecting their adversaries as well.

THE EASTERN FRONT

On the eastern front as well, what mattered was not only the Soviet Union's superior economic capacity, reconstructed after the devastation of the initial German offensive, but the way this capacity was deployed and the way the Red Army adjusted its strategy. Owing to the experiences of the 1930s, the Soviets already had the capacity to undertake brutally fast industrial initiatives, but it took time to redirect this capacity to effective military ends. During 1942 and early 1943, the general staff reorganized the army around powerful tank corps, copying the German model that relied on concentrations of tanks to break through enemy lines. At the beginning of the war, the Soviets had lost six to seven tanks for every German one they took out. By late 1944, the ratio was one to one.

These changes were evident in the next great conflict after Stalingrad, centered on the city of Kursk, some 350 miles south of Moscow. The Germans had 3,000 tanks and 1,800 aircraft. The Red Army countered with 3,600 tanks, nearly 2,800 aircraft, and a stunning 1,300,000 infantry. Soviet forces at Kursk held, shattering the Nazi offensive. The Soviets could now continue pushing the Germans back out of their territory, even as they continued to take frightful losses.

THE INVASION OF ITALY

The only way to relieve the ferocious pressure on the Soviets was for the western Allies to open a second front, to divert German resources from the east. But where would the western Allies strike? Stalin continued to urge an attack on German forces in France. The British, however, saw a more immediately tempting target that would distract the Germans without requiring the immense concentration of force necessary for an invasion of France—a concentration they believed was not yet possible. Instead, they looked to Italy. Mussolini had come unwillingly into the war, had gained little from it, and faced weakening support among the Italian population. The Americans initially were reluctant, wishing to conserve resources for the eventual attack through France, but Churchill prevailed upon Roosevelt.

In July 1943, the Allies successfully invaded the island of Sicily. Soon afterward, the Fascist Grand Council turned against Mussolini and arrested him, while King Vittorio Emmanuel III took control over the armed forces. The new government signed an armistice with the Allies on September 3. Five days later, American general Eisenhower began landing his troops near Naples. Italy would not prove so easy to subdue, however, for Hitler immediately sent divisions of his own to occupy the peninsula, and SS officers staged a daring rescue of Mussolini by using gliders. Allied forces only reached Rome in June 1944 and did not liberate parts of northern Italy until nearly the end of the war, at which point the Italian resistance captured and executed the dictator who had launched the fascist movement a quarter of a century before.

HOME FRONTS

The war brought the greatest suffering to the vast areas of the continent under Axis military occupation. But even more than in World War I, conditions of total war also transformed daily life beyond recognition for millions behind the front lines in the combatant countries. Not only did millions of men and women experience the horrific bombing campaigns discussed above; they also found themselves required to participate in the most ambitious mobilization of social resources ever attempted by European states.

WARTIME BRITAIN, GERMANY, AND THE USSR

Although never invaded by the Axis, Great Britain experienced enormous changes in the war. As the Allies carried out their invasion of Italy and planned for an invasion of France, the British Isles became their staging ground. By mid-1944, there were over 1.6 million American personnel in Britain. New military bases proliferated, and the British were exposed to American culture as never before. Over 70,000 British women became brides of American servicemen by the end of the war.

Other changes were reminiscent of what Britain had experienced in World War I. Rationing began almost immediately and affected nearly every consumer product, including foodstuffs, textiles, and fuel. The government urged civilians to donate aluminum cookware to the war effort to produce airplane parts, and millions complied. Blackouts, as a precaution against bombing, left nighttime streets dark and empty. Censorship of the news media and popular entertainment, while not comparable to that experienced in Germany or the Soviet Union, increased dramatically. The film industry in particular became virtually an arm of a new Ministry of Information. Even more quickly than in World War I, government ministries effectively took over large parts of the economy, setting production and consumption quotas, fixing wages, and organizing manufacturing.

In addition to conscripting able-bodied men for the military, in late 1941 Parliament passed a law conscripting single women in their twenties for service in industry, civil defense, or women's auxiliary corps attached to the armed forces. The proportion of women in the civilian workforce rose from 26 percent before the war to nearly 40 percent. Feminists again hailed the evidence that women could perform as well as men in jobs previously closed to them, and expressed the hope that this time the new opportunities would remain in place permanently.

In Germany and the Soviet Union, wartime daily experience more closely resembled that of the pre-war period in some ways. In both countries, totalitarian governments had already attempted massive reconfigurations of society. In the USSR the government already had virtually total control of the economy, and in Germany it set economic policy to an extent unknown in the Western democracies. Both states already exercised total control over the media,

WOMEN OF BRITAIN COME INTO THE FACTORIES

As in World War I, during World War II women were called on to fill jobs in industries that had previously been held by men, working in factories, hospitals, government offices, and on farms. In Britain, many women also served in noncombatant roles in the military as drivers, pilots, clerks, radar operators, and code-breakers.

To encourage women's participation in the war effort, the British government produced hundreds of posters that celebrated women's roles in fighting Nazi Germany. This poster from December 1941 calls for women to work in munitions factories. Flanked by a factory and a pair of advancing tanks, a woman worker assumes a powerful stance, her outstretched arms seeming to command forward a squadron of bombers. The text at the bottom encourages women to ask at centers managed by the Ministry of Labour about employment opportunities in factories. Such posters appealed to women's sense of patriotism and their status as British subjects.

QUESTIONS FOR ANALYSIS

1. What forms of work related to the war effort were available to women in Britain?
2. How does this poster attempt to persuade women to seek employment in factories?
3. How might this poster have tied into feminist views of women's place in society?

797

engaged in constant large-scale propaganda campaigns, and made use of enormous police apparatuses to stifle any significant dissent. In the USSR, women already participated in the labor force to a higher proportion than any other European state.

But in both countries the war nonetheless brought massive disruptions and changes. Both countries introduced extensive rationing, and in both the specter of malnutrition and even famine soon arose. As we have seen, Soviet women were conscripted along with men, and served extensively in combat positions. Soon after the German attack, Stalin ordered the deportation to the East of hundreds of thousands of "Volga Germans"—descendants of Germans who settled in Russia at the invitation of Catherine the Great in the eighteenth century. During the war, other Soviet nationalities suspected of sympathy for the Nazis suffered a similar fate, including hundreds of thousands of Crimean Tatars (the original Muslim inhabitants of the Crimean Peninsula in the Black Sea), who mostly ended up in Uzbekistan. Germany, meanwhile, made use of millions of slave laborers, including prisoners of war, to keep its domestic economy functioning. By 1944, more than seven million men and women from across Europe were working as forced labor in Germany.

RESISTANCE MOVEMENTS

As the Allies built up their strength in Britain, planning for an eventual invasion of France, Hitler's support outside of Germany weakened. In the occupied countries, collaborations grew more isolated, while resistance movements gained adherents and undertook bolder campaigns. To a large extent, the success of these movements depended on geography. Lowland countries like the Netherlands, Belgium, and Denmark had few territories in which partisans could hide from the Germans. The mountains of Yugoslavia and the deep forests of Russia, Ukraine, Norway, and Poland offered considerably safer terrain. The effectiveness of resistance forces also depended on organizational ability, and here communist groups, in some cases drawing on long experience of covert, underground organization before the war, had a decisive advantage. The Allies attempted where possible to drop supplies as well as personnel to help resistance groups.

In Yugoslavia, communist and non-communist partisans fought Germans, Italians, Croatian and Serbian fascists, and one another, with the bitter conflicts ultimately taking the lives of perhaps a tenth of the pre-war population. The Communist leader Josip Broz, who called himself Tito (1892–1980), eventually came out on top. Meanwhile, behind German lines on the eastern front, the numbers of partisans fighting in the forests steadily grew: in Ukraine, from 17,000 in mid-1943 to 140,000 a year later. Although poorly armed, these fighters did manage to disrupt German supplies and kill or wound tens of thousands of German soldiers. The Germans responded with vicious scorched-earth tactics and the slaughter of civilians.

It was in France where "the **Resistance**" was most systematically celebrated after the war. It had its heroes and martyrs: most famously Jean Moulin (1899–1943), a high official dismissed by Vichy who fled to Charles de Gaulle's Free French forces in London and then returned to unite and organize the disparate non-communist Resistance forces. Captured by the Germans in June 1943, he was most likely tortured to death. By July 1944, the French Resistance may have numbered as many as 116,000 men and women, but in truth its exploits are often exaggerated. Through most of the war, the Germans, reinforced by an unpopular French Militia, needed no more than a security force of 6,500 to guard against Resistance activity in France. Through at least mid-1942, the majority of the French population continued to support Pétain's Vichy regime.

In some ways, the single most impressive act of resistance to the Nazis was also the most hopeless, and it took place in the heart of Hitler's darkness: the Warsaw Jewish ghetto. In January 1943, as the Germans carried out

Warsaw Ghetto Uprising Following the defeat of the January 1943 uprising, German soldiers round up for deportation the inhabitants of the Warsaw ghetto, who raise their hands in surrender.

yet another sweep aimed at deporting Warsaw's Jews to the death camps, a secret Jewish Combat Organization attacked with a motley collection of pistols, ancient rifles, grenades, and Molotov cocktails. Taken by surprise, the Germans withdrew, enabling the insurgents to fortify themselves in a series of underground bunkers. A German SS and police force counterattacked in force in April, but it finally succeeded only by literally burning the entire section of the city to the ground. Some 13,000 Jews died in the uprising. Of the remaining 50,000 Jews of Warsaw, most ended up in the Treblinka death camp.

LIBERATION

Since 1940, Winston Churchill had made clear that he would only accept one outcome for the war: Germany's unconditional surrender. Stalin and Roosevelt concurred. Adolf Hitler, meanwhile, after invading the Soviet Union, made no further serious peace overtures, even when an Allied victory came to seem inevitable after the battles of Stalingrad and Kursk.

THE BEGINNING OF THE END

In February 1943, after the surrender at Stalingrad, Hitler's propaganda chief, Joseph Goebbels, gave a hallucinatory speech at the Berlin Sports Palace in which he screeched: "I ask you: Do you want total war? Do you want it more total and more radical than we can even yet imagine?" Hitler himself turned increasingly disjointed in his speech and dependent on drugs, including narcotics and amphetamines, administered by his personal physician. More and more he put his faith in a miraculous reversal of fortunes, perhaps thanks to new super-weapons.

BUILDING AN ATOMIC BOMB Both sides attempted to develop such weapons during the war. German scientists managed to develop two important new weapons: a pilotless flying bomb (the V-1), followed by the first workable ballistic missile (the V-2). However, in another triumph of intelligence work the Allies discovered the V-program's center of operation and destroyed it. In 1944, the Germans finally managed to start producing V-1's and V-2's in large numbers and launched them toward London, killing some 2,500 people. But the weapons came too late.

The Germans also worked on atomic weapons, but their efforts were hindered by insufficient coordination and the fact that many Jewish physicists had fled before the war. As a result they fell far behind the large-scale **Manhattan Project** run by British and American physicists in the United States. Even before the war, émigré scientists Albert Einstein (1879–1955) and Leo Szilárd (1898–1964) had urged President Roosevelt to begin a nuclear weapons program, lest Germany develop such weapons first. After Pearl Harbor, the Americans and British devoted massive resources to the project, eventually spending over $2 billion and employing some 130,000 scientists and staff. It was the Allies who would test the first nuclear weapon—in New Mexico in July 1945.

PLANNING A CROSS-CHANNEL INVASION The war now approached its final stages. In the Pacific, the Americans continued their advance and in June 1944 captured the island of Saipan, from which American bombers could strike at the Japanese home islands. Meanwhile, through the first half of 1944 the Red Army continued its own advance westward. By June, it had driven the Germans out of almost all of Russia and eastern Ukraine. Another major offensive would push them back to the 1939 border line by August.

Even as these events were taking place, planning for the second front was reaching fruition. Churchill, Roosevelt, and Stalin agreed at a summit meeting in Tehran in November 1943 to launch an invasion of France across the English Channel the next spring. By this point, Churchill had put aside his earlier reluctance to commit to such a massive project. He and Roosevelt had always wanted to defeat Germany as quickly and decisively as possible, but now they also realized that if they did not soon strike in the west, the Red Army might well end up liberating the entire Continent and install governments sympathetic to Stalin from Poland to Provence. Churchill in particular had few illusions about the durability of the western democracies' alliance with Stalin (he tellingly once remarked: "If Hitler invaded Hell I would make at least a favorable reference to the Devil in the House of Commons"). And so, ironically, he and Roosevelt now acted to restrain Stalin's future success by granting him his long-standing demand: the invasion of France.

D-DAY AND THE INVASION OF FRANCE

The Allied invasion across the English Channel was a massive operation. In November 1943, Hitler had ordered the construction of an Atlantic Wall involving some 3 million mines, half a million obstacles on beaches, and the reinforcement of German divisions in France and the Low

Countries. The Allies, meanwhile, steadily built up their forces in Britain, while doing their best to confuse the Germans about the eventual site of the landing. Overall command of the operation was given to American general Dwight D. Eisenhower (1890–1969), a steady, cautious commander who managed to contain considerable squabbling among his multinational subordinates.

When the invasion force actually appeared off the coast of Normandy on June 6, 1944—**D-Day**—it took the Germans at least somewhat by surprise. The very size of the Allied fleet had shock value: some 5,000 ships ranging from battleships to small landing craft, carrying 100,000 predominantly American and British soldiers to five beaches spread out over some thirty miles, heavily supported by air power. On the beach code-named Omaha, American forces had to advance under murderous German fire. Yet in the end, D-Day casualties numbered around 10,000—far less than the supreme commander, Eisenhower, had feared—and the Allies successfully established a beachhead.

Breaking out of Normandy's small Cotentin Peninsula still took two months of hard fighting. But during July alone, the Allies landed more than 1 million men, 171,000 vehicles, and 560,000 tons of supplies. In early August, the hard-driving American general George Patton (1885–1945) finally cut through German lines to the south, and his Third Army embarked on a virtual blitzkrieg of its own. By late August, Allied forces were approaching Paris. Hitler angrily ordered the city destroyed, but his commander in Paris refused to obey the order. In mid-August, Parisian police and Resistance units rose up in revolt against the Germans, who soon began pulling out. In a gesture

D-Day U.S. soldiers disembarking from a landing craft rush through water to the beaches of Normandy on June 6, 1944.

to the Free French forces under De Gaulle, Eisenhower allowed the actual liberation of Paris to be conducted by the French Second Armored Division, and on August 23 its first three tanks entered the city. By mid-September, the Allies had liberated Belgium and Luxembourg and had penetrated as far as the French border with Switzerland.

In fall 1944, the Allied push to the east briefly faltered. The liberation of the Netherlands took far longer than planned, and German resistance stiffened noticeably as the Wehrmacht retreated back toward its home territory. The success of Hitler's deputy, Albert Speer, in dispersing industrial production to avoid bombing temporarily enabled Germany to manufacture record amounts of war materiel. Between September and December, the Allied front line did not advance significantly, and in mid-December Hitler launched his last major offensive in the west. Still, by New Year's it was clear that the Germans had lost the so-called Battle of the Bulge, and by March 1945 the Allies had captured most of the German Rhineland.

LIBERATION AND POWER STRUGGLES

With the Allies advancing toward Germany from both sides, the countries that had suffered under the Nazi yoke celebrated their liberation. But this liberation came with significant pain and strife. Everywhere, but especially in the east, the front often rolled back over cities and towns like a steamroller, leaving rubble behind. While some occupied cities largely escaped damage in the war—Paris, Prague, Copenhagen, Kraków—they were in the minority. Now, with Nazi rule finally crumbling, the resistance forces throughout occupied Europe achieved their greatest importance as they harried the demoralized Germans and maneuvered to take control of the liberated areas.

The liberation brought bloody score-settling and vicious struggles for power in many countries. In Greece, communist and non-communist resistance forces, who had barely managed to cooperate beforehand, fell into a full-fledged civil war that lasted, with interruptions, until a final communist defeat in 1949. In France, the Resistance took revenge on the more visible and vulnerable collaborators: thousands died, and women who had slept with German soldiers sometimes had their heads shaved as a sign of shame. The restored French Republic Marshal Pétain, now in his late eighties, was put on trial and sentenced to life imprisonment. Other collaborators died in front of firing squads. Still, many highly placed ones, particularly those who had managed to slide over to the

Victory Townspeople flood the streets of Prague to celebrate, here gathering around a soldier playing the accordion, after the Red Army's liberation of Prague in 1945.

Resistance in time, remained in prominent positions in public life, including police officials who had helped round up French Jews for deportation to the death camps.

Where the Red Army advanced in eastern Europe, it sought to place its friends in power. Stalin attached particular importance to Poland, which he insisted become a pro-Soviet buffer against any new invasion of his country. As the Red Army moved into Poland in the summer of 1944, Stalin recognized a pro-communist group in the eastern city of Lublin as the legitimate government, even though the government-in-exile in London had the loyalty of the largest Polish resistance group, the **Home Army**. The Home Army itself desperately wanted to avoid communist rule, and as the Red Army approached Warsaw at the end of July 1944, fully 20,000 of its fighters revolted against the Germans in an attempt to seize the city. They acted prematurely, however. While a German counterattack initially kept the Soviets pinned down across the Vistula River, German army and SS divisions set about systematically destroying Warsaw. By early October, the city center no longer existed, and its population was dispersed or imprisoned. The Soviets, who had little desire to rescue the Home Army, only captured the ruins of Warsaw in the winter.

Amidst these tensions and conflicts, the liberation continued. In the fall, Romania and Bulgaria abandoned their German allies and opened their frontiers to the Red Army. The Germans retreated from Greece, and Yugoslavia fell, with Tito's resistance seizing power. By January 1, 1945, Soviet forces stood inside the boundaries of German East Prussia.

But Germany did not surrender. The last chance for an early end to the war had been lost on July 20, 1944, when a group of high-ranking German officers failed in an attempt to assassinate Hitler and seize power. An aristocratic Catholic officer, Count Claus von Stauffenberg, smuggled a bomb into Hitler's bunker in East Prussia inside a briefcase. But when it exploded, Hitler was on the other side of a heavy oak conference table and suffered nothing but a burst eardrum. The plotters were quickly discovered and killed.

A VIOLENT CONCLUSION

The final chapter of World War II in Europe had an otherworldly quality. Cities that six years before had been a part of the modern world, with electric light and factories, automobiles and department stores, had been reduced to smoking rubble where dazed survivors scrounged for food and fuel, and callous soldiers killed, raped, and stole like a mythical barbarian horde. The British poet Stephen Spender (1909–1995), upon seeing the ruined German city of Cologne in July 1945, wrote:

> My first impression on passing through the city was of there being not a single house left. There are plenty of walls, but these walls are a thin mask in front of the damp, hollow, stinking emptiness of the gutted interiors.... The ruin of the city is reflected in the internal ruin of its inhabitants, who, instead of being lives that can form a scar over the city's wounds, are parasites sucking on a dead carcass, digging among the ruins for hidden food.

Refugees choked the roads of Europe. According to some estimates, as many as 10 million people struggled to make their way home in spring and summer 1945. The Allies uncovered crimes so hideous that Europeans did not fully come to terms with them for decades.

Much of the violence that accompanied the fall of Nazi Germany had of course been provoked by the Nazis' own barbarization of warfare. In a speech to his men as they stood on the boundaries of Germany, Marshal Zhukov gave voice to the Soviet people's deep hatred and desire for revenge:

> We have not forgotten the pain and suffering done to our people by Hitler's cannibals. We have not forgotten our burned-out cities and villages. We remember our brothers and sisters, our mothers and fathers, our wives and children tortured to death by Germans. We shall avenge those burned in the

devil's ovens, avenge those who suffocated in the gas chambers, avenge the murdered and the martyred. We shall exact a brutal revenge for everything.

In their advance, Soviet forces made little attempt to spare the German civilian population. Soviet soldiers routinely raped German women and girls, stole from the population, and killed Germans out of hand. Their officers generally made little attempt to control them.

BORDERS AND REFUGEES

The violence and disruption in 1945 were also shaped by decisions taken collectively by the Allies at their wartime conferences. At the Tehran meeting with Stalin in November 1943, Churchill and Roosevelt had reluctantly agreed that in compensation for the massive Soviet losses, after the war the Soviet Union would keep the territories it had seized in 1939–40: the Baltic states and eastern Poland. In addition, the Allies discussed compensating Poland for this loss with territory taken from Germany.

At the Crimean resort town of **Yalta** in February 1945, the Big Three met again and confirmed these decisions. Roosevelt was especially anxious to please Stalin so as to secure Soviet support for the ongoing war in the Pacific. They further agreed to demilitarize and denazify Germany, to divide both the country as a whole and also Berlin and Vienna into occupation zones, and to restore Austrian independence. At Yalta they also agreed to free elections in Poland to choose between the two competing claimants to power: the government-in-exile that had established itself in London in 1939, and the Soviet-backed provisional government based in Lublin.

The Allied decisions meant expulsion or worse for the more than 12 million Germans living in what was now Poland and for millions of other ethnic Germans throughout Europe, notably 3 million in the Czech Sudetenland. More than half of them fled ahead of the Red Army, and as many as 2 million died or disappeared in the process amid terrible scenes. On January 30, 1945, as the German passenger ship *Wilhelm Gustloff* steamed into the Baltic from the port of Gdynia carrying more than 9,400 panicked German refugees and also some German military personnel, it was torpedoed by a Soviet submarine and sank. Nearly all the passengers died, close to half of them children, in what still stands as the greatest maritime disaster in history.

The German refugees were just part of a larger flood tide of refugees from every part of the Continent. It included Cossacks and other minority groups in the Soviet Union whom Stalin—with the tacit support of Roosevelt and Churchill at Yalta—ruthlessly expelled to Siberia in revenge for their initial support of the German invasion. It included 5.7 million men and women who had volunteered or been forced into working in Germany, as well as hundreds of thousands of surviving Jews whose homes had been destroyed or who did not dare return to them for fear of further pogroms—a real threat in Poland. To these groups must also be added the millions of Europeans who had seen their homes destroyed. It was human disruption on an unbelievable scale, amid the ruins of a civilization.

THE GERMAN SURRENDER AND THE LIBERATION OF THE CAMPS

The final act of the war in Europe took place in the city where it had started with Hitler's seizure of power twelve years before: Berlin. In the late winter and spring of 1945, the Soviets made a final push for the city. Hitler continued to deny reality, seizing at any wisp of good news (most notably, Franklin Roosevelt's death on April 12) as proof that Germany's deliverance was at hand. The Nazis forced old men, and boys as young as twelve or thirteen, into the fray and hanged suspected traitors and cowards. But the city was lost. In late April, even as American and Soviet troops met on the Elbe River, the Red Army forced its way through Berlin's suburbs, fighting building by building.

In a bunker near the Reichstag where he had lived for much of the year, Hitler finally recognized what had happened, castigated the German people for failing him,

The Big Three Churchill, Roosevelt, and Stalin meet at the Yalta conference in February 1945.

Europe at the End of World War II, 1945 Amid the ruins to which many parts of Europe had been reduced, the Allies redrew the map. They reconstituted Poland, Czechoslovakia, and other countries Hitler had invaded, and they divided Germany into four zones of occupation, with Berlin and Vienna governed jointly by the four Allied powers.

and solemnly prepared his death. "I must now obey the dictates of Fate," he told his aides. "Even if I could save myself, I would not do so." After marrying his long-time mistress, Eva Braun, he shot himself and she took poison. His aides then doused the bodies with gasoline and burned them. Joseph Goebbels, ever the fanatic, along with his wife poisoned their six children as they slept in the bunker, and then committed suicide in their turn. Admiral Karl von Dönitz, named by Hitler as his heir, acceded to Allied demands and after a week signed the acts of unconditional surrender. The war in Europe was over.

Even as this final act of the Third Reich was taking place, on April 15, 1945, British and American troops liberated the concentration camp of Bergen-Belsen in northern Germany. They found thousands of bodies lying unburied on the ground and thousands of prisoners in a state of advanced starvation: hideous living skeletons. The reports shocked even a war-hardened western public. In January, the Red Army had liberated Auschwitz, which the Germans had abandoned shortly before, herding the surviving prisoners back toward Germany in a death march. In May, the Soviets made public what they had found there,

Liberation Survivors liberated by Allied forces at a concentration camp in Ebensee, Austria in 1945.

although they neglected to specify that the large majority of victims had been Jews. In some camps in Germany, Allied commanders forced the inhabitants of nearby towns to come see what had been done in the name of Germany and to help bury the dead.

THE WAR IN ASIA AND THE POTSDAM CONFERENCE

The war was over in Europe. But in Asia, it dragged on and continued to affect European developments. The long and brutal push to dislodge Japanese forces from a series of island fortresses continued, along with saturation bombing of Japan that took lives on the same scale as the bombing of Germany. The Allies began to plan for a massive invasion of the Japanese home islands, while hoping that Japan, starved of resources by the ongoing blockade, might be driven to surrender without it. Britain and the United States continued to press the Soviets to declare war on Japan. Although liberated France now reestablished control over its African colonies, the European colonies in Southeast Asia remained battlefields.

This was the atmosphere in which Churchill, Stalin, and the new U.S. president, Harry Truman, met in Potsdam, outside of Berlin, in mid-July 1945. They finalized the details of the occupation zones of Germany and Austria, agreed on policies to purge Nazis from German government and society, imposed reparations on Germany, and

planned to eliminate Germany's industrial war potential. They also agreed to war crimes trials for Germans, including many of the country's leaders.

These trials took place in the German city of Nuremberg from the fall of 1945 to the fall of 1946, and they resulted in long prison terms or death for much of the surviving Nazi leadership. Hermann Goering cheated the hangman by committing suicide, while Heinrich Himmler, head of the SS, killed himself before even coming to trial. During the **Potsdam conference**, the stubborn spirit of democracy expressed itself in an unexpected way: in British elections, voters weary of hardship and rationing threw the governing Conservatives out of office in favor of a Labour Party pledged to sweeping social reforms. Winston Churchill duly departed from Potsdam to be replaced by the new prime minister, Clement Attlee.

It was clear by this point that even as the Allies scrambled to end the Pacific War, they were also preparing for a future shaped by competition between a western bloc led by the United States and an eastern one led by the Soviet Union. These considerations, along with a desire to end the war without further loss of Allied life, fed into the final, momentous American actions of the summer of 1945. On August 6, four days after the end of the Potsdam conference, the United States dropped the first of two **atomic bombs** on Japan, vaporizing the city center of Hiroshima and killing between 60,000 and 80,000 people instantly, with a final death toll over 130,000. Three days later, even as the Americans dropped a second bomb

Hiroshima The devastation wrought by the atomic bomb on Hiroshima on August 6, 1945, included the leveling of most of the city. The Prefectural Industrial Promotion Hall, at right, was one of the very few structures to survive the bombing mostly intact, although everyone inside it was killed.

on Nagasaki, the Soviet Union went to war against Japan and rapidly seized large territories in Manchuria and Sakhalin Island. On August 12, 1945, Japan joined Germany in surrender.

UNPARALLELED VIOLENCE

World War II remains the greatest outbreak of violence in the entire history of humanity. Of the hundred bloodiest battles of modern times, a large majority took place during World War II, with most of those on the eastern front. The colossal death toll almost defies explanation, but it had at least three obvious sources. The first was the rise of an expansionist racial ideology in Germany that placed little or no value on the lives of those it dubbed "subhumans," including Slavs and particularly Jews. The Germans' murderous attempts to translate this ideology into military reality forced Germany's enemies to adopt ruthless means in response, something that came especially easily to Stalin's totalitarian dictatorship, which was faced with challenges far beyond what any other Allied power faced. Second, there was the state of military technology, which, despite the increasing prominence of tank and air warfare, still reserved a crucial place for the mass use of infantry. As a result, the contending powers mobilized a higher proportion of their populations than at any other time in history. Third, there was the ability of advanced industrial economies to produce the means of death on a hitherto unimaginable scale. The result was unimaginable horror. Germany paid a heavy price for unleashing it; but despite losing millions of people and a quarter of its territory, it still did not suffer as much as its victims.

The barbarization of warfare between 1939 and 1945 affected all the combatants. By 1942, the Allies had begun campaigns of "area bombing" against Germany that, despite the concentration on industry, entailed a frightful toll in innocent civilian life. During the war as a whole, the Allies dropped no less than 2.5 million tons of conventional explosives on Germany and Japan. Between 1943 and 1945, almost every major German city was left in ruins.

Still, it was the Germans who inflicted the greatest harm, and the Soviet Union that suffered the most. Of a Soviet population that numbered nearly 197 million in June 1941 (counting the recent annexations), more than one person in eight would lose their life over the next four years—over 27 million men, women, and children. Soviet military losses alone came to a staggering 10.7 million—more than thirty times the corresponding American figure. Soviet birth rates dropped sharply during the war, and the loss of young men was so severe that among Soviet women in their mid-twenties during the war, fewer than two-thirds ever married. The cities of the western Soviet Union were left, for the most part, smoking ruins. And the same was true of most of central and eastern Europe. This was the essence of World War II. For four evil years, the achievements of European civilization—its ingenious developments in technology, industry, and social organization—seemed to turn to this one terrible purpose of destruction.

UNDERSTANDING THE HOLOCAUST

And then there was the Holocaust, perhaps the single darkest moment in all of European history. Despite the impossibility of ever fully understanding it, historians have nonetheless tried to offer some explanations. Many have argued that the Holocaust was driven by impersonal processes, like some bureaucratic cancer that carried events beyond even the Nazis' conscious intentions. Yet such interpretations tend to distract attention from the men and women who actually carried out the killings. And they also discount the decade or more of intensive ideological indoctrination by which Hitler's state, building on and deeply intensifying long traditions of anti-Semitism, taught its citizens that Jews, Roma, and other "undesirables" were vermin who posed a mortal threat to Germany's survival.

Even this indoctrination might not have been enough to transform ordinary Germans and others into willing executioners. But when combined with the habits of obedience inculcated by an authoritarian state turned totalitarian, in the crisis atmosphere of total war, and with the killers' desire not to show weakness in front of their comrades or to let them down, this indoctrination sufficed to break the human bond and bring about the Holocaust. In October 1943, Heinrich Himmler, head of the SS, told a gathering of his colleagues: "Most of you know what it means to see a hundred corpses lying together, five hundred, or a thousand. To have gone through this and yet—apart from a few exceptions, examples of human weakness—to have remained decent fellows, this is what has made us hard. This is a glorious page in our history that has never been written and shall never be written."

In the face of these crimes, some Europeans did act, often at great risk, to hide the victims or help them escape. The Danish people and government ferried virtually their entire Jewish population to safety in neutral Sweden. The Bulgarian government, in response to widespread popular protest, refused to deport the country's 50,000 Jews. Individual Christians—like the ones in Amsterdam who hid Anne Frank's family—helped individual Jews. The Israeli government's Holocaust monument and museum has recognized 22,000 "righteous" individuals who acted to save Jews, including a disproportionate number of Christian clergy.

Yet at the same time, little was done to help by some who had considerable power to do so. By mid-1943, numerous credible reports of the Holocaust had already appeared in the American, British, and Swiss press. Pope Pius XII and the Catholic Church hierarchy knew well what was happening in German-occupied Europe. But the pope, who still had considerable sway over German and Austrian Catholics, failed to denounce the killings. As for the Allied powers, they did so only weakly, if at all, and made no serious effort to disrupt them—for instance, by bombing the death camps or the railroads leading to them. Many officials continued to dismiss reports of the slaughter, however well documented, as wild rumors, even as attempts by Jews to gain special treatment. Anti-Semitism undoubtedly played a role in these reactions, as did a misguided determination not to let anything interfere with the central goal of Allied victory. But in some cases, Allied inaction also stemmed from an inability to come to terms, even in the face of solid proof, with the enormity of what the Nazis were doing. Could "civilized" Europeans really commit such acts?

CONCLUSION

Overall, World War II marked the culmination of trends in European history that had been developing since the first Industrial Revolution and the almost simultaneous rise of racially tinged romantic nationalism. But the year 1945—what the Germans refer to as their Hour Zero—brought a sudden and definitive end to these trends, and to much else besides. The defeat of Nazi Germany, and the revelation of German crimes, overnight turned fascism and extreme conservatism into pariah ideologies preserved only by tiny fringe movements. The kindling of atomic light over Hiroshima made war of the sort just fought, with its confrontation of massive land, sea, and air forces, impossible to repeat. The joint triumph of the United States and the Soviet Union meant that in place of a continent dominated by a shifting and contentious constellation of native powers, there would now be a continent divided between two great and opposed political forces, led by nations outside the traditional European heartland.

Like the Napoleonic Wars and World War I, World War II would also have tremendous long-term consequences for Europe's relations with the rest of the world. Japan, with its program for an East Asian Co-Prosperity Sphere, tried to cast a veil of anti-imperialism over its own imperialist ambitions. In some of the European colonies that it overran, notably the Dutch East Indies, Japan installed puppet governments that claimed to represent local nationalist aspirations, and thereby strengthened these aspirations. More important, by driving European nations out of large areas of Asia, even as those same nations bled white in the European conflict, it damaged the structures of European colonialism, making them harder to reimpose in the war's aftermath. European authority also suffered in the French colonies left in limbo between Vichy and the Allies.

In Europe itself, amid the ruins, facing this unpredictable future and the long and wearying process of rebuilding, men and women had every reason to be apprehensive. Already in the spring of 1945, tensions between the West and the Soviet Union were clearly visible. In a letter to President Truman, Winston Churchill had already used the phrase *iron curtain* (which he would make famous in a speech a year later) to describe the division of Europe between East and West. Even so, to a remarkable extent this apprehension was *not* justified. The next fifty years would bring much trouble and tension. But overall, it would also bring something surprising: stability, prosperity, and peace. The most horrible chapter in European history was about to give way to one of the brightest.

[CHAPTER REVIEW]

KEY TERMS

blitzkrieg (p. 776)
Dunkirk (p. 776)
Vichy (p. 777)
Winston Churchill (p. 777)
Blitz (p. 779)
Lend-Lease (p. 780)

Holocaust (p. 781)
Operation Barbarossa
   (p. 782)
Einsatzgruppen (p. 784)
Pearl Harbor (p. 786)
battle of Stalingrad
   (p. 789)

Wannsee conference
   (p. 791)
Auschwitz-Birkenau
   (p. 792)
Resistance (p. 798)
Manhattan Project (p. 799)
D-Day (p. 800)

Home Army (p. 801)
Yalta conference (p. 802)
Potsdam conference
   (p. 804)
atomic bombs (p. 804)

REVIEW QUESTIONS

1. What were the results of the German offensives in western Europe in 1940?

2. In terms of its impact on civilians, how did World War II differ from World War I?

3. How did German occupation practices in Poland compare with those in western Europe?

4. How did the German invasion of the Soviet Union bring a new scale of destruction to World War II?

5. In what ways did the Japanese attack on Pearl Harbor change the global dimensions of World War II?

6. How did the systematic mass murder planned at the Wannsee conference mark a change from earlier Nazi measures against Jews and others deemed undesirables?

7. What factors contributed to the perpetration of the Holocaust?

8. Starting in 1942, how did the Allies harness their economic advantages to achieve military victories?

9. Why did violence follow liberation throughout Europe?

10. How did the Allied leaders decide to reshape Europe during their conferences near the end of the war?

CORE OBJECTIVES

After reading this chapter, you should have a solid understanding of the following core objectives. To strengthen your grasp of the core objectives, use the resources on the Student Site for The West.

- Describe the military tactics and occupation policies employed by Germany in the first two years of World War II.

- Assess the German invasion of the Soviet Union and its horrific impact on the Soviet people.

- Trace the spread of the war around the globe starting in 1941.

- Explain the origins, evolution, and culmination of the Holocaust.

- Analyze the late period of the war leading to Allied victory.

- Identify the major demographic, social, and cultural effects of the war.

 GO TO inQuizitive TO SEE WHAT YOU'VE LEARNED—AND LEARN WHAT YOU'VE MISSED—WITH PERSONALIZED FEEDBACK ALONG THE WAY.

1945
Nuremberg
trials

1947
Marshall Plan
announced

1947
India and Pakistan
become
independent

1948–1949
Berlin blockade and airlift

1948–1949
Communist regimes
established throughout
Eastern Europe

1948
State of Israel created

1948
George Orwell
publishes *1984*

1949
Simone de Beauvoir
publishes *The Second Sex*

1949
NATO formed

1949
Mao Zedong and
Communists take
power in China

1950–1953
Korean War

1954–1962
Algerian War
of Independence

1954
French defeat
in Vietnam

March 1953
Stalin dies

1955
Warsaw Pact
formed

1957
Treaty of Rome
creates the European
Economic Community

1956
Soviet Union invades
Hungary after the
Hungarian government
attempts to withdraw
from the Eastern bloc.

1956
Suez Crisis

1958
Fifth Republic
established
in France

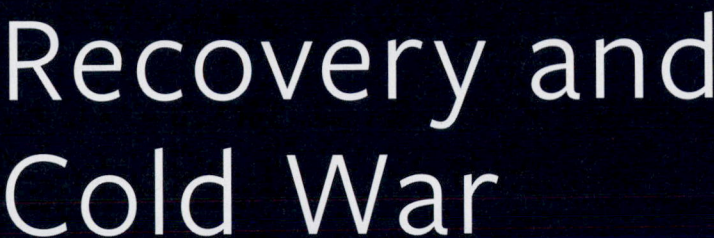

24

Recovery and Cold War

REBUILDING A DIVIDED CONTINENT

1945–1973

Spring 1968
Student protests
throughout Europe

1962–1965
Second Vatican
Council

1962
Algeria achieves
independence

1961
Berlin Wall
built

January 30, 1972
Bloody Sunday
in Ireland

1964–1975
Large-scale U.S.
military involvement
in Vietnam

I n July 1952, an American landing craft—one of the same that had brought American soldiers to Omaha Beach on D-Day seven years before—again hit a European shoreline. The target this time was Finland, a neutral country on the border of the Soviet Union, with which the United States and its allies were now locked in the ongoing confrontation of ideologies, and political and economic interests, known as the Cold War. And this time the craft did not carry soldiers or weaponry. Instead, it was loaded with salesmen, publicity material, and many thousands of bottles of Coca-Cola, all bound for the Olympic Games taking place in the Finnish capital of Helsinki. It was a publicity stunt connected to an aggressive plan by the American soft drink company to establish itself in Europe. The plan called for ninety-six bottling plants in western Germany by 1954, and sales of over a billion bottles a year on the European continent. As early as 1949, rumors had spread in France that Coca-Cola would try to advertise on the side of Notre Dame Cathedral or attach its famous logo to the Eiffel Tower. The French Communist newspaper *L'Humanité*, learning of the French sales goals, accused the company of seeking to replace wine with Coke and stridently asked: "Will we be Coca-Cola-Colonized?"

These incidents, while comic, illustrate a great deal about Europe's recovery from World War II. Coming so soon after the end of the fighting in 1945, they suggest just how

Protest in Prague In August 1968, Czechoslovakian protesters throng the streets to prevent Soviet soldiers in tanks from reaching the headquarters of the national radio station after the Soviets invaded so as to overturn the country's reform-minded Communist government.

FOCUS QUESTIONS

- Why was the aftermath of war so unsettled in Europe?
- What drove the speedy rebuilding of Europe?
- What caused the onset of the Cold War?
- What were the causes of decolonization in the post-war years?
- What were the major social changes in post-war Europe?
- How did the politics of Eastern and Western Europe differ in the 1950s?
- How did the crises of Suez and Algeria affect politics in Europe?
- How did the Cold War turn more threatening in the early 1960s?
- What caused the popular protests that spread across Europe in the late 1960s?

quickly European countries literally cleared away the war's rubble and rebuilt themselves. These incidents point to the new centrality of consumption, and consumers, in post-war European society and economics. And they also underline a startling reversal that Europe experienced in the aftermath of World War II. After several centuries in which the Continent had exported power, technology, and population to the rest of the world, now the currents were moving in the opposite direction.

Most immediately, Europe felt the powerful influence of the United States, whose industrial capacity in 1945 equaled that of the rest of the world put together. America had emerged from the war as the world's sole nuclear-armed power and quickly took on the role of Western Europe's protector against the Soviet Union. In 1949, the United States, Canada, and ten Western European nations would sign a formal military alliance, the North Atlantic Treaty Organization (NATO). At the same time, Central and Eastern Europe felt a different external influence—that of the Soviet Union—as the Cold War split the Continent in half. The Soviet Union and its satellite states would form an economic alliance called Comecon in 1949, and their own military alliance, known as the Warsaw Pact, in 1955. Although in 1945 the

Allies had created a new international organization—the United Nations—as a successor to the League of Nations, these rival Western and Eastern military alliances had greater importance in international affairs throughout the post-war period.

This period also saw a vast, rapid shift in Europe's relationship with the rest of the world. In an often-violent process, the formal European colonial empires almost entirely dissolved as countries around the world gained independence. Decolonization would not just affect the former colonies themselves. It would also have important effects on the societies, cultures, and politics of the former imperial homelands. Notably, it would mark the start of large-scale movements of populations back toward Europe from the overseas empires—both European colonists and also, increasingly, non-European immigrants and refugees seeking a better life for themselves.

THE AFTERMATH OF WAR

Much of Europe in mid-1945 gave the impression of a continent in ruins. Scores of cities—above all, in Germany, Poland, and the Soviet Union—had been largely or partially destroyed by aerial bombing and artillery. Many tens of millions of people were dead. Perhaps 40 million more—refugees, forced laborers, prisoners of war—were displaced and desperate to return to homes that, in many cases, no longer existed. Much of the Continent remained under the effective control of the Allied armies. Both Germany and its capital, Berlin, had been formally divided into American, British, Soviet, and French occupation zones, in accordance with plans finalized at the Potsdam conference in the summer of 1945.

REFUGEES

The speed of Europe's recovery from the war was all the more impressive because violent disruptions did not end with the May 1945 armistice. The cease-fire led to one of the largest movements of European populations in the modern period. The expulsion of German populations from Poland, Czechoslovakia, and other states continued, with the refugees washing into camps in the American, British, and French occupation zones of Germany. Meanwhile, the Soviets were expelling as many as

2 million Poles from the formerly Polish territories they had annexed during the war, with the majority moving west to formerly German cities and towns such as Breslau and Stettin, henceforth known by the Polish names of Wrocław and Szczecin. The Western allies were sending back to the Soviet Union, often forcibly, as many as 2.5 million Soviet citizens who had ended up on their side of the demarcation lines. Fully 20 percent of these men and women were imprisoned in the Gulag or executed, and whole ethnic groups were sent into inhospitable internal exile. Millions more prisoners of war and forced laborers took more months or even years to return home. The USSR, which had taken between 2 and 3 million Germans prisoner during the war, kept hundreds of thousands of them in captivity until as late as 1956.

Jews who had survived the Holocaust faced renewed persecutions and difficulties, despite the worldwide revulsion that had accompanied the exposure of the Nazi crimes. Several hundred thousand Jews hoping to leave Europe for Palestine found themselves trapped in "displaced persons" camps, including one located next to the Nazi concentration camp of Bergen-Belsen. The British government, nervous about aggravating tensions between Jews and Arabs in the Palestinian territory, which it had governed as a mandate since 1918, refused Jews entry there and kept them in limbo. A Palestinian Jewish organization attempted to smuggle refugees past the British blockade, but the British intercepted most of them and imprisoned over 50,000 Jews in camps on Cyprus. The refugee crisis, however, finally helped push the British to surrender control of Palestine. In 1947, it turned the problem over to the new United Nations, which voted to partition the territory into separate Jewish and Arab states. The new nation of Israel came into being in May 1948, succeeded in defeating an invasion by five Arab armies, and expelled Arab populations from many of the areas they controlled. Between 1948 and 1950, over 300,000 Jews from Europe, and another 200,000 from Muslim countries, immigrated to the new Jewish state.

RECKONING WITH WAR CRIMES

In addition to these massive movements of population, most European countries had internal reckonings to carry out with respect to former Nazis and Fascists, or their collaborators—especially in Germany, Italy, and countries that had suffered under Axis occupation. The Eastern bloc countries tried thousands for war crimes—both Germans and home-grown collaborators. Poland tried and executed or imprisoned former officials from concentration

European Refugees, 1945–1950 Mass movement of migrants and refugees followed the post-war redrawing of European borders, of which Jewish survivors of the death camps were a small minority. Ethnic Germans were moved from Poland and Czechoslovakia to Allied-run refugee centers in West Germany, and Soviet citizens were moved back to the Soviet Union. Many spent years in refugee camps (also known as displaced persons camps) across Western Europe.

camps—including the former commandant of Auschwitz, who died on a gallows at the camp itself in 1947. Norway, meanwhile, put all 55,000 members of the country's principal pro-Nazi organization on trial, and imprisoned some 17,000, or one out of every 175 of the country's citizens. In France, the immediate aftermath of the liberation saw violent, large-scale settling of scores, with some 80,000 arrests and over 10,000 summary executions. Once the chaos of this initial period passed, however, the desire to impose justice diminished in most countries. In the end, the French imprisoned fewer than one person in a thousand for helping the Nazis, and nearly all of them went free in a 1947 amnesty, although the senile Marshal Pétain received a sentence of life imprisonment and the collaborationist prime minister Pierre Laval was executed.

In the Axis countries, a full reckoning with Nazi and Fascist crimes was not really attempted. The Allies did make a serious effort to punish the most important Nazi leaders, whom they put on trial at Nuremberg in late 1945. While many had died in the war or escaped (including Adolf Eichmann, a chief organizer of the Holocaust, who went into hiding in Argentina), twenty-one were prosecuted at the **Nuremberg trials**. Ten—including former foreign minister Ribbentrop—went to the gallows in October 1946, while Hitler's deputy Hermann Goering committed suicide the night before his scheduled execution. A larger series of trials of leading figures in Nazi Germany followed over the next several years. They ended in more death sentences and established the principle that perpetrators of war crimes could not be exonerated on the grounds they had just "followed orders." But the numbers of defendants remained tiny in proportion to the 8 million Germans who had belonged to the Nazi Party, including the elites of nearly every profession.

The rapid onset of the Cold War increased the incentives for the United States, the Soviet Union, and their European allies to make use of experienced personnel, even those with tainted wartime records. Millions of former Nazis remained in leadership positions in both the Western and Soviet occupation zones of Germany, especially the former. When the Western zones consolidated into the new Federal Republic of Germany in 1949, no less than 43 percent of its new diplomatic corps had seen service in the SS. In Italy, where a referendum put an end to the disgraced monarchy in 1946, tens of thousands of former Fascists went to prison, but mostly for short periods. As for Austria, which had provided a higher proportion of SS members and war criminals than Germany itself, the Allies preferred, in restoring it as an independent state, to consider it "Hitler's first victim." Fewer people—and a far smaller percentage of the population—went to prison for war crimes in Austria than in Norway.

Most people in the Axis countries thought sufficient punishment had already arrived in the form of defeat, war deaths, territorial losses, and the massive physical devastation they had suffered. Germany, in addition to at least 5 million war dead (possibly many more), over 2 million soldiers still in captivity, and the amputation of its eastern territories, had lost 20 percent of its industrial capacity, 40 percent of its housing stock, and 90 percent of its railways. One American official there spoke of "complete economic, social and political collapse, the extent of which is unparalleled in history unless one goes back to the collapse of the Roman Empire." Of course, even this degree of destruction could not match what the Soviet Union had experienced, with its 28 million dead, and 70,000 villages and 32,000 factories simply wiped from the map. But Germans still refer to the immediate post-war period as Zero Hour.

REBUILDING

Throughout Europe, the immediate focus was less on coming to terms with the war than on simple rebuilding. And in rebuilding, Europeans looked more intently than ever to the guiding hand of the state.

THE ROLE OF THE STATE

No matter what the prevailing ideology, the war had everywhere led to government taking a larger role than ever before in the management of national economies—capitalist Britain, corporatist Vichy France, fascist Germany, and the communist Soviet Union all had similar experiences in this regard. Now facing the Herculean task of clearing away ruins, restoring infrastructure, and rebuilding homes and factories, few Europeans questioned the need for continued, massive state intervention. In November 1945, the British historian A. J. P. Taylor could write: "Nobody in Europe believes in the American way of life—that is, private enterprise."

Nuremberg Trials Soldiers guard Hermann Goering, Joachim von Ribbentrop, and two other Nazi leaders as they stand trial for war crimes and crimes against humanity at Nuremberg in 1945.

But the state role in reconstruction efforts varied greatly. In some countries, elaborate economic planning bureaucracies took shape, such as France's General Planning Commissariat, established in early 1946, which coordinated economic efforts by government, management, and labor. In other cases, what mattered most was state ownership of industry. In Great Britain, the Labour Party government that took power at the end of the war began an ambitious program to bring the "commanding heights" of the economy under state management. Between 1946 and 1949, it nationalized the Bank of England, telephone and telegraph service, the coal industry, iron and steel, the railroads, and electricity generation, with each henceforth run by quasi-independent public boards responsible to Parliament. In Czechoslovakia, even before the Communist takeover there, the state employed 93 percent of all transport workers and 78 percent of industrial workers. Throughout Europe, the state remained by far the largest source of public investment, and in the late 1940s nearly every state concentrated its investment efforts on the rebuilding of basic infrastructure: factories, railroad tracks, power generation stations, and the like.

INDUSTRY OVER CONSUMERS One result of this strategy was a relative neglect of the consumer sector. Food rationing remained in effect throughout much of Europe for years after the end of the war. In Britain, it actually expanded to previously unrationed commodities such as bread and potatoes, and finally came to an end only in 1954. In devastated Germany, the official daily food ration in the American occupation zone fell to only 860 calories per adult in 1945–46: close to starvation level. In the former Axis countries, the difficulties for consumers were worsened by the collapse of currencies, sometimes amid episodes of hyperinflation reminiscent of Germany after World War I. Hungary, in July 1946, experienced a theoretical monthly inflation rate of 42 quadrillion percent—the highest ever in world history (in fact the currency simply collapsed). In Germany, American Camel cigarettes temporarily took the place of the devalued reichsmark as the effective currency. Throughout Europe, real wages rose very little in the late 1940s. Yet the emphasis on infrastructure had the desired effect and was usefully reinforced by the experiences of wartime planning. Industry and transportation networks rapidly recovered from wartime damage. By mid-1946, over 90 percent of Germany's railways were again operational.

THE RISE OF THE WELFARE STATE An expanded role for the state produced many different tangible

UK Labour Party A staff member at Labour campaign headquarters sorts through election posters during the 1955 general election campaign. The photo of Clement Attlee on the wall bears the caption: "You can trust Mr. Attlee."

benefits for ordinary Europeans. Britain, under Clement Attlee's Labour Party, again led the way. While the newly established Coal Board moved to institute paid vacations and sick pay for miners, the government itself put in place enhanced unemployment benefits, retirement plans, and free public health care. The National Health Service, created in 1948, put most doctors and hospital personnel onto the public payroll and transformed medical services into an entitlement for all. Britain here followed the lead taken between the wars by Sweden and Norway, but substantially expanded on it. Similar policies followed across much of the Continent, marking the rise to maturity of the European **welfare state**—that is, a state that aims to guarantee a minimum level of services and subsistence for all citizens. In France, spending on social services as a proportion of gross domestic product rose by 64 percent from 1938 to 1949. A principal difference from earlier efforts was that the policies did not consist principally of "poor relief," but instead benefited the entire population.

BRETTON WOODS AND THE MARSHALL PLAN

The Continent also benefited in its reconstruction efforts from outside aid. Even before the end of the war, American officials, trained in the New Deal ferment of Franklin Roosevelt's Washington, had assumed that the United

Marshall Plan On this French poster, titled "To Reconstruct Europe," the flags of all the countries receiving Marshall aid hang from scaffolding, suggesting a sense of restored unity.

funded 50 percent of public investment. In Austria, it provided 14 percent of all national income. Overall, however, the Plan amounted to an average of less than 3 percent of national income in the countries that received it.

The program brought European managers and technicians to study in the United States, and it sponsored educational programs in Europe itself, including propaganda that touted the virtues of capitalist consumer societies. But this propaganda had relatively little impact and could even be counterproductive. In France, the Communist Party managed to convince a majority of the public (to judge by opinion polls) that the Marshall Plan was a blueprint for American domination. Similar suspicions led the Soviets to refuse Marshall aid, not only for themselves but for the Eastern and Central European states in their orbit as well. Instead, the Soviets moved toward the creation of Comecon, through which they would provide substantial aid to what became their satellite states.

COLD WAR

Between 1945 and 1949, the tensions between the emerging Western and Eastern blocs steadily worsened and finally brought about the period of prolonged ideological hostility and strategic competition that contemporaries soon came to call the **Cold War**.

TENSIONS BETWEEN THE UNITED STATES AND THE SOVIET UNION

Historians have long debated whether this turn of events was inevitable and who bears principal responsibility for it. Tensions between the Soviet Union and the West of course long predated 1945. As will be recalled, the United States and the United Kingdom had both sent supplies and small detachments of troops to fight against the Bolsheviks after the Russian Revolution. During the war, Stalin had repeatedly clashed with Churchill and, to a lesser extent, Roosevelt, especially over the timing of the Allied invasion of France. But through 1946 the victorious Allies all remained as concerned with the possibility of renewed German aggression as with an East-West confrontation. The United States drastically reduced its defense budget and continued to give considerable diplomatic support to Soviet actions. The Soviets, for their part, did not move immediately to subject the nations liberated by the

States would take a major role in rebuilding post-war Europe. In July 1944, representatives from all the Allied nations met in Bretton Woods, New Hampshire, to set up a new and stable international monetary system, based on a fixed price of gold in American dollars. The Bretton Woods system established fixed exchange rates among the major currencies, although Britain and France did not join the system until the late 1950s. It also created new institutions, located in Washington, to monitor the rules and provide liquidity: the International Monetary Fund and what would soon become the World Bank.

The United States also provided massive direct assistance to Europe, which Secretary of State George Marshall announced in a commencement address at Harvard University in 1947. "Our policy," he declared, "is not directed against any country, but against hunger, poverty, desperation and chaos." The **Marshall Plan** combined loans with $13 billion in direct aid to Europe, including the Western occupation zones of Germany. In France, the program

Red Army to Soviet political control. Yet at the same time, Joseph Stalin saw a certain degree of control as a legitimate spoil of war and also as a necessity for protecting the Soviet Union against future attacks along its western frontier. Millions of Soviet soldiers remained in the liberated nations.

The Western powers viewed Stalin as committed to the expansion of communism as a system. In a speech in Missouri in March 1946, Winston Churchill used memorable language to condemn Stalin for seeking the division of Europe: "From Stettin in the Baltic to Trieste in the Adriatic an iron curtain has descended across the Continent." The Soviets, he insisted, "desire . . . the fruits of war and the indefinite expansion of their power and doctrine." A year later, the influential American diplomat George Kennan published, anonymously, an article that laid out a fundamental new goal for U.S. foreign policy: the "long-term, patient but firm and vigilant containment of Russian expansive tendencies." As the only power possessing nuclear weapons, the United States could conceivably have launched a war of massive destruction against the Soviets or used the threat of nuclear attack to cow Stalin. But in the aftermath of the greatest military mobilization in American history, neither the administration of President Harry Truman (1884–1972) nor the American public had any stomach for such extreme measures.

As for Stalin, whatever his desires and tendencies, he was in fact relatively cautious in his immediate post-war policies. But disagreements with the Western Allies, especially over Germany, soon pushed him into a more aggressive stance. In part to avoid a repeat of the post–World War I economic debacle in Germany, the Western Allies wanted German reconstruction to take place as quickly as possible. France needed German coal to fuel its own heavy industries, while all the Western powers wanted Germany to recover as a market for their goods. Stalin, however, sought to strip Germany of its industry and impose heavy reparations. The Soviets actively pursued this policy in their occupation zone, moving thousands of factories eastward to the USSR. Stalin objected loudly to plans for a new German currency and a united economy.

At the end of 1946, after months of stalemate, the British and the Americans finally defied him and fused their two zones into a single economic region, leading Stalin to believe that the two Western powers were trying to transform Germany into an anti-Soviet puppet state. In 1947, he responded to these developments, and to the Marshall Plan, by bringing together Poland, Hungary, Romania, Bulgaria, and Yugoslavia into the so-called Cominform—a

Cold War Europe, 1950s The opposing alliances of NATO, joined by most Western European countries, and the Warsaw Pact of Soviet-allied states created an iron curtain roughly stretching from Stettin to Trieste across the European continent. The Berlin Airlift that followed the Soviet blockade of East Berlin in 1948 represented a rare confrontation along that hard border—and indicative of the particularly charged tensions in divided Germany.

partial revival of the pre-war Communist international organization, the Comintern.

THE SOVIETIZATION OF EASTERN EUROPE

The more Stalin sought to forge a united front against the West, the more he needed to transform the states on his side of the "**iron curtain**" into fully reliable—meaning Communist—allies. In none of them did the move find favor with a majority of the population. In early 1945, the Hungarian Communist Party still had fewer than 5,000 members, and the Romanian one barely 1,000. But just four years later, both of these states and four others (Bulgaria,

Czechoslovakia, Poland and East Germany) had become Soviet satellites, ruled by Communist regimes bent on creating smaller copies of Soviet government and society.

In Hungary, where the Communists still won less than a quarter of the vote in August 1947, despite committing massive election fraud, the Communist interior minister used his office to persecute political opponents and to take control of civil society. In 1946 alone, he banned some 1,500 unofficial civic associations and had hundreds of thousands of political opponents arrested. In 1948–49, the USSR forced the Hungarian Social Democrats to merge with the Communists and created a People's Front that duly passed a new, Soviet-style constitution. In Czechoslovakia, the Communists did better at the polls, but non-Communist President Edvard Beneš resisted a full takeover, forcing the Communists to carry out a coup d'état in February 1948. Romania and Bulgaria moved quickly into close Soviet orbit as well.

YUGOSLAVIA AND POLAND

The extent of sovietization did vary, however. Yugoslavia, led by the charismatic former resistance leader Josip Broz Tito, avoided absorption into the Soviet bloc altogether. Stalin broke with Tito soon after the war and never managed to reinstitute Soviet control over the Balkan state. While Yugoslavia remained dominated by its Communist Party and imposed a command economy similar to those in the Soviet bloc, Tito pursued a neutral foreign policy and abandoned the collectivization of agriculture. In later years, the Yugoslavs experimented with "worker self-management" in many industries. Tito also faced the considerable challenge of keeping intact the fractious union of peoples that constituted Yugoslavia, including Serbs and Croats who had fought bitterly against each other in the war.

Within the Soviet bloc, Poland remained in significant ways an outlier. Although at Yalta Stalin had promised that the Poles could hold free elections, the Red Army brought a Communist-dominated government, the so-called Lublin Committee, back to Warsaw. Then, with the help of a rigged referendum in 1946, the Communists further increased their power, sidelining forces who hoped for a return to democratic pluralism. In 1948, they banned or neutralized competing parties and turned the country into a People's Republic. But Polish agriculture remained largely in private hands, and the Catholic Church retained a large degree of autonomy. The Church continued to play a vital role in Polish life, and its Primate, or leading bishop, despite his opposition to the Communist regime, never suffered anything worse than three years' house arrest.

WESTERN REACTIONS

Western observers most often saw the clampdown on political dissent in what was coming to be called Eastern Europe, and the imposition of the Soviet model there, as confirming Churchill's warning about the iron curtain and fears of Soviet expansionism. The fact that a bitter civil war was continuing in Greece, with the Communists scoring significant gains in 1948, and that Communist parties remained strong in many parts of Western Europe, only added to the Western view.

In 1948, the British writer George Orwell gave lasting expression to Western anxieties in his novel *1984*, which presented a nightmarish vision of a totalitarian Britain ruled by a mustachioed dictator known only as Big Brother. Its miserable inhabitants lived under twenty-four-hour surveillance, while an all-powerful Party controlled every last scrap of information they received and used a sinister Thought Police to enforce its will. The Party aimed not simply at obedience but at the complete subordination of the human spirit. "If you want a picture of the future," a member of the ruling elite tells Orwell's defeated hero, Winston Smith, "imagine a boot stamping on a human face, forever." Orwell himself insisted that despite the obvious resemblance of his dystopia to the Soviet Union, he meant the book as a cautionary tale about all totalitarianisms, fascist as well as communist, and his own staunchly socialist background supports the claim. But in the chill political climate of 1948, most readers read *1984* as a warning of the dangers from the East.

BERLIN

In 1947, American president Harry Truman, in promising significant new aid to anti-Communist forces in Greece, declared defiantly that the United States would provide support to "free peoples" against what he labeled totalitarian regimes. The United States, even before the formation of NATO, was laying claim to leadership of what it called the free world. It faced little competition for the role. In addition to its military dominance, it also possessed by far the largest economy in the world and deserved to be called a superpower. Britain, still recovering from its wartime sacrifices and expenditures, was also confronting in South Asia the first great episodes of decolonization. The USSR lagged behind the United States economically, but owing to its military strength it could also be seen as a superpower. The confrontation between it and the United States would dominate international politics around the globe for the next four decades.

Berlin Airlift Spectators watch as an American military aircraft lands at Berlin's Tempelhof Airport in August 1948, delivering food and supplies to the West Berliners cut off by the Soviet blockade.

If the Cold War had a symbolic opening drama, it took place in the divided capital of defeated Germany. In early June 1948, faced with stalemate on the issue of Germany's future, the United States and Great Britain decided to reorganize the areas of the country under their and France's control into a new, separate state. On June 18, they gave it a currency: the so-called deutsche mark, which replaced the devalued and useless reichsmark. In response, at the end of the month the Soviets began a blockade of the three Western zones of Berlin, cutting off all surface communications with the surrounding, Soviet-occupied territory. By starving West Berlin, Stalin hoped either to force the Western Allies out of the German capital altogether or to abandon the idea of a separate Western German state. But the Allies mounted a huge airlift to supply the city with canned and dried food and other necessities. Over the next eleven months of the **Berlin Airlift**, Allied planes arrived in the city at the astonishing rate of over two per minute—over 278,000 flights in all, many making dangerous landings on hastily built runways next to crowded apartment blocks.

In May 1949, the Soviets finally abandoned the blockade. Soon afterward, with France joining its occupation zone to the British and American ones, the Western-supported Federal Republic of Germany formally came into being, with its capital in the small, sleepy, Catholic Rhineland town of Bonn—socially and culturally the opposite of massive, Protestant, Prussian Berlin.

Its founders gave the new state a democratic constitution and a decentralized governing structure in which ten large regions (*Länder*) possessed considerable autonomy. The Soviets soon matched West Germany with an East Germany, turning their own occupation zone into the German Democratic Republic, built, like the other states in the Soviet bloc, on the Soviet model. The new states quickly received international recognition, although it would take until 1973 for them to join the United Nations. Germany was now officially divided, which did not displease those who feared a revival of German nationalism. "I love Germany so much," the French novelist François Mauriac quipped, "that I am delighted there are two of them."

A DIVIDED CONTINENT IN A DIVIDED WORLD

The splitting of Germany served as the wedge, but the crack that it drove between the Western Allies and the Soviet bloc reached far beyond Central Europe. In April 1949, as we have seen, the United States, Canada, and ten Western European countries came together to form the **North Atlantic Treaty Organization (NATO)**, a new military alliance. The Communist countries constituted a de facto alliance as well, and in 1955 it took official form as the **Warsaw Pact**. Other events in 1949 heightened the tensions between these developing blocs. Communists led by Mao Zedong took power in China, the most populous country on earth, while the Soviets successfully tested an atomic weapon, having acquired the technology in part through espionage. In the United States, partly in reaction to this espionage, a wave of anti-Communist hysteria developed, led by Wisconsin senator Joseph McCarthy, bringing about widespread persecutions of suspected Communists. And a year later, in East Asia, after the USSR's client state North Korea invaded its southern neighbor, Western forces mobilized to repel it, led by the United States and acting under the banner of the new United Nations.

A period had begun in which the earth seemed divided between opposing camps—the Western "First World" and the Communist "Second World"—each armed with steadily expanding arsenals of atomic weapons. Europeans now had to confront the possibility of a new conflict whose horrors might, incredibly, overshadow those of the war just past, a conflict that might literally bring about the extinction of human life on the Continent.

DECOLONIZATION: THE FIRST STEPS

The coming of the Cold War signaled clearly that Europe no longer dominated the world as it had done in the past. The continent's future would now depend in large part on the conflict between the two "superpowers." But the influence of the European states had also begun to fray in regions that, for the moment, still belonged in large part to their colonial empires. France, Belgium, and the Netherlands struggled to reestablish their authority in overseas territories from which Nazi and Japanese occupations had cut them off, such as the French colonies in West Africa, the Belgian Congo, and the Dutch East Indies. But they were resisted by newly powerful independent movements in what would soon come to be called the Third World. Scarcely sixty years after the chaotic "scramble for empire" of the late nineteenth century, an even more chaotic process of decolonization was now beginning.

THE SUN SETS ON THE BRITISH EMPIRE

In the immediate post-war period, the most dramatic episodes of decolonization took place in the most powerful and extensive empire of all: Great Britain's. The

Indian Independence A parade in Bombay (Mumbai) on August 15, 1947, celebrates the declaration of Indian independence. Marchers wearing white carry instruments and the new Indian national flag, while crowds of spectators look on.

desperate fight against Germany and Japan had left the British Empire with vastly reduced strength, and nowhere was this weakness more apparent than in the "jewel in the crown"—India. In the 1930s, British India had roughly one British soldier for every two Indian soldiers; by the end of the war, the ratio had fallen to less than one to six. Britain had also proven woefully unresponsive in face of the great famine in Bengal in 1943, which took some 3 million lives. Meanwhile, the Indian nationalist movement had continued to grow in strength. Britain's Labour Party had a tradition of sympathy for Indian aspirations toward self-rule, and after its victory in the 1945 elections its leaders generally agreed that Indian independence had become inevitable. In early 1947, the British government sent a distant relation of the royal family, Lord Mountbatten, to India with instructions to negotiate the process.

The subsequent British retreat from India exemplified both the promise and the perils of decolonization. In theory, the rise of an independence movement committed to nonviolence, led by the renowned figure of Mohandas Gandhi (1869–1948), should have ensured a smooth transition of power. Gandhi's ally in the Indian National Congress, the suave, Cambridge-educated Jawaharlal Nehru (1889–1964), who spoke Hindi with a British accent, stood poised to become a prime minister with whom Great Britain could work. But not all subjects of the British possessions in South Asia wanted to be part of a united, independent India dominated by Hindus such as Gandhi and Nehru. A Muslim League led by Mohammad Ali Jinnah (1876–1948), who like Gandhi was trained in Britain as a barrister, demanded partition of British India into separate Hindu and Muslim states, and threatened civil war if Britain did not agree. The British, to Gandhi's despair, gave in.

On August 14, 1947, Nehru announced on radio that "at the stroke of the midnight hour, while the world sleeps, India will awake to life and freedom." But well before then, two huge, violent exoduses had begun—of Hindus from Muslim territory (which would become the Republic of Pakistan) and vice-versa. It recalled the bloody forced migrations in Europe after World War I. Eventually, some 11 million people would leave their homes and as many as 1 million would be killed in communal violence. The new, diminished state of India still had a significant Muslim population. The new state of Pakistan (meaning "land of the pure"), divided into western and eastern portions on either side of India, was far more religiously homogeneous. Lord Mountbatten and his wife presided over colorful, dignified independence ceremonies and then sailed serenely

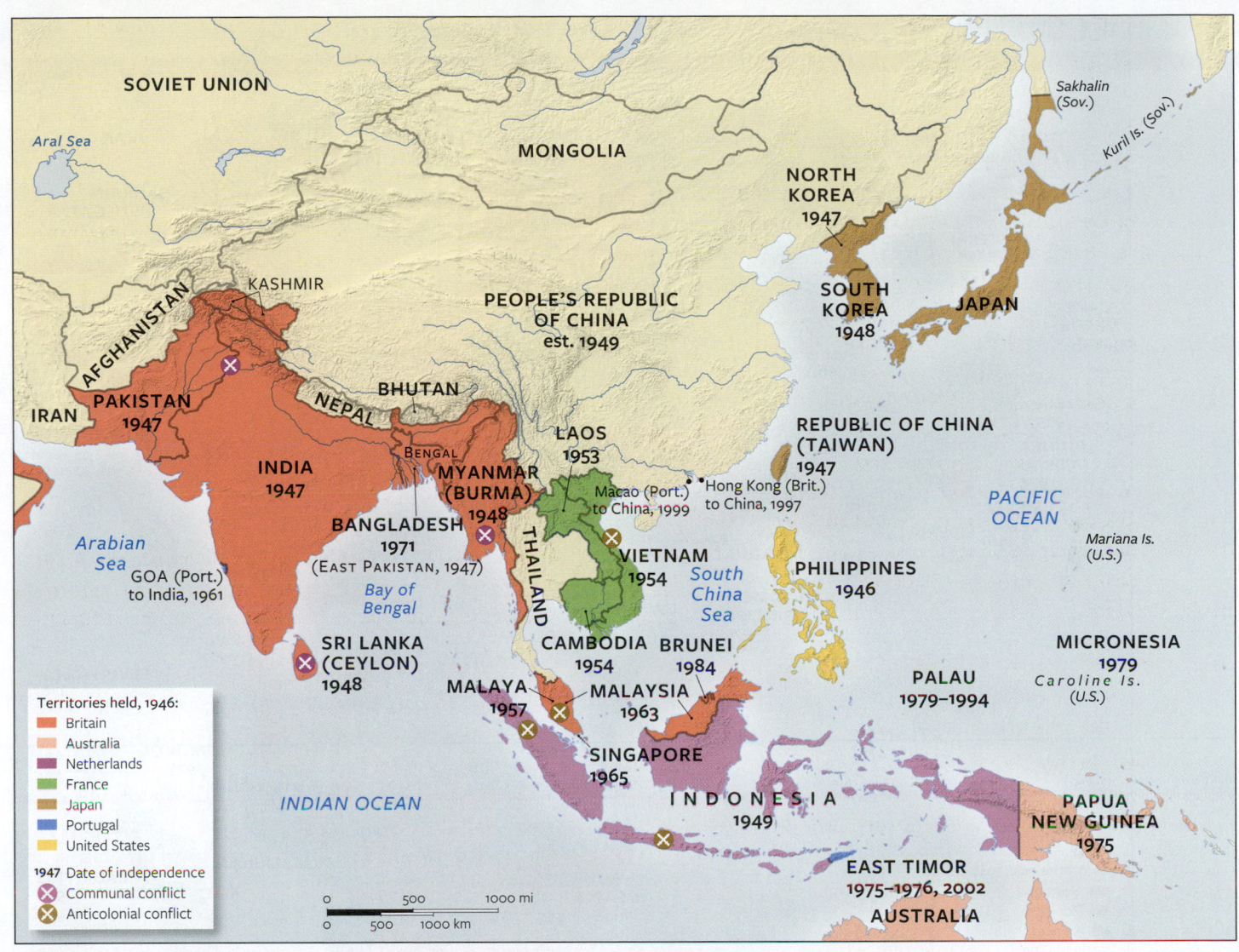

Decolonization in Asia The beginning of the end of European empires in Asia came with the independence of British India, subsequently partitioned into modern-day India and Pakistan. The war's aftermath also brought the end of the Dutch Empire in Indonesia, France's rule in Indochina, and U.S. control of the Philippines. Many smaller colonies did not become independent until decades later.

away from the carnage and chaos. In 1948, Gandhi himself fell victim to a radical Hindu assassin.

Britain quickly washed its hands of communal conflict in many other places as well. In early 1948, it officially granted independence to Ceylon and Burma, and in both these countries massive violence followed, including the assassination of the popular Burmese nationalist Aung San (1915–1947) by political rivals in 1947. On the Malay Peninsula, plans for an autonomous confederation foundered, leading to a long insurgency that the British doggedly worked to repress. The new state of Malaysia only attained independence in the late 1950s. And as we have seen, in 1948 Britain withdrew from the Palestine Mandate,

leading immediately to a full-scale war between the new state of Israel and several large Arab armies. Movements for greater autonomy, or even independence, also gained strength in Britain's African colonies, especially Kenya, leading, as we will see, to considerable violence.

THE DUTCH EMPIRE

The Netherlands saw an even more dramatic collapse of its overseas empire. The Dutch East Indies had long generated wealth for the Netherlands through its exports of rubber, oil, timber, metals, and spices. During World War II, the

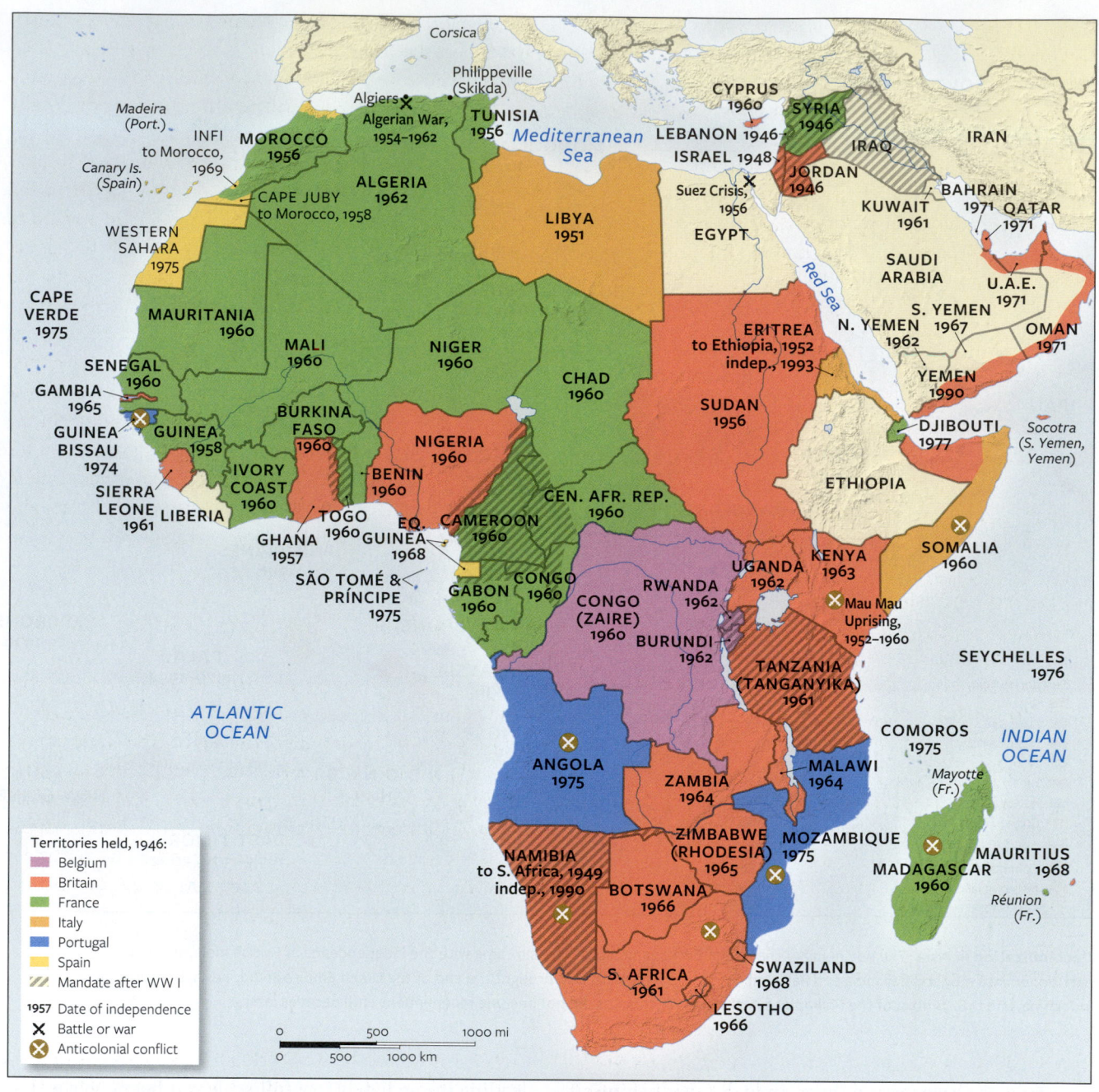

Decolonization in Africa French Northwest Africa became a series of independent nation-states beginning in the 1950s and culminating with the end of the bloody and divisive Algerian War in 1962. By 1970, all of the British East African territories that had stretched "from Cape to Cairo" were also independent, though many—most notoriously South Africa—remained riven by racial divides. Portugal was the last European power to leave its colonies, withdrawing from Angola and Mozambique amid anticolonial violence in the 1970s.

Japanese occupied nearly the entire archipelago and sponsored an independence movement under the leadership of a Javanese architect known as Sukarno (1901–1970). As the Japanese position in the islands collapsed, the movement tried to claim full control. On August 17, 1945, just two days after the Japanese surrender to the Allies, Sukarno's forces issued a Declaration of Independence for a new state they dubbed Indonesia. With the Netherlands still recovering from its own occupation by the Nazis, it was the British who initially moved in to reassert Allied control.

They tried to reach an accommodation with Sukarno and his allies; but as Dutch forces returned, these efforts collapsed. The Dutch began a series of aggressive "police actions" to restore their imperial authority, until they had close to 150,000 soldiers bogged down in the islands. In the resulting chaos, the threat of a communist insurgency grew, and as it did the United States put increasing pressure on the Dutch to recognize Indonesian aspirations. Indonesian independence was finally granted at the end of 1949.

THE FRENCH EMPIRE AND THE FRENCH UNION

The French Empire was weakened as well by the disruptions of World War II. Japan had occupied French Indochina (present-day Laos, Cambodia, and Vietnam), while France's massive possessions in sub-Saharan Africa (from present-day Mali and Niger down to Congo and Gabon) had initially come under the rule of Vichy, which tried to impose more explicit forms of white rule on them than France's Third Republic had done. In 1942–43, with Allied victories in North Africa and signs of an eventual German defeat, the French colonies mostly shifted their allegiance to the Free French led by Charles de Gaulle. But it took time for de Gaulle to establish effective control of the empire. In some areas, notably Indochina, movements that originally came together to fight the Axis transformed themselves, upon the Allied victory, into armed movements for national independence.

In 1945–46, the founders of the new French Fourth Republic sought to forestall the growth of these independence movements by transforming the empire into a cumbersome new structure called the French Union. In theory, this entity would give a greater political voice than before to the native peoples under French rule. France also formally designated several overseas possessions, mostly in the Caribbean, as integral parts of the French Republic—coastal Algeria, where political participation remained largely limited to European settlers, already had this status. The new "departments" became bound closely enough to France that they still form an equal, integral part of the French Republic today, much as Hawaii forms part of the United States.

The French Union, however, was most often greeted as an unworkable compromise, or as thin camouflage for the harsh realities of colonial exploitation. In Africa, in 1946 Félix Houphouët-Boigny of the Ivory Coast helped found a new movement that called for greater French support

for development and self-government in its African territories. The French government strongly opposed it, especially because it had the support of the French Communist Party. In Vietnam, the Viet Minh movement originally formed to fight Japan proclaimed an independent republic in 1945. Led by the veteran nationalist and Communist Ho Chi Minh (1890–1969), it was launched with a formal declaration modeled after the American Declaration of Independence and the French Declaration of the Rights of Man. Escalating violence would roil Indochina for the next thirty years, with the United States eventually replacing a defeated France as the major outside power struggling to limit the spread of Communist influence. And the Viet Minh's fight in turn made a lasting, powerful impression on the Algerian nationalists who came together in the late 1940s to form a paramilitary organization to fight for independence. So in the French Empire as well the British, it was becoming clear that decolonization would for the most part be a difficult, blood-soaked process.

POST-WAR PROSPERITY

Despite the anxieties of the Cold War and the retreat from empire, in the late 1940s and early 1950s Europe's broad loss of geopolitical dominance had relatively little impact on most day-to-day lives in Europe itself. British prime minister Harold MacMillan (1894–1986) spoke the truth when he declared in 1957: "Let us be frank about it—most of our people have never had it so good." The comment would have applied just as well to most of the Continent, including even the eastern portion.

STRUCTURAL CHANGE

A number of factors drove the quick return to prosperity after World War II. In Western Europe, states, employers, and powerful labor unions reached agreements whereby workers limited their wage demands in return for the entitlements of the new, expanded welfare states that were coming into being, including health care, old age pensions, generous guaranteed vacations, and a significant voice in economic planning. Their restraint freed up capital for high levels of long-term investment in industrial restructuring and new technologies. In addition, in many states the simple need for repairing war damage provided a powerful economic stimulus, as the theories of John Maynard Keynes suggested. Marshall Plan aid helped as well. In some cases, wartime destruction even provided a post-war boon. Whereas the British economy, despite new capital investments, remained hindered by aging, increasingly decrepit industrial plants, reconstructed West Germany could rely on largely new ones. In the Soviet Union, the factors were different because the entire economy was under state control, but the initial result was much the same. Simple reconstruction helped drive economic growth, as did the return to peacetime industrial planning. The Soviets benefited from the services of millions of prisoners of war who remained on its soil as laborers, and also from the industrial infrastructure and raw materials confiscated from Germany.

THE THIRTY GLORIOUS YEARS

The result, throughout Europe, was an economic boom. Just three years after the war, the Soviet economy had returned, amazingly, to its pre-war size. Between 1945 and 1950, the USSR managed an average growth rate of close to 15 percent, which fell to a still-respectable 5.8 percent over the subsequent decade. Eastern Europe took longer to start its recovery, but by the 1950s growth rates in the Soviet satellites had also taken off.

In Western Europe, the economic recovery started strong and remained at a remarkably high rate for decades. Today the French commonly refer to the thirty years following World War II as the Trente Glorieuses—the "Thirty Glorious Years"—and the phrase has resonance for Western Europe as a whole. Between 1950 and 1973, real per capita gross domestic product (GDP) there rose by an astonishing 163 percent. Even in Great Britain, burdened with an aging and inefficient industrial base, it went up by a remarkable 75 percent. Southern Europe managed particularly spectacular figures, with Italy rising nearly threefold between 1950 and 1973 and Spain more than threefold. West Germany's GDP expanded more than threefold as well, giving rise to the phrase "the West German economic miracle."

This growth in wealth and income per person took place in tandem with the greatest population boom in European history. After the war, as soldiers returned home and families were reunited, many countries experienced a **baby boom**. In the period 1945–50, the birthrate in Europe as a whole increased by 23 percent as compared to that of the war years. Overall, the Continent grew over 20 percent between 1940 and 1973, and its economies absorbed this growth without any negative effects on individual wealth. As late as the mid-1960s, the average unemployment rate in Western Europe remained just 1.5 percent.

Throughout this book, we have tried to highlight the continuing effects of economic hardship on European life, but the astonishing fact is that in the post-war period the threat of destitution diminished dramatically. By 1973, the percentage of Western Europeans experiencing real economic hardship had fallen to less than one-fifth. A large majority of the population, for the first time in history, now had the certainty of enough to eat, a roof over their heads, heat in the winter, and steady employment in the family. An increasing number of them could count on free public education, even up to university level; free health care; unemployment insurance, and a pension plan. An increasing number had a disposable income that allowed them to buy consumer products or to travel for recreation. Infant mortality in most European countries fell by more than half during the 1950s and 1960s.

A CONSUMER REVOLUTION IN THE WEST

Immediately after the war, the planners who tried to dictate economic priorities tended to emphasize growth in heavy industry—above all, coal and steel—over consumer goods. In Britain, these policies helped keep daily life feeling relatively pinched and poor, even for the middle class, through the early 1950s. Yet by the late 1950s, when Macmillan's boast became a Conservative Party campaign slogan, a flood of consumer goods, including such quintessentially American products as Coca-Cola, had inundated the Western half of the Continent and reached Britain as well.

The Soviet Union and its East European satellites proved unable to shift so nimbly toward a consumer economy. Their more rigid planning processes, coupled with large-scale economic inefficiency, meant that the consumer sector went largely neglected. Housing also lagged far behind. In Soviet cities, the state allocated all housing, and families faced years-long waiting lists, during which time they often had to share apartments with relatives or strangers, often three or more people per room. Even Tito's Yugoslavia, despite its experiments with worker self-management, could not match the West in consumer products. Throughout the late 1950s and early 1960s, the Eastern economies still continued to grow at a healthy pace, and men and women there had more to eat and better housing than at any time in their history. Nonetheless, they could only look on in envy at a Western prosperity that was beginning to dwarf their own.

The changes in the texture of daily life were radical. By

votre **réfrigérateur**

Consumer Society A 1957 French refrigerator advertisement speaks to the changes consumer goods brought to post-war society. "Never taken by surprise! Some friends for dinner…no problem!" reads the caption, as a housewife produces a roast from the fridge for her guests.

owned portable radios and television sets. Cinema attendance began to fall as Europeans increasingly took in their visual entertainment at home. Partly in reaction, and partly because the European film industry could not compete with Hollywood, important film directors such as Italy's Federico Fellini (1920–1993), Sweden's Ingmar Bergman (1918–2007), and France's François Truffaut (1932–1984) deliberately cast themselves as the "authors" of serious, difficult works of art that placed new demands on audiences. Like many other works of avant-garde art, these films often challenged conventional standards of morality and taste. Fellini's 1960 work *La Dolce Vita* ("The Sweet Life") earned condemnations both for irreligion (one scene parodied Christ's second coming) and for its frank depiction of sexuality. In France, Truffaut and other directors connected to the magazine *Cahiers du Cinéma* ("Cinema Notebooks") championed films shot in experimental styles that commented on current social issues, and that came to be known as the "New Wave."

NEW POSSIBILITIES FOR WOMEN

These changes in the texture of life had particularly important consequences for women. In Western Europe, the arrival of such conveniences as running water, central heating, and refrigerators, and later of washing machines and dishwashers, reduced the domestic drudgery that had dominated the lives of most young and married women. The same innovations reduced the need for domestic servants, even as the period's labor shortages enabled women to move out of service into higher-paid industrial jobs as well as office work and teaching. The provision of inexpensive child care as part of the growth of welfare states also contributed to the entry of women into the labor force in record numbers. The number of working women in Britain would more than triple between 1950 and 1990.

As these changes occurred, some formal legal restrictions on women vanished. French women finally received the vote at the end of the war, and by the 1960s they saw other expansions of their private rights. It took until this time for married women, for instance, to gain the right to publish books without their husbands' permission. The Labour Party in Great Britain appointed women to important cabinet positions. In Eastern Europe, the formal commitment of the Communist parties to sexual equalities meant an even higher level of female labor force participation and the rise to political prominence of several important women. Ana Pauker (1893–1960), born into

the 1960s, most Western Europeans had stopped shopping for food on a daily basis. In the Netherlands, the number of supermarkets rose from just seven in 1961 to 520 in 1971. In Italy, the number of households with refrigerators expanded from less than 2 percent in 1957 to 94 percent in 1974. Until the 1950s, European apartment buildings bristled with small storage shelves hung outside windows to keep food fresh during the winter months. By the 1960s, they had largely vanished. Houses in northern Europe gained central heating. Between 1951 and 1970, the temperature inside the average British house rose five degrees Fahrenheit. The numbers of cars on the road in Europe exploded ninefold in just seventeen years: 5 million in 1948; 44 million in 1965. Nearly all this increase came in the West.

The consumption of entertainment changed just as dramatically. If radios and record players (often hand-cranked) had been common in Western Europe before 1945, by 1970 most Western European families

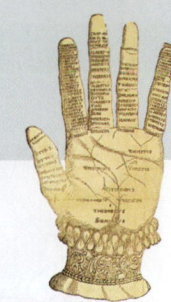

WOMEN'S INDEPENDENCE IN WEST GERMANY

The many changes in daily life in post-war Europe, from the timesaving conveniences of new housekeeping inventions to the hole in the labor force left by the ravages of war, contributed to shifts in attitudes toward women's roles in society. Immediately after the war, many women were left reeling in the midst of the destruction of their cities and families. At the same time, though, no longer simply confined to the care of their children, husbands, and households, women gained new rights and work opportunities.

In 1946, the West German radio host Walther von Hollander discussed the various ways in which women dealt with post-war life, and he received many letters from women in response—often expressing ambivalence. In the following note, a woman from an industrial region describes her relationship with her husband during the war, her living situation following his death, and her hesitancy about a new suitor.

We got married in 1934. My husband was an engineer in an airplane engine plant, a man highly talented in his field and utterly committed to his work. He had a good income. We had a small house…an hour's drive from the city; we had a car. Very soon we had two children. I saw my husband for an hour in the evening, when he came home from work dead tired. When he occasionally came earlier, he would sit at his drawing table half the night, brooding, and from my bed, I heard him talking to himself and cursing. He was a tough man in every regard. At least that's what those under him said, and his superiors didn't like him because he advocated his views brusquely and told everyone his opinion, even if it was unsolicited; I myself did not suffer from his gruffness. Toward me he was always consistently nice. But never affectionate, and he had no strong bonds with the children. How could he? He hardly ever saw them. Everything got worse during the war. He came out once a week, at most. Since he was working on mysterious weapons and there was nothing in his life other than his work, he became almost mute. Therefore, I don't know what kind of trouble there was in his factory. In any case, he was suddenly drafted into the army, even though he was completely indispensable. As a veteran, he was deployed immediately and was soon killed in action. My life changed little because of it. That may sound harsh, but that's the way it was. We had saved quite a bit. The house is rented out. We are living on the top floor, and I have a job as a secretary in the neighboring town. Everything could be fine. But a man has appeared. Again, a very capable man, an architect who is well employed and full of ideas that will surely lead to an excellent position soon. He loves me and wants to marry me. You are now going to say: Well, then! What good luck for this woman! My mother and girlfriends are saying the same. But I don't want to get married. Or, if I were to marry again, then it would be to a gentle person who needs me, whom I can guide and protect. For where did the men lead us? First, it was bleak working life—and now? Don't you think that the men have done a lot of stupid things and can't find their way out? And here I'm supposed to marry another man like that? Must I do that?

QUESTIONS FOR ANALYSIS

1. How was the letter writer affected by her husband's demanding work?
2. Why did her life change little after her husband's death?
3. How did the letter writer's attitude toward men and marriage change following the war?

Source: Walther von Hollander, "Women's Issues—Women's Worries" (1946), trans. Thomas Dunlap, in *Occupation and the Emergence of Two States (1945–1961)*, vol. 8, *German History in Documents and Images*, eds. Volker Berghahn and Uta Poiger (Washington, DC: n.d.), pp. 1–2.

Expanded Women's Rights Ana Pauker in front of a portrait of herself during her tenure as foreign minister of Romania in 1947–52. This was one very prominent example of a woman benefiting from the Communist commitment to sex equality.

an Orthodox Jewish family in Romania, became the effective leader of the Romanian Communist Party for a time after the war. She served as the country's foreign minister from 1947 to 1952 before falling prey to an anti-Semitic purge.

COUNTRYSIDE AND CITY

Even as women benefited in these diverse ways, the peasantry—the largest component of European society throughout history—began to vanish. A worldwide Green Revolution was taking place, involving the sophisticated use of fertilizers and mechanization, and the introduction of new, high-yield cereal grains. This made it possible to grow food more efficiently than ever before with

much less labor, reinforcing trends in European farming that had begun in the early modern period. By the early 1970s, the percentage of the population engaged actively in agriculture had fallen to less than 10 percent in France and West Germany; less than 5 percent in Belgium, the Netherlands, and Great Britain; and even in relatively undeveloped Spain to just 20 percent. In Spain, France, and Italy, whole villages sometimes stood largely abandoned, their former inhabitants now living in cities and suburbs.

Meanwhile, European cities, both East and West, expanded at a record pace, with newcomers from the countryside (and in some countries, increasingly, from abroad) mostly housed in long rows of nondescript concrete high-rise apartment blocks. These structures, and the office blocks that sprang up as well, had mostly plain, geometrical architecture in line with the aesthetic of the Bauhaus movement and the need for cheap, utilitarian construction. In Western Europe, suburbs around major cities also expanded. In the East, the Communist regimes deliberately drove the process of urbanization forward, with cities such as Bratislava in Czechoslovakia marked for large-scale industrial development. In 1949, the Polish regime founded a new steel city dubbed Nowa Huta next door to the old university town of Kraków, hoping in part to develop a politically reliable proletarian population there. In the next eleven years, its population climbed to 100,000 inhabitants.

POPULATIONS ON THE MOVE

People moved not only between rural and urban areas within the same countries, but across national borders as well. The movement led to rapid and dramatic changes in the demographic makeup of many European states, with important economic, social, and political consequences.

EUROPEANS From early in the 1950s, significant movement took place between European states, mostly from south to north, and into Europe from the crumbling colonial empires. Seven million Italians (mostly men) went abroad in search of temporary work between 1945 and 1970, as did a quarter of active Greek workers. By the early 1960s, Italians made up close to one-quarter of the labor force of neighboring Switzerland, while Germany sought to compete for the same supply of manpower by offering free transportation north. In France, which had led Europe in its openness to immigrants before World War II, waves of newcomers from Portugal and Spain added to existing populations of Poles, Italians, and Jews, while arrivals from France's colonies in Africa and Muslim North Africa steadily increased.

A different sort of population flow took place in the center of Europe, between the two German states that had come into being in 1949. Over the next twelve years—until the construction of the Berlin Wall—no fewer than 2.5 million East Germans, disproportionately young and well educated, left the Communist state for West Germany. In 1960 alone, some 200,000 East Germans emigrated out of a population of less than 18 million. They did so because of the repressive rule of the Communist East German government and the lure of prosperity across the border. By the end of the 1950s, only a tiny percentage of East Germans yet owned cars, televisions, or other consumer products common in the West. Most still heated their houses with coal. The East German state guaranteed employment and free child care to its citizens, but standards of health care lagged behind those in the West, and most East Germans had few opportunities for travel. When the East German state moved to collectivize agriculture, some 20,000 farmers emigrated to West Germany.

GUEST WORKERS European prosperity also lured millions of non-European migrants from former European colonies, and other non-European nations to Europe itself. The phenomenon had deep roots but became particularly significant in the 1960s, when for the first time in modern history more people came to live in Europe from outside the Continent than left it to live somewhere else. Most of the newcomers came as supposedly temporary **guest workers** to fill low-level jobs that prosperous native Europeans increasingly refused to take. The number of foreigners working in West Germany, for example, rose from 1.2 million to 4 million (accounting for 7 percent of the population and 12 percent of the labor force) between 1964 and 1973. Some 600,000 guest workers from Turkey formed the largest migrant group in Germany. In France, the largest numbers came from former colonies in North and West Africa; and in Britain, above all from India, Pakistan, and the Caribbean.

The governments of Western Europe initially gave the migrants a warm welcome, seeing them as crucial to continued economic development. The migrants found it easy to bring families to join them, and in most states they enjoyed the protection of the newly robust European welfare states. This welcoming attitude, however, was not always shared by ordinary citizens, who often greeted the newcomers with considerable suspicion and prejudice. As early as 1958, two weeks of rioting took place in the Notting Hill area of London, where white gangs fought with blacks of West Indian origin.

POLITICAL STABILIZATION

On both sides of the iron curtain, the 1950s saw a stabilization of the political patterns set in motion in the initial post-war period. But whereas in the East this stabilization involved considerable violence and repression, in the West it initially took place with relatively little disruption or even notice. The most important political challenges of the decade in Western Europe involved foreign policy and decolonization. Only at the end of the 1950s, as the collapse of more of France's overseas empire destabilized its government, did the threat of large-scale civil violence again, and only briefly, touch the soil of Western Europe itself.

DESTALINIZATION IN THE EAST

The repression in the East began with Joseph Stalin. By 1950, he was in his early seventies and had wielded absolute power for more than a quarter century. The years after the war did not see a repetition of the horrors Stalin had overseen before 1939, but as he grew old he turned increasingly suspicious, and the horrifying possibility of mass death again loomed over the Soviet population. Even as Stalin continued to support and encourage North Korean dictator Kim Il Sung (1912–1994) in direct military conflict with the United States, at home he started to warn against a dangerous plot by "Jewish nationalist" doctors, whom he called agents of American imperialism. But before he could take any action against the Jews, in March 1953 he suffered a stroke and died. Millions of communists throughout the world, swept up in his cult of personality, mourned his death as if it were that of a family member.

At first, power in the USSR passed in large part to the head of the secret police, Stalin's Georgian crony Lavrenti Beria. Beria stopped the persecution of the Jewish doctors and ordered the release of hundreds of thousands of prisoners from the Gulag. But the other survivors of Stalin's inner circle deemed Beria (quite correctly) psychotic, and within months they conspired to have him arrested and executed. Soon afterward, Nikita Khrushchev (1894–1971), a long-standing party functionary, emerged as the leading figure in the government. A coarse-mannered Ukrainian with a strikingly bald head,

Nikita Khrushchev
The Soviet premier famous for his campaign of destalinization gives a speech to workers in Azerbaijan (a constituent republic of the Soviet Union) in 1960.

Khrushchev quickly followed Beria's lead in what would become known as **destalinization**. He released more prisoners from the Gulag—ultimately, some 5 million. He pursued more stable relations with the West. He also moved carefully toward a repudiation of Stalin himself. It culminated in a highly critical, secret speech delivered to party elites in February 1956. Without abandoning the Communist ideology that had prevailed in its broad outlines since Lenin's day, Khrushchev denounced Stalin's "deviations" from that ideology and his crimes. Within days, newspapers in the West were reporting on the speech, and in the Eastern bloc the electrifying news quickly spread by word of mouth.

EASTERN BLOC REVOLTS

Khrushchev hoped that an end to the most severe Stalinist repression and a dose of moderate, rational reform would stabilize the Communist system, allow it to flourish, and, not least, secure his own power. But Khrushchev found that reform in fact released uncontrollable hopes and created dangerous new pressures. Soon after Stalin's death, thousands of prisoners in Gulag labor camps in Siberia began to strike for better conditions, and in one camp scores died when panicked officials ordered guards to open fire.

EAST GERMANY AND POLAND In June 1953, East German workers began striking for better conditions, and the strikes quickly turned into political protests, with demands raised for the government's resignation. Finally, the East German leadership called on Soviet troops to help quell the nascent insurrection, and they did so at a cost of scores, perhaps hundreds, of deaths. The German poet and playwright Bertolt Brecht (1898–1956), who had returned from the United States to live in East Germany, composed a satirical poem that cited a Communist functionary's statement that the people had forfeited the confidence of the government. "Would it not be easier in that case," Brecht wrote, "for the government to dissolve the people and elect another?"

In the summer of 1956, after Khrushchev's secret speech had become common knowledge, Polish security

forces bloodily suppressed riots by workers protesting food shortages. The alarmed government moved to placate the workers, and Władysław Gomułka, a leading Communist reformer whom the party had expelled just a few years before, was installed as party leader. He purged a hard-line Soviet marshal from the Polish politburo, a move that led Khrushchev and his associates briefly to consider an invasion.

HUNGARY These events helped to precipitate a full-fledged revolt against Communist rule in another Eastern bloc country. Since 1948, power in Hungary had swung back and forth between a hard-line faction dominated by Mátyás Rákosi and reformers led by Imre Nagy. Rákosi presided over the execution of nearly 500 political enemies and the imprisonment of more than 1.5 percent of the population. The Soviets ordered him deposed in the summer of 1956, but his Stalined allies remained in power. But in October, after news of events in Poland broke, students in Budapest began staging protests, inspiring much of the city's population to come out into the streets. In the hopes of forestalling an insurrection, the Communist leadership brought back Nagy as prime minister.

The protests, however, only continued to grow, and on October 28 Nagy announced that he would abolish the hated secret police and demand the departure of Soviet troops from the country. Two days later, encouraged by this remarkable cascade of events, Hungarian crowds attacked secret police headquarters, killing some twenty-four agents. Nagy himself now took command of what had become an open revolt against Communism,

Hungarian Revolt A crowd of Hungarian freedom fighters mount a Soviet tank in Budapest in November 1956.

"THE PATH FROM EARTH TO THE STARS"

The successes of the Soviet space program marked a realization of Communist goals for modernization. Following the 1957 launch of the first satellite, *Sputnik*, in April 1961, the Soviet Union successfully sent the first human into space, the cosmonaut Yuri Gagarin. These achievements inspired people living in the East and caused alarm in the West (the first American entered space in May 1961).

This propaganda poster from 1963 is one of many meant to sustain patriotism, optimism, and faith in the Soviet Union. Illustrated in bright Soviet red, it shows a giant hand boosting the launch of a rocket emblazoned with "USSR" and the Communist hammer and sickle. The rousing caption reads: "Be proud, Soviet person, you have opened the path from Earth to the stars."

QUESTIONS FOR ANALYSIS

1. What do you think the hand represents, and why was it was used as a symbol on this poster?
2. Why do you suppose the caption gives Soviet citizens credit for the space program's success?
3. How does this depiction of the space program relate to the Soviet Union's approach to industrialization in the twentieth century?

828

declaring an end to one-party rule and the rebirth of a "free, democratic and independent Hungary" that would immediately withdraw from the Warsaw Pact. With this as the final straw, the Soviet Union invaded and within days crushed desperate armed resistance and restored a reliably Communist government. Some 3,000 Hungarians died in the invasion and subsequent executions, while hundreds of thousands fled across the border to neutral Austria. Nagy himself was executed in 1958.

The Soviets' brutal action in Hungary succeeded in mostly stopping the momentum of Eastern European reform, although it did not entirely kill off enthusiasm for the Communist regimes. Improving living conditions and Khrushchev's limited liberalization somewhat increased support for these regimes in the late 1950s, while the USSR's successful 1957 launch of *Sputnik*, the first human artifact ever put into earth orbit, stirred genuine patriotic enthusiasm in the USSR (so did the first launch of a human being, Yuri Gagarin, into earth orbit in 1961). But in Western Europe, news of the invasion of Hungary hurt Communist parties more than anything since the Hitler-Stalin pact of 1939. Thousands resigned their memberships in disgust, and the Italian Communist Party split openly over the event.

WESTERN EUROPEAN STABILITY

In contrast to the violence in the East, most of Western Europe in the 1950s experienced a greater degree of political stability than at any time since the beginning of the century. In Great Britain, Winston Churchill and the Tories returned to power in 1951, but they did relatively little to deconstruct the welfare state put in place by Attlee and the Labour Party. Promises to re-privatize nationalized industries went largely unfulfilled, in part because the industries in question (especially coal and steel) appeared too unprofitable to potential buyers. In Italy, an intellectually lively Communist Party showed great electoral strength, especially in the north, but the right-wing Christian Democrats kept control of the government throughout the decade. Italian corruption was rampant by northern European standards, but the Christian Democrats did manage to divert some of the output from the post-war economic boom toward development of the woefully impoverished south of the country.

In France, the Fourth Republic (1946–58) largely re-created the politics of the Third, with a great deal of surface instability that did little to disrupt the economic progress of the Thirty Glorious Years. The period saw, on average, a new French government every six months, with power shifting back and forth among the old center-left parties, the new center-right Popular Republican Movement, and the Socialists. A new movement led by a shopkeeper named Pierre Poujade briefly emerged as a powerful force in the mid-1950s, appealing especially to the resentments of small business owners feeling threatened by economic transformations. But its appeal soon fizzled. The French Communist Party, rigidly loyal to Moscow, had formidable political appeal, attracting up to a quarter of the electorate, but it never came into power.

In the 1950s, certain parts of Western Europe demonstrated a political stability that verged on petrification. Spain and Portugal remained under their conservative, Catholic, protectionist dictators, Salazar and Franco, and both countries saw little relief from isolation and impoverishment during the decade. Greece, meanwhile, recovered from its brutal civil war and remained a fragile democracy. The Scandinavian countries largely saw steady Social Democratic rule and a further consolidation of their welfare states. Sweden's Social Democratic prime minister held office for a European record-setting twenty-three years, from 1946 to 1969. Finally, the German-speaking countries in the West saw a return to the sort of stability they had not known since before World War I. The Christian Democrats remained in power throughout the decade in West Germany, in alliance with Bavaria's Christian Social Union. The Communist Party, officially banned, had virtually no influence, and even the Social Democrats formally renounced Marxist orthodoxy in 1959. In Austria, the Soviets and the Western powers quietly agreed to an end to occupation in 1955 and a transition to a democratic, limited free-market system.

FIRST STEPS TOWARD EUROPEAN UNITY

Against this background of stability and peace, the Western European countries also moved toward unprecedented economic and political cooperation. In 1951, France, West Germany, Italy, and the Low Countries (Belgium, Luxembourg, and the Netherlands) entered into an agreement to abolish tariffs and create a common market for coal and steel. France in particular saw the move as a means of binding West Germany closely to it and increasing French political influence with Britain and the United States. But all the countries saw benefits for their economies and considered the agreement as only a first step. In 1957, after lengthy negotiations, the same six countries signed the

Treaty of Rome, which created a broader common market known as the European Economic Community—direct predecessor to the present-day European Union. Britain joined in 1973, along with Ireland and Denmark.

While the image of the 1950s as a decade of complacency only came after the fact, and as a caricature, it remains true that the period saw a quick ebbing of the ideological tides that had dominated European politics and culture from the 1930s through the early post-war period. By the middle of the decade, the prospect of Communist takeovers in Western Europe already seemed remote, and the economic boom and rising standards of living had diminished the desire for radical change on the part of millions of Europeans who now saw themselves as comfortably middle class. Even in France and Italy, the powerful Communist parties did not manage winning majorities of the vote. Meanwhile, despite the brief successes of figures like Poujade, the radical right, indelibly associated with fascism, remained a discredited and largely impotent political force throughout most of the West. In 1955, the liberal French sociologist Raymond Aron could write of "the end of the age of ideologies."

CULTURAL FERMENT

In keeping with this new political climate, the leading cultural movements of the 1950s often avoided direct ideological commitments. In the Soviet Union, the period marked a hiatus between patriotic wartime literature and the dissident writing that would flower in the 1960s. The most important Soviet novel of the decade, the melodramatic *Dr. Zhivago* written by Boris Pasternak (1890–1960), did not pass muster with the Soviet censors but nor did it directly challenge the regime. Smuggled to the West, it became one of the great bestsellers of the decade and the basis for a blockbuster film.

Other Soviet writers were at work on masterpieces that would blisteringly depict the crimes of Stalinism, but these did not appear until later. The great poet Anna Akhmatova (1889–1966) was finishing the long, brilliant elegy entitled *Requiem*, centered on the tragic figures of women who stood outside prisons waiting for news of arrested relatives—a role that Akhmatova herself had played after the arrest of her husband and son. Alexander Solzhenitsyn (1918–2008) was completing the harrowing *One Day in the Life of Ivan Denisovitch*—a brilliant account of the struggle to survive in Stalin's Gulag, based on his own experiences. Solzhenitsyn's novel was allowed to appear in print under Khrushchev. *Requiem* was only published abroad.

In the West, many of the most famous intellectuals continued to support the Communist Party, at least in name, until 1956, but without hewing mechanically to any line laid down in Moscow. More intellectual excitement bubbled up over the broad movement known as existentialism, associated above all with France's Jean-Paul Sartre (1905–1980). The existentialist movement explored the need of individuals to become free, willful actors in the midst of the world's absurdity, violence, and unreason. Sartre, the most famous intellectual of the decade, himself retained a fascination with cathartic, cleansing violence, which led him to express sympathy with anti-colonialist guerrilla and terrorist movements. His friend, the Algerian-born novelist Albert Camus (1913–1960), broke with Sartre over this aspect of his thought and over his political loyalty to the USSR. In Camus's own novels, notably *The Stranger* (originally published in 1942), he promoted a more humanist, apolitical ethic of responsible action. Playwrights, meanwhile, pushed the theme of the confrontation with the irrational to an extreme in the so-called theater of the absurd, which sought to provoke, perplex, and unsettle audiences by rejecting conventional notions of plot and character.

Many of the most daring intellectual experiments of the period became major cultural phenomena in the 1960s and 1970s. *The Second Sex*, first published by Sartre's long-time partner **Simone de Beauvoir** (1908–1986) in 1949, became a founding text of modern feminism.

Sartre and de Beauvoir Writers and romantic partners Jean-Paul Sartre and Simone de Beauvoir are caught in conversation in this candid photograph from 1945. Both had a major influence on developing intellectual movements—Sartre on existentialism, de Beauvoir on feminism.

EUROPE'S OTHERS WRITE BACK

In the cultural dislocation of post-war Europe, women, minorities, and other marginalized members of society challenged their exclusion from civil and cultural equality. Feminist writers such as Simone de Beauvoir criticized women's second-class status and demanded equal opportunities for women in political and social life. Artists and writers from racial minorities, both in imperial centers like London and Paris and in the colonies themselves, attacked the racism and hypocrisy of the European empires and demanded democratic reforms. These sidelined groups questioned the justness of the societies that for so long had been centered around and directed by white men.

Simone de Beauvoir, from *The Second Sex*

In this passage from her trailblazing feminist book *The Second Sex* (1949), de Beauvoir argues that throughout history woman has been seen as an inferior "Other."

Woman has ovaries and a uterus; such are the particular conditions that lock her in her subjectivity; some even say she thinks with her hormones. Man vainly forgets that his anatomy also includes hormones and testicles. He grasps his body as a direct and normal link with the world that he believes he apprehends in all objectivity, whereas he considers woman's body an obstacle, a prison, burdened by everything that particularizes it. "The female is female by virtue of a certain *lack* of qualities," Aristotle said. "We should regard women's nature as suffering from natural defectiveness." And Saint Thomas in his turn decreed that woman was an "incomplete man," an "incidental" being. This is what the Genesis story symbolizes, where Eve appears as if drawn from Adam's "supernumerary" bone, in Bossuet's words. Humanity is male, and man defines woman, not in herself, but in relation to himself; she is not considered an autonomous being. "Woman, the relative being," writes Michelet. Thus Monsieur Benda declares in *Le rapport d'Uriel* (Uriel's Report): "A man's body has meaning by itself, disregarding the body of the woman, whereas the woman's body seems devoid of meaning without reference to the male. Man

thinks himself without woman. Woman does not think herself without man." And she is nothing other than what man decides; she is thus called "the sex," meaning that the male sees her essentially as a sexed being; for him she is sex, so she is it in the absolute. She is determined and differentiated in relation to man, while he is not in relation to her; she is the inessential in front of the essential. He is the Subject; he is the Absolute. She is the Other.

Aimé Césaire, from "Discourse on Colonialism"

Césaire (1913–2008) was a poet and a politician from the French Caribbean possession of Martinique. In this excerpt from his 1955 essay "Discourse on Colonialism," he attacks the dehumanizing processes of colonization.

First we must study how colonization works to *decivilize* the colonizer, to *brutalize* him in the true sense of the word, to degrade him, to awaken him to buried instincts, to covetousness, violence, race hatred, and moral relativism; and we must show that each time a head is cut off or an eye put out in Vietnam and in France they accept the fact, each time a little girl is raped and in France they accept the fact, each time a Madagascan is tortured and in France they accept the fact, civilization acquires another dead weight, a universal regression takes place, a gangrene sets in, a center of infection begins to spread....

And then one fine day the bourgeoisie is awakened by a terrific reverse shock: the gestapos are busy, the prisons fill up, the torturers around the racks invent, refine, discuss.

People are surprised, they become indignant. They say: "How strange! But never mind—it's Nazism, it will pass!" And they wait, and they hope; and they hide the truth from themselves, that it is barbarism, but the supreme barbarism, the crowning barbarism that sums up all the daily barbarisms; that it is Nazism, yes, but that before they were its victims, they were its accomplices....

...What [the Christian bourgeois] cannot forgive Hitler for is not *the crime* in itself, *the crime against man*, it is not *the humiliation of man as such*, it is the crime against the white man, the humiliation of the white man, and the fact that he applied to Europe colonialist procedures which until then had been reserved exclusively for the Arabs of Algeria, the coolies of India, and the blacks of Africa.

QUESTIONS FOR ANALYSIS

1. According to de Beauvoir, how are women and men seen in relation to each other?
2. What link does Césaire draw between colonialism and Nazism?
3. How do both of these works expose the assumptions behind Europe's claim to having a superior form of civilization?

Sources: Simone de Beauvoir, *The Second Sex*, trans. Constance Borde and Sheila Malovany-Chevallier (New York: 2010), pp. 5–6; Aimé Césaire, *Discourse on Colonialism*, trans. Joan Pinkham (New York: 1972), pp. 13–14.

Written just as the post-war landscape began to offer new possibilities for European women, the book eloquently denounced traditional sex roles as the social and cultural inventions of men, rather than simple reflections of nature. "One is not born, but rather becomes, a woman," de Beauvoir wrote, and she challenged women to assert different identities and roles for themselves. The work of the black French thinker Frantz Fanon (1925–1961), culminating in his 1961 book *The Wretched of the Earth*, laid the basis for much subsequent thinking about race and violence. A psychiatrist who keenly analyzed the psychological effects of racism on blacks, Fanon spent much of the 1950s in French Algeria, joined the independence movement there, and found justification for extreme violence against colonial oppression.

DECOLONIZATION AND POLITICAL CHANGE

The major international crises afflicting Western Europe in the 1950s involved the continuing wave of decolonization that Fanon supported. Britain successfully tested nuclear weapons in 1952, and France in 1960, but these events had less practical effect on their geopolitical standing than the continuing crumbling of their empires. One dramatic European defeat occurred in Vietnam, where the French lost the battle of Dien Bien Phu to Ho Chi Minh's forces in 1954. The French quickly pulled out of Vietnam altogether, and following an international conference in Geneva, two independent Vietnamese states came into being in 1955: a North Vietnamese state under Ho Chi Minh and a pro-Western South Vietnam.

THE SUEZ CRISIS OF 1956

The most important flashpoint of the decade was Egypt, where young nationalist officers overthrew the pro-British monarchy of King Farouk (r. 1936–1952) in 1952. Egyptian nationalists then started to insist on control of the country's resources, including the **Suez Canal**—the crucial waterway that allowed shipping to pass from the Mediterranean toward the Indian Ocean. In 1954, Britain reluctantly agreed to begin withdrawing its military forces from the canal zone.

Matters came to a head in 1956 when the hot-tempered new Egyptian leader, Gamal Abdel Nasser (1918–1970), abruptly nationalized the Suez Canal. France, Britain, and Israel—which had never signed a peace agreement with Egypt—planned a joint military operation that they hoped would lead to a reoccupation of the canal zone and the fall of Nasser's government. But the Egyptian army put up an unexpectedly tough fight, and then both the United States and the Soviet Union began to pressure the Western countries to withdraw. U.S. president Dwight Eisenhower in particular resented what he saw as the Europeans' selfish and deceptive conduct, and he privately accused them of risking Middle East peace for their own economic benefit. With American financial pressure undermining the stability of the British pound, the British and French gave in by early November and withdrew their forces. The Suez Crisis led Britain to question its imperial role even further.

ALGERIA

In France, Suez—following on the final French defeat in Vietnam in 1954—further damaged a weak Republic that was already struggling with another crisis in the Arab world. Most of the French considered Algeria, which had over a million inhabitants of European descent, an intrinsic part of their nation.

THE WAR FOR INDEPENDENCE
That feeling was not shared, however, by the more than 8 million Algerian Muslims who remained largely shut out of political participation and deprived of most chances for social or economic advancement. An armed insurrection against France broke out in 1954, led by young Algerian nationalists inspired in part by events in Egypt. Unable to confront the French army militarily, their **National Liberation Front (FLN)** instead turned to guerrilla and terrorist tactics, including the massacre of 123 civilians in the Algerian town of Philippeville (now Skikda) in 1955. Such actions pushed the French to ever more desperate attempts at counterinsurgency, with the army carrying out massacres of its own and torturing prisoners to uncover the whereabouts of FLN units.

In the so-called battle of Algiers in 1957, the FLN carried out bombings and shootings in the Algerian capital and staged a general strike. French forces finally crushed the Algiers insurgents, but only after a costly campaign lasting the better part of a year. The FLN's attacks continued elsewhere in the territory. Algerians of European descent, known as *pieds noirs* ("black feet"), grew ever more suspicious of the government in Paris and ever more ready to take up arms themselves. Segments of the French army in Algeria openly sympathized with them.

The French leadership desperately considered different options. They granted full independence to the neighboring countries of Tunisia and Morocco, which had been French protectorates. They also developed the idea of giving full French citizenship to Algerian Muslims and introducing affirmative action for them in certain segments of French government. This plan violated the strict individualist principles underlying France's republican constitution. But by 1957–58, these principles mattered less than restoring order in Algeria—and preventing the disorder there from spreading back across the Mediterranean to France itself.

ALGERIA AND THE FALL OF THE FRENCH FOURTH REPUBLIC

The French leadership failed in this goal. In 1957–58, three successive French governments fell because of the Algerian issue. Then in May 1958, a group of army officers in Algiers staged a coup there and took control of the territory, demanding **Charles de Gaulle**'s return to power. When paratroopers loyal to these officers seized control of the French Mediterranean island of Corsica on May 24, the threat of bloodshed in France itself turned very real. To prevent it, the French president appointed de Gaulle, hero of the wartime Free French, as prime minister. The National Assembly voted him extraordinary powers for six months, along with the authority to prepare a new constitution. De Gaulle immediately flew to Algeria, and before a huge crowd he delivered the deliberately ambiguous words: "I have understood you." The new constitution he largely devised, which gave France its Fifth Republic, replaced the country's weak parliamentary system with a strong executive one. In December 1958, de Gaulle himself won election to the newly powerful office of president.

De Gaulle did not, however, save French Algeria. By the time he took office, he already realized that France had little hope of keeping the territory. The FLN continued its resistance campaign, including terrorist attacks in France itself. In October 1961, French police in Paris killed scores—perhaps as many as 200—of peaceful, mostly North African protestors, in a massacre that the French state covered up until the late 1990s. The police prefect who bore ultimate responsibility was Maurice Papon, who during the war had helped organize the deportation of French Jews to the Nazi death camps—like many other such officials, he had avoided post-war punishment and continued his successful administrative career.

But even before these events, de Gaulle had entered into secret negotiations with the FLN that concluded in 1962 with an agreement to give Algeria full independence. Enraged at this supposed betrayal, French generals

Algerian War French soldiers stand guard over members of the FLN whom they have taken prisoner following a confrontation during the Algerian War of Independence.

in Algiers staged another coup and planned to land paratroopers in Paris. The plot failed, and its leaders went underground into the so-called Secret Army Organization, which itself carried out terrorist acts including a failed assassination attempt on de Gaulle in August 1962. Meanwhile, the European settlers in Algeria fled to France, along with significant numbers of Arabs and Berbers associated with the French regime.

The loss of a territory that the French had considered part of their nation for more than a century had a traumatic effect, and ironically led prominent intellectuals to abandon earlier visions of French identity as "universal." In its place, they adopted a more limited, ethnically-exclusive vision of France. This shift would make it much harder for the country to absorb the wave of Muslim immigration that was just beginning.

THE SCRAMBLE OUT OF AFRICA

Even as the crises in Algeria and the Suez shook Western Europe, both France and Britain continued to wrestle with the forces of decolonization in sub-Saharan Africa. In Kenya, a widespread insurrection known as the Mau Mau Uprising took tens of thousands of lives and involved widespread atrocities by British forces, including the forced imprisonment of hundreds of thousands of members of the Kikuyu tribe in camps where torture and sexual assault were common. While the British ultimately suppressed the revolt, the events made clear that Britain could not hold on to its African colonies except at an impossibly high cost in money, blood, and the Britons' own principles.

By the mid-1960s, Britain and France had granted independence to most of their colonies in Africa, including Kenya, where the British government bought out the property of white settlers. Belgium likewise pulled out of its colony in the Congo, where some of the worst excesses of European imperialism had taken place. All in all, between 1957 and 1967 over thirty new African states joined the United Nations. White rule in Africa remained principally in the Portuguese colonies of Angola and Mozambique, and in the racist white settler states of South Africa and Rhodesia. The rulers of the latter unilaterally declared independence from Britain in 1965.

The new African states generally came into existence with democratic, European-style constitutions, grand hopes for development, and promises of aid and assistance from the former imperial powers. In most cases, these hopes and promises were soon largely dashed. In the subsequent fifty years, virtually none of them preserved their original democratic systems, and all had to contend with woeful economic underdevelopment, a catastrophic collapse in physical infrastructure, and a host of other afflictions, including the AIDS epidemic. Historians and social scientists debate the extent to which European imperialism directly caused these problems, but there is no doubt that the combination of imperialism and rapid decolonization left the African continent in desperate straits.

It is worth noting, however, that decolonization did not always mean real disengagement. The United States and the USSR both cultivated allies in Africa and sent advisers and aid to the new states. France retained a strong military presence in its former colonial region of West Africa, and all European states remained deeply involved in exploiting the African natural resources that had drawn them to the continent in the first place. In 1980, France had more citizens living in the Ivory Coast than twenty-five years before, during colonial rule.

SHIFTING COLD WAR DYNAMICS

Even as the former European imperial states continued to confront decolonization, the threat of war again loomed over Europe itself. In the early 1960s, at several frightening moments, it seemed as if the Cold War might turn very hot indeed.

COLD WAR CRISES

On Sunday, August 13, 1961, citizens of Berlin woke up to find the border between the two halves of the city closed. East German soldiers and police were tearing up pavement and erecting barbed wire fences around the enclave of West Berlin. The Communist regime, faced with the continuing flight of its citizens—especially younger, productive adults—had decided to keep them in the country by force. Within a few years, the **Berlin Wall** had evolved into a massive, forbidding symbol of Communism's failure: a 12-foot high, 87-mile-long concrete barrier studded with 116 watchtowers. It was separated from East Berlin by a "death strip" patrolled by armed border troops.

While several thousand East Berliners did manage to escape across the wall during its twenty-eight years of existence—including by tunnel, balloons, and wires stretched over to West Berlin buildings—they did so mostly at the start. At least 136 East Germans died trying to flee. The regime also massively reinforced its entire border with West Germany, laying minefields and setting automatic gun traps. The moves provoked angry rhetoric from the West and particularly from the young American president, John F. Kennedy (1917–1963), who extravagantly promised in his inaugural address in January 1961 to "pay any price, bear any burden . . . to assure the survival and the success of liberty." In 1963, Kennedy came to West Berlin, expressed his solidarity with its citizens, and laid down a stark challenge to the East: "There are some who say in Europe and elsewhere we can work with the Communists. Let them come to Berlin."

In 1962, the United States under Kennedy and the Soviet Union under Nikita Khrushchev came closer to open warfare than at any other time during the Cold War. In October of that year, after the Americans discovered that the Soviets were placing nuclear missiles in Communist Cuba, just ninety miles off the coast of Florida, they imposed a blockade of the island, and for several days the world feared the conflict might escalate into a nuclear exchange. The crisis ended with a deal by which the Soviets removed missiles from Cuba and the Americans secretly promised to do the same from Turkey.

The progress of a Communist insurgency in South Vietnam led the U.S. government to send advisers and material support to the Western-backed regime there. The growing American commitment in Vietnam was influenced by the Cold War strategy often referred to as the domino theory, which held that the fall to Communism of one pro-Western regime in the region would

COLD WAR BERLIN

> Berlin [has] now become—as never before—the great testing place of Western courage and will, a focal point where our solemn commitments stretching back over the years since 1945 and Soviet ambitions now meet in basic confrontation.
>
> PRESIDENT JOHN F. KENNEDY, TELEVISED SPEECH, JULY 25, 1961

BUILDINGS
1. Friedrichstrasse Station
2. Soviet Embassy
3. SED headquarters
4. Checkpoint Charlie
5. Brandenburg Gate

Legend
- Road
- Wall
- Railroad
- Checkpoint
- Sector boundary
- Plaza
- Mixed residential/commercial use
- Industrial use
- Park or open area

A group of East German workers' militiamen stands, armed, in front of the Brandenburg Gate on August 14, 1961, a day after the borders between East and West Berlin were sealed.

EAST GERMANS FLEEING TO THE WEST

1949–1961	2.8 MILLION*
May 1961	17,791
June 1961	19,198
July 1961	30,415
August 1–12, 1961	22,000

*16 percent of the German Democratic Republic's population, most of them young and well educated

The Bernhauer Strasse lay directly on the border of East and West Berlin. Many East Germans fled across this street, escaping through their apartment windows to the opposite sidewalk on the Western side.

"OPERATION ROSE," 1961

JULY 6

Soviet premier Khrushchev's approval of "Operation Rose," the East German plan to close the borders to West Berlin

AUGUST 13

"Barbed-Wire Sunday": border sealing begins at 1:00 a.m.; complete by 6:00 a.m.

The Berlin Wall, a symbol of the Cold War, eventually extended for almost 100 miles with 300 watchtowers.

Over two decades later, it was dismantled by Berliners on November 9, 1989.

QUESTIONS FOR ANALYSIS

1. How did the location of a divided Berlin make it a flashpoint in the ongoing hostilities of the Cold War?

2. What connections do you see between the flight of East Germans to the West and the plan of East German and Soviet officials to close off the Western sectors of the city?

3. What evidence do you see that the sealing off of West Berlin disrupted neighborhoods and families in the city?

lead to the loss of others in a series. By the mid-1960s, the United States had started to send troops in large numbers, fighting unsuccessfully against both the insurgent Viet Cong and Communist North Vietnam, with the conflict spilling over into other Southeast Asian states as well. Europeans waited and watched nervously to see which, if any, of these flashpoints might send dangerous sparks flying in their direction.

CHALLENGES TO COLD WAR IDEOLOGIES

Yet the Cold War in the 1960s did not amount to a simple continuation of the conflict that had begun in the late 1940s. Through at least the early 1950s, the ideological stakes on both sides had still seemed enormously high. Western and Soviet leaders each saw the other side as bent on the destruction of the opposing social and political system. Soviet actions in Central and Eastern Europe convinced a large portion of Western public opinion that their leaders were right. Societies, as well as governments, remained psychologically prepared for war. By the early 1960s, however, things had changed.

The Soviet Union continued the retreat from rigid ideology signaled by Khrushchev's secret speech of 1956. Although Khrushchev proclaimed that same year to a group of Western ambassadors that "we will bury you" and frequently predicted that the Soviet Union would soon surpass the West economically, at home he tolerated small but telling retreats from Communist orthodoxy. In the economy, he gave increased freedom to small private farmers who, while only working 3 percent of the country's available farmland, produced a third of its total agricultural output in the early 1960s. He also permitted Hungary greatly to enlarge its private sector. Politically, he allowed the Gomułka regime in Poland to continue cautious political liberalization. And in 1962, the Soviet regime itself allowed a literary magazine to publish Solzhenitsyn's *One Day in the Life of Ivan Denisovitch*. In foreign policy, divisions opened up between the USSR and the more radical Chinese regime of Mao Zedong (1893–1976). The Sino-Soviet split opened in part because of what Mao saw as Khrushchev's overly conciliatory policies toward the West, although it also echoed long-standing historical tensions between Russia and China. A full-fledged split took place in 1964, with Mao denouncing Khrushchev as a capitalist counter-revolutionary.

This major splintering of the Communist bloc, worsened by China's successful test of a nuclear weapon in 1964, undermined the standing of Khrushchev himself with the Soviet party leadership. In October 1964, they removed him from office, and the gray functionary Leonid Brezhnev (1906–1982) replaced him as party general secretary. Despite momentary fears in the West of a return to the Stalin era, Khrushchev's fall did not bring about any major changes of direction in Soviet policy, even if Brezhnev and his cautious colleagues showed less tolerance for dissent.

The idea that Western Europe had to follow the United States unquestioningly in a rigid ideological conflict with the Communist bloc also came in for serious political challenges. In 1958, a group of prominent left-wing British cultural figures founded the Campaign for Nuclear Disarmament, calling for Britain unilaterally to give up nuclear weapons and perhaps disengage from NATO altogether. Its protest marches attracted hundreds of thousands of supporters. French president de Gaulle (1890–1970) repeatedly signaled his disagreements with American policies and sometimes spoke of France as an independent power between East and West. In 1966, he followed through on this rhetoric by withdrawing French military forces from the unified NATO command structure although France remained a part of the overall alliance.

The deepening American involvement in Southeast Asia during the 1960s also stirred opposition in Europe. Although six Western European nations had sent at least token forces to fight in the Korean War in the early 1950s, none participated in the tragic Vietnam conflict (although Australia and New Zealand did). By 1967, polls showed that large majorities of Western Europeans opposed America's actions. Also in 1967, Britain's most prominent philosopher, Bertrand Russell (1872–1970), who had opposed British involvement in World War I fifty years earlier, presided over a mock tribunal in Stockholm that found the United States guilty of "war crimes." By 1968, every major Western European capital had experienced large-scale protest marches against the war.

THE DECADE OF YOUTH REVOLT

The increasing opposition to American policy had its origins not only in the waning of Cold War ideologies but also in the explosive and turbulent youth culture of the 1960s. Europe had of course seen generational tensions before.

They had a particular importance in the era of the French Revolution and at the birth of the romantic movement in art and literature. But in the 1960s, for the first time in European conflict, generational tensions came to be seen as one of the main forces driving political, cultural, and social change.

POST-INDUSTRIAL SOCIETY

As in the United States, the youth culture was linked to the baby boom that had followed the war and the coming to maturity of a huge cohort of men and women raised in unprecedented comfort and prosperity. More explicitly than ever before, the tastes and behavior of people in their teens and twenties—involving music, clothing, hairstyles, drugs, and sexual behavior—became politicized. And while the slogan "Never trust anyone over thirty" came from the youth movement in the United States, it had just as much resonance in Western Europe. Young people in Eastern Europe often aspired to develop their own versions of rebellious youth culture, but they had much less opportunity than their Western counterparts because of the regimented nature of the Eastern political regimes.

The transformation of youth culture would have been unthinkable had economic growth not continued. In the 1960s, it was not only continuing but bringing further structural changes to societies and economies of the West. Just as the proportion of the population employed in agriculture had been falling since the nineteenth century, now the proportion employed in manufacturing began to decline as well, to the profit of service and knowledge industries. Western Europe was experiencing what the sociologist Daniel Bell called "the coming of post-industrial society." The East, as we have seen, had much more difficulty making the transition away from heavy industry.

Educational patterns in Western Europe changed markedly as a result. As late as 1950, most Western European children left school by the age of fourteen to begin vocational training. British grammar schools and public schools (which were actually private), French *lycées*, and German *Gymnasiums* were all elite institutions catering to less than 10 percent of all teenagers. But in the 1960s, the numbers going through secondary education and higher education exploded. In 1950, West Germany had only 108,000 full-time university students. By 1968, the number had increased almost fourfold. Other European countries experienced similar rates of expansion. Nearly all the European universities were public and free, and many were open to anyone with a baccalaureate (high school) degree. Educational bureaucracies shoehorned students into existing facilities and oversaw the construction of new campuses.

THE DECLINE OF RELIGIOUS OBSERVANCE

These students came to universities with different outlooks and habits from even their immediate predecessors. Most striking, they were far less religious than their predecessors. During the 1960s, the number of children enrolled in religious education in Great Britain fell by half, and the number of children baptized fell to under 50 percent. Throughout Europe, weekly attendance at church was declining as well, especially among those under age thirty. In both the Catholic Church and the numerous Protestant denominations, the number of men and women entering religious life fell dramatically, too, forcing religious schools to hire greater numbers of secular teachers. A similar fall in religious observance took place in the officially atheist Eastern European states.

The established churches were trying to adapt to their changing societies, but often in a hesitant or reluctant manner. Most dramatic was the action of the Catholic Church. In 1958, the conclave of cardinals elected the seventy-six-year-old Italian Angelo Roncalli as pope. He was expected to serve as a passive placeholder after the controversial pontificate of Pius XII (r. 1939–1958), whose tolerance of the Fascists in Italy and Germany during the war had earned the Church considerable criticism. Instead, Roncalli, taking the name John XXIII (r. 1958–1963), embarked on an ambitious reform program that culminated in the **Second Vatican Council** of 1962–65. This body produced the greatest change in Church liturgy since the Middle Ages. Henceforth, priests would say the Mass in the local language, not in Latin, and while facing the congregants, not with their backs turned. Congregants no longer kneeled to receive Communion. The Church formally withdrew its accusation that the Jews had killed Jesus Christ.

But Church reform had its limits, as was evident in the explosive issue of birth control. In 1968, a new, more cautious pope, Paul VI (r. 1963–1978), reaffirmed the Church's ban on the practice. Sexual intercourse had only one purpose, he stated in an encyclical: human reproduction.

The declaration deeply disappointed a large proportion of the Catholic population, especially younger people in northern Europe, and hastened the decline of religious observance.

YOUTH CULTURE

The spread of birth control itself amounted to another broad cultural shift with particular significance for European youth. Europeans had employed forms of contraception for centuries—especially coitus interruptus, primitive prophylactic sheaths, and abortion-inducing drugs. While abortion remained illegal in nearly all of Europe through the 1960s, more efficient prophylactics for men were widely available. And starting in Britain in 1961, birth control pills for women became available as well. The risk of unplanned pregnancies fell dramatically, and rates of premarital sex rose just as dramatically. At the same time, many European states began loosening censorship laws on pornography. D. H. Lawrence's explicit *Lady Chatterley's Lover*, which had first appeared in print in Italy in 1928, finally made it to publication in the novelist's native Britain in 1960. Sex, in short, was becoming more visible in the public life of the West.

Beatlemania Young fans excitedly pose with Ringo Starr, John Lennon, Paul McCartney, and George Harrison at a concert hall in Edinburgh in 1964, at the height of the Beatles' fame.

All of these cultural changes left their mark on the vastly increased numbers of students who crammed into European universities in the 1960s—students who already had more free time and disposable income than their predecessors. Companies eagerly competed to sell them distinctive youth products: clothing, much of it marketed as sexually appealing (notably blue jeans and miniskirts), books, magazines, and above all music.

The most famous representatives of the new generation were four young working-class men from the grimy English industrial city of Liverpool, who came together as a band in the early 1960s playing music inspired by American rock and roll. The Beatles exploded onto the British and American music scenes in the fall of 1962. By early 1964, Beatlemania had grown so fevered that as much as half the American population tuned in to television to see the group perform on *The Ed Sullivan Show*. The group would go on to sell over a billion albums. The Beatles were only one of many rock groups to transform popular music in the 1960s, but they were almost certainly the most important. In 1966, John Lennon boasted that the group had become more popular than Jesus Christ—words that had a certain plausibility, given the fall-off in religious practice.

STUDENT REBELLIONS: 1968

Despite being packaged and sold by profit-seeking corporations, rock music and other elements of the 1960s youth culture breathed a spirit of rebellion. The flouting of sexual conventions by the youth culture, and its embrace of recreational drug use—especially marijuana and psychedelic drugs such as LSD—only intensified the tensions it generated. The Beatles boasted of smoking marijuana in the toilets in Buckingham Palace, and their fans widely took the surreal lyrics of "Lucy in the Sky with Diamonds" as a paean to LSD. The uncertain career prospects for the glut of new college graduates contributed to the tensions in a different way. As early as 1955, the British journalist Henry Fairlie had coined the term *the Establishment* to describe the constellation of individuals and institutions that exercised real control over British society. He used the word sardonically, but by the late 1960s it had become a term of abuse, not just in Britain but also throughout Europe and the United States, for young people at odds with their elders.

The tensions exploded in the year 1968. Throughout Western Europe and the United States, university students protested, staged sit-ins, went on strike, occupied

Violent Protests The French protests in May 1968, turn violent when a group of students rip pavement stones out of the Boulevard Saint-Germain, in the Latin Quarter of Paris, to throw at the police.

campus buildings, and took part in violent clashes with riot police. The great common cause was the war in Vietnam. Some 10,000 students in West Berlin held a sit-in to protest American involvement there, and Italian students forced the closure of the University of Rome for twelve days for the same reason. In West Germany, students also protested the continuing presence of former Nazis in prominent positions in government and society. It did not help that in 1966 a former Nazi propagandist had become chancellor of West Germany. In Spain, students protested against the repression of the Franco regime, and in response the regime closed the University of Madrid for a month. At the University of Belgrade, in Communist but non-aligned Yugoslavia, students went on strike for seven days and won some concessions from the Tito regime.

The protests of 1968 were most serious in France, where Charles de Gaulle had now been president for ten years. His Fifth Republic, with its powerful executive, enjoyed a degree of political stability known by no previous democratic regime in France. But this very success had left the elderly president dangerously complacent. On New Year's Eve 1967, he had declared in a national broadcast that "I greet the year 1968 with serenity. . . . It is impossible to see how France today could be paralyzed by crisis as she has been in the past." University students soon taught him a lesson.

Unrest first spread at the desolate, overcrowded, modernist campus in the Parisian suburb of Nanterre and soon spread to the Sorbonne, heart of the University of Paris. In April, the government closed the school and arrested some 600 students. On May 6, the escalating troubles turned bloody—students fought back against riot police, throwing cobblestones and improvised gasoline bombs,

and engaging in that most traditional of Parisian revolutionary actions: building street barricades. The rioting continued for a solid week, with thousands injured, at which point the heavily Communist trade unions took a role as well, declaring a national general strike for better pay and working conditions. A remarkable utopian spirit briefly appeared in Paris, expressed in slogans such as "Be Realistic: Demand the Impossible." In panic, de Gaulle briefly fled the country for a military base in West Germany. However, the students and workers failed to make common cause. De Gaulle called for new parliamentary elections, and on May 30 up to a million demonstrators flowed down the wide boulevard of the Champs-Élysées in support of his government. So in France, as throughout Western Europe, the events of 1968 led to surprisingly little violence, and little permanent political change, although much larger degrees of social and cultural change.

SPAIN AND NORTHERN IRELAND

The worst violence in the late 1960s and early 1970s in Western Europe had relatively little to do with the student movement. In Spain, the slow easing of Francoist repression enabled the regime's most viciously repressed victims—the country's large ethnic minorities—to start organizing and campaigning for greater rights. In the northern Basque country in 1958, radicals founded an armed movement called ETA (for the Basque initials for "Basque Country and Freedom") that aimed at full Basque independence, and in the late 1960s they started a campaign of assassination and bombings against police, government officials, and moderate Basque politicians.

In Northern Ireland, the Catholic minority campaigned for civil rights such as an end to discrimination against them in housing and employment. Growing Catholic support for a violent Provisional Irish Republican Army led to a noisy and brutal backlash from the province's dominant Protestants. In response to these so-called **Troubles**, in 1969 the London government deployed the British army to take over security from the autonomous Northern Irish government. But the army, sent largely to protect the Catholic population, came increasingly into conflict with it, culminating in Bloody Sunday in January 1972, when British paratroopers killed thirteen civilians in the town of Derry. As the so-called Provos gained support and started a full-fledged guerrilla campaign against the army, along with terrorist attacks in mainland Britain, the Conservative prime minister dissolved the Northern Irish government in 1972 and asserted direct control over

POLAND AND CZECHOSLOVAKIA

The late 1960s also brought considerable turmoil in the Soviet bloc. Students initially led the way in Poland, with protests for more freedom of expression and better living conditions. Police attacked them brutally, leading to much larger protests in Warsaw that were joined by workers. But in response, the relatively liberal Gomułka regime turned repressive, dismissing dissenting intellectuals from academic jobs and closing university campuses. The powerful interior minister, Mieczysław Moczar, blamed the crisis on Jews and used it as an excuse to begin purging them from the universities and the professions. Between 20,000 and 30,000 Jews—the majority of Poland's post-Holocaust Jewish remnant—fled the country. Gomułka himself struggled on for another two years. After police shot and killed protesting shipyard workers in the port city of Gdańsk in 1970, he was forced to resign. Polish workers

Czech Counterculture In 1965, students in costume pose on a festival stage with the American poet Allen Ginsberg (seated), whom they have just crowned King of the May. The gathering indicated the influence of Western counterculture on Czechoslovakian youth radicalism, much to the disapproval of the Communist authorities.

and students would continue to search for ways of putting pressure on the regime, and they received considerable support from the one institution in the country that maintained real autonomy during the decades of Communist rule: the Roman Catholic Church.

A much greater confrontation took place to the south. Czechoslovakia had also felt the currents of youth rebellion, with a vibrant student movement that eagerly embraced symbols of avant-garde Western culture. When the American "beat" poet Allen Ginsberg (1926–1997) visited Prague in the spring of 1965, students elected him King of the May. But the Communist authorities quickly expelled Ginsberg from the country, and students who protested openly against the regime found themselves blacklisted from promising careers or even imprisoned.

In January 1968, the Party Central Committee elected the forty-seven-year-old Slovak Alexander Dubček (1921–1992), a former member of the resistance against the pro-Nazi wartime government of Slovakia, as first secretary. He revived a stalled economic reform program, and this in turn encouraged public demands for greater press freedom. Seeking to build popularity for the regime, Dubček made further concessions, and his supporters began to speak of building "socialism with a human face." Dubček insisted on the primacy of the Communist Party and on remaining within the Warsaw Pact, believing that as long as he made these concessions the USSR would have no reason to fear Czechoslovak reform. But he was wrong.

The Soviets, and Communist leaders elsewhere in Eastern Europe, quickly grew concerned that events in Czechoslovakia would infect their own states. They issued steadily more dire warnings; and when the Czechs proved unwilling to rein in the reform movement, they resorted to force. On August 21, some 500,000 Warsaw Pact troops crossed the Czech frontier and quickly overcame a largely passive resistance. The Soviets allowed Dubček to remain in office, a humiliated figurehead, for one more year and then replaced him. For the next twenty years, Czechoslovakia would strike visitors as the most repressed of all the Soviet bloc states.

In both East and West, then, the youth revolutions failed to live up to the often-apocalyptic fears of conservative critics. The year 1968 did not turn out to be another 1848—a year of revolutions setting one another off across Europe like a chain of firecrackers. They did not even, for the most part, lead to the formation of durable new political parties. Instead, in Western Europe, most of the protesting students left their universities peacefully, accepted the jobs that the still-booming economy was offering them, and moved on into the middle classes. In the East, the protestors mostly withdrew into enforced silence, although a significant minority would become leaders of the growing dissident movements of the 1970s.

TOWARD NEW FORMS OF LIBERATION

Yet the events of 1968 had significance nonetheless, particularly in the West. In universities, and more broadly in national educational systems, they marked a partial collapse in old hierarchies, whether of the powerful bureaucrats who controlled French higher education or of the elite public grammar schools in the United Kingdom. Educational systems removed some of the competitive exams that tended, in practice, to benefit social elites. Teachers sought more explicitly to make schools an instrument not just of social mobility but also of social leveling. Even more important, the shaking up of sexual hierarchies led directly to the birth of movements for the rights of women. In 1970, a group of French women, mostly veterans of the student movement and inspired by the earlier works of figures like de Beauvoir, founded the Movement for the Liberation of Women. As we will see, it would flourish in the 1970s, along with similar groups in other Western European states, and build on the important social changes that the post-war period had already introduced to help bring about a permanent transformation of gender roles.

If most veterans of the youth movement greeted the lack of larger political change with acceptance or resignation, a radical minority did not. Some of them, infatuated with Third World guerrilla movements such as the Palestinian Liberation Organization, became convinced that only terrorist violence could shake existing power structures. In Germany, the year 1970 saw two young radicals, Andreas Baader and Ulrike Meinhof, form the terrorist Red Army Faction, which carried out a haphazard program of bombings, shootings, and kidnappings, especially of prominent businessmen and politicians with Nazi pasts. In Italy, the Red Brigades came into being with similar goals. Throughout the 1970s, as we will see, these and other groups would garner attention far out of proportion to their tiny numbers with a series of spectacularly brutal, if often clumsily executed, actions that harkened back to the anarchist terrorism of the late nineteenth century.

Even as they criticized the greed and materialism of Western society, the student rebels continued to behave as good Western consumers, buying Beatles albums and American blue jeans and swigging Coca-Cola. Some of the more profound and sympathetic artistic portrayals of the movement pointed to this contradiction: Jean-Luc Godard's 1967 film *La Chinoise* concentrated on a group of self-described Maoist youth who, very much unlike earlier generations of French students who had risked their lives on the barricades, earnestly debated theories of political violence amid middle-class comfort in Paris.

The student protests of the late 1960s found sharp and lasting expression in more intellectual forms of radicalism that were developing within the universities. Centered around forms of cultural analysis known as **structuralism** and post-structuralism, they raised questions about whether fixed, timeless intellectual frames of reference really exist: was there even such a thing as "human nature" that remained essentially the same across different cultures and time periods? They also explored the ways that forms of knowledge, by determining the boundaries of "truth" and "error," can structure relations of power within societies. These new ideas had particular appeal in a decade when fixed frames of reference seemed everywhere to be collapsing and many forms of authority were under assault.

One key figure was the radical French philosopher Michel Foucault (1926–1984). In several works, he advanced the seductively counterintuitive claim that the great Enlightenment movements for more humane treatments of criminals and the insane in fact represented a facet of increasingly insidious, faceless systems of social repression that forced people into rigid and fixed patterns of behavior and belief. This idea found a powerful echo in the youth movement, among those angrily attacking the prosperous, open, democratic societies of Western Europe as in fact deeply repressive of individual expression. In the 1970s and 1980s, the post-structuralists who emerged out of this intellectual climate would eclipse the Marxists as the dominant current in Western European thought. And they would challenge, more effectively than any other intellectual movement of the twentieth century, the idea that European history was a story of progress that would continue indefinitely into the future.

CONCLUSION

Despite the legacy of wartime devastation, the tensions of the Cold War, and the dislocations and violence of decolonization, the decades after the war were still, overall, ones of prosperity, peace, and stability for the European continent. The Thirty Glorious Years had transformed the Continent almost as much as the previous thirty years of war and destruction. In the lands of the Warsaw Pact, the politics of the Cold War weighed much more heavily than in Western Europe; but even here, living conditions had improved dramatically, not just since the war but in comparison with the pre-war period.

But already in the late 1960s, Europeans were being forced to confront the question of whether they could keep all they had rebuilt since the war, or whether their remarkable recovery would now start to crumble between their fingers. Could the prosperity of the post-war boom continue? Could the new welfare states continue to provide generous benefits? Warning signs were already present in the form of higher inflation and slowing rates of job creation. The new terrorist movements, in combination with the disruptions and protests of 1968, raised the question of whether political stability would continue. And the shadow of the Cold War remained deep and menacing.

[CHAPTER REVIEW]

KEY TERMS

Nuremberg trials (p. 812)
welfare state (p. 813)
Marshall Plan (p. 814)
Cold War (p. 814)
iron curtain (p. 815)
Berlin Airlift (p. 817)

North Atlantic Treaty
  Organization (NATO)
  (p. 817)
Warsaw Pact (p. 817)
baby boom (p. 822)
guest workers (p. 826)

destalinization (p. 827)
Treaty of Rome (p. 830)
Simone de Beauvoir
  (p. 830)
Suez Crisis (p. 832)
National Liberation Front
  (FLN) (p. 832)

Charles de Gaulle (p. 833)
Berlin Wall (p. 834)
Second Vatican Council
  (p. 837)
Troubles (p. 839)
structuralism (p. 841)

REVIEW QUESTIONS

1. In the immediate aftermath of World War II, how did the government's role in the economy change in many European states?

2. How did disagreements over the future of Germany escalate tensions between the Soviet Union and the other Allies?

3. What were the characteristics of the Communist governments that had been imposed in most of Central and Eastern Europe by 1948?

4. What caused the wave of decolonization in the British, Dutch, and French empires?

5. What factors contributed to the spectacular growth in European standards of living in the decades following World War II?

6. Following the Eastern bloc revolts of the 1950s, how did the Soviet Union reassert control over Eastern Europe?

7. Why did post-war Western Europe achieve such unprecedented political stability during this period?

8. What events led to the dissolution of the European empires in the 1950s and 1960s?

9. What challenges to Cold War ideologies arose in the 1960s?

10. What changes in post-war Western society contributed to the emergence of a distinctive, politicized youth culture?

CORE OBJECTIVES

After reading this chapter, you should have a solid understanding of the following core objectives. To strengthen your grasp of the core objectives, use the resources on the Student Site for The West.

- Assess the condition of the nations of Europe in the immediate aftermath of World War II.

- Explain the onset and development of the Cold War.

- Describe the decolonization process around the world in the decades that followed the war.

- Evaluate the economic and political developments that took place in post-war Europe.

- Analyze the social and cultural ferment of the period.

- Trace the evolution of politics and political ideologies in the 1960s and 1970s.

 GO TO inQuizitive TO SEE WHAT YOU'VE LEARNED—AND LEARN WHAT YOU'VE MISSED—WITH PERSONALIZED FEEDBACK ALONG THE WAY.

CHRONOLOGY

1967–1974
Military junta
rules Greece

1972
Munich
Olympics
massacre

1973–1974
Oil shock
1973
Solzhenitsyn's
The Gulag Archipelago
published in the West

1978
Pope John
Paul II
elected

1980
Solidarity forms
in Poland
1981
Martial law
in Poland

April 1986
Chernobyl disaster

October 1990
German reunification
Nov.–Dec. 1989
Velvet Revolution
in Czechoslovakia
November 9, 1989
Fall of the Berlin Wall

1971
Collapse of the
Bretton Woods
system

1975
Helsinki Accords
1976
Spain transitions
to democracy

1979
Soviet Union
invades
Afghanistan
1979
Margaret Thatcher
becomes British
prime minister

1985
Mikhail Gorbachev
rises to power
in Soviet Union

1988
Earthquake
in Armenia

1990s
Wars in
Yugoslavia
June 1991
Boris Yeltsin
elected president
of Russian Federation
August 1991
Coup in Soviet Union

Reunion

EUROPEAN UNIFICATION AND THE END OF THE COLD WAR

1973–1999

O n December 10, 1989, a team of coal stokers working for the Prague metro once again found themselves a man short. For several weeks, fifty-two-year-old Jiři Dienstbier had largely neglected his job. Now he sent word that he was quitting, effective immediately. He explained that an interesting new employment opportunity had come up for him: foreign minister of Czechoslovakia. Dienstbier, a prominent former journalist and dissident whom the Communist regime had forced to work as a stoker since the end of a prison term seven years earlier, was suddenly part of the first Czechoslovak government since 1948 that was not dominated by Communists. Just a week later, he would stand on the Czechoslovak-Austrian border with Austrian foreign minister Alois Mock, the two men together grasping a huge pair of wire cutters, and snip through the strands of barbed wire separating the countries—literally tearing down the iron curtain. Twelve days after that, the most famous Czechoslovak dissident of all, writer Václav Havel, would take the place long held by career Stalinists and become the country's president.

Jiři Dienstbier's rapid job change stands as one of the more remarkable events of the remarkable year 1989. But the truly remarkable thing is that by the time it occurred, it seemed almost humdrum. The year had begun with the Hungarian Communist Party allowing true opposition parties to form. In the spring, the Polish government agreed to allow partially free elections, which took place in June and resulted in the Communists' crushing

Berlin Wall A crowd of people sits atop the Berlin Wall on November 10, 1989, the day after the Wall fell.

SEASONS OF DISCONTENT

In the early 1970s, this favorable turn of events seemed almost unimaginable. Indeed, as the decade began, European democracy and prosperity seemed far more fragile than resurgent.

COUPS AND TERRORISM

Spain and Portugal remained under ineffective, authoritarian right-wing rule. Greece had retreated violently from democracy after a 1967 military coup. The new junta of conservative generals there arrested an estimated 8,000 political opponents and banned an almost comic range of supposed threats to Christian Greek culture, including the works of Aristophanes and the academic field of sociology. In Northern Ireland, the continuing Troubles saw terrorist attacks and heavily armed soldiers on the streets of Belfast. And in West Germany and Italy, the home-grown terrorists of the Red Army Faction and Red Brigades carried out a series of spectacular assaults on prominent figures in business and politics. In 1978, a former Italian prime minister was found shot dead in the trunk of a parked car, two months after his kidnapping by

Munich Olympics Massacre One of the terrorists looks down from the apartment in Munich's Olympic Village where nine Israeli athletes were being held hostage on September 5, 1972.

defeat. The following months only saw events accelerate, with the most momentous of all occurring on November 9: the opening of the Berlin Wall. In mid-November, Czechoslovakia's so-called Velvet Revolution began.

These events, followed two years later by the collapse and breakup of the Soviet Union, remain the most important in European history since 1945. They involved, to be sure, considerable economic dislocation and hardship. They also led directly to the violent breakup of Yugoslavia and to a series of Balkan wars that took hundreds of thousands of lives in the 1990s. Yet overall, the end of Communism and the Soviet Empire took place with relatively little bloodshed and oppression. In a short time, they brought the former states of Eastern Europe toward the unprecedented peace and prosperity enjoyed by their Western neighbors since the immediate post-war period.

Today more than 510 million Europeans live in a twenty-eight-member Union that covers nearly the entire continent west of the former Soviet Union; and despite many challenges, they still enjoy a remarkable degree of comfort and freedom. As we will see in the next chapter, today these achievements seem less durable than they did in the early years of the twenty-first century, but they remain impressive. The events of 1989 both reflect the

the Red Brigades. Both groups were eventually broken up by police forces.

The event that best symbolized the 1970s' seasons of discontent was the terrorist massacre at the 1972 summer Olympic Games in Munich. For West Germany, the chance to host the Olympics for the first time since the infamous 1936 Berlin Games had initially seemed a chance to demonstrate the country's full return to the company of civilized nations. But on September 5, a team of Palestinian terrorists attacked the Olympic Village, killed two members of the Israeli team, and took nine others hostage. An attempted rescue by the West German authorities went horribly wrong, and in a chaotic confrontation at a military airport all the hostages died. The games would now be remembered for an act of terrorism and the murder of Jews on German soil.

THE OIL SHOCK OF 1973–1974

The next year, strife in the Middle East contributed to European discontent in a more lasting manner and showed that European countries were becoming more economically vulnerable to global events beyond their control. In October 1973, Egypt and Syria launched a surprise attack on Israel during the Yom Kippur holiday, and the United States began an intensive effort to resupply Israel, enraging the Arab states. Within a week, the leading Arab oil exporters declared a complete embargo of oil shipments to the United States, followed by a general cutback in oil production. Over the next two years, the price of crude oil on the world market nearly quadrupled to a then-unimaginable $12 per barrel. Just twenty years before, Western Europe had mostly relied on coal for energy; but now oil, primarily imported from the Middle East, supplied over 60 percent of its energy needs, and the **oil shock** caused serious economic damage. Several European states took drastic measures to cut consumption, including the rationing of gasoline.

Worse, the shock came at a moment of particular economic fragility. In 1971, the Bretton Woods system, which had pegged major currencies to the price of gold and the U.S. dollar at fixed rates, had fallen apart. The value of most major currencies fell, contributing to inflation. The oil shock drove many countries into recession without reducing inflation, a deadly economic combination that afflicted the Continent for many years. Stock markets crashed across the Western world in 1973–74. In London the major stock index fell by 73 percent. Inflation

in Britain reached a height of nearly 27 percent per year in 1974–75. Similar patterns developed over much of the Continent.

WELFARE STATES UNDER PRESSURE

Even before 1971, the expansive welfare states created after World War II had been coming under increased pressure. With generous pension plans in place, European workers were retiring earlier, while advances in health care meant they now lived longer. In France, many workers for the national railroads retired before age fifty-five, even though few of their jobs still required hard physical labor. And at the same time, birthrates across Western Europe were steeply dropping as a result of the cultural changes discussed in the last chapter, including the decline in religious observance and the increased use of birth control. This meant that fewer workers would be available in the future to pay into the system and cover the swelling costs of pensions. A birthrate of 2.1 children per woman is needed for a population to remain stable. By the 1980s, in West Germany the figure had fallen to just 1.4. By the end of the century, in Italy it would hit 1.3. The economic crisis of 1973–74 signaled that the mechanisms Western European states had used to finance welfare-state benefits were no longer sufficient. But it took a long time for European politicians to understand this shift and develop responses to it.

This economic crisis hit most sharply in Great Britain, where after the war unions, industry, and government had developed effective forms of cooperation, and where entitlements such as health care, public education, and mass transit had expanded broadly. Now threats to strike by the country's powerful trade union movement made it difficult for industries, especially nationalized ones, to cut even obsolescent jobs or to reduce benefits for their workers. Although particularly hostile to Edward Heath's Conservative government of 1970–74, the unions came into conflict with Heath's Labour successors as well.

By 1976, the economic crisis in Britain had grown so severe that stringent austerity measures were necessary to restrain inflation—measures that lowered overall economic demand and thereby forced firms to lay off workers. The unions reacted by staging increasingly disruptive strikes. In the city of Liverpool, even gravediggers walked off the job, leading cadavers literally to pile up in the morgues. In many cases, the government gave in to the unions, providing wage increases of as much as

Public Housing Built during the period 1962–75 south of Naples, Italy, the Vele di Scampia housing project was intended as a utopian community. By the 1980s, however, the tower blocks were in poor shape, with many residents living in slum conditions amid drug trafficking and gang violence.

20 percent, which only added to inflationary pressures. Finally, in March 1979 Labour lost a no-confidence vote in Parliament and agreed to hold new elections.

The most visible symbol of the fraying welfare state was public housing. In the 1960s and early 1970s, Socialist and Conservative governments alike were continuing to sponsor the construction of millions of units of cheap residential housing for poor and lower-middle-class families. These mostly took the form of huge agglomerations of Bauhaus-style apartment blocks on the outskirts of major cities, owned and managed by the government. In France, the period saw more than 6 million people move into such housing units, and in Britain, by the mid-1970s, one-third of the population lived in them.

Although these new structures often represented a great improvement over their inhabitants' previous accommodations, critics denounced their stark, unlovely architecture and lack of greenery. More serious, rates of crime and unemployment in these new urban areas quickly rose high above national averages. By 1982, the British rock band The Jam could sing: "They were gonna build communities / It was going to be pie in the sky / But the piss stench hallways and broken down lifts / Say the planners' dream went wrong." Beyond housing, public systems of health care, education, and mass transit remained in place, with overwhelming support from the populations, but they too showed increasing strain as budgets tightened.

SOUTHERN EUROPE'S BUMPY ROAD TO DEMOCRACY

In southern Europe, politics and society in the 1970s moved in a more hopeful direction, but haltingly and at high cost. In Greece, the rule of the military junta ended in 1974, but in the context of a bloody dispute over the eastern Mediterranean island of Cyprus, where the Greek majority and Turkish minority had shared uneasily in a common government since independence fourteen years before. In the summer of 1974, Cypriot Greek officers, with the support of the Athens junta, staged a coup, triggering a Turkish invasion and occupation of the north of the island, which remains divided to this day between the Greek Cypriot state and a so-called Turkish Republic of Northern Cyprus recognized only by Turkey.

Even worse strife, linked to decolonization, was greeting the return of democracy to Portugal. Unlike France and Britain, Portugal had never given up its major African colonies, and by the early 1970s it found itself embroiled in increasingly costly struggles against insurgents in Angola and Mozambique. As many as one-quarter of adult Portuguese males fought in Africa during the 1960s and early 1970s, and the country lost a higher proportion of soldiers than the United States did in Vietnam. The aged dictator António de Oliveira Salazar (1889–1970) died in 1970, but his regime lingered for another four years until finally left-wing military officers staged a coup. There followed a period of violence in which radical military factions, allied with the Communist Party, threatened to seize power. Finally, in 1976, a democratic government prevailed in free elections and consolidated its authority.

Dictatorship also finally came to an end in Spain. In 1969, the seventy-six-year-old Francisco Franco (1892–1975) had promised to restore the monarchy, and he named as his successor the young prince Juan Carlos, grandson of the last king. Franco did so on condition that Juan Carlos swear to preserve the ultraconservative regime and society that he had built up since the Civil War of the 1930s. When Franco died in November 1975, Juan Carlos quickly broke this promise, legalizing the Socialist and Communist parties and allowing free elections.

Yet even in Spain the transition from dictatorship brought significant turmoil. Basque and Catalan nationalist movements demanded and received considerable autonomy for their regions in northern and northeastern Spain, while the Basque terrorist group ETA continued to carry out bomb attacks and assassinations. Most dangerously, in 1981 renegade officers loyal to Franco's memory took over the Parliament in an attempted coup. But they had little popular support, and the new king gained enormous popularity by insisting, in a television broadcast, on support for Spanish democracy. The coup failed, and Spain has remained a stable democracy ever since.

SHIFTS IN THE POST-WAR SOCIAL CONSENSUS

During the three decades after the end of World War II, the Western European consensus about the proper way to organize a society had seemed almost unchallenged. Its principal tenets were a generous, all-inclusive welfare state, nationalization of major industries, tax policies aimed at a limited redistribution of income, and a significant role for government in managing a country's economy. Economists generally argued that governments could maintain high levels of employment and growth by careful management of the money supply and interest rates, coupled with ambitious spending programs where necessary. Even conservative political leaders in Western Europe did little, if anything, to dismantle the extensive welfare states and planning mechanisms created earlier in the century in part as a result of wartime pressures. By the late 1970s, the top marginal income tax rate in Great Britain stood at 83 percent.

But the consensus was never total. In 1944, the Austrian-born economist Friedrich von Hayek, a refugee from Hitler in Britain, had published a book entitled *The Road to Serfdom,* which insisted that central planning threatened individual freedoms. During the 1950s and 1960s, Hayek's followers developed an extensive critique of close government management and regulation of economies. These **neoliberals**, as their critics would come to call them, advocated something closer to the classical laissez-faire liberalism of the nineteenth century. Through the end of the 1960s, they had relatively little political influence outside the United States—and even there, little outside of the Republican Party. But in May 1979, in Britain, this all changed.

MARGARET THATCHER'S ATTACK ON THE WELFARE STATE

If the British elections that month made headlines around the world, it was less because of the Conservative victory than because, for the first time, a woman had become head of a major European government. But **Margaret Thatcher** had not campaigned on a platform of woman's rights. Her first cabinet consisted of herself and twenty-four men. Her real significance lay elsewhere. Born in 1925, the daughter of a stern Methodist grocer, she won election to Parliament as a Conservative in 1959. An outsider to the party's cozy, wealthy establishment on account of both her sex and her class origins, she developed considerable scorn for it. Thatcher was temperamentally a radical, who once declared that "there is no such thing as Society. There are individual men and women."

Upon her election, she quickly made clear her intention to dismantle the British welfare state and managed economy as they had existed since the war, even if this entailed a very high social cost. Her government slashed income tax rates and began auctioning off state-run industries such as telecommunications and aerospace to the private sector. She also started an ambitious program of selling public housing units to the people who lived in them, arguing that people would take better care of homes they actually owned. In the midst of a deep recession, these actions proved deeply unpopular, and moderate Conservatives urged her to reverse her policies. Speaking to a party conference, she refused to budge: "You turn if you want to. The lady's not for turning."

Thatcher was bolstered by an economic recovery that began in 1982 and also by an unexpected military conflict that developed when Argentina seized the British-owned Falkland Islands in the South Atlantic. A British naval task force quickly defeated the Argentinians, and Thatcher's approval rating nearly doubled. Meanwhile, the Labour opposition underwent a destructive split, which Thatcher capitalized on to hold an election in June 1983. Labour refused to modify its long-established policies, including a demand for "common ownership of the means of production, distribution and exchange." One party member called this platform "the longest suicide note in history," and the Conservatives, despite seeing their share of the vote decline slightly, won a massive parliamentary majority.

During her second term in office, Thatcher grew even more ambitious and confrontational, fully earning her nickname of The Iron Lady. In 1984, when the National Coal Board decided to close inefficient mines and put some 20,000 miners out of work, even as unemployment rates remained high, the National Union of Mineworkers went on strike in protest. But Thatcher refused to make concessions, while railing against the union leaders as "the enemy within." After nearly a year, the miners surrendered. Thatcher won other battles with unions and permanently weakened the British labor movement. She also tried to weaken local governments, in part by replacing their funding with a deeply unpopular, nationally assessed poll tax. Her government deregulated London's financial markets and opened them up to world competition in what financiers referred to as the 1986 Big Bang. Finally, in 1990, Conservative leaders concluded that her policies—especially the poll tax—and her abrasive personal style had become liabilities, and forced her out of office. But the political transformation she had carried out proved enduring. The Labour Party would only regain power in 1997, after abandoning its commitment to public ownership, tacitly accepting many of Thatcher's neoliberal reforms.

IDEOLOGICAL SHIFTS

Elsewhere in Western Europe, the retreat from the post-war consensus was less dramatic. In Sweden, the Social Democrats lost control of the government in 1976 for the first time in forty years, but the new, centrist governing coalition did little to challenge Sweden's formidable welfare state. In West Germany, the government remained in Social Democratic hands through the 1970s and early 1980s, and even after a shift back to the right West German social welfare programs remained essentially intact. Despite neoliberal prophecies of doom, the Scandinavian and West German economies remained robust. And strong growth allowed these states to continue to support their swelling numbers of retirees.

COMMUNISM IN DECLINE Yet the political complexion of Western Europe had nonetheless changed for good, as shown not only by Thatcher's reforms but also by the decline and transformation of Communist political parties. In southern Europe, the Communists attempted to retain their electoral position by renouncing their Stalinist pasts and fidelity to the Soviet Union, and promising to move toward a socialist economy by persuasion rather than force. The Italian Enrico Berlinguer became the embodiment of a so-called Eurocommunism that even tried to reconcile with the Catholic Church. But even he could not stop a steady erosion of popular support after 1976 as the traditional industrial working class shrank in the transition to a post-industrial economy. In France, where the Communist Party refused to budge from its Stalin-era policies, support fell dramatically. To the dismay of mainstream European parties, many Communist voters did not turn toward the center but instead defected to the extreme right parties, which, as we will see, pandered to white working-class resentment of expanding immigrant populations.

Communism was also rapidly losing its appeal to Western European intellectuals—even in countries such as France, where so many leading thinkers and artists, such as Jean-Paul Sartre and the poet Louis Aragon, had belonged to the party or supported its goals. The year 1973 saw the hugely successful publication in French translation of Alexander Solzhenitsyn's devastating portrait of Soviet repression, *The Gulag Archipelago,* which, like his earlier *One Day in the Life of Ivan Denisovitch,* drew on his own experiences. Over the next few years, a succession of young French "New Philosophers" published strong, if not particularly original, attacks on Soviet totalitarianism, also to considerable acclaim. The influential historian François Furet worked to resuscitate a native French liberal tradition. In short, by the early 1980s it had become clear that while social and economic divisions had hardly disappeared from the European scene, orthodox Marxism, as a means for addressing them, no longer attracted much support from European politicians and intellectuals.

FRANCE'S "PARENTHESIS IN THE HISTORY OF SOCIALISM"

Despite these shifts, it initially seemed as if the political currents in France were turning in a very different direction from those in Britain. In 1981, the left-wing Socialist opposition took power for the first time since the 1950s. But the new French leader was no doctrinaire leftist. François Mitterrand (1916–1996), a cultured, sly, long-time politician who enjoyed the nickname The Sphinx, came from a right-wing Catholic milieu in southwestern France and had even flirted with a far-right terrorist group as a student in the 1930s. Only after the war did he become a fixture of the moderate left and eventually forge a "common program" with the fossilized French Communists.

The Mitterrand presidency initially seemed to signal a renewal of French socialism. Upon the 1981 election victory, as ecstatic supporters danced in the streets of Paris, Mitterrand visited the Pantheon, burial place of the "great men of the fatherland." (In one of his last acts as president in 1995, Mitterrand arranged for the first woman, Marie Curie, to be interred there. As of this writing, there are three and soon to be four: in addition to Curie, two were active in the French Resistance during World War II, and the fourth is Simone Veil, Holocaust survivor and minister of health who fought to legalize abortion in France.) At the Pantheon Mitterand laid red roses on the tombs of three of his left-wing idols, including the nineteenth-century abolitionist Victor Schoelcher—an apparent sign of his commitment to serving an increasingly multiracial population. Over the next year, his government (which included four Communist ministers) nationalized numerous large banks and firms. But these actions panicked French

Mitterrand's Paris The president's building projects included I. M. Pei's glass pyramid, installed at the Louvre Museum in 1989. Many Parisians initially saw the structure as ostentatious and unfitting for the site.

financial circles, leading to an abrupt worsening of the French economy.

Scarcely a year after taking office, Mitterrand executed an almost complete policy U-turn, implementing austerity measures, introducing income-tax cuts, and expressing support for private enterprise. Mitterrand himself claimed he was simply introducing a "parenthesis in the history of socialism"—but in fact the parenthesis never closed. And despite Mitterrand's nominal socialism, he grew increasingly regal in his manner during his fourteen years in office, concentrating much of his energy on massive, controversial construction projects such as the gleaming glass and steel pyramid designed by I. M. Pei in the courtyard of the Louvre Museum.

CULTURAL OPENINGS

President Mitterrand intended his grand projects to leave as great a mark on his capital city as those of some of his royal and imperial predecessors, such as Louis XIV and Napoleon Bonaparte. But the projects had little in common with theirs besides grandiosity, and few mustered much public support. Critics complained that European cities were turning into giant museums that no longer added to the glories of the past. Tellingly, the most successful of Mitterrand's projects, the addition to the Louvre Museum, drew millions of new spectators to view collections that dated almost entirely from before the twentieth century.

THE ARTS There was a settled, institutional quality to much of cultural life throughout Western Europe during the period. As had been the case for centuries, relatively few artists and writers managed to earn a living from their work. Now, in place of private or princely patrons, financial support mostly came from government fellowships or teaching positions in universities. No fresh artistic and literary movement or style developed that could compare in coherence, originality, or broad appeal with romanticism or modernism. Some figures, especially in architecture, embraced a post-modern style that resisted definition but

A POST-MODERN SKYSCRAPER

The Messerturm (Market Tower) in Frankfurt, Germany, was completed in 1991, and for several years claimed the title of the tallest building in Europe. The architect, Helmut Jahn (1940–), was born in Nuremberg, Germany, and grew up watching the city rebuild itself in the wake of World War II. He has studied and practiced architecture in both Germany and the United States, and his work is representative of the post-modern style of art and architecture that has in many ways characterized late-twentieth-century art.

This iconic skyscraper is based on the elements of a classical Greek column: with a plinth at the bottom, column shaft in the center, and pinnacle on top. In this case, the pinnacle is a glass pyramid similar to the Louvre Pyramid by I. M. Pei, blending classical and ancient architectural elements in a single, post-modern structure. The exterior façade is constructed of stones quarried in Sweden, polished in Italy, and assembled on the Danube—an international effort designed to look like the traditional Frankfurt sandstone used in many of the city's major buildings for centuries.

QUESTIONS FOR ANALYSIS

1. What elements of post-modernism are visible in Jahn's design?
2. How does the Messerturm reference classical and ancient motifs in its architecture?
3. In what ways does the Messerturm strive to be a primarily German building, and in what ways is it a composite of international efforts?

that usually involved a playful, ironic reintroduction of classical motifs into works that remained fundamentally abstract in form, such as the 1991 Messerturm (Market Tower) in Frankfurt. The so-called New Wave of cinematic *auteurs* such as Jean-Luc Godard who had attracted such attention in the 1950s and 1960s had few clear heirs in subsequent decades, while symphonies and operas overwhelmingly preferred the classical canon to the performance of new works.

In the arts, including film and television, censorship declined rapidly in this period. In 1972, the Italian director Bernardo Bertolucci (1940–) provoked a scandal with his film *Last Tango in Paris*, which graphically depicted the sexual relationship between a middle-aged American and a young French woman. But the film was widely distributed, and by the end of the century similarly graphic depictions of sexuality were commonplace in film and on cable networks. By contrast, the Communist governments of the Eastern bloc continued to impose much stronger restrictions on sexual expression of all sorts.

Many important cultural developments of the period derived from the neighborhoods of large cities where immigrant populations, especially from Africa and the Caribbean, helped to generate distinctive musical, visual, and literary styles. Events like the annual Notting Hill Carnival in London attracted hundreds of thousands of visitors each year to its vibrant displays of Caribbean dancing and musical performances. These developments showed that in culture, just as much as in economics, Europe was growing less isolated from larger patterns of global interaction.

GENDER AND SEXUALITY

Overall, the most important cultural changes of the late twentieth century were linked to changing attitudes toward gender and sexuality. The feminist movements that had taken on such strength in the 1960s continued to evolve and to push further demands for equality. One of their principal aims was the legalization of abortion. Already in 1967, Great Britain had legalized abortion under certain circumstances, including preserving the physical or mental health of the mother. Many other countries, including France and Italy, followed in the 1970s. In Spain, after Franco's death, the Parliament legalized contraception and adultery, which the law had previously forbidden.

Women's professional opportunities continued to expand, although unevenly across the Continent. By 1990, women constituted at least one-third of the members of Parliament in all of the Scandinavian states, but under 10 percent in France and Britain. In response, French feminists succeeded in passing a law, in 2000, mandating that political parties field equal numbers of male and female candidates in most elections or pay fines. The leading parties, however, often chose to pay the fines. In nearly every European country by the year 2000, women made up at least 40 percent of the labor force.

Also by the year 2000, laws against homosexual behavior had almost entirely vanished from the books in most of Europe. Homosexuals, while still disproportionately victims of hate crimes, achieved new levels of toleration and visibility. Prominent intellectuals and artists such as the philosopher Michel Foucault (1926–1984) and the singer Elton John (1947–) no longer hid their sexuality. In 1999, France allowed homosexual couples to enter into formal civil unions, but same-sex marriage would not receive acceptance in Europe until the twenty-first century.

EXTERNAL AND INTERNAL PRESSURES ON THE EASTERN BLOC

Even as these cultural differences between the Western and Eastern blocs were growing, their political relations were again turning confrontational. In the 1970s, following the end of the Vietnam War, U.S. president Richard Nixon had reached out to Communist China and also helped initiate a process of **détente** (relaxation of tension) with the Soviet Union. The two countries signed trade, sports, and arms control agreements and began to reduce their nuclear arsenals. Regular summits continued through the 1970s. But in 1979, the Soviet Union invaded Afghanistan on its southern border so as to shore up the wobbling new Communist government there, and quickly became embroiled in a costly struggle against Muslim insurgents. The U.S. government under President Jimmy Carter reacted strongly. It reinstated draft registration for young men, boycotted the 1980 Moscow Olympics, and moved ahead with a plan to station medium-range nuclear missiles in Great Britain and West Germany to counter the Soviet deployment of similar weapons.

RONALD REAGAN AND THE EUROPEAN PEACE MOVEMENT

In 1981, Ronald Reagan succeeded Carter as president. A long-time advocate of "rolling back" Communism rather than simply containing it, Reagan raised anxiety in much of Western Europe by denouncing the Soviet Union as an "evil empire," vastly increasing the U.S. defense budget, and providing substantial aid to the Afghan insurgents and to right-wing guerrillas in Central America. He also continued the deployment in Europe of medium-range missiles, which had the strong support of both the British and West German governments. Later in his term, he promoted the development of the so-called Star Wars missile shield to defend the United States against Soviet ballistic missile attacks.

The peace movement in Western Europe, which had declined after the end of the Vietnam War, quickly revived in response to these developments. In Britain, large anti-nuclear protest marches took place, and a permanent Women's Peace Camp was founded outside the gates of the Royal Air Force base at Greenham Common, one of the sites for the new missiles. In Germany, a powerful environmental movement, which had already spun off an important new political party known as the Greens, embraced the cause of nuclear disarmament and drew strength from it in turn. West German protest marches in the early 1980s attracted as many as a million people. Berlin, the focal point of Cold War tensions, ironically became the center of opposition to the missile deployment. In the West Berlin district of Kreuzberg, wedged up against the Berlin Wall, street murals portrayed Reagan as a cowboy with a giant missile protruding from his trousers,

while leaflets and posters claimed the deployment would lead to a devastating nuclear exchange on Western European soil. But in the end, the deployment took place.

DISSIDENT MOVEMENTS IN THE EAST

The peace movement had little equivalent on the other side of the iron curtain, despite the valiant attempts of some East German Lutheran churches to organize one. Instead, the most important political developments in the Eastern bloc during the 1970s involved the slow, halting revival of **dissident movements**. In 1974, the Soviet government sent its most prominent dissident writer, Solzhenitsyn (who had won the Nobel Prize for Literature in 1970), into exile abroad. Andrei Sakharov (1921–1989), a noted physicist and father of the Soviet hydrogen bomb, managed to avoid this fate, but his protests against the invasion of Afghanistan led to his arrest and internal exile. Sakharov's celebrity at least ensured him a measure of protection, but the secret police brutally hounded lesser-known dissidents, throwing thousands into labor camps or psychiatric hospitals. It also persecuted Russian Jews who were demanding the right to emigrate to Israel.

The Soviet satellite states, meanwhile, followed different courses on dissent. In Romania and Bulgaria, what little dissident activity that emerged was ruthlessly suppressed. In the former, party leader and president Nicolae Ceaușescu deliberately pursued a maverick, independent foreign policy, and in return the Western powers generally turned a blind eye to his increasingly baroque domestic tyranny. Like despots of legend, he razed large sections of Bucharest to build an elaborate palace for himself, while imposing drastic austerity policies on ordinary Romanians so as to pay off the country's foreign debt. He filled so many positions in the government with relatives that Romanians, referring to Stalin's slogan of "Socialism in a Single Country," joked that Ceaușescu wanted "Socialism in a Single Family."

The East German dissident movement remained weak as well, but for a different reason. After decades of relatively little official contact between the two Germanies, in the early 1970s West German chancellor Willy Brandt (1913–1992), on the view that both states would benefit from a stable relationship, began a series of cautious moves toward reconciliation and coexistence that came to be known as Ostpolitik ("East Policy"). By the early 1980s, West Germany's conservative Christian Democrats had come to agree, and in 1987 they even invited East German leader Erich Honecker (1912–1994) to visit his native

Greenham Common Members of the Women's Peace Camp at Greenham Common in 1983 participate in an "embrace the base" action, joining hands to encircle the perimeter of the Royal Air Force base. The colorful, hand-sewn banners on the fence became emblematic of the camp.

THE INDIVIDUAL AGAINST THE STATE

The social and cultural upheavals of the late twentieth century from both the left and the right emphasized the importance of individual freedom over the strictures of society and government. The economic malaise of the 1970s contributed to a questioning of the power of the state to manage the economy, helping lead to conservative governments in the West and contributing to the eventual collapse of Communism in the East. Dissident movements, such as the Czechoslovakian Charter 77 group led in part by future president Václav Havel, criticized Communist governments for betraying both individual freedoms and the ideals of socialism. Meanwhile, Margaret Thatcher led British Conservatives in attacking what they saw as state overreach and advocated a return to laissez-faire economic principles. Though differing in ideology, both movements aimed to prioritize the needs of the individual over state control.

Václav Havel, from "The Power of the Powerless"

In this passage from a 1978 essay, Havel describes the necessity of dissent within the Communist system.

A spectre is haunting eastern Europe: the spectre of what in the West is called "dissent." This spectre has not appeared out of thin air. It is a natural and inevitable consequence of the present historical phase of the system it is haunting.... The system has become so ossified politically that there is practically no way for such nonconformity to be implemented within its official structures....

...This is why life in the system is so thoroughly permeated with hypocrisy and lies: government by bureaucracy is called popular government; the working class is enslaved in the name of the working class; the complete degradation of the individual is presented as his or her ultimate liberation; depriving people of information is called making it available; the use of power to manipulate is called the public control of power, and the arbitrary abuse of power is called observing the legal code; the repression of culture is called its development; the expansion of imperial influence is presented as support for the oppressed; the lack of free expression becomes the highest form of freedom; farcical elections become the highest form of democracy; banning independent thought becomes the most scientific of world views; military occupation becomes fraternal assistance....

...If living within the truth is an elementary starting point for every attempt made by people to oppose the alienating pressure of the system, if it is the only meaningful basis of any independent act of political import... it is difficult to imagine that even manifest "dissent" could have any other basis than the service of truth, the truthful life and the attempt to make room for the genuine aims of life.

Margaret Thatcher, from "Speech in Finchley"

On May 2, 1979, Thatcher gave a speech to constituents in Finchley, the area of North London that she represented in Parliament. In this excerpt, she presents "independence of the individual" as a favorable alternative to the "big government" of the Labour Party.

...We stand for the independence of the individual, for the fundamental freedom of the individual....I've travelled many miles, visiting many constituencies, and we find everywhere we go that there is an overwhelming feeling throughout the country that it's time for a change. People say, "Look, we can't go on like this. We can't go on as we are. We don't like the decline in Britain. We don't like our neighbors overseas doing very much better than we are. We don't like it that Britain has fallen in the prestige of nations." And so frequently they say to me, "Give us back our national pride."...

...We must remember that Labour has ruled the country for eleven out of fifteen years....It's a philosophy of big government, big battalions, big taxation, big bureaucracy, until the individual says, "Goodness me, do I count for anything? Can I make any of my own decisions? Am I entitled to keep the fruits of my own labour in my own pocket to look after my own children?" And today, people long to be protected from the big battalions, and the world over there is a revolt against heavy taxation by government, there is a revolt against big government, and it is happening too in this country....

...Being Conservative, we found our policies on fundamental individual rights, the rights of families, the rights of men and women and their families, to lead their own lives in their own way with minimum interference by the state, but under a rule of law, under the firm protection of the government and the independence of the judges. So we see the process of recovery in Britain, the recovery of Britain, as the work of individuals.

QUESTIONS FOR ANALYSIS

1. According to Havel, why is dissent based in "the service of truth"?
2. According to Thatcher, how had the welfare state, as represented by the Labour Party, stifled the individual?
3. What are the similarities and differences between Havel's and Thatcher's interpretations of individual freedom?

Sources: Václav Havel, "The Power of the Powerless," trans. Paul Wilson, *International Journal of Politics* 15, no. 3/4 (London: 1985–1986), pp. 23, 30–31, 67; Margaret Thatcher, "Speech in Finchley" (May 2, 1979), Margaret Thatcher Foundation (website), www.margaretthatcher.org/document/104072.

western Germany. West Germany began to pay substantial sums to East Germany to "buy" dissidents and move them to the West, leaving relatively few opposition leaders behind the Wall for long.

In Hungary, and especially in Czechoslovakia, stronger dissident groups slowly emerged. They took particular advantage of the fact that in 1975 the Soviet bloc had joined with the Western states to sign the **Helsinki Accords**, pledging to respect current European borders—including the wartime Soviet annexations—but also fundamental human rights. Initially denounced by many Western conservatives as a propaganda victory for the Soviets, Helsinki in fact gave Eastern bloc dissidents a tool for holding their own governments to account. In January 1977, a group of dissidents in Czechoslovakia published a manifesto—soon called Charter 77—that denounced the Czech government for failing to live up to the Helsinki Accords. More broadly, the Accords marked a moment when states and international organizations increasingly oriented their foreign policies around issues of human rights, claiming the right to act on behalf of people throughout the world in the name of these rights.

"SOLIDARITY" IN POLAND

The biggest changes in the Soviet bloc took place in Poland. In 1976, large-scale protests forced the Communist government to repeal planned food price increases. Two years later, Polish cardinal Karol Wojtyła unexpectedly won election as Pope John Paul II (r. 1978–2005). A charismatic personality as well as a forceful theological conservative, John Paul drew huge, adoring crowds when he visited Poland in 1979, and he greatly strengthened the position of the Church as an autonomous force in Polish society.

These events emboldened ordinary Poles to defy the government, and in the summer of 1980, when the government attempted to raise the price of staple goods such as meat and gasoline, a wave of strikes broke out. In the port city of Gdańsk, striking shipbuilders formed a trade union they named **Solidarity**, led by a then-unknown electrician named Lech Wałęsa, and branches quickly spread across the country. The government retreated in disarray, and in November it tried to ease the ongoing unrest by giving Solidarity unofficial recognition. There followed thirteen astonishing months in which Solidarity, under Lech Wałęsa's charismatic leadership and in partnership with dissident intellectuals and a large section of the Polish clergy, effectively carved out a semi-free civil society in the middle of a Soviet satellite state.

Solidarity Lech Wałęsa takes up a microphone to address a crowd of workers during the shipyard strikes at Gdańsk in the summer of 1980.

All too aware of the suppression of reform movements in Hungary in 1956 and Czechoslovakia in 1968, the leaders of Solidarity proceeded with caution. They did not demand free elections or the dismantling of the socialist system. Nonetheless, the Communist authorities soon came to see the situation as dangerously unstable. General Wojciech Jaruzelski, who became prime minister in early 1981, felt that Solidarity would inevitably end up challenging Communist control and possibly provoke a Soviet invasion. To prevent this, in December 1981 his government outlawed the union, arrested its leaders, and imposed martial law. The crackdown engendered outrage in the West and contributed to increasing tensions between the blocs.

CRACKS IN THE EASTERN BLOC

By the mid-1980s, the rigidity of the Communist systems, to which the previous chapter already drew attention, had reached crisis proportions. In each of the Eastern European states, as in the USSR, the Communists had accomplished a rapid industrialization and urbanization of society. They had also managed to provide employment and basic services—including housing, health care, child care, elder care, and education—to virtually all their citizens. But they had proven unable to put in place the post-industrial shifts to a service and consumer economy that had taken place in the West. Inefficiency and corruption affected the distribution of even basic consumer goods, leading to endless lines for such commodities as bread, fruit, and toilet paper. While Eastern bloc

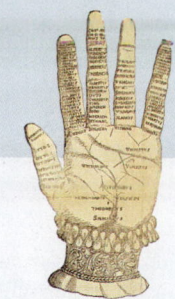

THE POWER OF LIPSTICK

In the 1970s and 1980s, chronic shortages and long lines for basic consumer goods were commonplace in Eastern Europe. Cosmetics and Western clothing were luxuries, difficult to obtain. In her essay "Make-Up and Other Crucial Questions" (1992), the Croatian journalist Slavenka Drakulić (1949–) describes the lengths to which Yugoslavian women went to appear fashionable, adding a personal dimension to the struggles of planned economies. Official Communist ideology dismissed consumerism as frivolous and decadent, yet, as Drakulić suggests, the wearing of lipstick or jeans could be integral to individual expression. And to present oneself as an individual in a collective state was not only difficult but potentially subversive. Drakulić blends a feminist critique of beauty standards for women with an observation of the Communist system, revealing the power of having control over one's own appearance.

The young communist states at that time—and until they ceased to exist—had more important tasks than producing make-up, tasks like rebuilding countries devastated by war, like industrialization and electrification. …Aesthetics were considered a superficial, "bourgeois" invention.…A nicely dressed woman was subject to suspicion, sometimes even investigation…

…Without a choice of cosmetics and clothes, with bad food and hard work and no spare time, it wasn't at all hard to create the special kind of uniformity that comes out of an equal distribution of poverty and the neglect of people's real needs. There was no chance for individualism—for women or men.…

To avoid uniformity, you have to work very hard: you have to bribe a salesgirl, wait in line for some imported product, buy bluejeans on the black market and pay your whole month's salary for them; you have to hoard cloth and sew it, imitating the pictures in glamorous foreign magazines.…To be yourself, to cultivate individualism, to perceive yourself as an individual in a mass society, is dangerous. You might become living proof that the system is failing. Make-up and fashion are crucial because they are political.…

Walking the streets of Eastern European cities, one can easily see that women there look tired and older than they really are. They are poorly dressed, overweight, and flabby. Only the very young are slim and beautiful, with the healthy look and grace that go with youth. For me, they are the most beautiful in the world because I know what is behind the serious, worried faces, the unattended hair, the unmanicured nails; behind a pale pink lipstick that doesn't exactly go with the color of their eyes, or hair, or dress.…They deserve more respect than they get, simply because just being a woman—not to mention a beauty—is a constant battle against the way the whole system works.

QUESTIONS FOR ANALYSIS

1. Why are such seemingly inconsequential goods as lipstick and blue jeans so important to the women of Eastern Europe, according to Drakulić?
2. How does Drakulić both celebrate and critique the pursuit of fashion?
3. What did women risk in being seen as too fashionable?

Source: Slavenka Drakulić, *How We Survived Communism and Even Laughed* (London: 1992), pp. 22–23, 26, 31–32.

---

consumers did gradually begin to acquire products like televisions and automobiles, they often had to wait years and paid a far higher percentage of their salaries for them than their Western counterparts did.

In their intensive pursuit of industrialization, the Eastern bloc states also ravaged the environment. In Slovakia, by the early 1980s nearly half the rivers were dangerously polluted. In the Soviet Union, the diversion of rivers to provide irrigation for industrial-scale agriculture literally dried up the Aral Sea, which eventually shrank to less than 10 percent of its original size—an unprecedented ecological disaster. In Poland, factories in the new industrial city of Nowa Huta pumped vast quantities of unfiltered smoke and gas into the air, much of it settling on neighboring

Environmental Devastation By the 1990s, much of the Aral Sea had disappeared as a result of Soviet irrigation projects. Here abandoned ships sit rusting on a dry, deserted former seabed.

bloc in the 1980s through its aggressive strategic moves and strong rhetoric. Most give particular credit to Soviet leader **Mikhail Gorbachev** and the policies of liberalization that he set in motion. In the words of the historian Tony Judt: "It was Mr. Gorbachev's revolution."

In fact, these various factors all worked together. The dissidents, by themselves, could never have overturned powerful police states. Yet their activities did more than anything else to discredit these states and to dramatize the need for reform—including to Gorbachev. The U.S. government's military buildup of the 1980s did not, by itself, push the Soviet Union to the breaking point, but it did help convince Gorbachev that his country could not compete with the United States without undergoing fundamental changes. Gorbachev himself did not set out to destroy the system—far from it. But without him, the events of 1989–91 would have been inconceivable.

NEW SOVIET LEADERSHIP: MIKHAIL GORBACHEV

In the early 1980s, the Soviet Union's decay seemed to express itself most directly in its leadership. Leonid Brezhnev, an aged and infirm seventy-five, died in 1982. He

Cracow, where the facades of beautiful early modern buildings crumbled and turned black from the pollution.

These failures caused support for Communist regimes to fall to the lowest levels ever, which only increased their political rigidity. Communist elites, desperate to stay in power, continued to deny the population both elementary freedoms and the rule of law. Rigged elections routinely ended with 98 percent of the votes supposedly cast for the same slate of career officials. Secret police forces no longer murdered on a vast scale, as in Stalin's USSR, but they could still prove enormously oppressive, and not just toward dissidents. The East German Stasi, or state security service, had some 85,000 employees, who in turn worked with over 650,000 collaborators and informers of various sorts. Altogether, they kept files on 6 million people—one-third of the East German population. Co-workers and neighbors routinely informed on each other, and in some cases so did family members, even spouses.

THE COLLAPSE OF COMMUNISM

The reasons for the collapse of the Communist system are still the subject of lively debate. With hindsight, historians recognize the system's weakness, but they also argue that the repressive state apparatuses of the Soviet bloc, combined with sheer inertia, could have kept the system going for decades more. Why did it fall apart when it did, and so quickly? Some scholars single out the heroic role of dissidents. Others credit the pressure that the administration of U.S. president Ronald Reagan put on the Eastern

Reagan and Gorbachev U.S. president Ronald Reagan looks on as Soviet leader Mikhail Gorbachev makes a speech at the signing of a treaty to reduce nuclear armaments, on December 8, 1987.

was succeeded as general secretary of the Communist Party by the sixty-eight-year old Yuri Andropov, a former head of the KGB. Three months later, Andropov's kidneys failed, and he spent most of the next year in the hospital before dying in early 1984. The leadership then fell to the seventy-three-year-old Constantin Chernenko, who also lasted barely a year in the job, much of it in the hospital.

Upon Chernenko's death, a long-awaited generational shift finally took place with the rise to power of Mikhail Gorbachev (1931–). Then just age fifty-four, Gorbachev, from Stavropol in southern Russia, had moved steadily up in the Soviet apparatus since obtaining a law degree from Moscow State University in 1955, gaining a reputation for energy and intelligence. As he rose, the failings of the system became all too clear to him; but on becoming general secretary his immediate goal was to reform the Soviet Union and make it more competitive with the West, not to change it radically. As the Yugoslav dissident Milovan Djilas wrote about him: "Gorbachev, unlike Brezhnev, strikes me as a true believer." His first major initiative was an attack on the perennial Russian phenomenon of alcoholism, in the hope of increasing productivity. He began to develop a program he would later call **perestroika**, or "restructuring"—in this case, of Soviet society and government.

Yet events quickly convinced him of the need for more dramatic action. In April 1986, a nuclear power plant in **Chernobyl** (Soviet Ukraine) suffered meltdown, releasing huge quantities of radiation into the atmosphere, hundreds of times more than the Hiroshima atomic bomb. Scores died, hundreds suffered severe radiation poisoning, over 130,000 were evacuated from the region, and the plant itself had to be encased in a thick shell of concrete. Reports widely attributed the accident to incompetent management, and Gorbachev was reported to have told his wife, the same evening: "We cannot go on like this." Two and a half years later, a horrific earthquake in Soviet Armenia killed at least 25,000 people; their deaths mostly resulted from the widespread collapse of shoddily constructed buildings. Meanwhile, the war in Afghanistan, increasingly called the Soviet Union's Vietnam, dragged on, with the Soviet forces no more able than the British in the nineteenth century to suppress Afghan resistance, despite a massive deployment of personnel. And the Soviet economy, which had become increasingly dependent on oil revenue, was suffering from falling oil prices.

Gorbachev still resisted any major retreat from Communist central planning, concentrating instead on

Chernobyl An aerial photograph shows a cloud of smoke rising from the rubble of the Chernobyl nuclear reactor after the meltdown in April 1986.

political changes. For the first time since Lenin's early days in power, the government encouraged public debate and criticism under the banner of **glasnost** ("openness"). It eased up on the persecution of dissidents, and at the end of 1986 allowed the dissident physicist Andrei Sakharov to return to Moscow. It rehabilitated Stalin's most prominent purge victims and cancelled high school history exams because textbooks could not keep up with the rapidly changing past. By 1988, Gorbachev was experimenting with limited free enterprise in services and small-scale manufacturing. In foreign policy, he forged a surprisingly cordial relationship with President Reagan and negotiated the most important nuclear arms reductions since the start of the Cold War. A 1987 treaty led to the elimination of thousands of intermediate-range nuclear missiles, and the START treaty—which Gorbachev signed with Reagan's successor, George H. W. Bush, in 1991—set a ceiling on the total number of warheads each side could possess. Throughout the reform process, Gorbachev remained confident about keeping it under control. As one of his deputies remarked, after implementing a measure that removed decades-old controls on the Russian Orthodox Church: "Since the power belongs completely to us, I think we are capable of pointing this track in whatever direction is to our interest." In fact, nothing could have been further from the truth.

Collapse of the Eastern Bloc, 1989–1990 One Communist government after another collapsed quickly in the summer and fall of 1989: in Poland, Hungary, Czechoslovakia, Bulgaria, Romania, and East Germany. The Berlin Wall fell in November. Within two years, the Soviet Union and Yugoslavia would experience not only the fall of communism but also the breakup of thier multi-national states.

THE END OF COMMUNISM IN POLAND AND HUNGARY

The most immediate challenge to the system did not come from Gorbachev himself, but from men and women far from Moscow who were encouraged by glasnost and perestroika to push a radical agenda. These men and women were located in the satellite states and also, increasingly, in the constituent republics of the USSR itself. As the grip of the Communist Party loosened, the idea that non-Russian nationalities in the USSR might achieve a greater degree of autonomy—perhaps even independence—suddenly seemed possible. Movements began to form first in the

Baltic states, annexed by Stalin only in 1940. They were then copied elsewhere, including in the six Muslim republics that lay to the south of Russia.

But Soviet control first cracked in what was still called Eastern Europe—a label the Czech dissidents in particular strongly rejected, feeling that they belonged to the heartland of the Continent, Central Europe. On December 7, 1988, Gorbachev spoke before the United Nations in New York and effectively renounced the "Brezhnev doctrine" by which the USSR had reserved the right to keep its satellite states in check by force, as in Czechoslovakia in 1968. In Hungary, the speech gave new confidence and energy to a reform movement that was developing within the Communist Party there. Its new leadership had already moved to legalize opposition movements, authorize free trade unions, and free the press. Now it began to move toward free elections.

The Poles then raced ahead of Hungary. Throughout the late 1980s, the government of General Jaruzelski had struggled without success against a continuing economic crisis. The cause was, above all, Poland's massive foreign debt to the Western countries, which the government had incurred in order to revamp Polish industry and purchase consumer goods. As the inflation rate rose steeply, approaching 1,000 percent in early 1989, labor protests again spread across the country. In desperation, the government entered into negotiations with the banned Solidarity union, leading to the legalization of free trade unions, economic reforms in favor of private enterprise, and partially free elections to be held in June.

These elections effectively marked the demise of Communism in Poland, as Solidarity won all but one of the freely contested seats. From Moscow, Gorbachev indicated his acceptance of the result, and in September 1989 a non-Communist prime minister took power in Poland for the first time since the 1940s. His government immediately began planning for full parliamentary democracy and a transition from Communism to a free-market economy. The handover took place with remarkable smoothness, not least because of the enormous restraint shown by the leaders of Solidarity. In part, Lech Wałęsa and his supporters still feared the possibility of Soviet military intervention, but more broadly these workers and intellectuals wanted to break with an older model of European political change. As the dissident intellectual Jacek Kuroń explained in an article for a French newspaper, what was happening in Poland was *not* a revolution. Revolutions, he insisted, with pointed reference to the bicentennial of the French Revolution of 1789 then being celebrated in Paris, involved too much bloodshed. The age of revolutions was over.

The Hungarian leadership practiced the same restraint. Free elections did not come to Hungary until the spring of 1990, but already in 1989 the Hungarian Communist Party gave up its formal "leading role" in the state, adopted a new constitution with a Bill of Rights modeled on that of the United States, and began planning for the transition to free-market democracy. Its loss of power was already a certainty. The Hungarians carried out another momentous change by removing the electrified fences that had lined its border with Austria. Now Hungarians—and also the citizens of any Eastern bloc country who could travel freely to Hungary—could cross into the West without hindrance.

EAST GERMANY AND THE FALL OF THE BERLIN WALL

The events in Hungary sparked the next major phase of the collapse of Communism. East Germans did not need visas to visit Hungary, and during the summer and early fall of 1989 tens of thousands of them traveled there and simply walked into the West. Tens of thousands more sought refuge in West Germany's embassies in Budapest and Prague. In East Germany itself, dissidents founded an opposition group called New Forum. Encouraged by clear signals of support from Gorbachev, street demonstrations swelled in Berlin and Leipzig, with hundreds of thousands of protestors chanting the slogan "We are the people." Younger Communists forced the elderly party leader Erich Honecker out of office and announced a program of cautious reforms—but these came far too late.

On November 9, in a last attempt to stabilize the situation, the new leaders announced that East Germans could now freely travel into West Germany. At a news conference, an official was asked when the new law would take effect, and, taken off guard, he replied: "immediately." Within hours, huge crowds had converged on the Berlin Wall from both sides. East German border guards, trained to kill anyone who crossed without authorization, stood by in confusion as tens of thousands of East Germans simply walked past them, or climbed up on the Wall in wild celebration, or started to dig into it with hammers and chisels. Fifty thousand East Berliners, most of whom had never seen the Western city that lay just yards away, ambled in delight past the brightly lit, well-stocked storefronts of West Berlin. Televised images of the event spread instantly around the entire world. Commentators correctly interpreted it as Communism's death knell.

CZECHOSLOVAKIA, ROMANIA, AND BULGARIA

With the Wall in ruins, the collapse of Communism in the three other satellite states became a foregone conclusion. True, Czechoslovakia, Romania, and Bulgaria did not have religious and independent organizations like Solidarity that were united in defiance of the Communists, as Poland did. They did not have a reforming Communist Party, as Hungary did. And they did not have a sister state in the West to escape to, as East Germans did. But their regimes had no more support from the population than in those three countries, and it had now become obvious that without support from Moscow, Communist regimes simply could not remain standing.

In Czechoslovakia, where memories of pre-war democracy and of the abortive 1968 experiment with "socialism with a human face" were strong, massive demonstrations quickly began. Veteran dissidents, led by the charismatic **Václav Havel** (1936–2011), a playwright and philosopher who had criticized the regime in absurdist plays and taken on a leading role in Charter 77, founded a broad-based opposition movement called the Civic Forum. On December 10, 1989, as demonstrations swelled, the Czech Communist leaders simply gave up and resigned in favor of a new largely non-Communist government, which Havel would soon head as president. The events had taken place in so quick, nonviolent, and smooth a manner that they were soon dubbed the **Velvet Revolution**.

Velvet Revolution Attendees at a vigil in Prague in 1989 light candles and display Czech flags. Such gatherings were typical of the peaceful demonstrations that accompanied the transfer of power in Czechoslovakia.

The transition in Romania was also quick, but in no way nonviolent or smooth. In November, the megalomaniacal Nicolae Ceaușescu could still count on some sixty-seven standing ovations from Party members after his reelection to the office of secretary general. But on December 21, the previously unthinkable happened: during a public speech Ceaușescu was openly booed by protestors, and he visibly faltered as if struck. The next day he fled the capital, while a group from within the government hastily announced the formation of a National Salvation Front. Scores died in street battles that broke out in Bucharest between its supporters and members of Ceaușescu's hated secret police, the Securitate. Ceaușescu himself was captured, hastily tried, and executed by firing squad, along with his wife. During the same period, Todor Zhivkov, longest serving of the East European leaders, fell from office in neighboring Bulgaria. The last Communist "domino," non-aligned Albania, turned out the Communists in 1990–91.

THE "THIRD WAY" REJECTED

Although the formal Warsaw Pact treaty organization would last until 1991, the Eastern bloc had effectively ceased to exist by 1990. American policy-makers had long warned of a domino effect in which the fall of one country to Communism might lead its neighbors to suffer the same fate. But in the end it was the fall of Communism that offered the most dramatic example of the domino effect in the twentieth century. The only real question, by the end of 1989, concerned what path the newly liberated satellite states would follow. Would they simply join the Western bloc and move as rapidly as possible to duplicate its political and economic systems? Or would they attempt to find a "third way" between socialism and capitalism, preserving the state ownership of industry and a comprehensive social welfare system while introducing democracy and limited markets?

Despite the hopes of some intellectuals on both sides of the Continent, the answer was a resounding endorsement of Western European free-market democracy and a decision to erase the Communist past. Solidarity leader Lech Wałęsa made this erasure dramatically clear when, in late 1990, he became president of Poland. Rather than accept the seals of office from his predecessor, General Jaruzelski, he reached out to the Polish government-in-exile in London, which had carried on a lonely and mostly ignored existence since it had refused to accept the Communist government in the late 1940s. Throughout the bloc, and most thoroughly in Czechoslovakia, anyone involved with the Communist secret services was banned from holding public office. Wałęsa, Havel, and most of the other new Eastern European leaders, who were by no means Thatcherites, wanted to retain strong social services. But they also believed that the path to Western levels of prosperity demanded mainly free markets and the private ownership of most of the economy.

THE REUNIFICATION OF GERMANY

The Germans, meanwhile, took the idea of a return to the past to its logical conclusion: a reunification of Germany. Even before the fall of the Wall, it was already being asked whether the small East German state (population 17 million) could possibly survive on its own as a democracy, or whether it would inevitably merge with its much larger Western neighbor (population 61 million). Erich Honecker's battered successors pushed for a "third way" and were joined, ironically, by many former dissident intellectuals, who had resisted emigration to the West and remained committed to socialism in some form. But a far larger number of East Germans simply wanted the freedom and prosperity of West Germany, as fast as possible. After the Wall came down in 1989, street demonstrations continued, but now the slogan "We Are the People" pointedly became "We Are One People." In March 1990, elections took place, and supporters of reunification won a decisive victory over the newly reformed Communists. The dissidents' New Forum received just 2.8 percent.

It was West German chancellor Helmut Kohl who, above all others, brought about unification. Kohl, a Christian Democrat from the Rhineland, feared that if unification did not take place quickly, it might never come about at all. The former World War II Allies, still nervous about a united, powerful Germany, might block it, or the East Germans themselves might grow reluctant. So Kohl pushed reunification through at breakneck speed, committing the West German state and economy to vast expenditures in the process and risking massive social disruptions in the East. To ensure their support, he allowed East Germans to convert large sums of their nearly worthless currency to solid West German deutsche marks at a rate of 1:1. To assuage the Soviets, he agreed to over $100 billion in direct transfers to their ailing economy. He also won over the Western allies by raising the prospect that anything other than speedy unification might eventually threaten the position of West Germany in NATO. When the American negotiators, President George H. W. Bush and his secretary of state, James Baker, promised that NATO would now become more of a political than a military alliance, Mikhail Gorbachev conceded that a united Germany could be part of NATO.

Under the treaty of unification in September 1990, Berlin finally lost the status of occupied city. The Soviets withdrew the 360,000 soldiers they still had stationed on East German soil. In October, unification formally took place. The Berlin Wall had already become a tourist attraction, with chunks sold off to adorn bookshelves and mantelpieces around the world.

THE END OF THE SOVIET EMPIRE

Less than two months after the fall of the Berlin Wall, a smaller but deeply symbolic event took place on Pushkin Square in the center of Moscow: the opening of a McDonald's restaurant. In order to ensure reliable supplies of beef and potatoes to its new Russian outpost, the company involved itself in every aspect of the food's production and distribution, from field and feedlot to cash register. It also charged higher prices than most competing restaurants. Nonetheless, it was immediately overrun with customers and for years remained one of the busiest McDonald's in the world. Some Soviet citizens craved this literal taste of the West so badly that they had Big Macs flash-frozen in Moscow and shipped by air as far as Vladivostok.

The opening of the restaurant raised the question of whether the USSR, too, could transform itself from an authoritarian state with a command economy into a democracy that allowed the operation of free markets. The hurdles were certainly much greater. In the former Eastern bloc, where the very different pre-war political systems were still part of living memory, Communism could be conveniently stigmatized as an alien imposition. In the USSR, however, Communism not only was home-grown but had been searingly affirmed by the massive sacrifices and ultimate victory of what Russians called the Great Patriotic War against Hitler. In the USSR, no one under age eighty had much recollection of any other sort of social system—and while the Russia of the tsars had permitted private enterprise, it had been no democracy. Soviet society was firmly organized along collectivist lines, with the result that an independent restaurant like McDonald's could not even count on getting a reliable supply of high-grade potatoes from Soviet farms without its own close supervision.

Free Market in Moscow Crowds pack Russia's first McDonald's as supervisors train the cashiers in taking orders shortly after the restaurant's opening in 1990.

NATIONALIST CHALLENGES

Yet even as the Soviet leadership started to grapple with these issues, it was increasingly distracted by the challenge of nationalism. In 1987, Mikhail Gorbachev had unwisely boasted: "We can truly say that for our country the nationalities issue has been resolved." But dreams of independence were already stirring in the Baltic states, encouraged by the collapse of Communism in Eastern Europe. In August 1989, as many as 1.8 million people—one-quarter of the combined populations of Estonia, Latvia, and Lithuania—formed a human chain through the three republics in a demonstration in favor of the republics' independence. In March 1990, the Lithuanian Supreme Soviet unanimously voted to secede and restore the country's pre-war constitution, although it hesitated to implement its decision.

And this nationalist unrest eventually reached into all the republics of the USSR. In the south, it affected Armenia and Georgia, which possessed strong national cultures and a long history of conflict with Russia. It affected Ukraine, which most Russians viewed as the birthplace of their own nation. The eastern half of Ukraine was predominantly Russian in ethnicity, language, and religion; its western half, much of it annexed from Poland during the war, was predominantly Ukrainian in language and ethnicity, and Catholic or other non-Orthodox Christian in religion. The nationalist upsurge even affected Byelorussia, which had never seriously aspired to independent status. And it affected the Muslim republics of Central Asia.

NATIONALISM IN PERSPECTIVE This apparently sudden emergence of nationalism, both in the USSR and beyond, needs some explanation. As we have seen, nationalism, which mostly began to take shape in Europe in the late eighteenth and early nineteenth centuries, had remained a potent political force throughout the twentieth century. It had driven the breakup of the Austro-Hungarian and Ottoman Empires after World War I, and the near breakup of the Russian Empire at the same time. It provided the pretext for Hitler's aggression in the 1930s and shaped the process of decolonization after World War II. But the Cold War, and the division of the Continent into two opposing camps, had muted its presence in Europe between 1945 and 1989.

Commentators in the 1990s overwhelmingly treated nationalism as a timeless, somewhat archaic phenomenon. They therefore interpreted its resurgence as the expression of "ancient" or "natural" ethnic sentiments that Communism had supposedly "frozen" and "suppressed" but that were now bursting out from under its melting ice. Yet there was nothing ancient or natural about nationalism. And the USSR, far from suppressing national identifications, had encouraged them as a means of placating its many non-Russian minorities and managing its vast, multicultural territory. It required that every citizen have a formal nationality, and it divided its territory along national lines, both on the scale of the Union and also within some of its constituent republics.

RUSSIAN NATIONALISM In fact, it was precisely these Soviet policies that helped drive the reassertion of nationalism when central authority in the USSR began to weaken. Until the very end, with the exception of the Baltic states, national independence movements gained relatively little popular support, even in the Muslim republics that bordered Afghanistan. In March 1991, Gorbachev sponsored a Union-wide referendum on whether the USSR should be preserved, and over 70 percent of participants voted yes. In some of the Muslim republics, the figure topped 90 percent. But as central government authority diminished, leaders of the dominant ethnic groups in the non-Russian republics feared challenges to their own privileged positions, both from above (Moscow) and from below (their own ethnic minorities). These fears were reasonable, since each republic was itself a mosaic of ethnic groups, with the largest minority, in most cases, being Russians who had settled there since 1917. In Baltic Latvia, for example, only 54 percent of the population was ethnically Latvian. In these circumstances, members of the different groups quickly started to embrace nationalist ideas, reviving or inventing ethnic traditions as a way to preserve or enhance the status quo.

Nationalism of this sort even emerged in Russia itself. The Russian Federation (RSFSR), which extended from Kaliningrad (the former German city of Königsberg) on the Baltic to Vladivostok on the Pacific, was by far the largest constituent republic in terms of surface area. Its 148 million people made up more than half of the Soviet population. In the period of glasnost and perestroika, Russian opponents of the regime found it increasingly useful to stoke nostalgia for pre-Soviet political forms and symbols—which meant Russian national ones. Peter the Great's red, white, and blue Russian flag, almost entirely forgotten, began to reappear in opposition marches, as did symbols of the long-dead tsarist family, the Romanovs.

Politically, the key advocate of Russian anti-Soviet nationalism was **Boris Yeltsin** (1931–2007), a strong-willed, impulsive, career Communist whom Gorbachev had initially treated as a protégé and appointed both to the Politburo and to head the Communist Party in Moscow. In 1987, after Yeltsin publicly denounced the slow pace of reforms, Gorbachev demoted him. But as central party control over Soviet elections declined, Yeltsin won an office in the Congress of People's Deputies, and then in the spring of 1990 he became chair of the Presidium of the Russian Federation's Supreme Soviet. He then led the RSFSR to declare the supremacy of its laws over those of the USSR, setting up a potential constitutional crisis.

THE CRISIS OF 1990–1991

Throughout late 1990 and early 1991, these nationalist tensions continued to grow, and Gorbachev's authority withered. In January 1991, an attempt to restore central authority in the Baltics led to serious bloodshed, including fourteen dead in the Lithuanian capital of Vilnius. Some 150,000 people marched in Moscow to protest, and Yeltsin defiantly signed bilateral agreements with the Baltic states, recognizing their sovereignty in the name of Russia. Desperately, Gorbachev staged the referendum on the preservation of the Union and then promulgated a new USSR constitution that gave republics the right of secession. In June 1991, in the first free elections ever held for a Russian leader, Yeltsin won the presidency of the RSFSR. The USSR now seemed on the brink of chaos.

At this point, far too late, conservatives within the Communist Party finally decided it was time to overthrow Gorbachev and restore the Soviet system in its entirety. On August 19, 1991, after the Soviet leader had left for his

Boris Yeltsin During the August 1991 coup led by the Emergency Committee, Yeltsin (center) stands on a tank and speaks to reporters in front of the Russian Parliament building.

annual vacation in the Crimea, a self-styled Emergency Committee in Moscow that included the prime minister, the defense minister, and the head of the KGB demanded that Gorbachev surrender his powers to them. He refused angrily, upon which they declared him incapacitated for reasons of health, and announced a state of emergency. They gave out extra pay to all KGB personnel and prepared for wide-scale arrests.

In Moscow, Yeltsin condemned the coup and called for a general strike to support Gorbachev. Ordinary Muscovites immediately flocked to the Russian Parliament building (the "White House") and started to build barricades around it. Yeltsin himself gave interviews to the foreign press while standing atop a tank. The stage was set for a violent conflict. But it never came, owing above all to the farcical incompetence of the coup plotters, at least one of whom allegedly spent most of the crucial period in an alcoholic stupor. The armed forces, rather than rallying to the conservatives, vacillated. Estonia and Latvia joined Lithuania in declaring full independence from the USSR. Yeltsin remained defiant, in full view of the world media, and collected expressions of support from world leaders. After just four days, the plotters gave up and submitted to arrest. One of them committed suicide.

Gorbachev himself quickly returned to Moscow and tried to regain the initiative by suspending the Communist Party. But the coup had already effectively completed the USSR's dissolution. Over the next month, the remaining Soviet republics declared independence, often with long-standing local Communist Party leaders reinventing themselves as anti-Soviet nationalists. The Russian Federation asserted control of state institutions on Russian soil and gave Leningrad back its original name of Saint Petersburg. In October, the KGB was formally abolished. And in December, the leaders of Russia, Ukraine, and Belarus met in Minsk to propose the formal end of the Union and its replacement by a loose Commonwealth of Independent States. Gorbachev protested and blustered, yet ultimately he had no choice but to agree to the dramatic end of a process that he himself had set in motion. On December 31, 1991, the Soviet Union ceased to exist.

And so, between 1989 and 1991 the borders of Europe, seemingly set in stone by the Cold War, shifted again. The three Baltic states of Lithuania, Latvia, and Estonia that had existed between the wars came back into being. New independent states of Ukraine, Belarus, Moldova, Georgia, Armenia, and Azerbaijan were created and received international recognition, as did the former Soviet republics in Central Asia. The Russian Empire, of which the Soviet Union had been the inheritor, finally ceased to exist.

Communism was simultaneously disappearing as a worldwide force. In China during the 1980s, although the Communist Party remained in power under the leadership of Deng Xiaoping (1904-1997), it abandoned its earlier ideology almost completely and embraced private enterprise. The Southeast Asian states moved away from Communism as well. At the end of the century, only Cuba and North Korea still retained the communist systems they had developed during the Cold War.

"RETURNING TO EUROPE"

Despite the theatrics around the August 1991 coup in Russia and the violence in the Baltics, the USSR met its end in what was, by historical standards, a remarkably orderly manner. Never before in history had such a large, multinational empire come to an end with so little loss of life. Credit belonged in the first place to Gorbachev and Yeltsin, who both behaved with considerable restraint. The Western alliance offered support where possible and otherwise refrained from counterproductive interference. But above all, the peaceful transition showed that in a crucial respect Russia and its neighbors, too, were finally, in a phrase much used in these countries at the time, "returning to Europe." Just as the Western European nations had lived in peaceful coexistence since 1945, so in 1989–91 the nations of the USSR showed themselves ready to observe the same standards.

As a result, the period's surge of nationalism played itself out in a very different manner from earlier periods.

The Former Soviet Union, 1992 New independent nation-states emerged from the breakup of the Soviet Union. These ranged from Eastern European countries like Estonia and Lithuania to those in central Asia bordering China, like Kazakhstan and Kyrgyzstan. The largest new state was the Russian Federation, itself experiencing resurgent nationalism and covering a vast territory.

The existence of large Russian minorities throughout the former Soviet republics did not lead to wide-scale violence or the readjustment of borders (although such violence would occur much later in Ukraine). Even newly independent Moldova, which had never existed as a state of its own and which had deep historical and linguistic ties to neighboring Romania, remained separate. One reason, tellingly, was that if Romania remained desperately poor by Western European standards, Moldova made it look rich in comparison, and few Romanians wanted the burden of absorbing their impoverished cousins. In this corner of the Balkans, as in most of the Continent, the desire for peace and prosperity outweighed national longings.

In the early 1990s, the same logic governed the development of nationalism elsewhere on the Continent. Slovakia and the Czech Republic parted ways without violence—the Velvet Revolution giving way to a Velvet Divorce. And

the example of nationalist success in the former Eastern bloc encouraged renewed pushes for autonomy in areas of Western Europe as well. In Italy, northerners angry at the central government for decades of subsidies to the southern part of the country founded a party called the Lombard League to push for autonomy or even independence. Belgium at several moments seemed ready to split between Flemish-speakers and French-speakers, who worked out ever more complex arrangements for sharing power. In Spain, the Catalans and Basques pressed successfully for a greater degree of local authority. In Great Britain, Scotland gained a Parliament of its own with significant control over education, health, and the justice system, while Wales obtained a less powerful local assembly (these reforms went by the name "devolution"). And in Northern Ireland, protracted negotiations brokered by American senator George Mitchell finally produced an uneasy settlement, the renunciation of violence by the Irish Republican Army, and the establishment of a new Assembly in Belfast, giving the province a degree of political autonomy. The violence that had begun in the late 1960s finally petered out.

The apparent consensus around peace, democracy, and a limited free-market economy was so striking that as early as 1989, the American political scientist Francis Fukuyama could publish an influential article predicting not just the end of empire but "the end of history." By this, he essentially meant an end to conflicts over the proper form of society. As more and more countries agreed that their societies should take the form of representative democracies with limited free markets, their public lives would supposedly turn increasingly dull, with technocrats tinkering with the universally accepted mechanisms for social development rather than ideologues engaging in dramatic struggles. Other social scientists amplified the message, arguing that since democracies (supposedly) did not go to war with one another, the spread of democracy would bring about an age of universal, perpetual peace.

But events did not work out as predicted. Even as the United States drew down its forces in Europe, it was increasingly drawn into conflicts in the Middle East. In 1990–91, it fought its first war since Vietnam, in alliance with several Arab countries, to liberate Kuwait, which Iraqi dictator Saddam Hussein had invaded. And in one corner of Europe, the 1990s saw the worst violence on European soil since World War II. Commentators mostly blamed it on the new nationalism that had burst out following the collapse of Communism. But most of the bloodshed occurred between warring religious groups as well as national ones. The fault line that now threatened the peace of Europe was the divide between Christianity and Islam, along which history returned to the Continent with a vengeance.

THE NEW BALKAN WARS

For much of the forty years after World War II, Yugoslavia, by the standards of Communist Europe, was a success story. Tito, its leader until his death in 1980, ruled with a relatively light hand after breaking with Moscow at the start of the Cold War. He allowed Yugoslavs to travel freely and permitted a wider range of political and cultural expression within the country than his Communist neighbors did. Economically, he broke with the prevailing Eastern bloc model of centralization by experimenting with various forms of worker self-management. And he

helped ensure a degree of coexistence among the country's principal ethnic groups (Serbs, Croats, Slovenes, Bosnian Muslims, Macedonians, Hungarians, and Albanians) by dividing the spoils of government among them and harshly repressing nationalist movements that threatened the arrangement. Intermarriage increased, and with each census a larger share of the population—although still a minority—described themselves simply as "Yugoslav."

YUGOSLAVIA'S COLLAPSE

Still, there were tensions within this composite state, assembled in 1919 after the peace conference at Versailles. The relatively wealthy Slovenes, who had once belonged to Austria and still considered themselves the efficient "Germans of Yugoslavia," resented subsidizing the poorer areas of the south. With just 8 percent of the population, Slovenia produced 29 percent of the country's exports, while the predominantly Albanian autonomous region of Kosovo, with the same-size population, produced 1 percent. Citizens of Serbia, with its powerful nationalist traditions dating to before World War I, resented the fact that despite having the most populous of the six Yugoslav republics and two autonomous regions, the 1974 constitution gave them no more representation in the federal government than tiny Montenegro, with barely one-tenth the population.

Tensions also arose over the boundaries of Yugoslavia's republics and regions, which were mostly derived from nineteenth-century international borders rather than the actual distribution of ethnic groups. Nearly 3 million Serbs lived outside the borders of Serbia. Yugoslavia's religious divisions compounded these tensions. In the regions ruled longest by the Ottoman Empire, Bosnians and Albanians had largely embraced Islam. In return, they had received favors from the Turks, which heightened the resentment felt toward them by the Serbs. Croats and Slovenes were largely Catholic; Serbs, Montenegrins, and Macedonians were largely Orthodox. The combination was potentially explosive.

After Tito's death, the system lumbered on for another eight years, even as the country's huge foreign debt triggered a powerful economic crisis. But by the mid-1980s, the simmering resentments had become more vocal, and the Serbs in particular began to push for a greater influence over federal affairs. In 1986, a memorandum of the Serbian Academy of Sciences and Arts stirred controversy by accusing Slovenes and Croats of systematic oppression and denouncing the genocide of Serbs by the Albanian majority in the region of Kosovo. The site of an

Yugoslavia, 1988–2000 When the composite state of Yugoslavia collapsed in 1991, Slovenia and Macedonia were able to establish their independence quickly. But Serbia responded to the secession of Croatia, and especially of Bosnia-Herzegovina, with bloody and drawn-out conflict.

Map labels:
Boundary of Yugoslavia, 1991
June 1991 Date of independence
Massacre
War

AUSTRIA
HUNGARY
SLOVENIA
June 1991
Ljubljana
Zagreb
ROMANIA
VOJVODINA
1991–1996
CROATIA
June 1991
BOSNIA-HERZEGOVINA
Apr. 1992
Belgrade
Srebrenica, 1995
Sarajevo
besieged, 1992–1996
1992–1995
SERBIA AND MONTENEGRO
BULGARIA
Mostar
MONTENEGRO
1999
Pec
Pristina
Kosovo
Dubrovnik
Adriatic Sea
ITALY
Skopje
MACEDONIA
Nov. 1992
ALBANIA
GREECE
EUROPE
AFRICA
0 100 200 mi
0 100 200 km

epic Serbian defeat at Turkish hands in 1389, Kosovo had strong symbolic value for Serbs, many of whom liked to see themselves as the vanguard protecting Christendom from Muslim invaders. The Academy's sentiments were tacitly encouraged by Slobodan Milošević, a fierce nationalist and ambitious Serbian politician who became president of the republic in 1988. Within a year, he destroyed Yugoslavia's constitutional stability by eliminating the autonomy of the regions of Kosovo and Vojvodina within Serbia—thereby increasing Serbia's size and influence within the federation. He also backed a peaceful uprising in Montenegro that put a pro-Serbian government in power there. With Serbia now in control of four of eight republics and regions, independence movements surged in Slovenia, Croatia, Bosnia-Herzegovina, and Macedonia.

Before the late 1980s, unrest of this sort in a neutral state strategically located between the Eastern and Western blocs would have resulted in great-power pressure to preserve the status quo. But now, with the Soviet Union moribund, the United States no longer had as significant a strategic interest in the region as it once did. Calls from the United Nations for peace were ineffectual. And so,

with nationalism sweeping across the region with apparent inevitability, no pressure materialized and Yugoslavia quickly followed the USSR into dissolution. Slovenia and Croatia, where multi-party elections had already turned the Communists out of power, declared independence in 1991, and Macedonia soon followed. A Serbian attack on Slovenia lasted less than two weeks and ended with the Serbians withdrawing and recognizing Slovene independence. Slovenia quickly made the transition to free-market democracy and prospered, subsequently joining NATO and the European Union. In a longer, messier conflict, ethnic Serbs in Croatia attempted to secede, leading to two rounds of large-scale violence.

THE WARS IN BOSNIA-HERZEGOVINA AND KOSOVO

These struggles were dwarfed, however, by the two wars involving the Muslim-Christian fault line: in Bosnia-Herzegovina, and then in Kosovo. In the first of these, the proclamation of independence in March 1992 led to a rebellion by ethnic Serbs—Christians by faith—who declared a separate Serb Republic supported by Milošević's government in Belgrade. Heavily armed bands of Serbian irregular forces aimed less at overturning the Bosnian government than at **"ethnic cleansing"** of the territories they claimed, adding through terrible violence a chilling new phrase to the world's long lexicon of horror. They also carried out a long and bloody siege of the Bosnian capital, Sarajevo.

The UN, the EU, and NATO condemned the violence

Siege of Sarajevo UN peacekeeping forces stand guard as Sarajevo residents take cover from sniper fire behind an armored vehicle in 1993—just a few of the many civilians affected by the ongoing violence in the former Yugoslavia.

but did little to intervene beyond the creation of a series of ineffective "safe areas." European peacekeepers stood by helplessly in July 1995 as Bosnian Serb forces slaughtered 7,400 defenseless Bosnian Muslim men and boys in the town of Srebrenica, part of a supposed safe area. Only in the late summer of 1995, after Bosnian Serbs had shelled the main marketplace in Sarajevo, did the U.S. government finally authorize a sustained bombing campaign by NATO against Serbia, which then agreed to peace talks at the U.S. Air Force base in Dayton, Ohio. The agreement negotiated there and signed in December 1995 ended up preserving a fragile but united Bosnia, in which Muslims, Croats, and Serbs had substantial autonomy.

During the Bosnian War, the Serbs repeatedly appealed to the late medieval struggles of Serbia against the Ottoman Turks and posed as the front-line defenders of Christendom against Islam. Many Muslim countries gave expressions of support to the embattled Bosnian government. Still, for the most part religion mattered in the conflict mostly as a badge of identification, not as a source of fervent belief. Most of the leaders on both sides had grown up in officially atheist, Communist Yugoslavia. But throughout the late 1980s, much of the Serb media presented an unrealistic picture of Serbs in danger of genocide from an expanding Yugoslav Muslim population. Milošević, and the Bosnian Serb leaders, felt threatened by Muslims in a way that they did not feel threatened by Catholic Croats or Slovenes, and at the same time they felt free to treat Muslims more brutally. It was these factors that allowed ethnic strife to explode into all-out violence.

And then, at the end of the 1990s, the former Yugoslavia again became the scene of appalling violence—this time in the region of Kosovo, once the symbolic heartland of Serbia but now home to an Albanian Muslim majority. Milošević, unconcerned with his international reputation as a butcher, turned a blind eye to massacres of Albanians by Serbian police units. Hundreds of thousands of Kosovars fled for safety to Macedonia and Albania. This time, the United States and NATO reacted more quickly. In the spring of 1999, they carried out an intensive, three-month-long bombing campaign against Serbia, at the end of which Milošević gave in and withdrew his forces from the region.

With the conclusion of this last Balkan war, the parts of the former Yugoslavia finally began a slow process of healing and started to follow the former Soviet bloc nations in the path of European integration. In September 2000, after Milošević lost a presidential election and tried to contest the results, popular protests drove him from office. The new democratic government handed him over to a war crimes tribunal in the Hague, set up on the model of the post-war Nuremberg tribunal. He died during his prolonged trial.

CHECHNYA

Several other armed confrontations took place in Europe following the collapse of Communism. Each had its own particular causes, but in broad terms they followed the same pattern of ethnic-religious conflict seen in the Balkans: the worst violence took place on the fault line between Christianity and Islam. In the Caucasus Mountains south of Russia, not far from where the Armenian genocide had occurred during World War I, a war took place between Christian Armenia and Muslim Azerbaijan over a majority-Armenian region within the latter. The conflict badly damaged the new Armenian state and ended with an uneasy truce in 1994.

Even worse fighting erupted to the north, within Russia itself. Although ethnic Russians composed nearly 80 percent of the population of the Russian Federation, scores of other nationalities—Tatars, Chechens, Ossetians, and many others—also occupied portions of its vast territory, with many of them having autonomous republics of their own. In predominantly Muslim Chechnya in the north Caucasus, a serious independence movement had developed during the late 1980s. Stalin had deported virtually the entire Chechen population to Kazakhstan during World War II, and even after their return in the 1950s

Chechen War A team of fighters transports an injured companion on a stretcher, in the midst of the violence in Grozny, in the 1990s. The Russian campaign against the Chechens laid waste to the city and left nearly half of the population dead.

they remained bitter toward the Moscow regime. In the early 1990s, Chechnya tried to secede but President Yeltsin refused to let the Federation suffer the same fate as the Soviet Union. Russia's disorganized military campaign against Chechnya dragged on for two years, left the capital city of Grozny a smoking ruin, and ended indecisively. In 1999, the Russian authorities blamed Chechen terrorists for a series of attacks in Russian cities that killed hundreds of civilians. They then unleashed a more effective campaign that destroyed the Chechen military, killed many of their leaders, and set up a compliant regime in the territory. Altogether, the Chechen War left at least 40,000 civilians and soldiers dead in a region with a population of little over a million and, as we will see, only strengthened hostility toward Russia.

In Chechnya as in Yugoslavia, religious identity did not initially play the decisive role in the conflict. But religious difference and the memory of past conflicts quickly heightened existing tensions and lowered the threshold at which violence could occur. As in Yugoslavia, the orchestration of Christian fears played a greater role in sparking the conflict than radical Islam. But then, in Chechnya, thousands of Muslim volunteers flocked from other countries to join the rebel forces. These fighters had a very strong religious motivation. They saw the conflict as part of a larger battle between Islam and the West, into which they also grouped the Soviet war in Afghanistan, the Bosnian War, and the Arab-Israeli conflict. And so the Chechen War helped to spur the development of radical jihadist movements—dedicated to the struggle against what they considered enemies of Islam—that would become increasingly important over the subsequent decades.

CONNECTIONS

The conflicts in the former Yugoslavia and Chechnya, violent as they were, had little direct impact on the everyday lives of most Western Europeans. The refugee crises that accompanied the war mostly did not spill over the

War in the Caucasus, 1998–1999 The Caucasus region was the site of ethnic and religious tensions that erupted into conflict in the 1990s: both on the border between Christian Armenia and Muslim Azerbaijan, and in the majority-Muslim region of Chechnya in the north Caucasus, whose attempts to seek independence from Russia led to reprisals.

borders of the former Yugoslavia. The main challenge for most of Europe in the 1990s was to navigate the more general problems posed by ever thicker, more intense sets of connections between the Continent and the wider world, and within the Continent itself.

THE CHALLENGE OF ECONOMIC GLOBALIZATION

These global connections, as we have already seen, involved the movement of both capital and people. In the 1980s, international bank lending, centered in the United States but flowing across the world, grew nearly twentyfold, and it continued to expand strongly in the next decade as well. Some European countries profited enormously from this change. Ireland, for instance, which did not have an antiquated industrial base dragging down its economy, and which possessed a well-educated population fluent in the main language of international commerce, saw its services and high-technology sectors expand at blazing speed, powered also by low taxes. Between 1990 and 2000, the "Celtic tiger's" economy doubled in size, copying the success of "Asian tigers" such as Taiwan, Singapore, and South Korea. Business centers such as London, Frankfurt, and Hamburg also benefited enormously.

Elsewhere in Europe, however, the same process of globalization made it all the more difficult to support obsolescent economic sectors, and the sort of labor disruptions seen in Britain in the Thatcher years repeated themselves across the map. Companies increasingly moved themselves across borders in search of lower operating costs, especially cheaper labor. Goods and people circulated more intensively. And in the mid-1990s, the development of the World Wide Web began to spark a new revolution in communications and commerce. France had initially taken the lead in new forms of telecommunication, with its state telecom company providing users with free terminals called "Minitels," through which they could access an extensive text-only data network. But the system could not compete with the internet, and the government's attempts to preserve it ended up delaying the spread of internet technology in France

IMMIGRATION AND RIGHT-WING POLITICS

Part of this newly intense phase of globalization involved immigrant communities. In the last quarter of the twentieth century, the populations of non-European origin on the Continent continued to expand, thanks both to high birthrates and to continued immigration. Between 1980 and 1992, fully 15 million immigrants came to Europe from around the globe. In Britain, the proportion of ethnic minorities rose by 50 percent in the 1990s. By 1995, in Germany, Austria, and Belgium, some 9 percent of the population was foreign-born. These new communities mainly fit into patterns set by earlier waves of migration: Turks moved to Germany, South Asians and Caribbean blacks to Great Britain, North Africans and sub-Saharan Africans to France.

Any pretense that the new groups were mere guest workers disappeared as the migrants had children who grew up speaking European languages as their native tongues and retained only distant connections to their parents' birthplaces. In many poorer areas of major industrial cities, such as Brixton in London or the poor suburbs around Paris, these populations became the majority, and right-wing politicians profited from white suspicions and fears of criminality. In France, the National Front of the blustery former paratrooper Jean-Marie Le Pen won over 10 percent of the vote in several national elections, often gaining the support of working-class voters who had previously backed the Communists. In Austria, the anti-immigrant politician Jörg Haider's Freedom Party won 28 percent of the vote in 1997. Both Haider and Le Pen also stirred up the embers of European anti-Semitism, with Le Pen calling the gas chambers a mere "detail" in the history of World War II and Haider expressing admiration for aspects of the Nazi regime.

Most mainstream European politicians denounced these extremists, but at the same time most Western European regimes moved to rein in illegal immigration and place stricter limits on the legal kind as well. Immigration to the Netherlands, mainly from the former Dutch colony of Indonesia and, increasingly, Morocco and the Middle East, became a political target when Pim Fortuyn, an openly gay politician, called Islam a "backwards" religion, in part because of its attitudes toward homosexuality.

Brixton Large numbers of immigrants from Jamaica and other parts of the Caribbean transformed the London neighborhood of Brixton in the 1990s.

Fortuyn founded a mass movement committed to restricting immigration.

TOWARD EUROPEAN UNION

Even as globalization was binding economies around the world closer together, many Europeans believed the destiny of the Continent would be found in its own political and economic integration. In 1985, five European countries signed the so-called Schengen agreement that drastically reduced the extent of border controls between them. The "Schengen Zone" has since grown to 26 countries. By the end of 1986, the European Community had grown to twelve members with the addition of Greece, Spain, and Portugal, but significant economic barriers remained among them. France and West Germany in particular pushed strongly for additional degrees of union, not only to cement their own relationship but also to allow Europe as a whole to compete more effectively with the United States and the rising Asian economies. Britain, where a significant portion of the Conservative Party remained opposed to the nation's membership in the Union altogether, seeing it as an infringement of British sovereignty, was much less enthusiastic. But the desire for closer union prevailed.

In early 1986 the member countries adopted a Single Europe Act, and in 1992 they signed the Maastricht Treaty. Together, these agreements created a fully open European market, opened all borders, renamed the Community the **European Union (EU)**, and committed the member states to adopting a single currency by the end

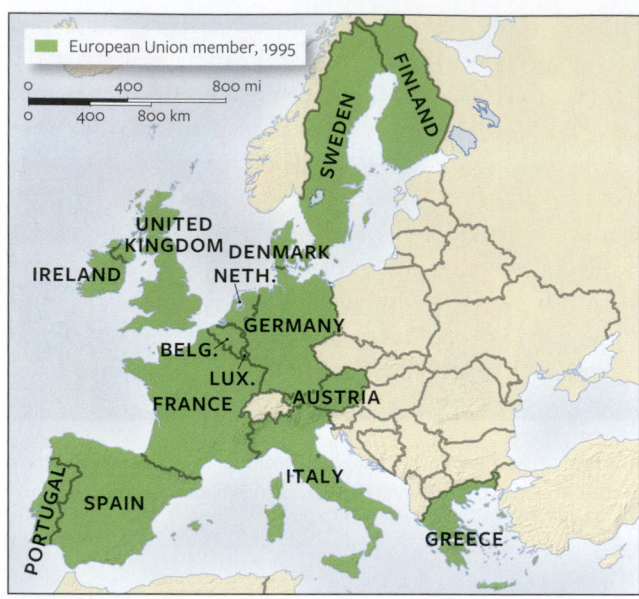

The European Union, 1995 Three years after the signing of the Maastricht Treaty, the EU comprised fifteen member states, including almost every country in Western Europe—though Norway and Switzerland remained notable exceptions.

of the twentieth century. They gave expanded powers to the executive European Commission in Brussels, which is joined in the constellation of European institutions by a European Parliament and Court of Justice. In 1995, after the end of the Cold War, the formerly neutral countries of Austria, Sweden, and Finland joined the Union as well.

The increasing strength of the EU certainly provoked opposition. British "Euroskeptics" liked to point to the endless bureaucratic regulations that seemed to pour out of Brussels, such as the jargon-filled Regulation 2213/83 that took eleven pages to define standards for onions. They criticized the Union for subsidizing uncompetitive farmers, especially in southern Europe, at a cost of tens of billions of dollars a year and "mountains" of unsold products. At times in the early 2000s, this EU "public stock" included nearly 100 million gallons of alcoholic beverages, mostly wine, sitting in storage.

At the same time, many Europeans, especially wealthy and well-educated ones, benefited from their new freedom of movement. Young French businessmen, stymied by their own country's legacy of heavy regulation, flocked to London's booming financial district. University students across the Continent benefited from the Erasmus exchange program, which gave them the ability to do part of their degrees in another EU state. EU citizens also appreciated the virtual disappearance of physical borders, freely moving back and forth across lines that had once bristled with police and fortifications.

ECONOMIC CONNECTIONS

And it was not only political changes that encouraged increased movement. In 1981, the French national railway inaugurated high-speed train service that cut travel time between Paris and Lyons by half. The so-called TGV (*Train à grande vitesse*, or "high-speed train") initially traveled at over 120 miles an hour—faster than Japan's pioneering bullet train. Since then, high-speed networks have spread over the western half of the Continent (including much of Italy and Spain), and speeds have increased on some lines to 180 mph. In France itself, the trains largely eliminated internal air travel and spawned a new species of long-distance commuters who might, for instance, live in Paris but work in the northern French city of Lille—130 miles away but just an hour by TGV. The best-known TGV line, meanwhile, connected Paris and London: it did so through the Channel Tunnel, an engineering marvel built as a joint effort of French and British companies, subsidized by the two governments. Construction began in 1988, and President Mitterrand and Queen Elizabeth

Reunified Berlin Once divided by the Berlin Wall, Potsdamer Platz in central Berlin now features twenty-first-century office blocks and a new train station, harkening back to the square's pre–World War II importance as a commercial hub and transit center.

II formally opened it in 1994. In the late 1990s, Europe followed the United States in deregulating airline travel. Fares tumbled, and discount airlines proliferated.

Connections grew across the former iron curtain as well. In Berlin, the new, united city government quickly moved to knit the former Eastern and Western cities together, reconnecting streets and subway lines and rebuilding the old central train station in East Berlin, which became the hub of yet more high-speed train lines. The Wall had physically bisected the city's great central square, the Potsdamer Platz, which had lain in ruins since the war. The city now hired a firm of Munich architects to transform it into a vast new commercial complex, including a new headquarters for the auto giant Daimler-Benz.

THE TRANSITION TO CAPITALISM IN THE FORMER EASTERN BLOC

Integrating the former Eastern bloc countries into a democratic, capitalist Europe proved considerably more difficult. These countries had to build new representative institutions even as they opened up their economies to private enterprise and sold off their inefficient state-owned industries—processes that came at considerable human cost. Strategies for accomplishing the transformation varied significantly. Some countries, such as Poland and Estonia, opted for a Big Bang strategy of immediately privatizing industry, allowing inefficient firms to fail, removing subsidies for basic consumer goods, and encouraging new private enterprise. In Poland, where industrial workers and farmers now found themselves competing in a worldwide market, real wages (that is, adjusted for inflation) fell by 40 percent almost overnight, and millions of workers incapable of retraining faced difficult times as they lost their jobs. Whereas the Communist system had guaranteed everyone a job, now unemployment spiked to over 15 percent by 1995. Polish street markets filled with pensioners and the unemployed desperately selling off their valuables to make ends meet. But after several hard years, Poland and Estonia managed the readjustment. In Estonia, economic growth hit 11 percent in 1997 and then remained consistently above 7 percent between 2000 and 2007. Countries such as Slovakia, Romania, and Ukraine, which tried to soften the transition and preserve subsidies to industry and consumer goods, generally lagged behind in terms of growth: by the late 1990s, real wages in Poland were five times that of neighboring Ukraine.

Building up democratic institutions could be just as difficult in the former Eastern bloc countries, which had little experience with genuine multi-party systems and a free press. Moreover, the former Communist parties often retained considerable strength and organization. During the 1990s, many of them took advantage of popular resentment at the economic dislocations to regain support, and in some cases, notably in Hungary, they won elections. But in most of the new states, a common desire to emulate the institutions of the West worked to preserve the new freedoms. In no case did a former Communist Party try to reverse the political and economic changes that had followed the events of 1989. Similarly, outside of the former USSR the dislocations did not threaten the transition to democracy. By the end of the century, the former satellite nations and the Baltic states all had functioning democratic systems with regular, free elections between rival parties.

Ironically, the country that experienced the greatest difficulties in making the transition to capitalism, outside of the former USSR and Yugoslavia, was the one with the greatest apparent advantages: East Germany. Even before its full absorption into the Federal Republic, the territory had received huge subsidies from West Germany, and the common language made it all the more attractive to West German investment capital. But through the transition, West Germans often showed little respect to Ossis ("Easterners") and were in turn angrily denounced as arrogant "colonizers." In the university system, whole cadres of professors were simply dismissed from their jobs if judged unqualified by West German standards and replaced by Western nominees. West German firms setting up or purchasing Eastern firms often sent in their own personnel to manage them. Within a few years, a wave of "Ostalgie" for the former regime had grown up (*ost* is German for "East"). It was gently spoofed in the film *Goodbye, Lenin!*, whose protagonists try to hide the end of East Germany from their fervently Communist but desperately ill mother, who has just awakened from a long coma and who they fear might drop dead from shock if she learns the truth.

RUSSIA'S DECADE OF DISRUPTION

East Germany's troubles paled, however, in comparison to those of Russia. Boris Yeltsin remained president throughout the decade but often seemed to be stumbling from one crisis to another. In the year following the end of the Soviet Union, he promoted an ambitious program of economic privatization, only to run into sustained opposition

Crisis in Russia A soldier stands atop a tank outside the "White House" in Moscow as fires blaze inside after Yeltsin ordered troops to fire on his political opponents in October 1993.

from the Russian Supreme Soviet. In 1993, he demanded special powers to push the program through and barely escaped impeachment. As the conflict with the Parliament escalated, Yeltsin ordered tanks to fire on the same "White House" building he had helped defend during the 1991 coup, and then he ordered elections for a new Parliament. The voters decisively rejected his policies of rapid privatization, giving a plurality to ultra-nationalists, while the Communists made a strong showing as well. However, the voters also approved a new constitution that gave the president expanded powers, which did allow Yeltsin to proceed with the economic transition. The next year, with Russian domestic politics still unstable, the first Chechen War broke out.

Thanks to these troubled conditions and Russia's lack of experience with democratic institutions or private markets (at least within living memory), Russian privatization took place in a chaotic, corrupt manner that enabled a small number of entrepreneurs—mostly with strong connections to the former regime and KGB—to seize control of vast sectors of the economy, including most of the crucial oil industry. By 2004, just thirty-six men—the so-called oligarchs—controlled wealth in excess of $110 billion, or one-quarter of the country's domestic product.

And unlike Poland or the Czech Republic, Russia did not rebound quickly from these immediate difficulties. Indeed, the country suffered an economic and demographic catastrophe in the years that followed the change in regime. In what was a boom decade for most of the Western world, the Russian economy *shrank* by over 40 percent between 1990 and 1996, and by 14.5 percent in

1992 alone. Overall life expectancy in the country tumbled, according to World Bank indicators, from 69.5 years in 1988 to 64.5 in 1994—a decline without parallel in modern history outside of wartime. The number of children born dropped precipitously, while rates of death from infectious disease, cardiovascular disease, and accidents all skyrocketed—all of them linked strongly to alcoholism. Death rates from alcohol poisoning (particularly from cheap homebrew) were estimated at 100 times the American rate. Boris Yeltsin, himself prey to alcoholism, nonetheless won a second term as president in 1996. Ordinary Russians, however, at the same time expressed increasing nostalgia for the Soviet Union and bitterness at Russia's decline. The entry of Poland, the Czech Republic, and Hungary into NATO in 1999 only strengthened these feelings, as did NATO's bombing of Serbia, a fellow Slav country and traditional Russian ally.

CONCLUSION

Russia's troubles, along with the Balkan wars and other episodes of ethnic and religious conflict, provided dark and unsettling codas to the story of Communism's collapse. By the year 2000, the exhilaration that had greeted the end of the Cold War had largely faded. The backlash against immigrant communities and concerns about globalization only darkened the mood further, as did the strains on social welfare systems. Despite a decade of relatively robust economic growth in most of the Continent, and despite the success of many former Eastern bloc countries in transitioning to Western-style limited free-market democracy, most Europeans greeted the new millennium with, at best, muted hopes. The ideological commitments and utopian visions that had flourished between the French Revolution and World War II had largely evaporated.

Even so, the prosperity and social-support systems that had been built up since the war still provided basic levels of comfort and security for most people on the Continent. The violence that followed the collapse of Communism had been contained without anything like the loss of life seen in earlier parts of the twentieth century. Globalization offered the prospect of new wealth and cultural enrichment as well as the threat of economic dislocation. And so, at the start of the twenty-first century, Europeans could still hope that the extraordinary social and political progress made since the war would not soon be reversed.

[CHAPTER REVIEW]

KEY TERMS

oil shock (p. 847)
neoliberalism (p. 849)
Margaret Thatcher (p. 849)
détente (p. 853)

dissident movements
  (p. 854)
Helsinki Accords (p. 856)
Solidarity (p. 856)
Mikhail Gorbachev (p. 858)

perestroika (p. 859)
Chernobyl (p. 859)
glasnost (p. 859)
Václav Havel (p. 861)
Velvet Revolution (p. 861)

Boris Yeltsin (p. 864)
ethnic cleansing (p. 868)
European Union (EU)
  (p. 871)

REVIEW QUESTIONS

1. In the early 1970s, what developments threatened the long period of prosperity and stability in the post-war West?

2. During the 1970s and 1980s, in what ways did Western European states shift away from the post-war social and political consensus?

3. What characterized the cultural developments of the late twentieth century?

4. How did the dissident movements of Eastern Europe fight against Soviet control?

5. During the 1980s, what Soviet policies and structural weaknesses foreshadowed the collapse of Soviet power in the Eastern bloc?

6. How did the events of 1989 lead to the end of Communism in Eastern Europe?

7. What major factors caused the collapse of the Soviet Union?

8. In the 1990s, why did ethnic violence arise in the former Yugoslavia?

9. From the 1980s onward, what challenges did globalization pose to European states?

10. What new economic connections developed among European countries at the end of the twentieth century?

CORE OBJECTIVES

After reading this chapter, you should have a solid understanding of the following core objectives. To strengthen your grasp of the core objectives, use the resources on the Student Site for The West.

- Examine the economic and political shifts of the 1970s and 1980s.
- Identify the trends that undermined the stability of the Soviet bloc.
- Evaluate the collapse of Communism in Eastern Europe.

- Explain the demise of the Soviet Union.
- Analyze the aftermath of the collapse of Communism.
- Assess the growth of global economic and political connections that transformed Europe in the 1980s and 1990s.

 GO TO inQuizitive TO SEE WHAT YOU'VE LEARNED—AND LEARN WHAT YOU'VE MISSED—WITH PERSONALIZED FEEDBACK ALONG THE WAY.

CHRONOLOGY

2004
French Parliament bans conspicuous religious symbols from schools

2004
European Council proposes constitutional treaty

2004
Seven former Eastern bloc countries join NATO

2001
Same-sex marriage legalized in the Netherlands

January 2002
Euro currency comes into use

2004
Ten countries join the EU, eight from former Eastern bloc

2007–2009
Great Recession

2007
Lisbon Treaty

2010
Conservative-led coalition in Britain ends New Labour era

2001
Afghan War begins

Sept. 11, 2001
Al-Qaeda launches terrorist attacks on the World Trade Center and Pentagon

2003–2011
Iraq War

2005
Angela Merkel becomes German chancellor

2009
Beginning of Greek debt crisis

2011
Syrian civil war begins

26

Under Pressure

EUROPE'S UNCERTAIN PRESENT

Since 2000

October 2016: On the outskirts of the French town of Calais, on the English Channel, a refugee camp had grown up. At least 7,000 asylum-seekers—a majority of them young men, about 10 percent of them minors—lived in tents, shipping containers, and makeshift huts, waiting for the chance to cross through the Channel Tunnel into Great Britain. Some had relatives there; others believed they would have a greater chance of receiving permanent asylum in Britain than elsewhere in Europe. Many looked for a chance to stow away in a truck or train heading through the tunnel, and already in 2016 at least thirteen had died in the attempt. They came from across the world, but especially from troubled areas of Africa and the Middle East. The British press, in a racially tinged phrase, called the place "the Jungle."

For the moment, the British had refused them entry, but still they waited. Residents of Calais complained about the threats of disease and violence, and about a drop-off in visits from British shoppers. Marine Le Pen (1968–), leader of France's far-right National Front Party, visited Calais and promised to sue the French government to close the camp. Aid workers and the refugees themselves complained about crowding, unsanitary conditions, and insufficient shelter. Finally, in October the French government forcibly dispersed the camp and moved the refugees to reception centers elsewhere in France. But newspapers

Refugee Crisis Volunteers on the Greek island of Lesbos helping refugees on a small boat just arrived from Turkey. In the fall of 2015, over 7,000 refugees, mostly Syrian, landed on Lesbos every day.

FOCUS QUESTIONS

- How did terrorism and war in the Middle East affect European society and politics?
- What were the major gains and setbacks in European integration?
- What impact did the Great Recession have in the EU?
- What were the major causes of the crisis in Ukraine?
- Why did an illiberal populism spread through Europe after 2010?
- What impact did the refugee crisis have in Europe?

soon reported that many of the former residents of the camp—possibly thousands—had ended up sleeping in the streets of Paris.

Calais, owing to its strategic location on the narrowest stretch of the English Channel, has long had a significant place in the European story. It was from here that Julius Caesar set off for his invasion of Britain, and here that England's Richard II landed in France on his way to the Crusades. Captured by England during the Hundred Years' War of the fourteenth and fifteenth centuries, the town remained the last piece of the European continent under English rule, returning to France only in 1558. During World War II, the Allies deceived the Germans into thinking that their cross-Channel invasion would take place at Calais, a ruse that helped the actual invasion, in Normandy, succeed.

But in 2016, the Calais refugee camp stood as an illustration of many of the problems facing Europe in the first decades of the twenty-first century. Most obviously, it illustrated how what is often called globalization—the increasingly intense and interconnected movement of people, goods, capital, and ideas across the world—has affected European communities and governments. In particular, civil wars and economic misery have sent millions of refugees and economic migrants heading toward many different European destinations. Over a million refugees arrived in Europe in 2015 alone, a majority of them fleeing the civil war in Syria. Globalization in turn helped fuel the rise of populist nationalism. The far-right leader Le Pen held up the Calais camp as a supposed example of the ways out-of-touch

French elites were disregarding the will of ordinary people by allowing migrants into the country, and the message resonated in Calais itself. In the French presidential election of May 2017, Le Pen won a large majority there even as she lost the country as a whole by a landslide. A month later, she was elected to a parliamentary seat from the Calais area.

The presence of refugees in Calais demonstrated as well the halting, uneven progress of European unification. As we have seen, by the year 2000 many members of the European Union had adopted the same currency and had virtually dismantled their intra-European border controls. But other countries resisted this trend, including Great Britain, which continued to enforce passport controls for everyone seeking to enter the country. Refugee status in the EU remained governed by a confusing welter of regulations, with ultimate control still belonging to the member states. As a result, the desperate refugees hoping to resettle in Britain found themselves stopped at Calais. The refugee crisis itself, as we will see, proved to be a boon to those in Britain who wanted to leave the EU altogether.

But the crisis in Calais also testified to something else. It showed that in 2016, for all the problems facing the Continent, Europe was seen by people from around the world as a destination worth considerable risk to reach. Throughout most of its modern history, Europe was a place that itself generated refugees. Hunger, war, and religious and political persecution drove desperate men and women to undertake migrations across the Continent and beyond. From the Puritan migrants of the 1600s, to survivors of the Irish potato famine in the 1840s, to victims of Nazism in the 1930s, Europeans fled across the oceans. In the early twenty-first century, the tide was reversed. The refugee issue, a source of crisis in the immediate political context, was also, in longer historical perspective, a sign of success.

In this final chapter, we will survey the history of Europe between 2000 and 2017, showing how the consensus that seemed to develop at the end of the twentieth century around liberal democracy, limited free markets, and strong social safety nets has come under pressure. But we will also consider how the social and political progress of the post-war decades has, at least for the moment, withstood this pressure. We will look briefly at the state of Europe today and offer some thoughts on where the Continent stands at this point in its history.

TERRORISM AND WAR

At the start of the twenty-first century, even as the former Soviet bloc countries were completing the first stage of their transition from Communism and the EU was preparing to introduce its single currency, a new challenge suddenly arose in a distant and unexpected quarter: the mountains of Afghanistan. There the terrorist network known as Al-Qaeda ("the base" in Arabic) planned an audacious attack on the United States. Its members were largely Arabs committed to a radical, violent version of Islam and a hatred of the West that had developed over the course of the Arab-Israel conflict, the Soviet invasion of Afghanistan, the Gulf War, and conflicts in Chechnya.

SEPTEMBER 11 AND ITS AFTERMATH

On September 11, 2001, the attack took place, with terrorists hijacking four American airplanes. They crashed two of them into the twin towers of the World Trade Center in New York City, destroying both with enormous loss of life, and one into the Pentagon in Washington, badly damaging it and killing many more. Passengers fought for control of the fourth plane, targeted either for the White House or for the Capitol building in Washington, and it crashed into a field in rural Pennsylvania. All told, nearly 3,000 people were killed.

Most Europeans reacted to the attack with outrage and sympathy. The headline in the leading French daily, *Le Monde*, ran: "We Are All Americans." True, some European commentators suggested that **9/11** had come as a response to aggressive U.S. policies in the Middle East, and the German composer Karl-Heinz Stockhausen was widely quoted calling the attack "the greatest work of art imaginable for the whole cosmos"; but these were very much minority voices. When U.S. president George W. Bush asked for European support to invade Afghanistan, overturn the Taliban regime that had supported Al-Qaeda, and destroy the terrorist organization itself, he received immediate aid from Britain. Eventually, the NATO alliance itself formally invoked its principle of collective defense (enshrined in Article 5 of the North Atlantic Treaty) and committed itself to the Afghan war. The Western forces met with early success, replacing the Taliban with a pro-Western government. However, these forces subsequently became bogged down in a long guerrilla conflict, and it took until 2011 for U.S. special forces to locate and kill the leader of Al-Qaeda, Osama bin-Laden.

Memorializing Tragedy People worldwide responded with shock and sympathy to the tragedy of the September 11, 2001, terrorist attacks. Here Prague residents flock to an impromptu public gathering on September 12 to remember the victims.

Europe itself had a central part in the story of the rise of jihadist terrorism. Several of the 9/11 attackers had lived for long periods in Germany, including one of the ringleaders, the Egyptian Mohammed Atta (1968–2001), who had studied at the Technical University of Hamburg. Alienated and isolated, feeling at home neither in his birthplace nor in Europe, Atta found meaning for his life, and a cause, in Al-Qaeda's hate-filled doctrines. And while Atta targeted the United States, other terrorists with similar backgrounds sought victims in Europe itself. On March 11, 2004, jihadist terrorists set off explosives on board trains in Madrid, killing 192. On July 7, 2005, four British-born terrorists blew themselves up in London subways and buses, killing 52. Such attacks would continue through the second decade of the century.

Nor did terrorism spare Russia, although in this case it was connected first and foremost to the brutal conflict in Chechnya rather than to a more general jihadist hostility toward the West. The worst incident was the **Beslan attack**: on September 1, 2004, a large group of terrorists, principally from the Muslim-majority autonomous southern Russian republics of Chechnya and Ingushetia, attacked a school in the town of Beslan in the southern autonomous republic of Ossetia. They took over 1,100 hostages, a majority of them schoolchildren. Two days later, Russian security forces attempted to end the standoff by force. In the fighting, much of the school burned and 330 people died, including 186 children.

THE IRAQ WAR

The initial solidarity of the European powers with the United States in what President Bush called the war on terror soon fractured. In 2002, the Bush administration began to plan for a war against Iraq. Although Iraqi dictator Saddam Hussein had no connection to Al-Qaeda and the 9/11 attacks, the Bush administration nonetheless saw him as a threat and charged Iraq with harboring weapons of mass destruction. Both the United States and France had given support to Hussein's regime in the 1980s; but following the Iraqi dictator's attempt to conquer Kuwait in 1990, which a broad Western and Middle Eastern coalition reversed in the Gulf War, he had become one of the United States' chief enemies. Bush and his team also thought that replacing Hussein with a democratic regime could spark a wave of liberalization throughout the Muslim world.

On February 5, 2003, U.S. secretary of state Colin Powell appeared before the United Nations and presented evidence allegedly proving the existence of a dangerous, clandestine Iraqi weapons program. But he did not convince all of America's European allies of the need for war. Britain, under the moderate New Labour government of Tony Blair, agreed to join the United States, as did many of the former Communist bloc countries that had now become part of NATO, including Poland, Hungary, and the Czech Republic. Germany and France refused, leading U.S. defense secretary Donald Rumsfeld to deride these countries as "old Europe." In response, on February 14 French foreign minister Dominique de Villepin delivered a passionate speech to the UN against the war. "This message," he declared, "comes to you today from an old country, France, from an old continent like mine, Europe, that has known wars, occupation, and barbarity."

In March 2003, despite the French and German objections, the **Iraq War** began. And although the U.S.-led "coalition of the willing" initially had great success, it found no weapons of mass destruction and was soon bogged down in a debilitating guerrilla conflict in which the Iraqi civilian population suffered enormously. European governments that supported the war, particularly Blair's in Great Britain, lost popular support. Triumphantly reelected to a second term in 2001, Blair eked out a third victory in 2005, but with a considerably reduced majority in the House of Commons. Two years later, amid accusations that he had deceived Parliament to bring Britain into the war, he resigned.

THE RESPONSE OF THE RIGHT

Only a very small percentage of European Muslims sympathized with terrorism. However, the events that followed from 9/11, particularly the U.S.-led war in Iraq, made it easier for radical Muslim preachers to recruit followers, especially among alienated Muslim youth, by claiming that an apocalyptic conflict between Muslims and unbelievers had begun. Similar rhetoric of a "clash between civilizations" also appealed to some non-Muslim politicians and cultural figures, especially on the far right.

The two countries where the temperature rose the highest were France and the Netherlands. In 2002, the veteran French far-right leader Jean-Marie Le Pen (father of Marine) shocked France by squeaking past a divided left to make his way into the second, run-off round of the presidential election campaign against the conservative Jacques Chirac, who led the party that had descended from the Gaullists. A crushing majority of voters (82 percent) supported Chirac in the second round, rather than vote for a man known for racism and anti-Semitism. Still, Le Pen's initial success raised fears that his xenophobic, anti-immigrant program was becoming more popular in the wake of 9/11.

Then in November 2005, following the deaths of two Muslim teenagers running from the police, a wave of youth rioting broke out throughout the dilapidated suburbs around major French cities in which Muslim immigrant communities were concentrated. The members of these communities, although increasingly French-born and French-speaking, remained subject to discrimination and found it difficult to integrate fully into French life. The rioters burned over 8,000 automobiles, and the French government restored order by imposing a formal state of emergency granting the police extraordinary powers. These events in turn helped Nicolas Sarkozy (1955–), who had gained a hard-line reputation as Chirac's interior minister, win the French presidency in 2007. Sarkozy

Rise of the Far Right National Front leader Jean-Marie Le Pen addresses a gathering of supporters at a rally calling on French voters to say "non" (no) in the 2005 referendum on a constitution for the European Union.

brought his party closer to the **National Front**'s positions on immigration, loudly insisting that French Muslims "integrate" fully despite the difficulties they faced.

In the Netherlands, the early years of the century were marked by two sensational assassinations. In 2002, the populist politician Pim Fortuyn was shot dead by a Dutch Christian who objected to his Islamophobia. Two years later, a Dutch Muslim of Moroccan descent shot the filmmaker Theo van Gogh, who had recently directed a film entitled *Submission* that viciously attacked Muslim treatment of women. These events helped spur the rise of the far-right Party for Freedom, led by the populist Geert Wilders, which in subsequent years became the second-largest party in the Dutch Parliament.

EUROPEAN CONSTRUCTION AND ITS DISCONTENTS

Suspicion of immigrant communities frequently formed part of a more general hostility to globalization in Western Europe. Populist politicians like Jean-Marie Le Pen stoked this hostility, warning that their countries' national identity and sovereignty were at risk. And in the first decade of the new century, this hostility increasingly focused also on the European Union, drawing on and intensifying the Euroskepticism of previous decades.

THE EU AND NATO

For the first few years of the new century, the process of what was widely called European construction had seemed to be continuing apace. On January 1, 2002, a major symbolic threshold was crossed when twelve member countries of the EU began using the same euro coins and bills. The currencies had been effectively joined since 1999, when conversion rates among them were fixed (initially for eleven states; Greece joined later) and control of their monetary policies passed largely to the European Central Bank. From then on, the member countries were in theory bound by a set of strict conditions, including keeping their budget deficits under 3 percent of gross domestic product (GDP). But for most ordinary Europeans the real shift came in 2002, when they could start to use the same physical money in countries from Portugal to Finland. By 2017, nineteen countries had adopted the euro as their currency. Among the largest European economies, Britain remained the major holdout. Many economists criticized the euro as a dangerous and unworkable innovation because it forced countries with very different economies and political systems to follow the same monetary policies. But the desire for political progress outweighed purely economic considerations.

Two years after the introduction of the euro, another major transformation of the EU took place when it admitted ten new member states, all but two from the former Eastern bloc. In terms of population, the expansion was the largest in the Union's history. The new states included Poland, whose 38 million people made it the EU's sixth-largest member. But the expansion also introduced a new level of inequality among EU countries. Latvia, the poorest new member, had a GDP per capita of just $10,000 per year—less than one-third that of the richest members, Denmark and Austria. Poland's was only slightly larger, at $11,000 per year. With citizens of the new member countries eligible to live and work in other member states within a few years, large-scale labor movement began. By 2007, some 2.3 million Polish citizens were living abroad—nearly 400,000 in the United Kingdom alone. The figure of the so-called Polish plumber—willing to work for less than his British competitors—became a fixture of British popular culture, and indeed employment levels among the least skilled elements of the British workforce stagnated during these years. In the decade after 2004, Bulgaria,

Romania, and Croatia also joined the EU, bringing total membership to twenty-eight states.

The first decades of the century also saw a further expansion of NATO. In 2004, seven states from the former Eastern bloc joined the alliance, including the three Baltic states of Estonia, Latvia, and Lithuania. With this enlargement, NATO came to include not only all of the former Soviet satellite states of Central and Eastern Europe, but also these three former republics of the Soviet Union itself. Although the Russian government did not object strenuously to the change at the time, over the next decade Russian resentment of the alliance would grow steadily more powerful.

POLITICAL INTEGRATION

In the Western European states where the EU had been born, the next step in the so-called construction of Europe was a greater degree of political union. In 2002, the European Council convened a constitutional convention, chaired by former French president Valéry Giscard d'Estaing. Some of the participants hoped that the convention might produce a document similar to national constitutions, combining a grand statement of principles with articles that would clearly and simply delineate the powers of the Union and its principal institutional branches: the executive European Council, the Parliament, and the Court of Justice.

However, after protracted negotiations, the participants could not come to a consensus around such a document. Instead, in 2004 they produced a Treaty Establishing a Constitution for Europe, nearly five hundred pages long, which spelled out in far more detail the functions of European institutions and the relation between the Union and its member states. It strengthened the powers of the Union government, but only incrementally, and did not offer a major departure from established practice. Among other things, it created new offices for a president of the European Council and a Union minister for foreign affairs.

To take effect, the new constitutional treaty needed ratification by all members of the Union: at the time, twenty-five separate states. In most cases, the member Parliaments complied without substantial debate. But then something very unexpected took place. In France in 2005, President Chirac decided to submit the decision to a national referendum, hoping that a large "yes" vote would serve as a vote of confidence in his own government. Both his own party and the opposition Socialists announced their approval. But an unexpectedly strong "no" campaign took shape in response. Dissident Socialists, the Communist Party, and several other small parties on the left opposed the treaty on the grounds that it would make it harder for France to resist Europe-wide free-market policies. Dissident neo-Gaullists and the far-right National Front led by Jean-Marie Le Pen claimed that the treaty would allow the Union to infringe on French sovereignty. Both sets of opponents suggested that increasing European integration would enable yet more migrants from Central and Eastern Europe to take jobs away from French citizens. And on May 29, in a turn of events that shocked most members of the French social elite, 54.7 percent of voters rejected the treaty. Three days later, following a similar debate, an even larger proportion of Dutch voters (61.5 percent) voted "no" in their own referendum.

Following this failure, a different strategy came into play. Instead of proposing a new treaty that would supersede earlier European agreements, in 2007 negotiators from the member countries devised the so-called **Lisbon Treaty** that would function as a series of amendments to those agreements. In practice, many of the changes proposed in the earlier treaty were incorporated into the new one, including the offices of Union president and foreign minister. But it was much harder to characterize the Lisbon Treaty as the foundation stone of a new, pan-Union government threatening the sovereignty of individual member states, and this time the French and Dutch governments prudently declined to hold referenda on ratification. The member states all formally signed the treaty in 2007, and it came into effect in 2009. But given the difficulty of getting any treaty approved, and the opposition in many member states to further European integration, it seemed unlikely that any additional major steps would take place in the construction of Europe for some time. In Great Britain, the Lisbon Treaty strengthened the Euroskepticism that had long flourished in the Conservative Party.

The country that remained most committed to the European ideal was Germany. There, given the weight of the past, a strong commitment to Europe seemed the surest guarantee against any resurgence of xenophobic nationalism. But in addition, as the European country with the largest population (81.9 million people in 2000) and the largest economy ($1.95 trillion in 2000), Germany could count on exercising more influence in the Union than any of its partners. In 2005, after elections that left the center-right Christian Democrats as the largest party, the chancellorship passed to Angela Merkel (1954–): the country's first female leader, and the first leader of the newly united Germany from the former East. A chemist

Angela Merkel Leader of the opposition party in the German Parliament, Angela Merkel campaigns in the days prior to the September 2005 election that made her chancellor.

by training, a cautious and methodical leader, Merkel consistently advocated the strengthening of European cooperation and European institutions. She knew well that Germany, as Europe's leading exporter, benefited disproportionately from the expansion of European markets.

SOCIAL AND CULTURAL CHANGE

The debates over increased European integration took place simultaneously with the ongoing transformation of European countries into post-industrial societies, in which the service and information sectors of the economy came to dwarf manufacturing in importance. In Great Britain, the country that had led Europe's industrial development in the nineteenth century, manufacturing jobs still accounted for 45 percent of all employment as late as 1970. But by 2015, that figure stood at just 19 percent. Most other Western European countries had fallen to similar levels. In Central and Eastern Europe, manufacturing was also in decline, although not as steeply: in the Czech Republic in 2015, for example, manufacturing still accounted for 38 percent of

all jobs. Large areas of Europe were also becoming more educated. In Scandinavia, the British Isles, and the Low Countries, over 40 percent of thirty-year-olds had completed some form of post-secondary education. The same was true in large portions of France, Spain, and Poland.

Among these highly educated Europeans, especially those in the service and information sectors of the economy, support for European integration, and globalization more broadly, was high. In general, these men and women benefited from the free movement of people and capital across borders. But workers attached to the industrial sector feared—often correctly—that this free movement would enable their employers to close factories and outsource their jobs to cheaper labor markets elsewhere. They provided the core of support for the "no" votes in the French and Dutch referenda on the European constitutional treaty.

But not all changes in the economy in this period were so divisive. Some—in particular, those related to new means of communication and information—quickly spread to all sectors of the population. By 2015, an estimated 77 percent of all Europeans had regular Internet access. In most countries, over 50 percent of the population owned a smartphone, and in wealthy Sweden and Switzerland the proportion topped 70 percent. By the end of 2016, over 40 percent of all Europeans used Facebook.

A broad European consensus also spurred the development of renewable energy sources in the face of climate change. Between 2000 and 2016, overall energy production from renewable sources (such as solar, wind, and

Renewable Energy Windmills tower over a power plant in Copenhagen, Denmark, indicative of the country's increasing reliance on renewable forms of energy and on wind in particular.

geothermal) more than doubled in the states of the European Union. Energy from wind power expanded nearly twelvefold, as vast wind farms sprang up in locations ranging from the Baltic Sea to the plains of southeastern Romania. Wind power produced nearly 40 percent of Danish domestic energy consumption and 8 percent of European consumption overall. Consumption from all renewable sources together roughly equaled the consumption from oil. Few voices in Europe challenged the reality of climate change, and all the European states signed on to the 2015 Paris accord, in which nearly all the nations of the world pledged to work to reduce their output of carbon dioxide.

Among cultural changes during this period, one in particular took place with striking speed—and also caused deep divisions. As of the year 2000, not a single European country had yet recognized marriage between members of the same sex. But the Netherlands took this step in 2001, followed by Belgium in 2003 and another twelve countries—including Great Britain, Spain, Germany, and France—by 2017. Eleven other countries, including Italy, recognized some sort of domestic partnership arrangement.

Religion played a part in the conflicts over the issue. Nearly every Protestant country legalized gay marriage, while Catholic ones were split. But the major division occurred across the former iron curtain. Not a single former Communist country recognized gay marriage as of mid-2017, and only three—the Czech Republic, Hungary, and Slovenia—allowed a form of domestic partnership. In fact, between 1990 and 2015 thirteen countries formerly under Communist rule took the step of formally defining marriage as heterosexual. But even in Western Europe, the change did not come without significant opposition. In France, opinion polls as late as 2016 showed 30 percent of respondents disapproving of gay marriage and 40 percent disapproving of adoption by homosexual couples. Large protests erupted after France legalized what proponents called "marriage for all" in 2013, and these protests helped push the cultural conservative François Fillon to the presidential nomination of the conservative party, now called the Republicans, in 2017.

THE GREAT RECESSION AND THE EUROZONE CRISIS

In the midst of these social and cultural changes, in 2007–8 Europe suddenly found itself confronting the largest economic challenge since World War II. As with the Great Depression of the inter-war period, the initial shock came from the United States, where a real estate bubble fueled by lax lending policies collapsed, leading to the failure of a major investment bank, a spectacular stock market crash, and the worst economic downturn since the Depression itself seventy years before. Dubbed the **Great Recession**, this new downturn quickly spread to Europe, whose countries had generally experienced robust growth since the start of the century, but where banks' lending policies had often imitated the dangerous U.S. examples.

In Europe, the effects of the crisis varied considerably from country to country. While Germany experienced a moment of severe economic contraction in 2008–9, by early 2010 its economy had again begun to expand. France experienced only a mild recession, although its economy subsequently went into a long period of stagnation. But small Iceland, whose leading banks had gambled heavily on the continuation of high stock prices and easy access to credit, came close to economic collapse: its GDP declined from $21.3 billion in 2007 to just $12.9 billion two years later. A quarter of the population went into default on their home mortgages. Finland also saw a severe contraction, in part because its economy had become dependent on the success of a single corporation—the cell-phone maker Nokia, which had unwisely dismissed smartphones as a momentary fad. Greece, Spain, Italy, and Ireland, all with overheated economies in the first years of the century, also experienced deep recessions. In Greece, as we will see in a moment, the political consequences—not just for the country itself, but for Europe as a whole—were especially dire.

TENSIONS WITHIN THE EUROZONE

Europe had of course experienced such downturns before, but one particular factor made this economic crisis strikingly different from earlier ones: the existence of the **Eurozone**. By joining the common currency, its member countries had effectively surrendered much of the direction of their own economies to the European Central Bank. They could not devalue their own national currencies to make their exports cheaper, nor could they print more money to pay off their debts. They had no control over interest rates. And keeping their commitment to maintain their budget deficits at less than 3 percent of their GDP would prohibit them from compensating for low economic demand in the classic manner prescribed by John Maynard Keynes: through government stimulus spending.

Worse, the leading country in the Eurozone—Germany—showed little inclination to relax these rules to

A CRISIS IN UNITY

The end of the Cold War in 1989 presented a utopian moment for the architects and advocates of a unified Europe. For its proponents, the EU represented an opportunity to put a century of wars, ethnic genocide, and political division definitively behind them. The new "United States of Europe" would work toward a free, prosperous, and tolerant society unburdened by the prejudices and horrors of the past. At the same time, many Europeans distrusted the new institution as a bureaucratic power grab that was subservient to the interests of political and economic elites and not responsive to those of ordinary citizens. Disputes culminated in the 2016 referendum in which British citizens voted narrowly to withdraw from the EU. The prospects for a unified Europe, which seemed so certain in 1993, now seemed quite gloomy.

Angela Merkel, from "Speech at the ceremony commemorating the 100th anniversary of the battle of Verdun, 5/29/16"

Angela Merkel (1954–) has served as chancellor of Germany since her election in 2005. She has emerged as Europe's leading politician and an adamant defender of the European Union. In this speech, delivered to commemorate the deaths of hundreds of thousands of French and German soldiers at Verdun in 1916, she emphasizes the importance today of leaving behind "the trenches of enmity" and maintaining full European integration.

Only by opening up to one another can we also learn and benefit from each other. That precisely is the key to Europe's success. It is particularly apparent these days, when we are also witnessing weaknesses in our community. Still, I maintain that the 21st-century challenges we face can only be tackled together.

With European integration, we have left behind us the trenches of enmity. We have gained peace and prosperity. We have overcome quite a number of crises during which we feared the many things we've accomplished through integration may forever be lost. After the recent Franco-German Council of Ministers, President François Hollande said: "We have always managed to overcome the obstacles in our path." That is exactly why today, as well, despite numerous difficulties and setbacks, we can confidently set our sights on the future.

In the European Union, we will at times [have] different opinions on certain issues. That is only natural. However, all sides will benefit if, in the end, we always prove that we are able to reach compromises and adopt common positions. Thinking and acting as pure nation states would set us back. We would not be able to successfully defend our values or promote our interests, neither internally nor abroad. This is true for overcoming the European sovereign-debt crisis, for dealing with the many people who have come to Europe seeking refuge, and for all other great present-day challenges.

We must visibly demonstrate on a daily basis our shared commitment to the fundamental values of freedom, democracy and the rule of law.

Nigel Farage, from "Speech to the European Parliament, 6/28/16"

Nigel Farage (1964–) has been a member of the European Parliament and leader of the United Kingdom Independence Party (UKIP), a Euroskeptic organization. In this address to members of the EU governing body, he speaks on behalf of British voters who rejected what they saw as an unwelcome, imposed political union.

You, as a political project, are in denial. You are in denial that your currency is failing.…Just look at the Mediterranean.…As a policy to impose poverty on Greece and the Mediterranean you have done very well.… You are in denial over Ms Merkel's call last year for as many people as possible to cross the Mediterranean into the European Union, which has led to massive divisions between countries and within countries. But the biggest problem you have got, and the main reason the United Kingdom voted the way that it did, is that you have, by stealth, by deception, without ever telling the truth to the British or the rest of the peoples of Europe, imposed upon them a political union.…

…What the ordinary people did, the people who have been oppressed over the last few years and seen their living standards go down, [was] they rejected the multinationals. They rejected the merchant banks, they rejected big politics, and they said, actually, we want our country back. We want our fishing waters back, we want our borders back, we want to be an independent, self-governing normal nation, and that is what we have done and that is what must happen. And in doing so, we now offer a beacon of hope to democrats across the rest of the European continent. I will make one prediction this morning: the United Kingdom will not be the last Member State to leave the European Union.

QUESTIONS FOR ANALYSIS

1. According to Merkel, why is openness so important for Europe's future?
2. In Farage's account, how did the 2016 British referendum vote express the voice of ordinary Europeans?
3. Based on these two speeches, what issues are dividing Europeans and how might the European Union resolve or worsen them?

Sources: Angela Merkel, "Speech at the ceremony commemorating the 100th anniversary of the battle of Verdun, 5/29/16," The Press and Information Office of the [German] Federal Government (website); Nigel Farage, "Speech to the European Parliament, 6/28/16," European Parliament, Debates, Tuesday, 28 June 2016, Brussels (website).

help the countries in greatest difficulty, still less to provide the sort of generous economic bailout that the Germans themselves had benefited from after World War II. German economists, reasoning from their country's own position, believed that the problem with the worst-affected countries lay not in low economic demand but in profligacy and waste stimulated by overly easy access to cheap credit. These economists did not prescribe deficit spending, but rather severe austerity measures to *cut* public spending and restore fiscal responsibility. Chancellor Merkel fully shared these views. In her speeches, she frequently referred to the legendary figure of the so-called Swabian housewife—a frugal domestic manager from the German province of Swabia who hated debt and could always make do with less. Following Merkel's lead, the EU insisted that the countries in economic distress tighten their belts.

THE CRISIS IN GREECE

But in many countries, especially in southern Europe, such **austerity policies**, coming on top of the constraints of the Eurozone, only deepened the economic misery. And in Greece they came close to causing social collapse. Up until 2007, Greece had routinely reported budget deficits of just over 3 percent of GDP—a level in keeping with Eurozone rules. But after the financial crisis, Greek officials confessed that this figure had been calculated using accounting tricks. The true figure was over 15 percent. Fiscal trickery had a long history in Greece, which had been in default on its national debt in over half the years since its independence in 1832.

The new revelations led to the wholesale collapse of the Greek banking sector and one of the worst economic contractions in European history. The country's GDP, which stood at $354 billion in 2008, fell precipitously and kept falling, reaching just $195 billion in 2015. It was unclear whether the country could remain in the Eurozone, even though its withdrawal might prompt other countries such as Spain to follow and ultimately lead to the collapse of the common currency altogether. In the end, European institutions and the International Monetary Fund agreed to a bailout, but—taking the lead from Germany—only on the condition that the Greek government impose even more severe austerity policies. They also overestimated the total amount of the Greek debt, thereby calling for even harsher austerity than their own theories prescribed. For ordinary Greeks, the crisis was punishing. The unemployment rate reached 25 percent, and the youth unemployment rate twice that. State pensions fell by nearly half,

Economic Crisis Protestors and riot police clash on the streets of Athens on June 28, 2011, during a two-day strike against the government's economic failings. The harsh austerity policies occasioned by the Greek economic crisis incited widespread demonstrations and strikes.

while the homelessness rate rose by more than a quarter. The population's suicide rate rose by 45 percent.

It was a testimony to Europe's newfound social and political stability that despite this severe test, even in Greece the Great Recession and Eurozone crisis did not provoke anything like the social and political upheavals that occurred during the Depression of the 1930s. While the downturn grievously stretched social safety nets, they did not break. In England in 2011, the shooting of an unarmed black man by police prompted a wave of riots, with large-scale arson and looting by racially mixed crowds, and five deaths, but no large-scale threat to social order. Greece experienced a wave of violent protests against austerity policies but saw no fundamental challenge to its democratic system. And while the **Greek crisis** spurred the rise of a new left-wing party called Syriza, when its leader came to power in 2015 he continued to cooperate with the European Union, accepted modified austerity policies, and remained committed to Greece's membership in the Eurozone.

CONFLICT IN THE FORMER SOVIET UNION

While the EU countries remained politically stable even under the pressure of the Eurozone crisis, other parts of the Continent did not avoid large-scale violence between

2000 and 2017. As in the 1990s, the trouble broke out along the former internal boundaries of a multi-ethnic Communist state. But this time the state in question was not Yugoslavia, but the Soviet Union. The level of destruction did not approach that of the earlier Balkan wars, but at many points it threatened to do so.

PUTIN'S RUSSIA

The dominant figure in these conflicts—and the most important European political figure of the twenty-first century to date—was the new president of the Russian Federation, Vladimir Putin (1952–). Born in Leningrad, as it was then known, Putin made his early career in the Soviet secret police, the KGB, serving for many years as a high-ranking officer in East Germany. In the 1990s, following the collapse of the Soviet Union, he entered Russian political life and soon became a favorite of President Boris Yeltsin, who named him prime minister in mid-1999.

In this role, Putin made a reputation for ruthless and decisive action by directing a new campaign against the rebellious region of Chechnya after a series of terrorist attacks in Russia that the security services blamed on Chechens. This time, unlike in the earlier Chechen conflict, the Russians won a decisive victory and restored a pro-Russian government there. At the end of 1999, upon Yeltsin's resignation, Putin became acting president and Yeltsin's designated heir. He won election to a full term three months later. He has remained in power ever since, although term limits set by the Russian constitution forced him formally to step out of the presidency between 2008 and 2012, becoming prime minister but retaining real power.

After the chaos, economic disruption, and political freedom of the 1990s, Putin aimed to restore order to Russia, along with a large measure of authoritarianism. And he largely succeeded, thanks to a combination of often-brutal repression and a spike in oil prices that generated massive new wealth for the Russian economy. The repressive tactics included the placing of state media—especially television—firmly under Putin's control, while intimidating and marginalizing independent media. It also extended to beatings of protestors by police and even, allegedly, to the murder of opponents, including a prominent opposition journalist who was mysteriously shot on Putin's birthday in 2006, and the deliberate radiation poisoning—in London—of a former intelligence officer turned dissident. Putin also gave new powers and resources to the police to cut down on crime, and he cultivated an image of personal strength: a physical fitness enthusiast, he liked to pose for pictures bare-chested. Putin cultivated an alliance with the Russian Orthodox Church, reconstructing church buildings destroyed under Communism and banning proselytism by competing Christian denominations. In return, the Church gave him its enthusiastic support.

As for the oil wealth, much of the country saw relatively little of it; but Moscow and Saint Petersburg boomed with new construction, while their streets flooded with new Western automobiles that caused virtually permanent traffic jams. As late as 1980, even in Moscow, fewer than one person in thirty had owned a car. By 2012, nearly half of all Russians owned one. Russians experimented with new tastes and developed a particular love for sushi. By 2014, Moscow had nearly 1,000 Japanese restaurants—twice the number to be found in New York City. A new, capitalist middle class was emerging, and its members largely credited Putin for the country's new stability and prosperity.

Putin did not put an end to the influence of the so-called oligarchs who had siphoned vast state resources into their own pockets after the collapse of the USSR. However, he

Putin's Russia Russian president Vladimir Putin walks with senior Russian Orthodox clerics in Moscow in May 2017. Warm relations with the Russian Orthodox Church have been an important aspect of Putin's distinctive brand of nationalism.

broke the power of the wealthiest and most independent of them, including the head of the Yukos oil company, Mikhail Khodorkovsky, who was arrested in 2003 and spent the next ten years in prison on corruption charges. In their place, Putin developed a new class of oligarchs, loyal to himself and drawn in many cases from a close circle of boyhood friends. Arkady Rotenberg, who had the good fortune to meet Putin in a judo club at age twelve, made a fortune estimated at $2.5 billion from infrastructure contracts awarded by the Russian government. Putin's own personal fortune remained a matter of speculation, but it almost certainly amounted to billions of dollars as well.

From the start of his rule, Putin set as a key goal the restoration of Russian influence over the territory of the former Soviet Union. Although he could not prevent the Baltic states from joining NATO in 2004, over the next few years he successfully put pressure on Ukraine and Georgia, which were dependent on Russian oil and natural gas, to prevent them from taking the same step. In 2008, when Georgia tried to repress an uprising in its pro-Russian region of South Ossetia, Putin sent in the Russian army, which occupied part of Georgia and briefly bombarded its capital city. South Ossetia subsequently declared independence, although only Russia and a few small allies gave it diplomatic recognition.

CRISIS IN UKRAINE

Five years later, a major crisis erupted in the largest of the non-Russian former Soviet republics: Ukraine. After achieving independence at the end of 1991, the country had experienced a difficult transition to democracy. Former Soviet officials remained in positions of power amid widespread charges of corruption. And Ukraine suffered from sharp divisions between Russian-speaking, Russian Orthodox groups, largely in the east, who felt a strong bond of identification with Russia, and Ukrainian-speakers, many of them belonging to other Christian denominations, largely in the west. In 2004–5, after the pro-Russian Viktor Yanukovych (1950–) claimed victory in the presidential election, opponents alleging voter fraud staged a series of large protests. The Ukrainian Supreme Court ordered a second vote, which Yanukovych lost. This bloodless transition of power became known as the Orange Revolution, the color adopted by the opposition campaign.

Yanukovych became president after a fair election in 2010 and tried to steer a middle course between Russia and the West. But in 2013, under pressure from Putin, he decided not to sign a trade agreement with the EU that

Ukrainian Crisis A protestor throws a stone at a police vehicle in a confrontation between protestors and police during outbreaks of violence in Kiev in January 2014—part of widespread popular protest against Viktor Yanukovych's government.

hopeful Ukrainians had viewed as a first step toward the country's membership in the Union. Protests erupted, and student demonstrators set up a protest camp in Independence Square in the capital, Kiev. Police attempts to break up the camp only drew more protestors to what became known as the **Euromaidan** (after the Ukrainian word for "square"). In February 2014, the violence spiraled out of control as police fired on protestors (a small number of whom were armed), causing as many as a hundred deaths. On February 22, Yanukovych resigned and the Parliament set a date for new elections. It seemed that a second post-Soviet revolution had taken place.

THE CRIMEAN PENINSULA But the **Ukrainian crisis** had only begun. The Crimean Peninsula was an ethnically Russian region of Ukraine that traced its Russian history back to its seizure by Catherine the Great from Muslim Tatars in the eighteenth century. Nearly entirely Russian-speaking, and a favorite Black Sea destination of Russians, the Crimea had only been joined to Ukraine in the 1950s by Communist Party leader Nikita Khrushchev. Just days after Yanukovych's resignation, crowds in Crimea flying Russian flags called for the peninsula to secede from Ukraine. Gunmen, most of them Russian army soldiers in disguise, took control of government buildings in the Crimean capital, Simferopol. On March 16, 2014, in the face of international condemnation of this military action, local authorities in Crimea staged a referendum and announced that 96 percent of the voters favored immediate union with Russia. Two days later, President Putin signed a hastily passed law annexing the region. With Crimea tied to mainland Ukraine only by a narrow land bridge, the new Ukrainian government did not attempt to reassert control.

EASTERN UKRAINE In April, the process seemed to repeat itself in Russian-speaking areas of eastern Ukraine, on the Russian border. Protestors in several Russian-speaking industrial cities, such as Donetsk and Luhansk, again supported by Russian soldiers in disguise, seized control of government buildings. In May, two People's Republics in the region (the name a deliberate nod to Communist-era titles) declared independence. But this time, the Ukrainian army responded, and widespread fighting broke out. Over the next year, an estimated 6,000 people would die as the Ukrainians battled local militias aided by the Russian army. International observers fretted that the conflict might explode into a full-scale war and warned that Putin's Russia might attempt similar moves against other former Soviet Republics—notably the Baltic states, which had large minorities of ethnic Russians. The EU and the United States passed a series of stringent economic sanctions to punish Russia for its role in the crisis and to pressure it to withdraw support for the rebels.

Ukraine and Crimea, 2014–2017 Tensions on the Russia-Ukraine border simmered throughout the 2010s. In 2014, Russia occupied and annexed the Crimean Peninsula. Territory on the eastern border of Ukraine changed hands repeatedly, amid fighting between the Ukrainian army and separatist militias aided by Russia.

In fact, the worst fears of Putin's Western critics, some of whom compared his actions to those of Hitler in the 1930s, did not materialize. The Ukrainian crisis coincided with a 50 percent fall in the worldwide price of oil, which sent the oil-dependent Russian economy into a recession that the Western sanctions worsened. The fighting in eastern Ukraine gradually died down, and a weakened Russia did not make aggressive moves elsewhere in the former USSR. The most blatant Russian aggression did not occur on the ground with troops, but in cyberspace with hackers, as Putin's intelligence services attempted to destabilize the political systems of their adversaries. Most notoriously, in 2016 Russian hackers allegedly interfered with the U.S. presidential election campaign on behalf of Donald Trump, stealing e-mails from Democratic Party and other servers and making them available to leakers.

A RISING ILLIBERALISM

Vladimir Putin, the point bears repeating, was no Hitler or Stalin. He had no ambition to transform Russia—still less other areas of the world—in accordance with any sort of totalitarian ideology, and he did not develop a powerful ideological party apparatus. While his regime flagrantly violated the norms of human rights that had developed in most of Europe by the year 2000, the level of political repression remained well below what Russia had experienced under Stalin's Soviet Union, or Germany under the Nazis.

But Putin nonetheless represented a model of sorts for a new, powerful current of **illiberalism** that flourished in Europe after 2010. Elements of the model included strong doses of nationalism and anti-Americanism, a disdain for democratic constitutionalism, an admiration for the naked exercise of power, and a cultural conservatism that expressed itself especially in hostility to homosexuals and gay marriage. (In 2013, Putin's tame Parliament passed a law outlawing so-called homosexual propaganda that might allegedly influence minors.)

HUNGARY AND POLAND

This current of illiberalism found a strong echo in two states of the former Eastern bloc: Hungary and Poland. In the former, the driving force was the politician Viktor Orbán (1963–), the long-time leader of the Fidesz Party, which had emerged out of dissident student movements at the end of the Communist period. Under Orbán's leadership, the party took on an increasingly conservative, nationalist character. In 2010, in coalition with the Christian Democrats, it won an overwhelming majority in Parliament, bringing Orbán to the premiership and allowing him to pass constitutional changes that, notably, reduced the independence of the Hungarian judiciary and the central bank.

The government then purged the heads of cultural institutions such as the Budapest New Theater, replacing them with strident Hungarian nationalists. It did little to stop right-wing gangs who were assaulting Roma encampments and desecrating Jewish cemeteries. It also passed laws banning gay marriage and defining conception as the beginning of life (although to date it has not banned abortion). During the refugee crisis of 2014–15, as we will see, it attempted to close Hungary's border to prohibit the entry of asylum-seekers from the Middle East. Orbán assumed close control over state-run media, and soon after a leading opposition newspaper criticized his personal corruption, it was closed, most likely because Orbán had threatened its owners. Orbán also attacked the EU, especially after its officials criticized his tendencies toward authoritarianism, and in 2017 the Hungarian Parliament attempted to close Budapest's independent Central European University. In his speeches, Orbán called for Hungary to become a "non-liberal democracy" and expressed admiration for Vladimir Putin.

Poland seemed to embark on a similar course after the conservative, nationalist Law and Justice Party took power after elections in October 2015. Led by Jaroslaw Kaczyński (1949–), the party restricted the independence of the highest Polish court and asserted control over state-run media. The government cracked down on public protests, with the police using tear gas to break up peaceful demonstrations. Kaczyński, like Viktor Orbán, frequently attacked Western cultural attitudes, especially the toleration of homosexuality. The government insisted that state schools and museums convey a strongly nationalist view of Polish history, and it threatened to prosecute a Polish-born American historian, Jan Gross, who had published evidence about the murder of Polish Jews by Polish Christians during the Holocaust. The same strong Polish nationalism, however, kept Kaczyński and other party leaders from seeking a close relationship with the leader of Poland's traditional adversary, Russia.

WESTERN EUROPE

The nationalist **populism** seen in Hungary and Poland bore a striking similarity to that of right-wing populist parties in Western Europe. Populism can take many forms, but it always involves a sharp hostility to social and cultural elites. In recent times, it has also almost always incorporated a bitter opposition to international free trade and international organizations such as the EU.

FRANCE In twenty-first-century Europe, the most prominent European populist party has been France's National Front. In 2011, Jean-Marie Le Pen gave up its leadership and was replaced by his daughter, Marine. She immediately began a process that the French press called the "de-demonization" of the Front, notably by renouncing her father's anti-Semitism. Indeed, she actively cultivated Jewish support while maintaining her father's hostility toward recent immigrant communities, especially those from Muslim North Africa. She was hoping to profit from rising tensions between Jews and Muslims in France and from several cases of anti-Semitic violence by Muslim extremists, including the murder of a rabbi and three schoolchildren outside a school in 2012. She also took an increasingly conservative line on social issues, including gay marriage.

Marine Le Pen called for France's withdrawal from the EU and praised Putin on several occasions. Russia, it was alleged, was providing the National Front with direct financial support. The Dutch populist Geert Wilders did not show the same approval of Putin and took a more liberal line on social issues than Le Pen, but he shared the National Front's stance on immigrant communities and the EU.

BREXIT In Great Britain and Germany, populist movements failed to gain comparable support. The right-wing Alternative for Germany Party, with a program broadly similar to the National Front's, rarely topped 15 percent in opinion polls and by 2017 had fallen to less than half of that. In Britain, the United Kingdom Independence Party (UKIP) campaigned largely on a single issue: British withdrawal from the EU. It did well in the 2014 European elections but never managed to elect more than two members of the British Parliament.

UKIP did, however, play an important role in forcing the British Conservative Party to confront the issue of EU membership. Euroskepticism had long had considerable influence in the party, as we have seen; but for forty years after Britain joined the EU, the skeptics had managed to do little more than limit the extent of Britain's participation in EU and other pan-European initiatives: Britain had remained out of the common-currency Eurozone and the Schengen "open borders" zone created in 1985. But UKIP's

ERASING BRITAIN FROM EUROPE

Banksy is an internationally renowned, but anonymous, artist whose work draws on graffiti and street art traditions to address contemporary social and political concerns. Banksy's work has appeared in cities and locations worldwide and has highlighted issues ranging from mass surveillance to police brutality to consumer capitalism to the rights of Palestinians. This recent piece, which depicts the EU flag, responds to the 2016 Brexit referendum, in which a narrow majority of British citizens voted to leave the European Union. Bansky placed the mural on the side of a building in Dover, England, not far from where the Calais ferry and the so-called Chunnel rail tunnel link Britain with continental Europe. In a crucial twist, Banksy has painted a workman standing on a ladder, chipping away at one of the stars on the EU flag.

QUESTIONS FOR ANALYSIS

1. What is the significance of the workman's actions in Banksy's mural?
2. Why do you suppose Bansky placed this image in Dover, England?
3. What is Bansky communicating about Britain's decision to leave the EU?

strident attacks on the EU, especially after the Lisbon Treaty came into effect in 2009, strengthened the hand of EU opponents in the Conservative Party and forced the party leadership to take on the issue.

Matters came to a head in 2015, when incumbent Conservative prime minister David Cameron (1966–) promised, in his successful reelection campaign, that the party would hold a referendum on a British exit from the EU, or **Brexit**. In the campaign leading up to the June 2016 referendum, the conservative British tabloid press issued dire warnings about the loss of British sovereignty and

promised that if Britain withdrew it would gain full control of its borders, expel much of its foreign labor force, and save the money that it contributed to the Union. Opponents of Brexit including Cameron vehemently challenged these arguments and emphasized the economic and political benefits Britain received from its EU membership, including the greater weight Britain enjoyed on the world stage as part of this larger whole. The vote, taking place in the middle of the Calais refugee camp crisis, produced a narrow victory for Brexit. Cameron resigned, and a year later his successor, Theresa May (1956–), initiated the

Brexit Demonstrators gather near Parliament to urge the British government to follow through on its promise to leave the European Union following the divisive June 2016 referendum. They hold signs from the "Vote Leave" referendum campaign and from the United Kingdom Independence Party, which supported the campaign.

characteristic of so much earlier European nationalism. In 2007, an alliance with the Scottish Greens allowed the Scottish National Party (SNP) to form a government in the Scottish assembly created as a result of the Blair government's decentralizing initiatives in the late 1990s. In 2011, they achieved an absolute majority, enabling them to push for a referendum on independence, which took place three years later.

In the referendum campaign, the nationalists pledged to develop stronger ties between an independent Scotland and the EU, and to preserve social welfare policies that they accused the Conservative British government of undercutting. The "no" forces warned of possible economic chaos if Scotland seceded from the United Kingdom, while promising a greater degree of autonomy for the Scots. Voters ended up defeating the proposal for independence by 55 percent to 45 percent, but in the next year's general election the nationalists under First Minister Nicola Sturgeon won fifty-six out of Scotland's fifty-nine seats in the British Parliament. And as the possibility of a British exit from the European Union rose, so did the

lengthy process of negotiating Britain's actual withdrawal from the EU.

SPAIN Although populism largely expressed itself through nationalist, right-wing parties during this period, in a few countries a left-wing populism made considerable strides as well. The most important case was Spain, which had suffered terribly from the Eurozone crisis, if not to the same extent as Greece. In 2013, Spanish youth unemployment topped out at more than 55 percent. In 2014, a group of left-wing Spanish academics founded a new political movement called Podemos ("We Can"), which initially committed itself to a repeal of austerity policies and a guaranteed basic income for all citizens. While not favoring Spanish withdrawal from the EU, it called for a democratization of European institutions and opposed the EU's promotion of free-market policies. Its leader, Pablo Iglesias, also criticized the EU's "aggressive" support of Ukraine in the conflict with Putin's Russia. Within a year, Podemos was polling ahead of the Socialists and the conservative Popular Party, and in the 2016 elections in alliance with other left-wing parties it captured nearly a quarter of the vote.

SCOTLAND In Scotland, the nationalist movement that had campaigned for independence from the United Kingdom since well before the start of the century flourished in large part because it moved away from the xenophobia

The European Union, 2017 By the early twenty-first century, the EU had twenty-eight member states, including the former Eastern bloc countries that had joined in 2004. But several members did not participate in the Schengen immigration agreement or use the euro as their currency. One such long-time EU member was the United Kingdom, which in 2016 voted to withdraw from the Union.

Legend:
- European Union member, 2017
- European Union Eurozone
- Limit of Schengen area
- Scheduled to leave EU in 2019 (Brexit)

possibility that the enthusiastically pro-European Scots might rethink their decision to remain within the United Kingdom.

FROM FRICTION TO VIOLENCE: EUROPE AND ISLAM

The rise of populist movements was fueled in part by continuing disputes over the place of Islamic immigrant communities in European life. France, home to the largest Islamic population in Western Europe—an estimated 5 million people—once again drove these disputes.

CULTURAL CONFLICT

Disputes often arose over cultural and religious practices. For instance, did girls have the right to wear Islamic head coverings in school? Since the 1990s, many leading French cultural critics and politicians had insisted that the practice violated French republican principles of church-state separation, which—more stringently than the U.S. variety—demanded the removal of all forms of religious observance from public spaces. While few schools had actually reported problems with the practice, advocates of a ban on headscarves argued that it would further the "integration" of Muslims into French life, notably by requiring young French-born Muslim women to give up at least one of the allegedly misogynistic customs their parents had brought from their homelands.

In 2004, the French Parliament passed a law banning "conspicuous religious symbols" from schools—presumably including not only the headscarf, or hijab, but also Sikh turbans and Jewish yarmulkes, although nearly all the debates only mentioned headscarves. In 2010, it added a law banning full-face coverings such as the burqa, this time with the argument that obscuring the face did damage to French communal life. In 2016, several French seaside towns also tried to ban so-called burqinis—full-body swimsuits preferred by some Muslim women—even though these garments resembled nothing so much as the wetsuits worn by surfers. Critics insisted that despite the stated purpose of "integration," these measures in fact sent French Muslims the message that if they followed their consciences as to religious observance, they would not be welcome in France.

Other countries pursued different strategies. The Netherlands, home to an increasing number of Muslim

Cultural Conflict Muslim women draped in French flags protest on the streets of Paris on January 17, 2004, rallying against the French government's decision to ban the hijab from schools in France.

immigrants from North Africa as well as from the former Dutch colony of Indonesia, established a new entrance examination for would-be immigrants in 2006. Part of it involved the viewing of a movie that showed gay men kissing and topless women sunbathing as examples of tolerant Dutch values. Denmark, under pressure from a right-wing populist party, significantly tightened its immigration laws, requiring that would-be migrants demonstrate "an active commitment to Danish society" and financial independence, even for those hoping to gain citizenship because of marriage to a Dane. In 2015, in Denmark, social benefits to immigrants and refugees were cut, and the government was empowered to confiscate assets from asylum-seekers to pay for their resettlement.

THE ISLAMIC STATE AND TERRORISM

The challenge that these issues posed for Europe was intensified by terrorism, which became more of a threat thanks to the ongoing crises in the Middle East. Continuing violence in Iraq, followed by the catastrophic civil war in Syria that began in 2011, spurred the birth of the so-called Islamic State, a radical group located across the border of the two countries and south of the border with Turkey. Its leaders declared that they were establishing a new caliphate to rule all Muslims, invoking the examples of the great Umayyad and Abbasid caliphates of the Middle Ages. They also called for Muslims everywhere to strike against "unbelievers" through acts of terrorism. Several thousand European Muslims traveled to Syria to fight for the Islamic State and for branches of Al-Qaeda, and many received terrorist training there.

On January 7, 2015, two young French Muslim brothers of Algerian descent with ties to these Syrian-Iraqi networks walked into the offices of a satirical French magazine, *Charlie Hebdo* ("Charlie Weekly"), which had published obscene cartoons of the Prophet Muhammad. Armed with assault rifles, the men killed twelve people, mostly members of the magazine's editorial staff. Two days later, even as police caught up with the brothers and killed them in a firefight, a companion of theirs shot and killed four more people at a Jewish supermarket in Paris and engaged in a lengthy hostage standoff with police. The attacks deeply shocked the French public and prompted one of the largest demonstrations in the country's history in solidarity with the victims. The slogan "Je suis Charlie" ("I am Charlie") went viral on social media in France and around the world. Socialist president François Hollande (1954–) imposed a state of emergency and declared that France was at war with the terrorists. He also promised, in a choice of words that unwisely recalled late-medieval conflicts between Christians and Muslims in Spain, to "reconquer" the predominantly Muslim suburbs that had allegedly nourished the terrorists' hatreds.

Over the next two years, such attacks continued, and not just in France. Some of the attacks involved men trained in terror tactics in Syria and Iraq. Others involved inexperienced "lone wolves"—mostly alienated and confused young men driven to terrorism by online propaganda from the Islamic State or other jihadist organizations. In the single most bloody episode, several teams of terrorists, from both France and Belgium, killed 130 people in

"Je Suis Charlie" Demonstrators wave French flags and carry a banner with *Charlie Hebdo*'s logo as a gesture of national unity at a rally in solidarity with victims of the Paris terrorist attacks in January 2015.

coordinated attacks in Paris in November 2015, including 89 at a rock concert in a theater once owned by Jewish supporters of Israel. On July 14, 2016, a lone wolf drove a heavy truck at high speed into dense crowds celebrating the French national holiday on the seaside promenade in the southern city of Nice, killing 86 and wounding hundreds of others. Bloody attacks occurred in Belgium, Spain, and Britain as well, including a suicide bombing by a Muslim Briton of Libyan descent who blew himself up outside a Manchester concert hall where an American pop star popular with young girls had just finished performing in May 2017. Twenty-two people died, including several girls.

While intelligence services had some success in disrupting terror networks in these countries, they could do little against the lone wolves. Authorities throughout much of Western Europe warned that for the foreseeable future the population would have to expect more such attacks and also tolerate more police presence and possible limits on civil liberties. The attacks did not generally provide immediate electoral benefits for the right-wing populist parties, but they certainly contributed to the atmosphere in which these parties could build support.

THE REFUGEE CRISIS

The Syrian civil war also did more than any other factor to create the **refugee crisis** that threatened to overwhelm Europe's capacity to receive newcomers in 2015. That year, over a million refugees reached Europe, mostly by sea—from Turkey to Greece and from North Africa to Italy and Spain. In the fall of 2015, over 7,000 refugees, mostly Syrian, landed on the small Greek island of Lesbos, just off the Turkish coast, every day. But the EU as a whole managed to approve only 292,000 asylum applications in 2015, with the other applicants kept in limbo, many in temporary camps. At the Keleti train station in Budapest, Hungary, thousands of men, women, and children—mostly from Syria, Iraq, and Afghanistan—crammed into tents and makeshift shelters, hoping for permission to continue on the land route to northern EU nations, especially Germany and Scandinavia. As would be the case in Calais the next year, the plight of the refugees at Keleti received worldwide attention.

In 2015, this plight also provoked a dramatic humanitarian gesture from German chancellor Merkel, who announced that Germany would welcome all Syrian refugees who arrived at its border. Germany did ultimately accept up to 1 million of them. Although controversial, the announcement was also a highly symbolic statement from

A REFUGEE'S PERILOUS JOURNEY

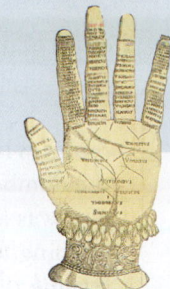

Since 2011, millions of refugees from Africa, the Middle East, and Central Asia have undertaken dangerous journeys to reach the relative peace and prosperity of Europe. Thousands have died in the attempt, either drowned in the Mediterranean after overcrowded boats capsized or asphyxiated in sealed shipping containers. The story of Hosein, told to an aid worker with the United Nations Refugee Agency, is sadly typical. An Afghan engineering student fleeing the ongoing Afghan civil war with his mother and sister, he boarded a smuggler's boat bound for Samos, Greece. The boat overturned in rough seas, and although Hosein survived, his family is still missing. Hosein's account speaks to some of the dangers that threaten millions of refugees and migrants seeking safety in Europe.

International organizations have criticized the responses of the European government to the refugee crisis, which is one of the largest humanitarian crises since World War II. Despite being bound under both international and EU law to aid refugees, many governments have responded to fears about Islamist radicalism by expelling migrants or holding them in transfer camps, making the perilous journey to Europe only one hurdle in a long succession of dangers that refugees face.

The past ten days were the most agonizing days of my life. On 10 July, along with my mother Fatme and my sister Shokoufeh, we sailed off in a 12 meter [40-foot] boat after having paid 9,000 Euro for the three of us. It was overcrowded as the smugglers had crammed around 40 men, women and children on that little boat.

After several hours at sea, the captain informed us that he was no longer in command of the boat, which suddenly started taking in water.

Among terrified screams, I tried to elbow myself to reach the small cabin where my mother and sister were, but I was hurled overboard by panicking passengers. I was very desperate. In the sea, the currents were so strong that I could hardly swim. It was only until several hours later, namely on Friday 11 July at noon, that I along with another, almost unconscious passenger, were spotted by an Italian sailing boat and were transferred to Chios Island. Other survivors were brought to Samos. Fifteen Syrians and Afghans have been rescued. The shipwreck so far claims the lives of six persons who were found by the Greek and Turkish Coast Guards while the rest are still missing.

Other family members of missing people with whom we were in the same boat, are in Germany and in Denmark while I am currently in France with my two sisters and their families. I traveled legally on a travel document issued by the French Embassy in Athens. All the families of missing people are appealing that the search and rescue operations of the authorities continue unabated. We urge the Greek authorities to bring up the boat as there were women and small children in the cabin who may have been trapped.

As for my missing mother and sister, another passenger who left the boat after me told me that they were not trapped in the cabin. Since they had very good life jackets, they must have survived. I am sure they are alive. I will not abandon the search. I expect and hope for good news. But even if the news were bad I still want to know!

QUESTIONS FOR ANALYSIS

1. Reading Hosein's story, how would you describe the kinds of conditions that refugees face in their attempt to reach Europe?
2. How have European governments both helped and failed migrants like Hosein?
3. Why does Hosein refuse to give up hope?

Source: UNHCR Stories, "Hosein's Story, Greece," recorded by Ketty Kehayioylou UNHCR/2014 (website), http://stories.unhcr.org/hoseins-story-greece-p13163.html.

---

the leader of the country that had, within living memory, attempted to exterminate minority populations deemed racially inferior.

But Germany also found it difficult to absorb such a vast new number of refugees. Within a year, Merkel was admitting that the country had not properly prepared for the influx and was working to cut down sharply on new arrivals. In 2016, the EU reached an agreement to send refugees landing in Greece back to Turkey, and as a result the numbers reaching Europe fell by two-thirds. But the deal was a fragile one, and with the Syrian civil war still ongoing, the possibility remained that the flood might resume.

A CENTRIST RESPONSE

The events of the new century placed liberal democracy in Europe under greater pressure than at any time since World War II. Despite this, voters in several European countries proved capable of resisting the populist candidates seeking to exploit the pressure and discontent for their own benefit.

In May 2017, as most observers had predicted, Marine Le Pen made it into the second round of the French presidential election campaign. But she faced an unexpected opponent. Following a decade of economic stagnation and political paralysis, the mainstream parties, the Socialists and the neo-Gaullist Republicans, both saw their support collapse. (The Republican candidate was also mired in a corruption scandal.) Instead of one of their candidates, Le Pen found herself running against the thirty-nine-year-old free-market centrist Emmanuel Macron (1977–), who had never held elective office, although he had briefly served as Hollande's economics minister. Handsome, eloquent, and charismatic, Macron crushed Le Pen in a televised debate and went on to defeat her by a 2 to 1 margin in the second round. Then, in June, his brand-new centrist political party, called Republic On the Move, won a landslide victory in legislative elections.

Like populists across Europe, Macron benefited from popular disgust with politics as usual. But instead of appealing to xenophobic nationalism, he called for further integration of France into Europe while also denouncing his own country's earlier imperialist ventures in Algeria as a "crime against humanity." While promising to renegotiate the conditions of France's membership in the Eurozone, Macron also appeared as a natural partner for Germany's chancellor Merkel. In the same month, June 2017, Britain's Conservative Party lost its majority in a

Peril at Sea A Muslim girl wades through the water of the Mediterranean Sea on November 15, 2015, having just disembarked from the small boat that brought her from Turkey to the Greek island of Lesbos.

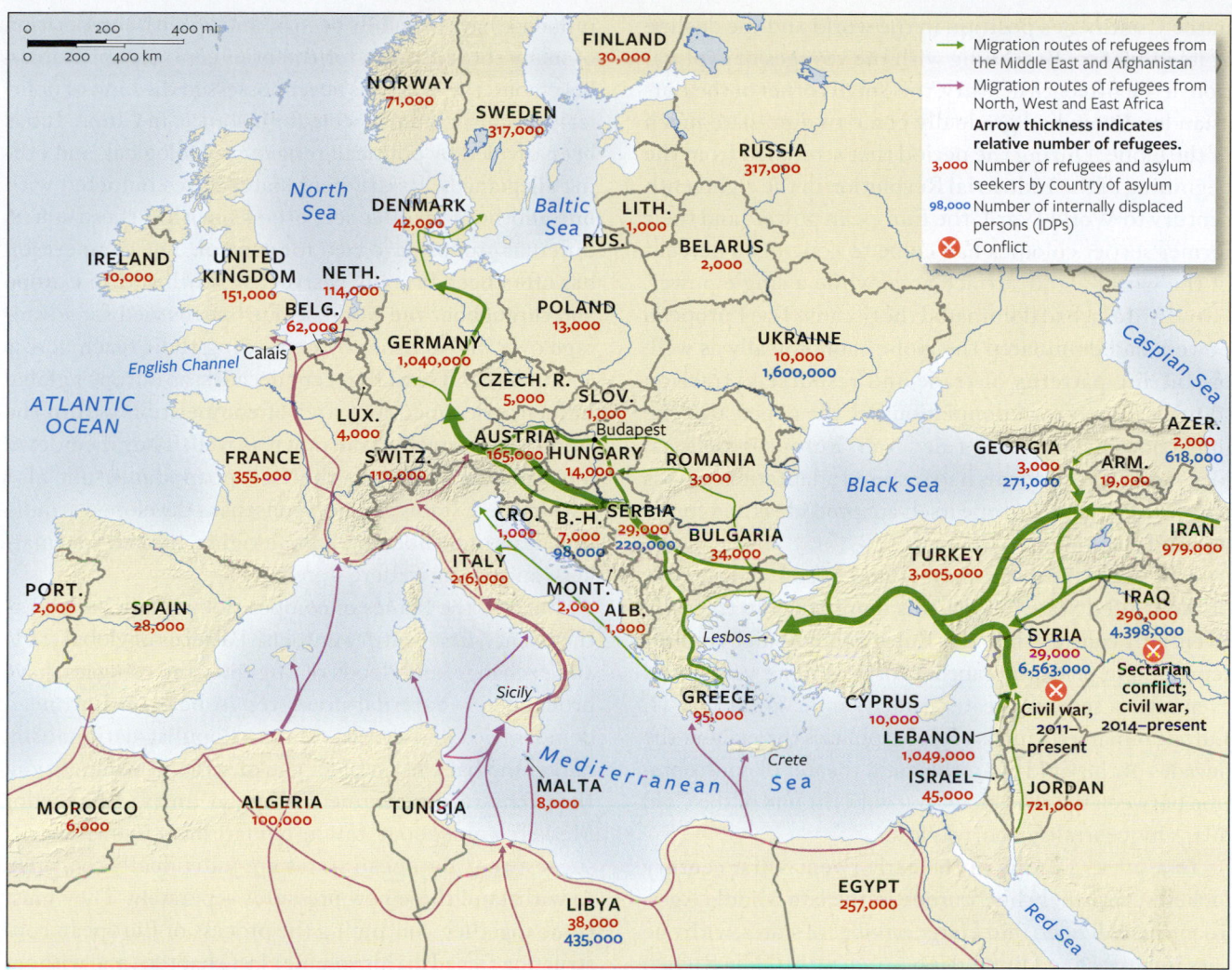

Refugee Crisis, ca. 2016 Fleeing civil war and sectarian conflict in the Middle East, and famine and war in sub-Saharan Africa, millions of displaced people entered Europe in the largest refugee crisis since World War II. Their typical routes involved crossing the Mediterranean or coming by land from Turkey before entering the European Union in Italy, Greece, or Bulgaria, and then traveling northward to Germany, France, and Scandinavia.

general election, weakening its hand in the Brexit negotiations that were just beginning.

European resistance to populism was also strengthened, ironically, by the rise of populism in the United States. In 2016, the winner of the U.S. presidential election, Donald Trump (1946–), criticized European NATO members for not contributing enough financially to the alliance's overall budget. He refused to say whether the United States would come to the aid of European allies under attack, and he hinted that the alliance as a whole had outlived its usefulness. As president, at a NATO summit in May 2017 he again failed to confirm Article 5 of the North Atlantic Treaty, which binds each member state to support others if attacked (he has subsequently confirmed it, however). Trump's remarks spurred new support throughout the Continent for European cooperation on defense matters. Chancellor Merkel declared in a speech that Europe needed "really to take our fate into our own hands." She added: "The times in which we could rely fully on others—they are somewhat over."

CONCLUSION: THE PRESENT MOMENT IN HISTORICAL PERSPECTIVE

Overall, the various pressures on European liberal democracy in the second decade of the twenty-first century reminded Europeans on a daily basis of the changes in the Continent's position in the world and the decline of its influence. Beginning with the voyages of exploration in the fifteenth century, this small corner of the Eurasian landmass had gradually come to dominate much of the globe. During the period that stretched from the beginning of the Industrial Revolution in the eighteenth century to World War I, the European powers and their former settler colonies had come to control 84 percent of the world's land surface area, while a single power, Great Britain, had dominated the oceans. The European powers had dominated the globe economically as well, organizing patterns of trade and resource extraction to benefit their own populations, at the expense of the indigenous peoples they ruled over. European political ideas and cultural forms had inspired adaptations across the world, even as Europe itself adapted ideas and forms it found elsewhere.

The suicidal cataclysm of World War I and the rise of the United States shook this dominance in the early twentieth century, but the European colonial empires remained in place for another forty or more years. And even after a second, greater cataclysm in World War II, Europe remained a focus of global politics throughout the decades of the Cold War: the main theater of confrontation between the rival blocs. But with the end of the Cold War, this centrality, too, was lost.

In a sense, Europe in the early twenty-first century looked surprisingly like Europe in the late Middle Ages: a continent divided into a large number of states, with one very imperfect and limited large union (the Holy Roman Empire in the earlier period, the EU in the present one); a continent that looked like a backwater compared to more populous and powerful states elsewhere on the globe.

But in another sense, Europe in this period, for all the pressures and challenges it was facing, still represented a significant human achievement. For over seventy years since the end of World War II, despite the divisions caused by the Cold War and its troubled aftermath—and despite the bloody conflicts that the Cold War spawned elsewhere in the world—the Continent itself had remained largely at peace. For over seventy years, despite many economic challenges, it had maintained a remarkably high level of material comfort and social welfare. For over seventy years, despite many setbacks, democracy and protection for human rights had advanced across the Continent.

But even as Europe achieved new levels of peace and prosperity, its influence on the global stage waned. Since the time of the Greek city-states, Western power and influence have generally been bound up with competition of many sorts. Except for the brief centuries of Roman hegemony, the West has never possessed the kind of political and cultural unity seen, for instance, in China. It has been divided by political, religious, ideological, and ethnic allegiances. Its different states have competed with one another for influence, even as, within these states, different groups have vied for control. The competition has often been brutally destructive, both within Europe and throughout the world, as Europeans vied for advantage over one another by expanding their reach across continents and seas. In recent decades, as Europe's global influence declined, the fires of competition within the Continent seemed to die down as well. They died down most obviously among the European states, but also within these states as a new consensus developed around the ideals of democracy, human rights, limited free markets, and strong welfare states.

But will the flames of competition remain banked as the twenty-first century unfolds? Patterns of global trade and exchange, and floods of migrants and refugees, have brought new external pressures to bear on European democracies and welfare states. Populist nationalism, harkening back to an older age of strident competition, threatens to undermine European unity. Chancellor Merkel's words about "taking our fate into our own hands" suggest that European states are individually too small to withstand these new pressures separately. They must come together, continuing the process of European construction traced in this volume's last chapters, and without relying on the United States to the degree they did after World War II. But others fear that a more united Europe will inevitably be a Europe dominated by its most populous and economically powerful state: Germany. The long, deeply fraught question of Russia's relation to the rest of the Continent also remains volatile.

In the face of this uncertainty, Europeans have many reasons for discontent and anxiety. They also have reasons to feel shame for what has been done in the name of their societies in the past. But they can take pride in having created societies whose people enjoy more comfort and freedom than at any point in the past. In Europe, the epic story of the West, after a period of almost unfathomable horror in the first half of the twentieth century, took a surprisingly calm and happy turn in the subsequent decades, and even the disturbances of the early twenty-first century have not reversed this turn. The question is whether this achievement can be preserved.

[CHAPTER REVIEW]

KEY TERMS

9/11 (p. 879)
Beslan attack (p. 880)
Iraq War (p. 880)
National Front (p. 881)

Lisbon Treaty (p. 882)
Great Recession (p. 884)
Eurozone (p. 884)
austerity policies (p. 886)

Greek crisis (p. 886)
Euromaidan (p. 888)
Ukrainian crisis (p. 888)
illiberalism (p. 889)

populism (p. 890)
Brexit (p. 891)
Charlie Hebdo (p. 894)
refugee crisis (p. 894)

REVIEW QUESTIONS

1. In what ways did European countries respond to the rise of terrorism in the wake of 9/11?

2. How did the EU and NATO expand and develop in the early twenty-first century?

3. Why did the Eurozone sharpen the effects of the Great Recession across Europe?

4. What risks did the economic crisis in Greece pose to the EU itself?

5. What factors contributed to increased Euroskepticism in the early twenty-first century?

6. How did Vladimir Putin change the social, political, and economic order of Russia?

7. What factors contributed to the crisis in Ukraine?

8. What were the characteristics of the illiberalism that gained traction in Europe after 2010?

9. In what ways did populism manifest itself in Britain and elsewhere in Europe?

10. What challenges did the refugee crisis present, and how did individual European countries respond to them?

CORE OBJECTIVES

After reading this chapter, you should have a solid understanding of the following core objectives. To strengthen your grasp of the core objectives, use the resources on the Student Site for The West.

- Analyze the conflicts that arose throughout the world in the aftermath of 9/11.
- Consider the evolution of, and disruptions to, the European Union in the last two decades.

- Explore developments in Russia under Vladimir Putin.
- Explain the growth of right-wing populism in Europe.
- Evaluate the crises arising from terrorism.

 GO TO inQUIZITIVE TO SEE WHAT YOU'VE LEARNED—AND LEARN WHAT YOU'VE MISSED—WITH PERSONALIZED FEEDBACK ALONG THE WAY.

CHAPTER 1 Origins (12,000–600 BCE)

Assmann, Jan, *The Mind of Egypt: History and Meaning in the Time of the Pharaohs*. New York, 2002.

Cline, Eric, *1176 B.C.: The Year Ancient Civilization Collapsed*. Princeton, 2014.

Damrosch, David, *The Buried Book: The Loss and Rediscovery of the Great Epic of Gilgamesh*. New York, 2007.

Foster, Benjamin, and Karen Pollinger Foster, *Civilizations of Ancient Iraq*. Princeton, 2009.

Liverani, Mario, *The Ancient Near East: History, Society and Economy*. New York, 2014.

Podany, Amanda, *The Ancient Near East: A Very Short Introduction*. Oxford, 2013.

Romer, John, *A History of Ancient Egypt: From the First Farmers to the Great Pyramid*. London and New York, 2012.

Shapiro, H. A., ed., *The Cambridge Companion to Archaic Greece*. Cambridge, 2009.

CHAPTER 2 "The School of Greece" (600–400 BCE)

Beard, Mary, *The Parthenon*, rev. ed. Cambridge, Mass., 2010.

Lloyd, Geoffrey, *Early Greek Science: Thales to Aristotle*. New York, 1970.

Missiou, Anna, *Literacy and Democracy in Fifth-Century Athens*. Cambridge, 2011.

Ober, Josiah, *Democracy and Knowledge: Innovation and Learning in Classical Athens*. Princeton, 2008.

Ober, Josiah, *Mass and Elite in Democratic Athens: Rhetoric, Ideology, and the Power of the People*. Princeton, 1989.

Ober, Josiah, *The Rise and Fall of Classical Greece*. Princeton, 2015.

Pomeroy, Sarah, *Goddesses, Whores, Wives, and Slaves: Women in Classical Antiquity*. New York, 1975.

Pomeroy, Sarah, et al., *Ancient Greece: A Political, Social, and Cultural History*, 3rd ed. New York, 2012.

Samons, Loren J., II, ed., *The Cambridge Companion to the Age of Pericles*. Cambridge, 2007.

Waterfield, Robin, *Why Socrates Died: Dispelling the Myths*. New York, 2009.

CHAPTER 3 From Classical Greece to the Hellenistic World (400–30 BCE)

Barnes, Jonathan, ed., *The Cambridge Companion to Aristotle*. Cambridge, 1995.

Bartlett, John, and Ronald Williamson, *Jews in the Hellenistic World*, 2 vols. Cambridge, 1985–89.

Bugh, Glenn R., ed., *The Cambridge Companion to the Hellenistic World*. Cambridge, 2006.

Casson, Lionel, *Libraries in the Ancient World*. New Haven, 2001.

Kraut, Richard, ed., *The Cambridge Companion to Plato*. Cambridge, 2006.

Lloyd, Geoffrey, *Greek Science after Aristotle*. New York, 1973.

Parsons, Peter, *City of the Sharp-Nosed Fish: Greek Lives in Roman Egypt*. London, 2007.

Pomeroy, Sarah, *Women in Hellenistic Egypt: From Alexander to Cleopatra*. New York, 1984.

Rice, E. E., *The Grand Procession of Ptolemy Philadelphus*. London, 1983.

Shipley, Graham, *The Greek World after Alexander*. London, 2000.

CHAPTER 4 Rome (1000 BCE–14 CE)

Beard, Mary, *SPQR: A History of Ancient Rome*. New York, 2015.

Cornell, Tim, *The Beginnings of Rome: Italy and Rome from the Bronze Age to the Punic Wars (c. 1000–264 B.C.)*. London and New York, 1995.

Erdkamp, Paul, ed., *The Cambridge Companion to Ancient Rome*. Cambridge, 2013.

Flower, Harriet, *Roman Republics*. Princeton, 2010.

Flower, Harriet, ed., *The Cambridge Companion to the Roman Republic*. Cambridge, 2014.

Galinsky, Karl, ed., *The Cambridge Companion to the Age of Augustus*. Cambridge, 2007.

Stevenson, Tom, *Julius Caesar and the Transformation of the Roman Republic*. London and New York, 2015.

CHAPTER 5 The Roman Empire and the Rise of Christianity (14–312 CE)

Beard, Mary, *SPQR: A History of Ancient Rome*. New York, 2015.

Burkett, Delbert, *An Introduction to the New Testament and the Origins of Christianity*. Cambridge, 2002.

Erdkamp, Paul, ed., *The Cambridge Companion to Ancient Rome*. Cambridge, 2013.

Fredriksen, Paula, *Jesus of Nazareth, King of the Jews: A Jewish Life and the Emergence of Christianity*. New York, 1999.

Heffernan, Thomas, *The Passion of Perpetua and Felicity*. New York, 2012.

Kulikowski, Michael, *The Triumph of Empire: The Roman World from Hadrian to Constantine*. Cambridge, MA, 2016.

Mitchell, Margaret, and Frances Young, eds., *The Cambridge History of Christianity*. Vol. 1, *Origins to Constantine*. Cambridge, 2006.

CHAPTER 6 The Late Roman Empire and the Consolidation of the Church (312–476)

Beard, Mary, *SPQR: A History of Ancient Rome*. New York, 2015.

Brown, Peter, *The Rise of Western Christendom: Triumph and Diversity, A.D. 200–1000*. Chichester and Malden, 2013.

Canaday, Augustine, and Frederick Norris, eds., *The Cambridge History of Christianity*. Vol. 2, *Constantine to 600*. Cambridge, 2007.

Herrin, Judith, *Byzantium: The Surprising Life of a Medieval Empire*. Princeton, 2007.

Herrin, Judith, *Unrivalled Influence: Women and Empire in Byzantium*. Princeton, 2013.

Lenski, Noel, ed., *The Cambridge Companion to the Age of Constantine*. Cambridge, 2012.

O'Donnell, James, *Pagans: The End of Traditional Religion and the Rise of Christianity*. New York, 2015.

O'Donnell, James, *The Ruin of the Roman Empire*. New York, 2007.

Ward-Perkins, Bryan, *The Fall of Rome and the End of Civilization*. Oxford, 2005.

CHAPTER 7 Between Worlds (476–900)

Berkey, Jonathan, *The Formation of Islam: Religion and Society in the Near East, 600–1800*. Cambridge, 2003.

Brown, Peter, *The Rise of Western Christendom: Triumph and Diversity, A.D. 200–1000*. Chichester and Malden, 2013.

Geary, Patrick, *Before France and Germany: The Creation and Transformation of the Merovingian World*. New York, 1988.

Herrin, Judith, *Byzantium: The Surprising Life of a Medieval Empire*. Princeton, 2007.

Herrin, Judith, *The Formation of Christendom*. Princeton, 1988.

McKitterick, Rosamund, *Charlemagne: The Formation of a European Identity*. Cambridge, 2008.

Noble, Thomas, and Julia Smith, eds., *The Cambridge History of Christianity*. Vol. 3, *Early Medieval Christianities, c. 600–c. 1100*. Cambridge, 2008.

Wickham, Chris, *Medieval Europe*. New Haven and London, 2016.

CHAPTER 8 Europe Revived (900–1200)

Colish, Marcia, *Medieval Foundations of the Western Intellectual Tradition, 400–1400*. New Haven, 1997.

Epstein, Stephen, *An Economic and Social History of Medieval Europe*. Cambridge, 2009.

Herrin, Judith, *Byzantium: The Surprising Life of a Medieval Empire*. Princeton, 2007.

Jordan, William, *Europe in the High Middle Ages*. London, 2001.

Noble, Thomas, and Julia Smith, eds., *The Cambridge History of Christianity*. Vol. 3, *Early Medieval Christianities, c. 600–c. 1100*. Cambridge, 2008.

Partner, Peter, *God of Battles: Holy Wars of Christianity and Islam*. London, 1997.

Rubin, Miri, and Walter Simons, eds., *The Cambridge History of Christianity*. Vol. 4, *Christianity in Western Europe, c. 1100–c. 1500*. Cambridge, 2009.

Thompson, John, *The Western Church in the Middle Ages*. London and New York, 1998.

Tierney, Brian, *The Crisis of Church & State, 1050–1300*. Englewood Cliffs, NJ, 1964.

Wickham, Chris, *Medieval Europe*. New Haven and London, 2016.

CHAPTER 9 Consolidation and Crisis (1200–1400)

Baldwin, John, *Paris, 1200*. Stanford, 2010.

Colish, Marcia, *Medieval Foundations of the Western Intellectual Tradition, 400–1400*. New Haven, 1997.

Epstein, Stephen, *An Economic and Social History of Medieval Europe*. Cambridge, 2009.

Gimpel, Jean, *The Medieval Machine: The Industrial Revolution of the Middle Ages*. New York, 1976.

Herrin, Judith, *Byzantium: The Surprising Life of a Medieval Empire*. Princeton, 2007.

Jordan, William, *Europe in the High Middle Ages*. London, 2001.

Rubin, Miri, and Walter Simons, eds., *The Cambridge History of Christianity*. Vol. 4, *Christianity in Western Europe, c. 1100–c. 1500*. Cambridge, 2009.

Tierney, Brian, *The Crisis of Church & State, 1050–1300*. Englewood Cliffs, NJ, 1964.

Wickham, Chris, *Medieval Europe*. New Haven and London, 2016.

CHAPTER 10 Renaissance Europe (1400–1500)

Andrade, Tonio, *The Gunpowder Age: China, Military Innovation, and the Rise of the West in World History*. Princeton, 2016.

Baxandall, Michael, *Painting and Experience in Fifteenth-Century Italy*, 2nd ed. Oxford, 1988.

Fernández-Armesto, Felipe, *1492: The Year the World Began*. New York, 2009.

Fletcher, Catherine, *Diplomacy in Renaissance Rome: The Rise of the Resident Ambassador*. Cambridge, 2015.

King, Margaret, *The Renaissance in Europe*. London, 2003.

Kraye, Jill, ed., *The Cambridge Companion to Renaissance Humanism*. Cambridge, 2006.

Pettegree, Andrew, *The Book in the Renaissance*. New Haven, 2011.

Rubin, Miri, and Walter Simons, eds., *The Cambridge History of Christianity*. Vol. 4, *Christianity in Western Europe, c. 1100–c. 1500*. Cambridge, 2009.

Skinner, Quentin, *Foundations of Modern Political Thought*. Vol. 1, *The Renaissance*. Cambridge and New York, 1978.

CHAPTER 11 Reformations (1500–1600)

Benedict, Philip, *Christ's Churches Purely Reformed: A Social History of Calvinism*. New Haven, 2002.

Eire, Carlos, *Reformations: The Early Modern World, 1450–1650*. New Haven, 2016.

Greengrass, Mark, *Christendom Destroyed: Europe 1517–1648*. London, 2015.

Holt, Mack, *The French Wars of Religion*. Cambridge, 2005.

Hsia, R. Po-chia, ed., *The Cambridge History of Christianity*. Vol. 6, *Reform and Expansion, 1500–1600*. Cambridge, 2007.

Kaplan, Benjamin, *Divided by Faith: Religious Tolerance and the Practice of Toleration in Early Modern Europe*. Cambridge, MA, 2007.

Kraye, Jill, ed., *The Cambridge Companion to Renaissance Humanism*. Cambridge, 2006.

Pettegree, Andrew, *Brand Luther*. London, 2016.

Richardson, Glenn, *Renaissance Monarchy: The Reigns of Henry VIII, Francis I and Charles V*. London, 2002.

Skinner, Quentin, *Foundations of Modern Political Thought*. Vol. 2, *The Reformation*. Cambridge and New York, 1978.

CHAPTER 12 Things Fall Apart (1600–1640)

Elliott, John H., *The Old World and the New, 1492–1650*. Cambridge, 1970.

Hufton, Olwen, *The Prospect before Her: A History of Women in Western Europe*. New York, 1996.

Parker, Geoffrey, *Global Crisis: War, Climate Change and Catastrophe in the Seventeenth Century*. New Haven, 2013.

Underdown, David, *Fire from Heaven: Life in an English Town in the Seventeenth Century*. New Haven, 1994.

Wilson, Peter H., *The Thirty Years War: Europe's Tragedy*. Cambridge, MA, 2009.

CHAPTER 13 Ordering the World (1640–1680)

Beik, William, *Absolutism and Society in Seventeenth-Century France: State Power and Provincial Aristocracy in Languedoc*. Cambridge, 1985.

Elliott, John H., *Richelieu and Olivares*. Cambridge, 1984.

Rabb, Theodore, *The Struggle for Stability in Seventeenth-Century Europe*. New York, 1975.

Schama, Simon, *The Embarrassment of Riches: An Interpretation of Dutch Culture in the Golden Age*. New York, 1987.

Shapin, Steven, *The Scientific Revolution*. Chicago, 1998.

Worden, Blair, *The English Civil Wars, 1640–1660*. London, 2009.

CHAPTER 14 From Court to City (1680–1740)

Bell, David A., *The Cult of the Nation in France: Inventing Nationalism, 1680–1800*. Cambridge, MA, 2001.

Brewer, John, *The Pleasures of the Imagination: English Culture in the Eighteenth Century*. New York, 1997.

Cracraft, James, *The Revolution of Peter the Great*. Cambridge, MA, 2003.

Harms, Robert W., *The Diligent: A Voyage through the Worlds of the Slave Trade*. New York, 2002.

Israel, Jonathan, *Radical Enlightenment: Philosophy and the Making of Modernity, 1650–1750*. Oxford, 2001.

Pincus, Steve, *1688: The First Modern Revolution*. New Haven, 2009.

CHAPTER 15   Enlightenment (1740–1780)

Brewer, John, *The Sinews of Power: War, Money and the English State, 1688–1783*. London, 1989.

Colley, Linda, *Britons: Forging the Nation, 1707–1837*. New Haven, 1992.

Darnton, Robert, *The Great Cat Massacre and Other Episodes in French Cultural History*. New York, 1984.

Edelstein, Dan, *The Enlightenment: A Genealogy*. Chicago, 2010.

Goodman, Dena, *The Republic of Letters: A Cultural History of the French Enlightenment*. Ithaca, 1994.

Robertson, John, *The Case for the Enlightenment: Scotland and Naples, 1680–1760*. Cambridge, 2005.

CHAPTER 16   Revolution (1780–1799)

Blanning, T. C. W., *The French Revolutionary Wars: 1787–1802*. New York, 1986.

Edelstein, Dan, *The Terror of Natural Right: Republicanism, the Cult of Nature and the French Revolution*. Chicago, 2009.

Hesse, Carla, *The Other Enlightenment: How French Women Became Modern*. Princeton, 2001.

McPhee, Peter, *Liberty or Death: The French Revolution*. New Haven, 2016.

Mokyr, Joel, *The Enlightened Economy: An Economic History of Britain, 1700–1850*. New Haven, 2009.

Thompson, E. P., *The Making of the English Working Class*. New York, 1966.

CHAPTER 17   The Age of Napoleon (1799–1820)

Bayly, Christopher, *The Birth of the Modern World, 1780–1914: Global Connections and Comparisons*. Oxford, 2004.

Bell, David A., *The First Total War: Napoleon's Europe and the Making of Warfare as We Know It*. Boston, 2007.

Englund, Steven, *Napoleon: A Political Life*. Cambridge, MA, 2004.

Hochschild, Adam, *Bury the Chains: Prophets and Rebels in the Fight to Free an Empire's Slaves*. Boston, 2006.

Lieven, Dominic, *Russia against Napoleon: The True Story of the Campaigns of War and Peace*. New York, 2010.

CHAPTER 18   Acceleration (1820–1845)

Beckert, Sven, *Empire of Cotton: A Global History*. New York, 2014.

Blanning, T. C. W., *The Romantic Revolution: A History*. London, 2010.

Evans, Richard J., *The Pursuit of Power: Europe, 1815–1914*. London, 2016.

Pomeranz, Kenneth, *The Great Divergence: China, Europe, and the Making of the Modern World*. Princeton, 2000.

Vick, Brian E., *The Congress of Vienna: Power and Politics after Napoleon*. Cambridge, MA, 2014.

CHAPTER 19   Growing Pains (1845–1880)

Figes, Orlando, *Crimea: The Last Crusade*. London, 2010.

Judson, Pieter, *The Habsburg Empire: A New History*. Cambridge, MA, 2016.

Koven, Seth, *Slumming: Sexual and Social Politics in Victorian London*. Princeton, 2004.

Sperber, Jonathan, *The European Revolutions, 1848–1851*. Cambridge, 2005.

Stern, Fritz, *Gold and Iron: Bismarck, Bleichröder and the Building of the German Empire*. New York, 1977.

CHAPTER 20   Apogee (1880–1910)

Cohen, Deborah, *Household Gods: The British and Their Possessions*. New Haven, 2005.

Hochschild, Adam, *King Leopold's Ghost: A Story of Greed, Terror and Heroism in Colonial Africa*. Boston, 1999.

Hull, Isabel, *Absolute Destruction: Military Culture and the Practices of War in Imperial Germany*. Ithaca, 2005.

Mayer, Arno, *The Persistence of the Old Regime: Europe to the Great War*. New York, 1981.

Schwartz, Vanessa, *Spectacular Realities: Early Mass Culture in Fin-de-Siècle Paris*. Berkeley, 1998.

Walser Smith, Helmut, *The Butcher's Tale: Murder and Anti-Semitism in a German Town*. New York, 2002.

CHAPTER 21   Things Blow Up (1910–1922)

Clark, Christopher M., *The Sleepwalkers: How Europe Went to War in 1914*. London, 2012.

Fitzpatrick, Sheila, *The Russian Revolution*. Oxford, 1982.

Hochschild, Adam, *To End All Wars: A Story of Loyalty and Rebellion, 1914–1918*. Boston, 2011.

Strachan, Hew, *The First World War*. New York, 2001.

Tooze, Adam, *The Deluge: The Great War and the Remaking of Global Order, 1916–1931*. London, 2014.

Winter, Jay, *Sites of Memory, Sites of Mourning: The Great War in European Cultural History, 1914–1918*. Cambridge, 1995.

CHAPTER 22   Ideologies (1922–1940)

Hobsbawm, Eric, *The Age of Extremes: A History of the World, 1914–1991*. New York, 1994.

Kershaw, Ian, *Hitler*. New York, 1991.

Kotkin, Stephen, *Magnetic Mountain: Stalinism as a Civilization*. Berkeley, 1995.

Maier, Charles S., *Recasting Bourgeois Europe: Stabilization in France, Germany, and Italy in the Decade after World War I*. Princeton, 1975.

Mazower, Mark, *Dark Continent: Europe's Twentieth Century*. New York, 2000.

Pedersen, Susan, *The Guardians: The League of Nations and the Crisis of Empire*. New York, 2015.

CHAPTER 23   The Abyss (1940–1945)

Browning, Christopher R., *Ordinary Men: Reserve Police Battalion 101 and the Final Solution in Poland*. New York, 1998.

Hitchcock, William, *The Bitter Road to Freedom: A New History of the Liberation of Europe*. New York, 2008.

Krylova, Anna, *Soviet Women in Combat: A History of Violence on the Eastern Front*. Cambridge, 2010.

Overy, Richard J., *Why the Allies Won*. New York, 1996.

Paxton, Robert O., *Vichy France: Old Guard and New Order*. New York, 1982.

Snyder, Timothy, *Bloodlands: Europe between Hitler and Stalin*. New York, 2010.

CHAPTER 24   Recovery and Cold War (1945–1973)

Elkins, Caroline, *Imperial Reckoning: The Untold Story of Britain's Gulag in Kenya*. New York, 2005.

Judt, Tony, *Postwar: A History of Europe since 1945*. New York, 2005.

Kynaston, David, A World to Build: Austerity Britain, 1945–48. London, 2008.

Sheehan, James J., *Where Have All the Soldiers Gone? The Transformation of Modern Europe*. Boston, 2008.

Shepard, Todd, *The Invention of Decolonization: The Algerian War and the Remaking of France*. Ithaca, 2006.

Zahra, Tara, *The Lost Children: Reconstructing Europe's Families after World War II*. Cambridge, MA, 2011.

CHAPTER 25   Reunion (1973–1999)

Ash, Timothy Garton, *The Magic Lantern: The Revolution of '89 Witnessed in Warsaw, Budapest, Berlin, and Prague*. New York, 1990.

Gillingham, John, *European Integration, 1950–2003: Superstate or New Market Economy?* Cambridge, 2003.

Kotkin, Stephen, *Armageddon Averted: The Soviet Collapse, 1970–2000.* New York, 2001.

Sarotte, Mary, *1989: The Struggle to Create Post–Cold War Europe.* Princeton, 2009.

Young, Hugo, *One of Us: The Life of Margaret Thatcher.* London, 1993.

CHAPTER 26 Under Pressure (since 2000)

Bowen, John R., *Why the French Don't Like Headscarves: Islam, the State, and Public Space.* Princeton, 2007.

Camus, Jean-Yves, and Nicolas Lebourg, *Far Right Politics in Europe.* Cambridge, MA, 2017.

Gessen, Masha, *The Man without a Face: The Unlikely Rise of Vladimir Putin.* New York, 2012.

Mueller, Jan-Werner, *What Is Populism?* Philadelphia, 2016.

9/11: An attack carried out by the terrorist group Al-Qaeda against the United States on September 11, 2001, destroying the World Trade Center, damaging the Pentagon, and killing nearly 3,000 people. The attack initiated a NATO alliance committed to combating jihadist terrorism.

absolutism: The expansion of royal authority, the dominant political trend among European monarchies of the seventeenth and eighteenth CENTURIES. Absolute monarchies generally reduced the political autonomy of the nobility, limited the role of independent political institutions, and involved the state in broad areas of social and economic life.

Acropolis: The steep hill dominating the center of Athens that is home to many famous structures, most notably the Parthenon. More generally, an acropolis is the uppermost part of a city, usually where a fortress or citadel is positioned.

Adrianople: The site in Thrace of a 378 CE battle in which the eastern Roman emperor Valens suffered a devastating defeat to the Goths.

agricultural: Relating to the cultivation of plants and animals. On a large scale, agriculture produces food surpluses, which enable people to settle in one place and develop a level of culture not found in nomadic societies.

Alberti, Leon Battista (1404–1472): A renowned Italian humanist with a wide range of talents and interests, mainly in the arts. He is best known as the author of important and influential fifteenth-century treatises on painting, sculpture, and architecture.

Alexander (356–323 BCE): The son of Philip II of Macedon, and a brilliant general who conquered an area spanning from Greece and Egypt in the west to India in the east. He is known to history as Alexander the Great, and his empire promoted the diffusion of Greek culture throughout the eastern Mediterranean and Middle East.

Alexander II (r. 1855–1881): The tsar who ended Russian serfdom in 1861 as part of his program to modernize Russia's economy and society. He remained committed, however, to retaining Russia's autocratic form of government and to expanding the empire's boundaries and influence.

Alhambra Decree (1492): A decree issued by Ferdinand and Isabella that gave Jews four months to convert to Christianity or leave Spain.

Alighieri, Dante (1265–1321 CE): Usually referred to simply as Dante, an Italian poet and writer who lived from 1265 to 1321 CE. His most famous work is *The Divine Comedy*, an epic poem describing his allegorical journey through Hell, Purgatory, and Heaven.

ambassadors: Beginning in Italy in the mid-fifteenth century, diplomats sent to capitals to represent their state's interests, gather information, and convey official communications.

American Revolution (1775–1783): The successful revolution of the American colonies against the British, which promoted principles of liberty and the rights of the common man.

Anabaptists: A radical Protestant denomination found primarily in Switzerland and Germany starting in the sixteenth century. Anabaptists constituted an apocalyptic sect that rejected infant baptism in favor of adult baptism and that argued the Bible was a blueprint for creating the perfect society. Members of this faith were often persecuted by both Catholics and more mainstream Protestant groups.

Aquinas, Thomas (1225–1274): A Dominican friar and Catholic priest who was one of the leading philosophers and theologians of the Middle Ages. His *Summa Theologica* is considered the high point of scholastic theology, a philosophical and theological movement that aimed to apply Aristotelian logic to the study of faith.

Arianism: Defined as the teachings attributed to the Egyptian Christian priest Arius in the third and fourth CENTURIES CE. Arianism's main departure from standard Christian dogma is on the matter of the Trinity. Arius argued in his concept of Christ that the Son did not always exist and was therefore distinct from the Father. This went against the orthodox teaching established at the Council of Nicaea, which marked Arianism as heretical.

Aristotle (382–322 BCE): A student of Plato and a key figure of classical Greek philosophy. Breaking with Plato over the idea of the forms, he instead argued that the essence of an object can be found in the object itself.

Armenian genocide (1915–1917): In response to an Armenian nationalist movement, brutal repression by the Turks in which at least 600,000 Armenians perished.

Athena: The Greek goddess of wisdom and the patron goddess of Athens.

atomic bomb: The nuclear weapon dropped by the U.S. government on the Japanese cities of Hiroshima and Nagasaki in August 1945, ending World War II. The Soviet Union tested its first atomic bomb in 1949.

Augustine (354–430 CE): Arguably the most important of the early church fathers, Augustine lived in North Africa. He was highly influential on Christian theology, especially on the matters of God's grace and original sin. His writings, including *The City of God* and *Confessions*, are cornerstones of the Christian worldview.

Augustus (63 BCE–14 CE): The great-nephew and adopted son of Julius Caesar, Augustus defeated the enemies of Caesar, and his former allies in the Second Triumvirate, to become the unquestioned leader of Rome following the battle of Actium in 31 BCE. Born Octavian, he was renamed Augustus, or "the revered one." Augustus brought stability to Rome and ushered in the beginning of the Roman Empire.

Auschwitz-Birkenau: The largest German concentration camp during the Holocaust. Some of the prisoners deported there were used as slave labor; but the vast majority, including nearly 1 million Jews, were killed in the gas chambers and their bodies burned in crematoria.

austerity policies: Measures taken to significantly curtail government spending and reduce government debt.

Austerlitz: Napoleon's defeat, in 1805, of combined Austrian and Russian forces. The decisive victory permitted Napoleon to impose a peace that greatly diminished Austria's role and increased French influence in Germany.

Avignon papacy: Also known as the Avignon Captivity, the period lasting from 1309 to 1377 during which popes resided in Avignon instead of Rome. During this time, the papacy was widely criticized for being corrupt and being dominated by the French.

baby boom: The marked increase in birth rate after World War II as families were reunited and wealth and income per person grew. In the period 1945–50, the birthrate in Europe increased by 23 percent as compared to that of the war years.

Bacon, Francis (1561–1626): A British philosopher and scientist who pioneered the scientific method and inductive reasoning. He argued that thinkers should amass many observations and then draw general conclusions or propose theories on the basis of these data.

barbarians: A term originally used by the Greeks to describe people who did not speak Greek and were therefore considered "uncivilized," the word was also used by the Romans to describe the various Germanic tribes that lived along their northern border.

Baron Montesquieu (1689–1755): An Enlightenment *philosophe* whose most influential work was *The Spirit of the Laws*, in which he investigated different types of government and connected each to the physical environment, especially climate, in which it predominated. His fictional *Persian Letters* critiqued despotic political authority.

Baroque: A seventeenth-century artistic style that featured dramatic displays of monarchical and religious grandeur, exemplified in the works of Peter Paul Rubens and Gian Lorenzo Bernini.

Bastille: The fortress at the eastern edge of Paris that was destroyed on July 14, 1789 by a crowd of Parisian citizens seeking ammunition to use against troops believed to be threatening the city. The success of the attack heralded the loss of royal control of Paris.

battle of Stalingrad: In the summer of 1942, the Germans launched a major offensive against the Russian city of Stalingrad on the banks of the Volga River. Although the Germans at first captured almost the entire city, a Soviet offensive drove them back and eventually forced the surrender of a large German army—but only after staggering loss of life on both sides.

battle of the Somme: An effort by Britain and France beginning in the summer of 1916 to turn the tide of World War I through a large-scale offensive involving massive artillery bombardment of German positions followed by coordinated infantry assaults. By mid-November, the plan had failed due to the defensive advantages of the German entrenchments.

battle of Verdun: A battle sparked by a major German offensive against a key point in France's defenses in 1916. The battle cost hundreds of thousands of lives on both sides, but by its conclusion the Germans had failed to advance.

Bauhaus School: A school of architecture that emerged in Germany during the 1920s, generally incorporating steel-reinforced concrete, simple geometrical forms, little ornamentation, and large windows.

Bayle, Pierre (1647–1707): A French Protestant who fled to the Netherlands, Bayle edited and wrote for the periodical journal *News from the Republic of Letters*. His *Historical and Critical Dictionary* took a critical approach to biblical texts and used satire to question the compatibility of received doctrines and reason.

Beer Hall Putsch: An unsuccessful Nazi coup launched from a Munich beer hall in 1923. For his role in the plot, Hitler served one year in prison.

Benedict (480–545): Benedict of Nursia, later canonized by the Catholic Church as Saint Benedict, lived in Italy. He is famous for writing the *Rule of Saint Benedict*, which became the foundation for most religious communities in Europe during the Middle Ages. Because of this, he is often referred to as the founder of Western monasticism.

Berlin Airlift: In response to a Soviet blockade of the three Western zones of Berlin, the Americans and British airlifted massive amounts of food and other necessities into the city during the period 1948–49.

Berlin Conference of 1884–1885: A meeting at which major European powers divided up African territories and established boundaries for future expansion.

Berlin Wall: The wall built in Berlin in 1961 by the East German Communist regime to prevent citizens of East Germany from fleeing to West Germany. It was torn down in 1989.

Beslan attack: An attack in Russia on September 1, 2004, in which terrorists primarily from southern Russian republics of Chechnya and Ingushetia took over 1,100 people hostage at a school in Beslan, Ossetia, leading to 330 deaths.

bishop: An ordained member of the Christian clergy who holds a position of leadership within their community. Bishops claim a direct historical lineage back to the original twelve apostles, thus justifying their authority within the religion. Bishops have several main responsibilities, including preaching, performing religious instruction, raising and controlling funds, carrying out administrative duties within their district, and representing their communities within the Christian world.

Bismarck, Otto von (1815–1898): The prime minister of Prussia and later the first chancellor of a unified Germany, Bismarck was the architect of German unification and helped to consolidate the new nation's economic and military power.

Black Death: An outbreak of bubonic and pneumonic plague that migrated from China along the Silk Road, eventually reaching the port city of Genoa in 1347 CE. The disease killed approximately half the population of Europe in the first four years of the pandemic.

Blitz: The German bombing of London from September 1940 through May 1941. Despite the destruction inflicted on the city, the campaign failed to weaken Britain's industrial capacity or civilian morale.

blitzkrieg: The German "lightning war" strategy used during World War II. The Germans invaded Poland, France, the Soviet Union, and other countries using fast-moving and well-coordinated attacks involving aircraft, tanks, and infantry.

Boers: Ethnically European settlers in South Africa. In the Boer War (1899–1902) with Britain, both sides suffered terrible casualties, with many Boer families being confined to concentration camps.

Bohemians: During the 1830s and 1840s, an ill-defined group of struggling artists and writers who defied middle-class social and moral conventions.

Bolshevik Revolution (1917): Also known as the October Revolution, the 1917 uprising in which Bolsheviks overthrew the Provisional Government and seized control of Russia.

Bolsheviks: Radical former members of the Russian Social Democratic Party who advocated for violent revolution and rule by the proletariat, and who started the Russian Revolution. Prominent Bolsheviks included Vladimir Lenin, Joseph Stalin, and Leon Trotsky.

Bonaparte, Napoleon (r. 1799–1814): The Corsican-born French general who seized power and ruled as dictator and emperor after the French Revolution. Following the successful conquest of much of Europe, he was defeated by Russian and Prussian forces and died in exile.

bourgeoisie: A term for the middle class—people who fell in between those who lived by manual labor and those who had inherited titles of nobility or vast wealth, originally designating non-noble town-dwellers.

Brexit: A referendum passed by British voters in June 2016 to exit from the EU.

Burke, Edmund (1729–1797): A prominent English political figure who argued in his *Reflections on the Revolution in France* (1790) that the French Revolution was doomed to end in bloodshed and the destruction of European tradition. Burke's book had a major influence on modern conservatism.

Caesar, Julius (100–44 BCE): A brilliant general, politician, and author, Julius Caesar used his victories on the battlefield to propel himself to the height of power at the end of the Roman Republic. Caesar was a *populare* who assumed the title "Dictator in Perpetuity" before he was assassinated on the Ides of March by the senators Brutus and Cassius.

caliph: The title used by the spiritual and political leader of the Muslim community. The term means "successor," indicating that the caliph had taken on the authority of the original leader of the followers of Islam, the prophet Muhammad. The split between Sunnis and Shiites originated in a dispute over who was the rightful successor as caliph following the death of Muhammad.

Calvin, John (1509–1564): An important figure in the Protestant Reformation, Calvin created a branch of the church that came to bear his name. His most important theological contributions were ideas about predestination. Calvin became the de facto ruler of the city of Geneva for twenty years in the mid-sixteenth century.

Carbonari: From the Italian word for "charcoal-burners," Carbonari were members of Italian secret societies, originally formed to resist Napoleonic rule. After 1815, they worked against the restored Austrian rule in the north and the Bourbon monarchy in the south to establish a united Italy based on democratic principles.

Carolingian Renaissance: A cultural and intellectual flowering that took place around the court of Charlemagne in the late eighth and early ninth centuries.

Carolingians: Named after the king Charles Martel, the Carolingian family replaced the Merovingians as leaders of the Franks. This royal house ruled from 750 to 987 CE.

Carthage: A Phoenician settlement on the coast of North Africa in the area of modern-day Tunisia. The Carthaginians controlled vast areas of the western Mediterranean in the middle of the first millennium BCE and ultimately became a major rival of Rome. Carthage lost its empire in a series of clashes with Rome known as the "Punic Wars" (264–246 BCE).

Cathars: Members of a Christian religious sect in northern Italy and southern France that rejected important elements of Catholic doctrine. Deemed heretics by the papacy, the Cathars were subject to a crusade and multiple inquisitions and were essentially destroyed by the mid-thirteenth century CE.

di Cavour, Camillo (1810–1861): The prime minister of Piedmont-Sardinia who played a key role in the movement for Italian unification under the Piedmontese king Victor Emmanuel II.

Charlemagne (r. 768–814): The second of the Carolingian kings, Charles the Great is known to history as Charlemagne. Crowned Holy Roman emperor in the year 800 by Pope Leo, Charlemagne was instrumental in reviving the classical liberal arts education, modernizing the Latin language, spreading Christianity throughout the Germanic lands, and unifying western Europe for the first time since the fall of Rome.

Charles I (r. 1625–1649): The king of England who clashed repeatedly with Parliament, preferring the continental absolutist model of government. Charles tried to rule without Parliament altogether from 1629 to 1640, thereby breeding conflicts that set the stage for civil war throughout the British Isles.

Charles V (r. 1519–1556): Heir to three of Europe's largest royal houses, Charles V was also Holy Roman emperor in the first half of the sixteenth century. Charles saw it as his duty to defend the Catholic faith against the Protestant reform movement. Because of his vast empire, he was in nearly constant warfare with the other major states of Europe.

Charlie Hebdo: A satirical French magazine that was attacked by terrorists in 2015 after publishing offensive depictions of the Prophet Muhammad. The slogan in solidarity with the victims, "Je suis Charlie," echoed across France and around the world, and the event mobilized France to join in the war against terrorism.

Chartist movement: An English radical movement supporting the People's Charter (1838), which called for universal adult male suffrage and annually elected parliaments. Although the Chartists for a time gained considerable public support for their program, the movement failed to achieve its goals.

Chernobyl: A Soviet nuclear power plant that suffered a meltdown in 1986. The accident killed at least thirty-one people, exposed hundreds to severe radiation poisoning, forced the evacuation of more than a hundred thousand more, and raised concerns throughout Europe about the release of nuclear radiation. The disaster highlighted inefficiencies and incompetence in the management of the Soviet economy.

chivalry: An ethic forged during the twelfth century, chivalry was a code that set forth the qualities found in the ideal knight. These included courage, honor, piety, learning, and the willingness to protect women and others seen as weak.

Chmielnicki, Bogdan (1595–1657): A Cossack leader who began a 1648 uprising against the Poles, targeting Jews and Christians.

cholera: A water-borne disease that reached epidemic proportions in the crowded cities of the 1830s and 1840s. Sanitary efforts to reduce outbreaks marked a sharp break with earlier medical models that had focused on the physical or moral characteristics of individual patients.

Churchill, Winston (1874–1965): The British prime minister who led the country during World War II.

Cistercians: Members of a religious order founded in 1098 at Cîteaux in France and based on a return to strict observance of Benedict's teachings. Leaders such as Bernard of Clairvaux emphasized humility and the power of the Virgin Mary.

city-state: A political entity based on an urban center and surrounding territories. Ancient city-states were sovereign and were connected internally through politics, economics, culture, and infrastructure.

Civil Code: Also known as the Napoleonic Code, a national legal system devised under Napoleon and based on Roman law. Although it stated the equality of all citizens before the law and confirmed the redistribution of property, including to peasants, it asserted the legal subordination of married women and recognized Catholicism as the dominant religion in France.

civilization: Society characterized by a social hierarchy, written communication, domestication of plants and animals, political and economic centralization, and advanced forms of culture, such as religion and monumental architecture.

Code of Hammurabi: A written collection of statements that describe 282 laws covering criminal, civil, and commercial activities. Recorded around 1700 BCE, the code portrays Hammurabi as the protector of divine justice.

Cold War (1945–1991): The ideological, political, and economic conflict in which the Soviet Union and Eastern Europe opposed the United States and Western Europe in the decades after.

collectivization: The forced replacement of private agriculture with state-managed collective farms in the Soviet Union.

coloni: The plural term for a *colonus*, a tenant farmer in late antiquity and the early Middle Ages. The *coloni* paid landowners a portion of the crops in exchange for the use of their farmlands. The growing numbers of *coloni* signified the decline of the independent farmer in the Roman Empire; they were comparable to medieval serfs.

Columbus, Christopher (1457–1506): The Genoese mariner Columbus received a commission from the monarchs of Spain to chart a new route to the East Indies in 1492. Over the course of a decade and four voyages across the Atlantic, Columbus established settlements throughout the Caribbean Sea and ushered in the era of Spanish colonization in the New World.

Comintern: Also known as Communist International, a united party formed by the Soviet Union in 1919 to advocate for international communism.

Committee of Public Safety: An executive authority formed by the French legislature in April 1793 to meet the immediate threats of invasion and counterrevolution. Under the leadership of Robespierre, the Committee exercised almost unlimited emergency authority during the Reign of Terror.

common law: The body of English law that is derived from custom and judicial precedent, unlike statutory law, which is created through the legislative process.

communes: Groups of noblemen in eleventh-century Italian cities who formed new governments independent of their bishops or local lords.

Communist Manifesto: An 1848 political pamphlet by German radicals Karl Marx and Friedrich Engels calling for a new socialist order, driven by an uprising of the proletariat, to replace the inherently unjust capitalist order.

composite monarchies: Early modern empires in which several countries were ruled by a single ruler, who governed each territory separately and distinctly according to the local government, laws, and customs.

Concert of Europe: An agreement among the major powers gathered at the Congress of Vienna to cooperate in the settlement of international disputes. For about forty years, this system prevented any wars among the major powers, and no total war broke out in Europe for one hundred years.

Concordat of Worms: The 1122 agreement between Henry V and Pope Calixtus II that formally ended the Investiture Controversy, though the struggle between church and state continued.

confraternities: Lay Christian associations founded beginning in the Middle Ages as charitable organizations or as groups to conduct rituals and worship.

Congress Poland: A sovereign state of Poland created by the Congress of Vienna in 1815. Congress Poland tried unsuccessfully to claim full independence from Russia in 1831, leading to its complete dissolution in 1832.

Congress of Vienna: The international conference held in 1814–15 to reorganize Europe after the downfall of Napoleon. European monarchies restored the Bourbon family to the French throne and agreed to respect one another's borders.

conservatism: A political and social movement starting in the nineteenth century and opposed to liberalism and revolutionary politics. Conservatives sought stability and incremental change that strengthened structures of authority.

Constantine (r. 312–337 CE): The leader who emerged from the last tetrarchy to become sole ruler of the Roman Empire in 312 CE until his death. He was the first Christian emperor of Rome, and his conversion was the first step toward Rome becoming a Christian state.

Constantinople: The capital city of the Roman Empire and subsequent Byzantine Empire built by the emperor Constantine I in the fourth century CE. Constantinople was the political, religious, and economic hub of these empires and remained so until it was captured by the Ottomans in the fifteenth century. Constantinople lies at the meeting point of Europe and Asia and is now the modern-day Turkish city of Istanbul.

Continental System: The economic embargo of Britain that Napoleon imposed in 1806 on the European territories under French control. Because it proved impossible to effectively patrol thousands of miles of coastline, the boycott failed to trigger the economic collapse of Britain.

Cook, James (1728–1779): An English explorer who undertook three expeditionary voyages during the period 1758–79. During his journeys in the Pacific Ocean, he and the scientists who accompanied him investigated indigenous populations as well as the flora and fauna of these regions.

Copernicus, Nicolaus (1473–1543): The Polish astronomer who advanced the idea that the earth revolves around the sun.

corporatism: The model of social organization, imposed by Mussolini in Italy, in which the various sectors of the economy were managed by corporations that supposedly represented both capital and labor, with the state serving to reconcile the divergent interests.

Corpus Iuris: A new law code for the Roman world that was produced by a ten-man commission established by Justinian. This "Body of Civil Law" contained the existing statues of the emperors, the legal opinions of leading Roman jurists, and new laws added by Justinian. The code provided a systematic approach to law with a focus on justice as its underlying principle.

Cortés, Hernán (1485–1547): The Spanish *conquistador* who defeated the great Aztec Empire of mainland Mexico in the early sixteenth century. His victory enabled the Spanish to claim lands throughout Central America, Mexico, and the area known today as the United States. Cortés was the first governor of the colony known as New Spain.

Council of Constance (1414–1418): A council of the Catholic Church called to end the dispute between French and Italian claimants to the papacy. The result of the Council was the removal of the two rival popes and the ascension of Pope Martin V to the papal throne.

Council of Nicea (325): Assembled by Constantine, the first general council of the Catholic Church, held in 325. The bishops at the council ruled against Arianism and in favor of Jesus's divinity, a decision that shaped the core beliefs of the Catholic religion.

Council of Trent (1545–1563): An ecumenical council of the Catholic Church held in the Italian city of Trent. The Council sought to clarify Catholic doctrine and answer criticisms of the Church brought forth by the Protestant movement.

Court of Star Chamber: An English court of law that met secretly and passed harsh sentences on Puritans and others who were thought to be disloyal to the monarchy. The Court was abolished in 1641 by the Long Parliament under King Charles.

Crimean War (1853–1856): The invasion by Britain and France of Russia's Crimean Peninsula to protect the Ottoman Empire from Russian expansion. Although the British and French were victorious, the peace treaty did not result in any major changes in boundaries.

Cromwell, Oliver (1599–1658): The commander of Parliament's new Model Army during the British Civil Wars and Lord

Protector of England following the execution of Charles I.

Crusades (1095–1291 CE): Military campaigns called for by the Catholic Church against Muslim "infidels," the Crusades lasted for two CENTURIES. The main goal of the Crusades was to conquer and claim the Holy Land for the Christian west.

cult of domesticity: Gender roles connected to the economic and social changes of the nineteenth CENTURY. In particular, because middle-class men increasingly worked in larger businesses or government offices, maintaining the home and caring for children became more exclusively the responsibility of women.

cuneiform: A writing system that developed in Mesopotamia (specifically, Sumer) during the third millennium BCE and that was characterized by wedge-like symbols pressed into clay tablets.

Darwin, Charles (1809–1882): A British naturalist whose *On the Origin of Species* (1859) developed the theories of natural selection and biological evolution.

D-Day: The Allied amphibious invasion of Normandy, France, on June 6, 1944, which opened up a long-awaited second front against the Germans.

de Beauvoir, Simone (1908–1986): The French author whose influential book *The Second Sex* (1949) questioned traditional gender roles as cultural norms imposed by men, rather than as reflecting innate differences between the sexes. Her book played a foundational role in the feminist movement following World War II.

De Gaulle, Charles (1890–1970): The leader of the Free French during World War II and founder of the Fifth Republic of France in 1958. In 1962, de Gaulle and the FLN came to an agreement to give Algeria full independence.

Decembrists: Nineteenth-century Russian army officers who were influenced by events in France and formed secret societies that espoused liberal governance. Their protest in December 1825 was put down by Nikolai I.

Declaration of the Rights of Man and Citizen (1789): Issued by the French National Assembly, the Declaration enumerated the rights of all male citizens on the basis of their civic equality. The Declaration also asserted the nation as a whole, rather than just the king, to be the source of all legitimate authority.

Defenestration of Prague: A 1618 event in which Protestant deputies of the Bohemian Estates threw three representatives of the Catholic king Ferdinand from the windows of Prague's royal palace, igniting the Thirty Years' War.

deism: A set of beliefs that holds that a single, non-Christian God figure created the universe and then left it to its own devices.

Delian League: An alliance created by the Athenians in 478 BCE to evict the Persian fleet from the Aegean Sea. Named after the island of Delos, where the member city-states conferred, the league eventually became the basis for the growing Athenian naval empire.

deme: A local unit or ward of ancient Athens.

democracy: A form of government in which citizens participate in the creation of the laws and institutions of their society. Fifth-century BCE Athens is typically cited as the world's first democracy. From the Greek words *demos* ("people") and *kratos* ("rule").

Democracy in America: The French liberal Alexis de Tocqueville's reflections on his visit to the United States during the 1830s. Unlike most European aristocrats, who saw America as immature in its development, Tocqueville presented American democracy as the wave of the future.

Deroin, Jeanne (1805–1894): A French feminist and socialist who advocated for equal rights for women, founding women's clubs and newspapers and unsuccessfully running for the French Assembly in 1849.

Descartes, René (1596–1650): The French philosopher who maintained that the universe could be understood not on the basis of received truths but, instead, only through principles that could be established without doubt.

destalinization: Following the 1953 death of Joseph Stalin, the Soviet Union's self-distancing from his policies. Destalinization included the release of millions of prisoners from the Gulag, the stabilization of relations with the West, and Soviet premier Nikita Khrushchev's 1956 denunciation of Stalin in his "secret speech."

détente: The relaxation of Cold War tensions between the United States and the Soviet Union during the 1970s.

Diderot, Denis (1713–1784): The French *philosophe* and author who was the guiding force behind the publication of the first encyclopedia. His *Encyclopedia*, edited with Jean le Rond d'Alembert, showed how reason could be applied to nearly all realms of thought and aimed to be a compendium of all human knowledge.

Diet of Worms (1521): A meeting of the imperial parliament called by the Holy Roman emperor Charles V to address the growing Protestant movement. Luther refused to renounce his views and was arrested afterward.

Diocletian: A decorated soldier from a lower-class family who ascended to the rank of Roman emperor in 284 CE and reigned until 305 CE. Rising to power after a CENTURY of chaos and instability in Rome, Diocletian pushed through important political, economic, and military reforms that stabilized the Empire.

Directory: The five-member executive that governed France from 1795 to 1799. Although it repudiated the egalitarian policies of the Jacobins, the Directory remained committed to maintaining republican government and "exporting" the Revolution through a policy of French expansion.

dissident movements: In the Eastern bloc during the 1970s and 1980s, groups of artists, scientists, politicians, and thinkers, including the famous writer Alexander Solzhenitsyn, who spoke out against the ideology and policies of their states' Communist governments.

divination: The practice of attempting to predict the future by looking for messages imprinted in the natural world.

Domesday Book: The extensive survey of English landowners' property conducted by William I.

domesticated: In terms of wild plants or animals, the condition of having been brought under human control.

Dominican Order: Founded by the Spanish priest Dominic de Guzmán in 1216 CE, an order consisting of friars and nuns with a special focus on preaching, education, conversion, and combating heresy. The Dominicans are considered a mendicant order: they wander through cities and countryside as opposed to staying cloistered.

Donatists: North African Christians who in the fourth CENTURY denounced bishops who survived persecution by compromising their faith. The Donatist church demanded adherence to a strict set of principles.

Dreyfus Affair: Beginning in 1894, the French scandal surrounding accusations that a Jewish officer, Alfred Dreyfus, had sold military secrets to the Germans. Convicted, Dreyfus was sentenced to confinement for life. However, after a public outcry it was revealed that the trial documents were forgeries, and Dreyfus was fully exonerated in 1906 after a long series of trials.

Duma: The Russian national parliament, created in response to the Revolution of 1905.

Dunkirk: The French port on the English Channel from which a makeshift fleet of British naval and civilian vessels evacuated 337,000 troops surrounded by the Germans between May 27 and June 4, 1940.

Dutch "Golden Age": The period during the mid-1600s when the Dutch Republic dominated European trade and enjoyed the highest standard of living in Europe. The Golden Age gave rise to a new style of painting by artists such as Dirck Hals (1591–1656), Jan Vermeer (1632–1675), and Rembrandt Harmenszoon van Rijn (1606–1669), who drew inspiration from scenes of everyday life.

Dutch Revolt (1566): The largely Calvinist population of the Dutch provinces of the Spanish Empire began a revolt against what they saw as the increasing repression of Philip II's rule. The Dutch broke free and formed the United Provinces in 1581, finally achieving officially recognized independence in 1648.

East-West Schism: Also known as the Schism of 1054, the divide between the Roman and Orthodox churches that was driven in part by disagreements about the nature of the Holy Spirit.

Edict of Milan (313): The decree passed by the emperor Constantine I that allowed for religious tolerance in the Roman Empire. It was specifically geared toward the growing Christian community, which had suffered great persecution under many previous emperors. The Edict was the first step toward Rome accepting Christianity as its official religion.

Edict of Nantes (1598): Signed by the French king Henry IV, the Edict granted the Huguenots substantial rights within the state and allowed for a greater degree of toleration after the French Wars of Religion of the sixteenth century.

Edict of Restitution (1629): Signed by Holy Roman Emperor Ferdinand II, the Edict returned to the Catholic Church all its property that had been seized by Protestants since 1552, stoking Protestant fears and expanding the scope of the Thirty Years' War.

Einsatzgruppen: Special German military task forces whose sole purpose, beginning in the summer of 1941, was to exterminate Jews, Roma, homosexuals, the mentally handicapped, and Communists and other political opponents of the Reich.

Einstein, Albert (1879–1955): The German scientist who posited that time could flow at different rates for different bodies, depending on their relative motion, and whose groundbreaking theory of relativity linked mass and energy, thereby opening up the theoretical possibilities of nuclear fission and fusion.

empirical: A method of study favored by Aristotle in which evidence is attained through the observation of nature. Focusing on experimentation, empirical study later became the foundation of the modern scientific method.

enclosure: In eighteenth-century Britain, the practice through which wealthy landowners appropriated lands previously used for common grazing. Through the application of new agricultural techniques, these lands contributed to a tremendous growth in agricultural production and productivity.

Engels, Friedrich (1820–1895): A German socialist thinker and journalist who collaborated with Karl Marx on many publications, including *The Communist Manifesto*.

enlightened absolutism: An absolute monarchy, inspired by Enlightenment thought, in which absolute rulers held to the tenets of rationalism and utilitarianism to curtail the power of the Church and introduce Enlightened reforms.

Enlightenment: The intellectual movement in eighteenth-century Europe that reflected a belief in human betterment through the application of reason to solve social, economic, and political problems.

epic: A form of literature that was a foundational part of the unified Greek culture that developed during the archaic age. Homer's great epic poems, the *Iliad* and the *Odyssey*, recorded around 800 BCE, are set in the Mycenaean period and deal with events surrounding the Trojan War.

Epic of Gilgamesh: An Akkadian poem from Mesopotamia about the hero Gilgamesh and his encounters with various gods and goddesses as he tries to discover the path to eternal life. It was compiled in the eighteenth century BCE from earlier Sumerian stories.

Epicureans: Followers of the Hellenistic philosopher Epicurus (314–270 BCE), who broke from the classical Greek model of an ordered and rational universe and argued for something more chaotic and random. Epicureans tried to gain peace of mind through the rational pursuit of pleasure.

Erasmus, Desiderius (1466–1536): A Dutch teacher, scholar, theologian, and humanist. He is considered one of the most important forerunners of the Reformation owing to his criticisms of the Catholic Church, although he himself did not leave the faith.

Estates General: The representative body of the three estates in France. In 1789, King Louis XVI summoned the Estates General to meet for the first time since 1614 because it seemed to be the only solution to France's worsening economic crisis and financial chaos.

ethnic cleansing: A term coined during the Bosnian War (1992–1995) to describe the systematic murder or deportation of all members of an ethnic or religious group from a region. During the Bosnian War, Serbian troops slaughtered thousands of defenseless Bosnian Muslims.

Etruscans: A people of unknown origin who settled the Po River valley of north-central Italy and were the dominant power in the area for approximately three centuries, from around 800 to 500 BCE. The Etruscans strongly influenced the culture of ancient Rome, specifically in architecture, art, and dress.

eugenics: A term devised by the English scientist Francis Galton (1822–1911), referring to efforts to improve the human race through selective breeding, generally of Europeans.

Euromaidan: After the Ukrainian word for "square," a surge of demonstrations in Kiev, Ukraine, in late 2013 through early 2014, protesting President Viktor Yanukovych's refusal to sign a trade agreement with the EU and signaling the start of the Ukrainian crisis.

European Union (EU): The successor organization to the European Economic Community, formed by the Maastricht Treaty of 1992. The member states of the European Union share an open market; open borders among members; a single currency, the euro; and certain political institutions, including a European Parliament and Court of Justice.

Eurozone: The group of nations in the European Union whose currency is the euro. As of 2017, the Eurozone includes nineteen countries.

Eusebius: A Caesarean Christian cleric who compiled complex histories of the world and the Church; lived from around 260 to around 339.

excommunication: A decree from a high-ranking church official, usually a bishop or even the pope himself, that prohibits a parishioner from participating in the sacraments of the Church. The excommunicated were also subject to isolation from the social community.

factory towns: During the Industrial Revolution, towns sustained by factories, mills, mines, and foundries, made notorious by contemporary literature for their cramped and filthy living conditions.

fascism: The doctrine, formulated by Benito Mussolini, that emphasized three main ideas: absolute state control, nationalism, and militarism.

fealty: Beginning in the early Middle Ages, the practice of vassals swearing loyalty to a lord, who in turn granted protection.

Five Pillars of Islam: These are the basic duties of every observant Muslim. They include: acknowledging the oneness of God, praying five times a day, fasting during the holy month of Ramadan, providing alms to the poor, and making a pilgrimage to Mecca at least once in one's lifetime.

Five-Year Plan: A Soviet effort launched in 1928 in which Stalin set goals for the rapid industrialization of the still largely agrarian Soviet Union. The plan did indeed result in increased industrial production, an explosion of the urban population, and a state-managed economy. But the forced collectivization of the countryside to increase agricultural output led to millions of deaths by execution, deportation, and starvation. Starting in 1933, subsequent Five-Year Plans followed the first.

forms: The Platonic term for eternal, unchanging absolutes that exist separately from matter. Plato argued that forms constitute ultimate reality and are accessible through meticulous and careful reflection and study.

Fourteen Points: U.S. president Woodrow Wilson's plan to establish peace after World War I on the basis of a new world order. The points included redrawing the map of Europe according to the principle of national self-determination and creating a League of Nations to settle international disputes.

Fourth Lateran Council: The Church council convened by Innocent III in 1215 CE that created rules firmly separating secular and church authority and required all Christians to confess once per year.

Franciscan Order: Founded by the Italian clergyman Francis of Assisi in 1209 CE, this order had a strict vow of poverty and, like the Dominicans, was a wandering order. The Franciscans were effective preachers of the Crusades, agents of conversion, and missionaries on the borders of the Catholic world.

Franco-Prussian War (1870–1871): Following Prussian chancellor Otto von Bismarck's provocations, Napoleon III declared war. Prussia's more mobile army proved victorious, and the southern German states that had supported Prussia formed a German Empire ruled by the king of Prussia.

Franks: A group of Germanic tribes originating in the lower Rhine region in the third CENTURY CE. Eventually, the Franks became rulers of northern Gaul and reached the peak of their territorial gains under Charlemagne in the ninth CENTURY. They are credited with halting the Muslim advance into continental Europe as well as becoming the successors of the emperors of the western Roman Empire. Modern-day France derives its name from this group.

Freemasons: An eighteenth-century society that developed into a network of "lodges" throughout Europe. Masons engaged in complex rituals and devoted themselves to ideals of the public good derived from radical ideas of the English Civil War.

Freud, Sigmund (1856–1939): The Austrian physician who founded the discipline of psychoanalysis and who suggested that human behavior is largely motivated by unconscious and irrational forces.

Fronde: A revolt against royal authority that began in Paris in 1648, originating in protests by the magistrates of high court against new taxes and CENTRALIZING policies.

Fugger, Jacob (1459–1525): A wealthy German banker who lent money to the Habsburgs and other monarchs in exchange for mining and trading rights; lived from 1459 to 1525.

Gallipoli Campaign: The unsuccessful 1915 plan devised by Winston Churchill to knock Turkey out of the war by capturing the Dardanelles. About half of the invasion force of 400,000 were killed or wounded before the Allies withdrew.

Gandhi, Mohandas (1869–1948): The Indian leader who advocated nonviolent noncooperation to protest colonial rule and helped win home rule for India in 1947.

Garibaldi, Giuseppe (1807–1882): The Italian revolutionary leader who led the fight to free Sicily and Naples from the Habsburg Empire.

German Confederation: Founded in 1815, a weak collective of German states led by Prussia and Austria that succeeded the Holy Roman Empire.

Girondins: Members of a Jacobin faction during the French Revolution, led by Jacques-Pierre Brissot. In 1792, they were strong advocates of war against Austria. Following the overthrow of the monarchy, they opposed *sans-culottes* demands for strict price control and sought to reduce the influence of Parisian radicals on the government.

glasnost: Meaning "openness," the policy introduced in 1986 by Soviet leader Mikhail Gorbachev allowing public debate and criticism, with the aim of reforming the Communist system. Instead, such open discussion undermined the authority of the Communist Party and contributed to the collapse of the Soviet Union.

globalization: The integration of world economic networks. These global exchanges are not limited by nation-states and in recent decades have become associated with new technologies, such as the Internet.

Glorious Revolution (1688): The events surrounding the nearly bloodless overthrow of King James II of England, after which William III and Mary II were granted rule. In the subsequent Bill of Rights, Parliament asserted its indispensable role as part of the government and explicitly limited the monarch's authority.

Gnostics: Taking their name from the Greek word for "knowledge," *gnosis*, Gnostics were identified by their rejection of the material world and their connection to Platonic thinking. There were many gnostic Christian groups in the first CENTURIES of the religion, often at odds with orthodox thinking around the nature of God, the resurrection, and the interpretation of scripture. Gnostics emphasized the importance of hidden truth.

Gorbachev, Mikhail (1931–): The Soviet leader who attempted to reform the Soviet Union through his programs of glasnost and perestroika in the late 1980s. He encouraged open discussions in other countries of the Soviet bloc, which led to the end of Communism throughout Eastern Europe. Eventually, the political, social, and economic upheaval he unleashed led to the breakup of the Soviet Union.

gospels: Deriving from the Old English word *god-spell*, meaning "good news," the four Gospels are narratives of the life, teachings, death, and resurrection of Jesus Christ. There were many different gospels written in the late first to early second CENTURIES BCE, but only those attributed to Matthew, Mark, Luke, and John are considered canonical and form part of the Christian Bible.

Gothic: The architectural style that came to supplant Romanesque as the most popular style in Europe and lasted until the fifteenth CENTURY. Gothic architecture is characterized by pointed arches, ribbed vaults, and thin walls with large expanses of stained glass.

Goths: An east Germanic people whose two main branches, Visigoths and Ostrogoths, were instrumental in the downfall of the western Roman Empire in the fifth CENTURY CE. The Goths and other Germanic tribes had an uneasy peace with the Romans for CENTURIES, but it was shattered with the introduction of the Huns, a nomadic group from Central Asia who moved into CENTRAL Europe in the fourth CENTURY, displacing the Goths.

Gracchi: Two brothers from the Gracchus family, Tiberius and Gaius, who rose to power in the second CENTURY BCE with a reform agenda appealing to the mass of Roman citizens, specifically involving land reform. Both men were assassinated by rival factions in the Senate, who felt the brothers' policies were too radical.

Great Depression: The global economic crisis following the U.S. stock market crash on October 24, 1929, and ending with the onset of World War II.

"Great Fear": Following widespread rumors of imminent attacks by gangs of brigands in the summer of 1789, this panic caused many French peasants to attack nobles' property and destroy records of the peasants' feudal obligations.

Great Persecution: The Christian persecution ordered by Diocletian in 303 CE, destroying churches and attacking Christians throughout the Roman Empire.

Great Recession: A massive, prolonged economic downturn from 2007 to 2009, sparked by the collapse of the U.S. housing market and risky bank lending policies worldwide.

Great Schism: A divide in the Roman Catholic Church lasting from 1378 to 1417 CE and caused by two—and at one point three—simultaneous claims to the papacy. The division between Italian and French claimants was largely driven by politics as opposed to theology and did great damage to the reputation and power of the Church.

Great Terror: The series of anti-counter-revolutionary purges in the Soviet Union between 1936 and 1938 during which thousands were executed or imprisoned in the Gulag.

Greek crisis: The collapse of the Greek banking sector during the Great Recession in part due to misreported budget deficits, jeopardizing Greece's membership in the EU. Greece was bailed out by European institutions and the International Monetary Fund after agreeing to adopt severe austerity policies.

Gregorian Reform Movement: Late eleventh-century efforts of Pope Gregory VII and his associates to codify the preeminence of the pope, ordained by God, above all others both within and outside of the Church. Imperial theologians responded by arguing the absolute authority of secular rulers.

Gregory (r. 590–604 CE): Commonly referred to as Saint Gregory the Great, he was pope from 590 to 604 CE. A prolific writer, Gregory was known as the "Father of Christian Worship" for his work on the liturgy and rites of the Catholic Church. He was also instrumental in spreading Christianity to the British Isles.

Grumbach, Argula von (1492–ca. 1554): A Bavarian noblewoman whose pamphlets in defense of Luther and Protestantism were printed as many as 29,000 times.

guerrilla warfare: Spanish for "little war," originally used to describe Spanish irregulars' insurgency against French forces during the Peninsular War. Guerrilla forces generally attack by surprise in small groups and then blend back into the countryside.

guest workers: In the second half of the twentieth CENTURY, supposedly temporary workers from former colonies and the Middle East who filled low-level jobs in Europe. These newcomers often encountered suspicion and prejudice on the part of citizens of European countries.

guild: A professional organization in commercial towns that regulated business and safeguarded the privileges of those practicing a particular craft.

Gutenberg, Johannes (1398–1468): A German metalsmith and printer, Gutenberg is credited with introducing the printing press to Europe in the 1450s. The printing press allowed for the rapid and inexpensive production of books and made them accessible to people at all levels of society.

Habsburg dynasty: One of the most influential royal houses in Europe, the Habsburgs ruled over Austria, Spain, and various other European states from the eleventh to the twentieth CENTURY. They also controlled the title of Holy Roman emperor for most of the early modern era.

Hanseatic League: Beginning in the twelfth CENTURY, a loose but powerful network of trading cities in northern Europe that were CENTERS of manufacture, including silk and linen cloth, armor, and religious art.

Havel, Václav (1936–2011): The playwright and philosopher who led an anti-Communist movement in Czechoslovakia, later becoming the last president of Czechoslovakia (1989–1992) and the first president of the Czech Republic (1993–2002).

Hellenistic: The term used to describe the Greek-based culture that developed in the wake of Alexander's conquests. Hellenistic means "Greek-like" and refers to the fusion of existing cultures with Greek language and culture.

helot: A member of a Greek-speaking Messenian culture of the southwestern Peloponnesus enslaved by the Spartans in the eighth CENTURY BCE. Helots were tied to the land and forced to produce food so that their Spartan masters could focus their efforts on military training and conquest.

Helsinki Accords: A 1975 agreement in which nearly all European states as well as the United States recognized the de facto post-war boundaries established in Europe. Although the recognition of wartime annexations seemed a major gain for the Soviet Union, dissident groups soon referred to Helsinki to hold their governments accountable.

Henry VIII (r. 1509–1547): The second monarch of the Tudor dynasty, Henry ruled England from 1509 until his death in 1547. Although he was famous for his marriages, his most consequential policy was to break with the Catholic Church in the 1530s and establish the independent Church of England.

heresy: A teaching of belief not considered to be orthodox, usually referring to violations of important church teaching. Someone who challenges orthodox teaching is called a "heretic."

hetairai: Professional female companions who entertained elite men during the classical and Hellenic periods in Greek culture. Hetairai were educated, sophisticated, relatively independent women who were welcomed out in public and in the social circles of prominent men.

hieroglyphs: A system of writing from ancient Egypt in which pictographs represent both sounds and objects.

Hitler, Adolf (1889–1945): The leader of the Nazis who became chancellor and subsequently dictator of Germany. Hitler and the Nazi regime started World War II and orchestrated the systematic murder of over 6 million Jews, 250,000 Roma, and tens of thousands of homosexuals and political prisoners.

Hobbes, Thomas (1588–1679): The English philosopher whose *Leviathan* discussed the origins of government and the effective exercise of political authority. Hobbes maintained that government rests on a social contract with its subjects, formed to prevent the violence and uncertainty of man's natural condition. This contract requires subjects to subordinate themselves to a sovereign authority.

Holocaust: The genocide of 5.4 million Jews and the murder of around 250,000 Roma, tens of thousands of homosexuals and political prisoners, and millions of Soviet prisoners of war by Nazi Germany.

Holy Roman Empire: The name used for the old eastern Frankish Empire starting in the twelfth CENTURY, a multi-ethnic federation of states in central Europe nominally under the control of the Holy Roman emperor. The empire lasted until the nineteenth CENTURY, when it was dissolved by Napoleon I.

Home Army: The largest Polish resistance group during World War II. Because the Home Army supported the non-Communist government-in-exile in London, the Soviets did not support its unsuccessful July 1944 uprising in Warsaw.

home rule: Self-government sought by Irish nationalists, who in the nineteenth CENTURY called for repeal of the 1801 Act of Union between Great Britain and Ireland.

hoplite: A citizen-soldier of a Greek city-state of the seventh to fourth CENTURIES BCE. Hoplites were armed with helmet, spear, and large wooden shield, and they fought in a tightly packed infantry formation called a "phalanx."

Huguenots: French Calvinists. The Edict of Nantes led to increased toleration of the Huguenots, but Louis XIV reversed it in 1685 when he abolished all legal recognition of Protestantism in France.

humanism: The intellectual worldview held by leading figures of the Renaissance, who were attempting to revitalize classical culture. Humanists celebrated reason and rationality, the liberal arts, and civic engagement. Humanism emphasized the value and potential of mankind.

Hume, David (1711–1776): A leading philosopher of the Scottish Enlightenment who championed rigorous skepticism and argued in *The Natural History of Religion* that belief in God was rooted in superstition.

Hundred Days: The three months in early 1815 during which Napoleon regained control of France following his escape from Elba. After his defeat at Waterloo by the British and the Prussians, Napoleon was exiled to the remote island of Saint Helena.

Hundred Years' War (1337–1453): A long series of battles between the English and French. The conflict was in part about succession to the French throne as well as control over various territories such as the duchies of Aquitaine and Normandy.

Huns: A nomadic people who originated in Central Asia, the Huns were skilled horsemen and fearsome warriors. The arrival of the Huns into the heart of Europe displaced many Gothic tribes and helped hasten the fall of the western Roman Empire.

iconoclasm: The rejection or destruction of religious images as heretical. The concern of iconoclasts is that worshipers venerate the object rather than God. The emperor Leo III initiated a policy of iconoclasm in the Byzantine Empire starting in 731 CE, furthering the schism between eastern and western branches of the Christian church.

illiberalism: An ideology that gained support across Europe after 2010, consisting of fervent nationalist and anti-American sentiment, a disdain for democratic constitutionalism, an admiration for the naked exercise of power, and a cultural conservatism that was most manifest in issues relating to homosexuality.

impressionism: A nineteenth-century artistic movement that experimented with light and color, eschewing the precise forms of realism.

indulgence: A donation made to the Catholic Church for the remission and forgiveness of sins. Abuse of the sale of these indulgences, as well as the question of their validity, was the subject of Luther's Ninety-Five Theses.

Industrial Revolution: The gradual accumulation and diffusion of technical knowledge that accelerated in the nineteenth CENTURY, spurred by a state-supported culture of innovation and by developments in coal power, finances, and agriculture. The Industrial Revolution changed the economic landscape of northwestern Europe and North America, catapulting industrialized areas ahead of the rest of the world in manufacturing, agricultural output, and standard of living.

Innocent III (r. 1198–1216): A pope who held a deep belief in human sin and sought to reform the Church, most notably through the Fourth Lateran Council, to set stricter bounds on the behavior of clergy. He also revived the Crusades, beginning with the Fourth Crusade of 1202–4.

inquisition: An ecclesiastical court established by the pope in the thirteenth CENTURY to combat heresy. Mainly from the Dominican order, clerical inquisitors targeted Cathars, Jews, Muslims, and eventually Protestants.

intendants: French royal agents who since the late Middle Ages had been sent to the provinces with powers to act on the king's behalf. In 1635 Cardinal Richelieu, adviser to Louis XIII, made them permanent fixtures of royal administration.

Investiture Controversy: The name given to a series of debates over the limitations of spiritual and secular power in Europe during the eleventh and early twelfth CENTURIES, it came to a head when Pope Gregory VII and Emperor Henry IV of Germany both claimed the right to appoint and invest bishops with the regalia of office. After years of diplomatic and military hostility, the controversy was partially settled by the Concordat of Worms in 1122.

Iraq War (2003–2011): A conflict initiated by a U.S.-led coalition backed by Britain and many former Communist bloc countries in NATO, who attacked on the grounds that Iraq possessed weapons of mass destruction. The alleged weapons were never found, and the war devolved into a taxing and unpopular guerrilla conflict.

Irish famine: The period of agricultural blight in Ireland from 1845 to 1849. Because of inadequate relief efforts by the British government, hundreds of thousands died from hunger or disease. The economic collapse also led to the emigration of another million Irish.

iron curtain: A term coined by Winston Churchill in 1946 to refer to the borders of Eastern European nations that lay within the zone of Soviet control.

Jacobins: Members of a radical political group during the French Revolution that took power after 1792, executed Louis XVI, and sought to remake French culture.

Jansenism: An ascetic Catholic movement in France and the Low Countries during the seventeenth CENTURY. Jansenists criticized the lavish decoration of Baroque churches and what they saw as an undue emphasis in the Catholic Reformation Church on the role of free will in the process of salvation.

Jerome (ca. 345–ca. 420): One of the most important of the early church fathers who became a "Doctor of the Church," Jerome was a theologian and priest who lived from around 345 to 420 CE. Jerome was a prodigious writer who became most famous for his translation of the Bible into Latin.

Jesuits: Officially known as the Society of Jesus, the Jesuit religious order was founded by Ignatius Loyola and recognized by the pope in 1540. The Jesuits were particularly active in education and missionary activity and were leaders of the Catholic Reformation.

Jesus (ca. 4 BCE–ca. 33 CE): A Jewish religious leader who lived from around 4 BCE to around 33 CE, Jesus was the founder of the Christian religion. A wandering teacher and prophet who was believed to be the Son of God by his followers, Jesus was executed by the Romans by the method of crucifixion. Jesus is called the "Christ," which means the "anointed one," and Christians believe his death and resurrection make possible the cleansing of sin and entrance to the afterlife.

July Revolution (1830): A revolt beginning on July 27, 1830, during which Parisians overthrew Charles X and installed his cousin, Louis-Philippe, who ruled in cooperation with bourgeois advisers and expanded the size of the electorate.

justices of the peace: Beginning in the fourteenth CENTURY in England, justices of the peace were unpaid local officials, serving terms of one year, that oversaw juries, kept public order, and enforced legislation.

Justinian: Emperor from 527 to 565 CE, Justinian is considered one of the most consequential leaders of the Byzantine Empire. His many accomplishments include reclaiming lost territory in the west, instituting major building programs, and creating a comprehensive law code.

Kaaba: Located in the holy city of Mecca in modern-day Saudi Arabia, the Kaaba is the most important shrine for the Muslim community. During their pilgrimage to Mecca, observant Muslims circle the Kaaba seven times. Islamic tradition states that the shrine was originally built by Abraham in the city of Muhammad's birth.

Keynes, John Maynard (1883–1946): An influential British economist who argued that in order to maximize the growth of free markets, public spending by the government is needed to stimulate economic demand.

laissez-faire: Also known as free-market capitalism, an economic system in which the state does not regulate or interfere with the workings of the market, and most economic activity is controlled by private individuals and privately owned corporations.

latifundia: From the Latin word meaning "widespread estates," *latifundia* were extensive parcels of land privately owned by wealthy Roman patricians. The produce on these massive farms was grown with slave labor and was typically used for export.

Latin right: After 338 BCE, the right of Latins to marry and trade with Romans and gain citizenship if they settled in Rome.

Law of the Twelve Tables: The set of laws published around 450 BCE that defined the legal rights and procedures of the Roman Republic.

League of Nations: An international organization founded after World War I to resolve international disputes through arbitration. It was dissolved in 1946 and its assets were transferred to the United Nations.

legions: Disciplined detachments of around 5,000 soldiers in the Roman army. Legions also built camps, roads, and bridges throughout the empire.

Lend-Lease: A program, beginning in 1941, through which the United States provided war materiel first to Britain in exchange for leases on military bases and then to other Allied nations on the promise of eventual repayment.

Lenin, Vladimir (1870–1924): Born Vladimir Ilich Ulyanov, Lenin was the head of the Bolshevik Revolution (1917) and the first leader of the Soviet Union.

Levellers: A radical group in the English New Model Army who called for granting all adult men the right to vote.

liberalism: A political and social movement starting in the nineteenth CENTURY and adopted by those who favored democratic, representative government, the principle of human rights, and the reduction of government control over the economy.

Lisbon Treaty (2009): A series of amendments to the former European Union agreements, formally establishing the offices of Union president and foreign minister. Ratified by all EU member states in 2007, the treaty took effect in 2009.

Little Ice Age: A period of global cooling from the sixteenth through the early nineteenth CENTURIES, which reached its greatest intensity during the seventeenth CENTURY. It played a role in harvest failures that were responsible for the death of millions from starvation and from lowered resistance to epidemic diseases.

Locke, John (1632–1704): The English philosopher and political theorist who maintained that government originated when people formed a social contract to overcome the uncertainties of living in the state of nature, but that the people retained most of their natural rights and thus had the right to resist and even depose tyrannical rulers.

Louis XIV (r. 1643–1715): Known as the Sun King, Louis greatly strengthened the monarchy in France by establishing a highly CENTRALIZED, absolutist government.

Louis XVI (r. 1774–1792): The well-meaning yet weak-willed king of France who was finally deposed and executed by guillotine during the French Revolution.

Low Countries: The coastal region of northwest Europe, including the area of the modern-day Netherlands and Belgium, which was a CENTER of trade and manufacturing in the fifteenth CENTURY.

Luddites: English textile weavers who in the early 1800s organized to destroy the new power looms and workshops that threatened their livelihoods. They claimed to be following the example set by the semi-mythical Ned Ludd, said to have smashed looms thirty years earlier.

Lusitania: A large ocean liner that was sunk by a German U-boat in May 1915. Although the ship was in fact carrying munitions, the heavy loss of civilian life, including many Americans, led to widespread condemnation of Germany by the American press.

Luther, Martin (1483–1546): A monk and professor with a doctorate in theology who was the primary figure in the early Protestant Reformation. Luther's criticisms of the Catholic Church ended that institution's dominance over the religious culture of western Christianity.

Lyceum: The school founded by Aristotle around 335 BCE on the outskirts of Athens. Dedicated to the god Apollo, the school focused on both debate and the study of textual sources.

ma'at: A complex concept from ancient Egypt describing the fundamental cosmic order established by the gods, and also encompassing justice, truth, and balance.

Maccabees: The leaders of a Jewish rebel army who overthrew the Seleucids in 166 BCE. The Maccabees established the Hasmonean dynasty, which ruled over Judea for the next CENTURY.

Machiavelli, Niccolò (1469–1527): An Italian Renaissance diplomat, historian, and political theorist most famous for his work *The Prince*. Machiavelli is considered one of the most influential political thinkers of the early modern era due to his essays concerning the nature of power and leadership.

Magna Carta: Latin for "The Great Charter," the Magna Carta is considered the foundational document of the English constitutional tradition. In 1215, members of the English nobility forced King John to sign the charter, which pledged the king's respect for the traditional privileges of the nobility, free cities, and the clergy.

mandates: Middle Eastern territories, including Palestine, Iraq, Syria, and Lebanon, ostensibly subject to the League of Nations following World War I but directly administered by Britain and France.

Manhattan Project: The secret American and British government research project that developed the first nuclear bomb, first tested in New Mexico in July 1945.

Mani (216–276): A Persian Christian mystic whose dualist belief system argued that the evil realm of matter had invaded the good realm of spirit, dooming humans to sin. His followers, known as "Maniche-ans," continued to challenge conventional Christianity after his death.

manorialism: The dominant socioeconomic system of medieval Europe. Centered on the manor, a parcel of land controlled by a lord, the manorial system placed legal and economic power with a lord who had control over, and responsibility for, the local peasantry.

Marshall Plan: Announced in 1947, an American economic plan pledging billions of dollars in direct aid and loans for the post-war reconstruction of Europe. Suspicion of American motives played a role in the formation of a rival system of cooperation, COMECON, between the Soviet Union and the regimes it had established in Central and Eastern Europe.

Marx, Karl (1818–1883): A German socialist writer, organizer, and economist who believed that a revolution of the working classes would overthrow the capitalist order and create a classless society. Author of *The Communist Manifesto* (with Friedrich Engels) and *Capital*.

Maximillian I (r. 1508–1519): The Holy Roman emperor who established Habsburg claims over much of Burgundy, Aragon and Castile, and Milan, while leading an ambitious effort to reform the empire.

Medici family: An Italian banking family and political dynasty that dominated Renaissance Florence. The Medici were also important patrons of the arts and proponents of civic humanism, which made them instrumental to the Renaissance.

Mehmed I (r. 1413–1421): The Ottoman ruler who expanded the empire's territory throughout Europe and Asia Minor, conquering Constantinople in 1453.

Mensheviks: A moderate faction, formerly of the Russian Social Democratic Party, whose members advocated slow changes and a gradual move toward socialism.

mercantilism: Economic policies shaped by the assumption that one country's commerce could only grow at the expense of another's because of limits in the world's economic resources.

metics: Resident aliens of a Greek city-state who lived there legally but were not considered citizens. Many were invited to settle in Athens if they were skilled in trade, arts, crafts, or teaching.

middle passage: The trans-Atlantic route from Africa to the Americas, along which over 11 million Africans were transported in grueling conditions to be sold into slavery.

Mill, John Stuart (1806–1873): An English philosopher whose faith in human reason led him to support a broad variety of civic and political freedoms for men and women, including the right to vote and the right to free speech.

Mississippi Company: A French overseas trading corporation established by the Scot John Law, who became France's finance minister in 1716. The price of shares rose dramatically until 1720, when the investment bubble burst because speculation far outstripped actual profits from Louisiana. The collapse of the company, and with it the banking system introduced by Law, set back French economic development.

modernism: In the late nineteenth and early twentieth centuries, a movement in art, literature, and music that included the following beliefs: that the world had radically changed and that this change should be embraced; that traditional aesthetic values were ill suited to the present; and that art should emphasize expression over representation and value novelty, expression, and creative freedom.

monastic: A term describing communities that were created throughout the Christian world as places where men and women could pursue a life of spirituality. The monastic life was built around work, prayer, and an ascetic lifestyle.

Mongols: A nomadic people from the steppes of Central Asia who were united under the ruler Genghis Khan. His conquest of China was continued by his grandsons, whose armies also seized Muscovy and then moved through Hungary and Poland, reaching as far as the gates of Vienna.

monotheistic: A term describing a religious system that espouses a belief in only one god, or the oneness of God. The three major Western faiths—Judaism, Christianity, and Islam—are all monotheistic religions.

More, Thomas (1478–1535): An English scholar, lawyer, politician, and humanist. More wrote *Utopia* and was the lord chancellor of England before being executed for refusing to recognize Henry VIII's Church of England. He was also one of the most vocal and harshest critics of Luther.

mosques: Islamic houses of worship, often serving as centers of communities.

Mountain: A radical Jacobin faction—so named for the high seats its members occupied in the Assembly hall—that held power during the Reign of Terror. Under the leadership of Robespierre, they successfully pushed for the execution of Louis XVI, vigorous prosecution of the

war effort, government regulation of the economy, and ruthless suppression of counterrevolution.

Muhammad (570–632): The founder of the Islamic religion. It is said that he was approached by the archangel Gabriel with the word of God that formed the holy book of Islam, the Qur'an. Muslims believe that Muhammad was the last in a line of prophets dating back to Abraham and that the message he received was the culmination of God's word to mankind.

Mussolini, Benito (1883–1945): The leader of Italian fascism, Mussolini consolidated his hold on Italy between 1922 and 1925, staging a "March on Rome" with his paramilitary black shirts. After 1925 Mussolini ruled Italy as head of a party dictatorship, until he was deposed in 1943, captured, and executed in 1945.

Mutiny (1857): The British term for the Indian uprising that was sparked when Hindu and Muslim soldiers refused to use rifle cartridges they believed to be coated with beef and pork fat and were harshly disciplined by their British commander. Protests against the cartridges fed into widespread resentment of British policies, and soon the episode became a full-fledged rebellion before being violently suppressed by British troops.

Napoleon III (r. 1852–1870): The nephew of Napoleon Bonaparte, Napoleon III was elected president of the French Second Republic in 1848 and made himself emperor of France in 1852. During his reign, he rebuilt the French capital of Paris. Defeated in the Franco-Prussian War, he went into exile.

National Assembly: The governing body of France that succeeded the Estates General in 1789 during the French Revolution. It was composed of, and defined by, the delegates of the Third Estate.

National Convention: The governing body of France from September 1732 to October 1795, charged with writing a new constitution. It declared France a republic and then tried and executed Louis XVI. The Convention also confiscated the property of enemies of the Revolution, instituted a policy of de-Christianization, and placed a cap on the price of necessities.

National Front: The most prominent political party in twenty-first-century France, known for its conservative policies and anti-immigrant rhetoric; led first by Jean-Marie Le Pen, then by his daughter, Marine Le Pen.

National Liberation Front (FLN): A nationalist Algerian movement founded in 1954, using guerrilla and terrorist tactics to revolt against French control.

nationalism: A movement to unify a country under one government based on perceptions of the population's common history, customs, and social traditions.

Nazis: The National Socialist German Workers' Party, which under Adolf Hitler controlled Germany from 1933 to Germany's defeat in 1945. Nazi ideology was founded on violent anti-Semitism, anti-Marxism, and German nationalism.

Nazi-Soviet Pact: An August 1939 agreement in which Nazi Germany and the Soviet Union declared mutual non-aggression. Secret clauses divided eastern Europe into spheres of influence. The pact paved the way for the German invasion of Poland just a week later.

neoliberalism: The economic belief that free markets and restraints on budget deficits and social welfare programs are the best guarantee of individual liberties.

Neoplatonism: A school of philosophy heavily influenced by the Platonic tradition and developed largely by Plotinus in the third CENTURY. Neoplatonists conceived of a universe in which all matter is closely linked to the gods. Unlike Platonism, Neoplatonism held that philosophers were holy men who spoke directly to the gods, and instead of expressing their arguments in dialogues, they wrote treatises.

new imperialism: A push for colonial expansion beginning in the 1880s, in which major western European powers vied for territory in Asia and Africa for economic gain and material resources rather than for settlement. The new imperialism demonstrated Europe's economic and technological clout and led to the severe subjugation of indigenous populations.

New Testament: The collection of texts, taken together with the Hebrew Bible, or Old Testament, that form the Christian Bible. The New Testament took shape over the first two CENTURIES CE and contains the four Gospels, the Letters of Saint Paul, and other early Christian documents. All of the original books of the New Testament were written in Greek.

Newton, Isaac (1642–1727): An English physicist and mathematician who in his *Principia Mathematica* (1687) showed how objects act on one another through a law of universal gravitation. By using differential calculus, which he invented, he demonstrated how the same forces govern both terrestrial and planetary motion.

Nietzsche, Friedrich (1844–1900): The German philosopher who argued that both Christian morality and rationality had sapped Western civilization of its creative life force. In works such as *Thus Spoke Zarathustra* (1883–85), he maintained that a "superman" not bound by conventional morality could restore the vitality of the life force.

Nightingale, Florence (1820–1910): A British battlefield nurse who served in the Crimean War, established nursing as a profession, and worked to improve healthcare.

Ninety-Five Theses: Penned by Luther in 1517, the theses were a stinging criticism of the Church's practice of selling indulgences and are considered the first event in the Protestant Reformation.

North Atlantic Treaty Organization (NATO): A military alliance created among the United States, Canada, and ten Western European countries in 1949 to counteract the growing influence of the Soviet bloc. Today NATO includes twenty-eight countries, including former members of the Warsaw Pact.

Nuremberg Laws: Laws enacted by the German government in 1935 that stripped Jews of citizenship, denied them entry into most professions, and required them to wear yellow Stars of David on their clothing.

Nuremberg trials: The prosecution of twenty-one leading Nazis in late 1945. Eleven were sentenced to death, including Hitler's deputy Hermann Goering.

oil shock (1973–1974): In retaliation for U.S. support of Israel during the 1973 Yom Kippur War, Arab states halted oil exports to the United States and cut back on oil production. Over the next two years, the fourfold increase in crude oil prices contributed to a severe economic recession in most of the West.

oligarchy: As first established in ancient Greece, particularly in Sparta, rule of the state by the few rather than by a monarch or all citizens.

Operation Barbarossa: Germany's invasion of the Soviet Union in 1941.

Opium War (1839–1842): The conflict between Britain and China that was ended by the Treaty of Nanking, which granted Britain access to Chinese ports and markets and control of the port city of Hong Kong.

oracle: A place or a person the ancient Greeks considered a vessel through which the words of the gods and goddesses could reach the public. Oracles were often asked for counsel and predictions of the future.

ostracism: A procedure in Athenian politics that gave the members of the Assembly an opportunity each year to vote to expel a citizen they deemed a danger to the state. From the Greek word *ostrakon*, a piece of pottery used as a ballot in the ostracism proceedings.

Ottomans: The Ottomans, first led by Osman I, were a nomadic, warrior people who originated in the area of modern Turkmenistan. By the end of the fourteenth CENTURY, they controlled most of Turkey; led by Mehmed II, they sacked Constantinople in 1453. Their empire lasted until their defeat in World War I and the emergence of the modern Turkish state.

pan-German parliament: An assembly, formed in March 1848, to draft a constitution for a united German state. Its goals were never realized, with the most powerful German states, Austria and Prussia, refusing to be governed under a constitutional monarchy.

Pankhurst, Emmeline (1858–1928): A British feminist and the founder of the Women's Social and Political Union, which championed women's suffrage. Pankhurst urged her followers to bring the issue to the fore by taking assertive action, including civil disobedience.

papyrus: An ancient Egyptian writing material made from reeds.

Paris Commune: The revolutionary government in Paris that was formed in the spring of 1871 by the Parisian National Guard, militant workers, and political radicals who were disenchanted with the new French Republic established following the defeat by Prussia and the overthrow of Napoleon III. When the French government sent troops to assert its authority over Paris, the result was a bloody conflict in which both sides killed prisoners.

parlement: Beginning in the thirteenth CENTURY, the French court that established in theory and enforced in practice royal authority.

parliament: From the French verb *parler*, "to speak," parliaments are legislative bodies with enumerated rights in a system of representative government. During the High Middle Ages, especially in England, Parliament came to be seen as representing the will of the realm as a whole.

Pascal, Blaise (1623–1662): The Jansenist mathematician and philosopher whose *Pensées* defended Christian faith and expressed skepticism about conventions regarding society and knowledge.

paterfamilias: Derived from the Latin term for "father of the family," the *paterfamilias* was the oldest living male in a household and held complete control over all other family members.

patricians: According to the Roman historian Livy, the patricians were the noble families of Rome that descended from the original 100 senators appointed by Romulus. Constituting the legally defined upper class of the Roman world, the patricians dominated the economy and political institutions of the state.

Paul: An educated Jew and Roman citizen, Saul of Tarsus, who changed his name to Paul, became one of the most important apostles of the Christian religion. Paul was instrumental in spreading Christianity throughout the eastern Mediterranean and is usually credited with writing fourteen of the twenty-seven books of the New Testament.

Pax Romana: Latin for "Roman Peace," the Pax Romana refers to the era of relative peace that began with the reign of Augustus and lasted until the end of the second century CE.

Peace of Augsburg: The 1555 settlement, reached between Charles V and the Schmalkaldic League (an alliance of Protestant German states), that created the policy of *Cuius regio, eius religio*: the rulers of the German states could decide the official religion of their territory.

Peace of God: A tenth- and eleventh-century movement that condemned violence against the innocent. The movement proclaimed the Truce of God, which forbade warfare during the days Thursday through Sunday.

Peace of Utrecht: Negotiated in 1713–14, an agreement that concluded the War of the Spanish Succession. The settlement left Philip V on the Spanish throne; but by partitioning Spain's European territories, it put an end to Louis XIV's ambitions of French expansion.

Peace of Westphalia: The set of treaties that in 1648 brought an end to the Thirty Years' War. The negotiators in effect replaced the notion of a Europe united by a common Christian religion with one of a continent based on mutual respect for the sovereignty of individual states.

Pearl Harbor: The American naval base in Hawaii that was attacked by Japan on December 7, 1941, bringing the United States into World War II.

Peasants' War (1523–1525): A widespread popular revolt of the German peasantry. The war was fueled by several factors, primarily centered on issues of class, economics, and the Reformation. The revolt was put down in particularly brutal fashion following Luther's denunciation of the peasants.

Peninsular War (1808–1814): The conflict that raged in Iberia following Napoleon's replacement of Spain's Bourbon monarch with Napoleon's own brother Joseph. Resistance from Spanish royal forces aided by the British and by bands of local irregulars prevented France from securing effective control of Spain, thereby weakening French efforts in Russia and elsewhere.

perestroika: Meaning "restructuring," Mikhail Gorbachev's plan to reform the Soviet Union and increase efficiency to make it more competitive with the West.

Pericles (r. 460–430 BCE): As a leading statesman and general, Pericles began many of the major building projects of classical Greece and was central in further democratizing the city-state.

Peter the Great (r. 1682–1725): The energetic tsar who transformed Russia into a leading European country by centralizing government, orienting elites more toward the West, modernizing the army, creating a navy, and reforming the economy.

Peterloo Massacre: The brutal attack by British cavalry on peaceful demonstrators in Manchester, England, on August 16, 1819. The incident occurred in response to a large popular demonstration demanding parliamentary reform and the repeal of laws that restricted foreign imports and kept cereal prices high.

Petition of Right (1628): A declaration by Parliament that limited royal power, establishing that only Parliament had the authority to levy taxes, that the king could not declare martial law during peacetime, and that prisoners had the right to appeal their detention before a court or judge.

Petrarch: Often referred to as the "Father of Humanism," Petrarch was an Italian scholar, linguist, and poet who was an important figure in the beginning of the Renaissance. He rediscovered many lost texts, which inspired him to work at revitalizing the study of classical Latin.

Pharisees: An influential group within the Jewish community of Palestine during the Second Temple period, the Pharisees consisted largely of "common" Jews as opposed to the more elite Sadducees. The Pharisees argued that law was the center of Jewish life, and their interpretation of the Torah and Hebrew legacy became the foundation of modern Judaism.

Philip II (r. 359–336 BCE): The leader of the northern Greek-speaking state of Macedon. Philip led Macedon to the peak of its power through his tactical military innovations, including a new, more lethal version of the phalanx.

philosophe: One of a group of leading public intellectuals who sought to teach as well as implement the ideas of the Enlightenment, especially religious toleration.

Phoenicians: A seafaring Semitic people based on the eastern coast of the Mediterranean Sea whose culture was particularly vibrant from the Bronze Age through the classical Greek era.

Picasso, Pablo (1881–1973): A Spanish painter and leading modernist artist, whose 1907 masterpiece *The Young Ladies of Avignon* incorporated African influences and reduced figures to basic shapes, a technique that he developed further in later cubist works.

pietism: A Protestant religious movement that began in Germany in the seventeenth century and flourished in the eighteenth. Pietists, such as Methodists, supported an emotional, enthusiastic form of religion that focused on the individual experience of salvation.

Plato (425–347 BCE): A student of Socrates, the teacher of Aristotle, and a central figure in Western philosophy who lived in Athens. Plato taught that absolute concepts and virtues existed on a higher level of reality compared with the everyday world.

plebeians: The general body of free Roman citizens who were not part of the patrician class. Plebeians made up the majority of the Roman citizenry.

pogroms: Anti-Jewish riots, typically occurring in nineteenth- and twentieth-century Russia.

polis: Singular form of *poleis*: independent cities in ancient Greece that developed formal constitutions between the eighth and sixth centuries BCE.

polytheistic: A term describing a religious system that involves the worship of multiple gods and goddesses. The religions of ancient Mesopotamia, Egypt, Greece, and Rome were polytheistic.

Poor Law Amendment of 1834: An attempt by the British Parliament to address the problem of poverty by instituting a national policy designed to impose more discipline on the poor through a nationwide system of residential workhouses.

pope: The head of the Roman Catholic Church.

populares: Roman political leaders in the late Republican period, usually from the upper classes, who garnered support among the common folk with their calls for land reform, public works projects, and government subsidies for the masses. The Gracchi brothers and Julius Caesar are examples of *populares*, which is Latin for "favoring the people."

populism: A political orientation that champions the common person, usually in bitter contrast to social and cultural elites, and often demonstrates a fierce opposition to international organizations and international free trade.

portolan chart: A detailed rendering of the coastlines, ports, and trade routes of Europe, Africa, and Asia created by fourteenth- and fifteenth-century European cartographers using compasses. These maps were incredibly accurate and helpful for establishing trading posts.

Potsdam conference: The 1945 conference where U.S. president Harry Truman, British prime minister Winston Churchill, and Soviet premier Joseph Stalin met to discuss making territorial changes to Germany and its allies and the question of reparations following World War II.

princeps: A Latin term usually translated as "first citizen," this title was first given to Octavian in the year 30 BCE. The term served to imply his position as a first among equals and to pay homage to the Republican past, but the new system, known as the "principate," put control of the Roman state ultimately into the hands of one man.

proletariat: A term for the industrial working class—people who worked for wages—beginning in the nineteenth CENTURY.

prophet: An individual who claims to have contact with the divine and acts as an intermediary between humans and God. Within the context of Judaism, prophets were religious reformers who argued that the Hebrew people were breaking their covenant with Yahweh and therefore needed to transform society in order to be more religiously pure.

protectorate: A form of imperial rule that was ostensibly created to protect indigenous populations but that in reality granted imperial governments even more power. Established by European colonizers including the British, French, and Germans during the scramble for Africa.

Protestant Reformation: The movement, starting in 1521 and inspired by Martin Luther, that called into question the theology and practices of the Catholic Church. Due to the decentralized nature of reform, many different Christian denominations emerged under the umbrella of Protestant churches.

Provisional Government: Following the abdication of Tsar Nikolai II in 1917, the unelected Russian government led by Alexander Kerensky that failed to gain widespread popular support.

Ptolemies: The dynasty established by Ptolemy that ruled a Hellenistic kingdom in Egypt for nearly three CENTURIES (305–30 BCE) as a successor to Alexander's empire. The Ptolemies epitomized the features of Hellenistic rule, as their society fused Greek and Egyptian customs, language, and institutions.

Punic Wars (264–146 BCE): A series of three wars fought between the Roman Republic and Carthage. These clashes were mainly over control of the western Mediterranean, with Rome eventually emerging victorious over its chief rival in the area. "Punic" comes from the Latin word for Phoenician, as Carthage was originally founded by the Phoenicians.

Puritans: A group of English Protestant reformers who felt that the reforms of the Church of England under the Tudor and Stuart monarchs did not go far enough to "purify" the English church of all vestiges of Roman Catholicism. Many Puritans left England for the North American colonies starting in the 1630s.

"putting out" system: An eighteenth-century textile manufacturing system in which urban merchants delivered wool to peasants in rural areas, who were paid for processing the wool into coarse cloth.

Quakers: A Christian group that emerged during the English Civil Wars. They refused any role for a clergy, rejected displays of social deference, and renounced military service.

Queen Victoria (r. 1837–1901): The influential queen of Great Britain who presided over the expansion of the British Empire as well as the evolution of English politics and social and economic reforms.

Qur'an: Literally meaning "the recitation," the Qur'an is the CENTRAL holy text of the Islamic faith. Muslims believe it to be the final revelation of God to the prophet Muhammad in the seventh CENTURY CE. To be considered truly authentic, the Qur'an must be in its original Arabic.

realism: A nineteenth-century artistic and literary style that sought to portray common situations as they would appear in reality.

Realpolitik: A political strategy based on advancing power for its own sake, with no regard for moral or ideological concerns.

Reconquista: Spanish for "reconquest"; the term refers to the period of approximately eight CENTURIES (711–1492 CE) when Muslim and Christian princes battled for control of the Iberian Peninsula.

Reform Bill of 1832: In response to strong popular support for electoral reform, the British Parliament passed this bill to expand the electorate, provide for free elections, and redraw the country's electoral map more fairly.

refugee crisis: The movement of over a million refugees—mostly from Syria, Iraq, and Afghanistan—to Europe, beginning in 2015. Such a large influx created tension across Europe as different countries responded to the humanitarian crisis in different ways.

Reign of Terror (1793–1794): The campaign at the height of the French Revolution in which violence, including systematic executions, was used to purge France of its "enemies" and to extend the Revolution beyond its borders. Radicals executed as many as 40,000 people who were judged to be enemies of the state.

Republic of Letters: An informal international community of intellectual figures that included the English scientist Francis Bacon, the French philosopher René Descartes, and the Dutch scholar Anna Maria van Schurman. Starting in the late sixteenth CENTURY, members of this community shared their ideas through correspondence in Latin.

republicanism: An Enlightenment current of thought inspired by ancient republics and developed by Rousseau and other writers; it called for austerity and a strict separation of sexes.

Resistance: Anti-Vichy French resistance forces during World War II.

Richardson, Samuel (1689–1761): An English novelist whose most famous novels *Pamela* (1740) and *Clarissa* (1748), written in the form of letters by the protagonists, had a strong influence on European culture.

Robespierre, Maximilien (1758–1794): The former lawyer who became a leader of the Jacobins and the Committee of Public Safety, and also the architect of the Reign of Terror during the French Revolution. He was executed at the beginning of the Thermidorian Reaction.

Robinson Crusoe: Published in 1719 and widely regarded as the first modern realist novel. In this purportedly factual account of the resourcefulness of a man who survives a shipwreck, author Daniel Defoe provided both an exotic adventure story and a protagonist with whom ordinary readers could identify.

Romanesque: An architectural style that spread throughout western Europe beginning in the late tenth CENTURY and ended approximately 200 years later. Romanesque buildings are characterized by rounded arches, barrel vaults, massive stone pillars, and thick walls.

romanticism: An artistic and literary movement that started in the late eighteenth CENTURY and was inspired by nature and sentiment rather than by science and reason.

Rousseau, Jean-Jacques (1712–1778): The French *philosophe* and radical political theorist whose *Social Contract* attacked privilege and inequality. Rousseau argued that true freedom could only be attained by submission to the "general will."

Saint Bartholomew's Day Massacre: The mass murder of French Protestants (Huguenots) instigated by Queen Catherine de' Medici of France and carried out by Catholics in Paris on August 24, 1572 (Saint Bartholomew's day).

salons: Beginning in eighteenth-century Europe, gatherings in urban aristocratic homes, frequently hosted by elite women, for discussion of new literature, current events, and more generally ideas associated with the Enlightenment.

sans-culottes: Working-class Parisians, so named for wearing trousers rather than breeches (*culottes*), who during the French Revolution formed a militant political movement led largely by educated professionals and artisans.

satrap: A provincial governor of the Persian Empire and its successor states. Upon conquering Persia in 330 BCE, Alexander installed his own governors but kept this traditional Persian title.

Schlieffen Plan: A German military plan developed by Count Alfred von Schlieffen in 1905, calling for a quick defeat of France by invading through Belgium and then a longer war against Russia. The plan nearly succeeded in August–September 1914 but failed in part because of unexpectedly heavy resistance by the Belgians.

scholasticism: Beginning in the eleventh CENTURY, an approach to Christianity that centered on teaching, learning, the study of scripture and commentaries, and debate.

scramble for Africa: The European rush to colonize parts of Africa at the end of the nineteenth CENTURY.

Second Industrial Revolution: The technological developments of the last third of the nineteenth CENTURY, which included new techniques for refining and producing steel; increased availability of electricity for industrial, commercial, and domestic use; advances in chemical manufacturing; and invention of the internal combustion engine.

Second Temple: The CENTER of Jewish life and worship during the Hellenistic and early Roman periods. The Second Temple (the first having been destroyed by the Babylonians in 586 BCE) was built on the Temple Mount in Jerusalem, remaining until its destruction by the Romans in 70 CE.

Second Vatican Council: A meeting of the Catholic Church convened by Pope John XXIII during 1962–65 that introduced far-reaching changes in practices and teachings, including having the Mass read in local languages instead of Latin and ceasing to blame Jews for the death of Jesus Christ.

Senate: An essential Roman political institution established soon after the city's founding in the eighth CENTURY BCE that survived throughout the Republican and imperial periods. Primarily an advisory body, the Senate was dominated by the Roman nobility.

September Massacres (1792): The name given to the week during which vigilante mobs of *sans-culottes* raided the jails of Paris and summarily tried and executed hundreds of alleged counterrevolutionaries.

Septuagint: The Greek translation of the Hebrew Bible made in the third CENTURY BCE. From the Latin word *septuaginta* ("seventy"), which refers to the legendary seventy Jewish scholars who worked on the project.

serf: In medieval Europe, a dependent agricultural worker who performed labor on a manor in exchange for the security and rudimentary government provided by the local lord.

Seven Years' War (1754–1753): A conflict involving fighting in Europe, North America, Africa, and India. Britain's naval superiority as well as its ability to raise funds to equip and move armies contributed to its victory over France and its allies.

Sevi, Shabbetai: A Greek Jew who during the 1650s and 1660s identified himself as the Messiah before being ordered by the Ottoman sultan to convert or face execution. His movement collapsed when he chose to accept Islam.

ship money: A medieval custom in England established by King Charles I that required coastal towns to supply ships, or the money to build them, to the crown as a means of generating royal income.

Silk Road: A network of trade routes spanning the Asian continent from the Mediterranean in the west to China in the east. The Silk Road extends over 4,000 miles and was essential for creating economic, political, and cultural connections among the various peoples of Asia. It was named after the lucrative silk trade CENTERED in China that lured merchants from around the region.

Smith, Adam (1723–1790): The Scottish philosopher and economist who proposed in *The Wealth of Nations* that competition among self-interested individuals led naturally to a healthy economy and that a division of labor would increase productivity and prosperity.

Social War: A revolt of Rome's allies on the Italian peninsula whose demands for full citizenship were denied by the Senate in the early first CENTURY BCE. The rebels succeeding in briefly forming their own state outside of the confines of Rome, but after a year of conflict they were haltingly re-assimilated back into the Roman state.

socialism: Originally meaning a social system that guaranteed decent living conditions and work for all people, a political ideology that calls for a classless society with collective ownership of all property.

Socrates (ca. 470–399 BCE): An Athenian teacher and one of the founding figures in Western philosophy, whose ideas come to us chiefly through his pupil Plato. Socrates was a passionate promoter of critical thinking, and his willingness to challenge conventional wisdom landed him in trouble with the Athenian authorities, who sentenced him to death for allegedly corrupting the city's youth.

Solidarity: Beginning in 1980 as an independent trade union formed by Polish shipyard workers under the leadership of Lech Wałesa, Solidarity grew into a political movement tolerated by the Communist government. Solidarity's dominance in elections in 1989 heralded the end of Communism in Poland.

Solon: The ruler of Athens appointed in 594 BCE and charged with ending the social and economic unrest plaguing the city. Solon brought major reforms to the Athenian system and was an important transitional figure on the road from aristocracy to democracy.

sophist: An itinerant teacher of philosophy and rhetoric during the archaic and classical periods. Sophists focused on the skills of argument and debate rather than the search for absolute truths. From the Greek word *sophia* ("wisdom" or "wise").

soviets: Local councils elected by workers and soldiers in Russia that formed in the early twentieth CENTURY. In the midst of World War I, the Petrograd soviet in the capital emerged as one of the CENTERS of power after the Russian monarchy collapsed in 1917. Thereafter, the soviets became increasingly powerful, pressing for social reform and the redistribution of land.

Spanish Armada: The fleet of warships sent against England by Philip II of Spain in 1588 but vanquished by the English fleet and bad weather in the English Channel.

Spanish Civil War (1936–1939): A military conflict between conservative Nationalists, led by General Francisco Franco (1892–1975), and leftist Republicans, a coalition of liberals, socialists, communists, and anarchists. Franco and the Nationalists triumphed by 1939.

Spinoza, Baruch (1632–1677): The Dutch philosopher of Jewish descent who shocked Jews, Protestants, and Catholics when he rejected the distinction between spirit and matter and propounded that the universe comprises only one substance. He further maintained that the workings of the universe could be understood only through scientific observation and logic.

Stalin, Joseph (1879–1953): The Bolshevik leader who succeeded Lenin as leader of the Soviet Union and ruled until his death in 1953.

Stoics: Followers of the Hellenistic philosopher Zeno (ca. 335–263 BCE), who argued that people must accept that their life is determined by fate, and that upon this acceptance they can devote themselves to duty. Stoicism later heavily influenced Roman society.

structuralism: A form of cultural analysis that emerged in the 1950s, positing that language and culture have no inherent meaning apart from their cultural setting. Michel Foucault, a French philosopher associated with structuralism, maintained that changes in "epistemological regimes" were arbitrary.

Struggle of the Orders: The conflict between patrician and plebeian orders beginning in the early years of the Roman Republic. The plebeians gradually won a greater share of political power as a result of these efforts, and the struggle greatly affected the development of the Roman constitution.

Suez Crisis (1956): A conflict following Egyptian leader Gamal Abdel Nasser's sudden nationalization of the Suez Canal, in which Britain, France, and Israel launched coordinated attacks to reoccupy the canal zone and destabilize the new regime. Unexpectedly strong Egyptian resistance as well as condemnation of the attacks by both the Soviet Union and the United States forced the British and French to withdraw.

symposium: An important Hellenic social institution that provided a forum for upper-class men to discuss important issues of the day, including philosophy and politics.

syndicalism: A movement that flourished in France during the late nineteenth and early twentieth CENTURIES in which unions took militant political action against capitalism through general strikes.

taille: Established as early as 1439 in France, a permanent tax used to support the military, collected from all those who were neither clerics nor nobles.

Talleyrand, Charles-Maurice de (1754–1838): The French foreign minister under the Directory, Napoleon, and Louis XVIII. Talleyrand played an important role in persuading France's allies to restore the Bourbon dynasty under Louis XVIII following Napoleon's first abdication.

Tennis Court Oath: An oath taken by the French National Assembly in June 1789 pledging to create a new, written constitution.

tetrarchy: One of the most important reforms of the emperor Diocletian was the creation of the tetrarchy in 293 BCE. Meaning "the rule of four," the tetrarchic system included two senior emperors, each called an *Augustus*, and two junior emperors, each called a *Caesar*. Each pair of emperors ruled over one half of the Roman Empire, split between east and west. This system was created to help end the battles for succession that plagued third-century Rome as well as to make administration of the empire more efficient.

Thatcher, Margaret (1925–2013): Prime minister of Great Britain during the period 1979–1990, Thatcher led a conservative government that emphasized individuality and limited government.

Theodora: Wife of the emperor Justinian, Theodora was arguably the most powerful woman in the history of the Byzantine Empire. She was Justinian's most trusted adviser and helped to shape religious and social policy from her position as empress.

Theodoric (r. 475–526): Leader of the Ostrogoths who established a Gothic realm that stretched from the area of modern France to the Balkans. Though officially a representative of the emperor in Constantinople, Theodoric ruled essentially independently.

theology: The study of religious faith, practice, and experience, especially the nature of God and God's relation to the world.

Thermidorian Reaction: The phase of the French Revolution, starting July 27, 1794, in which Robespierre was executed and the Reign of Terror was ended, marking the close of the most radical period of the Revolution.

Thucydides: An Athenian historian and general who wrote the definitive history of the Peloponnesian War before his death around 400 BCE.

tolerationists: Beginning in the seventeenth CENTURY, thinkers who argued for tolerance of other religious beliefs.

total war: First described during World War I, a war effort drawing on all of a society's military, economic, and civilian resources.

totalitarianism: A system of government based on complete state control over all aspects of public and private society.

trade unions: Beginning in the nineteenth CENTURY, collectives of workers that pushed for better working conditions and expanded suffrage.

tragedy: A form of Greek theater that reached its peak in fifth-century BCE Athens with the playwrights Aeschylus, Sophocles, and Euripides. Tragedies highlighted the suffering that underlies human society and provided lessons for the audience through the tribulations of their main characters.

treaties of Tilsit: Negotiated in July 1807 by Napoleon and the Russian emperor Alexander I, two agreements that divided Europe into mutually recognized spheres of influence, reduced Prussian territory, and established new satellite states in Westphalia and Poland.

Treaty of Rome (1956): The agreement in which six Western European states established the European Economic Community, a common market without trade barriers.

Treaty of Tordesillas (1494): A treaty to divide the newly explored, non-Christian lands of the New World between the Spanish and the Portuguese in the wake of Columbus's first voyage.

trench warfare: Weapons such as the machine gun and barbed wire gave tremendous advantages to defensive positions in World War I, leading to prolonged battles between entrenched armies in fixed positions. Eventually, thousands of miles of trenches and tunnels stretched across the western front.

triangle trade: The eighteenth-century commercial Atlantic shipping pattern that involved transporting rum from New England to Africa, trading it for slaves taken to the West Indies, and bringing sugar back to New England to be processed into rum.

Trinity: An essential element of Christian theology, the Holy Trinity consists of God the Father, the Son, and the Holy Spirit.

According to accepted Christian orthodoxy, all three members of the Trinity are equal, eternal, and of the same substance.

Triple Alliance: An 1882 alliance among Germany, Austria-Hungary, and Italy.

Triple Entente: An alliance that by 1907 included Britain, France, and Russia.

trireme: A military vessel used by the Athenians and later by the Romans. Its name derived from the three rows of oars on either side of the ship.

the Troubles: Decades of political and sectarian violence in Northern Ireland between the Protestant majority and the minority Ulster Catholics, led at times by the Irish Republican Army. The Good Friday Agreement, signed April 10, 1998, which provided for representation of Catholics and Protestants in a National Assembly, paved the way to a reconciliation.

Turgot, Anne-Robert (1727–1781): A physiocrat, or "economist," who advocated for a series of unpopular reform programs, including edicts that freed price controls on grain, ended the conscription of peasants, abolished guilds, and formed an elected assembly to advise the monarch.

Twelve Tables: Representing an important victory for the plebeians in the Struggle of the Orders, the Twelve Tables helped standardize basic legal proceedings in the Republic and formed one of the centerpieces of the Roman constitutional system. Completed around 450 BCE, the Twelve Tables, according to the Roman historian Livy, were based largely on Greek law.

Ukrainian crisis: A crisis that erupted in Ukraine after the pro-Russian president, Viktor Yanukovych, resigned following a series of protests known as the Euromaidan, which called for Ukraine to align with the EU rather than Russia. Yanukovych's resignation ignited violence in Crimea and later in parts of eastern Ukraine, as rebels aided by Russian soldiers called for secession from Ukraine and union with Russia.

Umayyads: Members of the seventh- and eighth-century Islamic caliphate that ruled an empire stretching from the Middle East to Spain. The Umayyad Caliphate saw the development of the Qur'an and other fundamental aspects of Muslim culture.

utilitarianism: A liberal school of thought that measures political good according to the welfare of individuals and holds that a government should always act to benefit the majority.

vassals: Typically, low-ranking knights or noblemen who swore an oath of fealty to bring both financial and military aid to their lord, usually in return for lands to support themselves. The lord–vassal relationship was the foundation of the medieval feudal system.

Velvet Revolution: Led by Václav Havel in November–December 1989, the peaceful transition in Czechoslovakia from a Communist to a mostly non-Communist government.

venality of office: The sale of government offices in France, especially judgeships, starting in the fifteenth CENTURY in response to the increased need for agents of the CENTRAL government. The practice brought both income and noble status to the purchasers, while at the same time providing revenue to the French state.

Vendée: The department of western France that served as home to the counterrevolutionary Royal and Catholic Army. During the Reign of Terror, government forces ruthlessly exterminated not only the rebels but also much of the civilian population of the region.

Versailles Peace Conference: The peace conference held by the victors of World War I; it resulted in treaties that redrew the map of Europe, forced Germany to pay reparations and to give up its colonies to the victors, and broke up the Austro-Hungarian Empire.

Versailles: The enormous palace built by Louis XIV outside of Paris and the new CENTER of French government in the late seventeenth CENTURY.

Vichy: The French government established after the surrender to Germany in June 1940, led by World War I hero Marshal Philippe Pétain (1856–1951). The authoritarian regime sought to remake France by pursuing ultra-conservative, anti-Semitic policies.

Voltaire (1694–1778): The French *philosophe* and satirist who championed the cause of human dignity against oppression by the state and the Church. His masterpiece, *Candide*, took aim at the belief of optimism.

Vulgate: A Latin translation of the Bible from the late fourth CENTURY CE written by Jerome. This was the most widely used Bible in the Latin-speaking west and became the official Bible of the Catholic Church during the Council of Trent in the sixteenth CENTURY.

Wannsee conference: A meeting of high-ranking Nazi officials in January 1942 to plan the systematic extermination of the Jews of Europe. Jews, as well as Roma, homosexuals, and those accused of political crimes were now to be deported to concentration camps, where most would be killed in gas chambers.

war communism: Radical economic policies adopted by the Bolshevik government during the Russian Civil War of 1918–1921. The policies included a top-down system of CENTRAL planning, the virtual abolition of cash, and the nationalization of heavy industry.

War of the League of Augsburg: An alliance formed in the 1680s by Protestant and Catholic powers, including Sweden, England, the Netherlands, Austria, Spain, and Bavaria, to resist France's expansionist policies. The ensuing war ended in a compromise peace in 1697.

War of the Spanish Succession: A conflict beginning in 1702 when, through the will of Charles II, the entire Spanish Empire was offered to Louis XIV's grandson, who became Philip V of Spain. The prospect of Spain's European and American territories coming under French control led Austria, the Netherlands, England, and other European powers to form a Grand Alliance to contest the succession.

Wars of the Roses (1455–1487): A series of wars waged between the Houses of Lancaster and York during the years 1455–87 CE for control of the English crown. The Lancastrian Henry Tudor emerged victorious and established his family's dynasty for the next CENTURY.

Warsaw Pact: A military alliance among the Soviet Union and other Communist states, established in response to the formation of NATO.

Weimar Republic: The democratic German government established after World War I, so named for the town in which the constitution was drafted in 1919. The Republic came to an end with Hitler's rise to power in 1933.

welfare state: A state structure, adopted by states such as Sweden, Norway, Britain, and France in the twentieth CENTURY, that aims to guarantee a minimum level of services and subsistence for all citizens.

What Is the Third Estate?: A widely distributed pamphlet, written by Emmanuel Sieyès, that attacked the idea of France as a kingdom comprising different orders, or estates. The pamphlet asserted that the Third Estate—the vast majority of French who were neither clergy nor nobility—constituted a complete nation with the authority to decide for the whole.

Wilkes Affair: The controversy following Parliament's removal of John Wilkes, a radical critic of the government, from his seat. The affair and subsequent movement to seat Wilkes led to British public opinion gaining a voice in politics.

William the Conquerer: Duke of Normandy and later King William I of England following his conquest of England in 1066. The first Norman king of England, he reigned until his death in 1087.

Yalta Conference: The 1945 meeting among U.S. president Franklin D. Roosevelt, British prime minister Winston Churchill, and Soviet premier Joseph Stalin in which they planned for the post-war order.

Yeltsin, Boris (1931–2007): A strong advocate of Russian anti-Soviet nationalism and the first president of Russia (1991–1999) following the collapse of the Soviet Union.

Young Turks: Members of the Committee of Union and Progress who launched a successful coup in 1908 with the goal of bringing constitutional government and modernization to the Ottoman Empire.

ziggurat: A monumental tiered or terraced temple found in ancient Mesopotamia beginning in the early third millennium BCE. Most ziggurats were built of mud brick, with ornamental facades and stairways and ramps for access to the shrines.

Zwingli, Ulrich (1484–1531): The leader of the Reformed church in Zurich, Zwingli broke from Luther over differing interpretations of the Eucharist. He argued that public behavior should be regulated by the Christian magistrate.

CHAPTER 1

Making Connections, p. 21 Excerpts from "I Will Praise the Lord of Wisdom" from *The Ancient Near East, Vol. II*, pp. 151–154, edited by James B. Pritchard, translated by Robert D. Briggs. © 1975 by Princeton University Press. Reprinted by permission of Princeton University Press.

Documenting Everyday Life, p. 27 "Pap. Kahun I, 1 (ca. 1900 BC)," http://www.stoa.org/diotima/anthology/wardtexts.shtml#I, translated by William Ward. Reprinted by permission of the Estate of William Ward.

CHAPTER 2

Documenting Everyday Life, p. 64 "77: Funeral Law. Ioulis on Keos, Late 5th Cent. BC" from Mary R. Lefkowitz and Maureen B. Fant, eds., *Women's Life in Greece and Rome: A Source Book in Translation, 2nd Edition*, pp. 58–59. © 1982, 1992 M.B. Fant & M.R. Lefkowitz. Reprinted with permission of Johns Hopkins University Press and Bloomsbury Academic, an imprint of Bloombsury Publishing Plc.

Making Connections, p. 66 From *Xenophon, Vol. VII*, pp. 479–481, translated by E.C. Marchant and G.W. Bowersock, Loeb Classical Library Volume 183, Cambridge, Mass.,: Harvard University Press, Copyright © 1968 by the President and Fellows of Harvard College. Loeb Classical Library ® is a registered trademark of the President and Fellows of Harvard College.

"The Berezan Lead Letter" from Michael Trapp, ed., John Chadwick, trans., *Greek and Latin Letters: An Anthology with Translation* (Cambridge: Cambridge University Press, 2003), p. 51. © 2003 Cambridge University Press.

CHAPTER 3

Making Connections, p. 86 Excerpts from *The Campaigns of Alexander*, by Arrian, edited by James Romm, translated by Pamela Mensch (New York: Pantheon Books, 2010), pp. 168–9. Originally published in *Alexander the Great: Selections from Arrian, Diodorus, Plutarch, and Quintus Curtius* (Indianapolis: Hackett Publishing Company, 2005), pp. 106–7. © 2005 Hackett Publishing Company. Reprinted with permission from the publisher, Hackett Publishing Company, Inc. All rights reserved.

Documenting Everyday Life, p. 93 "Woman scalded by bath-attendant" from Jane Rowlandson, ed., *Women and Society in Greek and Roman Egypt: A Sourcebook* (Cambridge: Cambridge University Press, 1998), pp. 172, 174. © 1998 Cambridge University Press.

CHAPTER 4

Documenting Everyday Life, p. 130 "The Humble Townspeople: From the Walls of Pompeii" from Naphtali Lewis & Meyer Reinhold, eds., *Roman Civilization, Selected Readings, Vol. II: The Empire, 3rd Ed.* Copyright © 1990 Columbia University Press. Reprinted with permission of the publisher.

CHAPTER 5

Documenting Everyday Life, p. 176 Excerpt from Allan Chester Johnson, Paul Robinson Coleman-Norton, and Frank Card Bourne, *Ancient Roman Statutes* (Austin, TX: University of Texas Press, 1961), p. 232. © 1961 by University of Texas Press. Reprinted by permission of the publisher.

CHAPTER 6

Making Connections, p. 194 "Goals and Laws of Marriage" from "Stromateis, Book Two" in *The Fathers of the Church, A New Translation: Clement of Alexandria, Books 1–3*, edited by Thomas P. Halton, translated by John Ferguson. Copyright © 1991 The Catholic University of America Press. Reprinted with permission.

CHAPTER 7

Making Connections, p. 239 "The Titles of the Patus Legis Salicae," from Katherine Fischer Drew, trans. and ed., *The Laws of the Salian Franks* (Philadelphia: University of Pennsylvania Press, 1991), pp. 59–63. © 1991 by the University of Pennsylvania Press. Reprinted with permission of the University of Pennsylvania Press.

Documenting Everyday Life, p. 243 Excerpts from Marcelle Thiébaux, trans. and ed., *Dhuoda, Handbook for her Warrior Son: Liber Manualis* (Cambridge: Cambridge University Press, 1998), pp. 101, 103, 105. © 1998 Cambridge University Press. Reprinted with the permission of Cambridge University Press.

CHAPTER 8

Documenting Everyday Life, p. 259 Excerpt from "The Survey of Huntingdonshire in Domesday Book," *English Historical Documents 1042–1189 2nd Ed,* edited by David C. Douglas & George W. Greenaway. Copyright © Eyre Methuen Ltd. 1953, 1981. Reproduced with permission of Taylor and Francis Books UK.

Making Connections, p. 265 "Quan vei la lauzeta mover" by Bernart de Ventadorn, translated by Keith Anderson in *Music of the Troubadors* by Ensemble Unicorn, 1996. Reprinted courtesy of Naxos Music Group.

Translation of "L'autrer jost' una sebissa," in *Marcabru: A Critical Edition*, edited by Simon Gaunt, Ruth Harvey, Linda Paterson with John Marshall (Cambridge: D.S. Brewer, 2000), pp. 379, 381. Reprinted by permission of Boydell & Brewer Ltd.

CHAPTER 9

Documenting Everyday Life, p. 299 "Regulating Prostitution in Marseilles," translated by Kirsten Schut. Based on *La prostitution à Marseille* (Paris: Librairie du la Societe des gens de lettres, 1882), pp. 365–366. Printed here by permission of Kirsten Schut.

Making Connections, p. 317 "Rabban Sâwmâ in Fransâ" from *The Monks of Kublai Khan, Emperor of China: Medieval Travels from China through Central Asia to Persia and Beyond*, by Rabban Sawma, translated by Sir E.A. Wallis Budge. Originally published by Harrison & Sons, Ltd. in 1928 for the Religious Tract Society. Reprinted by permission of Lutterworth Press.

CHAPTER 10

Documenting Everyday Life, p. 328 "The Declaration of Lorenzo Ghiberti, sculptor" from *The Society of Renaissance Florence: A Documentary Study*, edited by Gene A. Brucker (Toronto: University of Toronto Press, 1998). Reprinted by permission of Gene A. Brucker.

Making Connections, p. 332 "The Plight of the French Poor," translated by James Bruce Ross, from *The Portable Renaissance Reader*, edited by James Bruce Ross and Mary Martin McLaughlin, copyright 1953, 1968, renewed © 1981 by Viking Penguin Inc. Used by permission of Viking Books, an imprint of Penguin Publishing Group, a division of Penguin Random House LLC.

CHAPTER 11

Making Connections, p. 383 Excerpts from "The Twelve Articles of the Peasants" from Lowell H. Zuck, ed., *Christianity and Revolution: Radical Christian Testimonies, 1520–1650* (Philadelphia: Temple University Press, 1975). Reprinted with permission from the Estate of Lowell H. Zuck.

Excerpts from "Admonition to Peace" by Martin Luther, translated by Charles M. Jacobs in *Luther's Works: The Christian in Society III, Vol. 46*, edited by Robert C. Schultz. Copyright © 1967 Fortress Press. Reproduced by permission of Augsburg Fortress Press. All rights reserved.

CHAPTER 12

Documenting Everyday Life, p. 430 Excerpts from *The Essential Thirty Years War: A Documentary History*, edited and translated by Tryntje Helfferich (Indianapolis: Hackett Publishing Company, 2015), pp. 47–49. © 2015 Hackett Publishing Company, Inc. Reprinted with permission of Hackett Publishing Company.

Making Connections, p. 437 Excerpts from *The Galileo Affair: A Documentary History*, edited and translated by Maurice A. Finocchiaro (Berkeley: University of California Press, 1989). Copyright © 1989 by The Regents of the University of California. Reprinted by permission of the University of California Press.

CHAPTER 14

Making Connections, p. 491 "The Code Noir" reprinted from *Slave Revolution in the Caribbean, 1789–1804: A Brief History with Documents*, by Laurent Dubois and John D. Garrigus (New York: Palgrave Macmillan, 2006), pp. 51–54, © 2006 by Bedford/St. Martin's, with permission of Springer Nature.

CHAPTER 15

Making Connections, p. 526 Excerpts from "Sketch for a Historical Picture of the Progress of the Human Mind: Tenth Epoch," by Marquis de Condorcet, translated by Keith Michael Baker. *Daedalus* 133:3 (Summer 2004), pp. 74, 77–78. © 2004 American Academy of Arts & Sciences. Reprinted by permission of MIT Press Journals.

CHAPTER 16

Documenting Everyday Life, p. 558 Excerpt from *Women in Revolutionary Paris, 1789–1795*, edited and translated by Darline Gay Levy, Harriet Branson Applewhite and Mary Durham Johnson. Copyright © 1979 by the Board of Trustees of the University of Illinois. Used with permission of the University of Illinois.

CHAPTER 19

Making Connections, p. 656 Excerpts from *From Supplication to Revolution: A Documentary Social History of Imperial Russia*, edited by Gregory L. Freeze. Copyright © 1988, Oxford University Press, Inc. Reprinted by permission of Oxford University Press, USA.

CHAPTER 21

Documenting Everyday Life, p. 734 "Letter from a peasant to Bolshevik Leaders, 10 January 1918" from *Voices of Revolution, 1917*, edited by Mark D. Steinberg, translated by Marian Schwartz, pp. 302–303. Copyright © 2001 by Yale University. All rights reserved. Reprinted by permission of Yale University Press.

CHAPTER 22

Making Connections, p. 755 "The Doctrine of Fascism" by Benito Mussolini, from Michael Oakeshott, ed., *The Social and Political Doctrines of Contemporary Europe* (Cambridge: Cambridge University Press, 1939), pp. 166–168, 170–171, 177–178. © 1939 Cambridge University Press.

Documenting Everyday Life, p. 762 Excerpt from *Account Rendered: A Dossier on my Former Self* by Melita Maschmann, translated by Geoffrey Strachan. Copyright © Melita Maschmann. English translation copyright © 1964 by Harper & Row. Reprinted by permission of HarperCollins Publishers and Plunkett Lake Press; paperback and eBook editions at http://plunkettlakepress.com/ar.

CHAPTER 23

Making Connections, p. 790 Excerpts from "Russian Passion" from *A Stranger to Myself: The Inhumanity of War, Russia 1941–1944* by Willy Peter Reese, translated by Michael Hofmann. Copyright © 2011 by Hannelore Kern and Stefan Schmitz. Translation copyright © 2005 by Michael Hofmann. Reprinted by permission of Farrar, Straus and Giroux.

Excerpt from *Life and Fate* by Vasily Grossman, translated by Robert Chandler. Published by Collins Harvill. Reprinted by permission of The Random House Group Limited.

Documenting Everyday Life, p. 793 "Friday, September 4, 1942" by Josef Zelkowicz from *In Those Terrible Days: Writings from the Lodz Ghetto* (Jerusalem: Yad Vashem, 2002), edited by Michal Unger. Reprinted by permission of Yad Vashem Publications.

CHAPTER 24

Documenting Everyday Life, p. 824 "Women's Issues—Women's Worries," by Walther von Hollander. *Occupation and the Emergence of Two States (1945–1961), Vol. 8, German History in Documents and Images*. Edited by Volker Berghahn and Uta Poiger, translated by Thomas Dunlap. Originally published as "Frauenfragen—Frauensorgen," *Nordwestdeutsche Hefte*, 1946, H. 2, S. 21 ff. Reprinted by permission of Axel Springer Syndication GmbH.

Making Connections, p. 831 From *The Second Sex* by Simone de Beauvoir, translated by Constance Borde & Sheila Malovany-Chevallier, translation copyright © 2009 by Constance Borde and Sheila Malovany-Chevallier. Used by permission of Alfred A. Knopf, an imprint of the Knopf Doubleday Publishing Group, a division of Penguin Random House LLC. All rights reserved. And by permission of the Random House Group Limited.

From *Discourse on Colonialism* by Aimé Césaire (New York: Monthly Review Press, 1972). © 1972 Monthly Review Press. All rights reserved. Originally published as *Discours sur le colonialism* by Présence Africaine, © 1955 by Editions Présence Africaine. Reprinted by permission of Monthly Review Press.

CHAPTER 25

Making Connections, p. 855 "The Power of the Powerless," by Václav Havel in *The Power of the Powerless: Citizens Against the State in Central-eastern Europe* (M.E. Sharpe, 1985), edited by John Keane. © 1985 Taylor & Francis. Reprinted by permission of Taylor and Francis Group LLC.

"Speech in Finchley" (May 2, 1979), by Margaret Thatcher, http://www.margaretthatcher.org/document/104072. Reprinted by permission of the Margaret Thatcher Foundation.

Documenting Everyday Life, p. 857 From *How We Survived Communism and Even Laughed* by Slavenka Drakulić. Copyright © 1991 by Slavenka Drakulic. Used by permission of W. W. Norton & Company, Inc. and by permission of Copenhagen Literary Agency.

CHAPTER 26

Making Connections, p. 885 "Speech by Federal Chancellor Angela Merkel at the ceremony commemorating the 100th anniversary of the battle of Verdun," The Press and Information Office of the Federal Government, May 29, 2016. www.bundesregierung.de. Reprinted with permission.

Nigel Farage, "Speech to the European Parliament." Debates, Tuesday, 28 June 2016—Brussels. http://www.europarl.europa.eu. Reprinted with permission.

Documenting Everyday Life, p. 895 "Hosein's Story, Greece." UNHCR, The UN Refugee Agency, Stories (2014). http://stories.unhcr.org/hoseins-story-greece-p13163.html. Reprinted with permission.

A27

Romano, Rome, Italy/Bridgeman Images; p. 153 (left): Michele Falzone/Alamy Stock Photo; (right): The Art Archive at Art Resource, NY; p. 154: Alinari/Bridgeman Images; p. 155 (top): © The Trustees of the British Museum; (bottom): DEA Picture Library/De Agostini/Getty Images; p. 158: Yael Yolovich/The New York Times/Redux; p. 160: akg-images/André Held; 162: Lanmas/Alamy Stock Photo; p. 163: akg-images/CDA/Guillemot; p. 164 (top): akg-images/Pictures From History; (bottom): akg-images/André Held; p. 165: akg-images/André Held; p. 166: akg-images/Pirozzi; p. 167: Erich Lessing/Art Resource, NY; p. 171: akg/Bible Land Pictures; p. 172: akg-images/De Agostini Picture Library; p. 173: DeAgostini/Getty Images; p. 174: Staatliche Museen, Berlin/Johannes Laurentius/Art Resource, NY; p. 177: Album/Art Resource, NY; p. 178: The Art Archive at Art Resource, NY.

Chapter 6: Pages 180–181: Scala/Art Resource, NY; p. 183: Timothy McCarthy/Art Resource, NY; p. 184: © The Trustees of the British Museum, London; p. 185: DeAgostini/Getty Images; p. 186: akg/Bildarchiv Steffens; p. 188 (top): DeAgostini/Getty Images; (bottom): Wikimedia, public domain; p. 189: Album/Art Resource, NY; p. 190: akg-images/Rabatti – Domingie; p. 191: Museo Archeologico Nazionale, Naples/Bridgeman Art Library; p. 195: Bibliothèque nationale de France; p. 196: Alfredo Dagli Orti/The Art Archive at Art Resource, NY; p. 197: akg-images/Andrea Lemolo; p. 198: Werner Forman/Art Resource, NY; p. 199: akg-images/Interfoto; p. 200 (left): Ancient Art and Architecture Collection Ltd./Bridgeman Art Library; (right): Scala/Art Resource, NY; p. 201: De Agostini Picture Library/Getty Images; p. 202: Archiv Gerstenberg/ullstein bild via Getty Images; p. 203: DeAgostini/Getty Images.

Chapter 7: Pages 210–211: DeAgostini/Getty Images; p. 213: De Agostini/Getty Images; p. 214: Album/Art Resource, NY; p. 216: Scala/Art Resource, NY; p. 217: Artur Bogacki/Alamy Stock Photo; p. 218 (left): Erich Lessing/Art Resource, NY; (right): Ancient Art and Architecture Collection Ltd/Bridgeman Images; p. 219: Image copyright © The Metropolitan Museum of Art. Image source: Art Resource, NY; p. 223: Image copyright (c) The Metropolitan Museum of Art. Images source: Art Resource, NY; p. 224: halil ibrahim kurucan/Alamy Stock Photo; p. 228: Pictures from History/Bridgeman Images; p. 229: akg-images/De Agostini Picture Lib./G. Dagli Orti; p. 230 (top): Bildarchiv Steffens/Bridgeman Images; (bottom): SSPL/Science Museum/Art Resource, NY; p. 231: Gianni Dagli Orti/The Art Archive at Art Resource, NY; p. 232: Private Collection/Bridgeman Images; p. 234: Bibliotheque Municipale, Rouen, France/Bridgeman Images; p. 235 (left): DeAgostini/Getty Images; (right): akg-images/De Agostini Picture Lib./G. Nimatallah; p. 236: De Agostini Picture Library/G. Dagli Orti/Bridgeman Images; p. 237: © The Board of Trinity College, Dublin, Ireland/

Bridgeman Images; p. 241: RMN-Grand Palais/Art Resource, NY; p. 242: Gianni Dagli Orti/The Art Archive at Art Resource, NY; p. 244: Kunsthistorisches Museum, Vienna, Austria/Bridgeman Images; p. 245: © BnF, Dist. RMN-Grand Palais/Art Resource, NY.

Chapter 8: Pages 248–249 (from left to right): Kunsthistorisches Museum Wien, Kunstkammer (KK 5118); Landesmuseum Württemberg, Stuttgart (KK grau 53); Kunsthistorisches Museum Wien, Kunstkammer (KK 5088); p. 251: British Library, London, UK/© British Library Board. All Rights Reserved/Bridgeman Images; p. 255: Gianni Dagli Orti/The Art Archive at Art Resource, NY; p. 256 (left): Kharbine-Tapabor/The Art Archive at Art Resource, NY; (right): British Library Board/Robana/Art Resource, NY; p. 258: Universal History Archive/UIG/Bridgeman Images; p. 261: DeA Picture Library/Art Resource, NY; p. 263: Granger Collection; p. 264: akg-images/World History Archive; p. 266 (top): akg images; (bottom): Interfoto/Alamy Stock Photo; p. 267: Pictures from History/Bridgeman Images; p. 268: akg-images/André Held; p. 270: akg-images/De Agostini Picture Library; p. 272: © British Library Board/Robana/Art Resource, NY; p. 273: Pictures from History/Bridgeman Images; p. 274: Gianni Dagli Orti/The Art Archive at Art Resource, NY; p. 275: Stuart Whatling http://www.medievalart.org; p. 276 (left): Shutterstock; (right): Peter Willi/Bridgeman Images; p. 278: Hereford Cathedral, Herefordshire, UK/Bridgeman Images; p. 279: Archivo de la Corona de Aragon, Barcelona/Bridgeman Images; p. 281 (top): Gianni Dagli Orti/The Art Archive at Art Resource, NY; (bottom): Kharbine - Tapabor/The Art Archive at Art Resource, NY; p. 282: Ken Welsh/Bridgeman Images; p. 284: Photo12/UIG/Getty Images.

Chapter 9: Pages 286–287: Biblioteca Nazionale, Turin/Bridgeman Images; p. 289: Bibliotheque Nationale, Paris; p. 292: akg-images/De Agostini/A. Dagli Orti; p. 293: Private Collection/Bridgeman Images; p. 294 (top): Universal History Archive/UIG/Bridgeman Images; (bottom): Album/Art Resource, NY; p. 295: De Agostini Picture Library/G. Nimatallah/Bridgeman Images; p. 296: akg-images/British Library; p. 297: Universal History Archive/UIG via Getty Images; p. 298: © Bodleian Libraries/Douce 88 folio 111V/The Art Archive at Art Resource; p. 301: British Library, London/Bridgeman Images; p. 302: Album/Art Resource, NY; p. 304: Alfredo Dagli Orti/The Art Archive at Art Resource, NY; p. 305: Herzog August Bibliothek; http://creativecommons.org/licenses/by-sa/3.0/de/; p. 306: akg-images/British Library; p. 309 (top): DEA/G. DAGLI ORTI/Getty Images; (bottom): DEA/M. Seemuller/Getty Images; p. 310: akg-images; p. 311: akg-images/British Library; p. 312: akg-images/Tristan Lafranchis; p. 313: Granger Collection; p. 316 (left): akg-images/ullstein bild; (right): bpk, Berlin/Vatican Museum/Alfredo Dagli Orti/Art Resource, NY; p. 319 (top): Scala/

Art Resource, NY; (bottom): akg-images/VISIOARS; p. 321 (top): HIP/Art Resource, NY; (bottom): British Library/The Art Archive at Art Resource, NY.

Chapter 10: Pages 324–325: National Gallery, London, Bridgeman Images; p. 327: Scala/Art Resource, NY; p. 330: Alinari/Art Resource, NY; p. 333: Jean of Wavrin (1398–1474), manuscript/British Library, London, UK/De Agostini Picture Library/Bridgeman Images; p. 334: Bridgeman Images; p. 335: Album/Art Resource, NY; p. 336: Topkapi Palace Museum, Istanbul/Bridgeman Images; p. 337: Erich Lessing/Art Resource, NY; p. 338: World History Archive/Alamy Stock Photo; p. 339: akg-images/British Library; p. 341: bpk, Berlin/Art Resource; p. 342: Photo © AISA/Bridgeman Images; p. 344: Copyright of the image Museo Nacional del Prado/Art Resource, NY; p. 345: Gianni Dagli Orti/The Art Archive at Art Resource, NY; p. 346: Museu Nacional de Arte Antigua, Lisbon, Portugal/Bridgeman Images; p. 348: Tomasso Brothers Fine Art, UK; p. 349: bpk, Berlin/Staatsbibliothek zu Berlin, Stiftung Preussicher Kulturbesitz/Art Resource, NY; p. 351: PHOTOAISA/BEBA/Interfoto; p. 352: Granger Collection; p. 354: Biblioteca Medicea-Laurenziana, Florence/Bridgeman Images; p. 355: Library of Congress; p. 356: Scala/Art Resource, NY; p. 357: Biblioteca Medicea Laurenziana, Florence, Ms. Strozzi 50, 1 recto. By permission of the Ministero per i Beni e le Attivita Culturali with all rights reserved; p. 359: Sterling and Francine Clark Art Institute, Williamstown, Massachusetts/Bridgeman Images; p. 360: British Library, London/© British Library Board. All Rights Reserved/Bridgeman Images; p. 361 (left): Brancacci Chapel, Santa Maria del Carmine, Florence/Bridgeman Images; (right): Alinari/Art Resource, NY; p. 362: De Agostini Picture Library/A. Dagli Orti/Bridgeman Images; p. 363 (left): Baptistery, Florence/Bridgeman Images; (right): Image copyright © The Metropolitan Museum of Art. Image source: Art Resource, NY; p. 364 (left): National Gallery, London/Bridgeman Images; (right): Kunsthistorisches Museum, Vienna/Ali Meyer/Bridgeman Images; p. 365 (left): Scala/Art Resource, NY; (right): Vatican Museums and Galleries, Vatican City/Bridgeman Images; p. 366 (left): Vatican Museums and Galleries, Vatican City/Bridgeman Images; (right): Louvre, Paris/Bridgeman Images; p. 367: Scala/Art Resource, NY.

Chapter 11: Pages 370–371: akg-images/World History Archive; p. 373: (left): Erich Lessing/Art Resource, NY; (right): SZ Photo/Scherl/Bridgeman Images; p. 374: The Art Archive at Art Resource, NY; p. 375: Foto Marburg/Art Resource, NY; p. 376: British Library Board/Bridgeman Images; p. 378: Bibliotheque Nationale, Paris/Bridgeman Images; p. 380: Library of Congress; p. 381: © The Trustees of the British Museum; p. 382: akg/De Agostini Picture Library; p. 384: akg-images; p. 385: Roger-Viollet, Paris/

Viollet Collection/Getty Images; p. 643: Dagli Orti/ REX/Shutterstock; p. 645 (left): Granger, NYC; (right): Christophel Fine Art/UIG via Getty Images; p. 648: Pictorial Press Ltd/Alamy Stock Photo; p. 649: Pictures From History/akg-images; p. 652 (left): Florence Nightingale Museum, London/Bridgeman Images; (right): Private Collection/Bridgeman Images; p. 653: Schloss Friedrichsruhe, Germany/Bridgeman Images; p. 655: Granger, NYC; p. p. 657: Universal History Archive/UIG/ Bridgeman Images; p. 659: Granger, NYC; p. 660: Granger, NYC; p. 661: Private Collection/Bridgeman Images; p. 662: Kharbine-Tapabo/ REX/Shutterstock; p. 663: Bibliotheque Marguerite Durand, Paris/ Archives Charmet/Bridgeman Images; p. 667: Musee d'Orsay, Paris/Bridgeman Images; p. 668: Niday Picture Library/Alamy Stock Photo.

Chapter 20: Pages 670–671: Art Collection 3/ Alamy Stock Photo; p. 673: ullstein bild via Getty Images; p. 676: Heritage Image Partnership Ltd/ Alamy Stock Photo; p. 680: Archives Charmet/ Bridgeman Images; p. 681: akg-images; p. 683: Museum of the Revolution, Moscow/Sputnik/ Bridgeman Images; p. 685: Baker Street Scans/ Alamy Stock Photo; p. 686: Granger, NYC; p. 689: Private Collection/Photo © Ken Welsh/Bridgeman Images; p. 691: World History Archive/ Alamy Stock Photo; p. 692: Sueddeutsche Zeitung Photo/Alamy Stock Photo; p. 694: Library of Congress/Corbis/VCG via Getty Images; p. 697: © 2017 Artists Rights Society (ARS), New York/ADAGP, Paris; Les Demoiselles d'Avignon, 1907 (oil on canvas), Picasso, Pablo (1881–1973)/ Museum of Modern Art/ Bridgeman Images; p. 698: Heritage Image Partnership Ltd/ Alamy Stock Photo; p. 699 (left): INTERFOTO/ Alamy Stock Photo; (right): ANL/Vienna, LW 73.623-C; p. 700: Rue des Archives/Granger, NYC; p. 701:Images Group/ REX/Shutterstock; p. 702:© Ludwig Meidner-Archiv, Jüdisches Museum Frankfurt. akg-images.

Chapter 21: Pages 704–705: *The Menin Road*, 1919 (oil on canvas), Nash, Paul (1889–1946)/ Imperial War Museum, London/Bridgeman Images; p. 709: Mary Evans Picture Library/ Alamy Stock Photo; p. 710: Dagli Orti/REX/Shutterstock; p. 712: akg-images/Jean-Pierre Verney; p. 714: Trinity Mirror/Mirrorpix/Alamy Stock Photo; p. 715: Photo © Bonhams, London/ Bridgeman Images; p. 716: The Stapleton Collection/Bridgeman Images; p. 717: Everett Collection Historical/Alamy Stock Photo; p. 719: The Stapleton Collection/Bridgeman Images; p. 720: Science History Images/Alamy Stock Photo; p. 721: Granger, NYC; p. 722: 'Over the Top' 1st Artists' Rifles at Marcoing, 30th December 1917, 1918 (oil on canvas), Nash, John Northcote

(1893–1977)/Imperial War Museum, London, UK/© IWM (Art.IWM ART 1656)/Bridgeman Images; p. 723: James Kerr/Alamy Stock Photo; p. 725: Pictures from History/Bridgeman Images; p. 729 (top): Images Group/REX / Shutterstock; (bottom): The Print Collector/ Alamy Stock Photo; p. 735 (top): Granger, NYC; (bottom): Universal History Archive/UIG/ Bridgeman Images; p. 736: Granger, NYC.

Chapter 22: Pages 740–741: © 2017 Artists Rights Society (ARS), New York/ADAGP, Paris. *Fireside Angel* 1937 Max Ernst classicpaintings/Alamy Stock Photo; p. 744 (top): Godot13/ National Numismatic Collection, National Museum of American History https://creativecommons.org/licenses/by-sa/4.0/deed.en (bottom): Suddeutsche Zeitung/Granger, NYC; p. 747: Granger, NYC; p. 749: Art © Estate of George Grosz/Licensed by VAGA, New York, NY. *The Pillars of Society*, 1926 (oil on canvas), Grosz, George (1893–1959)/Nationalgalerie, Berlin, Germany/Bridgeman Images; p. 750: halpand/Alamy Stock Photo; p. 751: © SZ Photo/ Scherl/Bridgeman Images; p. 752: © Look and Learn/Elgar Collection/Bridgeman Images; p. 753: ullstein bild/akg-images; p. 757: ullstein bild/ akg-images; p. 759: AP Photo; p. 761: Galerie Bilderwelt/Getty Images; p. 763: United States Holocaust Memorial Museum, courtesy of Virginius Dabney; p. 764: Art Collection 3/Alamy Stock Photo; p. 766: Granger, NYC; p. 767: © 2017 Estate of Pablo Picasso/Artists Rights Society (ARS), New York *Guernica* 1937 (oil on canvas), Picasso, Pablo (1881–1973)/Museo Nacional Centro de Arte Reina Sofia, Madrid, Spain/Bridgeman Images; p.768: Universal History Archive/UIG/Bridgeman Images; p. 770: Associated Newspapers Ltd./Solo Syndication.

Chapter 23: Pages 774–775: CPA Media—Pictures from History/Granger, NYC; p. 777: Albert Harlingue/Roger Viollet/Getty Images; p. 779 (top): Daily Mail/REX /Shutterstock; (bottom): Trinity Mirror/Mirrorpix/Alamy Stock Photo; p. 781: Henryk Ross Polish, 1910–1991 Man walking in winter in the remains of the synagogue on Wolborska Street, destroyed by the Germans in 1939, 1940, gelatin silver print 12.7 x 18 cm (5 x 71/16 in.) Art Gallery of Ontario. Gift from Archive of Modern Conflict, 2007 2007/2365 ©Art Gallery of Ontario; p. 783: ullstein bild/Getty Images; p. 784: Sovfoto/UIG via Getty Images; p. 787: dpa picture alliance/Alamy Stock Photo; p. 789: Pictorial Press Ltd/Alamy Stock Photo; p. 792: © SZ Photo/Bridgeman Images; p. 794: David Harding/Alamy Stock Photo; p. 795: Images Group /REX/ Shutterstock; p. 797: The Stapleton Collection/Bridgeman Images; p. 798: REX/

Shutterstock; p. 800: Archive/UIG/REX/Shutterstock; p. 801: SPUTNIK/Alamy Stock Photo; p. 802: Prisma by Dukas Presseagentur GmbH/ Alamy Stock Photo; p. 804 (top): World History Archive/Alamy Stock 5/11/17Photo; (bottom): akg-images.

Chapter 24: Pages 808–809: Sovfoto/UIG via Getty Images; p. 812: Private Collection/Bridgeman Images; p. 813: Paul Popper/ Popperfoto/ Getty Images; p. 814: Deutsches Historisches Museum, Berlin, Germany/© DHM/Bridgeman Images; p. 817: akg-images/Tony Vaccaro; p. 818: Dinodia Photos/Alamy Stock Photo; p. 823: Rue des Archives/Granger, NYC; p. 825: Corbis via Getty Images; p. 827 (top): Images Group/ REX/Shutterstock; (bottom): Rue des Archives/ Granger, NYC — All rights reserved; p. 828: World History Archive/Alamy Stock Photo; p. 830: Bridgeman Images; p. 833: Photo 12/ Alamy Stock Photo; p. 835 (top): akg-images/ Universal Images Group/Sovfoto; (bottom): David Harding/Alamy Stock Photo; p. 838: ANL/ REX/Shutterstock; p. 839: Patrice Habans/ Paris Match via Getty Images; p. 840: CTK/ Alamy Stock Photo.

Chapter 25: Pages 844–845: Tom Stoddart/ Reportage by Getty Images; p. 846: Getty Images; p. 848: Pacific Press/Alamy Stock Photo; p. 851: age fotostock/Alamy Stock Photo; p. 852: Kai Pfaffenbach/REUTERS/Newscom; p. 854: Homer Sykes Archive/ Alamy Stock Photo; p. 856: Rue des Archives/Granger, NYC—All rights reserved; p. 858 (top): Eye Ubiquitous/REX/ Shutterstock; (bottom): Sputnik/Alamy Stock Photo; p. 859: Images Group/REX/Shutterstock; p. 861: Justin Leighton/Alamy Stock Photo; p. 863: Steven L. Raymer National Geographic /Getty Images; p. 865: ITAR-TASS Photo Agency/Alamy Stock Photo; p. 868: REUTERS/ Alamy Stock Photo; p. 872: Murat Taner/Corbis/ Getty Images; p. 869: David Brauchli/Sygma via Getty Images; p. 861: Greg Balfour Evans/Alamy Stock Photo; p. 874: Peter Turnley/Corbis/VCG via Getty Images.

Chapter 26: Pages 876–877: Antonio Masiello/ ZUMA Press/Newscom; p. 879: Sean Gallup/ Getty Images; p. 881: Jean-Francois Deroubaix/ Gamma-Rapho via Getty Images; p. 883 (top): AP Photo/Markus Schreiber; (bottom): Graham Mulrooney/Alamy Stock Photo; p. 886: Aris Messinis /AFP/Getty Images; p. 887: Alexei Druzhinin /SPUTNIK/KREMLIN POOL/ EPA/REX /Shutterstock; p. 888: AP Photo/ Evgeny Feldman; p. 891: Jonathan Bright/ Alamy Live News; p. 892: James Gourley/ REX/Shutterstock; p. 893: Pascal Le Segretain /Getty Images; p. 894: Vidon-white/Epa/REX/ Shutterstock; p. 896: AP Photo/Santi Palacios.

Page numbers in italics refer to illustrations, maps, and tables.